REAL ESTATE
INVESTMENT

REAL ESTATE INVESTMENT

Strategy, Analysis, Decisions

STEPHEN A. PYHRR
JAMES R. COOPER
LARRY E. WOFFORD
STEVEN D. KAPPLIN
PAUL D. LAPIDES

SECOND EDITION

WILEY

JOHN WILEY & SONS

New York ■ Chichester ■ Brisbane ■ Toronto ■ Singapore

Cover Designed by John Hite

Photo Credits
Part 1: Courtesy Skyviews Survey, Inc.
Parts 2 and 5: Courtesy JMB Realty
Parts 3, 4 and 6: Courtesy Trammell Crow Company

Library of Congress Cataloging-in-Publication Data

Real estate investment.
   Rev. ed. of: Real estate investment/Stephen A. Pyhrr,
   James R. Cooper. c1982.
   Bibliography
   Includes index.
   1. Real estate investment. I. Pyhrr, Stephen A.
II. Pyhrr, Stephen A. Real estate investment.
HD1382.5.P93 1989   332.63'24   88-27961
ISBN 0-471-87953-3

Printed in the United States of America

10 9

Printed and bound by Malloy Lithographing, Inc.

This book is dedicated to Weston Shank Pyhrr, fourteen-year-old son of Stephen and Daphne Pyhrr, who died tragically in September 1986. This book is also dedicated to Dr. James A. Graaskamp, who died in April 1987. His immeasurable influence on real estate investment theory and practice will not soon be forgotten.

Stephen A. Pyhrr is an Adjunct Associate Professor of Real Estate and Finance in the Graduate School of Business at the University of Texas at Austin. He earned his master's and doctorate in real estate and finance at the University of Illinois and is a graduate of the School of Mortgage Banking at Northwestern University.

Dr. Pyhrr is the author of numerous articles in the *Journal of the American Real Estate and Urban Economics Association, The Appraisal Journal, The Real Estate Appraiser and Analyst, Financial Management, Real Estate Review,* and *Mortgage Banking.* He speaks nationwide on real estate investment, finance, and taxation subjects for professional organizations such as the Society of Real Estate Appraisers, the Mortgage Bankers Association of America, and several state associations of Realtors. He is also widely known for his pioneering work in the development of computer simulation models for the financial analysis of income property.

Dr. Pyhrr is a partner with the real estate investment and property management firm of Davis and Associates in Austin, Texas, and is the director of its Investment and Marketing Division and its Research and Consulting Group.

James R. Cooper is Professor of Real Estate and Legal Studies at Georgia State University. A former member of the faculties of the Wharton School of the University of Pennsylvania, the University of Pittsburgh, the University of Illinois at Champaign, and the University of Wisconsin at Madison, Dr. Cooper received his J.D. from the University of Pennsylvania.

Dr. Cooper holds an SRPA designation from the Society of Real Estate Appraisers, has taught national courses in appraising for both the SREA and the American Institute of Real Estate Appraisers, and is past director of the American Real Estate and Urban Economics Association. He is a founder and honorary life member of the American Real Estate Society.

In addition to numerous articles on housing and housing policy, investment analysis, valuation, and usury, Dr. Cooper is the author of *Real Estate Investment Analysis,* an early book on computer simulation of real estate investment, the coauthor of *Real Estate and Urban Land Analysis,* and has produced real estate computer software including the Illini–Cooper and REIG, USA.

Dr. Cooper is a member of the bar of the District of Columbia and has been admitted to practice before the United States Supreme Court. He is an investor in numerous real estate projects and serves as a personal financial planner for selected clients.

Larry E. Wofford is President of C & L Systems Corporation and an adjunct professor in the Coll. of Architecture, University of Oklahoma. Formerly a Professor of Finance and Real Estate and head of the real estate program at the University of Tulsa, he also served as Distinguished Professor and Visiting Chairholder in Real Estate at the University of Hawaii during 1981 to 1982. He earned a doctorate in finance and real estate from the University of Texas at Austin.

Dr. Wofford is the author of the principles textbook, *Real Estate,* published by John Wiley & Sons. He has been a regular contributor of articles to such leading real estate journals as *Land Economics, Journal of the American Real Estate and Urban Economics Association, Housing Finance Review,* and *The Appraisal Journal* and has served as editor of *The Journal of Real Estate Research.* Dr. Wofford is the 1989 President of the American Real Estate Society, has served on the Board of Directors of the American Real Estate and Urban Economics Association, and consults on real estate matters with numerous private and public entities. He is a member of the American Institute of Certified Planners.

Steven D. Kapplin is Professor of Finance and Real Estate at the University of South Florida, where he directs the real estate program. Dr. Kapplin received his doctorate in real estate and urban affairs from Georgia State University and was instrumental in developing the real estate program at the University of South Florida.

Dr. Kapplin is the author of numerous articles on real estate investment analysis and valuation and has contributed to such publications as *The Appraisal Journal, The Real Estate Appraiser and Analyst, Journal of Condominium Management, The Journal of Real Estate Research, Journal of the American Real Estate and Urban Economics Association,* and *Real Estate Issues.* He is a past director of the American Real Estate Society and coeditor of the Research in Real Estate Monograph Series, jointly sponsored by the American Real Estate Society and JAI Press.

Paul D. Lapides, an Adjunct Assistant Professor of Real Estate at New York University, is a frequent speaker at industry meetings and conducts two-day seminars on real estate investment, management, and marketing. A CPA, Lapides is a graduate of The Wharton School at the University of Pennsylvania and received his M.B.A. from New York University.

In addition to numerous articles, Mr. Lapides is the author of *Managing Residential Real Estate* and *Computer Selection & Implementation for Property Managers.*

Mr. Lapides has had management experience with more than $3 billion in income-producing real estate and has acted as a consultant to more than 50 companies engaged in real-estate-related activities ranging from brokerage, investment, syndication, and management to lending and computerization. He currently serves on the Advisory Board of *Real Estate Accounting & Taxation* and *Guide to Real Estate and Mortgage Banking Software.*

PREFACE

The goal of the original edition of this text was to offer a high-quality advanced book that would help students and business professionals approach real estate investment decision making in a rational and systematic manner. Traditionally, most real estate investors concentrated on a few key assumptions about a property and its economic future, examined a few rules of thumb, mulled over the situation, and then decided, relying on the implicit decision-making apparatus of judgment, hunch, instinct, intuition, faith, and gut feel. As in the first edition, which was adopted by more than eighty universities and colleges and extended to eleven printings, the authors hope to continue participating in the movement that has brought real estate decision making to new and greater plateaus of knowledge and skills. To this end we have updated, reorganized, revitalized, and expanded the original text.

Six years is a mere byte in the virtual memory of the history of the world, but in the dynamic realm of business much has changed that directly or indirectly influences the nature of real estate investing and decision making. This text, therefore, integrates such important industry trends as institutionalization, financial deregulation, securitization, tax reform, globalization, and vertical integration. In the various parts of the book, the authors have sought to set forth a general normative methodology for analyzing investments in properties; to present the state of the art in institutional and individual portfolio management; and to apply the analytical techniques developed to different types of property.

Central Themes and Theories

The basic objective of this book is to develop an analytical framework by which individuals and institutions can make real estate investment decisions. The primary emphases of the book are on theory, concept building, financial modelling, and practical application. The framework considers the traditional methods of real estate investment analysis and the professional orientation of the majority of investors in the marketplace, as well as the modern methodologies, techniques, and computer applications preferred by sophisticated investors and analysts. One major case study and a number of short examples illustrate many of the concepts and techniques discussed throughout the text. Well received in the first edition, the updated Aspen Wood Apartments continuing case study analyzes this real estate investment over a period of fourteen years, from its initial acquisition through two ownership life cycles, numerous market cycles, and its restructuring and resyndication.

The cornerstones of the analytical framework developed are rate of return and risk concepts, which are related to the subtitle of the text as

- Strategy: return and risk *definition*
- Analysis: return and risk *measurement*
- Decisions: return and risk *evaluation*

The view of the investment decision process as a return–risk trade-off is not new, but as presented here, represents more than the traditional financial and quantifiable measures. Nonfinancial and financial considerations are integrated, with explicit attention given to market, marketability, legal, political, social, and physical factors affecting investment decisions and performance. Although they receive relatively little attention in most investment books, these factors are treated in this text as an integral and important part of the investment decision process. Because these factors can have dramatic impact on a project's returns and risks, they must be considered in the investment framework.

Underlying the return–risk framework is the definition of real estate investment as a process of identifying and structuring projects to maximize returns relative to risks. We therefore advocate the view that a decision maker can, to a substantial degree, control returns and risks through careful analysis and structuring of the financial and nonfinancial variables. Through greater expertise in the areas of market and marketability analysis, tax planning, and risk management, a decision maker can structure the purchase, operation, and termination of a property so that investment returns are increased relative to risks. Because real estate investments are, unlike stock investments, heterogenous and affected by a relatively inefficient marketplace, better-than-average performances are available to better-than-average real estate investment decision makers. In short, good strategic planning, market analysis, and financial analysis pay off in real estate investing! This book is designed to assist both the student and the professional through a learning process that will improve their judgmental and structuring capabilities. .

The normative methodologies developed here for analyzing investments consider the efficient allocation of human as well as financial capital resources. In contrast to investment theories that ignore the decision maker's time allocation problems when developing strategy, analyzing investments, and making investment decisions, we advocate a sequential investment analysis process that recognizes the multiple investment objectives and constraints applied by investors at different time stages in the process. We also recognize that different types of analysis (i.e., levels of sophistication) are appropriate for different types of property, different sizes of projects, and different phases of the analytical process.

Further, we make a distinction between existing projects and development projects because they differ in the nature and level of returns and risks and in the nature and extent of the analysis performed. Our focus is on existing or ongoing projects assumed to be absorbed in the marketplace and on turnkey projects for which the developer promises completion. Although the principles and concepts learned here are used to evaluate development and construction projects, a separate text or course on real estate development will provide a full treatment of these subjects.

Largely ignored in most investment texts, the dramatic impact of inflation and real estate cycles on real estate investment returns and risks is thoroughly discussed here. The importance of knowing how to handle these variables effectively was clearly demonstrated by the investment experiences of individuals and institutions during the real estate depression of the middle 1970s, the volatile inflation cycle of the late 1970s and early 1980s, and the overbuilding cycle of the middle 1980s. Learning through mistakes made in the real world is costly; thus, investment theory must demonstrate an effective approach to handling these variables if decision skills are to be improved through formal learning experiences.

Because the managing equity investor is the key decision maker responsible for the location, acquisition, operation, and termination decisions of a real estate venture, the authors have written with this role, and to a lesser degree that of the passive equity investor, in mind. And because the ability of the managing equity investor to operate successfully is influenced and often controlled by the decisions and preferences of lenders, developers, architects and engineers, accountants, attorneys, promoters, government administrators, and consumers of urban space, the views of these participants are also considered.

Indeed, real estate returns and risks cannot be assessed intelligently and accurately without a holistic and interdisciplinary approach. The successful decision maker possesses a generalist's knowledge of architecture and design, engineering, construction, marketing, and management as well as expertise in urban economics and financial analysis. Decision makers must learn to understand better the interrelations and linkages between these areas and their probable impacts on investment returns and risks. A sound assumption base for a financial analysis cannot be developed without this knowledge. Neither can a sound investment strategy be based on an analysis that employs bad assumptions. We stress that "The buyer should buy the assumptions that create the yield rather than the yield itself"; those who research a property and arrive at the most realistic set of assumptions will have the highest probability of success in real estate investing. Real estate investment analysis is thus a process of validating key assumptions such as those about income, expenses, financing, and resale. As the old GIGO principal teaches, if you put garbage in your investment model, you get garbage out!

The importance of applying modern capital-budgeting techniques and computer models to real estate investment analysis cannot be emphasized enough. After-tax cash flow analysis, discounted-cash-flow models, and ratio and risk analysis techniques are therefore explored in depth, and we stress the need for technical competence in measuring returns and risks in the early steps of the strategic framework. These techniques and models enable the investor to compare a project under analysis with the best alternatives available at the time, or with other projects in a portfolio. Computer models are illustrated, including those developed by the authors, and readers are encouraged to develop their own models or purchase commercially available software. Although background knowledge of computer software would be helpful, the illustrations used in the text to explain computer simulation techniques provide the reader with the skills required to use such programs.

One program for computer simulation analysis used by the authors and available to readers is REFINE: TWO. This program is designed for novice-to-intermediate computer users who are interested in doing sophisticated real estate analysis. REFINE: TWO evaluates the financial and investment feasibility of alternative real estate proposals by calculating value, return, and risk indices for each year of the ownership period, along with other necessary accounting output. Additional information concerning the REFINE: TWO program and the accompanying *Instruction Manual*, *Data Manual*, and VCR training tape can be obtained by contacting The Refine Group, Inc., Post Office Box 194, Blacksburg, Virginia 24063-0194. Other computer software programs are discussed in Chapter 7.

Suggested Readership and Background Knowledge

This book was designed to confront the continuing needs of students who are taking advantage of the stronger repertoire of courses on real estate principles offered in the nation's colleges and universities and who are ready for advanced studies in real estate. As well as providing an advanced lesson plan for investment analysis at the business undergraduate level and for graduate programs leading to the M.B.A. and M.S. degrees, this text is appropriate for some schools and colleges of architecture, planning, engineering, and accountancy. Updated and revised to include changes affecting the real estate industry, this edition should also continue to serve as an annotated reference for career development and professional continuing education courses. This study leads the student through the rudiments of real estate investing to the highest current state of the art, and as such can assist individual, corporate, and institutional investors in real estate in upgrading their analytical and decision-making skills. This edition, as the first, can be retained as a ready reference book for solving particular problems as they are encountered.

To take full advantage of this book, the reader should have some knowledge of real estate principles and practices, accounting, finance, and mathematics. Experience has indicated that, although desirable, a background course in real estate is not necessary for business students in graduate school. However, the student at the undergraduate level should have at least one background course in real estate before undertaking advanced real estate investment analysis. Review of *Modern Real Estate*, by Charles H. Wurtzebach and Mike E. Miles (New York: Wiley, 1987, third edition), or *Real Estate*, by Larry E. Wofford (New York: Wiley, 1986, second edition), or of a comparable text would lay a solid foundation appropriate to the entry level for this book.

Reorganization of the Text

In this second edition, some of the chapters were reorganized to improve the flow of the text and the presentation of the investment analysis and financial structuring process as advocated by the authors. We hope that the following listing comparing the chapter order of the two editions will provide appropriate guidance to instructors preparing course outlines.

Second Edition	Chapter Title	First Edition
PART 1	REAL ESTATE INVESTMENT: THE STATE OF THE ART	
1	The Nature and Scope of Real Estate Investment	1
2	Overview of the Investment Decision Process	2
3	Decision-Making Approaches to Real Estate Investment	3
PART 2	SYSTEMATIC INVESTMENT ANALYSIS	
4	Investment Strategy	8
5	Selecting the Ownership Entity	9
6	Preliminary Financial Feasibility Analysis	10
7	Discounted-Cash-Flow and Ratio Analysis	11
8	Risk Analysis and Risk Management: Single Projects	12
9	Financing and Refinancing Decisions	14
10	Tax Planning and Detailed Financial Analysis	13

Second Edition	Chapter Title	First Edition
PART 3	**ANALYZING REAL ESTATE MARKETS UNDER CHANGING CONDITIONS**	
11	Urban Analysis	4
12	Market Analysis	5
13	Marketability Analysis	6
14	Inflation, Deflation, and Real Estate Cycles	7
PART 4	**NEGOTIATIONS, MANAGEMENT, AND TERMINATION DECISIONS**	
15	The Art of Real Estate Negotiations	15
16	Property and Asset Management	16
17	Termination of the Investment	17
PART 5	**PORTFOLIO STRATEGY AND INVESTMENT OUTLOOK**	
18	Institutional Real Estate Portfolios	25
19	Developing a Personal Portfolio with Real Estate	26
20	The Real Estate Investment Outlook	27
PART 6	**PROPERTY SELECTION**	
21	Property Types and Selection	18
22	Apartments	19
23	Shopping Centers	20
24	Office Buildings	21
25	Industrial Buildings and Parks	22
26	Other Income-Producing Properties	23
27	Land Investments	24

May we ask that those who discover errors or have suggestions for making the next edition of the book more effective please contact us through our publisher: John Wiley & Sons, Inc., Real Estate Editor, 605 Third Avenue, New York, New York 10158.

December 1988

Austin, Texas	STEPHEN A. PYHRR
Atlanta, Georgia	JAMES R. COOPER
Tulsa, Oklahoma	LARRY E. WOFFORD
Tampa, Florida	STEVEN D. KAPPLIN
New York, New York	PAUL D. LAPIDES

ACKNOWLEDGMENTS

It would not be possible to recognize and thank separately all those individuals who have contributed to the development and preparation of this second edition and those whose work and suggestions benefited the first. Our indebtedness extends to a great number of colleagues in academia and business and to many former students.

We are, however, particularly indebted to the following colleagues and friends who offered insight, suggestions, and material throughout the evolution of this book. Their very substantial contributions are gratefully acknowledged: the late James A. Graaskamp, University of Wisconsin, Madison, Wisconsin; Charles H. Wurtzebach, The Prudential Realty Group; Kenneth M. Lusht, Pennsylvania State University; James P. Gaines, Rice Center, Houston, Texas; Ivan J. Miestechovich, Jr., University of New Orleans; Karl L. Guntermann, Arizona State University; George E. Moody, West Virginia University; J. Sa-Aadu, University of Iowa; Janet K. Tandy, Real Estate InfoSources, San Francisco; James T. Ross, Davis and Associates, Austin, Texas; Bonnie Bailey, B. Bailey and Associates, Atlanta, Georgia; Ivan Bloch, Bloch Realty Group Inc., New York; Allen Cymrot, Cymrot Realty Advisors, Inc.; Alan Parisse, Alan J. Parisse and Associates; Richard Silver, Shearson Lehman Hutton, New York; Paul Zlotoff, Uniprop Inc., Birmingham, Michigan; and William A. Bugg, Cushman and Wakefield, Atlanta, Georgia. The authors also gratefully acknowledge the efforts of Michael Mescon, James D. Vernor, and Timothy Sakhnovsky, Georgia State University; and Scott P. Cooper, Boeing Aerospace, Oklahoma City, Oklahoma.

The original authors, Stephen Pyhrr and James Cooper, thank the new coauthors, Larry Wofford, Steven Kapplin, and Paul Lapides, for joining the effort to complete this second edition. Although too many ingredients can spoil some brews, this text could not have been completed without all their good work. Special thanks are also due to Robert Allen, Arthur Young and Company, Boston, for his assistance with Chapter 10, "Tax

Planning and Detailed Financial Analysis"; to Waldo L. Born, Eastern Illinois University at Charleston, for his extensive work on Chapters 11 through 14, "Urban Analysis," "Market Analysis," "Marketability Analysis," and "Inflation, Deflation, and Real Estate Cycles"; to James R. Webb, University of Akron, who coauthored the revision of Chapter 17, "Termination of the Investment"; to George M. Hiller, George M. Hiller Wealth Management, Atlanta, Georgia, coauthor of Chapter 19, "Developing a Personal Portfolio with Real Estate"; and to Edwin J. Bomer, Davis and Associates, Austin, Texas, who provided the information for the comprehensive case study that appears throughout the text.

The authors, aware that this second edition would not have been possible without their editor, Judy Lummis, wish to express their special gratitude to her. We thank Eugene Simonoff for his instrumental role in bringing the first edition to fruition and for contributing greatly to the smooth transfer to our current publisher. We are also grateful for the significant editorial and production help from Priscilla Todd and Katharine Rubin, John Wiley, New York; and from Harvey Sussman, Northeastern Graphic Services, Inc., Englewood, New Jersey.

Lastly, the authors acknowledge the tremendous effect that their writing has upon their families. Stephen Pyhrr thanks his wife, Daphne, for her love, understanding, and support during the writing of this edition. James Cooper is grateful to his parents John and Isabella Cooper who were reunited in 1988. Larry Wofford is grateful for the support of his wife, Olivia, and of his parents, Charles and Wanda Wofford. Steve Kapplin wishes to extend appreciation to his wife, Andi, for her patience and support during the long hours. Paul Lapides thanks his son, John, who is ready, willing, and increasingly able to help.

Stephen A. Pyhrr
James Cooper
Larry E. Wofford
Steven D. Kapplin
Paul D. Lapides

CONTENTS

PART 1 REAL ESTATE INVESTMENT: THE STATE OF THE ART

1 THE NATURE AND SCOPE OF REAL ESTATE INVESTMENT   3

Defining Real Estate   Opportunities Created by the Real Estate Environment   Investor Motivations   Participants in the Investment Process   Framework for Real Estate Investment Studies   Summary

2 OVERVIEW OF THE INVESTMENT DECISION PROCESS   30

Investment Contrasted with Speculation   Investment Analysis, Feasibility Analysis, and Appraisal   Time Horizons for Investment Decisions: Life Cycles   Summary

3 DECISION-MAKING APPROACHES TO REAL ESTATE INVESTMENT   54

Popular "How-To" Approaches   Traditional Financial Decision Approaches   Modern Capital Budgeting Approaches   Summary

PART 2 SYSTEMATIC INVESTMENT ANALYSIS

4 INVESTMENT STRATEGY   85

Framework for an Investment Strategy   The Investment Analysis and Financial Structuring Process   Developing an Investment Strategy Summary   Appendix 4A. Selecting a Public Real Estate Partnership Aspen Wood Apartments

5 SELECTING THE OWNERSHIP ENTITY   125

Ownership Alternatives   Ownership Decision Model   Ownership
Selection Criteria   Noncorporate Forms of Ownership   Corporations and Trusts   A Matrix Approach to the Ownership Entity Decision   Summary   Aspen Wood Apartments

6 PRELIMINARY FINANCIAL FEASIBILITY ANALYSIS   170

Important Concepts, Principles, and Techniques   The Basic Financial
Feasibility Model   Application of the Basic Financial Feasibility
Model   Developing a Detailed One-Year Pro Forma
Summary   Aspen Wood Apartments

7 DISCOUNTED-CASH-FLOW AND RATIO ANALYSIS   210

Present Value and Internal Rate of Return   Discounted-Cash-Flow
After-Tax Analysis   Financial Ratio Analysis   Summary

**8 RISK ANALYSIS AND RISK MANAGEMENT:
    SINGLE PROJECTS**   247

Risk Analysis   Risk Management and Control   Summary
Aspen Wood Apartments

9 FINANCING AND REFINANCING DECISIONS   274

Financing Decision Model   Debt Financing Alternatives   Illustrations of Different Financing Techniques   The Refinancing Decision
Illustration of the Refinancing Decision   Equity Financing Alternatives   Syndication Offerings   Summary   Aspen Wood
Apartments

10 TAX PLANNING AND DETAILED FINANCIAL ANALYSIS   322

Tax Reform and Real Estate Investment   The Tax Law   Tax-Planning Alternatives and Issues   Tax Shelter Strategy   Summary
Aspen Wood Apartments

PART 3   ANALYZING REAL ESTATE MARKETS UNDER CHANGING CONDITIONS

11 URBAN ANALYSIS   373

Defining a Metropolitan Area   Urban Economic Analysis   Urban
Demographic Analysis   Patterns of Urban Growth   Summary

12 MARKET ANALYSIS   000

Elements of a Market Study   Real Estate Markets   Market Studies:
A Descriptive Analysis   Summary

13 MARKETABILITY ANALYSIS   425

Scope of Marketability Analysis   Guidelines for a Marketability
Analysis   Establishing the Boundaries   Immediate Market Area
(Neighborhood) Analysis   Site and Property Analysis   Field Sur-
vey of the Competition   Absorption and Capture Rates   Revenue
and Revenue-Related Expense Forecasts   Marketing Strategy and
Management Plan   Summary

14 INFLATION, DEFLATION, AND REAL ESTATE CYCLES   448

Framework for Analyzing Inflation and Cycles   Impact of Inflation
on Investors and Properties   Inflation Cycles and Investment
Strategy   Other Real Estate Cycles   Summary

**APPENDIX TO PART 3: SOURCES OF MARKET DATA FOR
REAL ESTATE INVESTORS   502**

PART 4   NEGOTIATIONS, MANAGEMENT, AND TERMINATION DECISIONS

15 THE ART OF REAL ESTATE NEGOTIATIONS   511

The Role of Negotiations   The Psychology of Negotiations
Achieving the Objectives of the Negotiating Parties   Ending the Nego-
tiations—Final Settlement and Closing   Summary   Checklist:
Guide to Real Estate Negotiations   Aspen Wood Apartments

16 PROPERTY AND ASSET MANAGEMENT   533

The Purpose of Property Management   The Management Function
The Need for Quality Property Management   Professional Property
Management versus Self-Management   Considerations for the Form
of Management   Selection of a Property Manager   Prepurchase
Consultations   Market Promotion and Leasing   Operation of the
Property   Administrative Responsibilities   Counseling and Com-
municating with the Investor   Asset and Venture Management
Summary   Aspen Wood Apartments

17 TERMINATION OF THE INVESTMENT   574

Disposal as Part of the Investment Cycle   Guidelines for Disposition
Strategy   Methods of Disposition   The Analytical Framework
Summary   Appendix 17A. Exchanges   Aspen Wood Apartments

PART 5   PORTFOLIO STRATEGY AND INVESTMENT OUTLOOK

18   INSTITUTIONAL REAL ESTATE PORTFOLIOS   625

Portfolio Choice   Real Estate Investing and Modern Portfolio
Theory   An Extended Development of Portfolio Theory   Impact
of Portfolio Theory on Large Institutional Investors   Summary

**19   DEVELOPING A PERSONAL PORTFOLIO WITH
REAL ESTATE**   661

The Purpose of Financial Planning   Collecting and Assessing Personal
and Financial Data   Identifying Financial and Personal Goals and
Objectives   Analysis of Financial Situation and Identification of Financial Problems   Implementing Strategies, Recommendations, and
Solutions   Periodic Review and Revision   Summary

20   THE REAL ESTATE INVESTMENT OUTLOOK   690

Global Attitudes   National Considerations   Strategic View of Real
Estate   Short-Term Overview   1988 Real Estate Investment Outlook   Considering the Longer Term   Conclusion

PART 6   PROPERTY SELECTION

21   PROPERTY TYPES AND SELECTION   733

Property Types   Property Selection   Summary

22   APARTMENTS   750

Track Record and Trends   Investing in Apartments   Preliminary
Analyses   Financing   Taxation   Discounted-Cash-Flow
Analysis   The Investment Decision   Selected References

23   SHOPPING CENTERS   767

Track Record and Trends   Investing in Shopping Centers   Preliminary Analyses   Financing and Refinancing   Taxation and Tax
Structure   Discounted-Cash-Flow Analysis   The Investment Decision   Selected References

24   OFFICE BUILDINGS   801

Track Record and Trends   Investing in Office Buildings   Preliminary Analyses   Financing   Taxation and Tax Structure   Discounted-Cash-Flow Analysis   The Investment Decision   Selected
References

25 INDUSTRIAL BUILDINGS AND PARKS 826

Track Record and Trends   Investing in Industrial Buildings and Parks
Preliminary Analyses   Financing   Taxation and Tax Structure
Discounted-Cash-Flow Analysis   The Investment Decision
Selected References

26 OTHER INCOME-PRODUCING PROPERTIES 855

Single-Family Homes, Condominiums, and Small Apartment Properties, 855
Track Record and Trends   Investing in Small Rental Properties
Preliminary Analyses   Financing Techniques   Taxation
Problems   Discounted-Cash-Flow Analysis   The Investment
Decision

Special-Use Properties, 869

Hotels and Motels, 871
Investing in Hotels and Motels   Preliminary Analyses   Financing
Taxation Problems   Discounted-Cash-Flow Analysis   The Invest-
ment Decision

Nursing Homes, 883
Investing in Nursing Homes   Preliminary Analyses
Taxation Problems   The Investment Decision   Selected References

27 LAND INVESTMENTS 900

Track Record and Trends   Investing in Land   Preliminary Analyses   Financing   Taxation and Tax Structure   Discounted-Cash-
Flow Analysis   The Investment Decision   Selected References

APPENDIXES

A The Time Value of Money: Problems for the Student   913

B Selected Compound Interest Tables   916

C Coefficients for Present Value of $1   940
Coefficients for Present Value of a $1 Annuity   941

D Mortgage Constant: Monthly Payment in Arrears   942

INDEX 945

REAL ESTATE INVESTMENT

The State of the Art

New York, New York.

The basic objective of this first part of the book is to develop an analytical framework for real estate equity investment decisions by individuals and institutions. The traditional methods of real estate investment analysis and the practical orientation of the majority of investors in the marketplace are discussed as well as the modern methodologies and techniques that are increasingly preferred by sophisticated investors and analysts.

The cornerstone of the analytical framework presented is rate of return and risk analysis, often referred to as *wealth maximization*. Investment decisions and the investment decision process are thus viewed as a return–risk trade-off process. However, the return–risk framework is not simply a financial and quantifiable phenomenon. Nonfinancial considerations are integrated into the framework, with explicit consideration given to market and location, legal, political, social, and physical factors affecting investment performance and investment decisions. Furthermore, it is argued that the decision maker can control to a substantial degree the returns and risks of a project through careful analysis and structuring of the financial and nonfinancial variables.

Chapter 1 examines the nature of real estate investment, its numerous advantages and disadvantages, and the various roles played by key participants in the investment process. Chapter 2 explains the strategy–analysis–decisions framework of this text and the importance of the life cycles that affect the return–risk relationship upon which the investor's decision is based. Chapter 3 compares and contrasts traditional "how to" approaches, traditional financial decision approaches, and modern capital-budgeting approaches to investment decisions. Together these chapters synthesize the current "state of the art" in real estate investment.

1

THE NATURE AND SCOPE OF REAL ESTATE INVESTMENT

A Neanderthal developer once rolled a rock to the entrance of his cave and created real estate, providing the natural void with some additional attribute not found in nature, such as warmth, security, or exclusiveness. He had successfully interfaced land (a finite natural resource) with an artifact (the rock—the first solid-core door) to serve an unmet need of a space consumer (a market). Eventually, his possession of the cave over many moons became institutionalized as artifacts for the delineation of space became more sophisticated with survey monuments, county records, and equity courts. Real estate is therefore a manufactured product of artificially delineated cubage with an institutional time dimension (square foot per year, room per night, cave per moon), designed to interface society with the natural resource land.[1]

JAMES A. GRAASKAMP

DEFINING REAL ESTATE

A real estate investment is often perceived as a physical product or entity. Since the dawn of history, we have been possessed with the need to own and control physical things, and many of us believe that land and the improvements made by human beings are the essence of real estate. To own or control a diversified portfolio of apartments, shopping centers, office buildings, and industrial or other real estate is the goal of many individual and institutional investors. This bricks-and-mortar concept is probably the most common approach to the definition of real estate.

As James Graaskamp has correctly pointed out, however, the essence of a real estate investment consists of the space or the void, not the solids. The walls, floors, and ceilings are worth very little; they are simply ways

[1]James A. Graaskamp, "A Rational Approach to Feasibility Analysis," *The Appraisal Journal* (Chicago: American Institute of Real Estate Appraisers), October 1972, p. 513.

of delineating cubage. In fact, brick and mortar are very clumsy standards for the delineation of space. For example, at the beginning of this century, high-rise office buildings were commonly built with five-foot-thick walls on the first floor and with load-bearing walls and columns extending throughout the building. As technology changed from brick to steel construction and as engineers discovered how to dispense with both bulky exterior materials and space-consuming interior walls and columns, buildings became more efficient and far more flexible. Developers have learned how to create more rentable square feet within the structure, how to reduce the bulk of the supporting structure and the weight of the building, how to simplify the foundation design, and how to erect buildings on sites that formerly could not be used because of troublesome soil types. In short, more artificially delineated space can now be created with less brick and mortar.

Real Estate as Space and Money over Time

The three-dimensional concept of real estate (i.e., as artificially delineated space) is basic to an understanding of its nature. The concept becomes far more relevant to the investor, however, with the introduction of a fourth dimension: time. Investors are most interested in renting space over time: an apartment unit per month, a motel room per night, or square feet of office space per year. Thus, real estate can be conceptualized as money flows over time.

Real estate investment analysis focuses on the conversion of space–time units into money–time units. Although engineers and architects may prefer to think of real estate in a space–time context, land economists and real estate investors prefer to consider money flows over time. Investors are concerned with the amount of money needed to acquire the asset and with the cash flows they may anticipate over some future time period. Indeed, investors have devised sophisticated computer models that utilize internal rate-of-return and present-value techniques to convert space–time concepts into money–time projections. The essence of real estate investment analysis, therefore, is learning the techniques by which we can develop reliable methods of converting space–time into money–time.

These space–time and money–time approaches reveal the perishable nature of real estate that should be considered at all times. That is to say, space–time cannot be stored; therefore, the managerial expertise to prevent or reduce vacancy is critical to any real estate enterprise.

Real Estate as a Dynamic Relationship

Success in converting real estate space into money flows over time depends on how well the investor operates within the real estate environment. This environment can be depicted as the dynamic relationship between the real

EXHIBIT 1-1.   Conceptual Model of the Real Estate Investment Environment

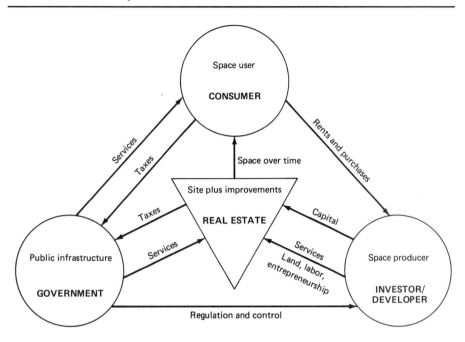

estate itself (site plus improvements) and three participant groups: (1) investors–developers, who provide real estate space over time; (2) consumers, who use or consume the space provided; and (3) government, which provides the public infrastructure within which all real estate transactions take place. This relationship is illustrated in Exhibit 1-1.

The goals of the three groups are seemingly incongruent (consumers want lower rents; investors want higher rents; the government wants to tax away as much of the rent as possible), yet they all have a vested interest in achieving a middle ground that provides for the financial solvency of all participants. The three parties must interact to find compromise solutions that permit them to operate successfully together over both the short and the long run. None of the three can require the others to make outlays that inevitably would lead to insolvency; the power to force insolvency on others is the power to destroy an enterprise. Although the war between private businesses is an integral aspect of free enterprise, it is not an acceptable relationship between public and private enterprises.[2]

[2]James A. Graaskamp, *Two-Day Workshop: Real Estate Feasibility Analysis for the Appraiser*, prepared at the request of the American Institute of Real Estate Appraisers, Seminar Committee, 1976, p. 3.

Real Estate as a Stewardship

We have been living in an era of tighter government controls on every front. The increased use by local governments of "police powers" to regulate private property is evidenced by the development of master plans regulating land use and of more rigorous zoning ordinances, building codes, and subdivision regulations.

At the state and federal levels, growing concern about how land use affects the living environment and the quality of life led to a barrage of legislation in the late 1960s and early 1970s, including the following federal acts as amended to date: National Environmental Policy Act of 1969, the Clean Air Act Amendment of 1970, the Federal Water Pollution Control Act of 1972, the Coastal Zone Management Act of 1972, and the Housing and Community Development Act of 1974. Most states also enacted land use legislation and delegated the task of implementation to regional and county governmental bodies. In recent years, greater emphasis has been placed on consolidation, modification, and, in some cases, retrenchment and simplification of the various existing land use programs at all levels of government.

Consumers have acted more on their own behalf as well as through the governmental bodies that represent them. The power of consumerism is evident in almost every real estate transaction today: in the case of real estate leases, the law has increased the enforceable rights of tenants and provides them with expedient legal remedies if the landlord fails to perform the duties required by the lease agreement; in the case of residential loan-closing statements, more effective advance disclosure of settlement costs to both buyers and sellers is required; and legislation on deceptive trade practices provides liberal legal remedies to consumers who feel that they have been deceived or cheated by real estate practitioners. Neighborhood groups have been organized in most metropolitan areas, and they are demanding their "sovereign" right to control land uses and to regulate development efforts that affect their neighborhoods.

As a result of these trends, ownership rights in land have been shifted from the private to the public sector. Fee simple ownership no longer commands the same complete bundle of rights possessed in the past by the owner of record. Private-sector businesses are being asked to assume broader social responsibilities than ever before and to serve a wider range of human values.[3] Whereas the primary function of business clearly remains in the making of profits, there is no question that profit maximization must be tempered by another objective: serving the current needs of society and providing for the needs of generations to come. Support is growing for the belief that a titleholder should act as a steward or a trustee

---

[3]James R. Cooper and Karl L. Guntermann, *Real Estate and Urban Land Analysis* (Lexington, Mass.: Lexington Books, 1974), p. xxi.

of the property for its future users. Today, the successful real estate investor should consider the words attributed to a Nigerian chieftain: "We have received this land from all those who have gone before and hold it for all those who are yet to come."

Real Estate as a Part of the Wealth Portfolio

Real estate can also be defined in terms of its relative importance in local, national, and world economies. For example, we can define real estate as a sector of the gross national product, as a component of the U.S. capital markets, or as an element of the world wealth portfolio.[4] Exhibit 1-2 shows these relationships.

Real estate, as a sector of the gross national product, exceeds 15% of the GNP, making it comparable to or larger than retail trade, wholesale trade, durable goods manufacturing, and other sectors that command the investor's attention (see Exhibit 1-2a). The real estate sector, defined here, includes construction, professional services and real estate finance accounts for designing, building, managing, brokering and financing residential, commercial and industrial properties that are built or traded for investment. Building materials and public facilities construction are excluded. While the industry definition may be debatable, one thing is quite clear: real estate is too large an industry and too broad in its scope to be ignored or considered an industry of secondary importance.

Real estate has a very important and growing role in the world economy, as shown in Exhibit 1-2b. Few investors realize real estate's dominant role in the global picture, and one that is becoming even more important as the world economy unifies. Nearly 60% of the world's capital market values are based on the real estate industry. The value of foreign real estate is twice that of the United States. Even with barriers to entry in many foreign real estate markets, the potential is tremendous for increased investment in properties worldwide.

Real estate's impressive scale in world capital markets is mirrored in the United States. Exhibit 1-2c shows that real estate is almost 50% of the total asset values that make up the U.S. capital markets, greater than the combined values of both bonds and equities. Mortgage debt represents 44% of this real estate market (Exhibit 1-2d). Active equity funds from REITs, public and private syndications, and pension funds represent less than 3% of this total, while "latent equity" represents almost 54%. The latent equity share, which exceeds over $2.5 trillion, is made up of real estate assets owned by corporations, other organizations, and individuals. While only

[4]Mahlon Apgar, IV, "A Strategic View of Real Estate," *Real Estate Issues*, Fall/Winter 1986, pp. 6–11; also Roger G. Ibbotson and Laurence B. Siegel, "The World Market Wealth Portfolio," *Journal of Portfolio Management*, Winter 1983, pp. 5–7.

EXHIBIT 1-2.   Real Estate as a Part of the Wealth Portfolio

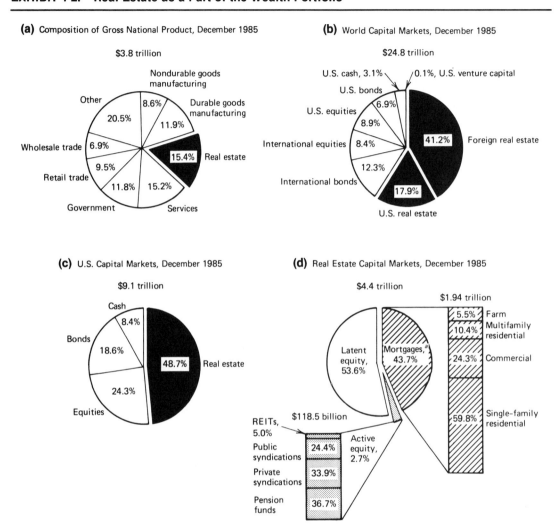

(a) Composition of Gross National Product, December 1985

$3.8 trillion

- Nondurable goods manufacturing 8.6%
- Durable goods manufacturing 11.9%
- Other 20.5%
- Real estate 15.4%
- Wholesale trade 6.9%
- Retail trade 9.5%
- Government 11.8%
- Services 15.2%

(b) World Capital Markets, December 1985

$24.8 trillion

- U.S. cash, 3.1%
- 0.1%, U.S. venture capital
- U.S. bonds 6.9%
- U.S. equities 8.9%
- International equities 8.4%
- Foreign real estate 41.2%
- International bonds 12.3%
- U.S. real estate 17.9%

(c) U.S. Capital Markets, December 1985

$9.1 trillion

- Cash 8.4%
- Bonds 18.6%
- Real estate 48.7%
- Equities 24.3%

(d) Real Estate Capital Markets, December 1985

$4.4 trillion

- Latent equity, 53.6%
- Mortgages,[a] 43.7%
- Active equity, 2.7%

$1.94 trillion

- Farm 5.5%
- Multifamily residential 10.4%
- Commercial 24.3%
- Single-family residential 59.8%

$118.5 billion

- REITs, 5.0%
- Public syndications 24.4%
- Private syndications 33.9%
- Pension funds 36.7%

Source: Mahlon Apgar—IV, "A Strategic View of Real Estate," *Real Estate Issues,* Fall–Winter 1986, pp. 7–8.
    [a]Excludes mortgage-related securities.

a fraction of these asset values can be traded in today's markets, compelling forces such as *securitization* of commercial property and *equitization* of corporate property assets are at work to unlock them and provide new investment opportunities for individual, group, and institutional investors.

OPPORTUNITIES CREATED BY THE REAL ESTATE ENVIRONMENT

The advantages and disadvantages of real estate as an investment stem from the nature of the asset and the markets in which it is bought and sold. The potential investor should first become acquainted with the many dimensions of the asset and of the marketplace.

One may argue that real estate is a relatively weak and feeble product. The sales of an average manufacturing firm exceed its total assets each year, but the average real estate property generates sales (rents) of only 10 to 20 percent of the total cost of the property. The cash inflows are so weak that it takes twenty-five to thirty years for the mortgage to be fully amortized.

One might also argue that real estate is a poor investment even in the long run. First, the investor buys a product in a fixed location; if people choose not to drive to that location next year, the investor is in trouble. Second, the product is built to last, so the investor is committed to an investment that has a physical life of fifty years, yet may become obsolete after only a few. In contrast, automobile manufacturers build and sell new cars each year in the hopes that the planned obsolescence will occur on schedule. Third, the real estate product purchased reflects the lifestyle and standards of the day; fifteen years down the road, the investor may find that the investment represents the wrong lifestyle.

At the same time, these inherent characteristics of real estate offer the entrepreneur numerous opportunities to generate extraordinary profits. By learning to analyze carefully and to assert some degree of control over the physical, legal, social, and financial aspects of real estate, the entrepreneur can then develop a strategy that will increase returns relative to risks. If the investor can identify the best locations in town, identify a product that can be adapted to changing lifestyles, leverage the investment with mortgage funds, structure a tax shelter package that generates tax savings, and manage the property professionally, that investor may very well be entitled to monopoly profits, or at least above-average returns.

The investor can also find many opportunities to take advantage of the imperfect market conditions that characterize real estate, including the following.

1. *Highly stratified local markets.* The stratification of markets gives an advantage to experts who can correctly assess demand within the submarkets of a city.
2. *Heterogeneous products.* Investors who can perform market analyses to determine the product needs of consumers in local submarkets can design "a better mousetrap."
3. *Poor information flows resulting from private transactions.* Developing a good data base through local contacts and research will provide a competitive advantage.

4. *Poorly educated and unknowledgeable investors and industry participants.* Highly ethical, well-educated, and trained professionals too often are a rarity in real estate. Such investors can quickly gain a competitive edge.

5. *An unorganized market with slow adjustments to supply and demand.* Historically, a market that adjusts slowly has caused relatively severe real estate cycles, with periods of overbuilding followed by periods of depression and underbuilding. Strategies can be developed for tracking these cycles more accurately and taking advantage of their upsides and downsides (see Chapter 14).

6. *A high degree of government control of the market.* Government controls reaffirm the need for more careful planning and for analysis of the political factors that may affect development and ownership. Consultants prosper as government regulation increases, because there is a greater need for effective feasibility and investment analyses.

Real estate is often described as the last bastion of entrepreneurship. The imperfections of the marketplace present small investors with opportunities that are not available in more organized, efficient marketplaces. Whereas the average size of firms is increasing and financial giants like Bank of America and Prudential-Bache are playing more significant roles, most of the firms concerned with real property development and ownership are small. Even in today's complex and highly regulated economy, there are still relatively few barriers to entry into real estate and almost anyone can become an entrepreneur in this field.

INVESTOR MOTIVATIONS

Investment incentives, motives, and returns are as diverse as the investors who acquire real estate. Some economists argue that individuals save a portion of their current income to provide for future consumption and thus face investment decisions regularly. Rarely, however, is the future-consumption argument stated by the real estate investors themselves. Instead, most cite the financial and nonfinancial advantages and disadvantages of real property investments. Furthermore, individual motivations differ significantly from corporate and institutional objectives.

Investment Advantages and Returns

The perceived advantages of certain real estate investments may vary over time and require periodic evaluation relative to changing attitudes and strategies. Some of the claims and myths will be discussed in later chapters, but the advantages and returns are generally considered to be combinations of the following.

Pride of Ownership. Real estate is a product that investors can feel and touch (the bricks-and-mortar concept). Real estate ownership is thus an emotional experience for many, and it is important for investors to recognize and deal with their attitudes toward such investments. Although pride of ownership is most often associated with single-family dwellings, it is also prevalent—sometimes overwhelming—within the environs of commercial properties. Some investors feel a need to own and control real estate for the sake of status or ego gratification, whereas others may visualize real estate as a measure of greatness, importance, or success. When taken to the extreme, the desire to create the most prestigious office building, corporate headquarters, or apartment complex, regardless of cost, has driven many an investor and developer into bankruptcy.

Personal Control. Real estate, unlike other investment assets such as stocks and bonds, affords the investor an opportunity to exercise personal and direct control over an asset. If the real estate is owned directly, the investor can control decisions regarding purchase terms and price, leverage, form of ownership, operations, refinancing, and disposal of the property. For many investors, the desire to exercise direct control over a property, without interference from partners or other investors, is a significant reason for participation in real estate.

Personal Use and Occupancy. Many investors acquire real estate for personal use. The purchase of a single-family dwelling or condominium unit is a form of investment that provides both physical shelter and tax shelter. In addition, the owner benefits from appreciation of property value and freedom from rent payments. An investor–occupant of a manufacturing plant benefits in a similar way, and medical doctors and dentists often prefer to own facilities designed to meet their particular needs.

Estate Building. Theodore Roosevelt argued that real estate was the surest and safest method of becoming independently wealthy. An investor can begin to build an estate by acquiring leveraged real estate, reinvesting the cash proceeds (which can be tax-sheltered), and building up equity over the long run through loan amortization and appreciation of property value. Periodically, properties can be refinanced and the funds reinvested tax-free into other properties, thereby repeating the process. Tax-free exchange techniques are used to pyramid small properties into larger ones, or to convert high-risk properties into low-risk properties that provide regular income during retirement. Real estate as a portfolio-building technique offers great flexibility for the investor.

Security of Capital. The safety of the principal is a primary concern to most investors. Mortgage investors attempt to secure their investments by recording liens against properties and requiring personal guarantees and pledged collateral. Compared to other investment forms, real estate generally is highly ranked in terms of security of capital: it tends to be permanent, indestructible, and relatively scarce; demand usually exceeds supply; and the price tends to be directly influenced by inflationary pressures.

High Operating Yield. Some experts have claimed that prime real estate would yield a before-tax return on total investment, including equity and debt, of 8 to 15 percent annually. Speculative real estate may show yields of 25 percent or more. Through leases, the investor is often able to obtain a reasonably certain return with a minimum of risk. Although such before-tax yields are attractive to pension funds, which are tax-exempt and generally prefer to buy debt-free properties, most investors prefer to evaluate properties on a leveraged basis and take tax shelter factors into consideration.

Leverage. One of the major attractions of real estate is the opportunities it offers to the investor to control a large asset with a small amount of equity capital. Whereas most large manufacturing operations boast conservative debt ratios (debt to total assets) of less than 50 to 60 percent, most real estate equity investors have debt ratios in the range of 70 to 80 percent. With a high degree of leverage, investors can use other people's money to parlay their equity yield to significantly higher levels. Leverage financing is thus a key factor in most real estate investments.

Tax Shelter Factors. The real estate investor often seeks to shelter from income taxation all cash flows earned by a property. In addition, the investor may try to generate tax losses that can be used to shelter other income. In addition, when the property is later sold, taxable gains on the (presumably) appreciated property value can be deferred through installment sales techniques or tax-free exchanges. In short, investors can utilize tax-planning techniques to maximize after-tax cash flows over the long run.

Capital Appreciation and Protection Against Inflation. In addition to other forms of return, the investor also desires to receive a return from increases in property value. Appreciation can be caused by one or both of two economic factors. First, it can occur as a result of an increase in demand relative to supply in a noninflationary economy. For example, a well-designed and professionally managed apartment property that is located in an improving neighborhood may substantially increase in value through the sheer pressure of demand. Second, price inflation may increase property prices dramatically. Historically, real estate has been a good inflation hedge, and diversified portfolios of real estate have generally outperformed stocks and other financial assets.[5] Without question, during the last decade the most significant portion of the investor's nominal return on leveraged real estate has come, on average, from the appreciation of property value due to inflationary pressure.

Investment Disadvantages and Risks

With so many advantages emanating from real estate investments, it seems logical for an investor to commit a large portion of his savings to them. After careful analysis, however, it becomes clear that many of the so-called advantages to real estate investment can become traps for the unwary. There are significant disadvantages, risks, and uncertainties associated with real estate investment (see also Exhibit 1-3).

Illiquidity and Time Constraints. Real estate is difficult to convert quickly into cash, and the presence of illiquidity in situations of financial stress can lead to investor insolvency, bankruptcy, and personal ruin. The product is not standardized or traded on an exchange, and the time required for an investor to analyze the purchase is relatively long. Even after a purchase decision has been reached, time is required for negotiation of the sale, title search, preparing the necessary legal docmentation, and arranging financing. Sometimes financing is not available or interest rates make the purchase uneconomical.

The Management Burden. Most real estate investments require a significant amount of personal attention. Whether a property is to be managed by a tenant on a net lease contract, by the investor, or through a management company, constant care must be given to the property to maintain its income and value. The property manager is responsible for achieving the investor's projected cash flow, upon which the investment decision was based. Many investors find property management an unpalatable aspect of real estate investment and one that can create severe mental and physical stress (see Chapter 16).

Depreciation of Value. Although inflation may be raising the monetary value of real estate properties, appraisers are quick to emphasize that the real value may actually be diminished as a result of physical, functional, or locational depreciation. Physical depreciation results from ordinary wear and tear as well as the actions of the elements; often it can be cured by an injection of dollars. Functional obsolescence may be curable (e.g.,

[5]For examples, see Robert H. Zerbst and Barbara R. Cambon, "Real Estate: Historical Returns and Risks," *Journal of Portfolio Management*, Spring 1984, pp. 5–20.

EXHIBIT 1-3.   Scenario of the Great Worldwide Real Estate Depression of 1974–1976

Descriptions and scenarios of the great real estate depression of 1974–1976 are convincing evidence of the disadvantages and risks associated with real estate investments. In 1974, as a result of escalation of interest rates and construction and operating costs without corresponding increases in rents and sales prices, real estate values fell below costs and mortgage balances.[6] Gibbons and Rushmore vividly illustrate the perverse 1974 situation, which continued through 1976 in most areas of the country.

> Monetary policy was used in a meat ax fashion, dismembering the economy so thoroughly that the nation now has a splendid chance to achieve depression conditions rivaling the best the 1930's could produce. In real estate development, which is a highly levered field, sensitive to interest changes, the escalation of borrowing rates wrought extraordinary havoc, producing so many bankruptcies and mortgage foreclosures that the industry ground to a halt. . . .
>   If one looks into the world of 1974, elicits interest rates being charged for various types of capital, and uses them to create overall capitalization rates, it will be apparent that application of such rates to property earnings will produce values far below costs to create the projects involved. So, feasibility died, and when it did, many incompleted realty projects failed financially and were abandoned. . . .
>   . . . existing properties came under pressure from escalations of operating expenses, which cut deeply into net bottom-line earnings. If an owner found himself in the unenviable position of having a building with such a severely reduced net income, yet was under some compulsion to dispose of his property immediately, there was no way he possibly could avoid taking a huge financial bath. In fact, throughout the year, if a prospective purchaser who planned to bring new capital into an existing income property venture employed an appraiser for valuation guidance, the resulting appraised value probably would fail to equal even the mortgage position of the seller's investment.[7]

The gloomy picture outlined above illustrates some of the downside risks and disadvantages of real estate investments. Contrary to the beliefs of many optimists, these downside situations tend to occur once or twice each decade.

---

[6]James E. Gibbons and Stephen Rushmore, "Using Total Project Analysis to Compete for Investment Capital," *The Appraisal Journal* (Chicago: American Institute of Real Estate Appraisers), October 1975, pp. 491–516. See also Nigel Enever, *The Valuation of Property Investments* (London: Estates Gazette. 1977); and Maurice T. Daly, *Sydney Boom, Sydney Bust* (Sydney: George Allen & Unwin, 1982).
[7]Ibid., pp. 492, 495 and 496.

the addition of air-conditioning to an office building) or incurable (e.g., extrawide corridors or other features that may be considered undesirable and are inherent to the structure of the building or cannot be modified). Owners of property located in economically declining areas can provide expert testimony on the adverse effects of location on value.

Government Controls. Rent controls, controls on foreign investment and ownership, land use and density-of-development controls, floodplain and water runoff controls, antipollution and other environmental controls, monetary and fiscal policy, and full-disclosure requirements impose constraints on the development and use of property. These sociopolitical decisions have the combined effect of limiting development, restricting acquisition, reducing cash flow, and arresting growth. In housing, government controls and regulations have added thousands of dollars to the cost of purchasing and owning a home.

Inflation, Deflation, and Real Estate Cycles. High rates of inflation made millionaires of many property owners in the late 1970s and early 1980s, and low rates of inflation and overbuilding bankrupted many in the middle 1980s. Since the values of existing properties tend to move with construction costs and the prices of new properties, investors who have enough carrying power to survive short-run down cycles will usually benefit over the long run in a growing economy when price inflation is occurring. This is of little consolation, however, to an owner of rent-controlled apartments in New York or Boston (or scores of other communities) when inflation raises operating costs by 9 percent a year and local authorities either refuse to or are slow to permit a pass-through of expenses to the tenants. Nor is inflation very helpful to the owner of a free-standing warehouse or retail facility leased for twenty-five years without escalation-in-rent provisions to offset rising expenses.

Legal Complexity. The contracts between owners, lenders, and promoters are complex and can make or break a transaction. Complexities also arise from the frequent and unpredictable changes in tax laws, which can adversely affect an investor who relies on tax benefits for a substantial portion of returns.

Lack of Information and Education. The information essential to good decisions is imprecise, difficult to find, and likely to be inaccurate.[8] Furthermore, investors often lack the interdisciplinary education required to

[8]Sherman J. Maisel and Stephen E. Roulac, *Real Estate Investment and Finance* (New York: McGraw–Hill, 1976), p. 6.

make sound investment decisions, and they must either expend considerable effort in time-consuming research or delegate responsibility to an expert.

Weighing Advantages and Disadvantages

Well-motivated investors can diligently assess the risks as well as the returns expected from a property investment. Successful investors consider many alternatives, then choose the best one and negotiate the best deal possible. This process requires a careful analysis of the inherent advantages and disadvantages of each investment, followed by a translation of these into a forecast of returns and risks. Successful investors make the necessary contingency plans to minimize the risks and to control the consequences of faulty judgment or imprecise forecasting.

PARTICIPANTS IN THE INVESTMENT PROCESS

Successful investing also requires an appreciation of the roles, motives, and personalities of the key participants in the real estate investment process and the relationships among them. A thorough investigation of the participants was performed by a federal government task force. Although the study focused on the housing process, the major participants and relationships are the same for any type of property, as can be seen in Exhibit 1-4. The participants are identified by their involvement in each of four phases of a project's investment cycle: (1) preparation or acquisition, (2) production or construction, (3) distribution or marketing, and (4) service or management. Most of the participants are risk-averse decision makers whose first concern is their own survival. It is rare for any one individual or firm to assume all the responsibilities and risks of an entire project. Instead, during the development and ownership periods, the responsibilities are spread among many individuals, each of whom exercises some degree of control over the project and seeks to achieve a return level that will compensate for the risks perceived.

Real Estate Investor Roles

An investor who packages, builds, or manages the property, in addition to investing equity capital, is classified as an active owner. On the other hand, an investor who invests equity capital only and otherwise does not take an active role, is classified as a passive investor. Within the active-investor category, three investor subtypes are identified.[9]

[9]Also see Stephen E. Roulac, "Understanding the Players," *Pensions and Investment Age*, June 8, 1981, pp. 40 and 45.

EXHIBIT 1-4. The Housing Process—Major Participants and Influences

Developer	Developer	Developer	Owner
Land Owner	Lending institutions (interim and permanent)	Real estate brokers	Maintenance firms and employees
Lawyers	FHA, VA, or private mortgage insurance company	Lawyers	Property mgt. firms
Real estate brokers	Contractors	Lending institutions	Insurance companies
Title companies	Subcontractors	Title companies	Utility companies
Architects and engineers	Craftsmen and their unions	FHA, VA or private mortgage insurance company	Tax assessors
Surveyor	Material manufacturers and distributors		Repairmen, craftsmen and their unions
Planners and Consultants	Building code officials		Lending institutions
Zoning and planning officials	Insurance companies		Architects and engineers
	Architects and engineers		Contractors
			Subcontractors
			Material manufrs. and distributors
			Local zoning officials
			Local bldg. officials

1 PREPARATION PHASE	2 PRODUCTION PHASE	3 DISTRIBUTION PHASE	4 SERVICE PHASE
A. Land Acquisitions B. Planning C. Zoning Amendments	A. Site Preparation B. Construction C. Financing	A. Sale (and subsequent resale or refinancing)	A. Maintenance and Management B. Repairs C. Improvements and additions

			Property taxes
			Income taxes
	Banking laws		Housing and health codes
	Building and mechanical codes		Insurance laws
Real estate law	Subdivision regulations		Utility regulations
Recording regulations and fees	Utility regulations	Recording regulations and fees	Banking laws
Banking laws	Union rules	Real estate law	Union rules
Zoning	Rules of trade and professional associations	Transfer taxes	Rules of trade and professional association
Subdivision regulations	Insurance laws	Banking laws	Zoning
Private deed restrictions	Laws controlling transportation of materials	Rules of professional association	Building and mechanical codes
Public Master plans			Laws controlling transportation of materials

Source: Report of the President's Committee on Urban Housing—A Decent Home (Washington, D.C.: U.S. Govt. Printing Office, 1968), p. 115.

1. *Builder–developer.* The primary objective of a builder–developer is to realize a profit from the sale of real property. The profit is measured as the difference between the sale price and the costs of creating the product.

2. *Packager–syndicator.* The primary objective of a packager–syndicator is to realize a profit from the sale to passive investors of equity interests in properties. This profit may be a share of investment returns and/or real estate commissions and packaging fees.

3. *Property manager.* The primary objective of a property manager is to realize a profit from managing real estate during the rental period. In the case of subdivision or condominium sales, the property manager may not play a significant role.

Key Decision Makers

Another method of analyzing investor roles is by examining the activities of decision makers who are responsible for the creation and ownership of the asset. Under this scheme, the importance of a packager–syndicator is diminished, for this type of investor is seen as an intermediary between the buyers and the sellers who make the decisions. In a similar way, a property manager is responsible for a property after acquisition but is not responsible for the decision to buy, sell, or develop. Although both parties may be influential in the development and investment decision—and, indeed, their roles are often critical—they are not the key decision makers.

There are six key decision makers: (1) the developer, (2) the joint-venture partner, (3) the construction lender, (4) the permanent lender, (5) the managing equity investor, and (6) the passive equity investor. One common goal links all these decision makers: each is attempting to maximize returns relative to associated risks. Although the primary focus of this book is on the managing equity investor and the passive equity investor, we will examine briefly the role played by each of the six (see Exhibit 1-5).

Developer. A developer wants the maximum possible return with the minimum financial and time commitments. The return generally consists of (1) development fees, (2) profits on the sale to equity investors, and (3) tax write-offs and possible operating cash flows prior to the takeover of the property by equity investors. Developers may, and frequently do, take a long-term equity position in the property. To the extent that they do so, their goals are the same as those of equity investors.

The developer often is not involved in the actual construction process. Hence, the concept of builder should be distinguished from that of developer. Many successful nationwide developers of commercial properties, such as the Dallas-based Trammell Crow, argue against an extensive role by the developer in the building and contracting processes. They believe

EXHIBIT 1-5.   Key Decision Makers

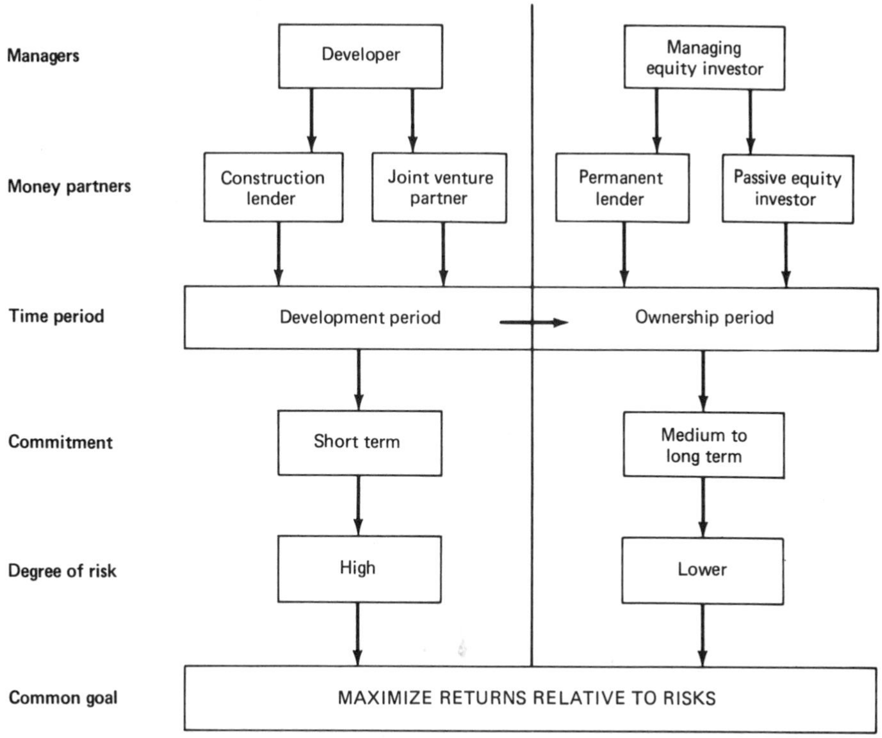

	Development period side		Ownership period side	
Managers	Developer		Managing equity investor	
Money partners	Construction lender	Joint venture partner	Permanent lender	Passive equity investor
Time period	Development period →		Ownership period	
Commitment	Short term		Medium to long term	
Degree of risk	High		Lower	
Common goal	MAXIMIZE RETURNS RELATIVE TO RISKS			

that developers should create new properties, minimize the size of their staff, and maintain maximum flexibility.

Developers typically have a short time horizon and wish to minimize the duration of their involvement. Because they sell time, in contrast to the passive equity investor who "sells money," developers are anxious to push fledgling projects out of the nest and move on to new projects. Few of these entrepreneurs have a long-run interest in selecting tenants, supplying management and maintenance, and meeting mortgage payments, unless they extend their roles.

The developer's financial exposure comes in two distinct ways. First, the developer must expend time and money before being assured that the project will be built; the developer naturally seeks to minimize such expenditures. Second, the developer may miscalculate the total cost of completing the project and perhaps also the value of the project once it has been completed. In many situations the developer will guarantee certain project occupancy and rental levels and will be penalized by the lenders and equity investors if these levels are not achieved.

Joint-Venture Partner. A joint-venture partner is an equity investor who provides a developer with equity funding during the development period in return for a share in the profits. The joint-venture partner attempts to achieve the maximum portion of the development period returns based on the minimum possible financial commitment. The partner's return is based primarily on the difference between project value and project cost, and on the amount and terms of the debt financing. The partner's equity generally serves to bridge a portion of the gap between project costs and available debt financing. Because most projects require substantial amounts of equity dollars to cover total project costs, the typical developer requires such an addition to the available interim financing.

The risk to the joint-venture partner depends on the extent of the equity investment if no personal liability is assumed for debts. In cases in which the joint-venture partner has personal liability on interim debt, the risk is much greater and relates to the amount of debt created as well as to the equity investment. Should the developer fail to perform properly, the joint-venture partner may bear the entire loss as well as the difficult managerial task of completing the project abandoned by the developer.

Construction Lender. A construction lender provides short-term funds and is concerned with (1) the total cost of completing the development according to plans and specifications, and (2) the commitment of a permanent lender to take over ("take out") the loan at the end of the construction period. Construction delays and cost overruns can easily push costs well above the developer's intended budget. The construction lender's risk is that these costs—or the portion financed by the lender—may exceed the amount of the permanent loan. When this occurs, the interim lender must look to the developer or utilize equity interests to cover the difference. If not, the construction lender must decide whether to foreclose or convert the construction loan into a long-term loan or equity interest as a solution to insolvency. The construction lender must weigh the risks of such undesirable consequences against the interest return (including origination fees and compensating balances) that might be earned by making the loan.

Permanent Lender. A permanent lender, like a construction lender, is concerned with maintaining the safety of the loan and achieving the maximum possible return. But although the construction lender has a short-term interest in the property and often a takeout guarantee from the permanent lender, the permanent lender is prepared to fund a long-term interest with no takeout source. Therefore, he is concerned with the long-term value of the project once it has been completed and is operational, and with the relationship of this value to the loan.

Permanent lenders, as well as construction lenders, usually are intermediaries acting as the fiduciaries of savers. As such, they are expected to comply with rigorous underwriting standards that are more conservative than the standards most equity investors or developers would apply to their own positions. Indeed, society depends on the lender to control the optimism of the developer and the equity investor.

In past years, the underwriting record of lenders has been erratic. When money was available, they often lent it without serious regard for a project's feasibility. Consequently, many office buildings, combination use buildings, apartment complexes, hotels, and industrial parks have been built throughout the nation without regard for the supply–demand trends that determine project feasibility. In the interest of ensuring a competitive return, the lender should be expected to assume—with the developer and equity investors—a portion of the responsibility for seeing that the project is successfully completed; after all, no commercial real estate project is complete or successful until it produces rental income sufficient to amortize the investment and provide a return to the lenders and equity investors.

Managing Equity Investor. A managing equity investor is responsible not only for *venture (asset) management*—that is, structuring the investment package for the purchase of an existing or new property and managing the asset over the ownership period—but also for *property management*, for hiring, firing, and overseeing the property management personnel. In the case of a new property, a managing equity investor often engages the services of a developer to build and deliver a completed project. This often is referred to as a turnkey job. Although the project can be bought during the planning or construction phase, funding generally will not take place until the project is complete and operating. Thus equity investors, like permanent lenders, will provide a takeout (purchase) commitment for the equity portion of a project. An equity investor who wishes to become a funding partner during the development period becomes, by definition, a joint-venture partner.

Managing and passive equity investors by definition do not take development period risks, nor do they participate in development period returns. Their primary sources of returns are cash flow from operations, tax savings, equity buildup through loan amortization, and property appreciation. The managing equity investor who is a syndicator–packager as well will also seek commissions and fees (or a proportionate amount of other benefits) as compensation for the amount of time spent analyzing and packaging an investment for sale to passive equity investors. A syndicator often becomes a managing equity investor by taking an equity interest in the property in return for the services performed. In any case, the managing equity investor should have substantial equity capital at risk.

The key distinction between managing and passive equity investors is the burden of management responsibility for the property and for the venture during the ownership period. Even if the day-to-day responsibilities of accounting, marketing, conserving, and enhancing the value of the property are delegated to professional property managers, the overall burden of property and venture management falls upon the managing equity investor, who must indeed continuously manage the property manager as well as the affairs of the venture that owns the property.

Both society in general and the mortgage lender in particular look to the managing equity investor for fulfillment of the responsibilities of ownership. Indeed, many individual and institutional investors prefer taking the active role of the managing equity investor, believing that they can significantly enhance the performance of the project and of their own returns by not delegating these responsibilities to others. On the other hand, many institutions, business organizations, and individuals prefer to avoid such risks and responsibilities.

In recent years the term "asset manager" has evolved and is used to describe an experienced professional who is responsible for performing the duties of a managing equity investor. An asset manager may be the de facto managing equity investor, or an independent contractor or employee who is hired to perform these duties on a fee basis. In this book the terms asset manager and venture manager are used interchangeably, and are discussed in Chapter 16.

Passive Equity Investor. A passive equity investor invests equity capital only and does not take an active role in packaging, building, or managing the property. Like that of the securities investor, the passive equity investor's investment decision consists primarily of whether or not to buy and, if so, how much. Like the managing equity investor, the passive equity investor makes a medium- to long-term commitment to a property. The primary sources of returns to such an investor are (1) cash flow from operations, (2) tax savings, (3) equity buildup through loan amortization, and (4) property appreciation. Since the risks of this form of investment are usually lower than those of other forms, the passive equity investor is usually satisfied with less return than the managing equity investor would be willing to accept.

Passive equity investors obviously need managing equity investors to provide them with structured investment alternatives. They may use legal contrivances to create a passive role and shift management responsibilities to others. They can become stockholders of a corporation, shareholders of beneficial interest in a real estate investment trust (REIT), limited partners in a partnership, and so on. Many institutional investors, such as pension funds, foundations, and churches, must act as passive investors in order to obtain advantageous tax treatment and maintain their status as special legal entities.

The Interrelationship of Decision-Making Roles

The concepts of developer, construction lender, permanent lender, joint-venture partner, managing equity investor, and passive equity investor presented here are simplified for academic purposes; in reality, these roles are complex and interrelated. The definitions are not perfect, and the separation of activities is not always clear-cut. Actors change roles and often play more than one role at a time. A developer, for example, may sell out only a fractional interest to equity investors, giving up all supervisory power and control but retaining the equity interest of a passive investor after the project has been completed. A construction lender may choose to take on the role of a joint-venture partner in the development phase, funding the construction loan and reverting to the role of long-term lender upon completion of the project. An owner of land may decide not to cash out by selling the land to a developer. Instead, the owner may seek either to exchange controlling interest for that of a joint-venture partner or to become a passive or managing equity investor and thereby avoid development risks. A wealthy individual seeking complete control over a project may choose to assume all the key decision making roles from developer through passive equity investor. The combinations are limitless.

As previously stated, this book focuses on the roles of managing and passive equity investors. The real estate investment world is seen primarily through their eyes, although these actors often switch hats and must understand the roles of all the others who influence their own decisions and investment activities.

Structural Changes in the Marketplace

The roles and interrelationships of the various participants in the real estate business may vary in the face of changes in the rules of the marketplace. For example, recent changes in regulations, tax laws, and economic unit aggregations led to a restructuring of these relationships. Financial deregulation, which began in 1975 and continued through the late 1980s, has had perhaps the most obvious impact.

Institutionalization and Vertical Integration. Financial deregulation has increased the competition for deposits among financial institutions, such as savings and loan associations and commercial banks. It has also led to the creation of a new financial market composed of organizations offering integrated services in all areas of finance and investment. The epitome of such organizations is the Sears Financial Network, which offers services ranging from insurance to banking and stock brokerage to real estate brokerage and financing. Merrill-Lynch offers a complete line of financial and investment services, as does Prudential-Bache. These organizations compete directly with traditional banks and savings associations as well as with small real estate developers, investors, and brokers.

Financial deregulation has also led to a vertical integration in the real estate market, where single organizations have the capability to handle every aspect of real estate from speculative land banking to financing, packaging, and selling.

The increased impact of institutional investors certainly will affect the ability of the small investor to compete as the institutions bring out more alternatives for attracting investor funds to large real estate ventures. The small developer will also find that the financial institutions can be more effective at influencing and controlling development. This is evidenced today by greater demands from the financial institutions for participation in new development. It even seems possible that one day the developer will no longer be the dominant character in real estate production, but instead will be a partner or employee of a large institutional investor.

There is little question that the impact of large institutions on the structure of the real estate market has become significant. These changes will continue into the future and will have to be taken into account by investors as real estate moves forward into the 1990s.

Securitization and Globalization. Direct investment in real estate is not a realistic alternative for many of the new players in the real estate investment game. This is particularly true for many institutional investors, such as pension plans, that have a need for flexibility and liquidity. Investing in real estate securities or a portfolio of these securities—as opposed to investing in the properties themselves or a commingled pool of properties—provides these investors with a significant advantage not previously available.[10]

Real estate securities can be defined as stocks and bonds issued by companies engaged in the ownership of income property. The most common real estate securities are the shares of real estate investment trusts (REITs) which have experienced a renewal of interest in the 1980's on the part of both Wall Street and investors. The REIT market now exceeds $10 billion in market value and has been joined by numerous other forms of real estate securities such as Master Limited Partnerships (MLPs), real estate mortgage investment conduits (REMICs), and other bonds collateralized by real property. A new generation of hybrid investment vehicles has been spawned in recent years, such as real estate mutual funds that combine securitization with daily portfolio supervision.

The securitization of real estate capital has been one of the major forces in the growth of the availability and importance of "global" real estate capital sources (foreign investment). Whether a property is an office building in London or a hotel in Los Angeles, it is now possible that the buyer will be from one country, the seller from another, and the lender from a third.[11] Salomon Brothers, a major Wall Street investment banking firm,

    [10]Martin Cohen, "Real Estate Securities Offer an Alternative to 'Sticks and Bricks,'" *Pension World*, February 1987, pp. 32, 34.
    [11]REF Symposium, "The 'Globalization' of Real Estate Finance," *Real Estate Finance*, Summer 1987, pp. 37–50; also Anthony Downs, "Foreign Capital 'Invades' U.S. Real Estate Markets," *National Real Estate Investor*, February 1987, p. 38.

estimates that total foreign investment in U.S. developed real estate is about $24 billion, or just over 1% of the total value of all developed property in the market.

Foreign investors who have been active in the United States and who are increasing their commitments include British, West German, and Dutch institutional funds; Canadian developers; and flight capital investors who go through the Netherlands Antilles and other tax-haven countries.[12] The country which has dramatically increased its involvement in American real estate since 1985 is Japan. Japanese investments have typically focused on first class office buildings in the central business districts of major U.S. cities such as Los Angeles, San Francisco, New York, and Chicago. Foreign investors are attracted to the United States because of its political stability along with the relatively high yields that have historically been realized on U.S. real estate investments. Increasingly, investors in this country will find opportunities for growth of their portfolios through partnerships with foreign investors who seek to invest capital in higher yielding U.S. properties but who need a managing equity investor to perform all the venture and property management functions necessary for successful performance.

FRAMEWORK FOR REAL ESTATE INVESTMENT STUDIES

In the preceding discussion we outlined the complex processes that make up the world of real estate investing and we described the many players of the real estate game. No single book can possibly do justice to the full scope of activities involved in real estate investing. It is our goal, however, to provide a rational framework for analyzing real estate investments.

The analysis of real estate investments requires diverse, interrelated activities such as market analysis, financial analysis, capital structure decisions, and tax strategies. The tools, techniques, theories, and concepts presented here relate to a fundamental analysis of the real estate investment within the context of a formal framework or methodology of analysis. With these, we believe we have established a framework that enables the investor to evaluate logically the returns and risks of real estate investment and thereby make sound investment decisions.

Although the focus of this text is the viewpoint of the individual equity investor, the methodology and material presented in the ensuing chapters are as applicable to the small investor purchasing a single-family rental house as they are to the sophisticated money manager making decisions for a large pension fund or public syndicate.

---

[12]*Emerging Trends in Real Estate,* prepared by Real Estate Research Corporation for The Equitable Real Estate Group Inc., 1986, 1987, 1988.

Elements of the Investment Framework

The four key elements that make up our framework for the study of real estate investment are *strategy, analysis, decisions,* and *investment transactions,* as shown in Exhibit 1-6. Continuous feedback of information is another underlying factor throughout the investment process. Because we believe that a systematic approach should be developed for analyzing real estate investment problems and arriving at sound decisions, this text focuses primarily on the strategies, analyses, and decisions necessary to solve investment problems and only secondarily on the transaction itself.

As a practical matter, a joint-venture partner or managing equity investor must have considerable expertise in the mechanics of real estate transactions, but a passive equity investor can get by with only a general familiarity with those mechanics. There are lawyers to guide the investor through the legal maze, mortgage bankers to act as experts in financial details, and tax accountants to help structure the best possible tax shelter package. More critical is the need for trained counselors, advisers, and investors who can devise sound investment strategies, perform better investment and feasibility analyses, and render more profitable investment decisions. Thus, the critical need is for more professionally trained generalists who can manage the entire investment process rather than for specialists who are expert in only one phase of that process.

Strategy. In making real estate investment decisions, the investor begins by establishing an investment strategy—*defining acceptable return and risk parameters* for a property. The investor's strategy should consist of four elements. First, the investor develops an *overall investment philosophy,* a set of general principles that can be used as guidelines in making investment decisions. Second, the investor defines *objectives* and establishes *decision criteria* that will determine when objectives have been achieved. Next, the investor develops *plans and policies* to maximize the probability of success with the least amount of time commitment. Finally, the investor determines a *strategy of analysis,* a plan that outlines how he or she will analyze properties and arrive at an investment decision. (In Chapter 4, these four elements of strategy are discussed in greater detail.)

Analysis. The analysis of a property is fundamentally a task of *measuring the return and risk parameters* that form the basis of the investor's strategy (see Chapters 6 through 10). In measuring returns and risks, the investor goes through various stages that become more sophisticated as the analysis progresses and more data are collected. Although the investor may begin with relatively simple, nonfinancial tests involving location and "curb appeal" criteria, the final analysis may consist of internal rate of return, present value, financial ratio, and risk calculations and evaluation. At each

EXHIBIT 1-6.   A Framework for the Study of Real Estate Investment

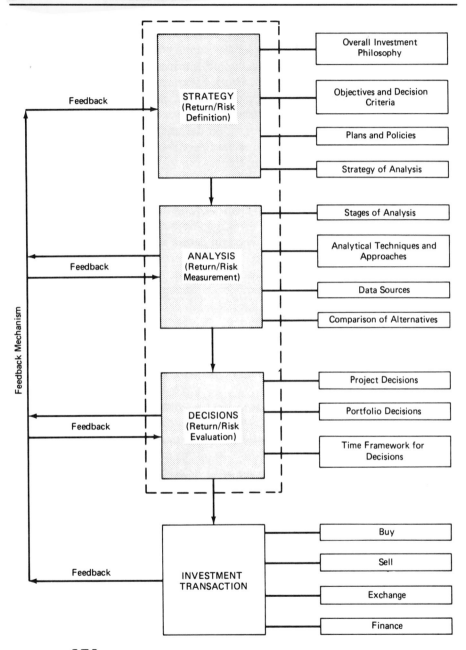

Attention is focused on these elements

stage of the analysis, alternatives are compared and evaluated with respect to the investor's objectives.

Decisions. Investment decisions require a *return and risk evaluation* of all the alternatives relative to the investor's strategy. In making decisions over a time horizon that includes both short- and long-run considerations, the investor must survive the short run in order to succeed in the long run. Although the majority of decisions may be go/no-go project choices, the investor may also be focusing on maximizing the value of an overall portfolio. For life insurance companies, pension funds, and other institutional investors that actively acquire and sell projects throughout the country, portfolio decisions are becoming increasingly important. (These subjects are addressed in Chapters 18 and 19.)

Investment Transaction. Often an investor decides to do nothing or to reject a project under consideration; in either case, no investment transaction results. In other situations an investment transaction will ensue and the investor will negotiate to buy, sell, exchange, or finance a property. Contracts and deeds will be drawn, closing arrangements made, and property management details arranged.

Feedback. Throughout the investment process, new information is being acquired constantly and may affect the investor's strategy, analysis, and decisions. The investor, operating in a dynamic, cyclical environment, must constantly revise and update data and the decision-making system itself in order to outperform competitors. After all, the object of this rigorous study is to develop better decision-making skills. Better investment decisions are the surest way to achieve higher investment returns while managing investment risks.

SUMMARY

Real estate can be defined in terms of artificially delineated space, a physical product or entity, or a series of money flows over time. Real estate investment analysis focuses on techniques for converting physical space into projections of money flows over future periods and on the evaluation of those money flows relative to investor objectives. For the investor, success largely depends on the ability to operate effectively in a complex environment.

Some people feel that real estate is too durable, becomes obsolete too quickly, and has too long a payback period relative to the total capital invested. However, the investor who makes good use of leverage and tax shelter provisions, chooses the "best" locations in town, and manages the assets professionally can consistently outperform the competition. The relatively inefficient real estate marketplace is often described as the last bastion of entrepreneurship.

Real estate investments have both advantages and disadvantages for the investor. The advantages include pride of ownership, personal control, self-use and occupancy, estate building, security of capital, high operating yield, leverage, tax shelter factors, capital appreciation, and protection against inflation. Often overlooked, however, are the inherent disadvantages and risks: illiquidity, the burden of management, depreciation of value, government control, real estate cycles, legal complexity, and lack of information and education. These must be carefully assessed and minimized whenever possible.

Investors can alter the nature of investment returns and risks by changing the nature of their involvement in a project. For developers and joint-venture partners, the returns and risks tend to be high. For lenders, whose interest returns are fixed by contract, the risks are significantly reduced. In contrast, an equity investor assumes ownership risks and is responsible for meeting debt service payments and operating expenses, but does not assume development and building risks. Thus, the investor's specific role tends to define the nature of the returns and risks as well as the investor's management responsibilities. The key roles analyzed throughout this book are those of the managing equity investor and the passive equity investor.

The formal analysis of real estate should proceed in a logical, rational fashion. Successful investing involves the development of an investment strategy. The investment should be analyzed using modern tools and techniques that provide investors with the necessary information with which to make sound decisions. Investments should then be monitored to provide feedback to the investor, allowing for the correction of mistakes and the improvement of future performance.

The next chapter will provide an overview of the investment decision process and will discuss time horizons for investment decisions.

2

OVERVIEW OF THE INVESTMENT DECISION PROCESS

Almost all real estate problems involve an investment decision—
whether to buy and what to buy, whether to sell and at what price,
whether to modernize or replace, whether to lend and how much to
lend under what terms. . . . This transaction is the generating force in
urban growth and change; it is the determinant of land use and thus
builds our cities.[1]

RICHARD RATCLIFF

Real estate investment is a complex and dynamic enterprise that requires
careful study and analysis in order to ensure financial success. In essence,
the investor is buying a new business with each property purchase, and
each investment has a distinct set of physical, market, legal, and financial
characteristics. The investor who has a good understanding of this complex set of attributes, and how they translate into investment returns and
risks, is far more likely to make successful investment decisions. Moreover, the investor who effectively manages the investment process has a
greater chance of success.

This chapter develops the concept of investment analysis as a tool for
the decision process, in contrast with feasibility analysis. In reality, investment analysis is a subset of feasibility analysis, but for the sake of clarity in
this text, we separate the two and emphasize the former. Investment analysis, as we define it, deals with the return–risk relationships associated
with *existing* projects. Feasibility analysis generally considers the return–

---

[1]Richard N. Ratcliff, *Real Estate Analysis* (New York: McGraw-Hill, 1961), p. v.

risk relationships in the *development and construction of new* projects. Both entail far more than the financial analysis of a project, generally involving market, marketability legal, and physical analyses. This chapter also examines the different life cycles—investor, property, and ownership—that affect investment performance, perceptions, and decisions.

INVESTMENT CONTRASTED WITH SPECULATION

The term speculation has historically conjured images of shady enterprises and possible evil doings, yet it has become increasingly difficult to define the elements that make up a speculative venture. Real estate strategies for maximizing an investor's returns relative to risks are significantly different for different types of equity investors. In the United States, the rules for responsible financial behavior derive from the Puritan ethic embodied in Ben Franklin's *Poor Richard's Almanac:* Work hard; be thrifty; don't borrow. This innate moral code has led the average American to draw a distinction between speculation (considered bad) and investment (considered good.)[2] One aspect of Poor Richard's theory of investment is that it be purchased and held for a substantial period. Buying and holding has been considered ethically superior and more financially rewarding than in-and-out speculative trading.

Webster's dictionary defines speculation as an act of "engaging in business out of the ordinary, dealing with a view to making a profit from conjectural fluctuations in the price rather than from earnings of the ordinary profit or trade, or by entering into a business venture involving unusual risks for a chance at an unusually large gain or profit."[3]

Speculative real estate, therefore, might be regarded as property purchased for the sole purpose of realizing a profit upon resale. Generally, no additional capital is invested in the property following the acquisition, and any income produced during the holding period is incidental to the measurement of profits. For example, agricultural land normally remains under cultivation after acquisition by a speculator. However, property taxes, interest, and other carrying charges usually offset any revenue generated from the operation of the farm during the interim period.[4] In contrast to speculative real estate, investment real estate may be defined as a property that produces, or is capable of producing, periodic revenue from its operation and ownership as part of the total return.

[2]Roger Klein and William Wolman, *The Beat Inflation Strategy* (New York: Simon & Schuster, 1975), p. 46.

[3]*Webster's Third New International Dictionary* (Springfield, Mass.: G. & C. Merriam Co., 1981).

[4]Lincoln W. North, *Real Estate Investment Analysis and Valuation* (Winnipeg, Man., Canada: Saults & Pollard, 1976), p. 3.

In view of the economic changes of past decades, however, the traditional distinction between speculation and investment has become blurred. Inflation and competition in today's economy have eroded the amount of current income that can be derived from a property. Investors must rely on future price appreciation for much of their return. Therefore, in order to achieve high returns and to control downside risks throughout the real estate cycle, investors must be willing to make changes in the asset mix of their portfolio over time. In addition, they should devise investment strategies that foster more accurate prediction of changes in property value, because this component of return and risk is often the most significant.

The current market environment and investor motivation call for a reevaluation of the concepts of investment and speculation, with the realization that price fluctuations—variables historically linked to speculation—may now be considered integral aspects of wise investment and investment analysis. Perhaps a better approach to determining whether a person is speculating or investing would be to consider the nature and the degree of the analysis performed. In this realm, it can be argued that an investor who evaluates a project in which the returns are not estimated, and who makes purchase decisions on the basis of hunch, instinct, or intuition, is partaking in a speculative venture. On the other hand, an investor who explicitly attempts to measure the return and risk parameters of a project and who bases the purchase decision on this analysis is performing an act of investment, even if the expected returns and risks are high. It is with this broader concept of investment that the remainder of the text is concerned.

INVESTMENT ANALYSIS, FEASIBILITY ANALYSIS, AND APPRAISAL

Investment and Investment Analysis

The act of investing involves the commitment of money (a capital outlay) for the purpose of earning future income or a profit on that outlay. *Investment analysis* is the systematic evaluation of capital outlays in relation to the expected income stream for the purpose of rendering an investment decision. An overview of the investment analysis concept for income property is shown in Exhibit 2-1.

Capital Assets. Real estate investment analysis begins with the study of the proposed real-property acquisition—that is, the *capital asset*. A capital asset can encompass various degrees of ownership and control of land and improvements. It can be a tangible asset, such as a rental house, a shopping center, or an industrial building, or it can be a financial or paper asset, such as a leasehold interest or mortgage note.

EXHIBIT 2-1. **Overview of the Investment Analysis Concept**

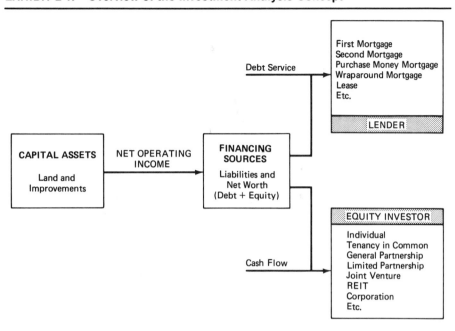

Equity. Capital assets are purchased by an *equity investor*, a buyer who invests through a variety of legal entities: individual, joint-venture partner, limited partner, corporation, REIT, pension fund, and so forth. The dollars that the equity investor spends to acquire the capital asset may be referred to as the *equity investment*, *equity*, *net worth*, *owner's cash investment*, or, simply, *total down payment*. Most of these terms are used interchangeably.

Debt. The term *debt* has numerous synonyms, including *liabilities, leverage, loans,* and *other people's money.* The debt alternatives available to investors are equally numerous, including first mortgages, second mortgages, purchase money mortgages, wraparound mortgages, and leases. Often the debt financing takes on the characteristics of both debt and equity, thus becoming hybrid. Such hybrid arrangements were particularly popular in the early 1970s and again in the early 1980s, when many large investment property transactions carried mortgages with kickers or equity participations.[5] These enabled lenders to take a "piece of the deal," that is,

---

[5] The right of a lender to share a gross profit, net profit, or cash flow from a property on which the lender has made a loan; an additional payment or amount that may be paid to a lender over and above periodic fixed interest or fixed rent. (Source: Alvin L. Arnold and Jack Kusnet, *The Arnold Encyclopedia of Real Estate* (Boston: Warren, Gorham & Lamont, 1978), pp. 226, 444.

to obtain a cash flow return in excess of the contract interest rate specified in the mortgage note.

Net Operating Income. A primary objective of owning or controlling a capital asset is the production of a stream of revenue or income. Both the lender and the equity investor depend largely on the *net operating income* (NOI) stream for that source of revenue—except in the case of such nonincome property as land, for which the appreciation of asset values is the primary income source. The NOI is divided, by contractual arrangement, between lenders and equity investors after all operating expenses have been paid. The portion of the NOI received by the lender is called *debt service;* the residual, if any, is received by the equity investor and is called *cash flow.* Some often-used aliases for the term *cash flow* are *cash throw-off, equity dividend, net income after debt service, cash flow before tax,* and *cash flow from operations.*

Both lenders and equity investors consider the NOI stream from the property to be the basis for their involvement. Their interests, however, seem to conflict because increasing the returns to one requires decreasing the returns to the other. An increase in debt service requires a dollar-for-dollar decrease in cash flow before tax. And because more is always preferred to less, each party negotiates to maximize its portion of the NOI. Consequently, one of the most difficult aspects of the investment process is locating a project that produces a sufficiently high NOI to service the debt and still provide an acceptable cash flow return to the equity investor.

Relationship of the Lender to the Equity Investor. The traditional economic role of the lender in relationship to the equity investor in real estate can be summarized as follows.

1. *Division of net operating income.* The lender receives debt service whereas the equity investor receives cash flow.
2. *Debt-to-equity ratio.* Generally, the lender supplies the larger fraction (e.g., 75 percent) of the capital to finance the asset, while the equity investor often seeks to acquire the asset with as little money down as possible. According to the "golden rule" ("Whoever has the gold makes the rules!"), the lender has controlled the rules and regulations of financing in the investment property arena.
3. *Certainty of income.* The lender seeks a contractually guaranteed income and expects such income to provide both a return *of* the investment (loan amortization) and a return *on* the investment at market interest rates. In contrast, a rational equity investor willingly accepts higher risks, but also expects a higher return. Although these are the usual expectations, they are not always realized.
4. *Priority of claim on income.* The lender has a senior or superior

claim to the income from the project, whereas the equity investor has a residual claim on the income. Basically, the equity investor gets whatever, if anything, is left over.

5. *Priority of claim on assets.* The lender also has the first or senior claim on the assets in the event of a default in debt service payments. The equity investor often loses all interest in the asset when foreclosure occurs. On the other hand, an inept lender may find the borrower still in control of the asset and may be forced to negotiate a settlement.

6. *A shorter investment time horizon.* In the past, a lender generally committed to a project for ten to forty years (the term of the loan), whereas the equity investor typically committed to a holding period of three to ten years. Lenders thus had a relatively long-run view when analyzing a mortgage investment, but most equity investors maintained medium- to short-run views. Recent inflation, interest rate, and supply-demand uncertainties, however, have forced both to pay more attention to short-run solvency and profit considerations. With inflation and interest rate uncertainties characterizing the marketplace, neither party is willing to make fixed long-term commitments.

Traditionally, equity investors have sought to maximize the use of leverage and often have "mortgaged out" by obtaining long-term financing in excess of the costs incurred through developing or buying a property. More recently, however, interest rates, operating expenses, and building costs have increased more rapidly than rents, and losses have resulted from undercapitalized (overfinanced) projects. Consequently, lenders have taken a more defensive position in financing real estate investments, demanding more conservative capital structures in which borrowers invest greater amounts of real equity dollars. They also are increasing their own interest in the equity investment by demanding equity participation in projects, either through joint-venture positions or through 100 percent equity ownership positions. Thus, institutions are accepting greater operating risks in return for greater yield expectations and protection against inflation. Additional measures being taken by lenders to guard against inflation and interest rate uncertainties include the use of creative mortgage instruments, such as variable-rate, renegotiable-rate and convertible mortgages. These, along with other hybrid financing devices, are increasingly common and are resulting in a blurring of the distinction between debt and equity and a narrowing of the difference in realized returns between debt and equity investors.[6]

---

[6]Stephen E. Roulac, *Modern Real Estate Investment* (San Francisco: Property Press, 1976), p. 18.

Maximization of Wealth. Investment decisions are made with some objective in mind. This book is written on the assumption that the primary financial goal is to maximize wealth by making capital investments that offer some optimum combination of returns and risks that satisfies the investor's preferences.[7] Generally, investors want their rate of return to be relatively high, preferring more return to less. At the same time, other things being equal, they prefer a return that is dependable and stable; that is, they prefer less risk to more. There probably is a group of people who ignore risk, evidently hoping that it will go away if its presence is not admitted. This group may be labeled "unbounded optimists" or "risk ignorers" and might find its citizens in Boot Hill, San Quentin, Las Vegas, or working for some land syndicators or development companies. This book ignores the risk ignorers.

The concept of wealth maximization through choosing the proper return–risk combinations is illustrated in Exhibits 2-2 and 2-3. Using this concept, the investor first *measures* the return and risk parameters for projects under consideration, then *evaluates* the projects by comparing them to one another and to his or her investment criteria, defined here as the investor's indifference curve or return–risk preference curve. In Exhibit 2-3, the investor's indifference curve is shown as line *ABC*. The investor is unwilling to accept any risk level in excess of "4," because the potential loss is too great to bear under any circumstances. At the same time, the investor is unwilling to invest in any projects that fall below line *AB*, because these represent undesirable combinations of return and risk. The acceptable projects ("yes" possibilities) appear above the indifference curve, with the most desirable combinations of return and risk being the projects farthest above and to the left of the *ABC* line. The most desirable projects are those that have the highest rate of return relative to the risks. For our purposes here, we can define risk as the probability of not achieving the expected rate of return.

Return and Risk Management. An integral part of investment and investment analysis is the management and control of risk. Many investors manage money, but "the really successful ones manage risk, the idea being not to avoid risk but to be skilled at identifying it, coping with it and then living with it under acceptable circumstances."[8] Risks can be managed and

[7]Stephen A. Pyhrr, "A Computer Simulation Model to Measure the Risk in Real Estate Investment," *American Real Estate and Urban Economics Association Journal*, June 1973, p. 48. Reprinted in *The Real Estate Appraiser*, May–June 1973, p. 15; also, Austin J. Jaffe and C. F. Sirmans, *Fundamentals of Real Estate Investment* (Englewood Cliffs: Prentice-Hall, Inc., 1986), p. 32.

[8]J. Thomas Montgomery, "Real Estate Investment Risk—Basic Concepts," *The Appraisal Journal*, January 1976, p. 14. Also see Robert Freeman, "Risk Management Concepts and Techniques," Chapter 6, *The 1984 Real Estate Valuation Colloquium, A Redefinition of Real Estate Appraisal Precepts and Processes* (Boston: Oelgeschlager, Gunn & Hain, in association with the Lincoln Institute of Land Policy, 1986).

EXHIBIT 2-2. Return–Risk Measurement

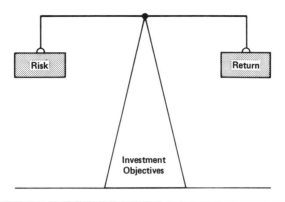

Source: J. Thomas Montgomery, "Real Estate Investment Risk—Basic Concepts," *The Appraisal Journal* (Chicago: American Institute of Real Estate Appraisers), January 1976, p. 12.

EXHIBIT 2-3. Return-Risk Evaluation

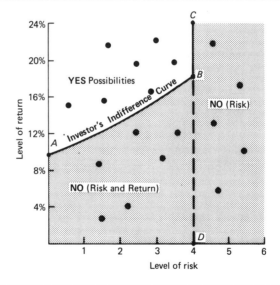

Source: J. Thomas Montgomery, "Real Estate Investment Risk—Basic Concepts," *The Appraisal Journal* (Chicago: American Institute of Real Estate Appraisers), January 1976, p. 20.

controlled through application of the techniques of avoiding, transferring and reducing. (The analysis and management of risk are discussed in Chapter 8.)

Fundamental to the return–risk wealth-maximization framework of this book is the assumption that the decision maker can control, to a substantial degree, the returns and risks of a project through careful analysis and structuring of financial as well as nonfinancial investment variables. Indeed, real estate investment analysis can be defined as the process of identifying and structuring projects in order to maximize returns relative to risks. Through greater expertise in the areas of market analysis, tax planning, financial analysis, and negotiation techniques (e.g., the negotiation of lease escalations and exculpatory clauses in mortgages), a decision maker can structure the purchase, operation, and termination of a project so as to increase the returns *relative to* the risks.

Feasibility and Feasibility Analysis

Investment analysis has traditionally focused on the financial aspects of real estate investments (maximizing returns), whereas feasibility analysis concentrates more on the nonfinancial aspects of the investment and tests the basic assumptions underlying the investor's financial analysis. Thus, feasibility analysis focuses on testing the marketing, legal, political, physical, and social dimensions of a real estate project in addition to the financial dimensions. (We acknowledge, however, the controversy concerning the use of these terms.)

A feasibility study is an analysis aimed at discovering whether a specific project or program can actually be carried out successfully.[9] In short, a feasibility study answers the fundamental question: "Will it work?" It explores every known alternative worthy of consideration in determining whether the economic and market climate is favorable for the effective implementation of a proposed real estate development. "In essence, a feasibility study is a forecast of things that will likely occur when the project is open for business. . . . It tells the complete story of the why, when and how of a project. Its conclusion will be critical to the investor, lender and all others constructively involved in the project."[10]

James Graaskamp, in his book *A Guide to Feasibility Analysis*, states

[9]Anthony Downs, "Characteristics of Various Economic Studies," *The Appraisal Journal*, July 1966, pp. 229–338. Reprinted in *Readings in Real Estate Investment Analysis* (Cambridge, Mass.: Ballinger, 1977), pp. 77–86.

[10]Lloyd D. Hanford, Sr., *Feasibility Study Guidelines* (Chicago: Institute of Real Estate Management, 1972), p. v. See also Stephen D. Messner, Byrl Boyce, Harold G. Trimble, and Robert L. Ward, *Analyzing Real Estate Opportunities: Market and Feasibility Studies* (Chicago: Realtors National Marketing Institute of the National Association of Realtors, 1977), pp. 78–86.

that a project is "feasible" when "the real estate analyst determines that there is a reasonable likelihood of satisfying explicit objectives when a selected course of action is tested for fit to a context of specific constraints and limited resources."[11] This definition is realistic, for it admits the presence in many situations of multiple investor objectives, both financial and nonfinancial. These objectives usually vary from one investor to the next and may be irrational in the narrow financial sense of maximizing financial wealth as defined in most finance textbooks. Certainly many facilities that are built as headquarters for major corporations are not designed to maximize financial return. Instead of maximizing anything, such investors are trying to find a "best fit." Relative to financial theory, this concept is similar to the goal of satisficing, in which investors attempt to satisfy numerous goals and objectives, thereby exceeding minimum standards of performance and living within a given set of constraints and resource limitations.

Distinction Between Existing and Development Projects. A useful distinction between investment and feasibility analysis is the one that can be drawn between existing and proposed projects. Feasibility analysis generally presumes a *development* situation in which the following conditions exist.

1. *A site or building is searching for a user.* The developer may be trying to determine the highest and best use for a tract of land that he or she owns or controls, or may be looking for a tenant for an empty office building that is nearing completion.
2. *A user is searching for a site and certain improvements.* This is the classic location decision. For example, a franchise hamburger operation may be looking for three new sites in a city, or a life insurance company may be seeking to locate a new regional office.
3. *An investor is looking for a means of participating in either of the situations just described.* The term "investor" here includes construction lenders, permanent lenders, and equity investors.

In contrast, investment analysis generally focuses on existing or "ongoing" projects that are assumed to be complete and already absorbed in the marketplace. The development period and its risks are ignored. Rather, various assumptions are made for an assumed time horizon regarding capital expenditures, rents, expenses, property value, and taxation; the inves-

[11]James A. Graaskamp, *A Guide to Feasibility Analysis* (Chicago: Society of Real Estate Appraisers, 1970), p. 4. Also see James A. Graaskamp, *Fundamentals of Real Estate Development* (Washington, D.C.: Urban Land Institute, 1981); and Terry V. Grissom, "A Feasibility Approach: Benefits of Land Economics and Risk Management," *The Appraisal Journal*, July 1984, pp. 356–374.

tor then tests the results of these assumptions against the investment objectives and criteria established at the beginning of the analysis. Although the analysis of "likelihood" and risk may and should be an integral part of investment analysis, the approach presumes a "going concern" rather than addressing the question: "How do we get the concern going?"

An important distinction should therefore be drawn between existing properties and development projects. The nature and level of returns and risks are significantly different for the two situations, as are the nature and extent of the analysis performed. Becoming involved in development activities (vs. existing projects) requires a critically different set of management skills and knowledge, risk-taking capacity, and analysis.

Types of Feasibility Analysis Reports. Various types of reports are often lumped together under the general term "feasibility study." Actually, a "complete" feasibility study might include seven types of studies, any one of which could be the analyst's total assignment in a particular situation.[12]

1. *Strategy study.* Determination of investment and development objectives, policies, plans, and decision criteria.
2. *Legal study.* Analysis of the various legal and political constraints and problems that may affect the project, including forms of organization, title, zoning, building codes, and so on.
3. *Compatibility study.* The compatibility of the project to surrounding land uses, city or county master plans, public policies, and environmental standards.
4. *Market analysis.* Macroeconomic studies, including regional analysis, economic base, and neighborhood or related aggregate—data reviews.
5. *Merchandising study.* Consumer surveys, analysis of competitive properties, sales and marketing evaluation, and strategy, price, and absorption rate studies, and the like.
6. *Architectural and engineering study.* Determination of alternative land use plans, structure, and design alternatives, soil analysis, utility availability, and so on.
7. *Financial–economic study.* Cash flow forecasts, tax and tax shelter planning, rate-of-return analysis, analysis of financing alternatives, holding-period analysis, and so on.

As can be seen, the nature and extent of the feasibility study performed is determined by the nature and extent of the problems that need to be solved. It also is determined by the sophistication of the decision maker who perceives the problems, the size of the project, and the budget avail-

[12]James A. Graaskamp, *A Guide to Feasibility Analysis,* p. 7.

able for such study. Too often, budgets for such studies are inadequate, and poor investment decisions are reached on the basis of inadequate information. The result may be financial disaster. Unfortunately, many of the approaches that have been used in the past to determine feasibility may be likened to consulting oracles, sticking one's head in the sand, calling in astrologers, or reading sheep's entrails.[13]

In light of the wealth of possibilities, it is necessary to define the concept being used and the nature of the study being done when using the term "feasibility study." Seldom does a developer, investor or analyst perform a complete feasibility study as defined here, in which investment analysis is actually a subset of feasibility analysis. Conversely, many studies called investment analyses are more truly a form of feasibility analysis.

Real Estate Appraisal

The appraisal process begins when an independent appraiser is contracted to carry out field research, collect and analyze data, and estimate the value of a specific property as of a specific date. The appraiser typically uses the income, cost, and market approaches to value and reconciles the findings to arrive at a final value estimate. This estimate becomes the conclusion of the appraisal report.

Clients have many reasons for engaging an appraiser, and the definition of "value" may vary depending on the objectives of the assignment. The most common definitions of "value" are *market value* and *most probable selling price*. A less common definition is *investment value*. Appraisers are sometimes required to appraise value using other special definitions, such as insured value, liquidation value, assessed value, and book value.

Market Value. As a result of considerable courtroom litigation, market value has acquired various definitions. According to the American Institute of Real Estate Appraisers (AIREA), the most widely accepted definitions of market value include the following.[14]

1. The highest price in terms of money that a property would bring in a competitive and open market under all conditions requisite to a fair

---

[13]Montgomery, "Real Estate Investment Risk," p. 11. For a discussion of problems with feasibility studies, see John R. White, "Non-Feasance with Feasibility = Failure: Improving the Quality of Feasibility Studies," *Urban Land*, October 1976, p. 6.

[14]American Institute of Real Estate Appraisers, Textbook Revision Subcommittee, *The Appraisal of Real Estate* (Chicago: AIREA, 1978), p. 23. The 1987 edition of this text expands the concept of market value and explores the controversial issues with respect to its definition; see pp. 16–19. Also see Peter F. Korpacz and Richard Marchitelli, "Market Value: A Contemporary Perspective," *The Appraisal Journal*, October 1984, and "Market Value: Contemporary Applications," *The Appraisal Journal*, July 1985; and Jared Shlaes, "The Market in Market Value," *The Appraisal Journal*, October 1984.

sale, with the buyer and seller each acting prudently and knowledge-
ably and under the assumption that the price is not affected by undue
stimulus.

2. The price at which a willing seller would sell and a willing buyer
   would buy, neither being under abnormal pressure.

3. The price expected if a reasonable time is allowed to find a purchaser
   and if both seller and prospective buyer are fully informed.

Certain conditions or assumptions implicit to the market definition are
noted in *Real Estate Appraisal Terminology*.[15]

1. Buyer and seller are motivated.

2. Both parties are well informed or well advised, and both are acting in
   what they consider to be their own best interest.

3. A reasonable time is allowed for exposure in the open market.

4. Payment is made in cash or its equivalent.

5. Financing, if any, is on terms generally available in the community
   at the specified date and typical for the property type in its locale.

6. The price represents normal consideration for the property sold, un-
   affected by special financing amounts and/or terms, services, fees,
   costs, or credits incurred in the transaction.

Unless the market is operating efficiently and producing equilibrium
prices, the market value is not the market price. Such market conditions
seldom exist.

Most Probable Selling Price. The use of the most probable selling price as
the proper measure of value has become increasingly popular because it
eliminates many normative assumptions about buyers and sellers, financing methods and costs, and current market conditions.[16] This definition
appears to be a realistic reflection of current market conditions, as contrasted with the market value definition, which attempts to define normal
medium-term equilibrium conditions. The most probable selling price is
defined as "that price at which a property would most probably sell if exposed to the market for a reasonable time, under market conditions prevailing as of the date of the appraisal."[17]

---

[15] American Institute of Real Estate Appraisers, Textbook Revision Subcommittee, Byrl
N. Boyce, ed., *Real Estate Appraisal Terminology*, rev ed. (Cambridge, Mass.: Ballinger,
1981).

[16] Richard N. Ratcliff, *Valuation for Real Estate Decisions* (Santa Cruz, Calif.: Demo-
crat Press, 1972), pp. 10–11; also *The Appraisal of Real Estate*, 1987 ed., pp. 18–19.

[17] AIREA, *Real Estate Appraisal Terminology*, p. 52.

Problems with Traditional Market Value Appraisals. Traditional market value appraisals have always played a key role in real estate financing and have been relied on heavily to verify the legality and economic soundness of loans underwritten by lending institutions. Many investors and developers consider appraisal data and conclusions when making investment decisions. Conversely, some argue that traditional appraisals are inherently limited in their usefulness to decision makers faced with complex investment and feasibility problems.

The basic problem with most appraisals from a decision-making standpoint lies in the assumptions made on the first page of the appraisal report. The appraiser, often assuming that the determination of market value is the central issue, adopts the perspective of "economic man," who is rational, intelligent, has good market information, and operates in an efficient market with the intention of maximizing the economic surplus of a single real estate property. In practice, market value is not usually the central issue. More often, investors are concerned with *investment* value, or the expected rate of return or profit from an investment expenditure; the goal of their study generally is to make some type of investment–feasibility decision. Unlike the appraiser, the investment–feasibility analyst sees a project from the perspective of a particular decision maker operating under a particular set of objectives and constraints. The decision maker may have noneconomic goals (including some that are irrational!), may work in a highly imperfect market in which accurate information is difficult to obtain, and may have considerable power to influence the final outcome. Indeed, the goal of an investor is to increase returns relative to risks through shrewd negotiation and investment structuring. Stated somewhat differently, the goal of an investor or entrepreneur is to create a monopoly (to whatever extent possible and for as long as possible) and thereby divert cash flows and other benefits to himself or herself. The imperfections of the real estate marketplace often make this possible.[18]

In summary, a market value appraisal often fails to solve many of the decision maker's important problems because it usually is not oriented to decision or action. In contrast, both feasibility and investment studies are action-oriented and can be structured to answer the specific questions facing investors and developers. In response to the need for more investment-specific evaluations, many appraisers are obtaining the additional education and skills necessary to carry out feasibility and investment assignments rather than traditional market value appraisal assignments, in which many problems are assumed away. Supporting this trend are lenders, investors, and developers, who are increasingly seeking market, merchandising, and other economic studies to aid them in rendering more

---

[18]For an example, see James E. Gibbons, "The Effect of Inflation and Tax Reform on Real Estate Valuation," *The Appraisal Journal*, July 1985, pp. 455–464.

profitable decisions, rather than demanding appraisal reports that are file cabinet fillers for decisions already locked into contracts, promises, and concrete-and-steel structures.

TIME HORIZONS FOR INVESTMENT DECISIONS: LIFE CYCLES

In analyzing any real estate investment, the investor should recognize the life cycles that affect the return–risk relationships on which investment decisions are based. Decisions based on techniques and forecasts that do not consider these life cycles often have surprising, disappointing, and possibly disastrous outcomes.

Three types of life cycles are of primary importance to investors. The first is an *investor life cycle*, which defines the type and amount of return and risk sought by the investor at different stages in his or her life. The second is the *property life cycle*, which encompasses the entire development and holding periods from the idea stage through the demise of the project at the end of its useful economic life. The third is the *ownership life cycle*, which consists of the holding period experienced by one ownership group from the day of purchase to the disposal of the property at the end of the holding period. Often, the point at which a person desires to enter the property and ownership life cycles depends on his or her stage in the investor life cycle.

Investor Life Cycle

It is commonly believed that investors experience personal "life cycles" related primarily to age, and that these cycles affect the types of returns and risks they are willing to accept at any given time.[19] Although the overall psychological and emotional makeup of an investor may remain unchanged throughout a lifetime, definite cycles tend to characterize investment preferences and behavior as a person becomes older. The average individual investor beginning a career after graduating from college passes through three key stages: (1) the young investor, (2) the middle-aged investor, and (3) the older investor nearing retirement.

Young Investor. According to Mark Twain, "The first half of life consists of the capacity to enjoy without the chance; the last half consists of the chance without the capacity." The young investor has relatively little eq-

[19]Jerome B. Cohen, Edward D. Zinbarg, and Arthur Zeikel, *Investment Analysis and Portfolio Management* (Homewood, Ill.: Richard D. Irwin, 1987), pp. 546–550; also Robert D. Milne, "Determination of Portfolio Policies: Individual Investors," in *Managing Investment Portfolios, A Dynamic Process*, eds., John L. Maginn and Donald L. Tuttle (New York: Warren Gorham & Lamont, 1983), p. 133.

uity capital or management experience, but can look forward to thirty or forty years of increasing income and investable surplus funds, and has the energy and risk-taking capacity to build wealth rapidly. Having little to lose, the young investor usually seeks highly leveraged projects that require minimal management expertise. Often a single-family residence is the first investment, followed by a rental house, a duplex, a quadruplex or a small apartment building. Because the young investor needs very little tax shelter, cash flow from operations, or equity buildup from loan amortization, he or she seeks instead to increase expertise quickly and to maximize property value appreciation.

Diversification is a difficult goal to achieve: the young investor usually builds a real estate portfolio one property at a time, and the property types and locations tend to be homogeneous as a result of a lack of expertise. In addition to mortgage debts, insurance premiums and monthly credit card payments exert considerable pressure on the young investor's cash resources; cars and furniture are usually debt-financed as well. Consequently, it is difficult to build up a substantial cash reserve for anything but emergencies, and the net-worth statement is but a gleam in the investor's eye.

Middle-Aged Investor. At this stage the investor has probably reached the economic prime of life. Although earnings may not have peaked, the middle-aged investor has built up substantial liquid resources and equities in properties, which provide greater financial mobility. With risk-taking capacity at its maximum, and having accumulated investment experience and expertise, the investor is now financially sophisticated and can become involved in development situations and commercial investments that are somewhat more complicated, such as shopping centers, office buildings, and motels.

Diversification will probably dominate the investor's strategy at this stage. Although the need for tax shelter has increased as the investor's income has risen, accumulation of wealth through property value appreciation continues to play a key role in the investor's strategy.

Older Investor. With advancing age, the investor generally demonstrates more conservative behavior and greater aversion to risk. Having passed the primary earning years, and now less inclined to pursue high returns, high risks, and capital accumulation alternatives, the older investor usually shifts his or her portfolio into properties that create high, current income, often used to augment retirement income. While still maintaining an interest in real property, the older investor may sell real estate equities or take back mortgage notes from purchasers as a means of shifting income and risk.

A successful investor who has built a substantial portfolio of real estate assets during a lifetime may experience little or no decrease in tax bracket after retirement. The amount of ordinary income may in fact increase if the portfolio is shifted into investments that provide steady, but ordinary income for tax purposes. Thus, the desire for tax shelter may be sustained after retirement. In contrast, a relatively unsuccessful investor may need to supplement income from retirement investments by cannibalizing the accumulated investment fund. Periodically selling off assets to supplement income eroded by inflation may be a means of maintaining a given life-style after retirement.

With age comes a certain weariness of investment and management responsibilities. Even the successful managing equity investor usually prefers to shift responsibility to younger and more aggressive individuals. The remaining portfolio can be restructured through an estate plan to accommodate the needs of family members, to give to charities and foundations, and so on. At this point, the individual's investing life cycle is over.

Institutional Investors. Little information is available to identify distinct life cycles for institutional investors. Life insurance companies, pension funds, REITs, and large-scale syndications are relative newcomers to real estate equity investment. They are constrained by their fiduciary responsibilities to their clients and by many legal and tax regulations that limit their investment flexibility. The goals and needs of institutions appear to change slowly relative to those of individuals; from a decision-making standpoint, therefore, the concept of an investor life cycle may be less relevant for the institutional investor. Institutional investors do have personalities, however, and they do change their return and risk preferences as they become more experienced in the real estate investment game. For example, a number of life insurance companies, such as Prudential-Bache, Metropolitan, and Aetna, have evolved from residential lenders to commercial lenders and then to commercial developers. In searching for greater returns, they have been required to participate in real estate activities that also produce a greater risk of loss.

Property Life Cycle

Every real estate investment has a property life cycle that evolves through several distinct stages: from its inception and development, through its operation, to the end of its productive life. Although the time spans may vary, this life cycle can be conceptualized as a pyramid and is explained by the acronym GLITAMAD, as shown in Exhibit 2-4.[20]

Investors can choose to invest at any stage of the pyramid. The upside

[20] Both the acronym and the concept were developed by Maury Seldin and Richard H. Swesnik, *Real Estate Investment Strategy* (New York: Wiley-Interscience, 1979), pp. 53–104. These authors were the first to identify clearly property life cycle stages in a return-risk decision-making framework.

EXHIBIT 2-4.   The Property Life Cycle Pyramid

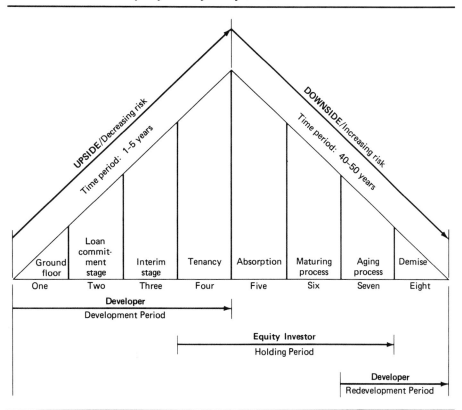

of the pyramid (which can span from one to five years) represents the development period, in which risks decrease as a project is developed and many of the uncertainties are eliminated. The developer is the dominant personality during this stage. The top of the pyramid (end of tenancy stage) represents a completed and fully occupied project with established income, expenses, and cash flow. By this point the risks are relatively low, and the equity investor typically becomes the dominant personality during the downside of the property cycle. The downside spans a long period, usually forty to fifty years, and is characterized by increasing risks as the project ages. At the end of its useful life, the property is often ready for a new use and will enter a new property life cycle, beginning the GLITAMAD pyramid once again. If the property and location will support redevelopment, the developer again becomes the dominant personality. If not, the property will be abandoned or left vacant until new development is feasible.

Investors may participate at any stage of the property life cycle, each of which represents a different return–risk situation and a different combination of returns: development profit, cash flow from operations, tax shelter, equity buildup through loan amortization, and appreciation (or depreciation) of property value. Since each stage appeals to a different type of investor, careful consideration should be given to the stage of the life cycle at which the investor chooses to become involved. Furthermore, once the life cycle stage has been chosen, many of the basic return and risk parameters are established and may be difficult to change.

The property life cycle is characterized here in terms of time, and each phase in the cycle has a suggested time frame. In reality, however, the life cycle of a property is more properly tied into the prevailing market conditions at any point on the property cycle, regardless of the actual calendar time. Changing market conditions can alter the life cycle completely by causing a shift. Therefore, the investor should rely on good market analyses to determine the current potential for an investment, regardless of where it may lie on the cycle as measured in time. For example, recently constructed property built for a nonexistent market may move very rapidly from the development period to its demise unless it can be remarketed. Conversely, older property, perhaps on the far end of the declining phase, may suddenly be lifted by a market boom, thus extending its life.

The Upside of the Property Life Cycle

The upside of the property life cycle corresponds to various stages of activity in real estate development. Since the uncertainties are many, the risks are very high during the early stages. There is little (if any) cash flow, relatively limited tax shelter, and no equity buildup or property appreciation. Any return is dependent primarily on entrepreneurial profit, the creation of a property value that is greater than the costs of development. For example, a developer might hope to invest $800,000 in land and improvements that, when rented, will be worth $1 million, thereby earning a $200,000 development profit.

An investor who chooses to become involved in the early stages of development (e.g., the ground floor or loan commitment stages) usually demands a portion of the development profit to compensate for the high risks. By definition, the investor who becomes involved in this manner is a joint-venture partner of the developer. The investor's alternatives include (1) fully sharing the development risks and returns with the developer, (2) requiring the developer to guarantee a return, (3) demanding a preferential return from the developer, or (4) combining several of these options to avoid or shift many of the development period risks to others. In any case, the investor should receive compensation in the form of development period returns (i.e., a slice of the development profit) in proportion to the development period risks taken.

As development progresses, construction and permanent loan commitments are obtained (loan commitment stage) and the project is built (interim stage). The risks diminish, and more people are committed to the successful completion of the project. Equity investors often become involved at this point, typically through syndications in which delivery of a completed and fully rented project is guaranteed by the developer; the equity funds raised are held in escrow until the project has been completed.

During the fourth stage (tenancy) the project is nearing the top of the pyramid. It is being leased to tenants and is producing income; the rents are at the top of the market because the project is new and desirable. In theory, the project is at the peak of its earning capacity at the end of the tenancy stage (top of the pyramid) and can then be sold at its highest price.[21] The rate of return required by equity investors in a competitive market is usually minimal because the risk is minimal. Clearly, the developer should be able to maximize expected profit by waiting until this point to sell the project, unless changing market conditions threaten to affect adversely the marketability of the project and discourage potential equity investors.

The developer who chooses to hold and own the project during the downside of the pyramid becomes, by definition, a long-term equity investor. Today, many developers choose to play dual roles, believing that they should not sell the valuable equities they create. Developers like Trammell Crow and Lincoln Properties seek to retain ownership of the properties they develop, except when financial partnerships are needed to raise the cash required for funding the difference between mortgage commitments and project costs.

The Downside of the Property Life Cycle

In a real economic sense, as a building and its neighborhood ages, the property value starts to decline and the risks become greater because the property is less desirable to an increasing number of investors. Although inflation may raise the property's monetary value, property improvements begin to wear out and, eventually, major replacements are needed.

Passive equity investors are most comfortable investing in the first two stages of the downside (absorption, maturing process), which typically span fifteen to twenty-five years of economic life after the project's completion. Many institutional investors, such as pension funds and life insurance companies, prefer relatively new projects with an established track record. Individuals and syndicates investing in real estate often prefer mature properties that may require some renovation but are located in highly desirable locations where incoming competition is limited.

The stages through which every property passes thus offer a variety of opportunities to investors with different objectives and preferences. Through subsequent purchases and sales of a given property, numerous

---

[21] This refers to the highest "real" price rather than the nominal dollar price, implies that the project is fully leased at the end of the tenancy stage, and ignores other real estate cycles.

investors or investment groups with different investment postures can be satisfied.

Eventually, every property deteriorates. Major repairs and renovations become necessary, and the forecasts of income and expenses are less certain. The risks of investing become greater, and the owner who does not maintain property may gain the title of slumlord. Real estate advisers recommend that only experienced investors be involved at this stage of the cycle. Also at this stage, a developer may enter the scene and undertake a major renovation of the property, seeking to bring it back to a new absorption period and return it to the topside of the pyramid. The property is thus kept from entering the demise stage, when bulldozers are brought to the site or the property is abandoned.

In the past attractive tax shelters could be created during the later stages of the life cycle, since the useful lives of improvements were considered very short and rehabilitation expenditures often qualified for favorable tax treatment. The Tax Reform Act of 1986 severely curtailed such tax shelters except for certain low-income housing investments. In any case, the risks are high and the problems more difficult than at any other stage of the downside.

Investment Strategy Implications

The stage of the pyramid at which the investor becomes involved is an important determinant of investment returns and risks. As the property life cycle pyramid suggests, there is a trade-off between return and risk, making it difficult to maximize returns *and* minimize risks simultaneously. In a free-enterprise system, the market generally works in a manner that requires investors, on average, to take greater risks to achieve greater returns. However, although this is true in a general market sense, it is not true for an individual investor operating in a relatively imperfect market. An equity investor or developer can often exert influence on both the return and risk parameters of a project through his or her own skills, expertise, and negotiating ability. Thus, the investor can choose an overall return–risk profile by selecting the stage of the project life cycle at which to become involved, and then alter that return–risk profile through entrepreneurship during the acquisition, operation, and termination stages of the project. These three stages make up the ownership life cycle, to which we now turn.

Ownership Life Cycle

The ownership life cycle is the period during which one person or group owns a real estate asset. An ownership life cycle generally encompasses a relatively short time span, although it can conceivably cover the entire property life cycle; for example, a developer may build and hold a property until it is razed forty years later. For an aggressive young investor seeking to build wealth quickly, the ownership life cycle may consist of a one- or two-year holding period, whereas a conservative wealthy investor purchasing an existing shopping center may analyze a project on the basis of a ten-year ownership period.

In recent years the rapid acceptance of discounted-cash-flow methods in real estate investment analysis has made the concept of ownership life cycles popular. The concept requires that all anticipated costs and benefits of an investment be considered for the expected ownership period, and that the time value of money be used to equate future expectations with today's values.

The stages of the ownership life cycle may be defined as follows.[22]

1. *Acquisition.* Organization of the venture and development or purchase of property.
2. *Operation.* Property management and management of the venture that owns the real estate.
3. *Disposal or termination.* Sale of the property and dissolution of the venture or property exchange, foreclosure, gift, and so on.

Since each of these stages has unique cash flow and tax effects, investment analysis should take into consideration the timing of these factors. Most analysts use a discounted-cash-flow procedure, projecting after-tax cash flows for each year of the expected ownership period and, in the final step, calculating an internal rate of return (or modified internal rate of return) on equity investment. Others advocate a discounted-cash-flow procedure for handling ownership life cycle considerations, but prefer a present-value approach (see Chapter 7).

There is considerable debate about which discounting techniques and investment measures should be used to measure and compare the returns and risks from real estate investments. These will be reviewed in the next chapter. However, although brokers and investors often emphasize only one-year pro forma results, most sophisticated investors agree that the entire ownership period should be evaluated when measuring project returns and risks.

Integration of Life Cycle Concepts

Knowledge of life cycles and their relation to one another is critical to the formulation of investment strategy. The interrelationship of the three life cycles discussed is pictured in Exhibit 2-5.

---

[22] See also Roulac, "Life Cycle of a Real Estate Investment," in *Modern Real Estate Investment*, pp. 297–306.

EXHIBIT 2-5.   Interrelationship of Life Cycle Concepts

INVESTOR LIFE CYCLE		PROPERTY LIFE CYCLE		OWNERSHIP LIFE CYCLE
Define amounts and types of returns and risks that are acceptable.	→	Choose stage of life cycle that represents acceptable returns and risks.	→	Analyze returns and risks using full life cycle cash flow forecasts.

The investor first determines the amounts and types of returns and risks that are acceptable (investor life cycle). On the basis of this knowledge, the investor can then choose the stages in the property life cycle (GLITAMAD) that represent acceptable return–risk situations. Properties are then located that meet the basic property and investor life cycle criteria; the investor analyzes each property using discounted-cash-flow methods that measure the return and risk dimensions over the entire ownership period (ownership life cycle). When these steps have been completed, the investor has integrated successfully the three life cycle concepts into the decision-making process.

Other types of real estate cycles are also important to the investor's evaluation of return and risk. Inflation cycles, business cycles, construction cycles, and neighborhood cycles are examples of others that must be carefully analyzed. These are addressed in Chapter 14.

SUMMARY

This chapter presented an overview of the investment decision process. Investment is defined to include the original commitment of capital by the investor, management of the investment to maximize returns, and disinvestment or liquidation. A capital asset is purchased by an investor and financed via a combination of debt and equity sources. Although the investor has traditionally sought to maximize the debt–equity ratio using fixed-rate, long-term mortgages, lenders have become more defensive and are requiring more substantial amounts of equity capital and various types of flexible-rate, shorter-term mortgages. The equity investor's primary financial objective is to make capital investments that will maximize wealth; that is, the investor seeks to identify, structure, and purchase projects that will maximize the return–risk ratio relative to personal preferences. Also emphasized is the need to develop techniques for better management and control of risks.

Feasibility analysis, in contrast with investment analysis, focuses on the development of new projects and explicitly considers the many nonfinancial objectives of investors. It seeks to test the marketing, legal, political, physical, and social dimensions of a project as well as its financial dimensions. A complete feasibility study is extensive and can be broken down into seven separate types of studies: strategy studies, legal studies, compatibility studies, market analysis, merchandising studies, architectural and engineering studies, and financial–economic studies. The investor should be able to distinguish between investment and feasibility studies and other studies, such as appraisals.

We also examined the importance of three types of life cycles that affect the return–risk relationships upon which the investor bases a decision. The investor life cycle tracks what risks and returns the individual investor seeks during different stages of his or her life. The property life cycle encompasses all the development and ownership periods of a property from its inception through its demise. An ownership life cycle encompasses only the purchase, operation, and termination of a property for one equity ownership group.

3

DECISION-MAKING APPROACHES TO REAL ESTATE INVESTMENT

The central theme of this book is that sound investment decision making based on a thorough return and risk analysis is the best strategy for maximizing one's wealth in the long run. However, most successful investors rely on personal formulas that often represent variations on more proven strategies. There are a variety of approaches and many investors choose to combine these. Indeed, there is as much to learn from successful school-of-hard-knocks entrepreneurs as there is from professional real estate managers who have completed advanced degrees in real estate and work for large, successful real estate companies.

Exhibit 3-1 provides an overview of the investment decision approaches discussed in this chapter. Applications of many of the theories and approaches developed here are illustrated in Chapters 4 through 10 and 15 through 17. Some textbooks ignore or disparage many of the popular and traditional approaches; however, we recognize that each approach has merits and can offer the investor an important perspective. Of those to be discussed here, the "how-to" techniques have historically dominated the popular real estate investment literature, including such best-selling titles of the past few decades as William Nickerson's *How I Turned $1,000 into Five Million in Real Estate*,[1] George Bockl's *How Real Estate Fortunes Are Made*,[2] and Robert G. Allen's *Nothing Down*.[3] By the 1970s, internal-rate-

[1]William Nickerson, *How I Turned $1,000 into Five Million in Real Estate* (New York: Simon & Schuster, 1980).
[2]George Bockl, *How Real Estate Fortunes Are Made* (Englewood Cliffs, N.J.: Prentice–Hall, 1972).
[3]Robert G. Allen, *Nothing Down* (New York: Simon & Schuster, 1980).

EXHIBIT 3-1. Decision-Making Approaches

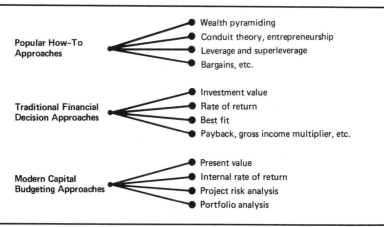

Popular How–To Approaches
- Wealth pyramiding
- Conduit theory, entrepreneurship
- Leverage and superleverage
- Bargains, etc.

Traditional Financial Decision Approaches
- Investment value
- Rate of return
- Best fit
- Payback, gross income multiplier, etc.

Modern Capital Budgeting Approaches
- Present value
- Internal rate of return
- Project risk analysis
- Portfolio analysis

of-return and present-value techniques, which were virtually unknown to real estate investors of the 1960s, became the accepted decision approaches. And today discounted-cash-flow approaches are studied by those enrolled in college and university investment courses as well as by those in trade organization courses leading to professional designations such as GRI, CCIM, SRS, CRE, MAI, SRPA, SREA, CPM, and CMB.[4]

POPULAR "HOW-TO" APPROACHES

The "how-to-get-rich" formulas, plans, schemes, and strategies, found in today's popular real estate investment literature portray real estate as the individual investor's best opportunity in this country to "get rich quick" and an activity for one's spare time. Although some of the authors of these how-to books may make considerably more money selling their books and seminars to the public than they do by investing in real estate, still, millions of investors firmly believe in the "how-to" approaches to real estate investing.

[4]The designations and their granting organizations are, respectively, Graduate Realtors Institute (GRI), awarded by state associations of Realtors; Certified Commercial Investment Member (CCIM), granted by the Realtors National Marketing Institute (RNMI), a subsidiary of the National Association of Realtors (NAR); Specialist in Real Estate Securities (SRS), an affiliate of NAR; Counselor of Real Estate (CRE), granted by the American Society of Real Estate Counselors (ASREC); Member of the Appraisal Institute (MAI), granted by the American Institute of Real Estate Appraisers (AIREA); Senior Real Property Appraiser (SRPA), granted by the Society of Real Estate Appraisers (SREA); Senior Real Estate Analyst (SREA), granted by the SREA; Certified Property Manager (CPM), granted by the Institute of Real Estate Management (IREM), a subsidiary of NAR; and Certified Mortgage Banker (CMB), granted by the Mortgage Bankers Association of America (MBA).

Pyramiding with Other People's Money

The key element of many "how-to" approaches is pyramiding with other people's money. Nickerson observed that most millionaires had borrowed most or all of their investment capital from others. Probably the world's most outstanding pyramider, according to Nickerson, was Henry Ford. Ford's billion-dollar enterprise is said to have grown faster than any other in history and eventually outstripped all but the Rockefellers'. Yet Ford himself had invested nothing in the business. One hundred percent of the investment capital was borrowed from others. Similarly, "big-time" operators buy millions of dollars' worth of property without a cent of their own money, and "big deals" are made by borrowing as much as possible from mortgages and the balance on personal and collateral notes.

The Wealth-Pyramiding Process. The Nickerson formula spells out a ten-step wealth-pyramiding process, beginning with the purchase of a single-family home. The leading example illustrated by Nickerson assumes an initial investment of $2,500, 75 percent leverage, *average* luck and market conditions, and investment in income-producing property, beginning with residential properties. The first step is to buy a somewhat rundown house that needs some "cosmetic" work. The purchase price is $10,000; the mortgage is $7,500, and the equity investment $2,500. The second step is to invest $600 from savings each year for two years to paint and renovate the house, thereby increasing the income and sales value of the property so that it can be sold at a profit. The third step is to sell the house for $14,000 (a 25% gross profit of $2,800 on the total investment of $11,200), paying the 5 percent sales costs of $700, which leaves a $2,100 profit *plus* the return of the original $2,500 investment capital *plus* the return of the $1,200 renovation capital. At the end of the second year the investor has accumulated $5,800 of investment capital ($2,100 + $2,500 + $1,200 = $5,800).

The fourth through tenth steps repeat the first three: Invest $5,800, borrow three times that amount (75% leverage), buy a larger property, renovate, hold two years, then sell for a 25 percent gross profit. By the end of the twentieth year the net worth or "estate" of the investor is $1,187,195, as shown in Exhibit 3-2. In theory, this pyramiding of income-producing property can be accomplished without substantial tax consequences through tax-free exchanges and tax sheltering by means of depreciation write-offs.

Clearly, the pyramiding formula is simply a mechanism used to generate high rates of return on the investor's equity through turnover operations. The rest is left to the theory of compound interest. In the case cited, the investor earns a compound rate of interest on successive investments of approximately 33 percent annually. This compounding factor, when applied against the original $2,500 investment (plus the two $600 renovation investments), builds up an estate of over $1 million in twenty years. These results may appear miraculous to the novice investor, but they are quite

EXHIBIT 3-2.   The Wealth-Pyramiding Process

Year	Net Worth (Estate)
0	$ 2,500
2	5,800
4	11,575
6	21,681
8	39,363
10	70,548
12	124,884
14	219,972
16	386,376
18	677,583
20	$1,187,195

elementary to a student who understands geometric progressions. There is absolutely no magic involved, only the well-known powers of compound interest and, according to Nickerson, average luck and market conditions.

Four Cardinal Principles. There are four cardinal principles of the Nickerson formula that, if followed, are said to produce (at least) the turnover profits just described.

1. Borrow the maximum that can be repaid safely.
2. Buy only property that needs improvement.
3. Make selective improvements that increase value.
4. Keep selling at a profit and reinvesting.

Nickerson's formula also implicitly assumes that the market will not be overbuilt and that the local economy will not contract. The base of the pyramid is built with rental housing properties, on the theory that the sustained growth of metropolitan areas promises a continually increasing demand for rental housing and, consequently, an ever-expanding choice of real estate investment opportunities.

The Conduit Theory and the Entrepreneurial Leverage Theory

George Bockl is among those authors who promote the use of entrepreneurial ability and creativity to generate high rates of return with low risks and who suggest the application of the related conduit and entrepreneurial leverage theories to the investment decision process.

A young investor can serve as a "conduit" for money flowing through from real estate projects. This theory assumes that youth is a valuable commodity and that a young person should learn to sell youth in a manner that will maximize investment returns. The young investor with management skills and time, but no money, can find elderly owners who seek security; the young person then convinces them to sell their real estate with nominal down payments and, usually, very generous financing terms. If the sale is structured correctly, both partners benefit and satisfy their personal investment goals: for the typical young investor a multimillion-dollar net worth built rapidly with nominal down payments; for the older investor, security, certainty of income, and peace of mind.

The entrepreneurial leverage theory argues that the formula for buying and keeping a real estate fortune requires youth, management skill, and imaginative borrowing. Any young person who becomes skilled in property management and learns how to borrow imaginatively will be worth at least as much as can be borrowed after debts are amortized. Through entrepreneurship, a thirty-year-old investor who could arrange to borrow $1 million on real estate would be worth $1 million by the age of fifty or sixty. If loans cannot be obtained from financial institutions, partners should be found to finance the cash needs. In addition, the entrepreneur–investor should develop good credit relationships with banks and other lending institutions. The investor will then be able to act quickly when opportunities arise and in situations in which a seller needs cash in a hurry.

To analyze the different sources of income that make up the full rate of return on a real estate investment, Bockl advocates the use of the "four-way benefit test."

1. *Cash flow return.* Before tax, after debt service.
2. *Amortization return.* As annual loan reduction.
3. *Gain from tax shelter.* Income saved via accelerated depreciation.
4. *Return from inflationary gains.* Increase in property value.

Compound Interest and Control

Authors like Mark Oliver Haroldsen advise investors to attain a thorough understanding of interest rates, compound interest, and leverage, and then search for investments that can be controlled.[5] Control is the critical ingredient of successful investing, a management tool that Haroldsen claims cannot be used in the stocks and bonds arenas, but can be applied to real estate investments. In addition, the small investor is said to have some distinct advantages in real estate investing. Having fewer financial resources, the small investor can compound money at higher rates of return by finding investments that are not of interest to larger and more sophisticated investors. Additionally, small investors generally do not have a vast

---

[5]Mark Oliver Haroldsen, *How to Wake Up the Financial Genius Inside You* (Salt Lake City, Utah: Mark O. Haroldsen, 1976).

amount of experience or knowledge; by exerting a little extra effort the individual can outdistance the competition.

Haroldsen's approach suggests that investment success depends on the decision to plan, save, invest, and compound. The *planning phase* requires "dreaming big," turning the financial dream into a plan, giving the plan details, making alternative plans when necessary, and putting the plan into action. The decision to **save** is explained by Haroldsen's *10 percent rule*: "You must save a minimum of 10 percent of your gross earnings. The second part of the rule is that you never, never, never spend that savings. Your capital is your savings and your capital must never be disturbed." The *invest* and *compound* stages of the decision are similar to those of the wealth-pyramiding approach.

The rate of return on real estate equity investments is the key to the compounding process and the source of wealth. Haroldsen measures that rate of return on the basis of the elements that appear in Bockl in the four-way benefit test: cash flow, equity buildup, inflation, and tax shelter. According to Haroldsen, annual rates of return of 25 to 225 percent are achievable in real estate when measured in this way.

Leverage, Superleverage, and Bargains

Many claim that leverage is the most important tool in the investor's bag, one formula for which is the OPM (other people's money) approach. Haroldsen's example of the effect of leverage on the investor's return is a 90 percent leverage situation in which inflation raises the total property value by 10 percent each year. As an example, a rental house is purchased with 10 percent down. If the property value rises by 10 percent annually (a reasonable amount, Haroldsen claims), the investor's rate of return is 100 percent annually. The effect is the same, whatever the size of the real estate investment.

Most "how-to" strategies rely on the discovery of "bargains" in the marketplace. Six types of properties are considered bargains.

1. Property that is undervalued.
2. Property that can be upgraded.
3. Property with rents that are too low.
4. Property with expenses that are too high.
5. Property whose basic use can be changed.
6. Property that can be purchased with little cash.

The key to achieving a 100 percent return compounded annually lies in finding "bargains" and then improving the real estate in some way. Raising rents or decreasing expenses has a tremendous multiplier effect, as illustrated by Haroldsen's "100 times formula." According to this formula, a $1 increase in rent per month adds, on an average, $100 to the property value (if the gross rent multiplier is 8.34):

The 100 Times Formula

$1 × 12 months =

12 × 8.34 gross rent multiplier =

$100 added value

Thus, improvements to a property that result in rental increases or expense decreases can easily raise property values and compound equity by 100 percent per year. With a 10 percent down payment, it takes only a 10 percent increase in value to make a 100 percent return on investment.

The ultimate leverage is superleverage, created by buying a property and, at the closing, or shortly thereafter, mortgaging out and perhaps generating extra cash to "pocket" in "Hip National Bank."[6] The investor most often achieves this degree of leverage by finding a "bargain" and refinancing, or by doing "cosmetic" work on a property, thereby raising both income and value. The investor can then refinance on the basis of the higher value.

Risks in Real Estate Investment

Underlying the theories of many who advocate the "how-to" approaches outlined here is the idea that risks in real estate investment are negligible if the investment is in housing. First, housing is a necessity; most other investments, such as stocks, bonds, motels, hotels, and most businesses, do not have this advantage. Second, there is a constant demand for housing as new families are formed through marriage and as individuals leave their parents' homes to set up their own households. Third, there is inmigration into many regions of the country, increasing the demand for housing in these regions. Finally, demand is innate to the "great American dream," which is manifest in the public's desire not only to own a home, but to periodically move up to a better one.

Critique of "How-To" Approaches

"How-to" approaches represent one view of real estate investment. Most of the "how-to" authors downplay risk, emphasize high rates of return,

---

[6]Ibid., p. 70.

offer simple formulas for success, and depend very little on analytical techniques or modern decision-making theories.

Great emphasis is placed on the upside of real estate investments: the tremendous rate-of-return potential available through shrewd purchasing, creative (highly leveraged) financing, and the imaginative management of properties. The powers of compound interest are believed to ensure an exponential growth rate for the value of an investor's portfolio. The investor's primary goal is assumed to be the creation of a monopoly, if only for a short while, which results in an increase in cash flow and property value.

The concept of taking advantage of imperfections in the marketplace is illustrated by these authors' strategies for finding bargains and using entrepreneurial leverage and conduit theory to keep the rates of return high and the estate growing at a pyramiding rate. Financing is usually through sellers who, for one reason or another, are in greater need of parting with their real estate than of receiving cash.

Extraordinary rates of return will be possible for some real estate entrepreneurs as long as "other" investors make irrational property decisions—decisions based on emotions rather than on economic analyses backed up by a thorough investigation of the facts. More than one nationally known real estate consultant has observed that the majority of real estate transactions are based on the emotions of individuals, not the economics of properties.[7] Consequently, an investor who can structure real estate solutions to solve the personal and emotional needs of the seller will frequently be able to raise the rate of return and simultaneously reduce the investment risks and the amount of cash necessary to acquire a property. High rates of return are presumed to occur if the formulas are followed.

To the innocent reader, everything seems simple; but the experienced reader should quickly recognize the need for research and detailed analyses, to which the authors allude only vaguely. Risk appears to be a forgotten dimension in the "how-to" approaches, and investors who employ them might be regarded as "risk ignorers." Real estate investment risks are assumed to be minimal if the given formula is followed religiously, and the employment of entrepreneurial effort is the recommended solution to any problem that arises. These theories further postulate that there are no risks in market cycles, competition, or life cycles—only opportunities. In fact, rent-producing properties are said to incur only negligible risks with a chance of success 1600 times better than that for starting a new business.[8] Nickerson calculates this 1600-times-safer factor from Department of Commerce statistics that show four in five new businesses fail within eight years, resulting in four-to-one odds that a new business will not survive. In contrast, mortgage statistics show that only one in every 400 properties is

[7]Robert W. Steele, *15 Ways to Buy-Sell-and-Control Real Estate without Using Cash* (Medford, Ore.: Newport, 1975), p. 18.
[8]Nickerson, *How I Turned $1,000 into Five Million*, p. 13.

foreclosed, putting the odds of succeeding in real estate at 400 to 1. Nickerson combines these statistics to produce odds of 1600 to 1 ($4/1 \times 400/1$) for success in income-producing property. With a little thought, one can recognize problems with these statistics and the conclusions that follow.

With all due respect, the "how-to" authors usually mention some of the more critical elements of successful investing, but only casually. Most offer advice on how to select properties utilizing simple rule-of-thumb techniques for both quantitative and qualitative analyses. The implication is that proper use of their respective "rules" and selection of the right properties bring riches very quickly and with minimal risks.

The central theme of *this* book is that sound investment decision making based on thorough return *and* risk analysis is the best strategy for maximizing one's wealth over the long run. In the "how-to" approaches, little emphasis is placed on the development of analytical techniques for forecasting rates of return, and no theoretical framework for decision making is developed. Instead, it is assumed that simple step-by-step formulas can be applied anywhere, at any time, and by anyone of average intelligence. The real estate calculation is simple, and thorough financial analysis is not required.

TRADITIONAL FINANCIAL DECISION APPROACHES

Unlike the "how-to" approaches, both traditional and modern capital-budgeting approaches concentrate on developing decision models that measure financial dimensions and provide quantitative data on which real estate investment decisions can be based. The following sections briefly examine both approaches to investment analysis.

Traditional methods of analysis can be classified as (1) investment value (income capitalization) models, (2) rate-of-return models, (3) best-fit models, or (4) other models, such as payback and gross income multiplier models. In the past, real estate analysts preferred income capitalization models because most appraisers in the field were trained to measure market value. However, recent years have seen a shift to the rate-of-return approach, which more accurately reflects the thinking of many investors and provides data that are more directly comparable. In contrast to modern capital-budgeting models, traditional approaches tend to be mathematically unsophisticated, contain few financial variables, and give little consideration to income taxes, changing cash flows over time, and the time value of money. Their use has remained popular, however, because of the ease of computation and the ease with which they can be explained to the less sophisticated investor. Furthermore, these approaches and models are important because they provide the historical and theoretical background for the development of modern capital budgeting models.

Investment Value Approach

Investment value is the present worth to the investor of expected future net returns capitalized at a rate that reflects the perceived investment characteristics of the property.[9] Investment value is contrasted with *investment cost* (e.g., total purchase costs or total capital assets), which is the total amount of money the investor has spent or expects to spend to acquire a new or existing property. Investment value also is contrasted with the market value and most probable selling price of a property. (See Chapter 2.)

Investment Value Decision Rule. Use of the investment value approach requires that the investor estimate the investment value and investment cost for each project being considered. According to the decision rule, projects are accepted only if the investment value is equal to or greater than the investment cost.

Investment Value Decision Rule

Invest if $\qquad\qquad V \geq C$

Reject or modify if $\quad V < C$

where V = investment value
C = investment cost

If numerous projects are considered simultaneously, a *profitability index* for each project can be computed by dividing investment value by investment cost. Projects can then be ranked on the basis of profitability indexes, with the highest indexes indicating the most desirable projects, and the lowest indexes the least desirable ones. Profitability indexes of less than 1.00 are unacceptable. Three models are commonly used to determine investment value.

Generalized Model of Investment Value. The basic model for computing the investment value of a real estate project is the general appraisal capitalization model ($V = I/R$), with the variables redefined to reflect the individual investor's view.

---

[9]Richard N. Ratcliff, *Real Estate Analysis* (New York: McGraw–Hill, 1961), p. 119.

Generalized Model of Investment Value

$$V = I/R$$

where V = investment value (present worth of future rights to income)

I = net operating income before depreciation and debt service (rental income less operating expenses)

R = capitalization rate (required rate of return on total capital to induce investment)

All the traditional valuation models (including direct capitalization, land residual techniques, building residual techniques, and property residual techniques) are variations of this basic model.

Because of its restrictive underlying assumptions, the generalized model of investment value usually produces a quick-and-dirty ballpark estimate that is appropriate for only the preliminary evaluation of a project. Those assumptions are[10]

1. All cash outflows occur at one time.
2. Productivity is defined as the annual net operating income from property before debt service and income taxes.
3. Income is often a "stabilized amount" derived from an assumption of declining or increasing income over the projection period.
4. The projection period is for the full useful life of the improvements, with no consideration of the ownership life cycle.
5. Capital is recaptured from income, except for land value, which is assumed to be constant. No explicit consideration is given to resale price changes or transaction costs.

Equity–Cash Flow Valuation Model. Another basic model for computing investment value is the equity–cash flow capitalization model, which more fully parallels the orientation of most investors.

---

[10]James A. Graaskamp, "Recent Trends in Real Estate Investment Valuation," in Arthur M. Weimer, Homer Hoyt, and George Bloom, eds., *Real Estate*, 6th ed. (New York: Ronald Press, 1972), p. 356.

Equity–Cash Flow Valuation Model

$$V_E = \frac{CFBT}{RROE}$$

$$V_P = V_E + V_M$$

where V_E = equity value
 CFBT = cash flow before tax
 RROE = required rate of return on equity investment before tax
 (before-tax "cash on cash" return)
 V_P = project value (investment value)
 V_M = mortgage amount

Like the generalized model, the equity–cash flow valuation model is a one-year model and does not explicitly consider the time value of money, equity buildup, changing revenues and expenses, income taxes, or property value increases or decreases over time. Nevertheless, as a "basic economics" testing model and preliminary evaluation technique, this model can be quite valuable. The basic financial feasibility model is presented in detail in Chapter 6.

Ellwood Valuation Model. Developed by L. W. Ellwood, a former chief appraiser for New York Life Insurance Company, the *mortgage equity technique* that bears his name expands on the generalized model of investment value.[11] It is the most sophisticated of the traditional models and was the forerunner of the modern present value approach. Originally used by real estate appraisers, it also gained popularity with brokers and investment counselors as a tool for investment analysis and marketing.[12] Ellwood's technique considers such diverse factors as the length of the holding period, property value change, income increase or decline, and differential rates of return between debt and equity. It differs from the previously discussed techniques in four important respects.

1. Income projections are made over the holding period of the investment rather than its economic life. Since the average period of prop-

---

[11]L. W. Ellwood, *Ellwood Tables for Real Estate Appraising and Financing, Part I*, 3rd ed. (Chicago: American Institute of Real Estate Appraisers, 1970).
[12]See, for example, Irvin E. Johnson, *Selling Real Estate by Mortgage-Equity Analysis* (Lexington, Mass.: Lexington Books, 1976).

erty ownership is eight to ten years, this assumption is more realistic.

2. Mortgage financing and mortgage terms, including equity buildup through loan amortization, are considered explicitly. Traditional capitalization methods tend to ignore the direct impact of mortgage financing on value.

3. The residual value of the investment (property value at the end of the holding period) is estimated rather than ignored or fixed by the underlying mathematical assumptions of the model.

4. The time value of money is considered in discounting resale proceeds and mortgage flows. In addition, net operating income is allowed to vary but must be converted into a stabilized annual amount before the value formula can be applied.

With the Ellwood technique, value is calculated using the basic appraisal capitalization model, $V = I/R$, where I is the stabilized net operating income of the property. Since I is assumed to be constant, the capitalization rate, R, is the critical variable and includes adjustments for all the complications just noted.[13] An overview of the Ellwood approach is presented in Exhibit 3-3. Although the formula for computing R (denominator in equation 3) looks complicated, in practice it is greatly simplified by the use of precalculated tables and programmable calculators. It has been shown by Wendt that the answer produced by the Ellwood model is identical to that produced by the discounted-cash-flow present-value model if identical input assumptions are used and a before-tax profile is assumed.[14]

Despite the sophistication of the Ellwood model as an appraisal technique, investment analysts have observed three deficiencies: (1) it does not consider the income tax effects of real estate ownership; (2) it ignores relative changes in rents, vacancies, and operating expenses over the ownership period; and (3) it does not consider selling expenses and loan prepayment penalties when a property is sold. As a result, most investment analysts prefer the more flexible present-value model, which can explicitly consider all these variables.

Rate-of-Return Approach

The rate-of-return approach is an alternative to the investment value approach for evaluating a real estate investment. Although the two approaches use the same basic formula and usually result in the same accept–

[13]An excellent overview of the Ellwood approach is presented by Peter F. Colwell and Philip J. Rushing in "To Ellwood and Beyond," *The Appraisal Journal*, July 1979, pp. 352–358.

[14]Paul F. Wendt, "Ellwood, Inwood and the Internal Rate of Return," *The Appraisal Journal*, October 1967, p. 563.

EXHIBIT 3-3. A Brief Overview of Ellwood

Ellwood's first premise is that value (V) equals the amount of the loan (L) plus the present value of equity (E):

$$V = L + E \qquad (1)$$

Ellwood's second premise is that the present value of equity is the present value of before-tax cash flow plus the present value of the future selling price minus the present value of the balance due on the mortgage at the time of the sale,

$$E = \sum_{t=1}^{m} \frac{d - VMf}{(1 + y)^t} + \frac{V(1 + app) - VM(1 - P)}{(1 + y)^m} \qquad (2)$$

where d = stabilized net operating income (NOI) and VMf = mortgage payment. Therefore, $d - VMf$ = stabilized before-tax cash flow (BTCF)

y = equity yield rate

m = number of period until property will be sold

app = proportion by which property is expected to appreciate during holding period

$V(1 + app)$ = projected selling price

P = proportion of loan paid off. Therefore, $(1 - P)$ = proportion not paid.

M = loan to value ratio

VM = loan size

$VM(1 - P)$ = balance due at time of sale

Substituting equation 2 into equation 1 and solving for V yields the familiar Ellwood basic equation:

$$V = \frac{d}{y - My + Mf - MP(1/s_m) - app(1/s_m)} \qquad (3)$$

Source: Peter F. Colwell and Philip J. Rushing, "To Ellwood and Beyond," *The Appraisal Journal* (Chicago: American Institute of Real Estate Appraisers), July 1979, p. 353.

---

reject investment decisions, their applications and uses do differ in practice. In traditional rate-of-return models, the concepts are simple: land and building returns do not have to be separated, and investment alternatives can be compared and ranked without first estimating the investor's required rate of return (capitalization rate). For investors who are unsure of their required rates of return, these models avoid the complexities of the value approach in which projects cannot be ranked without first estimating the required rate of return and then capitalizing net income to find value.

Rate-of-Return Decision Rule. The rate-of-return decision approach requires three steps to arrive at a go/no-go decision for a project. First, the investor estimates the expected rate of return. Second, the investor estimates the rate of return necessary to justify the investment and to compensate for the risks involved. Third, the expected and required rates of return are compared to make a go/no-go decision. If the expected rate of return (ROI) is greater than or equal to the required rate of return (RROI), the project meets the investor's financial criteria for a go decision.

Rate-of-Return Decision Rule

Invest if $ROI \geq RROI$

Reject or modify if $ROI < RROI$

where ROI = expected rate of return on investment
         RROI = required rate of return necessary to induce investment

---

Rate-of-Return Calculation Models. The expected rate of return can be measured in a variety of ways, not one of which is universally accepted. Given here are four of the more popular "accounting" or rule-of-thumb measures that can be computed on a before- or after-tax basis.

Traditional Rate-of-Return Calculation Models

1. $\text{Rate of return} = \dfrac{\text{net income before depreciation and debt service}}{\text{total capital invested (purchase price)}}$

2. $\text{Rate of return} = \dfrac{\text{annual cash flow after debt service}}{\text{cash equity investment}}$

3. $\text{Rate of return} = \dfrac{\text{annual cash flow } plus \text{ debt principal amortized}}{\text{cash equity investment}}$

4. $\text{Rate of return} = \dfrac{\text{annual cash flow } plus \text{ debt principal amortized } plus \text{ property appreciation}}{\text{cash equity investment}}$

Probably the most widely used return measure is the second one: cash flow relative to equity investment as measured on a before-tax basis. This measure is often referred to as the *cash-on-cash return*, the *cash throw-off rate*, or the *equity dividend rate*. Although most investors use these measures to calculate the rate of return for a one-year period only, it is beneficial to compute them for each year of a projected holding period on a before- and after-tax basis, as illustrated in Chapters 7 and 8. However, the simplicity of calculating a rate of return for one year only, using adjusted or normalized income and cash flow figures, appeals to many people. The Bockl approach, for example, advocates the calculation of the fourth rate-of-return measure just shown, using after-tax cash flows.

A less widely used rate-of-return measure is the *equity yield* (rate of return) calculated by the Ellwood model (see Exhibit 3-3), in which the investor solves for the equity yield rate y instead of the value of the property V. As is true with most investment value (income capitalization) models, redefining the dependent variable converts the model from an investment value model to a rate-of-return model. The reverse also is true.

Estimation of the Required Rate of Return. Estimation of the required rate of return, against which the investor measures expected return (and which is used as the capitalization rate in the investment value model), is a subjective judgment that the investor makes on the basis of experience, the available rates of return on alternative investment media, inflation expectations, and the riskiness of the property. The required rate of return should include (1) a real return, that is, a return for deferred consumption, (2) an inflation premium, and (3) a risk premium. Together, the "real return" and the "inflation premium" make up what is called a "risk-free" rate of return, representing the return an investor could expect from investments that are free of risk and of equal duration. The investor thus requires that the expected cash flows from a project compensate for deferred consumption, for the expected rate of inflation over the holding period, and for the chance that actual cash flow may not equal expected cash flow.[15] Defining and quantifying the investor's required rate of return has been a central problem in investment analysis for some time and tends to be ignored by the "how-to" authors.

Best-Fit Approach

Although the traditional investment value and rate-of-return approaches are widely used by investors and analysts, the assumptions associated with some of the models are unacceptable to many who feel they do not reflect

[15]Mike E. Miles and Arthur S. Estey, "The Relevant Required Rate of Return," *The Appraisal Journal*, October 1979, p. 513.

current investor objectives and motivations. Their use as decision models is limited because they inadequately account for such important variables as the time value of future cash flows, uneven cash flows, the after-tax value of proceeds from the sale of property, annual tax shelter benefits from depreciation, financing and refinancing alternatives and costs, inflation, possible holding periods, and risk.

However, investors can overcome these limitations in one of three ways. First, they can use more sophisticated discounted-cash-flow models and incorporate more of the relevant variables into a decision model. Second, they can develop a *best-fit* model, which involves a multiple-criteria analysis that considers both nonfinancial and financial variables. Using the best-fit model, investors analyze alternative investments and choose those that best fit the multiple objectives and constraints given. Third, investors can employ a combination of the two approaches, which involves the use of discounted-cash-flow models in conjunction with a best-fit model.

For example, an investor using a best-fit model identifies eleven basic *value* factors that are believed to affect the financial success of a property.[16]

1. Proper location.
2. High-quality construction.
3. Professional property management.
4. Good maintenance.
5. Amenities desired by tenants in the market area.
6. Attractive architecture and good land planning.
7. Good interior layout.
8. Properly selected target market.
9. Competent and reputable developer, owner, or both.
10. Sufficient cash from the project to cover operating costs and debt service.
11. Careful analysis and verification of project's income and expense figures, and determination of their reasonableness in light of recognized standards.

The investor is interested only in existing income properties. Each of the factors is weighed according to its relative importance to the investor, and each property analyzed is reviewed with respect to each factor listed.

After the basic value factors are defined and analyzed, potential returns

[16]William R. Beaton and Terry Robertson, *Real Estate Investment*, 2nd ed. (Englewood Cliffs, N.J.: Prentice–Hall, 1977); see also Lloyd D. Hanford, "Rating Guide for Real Estate Investments," *Journal of Property Management*, March–April 1972.

and risks can be analyzed in terms of *financial* factors and benefits. These benefits might include

1. Amount and stability of future equity cash flow.
2. Equity buildup from loan amortization.
3. Tax shelter benefits.
4. Mortgage-refinancing benefits.
5. Net proceeds from sale or termination of property.

Again, each of the factors is weighed according to its relative importance, and each property is reviewed with respect to each of the potential financial benefits. No sophisticated cash flow models are used. Instead, rule-of-thumb investment criteria can be established on the basis of investment experience for each of the financial variables considered.

Finally, the projects are compared to the multiple investment criteria, and the investor accepts those that have a reasonable or best fit.

Evaluation of the Best-Fit Model. Many of the investment criteria in the best-fit model are *underlying* value (return–risk) factors that influence the investor's cash flow projections and financial-yield calculations. As a vehicle for directly assessing the underlying assumptions that affect yield, the best-fit model is intuitively appealing to many investors because it is easy to use and can incorporate a significant number of complex financial and nonfinancial variables into an understandable decision format. However, two criticisms of these models are (1) that it is difficult to identify the relevant investment criteria and (2) that the process of assigning relative weights to investment criteria is highly subjective.

Other Traditional Approaches

In addition to the traditional financial decision approaches just discussed, two other models are popular with investors: *the gross rent multiplier* (GRM) and the *payback period* approaches. The gross rent multiplier approach advocates acceptance of projects in which purchase prices relative to gross rents are favorable. This method assumes a consistent relationship between the sales price of real estate and its gross rent. The multiplier is simply

$$\text{GRM} = \frac{\text{purchase price}}{\text{gross rental income}}$$

This model is exceptionally easy to use, but lacks sufficient detail to deal with such problems as varying operating expense ratios between properties and changing revenue streams over time. Despite these drawbacks, there is good evidence that such consistent market relationships often *do* exist and provide reliable valuation tools.

Based on the payback period approach, a project is deemed acceptable when there are adequate cash flows to pay back the investor's original capital in less than a specified number of years. The payback model is

$$\text{Payback period} = \frac{\text{investment cost}}{\text{cash flow}}$$

The major criticism of the payback model is that it does not calculate cash flows beyond the payback period. For example, one investment with a cost of $10,000 and producing cash flows of $2,000 per year for six years would pay itself off in five years. Another investment with the same $10,000 cost, but producing cash flows of $1,250 per year for twenty years would pay itself off in eight years. According to the payback period model, the latter would be less desirable because of its longer payback period, yet would continue to produce income for twelve years after payback; the first investment would produce only one additional year of income after payback. Consequently, the second investment, which should be preferred intuitively, would not be selected using the normal payback criterion alone.

MODERN CAPITAL BUDGETING APPROACHES

Modern capital budgeting approaches include present-value models, internal-rate-of-return models, risk analysis techniques, and portfolio analysis techniques. Many variables that are not dealt with explicitly in traditional models are incorporated in these more sophisticated capital-budgeting models, and many of the models have been adapted for computer systems and desktop calculators to make them more convenient for students and practitioners.

Present-Value Model

The present-value model, also called the discounted-cash-flow (DCF) valuation model, does not focus on measuring the capitalization rate as the Ellwood technique does, but instead emphasizes (1) defining income flows as after-tax cash flows, (2) placing cash flows in specific time periods, (3) accounting for each type of cash flow to reflect exposure to income taxes, and (4) relying on compound interest discounts only, rather than all-encompassing but fictional annuity factors.[17]

[17]James A. Graaskamp, "A Practical Computer Service for the Income Approach," *The Appraisal Journal*, January 1969, p. 51.

With the aid of financial tables or modern calculators, each year's net after-tax cash flow is "discounted" by applying a present-value factor derived from formulas based on the time value of money. (This model and the internal-rate-of-return model are fully presented in Chapter 7, along with the topic of time value of money.) The present value of each cash flow is computed, and all present values are added to get the total present value of the income stream generated by the investment during a specified holding period. The present-value decision rule is the same as that for the traditional models: if the investment value is equal to or greater than the cost, the investment is acceptable; otherwise, the investment is rejected or modified.

The following is the basic after-tax present value model.

After-Tax Present-Value Model

$$PV_E = \frac{CF_1}{(1+R)^1} + \frac{CF_2}{(1+R)^2} + \cdots + \frac{CF_n}{(1+R)^n} + \frac{SP}{(1+R)^n}$$

$$PV_P = PV_E + PV_M$$

where PV_P = present (investment) value of property

PV_E = present value of equity returns

$CF_1, CF_2, \ldots, CF_n$ = equity cash flow; annual after-tax cash flow to investor over the holding period (n)

SP = after-tax cash flow from sale of property (reversion cash flow)

PV_M = amount of debt borrowed to finance property (present value of mortgage)

R = required rate of return (IRR) on equity investment

n = holding period of investment

The after-tax cash flow received in each period (CF_1, CF_2, . . . , CF_n) is discounted back to the point of initial investment at the required (internal) rate of return on equity. The series of discounted cash flows is then totaled to measure the present value of the equity returns (PV_E). The present value of the property (PV_P) is then computed as the present value of the equity returns (PV_E) *plus* the amount of debt borrowed to finance the property (PV_M). If the present value of the property (PV_P) is *equal to or greater than* the total investment costs (C), the project is acceptable using the decision rule. If $PV_P < C$, the project should be rejected or modified either to raise PV_P or to lower C.

The investor can also use the basic present-value model to find the *net present value* (NPV) of any series of cash flows by subtracting the total investment cost (C) from the present value of the property (PV_P). As long as the net present value is zero or greater (NPV $\geq$ 0), the project is considered acceptable.

Internal-Rate-of-Return Model

Internal-rate-of-return (IRR) models, or discounted-cash-flow rate-of-return models, as they are sometimes called, have become popular in recent years for evaluating and comparing real estate investments. Many sophisticated investors and analysts consider this rate-of-return measure, or some modified version of it, the proper yardstick for comparing returns between real estate and other investment opportunities, such as bonds, stocks and annuities.[18]

The internal rate of return is the rate, expressed as an annual percentage, at which the present value of the net cash flows equals the present value of the equity investment. IRR can be calculated on a before- or after-tax cash flow basis on either total capital or equity capital invested. Most investors prefer an *after-tax* model, in which IRR is computed on the amount of *equity* investment. If it is computed on a *before-tax* basis on the equity invested and net operating income is held constant, it is identical to the *equity yield rate y* using the Ellwood approach. The basic model for performing this calculation is as follows.

After-Tax IRR on Equity Model

$$E_0 = \frac{CF_1}{(1 + IRR)^1} + \frac{CF_2}{(1 + IRR)^2} + \cdots + \frac{CF_n}{(1 + IRR)^n} + \frac{SP}{(1 + IRR)^n}$$

Solve for IRR,

where IRR = DCF (internal) rate of return on equity capital invested

E_0 = amount of equity investment

$CF_1, CF_2, \ldots, CF_R$ = annual after-tax equity cash flows

SP = after-tax cash flow from sale of property

n = holding period of the investment

---

[18]For an exposition of some of the common methods of measuring the internal rate of return, see Stephen D. Messner, Irving Schreiber, Victor L. Lyon, and Robert L. Ward, *Marketing Investment Real Estate: Finance, Taxation, Techniques* (Chicago: National Association of Realtors, Realtors National Marketing Institute, 1985), pp. 62–81.

The after-tax return on equity is generally recognized as the most significant measure of real estate returns because it explicitly considers the time value of money and the investor's ability to leverage the yield to a high degree, and then shelter the return from income taxes.[19]

The decision rule for investing is the same as the basic rule stated earlier: accept projects that have IRRs equal to or greater than the investor's minimum required IRR (IRR $\geq R$, where R is the investor's minimum required IRR on equity). Projects should be rejected or modified if IRR $< R$.

Risk Analysis Models

Internal-rate-of-return and present-value models are said to be *deterministic* in nature, in that a specific value for each input variable is entered into the model to calculate the desired output. In contrast, a risk analysis model is said to be *probabilistic;* that is, the values of many of the input variables are uncertain and must be defined as ranges with associated probability distributions, rather than as single-point estimates. A risk analysis model thus generates a range of possible returns rather than a single value and ideally will also compute the probability or chances of receiving different rates of return, depending on how the uncertain future unfolds.[20]

Real estate decision makers have always claimed to take calculated risks, but few have made it clear just how they calculate those risks. Without the knowledge of how to deal explicitly with risk in decision making, people typically concentrate on a few key assumptions about the future, examine a few rules of thumb, mull over the situation, and then make a decision. Although some of the risk considerations may be explicit, the mathematics of risk are often left largely to the four horsemen of the implicit decision-making apparatus: judgment, hunch, instinct, and intuition.

In contrast, financial theory has attempted to make risk analysis more explicit and to suggest some improved procedures. Three common methods of analyzing risk are (1) the payback decision rule, which focuses on how long it takes an investor to recover the initial cash investment; (2) the risk-adjusted discount rate, which attempts to account for risk by adding

[19]Paul F. Wendt and Alan R. Cerf, *Real Estate Investment Analysis and Taxation* (New York: McGraw–Hill, 1979), p. 53.

[20]Stephen A. Pyhrr, "A Computer Simulation Model to Measure the Risk in Real Estate Investment," *The Real Estate Appraiser*, May–June 1973, p. 18. (Also published in *American Real Estate and Urban Economics Association Journal*, June 1973, p. 57.) See also Steven D. Kapplin, "Financial Theory and the Valuation of Real Estate under Conditions of Risk," *The Real Estate Appraiser*, September–October 1976, pp. 28–37. See also R. B. Peiser, "Risk Analysis in Land Development," *American Real Estate and Urban Economics Association Journal*, 1984, p. 1.

some premium to the required rate of return demanded (i.e., to the investor's capitalization rate); and (3) conservative forecasts, which deal with risk by reducing forecasted returns to some more conservative level. These three methods, however, have been subjected to increasing criticism. Although they are simple and familiar, they contain assumptions that are not only unclear but may be erroneous and could lead to decisions at odds with the decision maker's own objectives and preferences. In addition, much information that could be valuable for sharpening the decision process is ignored or devalued by these procedures.

Ratio and Sensitivity Analysis. Additional project risk information can be calculated using the techniques of ratio and sensitivity analysis, as illustrated in Chapter 8. Ratios can be used to measure the level and trends of risk by comparing various output data from a cash flow analysis. Popular ratio measures of risk are the debt coverage ratio (the ratio of net operating income to annual debt service) and the breakeven point (the ratio of operating expenses and debt service to gross possible income). In contrast, sensitivity analysis measures risk in the cash flow model by assigning different values to the input variables that are considered to be uncertain, and then measuring their relative impact on the rate of return or other important output variables. With either ratio or sensitivity analysis techniques, if the data indicate a level of risk that is not commensurate with the expected level of return, the project is rejected or modified.[21]

Direct Utility Approach. In a classic article, Richard Ratcliff and Bernhard Schwab suggest that an investor can specify preferences for return and risk in the form of a utility, or preference, curve.[22] This curve can then be used to determine directly the desirability of an investment opportunity on the basis of the possible outcomes and the likelihood of their occurrence. The possible outcomes are calculated by using three estimates for each variable—high, most probable, and low—with corresponding probabilities of 10 percent, 80 percent, and 10 percent.[23] The outcomes produced are used as points on the preference curve to determine the acceptability of an investment.

Monte Carlo Risk Simulation Approach. The most sophisticated probabilistic approach applied to real estate analysis is known as the Monte Carlo risk simulation model. As the name implies, this approach attempts to imi-

---

[21]For a complete discussion of ratio and sensitivity analysis, see Chapters 7 and 8. See also Lawrence S. Thal, "Sensitivity Analysis—A Way to Make Feasibility Analysis Work," *The Appraisal Journal*, January 1982, pp. 57–62.

[22]Richard N. Ratcliff and Bernhard Schwab, "Contemporary Decision Theory and Real Estate Investment," *The Appraisal Journal*, January 1970, pp. 165–187.

[23]Ibid., p. 176.

tate how the variables that influence the investor's rate of return might combine as the future unfolds. That is, probability distributions are estimated for each uncertain factor that affects an investment decision, and the possible combinations of the values for each factor are then simulated to determine the range of possible outcomes and the probability of each.

A general model that synthesizes much of the earlier discussion on return–risk measurement and evaluation, as well as the material on modern techniques of investment analysis, is outlined in Exhibit 3-4. Risk analysis models usually incorporate a present-value or internal-rate-of-return model as a basis for measuring possible investment outcomes; the generalized model is important because it provides a framework for comparing risk measurement with other aspects of an investment decision.

The real estate investment decision process as described in the exhibit has five distinct stages or steps.

1. *Model specification.* The model uses a discounted-cash-flow procedure, such as the IRR on equity or total capital described previously. Input variables are defined as *control variables* or *state variables.* State variables are measured as probability distributions, and control variables are measured as single-point estimates.

2. *Information and estimation.* At this stage, the decision maker's uncertainty about the future is quantified by estimating probability distributions for the state variables. This requires forecasting possible values for each variable with their associated probabilities. The poor quality of data available in real estate makes this requirement difficult to fulfill. Factors and considerations that cannot be quantified (e.g., personal preferences or legal and environmental constraints) are placed in the *intangibles* category and explicitly considered in the final stage of the decision process.

3. *Calculations using Monte Carlo simulation.* In this step, the probabilistic information on state variables and the values of control variables are combined to produce a probability distribution for the expected rate of return on total capital (IRR_{TC}) and equity invested (IRR_E). In addition, liquidity or other measures (break-even point, payback, etc.) can be computed from yearly cash flow data generated during the simulation process.

4. *Project evaluation.* The information that by now has been generated enables the investor to compare projects in a number of ways. Projects can be ranked and compared through the use of risk profiles, probability-of-loss statistics, or desired liquidity measures. The measures used are a matter of personal preference.

5. *The investment decision.* On the basis of all the information generated, including intangibles that could not be quantified or were overlooked, the investor makes a decision to accept or reject the project

EXHIBIT 3-4. A Risk Simulation Model of the Investment Decision Process

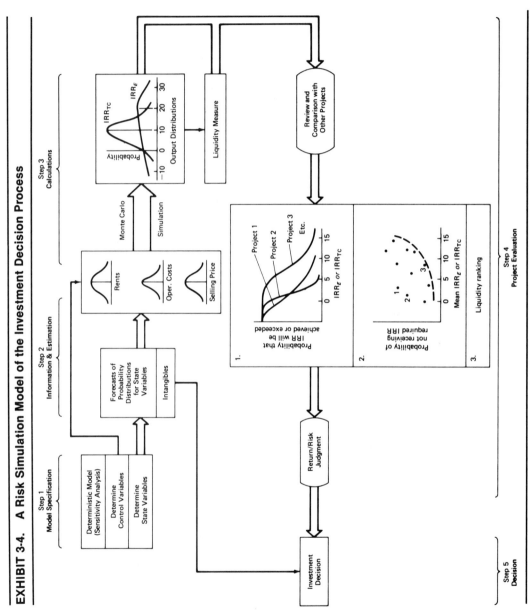

Source: Stephen A. Pyhrr, "A Computer Simulation Model to Measure the Risk in Real Estate Investment," *American Real Estate and Urban Economics Association Journal,* June 1973, p. 57.

during this final step in the investment decision process. At this stage, the investor must weigh all the data on return and risk against personal preferences (utility function) for the various combinations of return and risk.

It is hoped that a formal procedure like the one developed here will help the investor make better and more profitable decisions over the long run. Even if the procedure is not actually used (or a simplified version is used instead), understanding how to approach return and risk analysis and evaluation systematically will materially increase an investor's ability to make more educated judgments and wisely apply hunches, instincts, and intuitions when making investment decisions. Note, however, that investment situations often call for immediate action by the investor, precluding a lengthy period of analysis. When a market advantage can be gained, perhaps a monopoly position created, or a "bargain" taken advantage of, a decision maker must learn to apply the principles and concepts discussed here without the benefit of extensive analysis. Although advocates of the "how-to" approaches are at a disadvantage with their casual attitudes toward the return–risk trade-off, they often are out making deals while IRR analysts zealously rerun their numbers: analytical overkill has blown many a deal for would-be investors who overlooked the importance of flexibility in real estate investment.

Portfolio Analysis. Risk analysis in real estate can be divided into two categories: individual-project risk and portfolio risk. Analysis of individual-project risk, as shown in the Monte Carlo model, examines a single project and implicitly assumes that the risk associated with it can be considered independently of the risk in other investments. Analysis of portfolio risk, conversely, notes the interrelations of various investments. For example, the overall risk profile of a portfolio of diversified real estate projects with different cyclical characteristics may be significantly less than the mean of the individual-project risks because the contracyclical return patterns of some of the projects in the portfolio have a stabilizing effect.

Harry Markowitz developed the basic framework for portfolio analysis in the early 1950s.[24] By taking into account the extent to which returns from investments vary jointly, Markowitz developed a measure for the overall risk in a portfolio of investments. In the 1960s, William Sharpe further developed the general theory of portfolio analysis and asset pricing models. Sharpe introduced the single-index model that simplified Markowitz's model so it could be used by practicing professionals without access

[24]Harry M. Markowitz, *Portfolio Selection: Efficient Diversification of Investment* (New Haven, Conn.: Yale Univ. Press, 1959).

to a mainframe computer. The number of calculations necessary to use the model was significantly reduced.[25] The single-index model was soon super-ceeded by the multi-index model or arbitrage pricing theory (APT). Instead of relying on a single market index as the sole determinant of asset prices, analysts could account for the influence of multiple factors on asset prices and therefore on portfolio construction.[26]

More recently, the consumption-capital asset pricing model (consumption-CAPM), or consumption asset pricing model, was introduced. Research on the APT and consumption-CAPM are progressing at a rapid pace. However, whether these models will produce better results than the Markowitz model has yet to be determined. Most of the research using the APT or consumption-CAPM has been applied to financial assets not real estate assets.[27]

Mathematical portfolio analysis techniques, using the Markowitz and Sharpe models, have been examined and applied to real estate by a number of researchers, including Pellatt;[28] Friedman;[29] Findlay, Hamilton, Messner, and Yormark;[30] Brueggeman, Chen, and Thibodeau;[31] and Webb, Curcio, and Rubens.[32] Despite the proliferation of research in the area, current knowledge is not sufficient to answer many questions relevant to sound portfolio decisions. Several major issues remain open to further investigation. These issues, as well as a thorough examination of

[25]W. F. Sharpe, "A Simplified Model of Portfolio Analysis," *Management Science*, January 1963, pp. 227–93.

[26]D. Bower, R. S. Bower, and D. E. Logue, "A Primer on Arbitrage Pricing Theory," *Midland Corporate Finance Journal*, Fall 1984, pp. 31–40. See also R. H. Fogler, "Common Sense on CAPM, APT and Correlated Residuals," *Journal of Portfolio Management*, Summer 1982, pp. 20–28. See also R. Roll and S. A. Ross, "The Arbitrage Pricing Theory Approach to Strategic Portfolio Planning," *Financial Analysts Journal*, May–June 1984, pp. 14–26.

[27]D. T. Breeden, "An Intertemporal Asset Pricing Model with Stochastic Investment and Consumption Opportunities," *Journal of Financial Economics*, September 1979, pp. 273–96. See also D. T. Breeden, M. R. Gibbons, and R. H. Litzenberger, "Empirical Tests of the Consumption-Oriented CAPM," Research Paper No. 897, Graduate School of Business, Stanford University, 1986.

[28]Peter G. K. Pellatt, "A Normative Approach to the Analysis of Real Estate Investment Opportunities under Uncertainty and the Measurement of Real Estate Investment Portfolios," Ph.D. dissertation, Univ. of California, Berkeley, 1970.

[29]Harris C. Friedman, "Real Estate Investment and Portfolio Theory," *Journal of Financial and Quantitative Analysis*, April 1970, pp. 861–874.

[30]M. Chapman Findlay, Carl W. Hamilton, Stephen Messner, and Jonathan S. Yormark, "Optimal Real Estate Portfolios," *Journal of the American Real Estate and Urban Economics Association*, Fall 1979, pp. 298–317.

[31]W. B. Brueggeman, A. H. Chen, and T. G. Thibodeau, "Real Estate Investment Funds: Performance and Portfolio Considerations," *Journal of the American Real Estate and Urban Economics Association*, Fall 1984, pp. 333–354.

[32]James R. Webb, Richard J. Curcio, and Jack H. Rubens, "Diversification Gains From Including Real Estate in Mixed Asset Portfolios," *Decision Sciences*, Spring 1988, pp. 434–452.

mathematical portfolio analysis and planning, are the subjects of Chapter 18. Personal portfolio planning is addressed in Chapter 19.

SUMMARY

The primary goals of this chapter were to examine and contrast (1) popular "how-to" approaches, (2) traditional financial decision approaches, and (3) modern capital-budgeting approaches to investment decisions. "How-to" approaches tend to discount risk and to oversimplify decisions. They all stress pyramiding, in which the investor borrows the maximum that can be repaid, makes selective improvements to increase property value, then sells at a profit and reinvests in larger properties to start the process over again.

Other related theories and strategies include (1) the conduit theory, which shows how to take advantage of investor age differences; (2) the entrepreneurial leverage theory, which argues that the formula for creating a real estate fortune is youth, management skill, and imaginative borrowing; (3) the four-way benefit test, which advocates that investment returns be analyzed in terms of their component parts; (4) control of property, the key to raising the rate of return; (5) brain compounding, or the ability to increase returns through increased knowledge and expertise; (6) superleverage, in which the investor uses the multiplier effects of increasing rents to increase value and then refinances the property; and (7) finding bargains in the marketplace and improving them in some way.

Traditional and modern decision approaches concentrate on the financial and quantitative dimensions of real estate investment and the application of rate-of-return, present-value, and risk analysis theories. In addition, accept–reject decision rules can be developed for the investment value and rate-of-return approaches; these rules are valid regardless of the level of sophistication of the formula used. The decision rules apply to one-year accounting models, the Ellwood mortgage equity technique, and the internal-rate-of-return (IRR) and present-value (PV) models. Before-tax accounting rate-of-return models are used by the majority of investors, but after-tax models are preferred by sophisticated investors because they explicitly consider more of the variables that affect investment returns and risks. A best-fit decision model is recommended when the investor has multiple investment criteria and constraints and views nonfinancial as well as financial variables as important investment considerations.

Finally, we discussed how risk analysis and portfolio models can be used to sharpen the decision process, to make investment risk considerations more explicit, and to measure the interrelationships among projects over time. Real estate portfolio analysis and portfolio planning are emerging topics that are addressed in depth in Chapters 18 and 19.

SYSTEMATIC INVESTMENT ANALYSIS

Crocker Center South Tower, Los Angeles, California.

This part of the text develops a normative methodology for investment analysis and financial structuring that considers the efficient allocation of human, as well as financial, capital resources. Unfortunately, most investment theories ignore the time resource problems of the decision maker—the time allocation problems associated with performing investment analysis and making accept or reject decisions. Furthermore, most theories implicitly and naively assume a one-shot investment analysis process which results in a "go/no-go" decision.

In contrast, this text advocates a step-by-step investment analysis procedure, one which recognizes that knowledgeable investors develop "drop–continue on" points and have multiple investment objectives and constraints that they apply at different time stages in the project evaluation process. In addition, different procedures and levels of analysis are appropriate for different types of property and different sizes of projects. A "quick-and-dirty" analysis may be appropriate for a six-unit apartment project or a wealthy investor (given the return–risk trade-off preferences), but the professional documentation and standards of quantitative and qualitative analysis for a pension fund investing in a $50 million combination-use building would be very sophisticated.

The chapters in this part generally follow the sequential steps of the investment analysis and financial structuring process model that is presented in Chapter 4.

Chapter 4   Investment Strategy
Chapter 5   Selecting the Ownership Entity
Chapter 6   Preliminary Financial Feasibility Analysis
Chapter 7   Discounted-Cash-Flow and Ratio Analysis
Chapter 8   Risk Analysis and Risk Management: Single Projects
Chapter 9   Financing and Refinancing Decisions
Chapter 10   Tax Planning and Detailed Financial Analysis

A comprehensive case study, the eighty-six-unit Aspen Wood Apartments, is introduced at the end of Chapter 4. This case study, which is presented again at the ends of selected chapters in Parts 2 and 4 of the book, illustrates the application of the concepts and techniques discussed in these chapters.

4

INVESTMENT STRATEGY

Many real estate investors are motivated to develop a sound investment strategy only after they have experienced financial troubles. Even many of the major financial institutions and corporate giants that entered the real estate investment business during the last two decades have had poor performance records. There is considerable evidence that these disappointing results and unrealized expectations can be traced largely to deficient investment strategies.[1]

In this chapter a framework for a real estate investment strategy is defined, and the elements of that strategy for various types of investors are examined. A normative methodology will be developed to guide the investor through the investment analysis and financial structuring process. The focus of this process is on existing projects from the perspective of a managing equity investor. In the final section of the chapter a case study, Aspen Wood Apartments, illustrates the concepts and principles discussed. The case study is reintroduced in most of the chapters as the various facets of the ownership life cycle—acquisition, operation, and termination—are introduced. The Aspen Wood Apartments case provides a well-documented practical application of strategic planning and its successful implementation to achieve expected returns.

The appendix at the end of the chapter serves as a guide to partnership investing by outlining various considerations for selecting a public real estate partnership. As public and institutional types of investment vehicles become more predominant in the marketplace, investors must develop

---

[1] Stephen E. Roulac and Donald A. King, Jr., "Institutional Strategies for Real Estate Investment," *The Appraisal Journal*, April 1978, pp. 257–258; also Larry E. Wofford, "Cognitive Processes as Determinants of Real Estate Investment Decisions," *The Appraisal Journal*, July 1985, pp. 388–389.

better strategies for choosing among these types of indirect equity investments.

FRAMEWORK FOR AN INVESTMENT STRATEGY

We have argued that an investor's primary financial goal should be to maximize financial wealth over the long run. Real estate investment is thus viewed as a process of identifying and structuring projects in order to maximize expected returns relative to risks. As has been illustrated, the first step of this investment process is to develop a strategy—to define the nature and level of the returns and risks that are to be evaluated by the investor and how they can be achieved through the purchase of real estate. The strategy framework is shown in Exhibit 4-1.

Strategy can be defined as "skillful management in getting the better of an adversary or attaining an end."[2] Strategy can also be defined as forging investment goals, setting objectives for the investor's organization in the light of external and internal forces, formulating specific policies to achieve objectives, and ensuring their proper implementation so that the basic purposes and objectives of the investor will be achieved.[3] Strategy thus implies that management skills are developed in order to outperform the competition, skills that will "place the investor in the winner's circle." Such a strategy demands that four important elements be clearly identified and defined: (1) overall investment philosophy, (2) objectives and decision criteria, (3) plans and policies, and (4) a strategy of analysis.

Successful investors are fully aware that real estate investment strategies are carried out in an atmosphere in which "gut feelings," experience, and judgments about the impact of external events greatly affect the decision-making process and investment results. A formal planning system would seem to clash with the style of brilliant intuitive planners like William Zeckendorf, the flamboyant financial and entrepreneurial genius who remodeled whole sections of New York, Denver, Washington, Montreal, and Dallas, and moved the headquarters of the United Nations to New York.[4] A formal planning system, however, might have helped to avoid the "surprises" that destroyed some of Zeckendorf's visionary plans and eventually drove him into bankruptcy. A formal planning system is simply an effort to disclose fully the process of intuitive planning, not to eliminate intuition and judgment.

[2]*American College Dictionary* (New York: Random House, 1966), p. 1195.

[3]For examples, see John B. Miner and George A. Steiner, *Management Policy and Strategy* (New York, Macmillan Co., 1977), pp. 91–121; K. J. Redford, *Strategic Planning: An Analytical Approach* (Reston, Va.: Reston Publishing, 1980), pp. 1–21; and C. Robert Coates, *Investment Strategy* (New York: McGraw–Hill, 1978), pp. 543–544.

[4]William Zeckendorf, *Zeckendorf* (New York: Holt, Rinehart & Winston, 1970).

EXHIBIT 4-1.   Framework for an Investment Strategy

```
                    ┌──────────────┐        ┌────────────────────────┐
                    │              │────────│  Overall Investment    │
                    │              │        │     Philosophy         │
                    │              │        └────────────────────────┘
                    │   STRATEGY   │        ┌────────────────────────┐
                    │ (Return/Risk │────────│ Objectives and Decision│
                    │  Definition) │        │       Criteria         │
                    │              │        └────────────────────────┘
                    │              │        ┌────────────────────────┐
                    │              │────────│   Plans and Policies   │
                    │              │        └────────────────────────┘
                    │              │        ┌────────────────────────┐
                    │              │────────│   Strategy of Analysis │
                    └──────────────┘        └────────────────────────┘
                            │
                            ▼
                    ┌──────────────┐
                    │   ANALYSIS   │
                    │ (Return/Risk │
                    │ Measurement) │
                    └──────────────┘
                            │
                            ▼
                    ┌──────────────┐
                    │   DECISIONS  │
                    │ (Return/Risk │
                    │  Evaluation) │
                    └──────────────┘
```

A formal, systematic strategic planning system can improve on intuitive and judgmental planning and reduce the number and severity of decision-making mistakes. It will result in a strategy that considers the interrelationships among the external environment, social mores, investor resources, and personal values. As can be seen in Exhibit 4-2, only a relatively small number of strategies, those in the darkened area, will be successful. It is the interplay among "might do," "should do," "can do," and "want to do" that determines a successful strategy, one that over the long run will result in high returns relative to risks.

Terminology of Real Estate Investment Strategy

Real estate investment can be a confusing area of study for many people because no standard terminology is accepted by the various disciplines involved. Appraisers, tax accountants, attorneys, lenders, investors, and brokers all use specialized vocabularies, and some words tend to have many aliases. "Cash flow return" is also called "cash flow before tax on equity return," "equity dividend yield," or "cash-on-cash return." There

---

EXHIBIT 4-2.   Determination of a Successful Strategy

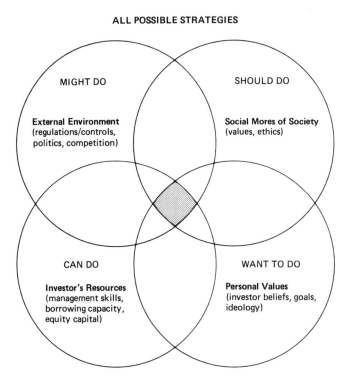

ALL POSSIBLE STRATEGIES

MIGHT DO

External Environment
(regulations/controls,
politics, competition)

SHOULD DO

Social Mores of Society
(values, ethics)

CAN DO

Investor's Resources
(management skills,
borrowing capacity,
equity capital)

WANT TO DO

Personal Values
(investor beliefs, goals,
ideology)

---

are large gaps between the disciplines, and a modern decision-oriented approach to real estate investment is yet to be developed. Such an approach would begin with the acceptance of basic decision terminology, including the following terms.

- *Investment Strategy.* A definition of the nature and level of returns and risks that are to be evaluated by the investor and how they can be achieved through real estate ownership. This is an all-encompassing term that includes as its subparts the determination of an overall investment philosophy, objectives and decision criteria, plans and policies, and a strategy of analysis.

- *Investment Philosophy.* A set of general principles and personal beliefs that guide the investor's behavior. An investment philosophy reflects the investor's financial and management resources and real estate knowledge and skills, the nature of the involvement sought, time availability, and so on. The philosophy determines the nature of the returns and risks that are acceptable to the investor.

- *Investment Objective.* A goal or end toward which investment efforts are directed consistent with the investment philosophy. Investors usually have multiple objectives: general and specific, financial and nonfinancial, short run and long run. Plans and policies are developed to achieve objectives.
- *Investment Criteria.* A standard by which to test whether a proposed course of action will achieve the investment objective. An investment criterion can be stated as a decision rule.
- *Plan.* A course of action or procedures that seeks to achieve agreed-upon objectives. Contingency plans are made should the original plans not result in the desired outcome.
- *Policy.* A rule or course of action used to control plan implementation. Policies are decision rules used during the investment process and are applied after the objectives have been established but before the investment criteria are applied. They act as screening devices that reduce the number of alternatives for consideration and analysis.
- *Strategy of Analysis.* A coordinated group of plans and policies that will guide the investor's behavior throughout the investment process.

Some of these terms are not used in the real estate investment literature; others are misused, not clearly defined, or used interchangeably. Agreement on essential terminology would greatly simplify the communication process and facilitate a systematic approach to investment strategy.

THE INVESTMENT ANALYSIS AND FINANCIAL STRUCTURING PROCESS

How should the investor proceed to acquire, operate, and terminate investment properties? An investor must learn to manage the investment process effectively in order to consistently achieve objectives with a minimum commitment of time and other resources. In short, each investor should have a strategy of analysis or model that outlines step-by-step procedures for acquiring, operating, and terminating a property (see Exhibit 4-3).

Basic Assumptions

This model was designed for a managing equity investor. It focuses on existing income property or properties bought from developers on a turnkey basis. No development period risks are present. The busy investor wishes to minimize the time commitment required for the acquisition and operation of properties, but also wishes to do thorough and systematic analyses. The strategy of analysis must therefore consider how human as

EXHIBIT 4-3.   A Model of the Ten-Step Investment Analysis and Financial Structuring Process

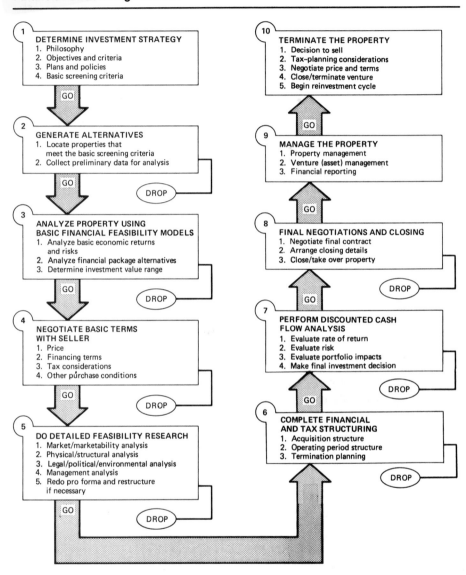

well as financial capital can be allocated effectively. In addition, over the long run the investor is interested in achieving varying degrees of return from each of the four cash flow sources: (1) operations, (2) tax savings, (3) equity buildup from loan amortization, and (4) appreciation of property value. Thus, the investor searches for leveraged properties that will be evaluated and compared on an after-tax basis. Although some investors may purchase on a before-tax and debt-free basis, most notably in the case of some pension funds, the basic principles and procedures are the same.

The Investment Process

The investment analysis and financial structuring process can be viewed as ten sequential stages, as shown in Exhibit 4-3. The separation of these activities is somewhat arbitrary because the stages are highly interrelated, but the model does represent a typical sequence of events that many experienced, knowledgeable, and successful investors follow. More important, it is a "normative" decision model that describes how a rational investor should behave in the situation given, rather than a "descriptive" model that explains how most investors actually behave. There is little reason to perpetuate the naive and intuitive models that are actually used by many investors in the marketplace if the investor's objective is to "do better than the competition."

The model covers the period from an investor's initial interest in a real estate investment through the purchase, operation, and termination of a property. The output from each step feeds into the next. If at any time during the process the investor reaches a point at which the investment being analyzed is no longer attractive in terms of increasingly stringent criteria, the project can be dropped or the information concerning its shortcomings can be used as feedback to restructure the deal. Then, after changes have been made in the assumptions and expected outcomes, the analysis is resumed several steps earlier.

The model describes a general process that is important to most equity investors in income property at any price range. Clearly, the purchase of a single rental house may not entail the explicit exercise of each step, but the thought process is basically the same. The ten steps may be summarized as follows.

Step 1. Determine an Investment Strategy. The investor determines his or her overall investment philosophy, objectives and criteria, plans and policies. From the list of investment criteria and policies, the investor specifies those that will serve as initial screening criteria. These criteria are used to disqualify from further investigation properties that have no reasonable chance of meeting the investor's objectives. Other investment criteria are applied at different stages of the process. Generally, the criteria become more specific and demanding as the investment analysis progresses. It is also common during this process for the criteria to be in a continual state of change as new information (feedback) is acquired and investor perceptions change. Many investors will make their form-of-ownership decision (see Chapter 5) at this stage of the investment process.

Step 2. Generate Alternatives. The investor attempts to locate properties that meet the basic screening criteria. This activity can be time-consuming, frustrating, and unproductive. Roulac's study of professionally managed investment programs showed that for every property purchased, 46 property submissions are considered.[5] Furthermore, for each property submission, many properties must be located and analyzed. Generating alternatives is a very creative and intuitive process, one that becomes more efficient as the investor gains experience in a variety of markets. Chapters 12 and 13 provide a general model for locating investment opportunities. In Chapters 21 through 27 the process is applied to specific types of properties.

Step 3. Analyze the Property Using the Basic Financial Feasibility Models. The basic financial feasibility model has traditionally been a single-period capitalization model that utilizes a one-year cash flow projection, and inputs data on the investor's return–risk requirements as well as the lender's basic loan underwriting requirements. More recently, the availability of computerized investment analysis and financial spreadsheet programs has brought into common use discounted-cash-flow analysis at this step in the investment process. Both types of models can be used to structure and test the basic economics of the project, the available financing alternatives, and the investment value range for the property. Properties that do not meet the investment criteria imposed at this stage of the analysis are dropped from further consideration or modified until the criteria are met. An acceptable financial structure can often be achieved through negotiation.

Step 4. Negotiate Basic Terms with the Seller. The buyer begins to discuss and negotiate the basic parameters of the deal with the seller, including price, terms, and tax considerations. The preliminary offer and negotiations are based on the objectives defined in step 1 and the analysis performed in step 3. The objective at this stage is to achieve a basic meeting of the minds before valuable time is spent on detailed feasibility research.

Before doing more work on the property, the buyer must take action to tie up the property. Later chapters deal with options, real estate contracts, letters of intent, and other ways of legally binding sellers while the buyer makes further investigations. In some situations it may require only a handshake for the buyer to obtain the seller's commitment to hold the property off the market until the feasibility research has been completed and negotiations can continue. Chapter 15 is devoted to the art of negotiation.

[5]Stephen E. Roulac, *Modern Real Estate Investment* (San Francisco: Property Press, 1976), p. 477.

Step 5. Do Detailed Feasibility Research. The investor collects and analyzes information in four areas: (1) market and marketability factors affecting the property; (2) the physical and structural condition of the property; (3) legal, political, and environmental considerations; and (4) management and operation of the property. Evaluation of these data, along with expectations regarding inflation and real estate cycles, enable the investor to make cash flow forecasts over the entire ownership life cycle. In most cases the new information brings about a reevaluation of the basic economics of the project (step 3) and, often, renegotiation of some of the basic parameters of the deal with the seller. Often projects are abandoned at this point because the new information places the property in an undesirable return–risk category.

Step 6. Complete Financial and Tax Structuring. The investor must fine-tune the financial and tax structure of the project before a complete discounted-cash-flow after-tax analysis of the property can be performed to determine its complete rate-of-return and risk characteristics. Financial and tax experts are consulted at this step to assure that all feasible structures are defined and tested. The three different "ownership life cycle" time periods produce differing tax and financing consequences and should be carefully analyzed.

1. Front-end tax deductions and financing costs affect cash flow in the year of acquisition.
2. Operating period tax deductions and financing costs affect cash flow during the period of ownership.
3. The termination period causes a "mixed bag" of tax and financing effects, including recognition of accrued tax liabilities, possible deferral of income through exchange and installment sales, payback of accrued interest expenses and prepayment penalties, and so on.

These subjects are discussed in Chapters 9 and 10.

Step 7. Perform a Discounted-Cash-Flow Analysis. The investor combines all the information and data generated from the previous steps and performs a rigorous discounted-cash-flow after-tax analysis of the property. A thorough analysis of the important rate-of-return and risk parameters of the project is performed, including a sensitivity analysis of key financial variables, and the results are compared to the most stringent investment criteria developed in step 1. Possible portfolio impacts are evaluated. At this point, the investment has successfully passed the hierarchy of other tests imposed at each step of the process and a final investment decision is made: either the project is abandoned or the investor enters final negotiations with the seller. These subjects are discussed in Chapters 7, 8, 18, and 19.

Step 8. Final Negotiations and Closing. At this point the investor knows what trade-offs affect the returns and risks associated with the property, what can be given up and what must be negotiated at the final bargaining session. The investor is in a good position to increase expected returns relative to risks through a final negotiation process that takes advantage of the personal preferences and biases affecting the positions of both the buyer and the seller. Ideally, the final purchase contract is drawn and closing details are arranged at this point. The buyer, the seller, and their attorneys go to a closing, review the final documents, sign the necessary papers; deeds are recorded and moneys disbursed. If the process goes smoothly, the investor has legally acquired the property. In many cases, however, the process does not follow the desired scenario: Disputes and arguments arise, tempers flare, and the deal falls through. Buyers and sellers should be prepared for "surprise negotiation tactics" at the closing. Coolheaded investors can still make good deals, in keeping with the investment strategy, through effective confrontation and conflict resolution. These concepts are discussed in Chapter 15.

Step 9. Manage the Property. After the acquisition, competent property and asset management becomes the critical aspect of successful ownership. Property management should have both authority and accountability for achieving the cash-flow projections on which the investment decision was based. Asset (venture) management is responsible for managing the property manager, reporting to the investors, monitoring the performance of the property, and refinancing or selling the property when such action is advantageous. The smaller investor may perform all management functions; larger institutions and syndicators often delegate responsibility to a number of specialists and professionals. These considerations are discussed in Chapter 16.

Step 10. Terminate the Property. Eventually the property is sold or exchanged, or is the subject of an involuntary conversion or foreclosure. The timing of a sale is critical if the investor is to obtain the most favorable price and terms. Like the original acquisition, the negotiations and the closing process can be problematic. After the closing, the venture is dissolved and final reports are issued to the investors. If an involuntary conversion, tax-deferred exchange, or installment sale takes place, the process is somewhat altered and deserves special consideration. Chapter 17 discusses these subjects.

The ten-step process just described is the subject of the next thirteen chapters. The greatest emphasis in this process is clearly on the acquisition phase of investment, which involves steps 2 through 8. Although excellence in all phases of the investment process is important for long-run success, it is especially important for the acquisition process. At this stage the returns and risks are analyzed and structured and the character of the investor's portfolio is established. If the process of acquiring properties is poorly structured and executed, good return–risk performance is unlikely to follow.

Although the ten-step process is dynamic and should be modified to fit each situation, it does provide a checklist of essential considerations for the investor wishing to participate in the real estate investment process. Like an airline pilot's preflight preparation, the ten-step investment checklist is a risk management and control device.

DEVELOPING AN INVESTMENT STRATEGY

The following sections detail the various elements of an investment strategy as described in step 1 of the investment process.

Investment Philosophy

An investment philosophy must address the nature and degree of the investor's involvement in real estate activity, including the following alternatives.

1. *Direct or indirect involvement.* Will properties be bought outright or owned through shares of a company or partnership that owns real estate? If indirect involvement is chosen, shares of an REIT, a development company, or a syndicate may be bought, or investments can be made in companies that provide services to the real estate industry, such as brokerage and appraisal.

2. *Time investment.* How much time should be devoted to investment activities? Perhaps investment will begin as a part-time venture and later become a full-time pursuit.

3. *Investor role.* Would the investor prefer to be a passive equity investor, managing equity investor, or joint-venture partner? On occasion he or she might choose to become a mortgage lender by selling a property and financing the sale in order to achieve installment sales treatment. A desire for a well-balanced portfolio may require numerous roles to be taken on simultaneously or a shift in roles to take advantage of real estate cycles.

4. *Management style and functions.* Will professional managers be hired or will the property be self-managed? Who will manage the financial affairs of the venture that owns the property? Will some or all of the tax, accounting, and legal work be done in-house or by outside consultants? Will management be a freewheeling one-man show, or will the investor seek to build a management team that gives continuity to the investment program?

The answers to these questions will be important aspects of the investor's overall investment philosophy. In addition, the investor should consider the types of returns and risks sought, given his or her financial resources and constraints, and whether the focus will be on portfolio analysis (estate building) or project analysis. Many astute investors have observed that portfolio values are created at the project level; the greatest emphasis, therefore, should be on project analysis, not portfolio analysis.[6] As Chapter 3 emphasizes, if projects are bought and sold in a way that generates, on average, high compounded yields, the theory of compound interest will take care of the portfolio over the long run. Although the ultimate goal may be to produce a multimillion-dollar estate or portfolio, the key to accomplishing this goal is analysis and control of individual properties.

Investment Principles

An important part of the investor's philosophy should be a set of principles like the following, which were developed by the Coldwell Banker Company.[7]

1. *"The buyer should buy the assumptions that create the yield rather than the yield itself."* Real estate investment is seen as a process of validating key assumptions, such as income, expenses, and resale. The investors who most thoroughly validate assumptions are the most successful.

2. *"The investor should be as concerned about what to offer the next buyer as with what he is buying."* Often real estate investment is based on speculation and reliance on the "greater fool theory." Sound investment philosophy is based on the assumption that the next investor, as well as the present one, will value the property on an economic basis using realistic economic assumptions.

3. *"The investor should price the property apart from the tax advantages."* The project should make sense from a "basic economics" viewpoint—cash in and cash out. Over the entire ownership life cycle, real gains are more important than tax gains produced by artificial tax losses. Ultimately, most tax losses turn into real losses if a project is not supported by real economic gains (e.g., price appreciation and cash flow from operations).

4. *"The investor should compare alternatives."* Investment analysis is

[6]Fred E. Case, *Investing in Real Estate* (Englewood Cliffs, N.J.: Prentice–Hall, 1978), p. 50.

[7]Robert M. Ellis, *Real Estate Investment Analysis* (Los Angeles: Coldwell Banker Company, 1976), p. 5.

the process of comparing assumptions and property alternatives. A real estate investment is good only to the extent that its assumptions are better than other alternatives. If the assumptions are analyzed incorrectly, the rate of return and risk projections will be incorrect.

5. *"The investor should understand the potential profit and risks in terms of dollars and cents."* Investors should not leave the measurement of return and risk to intuition and hunch. They should attempt to quantify their judgments and measure the impact of investment uncertainties on the expected after-tax returns of each venture. The final investment decision requires a comparison of project returns and risks with the investor's objectives, constraints and resources, and relative returns on other types of investments.

Thus, profitable real estate investing is seen as a process of finding properties that produce higher returns with more realistic assumptions. Profitable real estate investing is a critical balance among assumptions, alternatives, and yields.

Investment Objectives

The overall investment philosophy is a set of general principles that guide the investor's behavior, and objectives are ends toward which that behavior is directed. (The terms *goals* and *objectives* are often used interchangeably.) Investors generally develop a hierarchy of objectives, some long term and others short term, some financial and others nonfinancial, some very simplistic and others very sophisticated.

Each investor's objectives are unique to his or her personal, financial, and tax situation. As discussed in Chapter 1, investors have many general goals and objectives.[8]

1. Protection of purchasing power.
2. Diversification.
3. Tax shelter.
4. Regular return.
5. Capital gain.
6. Retirement income.
7. Estate building.

[8]See also Paul F. Wendt and Alan R. Cerf, *Real Estate Investment Analysis and Taxation* (New York: McGraw-Hill, 1979), pp. 333–334; James R. Cooper, *Real Estate Investment Analysis* (Lexington, Mass.: Lexington Books, 1974), p. 10; Mary Alice Hines, *Real Estate Investment* (New York: Macmillan Co., 1980), pp. 187–191; Austin J. Jaffe and C. F. Sirmans, *Fundamentals of Real Estate Investment* (New York: Prentice–Hall, 1986), pp. 4–5.

  8. Investment for use.
  9. Minimum equity.
 10. Rapid recovery of equity.
 11. Entrepreneurial profit.

A specific investor's objectives would logically be some subset of the ones in this list. The objectives of the pension investment fund founded in 1970 by the Prudential Life Insurance Company provide a good example. Currently the PRISA (Prudential Property Investment Separate Account) fund owns more than 900 properties with a value in excess of $2.75 billion.

> The objective of PRISA is to obtain an attractive rate of current income from the property investments which offer prospects of long term growth, in order to enhance the resources of participating pension plans to provide benefit payments. To fulfill that objective, Prudential invests PRISA funds primarily in the purchase of income producing real property including office and industrial buildings, shopping centers, other retail stores, apartments, hotels, and motels. Suitable diversification is maintained as to type of property and location. Particular attention is given to properties which are located in growth areas, may be leased on a basis permitting suitable rent revisions, and are considered to have good appreciation potential.[9]

Thus, PRISA's most important objectives are regular return, capital gain, and diversification, with the ultimate objective being retirement income to be provided by the individual pension plans around the country that participate in the PRISA fund. Little attention is paid to tax shelter because the pension plans themselves receive favorable tax treatment and because tax losses cannot be passed through to the individuals who contribute to the pension plans. In contrast, one of the main objectives of many limited-partnership syndications in the past has been to structure investments that provide a high degree of tax shelter for the participants, and to allocate tax losses that could be used to shelter other income earned by the investor. With the passage of the Tax Reform Act of 1986, which severely curtailed the tax shelter advantages of real estate and destroyed many tax-oriented syndications, surviving syndicators and partnerships have realigned their objectives more closely with investors such as PRISA. Thus, there has been (and until the next tax reform there will continue to be) a return to objectives that emphasize real, rather than legislated, economic returns.

Written Objectives. The investor's objectives should be carefully developed and committed to writing. Experienced investors do not deviate from their written objectives. They do, however, review these objectives fre-

___

[9]"A New Dimension in Pension Funding. PRISA—The Prudential Property Investment Separate Account."

quently in order to determine whether they are still valid and attainable in light of changing market conditions and changing personal net worth. If they are not, they are revised.

The Short Run Versus the Long Run. Historically, many individual and institutional equity investors have relied on one-year cash flow pro formas for their decision analysis. Syndicators and brokers have packaged investments and received all or most of their fees at the time of purchase rather than according to a formula based on property performance. Inadequate feasibility analysis of future trends and probable events has precluded the use of long-term forecasts as a basis for decision making. Nevertheless, successful real estate investing requires active, continuing, and prolonged involvement, and the responsibility should be delegated accordingly.

Although short-run solvency is necessary, overall long-run profitability is the paramount objective. In the ten-step model developed here, both short- and long-term objectives are addressed. For example, short-run return and risk criteria are emphasized in the basic financial feasibility models (step 3), whereas long-term (ownership period) return and risk criteria are emphasized in the discounted-cash-flow models (steps 3 and 7).

Unrealistic Objectives. Research studies have shown that real estate investors may be unrealistic in their return expectations. Most investors and managers indicate that they expect to outperform historical investment results. A survey by the Department of Housing and Urban Development, for example, found that 83 percent of the respondent investors expected an average annual return of 12 percent when, in fact, they had historically received only 10.5 percent.[10] In addition, Roulac has concluded that most investor objectives and criteria are little more than irresponsible hearsay and are totally lacking in trustworthiness.[11] The less-than-impressive real estate performance record is striking evidence of the broad gap between expectations and realizations. Investors must learn to eliminate this gap and to be more precise and realistic in establishing their objectives.

Financial Versus Nonfinancial Objectives. Investors consider numerous nonfinancial as well as financial objectives when developing an investment strategy. A HUD study of 137 investors of different types located in major cities around the nation analyzed both their financial and nonfinancial objectives. In rating financial objectives, all the investors ranked annual cash return (before tax from operations) as their most important objective. Tax

---

[10]U.S. Department of Housing and Urban Development, *Study on Tax Considerations in Multi-Family Housing Investments* (Washington, D.C.: U.S. Gov't. Printing Office, 1972), p. 43.

[11]Roulac, *Modern Real Estate Investment*, p. 89; also, Wofford, "Cognitive Processes," pp. 388–389.

shelter, capital appreciation, financial leverage, and low risk of loss were also ranked high, but were of secondary importance. Liquidity and cash fees were consistently ranked lowest by all types of investors. In rating nonfinancial objectives, active and passive investors compiled lists that varied widely and differed substantially. Generally, investors cited location as the most important nonfinancial factor but maintained that if any one of the factors—supply, demand, availability of mortgage financing, builder reputation—was out of line, the project might not be feasible.

Because the real estate investment industry is becoming more institutionalized and securitized, more information is becoming available on the explicit objectives and goals of investors and investment programs. For example, investment prospectuses for both public and private offerings by syndicators, REITs, and pension funds typically contain comprehensive discussions on real estate investment objectives and related investment policies for achieving those objectives.

Ranking Objectives. The investor must devise a ranking system when financial and nonfinancial objectives are numerous. A model must be developed for finding a "best fit" between property characteristics and investor objectives. Since not all the objectives can be achieved with equal success, the investor must decide the order in which they should be achieved and the relative importance of each. For example, in a period of rising inflation, investors should look increasingly to long-run capital gains and sacrifice some current income from operations. For most types of property it is difficult, if not impossible, to achieve both simultaneously.

Decision Criteria

Explicitly stated financial and nonfinancial objectives reveal the complex nature of the return–risk trade-off that the investor is willing to accept and the unfolding of his or her investment philosophy. The process of developing objectives provides insight into what types of real estate investments the investor will consider, how much to invest, what kind of financing will be acceptable, how much liability can be assumed, what the best legal form of ownership is, where in the property and real estate cycles the investor will invest, and how long the investment will be held. Objectives also provide insight into the things the investor will not do and does not want. The investor may not want an investment that is so risky or so dominant that it could jeopardize the entire portfolio and perhaps ruin the investor's credit and reputation. Or the investor may not want an investment that requires too much time.

Once the investor has specified the nature of the risks and returns that are acceptable, criteria are developed for judging the magnitude of the returns and risks measured. In short, objectives define where the investor is going, and the criteria signal when the objectives have been reached. For example, if the objective is cash flow from operations, the criteria will pin-point an amount of cash flow that will be acceptable in a given situation. The criteria might be that a shopping center purchase be structured to achieve a minimum of 8 percent cash flow before tax in the year of acquisition, with this rate equaled or exceeded each year for a minimum of five years.

Exhibit 4-4 illustrates various types of financial and nonfinancial criteria that have been used by investors in the past. However, these will be different for each investor and investment situation, and will be modified as the investment process produces new information.

Some of the criteria relate primarily to the rate-of-return dimension; others relate primarily to the risk dimension; and still others are indirect measures of both. The internal rate of return is clearly a measure of return, whereas a break-even point is clearly a measure of risk. A purchase price maximum of $90 per square foot for a shopping center, on the other hand, is a rule-of-thumb criterion that experience might show to be a reasonable maximum to pay in order to achieve an acceptable return–risk ratio for a specific investor operating in a local market. The nonfinancial criteria also relate, usually indirectly, to returns and risks. A "structurally sound" building with good "curb appeal" is presumed by some investors to have a more favorable return–risk ratio than one that lacks these characteristics. Dealing only with reputable sellers increases the probability of closing a deal, thereby reducing the risk of loss.

The various criteria will be applied at different stages in the investment process. Curb appeal may be an initial screening criterion and the internal-rate-of-return objective may be applied many steps later. Each criterion should also be ranked according to the importance of the investment objective it represents. Curb appeal may not be as important as the location of an office building. If a property has an excellent location, a relatively unimpressive facade may not be important enough to eliminate the project from consideration during the initial screening process.

Surveys and Studies of Investor Decision Criteria. Several researchers have undertaken studies to determine what decision criteria are used by investors in the acquisition process.[12] These studies have investigated the

[12] James R. Webb and Willard McIntosh, "Real Estate Acquisition Rules for REITs: A Survey," *The Journal of Real Estate Research*, Fall 1986, pp. 67–98; James R. Webb, "Real Estate Investment Acquisition Rules for Life Insurance Companies and Pension Funds: A Survey," *American Real Estate and Urban Economics Association Journal*, Winter 1984, pp. 495–520; Daniel E. Page, "Criteria for Investment Decision Making: An Empirical Study," *The Appraisal Journal*, October 1983, pp. 498–508; Edward J. Farragher, "Investment Decision-Making Practices of Equity Investors in Real Estate," *The Real Estate Appraiser and Analyst*, Summer 1982, pp. 36–41; Robert J. Wiley, "Real Estate Investment Analysis: An Empirical Study," *The Appraisal Journal*, October 1976, pp. 586–592.

EXHIBIT 4-4.   Examples of Investment Criteria

FINANCIAL CRITERIA

A. *Measures of Rate of Return*

1. A cash-on-cash return (cash flow/equity investment) of at least 8 percent.
2. A cash flow and equity buildup of at least 10 to 12 percent.
3. Appreciation of property value of at least 3 to 5 percent annually.
4. Front-end tax write-offs of at least 20 percent of each dollar invested.
5. Holding-period write-offs that shelter all cash flow.
6. An internal rate of return on the equity investment of at least 14 percent.
7. A net present value greater than or equal to zero.

B. *Measures of Risk*

1. A break-even point (operating expenses plus debt service divided by the gross possible income) less than 86 percent.
2. A coverage ratio (net operating income/debt service) not less than 1.20.
3. No all-bills-paid complexes; utilities pass through to the tenants.
4. A leverage ratio (debt/purchase price) not higher than 80 percent or, for a speculator, not less than 90 percent.
5. A strong rental occupancy history.
6. Payback period: all cash back within five years.

C. *Measures That Combine Risk and Return*

1. A gross rent multiplier less than 6.
2. A purchase price per unit maximum of $45,000 for apartments.
3. A purchase price per square foot maximum of $90 for shopping centers.

NONFINANCIAL CRITERIA

1. Structurally sound building.
2. Aesthetically pleasing design.
3. Age of building: five to seven years, no new buildings.
4. Size: more than 100 units for managerial efficiency, fewer than 20 for individual investor–managers.
5. Tenants: no special-use buildings; must be multitenant, general use.
6. Leases: must have good escalation clauses and be of relatively short duration.
7. Management burden of an acceptable level.
8. No flat roofs, gas air conditioners, or asbestos insulation problems.
9. Neighborhood: location must be promising—in path of growth and near major traffic arteries.
10. Must be able to obtain clear title with no complex legal problems.
11. Environment must be acceptable; pleasing landscape, no threat of floods.
12. Trustworthy seller with good reputation.
13. Type of property must be desirable and marketable.

---

decision-making practices of REITs, pension funds, real estate developers, insurance companies, and real estate companies. The results have clearly shown that decision-making practices have changed dramatically over the last fifteen years as a result of increased computer use, severe inflation cycles, deregulation of the financial markets, new investment and tax legislation, and rapidly increasing real estate values. In general, the decision criteria used have become more extensive and sophisticated, as real estate decision makers have become more educated and experienced in the application of modern capital-budgeting techniques.

Exhibits 4-5 and 4-6 show the comparisons of before-tax and after-tax investment criteria, and ratio and risk analysis techniques used by REITs, insurance companies, and real estate corporations. Some of the findings and conclusions of these studies are quite informative. First, most investors cite the importance of both before-tax and after-tax investment criteria, but they point out that after-tax criteria have become more important in recent years. The most popular before-tax rules of thumb are the equity dividend rate (cash flow/equity investment) and the overall capitalization rate (net operating income/total investment).

A second important conclusion is that the internal rate of return has become the most important investment criterion and the evaluation technique most widely used by all types of investors. This technique is used for before-tax analysis as well as for after-tax analysis, indicating the increasing importance of time value of money concepts. Third, the use of ratio analysis has become increasingly common and popular for evaluating a project's profitability and risk characteristics. The most popular risk ratios are the debt coverage ratio and the default ratio. The most commonly used profitability ratio is the return on equity (also called "equity dividend rate" and "cash-on-cash return"). Investors have increased their focus on this current-return measure since the moderation of inflation rates and recent tax legislation have eroded away the tax and appreciation benefits of real estate that were characteristic of the early 1980s.

A final conclusion is that more investors are using explicit risk adjustment techniques in their investment evaluation process, but that larger firms are more likely to employ this type of criteria than smaller firms. The three most popular techniques for adjusting risk are (1) adjusting downward the cash flows expected from the project, (2) adjusting upward the required rate of return, and (3) performing a sensitivity analysis. Of the three techniques, the second appears to have taken the lead in popularity in recent years. Webb's study of 111 REIT investors shows that 77 percent of them use this technique to adjust for risk.[13]

Plans and Policies

Every investor should have an investment plan that defines a step-by-step procedure for achieving objectives. The ten-step investment process that

---

[13]Webb and McIntosh, "Real Estate Acquisition Rules," pp. 83–84.

EXHIBIT 4-5.   Before- and After-Tax Investment Criteria

BEFORE-TAX

Before-Tax Measure	Percentage of 31 REITs	Percentage of 45 Insurance Companies	Percentage of 25 Real Estate Corporations	Percentage of 101 Respondents
Rules of thumb				
Payback period	7	17	6	12
Net income multiplier[a]	7	17	19	14
Gross income multiplier[b]	0	5	13	5
BTCF multiplier[c]	15	15	6	13
Overall capitalization rate[d]	26	66	25	45
Equity dividend rate[e]	26	39	31	33
Other	4	7	0	5
Discounted-cash-flow method				
before-tax IRR	48	66	50	57
No before-tax measure used	4	3	13	5

[a] Net income multiplier = total investment/net operating income.
[b] Gross income multiplier = total investment/gross income.
[c] Before-tax cash flow multiplier = equity investment/BTCF.
[d] Overall capitalization rate = net operating income/total investment.
[e] Equity dividend rate = BTCF/equity investment.

AFTER-TAX

After-Tax Measure	Percentage of 31 REITs	Percentage of 45 Insurance Companies	Percentage of 25 Real Estate Corporations	Percentage of 101 Respondents
Rules of thumb				
Payback period	6	13	7	11
After-tax rate[a]	0	29	0	17
After-tax multiplier[b]	17	11	14	14
Discounted-cash-flow techniques				
Net present value	6	18	36	20
Internal rate of return	22	61	43	50
Financial management rate of				
return	0	16	7	11
Profitability index	0	3	7	3
Tax shelter benefits	11	11	0	9
Other	6	3	7	5
No after-tax measure used	50	13	21	26

Source: Daniel E. Page, "Criteria for Investment Decision Making: An Empirical Study," *The Appraisal Journal,* October 1983, pp. 500–501. Also see James R. Webb and Willard McIntosh, "Real Estate Acquisition Rules for REITs: A Survey," *The Journal of Real Estate Research,* Fall 1986, pp. 81–83.
[a] After-tax rate = after-tax cash flow/equity investment.
[b] After-tax cash flow multiplier = equity investment/after-tax cash flow.

EXHIBIT 4-6. Ratio and Risk Analysis Techniques

RATIO ANALYSIS IN INVESTMENT DECISION MAKING

Do you use ratio analysis?	Percentage of 31 REITs	Percentage of 45 Insurance Companies	Percentage of 25 Real Estate Corporations	Percentage of 101 Respondents
Yes	72	78	47	70
No	28	22	53	30
Type of Ratios Used:				
Leverage ratios				
Mortgage debt to property value[a]	47	34	20	36
Debt coverage[b]	21	40	20	44
Default ratio[c]	21	29	20	25
Total asset turnover[d]	5	6	10	6
Operating expense ratio[e]	26	23	10	22
Profitability ratios				
Profit margin	0	0	10	2
Return on total investment	5	20	20	16
Return on equity	11	43	30	31
Other ratios used	21	14	20	17

[a]Mortgage debt to property value = mortgage outstanding/property value.
[b]Debt coverage = net operating income/debt service.
[c]Default ratio = operating expense + debt service/gross income.
[d]Total asset turnover = gross income/property value.
[e]Operating expense ratio = operating expenses/gross income.

RISK ADJUSTMENT TECHNIQUES

Risk Adjustment Technique	Percentage of 31 REITs	Percentage of 45 Insurance Companies	Percentage of 25 Real Estate Corporations	Percentage of 101 Respondents
Adjust upward the required rate of return for the project	33	28	31	30
Adjust downward the cash flows expected from the project	33	40	44	39
Use decision trees	4	0	0	1
Use sensitivity analysis	26	20	13	20
Use probability distributions	0	5	19	6
Other adjustments	0	8	0	4
No explicit adjustments for uncertainty	19	30	13	23

Source: Daniel E. Page, "Criteria for Investment Decision Making: An Empirical Study," *The Appraisal Journal,* October 1983, pp. 503–504. Also see James R. Webb and Willard McIntosh, "Real Estate Acquisition Rules for REITs: A Survey," *The Journal of Real Estate Research,* Fall 1986, p. 84.

has been described is a master plan to guide the investor's behavior throughout the investment and financial structuring process. At each stage of analysis investors should have a plan that will guide them through the maze of alternatives, help them compare the characteristics of the property to their criteria, and allow them to arrive at a logical decision of whether to go on or drop the project from consideration. Thus, an investment plan outlines how investors are to proceed to achieve objectives and apply the investment criteria. The plan should be flexible rather than rigid, and should provide for contingencies.

Investment policies are used to control plan implementation and act as a screening device to reduce the number of alternatives for consideration and analysis, as well as the amount of time required of the investor. A good example is the statement of purchasing policy developed by two full-time investor–developers in Washington, D.C., who started with a combined net worth of $60,000 and thirteen years later had a combined net worth of over $2 million. Their purchasing policies are shown in Exhibit 4-7.

Basic Screening Criteria

From the full set of investment criteria and policies, some basic screening criteria can be designated to disqualify a property early in the process, without further exploration. These criteria are used to evaluate the properties located during step 2 of the investment process. For example, some investors will not look at any property that is more than an hour's drive from their home, or will not consider student, military, or low-income housing. Many institutional investors are afraid to purchase commercial buildings in which asbestos products were used for insulation and fire-proofing. Other investors will not consider apartments because they are management-intensive; they prefer commercial properties that are relatively new, well located, and have plenty of "curb appeal" to impress limited-partner investors. Such preferences, and others, can be so overriding to a particular investor that they serve to eliminate many possible choices at the outset. Basic screening criteria should be foremost in the investor's mind as alternatives are located to avoid spending too much time investigating properties that have no chance of meeting the investor's needs.

Once investment properties have been located (step 2), the screening criteria serves to differentiate among them. If weights have been assigned to financial and nonfinancial criteria, potential acquisitions can be ranked according to the initial likelihood that they can fulfill investor objectives. The investor will want to continue investigating only the best opportunities.

Objectives and criteria developed in step 1 are used to judge acceptability throughout the investment process. At each step in the process, the project is evaluated against increasingly more demanding criteria. A proj-

---

EXHIBIT 4-7.   A Statement of Purchasing Policy

A. *Large Properties Only*

1. Office buildings having a minimum net rental area of 80,000 square feet.
2. Shopping centers in excess of 80,000 square feet of net rentable space or prime leasebacks.
3. Industrial leasebacks such as warehouses and research laboratories to AAA-1 tenants.
4. Apartment buildings having a minimum of 100 rental units.
5. Vacant ground to accommodate any of the structures listed above.

B. *New or Relatively New Properties Only*

1. To ensure an attractive property for loan purposes at the outset and for refinancing purposes after acquisition. This policy recognizes that many lenders, especially insurance companies, avoid making loans on older properties.
2. To ensure that amortization exceeds depreciation (*actual* wear and tear) so that the investor's equity is constantly increasing.
3. To provide a desirable property for sale after depreciation is no longer attractive enough in its tax consequences to produce tax-sheltered income. (This policy should not rule out properties that have been or may be completely restored through the installation of new mechanical, electrical, and air-conditioning equipment.)

C. *Large Equities, Never Thin*

The payment of sufficient equity capital above a conservative first deed of trust (mortgage) to ensure servicing of nonfluctuating debt service even in periods of economic recession.

D. *Limited to Washington, D.C., and Surrounding Area*

With approximately 50 percent of the employees in the metropolitan area employed by the Federal and District governments, and the other 50 percent occupied in providing goods and services for these personnel, the chances of a prolonged economic recession in the metropolitan area in Washington appear remote. We believe that Washington provides an atmosphere of economic stability enjoyed by extremely few metropolitan areas.

(Only very impressive factors concerning other metropolitan areas may dictate a variance from this policy.)

E. *No Speculative-Type Business Properties*

We do not buy any real property whose major source of income is derived from the operation of speculative-type business ventures such as hotels, motels, swimming pools, golf links or country clubs, amusement parks, bowling alleys, or stadiums; nor do we purchase single-purpose buildings, such as funeral homes, garages, or automobile retail locations.

Source: Maury Seldin and Richard H. Swesnik, *Real Estate Investment Strategy* (New York: Wiley–Interscience, 1979), pp. 5–6.

ect that proceeds through all the steps has met the investor's criteria in many ways and has a higher probability of achieving the investor's objectives.

Decision-Making Biases and Irrational Preferences

Investment decisions are subject to numerous biases and irrational preferences, which are difficult for an investor to overcome.[14] These biases and irrational preferences must be identified, understood, and explicitly dealt with by the investor as an integral part of developing a successful investment strategy.

Faulty Time Preferences and Biases. Investors frequently fail to consider important variables, such as property and ownership life cycles, in their decision-making process. Traditionally, because of the difficulties, dislike, or lack of knowledge about how to deal with these concepts, most investors have concentrated on a few key assumptions about the near-term future, examined a few of the rules of thumb, and then invested. Research studies have shown that most investors prefer and rely on short-run cash flow projections in their decision making. Many equity investors make decisions based on one-year "stabilized" cash flow forecasts, but others disregard financial forecasts altogether and purchase properties whenever current mortgage market conditions are favorable and lenders and partners are willing to invest with them.

Most decision makers overreact to current information. If the information is favorable, they tend to become too optimistic in their decision making, whereas unfavorable information causes them to make decisions that are too pessimistic. In other words, investors tend to capitalize or forecast the present market situation (and perceptions) into perpetuity. They also tend to overgeneralize about information received. If a business associate or friend is unsuccessful in motel investments, all motel investments are regarded as "bad investments."

Inability to Deal with Uncertainty. Extensive experiments and research have shown that many decision makers have irrational preferences and biases because they are unable to deal with risk and uncertainty, and their

---

[14]Amos Tversky and Daniel Kahneman, "Judgment under Uncertainty: Heuristics and Biases," *Science,* September 1974; Wofford, "Cognitive Processes," pp. 390–391; Mort La Brecque, "On Making Sounder Judgments," *Psychology Today,* June 1980, pp. 34–35; Paul Slovic, Baruch Fischhoff, and Sarah Lichtstein, "Risky Assumptions," *Psychology Today,* June 1980, p. 47; Daniel Kahneman and Amos Tversky, "The Psychology of Preferences," *Scientific American,* November 1980, pp. 160–163; Ward Edwards et al., "Probabilistic Information Processing Systems: Design and Evaluation," *IEEE Transactions on Systems Science and Cybernetics,* Special issue on Decision Analysis, September 1968.

ability to perceive and estimate uncertainty is not developed. Most people's *intuitive* ability to process uncertainty and arrive at rational conclusions is practically nonexistent. It is no surprise, then, that many real estate investors assume away many of the risk elements in their evaluation of real estate alternatives and thus have no need for the risk analysis techniques and criteria discussed previously in this chapter.

There are five reasons why investors tend to have biases in their decision making that make it difficult to arrive at rational investment decisions.[15]

1. *Investors think they know more than they do.* When investors forecast future events, they tend to be too narrow-minded. They fail to see the full range of possible outcomes with respect to various market conditions, rents, expenses, and so on and consequently are very often surprised; the unexpected happens, and they are caught off-guard. As a result, they usually end up taking bigger risks than they assumed in their initial evaluation.

2. *Investors overvalue easily accessible information.* They judge the likelihood of events on the basis of the ease with which they can recall or imagine such events; as a result they overvalue recent news. As previously noted, the riskiness of a motel investment rose sharply when the investor's friend went broke in the motel business.

3. *Investors do not revise their judgments in a rational manner.* They hold onto their initial opinions too long or throw them away too quickly. Most investors fall into the first classification: they are conservative information processors. They consistently fail to extract all the important information contained in data. In other situations, investors throw away all their initial opinions and use only the new information.

4. *Investor intuition cannot deal with complexity.* Most investors have difficulty in combining data about uncertain future events to reflect the overall risk and return of a property. They cannot deal simultaneously with more than three or four economic variables, and can handle even fewer when highly uncertain economic variables are introduced into the analysis.

5. *Investors are not clear about what they want.* They cannot decide on the level of risks they should take, and then they do not take the risks that they think they should. Investors often cannot keep their own particular objectives and preferences straight.

Overcoming Biases and Irrational Preferences. What does all this mean for investors? Too often it means confusion, ignorance, and disagreement

---

[15]Carl S. Spetzler, "The Development of a Corporate Risk Policy for Capital Investment Decisions," *IEEE Transactions on Systems Science and Cybernetics,* September 1968.

when intuitive decisions are attempted in the face of a highly complex and uncertain situation. Even so, it is possible for the investor to overcome the common biases and irrational preferences that lead to incorrect investment decisions.

The first step in dealing effectively with investment biases and irrational preferences is to accept their presence and understand the reasons for their existence and their impact on decisions. Wofford offers a model of these cognitive processes (Exhibit 4-8) that conceptualizes the information flows in the decision-making process and shows how perceptions and expectations are processed through various "filters" (heuristics, attitudes, beliefs, biases, etc.) and how investment goals and decisions are influenced during this process.[16] Developing a plan to eliminate decision-making problems and biases becomes much easier once the investor understands the psychological processes that cause these problems.

Developing a strategic approach to real estate investment decisions is a second major step in overcoming these biases and irrational preferences. The ten-step investment analysis and financial structuring process developed in this chapter is one such approach for forcing rationality and systematic decision processes on the investor. Such a planning process requires that investors clearly identify the overall investment philosophy, investment objectives and criteria, and plans and policies that make up a rational game plan for achieving investment success.

Finally, investors should consider their collection of investments as one portfolio rather than individual investments, and decisions should be made within the framework of an overall financial management plan. Each new investment acquired needs to be evaluated in light of its impact on the investor's current portfolio of real estate assets, its relationship to other assets in the portfolio, and their combined effects on the achievement of the investor's overall financial plan. These subjects are discussed in depth in Chapters 18 and 19.

SUMMARY

Disappointing investment results and negative experiences with real estate have often been caused by deficient investment strategies. This chapter outlines a framework for determining a sound investment strategy and presents a normative model of the investment analysis and financial structuring process that focuses on existing projects.

The first step of that process is to develop a strategy that defines the nature and measurement of the returns and risks that are acceptable to the investor. Such a strategy requires that the investor systematically identify

[16]Wofford, "Cognitive Processes," p. 393.

EXHIBIT 4-8.   Cognitive Processes in Real Estate Investment Decisions

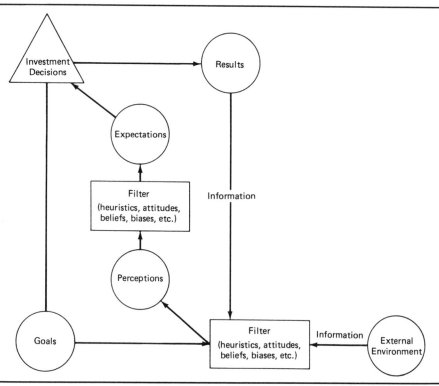

Source: Larry E. Wofford, "Cognitive Processes as Determinants of Real Estate Investment Decisions," *The Appraisal Journal*, July 1985, p. 393.

and define four important elements: (1) overall investment philosophy, (2) objectives and decision criteria, (3) plans and policies, and (4) a strategy of analysis.

The investment analysis and financial structuring process consists of ten sequential steps which require the investor to perform increasingly complex analyses. The ten steps are (1) determining an investment strategy, (2) generating alternatives, (3) analyzing the property using the basic financial feasibility models, (4) negotiating basic terms with the seller, (5) doing detailed feasibility research, (6) considering various financial and tax structures, (7) performing a discounted-cash-flow analysis, (8) engaging in final negotiations and closing, (9) managing the property, and (10) terminating the property. The acquisition phase is emphasized since the return and risk characteristics of an investment are largely established at this stage of the property life cycle. A project rather than a portfolio approach is also emphasized since ultimately wealth is accumulated through the analysis and control of individual properties. Portfolio analysis and approaches are the subjects of Chapters 18 and 19.

An appendix on selecting a public real estate partnership follows next. Then a comprehensive case study, Aspen Wood Apartments, is introduced. The 86-unit apartment complex will be discussed at the end of each chapter in this part of the book as the next nine steps of the investment process are analyzed.

APPENDIX 4A. SELECTING A PUBLIC REAL ESTATE PARTNERSHIP*

If you are interested in buying real estate in a partnership, you have over 130 public offerings to choose from. Some sponsors offer five or six different programs. How do you narrow down the field? What's right for you?

First, you determine your investment objectives. Then, you assess the risk you can take. Next, you match your objectives and risk tolerances with types of available programs. To simplify the task, use "Guide to Partnership Selection," given in Exhibit 4-9 to select the right type of partnership.

Step 1: Decide Your Investment Objectives

When you invest in a public real estate partnership, you are entitled to know approximately what economic benefits you may receive. The portfolio the sponsor intends to purchase will produce a relatively predictable pattern of taxable income or loss, cash distributions, and potential gains. Ask your advisor what you can expect.

The idea is to match up this stream of benefits with your investment objectives. Lower tax bracket investors might not be able to use tax loss effectively. Tax-free investors might prefer compounding high current return, available in insured mortgage loans. High-bracket investors might prefer limited cash distributions and a real chance at capital growth, available in leveraged partnerships.

Think about your income, net worth, age, and future income sources and requirements. This introspection should give you an idea of how much risk you can take and isolate your investment objectives. Particular real estate partnerships can accomplish any of the four investment objectives outlined below:

- *Shelter–Growth.* Some public real estate programs offer tax losses to shelter income from other sources. Leverage is the important factor in creating this tax loss. The more leverage in a real estate portfolio, the better the opportunity for capital appreciation. Current income is

*Source: The Stanger Report: A Guide to Partnership Investing, Sample Issue, (Shrewsbury, N.J.: Robert A. Stanger & Co., 1986), pp. 1–5. Reprinted with permission.

EXHIBIT 4-9. Guide to Real Estate Partnership Selection[a]

Investment Objective	Shelter–Growth	Growth	Growth–Income	Income
Partnership Type	Leveraged	Modestly leveraged/ participating second-mortgage loans	Unleveraged/ participating first-mortgage loans	Insured loans/ straight-rate loans
Maximum Risk	60–80% leverage	30–60% leverage 85–90% loan-to-value	0–30% leverage 65–75% loan-to-value	Noninsured–90% loan-to-value
	Under construction Single property type Regional 5 properties or fewer	Under construction Single property type Regional 5 properties or fewer	Under construction Single property type Regional 5 properties or fewer	Under construction Single property type Regional 5 properties or fewer
Moderate Risk	60–80% leverage	30–60% leverage 75–85% loan-to-value	0–30% leverage 65–75% loan-to-value	Noninsured–75% loan-to-value
	Rent-up phase 2 property types or more Limited geographic diversification 5 to 15 properties or more	Rent-up phase 2 property types or more Limited geographic diversification 5 to 15 properties or more	Rent-up phase 2 property types or more Limited geographic diversification 5 to 15 properties or more	Tenanted 2 property types or more Limited geographic diversification 5 to 15 properties or more
Lowest Risk	60–80% leverage	30–60% leverage 70–75% loan-to-value	0–30% leverage 65–75% loan-to-value	Insured loans
	Tenanted 2 property types or more National 16 properties or more	Tenanted 2 property types or more National 16 properties or more	Tenanted 2 property types or more National 16 properties or more	Tenanted Usually residential National 16 properties or more
Tax Status	10–25% of investment in tax loss during first twelve months	Equities: tax-free cash flow Loans: taxable	Equities: Partially tax-free cash flow Loans: taxable	Taxable
Current Yield	5% or less	Equities: 5–6% Loans: 9–10%	Equities: 6–8% Loans: 10–11%	11–13%

[a]Within each risk category, the type of property acquired or loaned against provides a further delineation of risk. The spectrum from most risk to least risk based on property type is (1) special-use facilities and hotels; (2) apartments and mini-warehouses; (3) smaller office buildings (less than 250,000 square feet) and community-strip shopping centers; (4) large office buildings and enclosed-mall shopping centers; (5) net leases. For instance, two partnerships could be ranked as Lowest Risk for Growth. If one purchased hotels and the other office buildings, the former would be more risky than the latter.

minimal for the first several years of investment in leveraged programs, say less than 4 percent.

▪ *Growth.* Some partnerships utilize modest leverage (30–60% mortgage debt). Here, the appreciation potential is significant but less than when more leverage is employed. But, current income is higher than for maximum leverage programs, say 5 to 6 percent. Generally speaking, the cash distributions will be tax-free (sheltered by depreciation). Some partnerships making participating second-mortgage loans are growth investments also—usually with less appreciation potential than modestly leveraged programs but higher current income, say 8 to 9 percent. For participating mortgage loan partnerships, all the income is fully taxable (no tax shelter).

- *Growth–Income.* Real estate can be acquired with no mortgage debt, so-called unleveraged real estate programs. Growth comes from property economics and not financial leverage. Here appreciation should equal or exceed the rate of inflation, and current income should be 7 or 8 percent. Most of the income will be tax-sheltered by depreciation. Other qualifying investments for growth–income are more conservative participating first-mortgage loan partnerships where current income is 9 or 10 percent (fully taxable). For this type of mortgage loan partnership and for unleveraged programs, a reasonable level of return is assured, and there are significant opportunities for both growth in income and capital values.

- *Income.* Some partnerships offer portfolios of government-insured, or other noninsured, straight-rate mortgage loans. Competitive levels of current return are available, and sometimes current yields are several percentage points above the prime rate, say 12 to 13 percent today (fully taxable). Modest capital growth, or enhanced return, is possible in some partnerships.

Obviously you could buy more than one type of real estate partnership to accomplish more than one investment goal. One partnership might be appropriate for your personal account, whereas another would be ideal for your IRA or Keogh plan. Participating first- and second-mortgage loan partnerships are more suitable for tax-free, or lower tax bracket, investors. Unleveraged and leveraged partnerships are more suitable for higher tax bracket investors. Determining up front what you are trying to accomplish with your real estate investment makes the appropriate selection easier later on.

Step 2: Assess Risk

Suitability requirements do not give you a clue about what risk you can afford in partnerships because legal suitability is essentially the same for most real estate partnerships. You need either a net worth of $75,000 exclusive of home, furnishings, and automobiles, or $30,000 of taxable income and $30,000 or more of net worth.

But, real estate partnerships can be characterized in terms of risk. You have to look at the kinds of investments the partnership will make. Real estate is like all other investments. The more risk you take, the higher the rate of return you expect to earn. Here are the four risk factors you should consider.

- *Leverage.* The greater the leverage, the greater the risk. Increasing the amount of leverage reduces current cash flow but increases your return from appreciation. The maximum leverage in public real estate partnerships is 80 percent of property purchase price, but may be set lower. Often the maximum allowable leverage stated in the prospectus is more than the partnership will borrow. So, ask the broker how much leverage the sponsor intends to use. For mortgage partnerships leverage is a risk factor in a different sense. Leverage is measured by the so-called loan-to-value ratio. The more you lend as a percentage of what the building is worth, the greater the risk. Loans of 60 to 70 percent of property value are not risky. Loans of 80 to 90 percent of property value are obviously much more risky. Moreover, some loans are second mortgages or wraparound mortgages. Here risk is greater because another lender has a first mortgage, a lien that comes before you in the event of default.

- *The User and the Lease.* Risk in real estate is also a function of the credit of the tenant and the length and terms of the lease. A building could be rented to a "credit tenant" like General Motors for a long period of time under what is called a net lease. Here the tenant pays all operating and maintenance costs and you receive a net rent check. Not much risk. Risk increases by property type in the following order. In a shopping center, typically 60 percent of the space is leased for a long period of time to "credit tenants" and smaller companies fill out the tenant roster, usually with leases of five years or less. In shopping centers, operating expenses are often passed through to tenants and are not paid by the landlord. Office buildings tend to have a mixture of large and small tenants with predominantly five- and ten-year leases. Sometimes for office buildings, increased operating costs are paid by the landlord. Apartments and mini-warehouses are rented for shorter periods, typically a year or less, and hotels must rerent all rooms every few nights, the typical length of stay. Here, the income stream is uncertain, the landlord pays all operating costs, and the credit behind the lease is an individual. Pretty risky. As you shorten the term of the lease and decrease the credit of the tenant, the return you expect rises, but your risk rises also. Special-use property, like a fast-food store, is more risky than general-use property, like an office building.

- *Construction Phase.* The earlier in the construction process you invest, the more risk you take. Real estate development has three phases. The first is the building phase, the time before the property is ready for occupancy. Risks include problems in completing the building, building costs exceeding budget, or construction delays, which increase interest-carrying costs. The second risk period occurs after completion of construction but before substantial occupancy. This is the so-called rent-up period. Here you will find out whether you have a good location, whether the rents you projected are realistic, whether you can hold the line on operating costs, and whether you have enough cash reserves to see the project through to substantial occupancy. The final risk phase is the operational period, the time between completion of rent-up and the ultimate sale of the property. During this period you have to negotiate with tenants and determine lease terms and rents, decide on repairs and improvements, maximize your return through effective management, and figure out when to refinance or sell a property. The more of these risks you assume, the higher return you should expect on your investment.

- *Diversification.* Some public real estate partnerships are comparatively small and buy just a few properties. Others raise over $200 million of investor capital and buy, say, $500 million of property. In general, the more buildings you own in one property pool, the less risk you are taking. Diversifying geographically spreads the risk of regional economics. Diversifying by property type also reduces risk. And in large property pools, you can buy more expensive, higher quality buildings.

The four risk factors apply whether you are buying properties or lending (making mortgage loans) because properties are the collateral if you are lending. The degree of leverage, the tenant, when you make the investment or the loan in relation to initial construction and portfolio diversification determine your risk.

The lowest risk ownership profile would be an unleveraged partnership with broad diversification in commercial buildings acquired when construction was complete and tenants have moved in. The most risky investment would be a nondiversified, highly leveraged portfolio of, for example, apartments or hotels in the early stage of development and construction.

Step 3: Understand Your Investment Alternatives

Five types of public real estate investments are typically offered today in terms of investment objective and risk.

- *Leveraged Partnerships.* When you buy leveraged real estate, your cash investment is a down payment on income-producing properties. The remainder of the purchase price is borrowed from a lending institution and perhaps even from the seller of the property. The investment appeal: You have many assets working per dollar of your cash, or equity, investment.

Leveraged partnerships will all fall in either shelter–growth or growth investment objective categories, depending on the amount of leverage. But the risk will vary considerably. Leveraged partnerships can buy properties under construction, which is riskier than buying completed, tenanted buildings. If the leveraged partnership buys apartments, there is more risk than with shopping centers. If the leveraged partnership's portfolio consists of a single property type, that is riskier than a diversified portfolio.

- *Unleveraged Real Estate.* To keep borrowing costs down, you can pay a larger percentage of the property purchase price in cash. Take this technique to its limit, and you have a pure, unleveraged real estate limited partnership. Unleveraged partnerships borrow no money and pay no debt service. The investment appeal: a competitive current yield and growth potential for both income and capital.

  Unleveraged partnerships are in either growth or growth–income categories of investment objective. If you buy commercial property, shopping centers or office buildings, growth of your principal is relatively assured because of rent escalation clauses in leases. If you buy apartments or hotels, your current income should be higher, but obtaining appreciation is less certain because higher rents must be earned in the marketplace. (Real estate risk considerations for unleveraged partnerships are the same as for leveraged partnerships with respect to phase of construction, property type, and diversification.) Obviously, on a comparative basis unleveraged partnerships will provide less appreciation and more current income than leveraged partnerships, but are less risky.

- *Participating Mortgage Loans.* Here the partnership lends your capital out in return for interest plus a participation in increases in cash flow and gains from property appreciation. The investment appeal: interest on a participating mortgage loan is generally higher in the early years than earnings on leveraged or unleveraged partnership investments. Participating first-mortgage loan partnerships are in the investment objective category of growth–income. The dominant part of the rate of return is the current yield, but the participating feature provides some growth. Participating second-mortgage loan partnerships are a little riskier, provide a little less current yield and somewhat greater growth potential. Their investment objective category is growth. (The degree of risk for both types is determined by the same four risk factors.) Comparatively, participating mortgage loan partnerships are much less risky than leveraged equity partnerships and a bit less risky than unleveraged equity partnerships.

- *Insured, or Straight-Rate Mortgage Loan Funds.* Insured-mortgage partnerships generally buy federally insured mortgages with a lower than current market interest coupon at a discount from principal (par) value. The investment appeal: competitive current yield with enhanced return from early mortgage payoff. There is almost absolute safety of principal where mortgage portfolios are federally insured. Insured loan partnerships are the least risky type of partnership and can provide 10 to 11 percent current yield.

Some partnerships make straight-rate mortgage loans either at fixed rates or at rates that fluctuate with the prime rate. Often these mortgages finance construction and development. Here the loans can be quite risky, but your current return can be above the prime rate.

Insured or straight-rate mortgage loan partnerships are in the income category of investment objective. Noninsured, straight-rate loan partnerships run the entire risk spectrum depending on the risk in the real estate they finance. For instance, construction and development loans on apartments are quite risky. Long-term loans on completed, tenanted commercial buildings are comparatively risk-free.

- *FREITs.* Finite life real estate investment trusts (FREITs) are alternatives to partnerships as vehicles for real estate investing. Cash distributions of a FREIT can be partially tax-sheltered by depreciation. FREITs are not taxed. They either purchase properties or make mortgage loans and can be leveraged or unleveraged. The primary advantage over partnerships is the liquidity of the shares in the secondary market. The primary disadvantage is that FREITs cannot pass through losses, only income.

FREITs can offer any of the four investment objectives that partnerships offer and any level or risk, depending on the types of investments they make. Because a secondary market develops for FREIT shares and not for most partnership interests, FREITs have liquidity and are less risky than partnerships. You compare FREITs with each other in terms of investment objective and risk by the same method outlined for partnerships.

ASPEN WOOD APARTMENTS

INTRODUCTION AND INVESTMENT STRATEGY

Good theory is good practice! If we are to prove this statement, it is important to illustrate how the framework developed in this chapter unfolds into practice when applied to real-world situations. Therefore, we have chosen to illustrate the model of the investment analysis and financial structuring process by applying it to a case history of a typical investment property. Aspen Wood Apartments was purchased in 1974 and sold in 1982. It was resyndicated in 1982 and in 1988 was nearing the end of its second ownership life cycle. Good data are available, and the history of the purchase, operation, and termination of the property through one of its life cycles is complete.

At the end of key chapters in Parts 2 through 4 of the book, the Aspen Wood case study will be reintroduced and the principles discussed in the chapter will be applied. It should be noted that the case study is based on actual fact; however, some of the names and information have been disguised to maintain the anonymity of the individuals involved.

The Aspen Wood property was originally syndicated in November 1974 under a joint-venture (general partnership) form of ownership by a Texas-based real estate firm known as D&B Associates. The firm engages in consulting, development, brokerage, syndication, and management of income properties. For the Aspen Wood property, the firm's primary role was that of managing equity investor.

The use of D&B Associates and Aspen Wood Apartments as a case study is not meant to imply that our investment model is useful only to syndicators of apartment complexes. Rather, it is felt that D&B Associates is a typical managing equity investor and that Aspen Wood Apartments is an understandable project of reasonable proportions. The general principles, concepts, and mechanics described in this study apply equally well to all types of residential and commercial properties.

DESCRIPTION OF THE PROPERTY

Aspen Wood Apartments is an 84-unit complex built in two phases in 1966 and 1967 in Austin, Texas, the state capital. The structure is approximately 75 percent masonry, with built-up roofs and about 55,000 square feet of rentable space. Aspen Wood is a well-designed, three-story walk-up, with a swimming pool in the middle of each phase and adequate parking surrounding the structures. The complex is situated in an excellent location for both students and state workers; it is adjacent to the University of Texas intramural fields and near the university campus and other state institutions.

General descriptive data are summarized in Exhibit 4-A. Additional information on Aspen Wood Apartments and its purchase will be presented as the case study develops.

EXHIBIT 4-A.   Aspen Wood Apartments

PROPERTY DESCRIPTION

Apartments:

	Type	Monthly Rental (1974)	
		Fall/Spring	Summer
64	1 Bedroom–1 Bath	$149.00	$129.00
14	2 Bedroom–1 Bath	$199.00	$159.00
6	2 Bedroom–2 Bath	$209.00	$179.00

Tenants pay electricity in individual units. Owner pays common electricity, gas heating, and hot water for all units.

Location: 4539 Guadelupe Street

Lots A and B in Huntington Place, a subdivision in the City of Austin, Travis County, Texas, according to the map or plat thereof as recorded in Plat Book 29, page 21, of the Travis County Plat Records.

Parcel size: Lots A and B of Huntington Place are rectangular in shape. Both average 208 feet in width and 131 feet in depth. Lot A contains 27,361 square feet and Lot B contains 27,374 square feet.

Year built: Phase I 1966; Phase II 1967

Construction: The complex is composed of two phases almost identical in structure, with built-up roofs and approximately 75 percent masonry construction.

Square footage:

	Floor		
	1	2	3
Phase I	7,463	10,367	10,367
Phase II	6,453	10,417	10,417

Real estate taxes (1974):

	Phase I	Phase II
City	$2,745.69	$2,740.45
School	$3,922.41	$3,914.93
County	$1,275.92	$1,414.54

7 Reasons Why You Should Live In Aspen Wood:

1. The Price The price of gasoline has gone up 5¢ in 5 months. When you live in Aspen Wood, you're miles closer to Highland Mall, UT, nightclubs and the airport. And, Aspen Wood is on the Shuttle Bus Route.

2. The Price The average cost of a one bedroom luxury apartment in Austin is $165/month. Our price is only $149.

3. The Price The average cost of a two bedroom luxury apartment in Austin is $230/month. Our price is only $199.

4. The Price Most other places can't boast a backyard with baseball diamonds, football fields and dozens of tennis courts. But we can! Aspen Wood wasn't built near the UT Intramural Fields by accident.

5. The Price Even with our low prices, we don't believe in wasting your time and money with long-term contracts. So, our contracts are for 6 months or 9 months.

6. The Price With the cost of eating out rising so rapidly, it's getting tough to find an inexpensive charcoal-grilled steak. Our price includes two outdoor fireplace grills for those special dinners with special friends. (It also means saving $15 to $20 on a new hibachi.)

7. The Price Our price includes furnished and fully carpeted apartments, two swimming pools, free cable hook-ups and landscaped courtyards. When you think about it, living at Aspen Wood *is* luxury. At the best price.

1 Bdr. $149.

2 Bdr. $199.

OVERALL INVESTMENT PHILOSOPHY

At the time of the purchase in 1974, D&B Associates, as a firm of real estate consultants, brokers, investors, and property managers, had a basic business objective of building a portfolio that would maintain growing profitability through all phases of real estate and economic cycles. Its investment philosophy focused on a plan to list or acquire income properties, package them, and offer shares to clients and members of the firm with the intention of maintaining control as partial owners, managers, and consultants. Substantial commissions on the purchase and sale of properties were expected to be forthcoming in times of high real estate turnover, but D&B relied heavily on the income from property and venture management agreements written into syndicated and other offerings, to carry it through downturns. In 1974, the firm managed over 2500 apartment units, of which a majority were syndicated using a joint-venture (general partnership) ownership vehicle. In addition, its investment program included purchases of shopping centers and office buildings. As a developer–investor, the firm engaged in the development of apartments, shopping centers, condominiums, and condominium conversions.

In 1974, D&B Associates was looking for apartment investments. It recognized the need for portfolio diversification, and an apparent overabundance of office space, shopping centers, and adult apartment projects in Austin led it to consider student apartment complexes. This market had been strong during the period from 1965 to 1972; only recently had overbuilding and expense increases, among other factors, disrupted the student market. D&B had substantial management expertise in this area and saw an opportunity to increase its control of apartment units, reap economies of scale in its property and venture management efforts, and develop an inventory of projects to meet clients' needs as well as provide inventory for future condominium conversions.

The principals of D&B Associates in 1974 were Charlie Davidson and Clyde Boomer. Davidson had been an active broker, investor, and syndicator for more than twenty years. Forty-five years old, he was responsible for the company's brokerage and syndication activities and venture management, including investor relations. Boomer, thirty-five years old, had been an executive with a major computer manufacturer and an active real estate investor for ten years. By this time, the five-year veteran of D&B Associates was responsible for the company's property management and administrative functions. He had recently installed a computer system that handled all the firm's management and accounting reports and provided a sophisticated software package for the financial analysis of income properties. The firm was employing more than fifty people, including professional and resident property managers, maintenance and repair personnel, and administrative and secretarial employees. Two of the property managers were CPMs (certified property managers, Institute of Real Estate Management), and the firm had recently achieved the professional designation of AMO (Approved Management Organization, Institute of Real Estate Management).

Davidson and Boomer took great pride in their professional approach to real estate investment and their use of modern capital-budgeting techniques to analyze proposed ventures. Projects were being analyzed on a before- and after-tax basis, using a discounted-cash-flow computer model. Extensive research and analysis were undertaken before the company committed itself to a project. This approach has apparently been successful, since the company has grown rapidly over the last fifteen years and enjoys an excellent reputation in the community.

INVESTMENT OBJECTIVES AND CRITERIA

Davidson and Boomer were selling shares in their joint ventures on the basis of three general objectives: (1) regular cash flow from operations that can be distributed quarterly to investors, (2) substantial tax shelter over the ownership period, and (3) substantial capital appreciation, to be realized through periodic refinancing or sale of the property at the end of a four- to seven-year holding period.

The specific investment criteria used by D&B in 1974 included the following financial and nonfinancial criteria.

Rate of Return. Most of D&B's investors seek a minimum 10 percent cash-on-cash return during the first year of ownership, increasing thereafter. D&B agrees that a property can be structured to offer that return to investors. In addition, to achieve its long-term rate-of-return objective, D&B seeks a minimum 18 percent internal rate of return (after tax). Although the investors did not specify this criterion (most are wealthy individuals who are not familiar with the IRR criteria), D&B believes that this is the single most important financial criterion to be utilized in the analysis of properties. Tax shelter criteria are also important both to D&B and to its investors: A project should be structured to generate front-end tax write-offs amounting to 25–50 percent of the equity investments and significant tax losses over the holding period by using component depreciation to increase tax deductions. Note that component depreciation was eliminated by the Economic Recovery Tax Act of 1981, and further restrictions were imposed by the Tax Reform Act of 1986.

Risk. D&B feels that it has a fiduciary responsibility to establish risk constraints on its syndicated projects. Its ventures must have a break-even point of less than 85 percent, a coverage ratio greater than 1.25, and a minimal chance of negative equity cash flows (cash calls). In addition, full multiperil insurance coverage must be established on each property, and the firm seeks mortgage loans that do not require the personal guarantees of the investors.

Leverage. Secondary or wraparound financing must be available at an acceptable interest rate. For financing the property, the leverage ratio could be 75–90 percent, but debt service must be limited, as evidenced by a coverage ratio greater than 1.25.

Location. The project must be visible, surrounded by a high-quality neighborhood, and close to shopping, transportation, and recreation.

Structure. The building must be well designed and appealing to an investor, structurally sound, usually less than ten years old, with more than 40 units (the most desirable size being 75–150 units). Tenants must pay their own utilities, and a strong rental history must evidence the attractiveness of the complex as a living environment.

These financial and nonfinancial criteria were initially chosen by D&B Associates to be used in selecting properties that would satisfy the explicit as well as implicit objectives of its clients. D&B has as an objective of earning commissions and management fees by pleasing clients. To do this, it must understand investor motivations and objectives and translate them into explicit investment criteria to be applied at various steps in the investment process.

PLANS AND POLICIES

D&B's investment plans and policies are action-oriented guidelines that reflect the investment philosophy and criteria enumerated earlier. Davidson and Boomer will use the ten-step investment analysis model as a guideline for their actions and will apply increasingly more demanding and stringent criteria as the investment analysis continues. Only properties that pass all the important hurdles will be acquired. We will see in later chapters how specific plans and policies evolve at each step of the investment process.

BASIC SCREENING CRITERIA

In the search for potential acquisitions, the nonfinancial criteria just noted tended to become the basic screening criteria, although the list was altered and refined over time. It is easy to determine by inspection whether a property meets these criteria. The financial criteria specified, on the other hand, call for more detailed analysis that is best performed later in the process. One financial criterion is of initial importance, however. This is the availability of secondary or wraparound financing. In 1974 very few deals were feasible without financing from a seller. New-mortgage money was extremely difficult to obtain, and interest rates on new mortgages were too high to achieve economic feasibility. At the same time, with overbuilding prevalent in most submarkets around the city and rent levels depressed, expenses were rising rapidly as a result of the energy crisis and general inflationary pressures.

After selecting the basic screening criteria, D&B have completed step 1 of the ten-step investment analysis process.

5

SELECTING THE OWNERSHIP ENTITY

In new real estate ventures and in reorganizations, one of the critical decisions the investor confronts is determining what form of business organization should be used, whether the property should be acquired and owned by the individual, by a general or limited partnership, or by a corporation or trust established by the investor. This decision has a direct impact on the investor's ability to achieve his or her objectives. The type of entity chosen and how it is structured affect the investor's rate of return and risks; it also often defines the nature of the investor's personal involvement and the degree of control that can be exercised over the venture and the property purchased.

The ownership entity decision will often be an integral part of step 1 of the investment strategy process (see Chapter 4), where the investment strategy is being determined. For example, an investor who seeks a high degree of tax shelter, flexibility, and complete control of a property may use the individual form of ownership to acquire properties. The entity is thus an extension of the investor's basic philosophy and objectives. Many syndicators use only the limited-partnership form in their business; no other alternatives are considered. In contrast, the ownership decision may be delayed until the financial and tax-structuring step is reached (step 6), or even later in the process if lenders and other investors can influence the decision. However, the ownership decision alternatives should be clearly understood at the outset and should be kept in mind throughout the study of this text.

OWNERSHIP ALTERNATIVES

The ownership vehicles that can be used to acquire and own real estate may be classified as follows.

- *Noncorporate Forms of Ownership.* Individual, joint tenancy, tenancy in common, general partnership, limited partnership, master limited partnerships, family partnership and joint venture.
- *Corporations and Trusts.* Regular corporation (C corporation), S corporation, REIT, pension trust, and other types of trusts.
- *Syndication.* Syndication is a generic term for various types of entities commonly thought of as a form of ownership, as well as a method of financing and marketing real estate investments.

Of all the forms of ownership used in real estate investments in recent years, the limited partnership and more recently the general partnership, Subchapter S corporation, and the REITs are the most commonly used because, with the exception of the general partnership, they offer investors the limited legal liability for tort and contractual liability exposure that a corporation offers, together with the tax benefits achieved from the pass-through of some tax losses and capital gains that a general partnership offers.[1] However, other ownership forms are appropriate for different situations, transactions, and investors. It now appears quite likely that REITs will be much more popular from 1988 forward. This is in part because of the curbs placed on using master limited partnerships as pass-throughs, in that their income will be treated as portfolio income in the future and they may be taxed as corporations. Tax policies are constantly changing.

No single type of entity is the best. The purpose of this chapter is to examine the various types of entities available and develop a general framework for evaluating the alternatives.

OWNERSHIP DECISION MODEL

A decision model for ranking alternatives has been developed to facilitate the choice of the ownership form that best fits an investor's return–risk objectives. Since the objectives of an equity investor will vary over time, the investment portfolio must be reviewed and revised periodically. Thus,

---

[1] James L. Kuhle and Carl H. Walther, "REIT vs. Common Stock Investments and Historical Perspective," *Real Estate Finance*, Vol. 3, No. 1, Spring 1986, pp. 47–84; and Jack Kusnet and Lee J. Holzman, "How to Choose a Form of Ownership Entity," Portfolio No. 14 (with supplemental updates) (Boston: Warren, Gorham & Lamont) are sources for the following pages, along with our own ideas. Errors or omissions are our own.

the optimal ownership form must be able to accommodate possible changes in the investor's strategy over the expected ownership period.

Exhibit 5-1 is a flow chart of the ownership decision model, beginning with a restatement of the investor's objectives as developed in Chapter 4. Next, the investor develops specific ownership selection criteria and ownership alternatives. Finally, the investor compares and ranks the alternatives according to their relative ability to satisfy investment objectives. He or she does so by assigning relative weights to the selection criteria and, through analysis, determining the degree to which each ownership alternative satisfies the defined criteria. Only then can the investor choose the optimal form of ownership—the one that best fits the return–risk criteria. Whether this process is intuitive or relies on a model like the one presented here, the essential elements are the same.

This chapter analyzes the various selection criteria for ownership decisions. Next, the ownership alternatives listed in Exhibit 5-1 are examined in detail. The last section of the chapter will illustrate the application of the ownership decision model to the Aspen Wood case study. Although the discussions may seem technical at times, they barely scratch the surface of the highly complex federal and state laws that govern the various forms of ownership. Before reaching any ownership entity decision, the investor should seek the advice and counsel of qualified legal and tax experts.

OWNERSHIP SELECTION CRITERIA

Criteria Defined

Tax considerations. Tax considerations are important and rank high in the list of selection criteria for determining the best form of ownership for a real estate venture. The most common choice here is between a form of ownership that offers the advantage of a single tax on income and a corporate form of ownership, in which income is subject to double taxation—first at the corporate level and again at the stockholder (investor) level. In addition to double taxation, other important tax considerations that should be evaluated are the following.

1. *Ability to pass through tax losses.* With some forms of organization, such as partnerships, tax losses can be passed through directly to the individual investor and used to shelter other income. With other forms of organization, such as a corporation or REIT, this ability is limited or does not exist.

2. *Maximum income tax deductions.* Some forms of organization are better suited to an aggressive tax shelter structure and can take liberal tax deductions without being disallowed or questioned by the

EXHIBIT 5-1. Ownership Decision Model

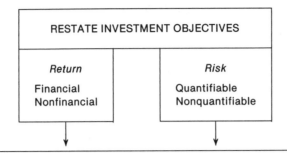

RESTATE INVESTMENT OBJECTIVES

Return	*Risk*
Financial	Quantifiable
Nonfinancial	Nonquantifiable

DEVELOP SELECTION CRITERIA

1. Favorable tax treatment
   a. Avoidance of double taxation
   b. Ability to pass through tax losses
   c. Maximum income tax deductions
   d. Capital gains treatment
   e. Flexibility in allocating gains and losses
   f. Estate tax treatment
2. Limited liability
3. Marketability and transferability of interest
4. Flexibility (allowed real estate activities)
5. Management control and expertise
6. Continuity of life
7. Degree of privacy
8. Favorable public image
9. Government controls and reporting requirements
10. Capital outlay requirements
11. Diversification
12. Regular return
13. Estate building
14. Retirement fund
15. Other

DEFINE OWNERSHIP ALTERNATIVES

1. Individual
2. Joint tenancy
3. Tenancy in common
4. General partnership
5. Limited partnership
6. Family partnership
7. Joint venture
8. Regular corporation
9. Subchapter S corporation
10. Nominee, straw, or dummy corporation
11. REIT
12. Pension trust
13. Other types of trusts
14. Syndication
15. Other

COMPARE AND RANK ALTERNATIVES

1. Assign weights to selection criteria.
2. Analyze ownership alternatives.
3. Choose ownership form that best fits return–risk selection criteria.

Internal Revenue Service. For example, liberal amounts of medical and dental expenses can be deducted for corporate officers, but a partnership cannot deduct such expenses for partners.

3. *Favorable capital gains treatment.* With some forms of organization, it is easier to achieve capital gains treatment on a sale, distribution, or liquidation of an interest in the entity, or a sale or other disposition of the real estate itself. Capital gains tax rates are generally at parity with other income tax rates; under the provisions of the 1986 Tax Reform Act, the distinction between ordinary and capital gains income remains intact. In addition, Congress is likely to provide favorable capital gains treatment to investors—through lower rates—when there is a need again to stimulate real estate investment.

4. *Flexibility in allocating gains and losses.* Investors may choose to allocate different items of taxable income and losses in a manner that meets their individual needs for tax shelter, capital gain, and cash flow. Such special allocations are possible with some entity forms but not with others.

5. *Estate tax treatment.* A burden could be placed on an investor's estate, requiring it to pay taxes on an interest in an entity that may be difficult to turn into cash.

To place too much focus only on avoiding or deferring taxes, however, and overlook the more important business, legal, and practical considerations, can lead to financial disaster. The price for tax savings is too high if the chosen form of ownership makes the property difficult to operate profitably or makes it difficult to dispose of the ownership interest. There are, in addition, many other considerations.

Limited liability. The probability and extent of exposure to tort and contractual liability are important. Limited partnerships offer limited legal liability to the investor with respect to the capital contribution, but they are subject to close government scrutiny. If the partnership is audited because tax deductions were too adventurous and if the deductions are disallowed, the investor may be confronted with greater tax liabilities than expected.

Marketability and transferability of interest. A publicly traded corporate share is generally more marketable than a partnership interest in the same property. With some forms of ownership, transferring an interest in real estate, or the real estate itself, is difficult; timely disposition with a minimum of legal hassle, price discount, and expenses may not be possible.

Flexibility and allowed real estate activities. REITs and pension trusts are limited in the scope and extent of real estate activities in which they can engage without jeopardizing their favorable tax status. In contrast, individuals have almost complete confidentiality and flexibility with regard to real estate activities.

Management control and expertise. The number of people required to run an entity, the type of management and expertise needed, and the degree of control exercised by the investor over the property vary for different forms of ownership. A substantial number of experienced people may be required to organize and operate a REIT, and the investor has very little direct control over the properties purchased. On the other hand, a general partnership may consist of only a few investors who each choose to exert considerable influence over the operations of the venture and the property.

Continuity. Some ventures are organized with a limited holding period in mind and would cease to exist if any of the key investors died. Other ventures are intended to span the lifetimes of many projects and investors.

Degree of privacy. Some investors seek privacy in their real estate activities and choose not to have their names appear in public records, such as recorded partnership agreements, or on deeds, deeds of trust, and so on. Use of certain types of trust devices (e.g., Illinois and Florida land trusts) and partnership agreements can easily accommodate such objectives.

Favorable public image. Some forms of organization have better public images than others. In general, the corporate form of organization inspires public confidence. In contrast, the REIT and limited-partnership forms of organization, because of widespread misuse in the past, are sometimes questioned or misunderstood by investors. As a result, some equity REITs and partnership interests have been undervalued.

Government controls and reporting requirements. Investors seeking a minimum of government scrutiny and controls might favor the individual or tenancy in common forms of organization, as opposed to a limited partnership, REIT, or the corporate forms of organization. These latter forms are more closely regulated and controlled, and the reporting requirements are significantly more complex and onerous. The IRS has improved its efficiency in auditing partnerships by requiring that a "tax partner" be designated and all auditing be centralized through that partner. Deficiency assessments and adjustments have been binding on all partners since 1982–1984.[2]

---

[2]Kermit Keeling, "Tax Treatment of Partnership Audits," *The Journal of Real Estate Taxation*, Fall 1987, pp. 36–73.

Capital outlay requirements. Some forms of organization are significantly more costly to handle than others. Since 1984, it has not been uncommon for a limited partnership to allocate 15 to 30 percent of the total equity raised to organization, promotion, sales and syndication fees, preacquisition costs, accounting, and legal fees. The changes in the IRS code in 1984 have diminished the front-end loading of expenses by requiring that they be accrued in the year in which the expenditure occurs. In contrast, a joint venture or a tenancy in common might limit such expenses to 5 to 10 percent of equity raised. Some forms of organization require large equity contributions (pension funds), whereas others seek to maximize the leverage ratio.

Diversification. Diversification by location, property type, management burden, and so forth can be achieved within one entity (REIT, corporation), or diversification can be prohibited by the entity agreement, as in the case of a joint-venture agreement that limits activity to the ownership and operation of a single property.

Regularity of return. Some forms of ownership are more conducive to regular distribution of returns than others. Investors seeking a regular current return may prefer a REIT or an unleveraged (100% equity) partnership that distributes all earnings, over a corporation that accumulates earnings and reinvests them in real estate equities.

Estate building. An investor who seeks to maximize the total value of real estate holdings over the long run, and is not seeking substantial current income and tax savings, may prefer a corporation or family trust form of organization.

Retirement fund. Many investors seek to build equity during their younger years so that property is owned free and clear at retirement. Often the individual form of organization best suits this objective. For a self-employed individual, a Keogh or other pension plan for retirement may be the best alternative.

Other selection criteria. There are many other criteria that may become important in individual situations. For example, an investor seeking to avoid double taxation and generate fringe benefits for his or her family may choose an S corporation as a form of organization. If prestige is desired, the investor may choose to organize as a C corporation, elect himself or herself chairman of the board and president, and have an advertising firm develop an impressive corporate logo and business cards that can be distributed to family, friends, and business associates. Attractive brochures and financial reports can please the ego, even though they do not generate immediate returns.

Assigning Relative Weights to the Selection Criteria

The importance of any given criterion in selecting a form of ownership may depend on the number of participants, their respective goals, the requirements imposed by the lender, and the nature of the transaction or operation. A tenancy in common, for example, might be desirable for two or a few people who know and have reason to trust one another. But this form of organization becomes less attractive with each additional person, for there may be title problems in the event of partition or conflict. Even when a lender does not dictate the type of entity, a demand for personal guarantees may reduce an investor's desire for a form of organization that shields him or her from personal liability. Guaranteeing only the mortgage debt does not expose a person to the third-party tort and contractual liabilities of a corporate entity; therefore, it may still be the preferred entity of the group.

How much weight is placed on any criterion is also influenced by the type of real estate investment. For example, new apartment projects are usually subject to substantial risk in their early stages, yet they present an excellent opportunity for tax losses to the investors. On the other hand, the purchase of a mature "cash cow" hotel that is generating substantial taxable cash flow returns (i.e., relatively little tax shelter) presents a different situation. It is an entity that could serve to keep its taxable income separate from the investor's taxable income. Thus, the investor should consider a computer analysis to determine whether the profits of the venture ought to be distributed to the investors or whether there may be a valid business purpose for accumulating the income. Obviously, if there is no valid business reason for accumulating income, a corporate entity that is subject to double taxation is a disadvantage to the investor and also exposes the investor group to the personal holding-company rules and possibly the accumulated-earnings tax.

Clearly, the process of assigning weights to selection criteria is highly subjective even though quite analytical, because it is based on uncertain future expectancies about unknown tax policies, interest rates, rent schedules, and so on. The Aspen Wood case history at the end of this chapter illustrates the dynamics of this process under tax policies that applied at the time of the investment.

NONCORPORATE FORMS OF OWNERSHIP

Seven noncorporate forms of organization are discussed in the following paragraphs: individual, joint tenancy, tenancy in common, general partnership, family partnership, limited partnership, master limited partnership, and joint venture. They have in common one important characteristic: they are all single-tax ownership entities that provide a flow-through of economic and tax benefits directly to individual investors. In general, they also lack continuity of life.

Individual Ownership

An individual ownership form (sole proprietorship) exists when a single investor acquires a property solely in his or her own name and is taxed on the income just once. The taxable income from the property each year is pooled with the other sources of income, and the investor is taxed at ordinary rates on total income for the year. If the property generates tax losses, they are used to reduce other income to the extent allowable under the three classifications of income: active, passive, and portfolio income.

Several distinct advantages characterize the individual form of ownership. First, this form is advantageous if the individual's tax rate is lower than the corporate tax rate. Second, tax losses from the property can be used to shelter other income earned by the investor. Third, the individual has complete control over the property rather than a fractional share. Finally, individual ownership is the most confidential form available.

The most significant disadvantage of individual ownership is that it subjects the owner to unlimited liability. Furthermore, illness, disability, and mortality can seriously disrupt the achievement of goals and objectives. Many investors choose not to subject themselves to this level of risk. Also, before choosing individual ownership, the investor should have decided that there would be no advantage in the limited legal liability and the possibility of fringe benefits offered by a closely held corporation, taking into account the double-taxation aspect of the corporation and the cost of organizing and operating under the corporate structure. Frequently a closely held corporation entity is preferred. In any case, individual ownership is usually recommended only for relatively small-scale real estate investments.

Joint Tenancy

In a joint tenancy, several people own the entire real estate. Each investor has the same ownership interest in a single parcel of real estate. Each owns an individual interest in the entire property, and, upon death of a joint tenant, the survivor takes the entire property—the survivor gets all! (subject to federal IRS taxes). The treatment of joint tenancy varies considerably from one state to another, so that it is difficult to make specific statements about this form of ownership. In some states there is a presumption that a joint tenancy is created when real estate is acquired by two or more people. In others, there is a presumption that the entity is a tenancy in common unless there is a specific disclaimer. Each joint tenant reports, for tax purposes, his or her share of income or loss generated by the property; but if one pays more than a pro rata share of the costs, the full amount of the payment may be claimed as a deduction. In contrast, some forms of organization (e.g., a tenancy in common) limit such deductions to the pro rata share of ownership.

The main advantage of joint tenancy is that ownership vests in the survivor. Thus, property does not go through probate when the investor dies, and much time and expense can be saved at the state level without interruption of management prerogatives. On the other hand, each joint tenant is personally liable for all expenses incurred on a property.

Tenancy in Common

The ownership of real estate by two or more people, each of whom has an undivided interest in the property with no right of survivorship, is called a tenancy in common. Whereas each tenant in common has an undivided interest in the entire property, the interests of the investors can be unequal; each investor may have any share of ownership that is agreed upon. When a tenant in common sells his or her interest (interest is freely transferable unless an agreement specifies otherwise), the buyer becomes a tenant in common with other tenants in common. When a tenant in common dies, the hiers (and not the other tenants in common) receive the ownership share. In many states there is a presumption that, in the absence of a written ownership agreement or provision to the contrary, a tenancy in common is created whenever real estate is acquired by two or more people.

Since each tenant in common owns an undivided interest in the property, there can be difficult problems when the tenants in common disagree and want to go their separate ways. A tenant in common is entitled to sue for partition of the property; if the property cannot be divided fairly, the court can order it to be sold and the proceeds divided among the investors according to their percentage interests.

A tenancy in common is considered by many investors to be a viable form of ownership only for smaller projects with relatively few investors. The property may not be sold, mortgaged, or even leased without the consent of all the investors. If the property is sold, all the investors must sign the deed to transfer the property. If one investor refuses, the others must enter into a costly legal process to enable the transfer to take place with a clear title, which may result in a distress sale. In addition, each tenant in common is personally liable for all expenses incurred on a property.

Each tenant in common reports income, gain, or loss from the property according to his or her share of ownership. One tax advantage of this form of ownership, as compared with a partnership, is that each investor reports only his or her share of gains and losses to the Internal Revenue Service each year. No partnership return (Form 1065) need be filed; the IRS must audit the investor and the property records if it wishes to scrutinize the depreciation and other tax methods and assumptions used. Furthermore, it is argued that because there is no formal record of partners in the property, privacy is maintained and the probability of a linked audit is reduced. Thus, one investor will not be audited as a result of owning a property with another partner who is being audited. Further, since a tenancy in common is not recognized for tax purposes, income and losses are divided according to agreement, and each investor can choose a depreciation method that suits his or her objectives and tax preferences. In contrast, each investor in a general partnership must accept the depreciation method chosen by the partnership entity.

In recent years the IRS has challenged the use of the tenancy in common as such for tax purposes. When the tenants in common are actively carrying on a trade or business (such as renting space and providing special services to tenants), the IRS may treat the entity as a partnership.[3] Consequently, a tenancy in common might be reclassified as a general partnership for tax purposes, be required to file a partnership return, which will subject investors to tax penalties that are onerous.

General Partnership

The general partnership is the most common form of noncorporate business association. It is very similar to a tenancy in common except for two major characteristics.

1. A partnership should have a partnership agreement; in numerous states a tenancy in common or other legal form is presumed to exist in the absence of such an agreement.
2. A partnership must file a federal tax information return (Form 1065), in contrast to a tenancy in common, which does not usually file a tax return.

Later we will see that some partnerships (which are entities formed under state law) can elect to avoid the partnership classification for federal income tax purposes.

According to the tax code, a partnership is a syndicate, group, pool, joint venture, or other unincorporated organization that carries on a business, venture, or other financial operation and that is not a corporation, trust, or estate.[4] The tax courts have ruled that a partnership exists if there is a voluntary association of the parties with the intent to carry out a business and each of the parties contributes property or service and shares in the profits of the organization. For federal income tax purposes, therefore,

[3] Ann Blair Furbush, "Real Estate Investment Administration, Is It Costing More Than It Should?," *The Real Estate Securities Journal* (Chicago, RESSI), Vol. 8, No. 1, 1987, pp. 25–30; Gerald J. Robinson, "Setting up the Real Estate Venture, An Overview," *The Journal of Real Estate Taxation*, Fall 1975, pp. 36–37.
[4] IRC Sec. 761.

a partnership can be an entity that is not recognized as a partnership under state law. The concept of a partnership is much broader under federal law than under state law, which in most states is patterned after the Uniform Partnership Act.

The Primary Advantage: Flexibility. Despite the problems that can arise from the unlimited personal liability of the members of a general partnership, the limited transferability of their interest in the partnership, and the limited continuity of the partnership, the partnership form of organization is popular because of its great flexibility. The investors have the freedom to structure an agreement that matches the rights and responsibilities of each partner to his or her particular risk–return objectives and areas of expertise. The partnership agreement may give more voting rights to some partners, delegate responsibility for property management to certain partners, and provide preferential returns and allocations to partners who require a return on capital before others get theirs.[5]

Flexibility is an important advantage, but it underscores the importance of a well-written partnership agreement that clearly defines the terms used and the rights and obligations of the investors. Terms like *cash flow, profits,* or *proceeds from sales or refinancing* all mean different things to different investors. These and similar terms used should be defined clearly so that little ambiguity remains and costly disputes can be avoided.

Tax Advantages. Partnerships have distinct tax advantages over corporations. First, the partnership form avoids double taxation: no tax is imposed at the partnership level. Second, the partnership can pass through tax losses to the investor, while the C corporation cannot. In a partnership, the very substantial tax deductions that real estate can generate (e.g., depreciation, interest, maintenance and repair, tax credits) are passed through directly to the investors and serve as a tax shelter for them to the extent they are applicable under the passive-loss rules. Each partner picks up the income and losses of the partnership as real estate passive income or losses, or as capital gains or losses, depending on their nature when realized by the partnership. Thus, a third tax advantage may be the ability to pass through favorable capital gains treatment to the investor when and if Congress makes the capital gains tax rate advantageous again. In the past this advantage was available to C corporate stockholders only under the very limited circumstances that the corporation was dissolved.[6]

---

[5]Thomas L. Dickens and Stephen L. Cash, "Treasury Provides Guidelines and Special Allocations in Real Estate Partnerships," *The Real Estate Securities Journal,* Vol. 8, No. 1, 1987, pp. 68–79.

[6]Daniel S. Goldberg, "The Passive Activity Loss Rules: Planning Considerations, Techniques, and a Foray into Never-Never Land," *The Journal of Real Estate Taxation,* Fall 1987, pp. 3–36.

The Tax Basis Problem. The amount of partnership losses that may be deducted on a partner's tax return is limited to his or her "basis." A partner's basis is the sum of two amounts: (1) the basis of his or her partnership (equity) interest and (2) his or her share of partnership mortgages and other qualified mortgage liabilities. For example, if an investor contributes $10,000 cash to the partnership and his or her pro rata share of liabilities is $40,000, the basis is $50,000. However, if property with a tax basis different from market value is contributed, the allowable depreciation deduction is based on the tax basis and not on the market value. For example, if a property with a tax basis of $30,000 and a five-year life is contributed at a market value of $50,000, the allowable deduction is $6,000 annually for five years ($30,000/5) rather than $10,000 annually ($50,000/5). If the contributing partner gets credit for the contribution at market value, the other partners will receive a reduction in tax benefits as a consequence. The tax disadvantage to investors who contribute cash rather than property may be rectified somewhat by allocating a larger depreciation deduction to those who contribute cash than to those who contribute appreciated property. Such an arrangement is called a special allocation.

Partnership Special Allocations. Special or disproportionate allocations are made when investors receive different amounts of cash flow, income, losses, deductions, or proceeds of sale or refinancing. Under tax law these allocations are valid for income tax purposes only if they have "substantial economic effect" and their primary purpose is not tax avoidance or tax evasion. For example, the IRS will not permit one partner to receive the benefit of all the partnership's depreciation deductions if that partner, whether there are either profits or losses, will receive cash flow and sale proceeds from the partnership as though no special allocation has been made. The 1988 Treasury guidelines substantially diminished artful special allocations resulting from abusive tax shelters in past years.[7]

Disadvantages. The three main disadvantages of a general partnership are said to be (1) unlimited liability, (2) limited transferability of interest, and (3) lack of continuity. In practice, these may or may not be disadvantageous. For example, the members of a general partnership are personally liable for the debts and obligations incurred by the partnership, and each partner is jointly and severally liable for these debts and obligations. In practice, such unlimited liability can be limited through property and liability insurance; exculpatory clauses in mortgages, which relieve investors of personal liability; indemnification clauses, which relieve certain partners of liabilities assumed by other partners; and so on. Consequently, a

[7]Stephen Jarchow, *Real Estate Syndication—Tax, Securities, and Business Aspects* (New York: Wiley, 1985); with supplemental updates, 1987), see p. 128.

general-partnership entity can be structured to have de facto limited liability, somewhat like a limited partnership. A partnership agreement can also be tailored to achieve almost any degree of continuity of life and transferability of interest desired by the partners.

Whereas a substantial degree of limited liability, continuity, and transferability of interest may be desirable attributes of an ownership entity, the partnership may face the substantial risk of tax reclassification if it assumes too many "corporate characteristics." Such structuring may cause it to be reclassified as a corporation for tax purposes and taxed twice: once at the entity level and again at the investor level. This problem is one usually faced by the limited-partnership form of organization, but it can also be a problem with a general partnership. The "Kintner regulations" about corporate characteristics are discussed in the next section on limited partnerships.

Yet another disadvantage of the general partnership, and other partnership forms, is a general lack of legal certainty about this form of ownership. Although corporate law is highly developed in most states, partnership law is subject to a mixed bag of legal precedents and case law. In short, in most states the legal risk with a partnership form of ownership is somewhat higher than with a corporate form.

Family Partnership

Family partnerships can be established to lower the overall tax burden of owning income properties that produce substantial taxable gains. One method of doing this is to divide the income from the property among low- or no-income members of the family. For example, the children may become the partners of the parent–investor, who is in a higher tax bracket. Simply stated, the parent makes an outright "no strings attached" gift of property to the children (or other family members), pays any applicable gift taxes, and effects a shift of tax from his or her relatively higher tax bracket to the lower tax brackets of the children. For example, if the marginal tax bracket of the parent is in the 28 to 34 percent range and the children's brackets are in the 0 to 17 percent range, there is a substantial reduction in the total tax burden. In addition, as long as the children and others materially and actively participated in the management of the real estate project, there could be more than one $25,000 current-year passive loss deducted in the early years of ownership, if generated by the real estate rental project and depending on the facts.

The IRS scrutinizes family partnerships very closely to see whether there is a genuine arrangement or merely a tax avoidance scheme or sham that should not be recognized for tax purposes. The tax code requires that donee partners actually own and control their interests in the partnerships;

this rule is designed to prevent the use of a family partnership as a means of dividing income among family members for work actually performed by one person.[8]

Limited Partnership

The limited-partnership form of ownership is often preferred by a real estate professional, because it gives the general partner–investor (i.e., managing equity investor) an opportunity to combine the financial resources of passive-equity investors with his or her own skills in an organization that allows flexibility of operation, limited liability for the investors, and direct pass-through of tax benefits to the investors. However, limited partnerships have a number of disadvantages, among them a sometimes poor image earned by past misuse of this ownership vehicle, tax problems, and the possibility of being reclassified as a corporation for tax purposes. As a general rule, limited partnerships also draw a considerable amount of attention from various federal and state agencies and are subject to numerous controls and regulations (e.g., securities laws) that are not usually imposed as rigorously on other types of partnerships. We will address this problem later in the chapter.

As defined under the Uniform Limited Partnership Act (ULPA), a limited partnership consists of at least one general and one limited partner. The general partner (or partners) manages the affairs of the partnership and is personally liable for the debts and obligations of the partnership, but the limited partners, who are passive investors, are not liable for partnership debts and obligations.

A limited partnership is actually a hybrid of a corporation and a general partnership. Like the liability of a corporate shareholder, the limited partner's liability is limited to his or her equity investment, and the status of limited partner does not allow him or her to control or actively participate in the affairs of the partnership. (A limited partner who actively participates in management legally becomes a general partner.) The general partner's roles and functions are very similar to those of corporate officers and directors. Just as a corporation must file a certificate of incorporation, a limited partnership is a statutory entity created in conformance with state law, and must file a certificate of limited partnership with the appropriate state authority, such as the county court. This certificate must contain the names and addresses of all the partners and the major provisions of the partnership agreement. Thus, the limited-partnership form of ownership does not generally afford a high degree of privacy to the investors as com-

[8]See Institute of Business Planning, *Real Estate Investment Planning*, (Englewood Cliffs, N.J.: Prentice–Hall, annual reporting service), paragraphs 56,240–56,245.

pared to a general partnership, tenancy in common, or individual form of ownership.[9]

In some respects, however, a limited partnership resembles a general partnership more closely than a corporation. In general, the rights and liabilities of the general partners in a limited partnership are similar to those of partners in a general partnership. Limited and general partnerships have similar problems with respect to continuity and transferability of interest. However, in recent years, many syndicators have sought to overcome these problems through the securitization process—by standardizing the partnership agreement and publically offering partnership shares through securities exchanges, for example the New York and American stock exchanges, which provide primary and secondary markets for such offerings.

Limited-Liability Considerations. Contrary to popular belief, limited partners may be liable for debts and obligations beyond their initial cash contribution. For example, limited partners are liable to the partnership for contributions that they have subscribed to make to the partnership in the future and for damages incurred because of any breach of the partnership agreement. On occasion, for example, a partnership agreement may require partners to make staged payments over several years (also called split down payments), or may require a capital contribution from the partners that is significantly above the cash down payment, which is compulsory in the year of property purchase. Although the liability is limited in both situations, nevertheless each imposes considerable liability on the investors beyond the initial capital contribution. Furthermore, when properties are distressed and NOI is insufficient to meet the debt service, the limited partners will face a very serious dilemma. They can abandon the partnership because they have no liability, and thus may earn a "phantom taxable gain" because early-year artificial losses reduce their basis excessively. Alternatively, they may meet a call for cash and try to preserve their capital if the property appears to have upside potential. Thus, limited legal liability is not necessarily limited business risk for the prudent investor.

Under the Uniform Limited Partnership Act, limited partners can perform certain limited management duties without incurring the taint of being a general partner and having unlimited liability. They can (1) elect to remove the general partner or partners, or (2) have a voice in determining whether and when the partnership properties should be refinanced or sold. On the other hand, the more rights that are granted to the limited partners, the greater the probability that they will be deemed by the courts to have

---

[9]If a high degree of privacy is desired by certain limited partners, trust agreements may be used.

the unlimited liability of general partners. Most important, however, limited partners should refrain from any active role in the day-to-day management of the partnership if they choose to maintain their limited-liability status.[10]

Continuity and Transferability of Interest. Although all partnerships have limitations with respect to continuity and transferability of interest, a limited partnership is usually structured to provide relatively more continuity and transferability than a general partnership. The death of a limited partner does not dissolve the partnership because clauses in the agreement provide for re-formation by the remaining general partners and the replacement of the decedent. The recipient of the limited-partnership interest (trustee or heir) has all the rights of the original partner, along with any additional liabilities. With regard to transferability of interest, the limited partner usually has more rights than a general partner. A limited partner's interest may be assigned at will, and the new partner has the same rights and obligations as the selling partner. Even though the partnership agreement may place some restrictions on the transfer to avoid too many corporate characteristics, the right to transfer an interest is ordinarily unrestricted. Securities laws allow that substantial long-term restrictions be placed on the rights of partners to sell or assign their partnership units to nonresidents of the state or to others without the consent of the general partners.

The Problem of Too Many Corporate Characteristics. If a partnership has too many corporate characteristics, it will be taxed as a corporation. The so-called *Kintner regulations* are used to determine when a group will be treated as a partnership and when it will be treated as an association (corporation) for tax purposes. In short, the IRS will classify a group as a partnership for tax purposes if it avoids at least two of these four corporate characteristics.

if not the IRS will classify you as a corporation. and double taxation.

fairly easy to avoid →

  1. Continuity.
  2. Centralization of management.
  3. Limited liability.

easy to avoid →

  4. Free transferability of interest.

In the past, tax experts have claimed that most limited partnerships qualify for partnership status because they lack the corporate characteristics of

---

[10]Recent case law and changes in the model code of the uniform state law proposal have enabled limited partners to enter into the day-to-day management of a "distressed property" in financial difficulties (e.g., threatened foreclosure) and still retain their limited-liability status so long as there is a clear and unambiguous understanding with third-party creditors.

continuity and limited liability (the general partner always has unlimited liability). In addition, tax experts have successfully defended the limited-partnership status in several instances, on the basis that centralization of management and free transferability of interest were not present.[11] Consequently, it is usually possible to structure an agreement so that the entity created will be classified as a partnership for tax purposes. There may be a problem, however, when a corporation is set up as the sole general partner, thus appearing to limit the liability of the general partner and giving the partnership entity the corporate characteristic of limited liability.

Use of a Corporate General Partner. The use of a corporation as the sole general partner of a limited partnership is a popular technique in limited-partnership syndications. The advantage of this arrangement is that it provides continuity of management that will survive the active managerial years of the individual general partner. A corporate general partner is not subject to ill health, death, insanity, or other human frailties. Specific requirements, known as the *safe harbor rules* (Revenue Procedure 72-13), have been set forth by the IRS for a partnership that seeks to avoid the limited-liability characteristic.

1. *Net worth requirements.* If the equity contributions to the partnership total less than $2.5 million, then at all times during the life of the partnership the corporate general partner must have a net worth equal to 15 percent of the total contributions or $250,000, whichever is less. If the total contributions are $2.5 million or more, the corporate general partner must have a net worth equal to 10 percent of total contributions.

2. *Ownership requirement.* The limited partners cannot own, directly or indirectly, more than 20 percent of the stock of the corporate general partner. Thus, the corporation must have substantial assets of its own in order to pass the limited-liability test.

Satisfying Investment Objectives Through Special Allocations. In a typical real estate limited partnership, the general and limited partners prefer to allocate accounting taxable losses (e.g., from depreciation deductions) in a different manner than they would allocate other items of distribution. Allocations may also be different for cash flow, refinancing proceeds, and sale proceeds. For example, passive losses incurred by the partnership in the early years of the investment might be allocated 95 percent to limited partners who will benefit from the carryover of such losses to other pas-

---

[11]Theodore S. Lynn, Harry F. Goldberg, and Daniel S. Abrams, *Real Estate Limited Partnerships* (New York: Wiley–Interscience, 1985; with annual supplements); see also Jarchow, *Real Estate Syndication*, pp. 20–40.

sive income sources, or to the terminal year when the gain occurs. Under post-1984 through 1986 tax changes, the general partner is more likely to deduct expenses and amortization of depreciation schedules as the events actually occur rather than to accrue them artificially in early years. Furthermore, the general partner is less likely to impose fees and charges that will produce business income in the early years, because the passive losses for the limited partners will not produce current-year deductions. General partners are more likely to impose their fees at the end of the ownership cycle, or upon a successful refinancing, when cash is actually produced from appreciated values. It is much more common now to give a preferred cumulative cash flow return to the limited partners, say, 6 to 8 percent, while the general partner seeks to obtain substantial compensation if the property performs well by taking a disproportionate share of the sale proceeds, say, 20 percent of the sale proceeds, or more, after the limited partners receive their invested capital back plus a 6 to 8 percent noncompounded cumulative return on invested capital.

These allocations must, as previously stated, have economic substance and not be motivated principally by the desire to avoid or evade taxes. If the allocation does not have "substantial economic effect," it will be disallowed, and each partner will receive taxable income (loss), cash, and so forth according to his or her partnership interest.

Basis Problems and Other Disadvantages. Deductions generated by the depreciation of improvements are usually based on the full cost of the improvements to the owner, including the amount of any mortgage loans from a qualified lender other than a purchase money mortgagee. A building purchased with a $100,000 down payment and subject to a mortgage loan of $900,000 produces $1 million of depreciable basis. The owner has purchased $1 million of depreciation with a $100,000 cash investment, thereby generating substantial amounts of tax shelter relative to a small down payment. Although this may produce an artificial "passive" loss which may not be currently deductible (unless the investor has other "passive income" sources), it may be carried over indefinitely. As such, all that is lost is the time value of the money benefit since it is a deduction deferred to the terminal year and so remains valuable.

A problem peculiar to the limited-partnership form of ownership is that the partner's basis in real estate is limited to the equity investment plus that partner's share of liabilities of the partnership, for which no partner (general or limited) is personally liable (nonrecourse qualified lender liabilities—generally from financial institutions not having an interest in the equity investment returns). For example, if the $900,000 loan were made by a local savings and loan association and contained personal guarantees by the general partner, only $100,000 of losses could be written off by the partnership. After the property basis reaches zero, no losses can be passed through to investors. In a tax-shelter-oriented investment, this might occur in two to three years, thus severely limiting the tax shelter benefits of the partnership. In the event of negative basis from excessive deductions, it may result in deficiency assessments by the IRS.

Another problem of the limited partnership is government regulation. Because limited partners are often unsophisticated and therefore at the mercy of the general partner, and because the limited-partnership form has been abused extensively by greedy and unscrupulous syndicators, the government sector has steadily increased its surveillance and regulatory controls over limited-partnership syndications. The Securities Exchange Commission and state securities commissions, as well as the IRS, have enacted numerous antifraud laws and regulations that seek to control the activities of promoters of real estate syndications. Although the laws apply to all legal forms of ownership, the focus is on the limited-partnership form.

Master Limited Partnership

Master limited partnerships (MLPs) are publicly registered partnerships with ownership interests—known as depository certificates—that can be traded publicly. In 1986 and 1987, master limited partnerships became increasingly popular. They appeared to offer investors wider diversification, a relatively secure cash flow, and, unlike single-property partnerships, their certificates (issued by the MLPs to the investors in lieu of active partnership interests) were traded on securities exchanges and therefore liquid. Thus, they appeared to retain the benefits of the limited partnership—avoiding double taxation and providing pass-through benefits without the unwieldiness of the REITs.

Several types of MLPs have been used. One, called the "rollup," is formed by consolidating several affiliated and possibly unaffiliated partnerships into one master limited partnership. Some distressed general partners have persuaded their limited partners to join in such a new venture rather than face the failure of their partnerships.

A second type of MLP is formed by using the IRS Section 1031 exchange powers to consolidate a number of partnerships into one MLP, with the former limited partners receiving depositary certificate shares in the new MLP.

A third type, a "developer's rollup," is formed by a national developer and is usually designed to use properties at various locations to raise equity capital through the public offering of the MLP. The proceeds of the offering may be used to buy down debt, thus refinancing the properties for the new equity holders in the MLPs, or the funds may be used to acquire more properties.

The fourth type, called a "rollout," is used by major corporations to spin off existing operations (e.g., Burger King restaurant locations). This procedure restructures the major corporation, produces liquid funds for redeployment, discourages hostile takeovers, and can raise the share price of the corporation by eliminating substantially undervalued real assets on the balance sheets.

At the time of this writing, it appears likely that the MLPs are an endangered species or at least will be less attractive. Future tax legislation is expected to recharacterize the partners' income from "positive" passive income (which could be matched against "negative" passive real estate income) to portfolio income, thus cutting down on the pool of potential investors. It also appears possible that the larger MLPs may not be permitted partnership status for tax purposes but will be required to comply with C corporation tax accounting rules, which will end the pass-through advantages and make them subject to double taxation. Moreover, trading in MLP shares has been less active than expected, indicating they are less liquid investments than previously believed.[12]

Joint Venture

A joint venture is a special type of general partnership formed by investors for the purpose of owning a specific property or set of properties. Although a joint venture is similar in most respects to a general partnership as already described, and is usually treated as such in many states, there is no intention on the part of the investors to enter into a continuing partnership relationship or to assume general partnership obligations and liabilities on any other enterprises of any of the partners. Such joint ventures are usually formed for projects that require large amounts of capital and specialized experience. Thus, it might be an ideal form for a managing equity investor who is short on investment capital or does not want to risk all his or her money in one project. For example, the Aspen Wood case study involves a joint-venture form of ownership in which the designated managing partner—that is, the managing equity investor—is both syndicator and property manager, and the investor's liability is limited by a nonrecourse wraparound mortgage. Still, all the partners remain liable in the event that the property becomes distressed because rents and occupancy are low, expenses are high, and so forth; in such financial straits, they may have to meet calls for cash to maintain the solvency of the project.

Tax Treatment. A joint venture is treated as a partnership for income tax purposes unless it is deemed to be a corporation, and therefore is taxed at both the entity and investor levels. A joint venture can elect, however, not to be taxed as a partnership if it qualifies for such treatment under the IRS guidelines. The IRS has set forth four conditions that must be met if investors choose not to be taxed as a partnership [Regulation 1.761–2(a)].

---

[12]Michael L. Fitzgerald, "Master Limited Partnerships," *The Real Estate Securities Journal*, Vol. 8, No. 1, 1987.

1. They must own the property as co-owners (undivided interest deeded to each of the investors).
2. They must reserve the right to own and sell their joint-venture interest separately.
3. They cannot at any time actively conduct a business.
4. One of the investors cannot irrevocably authorize the sale or exchange of the property.

If the joint venture qualifies for the election, it must report its election in a statement to the IRS before the end of the first taxable year of the joint venture. As a result, the venture will not file a Form 1065 partnership information return each year. In recent years, however, the IRS has actively opposed the use of this tax election and has defined and interpreted more narrowly the four conditions given. Consequently, to avoid the risks and costs of the IRS disallowing this tax election, most joint ventures choose to report as partnerships for income tax purposes.

The Fiduciary Relationship among Investors. Members of a joint venture, like partners, have a fiduciary relationship to one another that requires a significant degree of good faith and trust. As in all fiduciary relationships, each investor must fully disclose to the other investors all his or her dealings with the property and the venture. A binding written agreement that outlines all the rights and obligations of each investor and the housekeeping rules of the venture should be executed to prevent misunderstandings. Typically, the investors appoint one member to be responsible for venture management and property management while the others remain relatively passive, except for participating in major financial policy decisions. Of course, they have the power to remove the managing partner and take over active participation or choose another managing agent.

CORPORATIONS AND TRUSTS

Regular (Subchapter C) Corporation

The corporate form of ownership is not normally used as an investment vehicle by equity investors because of three tax disadvantages. The first is double taxation: corporate income is taxable first to the corporation when it is received or accrued, and again to the shareholders when it is distributed to them in the form of dividends. The second disadvantage is the inability of the corporation to pass through to its shareholders any tax losses generated by depreciation, interest, or other deductions. Third, it is difficult for a corporation to pass through capital gains income because dividends paid to stockholders are normally treated as ordinary income for tax purposes. However, under the 1986 act, this is no longer a disadvantage since capital gains income is taxed at the same rate as ordinary income. Unlike a partnership or joint venture, a corporation is a legal entity that exists separately and apart from its stockholders. It files its own tax return, as do the investors who own stock in the corporation. Despite these disadvantages, there are many advantages of the corporate form (also called a "C" corporation), and in some situations these advantages make the corporate entity the ideal choice.

Advantages of the Corporate Entity. Some of the advantages of using the corporate form of ownership flow from the basic corporate characteristics discussed earlier in the chapter.

1. *Continuity.* A corporation continues until dissolved by law (unless limited by state statute).
2. *Limited liability.* Stockholders have no individual liability for corporate debts and liabilities; a stockholder's losses are generally limited to his or her equity investment.
3. *Centralization of management.* Stockholders are not responsible for management; authority is vested in a board of directors. Corporate officers are hired as agents of the board and are paid to run the day-to-day operations of the corporation.
4. *Free transferability of interests.* Stock can ordinarily be sold or otherwise transferred at will. However, such transferability may be limited purposely by the organizers (e.g., a closely held or family corporation). Also, there may not be an active market for the stock.

Other advantages of the corporate form that are often cited by investors who use a corporate entity for their investments are the following.

1. *Diversification.* The corporation form allows the combination of several distinct properties into one entity, thus creating diversification and spreading the risks involved in investment properties.
2. *Favorable public image and legal certainty.* Lenders, investors, and the general public tend to view the corporation favorably. This gives an aura of solidity, strength, and continuity to the operations of the entity. In addition, a well-developed body of law regulates corporate activity and lends a high degree of legal certainty to this form of ownership.
3. *Control of large properties with minimum capital outlays.* Small investors can pool their money to buy larger properties through the corporation than they could individually. At the same time, they can maintain limited liability.

4. *Estate building or retirement fund.* A corporation can be used as a vehicle for building a portfolio of real estate assets by reinvesting accumulated earnings of the corporation. At the same time, the tax consequences to the corporation can be minimized by offsetting tax loss properties with tax gain properties, and through deductions allowed, such as salaries to stockholder-officers. Years later, when the stockholder-officer retires, the corporation can be liquidated or shares of stock can be sold; the capital gains income will pass directly through to the officer-stockholder without a tax at the entity level.

5. *Fringe benefits.* Principals, as officer-stockholders or employee-stockholders, can have a tax-favored retirement or pension plan set up for them. A corporation can carry insurance on the lives of employee- and officer-stockholders at a reduced annual tax cost and then, without any further income tax burden, realize the proceeds and make them available to pay estate taxes. Other fringe benefits could include group life insurance, full medical and dental insurance coverage for employee- and officer-stockholders and their families, disability insurance, pension plans, and death benefits to beneficiaries—all paid for by the corporation. These deductions are not generally available to the other forms of organization discussed.

6. *Financial and tax planning.* The corporate form can facilitate saving income and estate taxes by means of gifts to children or a family foundation. Corporate stockholders can often control the dividend process, dictating the year in which they will receive income and choosing years that yield the most favorable tax results. Frequently multiple corporations will be established, one for each property purchased, to limit liabilities and reduce the investor's overall tax burden. As Chapter 10 illustrates, however, there are strict controls on corporations formed primarily for tax avoidance purposes.

7. For a C corporation that is not closely held, is not a professional services corporation, and is not subject to the passive-loss rule limitations on rental income and loss, deductions may be offset against other income. However, the IRS has extraordinary latitude in characterizing passive losses according to congressional legislative records.

8. Major corporations have major assets in the present real estate markets in that both leaseholds and real estate assets of great magnitude on their balance sheets are currently undervalued. Securitization of the real estate assets by "spin-offs" can generate substantial capital for redeployment or provide more liquidity, as in the sale of Bank of America's major bank buildings.

In conclusion, the corporate entity may provide an ideal ownership entity for investors who seek to accumulate wealth and can minimize or avoid the problems of double taxation and limited tax shelter.

Problem Areas for Corporate Entities. Certain problems should be considered by the investor who is considering the corporate form as a vehicle for building real estate equities.[13] Careful tax planning can usually circumvent these problems before they occur.

The first is the *accumulated-earnings tax*. When a corporation accumulates earnings instead of distributing them as dividends to stockholders, it runs the risk of a penalty tax. The penalty is intended to discourage formation of a corporation for the purpose of avoiding double taxation by "unreasonably" accumulating earnings. This penalty tax becomes operative only when accumulated earnings exceed $250,000; the excess is taxed at 27.5 percent on the first $100,000 and 38.5 percent on the remainder. The investor can avoid the penalty tax by showing "reasonably anticipated needs of the business" as the purpose of the accumulation.[14] For example, if accumulated earnings are to be used to make mortgage payments, to buy additional properties, or as a reserve fund for the renovation of older properties, the accumulation problem can be avoided.

The corporation may have related penalty tax problems if it is classified as a *personal holding company*.[15] Prior to the establishment of the personal holding-company tax provision, there was a tax loophole, called the *incorporated pocketbook*, whereby an investor in a high tax bracket would form a corporation to furnish services to the investor. The corporation would then accumulate the income and obtain the benefit of the lower tax rates of the corporation. This tax shelter vehicle was closed by imposing a 50 percent penalty tax on all undistributed personal holding-company income, in addition to the regular corporate taxes. There are numerous tests and regulatory definitions that indicate what is considered a personal holding company. The investor who anticipates problems should perform a careful analysis and perhaps seek tax counseling.[16]

Multiple and Collapsible Corporations. A real estate investor may choose to operate with a separate corporation for each property (i.e., multiple corporations). If the legal entities are separate, the debts and obligations of one property will never be the responsibility of another. If one property becomes insolvent, creditors cannot look to the other properties for satisfaction of the debts. Investors also set up multiple corporations for tax purposes. Since the corporate tax rate in 1988 is only 34 percent, and lower tax rates for small corporations doing personal services are to be phased out, it appears that spreading the income from an investment program over as many low-tax-rate entities as possible will no longer be advanta-

---

[13] For an excellent discussion of corporate issues, see Arthur Andersen & Co., *Federal Taxes Affecting Real Estate* (distributed by Matthew Bender & Co.), December 1987 supplement.

[14] IRC Sec. 537.

[15] IRC Sec. 541.

[16] See IBP, *Real Estate Investment Planning*, paragraphs 56,315–56,320.

geous. However, even under current tax law this procedure may be disallowed if a major or principal purpose is to avoid income taxes. Special attention and scrutiny are given to the corporate form whenever multiple corporations are controlled by one person or by related individuals.[17]

Collapsible corporations can also create serious tax problems. When investors sell the property owned by a corporation, they can wind up with ordinary income rather than a capital gain if the corporation has held the property less than three years. The collapsible-corporation rule, as it is called, was enacted to prevent investors from setting up a corporation to purchase or construct real estate with a view to selling the property or stock of the corporation before the corporation realizes any substantial ordinary income from the property. Generally, the collapsible-corporation rule can be avoided provided most of the corporate property is depreciable property and the owners of the corporate stock are not "dealers" in real estate. The dealer classification and problem are discussed in Chapter 10.

Salaries of Stockholder, Employees. If corporate profits are distributed to shareholders as payments for services rendered to the corporation, the moneys are deductible by the corporation as expenses rather than being dividends to the shareholders and subject to a double tax. For example, investor-officers often attempt to adjust their bonuses or salaries at the end of each year in order to minimize corporate taxes. However, the IRS allows salaries and bonuses to be deducted by the corporation as an ordinary business expense only if they are "reasonable." If the purported salary or bonus is considered unreasonable, it cannot be deducted by the corporation. In addition, it will also be taxed as ordinary income to the shareholder, in the form of a "disguised dividend." The IRS uses a relatively elaborate set of principles and tests to ascertain reasonableness; basically, reasonable compensation is defined as the amount that would ordinarily be paid for like services by like enterprises under like circumstances. As with the other potential tax risks we have discussed, the salary reclassification risk can be reduced or minimized through good tax planning.

The "S" Corporation

The Internal Revenue Code, Subchapter S, allows certain small business corporations, called "S" corporations, to avoid corporate taxes. When a qualified corporation properly elects Subchapter S treatment, most of the tax consequences of its operations pass through to its shareholders. Thus, the investors enjoy the benefits of having a corporate entity offering them the usual corporate advantages (i.e., limited liability, continuity, central-

---

[17]IRC Sec. 1561; see also Sec. 385.

ized management, fringe benefits, good public image), and at the same time they enjoy many of the tax advantages of a partnership. Tax losses are passed through to stockholders, and each stockholder receives a pro rata share of those losses. Capital gains realized by the corporation are similarly passed through to the shareholders. Although there is some limitation on the pass-through of capital losses, which may require carryover, no tax is levied at the corporate level. In addition, the corporate problems of the tax on accumulated earnings and the personal holding-company tax are avoided.

A corporation can elect treatment as an S corporation only if it meets all the following requirements.

1. It must be a domestic corporation incorporated in the United States.
2. It must have no more than thirty-five shareholders (twenty-five prior to the 1984 tax act).
3. All stockholders must be individuals, estates, or special types of trusts.
4. Shareholders must all be U.S. citizens or resident aliens.
5. There may be only one class of stock; however, the existence of differences in voting rights among the shares of common stock alone may not be sufficient grounds for disqualification.
6. The corporation cannot be a member of an "affiliated group" of corporations; it cannot own 80 percent or more of the stock of another corporation.
7. Passive income in excess of 25 percent of gross receipts is taxed at the highest corporate rate, now 34 percent. Passive income includes, among other things, income from residential and commercial rents. Some types of rental income are not considered passive, such as that derived from hotel and motel operations, parking garages and lots, equipment rentals, and similar rents with which the lessor renders "substantial services" to the tenant.
8. It must use the calendar year as its fiscal year unless special consent is obtained from the IRS.

The Subchapter S election is made, assuming that the corporation meets all the requirements, by filing an election with the consent of all the stockholders. Once made, the Subchapter S election is effective for the taxable year of the corporation for which it is made, and for all subsequent tax years, unless the IRS revokes the election or the stockholders terminate it.

Use of the S Corporation in Real Estate Investment. Subchapter S treatment for real estate investors is severely restricted by the provision stating that pass-through deductions are limited to the shareholders' basis arising out of cash or property contributed, or the adjusted basis plus actual shareholders' loans to the corporation, thus barring the usual deductibility of a pro rata share of basis arising out of nonrecourse debt of qualified lenders. Despite this limitation, real estate investors can qualify for Subchapter S treatment by owning (1) motels and hotels; (2) shopping centers for which the corporate owner provides substantial promotional, maintenance, security, or other services; (3) a real estate brokerage or development company; or (4) any other business in which the investment income is from such special-purpose properties. Active real estate investors who own and manage several properties and actively and materially participate in management might create an S corporation to manage and lease properties, thus achieving limited liability from third-party tort and contractual liability, and to originate the debt on the property and make the loans to the corporation itself, and thus make themselves eligible for the deductions. The investors would therefore be legally liable on the debt as in a general trading partnership, but they would also achieve limited liability against other risks of the enterprise.

An S corporation may not be a wise choice for an investor, even if it can qualify. Under these circumstances the investor might prefer a partnership form of ownership. Moreover, an S corporation does not provide for transferability of stock or the flexibility of an ordinary corporation because of the limitations on the number and types of shareholders and classes of stock. These limitations may cause the investor to decide against the S corporation as an ownership entity, particularly when the following facts are considered: (1) tax losses can be deducted only to the extent of the shareholders' basis as indicated by the number of shares held (the corporation's debt to others is not included in this basis) and (2) special allocations of particular loss items are not possible. But the individual's tax rate at 28 percent is lower than the corporate tax rate, so the pass-through may prove attractive.[18]

Nominee, Dummy, and Straw Corporations

A nominee, dummy, or straw corporation[19] (the three terms are synonymous) can be organized to achieve a number of objectives, including the following.

1. Limiting the personal liability of the beneficial owners of the property.
2. Privacy—concealing ownership of property.

---

[18]Cherie J. O'Neil and Clarence C. Rose, "Real Estate Tax Shelters under the Tax Reform Act of 1986," *The Journal of Real Estate Taxation*, Winter 1987, pp. 115–126.

[19]For leading cases see IBP, *Real Estate Investment Planning*, paragraphs 56,310–56,315.

3. Simplifying the transferability of interest when there is a large number of beneficial owners.
4. Raising money to finance a property on which the rate of interest charged would be usurious were the loan made to an individual.

The tax and legal consequences of setting up a nominee corporation must be analyzed. From a tax standpoint, the corporate entity may be disregarded (not subjected to a corporate income tax) if it is the mere alter ego of its shareholders and beneficial owners, provided that it serves no other function and engages in no significant business activity. For example, a corporation that is created and used as a mere "dummy" to take title to property and hold that title blind in order to deter the creditors of a shareholder may avoid taxation at the corporate level: the income is taxed only at the shareholder level. On the other hand, if the corporation is not completely inactive, its income may be subject to double taxation. For example, if it engages in such real estate activity as executing leases, collecting rents, making improvements, maintaining a bank account, or negotiating sales, it may be treated as a taxable entity.

REITs: Real Estate Investment Trusts

A real estate investment trust (REIT)[20] is a specialized form of trust ownership created by congressional action, and its basic structure is defined by the Internal Revenue Code. Qualified REITs do not pay any federal income or capital gains tax on income or gains distributed to shareholders. Since they pass income through to shareholders without a tax at the trust level, REITs are often called conduits. The purpose of this favorable tax treatment is (1) to give small investors the chance to participate in large-scale real estate investments with professional management on a scale that was formerly available only to a few wealthy individuals, and (2) to stimulate the financing of the large-scale real estate developments needed in metropolitan and resort areas.

A REIT may be formed as either a corporation or a business trust. Because most REITs are publicly held and traded, they are organized by means of securities offerings made pursuant to registration under the 1933 Securities Act. Some REITs are organized through private placements under the securities law, but this is rare because a REIT must have at least 100 shareholders.

The REIT industry's dramatic rise and eventual collapse in the mid-

[20]Stephen P. Jarchow, *Real Estate Investment Trusts* (New York: Wiley, 1988) is a source for some of the following; also, Jarchow, *Real Estate Syndication*, especially the 1986 supplement (pp. 147–152), along with our own ideas. Any errors and omissions are our own.

1970s has been well documented and chronicled. After the collapse, several investment groups, seeing that traded stock prices were low relative to the underlying value of their assets, formed to operate as discount buyers of REIT shares. Southmark Corporation, itself a reconstituted REIT, followed this strategy of purchasing undervalued properties through REIT share purchases. Many foreign investors also formed REITs during the late 1970s and early 1980s and bought up these undervalued "property trusts."

REITs became popular again in 1985, with a flurry of blind pools being formed. The general trend seems to be toward more economically oriented transactions with an influx of pension funds and IRA/Keogh funds from investors who like the REIT format as a surrogate–fiduciary for their own diligence in asset selection and management.

There is also a new group of REIT sponsors who are utilizing the REIT entity as a captive real estate finance company to finance their real-estate-related activities, such as Rockefeller Center Properties, Inc., Lincoln (N.C.) Realty Fund, Inc., EQK Realty Investors, and Mellon Participating Mortgage Trust.

Eligibility Requirements for Conduit Tax Treatment. Unless the REIT meets all the requirements of the Internal Revenue Code, it will not receive the conduit tax treatment just described. Furthermore, the REIT may be disqualified if it does not continue to meet these requirements each quarter with a grace period; in some circumstances it may be assessed heavy penalty taxes. These requirements include the following.

1. *Corporation or trust.* The REIT must be a corporation or a common-law business trust. It cannot be a limited partnership.
2. *At least 100 beneficial owners.* With the exception of its first year of existence, the REIT must have at least 100 beneficial owners, who can be individuals, trusts, estates, partnerships, or corporations. It cannot be more than 50 percent owned by five or fewer individuals. The shares must be transferable.
3. *No real estate dealer activities.* The REIT may not be a dealer in real estate; that is, it may not hold property primarily for sale to customers in the ordinary course of business. Consequently, the REIT must not be an active participant in a real estate business such as development, property management, leasing, or brokerage. Any income from dealer properties is subject to a 100 percent penalty tax but does not disqualify the REIT. Yet, the REIT must engage the services of real estate professionals to manage its activities.
4. *Passive-income tests.* The REIT must derive at least 90 percent of its gross income from passive sources (e.g., dividends, rents from real estate, gain from the sale of real estate, stock, and securities) each year, and at least 75 percent of its gross income from rents from real

property, mortgage interest, gains from the sale and distribution of real estate, dividends or distributions from the ownership or sale of REITs, income or gain from foreclosure property, and mortgage loan fees—in effect, real estate sources. Instead of the REIT being disqualified by income exceeding these limits, a 100 percent penalty tax is charged against such income. Not more than 25 percent of the assets can be securities. Investments in the securities of one issuer may not exceed 5 and 10 percent of its outstanding securities.

5. *Dividend test.* A REIT loses its favored tax status and is treated like a corporation unless it distributes 95 percent or more of its income in the year the income is earned or in the following year.

6. *Asset tests.* At least 75 percent of assets must be in real estate and cash or cash equivalents.

REITs can own real estate, interests in real estate, and real estate mortgages. Mortgages can be pure loans or participate in excess cash flows and residuals. REITs are often referred to by the types of assets in which they invest.

- *Equity REITs.* Equity REITs invest in real estate equities on a long-term basis, with their principal sources of income being rents. They invest in real properties such as apartment buildings, office and industrial buildings, and shopping centers.
- *Mortgage REITs.* Mortgage REITs frequently finance every phase of a real estate venture, including acquisition of the land, its development, and construction of the building and other improvements. They also invest in permanent mortgages on residential and commercial properties.
- *Hybrid REITs.* Hybrid REITs make a combination of equity and mortgage investments in real estate.
- *Finite-Life REITs.* FREITs are closed-ended; they organize for a stated term of years, and additional equity offerings are not ordinarily used or permitted. They make one equity offering and terminate when the properties in the portfolio are liquidated.

The REIT is managed by trustees or directors who hold title to the property for the benefit of the shareholders. The majority must be independent outside trustees or directors. Serious problems in insuring and indemnifying directors and trustees against lawsuits have been encountered because of weighty responsibilities of due diligence and duties of investigation and the inadequacy of insurance coverage.

The trustees usually retain the advisory company that originally organized the REIT and selected the trustees. REITs have been organized by commercial bankers, mortgage bankers, real estate brokers, real estate

managers, and others with real estate experience. A large percentage of
REITs were sponsored and are advised by major commercial banks and
financial services companies.

Advisory firms generally provide portfolio strategy and acquisition recommendations, act as an agent in the event of buying or selling, and supervise day-to-day operations. It should be clear that the REIT is passive and
the trustees play a passive role, formulating and modifying and requiring
the implementation of REIT investment policies. The REIT must generally
engage the services of independent contractors to provide all essential services, including management of properties within the portfolio.

REITs pose obvious technical complications that inhibit their flexibility.
However, modern computer-assisted program management can correctly
implement the REIT approach.

REITs may not be traders in real property. Generally, they must comply
with a four-year holding period to avoid severe penalties. The 1986 act
relaxed this rule for foreclosed properties to allow the REIT to handle the
turnaround of such distressed properties, thus removing them from the
portfolio in a timely manner, rather than being forced into a distress sale
and the accompanying penalties. There are safe harbors for making expenditures on up to seven properties in order to ready them for resale
within four years, without penalties being imposed. This work must be
done by independent contractors.

Advantages Offered by REITs. The REIT is sometimes referred to as the
mutual fund for real estate investors. In addition to the advantage of being
a single-tax entity, REITs enable small investors to invest in large real estate enterprises and spread risk among many investors, and they provide
diversification, professional management, and liquidity in the form of a
public market for their shares. They are organized to earn immediate income and distribute that income to investors and, in equity and hybrid
REITs, to achieve appreciation in the value of their investment. REITs enjoy the corporate attributes of centralized management, limited liability
for their investors, continuity, and transferability of shares. At the same
time, for income tax purposes the investor–shareholders are treated in a
manner similar to that accorded partners, with the limitation that tax
losses cannot be passed through to them and used to shelter other income.

The REIT has been generally accepted by the investing public and, because of its broad base of shareholders and nationally recognized sponsor-
ing agents, has established a reasonably good market for its shares. In the
past the market for these shares has been stronger than the market for limited-partnership shares or other forms of ownership. Even large investors
may find the REIT an attractive vehicle because it has features not available in other forms of ownership. A REIT can be organized to acquire a
property that has limited market appeal as a single property but is more
easily marketed through the sale of shares. Thus, the unique advantages of

the REIT may be attractive to investors who can adapt these advantages to their return and risk objectives.

Disadvantages of the REIT. The REIT did not become a popular form of ownership until the early 1970s. From 1970 to 1974, many properties were built and financed regardless of their financial and market feasibility. The subsequent real estate crash of 1974–1976 was disastrous to the REITs, and they quickly fell from public favor. Much of the investment public continues to question the REIT as a desirable investment vehicle, despite the excellent track record of many of the well-managed mortgage and equity REITs.

Other disadvantages of the REIT form, which preclude it from consideration by many investors, are the following.

1. *Strict rules and regulations.* A REIT must comply with many federal and state regulations in addition to the ones cited earlier. There is not much freedom or flexibility in the real estate investment program; the accounting and legal requirements are onerous and entail substantial expense for the REIT.

2. *Probability of losing REIT status.* There is a significant risk of losing REIT status or incurring heavy penalty taxes. A tax rate of 100 percent may be imposed on prohibited real estate buy–sell transactions. If a REIT loses its status, it is treated as a regular corporation and incurs double taxation. Regaining the REIT classification is difficult. The 1986 IRS code changes did alleviate this situation in meaningful ways, but the risks remain.

3. *Limited tax shelters.* A REIT can shelter all cash flow produced by its properties, and therefore distribute "tax-free" cash, but it cannot pass through tax losses to the investor. The extraordinary change in the way passive real estate losses are now being handled for individual investors has, however, enhanced the attractiveness of the REITs because passive losses are less attractive than they were. Consequently, the REIT is now a more practical entity for investors who seek both income and capital gains. It should be noted that the income from an REIT is characterized as portfolio income and not as passive income, so income loss matching is not possible. After the demise of the master limited partnerships, one can expect greater interest in REITs in the investment banking and securities industry.

4. *Limited growth potential.* A REIT cannot significantly accumulate income and reinvest in properties. Thus, it is a relatively poor estate-building vehicle. However, one should not ignore the upside potential through appreciation of real estate assets in a low-leveraged or all-equity REIT; they may outperform zero-coupon bonds as they have in the past.

   5. *Limited use for syndication of a single property.* A REIT is not usu-
      ally the best form of organization for acquiring a single property be-
      cause of the substantial costs involved and the long time period re-
      quired to organize it.

In most real estate transactions time is of the essence. For an entrepreneur
who must quickly tie up property, set up an ownership form, and raise the
required equity with a minimum of expense and hassle, the REIT is not a
desirable form of ownership. The REIT is better suited to a larger institutional type of organization that can effectively manage the relatively cum-
bersome process of setting up and operating such an entity.

REITs have indeed experienced a resurgence; however, in 1988–1990 the
real estate industry as a whole faces serious liquidity problems. If one believes that the current problems are cyclical, it can be argued that substantial buying opportunities are at the bottom of the current real estate cycle,
and some equity REITs will reap the rewards as discount buyers. It is expected that more transactions will be conducted under all-equity formats
or with relatively low leverage, though only if the pension funds and individual investors can accept lower yields and lower levels of tax shelter.

In recent years well-managed equity and hybrid REITs have increased
earnings per share and asset values and have been excellent investments
for their shareholders.

Other Types of Trusts

The common types of trusts provide popular and flexible devices for indirectly controlling property while transferring the financial benefits to the
beneficiary, without taxation at the entity level.[21] The important feature of
any trust, including the REIT, is that legal title to property is held by trustees for the benefit of the shareholders or beneficiaries who possess rights to
share the income from the property or the proceeds from the sale of assets.
The authority of a trustee to purchase and sell real estate is established by a
recorded deed to the trustee from the grantor. Then a trust agreement that
spells out the rights and responsibilities of the beneficiaries and the trustee
is drawn up. Almost every trust agreement has control in the trustee,
transferability of shares, and continuance beyond the death of a participant. Therefore, it closely resembles a corporation and may be reclassified
as a corporation by the IRS if it does not meet certain tests.

Revocable and Irrevocable Trusts. A *revocable trust*, sometimes called a
living trust or grantor trust, may be terminated by the grantor during his

---

[21] See IBP, *Estate Planning* (Englewood Cliffs, N.J.: Prentice–Hall; reporting service),
Vol. 1, paragraph 16,901–17,200, for complete discussion of the use of trusts.

or her lifetime. This type of trust is desirable in that real estate placed in the trust may avoid probate procedure upon the death of the grantor. The trust also provides a measure of privacy and protects assets from outside creditors. It provides for continuity of management if the grantor becomes incapacitated. On the other hand, the revocable trust has the least favorable tax effects. The income is taxable to the grantor each year, and all real estate transferred to the trust is included in the grantor's gross estate for inheritance tax purposes. Thus, an owner in a high tax bracket is not able to shift taxable income to lower-bracket beneficiaries.

An *irrevocable trust*, in contrast, cannot be terminated by the grantor once it has been established and all property interests have been transferred to the trustee. This trust is the favored vehicle for tax planning of large estates because, if set up correctly, it provides more flexibility than a revocable trust and the income is not taxed to the grantor. It is often used (as are family partnerships) to redistribute income from real estate ventures to family members who are in lower tax brackets. In addition, the property value can be deducted from the gross estate of the grantor. One disadvantage of the irrevocable trust is that it usually triggers a gift tax at the time of the transfer. Six states have land trusts (e.g., Florida and Illinois), which have the added advantage of leaving very little duty or control in the hands of the trustee, converting the realty into personalty in the legal sense—secrecy—and enabling the beneficiaries to retain the powers of supervision and control over the property.[22]

Offshore Trusts. The ownership vehicle used in most "tax haven" (avoidance) strategies is an offshore trust set up in a low-tax country by a wealthy investor who wishes to accumulate profits and provide a channel for large deductions against U.S. taxation.[23] This device is frequently used by foreign corporate investors who seek to avoid paying taxes on operations conducted in the United States. If the trust is properly established in a country that has favorable tax treaties with the United States (e.g., Bermuda or the British Antilles), the income from operations is taxed at a relatively low rate (not subject to the regular graduated income tax), and the capital gains are not subject to any federal income tax. To qualify for these tax exclusions, the foreign trust must not be in a "U.S. trade or business" and its trustees cannot be physically present in the United States for 183 days or more during the taxable year.

In recent years the IRS has been discouraging the use of these vehicles to avoid taxes in the United States, especially if any of the beneficiaries are

---

[22]The Chicago Title and Trust Company has brochures explaining this attractive alternative form of ownership.

[23]Adam Starchild and John T. Kosarowich, "Using Tax Havens for U.S. Real Estate Investment," *The Journal of Property Management*, January–February 1978, pp. 000.

U.S. citizens, and further vigorous efforts to close these loopholes can be expected. Furthermore, during the next few years the IRS and state governments can be expected to make more aggressive efforts to tax foreign investors on real estate income and gains made on real estate assets located in the United States.

Pension Trusts. A pension trust is established for the benefit of employees and is similar to a tax-exempt foundation in that the beneficiaries (employees) are taxed on distributions of income that they receive while the trust itself is exempt from income taxes. Pension funds are becoming a significant factor in real estate investment markets, although they have traditionally restricted their purchases to publicly traded marketable securities. Because they have grown substantially over the past ten years, and because the stock market was volatile in the 1980s, pension funds have been required by law to diversify into real estate, investing in real estate equities as well as mortgages. Pension funds can commingle their funds with other pension funds and other entities, allowing them to invest in projects that are too large for a single pension fund. They can diversify their portfolios through the due diligence of professional real estate pension fund advisors and managers such as the National Life Real Estate Pension Fund Management Company. Pension funds that invest in real estate usually turn to private advisory firms, as well as banks, life insurance companies, and other financial institutions that have developed the real estate expertise required for such an investment program.

One significant problem that may be encountered by a pension fund investing in real estate is known as the "unrelated business income" problem. The use of debt to finance a property creates "unrelated-business taxable income," which may result in loss of tax-exempt status for a portion of the trust's income. For this reason some pension trusts have a policy of buying only debt-free properties. Other pension funds choose to buy mortgaged property and pay some taxes in exchange for the substantial benefits expected from leverage and the ability to diversify and control more properties with fewer equity dollars invested.

Individual Retirement Accounts and Keogh Plans. The 1986 revisions to the Employee Retirement Income Security Act (ERISA) and the Tax Reform Act modifications for individual retirement accounts (IRAs) and Keoghs, as well as 401(k)s, have allowed all individuals to set up their own IRAs or other qualified pension plans. Although such techniques remain an important source of equity funding, they will not be dealt with in this chapter. Chapter 19 discusses the importance of such savings methods in helping individual investors to accumulate wealth.

Numerous other types of pension plans can be established and used to channel before-tax dollars into real estate investments. For example, professional people—doctors, dentists, lawyers—can purchase real estate through the properly qualified plans of self-employed professional corporations that they administer. These can provide a very flexible vehicle for real estate investments compared with the IRA or Keogh plans. At the time of this writing it appears that the personal-services corporations will no longer have the favorable tax rates on the first $100,000 of their income; thus, it is even more likely that the professionals will use the qualified pension plans (Defined-Contribution Plans, Profit-Sharing Plans, and Defined-Benefit Plans) even more aggressively, probably saving the maximum to avoid current-year taxes. One should be forewarned of the tax act's provision that qualified plans may not properly receive unrelated business income without risking heavy tax penalties. Distributive shares of capital gains, or taxable income arising out of debt-financed properties, may be regarded by the IRS as unrelated business income.

REMIC

The Tax Reform Act of 1986 enacted a new type of investment alternative called a real estate mortgage investment conduit (REMIC). A REMIC holds a pool of mortgages and issues interests to investors. A REMIC is not actually an ownership entity but rather a tax-structuring device that permits multiclass pass-through mortgage securities to be issued without being subject to taxation at both the issuer and the investor levels. Any entity that meets specified requirements, including a corporation, partnership, or trust, can elect treatment as a REMIC. REMICs may hold any obligation secured by an interest in real property—residential or commercial—and need not be a separate entity. The first REMIC interests marketed have been consolidated mortgage obligations (CMOs) that have elected REMIC status.

The pass-through interests are mortgage-backed bonds requiring repayment of principal and interest in accordance with schedules arising out of the pooled mortgages. The issuer may originate any number of classes of "regular interests," which entitle the holder to receive the repayments of fixed principal from the pool of mortgages. Although the amount of principal is fixed, the timing of the payments is to a degree controlled by the repayment powers of the mortgagors of the underlying qualified mortgages in the pool.

The other interest sold is the "residual interest," of which there can be only one class. It arises from the interest income generated from the underlying debt (i.e., the pool of mortgages). Income allocated to the residual interests is generally fully taxable. Thus the REMICs are enabling the securitization of the flow of funds from the repayment of the principal and interest on mortgages, in accordance with their schedules (and earlier prepayments), into a variety of mortgage-backed securities that appeal to many investors with different risk trade-off and liquidity preferences.[24]

Real Estate Syndication

Syndication can be defined as a device by which a real estate professional—the syndicator or sponsor—obtains investors who provide the funds required to engage in a real estate enterprise.[25] Some people consider it to be a legal form of ownership, but others view it as a type of financing, one that offers smaller investors the opportunity to invest in real estate ventures that would otherwise be beyond their financial and management capabilities. A syndicate can be formed to acquire, develop, manage, operate, or market real estate, or to perform any combination of these functions. For example, a real estate syndicate might be organized to acquire income property and hold it for the cash flow and tax shelter it generates, or to acquire and hold real estate primarily for capital appreciation over a period of years, or for a combination of these objectives.

Syndicates are often formed to construct buildings or develop land, which is then sold to other investors. They can be formed to do virtually anything that any real estate enterprise might do. Syndicators benefit from the fees for their services, the interest they may retain in the syndicated property, and the ability to manage and profit from several ventures at the same time and thereby spread the risk. A syndicator who is also a real estate broker benefits from the increase of the market for the properties handled.

Syndication is discussed in Chapter 9 as a financing vehicle, but to the extent that syndication is a form of ownership, it utilizes the selection criteria and legal entities discussed in this chapter. A syndicator needs discipline and integrity to avoid the potential abuses of overvaluation, unreasonable accruals of inflated fees, and "puffing" of the wares by raising unreasonable expectations about upside potential of the properties purchased. The antifraud provisions of the Securities Acts of 1933 and 1934, Regulation D, and state securities laws make this a dangerous field for the unsophisticated and unscrupulous. Often, real estate syndications are small offerings that fall under the exemption provisions of private offerings, or they may be an intrastate offering. General solicitation, advertis-

[24]Misty S. Gruber and Susan Jacobsen, "The New REMIC Amendments and Mortgage-Backed Securities," *The Real Estate Securities Journal* (RESSI), Vol. 8, No. 1, 1987, pp. 7–25.

[25]Alvin Arnold (and Jack Kusnet), *The Arnold Encyclopedia of Real Estate* (Boston: Warren, Gorham & Lamont, 1985), or see most recent edition. See also Peter M. Fass et al., *Tax Aspects of Real Estate Investments: A Practical Guide for Structuring Real Estate Transactions* (New York: Clark Boardman Co., 1988); and Linda Wortheimer, *Securities and Partnership Laws for MLPs and Other Investment Limited Partnerships*, Vol. 14 (New York: Clark Boardman Co., 1988).

ing, and invitations to so-called seminars for potential investors may be incompatible with a private offering. Strict compliance with the federal and state securities laws is essential. Generally, an issuer must either disclose any and all information to a would-be investor that he or she needs for a prudent investigation before making an accept or reject investment decision, or else risk litigation under the antifraud provisions. Since the burden of proof is on the issuer and his or her broker–dealers that they do comply, there is great risk that a disgruntled investor will fall back on the protection of the securities law to seek a refund of the investment.

Syndicators must therefore be knowledgeable, skillful, ethical, and strongly committed to fulfill the investment objectives set forth in the offering documents. This should not be discouraging. Syndication has come of age: the *Stanger Reports* and Stephen Roulac & Associates indicate that even after the effects of the 1986 Tax Reform Act, billions of dollars of new equity funds are being invested each year in real estate partnerships and REIT syndications. There appears to be a good future for syndication.

A MATRIX APPROACH TO THE OWNERSHIP ENTITY DECISION

Many investors may feel overwhelmed by the complexity of the ownership entity decision. Such persons should develop their own systematic framework to facilitate overall comparison of the alternatives. A matrix approach could provide such a framework by allowing the investor to list the selection criteria and compare side by side the ownership alternatives. There are countless ways to perform matrix evaluation, but they all involve listing and weighting the selection criteria and assigning scores to each alternative. One such approach is outlined here to aid the reader in developing his or her own application.

Vertical Column

STEP 1. List all relevant decision criteria down the left side of the page.
STEP 2. Assign relative weights to each criterion by allocating, say, a possible 100 points over the various criteria.

Horizontal Columns

STEP 3. List the possible ownership alternatives across the top of the page for the kind of real estate investment contemplated.

Use of the Matrix—Subjective Analysis

STEP 4. Assign scores for each alternative on each criterion, using the relative weight assigned in step 2 as the maximum for that criterion.
STEP 5. Total the points and select the best ownership alternative.

EXHIBIT 5-2. Choice of Entity for Real Estate Ownership

The form of ownership of real estate assets is driven by a combination of many factors, including

- Tax implications
- Personal and business liability exposures
- Liquidity of ownership interests
- Managerial control
- Compensation and benefits
- Estate planning
- Capital requirements

Tax rate changes, the passive-loss limitations, the at-risk rules, and other provisions of the Tax Reform Act of 1986 change the tax focus regarding the most appropriate entity for acquisition, operation, and disposition of real estate assets. The following table summarizes key tax factors in comparing business forms.

	Partnership	S Corporation	Regular Corporation	MLP	REIT
Liability	Unlimited for general partners	Limited to amounts invested and loaned	Limited to amounts invested and loaned	Same as partnerships	Limited to amounts invested
Double taxation	No	No	Yes	No	No
Pass through profits and losses	Yes	Yes	No	Yes	Profits only
Losses deductible by owners	Limited to amount at risk (generally, investment plus prorated share partnership liabilities) or basis	Limited to amount at risk (generally, only amount invested and loaned to corporation) or basis	No	Same as partnership	No
Tax rates	Business income taxed to owners at their *marginal* tax rates	Business income taxed to owners at their *marginal* tax rates	Corporate tax rates apply	Same as partnership	Taxed as corporation if 95% of taxable income is not distributed
Special allocations	Yes, if substantial economic effect	No	No	Same as partnership	No

Fiscal year	Generally, calendar year required	Generally, calendar year required	Generally, any year-end is permitted	Same as partnership	Generally, calendar year required
Payments to owners	May be deducted in current year if paid within first 2½ months of year-end	Generally may not be deducted until the year paid	May be deducted in current year if paid within first 2½ months of year-end	Same as partnership	Not available
Tax-free fringe benefits	Limited	Most permitted	All permitted by law	Limited and unlikely	Not available
Public offering	Yes	No	Yes	Yes	Yes
Liquidity of interests	No	No	Maybe	Yes	Yes
Accumulated-earnings tax	No	No	Yes	No	No
Personal holding-company tax	No	No	Yes	No	No
Limits on tax-free cash distribution	Tax free to the extent of amount at risk	Tax free to the extent of amount at risk	Return of cash basis if dividends exceed E&P	Same as partnership	Tax free (to the extent of basis) if distribution exceed taxable income
2% limitation on investment expenses applies	Yes	Yes	No	Yes	No

Source: Coopers and Lybrand National Real Estate Group, "Special Analysis: Tax Reform Act of 1986," *Real Estate Newsletter*, October 1986, p. 36.

This approach provides an organized framework for matrix analysis, and it allows the investor to consider systematically all relevant financial and nonfinancial objectives and criteria in the ownership decision process. An example of a matrix approach is illustrated as part of the Aspen Wood case study, which follows.

SUMMARY

This chapter detail the various ownership alternatives available to investors and offers a general framework for evaluating these alternatives in relation to the investor's selection criteria and return–risk objectives. No single type of entity is necessarily best for a wide range of investment activities, and it is possible for investors to have a variety of ownership entities within one portfolio.

The numerous criteria for selecting ownership were examined. Although favorable tax treatment has traditionally been of paramount importance to most investors, many nontax considerations should also be taken into account in the ownership decision, including the cost of formation, the number of investors, the type of management needed, the degree of flexibility required, the extent and probability of exposure to liability, and the ease and transferability of interests.

Various types of ownership entities, their important characteristics, their advantages and disadvantages, and their possible use in achieving the investor's return–risk objectives were considered. Ownership vehicles were analyzed in three broad categories: (1) noncorporate forms of ownership, (2) corporations and trusts, and (3) syndication. Although syndication is not technically a legal form of ownership entity, it is commonly classified as such by investors. Exhibit 5-2 summarizes many of the factors used to compare ownership entities.

A matrix ownership decision model is developed as part of the Aspen Wood case study. This model compares and ranks the ownership alternatives being considered.

ASPEN WOOD APARTMENTS

APPLICATION OF THE OWNERSHIP DECISION MODEL

The preceding pages provided a discussion of a wide variety of selection criteria and ownership alternatives. From the list of possible selection criteria, an investor must define those that are most important given overall return and risk objectives, and then weight the relative importance of each. The investor must also be able to evaluate quickly the basic characteristics of each form of ownership and narrow the choices down to a manageable number. Normally this process is performed intuitively by experienced investors. However, a formal process using a decision model makes explicit all the variables being considered and enhances the rationality of the process. The results are more consistent and profitable decisions.

THE DECISION MATRIX

The decision matrix developed for Aspen Wood Apartments is shown in Exhibit 5-A. The managing equity investor–syndicator, D&B Associates, relies on twelve of the criteria listed in Exhibit 5-1, plus a thirteenth: ability to control the property, earn commissions, and retain the property management. After the desired holding period, D&B would, in many cases, form a new joint venture to buy the property from the existing joint venture and begin a new ownership and tax cycle. Some of the old joint-venture investors might also become partners in the new joint venture.[a] In this manner the property management company and the syndicator could assure themselves of repeat business and clients as long as the properties performed up to the expectations of the investors.

Each selection criterion is weighted according to its relative importance as perceived by the managing equity investor. The managing partners of the firm, Charlie Davidson and Clyde Boomer, had placed the greatest weight on five criteria that are extensions of the investor objectives developed in Chapter 4: (1) ability to pass through tax losses, (2) ability of the syndicator to control the property, (3) avoidance of double taxation, (4) limited liability, and (5) favorable image of the entity form among the target investor group. Of least importance to the investor were continuity and marketability of interest, assigned

[a]Under current (1986) tax law up to 80 percent of the owners of the selling entity can be partners in the buying entity without the IRS challenging the validity of the sale transaction. The advantages of selling a property and reinvesting in the same property are substantially less under the 1986 tax law, however, because (1) favorable capital gains tax treatment is eliminated; (2) deferral of gains through the use of the installment sales tax provision is limited; (3) depreciable lives for real assets have increased; and (4) the use of additional tax losses, resulting from the step-up in basis achieved by the resale of property at a higher price, is limited.

EXHIBIT 5-A.   The Ownership Decision Matrix

SELECTION CRITERIA	POINTS AVAILABLE	OWNERSHIP ALTERNATIVES					
		Tenancy in common	General partnership	Limited partnership	Joint venture	REIT	Regular corporation
1. Avoidance of double taxation	10	10	10	9	10	8	0
2. Ability to pass through tax losses	15	15	15	14	15	0	0
3. Maximum income tax deductions	8	8	7	6	8	4	4
4. Capital gains treatment	5	5	5	5	5	3	2
5. Limited liability	10	8	8	10	8	10	10
6. Marketability of interest	3	0	1	2	1	3	3
7. Flexibility and allowed activities	7	7	7	4	7	0	4
8. Ability to participate in management	6	6	6	2	6	1	1
9. Continuity of life	2	0	0	1	0	2	2
10. Favorable image—good track record	10	3	8	4	10	4	6
11. Minimum govt. controls and reporting	5	5	3	1	5	0	1
12. Minimum capital outlay	5	5	5	5	5	3	3
13. Ability of syndicator to control property	14	8	9	14	10	14	13
TOTALS	100	80	84	77	90	52	49

three and two points, respectively. The investors investing with Davidson and Boomer were expected to commit their capital for the entire ownership period, at the end of which, and as determined by a majority of the investors (who participate in major management decisions), the ownership entity would cease to exist. Investors usually achieve a high degree of limited liability, regardless of the ownership entity chosen, through the use of a nonrecourse mortgage and substantial liability insurance coverage. Consequently, all the entity forms shown have a high degree of limited liability.

When analyzing each ownership form, Davidson and Boomer were assigning to each some of the total points allocated for each selection criterion (ten for avoidance of double taxation, fifteen for ability to pass through tax losses, etc.). If an ownership form met the criteria perfectly, in their opinion, it was assigned the full number of points. If it did not meet the criteria to any significant degree, no points were designated. If an ownership form partially met the criteria, points were allocated accordingly. For example, the partners considered that three forms of ownership—tenancy in common, general partnership, and joint venture—completely meet the criterion of avoiding double taxation and thus were allocated the full ten points. In contrast, a corporation would be double-taxed and assigned zero points. A limited partnership (nine points) and a REIT (eight points) are subject to reclassification as corporations and, hence, to double taxation. Although this is not highly probable, these forms do not meet the criteria as well as the other forms do.

THE CHOICE OF A JOINT-VENTURE VEHICLE

After evaluating each of the ownership alternatives in terms of their selection criteria, Davidson and Boomer found that the joint-venture entity accumulated the most points, given their return–risk criteria and their subjective evaluation of each ownership entity. Because the joint venture is a type of general partnership formed for the purpose of owning a single property—Aspen Wood Apartments—the general partnership form of ownership is ranked second in the model, although it received an identical number of points in most categories.

Davidson and Boomer know their targeted investor market well and consulted with their tax attorney to evaluate the alternatives and assign weights. As with most models, the results are only as good as the input assumptions (garbage in, garbage out!). D&B has had excellent experiences with the joint-venture form of ownership as a syndication vehicle in the past. The firm has experienced relatively few problems with this entity form, and by insisting on nonrecourse mortgages and full-coverage liability insurance it achieved a high degree of limited liability for the investors. Thus, the joint venture already held a very favorable image among their investors and was readily accepted; in contrast, some of the investors had experienced poor results with limited-partnership investments formed by other syndicators in past years, and some of them preferred not to invest in such a vehicle again. When economic adversity struck in the mid-1970s, many limited partnerships quickly depleted their cash reserves and were unable to raise additional capital through the partners, who were not required to contribute moneys beyond their original capital contribution. Consequently, many good properties suffering from short-run difficulties were foreclosed or deeded back to lenders in lieu of foreclosure.

In contrast, joint venturers under D&B's direction have usually been able to decide jointly on the merits of the property. If the joint venturers decided to save the property from foreclosure, they approved the necessary "cash calls" to support operations until the real estate market improved.[b] In these instances, the joint-venture form proved to be more flexible than a limited partnership and allowed the investors to play a significant role in the investment decision process. These advantages have served as good marketing tools in the selling of the joint-venture shares. Most of D&B's investors are local and have enjoyed the opportunity of periodically evaluating their property's performance and making suggestions to the management.

[b]The same procedure can be achieved by a limited partnership in which the general and limited partners agree to such cash calls. Thus, the partnership agreement can be amended in a distress situation in order to solve such a financial problem.

6

PRELIMINARY FINANCIAL FEASIBILITY ANALYSIS

In Chapter 5 a methodology was developed for determining the form of ownership that would best fit the return and risk objectives of the investor. Steps 2 and 3 of that process consist of the following activities.

STEP 2. *Generate alternatives.* Locate properties that meet the basic screening criteria, and collect preliminary data for analysis.

STEP 3. *Analyze the property using the basic financial feasibility models.* These models are used to test the basic economics of the project, structure the financing alternatives available, and estimate the investment value range for the property.

This chapter develops a technique for analyzing the basic economics of an investment. Called the basic financial feasibility model (BFFM), it has several distinct advantages over more complex and technically correct models. First, it permits a quick analysis of an alternative to determine its worthiness of further investigation; second, the model allows a rapid evaluation of alternative financial structures that would require greater scrutiny using more sophisticated models.

However, the BFFM also has several disadvantages. It analyzes project cash flows for only one year, ignores future revenues and expenses, and does not incorporate present-value analysis. The model does not explicitly consider equity buildup through loan amortization, price inflation, and start-up or transactions costs, nor can it deal effectively with the erratic nature of net operating income (NOI)—and, hence, the "riskiness" of the project. Finally, the BFFM does not incorporate the effect of taxes and cannot accommodate modern "hybrid" mortgage instruments.

Discounted-cash-flow (DCF) models, which are more fully discussed in the next chapter, can provide the same and more information than the basic feasibility model; however, DCF models are problematic in that they require more detailed data input and more time to generate useful information. Thus, the BFFM, despite its obvious shortcomings, provides the investor with a "quick and dirty" method of analyzing many projects. It leads the investor to a better understanding of the return and risk parameters of a project and gives him or her a "feel" for its "worthiness" before entering into preliminary negotiations with a seller or mortgage lender. After preliminary negotiations have been completed, the investor will proceed to more sophisticated forms of analysis.

Working through the investment analysis process requires a proficiency in the basic mathematics involved in that process. It is important to know (1) how to prepare an accurate cash flow statement, the basis of all investment; (2) how to work with a mortgage constant (K) table and debt coverage ratios; and (3) how to compute rates of return on investment. Finally, (4) the concepts of leverage and risk should be mastered.

The rest of this chapter is divided into two major parts. In the first part the basic concepts are presented using an example property. In the second part the basic financial feasibility model is fully presented using the data and concepts developed in the first part.

IMPORTANT CONCEPTS, PRINCIPLES, AND TECHNIQUES[1]

The Cash Flow Statement

For an example, the cash flow statement of an existing sixteen-unit apartment complex that is for sale is presented here. Each unit is a 400-square-foot efficiency with central heating and air conditioning; utilities are paid by the tenant. The complex is twelve years old and the asking price is $180,000. The investors are seeking to refinance the property with a $144,000 loan (80 percent of the purchase price) from a local savings and loan association at 9.25 percent interest for twenty-eight years, resulting in a mortgage constant (K) of 10 percent. The required amount of equity is $36,000 ($180,000 − $144,000). On the basis of the past performance of the project, the cash flow is estimated as shown in Exhibit 6-1.

Note that the cash flow statement does not consider tax shelter factors, equity buildup through loan amortization, or property appreciation. These items would be added in a more sophisticated analysis, as discussed later. Note also that the cash flow statement is a one-year statement in which the *most likely* outcome is estimated. A more sophisticated analysis would attempt to measure cash flows for *each year* over the expected holding period of the investment. In addition, the investor may want to vary

[1]This discussion was largely developed in an earlier application by Stephen A. Pyhrr entitled "Mathematics of Real Estate Finance," in James A. Britton, Jr. and Lewis O. Kerwood, eds., *Financing Income-Producing Real Estate—A Theory and Casebook* (New York: McGraw–Hill, 1977), pp. 312–324.

EXHIBIT 6-1.   Cash Flow Pro Forma for a Sixteen-Unit Apartment Building

Gross rental income (16 units × $175/mo. × 12 mo.)	$33,600
Plus: vending income (16 units × $1.50/mo. × 12 mo.)	288
Gross possible income (GPI)	33,888
Less: vacancy and credit loss (7% of GPI)	(2,372)
Gross effective income (GEI)	31,516
Less: operating expenses (45% of GPI)	(15,250)
Net operating income (NOI)	16,266
Less: debt service (10% × $144,000)	14,400
Cash flow	$ 1,866

the assumptions to simulate a *pessimistic* and an *optimistic* set of outcomes, a technique used in risk analysis, which is discussed in a later chapter.

Despite its shortcomings, the one-year cash flow pro forma is widely used for investment analysis by equity investors, lenders, brokers, and developers throughout the nation.

Mortgage Constant, Debt Coverage Ratio, and Debt Structure

To understand fully the role of mortgage debt in the financial analysis of a real estate investment, the investor must first understand two basic terms: the mortgage constant and the debt coverage ratio. These terms are important both for the investor and the lender.

The *mortgage constant* (K) is defined as the amount of annual debt service necessary to pay interest at some stated rate and the entire principal over the amortization period. It is usually stated as a percentage. The mortgage constant is used to compute the annual debt service (principal plus interest) on a loan, as shown by the following formula:

$$\text{Annual debt service} = \text{loan amount} \times \text{mortgage constant}$$

The *debt coverage ratio* (DCR) is used by most large institutional lenders as a primary financial underwriting criterion for evaluating loans:

$$\text{Debt coverage ratio} = \frac{\text{net operating income}}{\text{debt service}}$$

Many institutional lenders have designated minimum coverage ratios for different types of property. For example, a lender may require a minimum coverage ratio of 1.3 for an apartment project and a coverage ratio of 1.5 for a motel (which is usually considered more risky). As the perceived risks associated with the property increase, the lender demands compensation in the form of a higher coverage ratio, and perhaps a higher interest rate and mortgage constant. Thus, the lender wants a cushion or buffer in case net operating income in any year drops due to a rise in vacancies, expenses, and so forth. The cushion (reflected in the DCR) should increase as the risk increases.

It will be helpful to expand on the example property described earlier in order to see the role of these two concepts. In that example the loan amount was $144,000 and the mortgage constant was 10 percent, resulting in debt service of $14,400. We found K by referring to the mortgage constant chart (Exhibit 6-2). Going down the left side of the chart to 9.25 percent, and across to twenty-eight years, resulted in a K of 10.01 percent, or roughly 10 percent.

Now suppose the interest rate rises to 11 percent and the lender will allow only a twenty-five-year term. What happens? The mortgage constant increases to 11.77 percent. Debt service increases from $14,400 to $16,949:

$$\text{Annual debt service} = \text{loan amount} \times \text{mortgage constant}$$

$$\$16,949 = \$144,000 \times .1177$$

EXHIBIT 6-2. Mortgage Constant (Constant Annual Percentage), Monthly Payments

Interest Rate	21 yr	22 yr	23 yr	24 yr	25 yr	26 yr	27 yr	28 yr	29 yr	30 yr		35 yr
9.00	10.62	10.46	10.32	10.19	10.08	9.97	9.88	9.80	9.73	9.66	...	9.41
9.25	10.82	10.66	10.52	10.39	10.28	10.18	10.09	10.01	9.94	9.88	...	9.64
9.50	11.01	10.86	10.72	10.60	10.49	10.39	10.31	10.23	10.16	10.10	...	9.86
9.75	11.21	11.06	10.93	10.81	10.70	10.60	10.52	10.44	10.38	10.31	...	10.09
10.00	11.41	11.26	11.13	11.01	10.91	10.82	10.78	10.66	10.59	10.54	...	10.32
10.25	11.62	11.47	11.34	11.22	11.12	11.03	10.95	10.88	10.82	10.76	...	10.55
10.50	11.82	11.68	11.55	11.43	11.34	11.25	11.17	11.10	11.04	10.98	...	10.78
10.75	12.03	11.88	11.76	11.65	11.55	11.46	11.39	11.32	11.26	11.21	...	11.02
11.00	12.23	12.09	11.97	11.86	11.77	11.68	11.61	11.54	11.48	11.43	...	11.25
11.25	12.44	12.30	12.18	12.08	11.98	11.90	11.83	11.77	11.71	11.66	...	11.48
11.50	12.65	12.51	12.40	12.29	12.20	12.12	12.05	11.99	11.94	11.89	...	11.72
11.75	12.86	12.73	12.61	12.51	12.42	12.35	12.28	12.22	12.16	12.12	...	11.95
12.00	13.07	12.94	12.83	12.73	12.64	12.57	12.50	12.44	12.39	12.35	...	12.19
12.25	13.28	13.16	13.05	12.95	12.87	12.79	12.73	12.67	12.62	12.58	...	12.43
12.50	13.50	13.37	13.26	13.17	13.09	13.02	12.96	12.90	12.85	12.81	...	12.67
12.75	13.71	13.59	13.48	13.39	13.31	13.24	13.18	13.13	13.09	13.05	...	12.91
13.00	13.93	13.81	13.71	13.62	13.54	13.47	13.41	13.36	13.32	13.28	...	13.15
13.25	14.14	14.03	13.93	13.84	13.77	13.70	13.64	13.59	13.55	13.51	...	13.39
13.50	14.36	14.25	14.15	14.07	13.99	13.93	13.87	13.83	13.79	13.75	...	13.63
13.75	14.58	14.47	14.37	14.29	14.22	14.16	14.11	14.06	14.02	13.99	...	13.87

Source: David Thorndike, *Thorndike Encyclopedia of Banking and Financial Tables*, rev. ed. (Boston: Warren, Gorham & Lamont, 1980), pp. 1–3.

As a result, the cash flow decreases by $2,549 and the value of the property will decrease by a multiple factor, as shown later. The reader should see that the mortgage constant (K) is actually a function of both the mortgage interest rate and the mortgage term. The constant is directly related to the interest rate and inversely related to the mortgage term. That is, an increase in the interest rate will cause the constant (K) to *increase*, and an increase in the mortgage term will cause the constant (K) to *decrease*.

In summary, the mortgage constant, which is determined by the mortgage term and interest rate granted by a lender, is used to compute the debt service on a loan; thus it affects the cash flow generated by the project. For each dollar increase in debt service, cash flow decreases by one dollar and the value of the project declines. An equity investor attempting to maximize cash flow—and, hence, the investment value of the property—would logically bargain with a lender for the longest term and lowest interest rate possible, thus keeping K to a minimum.

Two other useful formulas are the following (both derived from the debt service formula).

$$\text{Loan amount} = \frac{\text{annual debt service}}{\text{mortgage constant}}$$

$$\text{Mortgage constant} = \frac{\text{annual debt service}}{\text{loan amount}}$$

The first formula is used to calculate the maximum amount of loan a lender can grant, if the amount of debt service that the project can support is known. The second is used to compute the mortgage constant on an outstanding loan when the debt service and the loan amount are known.

Note that the mortgage constant will increase each year as a loan is amortized, because the denominator of the mortgage constant formula (loan amount) is decreasing as loan amortization occurs. In other words, although the interest rate and the amount of the debt service remain constant, the amount of the loan decreases because a portion of each debt service payment represents principal paid on the loan. From the equity investor's view, a rising K means an increase in the effective cost of borrowed money each year; it explains why investors periodically seek to refinance their properties, thereby raising the loan amount and term to more desirable levels. Real estate investors must consider periodic refinancing of their properties in order to maintain relatively constant debt–equity ratios. Corporations often avoid this problem because most of their debt is interest only (nonamortizing), thus providing a fixed debt–equity ratio over time (assuming no change in the firm's financial structure).

An Example. The sixteen-unit apartment complex illustrates the relation between mortgage constants and debt coverage ratios. The expected net operating income (NOI) was $16,266 and the equity investor was seeking a loan of $144,000 at 9.25 percent for twenty-eight years. The lender does not make loans that result in a coverage ratio of less than 1.3. Can the loan be granted? Obviously not, because the resulting debt coverage ratio is less than 1.3 and such a loan would be too risky for the lender to accept:

$$\text{Debt coverage ratio} = \frac{\text{net operating income}}{\text{debt service}} = \frac{\$16,266}{\$14,400} = 1.13$$

A combination of three approaches can be used to raise the coverage ratio and thus make the loan acceptable.

1. The mortgage constant and debt service can be reduced by increasing the amortization term of the loan.
2. The mortgage constant and debt service can be reduced by lowering the interest rate (which is generally the least desirable alternative to the lender).
3. The amount of the loan can be reduced, thereby decreasing the debt service.

A fourth possibility for raising the coverage ratio would be to raise the estimated net operating income by finding some realistic method for raising rental income, or reducing vacancies or expenses. For example, utilization of a professional property management company with a proven track record might convince a lender that *better-than-market* operating results are consistently possible and should be reflected in a higher net operating income estimate.

Maximum Loan Formula

Once the loan terms have been established, the debt coverage ratio may be used together with the loan amount equation defined earlier to determine the actual financial structure.

STEP 1. Use NOI and desired DCR to find maximum debt service:

$$\text{Maximum debt service} = \frac{\text{net operating income}}{\text{desired coverage ratio}}$$

$$\$12,512.31 = \frac{\$16,266}{1.3}$$

STEP 2. Use the loan amount equation to compute maximum loan:

$$\text{Maximum loan} = \frac{\text{maximum debt service}}{\text{mortgage constant}}$$

$$\$125,123 = \frac{\$12,512.31}{.10}$$

In the ongoing example, the project can support a loan no greater than $125,123, if the desired coverage ratio is 1.3. The loan request was for $144,000.

In step 1, maximum debt service is computed based on the desired debt coverage ratio of 1.3. The maximum amount of debt service is simply the net operating income divided by the desired coverage ratio, and is derived from this formula:

$$\text{Debt coverage ratio} = \frac{\text{net operating income}}{\text{debt service}}$$

In step 2, the loan amount is then computed by our earlier formula:

$$\text{Loan amount} = \frac{\text{annual debt service}}{\text{mortgage constant}}$$

In summary, the maximum loan formula is derived by combining and manipulating the debt coverage ratio and loan amount formulas.

A reduced mortgage constant can have a substantial effect on the maximum loan. For example, assume that K falls from 10 to 9.3 percent. (What loan terms would produce this result?) The lender can now make a loan of approximately $134,541.

STEP 1.

$$\text{Maximum debt service} = \frac{\$16,266}{1.3} = \$12,512.31$$

STEP 2.

$$\text{Maximum loan amount} = \frac{\$12,512.31}{.093} = \$134,541$$

Further, if the lender reduces the desired debt coverage ratio to 1.25, the loan can be increased to approximately $139,923, which is near the amount requested:

$$\text{Maximum debt service} = \frac{\$16,266}{1.25} = \$13,012.80$$

$$\text{Maximum loan amount} = \frac{\$13,012.80}{.093} = \$139,923$$

On the other hand, if interest rates increase to the levels seen during the late 1970s and early 1980s, and the mortgage term stays the same, the loan amount decreases significantly and equity investors are forced to invest more cash to purchase the property. For example, if the interest rate rises to 12 percent and the term of the loan is twenty-five years, the mortgage constant (K) rises to 12.57 percent and the maximum loan falls to $103,523. The equity required to purchase the property rises from $36,000

(80 percent loan) to $76,477, an increase of 112 percent from the original equity amount.

$$\text{Equity investment required} = \text{purchase price} - \text{loan amount}$$
$$= \$180,000 - \$103,523$$
$$= \$\ 76,477$$

Rising interest rates thus result in more conservative leverage ratios unless (1) a longer amortization term is negotiated, (2) a lower debt coverage ratio is accepted, (3) some form of secondary or "creative" mortgage financing is used, or (4) sellers are willing to reduce the price of their property. In most market situations a combination of all four tends to occur as interest rates rise. For example, in 1980 and 1981 numerous lenders increased their loan amortization terms from twenty-five or thirty years to thirty-five or forty years to offset partially the effects of rising interest rates. In some foreign countries amortization terms of fifty to seventy-five years are acceptable. An increase in the mortgage term from twenty-five to thirty-five years in the case described earlier will decrease the K from 12.57 to 12.19 percent; the maximum mortgage loan that can be justified increases from $103,523 to $106,750. Although the loan amount increases, the reader should observe that the increase is small, because extending a loan term from twenty-five years to a longer term has a small impact on both the mortgage constant and resulting mortgage amount.

In summary, the maximum loan formula may be used to compute how much of a loan a lender should be willing to grant if the investor knows the desired debt coverage ratio, the mortgage constant the lender will accept (this is to some degree negotiable), and the net operating income figure the lender will accept.

Risk and the Debt Coverage Ratio

Although other financial ratios may also be used (e.g., break-even ratios, loan per square foot), the debt coverage ratio tends to be the primary financial criterion used by most institutional lenders and is therefore the key to creating acceptable financial packages.

Risk is explicitly considered by the lender in establishing the minimum acceptable coverage ratio and mortgage constant. If a lender feels that a project is relatively risky but still wishes to make the loan, the lender can compensate by raising the desired coverage ratio and mortgage constant. The amount of the loan offered will then decrease. Conversely, anything the equity investor can do to convince the lender that the risks have been decreased should result in more favorable loan terms. For example, lease insurance or longer-term leases, evidence of a successful track record, strong anchor tenants with substantial preleasing, and a good feasibility study and mortgage submission package are factors that will decrease the perceived risks to the lender and increase the maximum loan amount for the equity investor.

The Break-even Ratio (Default Point)

Another ratio that lenders may look at when evaluating a loan proposal is the break-even ratio:

$$\text{Break-even ratio} = \frac{\text{operating expenses} + \text{debt service}}{\text{gross possible income}}$$

In our original example, in which a loan of $144,000 was requested, the break-even ratio is

$$\frac{\$15,250 + \$14,400}{\$33,888} = 87.5\%$$

In the restructured case, for which the mortgage loan is $125,123, the break-even ratio falls when debt service is reduced:

$$\frac{\$15,250 + \$12,512}{\$33,888} = 81.9\%$$

A break-even ratio of 82 percent means that a project can have a vacancy ratio of 18 percent before net operating income would not cover debt service payments. Thus, there is an 18 percent cushion for the lender before the possibility of default arises. Alternatively, the project must be 82 percent occupied in order to *break even*. After the break-even point has been reached, the cash flow will be positive.

As with the coverage ratio, the break-even point can be used as an underwriting criterion by the lender. For example, many lenders will not make a loan on a general-use income property for which the resulting break-even ratio is greater than 82 to 84 percent. The higher the break-even ratio, the higher the risk, and vice versa. Risk can be reduced by structuring a loan that reduces the break-even point.

The Equity Investor's Strategy

An equity investor must be aware of the "golden rule" (those who have the gold make the rules) and seek to understand the lender's point of view when developing a mortgage finance structure. Although the equity investor usually negotiates for the highest loan amount, the lowest interest rate, and the longest amortization term possible, the minimum objectives of the lender must simultaneously be achieved or exceeded. A mortgage loan proposal that does not explicitly meet the lender's interest rate, amortization term, coverage ratio, and break-even criteria has little probability of succeeding.

The equity investor, like the lender, can use the coverage ratio and break-even point as measures of risk. High coverage ratios and low break-even ratios indicate a low degree of risk (i.e., a lower probability of default on debt service obligations), whereas low coverage ratios and high break-even ratios indicate greater risk. If the equity investor wishes to control the degree of risk as evidenced by these ratios, he or she can structure the project price and loan terms to achieve the desired coverage and break-even ratios. This also can be achieved using the basic financial feasibility model, as discussed later in this chapter.

Computing Rates of Return on an Investment

Two important rate-of-return measures are critical for evaluating the debt–equity structure of a project. The first is the rate of return on total capital (ROI), sometimes referred to as the *free and clear return* or the *overall rate.*

$$\text{Rate of return on total capital (ROI)} = \frac{\text{net operating income}}{\text{total capital investment}}$$

This rate-of-return measure focuses on the productivity of the total capital invested, including both debt and equity capital. As presented here, it is used in conjunction with a one-year cash flow pro forma and should not be confused with the internal rate of return (IRR), which considers the cash flow for the entire ownership period.

The second important rate-of-return measure is the rate of return on the investor's initial equity investment (ROE), sometimes referred to as the *cash-on-cash return* or the *equity dividend rate.*

$$\text{Rate of return on equity (ROE)} = \frac{\text{cash flow}}{\text{equity investment}}$$

The ROE is the measure that investors use most frequently to evaluate proposed income property investments during the early stages of the investment process.

In the original example net operating income is $16,266, cash flow is $1,866, the total capital investment (asking price) is $180,000, and the equity investment is $36,000. ROI and ROE can be computed as follows:

$$\text{ROI} = \frac{\$16,266}{\$180,000} = 9.04\%$$

$$\text{ROE} = \frac{\$1,866}{\$36,000} = 5.18\%$$

This situation is generally undesirable for the equity investor unless net operating income can be raised over time (by increasing rents or decreasing expenses) and the ROE can be supplemented through property value appreciation and tax shelter. We noted previously that this situation is also unfavorable for the lender because the resulting coverage ratio is only 1.13. The basic problem here is *unfavorable* leverage (also called *negative* leverage).

Favorable and Unfavorable Leverage

Leverage exists whenever debt is present in the capital structure.[2] Simply stated, leverage means use of debt financing. The greater the use of debt financing relative to equity financing, the greater the leverage.

The situation described here is unfavorable because the ROE is only 5.18 percent whereas total assets are earning at a rate (ROI) of 9.04 percent. When leverage is favorable (*positive* leverage), increasing debt as a proportion of total capital will cause ROE to rise above ROI. The problem here is that the mortgage constant (K) is 10 percent. The equity investor can earn only 9.04 percent on each dollar of assets, but must pay 10 percent to the lender on each dollar of debt. Only 5.18 percent is left over for the equity investor on each dollar of equity invested. In this case leverage works against the investor; this condition is called unfavorable (*negative*) leverage.

Whether leverage is favorable or unfavorable can be readily determined by looking at the relation between the investment's ROI and the mortgage constant on debt. Whenever ROI is less than K (ROI $<$ K), leverage is unfavorable.[3] When the ROI is greater than K (ROI $>$ K), leverage is favorable. In other words, the rate of productivity for the total amount of money invested in a project (as measured by ROI) must be greater than the cost of debt (as measured by the mortgage constant) in order for leverage

---

[2]This definition refers to *financial leverage*, rather than *operating leverage*, as it is described in the business finance literature. See, for example, Eugene F. Brigham, *Fundamentals of Financial Management* (Hinsdale, Ill.: Dryden Press, 1978), pp. 373–383.

[3]A number of authors have criticized this definition and approach to favorable and unfavorable leverage. One author has argued that this approach must be rejected on both theoretical and practical grounds because it does not consider "the interrelationship among the interest rate, loan/value ratio, expected reversion value and the tax considerations involved, which determines the favorability of a given leverage situation. A complete discounted cash flow analysis is necessary to properly evaluate the effects of those relationships on return to equity" (Kenneth M. Lusht, "A Note on the Favorability of Leverage," *The Real Estate Appraiser*, May–June 1977, pp. 41–44. However, the basic fact remains that ROE may increase or decrease with increasing debt-equity ratios, depending on the ROI and the cost of debt. It goes without saying that a final determination of the positive or negative effects of high leverage rests with a complete discounted-cash-flow analyses. See also Robert H. Zerbst, Charlies E. Edwards, and Phillip L. Cooley, "Evaluation of Financial Leverage for Real Estate Investments," *The Real Estate Appraiser*, July–August 1977. See also Kenneth M. Lusht and Austin J. Jaffe, "Financing Decisions and Investment Analysis," in C. F. Sirmans, ed., *Research in Real Estate*, Vol. 3, *Issues in Real Estate Investment Analysis* (Greenwich, Conn.: JAI Press, 1983).

to be favorable (positive). When leverage is favorable, there is a positive relation between an increase in the debt–equity ratio and the change in the project's ROE. An equity investor should beware of any financing situation that creates unfavorable (*negative*) leverage for an extended period.

Chapter 7 reveals how leverage can be measured through an after-tax model using internal rate of return. Of course, the model presented in this chapter is a one-year, before-tax cash flow model that seeks to test the short-run economics of a property. The model's defects become apparent when trying to ascertain whether leverage is favorable or unfavorable, particularly when income taxes are concerned and NOI changes each year. In such cases, discounted-cash-flow models and annual-ratio analysis are required to evaluate the presence or absence of favorable leverage.

In summary, a comparison of K with ROI will indicate whether leverage is favorable or unfavorable. This is important because whatever net operating income is earned by the project goes to the lenders or to the equity investors. If too much is given to the lenders (ROI < K), there will be little left for the equity investors (ROE < K), and ROE will decline as the debt–equity ratio increases. As we saw in our example:

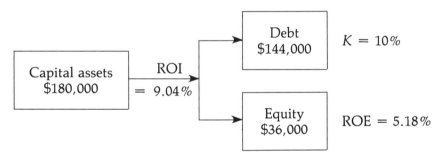

The relationship can also be expressed as follows.

1. *Conditions for favorable (positive) leverage:*
   Whenever   ROI > K
   then   ROE > K
   and   ROE > ROI
2. *Conditions for unfavorable (negative) leverage:*
   Whenever   ROI < K
   then   ROE < K
   and   ROE < ROI

Another possibility is that of *break-even* leverage, also called *neutral* leverage. Break-even leverage occurs when ROI is equal to K. When this condition occurs then ROE = K and ROE = ROI.

The illustrated situation (an ROE of 5.18% and a K of 10%) would not be acceptable to most knowledgeable investors except over a relatively short-run period when inflation or market conditions are expected to bail out the project over the long run by increasing rents and property values.[4] Basic economics are working against the investor and have resulted in a relatively high-risk (coverage ratio = 1.13) and low-return (ROE = 5.18%) investment. It therefore is necessary to raise ROI or lower K (or both) so as to achieve favorable leverage. The desired result can be achieved using the basic financial feasibility model.

THE BASIC FINANCIAL FEASIBILITY MODEL

The basic financial feasibility model incorporates all the concepts discussed up to this point and allows inclusion of an acceptable ROE level, a leverage advantage for the equity investor, and a coverage ratio that will satisfy both the lender and the equity investor. The investor's return–risk criteria are the inputs; the output is a financial structure that satisfies both the equity investor and the lender. The feasibility model presented in Exhibit 6-3 allows manipulation of the numbers in order to structure the economics of a project and simultaneously achieve the financial objectives of both the equity investor and the lender.

The final outputs of the model are estimates of (1) the maximum loan amount, (2) the maximum equity investment, and (3) the maximum project value or purchase price. The inputs are (1) estimates of rents, vacancies, and expenses, (2) the debt coverage ratio and mortgage constant desired by the lender, equity investor, or both, and (3) the desired rate of return on equity.

Use of the basic financial feasibility model can best be explained by referring again to the sixteen-unit apartment building, along with the following information.

1. The total leasable area in the buildings is approximately 6,400 square feet. The gross possible income per net leasable square foot is 44.13 cents per month, or approximately $5.30 annually (actually $5.295).

2. Vacancy and operating expenses are 52 percent of gross possible income (45 percent operating expense ratio and 7 percent vacancy ratio, as shown in Exhibit 6-1).

3. The required debt coverage ratio is 1.3 and the mortgage constant (K) is 10 percent (9.25 percent for approximately twenty-eight years). The investors are seeking a loan of $144,000.

---

[4]Such a climate existed in the late 1970s and early 1980s. Investors were accepting low or even negative ROEs on a current operating basis; they believed that continued inflation at high rates would result in higher rents and property values over the long run. In common parlance, they were "betting on the come." Today, lower rates of inflation coupled with less favorable tax laws should shift investor attention back to current operating results. High interest rates, however, could continue to make many real estate investments unattractive on a current-yield basis!

4. The equity investors require a 12 percent ROE. In the proposed sale of the property, a $26,000 equity price is asked.

The feasibility model (Exhibit 6-3) indicates that the project is worth approximately $156,400, not $180,000. If a debt coverage ratio of 1.3 is to be maintained, annual debt service cannot exceed $12,512, and a loan greater than $125,120 is not acceptable. With regard to the equity value, the investor cannot pay more than $31,283 if the goal is to achieve a 12 percent return and thus maintain a favorable leverage position. Using this model, the investor inputs the ROE required to make the investment and then capitalizes the cash flow to determine the equity value.

Illustration of the Model[5]

Box 1. *Gross income per leasable square foot.* This figure should be based on the history of comparable projects if the subject property is new. If the subject property is already in existence, its rental history will provide the number, *but rents on existing projects should be adjusted to reflect current market conditions.* Other income in addition to rents (e.g., vending income, income from laundry) should be included. In the example it is assumed that gross annual income per leasable square foot is $5.30.

Box 2. *Total leasable square feet.* This includes only the *leasable* square footage. It does not include, for example, the laundry room, foyers, lobbies, or the manager's office space. The example assumes 6,400 leasable square feet.

Boxes 3 and 4. *Gross possible income (GPI).* This is the product of box 1 times box 2: $5.30 × 6,400 = $33,888.

Box 5. *Ratio of vacancy and operating expense to gross income.* As with income, expenses as a percentage of gross income can, for new properties, be estimated on the basis of the history of comparable properties. For existing projects, expenses can be based on historical data *as long as the figures are adjusted for anticipated changes.* Note that both a vacancy and bad-debt allowance (usually 5 to 10 percent) *and* operating expenses (usually 35 to 55 percent) are included. Here the sum of vacancy and bad-debt allowances and operating expenses, as a percentage of GPI, is 52 percent.

Box 6. *Vacancy and operating expenses.* These expenses are the product of box 4 times box 5: $33,888 × .52 = $17,622.

Box 7. *Net operating income (NOI).* This is the remainder of box 3 less box 6: $33,888 − $17,622 = $16,266.

---

[5]Prepared with the assistance of Russell Welch, Murray State University, Murray, Kentucky.

EXHIBIT 6-3. The Basic Financial Feasibility Model

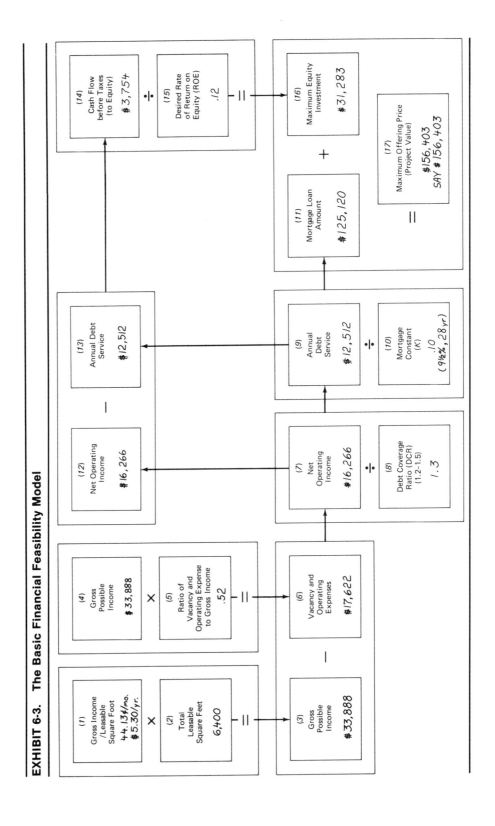

Box 8. *Debt coverage ratio (DCR).* In most situations the lender will indicate a minimum debt coverage ratio. In this example the DCR is assumed to be 1.3. As indicated earlier, the DCR may also be calculated as DCR = NOI/DS.

Box 9. *Annual debt service (DS).* This is the product of box 11 times box 10: $125,120 \times .10 = $12,512$. If the NOI (box 7) and DCR (box 8) are known, the maximum available debt service can be computed as

$$\text{Maximum DS} = \text{NOI}/\text{DCR}$$

In the example here, the NOI = $16,266 and the DCR = 1.3; therefore, DS = $16,266/1.3 = $12,512.

Box 10. *Mortgage constant (K).* Given the terms of the loan (assumed as 9.25 percent, twenty-eight years), K can be obtained from a table of mortgage constants. In our example $K = 10$ percent.

Box 11. *Mortgage loan amount.* The maximum may be predetermined by the lender (e.g., as a percentage of appraised value) or calculated if the maximum debt service and mortgage constant are known. The maximum loan amount for the example property is calculated as

$$\text{Loan amount} = \frac{\text{DS}}{K} = \frac{\$12,512}{.10} = \$125,120$$

Box 12. *Net operating income (NOI).* From box 7,

$$\text{NOI} = \text{GPI} - \text{vacancy and bad debt allowance} - \text{operating expenses}$$
$$= \$16,266$$

as before.

Box 13. *Annual debt service (DS).* From box 9, $12,512.

Box 14. *Cash flow before taxes (CF).* This is calculated as

$$\text{CF} = \text{NOI} - \text{DS}$$

or, if the maximum equity investment and desired ROE are known, as

$$\text{CF} = \text{equity} \times \text{ROE}$$

Here, CF = $16,266 − $12,512 = $3,754.

Box 15. *Desired rate of return on equity (ROE).* The desired ROE may be predetermined by the investor on the basis of the return available from alternative investments. The actual ROE is calculated as

$$\text{ROE} = \text{CF}/\text{equity investment}$$

Assume that an ROE of 12 percent is required.

Box 16. *Maximum equity investment.* The investor may be willing or able to invest only a given amount. If the price of the project is fixed and the maximum loan amount is known, the equity investment equals price less loan amount. Here, however, it is calculated as

$$\text{Maximum equity} = \text{CF/ROE} = \$3{,}754/.12 = \$31{,}283$$

Box 17. *Maximum offering price.* This is the sum of box 11 plus box 16: $125,120 + $31,283 = $156,403.

The significance of box 17 is that it illustrates that mutual equilibrium can be achieved. The lender has specified loan terms and a satisfactory debt coverage ratio and hence, presumably, is satisfied. The investor has determined that the desired rate of return on the equity investment (ROE) should be achievable, relative to an acceptable risk level (DCR of 1.3), and has calculated the maximum offering price for the property. Obviously, if the asking price is less than the maximum offering price, the property is more attractive. The equity investor should not offer *more* than the asking price.

The preceding example has assumed that the equity investor wishes to work forward through the model to determine the investment value of the project by capitalizing the cash flow. The model can actually be used in a combination of ways. For example, if the price is known, the investor can work backward to determine intermediate values, such as rents and expenses required to satisfy investor objectives. Thus, if the investor knows the basic formulas used in the model, the dependent variable can be changed and desired output data and values can be calculated. The various formulas used in the basic financial feasibility model are presented in Exhibit 6-4.

Restructuring the Financial Package

The financial model indicates that the apartment project is worth approximately $156,400, not the $180,000 asking price. If a coverage ratio of 1.3 is to be maintained, annual debt service cannot exceed $12,512 and a loan greater than $125,120 is not acceptable. Furthermore, as previously indicated, the equity investor cannot pay more than $31,283 for the equity if the goal is to achieve an ROE of 12 percent, maintain a favorable leverage position, and control risk with a DCR of 1.3.

The value of a project to both the equity investor and the lender is highly sensitive to the terms of the financial package, including the desired debt coverage ratio and the required K and ROE. The model allows for easy manipulation of the numbers and for restructuring the financial package in order to achieve a more desirable solution. In addition, sensitivity analysis can be performed quickly to test the impact of changes in input variables on the investment value or other desired investment parameters.

To demonstrate this, assume that the financial package and solution shown in Exhibit 6-3 are not acceptable to the seller. The seller demands a

---

EXHIBIT 6-4.   Formulas in the Basic Financial Feasibility Model

---

1. Gross possible income = gross income per net leasable square foot × total leasable square feet

2. Vacancy and operating expenses = gross possible income × ratio of vacancy and operating expenses to gross income

3. Net operating income = gross possible income − vacancy and operating expenses

4. Debt coverage ratio = $\dfrac{\text{net operating income}}{\text{annual debt service}}$

5. Annual debt service = 12 × (monthly interest + principal payment)

   $= \dfrac{\text{net operating income}}{\text{debt coverage ratio (DCR)}}$

   = mortgage loan amount × mortgage constant

6. Mortgage constant (K) = $\dfrac{\text{annual debt service}}{\text{mortgage loan amount}}$

7. Mortgage loan amount = $\dfrac{\text{annual debt service}}{\text{mortgage constant } (K)} = \dfrac{\left[\dfrac{\text{net operating income}}{\text{debt coverage ratio}}\right]}{\text{mortgage constant}}$

8. Cash flow before tax = net operating income − annual debt service

9. Rate of return on equity (ROE) = $\dfrac{\text{cash flow}}{\text{equity investment}}$

10. Maximum equity investment = $\dfrac{\text{cash flow}}{\text{desired rate of return on equity (ROE)}}$

11. Rate of return on total capital (ROI) = $\dfrac{\text{net operating income}}{\text{total capital investment}}$

---

minimum selling price of $175,000, and the current interest rate on new loans has risen to 14 percent. Is there a solution that is acceptable to the seller, the buyer, and the lender?

Clearly, with interest rates of 14 percent or more, conventional refinancing through an institutional lender is not feasible. However, in many situations sellers can provide financing in tandem with the assumption of existing notes. Assume that two mortgage notes exist on the sixteen efficiency units of the example. One of the notes is from an institutional lender and one is from a previous owner. The interest rates are 7.5 and 8.75 percent, respectively, but have relatively short maturities (twelve and eighteen years, respectively). The balances on the two notes total approximately $117,000.

If the investor can assume or "wrap around" the existing notes and take advantage of their low interest rates, he or she can arrive at an acceptable solution.[6] At the same time, the investor wishes to negotiate a relatively long mortgage term on the wraparound note in order to reduce the debt service payments and thus increase cash flow and the value of the project to the equity investors. In this example, there is no due-on-sale clause in either of the two underlying mortgage notes that would prevent this transaction and cause the underlying notes to be called (accelerated) when the property is sold.

Assume that the following solution was negotiated. The seller takes a 10 percent, thirty-year note for $145,000 on the property, and this note "wraps around" the two existing liens. A third-party trustee receives debt service payments on the $145,000 note, pays the debt service on the two underlying mortgage notes, and then pays the seller what is left over. In effect, the seller provides $28,000 of debt financing to the buyer ($145,000 − $117,000) and receives 10 percent on the entire $145,000 note whereas the underlying notes bear interest rates of 7.5 percent and 8.75 percent. The seller's effective yield on the $29,000 financing is significantly greater than 10 percent; in addition, the seller may qualify for installment sales treatment for tax purposes.[7]

Assume further that a preliminary market, marketability, and management analysis of the property reveals the following.

1. Apartment rents are low and have not kept pace with competitive properties in recent years. The investor believes that rents can be raised to an average of $.50 per square foot per month next year from a previous average of $.4413.

2. Past management practices have resulted in a vacancy ratio of 7 percent annually. The investor forecasts 5 percent in the future, thereby decreasing the vacancy and expense ratio from 52 to 50 percent.

---

[6]A wraparound mortgage, in this instance, is a form of third-lien financing in which the face amount of the third (wraparound) loan is equal to the balance of the first and second loans plus the amount of the new financing. Because the interest rate on the wraparound loan is normally greater than that on the first mortgage, upside (favorable) leverage is achieved on the new lender's return. In our case the new lender is the seller.

[7]For examples see Richard T. Garrigan, "Wrap-Around Mortgage Enhancing Lender and Investor Wealth," *Real Estate Issues*, Summer 1979, pp. 20–38; also, Donald J. Valachi, "Installment Sales of Mortgaged Real Estate and the Wraparound Mortgage," *The Appraisal Journal*, January 1980, pp. 9–14. Installment sales reporting has changed under the Tax Reform Act of 1986, and again in 1987. See *Tax Reform 1986: Analysis and Planning* (Arthur Anderson & Co., 1986), pp. 150–152, and the 1987 supplement. For an extended discussion of the impact on seller-financed transactions, read Barbara J. Childs and Caroline Strobel, "Seller Financed Real Estate Transactions after TRA 1986," paper presented at the annual meeting of the American Real Estate Society, 1987. The authors are from the University of South Carolina.

3. The overall risk of the property is perceived to be lower than originally estimated because of the excellent location and physical condition of the building. The investor is willing to lower the desired coverage ratio from 1.3 to 1.25 and the required return on equity from 12 to 11 percent to reflect this lower risk level.

Exhibit 6-5 shows the new solution, which produces a purchase price above the $175,000 minimum desired by the seller, satisfies the explicit financial objectives of the buyer–investor, and shifts the burden of some of the financing to the seller. The investor can compute the actual expected ROE by calculating the equity investment and dividing it into the expected cash flow. The equity investment is $30,000: the purchase price of $175,000 less the seller's wraparound loan of $145,000. The expected ROE is 12.8 percent:

$$\text{ROE} = \frac{\text{cash flow}}{\text{equity investment}} = \frac{\$3,840}{\$30,000} = 12.8\%$$

This example illustrates the pronounced effect of changes in the investor's perceptions of the market, in conjunction with changes in the financial package, on the investment value of a property. Further feasibility research will allow the investor to refine the inputs and evaluate their effects on project value. It is not uncommon to use the basic financial feasibility model over and over again to analyze and restructure the project in order to achieve a solution that is acceptable to all the parties involved in the transaction.

APPLICATION OF THE BASIC FINANCIAL FEASIBILITY MODEL

The financial feasibility model can be used to structure the basic economics of a property to achieve an acceptable return–risk ratio for the investor. In the last section the model was used to achieve three sets of short-run objectives.

1. *Equity investor objectives.* By achieving the investor's required ROE and DCR criteria and favorable leverage.
2. *Lender objectives.* By providing an acceptable mortgage loan amount, mortgage constant, interest rate, amortization term, and debt coverage ratio.
3. *Seller objectives.* By structuring an acceptable combination of sales price and terms that satisfy the seller's return–risk criteria.

Such a model, although it has numerous limitations, can be a tremendous aid to a managing equity investor by providing a framework for engaging in preliminary negotiations with the seller, discussing loan parameters with a potential lender, counseling passive equity investors or partners

190

EXHIBIT 6-5.   Basic Financial Feasibility Model, Revised

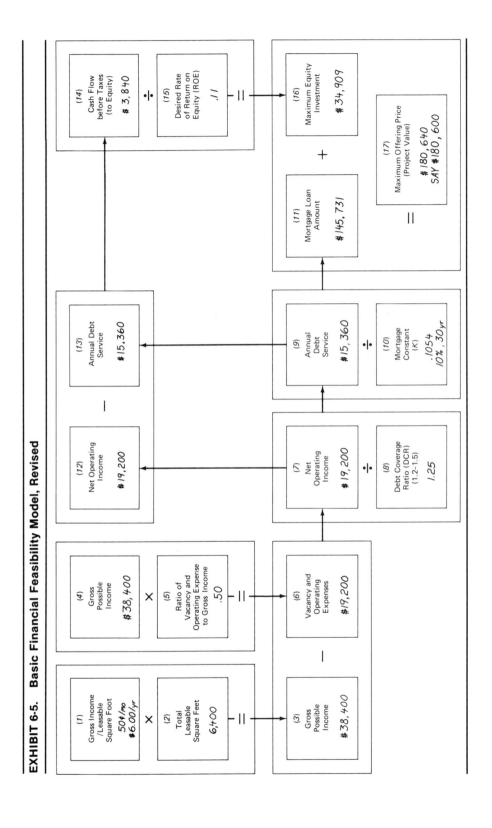

who do not understand more sophisticated financial techniques, and understanding the basic return–risk trade-offs of a potential property purchase. The return–risk trade-off is the relation between the return on equity (ROE) and the debt coverage ratio (DCR). Whenever the two are out of balance, it is beneficial for the investor to restructure and revalue the property using more desirable ROE/DCR combinations.

The following examples demonstrate some applications of the model to situations that frequently occur in the early stages of analysis. Again, valuable time can be saved if the "dogs and alligators" are identified and discarded early in the investment process.

Analyzing Rent and Expense Variability

There is a five-year-old retail center consisting of 14,000 square feet of leasable space located on a major thoroughfare. It is being offered for sale at $600,000. The facts are presented in Exhibit 6-6.

Using the data in the exhibit, and assuming a 5 percent vacancy and collection loss factor in the future, a minimum debt coverage ratio of 1.25, and an equity investor who is willing to purchase the center at an 8 percent ROE, the value of the center is approximately $641,000, as shown in Exhibit 6-7. The proposed $450,000 loan appears to be achievable and perhaps could even be increased to the $477,000 level calculated in the model.

The investor is willing to accept an 8 percent current ROE and unfavorable leverage (ROE < K) because of the potential for raising rents in the future and for increases in property value. A quick analysis of the effect of increasing rents and expenses, illustrated in Exhibit 6-8, demonstrates that a 25 percent rise in existing rents and expenses over the next five years

---

EXHIBIT 6-6.   Retail Strip Center: Facts

- *Facility.* 14,000-square-foot building, good location, high traffic count.
- *Asking Price.* $600,000. Owner says he has a commitment for a new mortgage at $450,000, 10.5 percent, thirty-year amortization term, no personal liability (K = 10.98 percent).
- *Tenants.* Regional chain furniture store, national chain drug store, beautician, and dentists. Lease rates average $.60 per sq. ft./month, or $7.20 per sq. ft./year.
- *Occupancy.* Present owner warrants that building is 100 percent leased on new five-year leases signed recently.
- *Operating Expenses.* Owner warrants that all tenants pay their own utilities and that escalation clauses allow for passing through all increases in operating expenses to tenants. Thus, property can be operated on about $2.16 per sq. ft./year, or about a 30 percent expense ratio.

EXHIBIT 6-7.   Retail Strip Center: Solution

- Gross possible income = 14,000 × 7.20 = $100,800
- Vacancy and operating expenses = .35 × 100,800 = $35,280
- Net operating income = 100,800 − 35,280 = $65,520
- Maximum debt service = 65,520/1.25 = $52,416
- Maximum loan possible = 52,416/.1098 = $477,377
- Cash flow = 65,520 − 52,416 = $13,104
- Equity value = 13,104/.08 = $163,800
- Maximum offering price = 163,800 + 477,377 = $641,177

---

would increase the equity value from $163,800 to $368,550 at the end of five years.

On the basis of this analysis and a thorough sensitivity analysis of the financial variables, the investor entered into a contract with the seller to purchase the property for $600,000, contingent on obtaining a loan of $450,000, bearing interest at 10.5 percent for thirty years, or better, and contingent on inspection of the seller's financial records and leases, and a physical inspection of the building. During the following two weeks of inspections, data collection and analysis, and other feasibility research, the investor discovered a number of important facts that substantially changed the data base used in the original analysis and cast doubt on the reliability of the seller's information and the value conclusions reached. This new information is shown in Exhibit 6-9.

On the basis of the new data the investor adjusted the inputs into the model and discovered that neither the proposed loan nor the purchase price was attainable. Vacancy was adjusted upward to 10 percent to account for the apparent certainty of losing the major tenant and the subsequent costs of releasing and remodeling the space. Estimated operating expenses were increased from $2.16 to $2.88 per square foot per year, or to 40 percent of gross possible income to account for rising utilities and other operating expenses that were not covered by the tenant escalation clauses. The coverage ratio was increased to 1.30, the interest rate on the loan was increased to 10.75 percent, and the term was lowered to twenty-five years

---

EXHIBIT 6-8.   Retail Strip Center: Value Five Years Hence

- Gross possible income (100,800 + 25%) = $126,000
- Vacancy and operating expenses = 35,280 + 25% = $44,100
- Net operating income = 126,000 − 44,100 = $81,900
- Cash flow = 81,900 − 52,416 = $29,482
- Equity value = 29,482/.08 = $368,550

EXHIBIT 6-9. Retail Strip Center: New Data

- *Utilities.* Actually paid for by the owner, not the tenants. The seller had apparently confused this property with another one.
- *Major Lease.* The major furniture store lease (65 percent of total space leased) was actually a two-year lease with one-year options. Discussions with the owners of the store and friends of the owners revealed that they were negotiating to build their own store and would most likely leave the center within two years. They were unhappy with the access to the property and the parking facilities.
- *Lease Escalation Clause.* A thorough reading of each lease revealed only partial escalation clauses.

($K = 11.55$ percent) to compensate for the increased risks of the venture; in addition, the equity investor increased the ROE requirement to 11 percent. As a result of all these changes, the property value dropped nearly $200,000, from approximately $641,000 to almost $441,000, as shown in Exhibit 6-10.

Even extensive sensitivity testing, restructuring, and subsequent negotiations failed to provide a possible solution that would be acceptable to both the seller and the investor. The investor was forced to drop the project and go on to the next-best alternative. Nevertheless, he had been able to identify an unacceptable project before spending substantial time gathering additional data and proceeding through a discounted-cash-flow analysis. There was simply no way of meeting the short-run economic criteria.

Multiple Loans and Joint Ventures

The basic financial feasibility model and concepts can also be applied to sophisticated multiloan packages and joint-venture situations. For example, a high-rise forty-story luxury apartment hotel is under construction in

---

EXHIBIT 6-10. Retail Strip Center: Revised Solution

- Gross possible income (unchanged) = $100,800
- Vacancy and operating expenses (.50 × 100,800) = $50,400
- Net operating income = 100,800 − 50,400 = $50,400
- Maximum debt service = 50,400/1.25 = $38,769
- Maximum loan possible = 38,769/.1155 = $335,662
- Cash flow = 50,400 − 38,769 = $11,631
- Equity value = 11,631/.11 = $105,736
- Maximum offering price 105,736 + 335,662 = $441,398

---

downtown Chicago, with eleven floors of office space preleased to AAA-rated corporate tenants. The apartment hotel is a relatively unique special-use concept catering to business people and travelers who wish to combine hotel services with the typically larger size and cooking facilities of a residential apartment. A customer might stay one week or three months; the cost would be significantly less per night than luxury hotel accommodations, yet would not require the relatively inflexible lease contract required for a normal luxury apartment rental in downtown Chicago.

The joint venturers and lenders agreed on the following pro forma and financial structure for the property, as shown in Exhibit 6-11.

The total cost of the project was $10 million and included a development fee and general contractor's profit to the developer–investor. Thus, the $49,626 cash flow left after all obligations were paid was a pure investment profit. The net operating income was conservatively projected to be $1,200,000; all parties to the transaction felt that actual operations would exceed this projection. A first-mortgage loan of $6,300,000 (conservative by most standards) was negotiated at a mortgage constant of 10.83 percent and required debt service of $682,290. After this loan had been deducted from the total project cost, $3,700,000 remained to be financed, and a cash flow of $517,710 remained after servicing the first loan. This resulted in a ROE of 13.99 percent ($517,710/$3,700,000). A second loan (K = 11 percent) was arranged with a REIT to cover furnishings, and the joint-venture partner, a national life insurance company, provided a third mortgage of

EXHIBIT 6-11. Financial Pro Forma for Luxury Apartment Hotel Property

Rate of Return	Income/ Cash Flow	Cost	Source of Financing
12.00% (ROI)	$1,200,000	$10,000,000	Total cost to be financed
10.83% (K)	682,290	6,300,000	First loan on building
13.99% (ROE)	517,710	3,700,000	Remaining equity
11.00% (K)	275,000	2,500,000	REIT second loan (for furnishings)
20.23% (ROE)	242,710	1,200,000	Remaining equity
16.00% (K)	160,000	1,000,000	Third loan by joint-venture partner
41.30% (ROE)	82,710	200,000	Remaining equity
			Joint-venture investment
16.54% (ROE)	33,084	200,000	(life insurance company)
∞ (ROE)	$ 49,626	$ 0	Remaining equity

ROI = 12%
Weighted-average DCR = 1.07
Weighted-average K = 11.40%
ROE to joint-venture partner = 16.54%
ROE to investor–developer = ∞

$1 million with a K of 16 percent. The joint-venture partner also invested the final cash equity of $200,000 and received 40 percent of the remaining cash flow, or $33,084 ($82,710 × 40 percent).

The project risk was high, as is evidenced by the low overall debt coverage ratio (1.07) and the nature of the proposed real estate activity, which remained untested in the Chicago marketplace. Nevertheless, there was favorable leverage at all stages of financing, and the remaining ROE was always greater than the K of the next loan. The weighted-average K was 11.40 percent (all loans), and the project ROI was 12 percent, again showing favorable leverage. The joint-venture partner received a 16 percent guaranteed return on the third-mortgage loan and an expected ROE of 16.54 percent on the $200,000 equity investment. The developer–investor had no cash equity; thus, the ROE was not meaningful as a decision criterion.[8]

The *value* of the equity can be computed should the developer–investor decide to sell his or her interest, if the ROE required by potential equity investors for a project like this one is known. If the required ROE were 17 percent (slightly above the joint-venture partner's ROE), the equity could probably be sold for approximately $292,000:

$$\text{Equity value} = \frac{\text{cash flow}}{\text{required ROE}} = \frac{\$49,626}{.17} = \$291,918$$

With the return–risk relationship apparently in balance, all parties agreed to the transaction as proposed. The developer–investor structured the project to receive a handsome development and contractor's profit, in addition to a holding-period investment return of over $49,000 annually. Actually, it was believed that the property would perform significantly better then the pro forma indicated, and the returns shown here would most likely improve as a track record was established.

Competition and Changing Property Usage

As the steel superstructure of the apartment hotel project was being erected, the owners were approached by a major international hotel chain. The chain was seeking a site in the immediate area for a luxury hotel, but because of the strong competition for prime sites it was unable to locate one that met its criteria. After months of negotiations, the owners agreed to lease to the hotel chain the entire space that was not already committed to office usage. The chain would guarantee a net rate (with possible future escalations) that would raise the NOI from $1,200,000 to $1,590,000. The total cost of the project would remain approximately $10 million. The $2.5

---

[8]Actually, as the equity investment approaches zero, the ROE approaches infinity. In mathematical terms, when the equity is zero the ROE is an "undefined" number.

EXHIBIT 6-12.   Revised Financial Pro Forma for Luxury Hotel–Office Property

Rate of Return	Income/ Cash Flow	Cost	Source of Financing
15.90% (ROI)	$1,590,000	$10,000,000	Total cost
10.50% (K)	661,500	6,300,000	First loan (10.75 to 10.5%)
25.09% (ROE)	928,500	3,700,000	Remaining equity
10.75% (K)	268,750	2,500,000	Second loan (11.02 to 10.75%)
54.98% (ROE)	659,750	1,200,000	Remaining equity
16.00% (K)	160,000	1,000,000	Third loan (same K)
250.00% (ROE)	499,750	200,000	Remaining equity
99.95% (ROE)	199,900	200,000	Joint-venture investment
∞ (ROE)	$ 299,850	$ 0	Remaining equity

ROI = 15.9%
Weighted-average DCR = 1.46
Weighted-average K = 11.12%
ROE to joint-venture partner = 99.95%
ROE to investor–developer = ∞

million of furnishings would not be needed, but about $2.5 million of structural changes and facility upgrading were required to meet the hotel chain's luxury standards.

The immediate result was a significant reduction in risk for all the parties involved in the project. Consequently, the owners renegotiated the first- and second-mortgage loan constants (K values) to reflect the reduced risk of AAA leases on the entire building. The net result is shown in Exhibit 6-12.

The return to the investor increased to $299,850 annually with no cash equity investment; the debt coverage ratio rose to 1.46; the entire net operating income was guaranteed by AAA credits; and profit potential was present as a result of escalator clauses in the long-term hotel chain contract and periodic renewals in the office space contracts. The joint-venture partner's return on his $200,000 equity investment rose from 16.54 percent in the previous case to 99.95 percent, and his risk was reduced significantly. In addition, the joint-venture partner continued to receive a K of 16 percent on the $1 million third loan, which was (at the time) significantly above the loan rates on competitive mortgages in a similar risk classification. If the equity investor–developer chose to sell his interest at this point, what would its value be? What would the required ROE be?[9]

[9]The required ROE would probably drop significantly due to the reduction in risk as compared to the original case. If the ROE dropped from 17 to 12 percent, the value of the developer's equity would be $299,850/.12 = $2,498,750.

Conclusion

Through their knowledge and expertise these managing equity investors have seemingly achieved the ultimate goal of investing: to identify and structure projects that produce maximum rates of return relative to the risks.

The vehicle used for analyzing these projects was the basic financial feasibility model. Although we recognize its limitations, we also need to recognize its advantages. It is easy to use; it is understandable; and it allows the investor to test quickly various combinations of economic variables. Most important, it appears to work in most income property situations in which investors have short-run positive cash flow objectives. Most sophisticated investors around the country are using this type of model in conjunction with the discounted-cash-flow models discussed in Chapter 7.

Postscript. A number of years after the project was completed and operating, the hotel chain encountered financial difficulties and defaulted on its lease. Soon thereafter the project became insolvent and went bankrupt. Ultimately, a second hotel chain took over the operation of the building at a reduced rental. The project never reached its long-run projected cash flow return to the original equity investors. Although the overall projected coverage ratio (1.46) appeared to provide adequate protection, it was based on assumptions that proved to be unsupported in the marketplace.

DEVELOPING A DETAILED ONE-YEAR PRO FORMA

The most critical number in any financial analysis of income property is the amount of NOI expected for the first year of operation. The first-year NOI projection, which includes estimates of gross possible income, vacancy and credit losses, and operating expenses, is the basic productivity estimate on which all financial structuring and rate-of-return estimates are based. Because all future-year projections are generally based on this first-year estimate, mistakes will usually be compounded in future years and result in multiple errors in the final property value estimates and rate-of-return calculations.

In the basic financial feasibility model, rules of thumb and aggregate estimates of income and expenses were used based on the investor's knowledge and experience, and on records for comparable properties that were available in-house or from property management firms. At some point in the investment process, however, a detailed income and expense statement must be constructed to verify the estimates used in the basic financial feasibility model. Investors who have ready access to management records for similar properties usually build this statement early in the investment process, before negotiating the basic purchase price and terms with the seller.

Other investors choose to enter preliminary negotiations with the seller and collect the necessary data to build a detailed statement only if preliminary purchase negotiations are successful. This procedure is said to minimize the investor's time commitment and data collection costs, but it can lead to many surprises after a "meeting of the minds" between the investor and seller has been reached.

Most books on real estate investment skim over the subject of developing a detailed pro forma, despite its great importance in the real-world investment environment. Most investors also skim over the importance of these calculations because they are time-consuming and require much detail work and patience. As a result, many investors buy properties on the basis of one set of numbers and then find that they operate on the basis of a completely different, more onerous set of numbers. Many surprises occur, and many unexpected risks are taken as a result of these miscalculations.

The remainder of this chapter offers some general ideas about the development of a detailed pro forma and the data sources that are required for its development. In Part 6 of this book detailed information is presented on estimating income and expenses for each type of property.

How Current NOI Can Be Distorted[10]

The financial records kept by an owner are the primary source of information about a property's NOI, but reading these records is an art in itself. In a variety of ways, and either deliberately or inadvertently, property records can mislead a prospective investor. There are many different ways in which the current NOI from a property can diverge from the property's true earning power, and many defenses that an investor should develop against problems of this nature. Here are eight such divergences, with the appropriate defense against each.

1. *Deferred maintenance.* In one of the most frequently met problems, deferred maintenance, maintenance and repair of the property have not been kept up. Simple examples include failure to paint at proper intervals and failure to periodically maintain the boiler and inspect and repair the heating, electrical, and plumbing elements. An owner may defer maintenance because the cash flow is inadequate or because he or she wishes to show the highest possible operating income to prospective purchasers.

   Investor's defense: A thorough inspection of the property by a competent engineer is the most obvious defense against this problem. Experienced investors will also have developed rules of thumb concerning the percentage of rental income that should be devoted to

10Major sections of this discussion were excerpted from *The Mortgage and Real Estate Executives Report* (Boston: Warren, Gorham & Lamont, bimonthly).

maintenance and repair each year (e.g., 10 percent of rental income). A financial statement that shows a much smaller percentage devoted to this purpose is suspect.

2. *Substantial capital improvements needed.* In addition to deferring necessary maintenance, the owner may have postponed needed capital improvements (thereby causing physical or functional depreciation). Capital improvements (e.g., a new roof) may be required to keep the property in good condition or may be necessary so that the building can remain competitive (e.g., an apartment building may require a swimming pool and other amenities to keep tenants from moving to newer buildings).

   Investor's Defense. Again, a complete inspection of the property is a must. In addition, the purchaser should do whatever market research is necessary to ascertain what the property needs to maintain its competitive position.

3. *Inadequate replacement reserves.* When personal property is a significant factor (as in motels or apartment buildings offering furnished units), adequate cash reserves should be maintained to replace short-lived items (furniture, carpets, etc.) A new investor may be forced to invest a substantial amount of additional capital soon after acquiring title to the property in order to replace short-lived items.

   Investor's Defense. The investor should deduct the amount necessary to fund the reserves to their proper level from the price he or she is initially willing to pay for the property.

4. *Improper capitalization of expenses.* The first three items all relate to actual inadequacies. But even when the owner has properly maintained the property, the financial records can be misleading if, in order to increase net operating income, the owner has capitalized (i.e., added to the capital account) expenditures that should properly have been deducted currently from gross rental income. In other words, by shifting actual expenditures (e.g., carpet repair and painting expenses) from the operating statement to the capital account statement, an owner can present an inflated net operating income and cash flow picture.

   Investor's defense. Although the distinction is sometimes difficult to make in practice, the general rule is that costs that do not increase the value of the property are to be regarded as expenses rather than capital expenditures. As already noted, experienced investors usually have their own rules of thumb for the percentage of gross income that should be devoted to repairs and maintenance. They substitute this figure for the one in the owner's financial statements.

5. *No provision for vacancies and credit losses.* An owner whose property is 100 percent rented will not hesitate to show gross rental income based on full occupancy and collections. Indeed, in their flyers (offering statements) many brokers assume full occupancy, even though this is not the fact (the gross rental income is then called *scheduled net*).

Investor's Defense. Astute investors reduce rental income to some extent to provide a cushion against future vacancies and credit losses, perhaps averaging 4 to 12 percent. This certainly should be done if there is a current oversupply of space in the neighborhood and any leases in the particular building will expire in the near future. For this purpose the investor should prepare a lease expiration schedule showing the precise dates on which each lease expires and the number of square feet that will become available. Also an analysis of the records of scheduled rents versus actual collections, and tenant credit evaluations, will provide a basis for estimating collection losses.

6. *Special concessions in leases.* In order to fill up a new building, or during periods of market weakness, many tenants are given leases with rent concessions (e.g., one rent-free month for each year of the lease) or step-down renewal options (the right to renew at a lower rental in the future). This may mean a substantial decline in rental income in the next few years.

Investor's defense. The investor should require the owner to provide a list of all leases and a summary of their rental provisions. The owner should also represent that there are no side agreements with tenants that contravene the lease terms. In addition, the purchaser or an attorney should read all leases to verify this information.

7. *Bona fide tenants.* When high vacancy rates are the rule, unscrupulous landlords will "pack" a building with short-term tenants or people paying no rent at all to give the appearance of full occupancy. Although not common today, this tactic remains a possibility that should be guarded against when dealing with unknown sellers. Another way for a landlord to defraud an investor is to enter into side agreements with some tenants, giving them free rent in the future in exchange for an immediate cash payment to the landlord. This is called "milking" the property.

Investor's defense. An investor who has doubts about the ethics of a seller should personally interview some or all of the tenants to verify their rent obligations. A more formal way to do this is to have the tenants execute *estoppel statements* in which they acknowledge their continuing obligation to pay rent according to the written lease terms.

8. *Management duties performed by the investor.* Property management and related expenses are often omitted or grossly understated if the seller performs property management and administrative duties. It is common for an investor–manager to render extensive property management and administrative services but never receive payment for them. Consequently, operating expenses will be understated by the value of the services rendered by the owner.

Investor's defense. To reflect the real cash flow generated by the property, the investor's financial projections should include a complete cost estimate for management services rendered, including resident and professional property management duties, accounting, payroll taxes, and expenses for income tax purposes; they should be included in the investment analysis.

The seller's financial records thus are subject to much distortion. These records may provide a basis for an NOI pro forma, but the investor must obtain data from other sources and make income and expense estimates that best represent how the property will perform for him or her during the first full year of operation.

On the other hand, historical data provided by the seller on rent rates, vacancies, and expenses can be a reliable basis for projections, if consistent accounting practices have been followed and a professional property management firm has been employed. Although NOI estimates are easily distorted in the short run, trend data for a period of years are less likely to be distorted significantly. These data, along with data from other sources, can provide an accurate basis for forecasting future income and expenses.

Other Sources of Data

▪ *Management Firms in the Area.* The investor should locate property managers who operate a substantial number of properties similar to the one being analyzed. Sharing information and expertise with other firms that have good data bases will solve many problems of data collection and forecasting. A professional property manager may be quite willing to share information and aid the investor in developing the one-year pro forma or budget if a fee or management contract may be offered for the services and expertise rendered.

▪ *In-House Data on Similar Properties.* Ideally, an experienced investor develops in-house accounting systems and data that are easily accessible for the purpose of analysis. Income and expenses are commonly kept on percentage and square-foot bases, and historical trends are figured on a line-item basis for a detailed one-year pro forma analysis.

▪ *Personal Interviews with Owners.* Personal contacts with other owners or through ownership associations can provide much needed information, as well as a format for discussions of market trends and changes that will directly or indirectly affect a property's performance.

■ *Published Data.* Numerous national and regional trade associations publish data on income and expenses for apartments, office buildings, shopping centers, hotels and motels, industrial buildings, and so on. The submarket data classifications are often useful in comparative and trend analysis. These will be discussed in detail when individual property types are discussed in Part 6.

■ *Market and Marketability Studies.* Studies of the market can be undertaken periodically by the investor to gather information and data for analyzing potential investments as well as evaluating existing properties in the portfolio. These studies are discussed in Part 3 and will be reviewed again in detail when individual property types are analyzed in Part 6.

SUMMARY

This chapter develops a financial model (1) to analyze the basic economics of the project with respect to the return and risk characteristics of a property, (2) to analyze the leverage alternatives and structure or restructure the financial package, and (3) to determine an investment value or range of value after having worked through the model with alternative assumptions. The model allows the investor to structure the economics of a project so that the financial objectives of the equity investor, lender, and seller are simultaneously achieved.

The basic financial feasibility model is a one-year cash flow model that incorporates a number of important relationships. The primary return measure used by the equity investor is the before-tax cash-on-cash return (ROE), and the primary measure of return to the lender is the mortgage constant (K). Both the equity investor and the lender can measure the risk level by computing a debt coverage ratio and a break-even point, and by analyzing the degree of favorable or unfavorable leverage. The most important overall measure of return is the ROI (net operating income relative to total capital invested), because it measures the overall productivity of the property. If the ROI is adequate, proper financial structuring can guarantee a mutually beneficial relation between the equity investor and the lender.

Intrinsic to the model are a number of weaknesses, the most important of which are utilizing a single net operating income and cash flow figure to represent the productivity of the property over its useful life and ignoring tax factors that affect the investor's return and risk. Although the model is easy to understand and the concepts are widely employed by real estate professionals, it is best used only in the early stages of analysis. If the basic economic criteria are met, a discounted-cash-flow after-tax analysis should follow.

After the basic model was applied to a number of investment situations, the development of a detailed one-year pro forma was studied.

In the Aspen Wood case study that follows, the basic financial feasibility model is used to generate financing alternatives for the proposed apartment building investment.

ASPEN WOOD APARTMENTS

GENERATING ALTERNATIVES AND APPLICATION OF THE BASIC FINANCIAL FEASIBILITY MODEL

In 1974, D&B Associates was seeking apartment, office, or retail properties that met their various investment criteria. In Chapter 5 were described the firm's basic apartment screening criteria: (1) locations: apartment properties that were highly visible, located in high-quality, stable neighborhoods, and close to shopping, transportation, and recreation; (2) a minimum of forty units, less than ten years old, well designed and appealing to the local investors as well as the renters, with utility charges paid by tenants on individual meters; (3) a good rental income track record, consistently high occupancy in recent years; (4) availability of secondary or wraparound financing to create a relatively high (75–85 percent) leverage position at a time when new financing was expensive and unavailable; and (5) tax shelter, the ability to structure the property in a way that generates a relatively high degree of tax shelter during the year of purchase.

Locating desirable properties proved to be a difficult task for Charlie Davidson and Clyde Boomer, the owners of D&B Associates. The years 1974–1976, often described as the great post-World War II real estate depression, presented such problems as (1) rapidly rising utility expenses as a result of the energy crisis; (2) low rents and high vacancy rates, because there was an excess inventory of apartment properties; (3) high interest rates and reluctance on the part of institutions to make any apartment loans in the city; and (4) a general economic recession, which, along with the depressed real estate conditions, discouraged investors from participating in syndication programs. Real estate became a buyer's market characterized by widespread mortgage defaults and negative cash flows.

Two members of D&B Associates spent nine months researching the desirable apartment areas in the city, writing down addresses, looking up ownership records, and contacting property owners. They also maintained active communication with other commercial brokers, commercial bankers, trust officers, tax attorneys specializing in real estate, builder–developers, owners of large properties in the city, and principals of other property management firms. After over one hundred properties had been analyzed, only two were purchased for D&B's syndication program. Locating properties that passed the basic screening criteria was not difficult, but few were able to pass the more rigorous return–risk criteria imposed in the basic financial feasibility model (step 3). In even fewer cases could successful negotiations be held with the seller (step 4).

In July 1974 Aspen Wood Apartments was located and appeared to meet the basic screening criteria (basic information was presented in Chapter 4).

1. It is adjacent to the Intramural Fields (forty tennis courts, track, baseball fields) and on the University's shuttle bus route. The neighborhood is pleasant and attractive to local workers as well as to students. The site is within three miles of two regional shopping malls, is visible from the inter-

section of two major traffic arteries, and is within one mile of numerous state office buildings.

2. Aspen Wood has eighty-four units, an acceptable number for managerial efficiency.

3. The building is durably constructed and well designed, including two swimming pools, laundry facilities, and adequate parking. The complex would appeal to investors and prospective tenants.

4. Electricity is paid for by the tenants.

5. The project had just undergone a complete refurbishing, including new drapes, carpet, furniture, and repainting inside and out. Over $100,000 was spent on these capital improvements in 1973–1974.

6. The seller was willing to accept a wraparound mortgage or secondary financing on the project. There was $650,000 of underlying liens and the asking price was approximately $1 million, depending on how the purchase was structured.

7. The seller was willing to offer tax benefits in the form of write-offs for 1974. This was important because the purchasing investors were tax-oriented professionals.

8. The project (allegedly) was 95 percent occupied and had an excellent occupancy record.

9. The seller was willing to sell on the basis of a 10 percent cash-on-cash yield (ROE) to buyers.

This list of investment criteria, though developed over fourteen years ago, would need to be modified only nominally to fit today's investment climate of moderate inflation rates and tax reform. If the list of criteria were redefined for the 1988 Aspen Wood environment, only criterion 7 (tax write-offs) would be eliminated. The others would still fit the investors' criteria of the late 1980s.

The seller of Aspen Wood Apartments was a limited-partnership syndication consisting of three general partners and numerous limited partners. The general partners were representing the syndication in the sale of the property. The limited-partnership syndication had originally overpaid for the complex and had borrowed (short term) $120,000 from local banks for the recent refurbishing program. The banks were now putting pressure on the general partners to repay the notes. The general partners had no experienced professional property manager on their staff; property records were practically nonexistent; and the current resident manager had stolen the last month's rental income and disappeared. Clearly, the sellers were motivated to sell.

THE SELLER'S OPERATING PRO FORMA

Exhibit 6-A shows the seller's operating pro forma. The rent schedule presented seemed reasonable to the buyer, but the so-called "scheduled net income" figure was distorted by a large "net deposits" figure and a 3 percent vacancy allowance. (Note that correct titles are given after the seller's terms.) Net deposits of such a large amount are usually a result of poor management, indicating a questionable

EXHIBIT 6-A. Seller's Operating Pro Forma, 9/1/74–8/30/75

INCOME

Scheduled gross rentals	$156,552	
Net deposits	3,000	
Net concessions	1,200	
Parking (18 spaces × $7.50)	1,620	$162,372
Less 3% vacancy		4,871
Scheduled net income (gross effective income)		157,601

OPERATING EXPENSES

Labor expense			
Resident manager	$ 3,600		
Maintenance	2,700	6,300	
Payroll taxes and insurance		1,194	
Electrical expense			
Materials and supplies	285		
Lamps	240		
Equipment maintenance	300		
Electricity	4,200	4,860	
Heating and air-conditioning expense			
Materials and supplies	285		
Equipment maintenance	600		
Gas	2,685		
Water	2,100	5,680	
General building expenses			
Materials and supplies	180		
Maintenance supplies	240		
Trash removal	816		
Exterminating	180		
Management fee (4.5%)	7,092		
Telephone	300		
Swimming pool	250		
General building maintenance	600		
Appliance repair	240		
Painting maintenance	480		
Plumbing maintenance	285		
Carpet repairs and replacement	120		
Cable television	1,560		
Advertising	1,800		
Legal and professional fees	800		
Miscellaneous	600	15,543	
Other expenses			
Real estate taxes	16,135		
Insurance	2,640	18,775	
Total expenses (33.2%)			52,342
Net cash flow before debt service (net operating income)			105,259
Debt service			66,591
Net cash flow before taxes (cash flow before tax)			$ 38,668

policy of not returning rent deposits to tenants who move, allowing too many tenant "skip-outs," or not requiring tenants to clean up their units at the termination of their leases. A 3 percent vacancy rate is not realistic for a long-run projection; few landlords in a student apartment market collect more than 95 percent of gross possible income, even when physical occupancy is 97 to 100 percent.[a]

Operating expenses were itemized in elaborate detail, but totaled to only 33.2 percent of gross possible income. This figure is unrealistically low; one might suspect that some bills were unpaid or "lost," maintenance was being deferred, expenses were being capitalized instead of expensed, or a combination of these. In addition, the seller's expense statement represented "last year's" expenses whereas the income represented next year's expectations.

Revision of these figures was necessary so that the buyer would have reliable data to feed into the basic financial feasibility model. A check of comparable well-managed properties led Davidson and Boomer to believe that rental rates were in line with the market, but that the vacancy allowance should be 5 percent and expenses about 40 percent.

SALE STRUCTURE PROPOSALS

The general partners made two initial presentations to D&B regarding sale structures that might be acceptable to both general and limited partners.

1. *Straight-sale proposal.* The asking price, which was derived by capitalizing the projected NOI of approximately $105,000 by a 10 percent capitalization rate, was $1,050,000. The buyer would make a total down payment of $414,000, to be paid $164,000 at closing (1974) and $250,000 one year later (1975). The buyer would assume the three existing notes on the property in the total amount of $636,000.

2. *Owner-financed sale proposal.* The asking price remained at $1,050,000, but the total down payment was reduced to $164,000. The remaining amount of the purchase price was to be financed by the seller using a wraparound mortgage bearing an interest rate of 8.875 percent, an amortization term of twenty years, and a fifteen-year balloon (remaining principal balance to be paid at the end of fifteen years). The seller was willing to accept over $100,000 of the down payment in the form of prepaid interest, points on the wraparound mortgage, and other fees that the buyer could deduct for income tax purposes (see Chapter 10). This proposal provided attractive tax shelters for the buyer (not available under current tax law).

The seller provided elaborate five-year projections of after-tax cash flows for each proposal. Both were reviewed carefully by Davidson and Boomer.

---

[a]Because of tenant turnover, broken leases, and collection losses, economic occupancy tends to be less than physical occupancy. Inexperienced investors often overestimate the amount of gross effective income (economic occupancy) that a property will produce because they underestimate the amounts of real vacancy and collection losses.

VALUATION USING THE BASIC FINANCIAL FEASIBILITY MODEL

In D&B's opinion neither of the seller's presentations was realistic. But the two presentations and some discussion provided useful information on which to base an offer. D&B felt that the general partners representing the property had two principal concerns: (1) appeasing the limited partners with a respectable selling price of approximately $1 million and (2) receiving an equity down payment of at least $160,000 to cover repayment of outstanding refurbishment loans. (The general partners had revealed that their creditors were pressing for repayment of about $120,000 in furniture liens and another $40,000 in other debts.

With this knowledge, D&B began to work the basic financial feasibility model both forward and backward, utilizing a $1 million minimum sales figure and an equity investment of $200,000 to $220,000 ($160,000 plus a $50,000 commission to D&B).

Exhibit 6-B shows a solution developed by Davidson and Boomer after numerous iterations. Although the maximum equity investment was somewhat less than the target amount of $210,000, the total project value of $1,036,000 was greater than the $1 million minimum specified; thus the numbers were "in the ballpark" from the point of view of the seller.

Gross rents were calculated on the basis of the seller's figures, but the vacancy and expense figures were adjusted as previously mentioned. As a result, the net operating income decreased to $89,305 from the $105,259 projected by the seller. Having specified the beginning and end values for the model, D&B began to specify values for other variables. A debt coverage ratio of 1.3 was felt to be minimum, as was a 10 percent desired (before-tax) rate of equity return (ROE). With a debt coverage ratio of 1.3, the maximum debt service that the project could support was $68,695 ($89,305 ÷ 1.3); with a debt amount of $830,000, the mortgage constant could be no greater than 8.3 percent. For this solution to be achieved, the seller had to be willing to provide wraparound financing of $830,000 with an interest rate and amortization term that would result in a mortgage constant no greater than 8.3 percent. In effect, the seller must pay for the high selling price with favorable mortgage terms.

At this point the seller has made a presentation regarding what he would like to receive if a sale were consummated, and D&B (the buyer) has completed a basic economic analysis of what it can offer. Now both parties must go over the facts and figures together to determine their bargaining positions and judge whether further efforts will be worthwhile. There is no reason to begin the exhaustive research and analysis called for in steps 5 to 7 (feasibility research, tax analysis, DCF analysis) if it appears that no agreement can be reached on the basic parameters of the sale.

At the end of Chapter 8 Davidson and Boomer are tracked through steps 4 to 7, beginning with negotiations with the seller and ending with a discounted-cash-flow analysis of the Aspen Wood property.

EXHIBIT 6-13.   The Basic Financial Feasibility Model—D & B's Solution

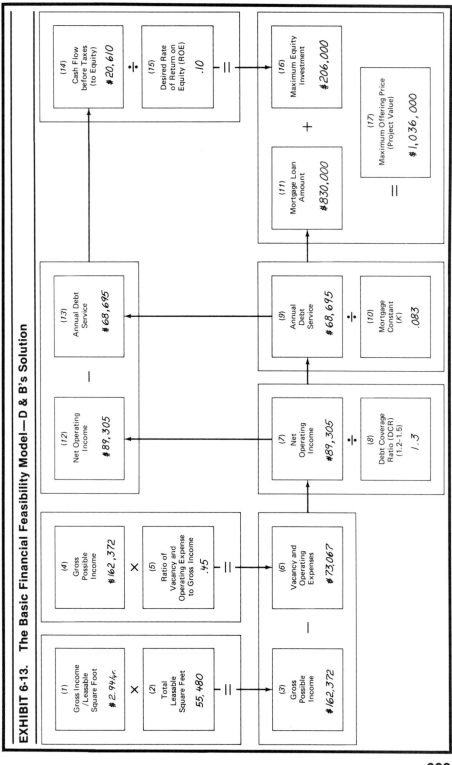

7

DISCOUNTED-CASH-FLOW
AND RATIO ANALYSIS

The use of the basic financial feasibility model to evaluate the performance of income-producing real estate was discussed in Chapter 6. Objections to the model focused on its inability to consider changes in economic variables over time, but as noted, the investor can use *present-value* (PV) and *internal-rate-of-return* (IRR) models, commonly known as discounted-cash-flow (DCF) models, to overcome many of these limitations. Indeed, the DCF models should be used extensively in the later stages of the investment process, as described by the ten-step model, before a final investment decision is made. Chapters 7 and 8 will provide an integrated framework for return and risk analysis using modern capital-budgeting techniques. Chapter 8 is actually an extension of this chapter.

This chapter opens with a review of the mathematics and economics of discounted-cash-flow (DCF) methods, including tax shelter impacts on cash flow. Then a complete after-tax cash flow analysis model is developed using DCF methods to analyze a project over a seven-year holding period. Third, a review is presented of types of annual financial ratios that can be used to evaluate a project's returns, risks, and the quality of the underlying assumptions used in the analysis.

Chapter 8 develops the concepts of sensitivity and risk analysis and illustrates how a computer simulation model can be utilized to evaluate the return–risk trade-offs in a real estate investment. Finally, we will again introduce the Aspen Wood case study and see how the concepts in both chapters were applied by D&B Associates in its investment analysis process.

Of course, the Economic Recovery Tax Act of 1981, the Deficit Reduction Act of 1984, and the Tax Reform Act of 1986 became effective during the time of the Aspen Wood case (1974 to 1988). Consequently, initial financial calculations are based on tax assumptions that applied to properties purchased before these acts became effective. However, the termination and resyndication analysis performed in 1983 (and presented at the end of Chapter 17) incorporated provisions of the 1981 tax act, but not the 1984 and 1986 tax acts. These situations are noted throughout, and the reader should refer to Chapter 10 for a complete discussion of the provisions of these tax acts and their impact on real estate investments.

PRESENT VALUE AND INTERNAL RATE OF RETURN[1]

The cliché, "A bird in the hand is worth two in the bush" clearly refers to the time value of birds, but the concept involved is equally applicable to money and real estate. Given the choice between a dollar today and a dollar a year from now, most people would choose a dollar today. Why is this so? Perhaps because immediate pleasure is preferable to future pleasure.

However, from the view of the real estate investor, the dollar today would be preferred not because an immediate pleasure can be gained but because the dollar can be put to work to earn a return. Should the investor choose to receive the dollar a year from now, it would mean forgoing the money that might be earned on that dollar over the course of the year; that is, there is an *opportunity cost* for passing up the cash flow that could be obtained by putting the dollar to work in an income property for a year.

Actually, a dollar received in the future can be less valuable for three reasons.

1. *Opportunity cost.* Earnings, the return that could have been earned had the money been available for immediate investment, are forgone.

2. *Inflation.* The purchasing power of a sum to be received in the future may be diminished by intervening increases in the price of goods and services.

3. *Certainty of payment (risk).* There is uncertainty about receiving payment in the future. For example, obligations of the U.S. government (e.g., Treasury bills) are considered free from the risk of loss. On the other hand, a lottery ticket bears a high degree of uncertainty. Most real estate investments fall somewhere between these extremes.

When determining the present value of future income, all three considerations must be evaluated in estimating a discount rate. A *discount rate* is simply the investor's required rate of return (or rate of interest), taking into account opportunity cost, inflation, and certainty of payment (risk).

---

[1] A good early discussion of this topic can be found in Robert Johnson, *Financial Management* (Boston: Allyn & Bacon, 1962), pp. 182–193; the present discussion is based on this earlier treatment.

Present Value

Perhaps the easiest way to understand *present value* (PV) is to first consider future value.[2] If an individual has $1.00 and deposits it in a savings account that pays 6 percent interest (compounded annually), at the end of one year the depositor will have $1.06 (the original $1.00 plus $.06 interest). If the $1.06 is left in the savings account, at the end of the two years it will have grown to $1.1236 (the $1.06 at the beginning of the second year plus $.0636 interest earned during the second year). After three years the original $1.00 will have increased to $1.191. The *future value* of $1.00 at 6 percent interest for three years is $1.191. The future value of any amount can be calculated as follows:

$$FV = A(1 + i)^n$$

where FV = future value
  A = original amount (here, $1.00)
  i = the rate of interest earned (here, 6 percent)
  n = the number of periods in the future (here, three years)

If $1.191 is the future value of $1.00 at 6 percent for three years, the *present value* of $1.191 to be received in three years, to someone whose opportunity cost or discount rate is 6 percent, must be $1.00. After all, if the $1.00 were available today, in three years it would increase to $1.191. The present value of any amount can thus be calculated by the reciprocal of the future-value equation:

$$PV = A\left[\frac{1}{(1 + i)^n}\right]$$

where PV = present value
  A = amount to be received in the future ($1.191)
  i = the rate of interest that could have been earned, or the discount rate (6 percent); also called the required rate of return
  n = the number of periods in the future (three years)

Fortunately, tables for the term inside the brackets in this equation are widely available, so extensive calculations are rarely necessary (see Appendix B). Present-value tables are fast becoming obsolete, however; today most students and analysts buy financial calculators that can compute present-value factors.

Using the 6 percent *annual* compounding table, we obtain 0.839619 as the present-value factor for three years. Multiplying this by the amount to

[2]This discussion was developed with the assistance of Russell Welch, Murray State University, Murray, Kentucky.

be received in the future ($1.191) gives $1.00: $1.191 × 0.839619 = $.99998623, or very close to $1.00. The difference is due to insignificant rounding. Again, to calculate the present value of an amount to be received in the future, multiply the amount by the present-value factor from the table, using the appropriate discount rate and the number of periods in the future.

Unequal Cash Flow Streams. The application of the notion of present value to real estate investment can be illustrated with another example. Suppose that a real estate investor has an opportunity to buy an income-producing property that is projected to provide an after-tax cash flow of $10,000 in the first year, $11,000 in the second year, and $15,000 in the third year.[3] The investor has determined that 12 percent is the appropriate discount rate for investments with risk levels comparable to that of this property. What is the present value of these cash flows? Clearly, it is *not* $10,000 + $11,000 + $15,000 = $36,000. Rather, it is calculated as follows.

Year	Cash Flow	×	PV Factor at 12 Percent	=	Present Value
1	$10,000		.892857		$ 8,928.57
2	11,000		.797194		8,769.13
3	15,000		.711780		10,676.70
				Total present value	$28,374.40

An analysis that values the cash flows at $36,000 is obviously misleading, because the calculated present value is almost $8,000 less. The present value may be viewed as the maximum offering price for a project on which a 12 percent discount rate is used. Alternatively, if $28,374.40 is paid for the project, a rate of return of 12 percent can be expected.

Equal Cash Flow Streams. Occasionally a real estate investor is presented with a situation in which an income stream will remain constant for several years (e.g., under a fixed-rate lease). Rather than applying a separate present-value factor to each year's cash flow, the investor can refer to a table that *accumulates* these factors and permits determination of the present value of a constant income stream with a single calculation. Such

---

[3] By convention, all cash flows are assumed to be received at the end of the year. This obviously is slightly misleading, but it reduces the number of calculations by a factor of 12 and is a well-accepted practice among financial analysts. However, if cash flow is received continuously, monthly, quarterly, or semiannually, other tables can be used. The present-value formula does not change, but all the terms in the formula are redefined in terms of the relevant cash flow period. For example, if we desire to discount cash flows on a monthly basis, i is the monthly rate and n is the number of months.

tables are known as *ordinary annuity* or *present value of one per period* tables (see Appendix B). For example, if an investor wants to compute the present value of a five-year net lease paying $1,000 per year, he or she could discount each year's lease payment at, say, 10 percent.

Year	Payment	×	PV Factor at 10 Percent	=	Present Value
1	$1,000		.909091		$ 909.09
2	1,000		.826446		826.45
3	1,000		.751315		751.32
4	1,000		.683013		683.01
5	1,000		.620921		620.92
			Total present value		$3,790.79

A simpler method is to multiply the amount by the table factor for the present value of one *per period* (10 percent column, Appendix B):

$$PV = \$1,000 \ (3.790787)$$

$$= \$3,790.79$$

One should note that the factor for the present value of one per period *is* the sum of all the years' factors for the present value of $1.00.

Now, what if the lease called for increased payments of $2,000 per year for years 6 to 10? How can the present value of this income stream be calculated? Each year's payment could be laboriously multiplied by the present-value factor and the resulting amount summed. However, use of the table can greatly reduce the computational effort. One way to determine the present value of this second stream of income would be to recognize that years 6 through 10 represent another five-year period, and that the present value of $1.00 per period for five years (again at 10 percent) yields

$$PV = \$2,000 \ (3.790787)$$

$$= \$7,581.57$$

However, this is the value of the income stream at the end of the *fifth* year (or the beginning of the sixth). Finding the *present value* necessitates discounting this amount by the five-year, *present value of $1.00* factor:

$$PV = \$7,581.57 \ (0.620921)$$

$$= \$4,707.56$$

The same result can be reached by subtracting the present value of $1.00 per period factor for *five* years (because the $2,000 payment will not be received until years 6 to 10) from the present value of $1.00 per period factor for *ten* years, and multiplying the difference by the amount of the income stream:

$$PV = A \text{ (tenth-year factor minus fifth-year factor)}$$
$$= \$2,000 \, (6.144567 - 3.790787)$$
$$= \$2,000 \, (2.35378)$$
$$= \$4,707.56$$

The Present-Value Decision Rule. The present value of an investment is the maximum amount an investor should pay for the opportunity of making the investment. If the calculated present value is *equal to* or *greater than* the investment cost, the decision rule is to *invest*, because there are net monetary benefits to be gained. If the calculated present value is *less* than the investment cost, the decision rule is reject or modify the investment, because the investment will not produce the required rate of return.

To illustrate the process better, assume that the required rate of return is 20 percent. The cash flows from a $100,000 investment have been estimated at $50,000 per year for three years. With the help of Appendix B or a calculator, the present value of this stream of cash flows, discounted at 20 percent, works out to be $105,324:

$$2.106481 \times \$50,000 = \$105,324$$

The proposed investment is worthwhile because the present value of the cash flows ($105,324) is greater than the cost of the investment ($100,000). The expected rate of return will be higher than 20 percent, because a 20 present value is greater than the investment cost, the expected rate of return is higher than the required rate of return. The reverse is also true. Chapter 3 presented the mathematical formulas and decision rules for the PV and other models discussed here. A review of these may be helpful.

Net Present Value (NPV). Exactly the same analysis can be carried out by subtracting the investment cost from the present value of the cash flows. If this difference is greater than zero, a net gain will be realized from the investment:

Present value of cash flows	$105,324
Investment cost	−100,000
Net present value	$ 5,324

The proposed investment is worthwhile because the net present value ($5,324) is positive. Computing NPVs for other investments enables the investor to rank them in order of desirability, from most to least. Investments with NPVs equal to or greater than zero are acceptable at the chosen discount rate (required rate of return).

Profitability Index (PI). When comparing or ranking investments of different sizes and costs, some investors prefer to calculate a profitability index rather than NPV, that is, the present value of cash flows divided by the cost of the investment. For example, the PI for the $100,000 investment would be 1.05:

$$PI = \frac{\text{present value of cash flows}}{\text{investment cost}} = \frac{\$105,324}{\$100,000} = 1.05$$

By computing profitability indexes for other projects, the investor can rank them in order of desirability, as shown in the following table. (A project with a PI of less than 1.00 would be undesirable; that is, its expected rate of return would be less than the 20 percent required rate of return.)

	Investment Cost	Present Value of Cash Flows	Net Present Value (NPV)	Profitability Index (PI)
Investment C	$ 80,000	$128,000	$48,000	1.6
Investment A	20,000	30,000	10,000	1.5
Investment B	100,000	130,000	30,000	1.3

Note that while investment B has a NPV greater than that of investment A, its PI is less. Thus, on a *relative* cost and profitability basis, investment A is more desirable than investment B; it produces higher net returns for each dollar invested. The PI method reduces the scale effects when comparing investments that have widely differing costs.

Given this conflict, which investment should be accepted if only one can be chosen? Stated another way, is it better to use the NPV or the PI approach? J. Fred Weston and Eugene Brigham suggest that, barring capital-rationing constraints, NPV is the preferred method.[4] However, their recommendation is based on portfolio selection decisions in which the investor is choosing more than one investment from among a group of alternatives and is seeking to maximize portfolio wealth. When the investor is making a mutually exclusive decision (selecting one and only one investment from a set of alternatives), either method can be used. Both methods produce the same accept–reject answer; investments that are acceptable under NPV are also acceptable under PI.

Internal Rate of Return

The internal rate of return (IRR) is defined as the rate of return that equates the present value of the expected future cash flows to the initial capital invested.[5] The IRR is also the discount rate that results in an NPV of zero.

[4] J. Fred Weston and Eugene F. Brigham, *Managerial Finance* (Hinsdale, Ill.: Dryden Press, 1978), pp. 327–329.

[5] An excellent survey of the literature on the IRR concept and its problems and limitations is provided by Austin J. Jaffe, "Is There a 'New' Internal Rate of Return Literature," *American Real Estate and Urban Economics Association Journal*, Winter 1977, pp. 482–502. See also Robert O. Kirby, "The Internal Rate of Return . . . It Does: The Reinvestment Rate Rethought," *The Real Estate Appraiser and Analyst*, Summer 1984, pp. 59–61.

The IRR formula is simply the PV formula solved for the unique value of the discount rate that results in an NPV of zero; the same basic equation is used for both methods.

Calculation of the Internal Rate of Return. In the earlier discussion, the required rate of return, or discount rate, was known and the present value of expected cash flows was being calculated. Now the expected cash flows and the investment cost required to achieve those cash flows are known, but in order to solve for the discount rate, the present value of the expected cash flows must be equated with the investment's original cost.

This technique is applied by calculating the rate of return on the $100,000 investment that produced cash flows of $50,000 per year for three years. The IRR can be estimated through a series of successive approximations, that is, by making guesses at its value. The goal is to find the one rate that will equate the $50,000 cash flows for three years with the $100,000 initial investment cost. The following equation demonstrates that a 20 percent rate produced a present value of $105,324:

$$2.106481 \times \$50,000 = \$105,324$$

In other words, if exactly $105,324 were invested in return for $50,000 each year for three years, the annual IRR would be 20 percent. But this much money need not be invested; the investment's cost is only $100,000. Therefore, the true IRR will be more than 20 percent. Discounting at 25 percent and using the present-value tables again, the investor calculates the present value of $50,000 received annually for three years to be $97,600:

$$1.952 \times \$50,000 = \$97,600$$

This calculation reveals that if $97,600 were invested in return for the $50,000 cash flows, the IRR would be 25 percent. Because in reality more than $97,600 must be invested, the IRR must be less than 25 percent but more than 20 percent. Moreover, it must be closer to 25 percent, because the actual required investment of $100,000 is closer to $97,600 than to $105,324. The actual rate can be approximated by interpolation.

Rate of Return		Present Value

$$
5\% \left\{ y \left\{ \begin{array}{l} 20\% = \$105,324 \\ \text{IRR?} = \$100,000 \end{array} \right\} \$5,324 \right\} \$7,724 \\ 25\% = \$\ 97,600
$$

$$\frac{y}{5\%} = \frac{\$5,324}{\$7,724}$$

$$y = (5\%) \times \frac{\$5,324}{\$7,724} = 3.45\%$$

$$\text{IRR} = 20\% + 3.45\% = 23.45\%$$

Observe that the calculated rate is, as we expected, closer to 25 percent than to 20 percent. In other words, a net cash inflow of $50,000 at the end of each year for three years is equivalent to an interest rate of about 23.45 percent *compounded annually* on an initial investment of $100,000.[6]

Actually, the IRR calculation using this interpolation method is only an approximation of the true mathematical solution. If one uses a preprogrammed calculator, the IRR is found to be 23.38 percent:

$$\text{Investment cost} = \frac{CF_1}{(1 + IRR)^1} + \frac{CF_2}{(1 + IRR)^2} + \cdots + \frac{CF_n}{(1 + IRR)^n}$$

$$\$100,000 = \frac{\$50,000}{(1 + .2338)^1} + \frac{\$50,000}{(1 + .2338)^2} + \frac{\$50,000}{(1 + .2338)^3}$$

Most calculators, as well as most computers, are programmed to find the IRR in a manner similar to that just illustrated—a process of trial and error. The process begins by choosing some discount rate as a starting point and computing the present value of the cash flows (CF_1, CF_2, CF_3, etc.). If the resulting PV on the left-hand side of the equation is greater than the investment cost ($100,000 in this case), a higher discount rate is chosen and the process is started again. This process is continued until the present value of the cash flows is just equal to the investment cost. Here, that occurs when the discount rate is 23.38 percent. *By definition, the IRR was found when the present value of the cash flow benefits is equal to the investment's cost.* Over a period of three years, the investor will receive the return of the original $100,000 investment plus a compounded annual return of 23.38 percent on that investment.

When the IRR is computed by hand through the interpolation process, rather than by a preprogrammed calculator or computer, errors occur because interpolation is a *linear* estimation that can only approximate a *geometric* progression. If the discount rates are far apart when the interpolation process begins, the resulting IRR approximation will be less exact than if the rates were closer together. As the discount rates come closer together, the error decreases and the estimated IRR converges on the actual IRR. For best results, the maximum spread between discount rates should be limited to about five percentage points.

Unequal Cash Flow Streams. Suppose that the investor discovers an opportunity to purchase a property that requires an equity investment of $10,000. The projected cash flows are for year 1, $2,000; for year 2,

---

[6]Observe also that the investor receives a *return* of the original $100,000 investment *in addition to* an annual interest rate of 23.45 percent. If the investment did not yield cash flows of at least $100,000 over three years, the calculated IRR would be negative; if the investment yielded exactly $100,000 over three years, the calculated IRR would be zero. Thus, an investment must produce cash flows that total *more than the initial investment cost* in order for the IRR to be a positive number.

$2,500; and for year 3, $3,000. The buyer anticipates selling the property at the end of the third year for a price that would result in net sale proceeds of $7,500. What is the IRR?

The true IRR is 17.43 percent using a programmed calculator, and the solution is

$$\$10,000 = \frac{\$2,000}{(1 + .1743)^1} + \frac{\$2,500}{(1 + .1743)^2} + \frac{\$3,000}{(1 + .1743)^3}$$

$$+ \frac{\$7,500}{(1 + .1743)^3}$$

If the investor were to guess at the IRR, however, and end up interpolating between 15 and 20 percent, the resulting IRR would be 17.53 percent:

Year	Cash Flow	Sale Proceeds	PV Factor at 15 Percent	Present Value
1	$2,000		.869565	$ 1,739.13
2	2,500		.756144	1,890.36
3	3,000		.657516	1,972.55
3		$7,500	.657516	4,931.37
			Total present value	$10,533.41

As before, the benefits are not being discounted at a high enough rate. Using a rate of 20 percent gives the following:

Year	Cash Flow	Sale Proceeds	PV Factor at 20 Percent	Present Value
1	$2,000		.833333	$1,666.66
2	2,500		.694444	1,736.11
3	3,000		.578704	1,736.11
3		$7,500	.578704	4,340.28
			Total present value	$9,479.16

The total PV of the benefits to the equity investor is now *less* than the required equity, so the IRR lies somewhere between 15 and 20 percent. Interpolating as before gives

Rate of Return   **Present Value**

$$5\% \begin{cases} y \begin{cases} 15\% = \$10,533.41 \\ \text{IRR?} = \$10,000.00 \end{cases} \$533.41 \\ 20\% = \$\ 9,479.16 \end{cases} \$1,054.24$$

$$\frac{y}{5\%} = \frac{\$533.41}{\$1,054.24} = (5\%) \times \frac{\$533.41}{\$1,054.24} = 2.53\%$$

$$\text{IRR} = 15\% + 2.53\% = 17.53\%$$

Internal-Rate-of-Return Decision Rule. The calculated IRR is then compared with the required IRR. If, for example, the investor determined that a 20 percent IRR was the lowest acceptable rate for this type of real estate investment, the project would be rejected or restructured until the calculated IRR was equal to or above the 20 percent required IRR. The suggested decision rule for investing is to accept projects that have IRRs equal to, or greater than, the investor's required IRR. Projects that are acceptable under the IRR method are also acceptable under the PV, NPV, or PI methods, provided that the minimum acceptable rate for IRR was also the discount rate used for PV, NPV and PI; they will all produce the same accept–reject answer for specific properties.[7]

Modified (Adjusted) Internal Rate of Return (MIRR)

Although IRR is widely used as a measure of investment return, there are a number of problems connected with reliance on IRR as an investment criterion.[8] Two of the commonly cited problems are the following.

1. *Multiple-rate-of-return problem.* Mathematically, the internal rate of return is calculated by solving an equation called an nth-degree polynomial [created by the denominator terms in the equation, $(1 + IRR)^n$]. In practice, what this means is that a project can have more than one IRR under certain conditions. In most situations there is only one IRR solution. However, if during the forecast period the expected cash flow changes from a positive to a negative and back to a positive number, more than one IRR solution may exist.[9]

2. *Assumed reinvestment at the IRR.* The IRR is an *internal* rate of return on capital *within* an investment. No mention has been made of a rate of return on cash flows withdrawn from the investment. However, there is an implicit assumption that the cash proceeds from the investment can be reinvested at the calculated IRR. If the timing of the cash flows differs among the investments being compared, and if the investor is choosing between mutually exclusive investment alternatives, the IRR may provide a misleading indicator of investment desirability. The go/no-go decision (accept–reject) will be the same

---

[7]See, for example, Weston and Brigham, *Managerial Finance*, p. 299.

[8]See Stephen D. Messner, Irving Schreiber, Victor L. Lyon, and Robert L. Ward, "Problems with the Use of IRR," *Marketing Investment Real Estate* (Chicago: National Association of Realtors, Realtors National Marketing Institute, 1985), pp. 69–74.

[9]For additional insights into the multiple-solution problem, see Donald J. Valachi, "Internal Rate of Return: A Note on the Arithmetic of Multiple and Imaginary Rates," *The Real Estate Appraiser*, March–April 1977, pp. 39–42; see also the classic article on the subject, William H. Jean, "On Multiple Rates of Return," *The Journal of Finance*, March 1968, pp. 187–191; also, James C. T. Mao, *Quantitative Analysis of Financial Decisions* (New York: Macmillan Co., 1969), Chap. 6.

using both the PV and IRR approaches, but the two may *rank* projects differently. In the PV approach, cash flows are assumed to be reinvested at the required IRR (discount rate); this is considered to be a more conservative and consistent assumption by many analysts.[10]

One solution to these two IRR problems is to assume a reinvestment rate equal to another, more realistic rate. Thus, annual cash flows (including sale proceeds) are equated with the original equity at the *modified (or adjusted) internal rate of return.* This MIRR is referred to as the *terminal-value IRR* by some analysts.

For instance, in the previous example, a $100,000 investment and annual cash flows of $50,000 for three years yielded a true IRR of 23.38 percent (23.45 percent using interpolation methods). But what if the realistic reinvestment rate for projects of similar risk levels is only 15 percent, rather than 23.38 percent? What is the MIRR if the investor assumes reinvestment at 15 percent? Obviously, the calculated IRR of 23.38 will fall to some number between itself and 15 percent, making the project appear somewhat less attractive:

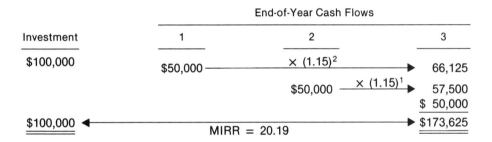

The MIRR procedure involves compounding all periodic cash flows to a terminal period (usually the year in which a property is sold) at the assumed reinvestment rate (or some other appropriate rate), and then finding the discount rate that equates the terminal value and the initial investment cost. In the example, the $50,000 cash flows received in the first and second years are compounded forward at 15 percent for two and one years, respectively. The $50,000 received in the third year is received at the terminal point, so no adjustment is needed. The *total terminal value* of the investment three years hence is therefore $173,625. The discount rate that causes the $173,625 to equal the investment cost of $100,000 is 20.19 percent. Said differently, the annual compound interest rate that causes the $100,000 investment to grow to $173,625 is 20.19 percent.

---

[10]See Eugene F. Brigham, "Conflicts between NPV and IRR," *Fundamentals of Financial Management* (Hinsdale, Ill.: Dryden Press, 1978), pp. 277–284. For an update on this discussion read Robert O. Kirby, "IRR vs. NPV: The Choice Is Yours," *The Real Estate Appraiser and Analyst*, Spring 1986, pp. 55–59.

As indicated, the IRR falls from 23.38 to 20.19 percent when cash flows can be reinvested at only 15 percent instead of the calculated IRR. If the holding period of the investment were longer or the calculated IRR higher, the difference between the IRR and the MIRR would be greater. Nevertheless, the project is still acceptable, because the MIRR is above the required 15 percent return.

The approach just described resolves the reinvestment problem, but as illustrated it does not resolve the problem of multiple IRRs caused by changes in the sign of the cash flows from positive (inflows) to negative (outflows) over the investment life. To accommodate this problem, the investor simply "discounts" negative cash flows back to the initial investment period, adds them to the initial outlay, and compounds all positive cash flows forward at the reinvestment rate, as was done in the previous example. By adding the discounted present value of the future negative cash flows to the initial investment, the investor explicitly creates a fund, accumulating interest at the reinvestment rate, which will be used to meet the cash outflows for the periods in which they exist. For example,

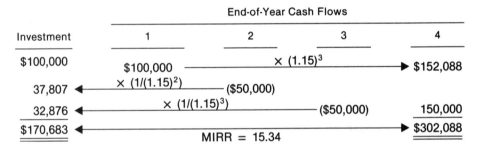

Note that outflows in periods 2 and 3 are discounted back at 15 percent, the reinvestment rate. By increasing the original investment to $170,683, the investor will have sufficient funds for purchasing the investment ($100,000), while leaving the remaining dollars in an account earning interest at 15 percent. There they will accumulate to the amounts needed to meet the cash outflows in periods 2 and 3. The remaining positive cash flows are compounded forward. The final terminal value is discounted to the total investment, producing the new modified IRR of 15.34 percent.

A critique of this method argues that negative cash flows should be discounted at some "safe" rate, rather than at the assumed reinvestment rate. The reasoning is that these future outflows are certain; thus, the invested funds used to meet these outlays should themselves be invested at a "certain" rate of return—the "safe" rate—rather than at the risky rate used for reinvestment of positive cash flows. Therefore, negative cash flows would be discounted at a rate representative of certainty, such as a savings account rate or treasury securities having maturities chosen to match the time periods when the negative cash flows must be paid.

Thus, the revised MIRR analysis requires discounting future outflows at some "safe" rate, while compounding positive cash flows at the chosen reinvestment rate. A further variation on this theme would have preceding positive cash flows reserved for paying future negative cash flows by reinvesting them at the "safe" rate and using the funds generated to offset a future negative cash flow. This technique, which is merely another version of modified IRR, has been called the financial management rate of return (FMRR) by its proponents.[11]

The Financial Management Rate of Return. The FMRR is a specialized form of MIRR in which it is assumed that

1. Only cash flows after financing and taxes from the property under evaluation are considered.
2. Funds can be invested at any time in any amount at a safe after-tax rate of i_L, and withdrawn when desired.
3. Funds can also be invested in "run of the mill" real estate projects of comparable risk at an after-tax rate of i_R. Such funds must be in minimum quantities of R dollars, however, and may not be withdrawn during the period to meet other requirements.

From these assumptions the FMRR is computed as follows.

1. Any positive cash flows that precede in time negative flows are employed (including compounding at i_L) to offset such negative flows. All remaining negative flows, including the initial outlay, are discounted to the present at i_L and added to become D_0^*.
2. The remaining positive flows are compounded at i_L until they sum to R, and they are then compounded at i_R. Subsequent flows continue the process toward a second investment of R. The compounded sum of these flows at the end of the project's life (year n) becomes T_n^*.
3. The basic FMRR is then defined as

$$\text{FMRR} = n\sqrt{\frac{T_n^*}{D_0^*}} - 1$$

4. This technique has been modified to determine optimal holding periods, select among mutually exclusive investment alternatives, and even deal with simple cases of rationing.[12]

[11]Stephen D. Messner and M. Chapman Findlay, III, "Real Estate Investment Analysis: IRR Versus FMRR," *The Real Estate Appraiser*, July–August 1975, pp. 5–20. Also see Messner, Schreiber, Lyon, and Ward, *Marketing Investment Real Estate*, pp. 69–81. In contrast to FMRR as an alternative rate-of-return measure, see Menachem Rosenberg, "An Adjusted Rate of Return on Real Estate Investments," *Real Estate Review*, Summer 1984, pp. 67–72.
[12]Guilford C. Babcock, M. Chapman Findlay, III, and Stephen D. Messner, "FMRR and Duration: Implications for Real Estate Investment Analysis," *American Real Estate and Urban Economics Association Journal*, Winter 1976, pp. 49–50. Also see Charles H. Wurtzebach and Neil G. Waller, "Duration: A Powerful New Tool for Managing Interest Rate Risk," *Real Estate Review*, Summer 1985, pp. 65–69.

The FMRR technique is taught widely in investment courses throughout the country; furthermore, at least one study has demonstrated mathematically that the reinvestment rate must be considered a major determinant of a project's rate of return and risk, especially when a long holding period is anticipated.[13] On the other hand, the technique has been criticized as a measure of investment performance that bears "a striking resemblance to the development of ancient cosmology."[14] In short, both the FMRR and the MIRR are said to be examples of mathematical overkill. The investor might better spend his or her time worrying about the underlying economic and market assumptions than worrying about multiple reinvestment rate assumptions that will rarely change an investment decision in the real world. As previously indicated, the IRR (or PV) is only one of many pieces of information that will be used to make the investment decision. Too exclusive a focus on any single investment criterion is generally a mistake.

In conclusion it can be argued that the problems inherent in IRR, which both MIRR and FMRR attempt to address, may be circumvented through the use of net present value, if the discount rate chosen represents the minimum acceptable rate of return or the investor's overall cost of capital. Under such assumptions, the difficulties associated with reinvestment and multiple rates of return are obviated. Of course, proponents of FMRR might argue that the cost of capital does not represent a "safe" rate to cover investments of funds needed to make up for future negative cash flows. In all likelihood such problems are nonexistent for small investors, coming into play mostly in land development and large-project development, to which most small investors are not exposed. Reinvestment is often a problem only for those investors who are concerned with portfolio effects and the need for continued investment of both new funds as well as funds thrown off by existing investments.

Conclusion

Present-value and internal-rate-of-return methods are adaptable to almost all income property situations. They can be utilized to evaluate cash flows on a before-tax or after-tax basis and to evaluate mortgage investments as well as equity investments. Moreover, they produce values that permit comparisons between projects and with other forms of investments.

The internal-rate-of-return approach seems to be preferred by real estate practitioners because (1) the calculated solution appears to be unique

[13]George W. Gau and Daniel B. Kohlhepp, "Reinvestment Rates and the Sensitivity of Rates of Return in Real Estate Investment," *American Real Estate and Urban Economics Association Journal*, Winter 1976, pp. 69–83.
[14]Michael S. Young, "FMRR: A Clever Hoax," *The Appraisal Journal*, July 1979, pp. 359–369.

and unambiguous; (2) the measure is the "standard" among most financial institutions and has been widely used for mortgage loan rates, bond rates, and the like; and (3) the measure provides a solution in a convenient form—a rate—that can be readily used as the criterion for comparisons with alternative investments.[15] In contrast, the present-value approach is preferred by many financial analysts and theorists because of the conservative reinvestment rate assumptions that underlie the model, and because it is said to be more consistent with the investor's primary financial goal of long-run wealth maximization.

In the following sections both approaches are applied to income property analysis. Like most "tools," they must be applied properly and accurately if they are to benefit the investor.

DISCOUNTED-CASH-FLOW AFTER-TAX ANALYSIS

Discounted-cash-flow (DCF) analysis focuses on valuation of the cash flows expected over the holding period of the investment. We generally consider three primary sources of after-tax cash flows.

1. Annual cash flow from operations (as measured previously).
2. Annual cash flow from tax savings (or taxes paid).
3. Cash flow from the sale of property after debts and income taxes (net reversion).

A fourth source, cash proceeds from refinancing the property, is also possible but is not generally considered in most cash flow projections.

The Aspen Wood Case

The Aspen Wood case, which in other chapters was treated as a separate section, demonstrates a typical DCF analysis and examines the effects of increasing rentals and expenses, loan amortization, accelerated depreciation, investor tax considerations, price appreciation, transactions costs, and the time value of money on the property's total investment value and rate of return. The analysis incorporates the following assumptions.

1. The first-year gross possible income of $166,980 increases by 4 percent annually (compounded). There are eighty-four units; the average unit, approximately 659 square feet, brings in $165.65 of gross income monthly (including other income).
2. The vacancy and credit loss allowance is expected to be 5 percent of gross possible income.

---

[15]Messner and Findlay, "Real Estate Investment Analysis," p. 6.

3. Total operating expenses are estimated to be 40 percent of gross possible income during the first year of operations, or $66,792. Thereafter, expenses increase at 7 percent per year (compounded).

4. The total cost of the project is $1 million. The land is valued at $100,000 and the improvements at $900,000. Because there are 55,356 leasable square feet in the building, the per-square-foot cost of the improvements is approximately $16.26.

5. A mortgage debt of $835,000 was negotiated at 7.5 percent for twenty-eight years. This results in annual amortization payments (debt service) of $70,574 and a mortgage constant of 8.55 percent. The time frame is 1974 and the loan wraps around two underlying mortgage notes that bear interest at 6.5 percent and 7.25 percent, respectively.

6. The improvements will be depreciated at the 125 percent declining-balance rate, and the remaining economic life of the improvements is twenty-two years. This economic life is an estimate of the average useful life of the building components, which have in fact been separated and individually depreciated by the investors, as noted in the next chapter. (Under the provisions of the Tax Reform Act of 1986, residential real property is depreciated using the straight-line method over 27.5 years, but land improvements (sidewalks, roads, and landscaping and so forth) may be depreciated over fifteen years using the 150 percent declining-balance method.)

7. The project value is expected to grow at 3 percent compounded annually, based on the original $1 million cost of the project. A selling expense (brokerage commissions and closing costs) of 5 percent is anticipated.

8. The investor's marginal income is taxed at 50 percent, and capital gains on the sale of the property are taxed at 25 percent. Although the actual capital gains rate would be 20 percent under the ordinary method using the 60 percent exclusion rule, the investor anticipates some rise in tax bracket during the year when the gain from sale is reported. In addition, there may be some minimum tax on the gain. Consequently, the investor prefers to use the more conservative 25 percent effective capital rate for the financial analysis. (The Tax Reform Act of 1986 reduced the income tax rate to 28 percent; capital gains are also taxed at the 28 percent rate.)

9. An after-tax (internal) rate of return on equity investment of 18 percent is sought. This is the IRR necessary to commit equity funds.

This analysis will provide information on the most likely consequences of the investment. As illustrated in Exhibit 7-1, our cash flow model incorporates five sets of input variables: investment outlays, operations, financing, reversion, and tax assumptions. The output of the analysis includes annual cash flow projections, discounted-cash-flow information,

EXHIBIT 7-1.   Project Analysis—Discounted-Cash-Flow Return Model

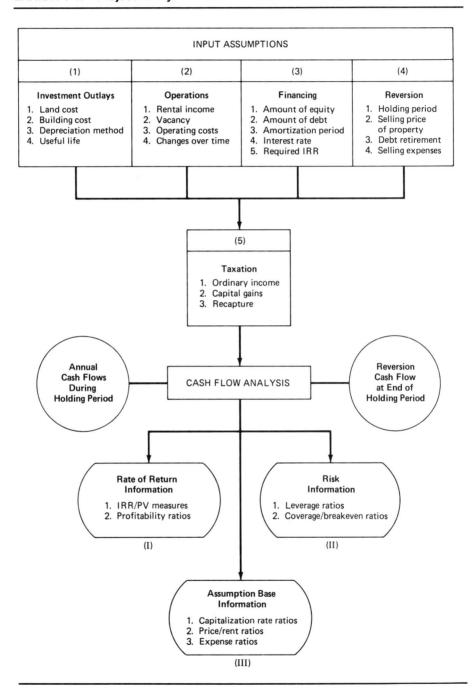

and various types of rate of return, risk, and assumption base information. Assumption base information consists of annual financial ratios that are used to test the underlying economic and market assumptions and relationships that have been presumed in the analysis but not explicitly tested.

Calculation of Cash Flow Data

The seven-year cash flow analysis illustrated in the following sections has been generated for us by a computer model known as RE001.[16] This model is one of many that is available to students and practitioners for use on three types of computers, minicomputers, desktop, and mainframe. Section 1 (Exhibit 7-2) is simply a recap of the data already given.

Property Information (Section 2). Exhibit 7-3 shows the balance sheet as of the purchase date. Also calculated is the *leverage position* as of the date of purchase, which is the total debt ($825,000) divided by the total property cost ($1,000,000). The project has a debt ratio of 82.5 percent. The equity investment of $175,000 thus represents 17.5 percent of the total property cost.

Depreciation Information (Section 3) (see Exhibit 7-4). The depreciation coefficient used to calculate annual depreciation expense is

$$\text{Depreciation coefficient} = \frac{1}{\text{useful life}} \times \text{depreciation method}$$

$$= \frac{1}{22} \times 1.25$$

$$= .056818$$

Depreciation for each year is calculated by multiplying the depreciation coefficient by the *beginning basis*. For example, the amount of *depreciation claimed* in year 1 is $900,000 × .056818 = $51,136. The beginning

---

[16]RE001 is a basic discounted-cash-flow computer model developed by Stephen A. Pyhrr at the University of Texas, Austin. The monograph that describes this model and the advanced model, RE004, was published by the Texas Real Estate Research Center, Texas A&M University, College Station, Texas 77843. The monograph, authored by Stephen A. Pyhrr and James A. Baker, is entitled *Computer Models for the Financial Analysis and Tax Planning of Income-Producing Real Estate Investments*, TRERC Technical Monograph No. 2. A new model is Planease by Feakens Analytical Association, Rolling Hills, California 90274. Many other new models are available from a variety of vendors. A specifically developed manual listing over 150 different real estate software vendors and detailing their products is available from Michael J. Hanrahan, President, Paradigm Real Estate Systems, San Francisco, California. Paradigm also operates the Real Estate Software Testing Center. Also active in developing computer spreadsheet software for income property analysis is Dr. Wayne R. Archer at the Real Estate Research Center of the University of Florida, Gainesville, Florida 32611.

EXHIBIT 7-2.   Aspen Wood Apartments: Computer Analysis—Section 1

---

1. RECAPITULATION OF INPUT DATA (SEPTEMBER 1974)

1. Type property (0. = residential, 1. = commercial)	1.
2. Total land cost ($)	100,000.00
3. Number of units in project	84.
4. Average square feet per unit	659.00
5. Square-foot cost of all improvements ($)	16.26
6. Depreciable life of improvements (years)	22.00
7. Depreciation method	1.25

    1.00 = straight line   1.75 = 175%
    1.25 = 125%   2.00 = double declining
    1.50 = 150%

8. Average monthly income per unit ($)	165.65
9. Expected occupancy rate (%)	.9500
10. Operating cost (% of gross possible income)	.4000
11. Annual growth rate of gross possible income (%)	.0400
12. Annual growth rate of operating costs (%)	.0700
13. Annual growth rate of property value (%)	.0300
14. Holding period (cash flow projection period, years)	7.
15. Selling expense (%)	.0500
16. Ordinary income tax rate (%)	.5000
17. Capital gains tax rate (%)	.2500
18. Required rate of return (IRR) on equity (%)	.1800
19. Amount of loan 1 ($)	825,000.00
20. Effective interest rate on loan 1 (%)	.07500
21. Amortization term of loan 1 (years)	28.00
22. Does this project involve secondary financing?	No

EXHIBIT 7-3.   Aspen Wood Apartments: Computer Analysis—Section 2

---

2. PROPERTY INFORMATION

Total square feet of improvements   55,356
Total property cost $1,000,000

Assets		Liabilities and Net Worth	
Land	$ 100,000	Total debt	$ 825,000
Building	900,000	Equity invested	175,000
Total	$1,000,000	Total	$1,000,000

Leverage position (debt/property cost) = .825

EXHIBIT 7-4.   Aspen Wood Apartments: Computer Analysis—Section 3

---

3. DEPRECIATION INFORMATION

Year	Beginning Basis	Depreciation Claimed	Undepreciated Balance	Straight-Line Basis	Excess Depreciation
1	$900,000	$51,136	$848,864	$859,091	$10,227
2	848,864	48,231	800,633	818,182	17,549
3	800,633	45,490	755,142	777,273	22,130
4	755,142	42,906	712,236	736,364	24,127
5	712,236	40,468	671,768	695,455	23,686
6ª	671,768	39,516	632,253	654,545	22,293
7	632,253	39,516	592,737	613,636	20,899

ªStraight-line depreciation amount exceeds accelerated depreciation amount, switched to straight-line depreciation.

basis is $900,000 and declines each year by the amount of *depreciation claimed* the previous year. The *undepreciated balance* at the end of the year is found by deducting *depreciation claimed* from the *beginning basis*. At the end of year 1, for example, the *undepreciated balance* is $900,000 — $51,136 = $848,864. Each year the depreciation amount declines until it becomes advantageous to switch to straight-line depreciation, which occurs in year 6.[17]

The *straight-line basis* calculation is made to determine the amount of excess depreciation, which is said to be *recaptured* and is subject to taxation at ordinary income tax rates. The *straight-line basis* is calculated by taking 1/22 of the *beginning basis* (1/22 × $900,000 = $40,909) and then subtracting this result each year from the *straight-line basis*. For example, *straight-line basis* at the end of year 1 is $900,000 — $40,909 = $859,091; at the end of year 2, $859,091 — $40,909 = $818,182; and at the end of year 3, $818,182 — $40,909 = $777,273.

The amount of *excess depreciation* each year is simply the difference between the *straight-line basis* and the *undepreciated balance* for that year.

Impact of 1986 Tax Reform Act. Recognize that under 1986 tax law the amount of depreciation would be substantially less: depreciation each year would be 1/27.5 × $900,000 = $32,727, assuming no allocation is made to land improvements or personal property that qualifies for accelerated depreciation over shorter useful lives. These concepts and tax provisions are fully explained and discussed in Chapter 10.

[17]Each year the computer calculates the actual amounts of straight-line and accelerated depreciation. When the amount of straight-line depreciation, which changes each year as the remaining basis and useful life change, exceeds the amount of accelerated depreciation, the depreciation method is changed.

Loan Information (Section 4) (see Exhibit 7-5). The amortization payment of $70,574 is calculated by multiplying the mortgage constant (8.55442 percent, shown as 8.55 percent in the output) by the loan amount ($825,000). Allocations are made each year to interest and principal, but are based on monthly payments (assumes monthly compounding). The *remaining principal* is calculated by taking the amount of *remaining principal* at the end of the previous year and deducting the *amortization of principal* during the current year. For example, *remaining principal* at the end of year 1 is $825,000 − $9,004 = $815,996; and at the end of year 2, $815,996 − $9,703 = $806,293. Note that the year 1 calculation begins with the original loan amount of $825,000. Various methods of calculating amortization schedules are discussed in Chapter 9.

The *effective mortgage constant* is calculated by the following formula:

$$\text{Effective mortgage constant} = \frac{\text{amortization payment}}{\text{remaining principal}}$$

Although the mortgage constant is originally 8.55 percent (70,574/825,000), it increases to 9.47 percent (70,574/745,237) in year 7 as the loan is paid down from $825,000 to $745,237. Thus, the effective cost of borrowing rises for the equity investor as equity buildup (loan amortization) takes place.

Like depreciation, interest deductions decrease as the loan is paid down, and this, as well as declining depreciation deductions, results in loss of tax shelter benefits.

EXHIBIT 7-5.   Aspen Wood Apartments: Computer Analysis—Section 4

---

4. LOAN INFORMATION

Loan 1 information

Amount	$825,000
Rate (%)	.0750
Term (years)	28.00
Mortgage constant (%)	.0855

Year	Amortization Payment	Interest Expense	Amortization of Principal	Remaining Principal	Effective Mortgage Constant
1	$70,574	$61,570	$ 9,004	$815,996	.08649
2	70,574	60,871	9,703	806,293	.08753
3	70,574	60,117	10,457	795,836	.08868
4	70,574	59,306	11,268	784,568	.08995
5	70,574	58,431	12,143	772,425	.09137
6	70,574	57,488	13,086	759,339	.09294
7	70,574	56,472	14,102	745,237	.09470

Cash Flow Analysis (Section 5) (see Exhibit 7-6). The calculation of net operating income (columns A–E) is self-explanatory.

EXHIBIT 7-6. Aspen Wood Apartments: Computer Analysis—Section 5

---

5. CASH FLOW ANALYSIS

Year	(A) Gross Possible Income	(B) Vacancy Allowance	(C) Gross Effective Income (A − B)	(D) Operating Expenses	(E) Net Operating Income (C − D)
1	$166,980	$ 8,349	$ 158,631	$ 66,792	$ 91,839
2	173,659	8,683	164,976	71,467	93,509
3	180,606	9,030	171,575	76,470	95,105
4	187,830	9,391	178,438	81,823	96,615
5	195,343	9,767	185,576	87,551	98,025
6	203,157	10,158	192,999	93,679	99,320
7	211,283	10,564	200,719	100,237	100,482

Year	(F) Interest Expense	(G) Depreciation Expense	(H) Taxable Income (E − F − G)	(I) Equity Cash Flow Before Tax (E − Amort. payment)	(J) Equity Cash Flow After Tax [I − (tax rate × H)]
1	$ 61,570	$ 51,136	$ − 20,867	$ 21,265	$ 31,699
2	60,871	48,231	− 15,593	22,935	30,731
3	60,117	45,490	− 10,503	24,531	29,783
4	59,306	42,906	− 5,596	26,041	28,839
5	58,431	40,468	− 874	27,451	27,888
6	57,488	39,516	2,316	28,746	27,588
7	56,472	39,516	4,494	29,908	27,661

Year	(K) Cash Flow to Total Capital After Tax	(L) Cumulative Cash Flow Before Tax	(M) Cumulative Cash Flow After Tax	(N) Property Value at End of Each Year
1	$ 71,488	$ 21,265	$ 31,699	$1,030,000
2	70,870	44,200	62,430	1,060,900
3	70,298	68,731	92,212	1,092,727
4	69,761	94,773	121,052	1,125,509
5	69,247	122,224	148,940	1,159,274
6	69,418	150,970	176,528	1,194,052
7	69,999	180,878	204,189	1,229,874

Important changes occur in net operating income (NOI) over the projection period. NOI increases each year, even though operating expenses are increasing at 7 percent while income is increasing at only 4 percent. This somewhat surprising result is not intuitively obvious to most people, but the explanation is quite simple: 7 percent of the operating expenses (a low dollar amount) is less than 4 percent of gross possible income (a high dollar amount). However, the *rate* of increase of NOI is *decreasing* each year. Eventually, as the expense ratio rises above a certain point, 7 percent increases in expenses will be greater than 4 percent increases in gross income, and NOI will begin to decrease. This is expected as a property gets older, and will usually continue until a property renovation is undertaken.

Taxable income (column H). Taxable income is calculated by deducting depreciation and interest expense from the NOI estimate each year. In this case the investor generates tax losses (negative taxable income) for five years and, thus, can shelter other income earned. In addition, all cash flows generated by the project (column I) are being sheltered as long as tax losses occur. Under 1986 tax law, tax losses can generally be used only to shelter other "passive income"; unused tax losses can be carried forward indefinitely.

Equity cash flow before tax (column I). Equity cash flow before tax is computed by deducting the amortization payment from the NOI estimate. For example, in year 1 the cash flow before tax is $91,839 − $70,574 = $21,265; in year 2 it is $93,509 − $70,475 = $22,935; and so on.

Equity cash flow after tax (column J). Equity cash flow after tax is different from the cash flow before tax by the amount of tax saving or taxes paid. In this example, during the first five years tax losses generate a tax saving equal to the tax rate *times* the amount of tax losses. In year 1 the tax saving is .50 × $20,867 = $10,434. Added to the $21,265 cash flow from operations, the after-tax cash flow is $31,699. In year 2 the tax loss declines to $15,593 and the cash flow before tax rises to $22,935 as a result of rising net income, but the *net result is a decrease* in the cash flow after tax to $30,731 [$22,935 + (.50 × $15,593)].

Of course, the underlying assumption in computing tax savings in this manner is that the investor has a substantial amount of taxable passive income from other sources to shelter and that these *artificial accounting losses* can be applied against the investor's other income, which is taxable at the rate assumed. In practice, future tax rates are difficult to estimate because all items of income and loss affect the marginal tax bracket, and tax law changes keep altering marginal tax brackets. A wealthy individual may have numerous projects that completely shelter income from other sources, and a substantial loss from a particular project can substantially lower the marginal tax bracket below that assumed in the analysis, or simply be unusable in that tax year.

Under these conditions, what are the proper tax bracket assumptions for analyzing any one specific project in the investor's portfolio? This problem is addressed in Chapter 10, together with an examination of how the 1986 Tax Reform Act alters the way in which the after-tax benefits of income property ownership are evaluated.

After year 5, *taxable income* (column H) becomes positive and the investor must pay taxes instead of receiving a tax saving. From this year on, unless the project is restructured to increase the tax shelter, *equity cash flow after tax* (column J) will be less than *equity cash flow before tax* (column I). In the example shown, the decline in tax shelter outweighs the increase in NOI from increasing rentals each year. The final, *bottom-line* result is a declining cash flow figure. *Equity cash flow after tax* declines from $31,699 in year 1 to $27,661 in year 7.

Cash flow to total capital after tax (column K). Cash flow to total capital after tax is computed in exactly the same way as *equity cash flow after tax*, but the former eliminates all leverage factors; it can be called the unleveraged cash flow after tax. If the project were 100 percent equity-financed, *equity cash flow after tax* would be identical to *cash flow to total capital after tax*. The reason for computing this cash flow figure is to show the unleveraged after-tax return on the total capital investment. In the internal-rate-of-return analysis, it will be used to calculate the unleveraged IRR on the $1 million total capital investment, which is useful for comparison purposes (and certainly would be an important rate of return figure to institutions that buy unleveraged properties). The formula used to calculate the *cash flow to total capital after tax* is the following:

Cash flow to total capital = equity cash flow after tax

+ annual amortization payment

− (ordinary tax rate × interest expense)

For example, in year 1 the cash flow to total capital after tax is $31,699 + $70,574 − (.50 × $61,570) = $71,488; in year 2 it is $30,731 + $70,574 − (.50 × $60,871) = $70,870; and so on.

Cumulative cash flows before tax and after tax (columns L and M). Cumulative cash flows before and after tax are calculated by adding the annual cash flow figures in columns I and J for the number of years specified. These estimates are useful for determining when the equity investor gets the *payback*. On a before-tax basis, the investor gets the original $175,000 back during the seventh year. On an after-tax basis, payback occurs during the sixth year. Some investors use this measure as one criterion for evaluating the investment. For example, an investor might reject a project if it has a payback greater than five years.

Property value at end of each year (column N). The final set of computations made in section 5 of the cash flow analysis is property value at the end of each year. Each year the property value is assumed to increase at a specified compounded annual rate based on the original total property cost. For example, at the end of year 1 the property value is assumed to be $1,030,000 [$1,000,000 $\times$ $(1.03)^1$]; at the end of year 2 the property value is assumed to rise to $1,060,900 [$1,000,000 $\times$ $(1.03)^2$]; and so on. The annual increase in property value is assumed at 3 percent—somewhat less than the increase in rents and expenses—for reasons to be explained later. Another method of determining property value each year, a method theoretically superior to the one just given, is to capitalize the NOI each year using an appropriate market capitalization rate.

Calculation of Proceeds from Sale of Property (Section 6). Proceeds from sale of property is also called the *reversion* cash flow and is shown in Exhibit 7-7. The selling expense is calculated at 5 percent of the selling price. The property is sold at the end of year 7 for $1,229,874. The remaining debt principal at this time is $745,237 (section 4, Exhibit 7-5), and taxes on the sale of the property amount to $124,136.

The *tax on the sale of the property* is computed by adding the capital gains tax to the ordinary income tax on excess depreciation. The four-step process for computing tax liability on the sale of this property is shown in Exhibit 7-8. The capital gains rate (25 percent) is applied to the difference between the *net selling price* and the *straight-line basis*, whereas the ordinary rate (50 percent) is applied to the difference between the *straight-line basis* and the *accelerated basis*. Under current tax law this methodology is still valid.

The cash flow that remains in the investor's pocket after all has been said and done is $299,007. We assume that it is received at the end of year 7 (in its entirety) when the property is sold. This cash flow will be used in computing the internal rate of return and present value of the investor's equity, and is indeed the largest cash flow received during the holding pe-

---

EXHIBIT 7-7.   Aspen Wood Apartments: Computer Analysis—Section 6

6. CALCULATION OF NET PROCEEDS FROM SALE OF PROPERTY

Selling price of property at end of holding period	$1,229,874
Less: Selling expense	61,494
Less: Remaining debt principal	745,237
Net proceeds from sale of property (before tax)	423,143
Less: Tax on sale of property at end of holding period	124,136
Net proceeds from sale of property (after tax)	$299,007

EXHIBIT 7-8.   Computation of Taxes on Sale of Property

---

1. COMPUTE BASIS OF PROPERTY USING 125% METHOD (END OF YEAR 7)

Undepreciated balance of improvements	$592,737
Plus: land value	100,000
Accelerated basis of property	$692,737

2. COMPUTE BASIS OF PROPERTY USING STRAIGHT-LINE METHOD (END OF YEAR 7)

Undepreciated balance of improvements	$613,636
Plus: land value	100,000
Straight-line basis of property	$713,636

3. COMPUTE NET SELLING PRICE

Gross selling price	$1,229,874
Less: selling expenses (5%)	61,494
Net selling price	$1,168,580

Tax Situation Graphically

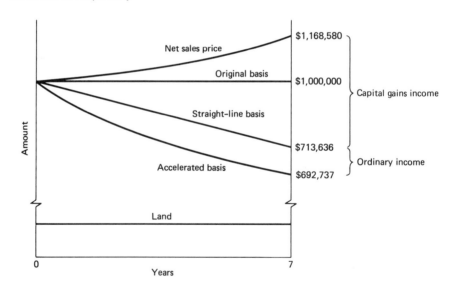

4. COMPUTE TOTAL TAX ON SALE OF PROPERTY

Capital gains tax = ($1,168,580 − $713,636) × .25 =	$113,686
Ordinary income tax = ($713,637 − $692,737) × .50 =	10,450
Total tax on sale of property	$124,136

EXHIBIT 7-9. Aspen Wood Apartments: Summary of Project Cash Flows

Year	Equity ($175,000) Cash Flow After Tax	Total Capital ($1,000,000) Cash Flow After Tax
1	$ 31,699	$ 71,488
2	30,731	70,870
3	29,783	70,298
4	28,839	69,761
5	27,888	69,247
6	27,588	69,418
7	27,661	69,999
7	$299,007	$1,044,244[a]

[a]The reversion in this case simply eliminates the debt principal repayment of $745,237. Tax liability is not affected by eliminating leverage factors. Consequently, this cash flow can be calculated by deducting selling expenses and taxes from the selling price ($1,044,244 = $1,229,874 − $61,494 − $124,136).

riod in this example. In an inflationary economy in which demand for real estate is strong, the reversion cash flow is the single most important factor affecting the internal rate of return and present value of the project.

Internal-Rate-of-Return and Present-Value Analysis (Section 7). So far, the equity investor expects to receive a total of eight cash flows during the seven-year holding period (Exhibit 7-9).

Present value. The *total present value of equity investment* (Exhibit 7-10) is found by multiplying the equity cash flows shown in Exhibit 7-9 by the present-value coefficients for each year at 18 percent (the required IRR), and adding together the resulting present values. The sum is $206,895.

EXHIBIT 7-10. Aspen Wood Apartments: Computer Analysis—Section 7

7. INTERNAL-RATE-OF-RETURN—PRESENT-VALUE ANALYSIS

Total present value of equity investment	$ 206,895
Plus: original mortgage balance	825,000
Total project value	$1,031,895

Internal rate of return
  On total capital invested   .0820
  On initial owners equity   .2214

Shown mathematically, the result is as follows:

$$\text{Present value} = \frac{CF_1}{(1 + RIRR)^1} + \frac{CF_2}{(1 + RIRR)^2} + \cdots + \frac{CF_n}{(1 + RIRR)^n}$$

$$= \frac{\$31,699}{(1 + .18)^1} + \frac{\$30,731}{(1 + .18)^2} + \frac{\$29,783}{(1 + .18)^3}$$

$$+ \frac{\$28,838}{(1 + .18)^4} + \frac{\$27,888}{(1 + .18)^5} + \frac{\$27,588}{(1 + .18)^6}$$

$$+ \frac{\$27,661}{(1 + .18)^7} + \frac{\$299,007}{(1 + .18)^7}$$

$$= \$206,895$$

Next, if the original mortgage balance (which already is a present-value figure) is added to the present value of the equity, the investor arrives at an estimate of the total project value. The total project value is therefore $\$206,895 + \$825,000 = \$1,031,895$.

The project is acceptable, using the present-value criterion, because its value (1,031,895) is greater than its cost ($1,000,000). Similarly, the *equity value* ($206,895) is greater than the *equity cost* ($175,000) by the same amount ($31,895). Comparing *equity value* to *equity cost*, the resulting *net present value* is positive and the *profitability index* is greater than 1. Thus, the investor will exceed the minimum criterion of an 18 percent IRR by investing in this project.

Internal rate of return. Because the project's cost is less than the project's value, we know that the actual IRR is greater than 18 percent. It is computed using the trial-and-error process described previously, with the *equity cash flows after tax* just given. Based on this approach, the IRR is about 22 percent. Using the same trial-and-error process, but to a much higher degree of accuracy, the computer calculates the IRR to be 22.14 percent. At 22.14 percent, the *present value* of the equity cash flows *just equals the cost* to acquire the equity ($175,000).

If an IRR calculation is performed on the total capital invested ($1,000,000) using the cash flows shown previously, the rate is 7.53 percent:

$$\text{Investment cost} = \frac{CF_1}{(1 + IRR)^1} + \frac{CF_2}{(1 + IRR)^2} + \cdots + \frac{CF_n}{(1 + IRR)^n}$$

$$\$1,000,000 = \frac{\$71,488}{(1 + .0753)^1} + \frac{\$70,870}{(1 + .0753)^2} + \frac{\$70,298}{(1 + .0753)^3}$$

$$+ \frac{\$69,761}{(1 + .0753)^4} + \frac{\$69,247}{(1 + .0753)^5} + \frac{\$69,418}{(1 + .0753)^6}$$

$$+ \frac{\$69,999}{(1 + .0753)^7} + \frac{\$1,044,244}{(1 + .0753)^7}$$

The 7.53 percent rate is the only rate that results in a present value of $1 million; this, by definition, is the IRR on total capital invested.

It is important that the unleveraged IRR is substantially *below* the leveraged (equity) IRR. That is, the effect of using leverage here is to raise the after-tax IRR from 7.5 to 22.1 percent; there is favorable (positive) leverage on an after-tax discounted basis. Assuming that the investor actually receives the equity cash flows projected, a 22.1 percent equity IRR is equivalent to putting money in a savings and loan association or bank, earning a 44.2 percent interest rate compounded annually, and then paying the federal government taxes equal to 50 percent of this return. Stated differently, it is equivalent to putting money in a tax-free municipal bond that pays a 22.1 percent annual interest rate.

FINANCIAL RATIO ANALYSIS

In section 8 of the DCF analysis, data for thirteen financial ratios are calculated. These are simple accounting ratios, calculated annually, with no consideration given to the time value of money. The ratios are shown in Exhibit 7-11.

Using financial ratios is beneficial for three primary purposes. First, they tell more about the nature of the *profitability* of the project—that is, how much of the IRR (relatively speaking) is from cash flow from operations, from tax savings, from equity buildup, and from appreciation—and the trends in profitability over time.[18] Second, they supply additional information about the *riskiness* of the project and trends in the future; included are ratios that help the investor analyze his or her leverage position each year and indicate when refinancing may be advantageous. Third, financial ratios are used to test the *underlying assumptions* used in the analysis, and to suggest when the investor has used assumptions that are inconsistent with conditions in the marketplace.

Profitability Ratios

NOI to Total Property Cost. The ratio of NOI to total property cost is the same as the ROI profitability measure described in Chapter 6, but it is calculated each year. As discussed earlier, whenever this ratio is less than the ROE (and therefore greater than the mortgage constant, K), a *favorable leverage* situation from operations exists, and vice versa.

---

[18]The investor should not attempt to use ratios as substitutes for the IRR measure. A discussion of this subject is provided by Kenneth M. Lusht, "Measuring Rates of Return: Two Rules of Thumb v. Internal Rate," *The Appraisal Journal*, April 1978, pp. 245–256. Also see Ronald E. Gettel, *Real Estate Guidelines and Rules of Thumb* (New York: McGraw-Hill, 1976).

EXHIBIT 7-11. Aspen Wood Apartments: Computer Analysis—Section 8

8. FINANCIAL RATIO ANALYSIS

Profitability Ratios

Year	(A) NOI/Total Property Cost	(B) Cash Flow Before Tax/ Initial Equity	(C) Cash Flow After Tax/ Initial Equity	(D) Cash Flow After Tax + Equity Buildup/ Initial Equity	(E) Cash Flow After Tax + Equity Buildup + Appreciation/ Initial Equity
1	.092	.122	.181	.233	.404
2	.094	.131	.176	.231	.408
3	.095	.140	.170	.230	.412
4	.097	.149	.165	.229	.417
5	.098	.157	.159	.229	.422
6	.099	.164	.158	.232	.431
7	.100	.171	.158	.239	.443

Risk Ratios

Year	(F) Debt Coverage Ratio	(G) Break-even Point	(H) Loan Balance (End of Year) as a Percentage of — Original Cost	(H) Loan Balance (End of Year) as a Percentage of — Property Value
1	1.301	.823	.816	.792
2	1.325	.818	.806	.760
3	1.348	.814	.796	.728
4	1.369	.811	.785	.697
5	1.389	.809	.772	.666
6	1.407	.809	.759	.636
7	1.424	.808	.745	.606

Assumption Base Ratios

Year	(I) NOI to Property Value	(J) Gross Rent Multiplier	(K) Operating Expenses as a Percent of — Gross Possible Income	(K) Operating Expenses as a Percent of — Gross Effective Income
1	.089	6.168	.400	.421
2	.088	6.109	.412	.433
3	.087	6.050	.423	.446
4	.086	5.992	.436	.459
5	.085	5.935	.448	.472
6	.083	5.877	.461	.485
7	.082	5.821	.474	.499

Year 1   91,839/1,000,000 = .092

Year 4   96,615/1,000,000 = .097

Year 7   100,481/1,000,000 = .100

The analysis here shows the ROI rising from 9.2 to 10 percent in year 7—the basic productivity of the property is rising each year relative to the total capital investment. Because the mortgage constant is 8.55 percent, a favorable leverage situation exists in each year; consequently, the ROE is greater than the ROI each year, as the following calculations show.

Cash Flow Before Tax to Initial Equity. The ratio of cash flow before tax to initial equity is identical to the ROE profitability measure used in Chapter 6, but it too is calculated each year. The cash flow increases each year and rises to 17.1 percent in year 7, indicating a very profitable situation for the equity investor; the initial level and trend are favorable.

Year 1   21,265/175,000 = .122

Year 4   26,041/175,000 = .149

Year 7   29,908/175,000 = .171

Cash Flow After Tax to Initial Equity. This profitability ratio takes the cash flow before tax, adds the amount of tax saving (or deducts the amount of taxes paid), and then compares the result to the initial equity invested. Alternately, it is the amount of *cash flow after tax* divided by the *initial equity investment*. It can be referred to as the *ROE after tax.*

Year 1   31,699/175,000 = .181

Year 4   28,839/175,000 = .165

Year 7   27,661/175,000 = .158

The analysis shows that cash flow *after tax* is decreasing each year because the declining tax shelter outweighs the effects of increasing cash flow from operations. Thus, whereas cash flow before tax *increases* from 12.2 percent to 17.1 percent in year 7, cash flow after tax *decreases* from 18.1 percent to 15.8 percent. After year 5 the investor must pay taxes (instead of receiving a tax saving), and the after-tax return falls below the before-tax return. Whenever taxable income is positive, the cash flow after tax will be less than cash flow before tax, and vice versa.

This ratio helps the investor understand the net impact of tax shelter items on the after-tax return, and can be used to indicate when a sale or refinancing of the property should be considered in order to achieve tax shelter objectives. For example, some equity investors would consider refinancing or selling after year 5, when taxable income becomes positive and tax liabilities result.

Cash Flow After Tax Plus Equity Buildup to Initial Equity. This ratio adds to the preceding one the impact of equity buildup (loan amortization). While the cash flow after tax is decreasing each year, the equity buildup is increasing because a larger part of each amortization payment represents amortization of principal.

Year 1	$(31,699 + 9,004)/175,000 = .233$
Year 4	$(28,839 + 11,268)/175,000 = .229$
Year 7	$(27,661 + 14,102)/175,000 = .239$

The net effect is that profitability, measured this way, decreases for four years and then levels off and starts increasing. Obviously, the effects of declining tax shelter are greater than the effect of increasing equity buildup in the early years. Then the situation is reversed. For all practical purposes, we might say that profitability remains fairly stable at 23 percent during the holding period, using this measure of return.

It is important to recognize that although the equity buildup adds to the investor's return, it is an unrealized gain until the time of sale or refinancing; consequently, the time value of money is ignored in its measurement.[19] The next ratio can be criticized for the same reason. Nevertheless, the ratio just presented can help us understand the *relative* impact of tax shelter and equity buildup on the investor's rate of return.

Cash Flow After Tax Plus Equity Buildup Plus Appreciation to Initial Equity. This ratio adds to the preceding one the impact of property value appreciation (or depreciation) that occurs each year. Property value appreciation is calculated as the difference between the property value at the end of the year and the value at the beginning of the year, as shown in column N of Exhibit 7-6.

Year 1	$[31,699 + 9,004 + (1,030,000 - 1,000,000)]/175,000 = .404$
Year 4	$[28,839 + 11,268 + (1,125,509 - 1,092,727)]/175,000 = .417$
Year 7	$[27,661 + 14,102 + (1,229,874 - 1,194,052)]/175,000 = .443$

Measured in this fashion, the total return rises from 40.4 to 44.3 percent in year 7, as contrasted with a 23 percent return before this factor is included. Property value increases add 17 to 20 percent to the investor's rate of return and further offset the effect of declining tax shelters.

It should be noted that this return measure makes no deductions for

---

[19]This point raises an interesting question. If "equity buildup" is not realized until the time of sale or refinancing, neither is the return of the *original* equity, on which these ratios are based. Thus, in making these ratio calculations, we presume that the original equity investment *will* in fact be realized. If it is not, the ratios do not fully represent a return on the original equity investment, and they may be misleading.

taxes and expenses resulting from the sale of the property. If, however, these expenses were deducted and then the time value of money discount were applied, an IRR on equity of 22 percent would result. Thus, the 40 to 44 percent *accounting rate of return* over seven years falls to a 22 percent *true yield*.

Risk Ratios

Debt Coverage Ratio. Analysis of the debt coverage ratio indicates an acceptable initial DCR, as well as decreasing risk and increasing project liquidity over the seven-year holding period. Each year, as net income increases, debt service remains constant.

$$\text{Year 1} \qquad 91,839/70,574 = 1.301$$
$$\text{Year 4} \qquad 96,615/70,574 = 1.369$$
$$\text{Year 7} \qquad 100,472/70,574 = 1.424$$

Break-even Point. Like the debt coverage ratio, the break-even point is used to analyze the risk and liquidity profile of a project. Risk is said to decrease as liquidity increases. Over each year of the seven-year projection period, a lower occupancy level is necessary to pay operating expenses and service the debt. In the example, both the initial level and the trend of the break-even point are favorable.

$$\text{Year 1} \qquad (66,792 + 70,574)/166,980 = .823$$
$$\text{Year 4} \qquad (81,823 + 70,574)/187,830 = .811$$
$$\text{Year 7} \qquad (100,237 + 70,574)/211,283 = .808$$

Loan Balance as a Percentage of Original Cost and Property Value. These two leverage ratios allow for a measurement of the impact of a declining loan balance relative to the original cost and property value.

Remaining Principal/Original Cost	Remaining Principal/Property Value
Year 1 815,996/1,000,000 = .816	Year 1 815,996/1,030,000 = .792
Year 4 784,568/1,000,000 = .785	Year 4 784,568/1,125,509 = .697
Year 7 745,237/1,000,000 = .745	Year 7 745,237/1,229,874 = .606

On a cost basis, the leverage ratio declines to about 75 percent in year 7; on a value basis, it declines to about 61 percent. To the extent that the loan is a decreasing percentage of either cost or value, the riskiness of the investment tends to decrease over time. In addition, the potential benefits of refinancing after the property has been held for a number of years are readily apparent from the ratios.

Assumption Base Ratios

NOI to Property Value. The critical ratio of NOI to property value is used to test the underlying assumptions used in the analysis. It is better known to students of appraisal as the *overall capitalization rate.* Specifically, this ratio tests our assumption of increasing property value over time. It is measured by dividing the NOI (column E) by the property value (column N) each year (from Exhibit 7-6).

Year 1	91,839/1,030,000 = .089
Year 4	96,615/1,125,509 = .086
Year 7	100,482/1,229,874 = .082

The analysis shows the capitalization rate falling from 8.9 percent to 8.2 percent in year 7. This might be a realistic assumption in a period of rising inflation rates (as explained in Chapter 14), but it is highly suspect in a period of stable or falling inflation rates, when capitalization rates tend to rise. Moreover, as a property gets older and uncertainties increase, this ratio tends to increase, reflecting the increasing risk associated with most older properties. In this example, the property value is probably rising too fast relative to net income. If this is true, the IRR on equity and total capital and any other return measure that includes capital appreciation have been overestimated. Additional analysis should be undertaken with more conservative property value assumptions, or the investor might want to reassess any assumptions affecting NOI increases per year, in order to bring this ratio to a higher (perhaps more realistic) level at the end of the holding period.

The capitalization rate data should be compared to data from comparable property sales. This information can be obtained from local appraisers. Such comparisons will enable the investor to determine whether the assumptions used in the analysis are realistic or whether adjustments should be made to the assumption base and the analysis redone. Still, the output information is only as good as the input assumptions.[20]

Gross Rent Multiplier. Like the expense ratios, the primary purpose of the gross rent multiplier is to test the underlying assumptions of the analysis. The ratio is calculated by dividing the property value at the end of each year by the gross possible income from the corresponding year.

Year 1	1,030,000/166,980 = 6.168

[20] This underlying theme is developed by Christopher A. Manning in the context of analyzing a syndication offering, "Correct 'Bottom Line' Analyses of Syndication Offerings", *Real Estate Review,* Summer 1986, pp. 42–50; also by Manning, "The Economics of Real Estate Decisions," *Harvard Business Review,* November–December 1986, pp. 12–23.

Year 4   1,125,509/187,830 = 5.992

Year 7   1,229,874/211,283 = 5.821

Generally, in a stable economic climate this ratio should decline over time as a structure gets older and becomes more expensive to maintain. An investor should be willing to pay more to acquire a dollar of rent from a new structure than from an older structure, other factors remaining the same. Because most experienced income property appraisers keep extensive data on gross rent multipliers, comparisons can be made with other properties to determine whether the forecasts are realistic. If not, the analysis should be redone.

As previously noted, the assumption of property value increases has a very substantial impact on the equity investor's IRR. In fact, comparative sales data from 1974 (the date of the original Aspen Wood analysis shown in the example) suggests that a 5.5 to 5.8, rather than a 6.1 gross rent multiplier in year 1 might have been more appropriate for the most likely data set. The investor should have rerun the analysis assuming a more conservative (lower) increase in property value, more rapid rent increases over time, or a combination thereof.

Operating Expense Ratios. Two operating expense ratios are calculated, one based on gross possible income, the other on gross effective income. These ratios are used primarily as comparative tools to test the underlying assumptions. As a project ages, the expense ratio usually increases, and the ratio that results should be consistent with ratios experienced by operators of comparable properties and with the statistics published by property owners' associations throughout the nation.

Operating Expenses/ Gross Possible Income	Operating Expenses/ Gross Effective Income
Year 1 66,792/166,980 = .400	Year 1 66,792/158,631 = .421
Year 4 81,823/187,830 = .436	Year 4 81,823/178,438 = .459
Year 7 100,237/211,283 = .474	Year 7 100,237/200,719 = .499

The many data sources that may be useful to investors in analyzing specific property types are discussed in Part 6.

SUMMARY

The concepts and mathematics of discounted-cash-flow and financial ratio analysis were developed in this chapter, beginning with a review of the time value of money concepts and an explanation of how present-value and internal-rate-of-return models are logical extensions of time value of money and compound-interest formulas. Whereas the PV and IRR models usually result in the same accept or reject investment decision, they can rank projects differently because they make differing assumptions about reinvestment rates. Various analysts have developed formulations, such as the modified internal rate of return (MIRR) and the financial management rate of return (FMRR), to overcome problems with the IRR, but there is still disagreement regarding the proper formula and approach to be used in evaluating proposed investments.

The second section of the chapter presented a full-scale after-tax cash flow model using the DCF methods developed in the first section. With the Aspen Wood property as an example, a seven-year projection was developed to include inflation estimates of rents, expenses, and property value. The price structure and wraparound mortgage package negotiated by the sellers in Chapter 6 were used. Various types of annual financial ratios were then calculated, explained, and used for further analysis of the project's profitability and riskiness. In addition, and perhaps most important, the ratios were used to analyze the underlying assumptions and economic relationships on which all the output data and return–risk measures are based.

Chapter 8 addresses the subjects of risk analysis and risk management and presents a sophisticated risk analysis model based on the DCF concepts developed here.

8

RISK ANALYSIS AND RISK MANAGEMENT: SINGLE PROJECTS

Chapter 7 showed how a discounted-cash-flow model provides valuable information not given by the basic financial feasibility model. It explicitly considers (1) changes in rents, expenses, and property value over time; (2) equity buildup through loan amortization; (3) income taxation; (4) transaction costs; (5) expected holding period; and (6) the time value of money. All these variables affect the rate of return and risk parameters of a proposed investment.

However, an important element that is not adequately measured by the DCF model is risk: the probability that the expected net operating income and cash flows will not be received. The following sections present concepts and techniques that attempt to harness the risk dimension and provide the investor with a better understanding of the possible consequences of risk and uncertainty. At the end of the chapter we show how the concepts and techniques developed here and in Chapter 7 are applied to the Aspen Wood case. Then in Chapter 18 we expand the risk analysis and risk management concepts to a portfolio framework.

RISK ANALYSIS

Nature and Definition of Risk

Risk exists in real estate because investors are unable to make perfect forecasts.[1] If they could, they would never make an investment that would yield less than the required rate of return, and investors could plan with precision to meet all financial obligations. Real estate investors and entre-

[1]G. David Quirin, *The Capital Expenditure Decision* (Homewood, Ill.: Richard D. Irwin, 1967), p. 199.

preneurs would cease to play their vital role as bearers of risks associated with economic, social, and political change.

Financial ratios, such as the debt coverage ratio and the break-even point, provide some information about the risk profile of a project. However, they do not provide information about the probable deviations from the *most likely* values used in the analysis. A *complete* risk analysis provides information about (1) the magnitude of possible deviations in cash flows that can occur under varying market and economic conditions, and (2) the probability associated with each of these projections.[2] None of the ratios discussed in Chapters 6 and 7 provides this information adequately.

Risk versus Uncertainty. Many economists distinguish between risk and uncertainty. One basis for this distinction is whether or not the probability distribution of outcomes (for rents, expenses, selling price, etc.) is known or can be estimated.[3] If the distribution is known or can be estimated, *risk* exists; if it is not known or cannot be estimated, *uncertainty* prevails. Such a distinction, however, has little meaning in most business situations. Most real estate decision makers have *some* feeling about the probability of the occurrence of future events, ranging from a high degree of confidence to a vague and ill-defined feeling. They neither are *completely ignorant* nor feel that they *completely know* the probabilities of future events.[4] In real-world decision making, the terms *uncertainty* and *risk* are used interchangeably. Both describe situations in which real estate analysts can assess the probabilities (objectively or subjectively) of future events.

Risk can be defined in a variety of ways. Here are five popular definitions.

1. The probability of loss.
2. The probability of not receiving what is expected.
3. The difference (or potential variance) between expectations and realizations.
4. The variance of returns relative to the expected or most likely return.
5. The chance or probability that the investor will not receive the expected or required rate of return on the investment.

[2] This statement refers only to the analysis of *project* risk as addressed in this chapter; it does not treat risk from a portfolio perspective. The relation between the two is explained by Steven D. Kapplin, "Financial Theory and the Valuation of Real Estate under Conditions of Risk," *The Real Estate Appraiser*, September–October 1976, pp. 28–37. Also see Chapter 17 of this volume.

[3] Famous for making this distinction are F. H. Knight, *Risk, Uncertainty and Profit* (Boston: Houghton Mifflin, 1923), and J. A. Schumpeter, *The Theory of Economic Development* (Cambridge, Mass.: Harvard Univ. Press, 1934).

[4] C. Jackson Grayson, Jr., "The Use of Statistical Techniques in Capital Budgeting," in Alexander A. Robichek, ed., *Financial Research and Management Decisions*. (New York: Wiley, 1967), p. 91. For an illustration of the application see K. B. Cady, C. S. Pettygrove, and D. K. Westby, "Quantifying Uncertainty in Investment Analysis," *Real Estate Review*, Spring 1986, pp. 85–89.

The last two probably make up the best operational definition. For example, an investor requiring an IRR of 10 percent is analyzing two apartment projects, both of which have an expected IRR of 20 percent. Because of the possibility of changes in the economy or competition in the future, project B has only a 5 percent chance of returning less than the required 10 percent IRR, whereas project A has a 30 percent chance. Clearly, if the investor is concerned with *downside* risk, project A is riskier than project B because there is a higher probability of not achieving the required 10 percent IRR. A probability distribution can be used to describe this hypothetical situation (see Exhibit 8-1). The distribution simply shows the possible IRRs (variance of IRRs) that could occur in the future. These distributions can be generated through computer simulation, and they may be used to estimate the probabilities associated with certain outcomes, as will be shown later.

Risk and Return—How Are They Related? As can be seen by the preceding discussion, risk can be defined as the variance of expected return. If an investment is risk-free, it has no variance; that is, the return is certain. Inasmuch as an investor can purchase an investment *without* risk, it is logical to assume that an investor who purchases a risky investment expects a return that is greater than the return on the risk-free investment.

The excess return over the risk-free rate is often referred to as a risk premium. The riskier the investment, the greater the risk premium the investor will demand to compensate for the added risk. In other words, the riskier the investment, the greater will be the investor's expected return and the greater will be the variance of that expected return relative to the risk-free investment. It should be noted, however, that a high rate of return on any particular investment does not necessarily mean that the investment was also very risky, nor does a low rate of return mean that the investment was virtually risk-free.

EXHIBIT 8-1. Distributions of Probable Rates of Return for Two Projects

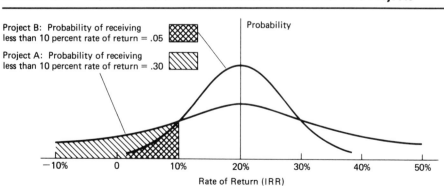

Project B: Probability of receiving less than 10 percent rate of return = .05

Project A: Probability of receiving less than 10 percent rate of return = .30

Probability

Rate of Return (IRR)

Types of Risk

Risk can be classified in several ways. One useful scheme is shown in Exhibit 8-2. The first distinction is between business and financial risk.

Business Risk. Business risk is the underlying asset risk: the probability that the expected level and pattern of productivity returns will not be received, or the uncertainty of the prediction of productivity. In other words, business risk is the *probability that the required rate of return on total capital* (IRR_{TC}) *will not be realized*. Business risk is related to expected changes over time in five variables: capital expenditures, gross possible income, vacancy and credit losses, operating expenses, and property value. (It ignores financing variables.) The greater the variance of the five variables, the greater the business risk. Moreover, if an after-tax cash flow model is used, income and capital gain tax variables affecting the property (excluding all financing impacts) will be among the business risk considerations.

Business risk can be further divided into static and dynamic (unsystematic and systematic) categories. *Static risk,* or its other term unsystematic risk, is related to physical cause and effect, occurs at random, and is beyond the control of the investor.[5] Static risk almost always results in a loss. Examples include damage to property caused by fire, storm, or flood,

---

[5]James A. Graaskamp, "An Approach to Real Estate Finance Education by Analogy to Risk Management Principles," *Real Estate Issues,* Summer 1977, p. 55.

EXHIBIT 8-2. Classification of Risk

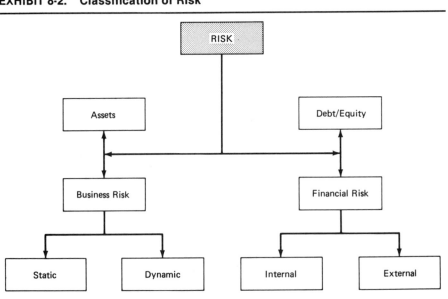

or losses caused by personal injury, theft, or "malicious mischief." Most of these risks are insurable because they are predictable over the long run. Consequently, investors can shift these risks by entering into an insurance contract with a property and casualty insurer. Static risk can be eliminated not only through insurance, but also through diversification of investments. The subject of diversification is discussed in greater depth in Chapter 18. Because static or unsystematic risk can be eliminated, it is not considered among the primary risks with which the investor should be concerned.

Dynamic risk, or systematic risk, can, on the other hand, produce either profit or loss. Dynamic risk is related to changes in general business conditions and the physical condition of the property. It is related to market demand and supply conditions, the age of the property, the quality of property and venture management, changes in the economic base and the environment, tax reforms, and so on. Dynamic risk is external; it is not under the direct control of the investor. Changes in these factors could alter the purchase price, the net operating income, the value of the property, related tax benefits, and, thus, the IRR_{TC}.[6] Systematic or dynamic risk cannot be eliminated through insurance or diversification. Consequently, investors expect compensation for this type of risk. In keeping with the earlier discussion of return and risk, the investor expects a risk premium to compensate for dynamic or systematic risk.

Financial Risk. Financial risk refers to the risks created by debt financing. Financial risk is additional to the underlying business risks and increases whenever the amount of debt service or related charges increase. Otherwise stated, financial risk is the *probability of not receiving the expected or required rate of return on equity* (IRR_E) *as a result of the investor's inability to meet fixed financial obligations created by debt financing.* The incurrence of debt reduces the expected net cash flows of the investment, but does not alter the variance of these cash flows (unless a variable rate debt financing source is used). However, if leverage is favorable, debt financing will increase the expected IRR_E and the variance of the IRR_E. Like dynamic or systematic risk, financial risk causes investors to demand additional premiums to compensate for the risk.

Since financial risk is essentially a cash liquidity or solvency problem that can be created by either internal or external factors, the investor must consider two types of financial risk. *Internal financial risk* relates to the ability of the project to generate enough cash to pay the monthly or yearly

---

[6]A somewhat different approach to risk classification is taken by other authors. See, for example, Herman Kelting, *Real Estate Investments* (Columbus, Ohio: Grid Publishing, 1980), pp. 71–75. Our classification scheme closely follows those that are commonly presented in business and corporate finance textbooks. To prevent confusion between our terminology and that used elsewhere, the authors have included common finance terms with the terminology used here.

debt service. For example, if the debt coverage ratio is low because of a high leverage ratio or mortgage constant, the project has a high internal financial risk. If this ratio *increases*, internal financial risk decreases. The second type of financial risk, *external financial risk*, is related to the investor's ability to obtain cash in the money markets or from other external sources. Thus, if an investor can readily finance a cash need of a property using funds from external sources, such as bank loans or additional equity cash investments, the project is said to have a low external financial risk. If funds from external sources become more difficult to obtain, external financial risk increases.

Relation Between IRR and Business and Financial Risk. The relation between financial risk and the IRR on equity (IRR$_E$) is not quite as simple as that between business risk and the IRR on total capital (IRR$_{TC}$). In reality, it cannot be said that financial risk is the probability of not receiving the expected IRR$_E$, because the IRR$_E$ depends both on basic productivity factors (IRR$_{TC}$) *and* on financial leverage. The IRR$_E$ is directly related to both business and financial risk; an increase in both types of risk can be directly linked to fluctuations (variance) in the IRR$_E$. Therefore, fluctuations in the IRR$_E$ can be considered a measure of *total* project risk, whereas fluctuations in the IRR$_{TC}$ are a measure of business risk only, unless there is no financial leverage.

One final, but important, relation between business and financial risk should be noted. Business risk should be the prime determinant of the amount of debt financing employed. The degree of business risk that is inherent in a project and the degree of financial risk incurred by the investor in financing the project should be inversely related. For example, if an investment is made in a neighborhood shopping center that has very high business risks (high vacancy rates, unstable neighborhood), the investor should use a relatively low degree of debt financing so that the total debt service will remain relatively low. Following this rule reduces the probability of insolvency in any given year and, thus, reduces financial risk. In situations in which there is less business risk, the investor might prudently justify higher ratios of leverage financing.

This normative relation between business and financial risk was illustrated in Chapter 6 during the discussion of the basic financial feasibility model. If the investor compensated for higher business risk (first-year NOI deviations) by raising the desired debt coverage ratio (DCR), the amount of debt service and the loan amount declined. In contrast, when using a DCF model the degree of total project risk was measured by simulating the possible variations in cash flows and IRR$_E$ under different states of nature and different capital (financial) structures. After analyzing the results, the investor determines the particular capital structure that best fits our return and risk preferences. Such a procedure for determining an optimal balance between business and financial risks is presented in Chapter 9.

Levels of Risk Analysis

There are five levels of risk analysis that can be performed by the investor. The investor should begin by applying simple one-year cash flow techniques and then apply more rigorous forms of evaluation as the investment analysis proceeds.

First Level: The Basic Financial Feasibility Model. Using this one-year cash flow model, the investor analyzes risk by analyzing the DCR and the favorable–unfavorable leverage situation. A low DCR indicates high risk unless NOI is known to be very stable. (This may be the case for an investment in property under a net lease to a AAA credit tenant.) The presence of unfavorable leverage is also an indication of high financial risk. No attempt is made to analyze the *probability* of different rate-of-return outcomes at this stage. At best, these are crude measures of total project risk.

Second Level: DCF Most Likely Outcome. At this stage annual data on the DCRs and break-even points are generated. By viewing these ratios over time, the investor can further analyze the level of risk, as well as how the trends in these ratios over time affect the level of risk. In addition, by comparing IRR_{TC} and IRR_E, the investor can evaluate the long-run, after-tax situation. If $IRR_E > IRR_{TC}$, a long-run, favorable-leverage situation is achieved. It can then be determined whether the IRR_E has increased sufficiently to compensate for the financial risk incurred.

Third Level: IRR Partitioning and Risk Absorption Analysis. Using DCF data, Valachi[7] and Zerbst[8] have presented methods for analyzing risk by partitioning the IRR into various components using present-value techniques. Three basic components of return are partitioned: annual cash flows, tax shelter, and cash proceeds of sale. The rationale for this type of analysis is that investors place different risk weights on different sources of return. The partitioned IRR can be used to determine whether the sources of expected returns from a particular property are consistent with their investment objectives. The more refined the categories (sources) of investor benefits, the more the partitioned IRR can add insight into the riskiness of an investment.

Exhibit 8-3 presents the results of a component analysis of the IRR. The IRR on equity was calculated to be 18.5 percent. The results of simple partitioning, having discounted each of the dollar amounts of return, indicate that total cash proceeds of sale represent 69.9 percent of the total 18.5 percent IRR (column 4). Of that 69.9 percent, *recapture of original equity*

---

[7]Donald J. Valachi, "The Three Faces of IRR," *Real Estate Review*, Fall 1978, pp. 74–78.

[8]Robert H. Zerbst, "Evaluating Risks by Partitioning the Internal Rate of Return," *Real Estate Review*, Winter 1980, pp. 80–84.

EXHIBIT 8-3. Component Analysis of the Internal Rate of Return

(1) Components of Total Return	(2) Present Value of Components	(3) Component as Percentage of Total	(4) Results of Simple Partitioning
Year 1 level of cash flow	$ 11,165	12.5%	
Growth in cash flow	9,075	6.7	
Total cash flow			19.2%
Tax savings	11,505	10.9	10.9
Recapture of original equity	53,848	51.0	
Loan amortization	5,809	5.5	
Expected net appreciation	14,265	13.4	
Total cash proceeds	$ 73,922		69.9
Total return	$105,666	100.0%	100.0%

Source: Robert H. Zerbst, "Evaluating Risks by Partitioning the Internal Rate of Return," *Real Estate Review,* Winter 1980, p. 83.

accounts for 51 percent, equity buildup through *loan amortization* for 5.5 percent, and *expected net appreciation* for 13.4 percent of the total return. The concentration of returns in the *total cash proceeds* from sale emphasizes the dependence of investment returns on the project's selling price and clarifies the relative sources of risk associated with the total IRR return.

Another DCF measure of risk is called the *risk absorption (RA) ratio.* This ratio, introduced by Wofford and Gitman, measures the amount of risk a project can absorb while still remaining acceptable to the investor.[9] The calculation of the RA ratio is illustrated in Exhibit 8-4. The ratio is based on the concept of annualized net present value (ANPV). The ANPV determines the maximum amount by which the cash flow each year could be reduced without reducing net present value below zero, that is, to a level that makes the investment unacceptable. The RA ratio is created by dividing the annualized net present value of equity cash flows by the equity investment required to initiate the proposal. Like the profitability index, the RA ratio is a relative measure used to compare projects of different sizes. *The RA ratio measures risk-absorbing ability per dollar of investment.* If all other risk and return measures are equal, the investment with the greatest risk-absorbing capacity will be preferred.

[9]Larry E. Wofford and Lawrence J. Gitman, "Measuring a Project's Ability to Survive Adversity," *Real Estate Review,* Spring 1978, pp. 91–94. For a nonmathematical approach to assessing risk, read Stephen E. Roulac and Robert C. Cirese, "A Risk Analysis Matrix to Improve Investment Decisions," *Real Estate Review,* Summer 1986, pp. 36–41.

EXHIBIT 8-4.   Calculation of the Risk Absorption Ratio

Investment A has the following equity cash flows:

Year	Cash Flow	Present Value of Cash Flow at 15 Percent
0	($25,000)	($25,000)
1	10,000	8,700
2	9,500	7,182
3	9,100	5,988
4	8,700	4,976
5	12,000	5,964
	Net present value	$ 7,810

The investor has a required IRR of 15 percent. The net present value of $7,810 can be annualized by dividing this amount by the factor for the present value of a five-year annuity discounted at 15 percent (i.e., by 3.352). The resulting annualized net present value is $2,230 ($7,810 ÷ 3.352 = $2,330). This means that if the investor experienced a reduction in annual cash inflows of $2,330, the investment would still be acceptable, since its net present value would then be zero. Any reduction in annual flows below $2,330 would leave the net present value positive. The risk absorption (RA) ratio is defined as follows:

$$\text{RA ratio} = \frac{\text{annualized net present value}}{\text{initial equity investment}}$$

$$= \frac{\$2,330}{\$25,000} = .093$$

The RA ratio thus is a *relative* measure of risk-absorbing capacity. The higher the RA ratio, the greater the risk-absorbing capacity of the investment. RA ratios for competing projects can also be computed and ranked from high to low.

Source: Larry E. Wofford and Lawrence J. Gitman, "Measuring a Project's Ability to Survive Adversity," *Real Estate Review*, Spring 1978, p. 93.

Fourth Level: Sensitivity Analysis. Sensitivity analysis is a technique that tests the impact of uncertainties on the investment decision. It is performed by varying the values of the input variables in the basic financial feasibility and DCF models to show how they affect the project value, the ROE, the IRR, the DCR, or other relevant output data.

If, through sensitivity analysis, it is discovered that certain variables have values that are uncertain but do not have a significant impact on rates of return, debt coverage ratios, or other outcomes, the investor can stop worrying about those uncertainties. There is no reason to worry about variables that "don't count." Equity investors are often surprised to discover which uncertain variables are important and which are not, because it is difficult to predict the results of the interaction among many complex economic and market interrelationships.

Exhibit 8-5 illustrates the final results of a sensitivity analysis on a 287-unit apartment property using computer model RE001. Through the analysis it was discovered that the four most important determinants of the investor's IRR on equity and coverage ratio over a ten-year period analyzed were (1) the growth rate of gross possible income, (2) the growth rate of operating costs, (3) the expected occupancy level, and (4) increases in property value. Exhibit 8-5 shows the effect of changes in these four variables on (1) IRR on equity investment, (2) IRR on total capital investment, (3) net operating income, (4) the break-even point, and (5) the debt coverage ratio.

The investor should conclude a sensitivity analysis with a set of computer runs representing optimistic, most likely, and pessimistic assumptions, as shown in Exhibit 8-5. This provides data that represent the possible range of results that can reasonably be expected if the inputs have been measured accurately. Clearly, the most crucial aspect of the whole process is generating accurate input information through market research.

In the example presented, the IRR on equity was acceptable to the investor. The most probable IRR was in the range of 21.24 to 22.63 percent, depending on the holding period of the investment. The coverage ratio averaged 1.4 to 1.6, considerably above the investor's desired 1.3 minimum. Only in the pessimistic case for seven- and ten-year holding periods does the coverage ratio drop below 1.0, where project revenues are insufficient to meet all expenses, and cash flow before tax is negative. The IRR on equity drops to the 6 to 7 percent range. In the optimistic case, the IRR on equity increases to 31.64 percent for the three-year holding period and falls to 30.1 percent for the ten-year holding period, with a coverage ratio above 1.6 in all cases. If the financial structure is perceived to be too conservative, the investor can increase the degree of leverage and raise the IRR on equity, as long as the coverage ratio and break-even points remain within acceptable limits.

Sensitivity analysis is a widely recognized form of *deterministic risk modeling*. A second deterministic risk-modeling approach that has gained acceptance in corporate risk analysis and bond risk analysis is based on a measure of elasticity between risk variables and such profitability measures as IRR_E. In contrast to sensitivity analysis, this approach does not depend on assumed changes in the risk (input) variables, but instead measures risk in the form of a single-value *elasticity coefficient*. Based on a property's operating and financial leverage, this analysis determines the elasticity of the equity return to changes in the independent variables. Investment risk is defined as the elasticity of the equity return with respect to changes in the cash flow (independent) variables.[10]

[10]Larry J. Johnson, James L. Kuhle, and Carl H. Walther, "An Elasticity Approach to Equity Risk Evaluation," *The Journal of Real Estate Research*, Fall 1987, pp. 41–49.

EXHIBIT 8-5.   Summary Table of Sensitivity Analysis Calculations, 287-Unit Apartment Complex

	I Optimistic	II Most Likely	III Pessimistic
A. INPUT VARIABLE ASSUMPTIONS			
1. Growth rate of gross possible income (%)	5	3	1
2. Growth rate of operating costs (%)	3	4.5	6
3. Growth rate of property value (%)	5.5	3	0
4. Expected occupancy level (%)	96	93	87
B. IRR ON EQUITY INVESTMENT (IRR$_E$)			
1. Year 3 (%)	31.64	21.24	5.75
2. Year 7 (%)	31.24	22.63	7.67
3. Year 10 (%)	30.10	22.05	6.94
C. IRR ON TOTAL CAPITAL INVESTMENT (IRR$_{TC}$)			
1. Year 3 (%)	11.46	9.07	6.01
2. Year 7 (%)	11.69	8.96	5.54
3. Year 10 (%)	11.89	8.95	5.23
D. NET OPERATING INCOME			
1. Year 3	$426,577	$369,336	$293,389
2. Year 7	$544,742	$395,583	$236,800
3. Year 10	$651,901	$414,931	$181,332
E. BREAK-EVEN POINT			
1. Year 3	.728	.768	.812
2. Year 7	.639	.754	.893
3. Year 10	.581	.747	.967
F. DEBT COVERAGE RATIO			
1. Year 3	1.686	1.459	1.159
2. Year 7	2.152	1.563	.936
3. Year 10	2.576	1.640	.717

Fifth Level: Monte Carlo Risk Simulation.[11] Sensitivity analysis is not a complete form of risk analysis. Although it can provide the investor with ranges of possible returns, or elasticities, it does not indicate the probability that the different returns will actually occur. A risk analysis simulation model attempts to overcome this problem. Such a model (pictured in Exhibit 8-6) measures the probability that various rates of return and liquidity positions will be achieved, if the probability distributions for uncertain variables can be measured.

The first step in using the risk simulation model is to designate the *control variables* (single-value estimates) and the *state variables* (probability distribution estimates). In the exhibit there are six control variables: (1) the square-foot dimensions of the property, (2) the equity investment ratio, (3) the depreciation method and useful life of improvements, (4) the existing tax structure, (5) the holding period of the investment, and (6) the loan amount.

The remaining state variables are assigned probability distributions by the analyst. Several methods for estimating these probability distributions have been developed and are used extensively in fields other than real estate. Some of these methods require that the real estate forecaster understand probability concepts, whereas some do not. Some methods allow the forecaster to estimate his or her own probability distributions, and other employ interview techniques. Space does not permit us to discuss these methods in depth, but it is important to recognize that past experiences with probability estimation are encouraging and reinforce the credibility of its use as a technique for quantifying risk. Experience has shown that decision makers and experts can realistically estimate probability distribu-

[11]See Stephen A. Pyhrr, "A Computer Simulation Model to Measure the Risk in Real Estate Investment," *American Real Estate and Urban Economics Association Journal,* June 1973, pp. 48–78; reprinted in *The Real Estate Appraiser,* May–June 1973, pp. 13–31. See also Richard U. Ratcliff and Bernard Schwab, "Contemporary Decision Theory and Real Estate Investment," *The Appraisal Journal,* April 1970, pp. 165–187. Also, an application in urban housing by James R. Cooper and Cathy A. Morrison, "Using Computer Simulation to Minimize Risk in Urban Housing Development," *The Real Estate Appraiser,* March–April 1973, pp. 15–26. Also, Michael S. Young, "Evaluating the Risk of Investment in Real Estate," *The Real Estate Appraiser,* September–October 1977, pp. 39–45. An operational risk simulation model for classroom use has been developed by George W. Gau and Daniel B. Kohlhepp. Entitled *OUPROB: A Discounted Cash Flow Model for Real Estate Investment Analysis* (User Guide and Instructor's Manual), it is available through the Center for Economic and Management Research, University of Oklahoma, Norman, Okla. 73019. Somewhat more specialized are Richard B. Peiser, "Risk Analysis in Land Development," *American Real Estate and Urban Economics Association Journal,* Spring 1984, pp. 12–29, and Joseph J. Del Casino, "A Risk Simulation Approach to Long-Range Office Demand Forecasting," *Real Estate Review,* Summer 1985, pp. 82–87.

EXHIBIT 8-6.   Project Analysis—Probabilistic Rate-of-Return Model

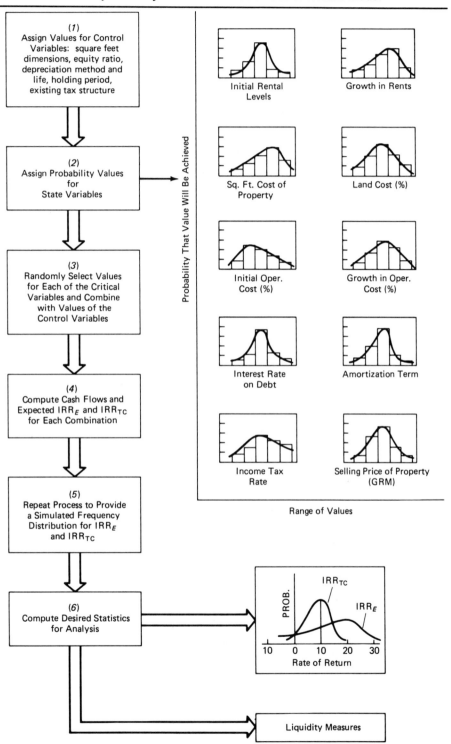

(1)
Assign Values for Control Variables: square feet dimensions, equity ratio, depreciation method and life, holding period, existing tax structure

(2)
Assign Probability Values for State Variables

(3)
Randomly Select Values for Each of the Critical Variables and Combine with Values of the Control Variables

(4)
Compute Cash Flows and Expected IRR_E and IRR_{TC} for Each Combination

(5)
Repeat Process to Provide a Simulated Frequency Distribution for IRR_E and IRR_{TC}

(6)
Compute Desired Statistics for Analysis

Probability That Value Will Be Achieved

Initial Rental Levels

Growth in Rents

Sq. Ft. Cost of Property

Land Cost (%)

Initial Oper. Cost (%)

Growth in Oper. Cost (%)

Interest Rate on Debt

Amortization Term

Income Tax Rate

Selling Price of Property (GRM)

Range of Values

IRR_{TC}

IRR_E

PROB.

10   0   10   20   30
Rate of Return

Liquidity Measures

tions for variables and, after some practice, become comfortable with the concept and process involved.[12]

Given the values of the control variables and the probability distributions for the state variables, the Monte Carlo simulation procedure is used to generate cash flows, DCF rates of return, and other statistical data. As shown in step 3 of the exhibit, a value for each of the ten uncertain variables is randomly chosen from the respective probability distributions and combined with the values of control variables. Then, in step 4, annual cash flows and the rates of return on total capital and equity are computed for that particular combination of input values.

This process is repeated a large number of times and a count is kept of the number of times various rates of return are computed. When the computer runs have been completed, the probability that various rates of return will occur can be calculated and plotted as shown at the bottom of Exhibit 8-6. Exhibit 8-7 is a detailed example of a cumulative probability distribution (risk profile) curve of the rate of return on equity (IRR_E) plotted from one hundred simulations. The vertical axis is the probability of IRR_E being achieved or exceeded, and the horizontal axis reflects IRR_E. For example, there is a 98 percent chance that a 7.5 percent rate of return will be achieved or exceeded over the ten-year holding period. Moving down the cumulative distribution curve shows that there is a 50 percent chance that a 10.3 percent rate of return will be achieved or exceeded. In this case the analyst desiring to know the probability of receiving less than an 8 percent rate of return can see on the graph that there is a 5 percent chance of this occurring. The graph also gives the expected (mean) IRR, its standard deviation, and range.

Additional information can easily be generated in whatever form the investor seeks. For example, liquidity measures can be computed from yearly cash flow data generated during the simulation process. If the investor is concerned with the probability of negative equity cash flows and their respective amounts for consecutive years, a summary statistical measure of these two dimensions can be specified and computed. Suppose an investor specifies that a negative cash flow of $25,000 in two or more consecutive years would cause insolvency. A measure of liquidity might be defined as the probability of receiving negative equity cash flows exceed-

[12]For examples see Carl S. Speltzer, "The Development of a Corporate Policy for Capital Investment Decisions," *IEEE Transactions on Systems Science and Cybernetics*, September 1968, pp. 279–300; Donald H. Woods, "Improving Estimates That Involve Uncertainty," *Harvard Business Review*, July–August 1966, pp. 91–98; David B. Hertz, "Risk Analysis in Capital Investment," *Harvard Business Review*, January–February 1964, pp. 95–106. For a complete treatment of the subject, see Larry Wofford, *A Simulation Approach to the Appraisal of Income-Producing Real Estate*, Ph.D. dissertation, University of Texas, June 1977. Also by Wofford, "Incorporating Uncertainty into the Data Program," *The Real Estate Appraiser and Analyst*, May–June 1979, pp. 30–38.

EXHIBIT 8-7. Cumulative Probability Distribution Curve of the Rate-of-Return on Equity (IRR$_E$)

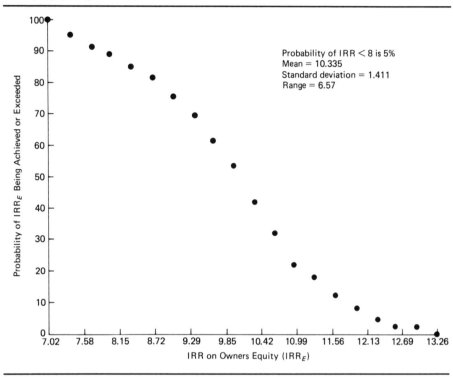

ing $25,000 in two or more consecutive years during the holding period. Instructions are given to the computer to calculate this liquidity measure.

A Simplified Probability Approach. The Monte Carlo technique provides an extremely sophisticated model for risk analysis, but its major drawback is that it requires extensive, often nonexistent, data and a sophisticated computer and the software. However, a technique similar to both Monte Carlo and sensitivity analysis can provide useful information for risk analysis without the extensive requirements of data, hardware, and software. This technique requires that the analyst assign probabilities to the optimistic, most likely, and pessimistic forecasts used in the sensitivity analysis. Then expected returns and variances can be computed on the basis of these probabilities.

For example, assume that the analyst uses the IRR$_E$ computations from the sensitivity analysis in Exhibit 8-5 for the ten-year holding period and assigns the following probabilities to their respective outcomes for the optimistic, most likely, and pessimistic categories.

	IRR$_E$ (Percent)	Probability (Percent)
Optimistic	30.10	20
Most likely	22.05	65
Pessimistic	6.94	15
	Total probabilities	100

Using these returns and their associated probabilities, the analyst can compute the expected IRR$_E$, its variance, and standard deviation. For this example the expected IRR$_E$ is 21.4 percent and the standard deviation is 6.8 percent. The method of computation is omitted here but is detailed in Chapter 18. Although this method is considerably cruder than the simulation model previously discussed, it does provide the investor with some idea of the distribution of possible outcomes. Here the analyst could construct a simple cumulative distribution curve or use available statistical tables to obtain estimates of the probability of returns being less than some desired minimum value. Using statistical tables the analyst can determine that in a quasi-normal distribution, 50 percent of all possible outcomes lie to the left of the expected or mean return and 50 percent lie to the right. Thirty-four percent of all outcomes lie within the first standard deviation (either to the right or to the left), about 47.3 percent lie within two standard deviations and 50 percent within three standard deviations. In this example there is a 10 percent probability that the IRR$_E$ will be less than 9.84 percent. Using the statistical table we find that 10 percent or less of all outcomes lies at a point about 1.7 standard deviations to the left (or the right) of the expected IRR$_E$. Thus,

$$\text{IRR}_{10\%} = E(\text{IRR}_E) - 1.7 \times \text{SD}$$

$$9.84\% = 21.4\% - 11.56\%$$

At three standard deviations to the left of the mean, virtually all possible outcomes are accounted for within the distribution curve. Because three times 6.8 percent (the standard deviation) is actually less than 21.4 percent, there is virtually no likelihood that the IRR$_E$ will drop below zero percent.

It is possible to extend the application of this technique to analyses of the income statement as well. By assigning probabilities to such variables as gross revenues or operating expenses, the analyst can perform a simulation of the investment that requires only the use of a calculator. This type of probability analysis is called Bayesian analysis. It is beyond the scope of this text to provide more complete detail on the development of such a risk analysis; however, the interested reader should consult the work of Peter Pellatt, who pioneered the application for real estate analysis. For an introduction to the technique (more extensive than that provided here) see Chapter 18.

Other Measures of Risk. A distinct advantage of models such as the Monte Carlo simulation model and the simplified model just described is that they can provide a measure of risk that is quantifiable and usable for ranking projects with respect to both return *and* risk. One very common measurement, the *coefficient of variation (CV)*, can be used. The CV is computed as the project's standard deviation divided by the project's expected return $[SD/E(IRR_E)]$. For the example just given that would be

$$CV = \frac{6.8\%}{21.4\%} = .32$$

The lower the project's coefficient of variation (CV), the less risky is that project. The advantage of the CV measure is that it is essentially independent of scale. Thus, one could rank projects using both their IRR_E and CV as a means of rating both return and risk. Another measure is called a *risk index (RI)*. It is computed by dividing the project's return by the project's standard deviation (the inverse of the CV). For the example just given the RI would be

$$RI = \frac{21.4\%}{6.8\%} = 3.15$$

The RI measures the amount of return per unit of risk, if risk is essentially measured by the standard deviation. A project with a high RI provides a greater return for a given unit of risk. A variation of the risk index, similar to that used in evaluating portfolio investments, measures the ratio of *excess return* to variability, $(IRR - R_f)/s$. Here R_f refers to the risk-free rate of return. If the risk-free rate of return is 8 percent, the computation just given would be

$$RI = \frac{21.4 - 8.0}{6.8} = 1.97$$

When the data from the Monte Carlo simulation example are applied, this project has a CV of .14 and an RI of 7.32:

$$CV = \frac{1.411\%}{10.335\%} = .14 \qquad RI = \frac{10.335\%}{1.411\%} = 7.32$$

The project described in the Monte Carlo model would be considered less risky than this second one. However, this second project has an expected IRR_E more than double that of the Monte Carlo model (21.4% versus 10.335%), whereas its standard deviation is almost five times that of the former (6.8% versus 1.411%). One might conclude that the second project produces considerably more risk than may be justified by its higher return, assuming that both projects produce acceptable returns. Using the second variation of the risk index, the second investment has an RI of 1.65, meaning that it produces less excess return per unit of risk than the first investment. Clearly the first investment with an RI of 1.97 is preferable using this measure of risk.

Which is the best measure of risk to use? Since the risk measures presented can produce different project rankings, the issue is one of concern to both theoreticians and practitioners. Unfortunately no definitive answers are available, and the choice of the proper risk measure to use is left to the individual decision maker.

The Future of Probabilistic Models. Will probabilistic models like those just described be utilized in the future? Psychologists and sociologists have demonstrated repeatedly that most people are reluctant to adopt new ideas that they find to be at variance with currently held beliefs. The successful development of a risk simulation model into a production model depends on acceptance of the model for planning and decision making and on the investor's ability to forecast and estimate probability distributions for uncertain variables. It may take considerable time before confidence in such a model evolves in the real estate field.

RISK MANAGEMENT AND CONTROL

Many investors manage money, but the really successful ones manage risk, the idea being not to avoid risk but to be skilled at identifying it, coping with it, and living with it.[13] Real estate investors who remain in business never risk more than they can afford to lose, never risk a great amount for a little, and always consider the odds. Before committing capital, investors should seek answers to the following questions.

1. What situations create the risk of loss?
2. Can they be avoided or eliminated?
3. Can the remaining risks be controlled?
4. How can losses be minimized?
5. Is there a need to shift the risk to others?
6. What are the trade-offs and costs involved?

Although there is some overlap, there are three general techniques for managing business and financial risk: avoiding or eliminating risk, transferring or shifting risk, and reducing the remaining risk.

---

[13]From J. Thomas Montgomery, "Real Estate Investment Risk—Basic Concepts," *The Appraisal Journal*, January 1976, pp. 9–22; revised and reprinted in James A. Britton, Jr. and Lewis O. Kerwood, *Financing Income-Producing Real Estate* (New York: McGraw-Hill, 1977), pp. 18–36. See also Graaskamp, "Approach to Real Estate Finance Education."

Avoiding or Eliminating Risk

The most basic risk management technique is "Don't make the deal." If the expected returns from a property do not compensate for the risks involved, and restructuring cannot correct the problem, reject the investment. Other examples are the following.

1. *Playing the real estate cycle.* The market is overbuilt and we are in a general economic recession. Avoid making the real estate investment; instead, wait until the time is right, when the bottom of the cycle has ended and conditions are beginning to improve. This eliminates a dynamic business risk.

2. *Nonrecourse mortgages.* An exculpatory clause in a mortgage will avoid the possibility of a lawsuit and a judgment if the property is unsuccessful. This shifts the burden of external financial risk wholly to the property and the lender. Of course in the event of default the investor may lose the property.

3. *Avoiding specific types of property.* To avoid insolvency that may result from rent controls, the investor can avoid apartment projects in certain communities. This eliminates a dynamic business risk.

4. *Avoiding market-indexed loans.* By avoiding the use of adjustable or renegotiated rate mortgages, or similar types of market-indexed financing techniques, the investor can reduce the dynamic business risk associated with inflationary affects on mortgage interest rates. (However, fixed-rate mortgages are often originated at higher interest rates than indexed mortgages. Thus, the investor risks being caught with a high-rate fixed mortgage (high internal financial risk) when interest rates are falling. Refinancing may be an acceptable alternative, but is not usually without cost.)

Transferring or Shifting Risk

As another risk management technique, the investor refuses to invest unless all or part of the risk can be shifted to someone else. Here are some examples.

1. *Insurance policy.* Fire and extended coverage, flood, rent loss, liability, mortgage, and title insurance are vehicles for shifting static business risks—but at a certain cost to the investor.

2. *Limited-partnership form of ownership.* The limited partners can shift the risk of unlimited liability and cash calls to the general partner. This can shift both some business and some financial risk to the general partner.

3. *Long-term leases with escalation clauses.* A long-term lease shifts the vacancy risk to the tenant, and contribution and rent escalation

clauses shift inflation risks and expense uncertainties from the investor to the tenant. A dynamic business risk is thereby shifted to the lessee.

4. *Land contract.* A land contract shifts a dynamic business risk by ensuring that, in the event the buyer defaults on the installment contract, possession of the property will revert quickly to the seller at a minimal cost. (Note that this is not always possible because some states require that recovery under a land contract follow the same regulations that govern mortgage foreclosures.)

Reducing the Remaining Risks

The investor can attempt to minimize any remaining risks through a variety of tactics. The following are examples.

1. *Loan amount and terms.* Reducing the amount of the loan and improving the mortgage terms, lowering prepayment penalties, eliminating the due-on-sale clause, and reducing origination costs are methods of reducing internal financial risks.

2. *Purchase price.* The investor can increase the expected rate of return and lower his or her equity investment exposure by negotiating better purchase terms. A dynamic business risk is reduced in this way.

3. *Diversification.* Risk can be spread through diversification with respect to size, type, and location of investments within a given portfolio. As a result, static (unsystematic) business risk is reduced. Becoming a limited partner in several different ventures or being a limited partner in a partnership that invests in a diversified portfolio are also means of accomplishing diversification.

4. *Good accounting controls and reporting system.* If problems are identified when they first occur and investors are informed, corrective actions can be applied faster and expenses reduced. In this way investors will be better informed, more content, and less likely to create trouble for the managing equity investor.

5. *Better financial feasibility research.* Better information will reduce perceived risk, because many uncertainties and financial surprises are due to ignorance of the facts rather than to any inherent unpredictability. More accurate pro formas can be developed, thus reducing the perceived business risks.

6. *Better property management and venture management.* A professional property management firm with skilled personnel should be able to generate a higher NOI from a property over a longer period. More skillful negotiations by the managing equity investor should also raise the returns relative to the risks of investment.

7. *Superior location.* Attracting and keeping good tenants who pay "top-of-the-market" rents through the purchase of superior locations

will reduce the dynamic business risks associated with rent collections and vacancy losses.

The risk management and control techniques described here should be an integral part of the investment decision process. Different types of risk management techniques can be applied at different points in the ten-step investment analysis process.[14] Using the basic financial feasibility model to structure acceptable return–risk parameters is a risk management technique. Developing an efficient investment analysis process, such as the ten-step process presented in Chapter 4, will reduce the amount of time expended in locating and purchasing a property that satisfies the investor's objectives. Clearly, risk management is critical to successful investing.

SUMMARY

This chapter presents various concepts and techniques of sensitivity and risk analysis for single projects and explains how, at different stages of the investment analysis process, the investor can apply risk management and control techniques to avoid, transfer, or reduce risk. Successful investors are generally good risk managers. Chapter 18 again addresses the topics of risk analysis and risk management, this time from a portfolio perspective.

In the Aspen Wood Apartments case study that follows, the concepts presented in this chapter are applied by D&B, and the basic negotiation techniques used by them are explained. In the next chapter we will turn our attention to the topics of financing and refinancing properties, and the use of DCF models to evaluate the impacts of alternative financing structures on the risk and return measures developed here.

---

[14]A comprehensive strategic planning framework for managing and controlling risk at various stages of a real estate decision process is presented by Mahlon Apgar, IV, "Commitment Planning: An Approach to Reducing Real Estate Risks," *The Appraisal Journal*, July 1976, pp. 412–427. Although the framework is applied to the real estate development process, the major elements and techniques of structuring and phasing apply equally well to equity investment. Another framework for conceptualizing and systematizing the risk management process, one that forces the decision maker to consider all the risk interrelationships between economic, financial, and physical variables, is presented by Stephen E. Roulac and Robert C. Cirese, "A Risk Analysis Matrix to Improve Investment Decisions," *Real Estate Review*, Summer 1986, pp. 36–40.

ASPEN WOOD APARTMENTS

NEGOTIATION, FEASIBILITY RESEARCH,
AND RETURN–RISK EVALUATION

In Chapter 6 Charlie Davidson and Clyde Boomer arrived at a proposed structure for the acquisition of Aspen Wood Apartments using the basic financial feasibility model. Among the major purchase parameters calculated were the following:

Estimated NOI	$ 89,305
Minimum acceptable debt coverage ratio	1.3
Maximum acceptable mortgage constant	8.3%
Minimum acceptable ROE	10.0%
Maximum mortgage loan amount	$ 830,000
Maximum equity investment	$ 206,000
Maximum offering price	$1,036,000

Davidson and Boomer planned to approach the seller with a $1 million purchase price offer, including an equity down payment of $175,000, from which a brokerage commission of $50,000 would be paid to D&B Associates for handling the transaction. The seller would be asked to provide wraparound mortgage financing in the amount of $825,000 at 7.5 percent, twenty-eight years, no personal liability, with a balloon (escalation-of-principal clause) at the end of ten years.[a] In addition, Davidson and Boomer would negotiate for the following mortgage clauses: prepayment of the note, without penalty and at the option of the buyer; and elimination of the standard due-on-sale clause. Elimination of the due-on-sale clause would give the purchasing joint venture the flexibility to sell the property in a future year and "wrap the wrap," that is, finance the next buyer by wrapping around the existing wraparound note and the underlying three mortgage notes.

The DCF analysis in Chapter 7 was based on the preceding assumptions. We found that the IRR_E was 22.14 percent, based on growth rate assumptions of 4 percent for rents, 7 percent for expenses, and 3 percent for property value. Although some possible inconsistencies in the assumption base relationships were noted (a falling overall capitalization rate over seven years), all the risk and return ratios looked favorable and were expected to improve each year over the seven-year projection period.

The ten-step investment process identifies three steps between application of the basic financial feasibility model and application of the DCF model.

[a]As will be indicated in Chapter 10, the use of seller wraparound financing with artificially low interest rates has been substantially limited by the tax reform acts passed since the original purchase of Aspen Wood Apartments in 1974.

- STEP 4. Negotiate basic terms with the seller.
- STEP 5. Do detailed feasibility research.
- STEP 6. Structure the financing and tax package.
- STEP 7. Perform DCF analysis.

In the following sections the Aspen Wood project proceeds through these four steps, showing the activities and thought processes leading up to the DCF analysis already presented, and the subsequent "surprises" that necessitated many reiterations of these steps.

NEGOTIATIONS WITH THE SELLER

D&B Associates presented its offer to the seller and was prepared to trade off various elements of price and terms as the negotiations proceeded. Davidson and Boomer began with an offer that maximized their returns relative to the risks, knowing that numerous concessions would be necessary. Using the basic financial feasibility model, they had performed an extensive sensitivity analysis on the price, mortgage package, and other terms of the purchase, and knew how different combinations of price and terms affected their before-tax return–risk position. Armed with this knowledge, they could bargain for a purchase structure that would simultaneously satisfy the personal needs and financial problems of the sellers and maximize the returns relative to risks for D&B. In addition, a number of preliminary DCF analyses were performed to test the after-tax consequences of the investment.

Mortgage Terms. Davidson and Boomer specified a maximum mortgage constant of 8.3 percent. What interest rate and term would be acceptable? A review of the K table shows that many combinations of rate and term will produce a K of .083—say, from 6.75 percent over 25 years to 7.5 percent over 30 years. A K value of less than 8.3 percent would not produce enough debt service on the wraparound to cover the debt service on the underlying three loans. A K of more than 8.3 percent would reduce the buyer's ROE to less than 10 percent, which was unacceptable. The sellers maintained that they would not accept less than the average interest rate (approximately 7 percent) on the three underlying loans and would prefer a higher rate to create a positive interest spread for their investors. A 7.5 percent interest rate was eventually agreed on. The sellers also agreed to a nonrecourse loan that provided for prepayment without penalty at the buyer's option.

Basic Tax Structure. In addition to negotiating a desirable price and mortgage package for the investors, Davidson and Boomer sought to create a tax package that would maximize tax shelter during the year of purchase and for each year during the expected holding period of four to seven years. Their basic objective, as detailed in Chapter 10, was to create the maximum degree of tax benefits over the ownership life cycle: acquisition, operation, and termination.

It was important for both parties to consider tax ramifications during the early negotiation stages. In any negotiations, if both the buyer and the seller are aware of and investigate all tax-planning alternatives, concessions can be made that cost one party little but provide a sizable benefit to the other. These benefits are reflected in the subsequent DCF analyses and negotiations leading to the final purchase contract.

Letter of Intent. A series of negotiations between the seller (general partners of the selling syndicate) and buyer (Davidson and Boomer, representing the buying syndicate) resulted in a September 30, 1974 letter of intent, which was written by Davidson and itemized the intended terms of purchase. Numerous other versions had preceded this one, and some changes had been made by both parties, but the offer reflected the price and terms outlined earlier. Total consideration (net price) to the seller was set at $980,000, which, with the $50,000 commission and syndication fee to D&B Associates, brought the total project cost to $1,030,000. The $980,000 cash paid to the seller was divided into cash, financing points, and prepaid interest. The buyer would be able to deduct the latter two items as expenses in the current tax year, 1974. (These benefits were subsequently eliminated by the 1976 Tax Reform Act, and are not allowed under current tax law.)

Although it was the end of September, the parties were planning to close the project *as of* September 1, 1974, and prorate all income and expenses as of that date.[b] The seller was to guarantee the cash flows equivalent to a 95 percent occupancy through the remainder of the calendar year but was allowed to refinance the wraparound obligation after five years, provided it could be accomplished within set mortgage constants of a magnitude that leave the buyer indifferent. The letter of intent spelled out the contingencies of the agreement and called for a rent roll, a profit-and-loss statement, and an on-site inspection, in addition to other evidence and reassurances. Upon accepting this offer, the seller was required to prepare the accounting records and property for inspection, enabling the buyer to pursue the detailed feasibility research that would be required before additional return–risk analysis could be undertaken.

DETAILED FEASIBILITY RESEARCH

The purpose of the detailed feasibility research is to gather the information required to further structure the financing and tax package and perform a more detailed discounted-cash-flow analysis. The negotiation process and the detailed feasibility research interact to a significant degree. In general, if new inputs into

---

[b]Investors who had agreed to purchase shares in Aspen Wood were expecting tax benefits based on a September 1 purchase—four months of depreciation instead of one or two. Under current tax law such backdating of contracts to close is no longer permitted. It was commonly practiced during this period as a technique to increase tax benefits to buyers during the year of acquisition.

the investment analysis result in a change in the investor's valuation of the property, more negotiation ensues. Seldom are everyone's cards laid on the table at one eventful meeting. The letter of intent, for example, only summarized the negotiations as far as they had gone; it is not usually an enforceable contract. The buyer may inspect, research, interview, and otherwise collect information until there are adequate feasibility data on which to base projections and a final return and risk analysis of the property. Chapter 22 provides a detailed analysis and checklist of apartment feasibility factors.

Feasibility Results. Davidson and Boomer had managed approximately eight hundred apartment units within a two-mile radius of Aspen Wood. Past experience and analysis convinced them that there was a strong market for this complex and that the location was favorable now and into the foreseeable future. Aspen Wood appealed to them because of its location, sound structure, and good floor plans and amenities. It was for these reasons that problems that arose when they researched the various items identified in the letter of intent were deemed worth working out.

On-site inspection revealed many inconsistencies. The "total refurbishment" program that allegedly had been completed had obviously missed many of the apartments. The flat roof had a number of serious problems, and the swimming pool filters and other major equipment were in questionable operating condition. The sellers were unable to produce an accurate rent roll, an inventory account, or other relevant details. The resident manager had recently been fired, and records were in disarray or missing. Vacancies, after freeloaders were evicted, amounted to 29 percent, not the reported 3 percent. The parking spaces shown in the seller's pro forma were seldom rented and deposits were unaccounted for. The management of this complex was clearly incapable of meeting any of the seller's projections.

The buyers also had questions concerning the legal and political efficacy of the transaction. A thorough reading of the note and deed of trust revealed that one of the underlying lienholders had an option to accelerate the loan, calling all remaining principal due when the property changed ownership. Securing the lender's permission to wrap around the existing mortgages would take an unknown amount of politicking and financial compensation. To consummate the sale, all the limited partners had to agree to sign the contract. This was difficult to arrange because the three general partners representing the limited partners disagreed among themselves regarding certain parameters of the sale.

Davidson and Boomer thus discovered that they were not going to receive the economic entity assumed in the analysis thus far; the complex, as represented to them, did not exist. Some of the adverse facts discovered during the research process were surprises to the sellers as well, and their bargaining position dwindled. As a result, Davidson and Boomer drew up a new operating pro forma that incorporated lower rental rates, a higher expense ratio, and no income from deposit forfeitures. They also required guarantees and escrows, to be described in the sales contract. Their revised selling price reflected the new information.

	Revised Purchase Structure	Structure as per Letter of Intent
Note	$ 793,400	$ 820,000
Down payment	160,000	160,000
Commission	50,000	50,000
Selling price	$1,003,400	$1,030,000

These revised figures and expectations were used for the remaining analyses of Aspen Wood.

DCF ANALYSIS

The DCF analysis was rerun to reflect the adverse changes that had occurred as a result of the feasibility research and subsequent negotiations.

1. *Price reduction.* from $1,030,000 to $1,003,400.
2. *Debt reduction.* from $820,000 to $793,400.
3. *Gross possible income reduction.* By approximately $3,000 per year to reflect the drop in rent required to attain 95 percent occupancy.
4. *Expense ratio increase.* From 40 to 42 percent to reflect the increased operating expenses necessary to improve and maintain the building in good condition.
5. *More detailed tax package.* To increase the front-end tax benefits and the annual depreciation write-offs, within the framework of the 1974 tax law.
6. *Increased IRR requirement.* From 18 to 20 percent on equity, because of the increased risk perceived as a result of the feasibility research.

Return–Risk Evaluation. The main output data for the most likely run (assuming a five-year holding period) included the following.

- IRR on equity invested = 24.01 percent
- IRR on total capital invested = 8.43 percent
- ROE before tax = 9.9 percent, increasing to 15.1 percent over five years
- ROE after tax = 20.1 percent, decreasing to 18.3 percent over five years
- Debt coverage ratio = 1.23, increasing to 1.35 over five years
- Break-even point = 85.2 percent, decreasing to 82.3 percent over five years

All the ratios indicated improving returns and decreasing risk over time and an acceptable IRR over a five-year period. Subsequent sensitivity and risk analyses confirmed this conclusion. The project, on average, met all the basic parameters set by the investors.

Some of the primary risk management tools used by D&B were revaluation and renegotiation of the purchase price and terms, the use of a nonrecourse wraparound loan with favorable terms and conditions, and an increased IRR requirement to compensate for higher risk. In addition, aggressive tax planning in conjunction with the renegotiated purchase price and terms increased the IRR on equity (after tax) from about 22 percent (see Chapter 7) to 24 percent after the process was complete, thereby offsetting the increased IRR requirement.

Although three months had passed since the initial screening process identified Aspen Wood apartments (it was by now late November, 1974), it appeared that the time spent would eventually pay off for D&B and the investors.

9

FINANCING AND REFINANCING DECISIONS

Financing and refinancing decisions have become critical aspects of the investment process in recent years. Because the availability of mortgage funds has fluctuated widely and their costs and terms have often become more onerous, equity investors are being forced to rethink their financing and refinancing strategies. The historically high interest rates of the early 1980s caused many institutional lenders to abandon fixed-rate, long-term mortgages in favor of short-term mortgages, variable and renegotiated-rate mortgages, and equity participations. In general, high inflation rates encouraged all investors to shift their portfolios out of fixed-rate and long-term debt investments and into short-term and equity types of investment vehicles.[1] Although interest rates in the latter part of the 1980s dropped to a level rivaling that of the late 1960s and early 1970s, there is no reason to believe that high interest rates may never again occur.

Although the equity investor had traditionally viewed financing as a problem of raising sufficient debt capital, now equal emphasis is placed on the process of raising sufficient equity capital and negotiating creative financial structures that "make the numbers work." This chapter emphasizes both debt and equity financing techniques, along with the many creative financing techniques that have evolved recently.

After a model of the financing decision process is presented, the two major sections of the chapter are devoted to debt and equity financing alternatives. Syndication is included as an equity financing alternative, and the various state and federal government laws regulating syndicate operations are discussed. The Aspen Wood case study illustrates the analysis of various debt and equity alternatives using a DCF model.

---

[1]See Anthony Downs, "With Inflation Rising, Does It Really Pay to Be a Lender?" *National Real Estate Investor*, October 1978, pp. 34–36.

FINANCING DECISION MODEL

The financing decision can be viewed as a submodel of the ten-step investment process model, as shown in Exhibit 9-1. Assuming that the investor has well-defined objectives and decision criteria, the financing process can be completed in four steps.

1. *Identify a project with an adequate NOI stream.* The most difficult aspect of the financing process is identifying a project that will produce a NOI stream sufficient to support a high level of debt financing. The NOI stream must be high enough to service the debt and provide sufficient cash after debt service to be competitive with other investment alternatives.
2. *Determine the financing alternatives.* Alternative financial packages must be defined and analyzed. A financial package can be defined as

EXHIBIT 9-1. The Financing Decision Model

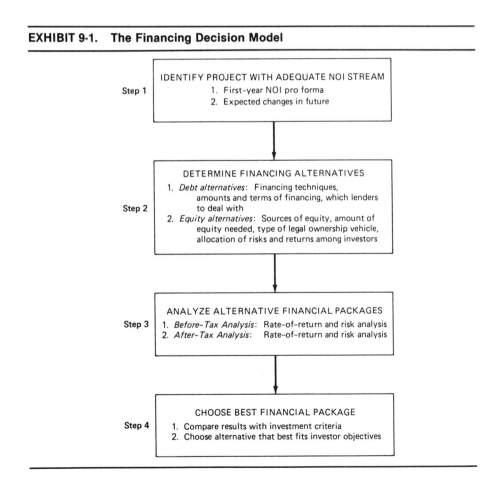

Step 1
IDENTIFY PROJECT WITH ADEQUATE NOI STREAM
1. First-year NOI pro forma
2. Expected changes in future

Step 2
DETERMINE FINANCING ALTERNATIVES
1. *Debt alternatives*: Financing techniques, amounts and terms of financing, which lenders to deal with
2. *Equity alternatives*: Sources of equity, amount of equity needed, type of legal ownership vehicle, allocation of risks and returns among investors

Step 3
ANALYZE ALTERNATIVE FINANCIAL PACKAGES
1. *Before-Tax Analysis*: Rate-of-return and risk analysis
2. *After-Tax Analysis*:   Rate-of-return and risk analysis

Step 4
CHOOSE BEST FINANCIAL PACKAGE
1. Compare results with investment criteria
2. Choose alternative that best fits investor objectives

any combination of debt and equity sources that is used to finance a project. Debt alternatives include the types of financing to be employed (first-mortgage loan, sale–leaseback, wraparound loan, etc.), the amounts and terms of financing, and the lenders with whom to deal. Equity alternatives include the various sources of equity (individuals, institutions, syndication, etc.), the amounts of equity needed, the type of legal ownership vehicle, and the allocation of returns and risks among investors. Discussions with mortgage bankers and other lenders and equity investors will often narrow the alternatives to a workable number. Further screening can be accomplished using the basic financial feasibility model.

3. *Analyze alternative financial packages.* The basic financial feasibility model can test the before-tax return and risk profile for each alternative financial package. Discounted-cash-flow models can be used as well and provide after-tax results. Alternatives that do not meet certain minimum requirements are dropped from consideration. The remaining alternatives should undergo thorough feasibility research and be analyzed using an after-tax model (such as the IRR model described in Chapter 7). After-tax rates of return, ratio and sensitivity analysis, and risk analysis will provide the investor with sufficient data for making the financing decision.

4. *Choose the best financial package.* The best combination of debt and equity financing is that package which best fits the investor's financial and nonfinancial objectives and risk-taking capacity. To a substantial degree the equity investor has control over the financial package created and can manipulate the return–risk relationship. However, the investor should also be aware that many external factors cannot be controlled, including changes in the money supply, reserve requirements, and open-market activities, which can markedly change the cost and availability of debt financing in the short run.[2] These factors would particularly affect the future interest costs of variable-rate mortgages.

DEBT FINANCING ALTERNATIVES

The first basic question of debt financing is how much leverage to employ. The leverage decision is a subject of considerable debate. The following section examines the leverage decision and then discusses debt financing techniques and the variables to be negotiated as an integral part of the debt financing package.

[2]See, for example, Halbert C. Smith and Carl J. Tschappatt, "Monetary Policy and Real Estate Values," *The Appraisal Journal*, January 1976, p. 20.

The Leverage Decision

Thus far the leverage on a before-tax "operations" basis has been analyzed using the basic financial feasibility model to structure a loan package that met desired DCR and ROE criteria. Leverage was favorable if the return on total capital was greater than the mortgage constant (ROI > K; when this occurred, ROE > ROI). However, it is important to recognize that over the holding period the relationship of ROI, K, and ROE will change as income and operating expenses change and as a result of changes in the interest rate or term of the mortgage (e.g., variable rate mortgage). Leverage can be favorable (positive) in some operating years and unfavorable (negative) in others. Therefore, in addition to analyzing leverage on a year-by-year, before-tax basis, one should test it on an after-tax basis using the IRR or PV approaches.[3]

Actually, three types of financial leverage should be considered:

1. *Operations leverage.* ROI, K, and ROE should be compared each year over the operating (holding) period.

2. *Tax leverage.* Interest and depreciation deductions produce tax benefits that generally increase the investor's return on equity. Although interest deductions are based on the entire mortgage value and depreciation deductions on the entire improvement value, the tax benefits accrue only to the equity contribution.

3. *Appreciation leverage.* Increases in property value work through the leverage factor to raise the investor's return on equity. For a 90 percent leveraged property, a modest 5 percent annual increase in value will result in a 50 percent annual appreciation return on the investor's equity investment.

Only through analysis of tax and appreciation leverage can one explain the recent widespread phenomenon of unfavorable leverage from operations

---

[3]Various approaches and techniques are presented and compared in the following articles: Kenneth M. Lusht, "A Note on the Favorability of Leverage," *The Real Estate Appraiser*, May–June 1977, pp. 41–44; Kenneth M. Lusht and Austin J. Jaffe, "On the Relevance and Irrelevance of Finance and the Market Value of Real Property," paper presented at the annual meeting of AREUEA, December 1981, and by the same authors, "Debt and Value: Issues and Analysis," *The Real Estate Appraiser and Analyst*, Fall 1983, pp. 5–18; William Dennison Clark, Jr., "Leverage: Magnificent Mover of Real Estate," *Real Estate Review*, Winter 1972, pp. 8–13; Raymond L. Erler, "Rejoinder on Leverage," *Real Estate Review*, Summer 1972, pp. 81–82; T. D. Englebrecht and Travis P. Goggans, "Leverage and After-Tax Returns," *Real Estate Review*, Summer 1980, pp. 15–18; Michael D. Farrell and Gaylon E. Greer, "Financial Leverage: A New Look at an Old Concept," *Real Estate Review*, Winter 1982, pp. 83–85; Robert W. Wilbur and James L. Short, "The Desirability of Leverage: Expanding the Concept," *Real Estate Review*, Summer 1983, pp. 41–47. Also see Ted L. Fisher, "Tax Leveraging and Real Estate Tax Shelters," *The Appraisal Journal*, July 1980, pp. 414–420, for a discussion of tax leveraging. A complete overview of real estate funds markets is found in Alvin L. Arnold and John Oharenko, *Guide to Real Estate Capital Markets* (New York: Warren, Gorham & Lamont, 1985).

(ROE < ROI). Properties are being purchased with low (even negative) ROEs on the basis of expectation of rising NOI and property values and the continued existence of some tax shelter benefits for real estate investors. The short-run risk of such investments is high (i.e., low coverage ratios and high break-even points), but investors expect to be "bailed out" of unfavorable leverage situations over the long run.

The effects of the three types of leverage can be illustrated by comparing before-tax and after-tax data for a property. For example, consider the analysis of Aspen Wood Apartments in Chapter 7. Ratios and IRRs were calculated for a seven-year holding period, as shown in Exhibit 9-2. The before-tax analysis compares ROI with ROE. Each year the leverage is favorable, and as NOI increases, it becomes more favorable. The after-tax analysis compares IRR on total capital (unleveraged position) with IRR on equity capital (leveraged position). The analysis shows that the net impact of leverage is to increase the IRR_E from 8.2 percent to 22.1 percent; this is a 170 percent increase in the investor's return as a result of the leverage structure.

Whenever favorable leverage exists (on either a before- or an after-tax DCF basis), increasing the loan-to-value ratio increases the ROE, the IRR on equity, and the present value of the property. In contrast, if unfavorable leverage exists (ROE < ROI; IRR_E < IRR_{TC}), increasing the loan-to-value ratio will decrease the ROE and the IRR on equity. Furthermore, it is quite common to have unfavorable operations leverage each year (ROE < ROI), yet favorable leverage over the long run when tax and appreciation leverage are considered (IRR_E > IRR_{TC}).

In sum, the leverage decision should be based on a combination of before- and after-tax DCF criteria. The investor should increase the lever-

EXHIBIT 9-2.   Aspen Wood Apartments: Summary of Financial Results

	BEFORE-TAX ANALYSIS ANNUAL FINANCIAL RATIOS		AFTER-TAX ANALYSIS DISCOUNTED-CASH-FLOW MEASURES	
Year	Net Income to Property Cost (ROI)	Cash Flow Before Tax to Initial Equity (ROE)	IRR on Total Capital Invested (IRR_{TC})	IRR on Equity Capital (IRR_E)
1	9.2%	12.2%		
2	9.4	13.1	Seven-year	
3	9.5	14.0	holding	
4	9.7	14.9	period	
5	9.8	15.7		
6	9.9	16.4		
7	10.0	17.1	8.2%	22.1%

age ratio until either short-term risk constraints (annual coverage ratio minimum, break-even point maximum, etc.) or long-term risk constraints (excessive variability of IRR) are exceeded. Finally, the investor should be aware that as the debt ratio approaches 100 percent, the amount of equity investment approaches zero and the rate of return on equity (ROE and IRR_E) approaches infinity. Since a *mortgaged-out* project cannot be evaluated by a rate-of-return-on-equity measure, other investment criteria must be used in the decision-making process; in such cases the NPV approach is usually preferred.

Erosion of Leverage Benefits

The benefits of financial leverage that used to be available to equity investors are no longer readily available.[4] Because lenders have limited the availability of traditional, nonrecallable, fixed-rate, long-term mortgage loans, the degree of leverage on operations and on appreciation has diminished. For example, a ROE rising through increases in NOI might be offset by the rising interest rate in a variable-rate mortgage; or the appreciation benefits might be diminished by a lender's participation in net sale proceeds. As a result, a property's expected IRR_E might be diminished substantially while its financial risk increases because of the cash flow uncertainties created by the lender's variable-rate or participation requirement.

Debt Financing Variables

The optimal amount of debt financing (leverage) involves not only the *amount* of financing but the *terms* as well.[5] As demonstrated by the negotiations for the wraparound mortgage on Aspen Wood Apartments (Chapter 8), an important trade-off exists between the amount of financing and the mortgage constant (interest rate and amortization term). Better financing terms allow the investor to increase the amount of the loan without adversely affecting the amount of debt service and the coverage ratio. In addition to these variables, many other financing terms affect the return–risk profile of a property.

A loan package typically includes two major provisions: a method of loan amortization and a rate of compound or simple interest. For example, a first mortgage at 12 percent interest may be payable monthly, fully am-

[4]Wayne E. Etter, "The Investor Loses His Leverage," *Real Estate Review*, Spring 1981, pp. 92–97.

[5]For a comparative analysis of loan terms by major lenders see James R. Webb, "Terms on Loans for Eleven Types of Income Property: A Comparative Analysis for 1967–1977," *The Real Estate Appraiser and Analyst*, July–August 1980, pp. 40–45. In a related vein see also Charles E. Edwards and Phillip E. Cooley, "Leverage Financing Choices for Real Estate Investments," *The Real Estate Appraiser and Analyst*, Summer 1984, pp. 73–78, for a discussion regarding the use of NPV to evaluate financing alternatives.

ortizing over a thirty-year *amortization term*, with a *loan term* (balloon) of five years. Although the lender is willing to base the payback of principal on a thirty-year period, he or she wants to be able to call in the remaining mortgage balance at the end of five years so that the money can be reinvested elsewhere if a higher return can be achieved.

In addition to these two important variables, mortgages usually include other provisions such as the payment of commitment fees, extent of borrower's personal liability, provisions for prepayment, requirement of escrow accounts for property taxes and hazard insurance, due-on-sale or encumbrance clauses as well as other acceleration clauses, and provisions for foreclosure. If the mortgage also covers lender participation, then the contract will include such relevant clauses.

Interest Rate. There are two kinds of interest: simple and compound. In most simple-interest loans the constant payment is determined by computing the total interest due on the loan as

$$\text{Total interest due} = \text{interest rate} \times \text{original principal} \\ \times \text{number of periods}$$

The total interest due is then added to the original principal and the result is divided by the number of payment periods:

$$\text{Payment} = \frac{(\text{total interest due} + \text{original principal})}{\text{number of periods}}$$

Under simple interest the interest cost is based on a constant outstanding loan balance. Simple interest usually brings the lender a higher yield. Current federal laws require that lenders restate the actual yield based on an assumption of compound interest.

Simple interest normally results in a substantially higher payment than compound interest in which the interest cost is computed on a declining balance rather than on a constant one. This concept of compounding was illustrated in detail through the discussions in Chapters 6 and 7.

Amortization Method. Loan amortization schedules can be customized in an endless variety of ways to meet the objectives and constraints of both lenders and equity investors. The equity investor will seek to negotiate repayment terms that will have the most favorable effect on cash flow and the IRR, relative to the risk imposed by such repayment terms.

Despite the many possibilities for creativity, most mortgage amortization arrangements fall into one of three basic categories.

1. *Straight-term mortgage.* Also referred to as an interest-only or standing loan, a straight-term mortgage calls for no amortization during its term; the entire principal becomes due at maturity.
2. *Partially amortizing mortgage.* Also called a balloon loan, a par-

tially amortizing mortgage, which is the most common arrangement today, calls for some, but not complete, repayment of the principal during the loan period. At maturity the borrower will have a substantial sum (balloon) still to be repaid, but less than the full amount.

3. *Fully amortizing mortgage.* Historically, a fully amortizing mortgage was the most common type of financing used for residential and commercial properties in the United States. Also called a self-liquidating loan, it employs periodic payments that provide for the full repayment of the principal (over twenty to forty years) along with interest payments based on the balance of the principal.

Ideally, an investor would like a mortgage calling for no repayment of principal (a cash payment not deductible for tax purposes), that is, *interest only* for the entire term of the mortgage. Better yet, the investor might prefer no payments of principal *or* interest. Zeckendorf describes such an arrangement as a *dormant mortgage*, which is a form of second-mortgage financing.[6] Neither interest nor principal is paid until the first mortgage on the same property is paid in full, at which time the owner of the dormant mortgage takes a first-lien position and begins to receive debt service payments. The maker of such a mortgage would possibly be an individual who seeks no current income but wishes to generate future income for retirement or some other purpose. The modern-day equivalent of the dormant mortgage is a zero-coupon bond, which has been used to finance several major properties and public syndications in recent years.

In most cases, however, the investor's strategy might be to choose the combination of interest costs and principal repayment that maximizes the loan amount while maintaining an acceptable debt coverage ratio, provide favorable leverage, and produce an acceptable IRR_E with respect to the combination of business and financial risk. Thus the optimum financial package is determined by subjecting the property to extensive DCF analysis using different financial packages and examining the results with respect to their risk–return trade-offs. In this way the investor can examine the impact of the loan terms on both project returns and risk. However, such an analysis does not provide much insight into the impact of other, nonfinancial terms of the loan.

Commitment Fees and Points. From the equity investor's point of view, commitment fees and points are the same. A first-mortgage loan commitment, for example, might require one point (1 percent of the loan balance) as a commitment fee and two discount points. The financial effect is the same: 3 percent of the loan balance must be paid in cash to secure the new loan. However, the legal effect is different. Usually the commitment fee pays for the lender's guarantee that loan funds will be made available on

[6]William Zeckendorf, *Zeckendorf* (New York: Holt, Rinehart & Winston, 1970), p. 147.

certain terms and conditions stipulated in the commitment. The fee may not be refundable if the borrower later fails to take the loan or fails to meet the conditions of the commitment. The fee may be refundable if the loan is made. Typically, the commitment fee is paid when the lender issues the loan commitment (*takeout letter*), and the discount points are paid at the loan closing. If some flexibility is permitted by the lender, the investor will negotiate payment of all three points at closing, or post a letter of credit in lieu of immediate payment of the commitment fee. A letter of credit guarantees payment of the fee to the lender, whether or not the loan is funded.

The investor should treat loan points and fees as a capital investment. They increase the investment cost and the tax basis of the property. Under the provisions of the Tax Reform Act of 1986 they can be capitalized separately and amortized over the term of the loan (the balloon period rather than the amortization period), thereby creating a tax shelter effect over the holding period. If the property is refinanced before the loan fees and points have been fully amortized, any remaining basis can be written off during the year in which the refinancing takes place. Frequently investors overlook this potential tax shelter; they simply forget to take these tax deductions in the year of refinancing.

Another way to treat loan points and fees is to consider them as an increase in the effective cost of financing. In some circumstances the lender may in fact deduct the fees from the requested loan amount. This is called a discount loan. Other lenders may add the loan fees onto the loan balance; this is called an add-on. If the total dollar amount of fees and points is deducted from the loan amount (to arrive at the net loan proceeds received), the effective interest rate (yield) on the mortgage can be computed by solving for the interest rate in the IRR formula.[7]

Participations. Also known as *equity kickers*, equity participations give the lender a share of the equity returns in addition to the normal debt service on a mortgage loan. Faced with inflation and tight money in the late 1960s, lending institutions often insisted on some form of equity participation. The lender's position was strong and equity kickers became the rage. Many different types were developed.

1. Contingent interest as a percentage of gross income.
2. Contingent interest as a percentage of net profit.
3. Contingent interest as a percentage of overages (shopping centers).

---

[7]The effective interest rate is the discount rate that equates the debt service payments over the term of the loan (or the holding period) with the net loan dollars received by the investor. The mortgage yield calculation is simply an application of the internal-rate-of-return procedure. As the amount of loan fees and points increase, the net loan proceeds decrease and the true mortgage yield (IRR) increases. For a discussion of IRR and NPV applications to the measurement of financing costs, see Christopher Cheatham, "Evaluating the True Cost of Mortgage Financing," *Real Estate Finance*, Spring 1987, pp. 75–82.

4. Contingent interest based on fixed step-ups, reappraisals of the property, or cost-of-living or similar index changes.
5. Participation in refinancing proceeds; a percentage of the new mortgage loan over the old one.
6. Participation in net sales proceeds; a percentage of the net cash realized when the property is sold.
7. Option to purchase an interest in the investor's real estate, stock, or partnership.

Equity investors have always resisted equity participations. They do not want lenders who are partners in profits but not in losses. They also fear that, because of the adverse effect on investment value, resale value will be hurt when a lender has an equity participation. In fact, lenders had serious problems with equity kickers in the 1970s. They were difficult to administer, usury problems developed, and the lenders received less overall return than expected. As a result, equity kickers lost much of their appeal and joint ventures began to replace them. In a joint venture the lender contributes some of the equity investment and assumes a risk of loss. Lenders also began to prefer the subordinated land leaseback, which gave them a preferred equity position and participation in future growth of income and property values. This technique is discussed later in this chapter.

Despite the problems just noted, equity kickers regained popularity among lenders in the early 1980s and will probably remain popular in the future. If so, the investor must be careful to measure the effects of such participations on projected cash flows and expected IRRs; often lender participations make a proposed investment infeasible. However, participations are often the only way an investor can secure high-leverage financing. Some lenders will provide nearly 100 percent financing with a good participation.

Miscellaneous Provisions. In addition to the four items discussed earlier, which are the most important financing variables, other loan provisions can affect the risk of debt. They include the following items.

1. *Degree of personal liability.* Personal liability is minimized by the use of nonrecourse debt. However, lenders today are less likely to provide nonrecourse debt unless the project is strong and the owner or purchaser has a good track record.[8]
2. *Prepayment provisions.* The following five prepayment provisions are the ones most commonly incorporated in mortgages.[9]

---

[8] An excellent article on the subject is Emanuel B. Halper, "People and Property: Mortgage Exculpation Clauses," *Real Estate Review*, Summer 1978, pp. 35–40.

[9] Normally the borrower cannot force prepayment by defaulting on the loan and then arguing that the acceleration clause comes into play and allows repayment of the principal balance. The relevant legal case on the subject is *Peter Fuller Enterprises* v. *Manchester Savings Bank*, 152 A. 2d 179 (Vt. 1959).

    a. Initial no-prepayment period. Also called a *closed* or *lock-in* period.

    b. Prepayment penalty. The lender receives a fixed fee if the loan is repaid early.

    c. Dates for prepayment. The lender may specify that prepayments take place on certain dates.

    d. Notice of prepayment. The lender requires that there be advanced written notice of prepayment.

    e. Partial prepayments. The lender may provide that prepayment can be made only in partial amounts without penalty.

Lenders are usually willing to negotiate prepayment provisions, generally one or more of these five. Sellers may be willing to negotiate better prepayment terms than institutional lenders.

3. *Required escrow accounts.* Lenders often require that escrows of property taxes and hazard insurance be established with them. This requirement is particularly prevalent in residential lending, less prevalent in commercial lending.

4. *Due-on-sale and due-on-encumbrance.* Used in particular since the 1960s, the first clause permits the lender to accelerate a loan in the event that the property is sold, and the second permits acceleration in the event that the borrower negotiates additional financing for the property.[10]

First-Mortgage Financing Alternatives

High inflation and uncertainties about interest rate fluctuations have caused many lenders to seek investment alternatives such as equity participations and joint ventures. Lenders have also developed various forms of alternative mortgage instruments (AMIs) in order to shift inflation and interest rate risks.[11]

1. *Adjustable-rate mortgage (ARM).* An ARM provides that the interest rate charged will be increased or decreased periodically on the basis of some predetermined interest index. In order to minimize the effects of the increase on the debt service payments, some versions of the ARM give the borrower the option of extending the term of the mortgage should the interest rate increase.

2. *Renegotiated-rate mortgage (RRM).* Also called a Canadian rollover (CRO), the purpose of an RRM is to achieve some of the bene-

[10]For examples see Alvin Arnold, *Real Estate Financing Techniques*, Portfolio No. 5 (Boston: Warren, Gorham & Lamont, 1974), pp. 38–39.

[11]For further discussion of the first five, see James H. Hammond, Jr., "Alternative Mortgage Instruments," *Mortgage Banker*, October 1978, pp. 44, 46, 50, 52, 54–56, 58.

fits of a VRM without departing substantially from the provisions of a conventional mortgage loan. The amount of debt service is fixed for a specific period, but at each renegotiation the interest rate is adjusted to a rate near the current market rate.

3. *Graduated-payment mortgage (GPM).* A GPM provides for periodic payments that increase one or more times during the term of the mortgage. During the early years of the mortgage, the amount of debt service may not be enough to pay the contractual interest rate (i.e., the mortgage constant is *less than* the contractual interest rate), resulting in an increase in the loan balance over time. The GPM is attractive to some borrowers because as time passes, the increased payments will be matched by the property's or borrower's increased income (at least in theory).

4. *Price-level-adjusted Mortgage (PLAM).* A PLAM provides for periodic increases or decreases in the loan amount on the basis of some price level index. The interest rate and term remain fixed. The debt service consequently will change when the loan balance changes. The PLAM approach has been adopted in several foreign countries that have experienced wide variations in inflation rates (e.g., Brazil). Only recently has it been used in the United States under the name *real rate mortgage.* A real rate mortgage is a fully amortizing mortgage that specifies a "real rate" of interest to be paid to the borrower (about 5 or 6 percent) and periodically adjusts the mortgage balance by the rate of increase or decrease in the consumer price index.

5. *Reverse annuity mortgage (RAM).* The RAM is designed primarily for owner–occupants who have large amounts of equity tied up in their property and seek annuity income. For example, an investor borrows the equity in his or her property, but instead of receiving a lump sum loan a monthly amount (annuity) is paid by the lender. In such a mortgage, the cash inflows and outflows are the reverse of those of a conventional mortgage. The borrower receives monthly payments and contracts to repay the lender the amount loaned, plus interest, at the maturity date of the mortgage or upon the death of the borrower (through settlement of the estate), whichever is sooner.

6. *Shared-appreciation mortgage (SAM).* An old idea with a new name, the SAM allows the borrower to pay a below-market fixed rate of interest in exchange for giving the lender a percentage of the property appreciation. This arrangement is identical to the equity participation mortgage loan discussed before, and is nothing more than an institutionalized version of the equity kicker.

The ARM, RRM, and GPM are being used in home ownership situations in many states. Though not widely used in multifamily and commercial lending, these and similar techniques have become common in the 1980s as a hedge against inflation and interest rate fluctuations. Cash flow forecasts are more difficult as interest rate and purchasing-power risks have shifted from the lender to the equity investor through the use of these new mortgage instruments.[12]

Government-Sponsored Loan and Grant Programs

All levels of government have been active participants in providing loan assistance (first-mortgage loans and related subsidies) for residential and commercial properties.[13] Most of the local, state, and federal programs have focused on providing housing loan assistance, although assistance to owners of commercial property is also available (e.g., through the Small Business Administration). The investor should be aware of these programs, because they may provide viable alternatives to financing properties for which conventional financing sources are limited.

At the local, county, and state government levels, there has been a surge in moneys loaned for the creation of single-family and multifamily units. Through the use of tax-free bonds, government agencies are able to grant loans at a lower effective rate than is possible through private sources. However, it is at the federal level, within the Department of Housing and Urban Development (HUD), that the great majority of loan programs are available.

Congress enacts a new housing statute, or amendments to one, every year, and HUD determines which section of the population or area of the country is being overlooked. Because of pressures from various interest groups and constant changes in HUD leadership, programs gain or lose priority over time. It is important for real estate investors to know what the priorities and funding capabilities of various programs are. An investor can spend countless hours and dollars learning to operate within a government subsidy program, and then have the entire investment plan undermined overnight by a congressional dictate. On the other hand, investments in a particular government-sponsored housing program that is subsequently eliminated could provide certain monopoly advantages to the investor who owns such properties. In any case the risks are high, and to compensate for them most investors require higher rates of return.

Active programs in recent years have included the following.

---

[12]The question of shifting interest rate risk through the use of such mortgages is addressed by Ravindra Kamath and Russell B. Raimer, "Do VRMs Transfer Interest Rate Risk?" *Real Estate Review*, Spring 1981, pp. 102–108.

[13]For an overview of government involvement in financing real estate investments and the myriad of related government programs, see "Financing" in the looseleaf service from the Institute for Business Planning, *Real Estate Investment Planning* (Englewood Cliffs, N.J.: Prentice–Hall, 1988, updated monthly), paragraphs 55,450–55,500. A very comprehensive treatment is provided by Warren, Gorham, & Lamont in their four volume information service entitled *Housing and Development Reporter* (Boston: Warren, Gorham & Lamont, 1988, updated twice monthly).

1. *The Section 8 housing program.* A program designed to stimulate privately constructed and financed housing, the principal thrust of Section 8, unlike previous housing programs, is to provide a direct subsidy to the tenant rather than to the owner of the project.[14] New and existing single-family houses, mobile homes, multifamily structures, and apartment hotels can qualify. However, preference is given to projects for the elderly and handicapped, and to projects with fewer than fifty units. Section 8 projects can be financed by conventional as well as FHA loans, and through public housing finance agencies.

2. *Community Development Block Grants and Urban Development Action Grants (UDAGs).* Federal support for these locally administered programs has been strong. The attraction of these funds is that they provide seed money for commercial and residential urban redevelopment, which reduces the private capital required to redevelop property that will be owned by private investors. A related program, the Housing Development Action Grant (HoDAG) program, provides a Federal subsidy (grant or low-interest loan) to investors for developing or rehabilitating multifamily housing in areas where shortages exist.

3. *Title V Farmers Home Administration (FmHA) rural housing.* Houses, condos, and rental properties can be financed through this program in small rural communities and cities with populations under 20,000. In the multifamily housing program, direct loans are made to the investor at subsidized interest rates and a forty- or fifty-year amortization term. The equity investor is limited to an 8 percent ROE (cash flow return) on the initial equity invested.

4. *Section 202 Housing Program.* Section 202 is a mortgage loan program to stimulate investment in housing for the elderly and handicapped. This program has increased in popularity, with Congress providing substantial amounts of funds, ranging from one to five billion dollars each year.

Legislation in most states now allows for joint public/private ventures between state agencies and private investors, and provides investors with low-cost financing, risk sharing, zoning concessions, and access to large assembled parcels of land in high-density urban areas. Between 1980 and 1985, eighty-four major mixed-use developments were completed under these new laws, and their importance is increasing.

Many government agencies and quasi-government agencies also have loan programs designed to stimulate housing and commercial investments.

---

[14]Jerome Y. Halperin and Michael J. Brenner, "Opportunities Under the New Section 8 Housing Program," *Real Estate Review,* Spring 1976, pp. 67–75. Also, Reference File 30—Section 8 and Public Housing, *Housing and Development Reporter.*

The Federal Housing Authority (FHA), Federal Home Loan Mortgage Corporation (Freddie Mac), Federal National Mortgage Association (Fannie Mae), and the Government National Mortgage Association (Ginny Mae), as well as state and local government finance authorities, offer a variety of programs to help investors access the money and capital markets for funds to finance various types of real estate. The investor should identify knowledgeable mortgage bankers to aid in defining and evaluating the plethora of alternatives available.

Junior Mortgage Financing Alternatives

Various methods of junior mortgage financing have always been popular with real estate investors who seek a high degree of financial leverage. There are many possible reasons for using secondary financing, including the following.

- To generate tax-free dollars while retaining favorable existing financing.
- As an alternative to syndication, a joint-venture partner, or other forms of equity.
- As an alternative to refinancing, when the current K exceeds the combined K that could be obtained by using junior lien financing.
- As a tax shelter vehicle, with lease rental payments, wraparound interest, or second-mortgage interest sheltering taxable income, while borrower's equity increases through first-mortgage liquidation.
- Larger loans may be obtained through unregulated commercial sources or through institutions if they grant a junior mortgage via "basket" funds—a device that allows them to exceed statutory or internal policy loan-to-value limits.
- Prepayment penalties are avoided, and the payment of financing fees is limited to the new funds obtained through the junior mortgage or leaseback.[15]

The essential advantage of secondary financing is to increase the "upside leverage" that exists. As long as the marginal cost of the additional debt is less than the rate of return on total capital invested, the additional debt will increase the rate of return on equity. However, as pointed out earlier, there may be a split effect from the extra debt. On a before-tax operations basis the debt may cause unfavorable leverage, whereas an after-tax DCF analysis may show very favorable leverage.

The majority of junior mortgage financing alternatives can be grouped into the following categories: (1) commercial second mortgages, (2) insti-

[15]William L. Ward et al., "Junior Lien Financing—Five Varieties and the Advantages They Offer," *Mortgage Banker*, May 1978, p. 41.

tutional second mortgages, (3) purchase money junior mortgages, (4) wraparound mortgages, and (5) subordinated land leasebacks.

Commercial Second Mortgages. REITs, commercial finance companies, and mortgage companies have provided most second-mortgage loans in recent years. These loans are relatively short term (three to five years), are priced on a floating-rate basis (4–5 percent over the prime), and usually allow prepayment without any statutory limitations and can accept higher loan-to-value ratios and lower debt coverage ratios than conventional institutional lenders. Combined first and second mortgages of 85 percent of appraised value are often acceptable. The lender's historical rule of thumb for such loans is "five times the bottom line"; that is, the amount of secondary financing is equal to the project's NOI, minus the debt service on the first mortgage, multiplied by five.

Institutional Second Mortgages. If available, the investor will usually prefer a second loan from a life insurance company, a pension fund, or a wholly owned subsidiary company that operates outside of insurance industry regulations. The interest rates charged are usually lower than with commercial second mortgages, and the amortization term is usually longer. On the other hand, depending on statutory limitations imposed on a particular lender, the loan-to-value ratios may be more conservative than those offered by commercial lending sources, and the prepayment privileges are likely to be more onerous.

Purchase Money Junior Mortgages. Probably the most common form of junior lien financing is the purchase money mortgage,[16] often termed *seller financing.* Purchase money mortgages become especially critical in real estate transactions when institutional financing is unavailable at a price and terms that are acceptable to the investor. Instead, the seller provides financing to the buyer and takes back a mortgage on the property. The mortgage can be a conventional second (or junior) or wraparound mortgage. For tax purposes, if such financing is nonrecourse in nature, it fails the "at risk" tests and may subject the investor to severe limitations on depreciation deductions (see Chapter 10).

Sellers are often motivated to provide purchase money mortgages for one or a combination of the following reasons.

1. *Installment sale tax treatment.* The seller wants to spread the taxable gain over a number of tax years.
2. *Facilitating the Sale.* The buyer may not be able to qualify for an institutional loan; institutional mortgages may not be readily avail-

---

[16]See Robert Bell, "Negotiating the Purchase-Money Mortgage," *Real Estate Review,* Spring 1977, pp. 51–58.

able; the interest rate and terms can be negotiated and the loan closed with few delays.

3. *Higher selling price and lower selling costs.* Providing favorable mortgage terms can create more value, which prior to the 1986 Tax Act resulted in favorable capital gains treatment. The requirements for appraisal, legal fees, and so forth are generally less than for institutional mortgages.

4. *A viable investment alternative.* The effective yield on the mortgage can be attractive to a seller who wishes to shift some of his or her portfolio into lower-risk investment vehicles. The loan may provide the seller with a comfortable annuity during retirement or with liquidity to protect other high-risk investments that have substantial negative cash flow possibilities.

The investor (buyer) also finds the purchase money route attractive. A high degree of leverage might be achieved with very favorable mortgage terms. Moreover, the mortgage clauses (timing of payments, personal liability, prepayment options, etc.) can be negotiated to fit the investor's needs and requirements. The mortgages and notes drafted by institutional lenders often permit little flexibility. Thus, a key advantage of this type of financing is flexibility.

A problem that often develops in purchase money mortgage situations could make a wraparound more desirable than a conventional second mortgage. The investor may not want to assume the first or other senior mortgages on the property for two reasons: (1) the effective mortgage constant may be too high to create favorable leverage, and (2) the payments may have an unfavorable interest–principal ratio, thereby creating tax problems. A wraparound mortgage can solve both problems.

Wraparound Mortgages. A wraparound is simply a junior mortgage loan that permits a second lender (e.g., a seller or institutional lender) to finance a borrower by lending an amount over and above the existing first-mortgage balance, which is not disturbed or paid off.[17] (If there are numerous senior mortgages already in existence, a wraparound could legally be a third, fourth, or fifth lien against the property.)

The important feature of a wraparound is that the face amount of the loan is equal to the balance of the existing loan(s) plus the amount of new financing. The wraparound loan (usually) calls for a higher interest rate than the existing loan, and that higher interest rate covers the entire amount of the loan, even though the wraparound lender provides only a relatively small amount of new money. For example, in the Aspen Wood

[17]See Alvin L. Arnold and Jack Kusnet, *The Arnold Encyclopedia of Real Estate* (Boston: Warren, Gorham & Lamont, 1978), pp. 893–896. Also, Arnold Leider, "How to Wrap Around a Mortgage," *Real Estate Review*, Winter 1975, pp. 29–34.

case a note for \$793,400 *wraps around three* underlying notes totaling \$636,000 (Chapter 8). In effect, the seller was providing junior lien financing (fourth mortgage) of \$157,400 (\$793,400 − \$636,000). The investors paid debt service on the entire \$793,400 note to the seller (actually, a trustee who was appointed to administer the loan), and the seller (trustee) sent to the senior lenders the debt service on the three underlying loans. The wraparound note carried an interest rate of 7.5 percent, and the underlying liens had interest rates in the 6.5 to 7 percent range. The effect is to leverage the wraparound lender's return on the \$157,400 investment. The seller received not only the 7.5 percent on the \$157,400 investment but also a 0.5 to 1 percent spread on the \$636,000 underlying liens.[18]

Four other situations might suggest the use of a wraparound mortgage.

1. The first-mortgage lender refuses to refinance, and prepayment is either prohibited or subject to heavy penalties.
2. The first-mortgage lender is unable to refinance (because of lending restrictions) and is not willing to allow prepayment.
3. The investor wants to reduce the debt service on an existing loan and cannot recast the first mortgage, and looks to the wraparound lender to refinance on a longer-term basis.
4. The borrower does not want to prepay a very favorable first mortgage, but needs additional short-term financing.

Probably the least-understood aspect of wraparound financing is that in most situations, while the underlying loan balance is amortizing, the wraparound loan balance (net funds loaned) actually increases. This happens because the loan amortization term on the wraparound is (usually) long compared to the remaining term on the underlying loan. Very little principal is being amortized on the wraparound, but a substantial portion of the debt service on the underlying lien represents amortization of principal.

The wraparound can present a serious tax problem to a seller. If a substantial portion of the wraparound interest received is used to amortize the principal on the underlying lien, the resulting tax liability on the net interest received by the seller (wraparound interest minus underlying loan interest) may approach or even exceed the amount of cash received by the seller. The wraparound can also present a serious tax problem to the buyer with respect to the "at risk" rules. If the wraparound lender does not meet certain qualifications, a buyer may not be able to include the loan amount as part of the depreciable basis for tax purposes, thereby limiting the amount of tax losses that can be used to shelter other income. See Chapter

---

[18]The computation of IRR before tax and after tax on a wraparound mortgage is illustrated by Egon H. Kraus in "Tax Advantages of Wraparound Financing," *Real Estate Review*, Spring 1981, pp. 11–17.

10 for a discussion on the "at risk" provisions of the tax law and its impact on equity investments.

As noted previously, a wraparound mortgage is often used as the financing vehicle of buyers and sellers and is thus a common form of purchase money mortgage. However, as a result of the gradual deregulation of financial institutions that has occurred in recent years, most federally and state-chartered financial institutions now have the authority to make wraparound loans. Many S&Ls and mortgage companies seek opportunities to make such loans, as do numerous life insurance companies, commercial banks, and REITs.

Subordinated Land Leasebacks. A subordinated land leaseback arrangement is created when an investor sells the land under an income property and then leases it back from the buyer on a long-term basis. Although the land fee ownership is transferred to the new buyer, the investor retains ownership of the improvements, control of the property, and the benefits of depreciation, equity buildup, and any operations related to the improvements. It is important that the equity investor (the owner of the improvements) negotiate a subordination clause with the land buyer to allow an institution to place a first mortgage on the improvements. Without a subordination clause, the fee owner of the land would hold the senior claim on the property and a subsequent mortgage loan placed on the property would be in a second-lien position. Mortgage financing on the improvements would be difficult to obtain and would require second-lien rates and terms.

The cost of the leaseback to the investor comes in the form of land rent, which is fully deductible for tax purposes. Land rent payments are normally payable monthly and have three principal components.

1. *Fixed rent.* A fixed rent is typically a fixed percentage of the selling price of the land; sometimes fixed rental increases are required during the life of the lease. Since subordinated land leasebacks are junior mortgages, the fixed percentage rates are generally from 1 to 4 percent above first-mortgage constants.

2. *Inflation hedge or percentage rent.* A percentage rent is generally pegged to the income stream generated by the property and is often about 10 to 15 percent of all gross rents collected over a certain base level. If the bargaining power of the land buyer is strong, a share of the refinancing or sale proceeds may also be demanded.

3. *Reimbursement for taxes.* Since the new owner of the land will be assessed for property taxes once the fee has been transferred, the leaseback agreement will usually provide for reimbursement by the lessee.

Sources of subordinated land leaseback financing include REITs, some pension funds and life insurance companies, and individuals who seek a relatively high level of current income but have no need for depreciation deductions. The financing criterion for land leasebacks is often stated as a land rent coverage ratio: the ratio of cash flow (left after debt service) to the land rental. The coverage ratio may be anywhere between 1.30 and 2.00. The normal range for the term of the lease is 50 to 99 years.

Two particular areas of concern for the equity investor who is buying a property that is subject to a land leaseback arrangement are (1) refinancing restrictions in the land lease that disallow refinancing the first mortgage on the improvements and (2) land rent escalations that are not limited to increases in the property's operating income or cash flow. Both may restrict the investor's flexibility and have severe negative effects on future cash flows over time.[19] In solving such problems, the investor should undertake extensive cash flow simulations to test the impact of various alternatives on returns and risks. Land leaseback arrangements will often dramatically increase the risk and reduce the marketability of the property. For this reason, many conservative investors avoid properties with land lease arrangements.

Other Creative Financing Techniques

Other financing techniques also allow an investor to achieve a high degree of leverage. These techniques include (1) sale–leaseback of an entire property or building, (2) sale–buyback, (3) sandwich lease, (4) collateralized or personal loan, and (5) high-credit lease loan.

Sale–Leaseback of Property or Building. The most frequent sale–leaseback situation involves the entire property. A developer sells to an institutional investor and simultaneously enters into a long-term net leaseback. Sale–leasebacks are also chosen by businesses and commercial firms that use real estate but do not wish to own it and have the related asset and debt shown directly on the balance sheet. The most important benefit to the seller of the property is that 100 percent (or greater) financing is attained and the investment is converted into cash. On the other hand, the seller loses all the depreciation deductions and the right to any future appreciation in the value of the property; in addition, the arrangement usually includes escalation clauses that periodically raise the lease payments and reduce cash flow. Normally, the lease will run anywhere from 25 to 99 years.

A sale–leaseback of a *building* occurs when the seller–lessee retains title to the land while selling and leasing back the building that is on the land. Traditionally, the purchaser of the building was an investor who was interested primarily in tax shelter (100 percent of the property purchased can be depreciated) rather than cash flow or long-term appreciation; the Tax

---

[19]An excellent discussion of the subject, including proposed solutions and examples, is provided by Arnold, *Real Estate Financing Techniques*, pp. 56–63.

Reform Act of 1986 has shifted investor interest to the latter benefits of ownership.

Sale–Buyback. A sale–buyback, like a sale–leaseback, allows the investor to mortgage out (100 percent financing). The investor sells the property to a lending institution with an agreement to buy it back under a long-term installment contract. The lending institution retains title, but the investor has an *equitable interest* in the title and therefore is entitled to take the depreciation deductions on the improvements. Whereas the investor in effect achieves 100 percent debt financing, the lender receives a fixed contract payment (interest and principal) and a contingent payment in the form of a percentage of the cash flow (or some other income figure).

A sale–buyback arrangement with a lender, like a sale–leaseback, is possible only if the investor has strong credit and a good track record. Both are relatively high-risk, high-return alternatives and are rarely used by conservative investors.

Sandwich Lease. A sandwich lease is a double-lease arrangement in which the investor creates a return without an equity investment. Simply stated, the investor leases an income property for a relatively long period, at a relatively low lease payment rate, and with the right to sublet the property at a profit. For example, an investor negotiates a twenty-year net lease on a vacant office building for $100,000 annually. The space is then sublet on the same net terms to numerous tenants (or, preferably, one high-credit tenant) at rentals that total $125,000. If successful, the investor will receive a $25,000 cash flow each year for twenty years (or more, if escalations are present). The investor is "sandwiched" in the middle, at a profit. Alternatively, the present value of the leasehold income can be estimated and the leasehold interest can be sold or mortgaged, or both, to equity investors.

The Empire State Building was syndicated under such an arrangement in 1961; the promoters sold $26 million of equity interests to investors at $10,000 per share. In essence, the promoters bought a leasehold interest in the land and building, which was owned by Prudential Life Insurance Company, and then created a sublease that guaranteed the passive equity investors a minimum ROE of 9 percent plus overages.

The primary risk for the owner of the leasehold interest is that some or all of the sublessees will default on their obligations. Ideally, the investor would seek a single high-credit sublessee on a lease term concurrent with that of the master lease, which would minimize the financial risk and management burden associated with such a financing technique.

Collateralized and Personal Loans. If a high-ratio loan exceeding the normal lending limit is sought by the investor, the lender can secure such a loan by taking a first mortgage on the property and a pledge of marketable securities (or some other collateral) for the amount that exceeds the normal lending limit. In this manner the investor can achieve a high leverage ratio from a single lending source. The same result can be achieved with a personal (unsecured) loan if the borrower has a substantial financial statement and good credit. For example, some equity investors will enter into syndications of property with equity investments that are 100 percent financed through short-term loans from their local commercial banks. In effect, they achieve 100 percent debt financing at the time of purchase.

High-Credit-Lease Loan. One key method of achieving a 90 to 100 percent loan is available when the investor has long-term, high-credit tenants occupying the property. A lender looks primarily to the credit of the tenants, and unless legal restrictions exist, a low debt coverage ratio and a high loan amount are acceptable. In general, the higher the credit of the lessee and the better the lease terms, the greater the loan amount that will be permitted. For example, a major food chain store on a triple net lease for thirty years, with periodic rent escalations based on the CPI, would provide an investor the maximum opportunity for high leverage.

ILLUSTRATIONS OF DIFFERENT FINANCING TECHNIQUES

To illustrate how different types of financing can affect an investment, the following section presents a "standard" property and applies four different financing methods.

1. Standard institutional loan.
2. Use of purchase money junior loan.
3. Subordinated land sale–leaseback.
4. Sale–buyback.

The example property currently produces a net operating income of $680,000. The project's total cost is $5.4 million.

Standard Institutional Financing. A commercial lender is willing to provide a $4.0 million loan at 10.5 percent for twenty-five years. The mortgage constant K is 11.33 percent. Debt service would be $453,220 and the DCR is 1.5. The equity requirement would be $1.4 million and cash flow before tax is $226,800. ROE would be 16.2 percent.

Use of Purchase Money Junior Loan. Second-mortgage financing is available for $320,000 at an interest rate of 13 percent for fifteen years. The mortgage constant K is 15.18 percent and debt service on the second mortgage would be $48,576. The total DCR would be 1.36 and total debt service would increase to $501,776. Cash flow before tax would be $178,224 and ROE would be 16.5 percent on an equity investment of $1,080,000.

The loan-to-value ratio would increase to 80 percent under this option, as opposed to 74 percent under the previous option.

Subordinated Land Sale–Leaseback. If the land under the building is separated from the total package, it can be sold to another investor such as an insurance company and then leased back by the developer. Assuming the land has a market value of $950,000 and the developer–investor can lease back the land under a long-term lease (say, forty years) at a fixed rental of 12 percent, the developer generates extra cash from the land sale, which reduces the required equity to $450,000. The land lease will require annual rental payments (which are fully deductible for tax purposes) of $114,000. Cash flow before tax will drop to $112,780, which is nearly a 25 percent ROE. The DCR (including the fixed cost of the lease) would be 1.2.

The land lease is subordinated to the original $4.0 million mortgage so as not to jeopardize the senior position of the first-mortgage lender. The purchaser of the land takes a risk that in the event of default on the first mortgage, the primary lender has a priority claim on the land. The land investor can increase the return on the land lease by adding participations to the lease agreement. This would increase the lessor return to compensate for the risk of the subordinated position.

Sale–buyback. Under a sale–buyback the developer–investor sells the project to an institutional investor and simultaneously buys it back under a long-term installment contract. The institution retains title to the property, but the developer–investor holds an equitable title and the right to depreciation deductions. In this illustration the institution receives installment payments consisting of principal and interest. The institution also receives a contingent interest payment based on cash flow before tax. Thus, if project revenues and operating income increase, the institutional investor will receive a proportionate share.

Assume that the institutional investor requires an 11 percent return, $K = 11.43\%$. Based on the purchase price of $5,400,000, the annual installment payment would be $617,220. In addition to installment payments the institution receives contingent interest based on cash flow before tax. The lender would receive 25 percent of cash flow while the developer–investor would retain 75 percent. The term of the contract is thirty years. In the first year the lender would receive an annual installment payment of $617,220 plus 25 percent of cash flow, $15,695 of contingent interest. The DCR for this deal is 1.1. The equity investment has been eliminated; therefore, the developer–investor's return on equity is undefined.

Comparison of Techniques. These four techniques, which have been simply illustrated, provide some insight into the impact that creative thinking about real estate finance can have on investor returns. However, investors must remember that increasing debt results in greater financial risk. The increase in returns provided by higher leverage must be sufficient to compensate for the increased risk.

The techniques just illustrated may not be feasible in markets in which interest rates are extremely high. Moreover, many institutions may not want to take part in these techniques because of increased risk, higher interest rates, and reduced profit margins. Investors are cautioned to subject all alternatives to a DCF analysis or IRR analysis before deciding between alternative financing structures. The examples illustrated merely looked at DCR, loan-to-value ratio, and return on equity before tax in the first year. A full analysis including sensitivity or risk analysis would be required before making a final choice.

THE REFINANCING DECISION

The rapid increase of property values over the last decade has directed considerable attention to the subject of refinancing existing mortgages on residential and commercial properties. Although historical data on the refinancing of mortgage loans on investment properties are not generally available, surveys of large U.S. life insurance companies and savings and loan associations indicate that their activity in refinancing mortgage loans has increased substantially.[20]

For many investors, refinancing is the preferred alternative to selling the property when the objective is to realize the benefits of increased property values. Many investors believe that a profitable property should never be sold. Rather, properties should be refinanced periodically and the refinancing proceeds used to achieve the investor's other objectives: expanding the portfolio, tax shelter, and so on. Such an attitude is little different from that of most business corporations, which usually refinance their debt rather than retire it.

Objectives of Refinancing

The specific objectives of refinancing can take numerous forms, including the following.

1. *Increasing personal liquidity.* Tax-deferred capital is obtained, because borrowing entails no ordinary or capital gains. The proceeds can be used to increase the liquidity of the investor's financial statement or to purchase consumer products and services.
2. *Expanding the portfolio (pyramid properties).* The refinancing pro-

[20]Perry Hayes, "Making the Right Refinancing Choice," *Real Estate Review*, Summer 1978, p. 92.

ceeds are used to purchase other properties and begin new cycles of cash flow, tax shelter, and appreciation.

3. *Diversifying the portfolio.* The tax-deferred cash is invested in other types of property, at different locations, using different ownership forms, investment interests, and so forth. The objective is to reduce the overall riskiness of the portfolio.

4. *Increasing cash flows.* A lower interest rate or extended term will increase the investor's cash flow from operations.

5. *Increasing tax shelter.* Refinancing will begin a new interest cycle, minimizing amortization while maximizing the interest portion of the debt service. In addition, an increased loan amount may substantially raise interest deductions and tax shelter. Moreover, any prepayment penalties and unamortized loan expenses on the original financing can be taken as deductions in the year of refinancing.

6. *Improving marketability and selling price.* Creating an attractive, high-leverage financial package for a potential buyer will make a property more salable and usually increase its market value. The risk of financing the property has been eliminated for the buyer.

7. *Funding a renovation or refurbishing program.* Periodically a property must undergo major renovations or refurbishing. Refinancing an existing first mortgage may provide an attractive alternative to securing secondary financing for this purpose.

Although refinancing is attractive in many situations, timing is critical. Too often refinancing proceeds are not available when the investor needs them. High interest rates and tight money conditions often prohibit refinancing. Tight money conditions will generally result in more conservative leverage ratios, higher points, higher interest rates, and more severe prepayment penalties. In addition, substantial prepayment penalties on existing mortgages, or the presence of a *closed period*, may make refinancing infeasible or unprofitable in relation to the risks involved.

A new loan may take a substantial amount of time to arrange, require personal liability, have substantial prepayment penalties, and contain other onerous mortgage clauses. The tax-free refinancing proceeds may be difficult to reinvest at a high IRR_E. Finally, as we illustrate in Chapter 10, the refinancing may create a serious tax problem at the time of sale, if the net proceeds are small but the tax liability from the sale is large.

Refinancing Alternatives

The key to solving a refinancing problem is the investor's ability to define or create alternatives. The number of possible alternatives is limited only by the creativity and imagination of the investor, as shown in Exhibit 9-3.

EXHIBIT 9-3. Twenty Techniques an Investor Can Use to Refinance Property

---

1. Sell the land and lease it back.
2. Obtain secondary financing to generate cash.
3. Pyramid with a second mortgage to gain buying power.
4. Refinance the existing financing into a new first mortgage.
5. Sell the entire property, lease back with an option to buy.
6. Renegotiate the existing financing to lower the mortgage constant.
7. Seek a moratorium on the existing financing for either interest or principal or both.
8. Refinance with use of real estate bonds.
9. Bring in a partner through a syndication or joint venture.
10. Plan addition and refinance total package.
11. Buy adjoining property and refinance total package.
12. Discount existing financing for cash.
13. Sell chattels (personal property) and lease them back.
14. Seek unsecured financing.
15. Refinance with a blanket mortgage adding other security.
16. Rent to cover expenses and debt service.
17. Prepay rent or mortgage to obtain better terms.
18. Sell only a portion of the property or interest.
19. Sublease a portion of the property or interest.
20. Look to a wraparound mortgage to generate required capital.

Source: From the book *Complete Guide to Real Estate Financing* by Jack Cummings, copyright © 1978, by Prentice-Hall, Inc., Englewood Cliffs, N.J. Published by Prentice-Hall, Inc.

Impact on Returns and Risks

The frequently stated principle, "Refinancing should be undertaken when cash flow becomes subject to tax as a result of the interplay between lower depreciation deductions and rising mortgage amortization," is incorrect for many, perhaps most, investment situations. Rather, the existing market environment and the expected returns and risks should determine the best refinancing strategy.

Various techniques for evaluating the refinancing decision have been proposed, including application of net present value and IRR models on both an after- and a before-tax basis.[21] Both techniques require that a pro-

---

[21]Ibid., pp. 92–96. See also Donald L. Valachi, "Analysis for Refinancing Decisions," *The Real Estate Appraiser and Analyst*, September–October 1978, pp. 42–47, and "Should You Refinance," in John T. Reed, ed., *15 New Real Estate Opportunities* (New York: Real Estate Investing Newsletter, 1980), pp. 25–27.

posed refinancing strategy be evaluated by comparing cash inflows and outflows assuming refinancing with those assuming no refinancing. If the returns relative to the risks are greater under the refinancing strategy (NPV > 0, or IRR_E > required IRR_E), refinancing should be undertaken; otherwise, it should be rejected or modified. The following is an illustration of the application of NPV and IRR to the refinancing decision.

ILLUSTRATION OF THE REFINANCING DECISION

The decision to refinance is based on a DCF analysis. The net cash flows from refinancing are compared with the net cash flows of retaining the existing financing. The analysis assumes equal holding periods. In the example that follows, the investor is deciding between retaining the property with existing financing or refinancing the property with a new loan. The IRR of the differential cash flows (the difference between the net cash flows from refinancing and the net cash flows of retaining existing financing) is computed. The decision to refinance is made if the IRR of the differential cash flows (the "cost" of refinancing) is less than or equal to the investor's opportunity cost (required IRR_E).

The property is an income-producing apartment investment which was originally purchased in 1981 for $150,000. It has an existing loan balance of $111,929. The existing loan carries an interest rate of 16 percent and has twenty-seven years remaining. The payment is $18,154 per year. The original loan also provides for a 4 percent prepayment penalty. The current market value of the property has been estimated at $185,000, and the property produces a first year NOI of $25,200. NOI is expected to increase at the rate of 2 percent per year over the five-year holding period. Depreciation deductions are based on a straight-line amount of $8,500 per year.

A new loan is available in the amount of $148,000 for twenty-five years at an interest rate of 14.5 percent. There is a 3 percent origination fee, and the loan provides for a prepayment penalty of 3 percent of the outstanding balance. The annual payment on this loan is $21,730 per year.

The property will be held for five years, at which time it will be sold for an estimated $237,000 with selling costs of 7 percent of the sales price ($16,590). The investor is assumed to be in the 40 percent marginal tax bracket and requires a minimum after-tax rate of return of 15 percent (IRR_E).

Exhibits 9-4 and 9-5 depict the expected net cash flows from operations for each of the alternatives. In addition to computation of the net cash flows under each of the alternatives, the net after-tax sales proceeds for year 5 must also be calculated. These are shown in Exhibit 9-6.

Once the cash flows from operations and sale have been estimated, the only remaining cash flow to be computed is that resulting from the refinancing itself. If the property were refinanced, the investor would receive

EXHIBIT 9-4.   Net Cash Flows—No Refinancing

	Year				
	1	2	3	4	5
Net operating income	$25,200	25,704	26,218	26,742	27,277
Less debt service	18,154	18,154	18,154	18,154	22,564[a]
Cash flow before tax	7,046	7,550	8,064	8,588	4,713
Plus tax (savings)	(484)	(266)	(42)	188	(1,337)
Cash flow after tax	7,530	7,816	8,106	8,400	6,050

[a]This amount includes the prepayment penalty on the existing loan if it is paid off at the end of the holding period.

EXHIBIT 9-5.   Net Cash Flows—With Refinancing

	Year				
	1	2	3	4	5
Net operating income	$25,200	25,704	26,218	26,742	27,277
Less debt service	21,730	21,730	21,730	21,730	26,115[a]
Cash flow before tax	3,470	3,974	4,488	5,012	1,162
Plus tax (savings)	(1,975)	(1,758)	(1,534)	(1,304)	(2,491)
Cash flow after tax	5,445	5,732	6,022	6,316	3,653

[a]This includes the prepayment penalty on the new loan if it is paid off at the end of five years.

EXHIBIT 9-6.   Net After-Tax Sales Proceeds

	No Refinancing	With Refinancing
Expected sales price	$237,000	$237,000
Less selling expenses	16,590	16,590
Net sales proceeds	220,410	220,410
Less mortgage balance	110,242	146,198
Profit before tax	110,168	74,212
Less taxes	22,146	22,146
Net after-tax proceeds	88,022	52,066

some cash proceeds from the difference between the new loan amount and the balance of the old loan. The calculations for determining the after-tax proceeds from the new loan are shown in Exhibit 9-7.

Now that all the relevant cash flows have been computed, the next step in the decision process is to compute the differential cash flows and estimate the IRR of refinancing (the "effective cost" of the newly borrowed funds). The pertinent cash flows are (1) the net cash flows from operations for refinancing and without refinancing, (2) the net after-tax sales proceeds from each alternative, and (3) the after-tax proceeds from the new loan. These respective cash flows are shown in Exhibit 9-8.

The results of the analysis indicate that the "cost" of refinancing is 11.25 percent. Because the investor's opportunity cost is 15 percent, it would be advantageous to refinance. The investor can presumably invest funds at a minimum IRR_E of 15 percent in other projects of comparable risk.

However, refinancing represents only one possible alternative for the investor. Other alternatives include outright sale and reinvestment and tax-deferred exchange. This analysis investigates only one refinancing alternative. Other alternatives should be identified and subjected to similar analyses. The investor would then choose the alternative that best achieves the investment criteria.

Although this example is somewhat simplified, it nevertheless illustrates the proper use of discounted-cash-flow analysis to evaluate investment alternatives.

EXHIBIT 9-7. After-Tax Proceeds from New Loan

New loan amount	$148,000
Less balance of old loan	111,929
Gross proceeds	36,071
Less prepayment penalty[a]	2,686
Less origination fees[b]	4,440
Plus tax savings[c]	0
After-tax proceeds	28,945

[a]The prepayment penalty on the old loan was 4 percent of the outstanding balance. The after-tax cost of the penalty is $(1 - t) \times$ penalty, where t is the investor's marginal tax rate.

[b]This is the origination fee for the new loan, 3 percent of the amount borrowed.

[c]This would be the savings resulting from the deduction of unamortized loan fees on the existing loan [$t \times$ (origination costs − accumulated amortization)]. In this example no origination fees were assumed for the existing loan.

EXHIBIT 9-8. Differential Cash Flows: Refinance versus No Refinance

Year	Cash Flow After Tax, With Refinancing	Cash Flow After Tax, No Refinancing	Differential Cash Flow After Tax
0	$28,945	$ 0	$28,945
1	5,445	7,530	(2,085)
2	5,732	7,816	(2,084)
3	6,022	8,106	(2,084)
4	6,316	8,400	(2,084)
5[a]	55,719 (3,653 + 52,066)	94,072 (6,050 + 88,022)	(38,353)

Computed IRR of differential CFAT = 11.25%
NPV of differential CFAT at 15% = +$3,926

[a]The amounts for the fifth year include cash flows from operations and net sales proceeds.

EQUITY FINANCING ALTERNATIVES

Thus far, this chapter has focused on the methods of debt financing that can be used to achieve the optimal or desired combination of returns and risks. By now broaching the issue of the equity portion of the capital structure decision, it will become obvious that many of the alternatives, like debt financing, are actually hybrid structures that mix elements of debt and equity.

Whenever a real estate project is organized under a multiperson form of ownership, it can be considered a syndication. In the following sections, syndication is treated as simply one form of equity financing; however, much of the general material on equity financing alternatives applies equally well to individuals, institutions, and syndicates. A later presentation on syndication offerings will extend this discussion and focus on security laws, regulations, and issues, and specific types of syndicate offerings.

Form of Ownership

To a substantial extent, the form of ownership chosen defines the legal and economic relationships between the parties involved in the equity structure. The various ownership alternatives were discussed in Chapter 5, but it is important to reiterate a few points. First, the form of ownership significantly affects the nature and level of returns and risks. Limited partners have limited liability, but they must sacrifice some of the property returns to the general partner, who is thereby compensated for accepting unlimited liability for the partnership. A joint-venture partner shares in the major management and financial decisions of the venture, but a corporate stockholder or limited partner has a very limited ability to affect ongoing management decisions.

In addition, the form of ownership chosen affects the ability of the managing equity investor (syndicator) to raise equity capital in the marketplace. For example, in comparison to a joint venture or tenancy in common, a limited partnership is generally a far superior pass-through tax vehicle for raising large amounts of equity capital from unrelated individuals over a wide geographic area. Finally, if an investor can define and weigh objectives and investment criteria, an ownership decision model can be developed to choose the best ownership form.

Sources of Equity Financing

Most equity real estate investments are sold to individuals or to groups of individuals. Increasingly, however, major industrial and manufacturing corporations seek involvement through joint ventures and other partnership arrangements with developers and institutional lenders. Similarly, major institutional lenders are increasing their investments in equity or hybrid positions as inflation continues to erode the traditional fixed-debt position. It is estimated that by the year 2000, 50 percent of all commercial real estate in the United States will be owned by institutions.[22]

In addition to the various forms of equity participations discussed earlier, lenders are developing new debt–equity combination vehicles. One of these is the convertible mortgage. Designed as permanent financing, the convertible mortgage progressively increases the lender's equity interest in the mortgaged real estate in lieu of cash amortization payments by the borrower.[23] The mortgage interest of the lender is converted into equity ownership over the amortization term of the financing. In effect, the convertible mortgage is a form of joint venture between the equity investor and the lender. Other combination debt–equity vehicles that are employed by lenders have been discussed throughout this chapter.

Institutional investors and developers are also seeking to increase their investments in long-term equity interests through joint-venture ownership arrangements. As a result, large projects can be planned, developed, and owned over the long term without any participation by outside equity in-

---

[22]William S. Reiling, "Lenders Seek New Financing Alternatives," *Mortgage Banker,* March 1981, pp. 36–39. Reiling presents an excellent overview of financing alternatives for the 1980s. For an excellent overview of contemporary financing techniques and analysis see Alvin L. Arnold and John Oharenko, *Guide to Real Estate Capital Markets* (Boston: Warren, Gorham & Lamont, 1985).

[23]Lois A. Vitt and Joel H. Bernstein, "Convertible Mortgages: New Financing Tool," *Real Estate Review,* Spring 1976, pp. 33–37.

vestors or syndicators.[24] Pension funds and foreign investors are competing with traditional investment groups and individuals. Local markets are disappearing as investor groups play an arbitrage game in which money is moved from low-return investments in one part of the country to higher returns in other geographic areas, including smaller towns, which heretofore have been overlooked by both individuals and institutions. Slowly the market is becoming more efficient as information flows and competition increases and the investment process becomes more systematic. Creative equity structures are becoming commonplace and today offer investors a wider variety of equity alternatives than ever before. Public ownership of real estate through passive equity investment vehicles (primarily equity REITs and limited partnerships) is becoming a standard practice as most of the major stock brokerage houses in the country have developed real estate securities offering divisions.

In short, the amount of equity money from all sources has increased dramatically, whereas the amount of pure debt financing has decreased. Managing equity investors need to tailor their financing structures to take advantage of these emerging trends.

Creative Equity Structures

Investors in corporate securities have a wide variety of choices that define particular return and risk classifications: common stock, preferred stock, bonds, puts, calls, and so on. Only recently have various classes of real estate equity interests been similarly developed.

Multiclass Equity Structures. In a multiclass equity structure, the benefits and risks are divided to coincide with different investor objectives. For example, some investors might receive a disproportionate allocation of the tax benefits, others a preferred cash flow, and still others appreciation returns. Such allocations may be disallowed for tax purposes if their principal purpose is found to be the avoidance or evasion of federal income taxes. Consequently, the equity ownership vehicle must be carefully structured to achieve the desired tax and economic benefits.

A multiclass equity structure should increase the total returns to the in-

---

[24]As institutional lenders gain more expertise in equity participations and development joint ventures, it is likely that more will choose to perform all the development and equity investment roles as well as the traditional lending roles. The developer may become an employee of the lender in these situations, working on a fee-plus-bonus basis. See Walter L. Updegrave, "Joint Venture: The Boom That's Reshaping the Industry," *Housing*, August 1980, p. 48.

vestors and, thus, the investment value of the property.[25] The packager can pass along this increase in value to the investors by offering equity shares with higher returns. Or, when the sum of the parts offered separately is greater than the price the property would bring if offered as a whole, the packager can take the benefits by selling different components. This concept of fractionalizing investment interests was pioneered by William Zeckendorf, who called it the Hawaiian technique.[26]

Three Approaches. Three general approaches to multiclass equity structures can be used.

1. *Different classes of ownership interest within the same ownership vehicle.* Two classes of interests are offered to investors, class A and class B. Class A is entitled to a preferential cash flow until a specified annual yield has been achieved, after which cash is distributed according to some formula between the two classes. Class B is entitled to a preference in the allocation of tax benefits in a similar fashion.

2. *The leasehold approach.* Two partnerships are created to own one property. Partnership A buys the property and leases it to partnership B for a rent equivalent to the mortgage payments on the property. Thus, partnership A investors realize a return consisting essentially of the tax deductions from depreciation on the property. Partnership B investors operate the building and enjoy a high (and perhaps increasing) cash return but little or no tax shelter.

3. *The loan approach.* This approach is similar to the leasehold approach except that partnership B (cash-flow-oriented investors) make a loan to partnership A (tax-shelter-oriented investors who own the depreciable assets). Payments on the loan, rather than rent payments, are made to partnership B, including some form of participation in the cash flow from the property.

In all three approaches tax and legal problems as well as conflicts of interest can arise. For example, during an economic downturn the tax-shelter-oriented investors may have increasing returns (more tax losses) while the cash flow investors have decreasing returns (less rents and cash flow). On the other hand, management decisions that result in increased cash flow (e.g., deferring maintenance expenses) may decrease the amount of tax shelter. Great care must be taken to define clearly the financial implications of the equity structure for all parties involved. In addition, changes in tax laws can cause severe problems for such multiclass equity structures. These problems are discussed in the following chapter.

[25]Stephen E. Roulac, "What's in Those Shiny New Syndication Packages?" *Real Estate Review*, Summer 1972, p. 79.
[26]Zeckendorf, pp. 143–148.

Compensation Schemes for Investors

In most equity investment structures the managing equity investor (who may be referred to as the general partner, the operating partner, the promoter, the syndicator, or the project sponsor) seeks compensation in the form of fees and commissions, as well as participation in the various forms of property return. There has been considerable debate in recent years regarding the compensation schemes used. Syndication sponsors have often been accused of structuring investments that benefit them handsomely, regardless of the economic consequences to the passive investors. Such structures are said to lack "goal congruency." An equity structure that has goal congruency is one in which the economic consequences to the sponsor closely parallel the economic consequences to the passive investors. That is, if the project does poorly, the sponsor receives a minimum return; if it does well, the sponsor is compensated proportionately (or more) for a job well done.

Various types of compensation schemes have been used or suggested.[27] The three in Exhibit 9-9 show varying degrees of goal congruency.

The first scheme, which is used by many real estate syndicators, has a high front-end load, including commissions that are paid regardless of a property's performance. The sponsor also takes a subordinated interest in both the cash flow and the proceeds of sale. Scheme II is similar, but the front-end fees and market and organizational costs are regulated by the amount of equity investor dollars going into the project (rather than being a percentage of the total purchase price, as in scheme I). Scheme III provides the most goal congruency; it has a low front-end load and market and organizational costs, but allocates a large sale participation interest (45 percent) to the sponsor if the property is successful. This scheme requires the promoter to maintain a continued interest in the operation and resale of the property, because the promoter's substantial profits are received only after the property has performed well for the passive investors.

Recently, a few innovative syndication offerings have even featured "no-front-end loads" to the investors; the syndicators claim that with this structure most of the equity investor's capital is put to work earning a return.

[27] See Gary K. Barr, "Compensation Schemes of Real Estate Securities," *The Real Estate Appraiser*, May–June 1974, pp. 4–9. Also, Stephen E. Roulac, "The Promoter's Participation Interest as a Form of Compensation in Real Estate Syndications," *The Real Estate Appraiser*, May–June 1973, pp. 33–40. For an up-to-date review of SEC position on compensation see Guide 5, Securities and Exchange Commission 17 CFR Parts 210, 231, and 249 (Release Nos. 33-6405 and 34-18787; File No. s7-908). The impact of tax reform on syndication structures is discussed in Richard N. Thielen, "Real Estate Syndications After Tax Reform: A Financial Advisor's View," *Real Estate Finance*, Winter 1987, pp. 67–74.

EXHIBIT 9-9. Investment Sponsor Compensation Schemes

Compensation scheme I: 6% real estate commission

Front-end load = 27.5% of money raised (6% sales commission)

Marketing and organizational costs = 1.7% of money raised

Subordinated cash flow = 10% of cash flow above an annual return of 6% on money raised (cash return)

Subordinated interest at sale = 10% of proceeds after a return of capital plus 6% annual return (cash return)

Compensation scheme II: Using guidelines adopted by the Midwest Securities Commissioners

Front-end load = 18% of money raised

Marketing and organizational costs = 15% of money raised

Participation = 10% of cash flow from operations

Participation at resale = 9% of proceeds after a return of capital plus a 6% annual return (cash return)

Compensation scheme III: Suggested method to provide goal congruency

Front-end load = 10% of money raised

Marketing and organizational costs = 10% of money raised

Participation in operation = 50% of cash flow above a 7% annual return. (cash return)

Participation at resale = 45% of net proceeds after a return of capital plus a 7% annual cumulative return (cash return)

Source: Gary K. Barr, "Compensation Schemes of Real Estate Securities," *The Real Estate Appraiser*, May–June 1974, p. 6.

Guaranteed and Nonguaranteed Returns. Equity investors often seek to limit the risks they take through some form of guarantee from the seller (or syndicator) of the property. This guarantee can take many forms, including the following.

1. *Rent-up guarantee.* The seller agrees to guarantee against a negative cash flow, or promises some positive cash flow for a specified period after purchase.

2. *Subordination of management fee.* The seller agrees to manage the property and subordinate the management fee until some specified cash flow is received by the investors.

3. *Minimum cash flows through leaseback arrangement.* A minimum cash flow rate is assured by a leaseback agreement with the seller for a limited period.

Clearly, the reduction of risk is proportionate to the type of guarantee, the length of the guarantee, and the quality of the guarantor. It should also be clear that while guarantees are desirable in many situations, they are usually paid for in the purchase price of the property. The risk reduction achieved in this manner usually results in some reduction of returns to the investors.

Staged Equity Investment Techniques. In many purchases the investor negotiates a staged-down payment arrangement in which the total equity is paid to the seller over several years. Thus, during the early years of ownership the relative returns are greatly magnified when measured by a cash-flow (or tax shelter) to equity ratio, and the marketability of the investment is increased substantially. For example, consider a highly leveraged property that can be purchased for an equity investment of $100,000 and is structured to produce tax losses of $50,000 in the year of acquisition. This structure provides the investor with a potential 50 percent tax write-off for each dollar of equity investment in the year of purchase. If, on the other hand, the equity down payment can be split into two equal payments, one this year and one next, the equity investor's tax shelter write-off doubles to 100 percent in the year of acquisition. The property becomes considerably more attractive to tax-shelter-oriented investors. However, the Tax Reform Act of 1986 severely reduced the tax benefits from this type of equity structure.

A staged equity investment can result when the exact purchase price is not know at the time the property is closed, because it is based on the property's performance (or some other event) after the closing. Then the equity (and debt) structure may be modified as the property does, or does not, perform according to the seller's pro forma guarantees.

SYNDICATION OFFERINGS

In the distant past, most real estate syndications involved a single property and a single class of investors, each of whom received a pro rata ownership interest in the syndicate. Purchasers of partnership units expected to hold their units until the property was sold and the partnership terminated. Today, managing equity investors frequently use a variety of new syndication concepts and vehicles. Syndications are becoming much larger in scope and size, are being offered through the public media, and consequently are being closely scrutinized and regulated by federal and state securities agencies.

Types of Syndication Offerings

Single- or Multiple-Property Offerings. An increasingly popular syndication concept is the multiple-property offering, or the fund approach, as it is often called. This type of syndication is said to offer investors the following advantages.

1. *Diversification of risk and type of return.* The syndicate may diversify by size and type of property purchased, geographic location, and so forth. In addition, high-cash-flow properties on net leases can be combined with appreciation-oriented investments.
2. *Economies of scale in the origination phase.* Marketing, legal, and administration costs are reduced (on a per-unit basis). Only one prospectus needs to be developed, instead of many.
3. *Economies of scale in operations.* Management and accounting costs can be reduced on a percentage-of-revenue basis as a result of operating efficiencies.
4. *Tax and cash flow planning among properties.* More control can be exercised to achieve the investment objectives.

If a syndicator offers shares to the public and must register the offering under federal and state laws, it makes sense to seek fewer registrations and raise more money per syndication. The minimum cost for a registration with the Securities and Exchange Commission (SEC) is about $50,000 and may run as high as $500,000 to $1 million for large syndications that register and sell shares in a large number of states.

The proponents of single-property offerings believe that the best theory is to "put all your eggs into one basket, then watch the basket like a hawk." They argue that it is more difficult to structure a multiple-property offering to meet the specific cash flow, tax, and other requirements of the investor. Investors can still achieve diversification by investing in several single-property offerings to fit specific needs and requirements.

Specified or Nonspecified Property Offerings. When an offering specifies its properties, it can be evaluated on the basis of the investment quality of the real estate itself; moreover, the exact amount of the sponsor's front-end compensation is known before the passive investors make their decision. Thus, assuming that projections are available, the investor can directly assess whether the investment is viable.[28] In the nonspecified investment offering, also called a *blind pool* or *blank check* offering, investors do not know which properties will be owned by the partnership. Consequently, they must rely solely on the general statement of the syndicate's

[28]For examples, see Christopher A. Manning, "Correct 'Bottom Line' Analyses of Syndication Offerings," *Real Estate Review*, Summer 1986, pp. 42–50; Adler and Lenz, "How to Evaluate the Offering Memorandum for a Real Estate Syndication," *Real Estate Review*, Spring 1985; Nourse, "Improve Investment Decisions By Breaking the DCF Habit," *Real Estate Review*, Winter 1986; also James L. Kuhle and Josef D. Moorehead, "Syndication Evaluation Using Equity Yield Analysis," *Real Estate Finance*, Summer 1985, pp. 79–85.

objectives and investment criteria, and on the reputation and track record of the syndicator.

Both approaches have advantages and disadvantages. Proponents of the nonspecified type feel that they can obtain better buys if they have the money in hand when they are negotiating. In addition, the syndicator does not have to use personal funds to tie up a property for an extended period of time while putting together a prospectus, going through the registration process (if necessary), and raising the funds for acquisition. On the other hand, there is the danger that a syndicator who is motivated to produce tax benefits before the end of the current tax year will be pressured to rush out and invest the money before the year ends. Having to invest money quickly does not usually give the investor a negotiating advantage and may mean accepting higher purchase prices and more onerous purchase terms.

Open- or Closed-End Offerings. Historically, most investment offerings have been closed. Partnerships were formed to own, operate, and sell real estate, and the partnerships were dissolved once the assets were sold. Although some provision may have been made for new partners, issuing new shares on a continuing basis was not usually allowed. However, a relatively new form of syndicate, called the open-end fund, has developed.

An open-end fund, like a common stock mutual fund, includes provisions to issue new ownership units on a continuing basis. These syndicates can acquire additional properties over time or, when a property is sold, replace it with another. Although the concept is relatively new, it will become more popular as increased government regulation and control drive up the costs of registration and legal compliance procedures. Furthermore, if the fund builds a track record, name identification can substantially aid in further marketing efforts.

An investor should be careful to evaluate the liquidity of the shares purchased in an open-end fund, because no orderly method of termination is provided. It is important to be able to dispose of shares to realize any appreciation in property values. The ability to trade shares in an organized marketplace and through organized exchanges and brokerage houses will be a key factor in evaluating such investments in the future.

The Master Prospectus.[29] This concept combines the economies of the multiple-property offering and the advantages of the single-property syndication. Investors buy partnership interests, which can later be converted into ownership shares in separate partnerships formed to hold each property. In one type of offering, for example, the investor specifies his or her investment objectives in the syndicate's subscription agreement. The syn-

---

[29]Roulac, "What's in Those Shiny New Syndication Packages?" p. 80.

dicator then allocates the investor's dollars to various individual partnerships according to the objectives and instructions contained in the subscription agreement. In another variation of the master prospectus approach, the investor purchases a participation interest and then selects a particular partnership.

A recent variation on this theme is the master limited partnership (MLP). An MLP is a large partnership that acts as a limited partner of several smaller partnerships. The smaller partnerships actually own property. The MLP is publicly registered and trades freely on one of the security exchanges, thus providing investors with considerably more liquidity than typical partnership interests provide. There are two basic kinds of MLPs, rollups and rollouts. In the first several existing limited partnerships are combined into a master partnership. In the second a corporation transfers some or all of its real estate assets to an MLP and then distributes limited-partnership interests to shareholders. MLPs are discussed in detail in Chapter 5.

Federal and State Regulation of Syndicates

The government imposes direct controls and regulations on real estate transactions whenever they are deemed to be "security" transactions. Many investors and syndicators have been surprised to learn that over the years their real estate transactions have actually been securities transactions and that they have not been complying with federal and state laws. Considering the many civil and criminal penalties that can be imposed, a syndicator today must begin with the assumption that all syndication activities are security transactions. Only by meeting certain exemption provisions will the syndicator be relieved of the onerous reporting requirements and procedures imposed by the SEC and, in most cases, state securities agencies.

A real estate interest is considered an "investment contract," and hence a security, if the "investors are induced to invest in a common enterprise in the expectation of profits which are to result solely from the efforts of the promoter or a third party other than the investor."[30] Most real estate syndications are therefore within the securities law. Passive investors receive investment interests in return for the funds they put into a common pool and are led to expect profit from the efforts of the syndicator.

The definition of "security" is constantly expanding and can be interpreted to include almost every real estate investment and brokerage activ-

---

[30]*How to Syndicate Real Estate*, Portfolio No. 11, prepared by the editorial staff of *Real Estate Review* with the assistance of Alan Parisse (Boston: Warren, Gorham & Lamont, 1977), p. 57. See also Alvin L. Arnold, *Real Estate Syndication Manual* (Boston: Warren, Gorham & Lamont, 1984).

ity.[31] In general, whenever a syndicator (regardless of the type of ownership form used) *sells* the ownership units and *management* of the property is an essential part of the transaction, there is a sale of a security. Thus, the crucial determinant of "security" is the manner in which the real estate asset is *marketed* and *managed*.

The Securities Acts of 1933 and 1934. The Securities Act of 1933 defines the basic federal law governing the sale and offering of securities. For this law to apply, the securities must be offered and sold in interstate commerce. However, interstate commerce is very broadly defined, and even the use of a telephone (which is regulated at the federal level) can mean that the offering will fall under the interstate commerce classification.

The regulation provisions call for the following.

1. *Registration.* To be filed with the SEC (Form S-11) before the securities are distributed.
2. *Full disclosure.* A prospectus disclosing all relevant information needed by an investor to make an assessment of the security and all risks involved.
3. *Discouragement of fraud.* Provides statutory remedies that are broader than those available under common law to discourage misrepresentation.

Under the Securities Exchange Act of 1934, securities exchanges are required to register with the SEC or to obtain an exemption from registration as a prerequisite for doing business. Before securities can be traded they must be registered with the SEC.

Fortunately, the federal government offers exemptions from full registration for certain classes of securities, including private offerings, intrastate offerings, and offerings aggregating under $1,500,000 (Regulation A).

Private offerings. To qualify for a private-offering exemption, the securities must be offered only to people who are believed to be financially strong enough to bear substantial investment risks. These offerees should be capable of making intelligent investment decisions or have access to an adviser who can assist in such a decision. The issuer and investor should be in direct contact so that questions can be answered, and no solicitation (e.g., advertising) that would attract an unsophisticated investor is permitted.

---

[31]For a complete discussion of securities laws in real estate, see *How Securities Laws Affect Real Estate Offerings*, Portfolio No. 12, prepared by the editorial staff of *Real Estate Review* and Jackson L. Morris (Boston: Warren, Gorham & Lamont, 1977), p. 72. Also, Stephen E. Roulac, "REF Special Report: Real Estate Securitization: Prologue and Prospects," *Real Estate Finance*, Spring 1988, pp. 15–24.

The private-offering exemption language in the Securities Act of 1933 was vague. However, in 1974 the SEC issued Rule 146 (known as the Safe Harbor Act), which specifically sets forth the exemption requirements. Under Rule 146 a private-offering exemption is achieved if *all* the following conditions are met.

1. There must be no more than thirty-five purchasers.
2. General solicitation and advertising to sell or offer securities are prohibited.
3. The offeree must be a knowledgeable investor, or be able to bear substantial economic risks.
4. A private-offering memorandum is required; the offeree must be given the same information that the formal registration statement would contain.

Although SEC Rule 146 clarified the guidelines for the private-offering exemption, many questions and issues still remain. For example, one might ask, What is a "knowledgeable" investor?[32] What constitutes being "able to bear substantial economic risk"? Since the passage of Rules 146 and Rules 240 and 242, which separately covered various exempt offerings, the SEC unified these three rules under a new, single rule, Regulation D. Regulation D, which went into effect on June 30, 1982, effectively combines into one regulation all revisions for exemptions from registration involving limited offers and sales. Under Regulation D, Rule 146 has been replaced with Rule 506, Rule 240 has been replaced with Rule 504, and Rule 242 has been replaced with Rule 505. In addition, Section 4(6) provides for an exempted offer with an aggregate price of $5 million and an unlimited number of investors, provided the investors are accredited (knowledgeable and experienced.)[33]

In any event, a syndicator who wants a private-offering exemption should proceed with caution and under the direction of experienced legal counsel.

Intrastate offerings. The Securities Act of 1933 exempted the issues of securities sold only to residents of the state in which the issuer is a resident and doing business. This exemption can be lost if even one offeree is an out-of-state resident. SEC Rule 147 (Safe Harbor for Intrastate Exemption) was adopted to implement the intrastate exemption; the requirements are very strict, and the exemption cannot be relied on unless *all* its qualifications are met. These include the following.

[32]A study of investor profiles and attitudes is presented by Wayne E. Etter and Donald R. Levi in "Investors' Views of Real Estate and Limited Partnerships," *The Appraisal Journal*, January 1978, pp. 112–121.
[33]Stephen P. Jarchow, *Real Estate Syndications: Tax, Securities, and Business Aspects* (New York: Wiley, 1985), Appendix 3, pp. 767–805. Also, W. L. Born, *A Guide to Real Estate Syndication* (College Station, Texas: Texas Real Estate Research Center, 1986).

1. The issuer is a resident and doing business (at least 80 percent of total assets) in the state in which offers are being made.
2. No part of the issue is offered or sold to nonresidents, or resold to nonresidents until nine months from the date of the last sale.
3. All documented precautions are taken against interstate distribution.

Offerings aggregating under $1.5 million (Regulation A). Regulation A is a "short-form" registration available for offerings under $1,500,000. The major benefit of this exemption is that the offering document is simplified and review is done at the regional SEC office, rather than in Washington, D.C. Theoretically, the processing time is less and the costs are reduced. The exemption has not been used frequently because the previous equity limit was $500,000. Moreover, syndicators of relatively small offerings tended to rely on the intrastate and private-offering exemptions. Raising the maximum equity amount to $1,500,000 should substantially increase the use of this vehicle in the future.

Consequences of failure to qualify for an exemption. When an exemption is lost, it is lost for the entire issue. Although there are no specific penalties against the syndicate, the syndicator must offer all investors a refund, and no sales can take place until the issue is registered. As a consequence, the syndication may be abandoned, or substantial costs and delays must be incurred to register the syndication. However, if a syndicator has made untrue statements, or has materially misrepresented the property, or has misled the investor, both civil and criminal penalties can be imposed.

State laws. State "blue-sky laws" have basically the same objectives as federal laws. Some states can even disqualify investments that are found lacking in merit under so-called *merit review* procedures. Satisfaction of the federal registration requirement does not automatically satisfy the state requirements. The toughest hurdle is often compliance with state regulations and "administrative" procedures. Each state has a distinct and usually different set of regulations. Thus, full registration in all fifty states can be time-consuming and expensive, ranging in cost from $500,000 to $1 million. For this reason, some syndicates register only in states in which they believe their potential investors reside and in states where the reporting requirements are not too stringent.

SUMMARY

This chapter presents a methodology for the financing decision process. This process begins with the identification of a property that will produce an adequate NOI stream. Next, the investor determines the financing alternatives, including debt and equity, that are possible. Third, the alternative financial packages are analyzed on a before- and after-tax basis. A financial package is defined as a particular combination of debt and equity sources used to finance a project. Finally, the results for each alternative are compared with the investment criteria, and the alternative that best fits investor objectives is chosen.

The bulk of the chapter was devoted to analyzing debt and equity alternatives. The analysis of debt alternatives included a discussion of the leverage decision, debt financing variables that can be negotiated, senior and junior mortgage financing techniques, creative debt financing techniques, and various government-sponsored loan programs. The refinancing decision was also discussed.

Later in the chapter equity financing alternatives were considered. Forms of ownership, sources of equity financing, creative equity structures, and syndication were discussed. The various federal and state laws regulating syndicates have become major factors in the design of syndicate marketing and management techniques.

The Aspen Wood case study is introduced again to illustrate the many principles and concepts developed in this chapter. With the DCF model presented in Chapter 7, a variety of simulations are undertaken to measure the impact of alternative financial packages on risk and return parameters.

ASPEN WOOD APARTMENTS

NEGOTIATING THE FINANCIAL PACKAGE

The financial package negotiated for Aspen Wood Apartments by syndicators Charlie Davidson and Clyde Boomer of D&B Associates is shown in Exhibit 9-A.

The basic parameters of the package were determined using the basic financial feasibility model. (See Chapter 6.) Given the basic return objective (ROE = 10 percent) and risk level constraint (DCR = 1.3), along with a best estimate of NOI ($89,305), D&B proceeded to determine an acceptable debt and equity structure. The original solution shown at the end of Chapter 6 included a maximum loan of $830,000, with a mortgage constant not to exceed 8.3 percent, a maximum equity of $206,000, and a maximum purchase price of $1,036,000. Later (Chapter 8), with additional information obtained during the feasibility research stages, the NOI decreased and a more conservative financial package was structured using a DCF model to test the after-tax impact of various financing alternatives. The complete and final financial package is illustrated in Exhibit 9-A.

INPUT ASSUMPTIONS FOR FINANCIAL PACKAGE ANALYSIS[a]

The basic project data for the DCF analysis were presented in Chapter 7. At that stage of analysis the total purchase price was $1 million, with debt of $825,000 and equity of $175,000. Using this data Davidson and Boomer analyzed the impact of various financial packages on the expected returns in different economic scenarios to determine the most desirable package. The critical financing variables tested were as follows:

1. *Leverage ratio.* 75%, 85%, and 95%.
2. *Interest rate.* From 6% to 12%, with 1.5% increments.
3. *Amortization term.* 20, 25, and 30 years.
4. *Economic scenarios.* Most likely (base case), pessimistic, and optimistic.

The three economic scenarios involved variations in vacancies, rents, expenses, and property value, as follows.

	Most Likely (Base Case)	Pessimistic	Optimistic
Occupancy rate	.95	.90	.975
Income growth rate	.04	.02	.08
Expense growth rate	.06	.10	.06
Property value growth rate	.03	.00	.08

[a]This analysis is patterned after a case presented by James R. Cooper and Stephen A. Pyhrr, "Forecasting the Rates of Return on an Apartment Investment: A Case Study," *The Appraisal Journal*, July 1973, pp. 312–337.

EXHIBIT 9-A.   Aspen Wood Apartments—Financial Package

DEBT STRUCTURE

1. *Amount of debt.* $793,400.
2. *Lender.* Seller (a limited partnership syndication).
3. *Type of mortgage.* Wraparound, junior to three existing mortgage loans.
4. *Interest rate.* 7.5% annually, payable monthly with principal.
5. *Amortization method.* Fully amortizing, level payment.
6. *Amortization term.* 26.5 years.
7. *Loan term.* Balloon at end of ten years. First payment due one month after closing.
8. *Commitment fees/points.* Two points paid to lender (seller) at closing.
9. *Degree of personal liability.* None (seller remains liable on underlying notes).
10. *Prepayment provision.* Seller can prepay at any time.
11. *Prepayment penalty.* Pay only specified penalties in underlying notes when they are prepaid.
12. *Required escrow accounts.* No escrows for taxes and insurance. Tax and insurance paid receipts to be provided to lender. Trustee account (for buyer and lender) is established and receives debt service on wraparound loan, pays debt service on underlying loans, sends overage to wraparound lender (seller).
13. *Due-on-sale clause.* None. Owners can sell subject to a wraparound loan.
14. *Due-on-encumbrance clause.* No restriction on additional financing. Lender (seller) can refinance the wraparound loan at terms that leave the owners financially indifferent. Approval will not be unreasonably withheld by owner.
15. *Other mortgage clauses.* No adverse clauses affecting buyer. One-month grace period on debt service payments before loan balance can be accelerated by lender.

EQUITY STRUCTURE

1. *Amount of equity.* $210,000.
2. *Form of ownership.* Joint venture (general partnership, essentially).
3. *Source of equity.* Private participation by individuals and syndicators.
4. *Allocation of return–risks.* All partners share equally in cash flow, tax benefits, refinancing and sale benefits, according to their percentage ownership.
5. *Property management.* D&B Associates (syndicators); 5% fee.

EXHIBIT 9-A. Continued

6. *Venture management.* D&B Associates. Attorney and tax accountants retained by venture. All direct costs paid by the joint venture.

7. *Registration.* None. Venture relies on private and intrastate exemptions under federal and state laws.

8. *Tax status.* No 1065 filed. Venture elects out of partnership tax reporting. (*Note:* Under current tax law, the venture must file a 1065 or be subject to substantial penalties.)

EXHIBIT 9-B. IRR$_E$ and DCR Data for Financial Package Analysis, Most Likely Scenario

	75% Leverage			85% Leverage			95% Leverage		
	20 Years	25 Years	30 Years	20 Years	25 Years	30 Years	20 Years	25 Years	30 Years
6%	18.0 (1.42–1.64)	18.9 (1.58–1.83)	19.5 (1.70–1.96)	25.0 (1.26–1.45)	27.0 (1.40–1.61)	28.5 (1.50–1.73)	49.3 (1.12–1.30)	59.5 (1.25–1.44)	67.0 (1.34–1.55)
7.5%	16.6 (1.27–1.46)	17.3 (1.38–1.59)	17.8 (1.46–1.68)	22.7 (1.12–1.30)	24.4 (1.22–1.41)	25.6 (1.29–1.49)	43.8 (1.00–1.15)	52.6 (1.09–1.26)	58.9 (1.15–1.33)
9%	15.1 (1.13–1.31)	15.6 (1.22–1.40)	16.0 (1.27–1.46)	20.2 (1.00–1.16)	21.6 (1.07–1.24)	22.5 (1.12–1.29)	37.7 (0.90–1.03)	44.8 (0.96–1.11)	49.8 (1.00–1.16)
10.5%	13.5 (1.02–1.78)	13.9 (1.08–1.25)	14.1 (1.12–1.29)	17.5 (0.90–1.04)	18.5 (0.95–1.10)	19.2 (0.98–1.14)	31.1 (0.81–0.93)	36.4 (0.85–0.98)	40.1 (0.88–1.02)
12%	11.8 (0.93–1.07)	12.0 (0.97–1.12)	12.1 (0.99–1.15)	14.6 (0.82–0.94)	15.3 (0.86–0.99)	15.7 (0.88–1.01)	24.1 (0.73–0.84)	27.6 (0.77–0.88)	29.9 (0.78–0.90)

Investment criteria:

1. Internal rate of return on equity (IRR$_E$) for 7-year holding period (top number shown in each box).

2. Debt coverage ratio range (DCR), years 1 and 7 (numbers in parentheses). In all cases the DCR increases each year for sever years; thus, the two DCR figures show the level and trend over the holding period.

Internal rate of return on total capital (IRR$_{TC}$): 7.64% in all cases. Variations in the financing variables do not affect the IRR$_{TC}$.

Especially important to D&B was the impact of the financial package on cash flow during an economic downturn (pessimistic case). Could the joint venture survive through bad times? The concern was to structure a financial package that would result in "tolerable" cash flow losses during such a period. It was clear to Davidson and Boomer that as the leverage ratio and interest rate increase and the loan term decreases, the DCR falls and eventually negative cash flows occur. What are the relationships among these changes, the IRR_E, the DCR, and other risk and return ratios?

OUTPUT DATA AND ANALYSIS

Altogether, the investor would need to perform 135 cash flow simulations to generate all the data required under the variations just described.[b] Exhibit 9-B presents the financial data for the most likely case only, using only the IRR_E and DCR range as financial criteria.

The results show IRR_E ranging from a high of 67 percent (95 percent leverage, 6 percent interest, thirty years) to a low of 11.8 percent (75 percent leverage, 12 percent interest, 20 years). The coverage ratios range from a high of 1.70–1.96 (75 percent leverage, 6 percent interest, thirty years) to a low of .73–.84 (95 percent leverage, 12 percent interest, twenty years). The results are not surprising, but they do show the relative magnitude of changes in the return parameters (IRR_E) and risk parameter (DCR) as the financing variables change. As expected, more aggressive leverage positions require the assumption of higher risks and increase the probability of negative cash flows (DCR < 1). However, in all cases there is positive leverage after tax in the long run, as evidenced by a comparison of the IRR_{TC} and the IRR_E. In all cases $IRR_E > IRR_{TC}$.

An analysis of the output data for the pessimistic economic scenario provided important information but is not presented here. As expected, all the data look substantially worse. The returns and the coverage ratios are consistently lower.

THE FINANCIAL PACKAGE DECISION

The investor's strategy is to negotiate a financial package that will produce the highest returns (IRR in this case) relative to the risks (DCR range in this case).

The financial analysis should provide enough data for two important determinations:

1. *Trade-off decisions.* What can be gained and lost during the negotiation process in order to leave the investor financially indifferent? The goal is to gain more than you lose, yet leave the negotiation table with the seller believing that he or she has achieved the same result.
2. *Minimum-cutoff-point decisions.* Certain financial packages are not acceptable to the investor and therefore should not be considered.

[b]Three leverage ratios, five interest rates, three amortization terms, and three economic scenarios will produce 135 simulations (3 × 5 × 3 × 3 = 135).

In the Aspen Wood situation Davidson and Boomer were not able to negotiate a high leverage ratio because of the seller's cash requirements, as explained in Chapter 6. However, a favorable interest rate and term were negotiated, along with very favorable mortgage clauses. All the minimum financial requirements of the venture were achieved, and the expected IRR_E was substantially above the required IRR_E.[c]

[c]Note that the required IRR_E might change for each financial package analyzed. The investor's required IRR_E should be increased when riskier financial packages are designed (e.g., higher leverage ratios and interest rates) and lowered when more conservative financial packages are designed.

10

TAX PLANNING AND DETAILED FINANCIAL ANALYSIS

In the days of the Indians there were no taxes—no debts—and the women did all the work. The white man thought he could improve on this system.

Death and taxes will always be with us; but there is a difference . . . death cannot get any worse.

HUGO H. LOWENSTERN[1]

The tax laws in the United States have become so complex and perplexing that more than one observer has exclaimed that "It takes more brains to make out income tax reports than it does to make the income." Tax laws, regulations, procedures, and guidelines become significantly more understandable when placed in an investment analysis framework and analyzed over the entire ownership life cycle. This chapter focuses not on the tax factors themselves, but rather on how they work through real economic variables and affect a property's investment value and expected rate of return and risk profile over both the short and the long run. It is especially important for the investor to understand how to manage and control tax variables within the framework of tax laws, regulations, and guidelines and thus increase or maximize the after-tax IRR relative to business and financial risks.

During the development of the ten-step model of the investment analysis process, it was noted that tax considerations are important in many of the steps. In fact, taxation considerations play an important role in each step as illustrated in Exhibit 10-1.

[1]*Tax Facts* (Amarillo, Texas: Tax Facts, 1972), pp. 117, 118.

Acknowledgment: The revision of this chapter was prepared with the assistance of Robert Allen of Arthur Young & Company, Boston.

EXHIBIT 10-1.   Overview of Tax Considerations in the Investment Analysis and Financial Structuring Process

Step in the Investment Process	Description of Relevant Tax Considerations
1 Determine Investment Strategy	Tax objectives and criteria are defined at this stage; plans and policies are developed to achieve these objectives. Basic screening criteria may be oriented toward achieving tax objectives.
2 Generate Alternatives	Properties are located that meet the basic tax criteria. The investor might seek properties with low land-to-improvement ratios, sellers who are willing to take low down payments, with interest-only financing terms, and so on.
3 Analyze Property Using Basic Feasibility Models	First runs of DCF analysis make basic tax assumptions and provide return–risk data for analysis and negotiations.
4 Negotiate Basic Terms with the Seller	The basic tax parameters of the purchase are negotiated with the seller. The purchase price, down payment required, and financing arrangements all have related tax impacts.
5 Do Detailed Feasibility Research	Basic data for arriving at the tax assumptions will be utilized to structure the tax package in step 6.
6 Complete Financial and Tax Structuring	Detailed analysis and structuring of tax benefits is undertaken. A tax package that considers all ownership phases—acquisition, operations, and termination—is developed.
7 Perform DCF Analysis	The impact of tax variables as they interact with other economic and financial variables is analyzed. The tax results are compared to tax criteria established in step 1 and a final investment decision is made.
8 Final Negotiations and Closing	Final negotiation of the contract and closing details are arranged, locking in all tax ramifications produced by the price, terms, and timing factors of the acquisition.
9 Manage the Property	Decisions regarding expensing or capitalizing cash expenditures, preventive maintenance programs, periodic refinancing and renovation, and leasing policies, among other factors, have important tax impacts each year.
10 Terminate the Property	Tax-planning considerations include recognition of gain, installment or outright sale, tax-free exchanges, income averaging, and balancing off gains or losses from other sources.

This chapter emphasizes step 6 of the investment process, beginning with a discussion of the various provisions of the federal income tax law as it affects real estate investors. Numerous tax-planning alternatives are then reviewed with a discussion of the issues that affect a property's return and risk parameters. Finally, a tax strategy framework and checklist will be developed, incorporating many of the complexities discussed. Then the Aspen Wood case is used to illustrate the principles presented, with detailed financial and tax analysis of that property.

TAX REFORM AND REAL ESTATE INVESTMENT

Before 1976, amendments to the federal income tax statutes were not followed by the general public with a great deal of interest. Since 1976 and particularly during the Reagan presidency, the constant tinkering with the federal revenue statutes has almost become an annual event. This continual, evolutionary effort has caused a consistently changing pattern of reducing tax burdens, closing loopholes, and making sure that everyone has paid his or her "fair share" of the federal income tax burden. A particular beneficiary of this process had been the real estate industry. Because of the various provisions, investors in real estate were able to enjoy accelerated depreciation to defer taxation of other forms of income and favorable taxation on the disposition of a real estate investment. The result was an unprecedented boom of prosperity for the industry. Critics charged that, because the tax law had such favorable bias toward the real estate industry, investment decisions were motivated more by perceived tax benefits than by real economic benefits. Part of the goal of Congress when it passed the Tax Reform Act of 1986 was to correct that perceived favorable bias.

Tax Reform Act of 1986

In 1986, the U.S. Internal Revenue Code was substantially revised in an effort by Congress to reverse the trend toward increased use of tax law to implement fiscal economic policy.[2] With the goal of removing the tax code as a significant factor in business and personal investment behavior, many

[2] A clear and concise analysis of the act is available in the Research Institute of America, Inc., *The RIA Complete Analysis of the '86 Tax Reform Act* (New York: The Research Institute of America, 1986). For a detailed analysis of the 1986 act, including the text of the law and relevant committee reports, see *Tax Reform Act of 1986: Law and Controlling Committee Reports* (Washington, D.C.: Commerce Clearing House Inc., 1986); see also *Explanation of Tax Reform Act of 1986* (Washington, D.C.: Commerce Clearing House Inc., 1986). A more investor-oriented analysis is provided by Alvin L. Arnold, *Real Estate Investments After the Tax Reform Act of 1986* (Boston: Warren, Gorham & Lamont, 1987). Most of the major public accounting firms have also published special reports on the 1986 act and its impact on real estate investments.

incentives such as investment tax credits and capital gains exclusions were removed from the law. Because of political factors, however, some incentive structures have remained, such as deductions for state and local taxes, charitable contributions, and home mortgage interest.

In addition to changing deductions and credits, the act significantly reduced tax rates for both individuals and businesses. The theory behind this change was that, with deductions and credits for investment incentives removed, the tax base would be larger and, therefore, the same amount of revenue could be raised with lower rates of tax. For individuals, the rate reductions were phased in. In 1987, the highest bracket was reduced from 50 percent to 38.5 percent. For 1988 and later years, the top rate is 28 percent. For corporations, the maximum rate of tax was reduced from 46 percent to 34 percent, effective July 1, 1987.

Several provisions have had a strong impact on the real estate industry: the repeal of the capital gains exclusion, the significant lengthening of cost recovery periods for real estate assets, and the introduction of passive-loss limitations. As of January 1, 1987, the 60 percent capital gains exclusion was repealed. The effective maximum tax rate for capital gains thus increased from 20 to 28 percent. Although this relatively small increase does not represent a significant disincentive for investing in real estate, the substantial incentive represented by the difference between the former maximum tax rate (50 percent) and the maximum effective rate of tax on capital gains (20 percent) was removed.

The vast scope of the changes in the tax law in 1986 has brought about a reevaluation of many traditional tax-planning ideas. Although some of the particulars of the new tax law, including revisions in 1987 and 1988, have not yet been resolved by Congress or the IRS, this chapter incorporates as many of the known variables and provisions as possible, compares them with the provisions of the prior law, and indicates how they are likely to affect real estate investment decision making. Investors should consult tax-planning literature to ascertain the current status of the new tax law as it is refined by the IRS and tested in the marketplace and through the federal court system.

THE TAX LAW

Real estate is taxed by all levels of government—federal, state, and local. The federal government taxes real estate investments through the income tax, the estate tax, and the gift tax. The primary emphasis here is on the federal income tax, since it has by far the most important influence on real estate investment decisions. As explained in Chapter 7, federal income taxes are levied on two forms of income: ordinary income and capital gains income. Gift and estate taxes are also relevant, but they will be discussed in Chapter 17.

In contrast to the federal government, most state governments do not rely on real estate as a primary source of revenue. Most states share in property taxes collected at the local level, and many states have an income tax, but the rates are quite low compared with federal rates. At the local level, the primary form of taxation is the real (ad valorem) property tax. For investment property such taxes are treated as operating expenses and, therefore, are deductible for purposes of federal income taxation.

The Income Tax Formula

Real estate investments, as contrasted with other investment media, generally have received relatively favorable tax treatment. One of the keys to understanding real estate taxation is to understand the general income tax formula. For individuals, this is encompassed by Form 1040, the individual income tax return. The details of the 1040 statement are extremely complex, but the basic formula contained therein is quite simple, as shown in Exhibit 10-2.

All Income. The income tax formula begins with the total income to the individual, including the following.

1. Wages, salaries, and tips
2. Interest income
3. Dividends
4. Capital gain or loss

EXHIBIT 10-2.   The General Income Tax Formula (Individual Taxpayer)

	All income
Less:	Exclusions
Equals:	Gross income
Less:	Deductions FOR adjusted gross income (AGI)
Equals:	Adjusted gross income (AGI)
Less:	Deductions FROM adjusted gross income (which consist of):
	1. The larger of
	▪ A standard deduction, OR
	▪ Itemized personal deductions, PLUS
	2. Personal and dependent exemptions
Equals:	Taxable income
Times:	Applicable tax rate(s)
Equals:	Gross tax
Less:	Tax credits and prepayments
Equals:	Net tax payable

Source: Raymond M. Summerfeld, Hershel M. Anderson, and Horace R. Brock, *An Introduction to Taxation* (New York: Harcourt Brace Jovanovich, 1979), p. 5-1.

5. Rents, royalties, partnerships, estates, or trusts
6. Scholarships, gifts, inheritances

Adjusted Gross Income (AGI). Deductions *for* AGI are subtracted from *gross income* to arrive at the *adjusted gross income.* Deductions *for* AGI include items such as business expenses and payments to a Keogh retirement plan, and in certain cases payments to an IRA retirement plan. After the investor has determined AGI, he or she must choose between itemizing personal deductions or taking the standard deduction. If the investor has substantial mortgage interest and property tax deductions on a *personal* residence, these will be deducted as itemized personal deductions. Deductions related to a personal residence are therefore adjustments *from* AGI, whereas tax losses on other types of real estate investments are adjustments in arriving at *all income.*

Taxable Income and Tax Rate Schedules. The tax rate is applied to *taxable income*, which is the net amount remaining after all exclusions and deductions have been taken. For example, the tax rate schedules for 1988 are as shown in Exhibit 10-3. The basic theory underlying the tax rate schedules is that the tax rate increases proportionately with the investor's income and wealth. In real estate the system sometimes works in reverse. For the investor who structures properties to produce tax losses, the tax benefit is directly related to the marginal income tax rate of the individual. If a married investor filing jointly reports taxable income in excess of $71,900 (Exhibit 10-3), the marginal income is taxed at 33 percent, and tax losses are used to shelter income that would otherwise be taxed at this rate.

For example, assume that a married investor has a taxable income of $149,250 in 1988 and subsequently purchases properties that produce tax losses of $149,250. By using these losses to offset the $149,250 in taxable income, the investor reduces net taxable income to zero.[3] Instead of paying $41,790, the investor receives a tax benefit of $41,790, and income through all the tax brackets (from 33 percent down to zero) has been sheltered. The greatest benefits, of course, are received at the higher tax brackets; lower tax brackets produce lower amounts of tax saving. In this example, the *effective marginal* tax rate used to calculate the tax savings (assuming that the tax situation shown remains unchanged over the holding period) should have been approximately 28 percent.

$$\text{Effective marginal tax bracket} = \frac{\text{taxes saved}}{\text{income sheltered (amount of tax loss)}}$$
$$= \frac{\$ \ 41,790}{\$149,250}$$
$$= 28\%$$

---

[3]Both the passive-loss limitation rules and the alternative minimum tax, which may increase taxes payable, will be discussed later.

EXHIBIT 10-3.   Tax Rate Schedules for 1988

SINGLE INDIVIDUALS			MARRIED FILING SEPARATELY		
Taxable Income Over	But Not Over	Rate	Taxable Income Over	But Not Over	Rate
$ 0	$ 17,850	15%	$ 0	$ 14,875	15%
17,850	43,150	28	14,875	35,950	28
43,150	89,560[a]	33	35,950	113,300[a]	33
89,560		28	113,300		28

MARRIED FILING JOINTLY			HEAD OF HOUSEHOLD		
Taxable Income Over	But Not Over	Rate	Taxable Income Over	But Not Over	Rate
$ 0	$ 29,750	15%	$ 0	$ 23,900	15%
29,750	71,900	28	23,900	61,650	28
71,900	149,250[a]	33	61,650	123,790[a]	33
149,250		28	123,790		28

[a]The 33 percent bracket will be broader than the amounts shown in the above schedules depending on the number of exemptions claimed. For each exemption, the upper limit of the bracket will increase by $10,920.

The investor should always consider the impact of new investments on the marginal tax bracket. In the present case, the marginal bracket went from 33 percent to zero, with the net impact being an *effective marginal bracket* of 28 percent for investment analysis calculations. If the original 33 percent marginal tax bracket were used (instead of 28 percent), the resulting cash flow projections (after tax) would overstate the amount of annual tax savings.

Net Tax Payable.   The gross tax minus tax credits and prepayments equals the *net tax payable*. Various tax credits have played an increasing role in real estate investments in recent years. Tax credits are often preferred by Congress when it seeks to stimulate capital investment, since individuals in lower tax brackets benefit equally with those in higher brackets. On the other hand, liberalizing investment expense deductions favors individuals in higher tax brackets. An increased depreciation deduction of $10,000 is worth $3,300 to a person in the 33 percent bracket, but only $1,500 to a person in the 15 percent bracket. A tax credit is thus a direct tax subsidy, whereas increased expense deductions are an indirect subsidy that works through the investor's tax bracket and favors persons in high tax brackets.

Corporations. Corporations use an abbreviated form of the tax formula to compute taxable income. They go directly from gross income to taxable income, with deductions allowed for all ordinary and necessary business expenses. Under the 1986 Tax Act the top corporate income tax rate is 34 percent; a graduated rate structure is provided for corporations with taxable income of less than $100,000.

CORPORATE TAX RATES	
Taxable Income	Tax Rate (Percent)
0–$50,000	15
$50,000–75,000	25
Over $75,000	34

Capital Gains Versus Ordinary Income

Since 1986, all taxpayers have been subject to new capital gains tax rules. The key distinction from prior laws is that the 60 percent long-term capital gains deduction for individuals, estates, and trusts is no longer available. Although long- and short-term capital gains have continued to be treated as distinct from other types of income, they will be taxed at the regular income tax rates as long as the 1986 rules remain in effect.

The repeal of the capital gains deduction eliminated capital gains as a preference item for purposes of the alternative minimum tax. Despite the repeal, taxpayers must still distinguish between ordinary income and capital gains, and they must continue to differentiate between long- and short-term gains. For tax years beginning after 1986, both net short-term capital losses and net long-term capital losses of individuals, trusts, and estates may be used to offset a maximum of $3,000 of ordinary income. Excess losses may be carried forward to an unlimited number of future years. The corporate rule of three-year carrybacks and five-year carryovers with no dollar limitation remains.

Necessary Conditions for Long-Term Capital Gain Treatment. There are four conditions that must be met to achieve long-term capital gains treatment on the sale of property. If they are not met, some or all of the gain recognized will be considered ordinary income.

1. The property must be considered a *capital asset* or *Section 1231 property* under the tax code definition.
2. The property must be owned for a period greater than six months.
3. The investor cannot be considered a *dealer* in real estate.
4. The straight-line depreciation (cost recovery) method must have been used.

Many real estate assets (e.g., raw-land investments) are considered *capital assets* by the tax code. However, a special provision of the tax code—Section 1231—allows for long-term capital gains treatment for real or depreciable property used in a trade or business, provided that the property has been held for more than twelve months and the net total of the transactions for the year for those properties shows a gain. Surprisingly, most rental property (e.g., apartments, office buildings, shopping centers) is classified as Section 1231 property for tax purposes. Exhibit 10-4 illustrates how gains and losses are netted in the various categories of capital assets and 1231 property.

Even though capital gains are currently being taxed at the same rate as ordinary income, for tax-planning purposes the distinction between the two categories has remained important. One reason is that favorable long-term capital gains treatment may be reinstated. Another reason is that individuals investing in real estate may want to avoid the limitations on use of capital losses to offset ordinary income. One way to achieve this would be for investors to qualify as dealers so as to avoid characterization of income or losses as capital gains and losses.

A dealer is one who holds property primarily for sale to customers in the ordinary course of a trade or business. A holder of property for long-term appreciation or to produce income is not a dealer. Many factors are considered in distinguishing a real estate dealer from an investor, including the following.[4]

- The seller's purpose in acquiring the property—whether for long-term investment or short-term resale.
- The purpose for which the seller actually used the property.
- The length of the holding period.
- Whether the property was promptly replaced with similar property, as is a dealer's inventory.
- Segregation of the investment property from business property on the owner's books.
- The extent of promotional or developmental activity: dealers, not investors, promote and develop their holdings.
- Whether the owner's intent at the time of sale was the liquidation of an investment, rather than turnover of inventory.
- The frequency of sales of the particular type of property sold: numerous sales point to a business rather than an investment.

[4]Mason J. Sacks, *Real Estate Tax Shelter Techniques*, Portfolio No. 13 (Boston: Warren, Gorham & Lamont, 1977), p. 36. See also John T. Reed, "Dealer Property" (Chapter 10), *Aggressive Tax Avoidance for Real Estate Investors* (Danville, Calif.: Reed Publishing, 1985), pp. 199–203; Richard P. Sills, "The Dealer-Investor Problem Revisted: Charting a Course to Avoid the Pitfalls," *Journal of Real Estate Taxation*, Fall 1976, pp. 24–40.

EXHIBIT 10-4   Taxation of Real Estate Asset Transactions[a]

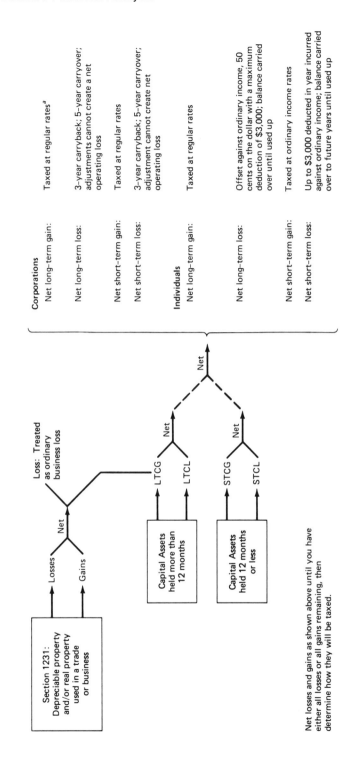

Net losses and gains as shown above until you have either all losses or all gains remaining, then determine how they will be taxed.

Source: J. Warren Higgins, *Tax Considerations in Real Estate Transactions* (Chicago: Society of Real Estate Appraisers, 1974), p. 1–8.
[a]Updated through the Tax Reform Act of 1986.

- Whether the gain realized resulted from the owner's development activities or was a long-term appreciation in value.
- The manner in which the property was sold and the purpose for which it was held at the time of sale.

Before the Tax Reform Act of 1986, the IRS would often contest the capital gains treatment if the investor was a real estate salesperson, broker, or developer, or had sold several properties within a reasonably short time. Real estate practitioners were especially vulnerable to IRS scrutiny of capital gains reported, but other professionals and business executives were also frequently challenged. For example, the following situations militated against favorable capital gains treatment for any investor: (1) several properties sold in one tax year, (2) the net gains from property forming a large part of the investor's total income, (3) the investor actively advertising and selling the properties without using a broker, and (4) a large percentage of the investor's time being devoted to real estate investment transactions.

Investors can take an aggressive position on the classification of their property. Even developers have been permitted capital gains treatment by the courts, provided they have been careful to segregate their books and list their investment separately from property suitable for development. Carefully kept books and records are essential to a successful investor defense.

Before 1986, the distinction between investor and dealer was very critical to the owner of real estate because of the very favorable taxation provided to investors in the disposition of their real estate investments (i.e., a maximum tax rate no greater than 20 percent). The repeal of the capital gains differential makes this distinction less important because the tax rates are the same. However, there is always the possibility that Congress will reinstate lower taxation for recognized capital gains and, therefore, it is still important for an investor to be concerned with avoiding the "dealer taint." Another reason for avoiding the dealer taint is that investors can qualify for favorable installment sale tax treatment when a property is sold; dealers cannot qualify for such favorable treatment under the Revenue Act of 1987.

Capital Gain and Depreciation Recapture. The amount of *total gain* recognized on the sale of real estate is equal to the difference between the depreciated basis of the property and the net selling price of the property (see Exhibit 10-5). If the owner used the straight-line method of depreciation and the property qualifies for long-term capital gains tax treatment, the entire difference $(B - D)$ is treated as a capital gain. However, if accelerated depreciation was claimed and the property is *residential* in character, the difference between accelerated and straight-line depreciation (called *excess depreciation* or *depreciation recapture*) is taxed as ordinary

EXHIBIT 10-5. Taxation of Total Gain upon Sale of Property

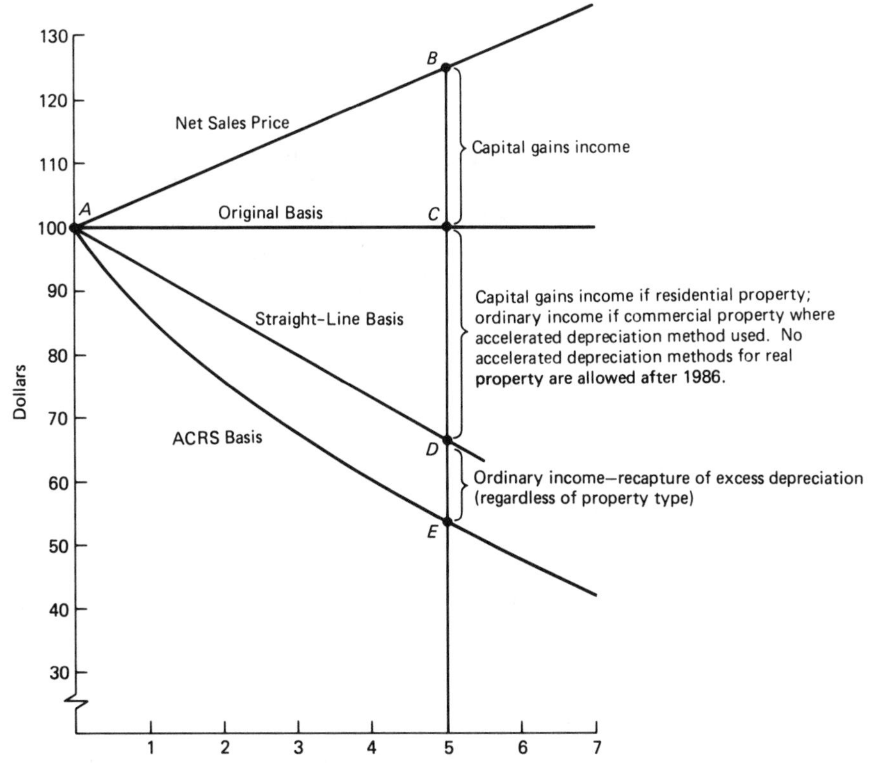

A = Purchase price = Original basis = $100,000
B = Net sales price = $125,000
C = Original basis = $100,000
D = Remaining basis using straight-line depreciation = $66,667
E = Remaining ACRS basis (175% declining balance depreciation) = $53,780

income. Sales of residential rental property and nonresidential real property acquired after 1986 will not be subject to the recapture rules because such property is required to be depreciated on a straight-line basis.

In 1981 the recapture rules were modified for nonresidential (commercial) properties when the investor elected an accelerated depreciation (cost recovery) method. In such cases, not only was the amount of excess depreciation $(D - E)$ treated as ordinary income, but the total amount of straight-line depreciation taken $(C - D)$ was also treated as ordinary income. Thus, for commercial properties such as buildings and shopping centers, the total amount of depreciation taken $(C - E)$ was taxed as ordinary income when the property was disposed of. However, if the straight-line depreciation method was used, the entire gain $(B - D)$ was a capital gain.

The recapture rules were also modified for government-qualified, low-income residential properties. For such properties, if the holding period was less than 100 months (8$\frac{1}{3}$ years), all excess depreciation was recaptured as ordinary income. For each month thereafter, a 1 percent credit was given toward capital gains treatment. After 200 months (16$\frac{2}{3}$ years), all excess depreciation would be converted to capital gains income. This phase-out provision for depreciation recapture was intended to provide a tax incentive for investment for low-income housing. The reader is reminded that, under the 1986 tax reform law, the difference in tax between capital gains and ordinary income has been neutralized. However, if Congress does reinstate the differential between these two categories of income, characterization of gain will once again become important to the real estate investor.

Exhibit 10-5 assumes purchase of a building (no land) at a cost of $100,000 with a depreciable life (recovery period) of fifteen years[5]; the building appreciates at the rate of 5 percent (noncompounded) per year. At the end of five years the property has a market value of $125,000 and is sold at that price. Line *AB* shows the annual market value of the property. Line *AC* shows the original basis of the property. Line *AD* shows the annual depreciated basis for the property assuming the investor used straight-line depreciation. The amount of gain represented by the distance between points *B* and *D* would be taxed as a capital gain, except in the case of a commercial property for which an accelerated depreciation method was used. Line *AE* shows the annual basis for the property, assuming the investor used the accelerated cost recovery system (ACRS). The amount of gain represented by the distance between points *D* and *E* is the portion subject to recapture and will be taxed as ordinary income, regardless of the property type.

Depreciation and the Accelerated Cost Recovery System

Certainly the most significant variable that creates tax shelter benefits for the investor is the allowance for depreciation. From the beginning, the federal tax laws recognized an investor's right to deduct from taxable income an amount representing the *using up* of assets. In essence, this is a recognition that a portion of the net operating income from a property represents not true income but a recoupment of the capital investment, measured by the depreciation of those assets.

The accelerated cost recovery system (ACRS) was introduced in the Economic Recovery Tax Act of 1981. The ACRS classified property into groups based on recovery periods. Generally, real property was depreciated over a period of nineteen years for property placed in service after

---

[5]The fifteen-year useful life was permitted for property that was placed in service after 1980 and before March 16, 1984. Current law requires a 31.5-year life for commercial property and a 27.5-year life for residential property.

May 8, 1985 and before 1987. For real property placed in service after March 15, 1984 and before May 9, 1985, the recovery period was eighteen years. A fifteen-year recovery period was available for low-income housing and property placed in service before March 16, 1984 and after 1980. Cost recovery rates reflected the 175 percent and 200 percent declining-balance methods.

Under the provisions of the Tax Reform Act of 1986, the modified accelerated cost recovery system (MACRS) must be used to depreciate most tangible assets placed in service after December 31, 1986. Residential real property is depreciated on a straight-line basis over a period of 27.5 years. Nonresidential real property is depreciated in the same manner, but over a period of 31.5 years. It is important to note that the first-year depreciation can be claimed only for the portion of the year that the property is in service. The concept of cost recovery eliminates the need to determine the depreciation method used for each asset, its useful life, and its salvage value. These determinations are greatly simplified and allow the investor fewer choices. (In the following sections, which focus on these issues, the terms *depreciation* and *cost recovery* will often be used interchangeably.)

Depreciable Basis. What capital expenditures can be depreciated over time? In general, if a property expenditure is capitalized, everything except land and salvage value can be depreciated. Since 1981, the tax law has allowed real estate investors to disregard salvage value. With regard to allocations between land and improvements, tax shelter maximizers are motivated to allocate the maximum amount of basis to improvements and a minimum to land, thereby maximizing the amount of potential depreciation over time.

The problem of allocations between improvements and land is especially difficult when land and improvements are acquired together for a lump sum. The IRS regulations are silent on the issue of how the respective values are to be ascertained. A professional appraisal is one approach to solving the problem, but few investors are anxious to incur the expense of a professional appraisal for this purpose alone. Other approaches used successfully by investors include the establishment of land and improvement values based on (1) the local tax assessor's allocation, (2) allocations specified by the seller and buyer in the purchase contract, and (3) valuation of the building from an investment perspective by capitalizing its cash flow.

When does depreciation begin? Since depreciation is allowed on property that is assumed to be decreasing in value because of physical wear and tear, depreciation of an asset should begin when the asset is placed in service. Depreciable property is usually considered to be placed in service when it has been completed and is ready to be occupied by renters.

Depreciation (Cost Recovery) Methods. Traditionally, the tax law permitted real estate investors to use one of three depreciation methods:

straight line, sum-of-the-years' digits (SOYD), and declining balance. Exhibit 10-6 shows the depreciation method limitations applicable to various categories of real assets acquired before 1981, from 1981 to 1986, and after 1986. The person property category (Section 1245 property) includes assets such as furniture, drapes, refrigerators, stoves, individual room air conditioners, coin-operated vending machines, maintenance equipment, and carpets not permanently attached to the floor. Thus, numerous items in both residential and commercial properties qualify as personal property.

Again, if the investor owns commercial property purchased between 1981 and 1986, and used an accelerated method, *all* recovery deductions taken will be treated as ordinary income when the property is sold. Only appreciation of property value will be treated as a capital gain. Consequently, the law provided a strong incentive for owners of commercial property to use the straight-line method. In comparison, owners of residential rental property were treated favorably: gain on the sale of property was ordinary income only to the extent that the accelerated deductions taken exceeded those using the straight-line method (see Exhibit 10-5).

The term *residential rental property* includes single-family and multi-family housing, apartments, and similar structures used to provide living accommodations on a rental basis. To qualify, at least 80 percent of the gross rental income must be from dwelling units. Hotels, motels, inns, or other similar establishments are not treated as dwelling units if more than one-half the units are used on a transient basis. If the investor owns a multiuse property, at least 80 percent of the gross income must be from the residential portion in order to qualify.

Low-income housing rehabilitation projects receive special treatment ment under the 1986 cost-recovery rules. Such expenditures qualify for a special 60-month amortization period for up to $40,000 per unit. To qualify, however, such projects must meet strict criteria that may appear onerous to potential investors.

Passive-Loss Limitation Rules

One of the factors that contributed to the popularity of real estate investments prior to 1986 was the ability to use depreciation, interest, and other expenses in excess of income of the investment to offset taxes due on the investor's other forms of income (most commonly, salary from employment). This was changed dramatically by the introduction of the *passive-activity rules* and was the cornerstone of the attack on tax shelters in the Tax Reform Act of 1986.[6]

[6]Coopers and Lybrand, "Tax Reform Act of 1986," *Real Estate Newsletter*, October 1986, pp. 8–14. For a critical analysis of these rules, see Daniel S. Goldberg, "The Passive Activity Loss Rules: Planning Considerations, Techniques, and a Foray Into Never-Never Land," *The Journal of Real Estate Taxation*, Fall 1987, pp. 3–35; also, Alvin L. Arnold, *Real Estate Investments After the Tax Reform Act of 1986*, pp. 43–51.

Commencing in 1987, income of noncorporate taxpayers is deemed to fall into three broad categories labeled *active, portfolio,* and *passive.* Active income generally includes a taxpayer's earned income—such as wages, bonus, and income from a business that the taxpayer manages. Portfolio income generally consists of income from such traditional investments as stocks and bonds and includes dividends, interest, and gains from the disposition of this category of assets. Passive income is derived from activities from the operation of the business in which the owner does not materially participate. One special inclusion in the passive–activity category is the rental of real estate. Unfortunately, the impact of this inclusion is that, regardless of the individual's participation, no real estate rental activity—with one exception—can be classified in the active category.[7] Rather, by law, it must be classified as passive.

The major change resulting from this classification is that losses from passive activities (e.g., depreciation and interest expense in excess of rental income) can be used only against income from other passive activities. Therefore, the provision for using tax losses from real estate investments to offset taxation on other forms of income no longer applies to the real estate investor. What happens to the passive losses? A taxpayer who incurs a passive loss must postpone deducting this loss until he or she has passive income. If the individual never generates passive income, then this loss plus passive losses incurred in subsequent years are deferred (or "suspended") until the investor disposes of the real estate investment. At this time he or she can deduct all the suspended passive losses against the gain, if any, resulting from the disposition of the property. Any excess loss can then be used to shelter portfolio or active income.

The effect of this change is that the tax benefits or savings from these losses cannot be included in the investor's after-tax cash flow return unless the investor currently has passive income from other sources. The real estate investor may not have such passive income and will have to carry forward these tax losses until they can be offset in future years. These considerations must be addressed when arriving at an "assumption base" for all DCF analysis.

Phase-in Rule. The passive-loss limitation rules apply to all new and existing passive-activity investments made after 1986. However, for investments in real estate made before October 22, 1986 (the date of enactment of the law), the rule is phased-in over a five-year period. In 1987 the investor could use 65 percent of the passive losses from these investments to shelter active and portfolio income; in 1988 the amount declined to 40 percent; in 1989, it declines to 20 percent; in 1990, 10 percent; after 1990, no passive losses can be used to shelter other income. The phase-in rule was

---

[7]Hotels, motels, and other similar transient lodging facilities are one exception to this rule. Operating such a facility where "substantial services are provided" is not considered a rental activity.

EXHIBIT 10-6.   Depreciation (Recovery) Method Limitations Applicable to Real Estate Assets

Type of Property	Property Acquired before 1981: Maximum Depreciation Method Authorized[a]	Property Acquired Between 1981 and 1986: Maximum Cost Recovery Method Authorized Under ACRS[b]	Property Acquired After 1986: Cost Recovery Method Required by Tax Reform Act of 1986
PERSONAL PROPERTY (Section 1245 property)			
A. If the property is new	200% declining balance if life is greater than three years	Statutory percentages approximate the 150% declining-balance method for years 1981–1984, the 175% method for properties acquired in 1985, and the 200% method for properties acquired after 1985. No distinction between new and used property. Assumes switch to straight-line or sum-of-the-years' digits method.	Statutory rates approximate 200% method with switch to straight-line method. No distinction between new and used property.
B. If the property is used	150% declining balance		

REAL PROPERTY (Section 1250 property)

A. If residential rental property is:		
1. Acquired new	200% declining balance or sum-of-the-years' digits	Statutory percentages approximate the 175% declining balance method with switch to straight line for all property except low-income rental housing. Low-income rental housing is permitted deductions based on the 200% declining balance method with switch to straight line. No distinction between new and used property.
2. Acquired used with an estimated life of twenty years or more	125% declining balance	
3. Acquired used with an estimated remaining life of less than twenty years	Straight line	Straight-line method only for a period of 27.5 years. No distinction between new and used property.
B. If commercial property is		
1. Acquired new	150% declining balance	Statutory percentages approximate the 175% declining-balance method with switch to straight line. No distinction between new and used property.
2. Acquired used	Straight line	Straight-line method only for a period of 31.5 years. No distinction between new and used property.

[a] For the declining-balance method, any rate *less than* that shown can be used in computing depreciation deductions.
[b] The investor can also choose a method of cost recovery based on the straight-line depreciation method. Other methods are not permitted.

intended to decrease the severity of the losses experienced by investors under the 1986 law and provides investors a reasonable time period in which to make portfolio adjustments.

Special Rule for Rental Real Estate. Individuals, other than limited partners, can deduct up to $25,000 of passive losses that are attributable to rental real estate activities in which the individual "actively" participates. This rule applies to individuals who own condominiums, rental houses, apartments, or commercial property and who actively participate in managing the property. This $25,000 allowance is phased-out for investors with an adjusted gross income (excluding passive losses, IRA contributions or taxable social security benefits) exceeding $100,000 and less than $150,000, and is completely eliminated for investors with adjusted gross income greater than $150,000.

The active participation requirements are subject to interpretation and debate. However, it is clearly stated in the tax law that a limited partner cannot meet the "active participation" requirement. In addition, an individual owning less than 10 percent interest in income property cannot be considered an active participant.

This special $25,000 deduction rules applies as well to an equivalent amount of tax credits, with some modifications. For example, with rehabilitation and low-income housing tax credits, the $25,000 deduction applies on a "credit equivalent" basis even if the investor does not actively participate in the management of the property or is a limited partner. The credit equivalent of the $25,000 deduction is $7,000 for an individual in the 28 percent tax bracket. These deductions are phased out for investors with adjusted gross incomes between $200,000 and $250,000.

Inability to Deduct Real Economic Losses. Prior to 1986, investors could use tax losses to shelter other forms of income. Tax losses can come from either real "out-of-pocket" losses (expenses in excess of income) or artificial accounting losses (depreciation and amortization). The Tax Reform Act of 1986 makes no distinction between cash losses and tax losses; except for the special rules just discussed, all unused passive losses from a property must be carried forward until passive income is generated and can be used to cover the losses. Many observers believe that this rule unjustly discriminates against real estate investors and should be changed to allow deductions of real (cash) losses against other forms of income.

Impact on Investment Structures. The passive-loss limitations have dramatically changed the structuring and marketing of investments and require more rigorous tax planning by investors seeking to maximize returns. As compared with investments structures of the past, current law places incentive on the following.

1. *Increased cash flow orientation.* Investors are more cash-flow-oriented and seek real economic income as contrasted with tax shelter income. Each project must now be evaluated primarily on its ability to produce adequate amounts of cash flow and capital appreciation, since tax shelter benefits are limited.

2. *Increased passive-income orientation.* The 1986 tax law increased demand for investments able to produce passive income that can be offset against otherwise disallowed passive losses. An investment can be structured as a passive-income generator (a so-called "PIG") through various means: (a) using all-equity or low-leverage capital structures, (b) using special partner allocations to provide disproportionate amounts of cash flow and passive income to certain investors; (c) reducing front-end fees by syndicators, thus compensating the general partner through a larger portion of the appreciation in the property, and (d) choosing investments that promise to generate substantial amounts of cash flow each year over the holding period.

3. *Higher-risk investments.* Condominium conversions, although risky, may become a popular way to create passive income, particularly in view of reduced tax rates. Many investors may become inclined to seek partnerships with developers in search of generating high amounts of passive income that is taxable at a low rate or can be used to offset passive losses.

4. *Longer holding period.* Previous tax law encouraged "churning" of investments—the periodic sale of property and reinvestment of funds to maximize tax benefits. Investors subject to the passive-loss rules may wish to hold "burned-out" shelters (those that generate taxable income in excess of cash flow) as a source of passive income.

5. *Forms of ownership shifting to corporations and institutional structures.* Corporations have a significant advantage over individuals and partnerships because they are exempt from the passive-loss rules. Institutional investors, such as pension funds and insurance companies, and foreign investors have become more important sources of capital for real estate investments, since their asset pricing is primarily determined by real economic variables rather than tax variables. In the past, many institutions believed that real estate properties were overpriced because they had favorable tax benefits which institutions did not enjoy, but which could be sold by syndicators to individuals in high tax brackets.

At-Risk Rules

The at-risk rules were designed by Congress to prevent certain taxpayers from deducting losses in excess of the actual economic investment in a project. Generally, an investor is considered "at risk" in a property to the extent of the cash amounts invested in the property and the amounts borrowed to finance the property for which the investor has *personal liability.*

Each year the amount at risk increases by any additional personal liability or cash invested, but decreases by the amount of cash flow distributed and tax losses from the project. In effect, an investor cannot use tax losses from a project in excess of his or her equity in the project and personal liability on loans. Once tax losses exceed these amounts, they must be carried forward until additional equity is contributed, additional personal liability on loans is created, or the property is sold.

The at-risk rules apply to real estate acquired after 1986, and to all taxpayers except widely held corporations. Application of these rules to real estate was originally considered to be a major threat to real estate investors, but fortunately the real estate industry lobbied and won an important exception to the rules. This exception provides that an investor can allocate nonrecourse loans to the amount at-risk if the loan is *"qualified* nonrecourse financing." Qualified nonrecourse financing is provided by an individual or institution that is "actively and regularly engaged" in the business of lending money (and is not the former owner of the property) or is made or guaranteed by a local, state, or federal government agency. Thus, seller financing, to the extent that loans are nonrecourse in nature and result in highly levered capital structures, can impose significant tax shelter limitations on a project and its investors. For example, the ability to sell troubled property may be constrained by the inability to include seller financing in amounts at-risk. This may be troublesome for banks and savings institutions attempting to sell foreclosed property. In addition, wraparound loans would be used less frequently since they are considered seller financing.

The at-risk rules may be modified in the future and create further problems for real estate investors. However, other provisions of the tax law, such as changes in ordinary and capital gains income tax rates, the passive-loss limitation rules, and depreciation changes have a much greater impact on the expected rate of return and risks of an investment than do the at-risk rules.

The Alternative Minimum Tax

Since 1982, individual taxpayers have been subject to the alternative minimum tax (AMT). The purpose of this "alternative" is to ensure that taxpayers, generally those with high-incomes, will pay a tax of at least 21 percent on their effective economic income. The AMT generally applies to those taxpayers who have overindulged in the various tax preferences allowed by the Internal Revenue Code.

The AMT is a separate computation the taxpayer performs after having computed his or her regular tax liability.[8] If this separate computation produces a greater liability, the taxpayer is required to pay the higher amount.

[8]For a detailed explanation and analysis of these computations, see Robert H. Lipsey and William C. Withers, "Applying the New Alternative Minimum Tax to Real Estate," *The Journal of Real Estate Taxation*, Winter 1988, pp. 124–144.

The starting point in computing a taxpayer's AMT is regular taxable income (see Exhibit 10-2). To this amount are added certain deductions that were allowed for regular tax purposes and not allowed for AMT purposes. (Common items are accelerated depreciation and passive losses.) Also added back are certain items of income that are not taxable for regular tax purposes but are for purposes of AMT. (Common items are income related to certain stock options and certain tax-exempt interest.) Finally, this amount is reduced for deductions and exemptions allowed by AMT. The resulting figure is the income subject to the AMT rate.

Corporations are subject to a 20 percent alternative minimum tax on regular taxable income increased by preference items and certain other adjustments. The 20 percent AMT is levied on AMT income in excess of a $40,000 exemption, but only if greater than the regular corporate tax. This $40,000 exemption is phased out after AMT income exceeds $150,000 and is completely eliminated when AMT income exceeds $310,000.

Tax Credits

The Tax Reform Act of 1986 repealed provisions for investment tax credits (ITCs). However, tax credits are still available for two categories of expenditures relevant to investors in real estate: rehabilitation of qualified historic structures, and investments in low-income housing.

Certified Historic Structures. A rehabilitation credit of 20 percent is available for qualified rehabilitations of certified historic structures. For rehabilitations of all other qualified properties, a 10 percent credit against tax is available. For a property to be "qualified," it must have been placed in service before 1936.

Investments in Low-Income Housing. Before the 1986 Tax Reform Act was passed, incentives for investment in low-income housing were provided by a fifteen-year cost recovery system employing the equivalent of the 200 percent declining-balance depreciation method, and by a provision for five-year amortization of certain rehabilitation expenditures. The 1986 act replaced these provisions with credits for construction or rehabilitation of low-income housing and for purchase of low-income housing.[9] The credits are set in order to provide a tax offset equal to 70 percent of the basis in buildings that are not subsidized by the federal government. For buildings that are federally subsidized, the tax credit is 30 percent. The credit is implemented via the application of annual percentages as provided in Internal Revenue Code Section 42(a). Over a ten-year period, the

---

[9]These tax credit provisions are considered by some observers to be the only true tax shelters left for real estate investors after the Tax Reform Act of 1986. For a detailed analysis, see Richard S. Goldstein and Charles L. Edson, "The Tax Credit for Low-Income Housing," *Real Estate Review*, Summer 1987, pp. 49–60.

total amount of credits used will be equal to the present value of 70 or 30 percent of the building's basis, whichever is applicable.

The tax credit has a maximum rate of 9 percent annually on property placed in service after January 1, 1987 for new construction and rehabilitation, and a maximum rate of 4 percent annually for the purchase cost of existing housing. To qualify for the credit on new construction or rehabilitation, such expenditures must exceed $2,000 per unit. For a residential rental property, several income tests concerning the average incomes of the residents relative to area median income must be met for a period of fifteen years. Otherwise, the tax credits are recaptured (must be paid back) according to a rather complex formula.

The rules for claiming tax credits related to low income housing are complex and subject to the passive-loss limitation rules. Nevertheless, these provisions of the tax law are considered one of the few true tax shelters remaining in real estate. Since corporations are exempt from the passive-loss rules, they are encouraged by the tax law to invest large amounts of cash in low-income housing projects that produce these tax credits.

Investment Interest Limitations

Investors view the deductibility of interest payments on loans as one of the key advantages of owning real estate. However, there is a noteworthy limitation on such deductions under the current tax law: the limitation on *excess investment interest.* The primary purpose of the limitation is to restrict the amount of the interest deduction to the amount of investment income the taxpayer receives in the same year; interest on loans to carry property that has the potential of producing future capital gains, but generates little current income, is not deductible until the gains are in fact realized. Thus, income and expenses are to be matched; this is a basic tax principle that has often been cited by the IRS and the tax courts.

Limitations Imposed. The general rule regarding deductibility of investment interest expense for noncorporate taxpayers is that the amount of the deduction cannot exceed the amount of the taxpayer's net investment income from rents, royalties, interest, dividends, and so on. It is important to note that investment interest consists only of interest paid or accrued on debt incurred to purchase or maintain property that is "held for investment." If the taxpayer materially participates in the conduct of the trade or business that incurs the interest expense, the interest will not be treated as investment interest; also if the trade or business is a "passive activity," the interest expense will not be treated as investment interest.

Properties Subject to Investment Interest Limitations. The limitation on the deductibility of interest applies only to interest paid or accrued on property "held for investment." For real estate investments this term can be classified and analyzed as follows.

1. *Trade or business property.* The investment interest limitation does not apply to most rental property (e.g., an apartment or office building *owned and operated* by the investor). Such property is considered trade or business property rather than investment property. It is therefore subject to the passive-loss rules but not to the investment interest limitations.

2. *Net-leased property.* The Tax Reform Act of 1986 transferred net-leased property from the investment interest category to the "rental activity" category so that net-leased property is subject to the passive-loss rules but not the investment interest limitations. In general, property will be considered subject to a net lease if business deductions are less than 15 percent of the rental income from the property. Business deductions do *not* include ground rents or expenses for which the taxpayer is reimbursed by the lessee.

3. *Raw land.* Another type of property that is considered to be investment property is raw land held for speculation. Thus, interest on loans used to finance such land is subject to the investment interest limitation. If an investor acquires land with the intention of erecting commercial property on it and the land remains undeveloped, it may be difficult to prove it is not investment property, unless the investor can show a history of maintaining an inventory of such property for development.

TAX-PLANNING ALTERNATIVES AND ISSUES

Some of the more interesting tax-planning alternatives and issues an investor may encounter are (1) timing of income as influenced by the choice of a tax year and accounting method, (2) operating deduction issues, including the great debate about capitalizing or expensing cash expenditures, and (3) the IRS audit. Each of these subjects will be addressed in the following pages. Since tax issues related to form of ownership were discussed in Chapter 5 they will not be discussed here.[10]

Timing of Income: The Tax Year

When is taxable income or loss reported to the IRS? Of course, this is done at the end of the tax year, which cannot exceed twelve months, but which can be different for different ownership entities.

- *Individuals and partnerships* usually report at the end of the calendar

---

[10]A very aggressive approach to tax planning, including these and other issues, is presented by Reed in *Aggressive Tax Avoidance for Real Estate Investors.*

year. Under certain conditions, a tax year other than the calendar
year can be elected.

- *Corporations* often choose a fiscal year that is different from the calendar year. For example, a corporation may choose to be a "February
  28 corporation," whose fiscal year runs from March 1 to the following February 28 (except for leap year!).

A primary reason for having a fiscal year that is different from the calendar year is to reduce or postpone taxes. For example, the owner of a "January 31" consulting and appraisal corporation can pay himself or herself a
$20,000 bonus from the corporation, thereby reducing corporate earnings
and taxes reported for the year ended January 31. When does the owner as
an individual report the taxable income? For most individual investors,
not until April 15 of the following year, 14.5 months later.

The tax law significantly restricts the ability of certain taxpayers to
choose tax years that are not calendar years. For tax years beginning after
1986, partnerships (including real estate syndications organized as limited
partnerships) must adopt the taxable year of the partner or partners having an aggregate interest of more than 50 percent in the partnership's
profits and capital. Because many partners are individuals, this provision
has the effect of usually requiring partnerships to adopt calendar years.
Exceptions to the general rule are difficult to obtain; the taxpayer must
convince the IRS that the use of a certain fiscal year would substantially
conflict with the organization's natural business year.

The aforementioned provisions also apply to S corporations and personal service corporations; these entities are corporations in form, but, for
tax purposes they function like partnerships. Regular corporations may
adopt any fiscal year for tax purposes, but a change in tax year can be
made only with IRS permission, or without such permission in certain narrowly defined circumstances.

Recent legislation has eased this calendar year requirement for certain
partnerships, S corporations, and personal-services corporations. The legislation enables businesses to retain the fiscal year, provided they adhere
to certain "enhanced payments" requirements. To comply, the entity must
deposit the tax resulting from the difference between the calendar year and
the fiscal year of the entity. If an entity desires a fiscal year solely for tax
deferral reasons, the deposit effectively nullifies this benefit.

Cash versus Accrual Accounting. Real estate investors basically use two
methods of reporting income, the cash method and the accrual method.
The cash basis investor reports income when cash is actually or constructively received and expenses when actually paid, as shown in Exhibit 10-7
and the following examples.

Example 1. An investor is holding a rental income check for $5,000 on
December 20 and trying to decide whether to deposit the check this year

---

EXHIBIT 10-7. Accounting Methods

CASH METHOD

Income: Reported when actually or constructively received.
Expenses: Deducted when actually paid.

ACCRUAL METHOD

Income: Reported when earned (an unconditional right to receive it exists).
Expenses: Reported when they are incurred (a legal obligation to pay exists).

---

and report it as taxable income, or wait until January to deposit the money and report the income the following year. Under the *constructive receipt* doctrine, the investor should report the income in the current year.

Example 2. An investor does "creative" year-end tax planning by writing a large number of checks to vendors and employees to increase current-year tax deductions. The investor does not actually have enough cash in the bank account and will not be able to cover the checks until January rents are received and deposited. The checks are placed in the top drawer of the desk until January 5 and then mailed. Are these expenditures valid deductions for the prior year? Upon audit, the deductions will be disallowed if they are discovered. There was no actual payment.

Example 3. You invest in a warehouse property on December 30 and prepay three years of property insurance to a local insurance carrier. The cash basis taxpayer could write off the whole expense in the current year. Under current law the cash basis taxpayer may not prepay expenses in order to accelerate a deduction; thus, the "deducted when actually paid" doctrine has been altered to meet the current needs of the IRS.

The cash method of accounting is generally preferred by most real estate investors because it is simple to understand, easy to use, and usually allows higher tax deductions and more flexible tax-planning alternatives. Because accrual accounting for real estate investment transactions is complex, it is usually avoided except by large corporations whose accounting policies require that all activities be reported on a consistent accrual basis. However, recent regulations require that all "tax shelters" use the accrual method. Because the interpretation of the term tax shelter in this context is quite broad and the penalties for noncompliance are quite high, many syndicators and sophisticated equity investors have switched to accrual accounting.

Actually, most real estate investors use a hybrid method of accounting. They use the cash method to report operating income and expenses, but the accrual method when reporting depreciation, which is an accrued expense. Whichever method the investor chooses, the election must be reported to the IRS in the first tax return after the property is purchased. Once adopted, the method must be consistently applied and cannot be changed without the consent of the IRS.

Operating Deductions

The cash flow examples presented throughout this book assume that the investor is a cash basis taxpayer and thus records expenses when they are paid. Clearly, the advantage of deducting expenses when they are paid, such as prepaying vendors, taxes, and insurance on December 31, is to produce the greatest possible tax write-off in the year in which it is needed the most. Investors usually prefer to take higher deductions sooner rather than later, except when taxable income is expected to rise sharply in future years or when resulting passive losses cannot be used because of the passive-loss limitations. Then the investor might prefer to capitalize operating expenses and produce deductions in the years in which they will produce the greatest tax benefit.

The Great Debate: Operating or Capital Expense? The great debate, which continues without end, is whether a cash expenditure should be expensed in the current year or capitalized and written off over a period of years.

Investor strategy. The tax-shelter-oriented investor expenses as much of the purchase price and as much of every cash expenditure each year after the property is purchased as can be justified. Such an investor might like to expense all new carpets and drapes; new air-conditioning units, roofs, water heaters, and refrigerators; parking lot repaving, and so on. Immediate tax benefits are preferred to depreciation write-offs in future years. Most investors recognize the time value of money!

IRS position. The IRS, on the other hand, tends to be very conservative and would like the investor to capitalize most of the items just listed. The IRS defines a capital expenditure as anything that adds value to, lengthens the life of, or changes the use of the property. The Tax Reform Act of 1986 introduced uniform capitalization rules that require capitalization of many items formerly expensed. Real estate investors are most affected by the requirement to capitalize certain direct costs related to the production or acquisition of property for the purpose of resale. One important item is construction period interest, which cannot be deducted currently but rather must be included in the basis of the real property for depreciation. The previous provision allowing for ten-year amortization of construction period interest has been repealed. The uniform capitalization rules have been designed to make the capitalization of costs as broad in scope as possible. Accordingly, real estate investors must monitor certain expenses closely to ensure that they are properly capitalized. For example, under the provisions of the interest allocation rules, any interest on debt incurred or continued in connection with property used to produce other property must be capitalized.

Realistic position. The many court rulings dealing with the distinction between operating and capital expenditures are not consistent. Since policy seems to change from one regional IRS office to another, to determine the optimal strategy, the investor should research the policies used by other ethical and aggressive investors who have been audited. For example, if the investor is aggressive and writes off all minor capital items, the worst thing that will happen is that the investor may be audited and required to pay back taxes plus interest. As more than one investor has stated, "You don't get what you don't ask for!"

In most situations, the best plan is to keep the property in excellent physical condition through regular repairs and maintenance. The related expenses are deductible in the year in which they are incurred, which means that the value of the property is higher when it is sold; this additional property value becomes a capital gain for the investor.

Debatable Deductions. Over the years many court cases have identified specific *tax traps* and problem areas relating to operating deductions. Some of the more important ones involve lease–purchase contracts, security deposits, and a transaction with a purchase price in excess of market value.

Lease–purchase contracts. The investor normally expects lease payments to be fully deductible as expenses for tax purposes. However, they may not be if a property purchase is structured as a lease with an option to purchase at a nominal price at the end of the lease term. Under this type of arrangement, the IRS will claim that a portion of the lease payment is actually a principal payment covering the cost of purchasing the property, and will disallow part of the lease payment as a deduction for tax purposes.

Security deposits. For a cash basis taxpayer, the IRS may argue that security deposits received are taxable income in the year received and tax deductions in the year paid back to tenants. The problem occurs most notably when the investor commingles security deposit funds with the bank accounts for operating income and expenses, but can usually be avoided if separate accounting for security deposits is maintained. A safer approach, and one required by some states, is to keep security deposits in a separate bank account and treat them as legally separate from the operating funds.

Price in excess of market value. Real estate tax shelter syndicates will often negotiate a price exceeding the *fair market value* of a property in compensation for high-leverage seller-created mortgage terms and a high property basis that allows liberal depreciation deductions. The courts have denied depreciation and interest deductions that are based on a purchase price far in excess of and having no relationship to the value of the building and land purchased.[11]

Other problem areas relating to expense deductions will be discussed later in the chapter when the concepts of tax shelter and tax shelter strategies are fully developed.

The IRS Audit

Investors are subject to periodic audits by the IRS. What is the strategy to be employed when the IRS audits your property returns? Experienced investors who are frequently defendants in the audit arena suggest that the development of a strategic plan that focuses on good records and a systematic, clear, and logical defense of all tax assumptions used in the property returns are the essential ingredients in successfully surviving an IRS audit. If the investor is unsuccessful, he or she will receive a tax deficiency statement from the IRS and must remit additional taxes, plus interest, and a penalty tax in some cases. The interest rates generally correspond to prevailing rates in the corporate finance markets. Penalties can be sizable, especially if the tax shown on the original return is "substantially understated," or if there was fraud or negligence in preparing returns.

Upon receipt of a deficiency statement, the investor has five basic alternatives.

1. Pay the additional taxes and interest requested.
2. Go to appellate conference and argue the case. If the case is lost, pay the taxes or choose among alternatives 3, 4, and 5.
3. Pay the additional taxes requested; sue the IRS for a refund in the federal district court. (The investor can request a jury trial if this appears to be more advantageous than a trial by judge.)
4. Do not pay the additional taxes requested; go to the tax court and argue the case.
5. Do not pay the additional taxes requested; go to the court of claims and argue the case.

---

[11] Arthur Anderson and Company, *Federal Income Taxes Affecting Real Estate*, 6th ed., (Albany, N.Y.: Matt Binder & Co., 1987), pp. 88–89. Under the provisions of the tax reform acts of 1984 and 1986, such tax shelter practices are severely limited by the passive-loss limitation rules, the at-risk rules, and the "original issue discount" and "imputed interest" rules. For a further discussion of these subjects, see Arnold, *Real Estate Investments After the Tax Reform Act of 1986*, pp. 8–10 and 36–40.

Ultimately, the case could be appealed up to the Supreme Court of the United States.

An investor should seek experienced legal and tax counsel when weighing the pros and cons of these alternatives, and should recognize that each regional IRS office differs somewhat in its orientation and audit practices. As with any investment decision, the basic question is: Are the returns worth the risks? The time involved and the "hassle" experienced by the investor are the key variables to be considered when measuring the risk associated with this decision.

TAX SHELTER STRATEGY

This and previous chapters have made frequent reference to tax shelters. The mechanics of tax shelters have been discussed from the standpoint of both financial leverage and depreciation; also discussed was the strategy of expensing cash payments instead of capitalizing them and the debatable deductions that are frequently challenged by the IRS. However, the term *tax shelter* has not been explicitly defined or the concept analyzed. The concept of tax shelter and a decision-making framework for analyzing tax shelter strategy will now be developed. The following analysis should be viewed in light of the various limitations Congress has imposed on the investor wishing to utilize tax shelter benefits. (See the preceding discussion of passive-loss rules.)

The Concept of Tax Shelter

Tax shelter can be defined in a number of ways; in fact, there appears to be little agreement on the proper definition to be used by investors. Here are a few possible definitions.

1. Any deduction or credit against income that is available only to a special category of taxpayer.
2. Any favorable tax treatment providing preferential tax relief of a particular investment under the Internal Revenue Code.

3. Transactions or investments that have one or more of three objectives: tax deferral, leverage benefits, and the conversion of ordinary income into capital gain.
4. Negative taxable income. That is, when tax losses are generated, they can be used to shelter other income.
5. Depreciation expense that is greater than amortization of principal. As long as this condition exists, at least part of the investor's cash flow from operations is sheltered.

The first two definitions are general in nature. Each definition thereafter becomes more specific. The fifth definition is the most useful one for understanding the nature and mechanics of tax shelter over the ownership period; this concept is based on the difference between the cash flow and the taxable income statements.

Comparison of Cash Flow and Taxable Income Statements. Consider the accounting statements shown in Exhibit 10-8 and assume that the investor is a cash basis taxpayer whose cash operating income and expense items are all allowable revenue and expense items in the statement of taxable income. As noted previously, some investors use a different method of accounting for income and expenses, although these methods may not be acceptable for tax purposes. For example, a capital expenditure that is deducted as an expense in the cash flow statement may be disallowed in the tax statement. In this illustration, the investor reports an NOI of $100,000 in both statements, and there is no difference between income and expense reporting policies.

As shown, the cash flow from operations is a positive $10,000. This amount can be distributed to the investor "tax free"; it is *not* reported to the IRS as income (contrary to the belief of some investors) because it is considered to be a recoupment of invested capital. At the same time, taxable income is negative, so the investor has an artificial accounting loss of $50,000 that can be used to shelter the investor's other income, subject to the passive-loss limitation rules. In effect, two sets of books are kept: one real economic set of books and one for tax purposes.

The only difference between the two statements is in depreciation and amortization of principal. Therefore, the key to the tax shelter concept must be the relation between these two variables, which in algebraic form can be expressed as follows:

$$\text{CFBT} = \text{TI} + \text{dep} - \text{amort} \quad \textbf{or} \quad \text{TI} = \text{CFBT} - \text{dep} + \text{amort}$$

$$\begin{aligned} \text{where CFBT} &= \text{cash flow before tax (cash flow)} \\ \text{TI} &= \text{taxable income} \\ \text{dep} &= \text{depreciation} \\ \text{amort} &= \text{amortization of principal} \end{aligned}$$

EXHIBIT 10-8. Statement of Cash Flow and Taxable Income

	Cash Flow	Taxable Income
Gross possible income	$ 200,000	$ 200,000
Less: Vacancy and credit losses	− 20,000	− 20,000
Gross effective income	180,000	180,000
Less: Operating expenses	− 80,000	− 80,000
Net operating income	100,000	100,000
Less: Interest	− 80,000	− 80,000
Amortization of principal	− 10,000	0
Depreciation	0	− 70,000
Cash flow before tax	$ 10,000	
Taxable income (loss)		$ − 50,000

For example, if depreciation is equal to the amortization of principal ($10,000), both cash flow and taxable income will equal $10,000. Every dollar of cash flow will be taxable; thus, there is *no tax shelter.* If depreciation is greater than amortization, then at least part of the cash flow is tax-sheltered. When depreciation exceeds amortization by the amount of cash flow ($10,000), taxable income is zero and the cash flow is completely sheltered. The investor receives a $10,000 cash distribution but reports no taxable income from the property. Once again, the IRS treats the $10,000 cash flow as a return *of* original capital to the investor; thus, it is not a taxable transaction. Finally, if depreciation is greater than amortization *by more than* the cash flow, a tax loss is produced and can be used to shelter other income, subject to the passive-loss limitation rules.

Game Plan of the Investor. The game plan of the investor with respect to tax shelter is to generate cash flow from operations (CFBT) and at the same time produce tax losses that are as high as possible for as long as possible. The goal is to produce artificial tax losses, not real economic losses. All "real losers" produce good tax shelter. Unfortunately, if tax losses are maximized through reduced rental income or increased operating expenses, real cash flow dollars are reduced commensurately; effectively, an investor in the 33 percent tax bracket must lose $1.00 to receive a $.33 tax saving. Most rational investors consider this a poor economic trade-off, but history has suggested that many investors purchase property without sufficient regard for its *real* economic performance.

Tax shelter should be considered from an investment analysis view. Such a view presumes that investors seek to maximize overall returns relative to risks, and that tax savings is only one of four cash flow benefits that can result from ownership: cash flow from operations, tax savings, refinancing proceeds, and net proceeds from disposition. To focus too much on tax shelter aspects is usually a mistake. In their book *Tax Planning for Real Estate Investors*, Kay and Sirmans offer several words of caution in this regard.[12]

1. Tax shelters generally have high risk. Does the expected rate of return compensate the investor for the increased risk?

2. Tax shelters may be the last outpost of *caveat emptor* (let the buyer beware). Investors should know with whom they are dealing and should read all relevant documents carefully. They should not be misled by the short-run benefits but should determine the total impact of taxation on the investment decision.

3. Most tax shelters have a sponsor–manager of the project. The ability, reputation, and past experience of the sponsor is a critical factor. Full and complete disclosure of the investment should be demanded by the investor.

The passage of the 1986 tax act greatly diminished the use of tax shelters and put many tax-oriented syndicators out of business. The tax benefits from these syndications have been substantially diminished by the lengthening of the depreciation periods allowed, the passive-loss limitation rules, and the elimination of the opportunity for "conversion" of ordinary deductions into tax-favored capital gains.

Stages of Tax Shelter. A distinct pattern of tax shelter emerges if a property has a stable or increasing cash flow from operations, there is a relatively high degree of traditional mortgage financing, and an accelerated (personal property) and straight-line (real property) form of depreciation (cost recovery) is used. This tax shelter pattern can be described in five distinct stages.

STAGE 1. *Excess tax shelter.* In the early years of ownership the entire cash flow from operations is sheltered from the payment of any income taxes, and there is *excess* tax shelter left over. Taxable income is negative; that is, there is a tax loss. At this stage depreciation exceeds amortization by an amount *greater than* the cash flow from operations.

STAGE 2. *Complete tax shelter.* The entire cash flow from operations is sheltered from income taxes, but there is no excess. Taxable income is zero. At this stage, which occurs at a point in time during a tax year, depreciation exceeds amortization by the amount of cash flow.

STAGE 3. *Partial tax shelter.* After a period of years the property shows a taxable income, and part of the cash flow from operations must be used to pay income taxes. Depreciation is still greater than amortization, but by an amount less than the cash flow.

[12]James B. Kau and C. F. Sirmans, *Tax Planning for Real Estate Investors* (Englewood Cliffs, N.J.: Prentice-Hall, 1980), p. 23. See also Don P. Holdren and George E. Moody, "Recognizing Abusive Tax Shelters," *Real Estate Review*, Spring 1986, p. 79.

STAGE 4. *No tax shelter.* Taxable income is equal to the cash flow. Thus every dollar of cash flow generated through rentals is taxable. At this stage depreciation is equal to amortization.

STAGE 5. *Negative tax shelter.* Because of ever-decreasing amounts of mortgage interest and tax depreciation, the IRS begins taxing the project on income that exceeds the cash flow generated by the property. Amortization, which is a cash expense but is not deductible for tax purposes, is now greater than depreciation. Historically, most investors felt very uncomfortable in this stage and took some action to correct the situation, if they had not done so earlier. However since 1986 many investors have suspended losses (unused tax losses carried forward from previous years) that can be used to offset the taxable income created in Stage 5. In such situations, Stage 5 provides desirable tax shelter benefits.

As the investor proceeds through the five stages, tax shelter declines and equity builds up through loan amortization. As more dollars are tied up in the property, leverage and tax savings decrease and opportunity costs rise. At some point, usually during the third stage, an investor can take one of several actions to reverse the tax shelter trend that is developing. First, the investor can refinance the property and start a new interest cycle on the property. The refinancing proceeds are tax-free and can be reinvested in other properties. Second, the property can be sold and the equity reinvested in other properties, thereby creating new interest and depreciation cycles on the properties purchased. Third, a major renovation program can be undertaken to create a new depreciation cycle and increase tax shelter. Fourth, a tax-free exchange can be structured to raise the investor's depreciable basis and interest deductions, thereby increasing tax shelter. Finally, the investor can combine any two or more of the four actions. As always, the returns must be carefully weighed against the risks, since each action is a complex investment decision in itself.

Tax Shelter Pitfalls. The key to the tax shelter concept just presented is depreciation working through the leverage magnification process. Although many other variables influence the investor's taxable income and taxes payable, as we have discussed throughout this chapter, the two most important variables are depreciation and leverage. The investor should consider the following tax shelter pitfalls related to these variables, in addition to the general statements made earlier:

1. *Depreciation write-offs create future taxable gains.* For each dollar of depreciation write-off during the holding period, a dollar of gain is realized upon the sale of the property. Depreciation is thus a method of deferring taxes; it does not eliminate them. The value of the deferral is totally dependent on the time value of money since capital gains are now taxed at the same rate as ordinary (active, passive, and portfolio) income.

2. *Some tax depreciation is real economic depreciation.* Tax depreciation is an artificial accounting loss, but it may also be a real economic loss if the property is actually declining in value. Even if the monetary value of the whole property is increasing as a result of price inflation, components wear out and must be replaced periodically. To the extent that depreciation is equal to actual wear and tear, no *net* benefit is created by the depreciation process.

3. *Greater leverage creates greater financial risks.* Tax shelter benefits are magnified through (a) the use of leverage and (b) periodic refinancing to balance the relationships of depreciation, amortization, and the amount of equity value tied up in the project. As seen in the basic financial analysis presented earlier, additional leverage also lowers the coverage ratio, raises the break-even point, and increases the probability of insolvency and the risk of ruin.

4. *Tax law reforms often reduce shelter benefits.* The structure upon which most tax shelter rules are built is very fragile. The laws are changed every two to five years, and the trend during the last two decades has generally been to chip away at the favorable tax treatment offered to real estate investors. In addition, tax shelters must now register with the IRS, and it is generally believed that they will be subjected to close scrutiny. The investor should test the impact of changing tax laws through sensitivity analysis of the tax variables. If such changes have a substantial impact on the investor's IRR and other investment criteria, the risks of tax reform should be weighed carefully.

Another problem that is often overlooked is the relationship of the amount of debt remaining, the market value of the property, and the tax basis of the property. Consider, for example, a property that is purchased for $1,000,000 and sold fourteen years later for $2,500,000. The depreciated tax basis at the end of fourteen years is $500,000. One year prior to the sale, the property was refinanced with a $2,000,000 loan. The "tax-free" refinancing proceeds were reinvested in other properties. Assuming, for simplicity, that the $2,000,000 loan is interest only, the situation at the time of sale can be described as shown in Exhibit 10-9.

Simply stated, the investor cannot afford to sell the property. The total taxable gain ($1,900,000) is more than four times the cash proceeds realized from the sale ($400,000). Those "tax-free" refinancing proceeds and "tax-free" cash flows during the holding period have come back to haunt the investor. They have become tax liabilities at the time of sale. Investors frequently overlook these common pitfalls and risks when they are designing tax shelter packages and refinancing properties.

Tax Shelter Strategy Checklist

The investor should develop a tax shelter strategy within the framework of the ownership life cycle: acquisition, operations, termination. Assuming

---

EXHIBIT 10-9.   Relationship of Sales Price, Loan Balance, and Tax Basis

---

Sales price	$2,500,000
Less: Commissions and closing costs (4%)	100,000
Net sales price	$2,400,000
Loan balance	$2,000,000
Depreciable basis of property	$ 500,000

A = Net sale proceeds received equals $400,000 ($2,400,000 − $2,000,000)
B = Total taxable gain equals $1,900,000 ($2,400,000 − $500,000)

---

that a high-tax-bracket investor would like to design an aggressive tax shelter package that would maximize the after-tax IRR over the holding period, which tax variables can be structured and controlled to achieve the goal? The following checklists will prove useful to the investor.

Acquisition Period. The objective in designing an aggressive front-end tax package is to create the maximum possible amount of tax deductions and tax credits in the year of acquisition. The effect would be to reduce the after-tax equity investment, since immediate tax benefits produce an immediate return of a portion of the investor's equity capital. In the past, investors have looked to the following variables to create tax shelter during the acquisition period:

	Available under Previous Tax Law	Available under 1988 Tax Law
▪ Prepaid interest	Yes	No
▪ Financing points	Yes	No
▪ Consulting fees	Yes	Very limited
▪ Organization and legal fees	Yes	No
▪ Prepaid management and leasing fees	Yes	No
▪ Construction period interest and taxes	Yes	Very limited
▪ Prepaid taxes and insurance	Yes	Limited
▪ Bonus depreciation (or special first-year expenses)	Yes	No
▪ Investment tax credits	Yes	Limited

Generally, the strategy was to convert "hard" dollars into "soft" dollars—to convert as much as possible of the purchase price into tax-deductible dollars. This could be accomplished by reducing the contract purchase price for the property and substituting various fees and expenses that would be paid to the seller. Unfortunately for the investor, tax reforms during the 1970s and 1980s eliminated most of the acquisition period write-offs. Except for certain tax credits, the IRS now requires that most or all of these amounts be capitalized and written off over the appropriate recovery period. Since few alternatives remain for acquisition structuring, emphasis has shifted to the operating period.

Operating Period. The objective in designing an operating period tax package is to create the maximum possible amount of tax deductions and tax benefits, *relative to the amount of cash flow and risk.* For example, although increasing the interest rate or prepayment penalties on a loan will create more tax deductions, it will also create *real* cash flow losses. Such actions are not usually worthwhile in the long run.

There are five categories of operating period tax variables that are subject to some control by the investor.

1. *Depreciation deductions*
   - Basis of improvements—as high as possible.
   - Useful life (recovery period)—as low as possible (fixed cost recovery classes under MACRS).
   - Depreciation method—maximum allowed by law (MACRS defines statutory percentages for property types).
   - Component depreciation—allocate as much as possible to personal property.
   - Change depreciation method—when advantageous (very limited because MACRS defines statutory percentages to be used).
2. *Interest deductions and leverage variables*
   - Amount of debt—as high as possible within risk constraints.
   - Interest rate—as low as possible generally (if too low, IRS will impute).
   - Term of loan—as long as possible, interest-only is ideal.
   - Refinancing—periodic refinancing is usually desirable.
   - Prepayment penalties—as low as possible.
3. *Operating expenses and revenue*
   - Expensing policies—expense rather than capitalize where possible.
   - Shift expenses and reserve to years in which needed most.
   - Repairs and maintenance—keep property in good condition to maximize gain.
4. *Tax credits*
   - Amount—as much as possible.
   - Timing—as soon as possible, can carry back or forward fifteen years.
5. *Marginal tax rate of investor*
   - Level—higher bracket receives more tax loss benefit.

▪ Stability—change variables above to take advantage of possible tax bracket changes.

Since the overall investment objective is to maximize return relative to risk, the investor should try various combinations of these tax shelter variables in order to best fit his or her objectives and risk-taking abilities.

Termination Period. At the end of the holding period the objective generally shifts to minimizing the tax consequences of the property disposition. Some of the more important variables to consider are

▪ *Price and Terms of Sale.* Obtaining the highest price will create capital gain.
▪ *Installment Sale Treatment.* To defer the taxable gain to the future.[13]
▪ *Tax-Free Exchange.* To defer the taxable gain, increase depreciable basis and leverage.
▪ *Gift or Trust.* To minimize capital gains and estate taxation.

Since termination period strategy is covered in Chapter 17, further discussion of these variables will be deferred to that chapter.

SUMMARY

Taxation and tax planning should be understood from an investment analysis view. The investor can learn to manage and control many of the important tax variables, thereby increasing a property's value and its rate of return relative to business and financial risks. The primary emphasis in this chapter was on the federal income tax and its impact on the investor over the entire ownership life cycle—acquisition, operations, and termination.

The first section of the chapter analyzed various aspects of the tax law, including the general income tax formula that determines the investor's tax liability, ordinary and capital gains taxation, depreciation and the accelerated cost recovery system, the passive-loss limitation and at-risk rules, investment tax credits, and investment interest limitations. Then, such tax-planning alternatives and issues as the choice of a tax year and accounting method and the great debate about capitalizing or expensing cash expenditures were detailed. Tax shelter strategy was the third major subject discussed. The ideal tax shelter game plan is to generate positive cash flow from operations while at the same time producing tax losses that are as

---

[13]For a discussion on this important subject, see Barbara J. Childs and Caroline Strobel, "Seller-Financed Real Estate Transactions After the Tax Reform Act of 1986," *The Journal of Real Estate Taxation*, Summer 1987, pp. 299–311. Also, Philip J. Holthouse and Karen Ritchie, "Installment Sales Update," *The Journal of Real Estate Taxation*, Summer 1988, pp. 341–357.

high as possible for as long as possible, during a period when the investor has other qualified income to shelter.

After a review of the various stages, pitfalls, and risks of tax shelter, a detailed plan for developing an aggressive tax shelter package was presented. Note that tax laws are fragile and that periodic changes in the laws tend to have substantial impacts on the investor's after-tax return. Also, the Tax Reform Act of 1986 eliminated many of the tax shelter benefits previously available to investors.

To complete this chapter, the Aspen Wood Apartments case study presents a more sophisticated DCF model that includes the many tax and financial variables discussed throughout this chapter.

ASPEN WOOD APARTMENTS

DETAILED FINANCIAL AND TAX ANALYSIS

This chapter sought to develop many of the tax concepts that influence investment returns and risks. A more sophisticated DCF model must now be developed to handle the many variables discussed. Although it need not be computerized, the analysis presented here was performed on a computer model known as "RE004: Detailed Financial Analysis and Tax Planning Model."[a] The project analyzed is the eighty-four-unit Aspen Wood Apartments. Recall that the analysis was prepared in the fall of 1974 and the acquisition (closing) date was projected to be November 1, 1974. Charlie Davidson and Clyde Boomer, the managing equity investors, projected a holding period through 1979, or roughly five years plus two months of 1974. (The property was not actually sold until the end of 1981 and closed in January of 1982, as explained in Chapter 17.)

CAPITAL EXPENDITURES (SECTION ONE)

The total cost to acquire the property, including all commissions, closing costs, and legal fees, was expected to be $1,003,400 (as negotiated in Chapter 7). The total equity cash required was $210,000, with a wraparound mortgage of $793,400. The detailed financial picture is shown in Exhibit 10-A.

For tax purposes, Davidson and Boomer sought to convert as much of the total purchase cost as possible into "soft" dollars, deductible in the year of acquisition. One full year's prepaid interest ($59,505) on the wraparound loan was negotiated with the seller; two financing points ($15,868) were paid to the seller; and a consulting fee of $15,000 was paid to D&B Associates by the joint-venture partners. The total expensed items amounted to $90,373. (Note that under current tax law all three deductions would be capitalized. The consulting fee would be capitalized as part of the depreciable basis of the property and written off over the recovery period of the two components (real and personal property), rather than expensed in the year of acquisition. However, prepaid interest and points on the wraparound loan could be capitalized as a separate component and amortized over the ten-year balloon period of the loan, rather than written off over the recovery period of the property.)

At the date of closing, which was moved back to November 1, 1974 as a result of the problems that developed, the book assets were estimated to be $913,027, which is the total cost of the property less all expensed items. Of the total book

[a]Stephen A. Pyhrr and James Arthur Baker, *Computer Models for the Detailed Financial Analysis and Tax Planning of Income-Producing Real Estate Investments*, TRERC Tecnical Monograph No. 2 (College Station, Texas: Texas Real Estate Research Center, Texas A & M University, 1979).

EXHIBIT 10-A. Aspen Wood Apartments: Capital Expenditures

SECTION ONE: CAPITAL EXPENDITURES

Total Cost to Acquire Property

Total equity cash required	$ 210,000
Total debt	793,400
Total cost	$1,003,400

Allocation of Total Equity Cash Required for Tax Purposes

Expensed items		
Prepaid interest	$59,505	
Financing points	15,868	
Consulting fee	15,000	
Total expensed items		$ 90,373
Capitalized items		
Total capitalized items		119,627
Total equity cash required		$210,000

Balance Sheet at Date of Closing

Total cost to acquire property	$1,003,400
Less expensed items	90,373
Total assets	$ 913,027

Assets		Liabilities and Net Worth	
Working capital	0		
Land	$ 84,027	Total debt	$793,400
Total improvements	829,000	Net worth	119,627
Total	$913,027	Total	$913,027

Allocation of Total Improvements for Tax Purposes

Item	Percentage of Improvements	Amount (Basis)	Percentage Depreciation	Useful Life (years)	Depreciation Method	Bonus Depreciation Applicable
Structure	55.5	$460,095	100	25	125	No
Paving, pool, etc.	5.5	45,595	100	4	100	No
HVAC	7.3	60,517	100	5	100	No
Appliances	5.3	43,937	100	3	150	No
Carpeting	2.4	19,896	100	4	100	No
Electrical and plumbing	19.0	157,510	100	9	100	No
Drapes and personal property	5.0	41,450	100	6	150	Yes
Total	100.0	$829,000				

assets, about $1,000 per unit was allocated to land and the remaining amount to depreciable improvements. As a result of the expensed items, *net worth* was shown to be only $119,627 at the date of closing. Net worth is simply the total equity cash investment ($210,000) *less* the amount expensed for tax purposes ($90,373). Each year the *"book"* net worth will decline by the amount of tax losses produced by the property; eventually it will become negative. At the same time, the investor expects the actual market value of the net worth (equity) to rise substantially.

The component depreciation method was used (as noted, this has been eliminated under the 1981 and 1986 tax acts), with no salvage value attributed to any component. Seven components were defined: six real property components and one personal property component. The basis allocations and useful lives were based on Davidson and Boomer's previous experience with such allocations, including numerous audits and negotiations with the IRS at the appellate conference level. At the time of acquisition, minimum tax provisions were less rigorous than they are now; therefore, D&B made greater use of accelerated depreciation methods. The maximum accelerated depreciation rates were taken on all components. Bonus depreciation was taken only on the drapes and personal items, although appliances could have been included. In 1974 each partner could receive up to $2,000 of bonus depreciation, or $4,000 for a joint return. Under the 1981 and 1986 tax acts, these items could not be deducted.

No property components qualified for tax credits, and no major capital expenditures were expected during the projected five-year holding period. The recent renovations were expected to maintain the property until the end of 1979, at which time a major renovation would probably be required. Increasing maintenance and repair costs would be expensed annually and would compensate for the increasing amount of wear and tear over the holding period. In addition, to compensate for the aging of the building, property value would be increased at a slower rate (3 percent) than gross possible income (4 percent) and operating expenses (7 percent).

DEPRECIATION SCHEDULES (SECTION TWO) AND LOAN SCHEDULES (SECTION THREE)[b]

A depreciation schedule was computed for each of the seven components for two months of 1974 and annually thereafter for five years. If capital expenditures during the holding period and tax credits had been applicable, these schedules would have been generated at this point.

A loan amortization schedule was computed for the wraparound loan. Payments for the partial year 1974 as well as five full operating years were computed. If refinancing or secondary financing were expected, these schedules would also need to be included at this point of the analysis.

[b]Because of space limitations these schedules are not shown.

OPERATING ASSUMPTIONS (SECTION FIVE)[c]

During the mid-1970s, inflation was averaging 5 to 7 percent. In their operating assumptions (Exhibit 10-B) Davidson and Boomer projected growth rates in rental income at 4 percent annually beginning in 1975, based on the assumption that rents in an aging building generally lag behind inflation rates. Occupancy was held constant at 95 percent, while increases in operating costs were projected at 7 percent. The growth rate in property value was projected at 3 percent annually. Actual experience during those five-plus years revealed the following comparison:

	Percentage Projected	Percentage Actual
Growth rate in revenue	4	8
Projected occupancy	95	96
Growth rate in operating cost	7	10
Growth rate in property value	3	7

In general, investors during the 1970s underestimated inflationary trends; D&B were no exception.

The ordinary income tax rate was assumed to be 50 percent and the (effective) capital-gain rate was 25 percent. (A 50% exclusion for capital gains was available in 1974.) Sensitivity analysis was also performed on the tax rates to test the impact on the different partners' IRRs. Surprisingly, varying the tax rates between 30 and 70 percent had minimal impact on the IRR. (Note that the top tax rate for individuals under the 1981 tax act was reduced from 70 percent to 50 percent. The 1986 Tax Reform Act provided for a decrease in the maximum tax rate to 33 percent.) Little further thought was given to placing investors with different tax brackets in the same joint venture, a problem previously of concern to D&B.

CASH FLOW ANALYSIS (SECTIONS SIX AND SEVEN)

Cash flow analysis is undertaken for the year of acquisition and five full tax years through 1979, as illustrated in Exhibit 10-C. With the very substantial expensed items in the year of acquisition, Davidson and Boomer thought the expected return, including the excellent year-end tax shelter, would attract many wealthy investors to the joint venture.

The annual cash flow projection indicated a steadily increasing cash flow before tax and tax losses each year through 1979. As a result of the rapidly decreas-

[c]Note that Section Four, which is a summary of capital expenditures and financing transactions over the holding period, has been omitted in this discussion because, in this case, no additional financing or capital expenditures are expected.

EXHIBIT 10-B.　Aspen Wood Apartments: Operating Assumptions

SECTION FIVE: OPERATING ASSUMPTIONS

Year

1974	Gross possible income	$ 26,620
	Operating expenses	$ 10,648
	Occupancy rate	95%
	Growth rate in property value during year	0%
1975	Gross possible income	$159,720
	Operating expenses	$ 63,888
	Occupancy rate	95%
	Growth rate in property value during year	3%

Year	Growth Rate in Revenue (%)	Projected Occupancy (%)	Growth Rate in Operating Costs (%)	Growth Rate in Property Value (%)
1976	4	95	7	3
1977	4	95	7	3
1978	4	95	7	3
1979	4	95	7	3

Cash flow projection period	6 years
Selling expense (percentage of sales price)	5%
Investors required IRR on equity	18%
Ordinary income tax rate	50%
Capital gains tax rate	25%

---

ing amounts of depreciation and mortgage interest, the cash flow after tax would decrease each year. Nevertheless, the IRR would actually increase each year over the holding period as a result of property appreciation, as will be explained.

Impact of Tax Reform. If the analysis were redone under 1988 tax law provisions, the analyst would need to make assumptions about the investor's other "passive-income" sources. If the investor had other passive-income amounts equal to or greater than the amounts of the tax losses projected each year, then the full amount of losses could be used to shelter income each year. If the investor did not have sufficient amounts of passive income to shelter, then the use of these tax losses would be deferred until later years. Clearly, the projection of tax savings under current tax law has become more difficult and risky because it depends on each investor's personal financial situation and income sources.

NET CASH POSITION ANALYSIS (SECTION EIGHT)

This is a summary of all capital and operating transactions affecting the cash position of the investor each year—cash flow from operations, refinancing pro-

EXHIBIT 10-C.   Aspen Wood Apartments: Cash Flow Analysis

SECTION SIX: CASH FLOW ANALYSIS FOR CURRENT TAX YEAR (two months, 1974)

Gross possible income	$ 26,620	Gross possible income	$26,620
Less: Vacancy	1,331	Less: Vacancy	1,331
Effective gross income	25,289	Effective gross income	25,289
Less: Operating costs	10,648	Less: Operating costs	10,648
Less: Expensed items	90,373	Net operating income	14,641
Net operating income	– 75,732	Less: Debt service	5,752
Less: Depreciation	18,802	Less: Lease payment	0
Less: Interest	4,959	Cash flow before tax	8,889
Less: Lease payment	0	Plus: Tax savings (taxes)	49,746
Taxable income	$ – 99,493	Plus: Investment tax credit	0
		Cash flow after tax	$58,636

Taxable income (loss) as a percent of total equity cash required = 47.38%

SECTION SEVEN: CASH FLOW ANALYSIS FOR FUTURE TAX YEARS

PROJECTED CASH FLOWS

	1975	1976	1977	1978	1979
Gross possible income	$159,720	$166,109	$172,753	$179,663	$186,850
Less: Vacancy	7,986	8,305	8,638	8,983	9,342
Effective gross income	151,734	157,803	164,115	170,680	177,507
Less: Operating costs	63,888	68,360	73,145	78,266	83,744
Net operating income	87,846	89,443	90,970	92,415	93,763
Less: Depreciation	98,380	85,723	81,267	68,355	51,716
Less: Interest	59,109	58,340	57,511	56,617	55,654
Less: Lease payment	0	0	0	0	0
Taxable income	– 69,643	– 54,619	– 47,808	– 32,558	– 13,607
Plus: Depreciation	98,380	85,723	81,267	68,355	51,716
Less: Principal payment	9,913	10,682	11,511	12,405	13,368
Cash flow before tax	18,824	20,421	21,948	23,393	24,741
Plus: Tax savings (taxes)	34,822	27,310	23,904	16,279	6,803
Plus: Investment tax credit	0	0	0	0	0
Cash flow after tax	$ 53,646	$ 47,731	$ 45,852	$ 39,671	$ 31,545

ceeds or deficits, capital expenditures, tax savings or taxes paid, and investment tax credits, as shown in Exhibit 10-D. Since the Aspen Wood Apartments analysis contained no capital expenditures, financing transactions, or investment tax credits during the period analyzed, the *net cash position after taxes* is identical each year to the *cash flow after-tax* figures shown in Sections six and seven (Exhibit 10-C). Consequently, the complete schedule of *net cash position after tax* is not shown here. The *net cash position after-taxes* amount is used each year to calculate the IRR and PV outputs. Essentially, the concept of cash flow has been expanded here to accommodate the additional variables shown in Exhibit 10-D.

PROJECTION OF NET SALE PROCEEDS (SECTION NINE)

For purposes of comparison, the project is assumed to be sold at the end of each tax year over the projection period. In essence, six possible holding periods are analyzed, 1974 through 1979. Transaction costs are deducted, loans are repaid with prepayment penalties, and the investor pays the capital gains and ordinary income taxes due on the sale. This analysis is shown in Exhibit 10-E.

DCF ANALYSIS (SECTION TEN)

For each possible holding period, 1974 through 1979, the investor calculates the present value of the property and the IRR after tax on total capital and equity invested (Exhibit 10-E). According to the projection, the IRR on equity, considered to be the most important investment criteria by Davidson and Boomer, would decline each year through 1979, reaching a low of about 34 percent. Clearly, the aggressive tax packaging paid off financially. The DCF analysis in Chapter 7 (using RE001) resulted in an IRR of 22 percent. Both analyses used the

EXHIBIT 10-D. Net Cash Position Analysis for Years 1974–1975

SECTION EIGHT: ANALYSIS OF NET CASH POSITION

	1974	1975
Cash flow before tax	$ 8,889	$18,824
Plus: Net refinancing proceeds*	0	0
Minus: Capital expenditures	0	0
Net cash position before taxes	$ 8,889	$18,824
Plus: Tax savings (taxes)	49,746	34,822
Plus: Investment tax credits	0	0
Net cash position after taxes	$58,636	$53,646

*Includes net loan transactions, less loan points and penalties, plus any recaptured prepaid interest.

EXHIBIT 10-E. Aspen Wood Apartments: Sale Proceeds and DCF Analysis

SECTION NINE: PROJECT NET RESALE PROCEEDS

	1974	1975	1976	1977	1978	1979
Gross resale price	$1,003,400	$1,033,502	$1,064,507	$1,096,442	$1,129,336	$1,163,216
Less: Transaction costs	50,170	51,675	53,225	54,822	56,467	58,161
Net resale price	953,230	981,827	1,011,282	1,041,620	1,072,869	1,105,055
Less: Loan principal	792,607	782,694	772,012	760,501	748,096	734,727
Less: Loan penalty	0	0	0	0	0	0
Plus: Prepaid interest	29,753	29,753	29,753	29,753	29,753	29,753
Proceeds from sale before tax	190,376	228,885	269,022	310,872	354,526	400,080
Less: Ordinary tax	1,268	7,657	7,717	6,770	6,834	6,409
Less: Capital gains tax	14,117	42,667	71,431	99,806	124,675	145,863
Net proceeds from sale	$ 174,990	$ 178,561	$ 189,874	$ 204,296	$ 223,016	$ 247,807

SECTION TEN: DISCOUNTED-CASH-FLOW ANALYSIS

	1974	1975	1976	1977	1978	1979
Present value if held until year indicated	$ 227,269	$ 248,471	$ 267,266	$ 282,717	$ 293,565	$ 300,450
Plus: Original mortgage	793,400	793,400	793,400	793,400	793,400	793,400
Total project value	$1,020,669	$1,041,871	$1,060,666	$1,076,117	$1,086,965	$1,093,850
Internal rate of return						
On equity	89.6%	41.7%	38.3%	36.7%	35.4%	34.2%
On total capital	22.2%	11.2%	10.4%	10.2%	10.0%	09.8%

same NOI and growth rate assumptions (see Exhibit 7-2). When compared to the 18 percent required IRR, the project looked very desirable.

RATIO ANALYSIS AND FINAL INVESTMENT DECISION (SECTION ELEVEN)[d]

Ratio analysis using the more sophisticated model turned out results consistent with those presented in Chapter 7. All the ratios indicated improving returns and decreasing risk over time. Front-end tax shelter was a substantial *sweetener* and effective sales tool. Because the project continued to meet or substantially exceed all the investment criteria set by D&B, few problems were anticipated in selling shares to investor clients, even in the depressed real estate market that characterized their city at that time. They believed they had found their "hole in the market," and then further capitalized on the situation through financial structuring and the application of appropriate risk management techniques. As a result, returns had increased and risks had been reduced.

The decision was reached to proceed to final negotiations and closing. Various delays occurred, but the property was finally closed and deeds delivered on December 30, 1974. The effective date of closing remained November 1, 1974.

[d]This section of the computer output is not shown.

PART 3

ANALYZING REAL ESTATE MARKETS UNDER CHANGING CONDITIONS

Madera Pointe Apartments, Mesa, Arizona.

Careful market studies are essential in the real estate investment process. Their importance, however, is too often shortchanged by investors or neglected altogether. Even when market analyses are performed, they may be incomplete, lack logical consistency, or fail to provide defensible input data on which the investor can base the return and risk analysis. Consequently, this section focuses on real estate market analysis topics and includes the subjects of inflation and real estate cycles.

The various steps of a *market analysis* (macromarket study) and a *marketability analysis* (micromarket study) are discussed. The output of such analyses is a revenue forecast for a projected ownership life cycle under alternative economic scenarios; this forecast provides input data for the investor's return and risk analysis. The process begins at a very macro level and converges to the micro, project-specific level.

Chapter 11 discusses the process and patterns of growth and decline in metropolitan areas, which must be carefully considered by the investor when choosing locations. Chapter 12 outlines the various steps involved in a market analysis, from the analysis of national and international trends to the comparison of neighborhoods. Chapter 13 on marketability analysis, begins with a neighborhood analysis and proceeds through a series of steps to generate specific revenue forecasts for a property. Finally, Chapter 14 addresses the very difficult topics of inflation and real estate cycles, and studies their complex effects on real estate investors and properties.

These subjects are not applied to the Aspen Wood Apartments at the ends of these chapters because they have been addressed in previous chapters.

11

URBAN ANALYSIS

Successful real estate investors understand the process of growth and decline in urban areas. They are aware of the many relationships between the growth and development of the urban area and the demand for various types of space, the basic product of the real estate industry. Knowledge of an urban area and its development processes provides a baseline for forming overall impressions of the area as a foundation for further research into investment potential. Certainly, population growth creates the need for additional housing, and increases in office employment creates the need for more office space. The same logic applies to space for industrial, retail, entertainment, lodging, and other types of real estate activity.

Investors should be aware of the impact of the legal, political, and sociological dimensions of an urban area on the demand for and the ability to provide space. For example, if urban growth is being fueled by increasing office employment and many of these employees are young, well educated, and affluent, the demand for particular housing types may increase much more rapidly than has historically been the case. In particular, there may be a demand for condominiums and apartments that offer extensive amenities and cause homeowners and renters few headaches. The ability of the real estate industry to provide an adequate supply of this type of space is related not only to the availability of land but also to the attitudes of the formal and informal power structures of the community toward growth and real estate development, and to the legal environment with respect to land use controls. Thus, the real estate investor must be attuned not only to the macrodevelopment of the community but also to the many other factors that effectively shape the balance between the supply of and the demand for particular types of space.

For urban analysis the investor also needs to understand land use patterns within the area. Are there patterns of land use that indicate where various types of housing will likely be built in the future? Are there patterns in the location of office space, shopping space, and industrial space?

If so, do these patterns satisfy space user and consumer demands, and are these patterns likely to continue? Why?

This chapter discusses the process of urban growth and its analysis for real estate investment decision making. The emphasis is on economic analysis of the urban area, although the demographic, legal, and political dimensions are also considered. The chapter also discusses land use patterns, their causes, and their analysis. The goal of the chapter is to provide a basic understanding of the concepts and techniques presented that is sufficient to direct the investor in the analysis of urban areas, using secondary data and reports prepared by professional demographers and market analysts.

DEFINING A METROPOLITAN AREA

In terms of real estate investment, what is an urban area? In many urban areas, the central city contains only a fraction of the urban area's total population, employment, retail sales, or any other commonly used measure of size or economic activity. For example, in 1985 the city of Atlanta had a population of 426,000, whereas the greater Atlanta urban area had a population of 2,472,000. In contrast, San Antonio had a population of 843,000 within its city boundaries and an urban area population of 1,236,000. An analysis of the city of San Antonio would tell much more about the San Antonio urban area than would an analysis of the city of Atlanta. The point is simple: with the growth of suburban communities, an investor must carefully define the area to be analyzed in order to avoid using misleading information in the urban analysis.

A metropolitan area is an integrated economic and social unit with a large population nucleus. The word "integrated" is critical to an understanding of urban areas because political boundaries often mean little with respect to the flow of people to shopping facilities, places of employment, and entertainment opportunities. Yet in other ways, political boundaries can be important. Differences in taxes and such services as schools and utilities, can be material considerations in analyzing communities. Also important are differences in public attitudes toward real estate development and the legal and political structure adopted to implement land use regulations. In such a system of communities, the investor must carefully assess whether consideration can or should be limited to a particular set of political boundaries.

Federal Government Definitions

Urban Statistical Areas. How can an urban area be defined more precisely? One approach is used for data collection and analysis by the Bureau of the Census of the Department of Commerce and the Office of Management and Budget. Since these data are often used in performing real estate research, the definitions are important. Exhibit 11-1 illustrates the geographical detail of metropolitan statistical areas (MSAs), consolidated metropolitan statistical areas (CMSAs), and primary metropolitan statistical areas (PMSAs).

A *metropolitan statistical area* (MSA) is defined as the county containing a central city (or twin cities) or an urban area of 50,000 or more inhabitants, plus adjacent counties that are economically and socially integrated with the central-city county. An MSA may include other cities of 50,000 or more inhabitants in addition to its central city, and it may include territory in more than one state. In New England the definition is slightly different because cities and towns, rather than counties, are used as the basis of the definition. In 1985 there were 332 MSAs and PMSAs, ranging in size from 76,000 to 8,466,000 inhabitants. The distribution of MSAs by size is summarized in Exhibit 11-2.

A *consolidated metropolitan statistical area* (CMSA) is an urban area with a population of one million or more and contains a component area called a *primary metropolitan statistical area* (PMSA). A PMSA is an area of significant interest and meets criteria specified for a MSA. For example, within the Denver–Boulder CMSA are the Denver and Boulder–Longmont PMSAs. Extensive data will be available for both the CMSA and PMSA. Other examples of CMSAs are San Francisco–Oakland–San Jose, California, and Miami–Fort Lauderdale, Florida.

An *urban place* has a population of 2,500 inhabitants or more in an area that is incorporated as a city, village, or borough, but it excludes persons living in the rural portions of extended cities. An *urbanized area* consists of a central city (or twin cities) with a total of 50,000 or more inhabitants, together with a contiguous, closely settled territory known as the *urban fringe.*

Finally, a *city* is defined as a political entity with clearly delineated boundaries in accordance with its charter of incorporation. There are approximately 18,000 cities in the United States, and there may be dozens of cities within a single MSA. The city of St. Louis, for example, is a political subsection of the St. Louis MSA.

Department of Labor Definitions. Another method of urban area delineation is the *labor market area* used by the U.S. Department of Labor. This concept relies heavily on transportation facilities and commuting time limits. A labor market is defined as an area with an average radius from the center of the market area of 30 to 40 miles, and with a maximum travel time limit of about 90 minutes.

Retail Trade Areas. A third possible system of classification is by primary–secondary–tertiary retail trading areas. These are defined by the U.S. Census of Business. Data are available from any federal or regional Department of Commerce office and are usually on file at local planning

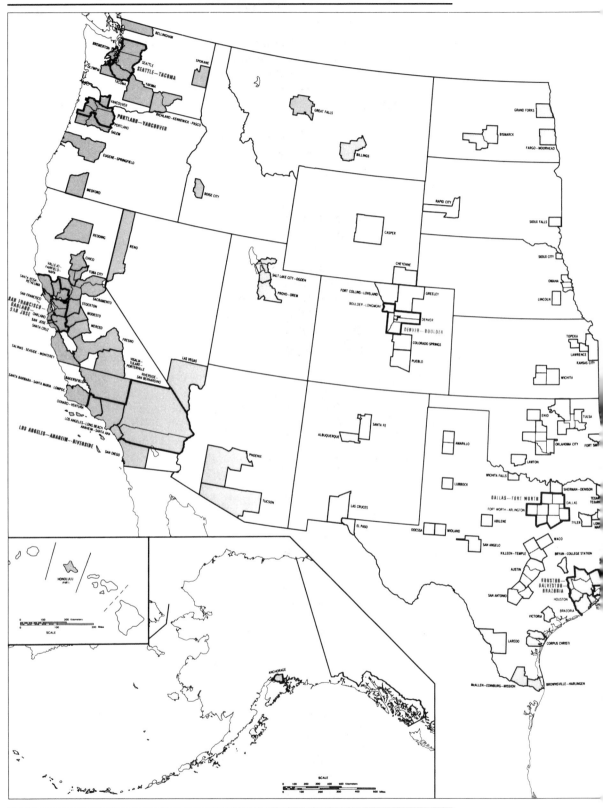

Source: U.S. Department of Commerce, Bureau of the Census, *State and Metropolitan Area Data Book* (Washington, D.C.: U.S. Gov't. Printing Office, 1986), pp. xvi–xvii.

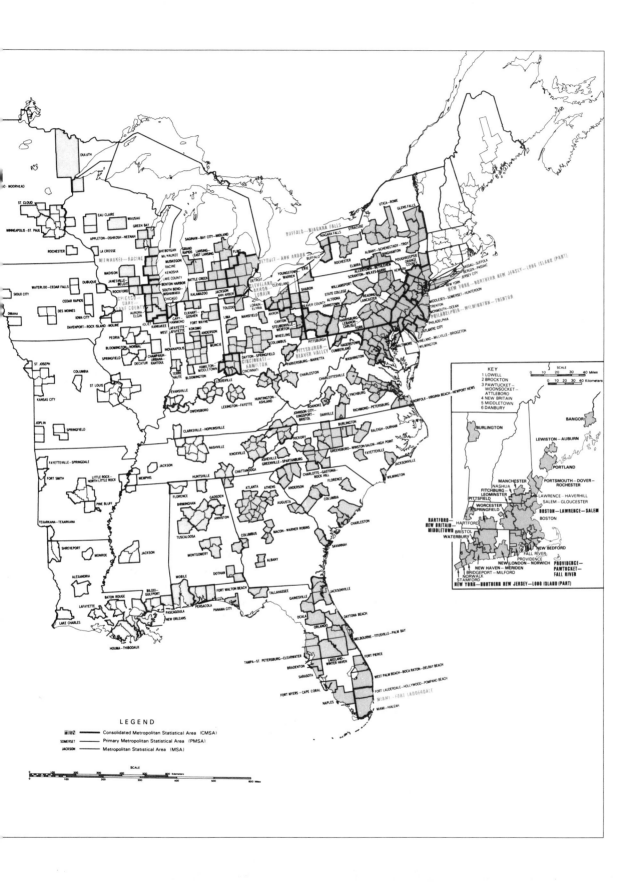

EXHIBIT 11-2.   Number and Population of MSAs, 1985

Number of MSAs	Population Class
9	2,500,000 or more
32	1,000,000–2,499,999
43	500,000– 999,999
72	250,000– 499,999
141	100,000– 249,999
35	Less than 100,000
332	182,500,000 total population

Source: U.S. Department of Commerce, Bureau of the Census, *Statistical Abstract of the United States, 1987* (Washington, D.C.: U.S. Gov't. Printing Office, 1987). This annual publication is an inexpensive source of statistics about urban places.

commission offices. Some state data centers, departments of commerce, and employment commissions provide useful reports on population and employment trends for economic development areas within the state.

As is true of many other social studies, establishing appropriate geographic limits is difficult. For convenience, market analysts often choose MSAs because of their rich statistical base. However, such geographic limits are not necessarily realistic for a specific type of real estate study. In any event, great care must be taken to evaluate the acceptability of the method of delineating the market area for the purpose of investment analysis.

URBAN ECONOMIC ANALYSIS

Changes in the economics of an urban area are directly related to the need for space of all types. Economic growth creates a demand for new office and industrial space for new employees to work in, homes for them to live in, and other types of space in which they can shop and be entertained. Associated with different types of employment are varying levels of income and expenditures by the employers and employees. For example, a semiconductor producer will require a different set of goods and services from the local community than will a steel plant. Similarly, the mix of administrative, research, and production employees will differ, as will their respective incomes and expenditure patterns.

One approach to urban economic analysis is economic-base analysis.[1]

[1]Ralph Pfouts, *Techniques of Urban Land Analysis* (Chandler–Davis, 1962). This is a classic compendium of articles on economic-base analysis techniques. More recent discussions can be found in Jerome Dasso, "Economic Base Analysis for the Appraiser," *The Appraisal Journal*, July 1969, pp. 374–385; and John M. Clapp, *Handbook For Real Estate Market Analysis* (Englewood Cliffs, N.J.: Prentice-Hall, 1987), pp. 107–125; and Neil Carn, Joseph Rabianski, Ronald Racster, and Maury Seldin, *Real Estate Market Analysis: Techniques and Applications* (Englewood Cliffs, N.J.: Prentice-Hall, 1988), pp. 26–45.

In its simplified form, economic-base analysis seeks to study the relation between basic and nonbasic economic activity. Basic economic activity is any economic activity associated with the production of goods and services sold outside the geographic area being studied. Thus, basic economic activity is analogous to export activity for a nation. Nonbasic economic activity is any activity associated with the production of goods and services to be sold within the geographic area being studied. Basic and nonbasic economic activity may be measured in different ways, such as by revenue and employment.

To understand the significance of basic and nonbasic activity, we should consider, in a very general way, the manner in which an urban area can grow. With no change in basic employment, the urban economy can grow only in a limited number of ways, such as through an increase in income that increases the demand for nonbasic goods and services, or by firms changing their production processes and demanding more local goods and services.

However, growth is more likely to come from a significant change in basic economic activity as new firms are created or are moved into the area. These changes are important because of the multiplier effect created by the spending of the firm and its employees; this spending creates nonbasic employment opportunities, which with related spending creates more nonbasic employment, and so on. The multiplier is the ratio of total change in employment (income) to the change in basic employment (income). For example, an increase in basic employment of 10 jobs may create a total employment increase of 100 jobs, thus a multiplier of 10. The basic employment increase leads to basic payroll increases of $300,000 and total area increases of $2,500,000, a multiplier of 8.3. Different pay scales will result in differences between employment and income multipliers. Thus, one objective of an economic-base study is to estimate the employment multiplier (or income multiplier if it is being used). At a minimum, economic-base analysis should classify economic activity in a geographic area into basic and nonbasic activities. Although critics have often found fault with the validity of the techniques used, economic-base analysis is still the best available tool for short-run forecasts.

The simplistic analysis just described allows the concepts of economic-base analysis to be discussed but would seldom be adequate support for most analyses. In a given urban area, the simple basic–nonbasic classification scheme does not provide enough detail about the composition of basic and nonbasic employment. Two cities with identical employment multipliers and numbers of basic and nonbasic employees may face very different economic futures because of the industries in each city. A city with a concentration of employment in growth industries is in a much different position from that of a city with a concentration of employment in maturing industries. For example, Seattle had a concentration of employment in the aerospace industry in the late 1960s and early 1970s that led to a sharp downturn in the local economy as that industry suffered substantial cut-backs from reduced national defense spending and fewer airline contracts for new equipment. More recently, Denver, Houston, and Tulsa, cities with concentrations of energy-related employment, suffered as oil prices dropped and exploration and production activities were reduced.

One measure of economic concentration, the location quotient, relates concentration of a certain activity (Industry A) in an area to the concentration of the same economic activity in a region, state, or the nation:[2]

$$\text{Location quotient} = \frac{\text{percentage of total employment in Industry A in urban area}}{\text{percentage of total employment in Industry A in U.S., region, or state}}$$

For example, if a city has 20 percent of its labor force in durable goods manufacturing whereas nationally only 10 percent of the labor force is employed in such endeavors, the location quotient is 2.0. Thus, relative to the nation as a whole, the area has a greater concentration of durable goods manufacturing employment. If the standard of comparison is the region and the region has 25 percent of its labor force employed in durable goods, the city location quotient is 0.8.

Location quotients are often used to compare the locational advantages of urban areas. Classifying economic activity in a standardized manner and calculating location quotients enables the relative concentration of employment to be assessed. Employment forecasts are often developed by considering the national or regional growth rates, or both, expected for different industry classifications, and then considering whether a specific urban area can be expected to experience a higher or lower rate of growth than the larger reference area. The growth rate of a community may be expected to be greater or less because it has locational advantages or disadvantages compared to other urban areas. For example, Austin, Texas, Raleigh-Durham, North Carolina, and San Diego, California, are predicted to experience a higher-than-national-average growth rate in semiconductor and other high-tech employment because these cities have unique locational advantages which attract firms in this industry.

Classifying Economic Activity

The Standard Industrial Classification (SIC) code defined by the Department of Labor is useful in classifying the local metropolitan economy into

[2]Werner Z. Hirsch, *Urban Economic Analysis* (New York: McGraw-Hill, 1973), Chapter 7; Edgar M. Hoover, *An Introduction to Regional Economics* (New York: Alfred A. Knopf, 1975), pp. 218–230; G. Vincent Barrett and John P. Blair, *How to Conduct and Analyze Real Estate Market and Feasibility Studies* (New York: Van Nostrand Reinhold, 1982), pp. 138–144; and Jerome Dasso, "Techniques of Area Analysis," *The Appraisal Journal*, October 1987, pp. 578–591.

its basic sector and its nonbasic, or service sector. This code enables the investor to compare MSAs and evaluate their relative potentials more efficiently. In the SIC system an economic activity is first classified as agriculture, mining, construction, manufacturing, transportation, wholesale and retail trade, finance, services, or government. Each of these divisions is broken down into major groups, which are assigned SIC numbers. Exhibit 11-3 is a table of the groupings with their SIC numbers. The two-digit designations of the major groups are broken down step by step to the four-digit level. Each successive digit represents a greater level of specialization within the group.

When employment and sales data are classified by SIC numbers, investors can compare rates of change from one metropolitan area to another. Unfortunately, in federal economic projections there is a strong bias toward analysis and reporting of import and export products based on manufacturing, agriculture, mining, and other extractive industries. The realization that over 50 percent of employment is in the service sector helps to explain the need to extend the analysis to the subclassifications of the SIC. Obviously, basic activities encompass both the production of goods and the provision of services to users outside the metropolitan area; thus, both an automobile manufacturer and a state capitol complex are basic activities.

Another reason for preferring analyses that use SIC codes is that every five years (e.g., 1985, 1990) the Bureau of Economic Analysis (BEA) publishes economic projections, called OBERS reports, that project personal income, business earnings, and employment for the entire nation, for 173 BEA economic areas, for water resource regions, for states, for all MSAs, and for other significant areas. These reports break down their data according to SIC groups. In addition to OBERS forecasts, the Department of Commerce produces the annual *U.S. Industrial Outlook*, an excellent source of trends and short-term projections of employment and activity by industries in the economy.

Limits to Urban Growth

The long-range viability of any metropolitan area rests on its capacity to innovate or to acquire in some way a new export base to replace older industries as they decline. It has been suggested, for example, that New York City may have exceeded its limits of growth. Diseconomies of scale appear to have occurred in its provision of certain labor-intensive municipal services, such as garbage removal and police and fire protection. On the other hand, the rich diversity of the greater New York economic base, coupled with a demonstrated capacity for innovation and change, suggests that New York City may simply be in a period of transition while it develops a new direction.

EXHIBIT 11-3. Industrial Groupings with Standard Industrial Classification Codes

All-Industry Total	SIC Code Number
Agriculture, forestry, and fisheries:	
Agriculture	01, 07
Forestry and fisheries	08, 09
Mining:	
Metal	10
Coal	11, 12
Crude petroleum and natural gas	13
Nonmetallic, except fuels	14
Contract construction	15–17
Manufacturing:	
Food and kindred products	20
Textile mill products	22
Apparel and other fabric products	23
Lumber products and furniture	24, 25
Paper and allied products	26
Printing and publishing	27
Chemicals and allied products	28
Petroleum refining	29
Primary metals	33
Fabricated metals and ordnance	34, 19
Machinery, excluding electrical	35
Electrical, machinery and supplies	36
Motor vehicles and equipment	371
Transportation equipment, excluding motor vehicles	37, except 371
Other manufacturing	21, 30–32, 38, 39
Transportation, communications, and public utilities	
Railroad transportation	40
Trucking and warehousing	42
Other transportation and services	41, 44, 47
Communications	48
Utilities (electric, gas, sanitary)	49
Wholesale and retail trade	50, 52–57, 59
Finance, insurance, and real estate	60–67
Services:	
Lodging places and personal services	70, 72
Business and repair services	73, 75, 76
Amusement and recreation services	78, 79
Private households	88
Professional services	80, 81, 82, 84, 86, 89
Government:	
Civilian government:	
Federal government	91, except fed. military
State and local government	92, 93
Armed forces	part of 91

Source: Executive Office of the President, Bureau of the Budget, *Standard Industrial Classification Manual* (Washington, D.C.: U.S. Gov't. Printing Office, 1987).

Indicators of Stability

Some metropolitan areas have a rich infrastructure that facilitates adjustment to change by providing the socioeconomic institutions and physical facilities needed to initiate new enterprises, to convert capital from old forms to new ones, and to retrain labor. These more stable economic bases are usually in the larger metropolitan areas. Such areas have been able to restructure old and dying bases to new and growing ones through activities that are not usually found in smaller urban areas. Universities and research parks, sophisticated engineering firms and financial institutions, public relations firms and advertising agencies, transportation networks, and utilities systems: all provide a much more diversified economic base than is found in the one-industry town. A diversified economy softens the shock of exogenous change by minimizing the impact of a dying industry on the urban area.

There appears to be a "ratchet" in urban growth in medium- and large-sized MSAs. Once the larger size has been achieved, sustained population decline is unlikely except in the largest MSAs—the megalopolises—where diseconomies occur because the economic and social environment deteriorates through transportation congestion, pollution, and inefficient application of resources.

Competition and Interdependence of Metropolitan Areas

The metropolitan areas of the United States simultaneously compete with and depend on one another.[3] Paradoxically, specialization is the key to both competition and interdependence. The past, present, and future roles of metropolitan areas are evident in their interdependence on their surrounding MSAs. A city usually sends its largest outflows of travelers and information to the city on which it relies most heavily for specialized services that are not available locally.

For instance, when the interflows of telephone calls and air passengers are mapped, it is clear that New York maintains a premier position among the twenty largest metropolitan areas. Only Detroit, St. Louis, Minneapolis–St. Paul, and Seattle are more closely linked to another one of the twenty metropolitan areas.[4] Chicago is clearly the nation's second most

---

[3]Edgar M. Hoover, *An Introduction to Regional Economics*, pp. 157–167 and 232–238, describes intraregional and interregional relationships and linkages between areas that support growth and create competition.

[4]John S. Adams, ed., *A Comparative Atlas of America's Great Cities: Twenty Metropolitan Regions* (Minneapolis: Association of American Geographers and the University of Minnesota Press, 1976). This represents a good source of information on competition and interdependence of metropolitan areas. More current relationships may be subjectively estimated using annual issues of the *Rand McNally Commercial Atlas and Marketing Guide*, which provide trends and projections of economic data and population, transportation, and communication data for over 128,000 places in the United States.

dominant metropolis, with Minneapolis–St. Paul, St. Louis, and Detroit dependent on it. Los Angeles, the nation's second most populous metropolis, had captured only Seattle's primary attention by the late 1960s.

The connection or subordination of major metropolitan areas to surrounding MSAs is a subject worthy of continued study. During the early 1980s Atlanta became the metropolis of the Southeast. The Dallas–Fort Worth metroplex, because of its links with adjoining southern states and Texas, profited from the South's rapid urban growth. On the other hand, cities like Hartford, Philadelphia, Pittsburgh, Cleveland, and St. Louis lost potential client cities to stronger or later arrivals, partly because of the shift in transportation and communication modes. The future offers relatively fewer growth opportunities for most of these cities, because with few client cities and no distinctive environmental amenities, the opportunities for expansion in specialized employment, which would attract more people, are limited.

New Orleans, Seattle, and Detroit also face a difficult future because the peripheral location of each reduces the number of subordinate MSAs that they might link up with. San Francisco, formerly in a dominant position in West Coast affairs, is increasingly ceding to Los Angeles. Minneapolis–St. Paul has only one metropolitan subordinate (Duluth), but it serves a large and productive agrarian hinterland. Miami, Houston, and Washington, D.C., are unusual cases. Miami has valuable climatic amenities and possible relationships with Latin American countries. Washington, D.C., almost fully a creature of the federal government, seems to be insulated from typical metropolitan competition and is capable of self-sustained growth in a way that no other city could be. Houston's prosperity and rapid growth have been based on petrochemical and aerospace industries, whose futures depend on the vagaries of international supply and demand forces and government support of aerospace programs.

URBAN DEMOGRAPHIC ANALYSIS

Demographics is the study of a population. The study begins with the compilation of the most reliable and current data available. Although much data is available through the Bureau of the Census, many independent research organizations also provide useful information.[5] Exhibit 11-4 is an example of data available on trends in population growth by state and region. As used in real estate analysis, demographics is the study of the particular population characteristics considered important to the demand for particular types of space. Demographic analysis provides richer

[5]For example, George Sternlieb, James W. Hughes, and Connie O. Hughes, *Demographic Trends and Economic Reality: Planning and Markets in the 80's* (New Brunswick, N.J.: Rutgers University, Center for Public Policy Research, 1982).

EXHIBIT 11-4. Population Trends by Region and State: 1975–1985

Region, Division, and State	1975 (1,000)	1978 (1,000)	1979 (1,000)	1980, April 1 (1,000)	1981 (1,000)	1982 (1,000)	1983 (1,000)	1984 (1,000)	1985, Preliminary Total (1,000)	Rank Order	Per sq. mi. of Land Area
United States	215,465	222,095	224,567	226,546	229,637	231,996	234,284	236,495	238,740	NA[a]	67
Region											
Northeast	49,411	49,194	49,160	49,135	49,268	49,329	49,535	49,728	49,859	NA	306
Midwest	57,890	58,604	58,783	58,866	59,000	58,942	58,918	59,078	59,197	NA	79
South	69,565	72,984	74,276	75,372	77,052	78,484	79,713	80,765	81,858	NA	94
West	38,600	41,313	42,348	43,172	44,317	45,241	46,117	46,924	47,826	NA	27
New England	12,163	12,283	12,322	12,348	12,416	12,432	12,491	12,578	12,660	NA	201
Maine	1,072	1,114	1,123	1,125	1,133	1,136	1,145	1,156	1,164	38	38
New Hampshire	829	892	909	921	937	948	959	978	998	41	111
Vermont	480	498	505	511	516	520	525	530	535	48	58
Massachusetts	5,758	5,736	5,738	5,737	5,755	5,747	5,766	5,798	5,822	12	744
Rhode Island	943	952	950	947	953	954	956	962	968	42	918
Connecticut	3,083	3,092	3,096	3,108	3,123	3,127	3,140	3,155	3,174	28	651
Middle Atlantic	37,247	36,911	36,838	36,787	36,852	36,896	37,044	37,150	37,199	NA	373
New York	18,003	17,681	17,584	17,558	17,567	17,587	17,685	17,746	17,783	2	375
New Jersey	7,338	7,351	7,367	7,365	7,408	7,430	7,468	7,517	7,562	9	1,013
Pennsylvania	11,906	11,879	11,888	11,864	11,877	11,879	11,891	11,887	11,853	4	264
East North Central	41,125	41,542	41,645	41,682	41,708	41,597	41,504	41,574	41,642	NA	171
Ohio	10,770	10,796	10,798	10,798	10,800	10,774	10,738	10,740	10,744	7	262
Indiana	5,366	5,470	5,501	5,490	5,489	5,483	5,474	5,492	5,499	14	153
Illinois	11,292	11,413	11,397	11,427	11,474	11,478	11,491	11,522	11,535	5	207
Michigan	9,118	9,218	9,266	9,262	9,210	9,117	9,054	9,058	9,088	8	160
Wisconsin	4,579	4,646	4,683	4,706	4,735	4,746	4,747	4,762	4,775	16	88
West North Central	16,765	17,062	17,138	17,183	17,292	17,345	17,415	17,504	17,555	NA	35
Minnesota	3,933	4,015	4,050	4,076	4,112	4,133	4,145	4,163	4,193	21	53
Iowa	2,881	2,918	2,916	2,914	2,918	2,907	2,904	2,903	2,884	29	52
Missouri	4,808	4,889	4,912	4,917	4,938	4,942	4,963	5,001	5,029	15	73
North Dakota	639	651	653	653	661	672	681	687	685	46	10
South Dakota	681	689	688	691	692	694	699	705	708	45	9
Nebraska	1,543	1,564	1,567	1,570	1,583	1,590	1,596	1,605	1,606	36	21
Kansas	2,281	2,336	2,351	2,364	2,388	2,408	2,427	2,440	2,450	32	30
South Atlantic	34,354	35,839	36,428	36,959	37,791	38,321	38,875	39,533	40,227	NA	151
Delaware	587	595	595	594	597	600	606	614	622	47	322
Maryland	4,139	4,184	4,191	4,217	4,257	4,273	4,301	4,349	4,392	20	447
District of Columbia	707	665	650	638	633	627	625	625	626	NA	9,931
Virginia	5,047	5,270	5,308	5,347	5,442	5,489	5,559	5,636	5,706	13	144
West Virginia	1,842	1,923	1,942	1,950	1,961	1,961	1,963	1,951	1,936	34	80
North Carolina	5,547	5,759	5,823	5,882	5,956	·6,016	6,077	6,166	6,255	10	128
South Carolina	2,902	3,044	3,090	3,122	3,187	3,226	3,258	3,302	3,347	24	111
Georgia	5,064	5,296	5,401	5,463	5,569	5,651	5,733	5,842	5,976	11	103
Florida	8,518	9,102	9,401	9,746	10,190	10,478	10,754	11,050	11,366	6	210
East South Central	13,822	14,416	14,576	14,666	14,788	14,868	14,945	15,033	15,122	NA	85
Kentucky	3,468	3,610	3,642	3,661	3,676	3,694	3,714	3,720	3,726	23	94
Tennessee	4,276	4,486	4,560	4,591	4,638	4,665	4,689	4,726	4,762	17	116
Alabama	3,679	3,832	3,866	3,894	3,927	3,942	3,960	3,989	4,021	22	79
Mississippi	2,399	2,488	2,507	2,521	2,547	2,567	2,583	2,598	2,613	31	55
West South Central	21,389	22,729	23,273	23,747	24,474	25,295	25,893	26,199	26,510	NA	62
Arkansas	2,160	2,243	2,271	2,286	2,300	2,307	2,325	2,346	2,359	33	45
Louisiana	3,886	4,069	4,138	4,206	4,300	4,383	4,441	4,461	4,481	18	101
Oklahoma	2,775	2,917	2,975	3,025	3,107	3,231	3,311	3,310	3,301	25	48
Texas	12,569	13,500	13,888	14,229	14,767	15,374	15,816	16,083	16,370	3	62
Mountain	9,849	10,733	11,129	11,373	11,749	12,066	12,339	12,563	12,789	NA	15
Montana	748	782	787	787	796	805	816	823	826	44	6
Idaho	832	911	933	944	964	978	988	999	1,005	40	12
Wyoming	382	433	454	470	494	510	516	513	509	50	5
Colorado	2,586	2,767	2,849	2,890	2,984	3,072	3,149	3,190	3,231	26	31
New Mexico	1,160	1,238	1,285	1,303	1,335	1,368	1,402	1,426	1,450	37	12
Arizona	2,285	2,515	2,636	2,718	2,814	2,897	2,977	3,072	3,187	27	28
Utah	1,236	1,368	1,420	1,461	1,515	1,558	1,595	1,623	1,645	35	20
Nevada	620	719	765	800	846	878	897	917	936	43	9
Pacific	28,751	30,580	31,219	31,800	32,568	33,175	33,778	34,361	35,037	NA	39
Washington	3,621	3,889	4,018	4,132	4,237	4,278	4,305	4,349	4,409	19	66
Oregon	2,330	2,518	2,588	2,633	2,669	2,669	2,660	2,676	2,687	30	28
California	21,538	22,836	23,257	23,668	24,265	24,784	25,311	25,795	26,365	1	169
Alaska	376	405	403	402	416	445	482	505	521	49	1
Hawaii	886	932	953	965	981	998	1,019	1,037	1,054	39	164

Source: U.S. Department of Commerce, Bureau of the Census, *Statistical Abstract of the United States, 1987* (Washington, D.C.: U.S. Gov't. Printing Office, 1987), p. 22.

[a]NA = not applicable.

insights than a purely economic analysis by examining the size and composition of the population and the impact of economic change on these variables. Demographic and economic analyses are not independent; rather, they are closely related.

Population forecasts are often predicated on expected changes in employment. Given an expected change in employment and unemployment, population change in an area is estimated using the following equation:

$$P = \frac{E + U}{N} \times F$$

where P = expected change in population
E = expected change in number of employed
U = expected change in number of unemployed
N = area average number of persons working per household
F = area average number of persons per household

Changes in employment and unemployment may be positive (increasing) or negative declining). In circular fashion, the size and characteristics of the population affect the potential for expected change in employment in the area. The availability of adequate numbers of workers with appropriate education, experience, or both is an important factor in the location decisions of many firms. Thus, local economic and demographic characteristics are related.

Population Projections

The Census Bureau periodically publishes several national population projections that reflect current population, assumed birth and death rates, and levels of migration and immigration. Sample projections through the year 2050 are presented in Exhibit 11-5. The numbers in Exhibit 11-5 reflect the uncertainty that surrounds population estimates through the use of four forecast series ranging from high to low. For example, even for the relatively short forecast period to the year 2000, the population forecasts range from a low of about 240 million to a high of about 285 million.

Population estimates and forecasts are also available for states, counties, and urban areas.[6] Such forecasts are made by the Bureau of the Census; state, regional, and local planning departments and agencies; various departments of colleges and universities; and others. As discussed earlier, these forecasts are often based on forecasts of employment for the urban

[6]Within the Bureau of the Census current population programs, United States and states "Population Estimates and Projections," P-25 series, are published monthly and annually. Data presented include population, age, sex, and race. "Local Population Estimates," P-26 series, are published irregularly for the United States, states, counties, MSAs, and subcounty areas.

EXHIBIT 11-5. U.S. Population Projections to 2050

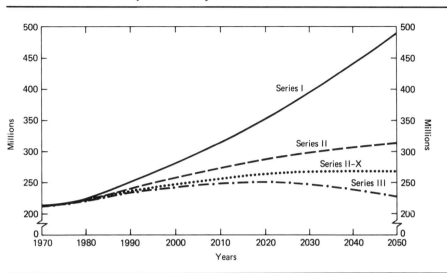

Source: U.S. Department of Commerce, Bureau of the Census, *Statistical Abstract of the United States, 1978* (Washington, D.C.: U.S. Gov't. Printing Office, 1978), p. 5.

area. Great care should be exercised to identify the source of these forecasts and the methodology used to make them. Further, as many forecasts as possible should be gathered and compared to capture the uncertainty inherent in such forecasts. One should be aware of the possibility of receiving estimates prepared by overzealous community boosters mistaking wishes for reality.

It should be clear that the underlying assumptions concerning population projections have a critical effect on assumed demand for various land uses. The problem—a very real one—is to find forecasts that are realistic and not motivated by ulterior objectives. In the long run, it is hoped that those who are interested in rational real estate investment decision making will encourage data-gathering and forecasting agencies to be more realistic. In the meantime, the overbuilding or underbuilding will continue, resulting, at least in part, from differences between anticipated and actual rates of growth.

Analyzing Other Aspects of the Population

For real estate investors, the number of people living in an urban area is only one guide to demand. A certain population level will, in general, generate a range of total demand for housing, shopping, entertainment, and other real estate space. Using demographic information to estimate this aggregate demand is a necessary and useful exercise to identify possible existing and potential differences for a market as a whole. However, aggregate numbers are of little help in estimating more precisely the needs of the population.

Limitless possibilities exist in demographic research, and there is a danger that such research will become mired in the detailed data available from federal, state, and local agencies and private firms. When there is no detailed conceptual model to identify the demographic variables of importance, a shotgun approach of gathering all types of data may develop. What follows is not an exhaustive discussion of all possible demographic data of interest, but rather a discussion of selected variables that may be significant in the general analysis of urban areas. Variables not discussed here may be appropriate in a number of specific situations. Further, the examples in the chapter are national in character, and it should be remembered that it is local levels and variations between urban areas that are usually of greatest interest.

Birthrates. The current U.S. birthrate is about 15 per 1,000, which is substantially lower than in recent decades. Even so, it is greatly inflated by the fact that females born during the baby boom (1945–1960) have reached reproductive age. Therefore, during the better part of the 1980s and 1990s, a sharp temporary increase in the underlying demand for housing and other goods is expected as the generation born in the 1950s produces record rates of grown children who wish to form households.

Fertility Rates. Fertility has been declining. During the 1950s the U.S. birthrate was nearly twice its level of the middle 1980s. Even as recently as 1970 it was nearly 40 percent higher. According to the latest surveys, the average American household now expects to have just over two children; that is a full child less than the three-plus expectation of the mid-1960s. The odds currently strongly favor subreplacement fertility. The skyrocketing costs of raising and educating children, a chronic expectation of job insecurity among younger workers, and the rapid increase in the number of two-income families all signal smaller families. With large numbers of women seeking their fortunes in the work force, there is a tendency to postpone and reduce childbearing.

Death Rates. From the standpoint of mortality, too, society appears to have entered an era that varies sharply with previous trends and expectations. Death rates for people under age fifty have become so low that further declines are unlikely. For example, if all male and female death rates between birth and age fifty suddenly dropped to zero, the gain in life expectancy from the current level of about seventy-three years would be only about four years—a change of less than 6 percent. Future declines in death rates are likely to come only through major breakthroughs against old-age diseases such as heart attack, cancer, and stroke.

Immigration. Natural increase is not alone in making demographic history. In recent years immigration has also been setting records. Legal immigration, which has reached a level of approximately 600,000 people annually, accounts for 25 percent of the country's approximate 2.3 million total annual growth. In addition, the net number of illegal immigrants is significant, estimated by some to be more than the number of legal immigrants. If we estimate illegal immigration to be about 500,000 persons annually and add that number to legal immigration, the ratio of total net immigration to total growth is about 50 percent. This is a greater level than that reached at the peak of European immigration a century ago. The combined impact of fertility rates, death rates, and immigration on population is shown in Exhibit 11-6.

Age. As a result of these changes in birth, fertility, and death rates, changes are occurring in the age composition of the population. Exhibit 11-7 illustrates the changes in composition of the population between 1960 and 1983 and forecasts through 2000. Sharp increases in the age groups forty-five and over, and similar decreases in the under-forty-five age groups occur as the "baby boomers" move through middle age. These changes have implications for the quality and quantity of space required to house, entertain, and provide workplaces for this population. Certainly, new demands for extended-care facilities of various kinds are to be expected.

EXHIBIT 11-6.   Components of Population Change: 1960 to 1985

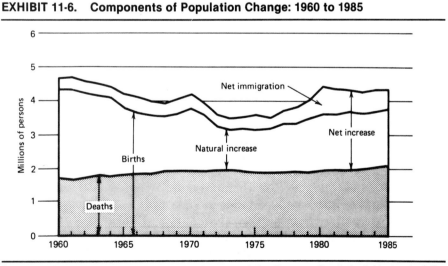

Source: U.S. Department of Commerce, Bureau of the Census, *Statistical Abstract of the United States, 1987* (Washington, D.C.: U.S. Gov't. Printing Office, 1987), p. 6.

EXHIBIT 11-7. **Age Distribution of United States Population, 1960 to 1983, and Projections to 2000**

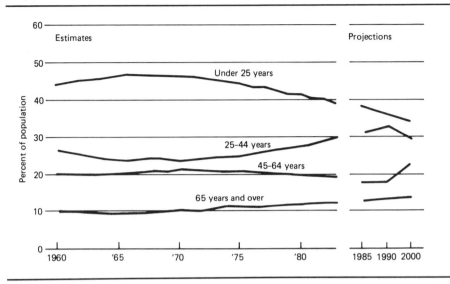

Source: U.S. Department of Commerce, Bureau of the Census, *Statistical Abstract of the United States, 1985* (Washington, D.C.: U.S. Gov't. Printing Office, 1985), p. 5.

Household Composition. All the changes noted thus far are having an impact on the size and composition of the average household. Statistically, if demand is measured by dwelling units, a decrease in average household size should stimulate the demand for dwellings of all types. For example, with 240 million people living in households, 80 million dwelling units would be needed if the mean number of persons per household were three, but 120 million units would be needed if the mean dropped to two—as long as income levels remained adequate to fulfill aspirations. This may seem like a drastic change; however, in only the fourteen years between 1960 and 1986, average household size went from 3.30 to 2.67 persons—a change of .63 persons. Exhibit 11-8 summarizes household size since 1960.

The fact that more and more households are being headed by single people is also implicit in Exhibits 11-7 and 11-8. The notion that housing is for families with children present is waning. With an average life expectancy of seventy-three years and a fertility rate indicating only two children per family, it appears likely that even if one becomes a parent, one can expect to live in a housing unit with children present for only about half of one's lifetime. The children will spend eighteen years with their parents and perhaps another eighteen with their own children—assuming, of course, no divorce.

EXHIBIT 11-8. Persons per Household

Year	Persons	Year	Persons
1960	3.30	1982	2.72
1970	3.14	1983	2.73
1975	2.94	1984	2.71
1980	2.76	1985	2.69
		1986	2.67

Source: U.S. Department of Commerce, Bureau of the Census, *Statistical Abstract of the United States, 1987* (Washington, D.C.: U.S. Gov't. Printing Office, 1987), p. 00.

Changes in Employment Rate and New-Job Formation. Since industrial and service employment are the key to economic-base analysis, this is an important and useful set of statistics. Comparative statistics on the rate of unemployment, the level of employment, and the rate of new-job formation are very useful in evaluating the health and vitality of an MSA. These statistics are however, substantially affected by short-run changes in activity and real estate cycles that do not necessarily affect the long-term need for real estate assets.

The Age of Migration

Population movements are the key to understanding the underlying demand for land use in a metropolitan area. Theoretical economists correctly argue that households are consumers and not producers. However, this theoretical position is of limited usefulness to a real estate investment decision maker. Del Webb's Sun City, Arizona, and the growth around Tampa–Sarasota, Florida, are due to retirement, not new jobs. Billions of dollars of real estate assets are dependent on income and credit flows that are not related in any way to migration in search of job opportunities. In an era of increasing uncertainty, there are substantial difficulties in forecasting population trends even using the best available economic and demographic statistics. Therefore, investors must be knowledgeable about the causes of population movements so that they can make their own demographic forecasts.

Migration as an Indicator of Change in the Demand for Real Estate. In- and out-migration are expressions of individual and family decisions to seek better economic and cultural opportunities. People move for many reasons: to begin a new career, to find a better climate for their retirement years, to leave an area where a plant has closed for another where their skills are in demand. In a market economy, migration is an interesting phenomenon. People generally do not choose to leave friends, relatives, and familiar surroundings unless they believe it is necessary to do so in order to fulfill their aspirations.

Each year about two out of ten Americans move from one state to another. In 1981 over 37 million people moved, almost 18 million of them within the same MSA. The most frequent movers, apart from college students, are young families in which the parents are twenty-five to thirty-four years old. For many of these families, an intracity move reflects an increase in family size. Older people are more inclined to move infrequently. This is especially true of those sixty-five years old and over, unless they are seeking a change at time of retirement. Middle-aged parents with children in high school move less often than families with younger children. However, younger families, middle-aged parents, and young singles seeking career opportunities all tend to move from one metropolitan area to another where economic opportunities appear to be greater.

The U.S. Bureau of Economic Analysis reported that, in general, the states in the South and West grew more rapidly than other areas of the nation, and some states in the Northeast and Midwest experienced a net out-migration.[7] A countertrend was evident in the New England states, where Connecticut, New Hampshire, Massachusetts, and Vermont have grown and are projected to grow faster than the United States as a whole through the year 2000. States with declining populations in the 1960s, such as West Virginia, the Dakotas, Mississippi, and Arkansas, are now experiencing some population growth.

Another study by the Census Bureau showed that in 1981, 83 percent of Americans did not move during the year. Eight percent had moved within the same metropolitan area, and 2.3 percent had moved from one metropolitan area to another. Only 1.6 percent had moved from *outside* an MSA *into* an MSA, and 1.1 percent had moved from inside an MSA to outside an MSA.

This brief recital of population trends should make it clear that identifying an MSA that would provide a desirable environment for a real estate investment requires some knowledge of the past, present, and future of that area compared with others. In the short run, an MSA's age and the time during which it experiences its most rapid growth are the major determinants of how many problems it has and how serious they are. Similarly, an investor considering a specific MSA must identify its growth prospects and forecast how well it can cope with its problems. Human and environmental problems are likely to be more intractable in stagnating places than in those where opportunities are expanding.

However, it should be noted that choosing a growing MSA is merely a risk management technique. It is quite possible to find good-quality invest-

---

[7]"Regional and State Projections of Income, Employment and Population to the Year 2000," *Survey of Current Business*, May 1985.

ments at well-selected locations in some slow-growing MSAs. Indeed, a mature, stable MSA should have high-quality real estate investments that could generate excellent cash flow with a minimum of risk over the ownership period. Obviously, choosing a prime location in slow-growing or stagnating MSAs requires more careful analysis and experienced judgment than is needed in a faster-growing MSA where external conditions provide growth to offset errors in decision making. The way growth and status are translated into a metropolitan area's collective feelings about itself, the confidence the average resident has that problems are solvable, and the decision to stay rather than move elsewhere are important qualitative factors used by residents and investors in evaluating an MSA's future.

Demand Indicators for Urban Space Use

In the absence of better data, population and employment estimates for MSAs can be used to forecast aggregate demand for various types of land uses. This process can be undertaken in six sequential steps.

1. *Total employment* for the metropolitan area at the end of the forecast period can be estimated using the ratio of basic employment to total employment *currently existing*. Then, this ratio is adjusted for expected changes and conditions, and a percentage rate of growth is selected depending on the information available about basic employment in the area over the forecast period. This derived ratio of future basic employment can be used to estimate the trend line of future total employment.

2. The *future population* of the entire metropolitan area may be estimated by applying the percentage of employment to the population that prevails in the base year and then using the selected percentage rate of growth for the forecast period.[8]

3. The *potential need for housing* is estimated by dividing the estimated total population increase by the projected average family size, taking into account adjustments for trends in fertility, birthrates, in-migration, and so forth.

4. For estimating the *growth of any geographic segment of the metropolitan area*, a percentage of the total growth can be allocated on the basis of new highways, new sewer and water extensions, new industries, vacant lands that may be available for residential use, and expected rates of growth in the area. The political climate in the

---

[8]For a theoretical treatment, see Michael Greenberg, Donald A. Krueckeberg, and Connie Michaelson, *Local Population and Employment Projection Techniques* (New Brunswick, N.J.: Rutgers University, Center for Public Policy Research, 1984). See also D. Pittenger, *Projecting State and Local Populations* (Cambridge, Mass.: Ballinger Publishing Company, 1976).

area, especially with respect to land use controls, should also be considered.

5. For calculating the *amount of land needed for new housing and retail service growth*, an estimation should be made of the number of people to be added through population growth. That figure is then separated into the need for ownership versus rental housing and, finally, into subclassifications such as apartments, row houses, detached single-family homes, and small estates. From this, the land areas for each of the required types of residences can be estimated. A potential investor can estimate the amount of land required for a new retail service center by calculating the square feet of floor area required for each type of store. This is done by estimating the volume of sales created by the buying power of the additional population in the trading area and allowing a 4:1 ratio between the parking and selling areas.[9]

6. The *amount of industrial space* required for the new growth can be estimated by ascertaining the amount of factory and yard space required for each employee in each of the specified types of industry. On the basis of the total increase in employment expected in each industry, the average number of employees per industry can be multiplied by the average space now used by each employee in modern factories, warehouses, assembly areas, and other productive facilities, along with parking requirements. This technique can also be applied to estimate office space needs.

Since jobs plus people provide the basis for land use, the steps just outlined have converted employment and population growth into gross crude indicators of the overall demand for land use in the appropriate residential, retail, office, and industrial categories.

The quality and usefulness of market studies depends largely on the skill and expertise of the producer of the study. The gross indicators set forth in the preceding list can be used by investors to spot-audit the estimates made by the market study. Failure to balance the expansion of urban land use and replacement of worn-out stock with actual population and employment growth has resulted in serious local real estate depressions. Many foreclosures and bankruptcies can be attributed in part to the unwarranted optimism of the population and space use projections made in market studies contracted for by developers and public agencies. Because investors generally must use secondary data and market studies prepared by and for others, they should treat them with a healthy skepticism and do careful analysis before accepting the forecasts.

[9]Current data are in *Dollars and Cents of Shopping Centers, 1988*, Urban Land Institute, published biannually. A 1981 study is in Urban Land Institute, *Parking Requirements for Shopping Centers* (Washington, D.C.: ULI, 1982).

Political and Legal Considerations

The political and legal environment of an urban area can have a direct and important impact on real estate investment decisions by affecting the overall environment for economic development and land use alternatives. A real estate investor should be aware of the impact of legal and political considerations along with the economic and demographic characteristics in order to complete the urban analysis. The objective in legal and political analysis is to identify their impact on the overall growth of the area and the extent to which they control the quantity, quality, and direction of growth and development.

Political and legal analysis begins with identifying the individuals and organizations that compose the formal and informal power structure. The formal power structure is made up of the elected officials who make legally enforceable decisions, establish policy, and determine how public funds are to be spent. Political structures differ from city to city around the country. Some areas have separate city and county governments and districts created for special purposes (e.g., flood control, utility and highway development, whereas others have a consolidated metropolitan government.

The analysis should go beyond identifying the official structure and into analyzing the actual political power structure—that is, those who are the real opinion leaders and decision makers in urban government. The informal power structure is composed of the nonelected individuals who influence public opinion and affect the way issues are addressed in the community. Informal power structures can be very influential in the attitudes toward economic development. During the 1970s, slow-growth or no-growth advocates were prominent in local affairs, and the economic development efforts of some communities were reduced or eliminated. In the 1980s, attention has turned from stopping growth to creating public–private partnerships to direct growth, which has many important ramifications for real estate development and investment.

Once the power structure is identified, attention can be focused on relevant attitudes toward the economic development of the urban area. What efforts are being made to promote economic development? Have firms been offered economic incentives to locate in the area, and will the practice continue? Have these efforts been successful? Does the power structure have stated criteria and is desired economic development possible within the criteria?

Formal and informal power structures affect not only overall urban development, but also the location of various types of space through zoning decisions, utility and road extension decisions, and other public infrastructure decisions and land use regulations. For a real estate investor, the difference between the amount of a given type of space demanded in a specific location and the amount the real estate industry is legally able to provide is a critical variable in decision making. For example, an investor considering investing in an existing office building may find it helpful to know that the officials responsible for making zoning decisions have refused to allow the construction of additional office buildings in the area. These decisions affect the extent to which supply will be affected in the future.

A Checklist for Urban Economic-Base Analysis

So far this discussion of urban market studies has considered the economic and demographic components of demand as well as the physical, social, legal, and political elements. Exhibit 11-9, a checklist for an urban analysis, serves as a useful review of all the components of a competent study of the economic and demographic characteristics of an MSA. Many studies purposely address only portions of the checklist. What is needed in each situation depends on the decision to be made.

Sources of Secondary Data

There are many sources of data for urban analysis. The following is a brief summary of some sources of valuable, low-cost materials.

Governmental Agencies. The U.S. Department of Commerce publishes many indicators of economic activity. For example, the Bureau of Economic Analysis publishes material on the investment and legislative climate in each of the fifty states and in Washington, D.C. The regional offices of the Departments of Commerce, Transportation, and Housing and Urban Development and the Federal Reserve Banks are rich sources of low-cost data on the level of economic activity and trends in their regions.

The various state departments of commerce, community affairs bureaus, housing and finance agencies, and industrial development authorities continually monitor economic activity and can provide at low cost many technical reports that are useful for comparative analysis of the MSAs in their regions.

Regional and local planning commissions and agencies are often excellent sources of data. In addition to supplying raw data, many agencies also do economic-base analyses and prepare transportation studies, master plans, and community renewal studies that are useful sources of data—if they are up to date. Much can be accomplished by contacting these sources by telephone. Many public employees treat such a contact as an opportunity to display their knowledge of the metro area.

Other Sources. In addition to governmental agencies, there are private sources that can be of significant assistance at low cost. Local newspapers and television and radio stations often develop excellent material about their trading areas. These data are usually available to interested individuals who visit their offices.

A list of various sources of data is provided in the Appendix following Chapter 14.[10]

A discussion of statistical methodology and reliability related to secondary data is not possible here. It is worth noting, however, that most federal, state, and local agencies provide technical appendixes to their statistics that explain the nature of their methodology and its reliability.[11]

PATTERNS OF URBAN GROWTH

Historically, the growth of cities has been related to the available modes of transportation and communication. This explains the vast differences between building-to-land ratios and lot sizes, for example, of Boston, which was built around its dock facilities and railheads, and Houston, which was built in the age of the automobile. In the past, limited resources led to the concentration of industry and commerce in relatively high-density areas.

Even today, urban areas tend to concentrate some types of land uses in order to minimize transportation or communication costs. Although workers often seek to minimize their journey to work, other space users in the same households, such as the shopping population or the school-attending population, may substantially affect the location of the family dwelling. Indeed, even the theater-going and library-using populations affect this choice.

Where goods rather than people are being moved, or where production serves local needs, such as the need for daily newspapers or bread, transportation costs are important and affect the selection of the site for activities. Indeed, over time, as transportation and communication modes change, a metropolitan area may restructure itself into an entirely different set of spatial arrangements.

The structure of metropolitan areas is affected by the maximum distance that users of the site would be required to travel to carry out daily activities. However, in selecting a location for a real estate investment, the investor should be aware that travel time and convenience, collectively called accessibility, are usually more important than actual distance. Ex-

---

[10] Also, an extensive compilation of publications, content, sources, and data validity are in two special reports: *Real Estate Market Research Data Publications*, Number 586, November 1987; and *Real Estate Market Research On-line Databases*, Number 626, February 1988. These reports are available from the Real Estate Center, Texas A&M University, College Station, Texas 77843-2115.

[11] A section in the back of the *Statistical Abstract of the United States* contains a broad discussion. Each federal government report will generally include a section discussing methodology and reliability.

EXHIBIT 11-9.   A Checklist for Urban Economic-Base Analysis

INTRODUCTORY INFORMATION

History
Climate, geography, geology
General factors

EXISTING LAND USE MAP

Commercial, industrial, residential
Boundaries
Comments on existing conditions (blight, deterioration)

POPULATION STATISTICS AND TRENDS

Total
Households (size, number)
Sex ratio, fertility ratio
Age distribution
Income distribution (per capita, per household)
Trends; compare MSA, state, national
Comments and evaluation

EMPLOYMENT STATISTICS

Male, female
Skills
Ratio (manufacturing, commercial, service)
Compensation levels for subclasses
Unemployment (structural, seasonal)
Comparison of employment levels, trends
Comments and evaluation

ECONOMIC TRENDS

Basic (primary)—classification, description, available statistics (sales)
Basic (secondary)—classification, description, available statistics (sales)
Nonbasic (tertiary)—classification, description, available statistics (sales); retail sales per capita; subclasses

Trends of sales and payroll statistics for each SIC classification
Trends; compare MSA, state, national
Comments and evaluation

COMMUNITY FACILITIES ANALYSIS

Hospitals
Water, sewage, utilities (adequacy, age)

EXHIBIT 11-9.   Continued

Fire, police (adequacy, age)
Schools (adequacy, age)
Recreational: parks, libraries, cultural, other
Comments and evaluation; compare MSA, state, national
Traffic patterns
Parking facilities
Streets
Lighting
Refuse collection
Comments and evaluation

TAX BASE STATISTICS AND TRENDS

Assessed valuation
Other taxes
Capital improvement program indebtedness
Revenues and expenditures
Comments and evaluation

POLITICS AND JURISDICTIONAL LIMITATIONS

Urban economy versus political boundaries
Stability of government (responsiveness to need, technical competence of offi-
    cials, capacity and willingness to carry out plans)
Comments and evaluation

COMMUNITY ORGANIZATION

Degree, quality, scope of community organization
Nature of civic organization (degree of awareness of problems, ability to mobi-
    lize, apathy)
Comments and evaluation

SOURCE ATTRIBUTION (this relates to the credibility of the report)

Adequacy

FORMAT, STYLE, APPEARANCE OF ACTUAL REPORT

Superior, excellent, good, fair, poor

Note: City planning departments, councils of government, regional and state planning
agencies, and others provide information on these subjects at very low cost. It is the user's
task to evaluate the quality and reliability of such reports. *Caveat emptor.*

EXHIBIT 11-10.   Ideal Maximum Distance to Daily Activities

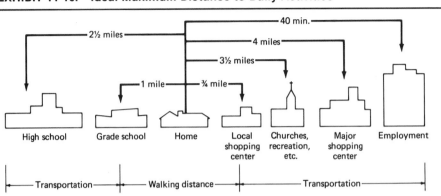

Source: Urban Land Institute, *The Community Builders Handbook* (Washington, D.C.: ULI, 1968, out of print), p. 33. Reprinted with permission.

hibit 11-10 illustrates typical accessibility standards for residences as deter-mined by the Urban Land Institute.

Theories of Land Use

Through the years, real estate practitioners and land economists have sought to identify patterns of land use. That is, have any patterns of land use developed in urban areas that may be useful in predicting the future development pattern of a given urban area? Through the observation of cities, several theories have been formulated. They are the concentric-ring, sector, axial-growth, and multiple-nuclei theories.[12]

Concentric-Ring Theory. Ernest Burgess developed the concentric-ring theory of land use by observing Chicago in the 1920s. His observations led

[12]For additional detail regarding urban growth theories see Fred E. Case, *Real Estate Economics, A Systematic Introduction* (California Association of Realtors, 1974), pp. 136–151; Dennis J. McKenzie and Richard M. Betts, *The Essentials of Real Estate Economics* (New York: Wiley, 1976), pp. 84–98; Thomas W. Shafer, *Urban Growth and Economics* (Reston, Va.: Reston Publishing Company, 1977), pp. 125–140; and G. Vincent Barrett and John P. Blair, *How to Conduct and Analyze Real Estate Market and Feasibility Studies* (New York: Van Nostrand Reinhold, 1982), pp. 120–128. Some of the classic texts are Ra-leigh Barlowe, *Land Resource Economics* (Englewood Cliffs, N.J.: Prentice-Hall, 1978); James Heilbrun, *Urban Economics and Public Policy* (New York: St. Martin's Press, 1974); Robert Murray Haig, *Major Economic Factors in Metropolitan Growth and Arrangement* (New York: Arno Press, 1974); Ernest Burgess, *The City* (Chicago: University of Chicago Press, 1925); Homer Hoyt, *The Changing Principles of Land Economics* (Washington, D.C.: Urban Land Institute, 1968); Richard B. Andrews, *Urban Land Economics and Pub-lic Policy* (New York: Free Press, 1971); and Richard U. Ratcliff, *Real Estate Analysis* (New York: McGraw-Hill, 1961).

Burgess to conclude that the various land uses array themselves in a ring-like fashion around a core, called the central business district (CBD). In the CBD are found office and retailing uses. Adjacent to the CBD is a ring containing manufacturing and other businesses. Low-income housing is in the next ring, and subsequent rings contain middle-income, and then high-income housing. The area that takes in manufacturing and low-income housing is a transitional area in which low-income housing is being consumed for increasing manufacturing activity. A basic premise of the theory is the idea of housing filtering; that is, new housing is added at the edge of the city and older housing is filtered, or passed, down to lower-income groups.

Sector Theory. The sector theory, developed by Homer Hoyt, also identifies a CBD and suggests that land use is generally uniform as one travels away from the CBD in a given direction. That is, if expensive housing is found immediately east of the CBD, then expensive housing will probably be found east of the CBD all the way to the edge of the urbanized area. The same is true for other types of housing and other land uses such as manufacturing. The rationale for this theory is that cities grow by adding development at the edges, and the most likely development for contiguous land parcels is more of the same land use; such a pattern is said to maximize the profitability of the developer and space user.

Axial-Growth Theory. In the 1930s the impact of transportation routes was integrated into urban development patterns with the axial-growth theory. Underlying this theory is the contention that development tends to occur first along or near transportation routes leading to the CBD. The savings in time and money afforded by these sites make them attractive. As a result, urban areas tend to develop by extending out along transportation arteries and then by filling in the accessible areas.

Multiple-Nuclei Theory. Chauncy Harris and Edward Ullman questioned the idea of a single center for urban areas.[13] Although they recognized the relative importance of the CBD, they suggested that other centers, or nuclei, may also affect the shape of the urban area. Harris and Ullman reasoned that these nuclei represent land uses that other businesses and individuals need or want to have close by. Competition for sites near a nucleus would cause land values to be greatest near a nucleus and decrease with distance away from it.

A major shopping center provides an excellent example of a nucleus and the land uses surrounding it. Other developers want to take advantage of the traffic generated by the center and attempt to purchase land to develop

---

[13]Chauncy D. Harris and Edward L. Ullman, "The Nature of Cities," *The Annuals*, 1945.

additional retail space. Developers of apartments, single-family homes, office buildings, movie theaters, restaurants, and banks also realize the benefits of being close to the center. The developers must compete for land around the center, with the profitability of the proposed use determining how much each developer can afford to pay for the land. Those with more intensive and more profitable uses will generally be able to acquire the better sites closer to the center. Thus, less profitable sites will be found farther from the center. It is in this manner that the multiple-nuclei theory explains land use patterns.

Analyzing the Land Use Theories. Increasing urbanization and the outward sprawl of metropolitan areas have complicated the land use patterns associated with cities of all sizes. Random observations of typical cities show that central business districts still attract intensive land uses. Whereas factory sites and industrial uses were in the past frequently located near the CBD, these activities are increasingly moving to outlying areas to gain improved access to highways, to provide parking facilities, and to allow conversion to single-story materials-handling processes. Commercial uses tend to follow the major arterial streets that flow out of the CBD; neighborhood shopping centers are often developed along these streets, and the areas between the major streets tend to be used primarily for residential purposes.

The critical issue is not whether any single land use theory discussed here is descriptive of an urban area, but rather what we can learn about existing and probable future land use patterns in a given urban area. The land uses in any urban area generally reflect a combination of the patterns. The real estate investor must attempt to identify the relevant patterns and ask whether they are likely to continue, and why. Personal preferences, zoning and other land use controls, topography, and other factors affect the likelihood of patterns continuing. By analyzing how individual decision makers—be they families, retailers, office firms, or manufacturers— make location decisions, the real estate investor can gain useful insights into probable future land use patterns.

Existing land use patterns can be analyzed using land use maps produced by many city planning departments and by aerial photographs available from private firms and, sometimes, through city planning departments. Aerial photographs can be especially useful in identifying existing land uses and the relationships between them, as well as parcels of undeveloped land. Aerial photographs can also indicate that urban land use patterns are substantially affected by topographic conditions, the age of the city, and the differing economic functions that these metropolitan areas are known to serve. They provide an uncommonly valuable perspective of the city. A time series of such photographs allows for a visual account of growth patterns in the city. Exhibit 11-11 gives aerial maps of generalized land use patterns for the metropolitan areas of Atlanta, Boston, Houston, and Washington, D.C.

In addition to generalized land use maps, urban geographers have adapted aerial photography to show economic and demographic data for metropolitan areas. These maps can provide additional insights into urban land use patterns. For example, they can show housing categorized by age, location of mobile homes, range in value and in rent per month, or location of single-family detached housing. Information can be provided on such socioeconomic characteristics as occupation, income, and household size. Maps showing population density and age distribution and other significant characteristics can also be found.

Location Concepts—The Source of Land Use Patterns

As discussed earlier, an understanding of how individual location decisions are made is at the heart of understanding urban development. In reality, urban form and land use patterns are simply the result of many individual development and investment decisions. Developers study the need for offices, shopping centers, industrial properties, and residences, and respond by locating projects where they are thought to serve best as evidenced by demand. Thus, understanding the basic concepts that affect a decision about location is invaluable to the real estate investor when assessing future urban growth patterns or a particular real estate investment opportunity.

Location decisions can be quite complex if all the data and considerations are explored in detail. It is easy to see that the detailed considerations and data requirements for a hotel are much different from those needed for a small shopping center. However, assuming that sites have been evaluated on the basis of size, topography, and legally permissible uses, all location research deals with a limited number of broad issues: accessibility, exposure, and price.

Accessibility. Accessibility is the cost in terms of time and money of moving people or products to a site from certain locations or from the site to certain locations. For example, in evaluating a site for a shopping center, a developer defines a primary market in terms of maximum driving time and then sets about analyzing the income and spending patterns of people within that area. An office developer may be concerned with the ability of prospective tenants to reach other businesses, hotels, eating establishments, and their homes. Regardless of how the destinations and origins of trips to and from the site are defined and how accessibility is measured, accessibiity is of critical importance.

Exposure. Exposure is the relation of the site to its surroundings. Favorable exposure increases a site's value, whereas unfavorable exposure decreases its value. What constitutes favorable and unfavorable exposure varies according to land use. For single-family homes, views, uncongested streets, clean air, quiet, and neighbors who maintain their properties may

EXHIBIT 11-11. Generalized Land Use Patterns: Atlanta, Boston, Houston, and Washington, D.C.

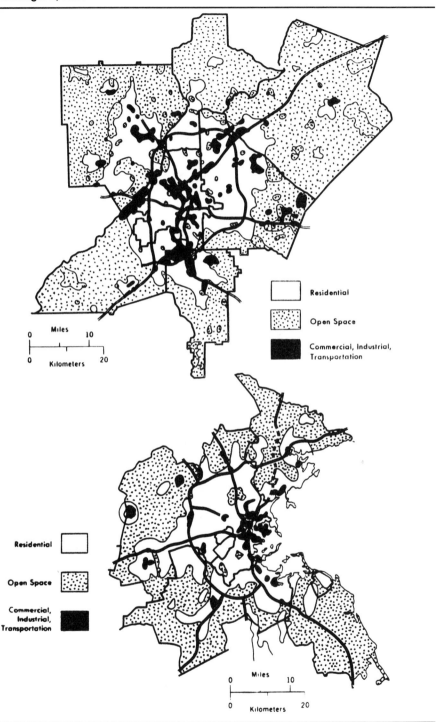

Source: John S. Adams, ed., *A Comprehensive Atlas of America's Great Cities: Twenty Metropolitan Regions* (Minneapolis: Association of American Geographers and the University of Minnesota Press, 1976), pp. 22, 198, 248, and 257. Reproduced with permission.

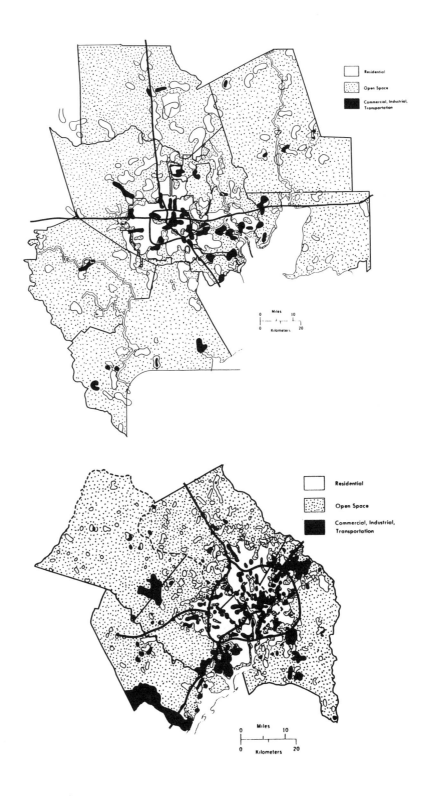

Residential

Open Space

Commercial, Industrial,
Transportation

Miles
0   10
Kilometers
0   20

Residential

Open Space

Commercial, Industrial,
Transportation

Miles
0   10
Kilometers
0   20

be considered favorable exposure. For a shopping center, views may not be important and uncongested streets may mean insufficient traffic to generate sales. For other land uses the definition of favorable and unfavorable exposure will vary, but the concept remains a critical one for successful real estate investment.

Price. Accessibility and exposure must be balanced with price. The best fast-food restaurant site will produce higher revenues for the restaurant than the second-best site. However, if the best site is more expensive, as it should be, does it produce enough additional return to justify the difference in price and risk? This is a question that must be answered for every site.

SUMMARY

Finding the target MSA is the first step in investment analysis. Investors need to understand the nature of growth and decline in urban areas in order to choose a target for investment analysis. Metropolitan areas compete for jobs and for people, as well as in the way land is used. Whereas some urban areas may be in a period of rapid growth, others may be mature and stable, and still others may be in a period of decline.

Defining an urban area requires careful consideration of available data, political boundaries, and economic and social integration. The Bureau of the Census defines a number of urban concentrations that transcend political boundaries, such as the metropolitan statistical area (MSA) and the consolidated metropolitan statistical area (CMSA). However, because of differences in taxes, services, and political processes, political boundaries may be quite important. How the investor defines an urban area is a function of the scope and perceived market area for a possible real estate investment.

Economic-base analysis was presented as a tool for analyzing the composition and vitality of the local economy. Standard Industrial Classification (SIC) codes were suggested as means of classifying economic activity in order to generate data and make comparisons between urban areas. Within the economic-base framework, the measurement of diversification, and the stability it generates, and growth potential are the goals.

Demographic characteristics play an important role in estimating the extent to which an urban area will demand particular types of space over the long and short run. Of importance is population growth, which is closely related to employment growth. Estimates of population change are produced by the Department of Commerce, local planning agencies, colleges and universities, and others. Birthrates, death rates, immigration, age of the population, and household composition constitute other important demographic information.

Estimates of economic and population changes, combined with identifying selected characteristics of these changes, enable investors to make rough estimates of the types and quantities of space necessary to support them. Such evaluations make use of relatively simple estimates of the quantity of space necessary to provide places to work, live, and be entertained.

Next, the question of where various types of space are located within an urban area was addressed through growth theories. Although none of these theories is capable of explaining or predicting all land use in an urban area, they collectively provide some valuable insights into land use patterns.

12

MARKET ANALYSIS

Real estate market analysis is the study of real estate markets at the macro level. It is not site- or property-specific but focuses on the current and likely future levels of the supply of and demand for a general type of real estate within a designated geographic area. The geographic area included in a market study may be an entire urban area or a subset of it. Similarly, the level of generality of property type may vary from the total office market for an entire urban area to a particular type of space such as suburban office buildings or a specific type of office building (e.g., high rise) in a particular area of the city.

Distinction Between Market Analysis and Marketability Analysis

The distinction between market analysis, the subject of this chapter, and marketability analysis, the subject of the next, is often blurred because of imprecise definitions and use of terminology in the real estate industry. In this book, marketability analysis deals with a particular property's marketability; that is, its ability to generate a revenue stream (gross effective income) that will satisfy the investor's financial objectives over a projected ownership cycle, along with an assessment of the impact of the specific property's attributes on vacancies and rental rates. Market analysis, on the other hand, may be the final objective of a market research effort, or it may be an intermediate step necessary to generate information for a marketability analysis. Market analysis evaluates aggregate demand and supply factors in a geographic area for the purpose of identifying unmet consumer needs and quantifies the amount of space that will be required to satisfy it.

Even with this distinction, it is not clear precisely where market analysis ends and marketability analysis begins. However, this confusion can be eliminated if one thinks of market analysis and marketability analysis as a continuum, with one flowing into the other, as shown in Exhibit 12-1. This model outlines various steps of a market analysis (macro market study)

EXHIBIT 12-1.   Conceptual Model of the Market Analysis and Marketability Analysis Process

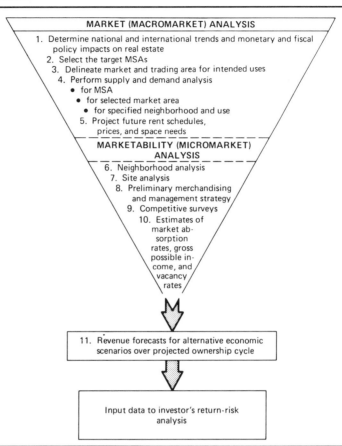

MARKET (MACROMARKET) ANALYSIS
1. Determine national and international trends and monetary and fiscal policy impacts on real estate
2. Select the target MSAs
3. Delineate market and trading area for intended uses
4. Perform supply and demand analysis
   ● for MSA
   ● for selected market area
   ● for specified neighborhood and use
5. Project future rent schedules, prices, and space needs

MARKETABILITY (MICROMARKET) ANALYSIS
6. Neighborhood analysis
7. Site analysis
8. Preliminary merchandising and management strategy
9. Competitive surveys
10. Estimates of market absorption rates, gross possible income, and vacancy rates

11. Revenue forecasts for alternative economic scenarios over projected ownership cycle

Input data to investor's return-risk analysis

and marketability analysis (micro market study). The final output of such analyses is a revenue forecast for a projected ownership life cycle under alternative economic scenarios that provides input data for the investor's return and risk analysis. The process is conceptualized as a funnel in which urban analysis, market analysis, and marketability analysis flow from the general to the specific, from the very macro level, including national and international trends and impacts of monetary and fiscal policy on real estate, to the very micro project-specific level at the end of the tenth step. The process flows from the large urban area, for which considerable secondary data are available, to the small market area, for which little or no data are available.

Faulty market analysis was a major contributor to the financial failure of real estate projects during the period from 1980 to 1989. The degree of fault ranged from no analysis to incorrect definitions of market size. In the worst cases, both lenders and borrowers become interminable optimists, following a herd instinct and chasing new construction and investment as long as money was available to finance projects.[1]

It is not unusual for market studies to be performed *after* the decision to invest has been made. Investors often choose to depend on casual observation and instinct in assessing market conditions. This is unfortunate because market research can help potential investors to avoid making poor decisions by providing a basis for making informed decisions: "The process of investing, as contrasted to gambling, presupposes a gathering, forecasting, and structuring of data upon which reasons for conclusions or decisions can be based."[2] Market analysis plays an important role in the information-gathering process.

The underlying assumption here is that the individual investor must cope with the constraints of time and budget limits in carrying out this critical function. Thus, existing published reports, secondary data, and professional real estate market analysts are of primary importance. The following discussion is intended to provide the investor with a sufficient understanding of market studies to evaluate such studies when performed by professional analysts. Professional real estate market analysts tend to be specialists in one or a few property types. The discussion here deals with general concepts, not with a particular property type. Later chapters provide additional details for specific property types.

Nature, Scope, and Depth of Market Analysis

A number of factors influence the nature, scope, and depth of market analysis. For example, is the property an existing one or a proposed one? Existing properties have an identifiable occupancy level and rent-generating capacity, but they are subject to change over virtually any extended time period. On the other hand, a proposed development must be totally concerned with the future; user profiles, competitive forces, site conditions, and other factors must be identified and analyzed.

Another important factor influencing the scope and depth of market analysis is the size of the investment opportunity. Obviously, the expenditure allocated for a multimillion-dollar project is usually vastly larger than is appropriate for a $250,000 investment. Finally, there is a significant difference between a preliminary market analysis undertaken prior to start-

[1]Waldo L. Born, "A Structure for Real Estate Market Research," research paper presented at the American Real Estate Society Meetings, San Francisco, April 16, 1988.

[2]Robert J. Wiley, *Real Estate Investment Analysis and Strategy* (New York: Ronald Press, 1977), p. 3. See also Stephen D. Messner, Byrl N. Boyce, Harold G. Trimble, and Robert L. Ward, *Analyzing Real Estate Opportunities: Market and Feasibility Studies* (Chicago: National Association of Realtors, 1977), pp. 5–10; the authors caution on page 6: "It is all too simple to carefully examine the present situation and then cavalierly extrapolate the present into the future without careful consideration of those variables which are most likely to change and thus affect any forecast of the 'status quo.' The whole point of examining the past and present is to provide insights as to the most likely future; it is not to assume that the future will be a duplication of the present or recent past."

ing negotiations with the seller, and a detailed market and marketability analysis conducted after a basic meeting of minds has been reached with the seller and a purchase contract has been signed.

ELEMENTS OF A MARKET STUDY

A real estate market study is a type of macro market analysis. Fundamentally, a market study involves the projection and analysis of the determinants of supply and demand. A study of all supply and demand indicators underlies the analysis of project rent levels, probable absorption rates, occupancy levels, and indirectly, the potential change in property value over some ownership cycle. The *supply* of real estate product is influenced by the availability of competing sites and land costs, the existing inventory of competing projects, demolitions, new construction, plans for comparable projects, building costs, and the availability of financing. The *demand* for real estate is determined from data on population, demographics, sales volume, rents, vacancies, turnover, consumer preferences, and real estate prices. Careful consideration should be given to the need for expansion demand and replacement demand—that is, whether there is demand for new facilities or whether there is continued demand for the use of existing facilities.

A market study is not merely a set of economic projections and ratio analyses; it also uses the planner's art of evaluating the ability of a metropolitan area to cope with its problems of growth and decline. Growth potential cannot be projected from analyses that are limited to economic activities. Investors cannot assume that political, legal, sociological, and physical forces will remain unchanged. By its nature, investment in real estate is long term and illiquid; failure to recognize adverse trends in a neighborhood can prove disastrous to a careless buyer—or recognizing them can be highly profitable for a more careful one. Investors need to know the urban area's priorities. Important considerations are the community's stance on growth issues, zoning, and capital improvement programs.

Essential Elements of a Market Study

A real estate market study uses demographic and economic trends to evaluate the present match or mismatch between the existing stock or inventory of facilities, on the one hand, and the demand for their use, on the other. A mismatch may signal an opportunity for investment in existing properties, development, rehabilitation, or conversion. As Dasso and Graaskamp have stated, market analysis applies to three types of situations: (1) a site or property in search of an appropriate use or user; (2) a use or user in search of an appropriate site or property; and (3) an investor looking for a means of involvement in either of these, given his or her goals, objectives, and return–risk constraints. This book is primarily concerned with this third situation.

The essential components of any competent market study include the following.

1. An overview and analysis of national and international economic conditions to determine whether current macroeconomic conditions (particularly economic growth, inflation, and interest rates) are favorable, or at least neutral, to entering into a real estate investment.
2. A summary of current economic, social, political, and demographic trends in the *region* and in the targeted *urban* area. This is a selective report of economic-base data that are relevant to the investment opportunity under consideration.
3. A delineation of the market or trading area to identify the geographical boundaries within which specified real estate facilities will be competing with one another to satisfy some market demand. This is the *location* of the real estate investment.
4. An analysis of the potential demand for the specified real estate facilities within the market or trade area.
5. An inventory report on existing competitive uses in the market or trading area.
6. An analysis of the potential competition to assess the nature of the various real estate products being offered to tenants in the would-be market and trading area.
7. Ideally, the study concludes with a thorough analysis of existing and projected levels of space needs, rents, vacancies, prices, and values in the market area under investigation. Implications and market opportunities for the investor should be outlined.

Limitations of Market Analyses

The questions to be answered by market analysis must be carefully defined, and the extent of the report will be determined by these questions. From an investor's view, the ultimate purpose of market analysis is to provide data for analyzing the return and risk characteristics of a property. With respect to risk, the investor must keep in mind that a market study is an analysis of current conditions and a forecast of an uncertain future based on imperfect data. In interpreting such information, the investor must recognize the limitations of the data as well as the sometimes loosely assumed or specified interrelation of the factors studied. Because of its forecasting nature and the uncertainty associated with such forecasting, real estate market analysis should be approached on a probabilistic rather than a deterministic basis.

REAL ESTATE MARKETS

Real estate markets are the arena in which the potential for a real estate investment is tested. It is in the market that the ability of the investment to attract tenants at various rental rates is determined. It is also in the market that the value of the returns the property generates is determined. It is in real estate markets that supply and demand for rental space and equity positions are brought together to produce prices. In simple terms, a real estate market is the composite of negotiations between buyers and sellers (and lessors and lessees), who communicate with one another to acquire or dispose of individual real estate products that, by their nature, are in some degree of competition with one another.

Importance of Submarkets

Investors are not usually concerned with supply–demand conditions in the overall real estate market because they perceive that a particular property competes with only a limited portion of the total market. For example, a suburban garden-style office building does not usually compete for tenants with large downtown high-rise office buildings. What is of interest is the submarket in which a property competes. A submarket may be defined in terms of location, price, property size, or any other characteristics believed to distinguish one property from another in the minds of potential tenants and equity investors. Each characteristic contributes to the overall attraction of a particular property compared with other competing properties.

Given the importance of submarkets, overall aggregated real estate market information must be extrapolated down to the submarket of interest. Many cities entered the mid-1980s with overall office occupancy rates of 75 to 85 percent, very low by most standards. Within many of these cities, however, there were office submarkets with much higher occupancy rates that produced premium rental rates and equity values and merited additional development activity. The importance of identifying and analyzing the appropriate submarket or submarkets cannot be overemphasized.

The submarket in which a particular property competes determines the spatial boundaries of the market area. As examples, a large regional shopping center competes for tenants with other shopping centers over a very large area—perhaps the entire urban area; a convenience store's market area boundaries may be no more than ten or twenty blocks in any direction; and a 1000-room national-chain convention hotel located in a commercial air carrier hub city may compete in a national market.

Trading Markets

The same concept applies to the market for equity interests in real estate. That is, the competitive forces affecting the value of a particular property type delineate the competitive market area. Investment locations may be regarded as links in a chain of substitutability. Thus, the market may be thought of as consisting of clusters of substitutes that are cross-linked in complex patterns related to buyer–seller behavior.

The lack of geographic focus and the absence of an organized exchange have caused some confusion in the minds of real estate investors about the nature of real estate markets. Understanding the nature of the trading market in which equity interests are bought and sold helps in the identification of buyers and sellers. Trading markets are concerned only with carrying out the transaction; they are not concerned with the quality of the product, which is a result of the interaction of supply and demand for the actual use of space.

It is useful to classify the real estate trading markets as national, regional, and local in nature. Although there is considerable overlap at the margins, these categories allow for a profile of the likely buyers and sellers for a particular transaction. More important, characterizing the market for a property as national–international, regional, or local facilitates the identification of which lenders or investors would be able to assist in the transaction.

National–International Markets. High-rise office buildings, industrial parks, large luxury apartment complexes, warehouse parks, recreational complexes, regional shopping centers, flagship hotels, and nationally franchised motels are traded in the national–international markets. The potential lenders and equity investors are large institutions such as transnational banks, mortgage bankers, life insurance companies, REITs, foundations, pension funds, and savings and loan associations.

Regional Markets. Community and neighborhood shopping centers, medium-rise office buildings, industrial buildings, professional buildings, fast-food franchises, smaller garden apartment complexes (fewer than 100 units), many warehouse projects, freestanding commercial buildings, and similarly sized properties trade in regional markets. Potential lenders are regional institutions such as banks, savings and loan associations, and pension funds.

Local Markets. Small, low-rise apartment buildings, small professional and commercial office buildings, freestanding retail locations in older areas, rehabilitation projects, and similar properties trade in local markets. The potential lenders are purchase money mortgagees, second mortgagees, and local banks and savings and loan associations that are knowledgeable about the specific area.

In international markets, buyers and sellers may come from virtually anywhere in the world by phone, letter, or airplane. At the other extreme, the local market for a small low-rise apartment building caters to the few buyers and sellers who are knowledgeable about neighborhood conditions and the prospects for loan commitments.

MARKET STUDIES: A DESCRIPTIVE ANALYSIS

Although an economic-base analysis would provide reasonable estimates of the rate of growth or decline of a metropolitan area, the impact of that economic change is the subject of market analysis. Market analysis is a detailed process requiring a set of skills and a time commitment that many real estate investors do not possess and are not willing to make. Therefore, the following description of the market analysis process is offered to guide the real estate investor in evaluating the professional competence of the market analyst and the quality of the market study.[3]

The description that follows may be implemented in virtually any level of detail. Not all situations require the same level of detail in market analysis; they can be expanded and contracted, depending on the availability of data and the size and type of decision being made. However, the framework and areas of analysis will remain the same. The discussion that follows is purposely not exhaustive; rather, it highlights the critical elements of market analysis. The elements to be discussed are:

1. Development of demand and supply models.
2. Market area definition.
3. Estimating present and future demand and supply.
4. Analysis of the relationship between demand and supply.
5. Salient facts and conclusions.

Development of Demand and Supply Models

One of the common problems with market studies is the use of a "shotgun" approach, in which large quantities of data are assembled in a rather loose manner to indicate the need for additional space. Such an approach is time-consuming and expensive, and it also often produces erroneous conclusions. Needed instead is a "rifle" approach that carefully defines the type of space to be analyzed and precisely identifies the factors creating potential demand for the particular kind of space. Further, the manner in which supply is to be estimated must also be detailed. Such an approach

---

[3]For more thorough analyses, see John B. Bailey, "Market Analysis," *The Appraisal Journal*, October 1972, pp. 644–699; and J. B. Bailey, P. F. Spies, and M. K. Weitzman, "Market Study + Financial Analysis = Feasibility Report," *The Appraisal Journal*, October 1977, pp. 550–577; G. Vincent Barrett and John P. Blair, *How to Conduct and Analyze Real Estate Market Feasibility Studies* (New York: Van Nostrand Reinhold, 1982), particularly Chapter 2; James D. Vernor, ed., *Readings in Market Research for Real Estate* (Chicago: American Institute of Real Estate Appraisers, 1985); John M. Clapp, *Handbook for Real Estate Market Analysis* (Englewood Cliffs, N.J.: Prentice-Hall, 1987); Neil Carn, Joseph Rabianski, Ronald Racster, and Maury Seldin, *Real Estate Market Analysis: Techniques and Applications* (Englewood Cliffs, N.J.: Prentice-Hall, 1988); Maury Seldin, "A Reclassification of Real Estate and Market Analysis: Toward Improving the Line of Reasoning," *Real Estate Issues*, Spring–Summer 1984.

will allow a systematic research effort that gathers only the necessary data and promotes an understanding of the results by eliminating unnecessary complexity and introducing a logical flow.

Demand Models. The determinants of demand for a particular type of space are often fundamentally simple to identify. For example, the need for retail space in an urban area is a function of the number of households in an area, their disposable income, and their spending patterns. The overall demand for office space is similarly a function of expected office employment and required space per worker. The demand for a particular type of office space—say, low-rise suburban office buildings—is a function of the particular types of office employment expected to be housed in such buildings. This is not to say that this process is one of certainty; it is not. Market research will often reveal only tendencies, but knowledge of these tendencies is very helpful.

Exhibit 12-2 illustrates an example of a demand model for housing. This model starts with total population and subtracts nonhousehold members of the population to calculate the household population. Nonhousehold members are those people living in group quarters such as nursing homes and fraternity and sorority houses. To derive the total demand for housing, the market analyst divides the household population by average household size. The result is the number of occupied housing units. Because there will always be vacant units as a portion of the population moves to satisfy its needs, a vacancy factor must be added to estimate the total number of housing units. It is easy to see that in forecasting housing demand, uncertainty about the population and average household size creates uncertainty about the demand for housing.

This aggregate demand number does not provide insight into whether this housing will be rental or owner-occupied, condominium or detached single-family, city or suburban, expensive or inexpensive. These considerations require additional research into housing trends in the city, the analysis of demographic data, and perhaps a survey of attitudes about alterna-

EXHIBIT 12-2.   Total Housing Demand Estimates for Market Analysis: 1989–1998

	1989	1990	1991	1992	1993	1998
Total population	63,293	65,635	68,064	70,582	73,194	81,365
Nonhousehold population	892	925	959	995	1,032	1,150
Household population	62,401	64,710	67,105	69,587	72,162	80,472
Household size	2.7	2.7	2.7	2.7	2.7	2.7
Demand for housing	23,111	23,967	24,854	25,773	26,726	29,804
Total demand with 4% vacancy factor	23,074	24,966	25,890	26,846	27,840	31,046

EXHIBIT 12-3. Projected Demand for Office Space, Metropolitan Area

	Actual			Projected		
	1970	1980	1985	1990	1995	2000
Total employment[a]	36.6	44.8	52.2	59.7	63.2	66.0
Percentage office-related	36.9%	42.2%	42.9%	43.0%	44.0%	45.0%
Office-related employment[a]						
Professional and technical	4.1	6.4	7.7	9.2	10.6	12.6
Managers and administrators	3.9	4.7	5.5	6.2	6.4	6.4
Clerical	5.5	7.8	9.2	10.3	10.8	10.7
Total	13.5	18.9	22.4	25.7	27.8	29.7
Space–employee ratio	256.5	265.7	273.6	280.0	285.0	290.0
Net rented area[a]	3462.8	5021.7	6128.6	7200.0	7900.0	8600.0
Vacancy allowance	8.3%	7.4%	13.0%	10.0%	10.0%	10.0%
Net rentable area[a]	3776.2	5423.0	7045.0	8000.0	8800.0	9600.0
Efficiency ratio	76.4%	78.3%	79.1%	80.0%	80.0%	80.0%
Gross building area[a]	4942.7	6925.9	8906.4	10000.0	11000.0	1200.0
Average annual increase in net rentable[a]		164.7	324.4	191.0	160.0	160.0

Source: Adapted from John W. McMahan, *Property Development: Effective Decision Making in Uncertain Times* (New York: McGraw-Hill, 1976), p. 185.

[a]In thousands. Projection calculations may not agree owing to rounding.

tive housing choices. In the example given, historical data may indicate that 55 percent of all housing units are rental housing and 45 percent are owner-occupied. If there is no reason, such as changing demographics, to expect this mix to change, the housing demand forecast could be allocated between rental and owner-occupied units. Similarly, by examining housing patterns, estimated and projected demographics, and household income, the market analyst allocates housing demand to geographical areas of the city and to rental price levels. It is important to note that the methodology for making such allocations should be stated before the research is started.

Exhibit 12-3 shows one approach for estimating the demand for office space. In the exhibit, historical data and projections are presented in the same framework. The framework is very similar to that for housing through the estimation of total net rentable area. From that point, the ratio between net rentable area and gross floor space, called the efficiency ratio, is used to estimate the gross building area necessary to satisfy the demand. Notice that the analyst uses employment projections reflecting changing proportions of professional, technical, managerial, administrative, and clerical employees. The projections also reflect an increasing number of square feet per employee, a trend the analyst had found from researching this and other markets.

The final product of the demand analysis shown is annual estimates of the average increase in net rentable area of office space needed for the metropolitan area studied. The projected annual demand for new office space between 1990 and 1995 is 160,000 square feet of rentable area, a substantial decrease from the demand during the years 1985 to 1990, when it averaged 191,000 square feet annually.

Demand and Supply Models for Specific Property Types. Numerous approaches and models have been developed for estimating demand and supply for different types of property. Although beyond the scope of this chapter, some of the approaches and models are discussed as appropriate in the chapters in which the various property types are treated separately (see Chapters 22 through 27).[4]

---

[4]There are a number of classic works, most of which apply specifically to retail properties but which contain principles basic to other property types. Such classics include William Applebaum, "Method for Determining Store Trade Areas, Market Penetration, and Potential Sales," *Journal of Market Research*, May 1966; J. Brummer and J. Mason, "The Influence of Driving Time upon Shopping Center Locations," *Journal of Marketing*, April 1968; L. Bucklin, "Trade Area Boundaries: Some Issues in Theory and Methodology," *Journal of Marketing Research*, February 1971; L. W. Ellwood, "Estimating Potential Volume of Proposed Shopping Centers," *The Appraisal Journal*, October 1954; David Huff, "A Probabilistic Analysis for Shopping Center Trade Area," *Land Economics*, February 1963; L. Mandell, "Quality of Life Factors in Business Location Decisions," *Atlantic Economic Review*, January 1977; Richard L. Nelson, *The Selection of Retail Location* (New

Market Area Definition

For a market study, the key objective in market area definition is to identify all the competitive geographic areas that will affect rent levels, vacancies, and prices, and that effectively represent alternative sites for the users of the prospective investment. The spatial size of the market area is affected by the characteristics of the property type under consideration. For example, class A suburban high-rise office buildings often compete with downtown high rises, and the market area for such properties may be the entire urban area or even the region (e.g., San Francisco versus Los Angeles). For smaller suburban office buildings, the market area may be all suburban office areas or, perhaps, only a particular suburban office area if the buildings are somewhat unique. The key is to determine all properties likely to compete in the property class under study. Of course, it is possible to define a market as the object of research; for example, an analyst might define the market under consideration as the suburban office market in the southeastern portion of the city.

An important objective of a market study may be to identify either the various submarkets or possible boundaries between a given property type. For example, the market analyst may be asked to determine whether all suburban office buildings compete with one another, or whether physical barriers such as hills, rivers, lakes, and distance or socioeconomic factors create different markets. The analyst must consider all factors that affect the definition of markets.

The geographic zones that are appropriate for investment are affected by various types of linkages—for example, the journey to work and access

---

York: McGraw-Hill Information Systems and F. W. Dodge, 1958); J. C. Goldstrucker et al., *New Developments in Retail Trading Area Analysis and Site Selection* (Atlanta: Georgia State University, 1978); and William Applebaum, *Guide to Store Location Research* (New York: Addison-Wesley, 1968). Other significant works include William C. Weaver, "Forecasting Office Space Demand with Cojoint Measurement Techniques," *The Appraisal Journal*, July 1984, pp. 389–398; Dan Conway, "Market Analysis: The Road to Profit, Prosperity and Peace of Mind," *Commercial Investment Real Estate Journal*, Fall 1987, pp. 8–14; R. L. Davies and D. S. Rogers, *Store Location and Assessment Research* (New York: Wiley, 1984), pp. 337–338; James A. Graaskamp, "Identification and Delineation of Real Estate Market Research," *Real Estate Issues*, Spring–Summer, 1985, pp. 6–12; Sean F. Hennessey, "Economic Studies for Hotels: A Guide to Gathering Basic Data," *The Appraisal Journal*, July 1986, pp. 443–459; B. A. Whitson, "Creating and Using Real Estate Data Bases," *Commercial Investment Journal*, Spring 1985, pp. 26–31; Kenneth T. Rosen, "Toward a Model of the Office Building Sector," *American Real Estate and Urban Economics Association Journal*, Fall 1984, pp. 261–269; Hugh F. Kelley, "Forecasting Office Space Demand in Urban Areas," *Real Estate Review*, Fall 1983, pp. 87–95; J. R. Kimball and Barbara S. Bloomberg, "Office Demand Analysis," *The Appraisal Journal*, October 1987, pp. 567–577; Daniel H. Lesser, "A Room Night Analysis of Lodging Demand," *Real Estate Review*, Winter 1983, pp. 67–73; and William B. Martin and Wilke D. English, "Forecasting Demand for Multitenant Office Space," *Commercial Investment Journal*, Winter 1985, pp. 7–9 and 27.

to essential community facilities. Consumer preference patterns may tend to produce social and economic groupings in certain areas of the MSA. In stratified housing markets, competitive forces may operate to establish widely separated neighborhoods that are more or less equidistant from a major place of work. On the other hand, the market study area for a retail service use, such as a grocery, drug, or apparel store, might well be limited to a specific trade area or neighborhood.

Estimating Present and Future Demand and Supply

When the market analyst estimates present and future demand, he or she applies the appropriate models using relevant secondary and primary data. It is here that the economic-base, population, and demographic analyses are actually applied, as shown in Exhibits 12-2 and 12-3. Care should be taken to ensure that all data are comparable in both time and geographic area. It is not unusual to find data collected at different times and for different areas to be incorrectly used together in a market analysis. The result of this part of the market analysis should be an estimate of current and projected *net demand* (demand minus supply) over a relevant time period. Of course, as the forecast period increases, so will the uncertainty surrounding the forecast.

Estimating present and future supply is generally more difficult than estimating demand. The initial impression of many investors is that estimating supply involves simply finding the appropriate secondary data about space or completing a survey on available space. This is an overly simplistic approach because much secondary information about supply is not available, or if it is available, it is out of date or of insufficient detail to be useful. For example, a listing of office buildings with locations and sizes may be available, but if data about age, quality, amenities, parking, and other aspects are not given, the listing may not be particularly useful without extensive primary research.

Primary research is also problematic; for one thing, it is costly. Gathering extensive market supply data is a time-consuming procedure requiring frequent audits on the quality of the data being gathered. Furthermore, finding and training field personnel is difficult and critical. Field personnel must make numerous qualitative judgments about quality, location, and amenities when gathering supply data.

The result of supply research should be the listing and analysis of all properties in the market area competing in the subject market. In addition, prospective additions to the supply of space must be identified. Interviews with developers, bankers, mortgage bankers, planners, brokers, utility companies, and others can provide a great deal of information about proposed properties. Researching local business and real estate publications is also a source of information. Zoning actions taken by the local planning board and building permit data can be helpful, but they may also be misleading. Many zoning actions do not lead to actual construction. Nor do all building permits lead to construction. Thus, prospective developers must exercise care and must visit prospective building sites in order to assess the likelihood of additional space becoming a reality.

Often, the existing inventory stock of residential properties is assumed to be equal to the inventory stock as defined in the last decennial census, modified by additions and conversions based on building permits, minus removals based on demolition permits. Unfortunately, the quality of the building and demolition permit data are generally so poor that this primary source should be supplemented with data from utility companies and local planning commissions.[5] In some states building permit data are flawed by incomplete geographic coverage, because some county governments do not have the authority to issue building permits.

Analysis of the Relationship Between Supply and Demand

Although the estimates of present and future supply and demand are of interest, it is the relation between them and the estimation of the net market position that are of critical importance. The investor contemplating an acquisition must be concerned with the competitive position of the subject property over the entire holding period, with special attention paid to those periods when leases expire on significant quantities of competing space. In the same regard, the investor must be concerned about renewal options in leases that may result in noncompetitive rental rates. The importance of lease analysis is considered in more detail in the next chapter on marketability analysis, but the impact of general leasing conditions on the future income-generating potential of the subject property is apparent and should be addressed in a market study.

Direct Estimation of Net Demand for Space. The most direct solution to the problem is simply to combine current and future estimates of supply and demand, and to look at the sign and magnitude of net demand. Exhibit 12-4 extends the demand analysis of Exhibit 12-2 by incorporating supply analysis to produce estimates of net demand. The analysis indicates an oversupply of units in 1989 (net negative demand of 866 units), virtually no opportunity for a new supply of units in 1990 (net demand of 26 units), and substantial net demand for new units beginning in 1991 (924 units). If care has been exercised in defining the market area and the type of space demanded, these results should allow the investor to compare future mar-

---

[5]F. W. Dodge, *Construction Potentials,* is an excellent source of detailed construction data. These data are far more accurate and complete for commercial building and construction than are building permit data. Inquire through a regional F. W. Dodge representative of the McGraw-Hill Information Systems Company of McGraw-Hill.

EXHIBIT 12-4.   Net Housing Demand Estimates for Market Analysis: 1989–1998

	1989	1990	1991	1992	1993	1998
Total population	63,293	65,635	68,064	70,582	73,194	81,365
Nonhousehold population	892	925	959	995	1,032	1,150
Household population	62,401	64,710	67,105	69,587	72,162	80,472
Household size	2.7	2.7	2.7	2.7	2.7	2.7
Demand for housing	23,111	23,967	24,854	25,773	26,726	29,804
Total demand with 4% vacancy factor	23,074	24,966	25,890	26,846	27,840	31,046
Less supply	24,940	24,940	24,940	24,940	24,940	24,940
Net demand	(866)	26	950	1,906	2,900	6,106
Change in net demand from preceding year		892	924	956	994	3,206
Net new units needed		26	924	956	994	3,206
55% Multifamily		14	508	526	547	1,763
45% Single-family		12	416	430	447	1,443

ket conditions with current ones and move on to consider how well a specific property will compete in such markets (marketability analysis).

A key economic indicator that must be derived from the available data is the prospective *market absorption rate*.[6] This is a product of supply and demand analysis, and it makes use of population movements, job formation, and other factors to estimate current and future demand, which is then compared with the standing stock and the number of units that are expected to become available during the forecast period. In this way the gap between supply and demand can be estimated, and the analyst can forecast the rate at which the market is likely to absorb any additional space—and the vacancy rate at given points in the future in the submarket in question.

Other Indicators and Measures of Net Demand.   In addition to this direct approach, the relation between demand and supply can be estimated by using other indicators. Such measures can serve as a check on current demand and supply estimates or as a means for a quicker, less rigorous estimate of current market conditions. For example, if demand is strong, unsold inventory, vacancies, and mortgage defaults should be at a low level.

---

[6]The absorption rate during a given period is
        Space vacant at beginning of period
   Plus: New space constructed during period
   Minus: Space vacant at end of period
For a discussion, see Carn, Rabianski, Racster, and Seldin, *Real Estate Market Analysis: Techniques and Applications*, pp. 79–81, 170, and 268.

If demand is weak, the indicators should be moving in the opposite direction. The ratio of unsold inventory to the stock of space for a specified use tracked over a period of time is a useful indicator of the market absorption rate. It has been said that vacancies are the equivalent of unsold inventory. This is imprecise. Some vacancies are necessary for normal turnover in income properties. The report should stratify vacancies by rent levels in order to discover the vacancy level for the market of interest. Overall vacancy rates for a particular category, such as housing or industrial uses, are inadequate for the real estate investor; the investor needs to know the vacancy level in the targeted market for competing properties.

In addition, analyses of the *nature of* the unsold inventory may prove quite helpful in evaluating the values, tastes, and attitudes of would-be users. Poor location is not the only reason for market rejection. Other reasons for market failure are a site with inadequate access and visibility; improvements that lack functional utility or have an unpopular architectural design; inadequate maintenance and repair; and bad management.

Current conditions in the mortgage market are also good indicators of the state of health of real estate markets. Usually, a small percentage of mortgages is in default because of death, divorce, or other difficulties of mortgagors. On the other hand, if current market conditions indicate an above-average level of defaults and foreclosures, this is a clear indicator of a market that is in trouble. A market analysis should also provide a discussion of relevant supply and demand cycles that impact on the market area, including general business and construction cycles, urban area and city cycles, and other macro real estate cycles that could affect expectations and estimates of rents, prices, and space needs. Because these cycle variables have a significant impact on returns and risks of properties in the market, investors should require a discussion of these issues in the reports of their market analysts, although such an inclusion is currently unusual. The subject of real estate cycles is addressed in depth in Chapter 14.

Summary of Salient Facts and Conclusions

The final component of a market study, a summary of salient facts and conclusions, should be self-explanatory. Some market studies also provide a financial feasibility analysis, which is a study of the *profit potential* of the proposed project or investment that takes into account market, physical, locational, legal, social, governmental, and financial factors. However, this book distinguishes market studies from marketability analyses and financial feasibility analyses, with the objective of clarifying and isolating the functions of these distinctly different types of studies.

The next chapter discusses marketability analysis, which is a *micro*-market analysis of the neighborhood and the specific property under study. Although the foregoing discussion has made it clear that a neighborhood analysis may be part of a real estate market study, it is discussed within the framework of the marketability analysis because it is normally the starting point of such a study.

SUMMARY

Careful market analysis is essential to success in real estate investing, but too often this step is neglected in the decision process. Generally, a market study should include a careful analysis of current economic, social, political, and demographic trends in both a national and a regional context. The trading areas in which demand for specific real estate facilities are likely to occur are then delineated, and potential supply and demand are analyzed. Aerial photography and computer mapping (which were discussed in Chapter 11) can significantly aid the real estate investor in understanding the growth and structure of market areas over time.

The skills of the market analyst are critical because the timing of the investment in relation to real estate building cycles will depend largely on the accuracy of the analysis. The investor should require the analyst to provide projections of future rents, prices, and space needs. The report should relate the type and amount of economic activity in the defined market area to the specific type of space as a useful indicator of the market absorption rate.

The gap between supply and demand should be estimated and a forecast provided regarding the rate at which the market is likely to absorb any additional space. If excessive vacancies exist in the submarket in question, this should be examined. Ideally, the market study will provide information on current financing practices, turnover rates in the specified use, the stability of the neighborhood, and competitive activities.

13

MARKETABILITY ANALYSIS

Marketability analysis is site- or property-specific market research and planning; it is a micromarket study. The marketability of a particular unit of space is the ability of the market to accept the transfer, sale, exchange, or lease or some or all of the rights in that space. Because of the importance of rent-generating ability to value and other financial consequences, a marketability study usually focuses on the leasing of space and attempts to answer questions about the possible levels and associated probabilities of rent and occupancy over a specified time period for a particular property or for a set of alternative uses. An alternative use may be defined as different types of space (e.g., office versus retail) or different quality and amenity levels associated with a specific type of space.

For example, marketability analysis may consider office space at various quality levels with attendant market baskets of amenities as alternative uses. Such an analysis may be useful for an investor who is considering acquiring an existing office building with major or minor rehabilitation potential, or for a developer considering a site for office development. Differences in marketing strategies or any other material aspect of a property may represent alternatives for which the expected rental and occupancy rates may be sought.

SCOPE OF MARKETABILITY ANALYSIS

Marketability analysis has been defined as

a study to determine to what extent a particular piece of property can be marketed or sold under current or anticipated market conditions. It is inclusive of a study (analysis) of the general class of property being considered.

425

Thus, a marketability analysis goes one step further than a market study by identifying the number of units that can most probably be absorbed within that specific trading area (market) and over a specified time period. Thus, the marketability analysis is not a project feasibility analysis in that it does not take into consideration development costs or profitability. In effect a marketability study is sandwiched in between the market study, on the one hand, and a basic financial feasibility analysis on the other.[1]

Marketability analysis may provide a variety of information, all of which should reflect the uncertainty inherent in the marketplace. Few, if any, certain conclusions can be drawn from a marketability analysis, and reports that fail explicitly to address the probabilistic nature of such findings should be viewed with suspicion until justified by the analyst.

The analyst should provide information about the following general areas with the goal of helping the investor understand more clearly the spectrum of expected-return and risk trade-offs with the various possible configurations of the existing property or site. That is, starting from a given product, a single assumption may be changed and its impact on rental rates and occupancy estimated. Thus begins the circular, iterative process wherein a product is tested, modified to create a new product, retested, and so on. The final product of this process is an understanding of return–risk trade-offs for gross rent rates and vacancies associated with alternative products, pricing strategies, and merchandising strategies.

1. *Market possibilities.* The range of reasonable real estate products and associated marketing strategies and, for sales efforts, relevant financing arrangements.
2. *Absorption (potential demand).* The total number of units of each real estate product that are estimated to be demanded in the immediate market area for each period of a specified time frame.
3. *Effective demand.* The difference between the potential demand for and the estimated number of new units of each real estate product during each year of the specified time frame.
4. *Capture.* The proportion of the potential demand for each real estate product that the subject is estimated to be able to attract.
5. *Lease analysis and necessary demand.* An analysis of existing leases for lease rates, escalations, renewal clauses, escape clauses, and other relevant provisions with the goal of estimating the income from existing leases and the amount of space likely to be leased in

---

[1]Byrl N. Boyce, *Real Estate Appraisal Terminology* (Cambridge, Mass.: Ballinger Publishing Company, 1975), p. 137. For more recent material, see Neil Carn, Joseph Rabianski, Ronald Racster, and Maury Seldin, *Real Estate Market Analysis: Techniques and Applications* (Englewood Cliffs, N.J.: Prentice-Hall, 1988), pp. 2–5.

each period as a percentage of demand the property is likely to capture.

Finally, for an existing property, the market analyst should estimate the gross possible income and vacancy rate under different economic scenarios for each year of the ownership life cycle. Related capital and operating expense estimates should also be developed in the marketability analysis since achievement of target gross possible income and vacancy levels is realistic only if certain expenses are incurred—for example, tenant improvements, advertising, and leasing commissions. In addition, the marketability study should provide information for evaluating alternative marketing strategies, if they are being considered.

GUIDELINES FOR A MARKETABILITY ANALYSIS

As noted before, the investor is a coordinator of a process designed to maximize returns relative to risk preferences. Since micromarket analysis is location-specific and requires extensive field survey work and time, the investor most likely contracts with a qualified real estate professional, such as a real estate counselor, to perform the marketability analysis. One of the most valuable qualities of such an expert is the fact that he or she may have access to data that are not generally available. Especially for out-of-town investors, it is important that whoever performs the marketability analysis be knowledgeable about the target real estate markets.

Because of the uncertainty inherent to real estate investment, marketability analysis should explicitly incorporate that uncertainty into the analysis. If the analyst perceives degrees of uncertainty about marketability results, these perceptions should be conveyed to the investor. The investor can only respond to risks of which he or she is aware, and a failure by the analyst to present a complete and accurate representation of the marketability of an investment can be disastrous. The tendency to report only the most likely, or expected results, masks the upside and downside potential of an investment. Analysts may use "optimistic," "most likely," and "pessimistic" estimates if unable to assign probabilities to the occurrence of each outcome. However, a range of possible outcomes along with associated estimates of the probability of each occurring is a more useful representation.[2]

[2]Donald H. Woods, "Improving Estimates That Involve Uncertainty," *Harvard Business Review*, July–August 1966, pp. 17–24. See Chapter 8 for a detailed examination of risk analysis and measurement techniques and for pertinent references.

The following is a list of the components of a thorough and complete marketability analysis.

1. Establishing the boundaries of the immediate market area (neighborhood).[3]
2. Immediate market area (neighborhood) analysis.
3. Site and property analysis.
4. Survey of competition, with interpretive analysis.
5. Absorption and capture rate analysis.
6. Revenue and revenue-related expense forecasts.
7. Marketing strategy and management plan.
8. Summary and conclusions.

All these components are interrelated; the economic–demographic profile, the competitive survey, the analyses of market absorption and capture rates, and the revenue and expense forecasts are based on the marketing strategy and management plans that the investor expects to adopt for each specific real estate product. Each of these elements is now discussed.

ESTABLISHING THE BOUNDARIES

Defining the immediate market area or neighborhood is often a difficult task requiring judgment and systematic analysis. The immediate market area is the area within which the subject property competes for tenants. For some properties, the market area will be a large geographic area; for others, it will be a small one. For example, a large class A high-rise suburban office building may compete for tenants with office buildings all over the city, in the CBD as well as in the suburbs. A small garden-style, single-story office building may compete for tenants only with similar office buildings within a short distance. Analogous situations exist for shopping centers, apartments, industrial properties, and other types of real estate. Market area identification is more fully developed for retail stores and shopping centers than for other types of real estate. Since time and budget constraints do not permit an analysis of all the possibilities, the market

---

[3]Although many writers prefer the term "immediate market area," it is used interchangeably here with the term "neighborhood." The traditional concept of neighborhood analysis evolved from urban economics and appraisal literature, often in reference to residential property only. However, commercial and industrial neighborhoods also exist, as do mixed-use neighborhoods. In fact, it is difficult to overstate the influence of the neighborhood (immediate market area) on a property's return and risk characteristics. For further discussion of this subject, see G. Vincent Barrett and John P. Blair, "Neighborhood Influences and Site Analysis," Chapter 4, *How to Conduct and Analyze Real Estate Market and Feasibility Studies* (New York: Van Nostrand Reinhold, 1982), pp. 115–137.

study should provide sufficient information to select the immediate market area that best conforms to the investor's philosophy and strategy.

Immediate market area boundaries are often established by *natural barriers*, such as hills or bodies of water, or by *legal–political barriers*, such as highways, rail lines, or green belts. Also affecting the definition of the immediate market area are demographic and economic factors and competitive properties. The key to practical immediate market area delineation is to keep in mind that it is the competitive forces of users, owners, and lenders that establish and change neighborhoods, and not the decisions of analysts, planners, or statisticians. On the other hand, time and budget constraints compel the investor to define an immediate market area to fit available secondary data, such as census tracts, blocks, or ZIP code areas.

In summary, the investor should establish the immediate market area with due regard for natural and political barriers, demographic and economic information, competitive forces, and the best available fit to data sources.

IMMEDIATE MARKET AREA (NEIGHBORHOOD) ANALYSIS

An analysis of the immediate market area should provide detail on the quality of access to public transportation, utilities, shopping centers, schools, religious and civic organizations, hospitals, community facilities, and recreational facilities, to the extent that they are pertinent to the use contemplated. Detailed information should be provided on the socioeconomic level and trends in the immediate market area by income, education, occupation, age, and population trends. There should be descriptive data on geological, topographic, climatological, and other environmental influences. There should be a narrative history and description of the nature of the immediate market area, how it came into being, and past, present, and future trends. Generally, the marketability report should provide the following information.

1. A statement of *what type of use predominates in the area*, the *degree of conformity or diversity*, and the *extent of inharmonious uses.*
2. An evaluation of the *area's reputation* and the qualitative factors in the area that measure the quality of the business and living environment.
3. The representative *range of sales and rentals*, and the *quality of improvements* relative to those in competitive and comparable submarkets.
4. An informed opinion on the *general remaining economic life of typical properties* in the neighborhood area. Signs of spot blight should be noted.

5. A comment on the *extent of neighborhood maturity and degree of neighborhood sprawl.* Is the location built up? Is it stable? Is it on the decline? Is it being rehabilitated? Is there pride of ownership? What is the quality of routine maintenance?

6. A report on the *typical source of financing and refinancing* in the neighborhood. The attitude of lenders toward the future of the neighborhood should be evaluated.

7. An evaluation of *how accessible the neighborhood is* to the municipal infrastructure, the urban economy, and essential services and amenities.

8. A report on *planning, zoning, and code controls.* Are there any restrictive covenants? Are occupancy permits required for new owners? Is code compliance activity adequate or overzealous? Are there any illegal or nonconforming uses in the area? Is a zoning variance, exception, or change necessary for the contemplated use?

9. An analysis of the nature and adequacy of *available utilities and necessary amenities* and other essential facilities *for the planned use.*

10. A report on the *level and trends of vacancy and occupancy rates* that exist in the neighborhood and the underlying factors that are influencing them. This report should be stratified as to tenure (owner–renter), price–income, and product-type categories.

11. A report on the *turnover rate* of ownership and occupancy.

12. A commentary on *any known hazards and nuisances* such as noise, air or water pollution, and traffic congestion. Historical uses should be reviewed to detect the potential presence of hazardous materials.[4]

13. A comment on *possible positive or negative effects of nearby major facilities,* such as schools, regional shopping centers, convention facilities, stadiums, and industrial districts.

14. An evaluation of *future neighborhood trends.* The analysis should provide a factual and objective opinion of both positive and negative influences, free from speculation or bias.

SITE AND PROPERTY ANALYSIS

Property analysis focuses on the physical and legal characteristics of the property. For unimproved land, the object of property analysis is to deter-

---

[4] A series of articles pertaining to hazardous and environmental issues were published in *Commercial Investment Real Estate Journal,* July–August 1988, pp. 16–38, including Shirley A. Ness, "Environmental Hazards in Real Estate"; Gary Andrews, "Asbestos: What You Don't Know Can Hurt You"; Robert F. Scoular, "Lender Liability—The Battle Moves into the Courts"; James R. Quince and Joseph W. Sheahan, "Protecting Assets Through Environmental Appraisals"; and Warren J. Drewes and Aleda Grahn, "Lenders Find Asbestos to be Risky Business."

mine appropriate land use and the optimum size of improvements. Improved property is analyzed to determine the physical condition of improvements, the expected operating expenses, and the possible limitations to rehabilitation, expansion, or conversion to another use.

The property analysis considers physical characteristics such as topography, soil types, drainage, public infrastructure available to the site, accessibility of the site, and other land improvements. Physical analysis also examines the condition of all building improvements. It provides reviews of legal factors such as zoning, environmental, storm water, and flood control regulations and floodplain criteria affecting the property. Public records are reviewed to identify pertinent restrictive covenants and other private legal restrictions. If the neighborhood analysis has made reference to hazards, nuisances, amenities, and the like, this part of the report should discuss their effect on the property and site.

Site Analysis Checklist

Generally, a site analysis should contain the following site-specific commentary.

1. The dimensions, shape, and area of the site.
2. Topography.
3. Soil and subsoil conditions.
4. Quality of drainage and storm water control.
5. Quality and adequacy of utilities.
6. The nature of on-site landscaping, paving, and other land improvements.
7. Is the site typical and representative in nature for the type of use in place or intended? If not, what is the extext of its nonconformity?
8. Quality, adequacy, and level of maintenance of the municipal infrastructure—streets, curbs, sidewalks, and so on. (Note: The immediate market area or neighborhood analysis should have provided information on the quality and level of police and fire protection, urban transportation, and sanitary hauling and sewage. However, some special comment may be necessary for a specific site. In a built-up area, the very reason for nondevelopment may often be the absence of or an inadequate level of some such service.)
9. Time and distance to urban services and amenities.
10. Comparison of the site with other competitive sites, using appropriate units of comparison (i.e., ratios such as real estate taxes per square foot or rents per square foot).
11. Condition of improvements.
12. Design and functional efficiency of improvements.

13. Current zoning classification and other pertinent land use control regulations.
14. Private restrictions on use of the site.

Site analysis can be extended by the use of *earth science maps.*[5] Covering anything from a city block to the entire planet, these maps have calibrated scales that are appropriate for urban applications. They provide the investor with valuable information, for example, on ease of excavation, landslide susceptibility, slope stability, seismic susceptibility, percolation rates, mineral potential, and solid-waste disposal. Neglecting site condition variables can be dangerous.

Economic and Demographic Profile of the Immediate Market Area and Site

Markets can be delineated in various ways: geographically, by political jurisdiction, or by time and distance radii. However, because of time and budget constraints the preferred choice is generally geographic delineation. A geographically oriented, areal, economic–demographic data base report can be conveniently produced at low cost by using a proprietary, computer-based data retrieval system of a firm specializing in such a service.[6] In 1970 the Bureau of the Census provided the Census of Population and Housing Summary in computer-readable form for the first time. Several organizations were formed to process the data and make them available to users. One such firm is CACI, which has developed the Siteline reports. The reports produced by CACI are used here to demonstrate the type of marketability information that is now available.[7] In the absence of

[5]G. D. Robinson and A. M. Spieker, eds., "Nature to be Commanded . . . ," Earth-Science Maps Applied to Land Use and Water Management, Geological Survey Professional Paper No. 950 (Washington, D.C.: U.S. Gov't. Printing Office, 1978). For another excellent discussion of land use data and its interpretation, see David Rhind and Ray Hudson, *Land Use* (New York: Methuen & Co., 1980).

[6]At least four nationally recognized firms offer this type of service: CACI Inc., On-line and Custom Data Services, 8260 Willow Oaks Corporate Drive, Fairfax, Va. 22031; Donnelley Marketing Information Services, A Company of the Dun & Bradstreet Corp., 1901 South Meyers Road, Oakbrook Terrace, Ill. 60148-5098; National Decision Systems, 539 Encinitas Boulevard, Box 9007, Encinitas, Calif. 92024-9007; and Urban Decisions Systems Inc., P.O. Box 25953, Los Angeles, Calif. 90025.

[7]We gratefully acknowledge the cooperation of Deborah A. Wilson, Sales Director, CACI, Fairfax, Va., for making this material available. Scholarly sources for the concepts imbedded in models such as CACI's are David E. Bell, Ralph L. Keeney, and John D. C. Little, "A Market Share Theorem," *The Journal of Marketing Research*, May 1975, pp. 136–141; Thomas J. Stanley and Murphy A. Sewel, "Image Inputs to a Probabilistic Model: Predicting Retail Potential," *Journal of Marketing*, July 1976, pp. 48–53; Stanley and Sewel, *Metro Markets* (Boston: Intercollegiate Case Clearing House, 1977), with teaching notes and program listings; and David L. Huff, "Defining and Estimating a Trade Area," *Journal of Marketing*, July 1964, pp. 34–38.

such a computer-based service, these data must be generated by time-consuming manual review and analysis of published data.[8]

Demographic Profile. The CACI system called *Siteline* provides a demographic data base covering 63,000 unique administrative or political units. In addition, special computer programs provide geographic cross-reference files for very small areas, such as block groups, census tract districts, and ZIP code identifiers, thereby enabling users to define areas of any size and shape desired. Ninety-eight key variables were selected for the system, including

- Total population.
- Population by race, age, and sex.
- Family income.
- Median income.
- Home values and rental prices.
- Major appliances.
- Occupation.
- Units in structure, including mobile homes.
- Automobiles.
- Education.
- Household and family composition.

[8]A broad array of economic and demographic data is available on tape and diskette from the Bureau of Labor Statistics, Department of Labor; Customer Services, Bureau of the Census; and the Bureau of Economic Analysis, Department of Commerce. In addition, a number of private firms offer data on diskette and on-line as well as in published form. These are listed and discussed in Waldo L. Born and Karla D. Svoboda, *Real Estate Market Research Data Publications*, Special Report No. 586, November 1987, and *Real Estate Market Research On-Line Databases*, Special Report No. 626, February 1988, both published by the Real Estate Center, Texas A&M University, College Station, Texas 77843. The most current census is the baseline from which estimates and projections are made. Private data vendors purchase data and intercensal updates from private firms such as telephone and survey companies, and from government agencies on the federal level, including the Bureaus of the Census, Labor Statistics, and Economic Analysis, and on the state level, particularly regarding vehicle registration, school attendance, and gross sales and tax information. These private vendors can provide packages of data tailored for market research and applicable to a user-defined market area. However, there are limitations to these data bases. Although census data may include a complete countdown to the block level, government intercensal data are almost never available below the county level. Most are collected by surveys that may be statistically valid only at the state or regional level. As a consequence, small-area analysis may provide insight for comparing two or more areas but will never replace on-site market analysis. In defense of the data collection system, far more data are collected in MSAs than outside MSAs. In other words, because the majority of people reside and the major portion of economic activity occurs in MSAs, almost as much intercensal data are available for MSAs as for states.

EXHIBIT 13-1.   Defining Geographic Market Boundaries

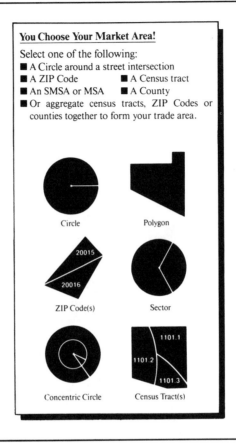

You Choose Your Market Area!

Select one of the following:
- A Circle around a street intersection
- A ZIP Code   ■ A Census tract
- An SMSA or MSA   ■ A County
- Or aggregate census tracts, ZIP Codes or counties together to form your trade area.

Circle   Polygon

ZIP Code(s)   Sector

Concentric Circle   Census Tract(s)

Source: Courtesy of CACI, Inc., Fairfax, Va.

The user first identifies a *site*. A site is a physical landmark, such as the intersection of two streets, that serves as a reference point around which a number of area boundaries may be geometrically defined. The populations of the subareas, called *cases*, are equal in sum to the total population of the site area. CACI enables the user to define up to twenty possible cases in any one computer run. Exhibit 13-1 illustrates a few of the ways in which a market area might be defined; the user can define a market area as one or more of the following: (1) the entire United States, (2) states, (3) counties, (4) MSAs, (5) ZIP code districts in MSAs, (6) census tracts, or (7) minor civil divisions. Exhibit 13-2 illustrates a few of the demographic, income, and area profile reports that are produced.

Sales Potential Profile. CACI provides another example of data retrieval capability with its sales potential system. With this system, users simply define a trading area of any size or shape. The system scans the CACI demographic base to determine the demographic characteristics of the residents of the trading area and then computes sales potential information using internal estimating equations. Although the sales potential system is most useful for retail or commercial investments, the methods and techniques of analysis are appropriate, with modifications, for all kinds of real estate investments.

The older, now outmoded, methods of developing such sales potential for an area were of only marginal value for smaller trading areas because the procedures did not take into account many factors that influence expenditures, such as ethnicity, occupation, income, family size, education, household composition, and regional effects. CACI and other computer data retrieval systems, however, analyze the relation between the expenditures of consumers and their demographic and socioeconomic characteristics.

The sales potential system can generate both a market growth index (MGI) and a market potential index (MPI) for the trading area, as well as for each line of merchandise (see Exhibit 13-2). The market growth index (MGI) compares the growth rate of total sales potential in the trading areas with the growth rate of the economic region in which the trading area is located. This is very similar to the technique of economic-base analysis. If the MGI of the trading area is 98.9, the total sales potential of the area has grown at a rate that is 1.1 percent *less than* the potential for the economic region. In comparison the market potential index (MPI) compares weekly per capita sales potential of the trading areas with that of the economic region in which the trading area is located. When, for example, the MPI is 141.9, the potential of the area is 41.9 percent higher than the average potential of the economic region.

The discussion of the CACI information systems has enabled us to review the nature of economic–demographic data base profiles and has provided a brief summary of how they are developed and made available. Once an immediate market area and site have been selected, such data retrieval systems can provide the demographic and socioeconomic characteristics that must be reviewed for any contemplated or existing use within that geographic area.

In addition to site evaluation, such data retrieval services might be used for market share analysis, in customer profiling, in tenant mix decisions, and as an aid in forecasting market absorption and capture rates. Some CACI reports are available by phone, and access to various subsidiary programs is available on several on-line data base time-sharing networks.

Keep in mind that such services provide more than just simple linear projections. The projections are controlled by the most recent estimates for census tracts and minor civil subdivisions. Some projections are

EXHIBIT 13-2. Custom Demographic Analysis of Market Area

1987 Demographic and Income Forecast

This report provides you with 1987 updates, actual 1980 census data and 1992 forecasts for age, household and family population, as well as household income.

Demographic and Income Forecast

```
ANTOWN, U.S.A.                    AREA REFERENCE: 38 52 10       RADIUS: OUTER  3.00
4TH & ELM                         LATITUDE:  38 52 10            DEGREES NORTH 38.87
0 - ANY SIZE RADIUS               LONGITUDE: 77  9 20            DEGREES WEST  77.16
```

	1980 CENSUS	1987 UPDATE	1992 FORECAST	1987-1992 CHANGE	ANNUAL GROWTH
POPULATION	152756	159740	159614	-126	0.0%
HOUSEHOLDS	61659	69734	73080	3346	0.9%
FAMILIES	39354	42194	42943	749	0.4%
AVG HH SIZE	3.06	2.24	2.14	-0.10	-0.8%
AVG FAM SIZE		2.90	2.79	-0.11	
TOT INC (MIL$)	1715.6	3078.0	3730.3	652.3	3.9%
PER CAPITA INC $	11231	19269	23371	4102	3.9%
AVG FAM INC $	32126	50064	57113	7049	2.7%
MEDIAN FAM INC $	29139	49943	63557	13614	4.9%
AVG HH INC $	27824	44140	51044	6904	2.9%
MEDIAN HH INC $	24092	41733	51401	9668	4.3%

HOUSEHOLD INCOME	1980 CENSUS	%	1987 UPDATE	%	1992 FORECAST	%
$ 0- 9999	9284	15.1	4948	7.1	3973	5.4
$10000-14999	7361	11.9	3869	5.5	2969	4.1
$15000-24999	17390	25.3	9472	13.6	8031	10.3
$25000-34999	10839	17.6	13619	19.5	12812	17.5
$35000-49999	5379	8.7	15209	21.8	15169	20.4
$50000-74999						
$75000 UP	1495	2.4	12152	17.4	22221	30.4

AGE DISTRIBUTION	1980 CENSUS	%	1987 UPDATE	%	1992 FORECAST	%
0-4	8431	5.5	7981	5.0	6872	4.3
5-16	10060	6.6	8996	5.6	8393	5.1
17-21	11583	7.6	9439	5.9	8666	5.4
22-29	25878	16.9	20549	12.9	17344	10.9
30-44	35551	23.3	44925	28.1	45203	28.3
45-54	16087	10.5	18162	11.4	22004	13.8
55-64	17224	11.3	16171	10.1	15531	9.7
65+	15920	10.4	21883	13.7	24204	15.2

	1980 CENSUS	1987 UPDATE	1992 FORECAST
AVERAGE AGE	36.0	39.0	40.5
MEDIAN AGE	32.7	37.1	39.0

RACE DISTRIBUTION	1980 CENSUS	%	1987 UPDATE	%	1992 FORECAST	%
WHITE	128006	83.8	131628	82.4	129255	81.0
BLACK	10722	7.0	12277	7.7	13377	8.4
OTHER	14028	9.2	15835	9.9	16982	10.6
HISPANIC	8536	5.6				

```
IMPORTANT: 1. HOUSEHOLD INCOME INCLUDES THE INCOME OF FAMILIES AND
              UNRELATED INDIVIDUALS. HOUSEHOLD INCOME IS THE TOTAL
              AVAILABLE INCOME FOR THE AREA.
           2. INCOME FIGURES ARE EXPRESSED IN CURRENT DOLLARS FOR 1980
              AND 1987. 1992 FIGURES ARE EXPRESSED IN 1987 DOLLARS.
```

1980 Census Profile

Over 290 information items on this multi-page report help you describe socioeconomic characteristics for your trade area.

1980 Census Profile

```
ANTOWN, U.S.A.                    AREA REFERENCE: 38 52 10       RADIUS: OUTER  3.00
4TH & ELM                         LATITUDE:  38 52 10            DEGREES NORTH 38.87
0 - ANY SIZE RADIUS               LONGITUDE: 77  9 20            DEGREES WEST  77.16
```

	1980 CENSUS	1987 UPDATE	ANNUAL CHANGE
POPULATION	152756	159740	0.64%
HOUSEHOLDS	61659	69734	1.77%
MEDIAN HSHLD INCOME	$ 24092	$ 41733	8.17%

POPULATION AGE BY:	MALE	%	FEMALE	%	TOTAL	%
WHITE	128006	83.8%				
BLACK	10722	7.0%				
OTHER	14028	9.2%				
TOTAL	152756	100.0%				
0-4	4284	5.8%	4147	5.3%		5.5%
5-9	4272	5.8%	4081	5.1%		5.5%
10-13	3808	5.2%	3570	4.5%		4.8%
14-17	4582	6.2%	4065	5.1%		5.7%
18-20	3467	4.7%	3212	4.1%		4.4%
21-24	5988	8.1%	6145	7.8%		7.9%
25-34	8781	10.8%	8240	9.8%		10.7%
35-44	7800	10.5%	7700	9.8%		10.5%
45-54	10042	12.7%	10024	12.5%		11.3%
55-64	7780	10.5%	8308	10.5%		11.3%
65-74	7692	10.4%	9532	12.1%		11.3%
75-84	4355	5.9%	6070	7.7%		6.8%
85+	1356	1.8%	2852	3.6%		2.9%
TOTAL	72266	100.0%	79915	100.0%		100.0%

	MALE	FEMALE
MEDIAN	34.32	35.96
AVERAGE	31.53	32.71

MARITAL STATUS (POP > 14 YRS)		
SINGLE	37738	29.8%
MARRIED	67624	53.4%
DIVORCED/SEPARATED	12812	10.1%
WIDOWED	8520	6.7%

HOME VALUE (NON-CONDO'S):		%
$ 0-20K	51	0.2%
$ 20-30K	192	0.3%
$ 30-40K	412	1.3%
$ 40-50K	8861	32.2%
$ 50-80K	8829	32.1%
$ 80-100K	7224	26.3%
$100-150K	1365	5.0%
$150-200K	530	1.9%
$200+	27551	100.0%
TOTAL	97105	
AVERAGE $	89497	
MEDIAN $		

OCCUPIED HSG UNITS	61659	95.8%
VACANT HSG UNITS:		
FOR SALE OR RENT	1880	2.9%
SEASONAL/MIGRATORY	11	0.0%
OCCASIONAL USE/OTHER	780	1.2%
TOTAL HSG UNITS	64330	100.0%

GROSS RENT (INCL UTIL):		
NO $ RENT	489	1.7%
$ <100	270	0.9%
$100-149	159	0.6%
$150-199	319	1.2%
$200-249	7365	25.6%
$250-299	9252	32.1%
$300-399	3980	13.8%
$400-499	3404	11.8%
$500+		
TOTAL	28821	100.0%
AVERAGE $	346	
MEDIAN $	327	

SINGLE PERSON HOUSEHOLDS		
MALE	6735	28.7%
FEMALE	10988	17.8%
	17723	

FAMILY HOUSEHOLDS	39354	63.8%
MARRIED COUPLE	32189	52.2%
SINGLE MALE HEAD OF HH	1623	2.6%
SINGLE FEMALE HEAD OF HH	5542	9.0%

CONDOMINIUM HOUSING:		
RENTED	972	24.7%
OWNED	2593	65.9%
VACANT	370	9.4%
TOTAL	3935	100.0%

```
AVG VAL OWN/OCC:$ 68846
OCCUPIED HOUSING UNITS:
  % OWNED       52.2%
  % RENTED      47.8%
```

TOTAL HOUSEHOLDS	61659	100.0%
TOTAL FAMILIES	39354	
AVERAGE SIZE	3.06	

Sales Potential

Choose any one of these 10 reports which measure potential customer spending in your trade area for your line of business.

Automotive Aftermarket	Home Improvement Center
Convenience Store	Investment Services
Department Store	Medical/Health Insurance
Financial Services	Restaurant
Grocery Store	Shopping Center

ACORN™ Area Profile Report

ACORN™—A Classification of Residential Neighborhoods—is `a state-of-the-art market segmentation and target marketing tool. The premise of ACORN™ is that people who share similar demographic, housing, and socioeconomic characteristics tend to live in homogeneous neighborhoods and share similar lifestyles, and thus present similar potential for products and services and react similarly to media, direct mail, and other promotions.

Sales Potential

```
ANYTOWN, U.S.A.        AREA REFERENCE: 38 52 10    RADIUS: OUTER   3.00
4TH & ELM              LATITUDE:  38 52 10         DEGREES NORTH  38.87
0 - ANY SIZE RADIUS    LONGITUDE: 77  9 20         DEGREES WEST   77.16
```

	1980 CENSUS	1987 UPDATE	ANNUAL CHANGE
POPULATION	152756	159740	0.64%
HOUSEHOLDS	61659	69734	1.77%
MEDIAN HSHLD INCOME	$ 24092	$ 41733	8.17%

MARKET POTENTIAL INDEX: 141.9
MARKET GROWTH INDEX: 96.9

ECONOMIC REGION: SOUTH METRO

TYPE OF EXPENDITURE	MPI (BASE=100)	ANNUAL TOTAL (THOU $)	ANNUAL $ PER HSHLD	ANNUAL $ PER CAPITA
1987 DEPT STORE MERCHANDISE	151.3	309300.	4434.00	1935.65
1980 DEPT STORE MERCHANDISE	150.0	234178.4	3379.96	1533.39
ANNUAL GROWTH RATE 1980-1987		4.05%	2.24%	3.39%
1987 DRUG STORE MERCHANDISE	128.3	111243.9	1595.26	696.41
1980 DRUG STORE MERCHANDISE	126.8	72954.2	1183.19	477.59
ANNUAL GROWTH RATE 1980-1987		6.21%	4.36%	5.54%
1987 GROCERY STORE MERCHANDISE	135.6	263815.1	3785.06	1551.53
1980 GROCERY STORE MERCHANDISE	134.0	188862.2	3063.01	1251.29
ANNUAL GROWTH RATE 1980-1987		4.89%	3.06%	4.22%
1987 RESTAURANTS (FOOD ONLY)	153.2	101125.5	1450.16	633.06
1980 RESTAURANTS (FOOD ONLY)	151.5	70564.1	1144.43	461.94
ANNUAL GROWTH RATE 1980-1987		5.28%	3.44%	4.60%
1987 APPAREL STORE MERCHNDSE	160.3	154746.9	2219.09	968.74
1980 APPAREL STORE MERCHNDSE	158.7	121042.9	1963.09	792.39
ANNUAL GROWTH RATE 1980-1987		3.57%	1.77%	2.91%
1987 FOOTWEAR STORE MRCHNDSE	127.0	33955.4	486.93	212.57
1980 FOOTWEAR STORE MRCHNDSE	126.2	27626.1	448.05	180.85
ANNUAL GROWTH RATE 1980-1987		2.99%	1.20%	2.34%
1987 HOME IMPROVEMENT STORE	100.4	15505.8	222.16	97.07
1980 HOME IMPROVEMENT STORE	99.4	11347.0	184.03	74.28
ANNUAL GROWTH RATE 1980-1987		4.56%	2.74%	3.90%
1987 AUTO AFTERMARKET	122.8	56644.9	812.30	354.61
1980 AUTO AFTERMARKET	121.6	42363.3	687.06	277.33
ANNUAL GROWTH RATE 1980-1987		4.24%	2.42%	3.57%
1987 HAIR SALON SERVICES	133.1	17874.7	256.33	111.90
1980 HAIR SALON SERVICES	131.6	12805.5	207.68	83.83
ANNUAL GROWTH RATE 1980-1987		4.88%	3.05%	4.21%

SEE NOTES ON NEXT PAGE

ACORN™ Area Profile Report

```
ANYTOWN, U.S.A.        AREA REFERENCE: 38 52 10    RADIUS: OUTER   3.00
4TH & ELM              LATITUDE:  38 52 10         DEGREES NORTH  38.87
0 - ANY SIZE RADIUS    LONGITUDE: 77  9 20         DEGREES WEST   77.16
```

ACORN TYPE	ACORN DESCRIPTION	POPULATION 1987	BASE %	AREA INDEX
A 1	ESTABLISHED SUBURBS	668	0.4	77
A 2	NEWER SUBURBS	13191	8.3	720
A 3	OLDER FAMILIES, HIGHER DENSITY	17331	10.8	504
A 4	NEWER SUBURBS: VERY HIGH INCOME	997	0.6	20
B 5	OLDER FAMILIES, POST-WAR SUBURBS	43495	27.2	1027
B 6	YOUNG FAMILIES, HIGH MOBILITY		0.0	7
B 7	FAMILIES WITH OLDER CHILDREN	635	0.4	4
B 8	MIDDLE INCOME, BLUE COLLAR	3660	2.3	51
C 9	UPPER-MID INC HIGH RENT/VALUE CONDO	4009	2.5	161
C 10	YOUNG ADULTS, MID & LOWER/MID INCOME	33436	20.9	431
C 11	COLLEGE UNDERGRADUATES		0.0	0
C 12	COLLEGE AREAS, OLDER STUDENTS	1201	0.8	52
D 13	HIGHRISE AREAS	4902	3.1	354
D 14	OLDER, MID-RISE AREAS	20124	12.6	1121
E 15	LOWER-MIDDLE INCOME, BLUE COLLAR	5657	3.5	140
E 16	YOUNG HISPANICS, SOUTHWESTERN STATES		0.0	0
E 17	OLDER POPULATION, ETHNIC MIX		0.0	0
E 18	POOR FAMILIES, VERY OLD HOUSING		0.0	0
F 19	HIGH RISE AND RACKS, MID-RISE, LOW RENT		0.0	0
F 20	LOWER-MID INCOME LOW VALUE HOUSE/APT.	417	0.3	7
F 21	OLDER POPULATION, OLD RENTAL HOUSING		0.0	0
F 22	VERY POOR BLACKS, LOW RENT HOUSING		0.0	0
G 23	MIDDLE INCOME, HIGHER VALUE HOUSING		0.0	0
G 24	YOUNG FAMILIES		0.0	0
H 25	YOUNG MOBILE FAMILIES		0.0	0
H 26	OLDER HOUSING		0.0	0
H 27	SEASONAL HOUSING AND FARMS		0.0	0
H 28	RURAL INDUSTRIAL		0.0	0
I 29	OLDER FAMS & RETIREES, HIGH MOBILITY	6609	4.1	91
I 30	OLDER HOUSING		0.0	0
I 31	SMALL TOWNS		0.0	0
I 32	EASTERN EUROPEANS, NORTHEASTERN U.S.		0.0	0
I 33	RURAL RETIREMENT AREAS		0.0	0
J 34	LOW AND VERY OLD HOUSING		0.0	0
J 35	SEASONAL HOUSING		0.0	0
J 36	MOBILE HOME AREAS		0.0	0
K 37	SELF EMPLOYED FARMERS		0.0	0
K 38	LARGE FARMS, LOW INCOME FARM WORKERS		0.0	0
L 39	LOW INCOME, POST-WAR HOUSING		0.0	0
L 40	POOR FAMILIES, HIGH UNEMPLOYMENT		0.0	0
L 41	V.LOW INC BLACKS & WHITES, LRGE FAMS		0.0	0
M 42	MILITARY AREAS	3408	2.1	238
M 43	INSTITUTIONS		0.0	0
		159740		

BASE DEFINITION:US

COPYRIGHT 1987 CACI, FAIRFAX, VA   (800) 292-2224   PRESS 2   DATE 7/14/87

Source: Courtesy of CACI, Inc., Fairfax, Va.

adapted for information from utility companies, the construction industry, and environmental groups.

A Shortcoming of Computer Generated Profiles. A major shortcoming of such profiles must also be kept in mind. The projections provided are based on past activities; they are not predictions of what will *actually* occur. No model can take into consideration changes such as the following.

1. Rapid intracounty economics and changes in population growth.
2. Rapid changes to higher and better land uses as a result of private or governmental action, such as demolition, highway construction, construction of public facilities, new industry in the area, or conversions from old to new uses.
3. Changes in technology or material shortages that are not yet reflected in consumption activities like mass transit or energy use.
4. Rapid changes in consumer buying patterns, such as those brought about by Kentucky Fried Chicken and McDonald's.
5. On an individual basis, such statistics are necessarily silent on the effects of competitors' plans.

These factors must be researched for the local area to determine whether changes that will cause the future to differ from the past have or are likely to occur.

FIELD SURVEY OF THE COMPETITION

A field survey of the competition is a determination, by competent professionals, of *existing and planned* real estate that would compete with the investment under consideration. Before proceeding with an acquisition, it is essential for an investor to discover how competitors are currently serving the area and how *additional* competitors are *planning* to serve it in the immediate future. With this information the investor can refine and improve the merchandising plan during the preacquisition stage. It is also possible that an investor will find that contemplated new construction is of such quantity and quality that interest in the particular property should be abandoned. Gathering such data can be time-consuming, costly, and difficult because virtually every piece of information must be verified. Such information can be cross-checked with utility companies, building contractors, mortgage lenders, and governmental agencies.

The data gathered from an appropriate competitive survey provide direct market comparisons of the subject property with alternative properties that are being offered to the tenants whom the investor seeks to capture. Information on the competition sharpens the investor's definition of customer profiles, potential rents, vacancies, and expenses and can test the kinds of amenity packages that competitors are providing. It provides an idea of the minimum standards for properties of the type being considered.

These critical data enable the investor to test his or her plans against what the market is already providing to tenants, and make it possible to identify the characteristics of properties that have recently received approval from lenders.

Exhibit 13-3 provides a summary, not intended to be exhaustive for all situations, of relevant factors that have been identified for the basic property types.[9] The material listed in Exhibit 13-3 is schematic in nature and lacks detail. Chapters 21 to 27 provide detailed definitions of many of the technical terms plus greater detail on the techniques of competitive analysis for each property type.

ABSORPTION AND CAPTURE RATES

Absorption Rate and Potential Demand

The absorption rate is the quantity of a given real estate product that the immediate market area demands over a specified time period. This demand represents *potential demand* for the subject property.

However, in order to realize this potential demand, the subject property must compete with other properties in the immediate market area. Potential demand represents the pool that must be divided between competing properties.

It is easy to become preoccupied with absorption rates and fail to place them in proper perspective. First, historical absorption rates can be misleading. Because a certain number of units or square feet of space have been absorbed on average in the past is not assurance that this trend will continue. The past should not be ignored, but marketability analysis must be future-oriented. An investor is buying a set of assumptions about the future, not about the past. Second, a concentration on absorption rates for overall market conditions can cause an investor to miss some excellent opportunities. For example, the expected overall absorption rate for office buildings may be quite low for the coming year. However, marketability research may indicate that the absorption for a specific type of office space is quite good. Thus, too much attention to overall rates may be misleading.

A marketability analysis should provide absorption rates and estimates of potential demand for *stratified* markets in small geographic areas. Because users can exercise a wide choice in deciding location—which is loosely defined in this context as time and distance from home to work—

---

[9]These guidelines are adapted from ideas presented in John McMahan, *Property Development* (New York: McGraw-Hill, 1976), a recommended book. See also John M. Clapp, "Evaluating Competing Properties," Chapter 10, and "Evaluating Competition with Regression Analysis," Chapter 11, *Handbook for Real Estate Market Analysis* (Englewood Cliffs, N.J.: Prentice-Hall, 1987), pp. 129–156.

EXHIBIT 13-3. Field Surveys of the Competition

RESIDENTIAL COMPETITIVE SURVEY

1. Map showing location of various competitive projects.
2. Number of existing or planned units in project.
3. Unit mix (i.e., number of bedrooms).
4. Square feet per unit (including balconies, patios).
5. Amenities of unit (carpet, drapes, appliances, security).
6. Nature and quality of project amenities (recreational facilities, clubhouse).
7. Price or rental range (sales price per square foot, expenses per square foot).
8. Tenants' lease terms.
9. Sales and financing terms of recent sales.
10. Vacancy and occupancy rates (stratified by unit mix).
11. Quality and nature of management and merchandising strategy (advertising, models, signs).
12. Rate of absorption of new or vacant units in recent months.
13. Nature of occupants (income, occupation, place of employment).
14. A judgmental rating of the overall competitiveness of the project on a scale from 0 to 10.
15. Date of field survey.

RETAIL–COMMERCIAL COMPETITIVE SURVEY

1. Map showing location of competitive projects (including time and distance indicators).
2. Gross leasable area (GLA) of competitive projects, broken down into major categories of goods and services.
3. Parking index—number of parking stalls or square feet of parking area per square foot of GLA.
4. Sales or rents per GLA, broken down into categories of goods and services.
5. Identification of major anchor tenants and competitive stores.
6. An evaluation of directly competitive users (comments on stores, appearance, personnel, advertising, and promotional techniques).
7. Opinion of the overall quality of the competitive center. This should be a consideration of the merchants' association, maintenance, shopping atmosphere, and so on.
8. An analysis of the area surrounding the center—presence of buffers, nearby uses, type and quality of nearby uses, transportation, growth trends. A rating scale of 0 to 10 should be used.

OFFICE COMPETITIVE SURVEY

1. Map showing location of competitive office buildings; the names of the office activity nodes where office uses cluster in the MSA.
2. Gross building area, net rentable area, net rented area, net occupied area of competitive buildings.
3. Schedule of rents per square foot, broken down by tenant and floor location of tenant categories.
4. Minimum lease duration.
5. Items normally included in tenant finish allowance (partitions, utility outlets, lighting, carpets, drapes).
6. Lease terms (building services included in base rent, escalation clauses, maintenance duties, risk of loss in the event of casualty).
7. Parking (provided, how, monthly charge).
8. Other building amenities (function rooms, restaurants).
9. General profile of major and minor tenants.
10. An evaluation of the overall competitiveness of the project (maintenance and management, appearance, locational advantages and disadvantages). A rating scale of 0 to 10 should be used.
11. Date of survey.

INDUSTRIAL LAND USE COMPETITIVE SURVEY

1. Map showing location of competitive projects.
2. Accessibility to various transportation modes (air, highway, rail, public transit), with time, distance, and frequency indicators.
3. Nature, quality, adequacy of various utilities (capacity, limits on utilization, surcharges, tap-in charges).
4. Development controls imposed.
5. Alternative site developments permitted (built-to-suit, general purpose only, sale–leaseback).
6. Acreage sold or rented to date, with annual absorption rate.
7. Acreage vacant or remaining to be sold or rented.
8. Profile of major and minor occupant firms.
9. Price or rental terms, per square foot, for various uses.
10. Lease terms (duration, escalation clauses, risk of loss in the event of casualty, rental options).
11. Project amenities provided by owner (landscaping, street maintenance, snow removal, lighting, conference facilities, recreational facilities, restaurants).
12. An evaluation of the overall relative competitiveness of the project. A rating scale of 0 to 10 should be used.
13. Date of survey.

the market absorption rate for, say, apartment space for an entire MSA can be forecast with more accuracy than the effective demand for apartment space within a smaller geographic area. Under such conditions, the usefulness of a proprietary type of demographic-economic data base profile for small areas is apparent, since it provides the means for comparing estimates of absorption rates with historical trends. Because the estimation of market absorption rates is subject to uncertainty, and is an exercise in human judgment as well as an objective process of quantification, the investor should forecast data under optimistic, most likely, and pessimistic conditions, or as a probability distribution.

Capture Rates and Effective Demand

The capture rate and effective demand are measures of the expected market share for a particular property.[10] The capture rate is the percentage of the potential demand the subject site is expected to garner in the market. Effective demand is the number of units or square feet available for the subject property over a specified time period. The estimation of effective demand requires estimates of and comparisons of supply and demand.

For an existing property, effective demand is a function of sharing demand, not necessarily equally, up to the capacity of supply. If supply exceeds demand, the allocation of demand will be a function of the relative attractiveness of the competing properties. Thus, the competitive analysis discussed earlier and a clear understanding of the preferences of space users, perhaps obtained through survey research techniques, are critical to estimating relative attractiveness. If projected demand exceeds supply, the allocation of demand among various competing properties is accomplished the same way, with particular attention paid to new developmet activity. Clearly, the greater the excess demand the lower the risk associated with a property. Situations in which excess demand does not exist provide a greater challenge to marketing and management personnel and generate increased risk. To the extent that the existing capture rate is less than the total demand for space, there exists an opportunity for the development of a real estate product to serve the need.

The development early in the analysis of a demand model that clearly identifies the sources of demand for a particular product is extremely useful. With such a model, absorption rates can be estimated by comparing the total potential for the immediate market area with the total number of existing units for the specified type of activity. Using the *summation estimating technique*, the marketability analysis would first establish the po-

---

[10]A thorough discussion of capture rates and their relation to absorption rates and other elements of market and marketability analysis is presented by Clapp, "Market Capture," Chapter 13, and "Market and Spatial Gap Analysis," Chapter 14, *Handbook for Real Estate Market Analysis*, pp. 167–188.

tential dollar expenditurres for the particular use that would be originated in the market area. To estimate a reasonable market share for an existing site, the investor could allocate the appropriate share of potential expenditures among the existing and planned competitive uses. The balance, divided by the site's revenue units (e.g., apartment units or gross leasable area of retail space), provides an estimate of the amount of expenditure per unit of space and can be used to evaluate the reasonableness of achieving various market shares.

A variation of this technique uses information produced by the field survey of the competition. Having identified the number of competing facilities within the market area, the investor proceeds to estimate the share of the market that the target site and the competitors have absorbed or are expected to absorb if the facilities are new. This is a judgmental process that takes into account competitive locational advantage, attractiveness of facilities, and the like. At this point the absorption rates can be multiplied by the expenditure for this type of consumption to provide an estimate of the sales that could be captured in this market area. When compared with estimates produced by the competitive survey, this acts as a check on the reasonableness of estimates.

In the case of a planned facility, the best available means of estimating a capture rate is to conduct primary behavior research to supplement information on consumer expenditure patterns arising out of the data base profile. This research is accomplished through personal interviews, phone interviews, or mail questionnaires. Attitudinal surveys of this kind are fraught with the possibility of error when conducted by amateurs; they should be conducted by experienced market researchers because of the special skills required.[11]

A crude measure of the potential demand for the contemplated use can be provided by an enumeration of how the respondents would want to use the facility. With a scientific sample, it is possible that an adjusted capture rate can be derived for the total projected population during the rent-up or sell-off period. Certainly such projections should be judgmentally adjusted for the effects of changes in the competition. The investor should also keep in mind that consumer surveys are an expression of wishes and desires; they are not necessarily good measures of actual or effective demand for the real estate product.

Formal methods for determining capture rates are in the early development stages. Therefore, the investor should use more than one of the meth-

---

[11] Survey methods for marketability analysis are discussed in Carn, Rabianski, Racster, and Seldin, "Primary Data," Chapter 14, *Real Estate Market Analysis*, pp. 309–347; see also J. Rabianski and J. Vernor, "The Use of Questionnaires in Marketability Research," in James D. Vernor, ed., *Readings in Market Research for Real Estate* (Chicago: American Institute of Real Estate Appraisers, 1985).

ods indicated here. In addition, a range of capture rates should be estimated, so that the reasonableness of the estimates can be assessed more effectively.

REVENUE AND REVENUE-RELATED EXPENSE FORECASTS

For existing properties, the conclusion of a marketability analysis forecasts (1) gross possible rental income and (2) vacancy rates for each year over the expected holding period of the investment. In addition, the marketability analysis should include a discussion of the capital and operating expenses that are necessary each year to produce the forecasted project rents and vacancy rates. For example, an aggressive marketing strategy calling for improving the physical condition of the rentable space and for the extensive use of leasing and management personnel to achieve higher-than-market-average rent and occupancy rates will result in capital and operating expenses unique to that marketing strategy and revenue forecast. Different marketing strategies will result in different revenue-related expense forecasts; consequently, the investor must evaluate the trade-offs between rent levels, vacancy, capital expenses, and operating expenses for alternative marketing strategies in order to determine the best marketing strategy. The marketability study therefore should be designed to provide forecasts of revenue-related expenses for each year over the expected holding period of the investment, although this practice is not common.

The marketability analysis should also account for the risks associated with the revenue–vacancy–expense forecasts through data projections for alternative economic scenarios and for different levels of confidence, either by assigning probability distributions to uncertain variables or by measuring dispersion using an optimistic–most likely–pessimistic range of values and sensitivity analyses. These data outputs from the marketability study are then used as input data for the investor's return and risk analysis.

MARKETING STRATEGY AND MANAGEMENT PLAN

The terms marketing strategy and management plan cover separate, but essential, management functions.

Marketing Strategy

Marketing strategy is defined as the investor's policy concerning the merchandising of the property. This policy is designed to achieve or maintain an adequate level of occupancy within acceptable market absorption rates and to produce a minimum rate of return at an acceptable level of risk. Although this definition differs from many, it is used in this text with the assumption that investment strategy, marketing strategy, and property management are all parts of a continuous process directed toward the goal of maximizing returns relative to risks. The functions should not be separated; their interrelationship should be carefully considered at all stages of the investor's analysis of a property.

The original market study identified market areas in an MSA where possible investment opportunities could be found. Once a site or property has been targeted, a merchandising program must be devised to exploit the opportunity at the site.

A merchandising program varies with the neighborhood and site, the nature of the location, the degree and nature of the competition, special advantages or disadvantages of the subject site, and the investor's evaluation of the effectiveness of other merchandising programs. Although a market analyst is sometimes asked to develop the marketing strategy and resulting merchandising plan, generally the investor devises the plan with the assistance of a qualified property manager, a real estate marketing–leasing agent, or both.

For the development of a merchandising plan, the characteristics and preferences of the target market must be described as precisely, simply, and definitively as possible. For example, the target market for an industrial park may be small-business firms, young or mature, that require a combination of office space, warehousing, nonpolluting manufacturing, or a laboratory. An apartment building might be aimed toward singles and empty nesters who earn $20,000 or more and are interested in security, close proximity to hospitals, and shopping. The target market for a boutique shopping center may be described as young executives and older couples with high disposable incomes who are interested in gourmet foods, art objects, high-fashion clothes, and other specialty items. As discussed in the preceding chapter, a demand model that clearly identifies the source of demand for a property is invaluable.

Definition of the target market early in the preacquisition stage forces the investor to ascertain whether or not the market currently exists in the targeted MSA market area. Clear characterization serves another valuable function in that the investor is required to formulate a merchandising plan that is consistent with the needs and resources of the target market. When the investor is purchasing an existing project with apparently adequate gross rents, this exercise is quite useful as a way of evaluating the representations made by the seller regarding the occupation, income, and other characteristics of the users.

Although a general model of a merchandising plan cannot be fully developed here, various decision points are important in evaluating and estimating market absorption and capture rates, given the merchandising plan. For example,

1. Once the typical space user has been defined, a shopping service might be engaged to compare the target with its competition.
2. Having considered the comparative advantages and disadvantages of the targeted use, the investor might consider what design, repairs, or improvements will be necessary. They could require amendment of the capital budget or renegotiation with the seller.
3. Every real estate project tends to develop an image in the market-place, even if it is so desirable that it is rented by word of mouth. Generally, however, it is necessary to promote a project in order to maintain high occupancy levels throughout the real estate cycle.
4. It must be decided who is to lease the property. This could be done by an in-house staff, a property manager, or a leasing firm.
5. The development of a model unit or model space and a sales or leasing center must be considered. A well-designed leasing center can be very effective in a leasing program. It can also be expensive.
6. The advertising program must be detailed. The media to be used and the theme of any campaign have to be identified.
7. Careful attention should also be given to the signage program, the way prospective user traffic will be handled, how sales models will be shown, and the sales–lease closing rooms.

The Management Plan

A management plan is defined as the tactical system that implements investment, marketing, and merchandising strategy in accordance with the investor's philosophy. It is the investor's supervisory control system over the property manager. In a newly developed or acquired property, property management is particularly important because of possible confusion and the need to attend to the details of completing construction on the development or rehabilitation undertaken. Chapter 16 presents a detailed discussion of property and venture management activities. The following is a list of some of the functions of the property manager, who acts as an agent of the owner. In general, the supervisory control system requires the property manager to provide analysis and recommendations in the following areas.

1. Space use planning to meet user preferences.
2. Market promotion policies, merchandising, and tenant selection.
3. Maintenance and replacement policy.
4. Policies for control of major construction and contractors.
5. Accounting policies and control of reserves.
6. Management policies for operation of the property.

The investor separates management of the property from investment management (also called asset management or venture management), which is concerned with acquisition, investment, and market analysis, with return-risk evaluation, with financing and refinancing, with tax planning, and with disposal or termination of the property. Although the investor may use an independent property manager to manage the property, control of the investment function should be retained by the managing equity investor.

SUMMARY

A marketability analysis is a micromarket study of the specific site and property being investigated for possible investment. Generally, marketability analysis requires the services of people who have technical qualifications beyond those of the typical equity investor.

The components of a marketability analysis include definition of the boundaries of the neighborhood, neighborhood analysis, site analysis, survey of the competition, identification and estimation of the market absorption and capture rates, revenue and associated expense forecasts, and development of a preliminary marketing strategy and management plan.

A careful, subjective analysis of the highest and best use of capital at the site must be made. To carry out such an analysis, the investor can use proprietary data retrieval computer services that generate economic-demographic trends for a chosen site. Although such data are essential, the dynamics of the urban environment are such that field surveys are also an essential part of a marketability analysis. Competitive surveys should be tailored to the type of site use contemplated and must analyze not only existing but also planned competition. Although the techniques for estimating market absorption and capture rates are still imprecise, the investor should ask the analyst for such data for the specific submarket. Capture rates should be stratified by user profile and limited to appropriate time and distance radii. The investor should also develop a preliminary marketing strategy and management plan so that decisions can be made about how the site will be used.

In conclusion, a real estate marketability analysis examines a specific property to assess its competitive position in the market, and estimates the amount of a specific real estate use that will be needed by the market, and at what price, within the forecast period. Much personal judgement enters into analyzing marketability because the techniques, concepts, and applications are not yet well developed, and because they deal with many complex variables over the uncertain future.

14

INFLATION, DEFLATION, AND REAL ESTATE CYCLES

THE WIZARD OF ID — By Parker

Inflation cycles were a strong underlying reason for the financial successes and failures of real estate investors in recent history. In the late 1970s and early 1980s, inflation dramatically increased rents and selling prices and, hence, the (nominal) rates of return of most existing properties. But inflation also dramatically increased interest rates, construction costs, and operating costs, and thus decreased the (nominal) rates of return for many new and some existing properties. High inflation rates created severe short-run solvency problems for many investors, although the long-run prospects for high returns were excellent if the short-run crises could be weathered. Disinflation followed, torpedoing expectations by depressing operating cash flows and sales prices of properties purchased at inflated prices, inflicting financial distress, and causing the investment rate of return to plummet.[1] In short, inflation cycles have a complex impact on real estate returns, risks, and investment values—an impact that should not be ignored or oversimplified.

Acknowledgment: The authors gratefully acknowledge the assistance of Waldo L. Born, Assistant Professor of Finance and Real Estate, College of Business, Eastern Illinois University, who co-authored this chapter.

[1]Inflation rate is the change in price level between periods. Inflation is characterized by increasing inflation rate, whereas disinflation is a decrease in inflation rate (price level still increasing). Deflation is a decrease in price level (negative inflation).

In earlier chapters the subjects of inflation and real estate cycles were treated only in a very broad sense. For example, Chapter 12 concluded with the point that market studies and marketability analysis must ultimately be translated into forecasts of cash inflows: sales and rent schedules, vacancy rates, absorption schedules, and the possible *variability* of these cash inflows. Inflation and real estate cycles have a dramatic effect on these variables and also on cash outflows, which the investor must recognize during investment analysis. The investor should also explicitly include inflation and cycle variables throughout the other steps of the ten-step investment analysis process.

FRAMEWORK FOR ANALYZING INFLATION AND CYCLES

This chapter develops a normative framework for incorporating inflation and inflation cycle variables into the real estate investment analysis and financial structuring process. The presentation of such a framework will include (1) identifying the important inflation and real estate cycle variables that influence investment returns and risks, (2) developing a basic understanding of the dynamics of inflation cycles, (3) suggesting a methodology for estimating inflation cycles and trends and their impact on investment variables, and (4) suggesting specific strategies for coping with inflation cycles. In addition to the effects of inflation, other types of cyclical impacts on real estate will be studied. International and national business cycles, construction and mortgage cycles, city and neighborhood cycles, and social change cycles are too often ignored or misinterpreted in investment analyses. Although they are difficult to analyze and estimate, these variables should be explicitly considered in the investor's cash flow projections and decision-making process.

Two major themes will evolve during this chapter. First, inflation and volatile real estate cycles will continue in the future. The cycles repeat periodically, and investors can take advantage of their ability to estimate these cycles to increase investment returns while decreasing risks. Second, timing is a key ingredient of successful investing.[2] As pointed out earlier, investors must be willing to make considerable changes in their portfolios over time in order to take advantage of constantly changing business and market conditions. Different assets will perform differently in the various stages of a real estate cycle. Thus, although there is no real estate asset for all seasons, there is a season for all real estate assets.

---

[2]Clayton P. Pritchett, "Forecasting the Impact of Real Estate Cycles on Investments," *Real Estate Review*, Winter 1984, pp. 85–89, discusses supply and demand cycles and strategies to use in real estate investment; Jack E. Harris and W. L. Born, *Real Estate Investment Timing*, Texas Real Estate Research Center Technical Report No. 502, College Station, Texas, 1985, and a modified version 1986, *Real Estate Review*, Summer 1986, pp. 79–83. The timing strategy presented is analogous to technical analysis of stock issues.

The Unanalyzed Factor

Several researchers have developed theoretical models to analyze the impact of inflation on asset values. Eugene Fama and William Schwert compared U.S. government bills, U.S. government bonds, real estate, human capital, and common stocks as hedges against inflation, and concluded that private residential real estate was the only asset that provided a complete hedge against both expected and unexpected inflation.[3] Analysis by other researchers supports the conclusion that real estate performed well during the 1950s, 1960s, and 1970s compared with financial assets.[4] Kenneth Lusht used a discounted-cash-flow, present-value model to demonstrate that the value of highly leveraged, nondepreciating assets benefited most from inflation.[5] Lewis Spellman analyzed the impact of inflation on the value of home ownership, with emphasis on the results created by changes in government policy (e.g., taxes and mortgage loan structure).[6]

Numerous articles and books address the subject of inflation's impact on real estate returns and values. As early as 1973, James Cooper and Stephen Pyhrr showed the impact of growth and inflation factors (rents, expenses, property values) on the investor's IRR on equity for various holding periods, loan terms, and depreciation methods.[7] Since then many

[3]Eugene F. Fama and G. William Schwert, "Asset Returns and Inflation," *Journal of Financial Economics*, November 1977, pp. 115–146.

[4]Paul F. Wendt and Sui N. Wong, "Investment Performance: Common Stocks versus Apartment Houses," *The Journal of Finance*, December 1965, pp. 633–646; R. Bruce Ricks, "Imputed Equity Returns on Real Estate Financed with Life Insurance Company Loans," *The Journal of Finance*, December 1969, pp. 921–937; James R. Webb and C. F. Sirmans, "Yields and Risk Measures for Real Estate," *The Journal of Portfolio Management*, Fall 1980, pp. 14–19; Thomas J. Coyne, Waldemar M. Goulet, and Mario J. Picconi, "Residential Real Estate versus Financial Assets," *The Journal of Portfolio Management*, Fall 1980, pp. 20–24; C. F. Sirmans and James R. Webb, "Investment Yields in the Money, Capital and Real Estate Markets: A Comparative Analysis for 1951–76," *The Real Estate Appraiser and Analyst*, November–December 1978, pp. 40–47, and a similar Sirmans and Webb article, "Yields on Commercial and Industrial Real Estate versus Other Assets," *Real Estate Issues*, Fall/Winter 1982, pp. 28–33; Dennis G. Kelleher, "How Real Estate Stacks Up to the S&P 500," *Real Estate Review*, Summer 1976, pp. 60–65; Roger G. Ibbotson and Laurence B. Siegel, "Real Estate Returns: A Comparison with Other Investments," *Journal of the American Real Estate and Urban Economics Association*, Fall 1984, pp. 219–242. Important results of other researchers have been summarized in Robert H. Zerbst and Barbara R. Cambon, "Real Estate: Historical Returns and Risks," *The Journal of Portfolio Management*, Spring 1984, pp. 5–20.

[5]Kenneth M. Lusht, "Inflation and Real Estate Investment Value," *Journal of the American Real Estate and Urban Economics Association*, Spring 1978, pp. 37–49.

[6]Lewis J. Spellman, "Inflation and Housing Prices," *Journal of the American Real Estate and Urban Economics Association*, Fall 1981, pp. 205–222; see also Douglas B. Diamond, "Taxes, Inflation, Speculation and the Cost of Home Ownership," *Journal of the American Real Estate and Urban Economics Association*, Fall 1980, pp. 281–298.

[7]James R. Cooper and Stephen A. Pyhrr, "Forecasting the Rates of Return on an Apartment Investment: A Case Study," *The Appraisal Journal*, July 1973, pp. 312–337.

real estate and corporate finance textbooks have incorporated discussions of inflation.[8] However, most of those discussions merely summarize and analyze historical data, treating in only a limited way the development of strategy and operational models for coping with inflationary effects.

In general, these authors place very little emphasis on real estate cycles.[9] There is almost no literature on how to develop a strategy that takes advantage of various types of real estate cycles; yet successful management of assets over various real estate cycles is the key to returns that are consistently above average. Unfortunately, most investors take a myopic view and capitalize the present situation into perpetuity when forecasting cash flows and making investment decisions. History has proved that such projections are more often wrong than right.

Perhaps the greatest competitive advantage for investors in the future will be gained by those who develop a systematic approach to incorporating inflation and other real estate cycle variables into their investment decision process.

Return–Risk Framework for Analyzing Inflation and Cycles

The impact of inflation and real estate cycles should be an explicit consideration in the investor's analysis of specific properties, as well as the entire investment portfolio. The investor must learn to understand the inflation and cyclical factors that influence the value of investments and the events that cause those factors to change. If the investor cannot develop such an understanding, his or her perceptions of the risks and returns involved are likely to be influenced greatly by the wrong media: the daily newspaper

---

[8]John McMahan, *Property Development—Effective Decision Making in Uncertain Times* (New York: McGraw-Hill, 1976), p. 83; Maury Seldin and Richard H. Swesnik, *Real Estate Investment Strategy* (New York: Wiley–Interscience, 1977), pp. 157–165; Paul F. Wendt and Alan R. Cerf, *Real Estate Investment Analysis and Taxation* (New York: McGraw-Hill, 1979), pp. 29–43; James C. Downs, *Principles of Real Estate Management* (Chicago: Institute of Real Estate Management, 1975), pp. 70–78, 113–117; Stephen E. Roulac, *Modern Real Estate Investment—An Institutional Approach* (San Francisco: Property Press, 1976), pp. 18, 82, 284; Sherman J. Maisel and Stephen E. Roulac, *Real Estate Investment and Finance* (New York: McGraw-Hill, 1976), pp. 181–183, 327–329; Michael Sumichrast and Maury Seldin, *Housing Markets* (Homewood, Ill.: Dow Jones–Irwin, 1977), pp. 157–165; Austin Jaffe and C. F. Sirmans, *Real Estate Investment Decision Making* (Englewood Cliffs, N.J.: Prentice-Hall, 1982), pp. 75–76; Eugene F. Brigham, *Financial Management Theory and Practice* (New York: Dryden Press, 1982), pp. 425–427; Thomas E. Copeland and J. Fred Westin, *Financial Theory and Corporate Policy* (Reading, Mass.: Addison–Wesley, 1983), pp. 61–65; Richard Brealey and Stewart Myers, *Principles of Corporate Finance* (New York: McGraw-Hill, 1981), pp. 448–454.

[9]Notable exceptions to this rule are provided by Downs, *Principles*, pp. 104–117. Also by Michael C. Halpin, *Profit Planning for Real Estate Development* (Homewood, Ill.: Dow Jones–Irwin, 1977), pp. 101–115; and Waldo L. Born, *A Framework and Model for the Analysis of Income-Producing Real Estate Investments under Cyclical Inflationary Conditions*, University Microfilms International, 1984, dissertation file No. 8421664.

headlines, the opinions of the six o'clock newscasters, and other highly subjective and shortsighted analyses. As a result, the investor is more likely to follow the crowd and buy and sell properties at precisely the wrong times.

The key to understanding how inflation and cyclical activity affect investment returns and risks is to understand how these macroeconomic variables interact to change the microeconomic real estate variables, namely, (1) property values; (2) rental income; (3) vacancies and credit losses; (4) operating expenses; (5) debt–equity financing alternatives, amounts, and terms; (6) the investor's required rate of return on investments; and (7) the overall market capitalization rate.[10] An understanding of interactions between macrovariables and microvariables includes knowledge of macrovariability sources, linkages to microvariables, and sensitivity of each microvariable to changes in each macrovariable. The knowledgeable investor can estimate values of these microvariables over time using conventional discounted-cash-flow analysis, sensitivity analysis, and risk analysis techniques. Thus, the investor can make investment decisions that will maximize returns relative to risk over time (i.e., maximize wealth). Furthermore, if estimates are made for a wide variety of real estate investments, as well as for non-real estate assets, the investor can begin to develop a strategy for shifting the portfolio to take advantage of cyclical developments.

It is our belief that economic history repeats itself.[11] Rapid inflation and volatile real estate conditions are frequent in the United States. High rates of inflation were characteristic of more than 20 percent of this century. Falling business activity has been almost as frequent, occurring in more than 15 percent of the period since the mid-nineteenth century. Although history never repeats itself exactly, most real estate and business factors have shown consistent patterns for centuries. The serious real estate investor should study these patterns and consult others who have experienced many years of real estate inflation cycles. The first step toward understanding the impact of inflation on future real estate returns and risks is to understand its history.

---

[10] Geoffrey H. Moore, *Business Cycles, Inflation, and Forecasting*, NBER Studies in Business Cycles, No. 24 (Cambridge, Mass.: Ballinger, 1983), is an excellent treatise on the linkage between macroeconomic and microeconomic factors. Also see Frank J. Fabozzi and Harry I. Greenfield, *The Handbook of Economic and Financial Measures* (Homewood, Ill.: Dow Jones–Irwin, 1984).

[11] The same line of reasoning is pursued by Beryl W. Sprinkel and Robert J. Genetski in *Winning with Money: A Guide for Your Future* (Homewood, Ill.: Dow Jones–Irwin, 1977), p. 248, and by Roger Klein and William Wolman, in *The Beat Inflation Strategy*, (New York: Simon & Schuster, 1975). The authors develop a series of policies and rules for winning at the inflation game, although very little emphasis is placed on real estate investment alternatives.

Measures of Inflation

Various statistical data on prices and inflation rates are available. Many of the aggregate data are collected and published by various federal, state, and local government agencies, or by industry trade associations like the International Council of Shopping Centers, Building Owners and Managers Association International, and the National Association of Realtors.

Measures of General Economic Inflation. Three commonly used measures of inflation (called series) are published by the federal government. The most comprehensive measure of the overall price level is the implicit price deflator (commonly known as the gross national product price deflator). This measure encompasses the behavior of prices paid by consumers, business, the government, and purchasers of U.S. exports. Less complete measures of inflation include the consumer price index (CPI), which tracks prices paid by consumers, and the producer price index (PPI). There is no single correct measure for inflation on which economists are agreed. Each measure covers a different scope of activity, and each is subject to various measurement problems and inaccuracies that bias the information it provides.

The consumer price index or some variation of it is the most common and most popular measure of inflation among investors. The CPI provides a monthly measure of the cost of goods and services purchased (expressed as an index with 1967 as the base year) by the "average urban American." It is based entirely on retail prices or imputed costs of goods and services to urban consumers obtained by a survey of over 60,000 respondents in eighty-five urban areas across the country. The Bureau of Labor Statistics (BLS) identified a fixed market basket of 382 items representing all goods and services purchased for everyday living by all urban residents, which are sampled, priced, and weighed to produce the index of consumer prices.[12] Indexes are published for the nation, for each of four regions, and for twenty-eight cities.[13]

The most pertinent CPI information for the investor is *percentage changes* in the CPI over time (see Exhibit 14-1). The annual *rate of inflation* is the comparative yardstick that is used to measure "real" returns

---

[12]U.S. Department of Labor, Bureau of Labor Statistics, *The Consumer Price Index: Concepts and Content over the Years,* Report 517 (revised) (Washington, D.C., May 1978); also see Bureau of Labor Statistics, *Handbook of Methods,* Bulletin number 2285, Chapter 19, April 1988. In January 1988, the base year for the CPI was changed from 1967 = 100 to 1982–1984 = 100. All references here to the CPI use the 1967 = 100 CPI series. For compatability, the two series must be spliced. The revised series may be obtained from the Prices and Living Conditions section of the Bureau of Labor Statistics.

[13]This information can be obtained directly from the current *CPI Detailed Report* (month, year), Bureau of Labor Statistics, U.S. Department of Labor (Washington, D.C.: U.S. Govt. Printing Office).

EXHIBIT 14-1. Consumer Price Inflation, Annual Rate: Four-Quarter Moving Average

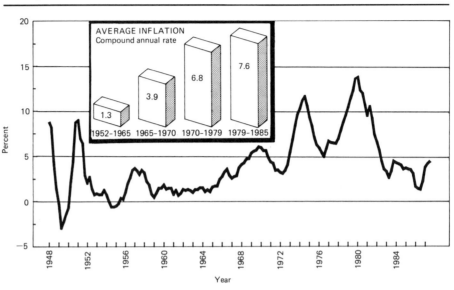

Source: Consumer price index, U.S. Department of Commerce, *Survey of Current Business.*

relative to "nominal" returns. However, some problems with the CPI should be recognized and understood. First, changes in prices may be accompanied by changes in quality of consumer goods and services. New products are introduced that bear little resemblance to products previously on the market. Direct comparison cannot be made. Second, the CPI represents the average movement of prices for the average urban wage earner but not necessarily in prices paid by any one family. In addition, the index is insensitive to changes in income and living standards. Third, the CPI measures only time-to-time price changes in a given area. City indexes do not show intercity difference in either price or living costs. The Bureau of Labor Statistics introduced an important improvement in the CPI in January 1983. The homeownership component was changed from an "asset" approach to a "flow-of-services" approach by employing a rental equivalence technique.

Measures of Real Estate Inflation. Real estate prices and values do not automatically move with the CPI. At best, the CPI gives the investor a general yardstick against which specific real estate inflation data can be compared. In many situations there is a low or negative correlation between the CPI and real estate values. Regional and local supply and demand forces often produce real estate prices and values that defy comparison with nationally based statistics like the CPI. For example, apartment rents in overbuilt metropolitan areas are not sensitive to changes in the prices of other goods in the short or medium run. The CPI may be increasing at 12 percent while landlords in such areas are lowering effective rents in order to increase occupancy and compete in the overbuilt market. Until the excess supply of units has been absorbed, there may be little or no relation between CPI movements and rent levels. Thus, local microeconomic factors can easily swamp macroeconomic factors.

Common Measurement Pitfalls. Investors are easily lured into making two mistakes when using published data. The first, mentioned earlier, is to assume that macroeconomic data apply directly to the micro situation. Usually much adjustment is necessary to develop project inflation rate and market assumptions from aggregate data series such as price, rent, and expense indexes. Certainly, *regional* and *city* data from the government-published series, if obtainable, would be far more appropriate (than national data) as a starting point for project cash flow projections.

The second classic mistake is to use *simple interest* rates of increase as a basis for projections that assume *compound interest* rate factors. Most builders of cash flow models use compound increase (decrease) factors for rents, expenses, and property values in their pro forma projections. Direct application of *ex post* trends (noncompounded) into the investor's *ex ante* model (assuming compounding of values) will seriously overstate (or understate) the cash flow returns and other financial data. This error is commonly observed in cash flow projections by students and practitioners alike. The obvious solution is to convert all inflation and growth data used in the analysis to a common statistical base. Frequently this requires the conversion of an index number to a compound interest number. For example, the CPI in January 1965 was 93.6, and twenty years later was 317.4, a 239 percent increase or an average annual increase of nearly 12 percent. But the compounded annual rate of change was only 6.3 percent. In another example, the purchase price of an existing single-family home increased by 96 percent from 1971 to 1980 (nine years). This is an average noncompounded annual increase of 10.6 percent. The compounded annual rate, however, is only 7.8 percent. Using 10.6 percent instead of 7.8 percent in a projection would lead to a substantial overstatement of investment return.

Real versus Nominal Returns. As with many aspects of life, the returns that an investor sees are not necessarily what he or she gets. Investors see nominal rates of return and interest rates, since these rates measure change in the dollar value of investments. But because of inflation (or deflation), dollar rates of return seldom reflect economic reality. Only *real* rates of interest (and return) measure real changes in an investor's economic well-being. Surprisingly, most investors never measure their real rates of return.

The classic work on the subject of real and nominal returns, Irving Fisher's *Theory of Interest,* was published in 1907.[14] According to Fisher, the relationship between nominal returns, real returns, and the expected inflation rate is approximately

$$\text{Nominal return} = \text{real return} + \text{inflation rate}$$

Using this equation, consider the plight of investors who held government savings bonds or invested money in savings accounts that yielded nominal interest rates of 5 to 6 percent in the late 1970s. With inflation rates of 10 to 13 percent, the real rates of return (before tax) were a negative 4 to 8 percent. In retrospect these were very poor investments.

The Fisher formula explains well the theory and concept of real versus nominal returns, but it is mathematically correct only in a simple-interest world. If the investor uses a compound-interest model (any discounted-cash-flow model), the formula must be adjusted as follows[15]:

$$\text{Real rate of return} = \frac{1 + \text{nominal rate}}{1 + \text{inflation rate}} - 1$$

For example, if a proposed office building investment was expected to yield an internal rate of return (IRR) of 18 percent annually over a five-year holding period and the investor expected the average annual inflation rate to be 10 percent (compounded) over the period, the real IRR would be 7.27 percent, computed as follows:

$$\text{Real rate of return} = \frac{1 + .18}{1 + .10} - 1 = 7.27\%$$

The investor will receive a real rate of return of 7.27 percent in addition to receiving a rate (10 percent) sufficient to compensate for losses in purchasing power attributable to price inflation.

The investor should use this measure of "real" rate of return for evaluating investment proposals or as a basis for establishing a required nominal rate of return. The formula can be rearranged to calculate the nominal rate of return (e.g., IRR after tax), given (1) the investor's required "real" rate of return (sufficient to compensate for the use of his or her money and the risks involved) and (2) the expected rate of inflation:

$$\text{Nominal rate of return} = (1 + \text{real rate})\,(1 + \text{inflation rate}) - 1$$

$$= \text{real rate} + \text{inflation rate}\,(1 + \text{real rate})$$

[14]Irving Fisher, *The Theory of Interest: As Determined by Impatience to Spend Income and Opportunity to Invest It* (New York: Macmillan Co., 1907), pp. 358–359.

[15]Frank K. Reilly, Raymond Marquardt, and Donald Price, "Real Estate as an Inflation Hedge," *Review of Business and Economic Research,* Spring 1977, p. 3. See also Thomas E. Copeland and J. Fred Weston, *Financial Theory and Corporate Policy* (Reading, Mass.: Addison–Wesley, 1980), p. 491, and Fisher, ibid.

If, for example, our office building investor desired a minimum *real* IRR of 12 percent, the required nominal IRR would be 23.2 percent [.12 + .10 (1 + .12)]. Investment proposals would not be acceptable unless the calculated IRR was 23.2 percent or greater.

IMPACT OF INFLATION ON INVESTORS AND PROPERTIES

Inflation does not necessarily destroy a nation, nor does it destroy investment opportunities. In fact, in many countries, price inflation that continues at a high rate is accompanied by a high savings rate, increasing productivity, a substantial rise in real economic output, and a rising standard of living for the average worker. Numerous researchers have concluded that other factors (e.g., investment and productivity) have a far more powerful effect on a country's growth rate than inflation.[16]

Winners and Losers

Although inflation may not by itself hurt a country or its investors in the aggregate, it does change the rules of the investment game and help determine who wins and who loses. Inflation may not destroy wealth or income, but it does redistribute it among competing elements through relative changes in asset prices. The winners receive the rewards of the redistribution, but largely at the expense of the losers. Successful investors learn to recognize inflation trends and to adjust their financial position so as to benefit from the redistribution.

During the 1970s inflation was generally higher than most equity investors and lenders expected. Certain types of investors and economic groups gained while others lost, as shown in Exhibit 14-2.

EXHIBIT 14-2.   Inflation's Impact in the 1970s

Winners	Losers
Borrowers	Lenders
Investors in real estate	Investors in financial assets
Skilled individuals and those with job mobility	Individuals on fixed incomes and those with no job mobility
Individuals employed in growth and high-technology industries	Individuals employed in mature and energy-inefficient industries
Government tax collectors	Most taxpayers and savers

---

[16]For examples, see Sprinkel and Genetski, *Winning with Money*, pp. 99–101. Also, Klein and Wolman, *Beat Inflation Strategy*, pp. 50–53.

Borrowers gain because they borrow money at interest rates that reflect inflation premiums which lenders underestimate. They pay off their debts with dollars that are worth less than was anticipated by the lenders. For each dollar gained by the borrower, a lender is losing a dollar. When the mathematics of this process are examined in the next section, this process is seen to reverse itself, which occurs when the inflation rate falls, and borrowers end up on the losing team. Two examples demonstrate the reversal process. Farm owners borrowed heavily during the early 1980s, using the inflated value of their agriculture land as collateral. The deflation in the mid-1980s and the drop in prices paid for agricultural produce reduced farm income and land values and loan collateral. The rate of foreclosure increased and forced many families off their property and out of farming. During the same period, inflated single-family home and commercial real estate values supported highly leveraged financing. When the local economies slackened, operating incomes were inadequate to cover debt service, and borrowers become delinquent in their payments. This chain of events led to foreclosures as lenders sought to cut their losses and eliminate non-performing loans from their books.

Empirical evidence shows that the prices of real and personal property (real estate, equipment, commodities, diamonds, gold, silver) increase during inflation while financial assets (currency, bank deposits, securities) lose value. Investors who have job mobility and are highly skilled are in a position to benefit from inflation, but those who are on fixed incomes and have little job mobility tend to lose. Similarly, there is a transfer of income and wealth from investors who work in industries and professions in which prices are rising more rapidly. Consequently, individuals employed in growth and high-technology industries do far better, on average, than individuals in mature and energy-inefficient industries. And finally, inflation raises nominal incomes and pushes more individuals into higher tax brackets, even if real incomes are declining. The beneficiary in this process is the government, which ends up with increased income and spending power at the expense of taxpayers and savers, in aggregate. Despite periodic "tax cutting" by the federal government, the percentage of personal income paid in federal taxes has climbed significantly over the last fifteen years.

The Economic Recovery Tax Act of 1981 indexed the federal government's tax rates to the benefit of taxpayers beginning in 1985. However, the government has changed the tax laws annually between 1981 and 1986, and indexing has been watered down. The Tax Reform Act of 1986 introduced considerable risk in the tax consequences of investment.

The Mathematics of Wealth Transfer

When the inflation rate increases, the prices of real assets increase. For example, as the inflation rate increased in the late 1970s and early 1980s, average home prices increased with (or exceeded) the inflation rate. However, the mortgage claim (a financial asset) against this real asset did not change in value, as long as the mortgage was not indexed to inflation in some way. The homeowner owes the same number of dollars, but these dollars purchase less for the lender. Consequently, the homeowner's net worth increases by the entire amount of the increase in asset value. In this manner inflation has worked to transfer wealth from the net monetary creditor, the mortgage lender, to the net monetary debtor, the homeowner.[17]

Investors who became wealthy during the 1970s maintained adequate cash reserves to protect against short-run liquidity problems, but invested a large proportion of their wealth in real property or other real assets (gold, diamonds, art, commodities, etc.). They kept up with inflation by purchasing assets and borrowing a large percentage of these invested funds from lenders who charged interest at rates that did not fully reflect inflation. The 1970s was a period in which lenders and equity investors underestimated the inflation rate. As a result, equity investors experienced windfall (unanticipated) gains at the expense of lenders, who experienced unanticipated losses. During the late 1970s and early 1980s, lenders began using indexed interest rates, shorter-term loans, and "equity kickers" or participations to hedge inflation, reducing the inflation-induced wealth transfer to borrowers.

The wealth transfer process works in reverse when inflation rates decrease (disinflation) after lenders have incorporated higher inflation expectations and premiums into the interest rates they charge. Disinflation in 1983–1986 tended to transfer wealth to lenders through periodic mortgage payments that were higher than the market rate. The wealth transfer process may not be evident in very strong or weak real estate markets in which supply and demand are in substantial disequilibrium and dominate the inflation effect. Furthermore, the process for new properties differs substantially from that for existing ones, as we will show later.

Impact on Leverage Strategy

The first key impact of inflation on real estate is rising interest rates. Changes in money and capital market expectations lag movements in inflation rates. Consequently, changes in interest rates lag both increases and decreases in inflation rate. High and volatile inflation leads to high and volatile interest rates. These effects are shown in Exhibit 14-3. *Real* interest rates are very low until lenders incorporate inflation expectations into *nominal* interest rates. Conversely, *real* interest rates are very high

---

[17]Rachel Balbach, "The Effects of Changes in Inflationary Expectations," *Review*, Federal Reserve Bank of St. Louis, April 1977.

EXHIBIT 14-3.   Consumer Price Inflation versus Conventional Mortgage Rates (Existing Home Purchases)

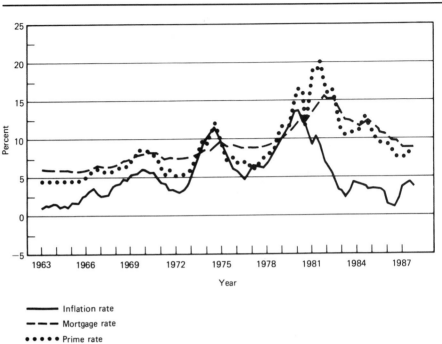

Source: Consumer price index, U.S. Department of Commerce, *Survey of Current Business.*

when inflation rates decline. Because real estate is generally a highly leveraged asset, small changes in financing conditions or terms have a substantial impact on project returns and risks.

Rising interest rates have several important effects on investors who seek an adequate return on their investment by building or purchasing existing real estate.[18]

1. *The amount of loan that can be supported by a project is reduced.* As more of a project's income stream must be used to pay for higher interest costs, the amount of loan must be reduced to compensate. In

[18]See Anthony Downs, "Interest Rate Rise Erodes Leverage and Appreciation," *The National Real Estate Investor,* September 1974, pp. 31, 98–99; also, Downs, "Inflation: A Two-Edged Sword for Realty Investors," *The National Real Estate Investor,* November 1974, pp. 31, 113; also, Richard D. Marshall, "Inflation Partially Negates Risk Position Yields," *Mortgage Banker,* December 1975, pp. 48–53.

addition, lenders tend to reduce the loan-to-value ratio that they will accept when interest rates are high, as a means of rationing funds and controlling risks. As a result, other things being equal, additional equity must be raised to finance a purchase, or the project must be rejected.

2. *There is more debt service and less cash flow.* Given a certain income stream from a property, more debt service to the lender means less cash flow to the equity investor. Not only is the return decreased, but the short-term risk is also increased as a result of the additional fixed financial obligation to the lender.

3. *Operating costs rise faster than rents.* Although operating costs have generally kept pace with inflation and increase immediately when inflation increases, rents tend to lag inflation and cause a profit squeeze for the investor. Rents are generally fixed by contract for various periods and prevent landlords from keeping up with cost increases by raising rents. For example, in real terms rents actually decreased from 1967 through 1980.[19]

4. *Construction loan costs soar.* Prime rates increase dramatically and raise the cost of construction. At the same time, high mortgage rates reduce the effective demand for real estate and tend to depress the prices people are willing (or can afford) to pay for real estate, as well as causing slower absorption rates for real estate in general.

These are primarily short-run effects, yet they can have a devastating impact on an acquisition or development program. In the long run, higher interest costs are like any other business cost and must be passed on to the consumer in the form of higher rents and asset prices. But it should be remembered that the short run must be survived before the long run can be reached.

Another indirect effect of high interest rates in the 1970s was to reduce the funds available for mortgage loans because of disintermediation. After 1979 the deregulations of depository institutions effectively eliminated the problem of disintermediation. By 1986 depository institutions had the tools necessary to match the duration of the lender's assets with the duration of liabilities on the balance sheet.[20]

Disinflation accompanied by a downturn in economic activity following an inflationary period may trap investors who earlier had employed high loan-to-value (L/V) ratios to financing real estate purchases. Furthermore, cash-rich lenders eager to originate loans had structured the debt

[19] *Real Estate Investing Newsletter,* November 1980, p. 1.

[20] Thomas E. Copeland and J. Fred Weston, *Financial Theory and Corporate Policy* (Reading, Mass.: Addison–Wesley, 1983), pp. 432–439; William W. Bartlett, "Duration and Immunization to Interest Rate Risk," *Executive Mortgage Report,* Bankers Research, Westport, Conn., February–March 1985, pp. 2–11.

repayment with "accommodating" debt coverage ratios (DCR) for borrowers. The combination of low DCR and high L/V ratios spelled disaster for investors who had falling revenues, falling property values, and insufficient reserves to refinance at more favorable terms.[21]

Theoretically an optimum L/V ratio exists for each inflation rate.[22] Assuming the traditional capital structure approach to capital budgeting and an interest rate on debt that increases as the L/V ratio increases, Exhibit 14-4 presents optimum L/V ratios for plus 4 percent inflation rate, zero inflation rate, and minus 4 percent inflation rate. The optimum L/V ratio is shown to be positively correlated with the inflation rate, assuming an interest rate on debt schedule (i) that does not shift upward when the inflation rate increases (as is the case with a fixed-rate mortgage). The optimal L/V ratio is that point where the weighted average cost of capital (ROI) is minimized and project value (v) is maximized.

Impact on New Properties

As a result of rapidly rising land and construction costs and rising interest and discount rates, the difference between project sales prices and total development costs becomes intolerably small and new development ceases or is significantly curtailed. Whereas higher construction and land costs may eventually be covered by higher sales prices and rental incomes, market prices do not respond immediately. Thus, the developer may have to survive an adjustment period until the market recovers and the product can be sold at a higher price. Unfortunately, with interim interest rates at a record high, holding costs increase and profitability declines rapidly.

In the early 1980s the growing availability of high-interest-rate savings deposits, coupled with deregulation of financial institutions, led lenders, especially thrift institutions, to make high-interest-rate (and high risk) loans for development, often at 100 percent loan-to-cost ratios. As a result, developers and builders could aggressively expand with no money at risk. A situation prevailed in which "as long as lenders lend, builders build and investors invest," regardless of project feasibility. Lenders had to lend aggressively to pay high interest rates on deposits and to "book" high rates of profit from the fees and points they charged borrowers. The lender's fundamental problem was one of poor evaluation of the risk and return potential of investment opportunities, coupled with greed. History recorded that in the 1982 to 1986 period many lenders were not good analysts or prudent underwriters.

[21]See Rocky Tarantello, "The Inflation Dependency of Leveraged Investments," *Real Estate Issues*, Fall–Winter 1985, pp. 7–12, for a more detailed discussion of the effects of cyclical inflation and a turbulent economy on financing and asset value.
[22]Born, *A Framework and Model*, pp. 122–127.

EXHIBIT 14-4.   Impact of Inflation and Leverage on Value: Traditional Capital Structure Approach

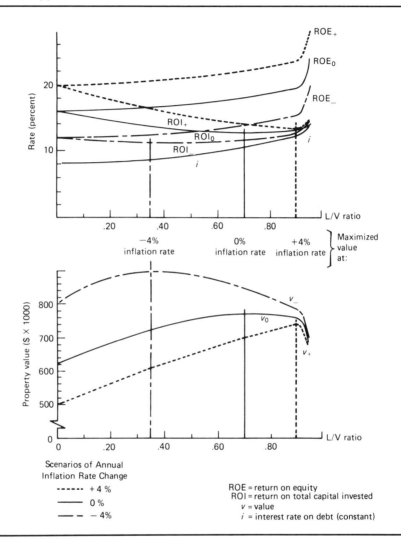

Scenarios of Annual
Inflation Rate Change

```
-------  + 4 %
————   0 %
— — — — 4%
```

ROE = return on equity
ROI = return on total capital invested
v = value
i = interest rate on debt (constant)

Impact on Existing Properties

Whereas high interest rates and decreasing new construction hurt builders and developers during years of high inflation rates, these years bring good times for owners of most existing properties. Decreasing construction starts reduces the supply of competing new products and, given a constant or rising demand for space resulting from population and income in-

---

EXHIBIT 14-5.   Effects of Inflation on Existing-Property Economics (10 Percent General Price Inflation)

CASE A: *Balanced supply and demand market:* vacancy = 5%; rental income increase = 10% annually; expense increase = 10% annually; capitalization rate = 10%.

CASE B: *Expanded demand over supply market resulting from unexpected inflation forces:* vacancy = 3%; rental income increase = 12% annually; expense increase = 10% annually; capitalization rate = 9%.

RESULTS:	TODAY	TWO YEARS LATER[a]	
	Base Case	Case A	Case B
Gross rental income	$100,000	$121,000	$125,440
Less: vacancy	− 5,000	− 6,050	− 3,763
Less: operating expenses	− 40,000	− 48,400	− 48,400
Net operating income	$ 55,000	$ 66,500	$ 73,277
Divided by: capitalization rate	÷.10	÷.10	÷.09
Market value of property	$550,000	$665,000	$814,187

[a]All increases in rents and expenses are compounded annually.

creases, vacancies decrease and rents are increased. In this situation, rent increases may keep up with inflation or often exceed the inflation rate. Subsequently, as long as expenses increase at the same rate or slower than rental income, the project's net operating income (NOI) will increase and property values will increase (assuming a constant or falling market capitalization rate).

The effects of the relationship of inflation rate, vacancy rate, and relative increases in rents and expenses are illustrated in Exhibit 14-5, assuming an overall inflation rate of 10 percent and two representative inflation situations. The point of departure is the base case, which assumes a gross possible income of $100,000, a vacancy rate of 5 percent, operating expenses of $40,000, and a capitalization rate of 10 percent, which is used to capitalize the NOI into an estimate of market value. Case A represents a marketplace in which supply and demand are balanced, vacancy remains at 5 percent, and rents and expenses keep up with the 10 percent rate of inflation. Case B represents the impact of a tight market caused by a rise in interest rates, reduced construction starts, and an increase of demand over supply. The vacancy rate drops to 3 percent over a two-year period; rents rise at 12 percent annually, and expenses increase at the 10 percent inflation rate. Investors shift their dollars away from the purchase of new properties and into existing properties, causing capitalization rates to fall from 10 to 9 percent.

In case A, the investor has increased the operating income by $11,500 over two years, and the property value has increased by $115,000. In case B, however, the income has increased by over $18,000 and property value has increased by over $264,000. Clearly, in case B the owner of the existing property, who has experienced these market shifts, has benefited from a windfall profit that was produced by unexpected inflation and decreasing construction starts. Many owners of existing properties benefited from these favorable market conditions during the 1978–1983 period.

Such increases in income stream and market value are not automatic, nor do they accrue to all owners of existing property in all cities. A number of factors affect the extent to which the owners of existing property enjoy rising operating income and property values during a period of high inflation rates like the one just described. Among the most important are the following.

1. *Strength of the real estate market.* Demand and purchasing power grow relative to the increase in supply. A very strong market would have significant pent-up demand; a market in equilibrium would have supply and demand increasing at about the same rate, while a weak market would have significant overbuilding or, simply, a supply of available space in excess of the demand.[23]

2. *Nature of lease contracts.* To take advantage of inflation pressures, owners do best by having short-term leases, in which rents can be increased frequently, or long-term leases indexed to the rate of inflation. Long-term leases with fixed rates, or short-term leases with options to renew at fixed rates, are usually undesirable and have an adverse impact on property values.

3. *Favorable financing rates and terms.* Owners who financed properties with high-leverage loans at fixed rates before high inflation premiums were included in the interest rate, and who can provide these favorable loans to the next buyer of a property, fare best. A seller who is willing to provide secondary financing to a buyer, where existing favorable loans can be assumed, can achieve the highest sale prices for property. Situations that require new financing have a negative impact on the selling price and marketability of the property.

The relationship between these factors and income property values during a period of price inflation can be viewed in Exhibit 14-6. The ideal situation for maximizing property values while minimizing inflation (pur-

[23]A comprehensive rating system for supply and demand factors for real estate markets throughout the country has been developed by Al Gobar, a California-based market analyst. See, for example, "Housing Demand Index, Fourth Quarter, 1980," *Housing,* October 1980, pp. 59–64.

EXHIBIT 14-6.   Key Factors Affecting Property Values and Inflation Risks

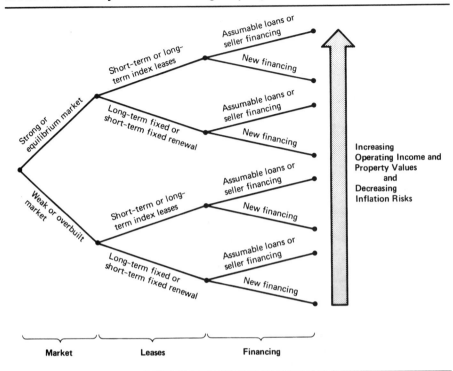

chasing power) risk is found in a very strong real estate market, with (1) short-term leases or long-term, inflation-indexed leases, or (2) favorable loans that are assumable, or (3) a seller who is willing to provide financing to the purchaser. In contrast, the most undesirable situation is found in a weak market, with long-term, fixed-rate leases (or short-term leases with fixed price renewals) and a selling situation that requires new financing at prevailing high interest rates. Although there are many exceptions to these general rules (e.g., in rent control situations), they do provide a guideline for understanding how inflation helps or hurts existing properties on a *relative* scale.

The ideal leasing and financing strategies during periods of disinflation or deflation for maximizing property values will be the poorest during periods of inflation. Long-term leases lock in higher lease terms as market rents decline. New financing takes advantage of reduced debt service payments as interest rates fall. An inflation cycle strategy will be a helpful tool for making decisions to shift from an inflationary posture to a deflationary situation. This strategy will be discussed in a following section.

Impact on Unimproved Land

It is important to distinguish between two types of unimproved land when inflation impacts are analyzed: (1) urban land that will be developed with improvements in the future, and (2) agricultural and forest land.

Urban Land. Inflation produces adverse short-run and positive long-run effects on well-located unimproved land in urban areas. In the short run, increasing construction costs and higher interest rates are quickly reflected in lower residual returns to developable land investments and in lower land prices.[24]

In the long run, however, if taxes and holding costs are a small percentage of profit when the land is finally developed, price appreciation can make the investment quite attractive.[25] The investor should consider that most types of land will not produce income until they are developed and that there are carrying costs as well as opportunity costs in holding a non-producing asset. Rapid appreciation of property value as a result of inflation pressures may not produce an attractive after-tax yield when all the costs and risks over the holding period are considered.[26]

Agricultural and Forest Land. Farm, ranch, and forest lands represent special types of investment in vacant land and have traditionally provided an excellent hedge against inflation. Exhibit 14-7 shows the relationship between the inflation rate and the increase in the average value per acre of farm real estate as reported by the U.S. Department of Agriculture. In every year from 1963 through 1980, except 1970 and 1971, the increase in land values exceeded the inflation rate. In numerous years the increase in land values more than doubled the rate of price inflation. Some land prices in specific states and regions increased at even more dramatic rates. From 1970 to 1977 the average price per acre of grain farmland in Iowa increased at an annual rate of 40 percent. After peaking in 1981, farm real estate values began a steep decline with the steepest drop occurring in 1985 and 1986.

Much farmland speculation by both Americans and foreigners took place during the 1970s, as investors shifted from financial to real assets as a hedge against inflation and foreigners sought to protect their wealth from political turmoil. As a result, gross income per acre increased at a much

[24]Paul F. Wendt, "Inflation and the Real Estate Investor," *The Appraisal Journal*, July 1977, p. 345.
   [25]Ben E. Laden, "The Impact of Inflation on the Investor," *Trusts and Estates*, January 1975, pp. 22–25.
   [26]See J. Bruce Lindeman, "Is the Land Boom Coming to an End?," *Real Estate Review*, Fall 1974.

EXHIBIT 14-7. Increases in Farm Real Estate Values Relative to Inflation

Year	Inflation Rate[a]	Annual Increase in Value[b]	Year	Inflation Rate[a]	Annual Increase in Value[b]
1963	1.2%	5.0%	1976	5.8%	13.7%
1964	1.3	6.6	1977	6.5	17.0
1965	1.7	5.5	1978	7.7	9.1
1966	2.9	7.8	1979	11.3	14.9
1967	2.9	7.3	1980	11.1	15.6
1968	4.2	6.8	1981	10.4	0.5
1969	5.4	5.6	1982	6.1	−4.3
1970	5.9	4.0	1983	3.2	−0.8
1971	4.3	4.3	1984	4.3	−13.2
1972	3.3	8.3	1985	3.6	−12.4
1973	6.2	13.0	1986	1.9	−7.9
1974	11.0	24.7	1987	3.7	2.9
1975	9.1	13.8			

[a]Calculated from annual percent change in the annual index CPI, adjusted annual rate, U.S. Department of Commerce, *Survey of Current Business.*

[b]Index number increases in average value per acre, U.S. Department of Agriculture, *Farm Real Estate Market Developments, Outlook, and Situation,* CD-80 series; then *Agricultural Land Values and Markets,* CD-90 series; followed by *Agricultural Resources: Agricultural Land Values and Markets Situation and Outlook Report.*

slower rate than land prices. This—combined with inflation-induced high operating costs and increased financing costs—caused severe cash flow problems for many farmers and ranchers. The disinflation that followed, plus reduced cash flow from agricultural produce, forced reductions in inflated land values. Over the long term, land prices must be supported by annual production yields adequate to cover operating costs, financing costs, and a profit to the operator.

Impact on the Homeowner

Exhibit 14-8 shows for each year the comparison between the annual inflation rate and increases in the median price of new and existing single-family homes. The primary years in which housing prices did not increase significantly faster than the inflation rate were the recession years of 1969–1970, 1974–1975, and 1980–1982. It can also be observed that new-home prices decline faster in bad years but increase faster in good years. Since new-home prices are a product of wide fluctuations in home construction activity each year, existing home prices are probably the best indicator of how most homeowners have fared. Even so, there are wide variations in prices in different parts of the country, in different seasons of

EXHIBIT 14-8. Percentage Increase in Prices of Single-Family Homes

Year	New Homes[a]	Existing Homes[b]	Inflation Rate[c]	Year	New Homes[a]	Existing Homes[b]	Inflation Rate[c]
1964	5.0%	n.a.	1.3%	1976	12.5%	7.9%	5.8%
1965	5.8	n.a.	1.7	1977	10.4	12.6	6.5
1966	7.0	n.a.	2.9	1978	14.1	13.5	7.7
1967	6.1	n.a.	2.9	1979	12.9	14.4	11.3
1968	8.8	n.a.	4.2	1980	2.7	11.7	13.5
1969	3.6	8.5%	5.4	1981	6.7	6.8	10.4
1970	− 8.6	5.5	5.9	1982	0.6	2.1	6.1
1971	7.7	7.8	4.3	1983	8.7	3.7	3.2
1972	9.5	7.7	3.3	1984	6.1	3.0	4.3
1973	17.8	8.2	6.2	1985	5.5	4.3	3.6
1974	10.5	10.7	11.0	1986	10.9	6.4	1.9
1975	9.5	10.3	9.1	1987	13.0	6.6	3.7

[a]*Median* price of new single-family residences, U.S. Department of Commerce, *Characteristics of New Housing,* Construction Reports, C25-(yr.)-(mo.).

[b]*Median* price of single-family homes, calculated from National Association of Realtors, Economics and Research Division, *Home Sales.* Data not available for years prior to 1969.

[c]Calculated from the annual percentage change in the annual index CPI, adjusted annual rate, U.S. Department of Commerce, *Survey of Current Business.*

the year, and in different neighborhoods within a particular MSA. The data shown can be used only as a very general guideline for the investor.

Studies have shown that owner-occupied homes have been a good financial investment and yielded a high after-tax rate of return on the equity capital invested.[27] For example, R. Bruce Ricks concluded that the typical Los Angeles homeowner would have realized an after-tax rate of return of 18.5 percent annually on an original equity investment of $6,000 over a ten-year holding period on a $26,500 home purchase in 1965. And this study was completed before rapid inflation rates came into play.

The average income property investor has also recognized the potential of the single-family home as a viable investment medium. Syndicators throughout the country have bought groups of single-family homes, have rented them, and have sold participation shares to equity investors. Single-family homes are said to be more marketable, are easier to finance, require relatively small down payments, and have more price growth potential compared with investment in other income properties, such as

[27]R. Bruce Ricks, "Managing the Best Financial Asset," *California Management Review,* Spring 1976. See also B. Jerrimad "The Best Real Estate Investment Ever?," *Real Estate Review,* Fall 1977, pp. 62–64, and Thomas P. Boehm and Joseph A. McKenzie, "Inflation, Taxes, and the Demand for Housing," *Journal of the American Real Estate and Urban Economics Association,* Spring 1982, pp. 25–38.

apartments, office buildings, and shopping centers.[28] However, such acquisitions have generally been accomplished in a fixed-rate mortgage market in which interest rates did not fully reflect the inflation rate. As discussed previously, the lenders have been the losers. If, however, the interest rate is increased to reflect fully higher rates of inflation, or the mortgage is indexed to inflation (e.g., through a variable-rate mortgage), the equity investor's benefits are decreased.[29]

Disinflation of the early and middle 1980s slowed the rise in the prices of housing.[30] In 1984, Douglas Diamond of HUD suggested that nearly all the inflation premium had been "wrung out" of housing prices in 1982 and 1983.[31]

Impact on Multifamily Income Properties

Apartments have had a turbulent history compared to single-family homes. Although many analysts have concluded that apartments have outperformed many other types of investment media over a long period,[32] other experts remind us that apartment investing is subject to wide cyclical fluctuations characterized by periods of overbuilding and underbuilding that are tied to construction cycles. In strong apartment markets prices rise faster than inflation, but during overbuilt periods prices rise slowly or actually decrease. Thus, the ability of an apartment investment to provide an inflation hedge depends to a substantial extent on the ownership period chosen relative to the apartment construction cycle.

During the period between 1977 and 1981, apartment construction was slow; the supply of existing apartments decreased as a result of condominium conversions; rents often rose faster than expenses, and market capitalization rates fell as more investors shifted to real estate assets. As a conse-

---

[28]A notable exception was the EPIC syndication operation, which collapsed in 1985 because of the inadequate performance of underlying properties, serious deficiencies in syndication structuring, and diversion of investment capital to investor payments. "EPIC Mess," *Wall Street Journal*, August 30, 1985, p. 1; "EPIC Was a Complex but a Lucrative Venture," *Wall Street Journal*, October 21, 1985, p. 6; "The Fast Buck Artist Is Alive and Well and Selling Dubious Investments," *Business Week*, December 30, 1985, pp. 143–144.

[29]For a discussion of the relative impact of inflation on lenders and equity investors, see David Rystrom, "Inflation and Real Estate Investment Value: A Comment"; also, Kenneth M. Lusht, "Inflation and Real Estate Investment Value: A Reply," *Journal of the American Real Estate and Urban Economics Association*, Winter 1980, pp. 395–403.

[30]John C. Weicher, "Disinflation and the Housing Market in the 1980's," *Real Estate Issues*, Fall–Winter 1984, pp. 6–14.

[31]Douglas B. Diamond, "The Impact of Inflation on New House Prices," *Contemporary Policy Issues*, May 1984, pp. 5–16.

[32]See, for example, the following studies: Paul F. Wendt and Sui N. Wong, "Investment Performance: Common Stocks versus Apartment Houses," *The Journal of Finance*, December 1965, pp. 633–646; Dennis G. Kelleher, "How Real Estate Stacks Up to the S&P 500," *Real Estate Review*, Summer 1976, pp. 60–65; Sheldon M. Blazar and Hugh G. Hilton, "Investment Opportunities in Existing Apartment Buildings," *Real Estate Review*, Summer 1976, pp. 47–52.

quence, price appreciation was exceptional, and investors who bought apartment properties after the real estate depression of 1974–1976 did exceptionally well, on average. In contrast, during the 1974–1976 period expenses increased rapidly through inflation and the impact of the energy crisis, a high rate of vacancies, and inability to raise rents until vacant units were absorbed. As a result, many investors became insolvent and distress sales and foreclosures were widespread.[33] A similar situation occurred during the recession of 1980–1982. In 1986–1988 sophisticated investors and syndicators formed "vulture funds" and took advantage of foreclosed properties in economically depressed metropolitan areas (e.g., Houston, Dallas, Tulsa, and Denver) by purchasing them at deep discounts and financing them on favorable terms at relatively low interest rates. Under these conditions of depressed rents and high vacancy rates, break-even or positive cash flow was still possible.

Many institutional investors and large syndicators have traditionally excluded apartment properties from consideration for two principal reasons. First, they view apartments as management-intensive. Second, they are afraid of the political effects of inflation on apartments. Landlords must raise rents frequently in order to cover higher operating expenses, rising interest rates, and higher loan amounts when properties are sold or refinanced. At the same time, inflation has been consistently outpacing the after-tax incomes of many tenants, who then protest by demanding rent controls and in many instances get them. Rent controls have been imposed in a number of large cities and urban counties, and even throughout whole states. Also, recent tax reform places increasing pressure for rent control in some cities as landlords raise rents to compensate for loss of tax shelter benefits.

As long as there is rapid inflation and renters outnumber landlords in local elections, rent control will be a definite long-run risk for apartment owners. In some nations, such as Brazil, which has experienced prolonged inflation, no developer builds residential rental property in the private sector of the economy. All new multifamily units are sold as condominiums.

Regardless of these management and political problems, institutional investors developed a renewed interest in apartment investments in the late 1980s as a result of decreasing yields on commercial properties, tax reform, and increasing pressures to diversify their portfolios and allocate increasing amounts of funds to all types of real estate investments.

Impact on Commercial Income Properties

Commercial income property, in the form of retail and shopping centers, office buildings, and industrial buildings, has been the focus of activity for

---

[33] A vivid account of the dynamics of the downside of the apartment cycle is provided in Howard W. Stevenson, "The Reason Behind the Real Estate Crash: A Case Study," *Real Estate Review*, Summer 1976, pp. 35–46.

major institutional investors and sophisticated individual investors. Such property is regarded as an excellent hedge against inflation and, in addition, avoids the management intensiveness and political problems associated with residential rental properties.

Shopping centers were especially popular in the 1970s and early 1980s because of their excellent and well-publicized financial track record with lenders (a very low foreclosure rate) and the rapid expansion in consumer sales experienced during this period. Even during periods of economic downturn and overbuilding of other types of property, the rate of new shopping center development has progressed steadily. Shopping center leases have been well indexed to inflation through percentage-of-sales rent clauses, so that as inflation has pushed up retail prices, the rental income (in established shopping centers) has increased immediately. In addition, shopping center investors and managers have been very successful in negotiating net lease contracts so that rising energy and other operating costs are passed directly on to tenants.

The demand for space in commercial income properties tends to be more sensitive to general business conditions and cycles than the demand for space in residential properties. Although consumers can easily delay purchases of new automobiles and durable goods, and businesses have less need for office and industrial space when economic activity declines, every family needs a place to live; new families are formed regardless of economic conditions.

The impact of inflation on investors and properties is the result of macroeconomic factors—factors that affect economic activity throughout the nation. However, microeconomic factors in a region or market area can be strong enough to swamp macroeconomic factor effects. The strength of the Sunbelt economy in the late 1970s and early 1980s is an example. However, the impact of plunging world oil prices in the mid-1980s reduced the strength of microeconomic factors in petroleum-based economy states, undermining the effects of the beneficial macroeconomic factors of reduced inflation and lower interest rates.

The United States is an integral part of a world market. Interest rates affect the currency exchange rates, which affect trade and investment. The U.S. economy is sensitive to the economic health of major foreign countries, in particular the economic health of its European and Asian trading partners. Consequently, the cause of macroeconomic and microeconomic changes affecting investors and properties in the future will increasingly be traced to world market economic and political forces and should be carefully considered by the investor.

INFLATION CYCLES AND INVESTMENT STRATEGY

The discussion so far has focused on rising inflation rates and their impact on investors and properties, addressing both a short-term rise in inflation rates and its impact on new and existing properties, and the long-term effects of a rising inflation rate on property values and rates of return. A closer examination of inflation data (Exhibit 14-1) reveals the presence of short-term cycles around a rising long-term trend line. This distinction has important strategy implications, which should be examined.

A history of inflation provides the investor with a framework for understanding the relevance of short-term cycles and long-term inflation trends. For example, there were four (short-term) inflation cycles from 1964 through 1981, although the long-term inflation trend line reveals an increase in the average inflation rate from about 2 to 10 percent.

1. Second quarter 1964–first quarter 1967. The acceleration phase of the cycle lasted about two years, and the deceleration phase lasted about one year.

2. First quarter 1967–first quarter 1972. The acceleration phase lasted almost three full years and the deceleration almost two years.

3. First quarter 1972–second quarter 1976. The acceleration phase of the third cycle lasted almost three years and reached double-digit figures in the fourth quarter of 1973. The deceleration phase occurred during 1975 and early 1976.

4. Second quarter 1976–fourth quarter 1982. In the most recent cycle inflation increased from 1976 to 1979 and peaked at the end of 1979. The deceleration phase occurred during the three-year period lasting through 1982.

By the end of 1983, the federal government was successful in reducing inflation; however, government expenditures were not controlled and deficits continued to increase. Reduced inflation depressed interest rates, reducing the cost of government debt financing. The short-term effect was aided by the Federal Reserve easing of credit restraints, which increased personal spending and consumption. Difficulty with fiscal policy measures cast doubt on the long-term trend of savings rates, money supply growth, productivity, and inflation. Since 1970 fiscal policy has been volatile, producing volatile inflation and interest rates. Although the 1970s were a period in which investors consistently underestimated inflation rates, the 1980s have been a period in which investors consistently underestimated the cyclical volatility of inflation rates in their analysis of real estate investments.[34]

An Inflation Cycle Strategy

Changes in the inflation rate will affect the relative prices of real and financial assets, as noted previously. Generally, in periods of rising inflation

[34] A. Steven Holland, "Does Higher Inflation Lead to More Uncertain Inflation?" *Review*, Federal Reserve Bank of St. Louis, February 1984, pp. 15–26; Jack L. Carr and Lawrence B. Smith, "Housing Finance Contracts and the Nonneutrality of Inflation," *Housing Finance Review*, January 1984, pp. 39–49.

rates real assets are the star performers, but financial assets like stocks and mortgages are the relatively best performers during a period of falling inflation rates. As a result, an investment strategy should dictate various portfolio changes over time. To understand why the portfolio should change, we must first analyze the dynamics of the inflation cycle itself.

Exhibit 14-9 illustrates the various stages that might make up a hypothetical inflation cycle. At each point of the cycle changes are taking place in the economy, and the investor should be making shifts in his or her investment portfolio in order to maximize wealth. The conservative investor will base investment strategy on the long-term trend line rate of inflation, whereas the aggressive investor will shift some or all of the portfolio to take advantage of accelerating and decelerating rates of inflation.

Klein and Wolman advocate a relatively simple and straightforward strategy for benefiting from inflation cycles.[35] Their major tenet is that the prices of real assets, such as commodities and gold, rise when the prices of financial assets, such as stocks and bonds, fall—and vice versa. (They did not consider real estate.)

The investor's general rule is to concentrate on investments whose prices are out of line with the expected long-term inflation trend. Exhibit 14-9 presents four points on a hypothetical inflation cycle and the investment rules that might be applied.

Point A. The actual inflation rate is still increasing but is near its peak and well above the long-term trend line rate. The stock market is depressed, interest rates are high, and bond prices are at an all-time low. Investors have been shifting into real assets for some time (the masses are jumping on the inflation bandwagon) and have bid these prices up. At this stage of the cycle the investor should sell real assets and buy short-term money market instruments. He or she should be prepared to shift into financial assets such as stocks and bonds.

Point B. The inflation rate is still above the long-term trend line rate but is decreasing. The investor has completely liquidated real assets and is selling short-term money market instruments and investing in a portfolio of stocks and bonds in order to take advantage of the falling inflation rates that will prevail in the deceleration stage. As inflation rates fall, interest rates will decline, bond prices will increase, and the stock market will revive as profit expectations increase.

Point C. The inflation rate is below the trend rate and is beginning to bottom out. The process now reverses itself. The investor is selling stocks and bonds and investing in liquid assets, and preparing to reinvest in real assets, which will ride the upward swing of the inflation cycle.

---

[35]Klein and Wolman, *Beat Inflation Strategy*, p. 162. The examples given do not include real estate alternatives. The emphasis is placed only on bonds, stocks, commodities, and foreign currencies as investment media.

EXHIBIT 14-9.   Stages of the Inflation Cycle

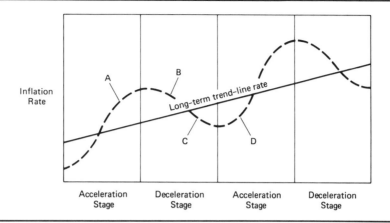

PoINT D. The inflation rate is in the initial stages of acceleration. The investor has liquidated all the stocks and bonds and is converting the liquid assets to real assets, such as commodities and gold.

For the real estate investor, this strategy may be of limited use. Because real estate assets are illiquid and transaction costs are high, rapid trading of assets is often not technically possible or financially feasible. Although some of the real estate portfolio can be shifted over the inflation cycle, many investors prefer to develop a strategy that primarily takes advantage of the long-term trend line of inflation. As long as the long-term trend line slopes upward, the portion of the portfolio in real estate investment increases. When the trend line shifts, or is expected to shift, downward, real estate investments are removed from the investment portfolio. Most real estate acquisition would logically take place between points C and D of the cycle, when interest rates are low, and expectations of low inflation rates result in lower asset prices. On the other hand, when the long-term trend line turns downward, most of the sales would logically take place between points A and B, when expectations of high inflation rates are incorporated into optimistic cash flow forecasts and cause values and prices of assets to rise.

The real estate investor can therefore use both the long-term trend line and short-term inflation cycle data as the bases of an investment strategy. The trend line projection causes shifts in the ideal mix of real estate and other assets in the portfolio and inflation cycle projections are used to implement the actual changes desired. Thus, correct timing in managing a real estate portfolio can be a product of both long-term trend line analysis and shorter-term inflation cycle analysis. As explained later in this chapter, this strategy does not assume that an investor is clairvoyant and can forecast inflation rates with a high degree of accuracy. However, it is assumed that investors will be knowledgeable and can evaluate inflation risks and develop rational inflation scenarios for real estate investment performance analysis.

Performance of Real versus Financial Assets. The inflation strategy just described is based on the assumptions that (1) volatile inflation cycles will continue and (2) financial asset prices and returns are negatively correlated with the inflation rate. The evidence presented by numerous researchers supports the thesis of a negative relationship between the returns on common stocks and inflation, and a positive relationship between inflation and real estate values (e.g., the value of farmland and private residential real estate, for which there are relatively good historical data).[36] However, the evidence does not clearly support the thesis that all types of financial assets do well in periods of moderate inflation or that all types of real assets do poorly in periods of moderate inflation.

Many investors will choose to remain fully invested in real estate assets over all phases of the inflation cycle. If such a strategy is adopted, the investor should seek property types and locations that will perform relatively well over the downward swing of the inflation cycle. Acquisitions should also be structured to benefit from this phase of the cycle. For example, an acquisition might be financed with a variable-rate mortgage that calls for a reduction in the interest rate and debt service when market interest rates fall as a result of lower inflation rate expectations. When the debt service declines, the investor will experience an increased cash flow and a higher investment value, other factors remaining constant.

---

[36] Fama and Schwert, "Asset Returns and Inflation"; John Lintner, "Inflation and Security Returns," *The Journal of Finance*, May 1975, pp. 259–280; Jeffrey Jaffe and Gershon Mandelker, "The 'Fisher Effect' for Risky Assets: An Empirical Investigation," *The Journal of Finance*, May 1976, pp. 447–458; Zvi Body, "Common Stocks as a Hedge against Inflation," *The Journal of Finance*, May 1976, pp. 459–470; Charles R. Nelson, "Inflation and Rates of Return on Common Stocks," *Journal of Finance*, May 1976, pp. 471–483; Reilly, Marquardt, and Price, "Real Estate as an Inflation Hedge"; Howard M. Kaplan, "Farmland as a Portfolio Investment," *The Journal of Portfolio Management*, Winter 1985, pp. 73–78; Roger G. Ibbotson, Laurence B. Siegel and Kathryn S. Love, "World Wealth: Market Values and Returns," *The Journal of Portfolio Management*, Fall 1985, pp. 4–23, Theodore E. Day, "Real Stock Returns and Inflation," *The Journal of Finance*, June 1984, pp. 493–502; H. Russel Fogler, Michael R. Granito, and Laurence R. Smith, "A Theoretical Analysis of Real Estate Returns," *The Journal of Finance*, July 1985, pp. 711–721; H. Russel Fogler, "20% in Real Estate: Can Theory Justify It?," *The Journal of Portfolio Management*, Winter 1984, pp. 6–13; Richard W. Kopcke and Peter C. Aldrich, "A Real Estate Crisis: Averted or Just Postponed?," *The Journal of Portfolio Management*, Spring 1984, pp. 21–29.

A Capital-Budgeting Approach to Inflation Cycle Strategy

A capital-budgeting approach can be used in carrying out the inflation cycle strategy presented in the last section. Theoretically, the use of present-value or internal-rate-of-return models would enable an investor to identify points A, B, C, and D on the inflation cycle. The investor must first complete three steps in analyzing each investment alternative.

1. Project inflation trend and cycle scenarios.
2. Estimate the impact of inflation on project income, expenses, property value, required rate of return (hurdle rate), and financing for each scenario over the projected holding period.
3. Use an NPV or IRR model to process the data, and apply sensitivity and risk analyses to incorporate the impact of alternate possible economic scenarios and arrive at an acceptable composite measure of return and risk.

The capital-budgeting model should be rejecting many real estate alternatives between points A and B and accepting them between points C and D, and vice versa for many financial assets, if the cycle strategy presented is indeed correct. Stated simply, as point A is approached, the expected IRR on a real estate project should be falling relative to the required IRR (NPV approaches zero). At point A they should be equal (NPV = 0), and between points B and C the expected IRR should be less than the required IRR (NPV < 0). The reverse should occur at the bottom of the inflation cycle.

A Framework for Projecting Inflation. The impact of inflation must be analyzed on several levels before it can be translated into estimates of changes in project rents, expenses, property value, and required rates of return, as shown in Exhibit 14-10. The investor begins with estimates of inflation at the national level.[37] Inflation is a macroeconomic variable; however, the amount at the regional or city level may be somewhat different from that reported on a national level. The international political and economic environment and national fiscal and monetary policy affect inflation expectations. The analysis of inflation and financing variables moves from national to region, city, and neighborhood estimates. The analysis of neighborhood historical rents, expenses, property values, and capitalization rates are compared with inflation to reveal the inflation sensitivity of each cash flow variable. Assumptions about the future should generate inflation scenarios falling between two rational bounds: the high-

---

[37]John A. Tatom, "Two Views of the Effects of Government Budget Deficits in the 1980's," *Review*, Federal Reserve Bank of St. Louis, October 1985, pp. 5–16.

EXHIBIT 14-10.   Framework for Predicting Impact of Inflation

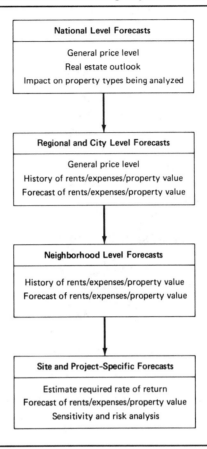

est expected inflation and the lowest. Finally, all the information analyzed must lead to a project-specific set of financial assumptions. The bottom line, and the most important part of the process, is an estimate of an inflation-adjusted required rate of return, plus forecasts of rents, expenses, and property value. Sensitivity and risk analysis techniques are used to test various possible inflation scenarios on the project's return and risk parameters.

The translation of national inflation trends and expectations into project-specific assumptions is difficult because price inflation is only one of many important supply and demand factors affecting a project's rent, expenses, and property value over time. Inflation analysis must be considered and structured as an integral part of the market and marketability analysis process described in the previous chapters if realistic input assumptions are to be estimated.

Mathematically Estimating the Impact of Inflation on Project Variables

There are two types of variables in a discounted-cash-flow framework: dollar-denominated and rate variables. Dollar-denominated variables are adjusted when the inflation rate is different from zero. Rate variables change only when the inflation rate changes. Dollar-denominated variables are gross possible income, operating expenses, and property sales price, and the amount of debt and equity required for property acquisition. The annual growth rates of gross possible income, operating expenses, and property sales price are related to dollar-denominated variables. The rate variables are interest rate, the investor's discount rate (required IRR), expected IRR, gross income multiplier, and overall capitalization rate.

The inflation rate is related mathematically to each of the cash flow variables through a unique inflation sensitivity measure.[38] The inflation sensitivity of the cash flow variables (specifically, gross possible income, operating expenses, gross income multipliers, overall capitalization rate, and property sales price) can be determined by comparing historical values of each cash flow variable with inflation. The effect of cyclical inflation on each cash flow variable may lead, be concurrent with, or lag the change in inflation. Intuitively, it is expected that changes in gross possible income caused by inflation will lag inflation changes, whereas changes in operating expenses, gross income multiplier, overall capitalization rate, and property sales price will be concurrent with inflation change. Changes in gross possible income, operating expenses, gross income multiplier, and property sales price are expected to be positively correlated with inflation change. However, change in overall capitalization rate is expected to be negatively correlated with inflation change. The correlation is negative be-

---

[38]The inflation sensitivity measure is the coefficient of the independent variable in a linear relationship between the cash flow variable (the dependent variable) and the inflation rate or price level (the independent variable),

$$y_t = \hat{\alpha} + \hat{\gamma} I_t$$

where y_t = cash flow variable

$\hat{\alpha}$ = constant term

$\hat{\gamma}$ = inflation sensitivity measure

I_t = inflation rate (price level)

When the dependent variable and the inflation rate (price level) are transformed by the natural log, the $\hat{\gamma}$ is the inflation elasticity of the dependent variable.

cause investors have incorporated expected changes in future income into the property sales price, although current net operating income has not changed to that extent. Changes in inflation rate influence interest rates and the IRR concurrently through the Fisher effect.[39]

Discounted-Cash-Flow Model Analysis. Since cyclical inflation scenarios can be developed and related to each cash flow variable separate from microeconomic effects in the local marketplace, estimation of future cash flow variable values can be made assuming inflation will be unchanged over the project holding period. This technique of separating the macroeconomic effects from the microeconomic effects simplifies future cash flow variable estimations.

An example will demonstrate the application of separating these effects. The current-year inflation rate is 4 percent and is assumed to be constant while evaluating microeconomic market supply and demand influences on cash flow variables throughout the investment holding period. Market analysis indicates that the gross rental income schedule will be

Year 1: $100,000
Year 2: $125,000
Year 3: $145,000
Year 4: $135,000 and so on

Remaining cash flow variables in the DCF model are evaluated over the holding period, using the assumed inflation rate of 4 percent. With these projected values for all cash flow variables, inflation cycle scenarios can be developed reflecting optimistic, pessimistic, and most likely economic conditions. Each inflation scenario is then used to adjust cash flow variables through several mathematic relationships.

The mathematical relationships between inflation and cash flow variables can be represented by four adjustment processes. For dollar-denominated variables, the adjustment is

$$CF_t = CF_{t-1}(1 + cf_t)(1 + \gamma_{cf}^t \, INF_{t+\lambda})$$

where CF = dollar-denominated cash flow variable
t = year, $t = 1, 2, \ldots, n$
cf = cash flow variable growth rate in period t caused by microeconomic factors
γ_{cf}^t = inflation sensitivity of dollar-denominated cash flow variable in period t

---

[39] The inflation sensitivity of these rates is $+1$; a one percent change in inflation rate causes approximately a one percent change in the interest rate.

INF_t = inflation rate in period t

λ = lead or lag; λ = . . . , $-2, -1, 0, 1, 2,$ . . . (years)

This adjustment procedure is applied to gross possible income, operating expenses, and property sales price.

The adjustment for gross income multiplier (GIM) and overall capitalization rate (OAR) is

$$R_t^{adj} = R_t^{unadj}\left(1 + \gamma_R^t\left\{\left[\frac{1 + INF_{t+\lambda}}{1 + INF_{t+\lambda-1}}\right] - 1\right\}\right)$$

where R_t^{adj} = GIM or OAR inflation-adjusted in period t

R_t^{unadj} = GIM or OAR before inflation adjustment

γ_R^t = inflation sensitivity of GIM or OAR in period t

The portion of the equation between { } is the change in inflation rate between period $t - 1$ and period t.

The inflation adjustment of market interest rate variables is

$$\text{Adjusted } r_t = (1 + r_{t-1})\left[\frac{1 + INF_{t+\lambda}}{1 + INF_{t+\lambda-1}}\right] - 1$$

where r = effective annual mortgage interest rate, or short-term borrowing rate on a line of credit, or reinvestment rate on invested annual cash flows. The r is unique to each application.

The inflation adjustment of the investor rate-of-return variable (r_1^d is the discount rate in the first period) is

$r_1^d = r^d$

$r_2^d = (1 + r_1^d)(1 + DINF_2) - 1$

$r_3^d = (1 + r_2^d)(1 + DINF_3) - 1 = (1 + r_1^d)(1 + DINF_2)(1 + DINF_3) - 1$

and in general,

$$r_t^d = \left[(1 + r_1^d)\prod_{j=2}^{t}(1 + DINF_j)\right] - 1$$

where $(1 + DINF_j) = \left[\dfrac{1 + INF_j}{1 + INF_{j-1}}\right]$

The average inflation-adjusted discount rate over the holding period of n years is

$$r^d = [(1 + r_1^d)(1 + r_2^d) \ldots (1 + r_n^d)]^{1/n} - 1$$

One final procedure is required for DCF analysis, the annual discounting procedure. After the annual cash flows have been adjusted for inflation in each year $t = 1, 2, \ldots, n$, and reinvested at an annually adjusted reinvestment rate, CF_n is the inflation-adjusted sum of the annuity plus the property reversion at the end of the holding period. CF_n must be discounted one year at a time from $t = n$ to $t = 0$, using the applicable r_t^d for each year.

Before the mathematical relationships given are applied, inflation sensitivities for cash flow variables are determined using historical data. Applying the inflation adjustments to cash flow variables in the DCF framework (PV or IRR model) provides the decision maker with purchasing power risk-adjusted investment return measures.

Sources of Information and Data. The appendix following this chapter lists the many sources of essential data for real estate investors, and from whom they can be obtained. At the national level, the most important sources of information on inflation are the major metropolitan banks and the Federal Reserve Bank of St. Louis. The Federal Reserve Bank of St. Louis has led the way in compiling useful data and analyses on monetary growth rates, short- and long-term interest rates, and growth in output and asset prices. Especially useful are its free publications, *Monetary Trends, U.S. Financial Data, Review,* and *Annual U.S. Economic Data,* which can be obtained by writing to the Federal Reserve Bank and requesting them.[40] Magazines like *Business Week* and *National Real Estate Investor* and monthly newsletters like *Real Estate Investing Letter* and *The Mortgage and Real Estate Executives Report* also contain many articles and ideas on inflation and its many effects on real estate investments by property type, location, and so forth.

At the regional and city levels, published information is disseminated by state, county, and city departments and agencies; by the business research departments of universities and local councils of government and state planning commissions; and by industrial development commissions and agencies.

In the private sector, state and local realtor organizations, banks, savings and loan associations, and land title companies and associations publish newsletters and information reports that are available to investors. Many of the researchers and writers for these organizations can be contacted directly and consulted for various inflation-related information that does not appear in the published documents.

At the neighborhood and project-specific levels, investors must often rely on individual contacts with real estate consultants, brokers, appraisers, and property managers who are intimately familiar with the history

---

[40]Major metropolitan banks employ staff economists who conduct research in international, national, regional, and local markets. Banks generally share results of their economic analyses with their customers and others as a means of expanding business.

and trends of properties comparable to the property being analyzed, and who collect data on individual properties. Without data and information from these individuals on project-specific trends in rents, expenses, vacancies, and property values, accurate projections for a property being analyzed are difficult to make.

OTHER REAL ESTATE CYCLES

The most important cycle affecting real estate investors in recent years has been the inflation cycle. However, from the individual investor's point of view many other cycles significantly affect rental income, vacancies, expenses, property values, and the cost and availability of mortgage financing. Homer Hoyt provided an early discussion of real estate cycle factors.[41] Later Alfred Ring and Jerome Dasso presented a concise description of the impact of supply and demand dynamics on real estate cycles.[42] Some of these cycles are closely related to inflation; others are not. Some are related primarily to new properties; others tend to affect existing properties. Some are not very important for investors operating on a national scale but are critical for individual investors operating in only one or a few local market areas.

The following section discusses the various types of cycles that can affect the investor, beginning with the macroeconomic cycles and working toward the microeconomic location- and property-oriented cycles. For making particular investment decisions, the local cycles are generally the most critical ones and therefore deserve the most attention from the investor.

The Macro Real Estate Cycle

Long Cycles. The most general form of real estate cycle that is of interest to historians and some investors is called the long cycle and is based on total real estate transactions or sales recorded in real estate markets throughout the United States. Roy Wenzlick, publisher of a famous but now defunct journal, *The Real Estate Analyst,* charted long cycles from 1795 through 1973 (when his publication was sold). In *The Coming Boom in Real Estate,* Wenzlick pointed out that the average duration of the long

---

[41] Homer Hoyt, "The Urban Real Estate Cycle—Performance and Prospects," *Technical Bulletin No. 35,* (Washington, D.C.: Urban Land Institute, 1960), pp. 8–16.
[42] Alfred A. Ring and Jerome Dasso, *Real Estate Principles and Practices* (Englewood Cliffs, N.J.: Prentice–Hall, 1977), pp. 50–56.

EXHIBIT 14-11.   The 18⅓-Year Real Estate Cycle, 1795–1973

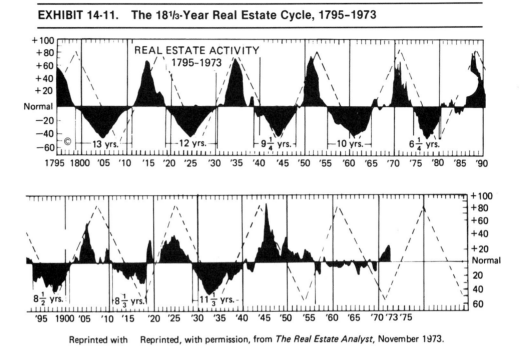

Reprinted with   Reprinted, with permission, from *The Real Estate Analyst*, November 1973.

Source: The Real Estate Analyst, November 1973. Reprinted with permission.

cycle from peak to peak (or trough to trough) averaged 18¹/₃ years.[43] Exhibit 14-11 shows Wenzlick's index, which was based on the number of voluntary transfers of property in relation to the number of families.

A similar long cycle of real estate activity was charted by Fred Case for Los Angeles County from 1850 to 1972.[44] Case's real estate cycle is a report of deed recordings per 1000 population in Los Angeles County. On average, the Los Angeles real estate cycles were found to occur every eighteen to twenty years, with a statistical average of 18²/₃ years. However, the cycles were longer or shorter on many occasions, and such deviations ap-

[43]Alan Rabinowitz, *The Real Estate Gamble* (New York: AMACOM—A Division of American Management Association, 1980), p. 238.

[44]Fred E. Case, *Real Estate Economics: A Systematic Introduction* (Los Angeles: California Association of Realtors, 1974), pp. 102–105. Also see Gordon T. Brown, "Real Estate Cycles Alter the Valuation Perspective," *The Appraisal Journal*, October 1984, pp. 539–549. William C. Wheaton, in "The Cyclic Behavior of the National Office Market," *Journal of the American Real Estate and Urban Economics Association*, Winter 1987, pp. 281–299, reviewed the post-World War I data on national office building construction and vacancy, revealing a ten- to twelve-year cycle.

peared to be tied to important historical events, such as wars, depressions, and major technological innovations like the automobile and railroads. Admittedly, since such historical events are difficult to predict, and since they disrupt the cycle for many years, precise forecasting methods are difficult to develop.

Short Cycles. In contrast to long cycles, short cycles last up to five years and are caused by shifts in the money markets, the availability of mortgage funds, and government housing programs like FHA and VA.[45] In his book on real estate cycles, Alan Rabinowitz notes that most attempts to involve the general public in income-producing real estate ventures (through security offerings) have been a failure and have resulted in five-year cycles of market acceptability. The examples cited are 1926–1931 for the sale of guaranteed mortgages, 1952–1957 for the great days of urban redevelopment finance, 1957–1962 for the first wave of publicly offered syndicate shares, 1960–1965 for the early land development securities, 1965–1970 for interest by big business in land development, and 1968–1974 for the Section 236 syndicates, REITs, and new communities.[46] A more recent cycle, the agressive tax shelter programs of 1981–1986, ended with the passage of the 1986 Tax Reform Act.

The Causes and Dynamics of a Real Estate Cycle

A real estate cycle is caused by shifts in supply and demand. Exhibit 14-12 shows the important relationships between the supply and demand forces that affect real estate activities. It is critical that investors understand the flow and sequence of these activities if they hope to understand the dynamics of the real estate cycle and learn how to cope with it. To that end, it will be useful to set out the various stages of a real estate cycle and follow through a typical sequence of activities that might occur to produce that cycle.[47] The starting point is the beginning of a new real estate upswing after the trough has passed and there is significant pent-up demand.

Stage 1. There is an imbalance between demand and supply. The unemployment rate is high, but the general business economy is expanding;

[45]Case, *Real Estate Economics*, p. 102.

[46]Rabinowitz, *Real Estate Gamble*, p. 237. For a more recent discussion of the flood of money into real estate investments, see "What Is Sending Property Prices through the Roof," *Business Week*, February 27, 1984, pp. 122–123.

[47]The stages of activity discussed here are based on a presentation by Case, *Real Estate Economics*, pp. 107–109; see also Sherman J. Maisel and Stephen E. Roulac, *Real Estate Investment and Finance* (New York: McGraw-Hill, 1976), pp. 183–188.

EXHIBIT 14-12.   Forces Affecting Real Estate Cycles

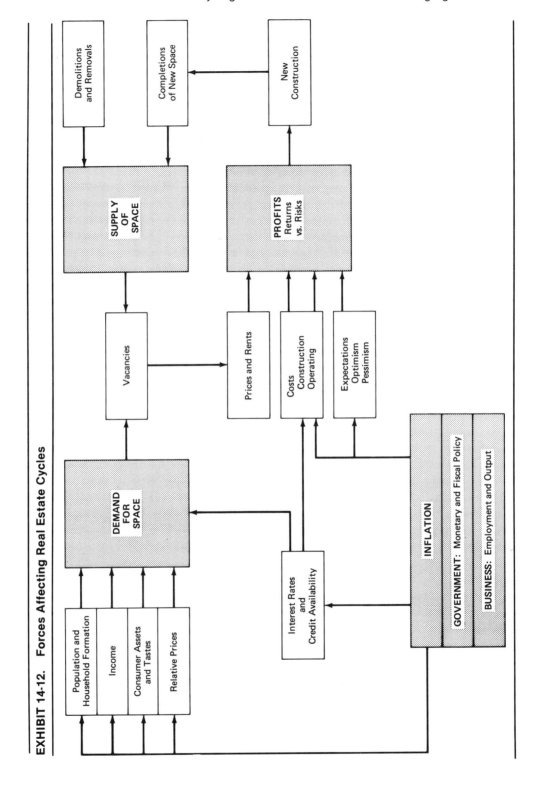

government monetary and fiscal policies are expansionary; inflation is moderate, and mortgages are available at relatively low interest rates. Population and family size are increasing, incomes are rising, and better employment increases demand for housing. The price of housing has not increased rapidly, and construction starts have been in the basement for some time. Thus, the supply of housing and other real estate is relatively fixed over the short run, with demolitions and removals offsetting completions of new space to some extent.

It should be noted that housing activity dominates the real estate market cycle, since the volume of housing activity is far greater than that of commercial property activity. Thus, most discussions of real estate cycles emphasize the role of the residential sector. Moreover, single-family residential construction activities generally lead multifamily and commercial property construction, as noted throughout this discussion.

When demand increases, vacancies decrease as existing vacant homes are sold and apartments are rented. Home prices and apartment rents rise sharply relative to operating and development costs. Builders of single-family homes become optimistic; profits are rising, and the construction of new single-family homes picks up and dominates the market. Ample construction mortgage credit is available at favorable rates, and builders respond by providing medium-priced housing in large quantities in subdivisions. As subdividers respond to increase home-building activity, vacant land near the city begins to disappear and subdivisions move farther out. Land prices begin to rise as a result. New apartment complexes have been planned, but the planning and construction cycle for them is much longer than that for single-family homes.

Stage 2. Sales activity rises sharply and the market is very active. The selling prices of homes are increasing, as are the costs of construction, and businesses of all types are expanding. Homes are sold very soon after they have been completed, and builders are building actively in all price ranges. Investors and speculators begin to enter the market to capitalize on the residential construction boom and the availability of mortgage credit at low rates. Multifamily housing projects begin to take off rapidly, followed by increasing numbers of commercial and industrial projects, which are developed to service the expanded residential areas. The demand for all types of space is high, and supply is increasing rapidly to meet the pent-up demand. All market indicators, rents and prices, mortgage recordings, building permits, and deed recordings increase to record levels. Inflation and interest rates are also rising, but building profits are still high and expectations are still optimistic. Investors are actively buying existing properties of all types and bidding up the selling prices of those properties.

Stage 3. Although demand increases at a steady rate, new construction tends to come onto the market all at once. Too many builders getting the same idea at the same time eventually cause an oversupply of space as projects are completed. Home markets become saturated, unsold inventory builds up, profits decrease, and builders begin advertising campaigns and offer additional amenities and financial inducements to buy at higher prices. Apartment projects and commercial properties are completed in large numbers and appear on the market. Inflation has increased rapidly, and the Federal Reserve is now applying the monetary brakes, causing interest rates to rise further. Credit controls reduce the available supply of loanable funds, and effective demand for homes is decreased. With high home prices, high interest rates, and greater difficulty in qualifying for loans, the attitude toward homeownership changes and rentals become preferable. The prices of older homes begin to fall; the average time between listing and sale increases, and builders become pessimistic. Rising land and interest costs further decrease profit expectations and building feasibility. Overexpansion of new apartment space results in higher vacancy rates, and rental income levels off or decreases as landlords compete for tenants.

Stage 4. General business activity is curtailed as the Federal Reserve continues to use monetary brakes to fight inflation. Real estate activity is beginning to decline, although the supply of commercial space is still increasing at a relatively strong pace. Builders are having trouble selling their properties and are taking second mortgages and offering concessions to facilitate sales. Holding costs are extremely high, as prime lending rates have increased to record levels. The apartment developers have overbuilt the market; as a result, renters are getting better services as landlords compete to avoid vacancies and turnover costs. Vacancies increase and, in overbuilt locations, reach levels as high as 20 to 30 percent. Cash flows and profitability decline; builders and owners have difficulty meeting mortgage obligations, and foreclosures become more frequent. Lenders become pessimistic and cease to make new permanent loans on properties, and interim lenders demand repayment of loans with accrued interest.

Stage 5. Business activity is slowing, unemployment increasing, and inflation continuing at a record pace and causing real incomes to fall. Credit is tight; interim and permanent mortgage interest rates are at record highs. Consumers and producers are pessimistic. The real estate cycle begins a rather sharp decline. Unemployment is high, especially in the building trades; renters double up to save money, and the rate of new household formation slows. Effective demand for all types of space is decreasing while substantial amounts of new space are being completed or are still under construction. How far down the real estate cycle goes depends on the degree of overbuilding that has taken place, any changes in restrictive monetary policies and lending practices, the degree to which lenders will work with developers and property owners to avoid foreclosures, and the degree to which real estate demand is decreased by the general economic recession. Stage 5 will end and a new stage 1 will begin only when there is an improvement in income and employment in the general business economy and consumers become more optimistic.

The Real Estate Cycle and the General Business Cycle

Clearly, there is a close (but not necessarily synchronized) relationship between the general business cycle and the real estate cycle. The character of the national real estate cycle is determined primarily by business conditions in the overall economy. These conditions are affected by factors such as variations in international money exchange, trade deficits, government debt, and monetary and fiscal policies.[48] The character of local real estate cycles is similarly determined by business conditions in local real estate markets. Basic business conditions influence real estate cycles directly. Real estate market activity increases when general business conditions become more favorable and decreases when business activity slows. As indicated, when the general economy is in an upswing, employment and income are up, consumption is up, and there is increased demand for all types of real estate space. The result is rising rents, sales prices, and expected profits and returns. The same is true in reverse. But this should be no great surprise to most students of real estate economics, who know that *real estate demand is a derived demand and, hence, depends on other economic activity for its substance.*

The Real Estate Cycle Is More Volatile. Real estate market activity tends to lag upward movements in business activity but goes to higher levels. During the downswing, real estate market activity tends to lead business activity, and it declines faster and goes down lower. Typically, business cycle changes are 20 percent above and below the long-term trend line of activity. In contrast, real estate cycles average 40 percent above and below the trend line.[49] It is no wonder that the real estate business is considered a boom-and-bust, rags-or-riches business.

Imperfect markets are one underlying reason for high volatility in real estate. Developers, equity investors, and lenders consistently misjudge market demand and overproduce space. Unlike the industrial sector, which can curtail production schedules and reduce output to the level of demand relatively quickly, the amount of real estate space in production

---

[48] An example of the pervasiveness of government policies is presented in Leland S. Burns and Leo Grebler, "Is Public Construction Countercyclical?" *Land Economics*, November 1984, pp. 367–377. They concluded that during the period 1950–1981 government public works projects were procyclical with the general business cycle aggravating the cyclical nature of the economy.

[49] Case, *Real Estate Economics*, p. 109.

cannot be curtailed easily, and once it is on the market it is too permanent. Moreover, like any durable good, real estate is subject to wide demand fluctuations because consumers can postpone the decision to buy when economic conditions are poor and pessimism prevails.

The Increasing Importance of National and International Cycles. In the past, real estate investors could largely ignore national and international business developments and concentrate on analyzing general business activity and trends in the particular MSA or urban areas in which they operated and on the investment projects under consideration. But because so many investors and developers have experienced serious setbacks in their local market areas as a direct result of actions at the national and international levels, they now attach more importance to having a national and international outlook in evaluating projects.

The booms and busts in new and existing properties will increasingly be generated by conditions outside the immediate market area, such as inflation, wide fluctuations in the availability and cost of mortgage funds, and the cost and availability of foreign crude oil. The investor does not have to be a trained economist to understand the implications of national and international events, since analyses and interpretations of these events are readily available through publications like the *Wall Street Journal*, *The Kiplinger Report*, *Business Week*, *Money*, and *Forbes*. However, the investor must learn to translate national trends and the forecasts of economists into usable information at the local level. Their implications with respect to the risk and return parameters of specific property alternatives must be analyzed and understood.

Increasing Recognition of Cycles by Investors. The importance of macro real estate and business cycles, and their impact on both investment performance and strategy, has gained the attention of many investors, especially the public and institutional real estate funds and programs. More investors are recognizing their pervasive impacts and the need to take advantage of them through portfolio revisions and effective structuring of individual projects. One example of a major investment partnership that has recognized cycles as an integral part of its strategic evaluation process is presented in Exhibit 14-13.

Other Cycles

There are nine other types of real estate cycles that may directly or indirectly affect investor returns and risks.

Construction Cycles. When money is plentiful and interest rates are low, builders build to satisfy pent-up demand from the period of limited con-

---

EXHIBIT 14-13. Real Estate Cycles

To evaluate the performance of investment programs, it is necessary to understand the real estate industry as a whole. Performance must be examined in context; a rise of 10 percent in a stock's price sounds good, but how would you rate that stock if the rest of the market had increased by 50 percent or had declined by 10 percent over the same period?

The real estate industry, much like the business world in general, has historically performed in a cyclical fashion, driven primarily by the laws of supply and demand. Levels of construction activity, absorption of space in office buildings, shopping centers, and apartment complexes, rental rates, and interest rates are all interrelated. They drive the performance of the entire real estate industry through an irregular four-phase cycle, which can be summarized as follows:

Phase I: Low Levels of Construction, High Absorption Rates

As demand begins to increase, vacancy rates decline and rental rates increase. Historically, the greatest escalation of rental income and property values has occurred during this phase. It is also typical of this phase for interest rates to be high and perceived to be going higher. At such times, lenders have significant opportunities to obtain equity participants from borrowers.

Phase II: Limited Availability of Space, Peak Demand

Demand is so high that it cannot be met with the available supply of rental space. Competition among tenants for space is sharp; this is a "landlord's market." Vacancy rates reach their lowest points, while rental rates remain high. Generally, loans in place during this phase perform well, and borrowers continue to be willing to offer equity participations.

Phase III: Excessive New Construction and Development

Construction levels rise and supply increases, exceeding the demand for additional space. Rental rates stabilize or even trend downward. Typically, interest rates are low, and funds for additional construction remain available, resulting in oversupply and increasing vacancy rates. Because loans are plentiful, borrowers are less willing to offer participations. As markets soften and properties fail to perform to expectations, borrowers begin to experience difficulty in meeting debt service obligations.

Phase IV: Demand Is Slow, Vacancies Reach Unacceptable Levels

Supply is so great, and demand so soft that rental rates decrease. This decline may be evidenced by actual rate reductions or by concessions, so called "free rent." This is a "tenant's market." Construction slows to a halt or to minimum levels. Borrowers, especially those who are inexperienced or who have become undercapitalized, are unable to support property operations and meet debt service. Lenders are forced to renegotiate some loans, and to foreclose on others in order to protect their invested capital. However, it is Phase IV that contributes to the start of another cycle, and leads to Phase I—demand first absorbs the supply created by overbuilding and then, in the absence of new construction, demand approaches available supply. However, until absorption begins to make inroads into the oversupply, real estate is in the trough of its cycle.

Source: The Balcor Company, An American Express Company, Skokie, Ill., 1987; publication entitled, *A Focus on Balcor's Mortgage Loan Partnerships.*

EXHIBIT 14-14.   Construction Supply–Demand Relationship

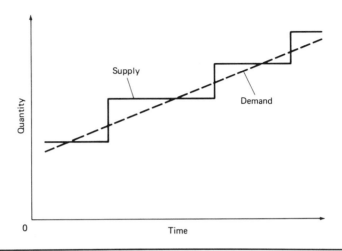

struction.[50] This is the most significant factor in housing construction. Many builders enter the market at the start of the cycle. Their success induces others to enter the market until supply equals or surpasses demand. Unless builders monitor supply and the absorption rate, they end up overproducing, which is precisely what occurred in the apartment and office building markets in 1973–1975, and 1984–1986.

The go–stop–go from all-out production to overbuilding and a construction halt creates a kind of ratchet effect. Demand increases rather smoothly, but supply tends to increase in steps, as Exhibit 14-14 shows. This step effect is easily identified and certainly more pronounced on a local level. Temporary oversupply is caused by the large number of small firms that are not very sophisticated in supply and demand research. Production is usually based on their demonstrated construction skill, the availability of workers, and their ability to obtain financing. If their bankers do not question the construction feasibility, the projects are built. Often a number of builders simultaneously initiate the same types of projects for completion in the shortest possible time, with little communication between them. Thus, the potential for continuation of this cyclical phenomenon seems to be built into the free-enterprise construction business.

[50]Rabinowitz, *The Real Estate Gamble*, pp. 240–243; Clarence D. Long, *Business Cycles as a Theory of Investment* (Princeton, N.J.: Princeton University Press, 1940); Homer Hoyt, *The Urban Real Estate Cycle—Performance and Prospects*, Technical Bulletin No. 38 (Washington, D.C.: Urban Land Institute, June 1960).

Mortgage Money Cycle. As noted previously, the mortgage money cycle is highly correlated with the business and construction cycle. During the contraction phase of the business cycle, Federal Reserve monetary controls almost always include credit controls in addition to tightening the money supply, which places upward pressure on interest rates. The imposition of credit controls means that fewer buyers are able to come up with the increased equity required to compensate for mortgages with a reduced loan-to-value ratio. In addition, rising interest rates result in higher mortgage payments and lower debt service coverage ratios; in turn, loans on income property are smaller and the feasibility of projects is reduced. With interest rates and debt service payments rising, fewer persons are qualified to buy homes because their incomes are too low to service the debt.

Two additional mechanisms that historically shut off permanent mortgage lending for single-family housing are disintermediation and usury ceilings. Disintermediation seems to have been moderated significantly by the deregulation of financial institutions. The federal government has taken steps to rescind state usury laws. With these two mechanisms becoming inoperative, the historic mortgage boom–bust cycle has been altered considerably.

Urban Area and City Cycles. Chapters 11 to 13 discussed at great length the growth and decline of metropolitan areas, the analysis of market area fluctuations, and strategies for dealing with these factors. It was shown that the character of the local real estate cycle is determined by business conditions in the local real estate markets. The driving force for increased real estate activity is the vitality of the business sector of the local economy, which is especially dependent on the basic industries that export products and services out of the metropolitan area and cause a multiplier effect throughout the service sectors.

The local business and real estate cycles can be substantially different from the national business and real estate cycles. To the extent that the mix of basic and nonbasic industries differs from the mix in the national economy, a city's cycles will have different characteristics and timing. Indeed, some local cycles will be countercyclical to the national cycle and those of other cities. In the middle of the energy crisis, from 1974 to 1976, which created serious economic problems for "Frostbelt" cities on the East Coast and in the Midwest, cities like Houston and Midland-Odessa, Texas, and Anchorage, Alaska—all of which are oil cities—were experiencing strong upswings in economic activity, population growth, and real incomes. Then, in the mid-1980s, the oil glut and OPEC loss of monopoly price control pushed oil cities and states into a recession; however, areas with a strong human capital and diversified economic base continued to grow. Cities dominated by industries that produce consumer and producer durable goods experience the widest business and real estate fluctuations, whereas cities that specialize in consumer necessities and services have the most moderate fluctuations. As a city grows and its industrial mix becomes more diversified, its cycles begin to approximate the behavior of the national cycles.

Neighborhood Cycles. Each neighborhood has its own specific land use life cycle that affects real estate activity. Exhibit 14-15 shows a life cycle scenario for a typical neighborhood or urban area. The public sector events that characterize the cycle are shown in lowercase letters on the outside of the cycle, and the private sector real estate activities are shown in capital letters on the inside of the cycle. Although this is a typical sequence of activity, each neighborhood is unique and differs to some degree in its development and characteristics.

The best opportunities for increases in value appear in the early stages of neighborhood development, when new uses come into existence and there is a high level of building and construction activity. The risk is also relatively high during these stages because of potential competition from other vacant sites and other builders and investors. As the neighborhood

EXHIBIT 14-15.   Stages in the Land Use Life Cycle

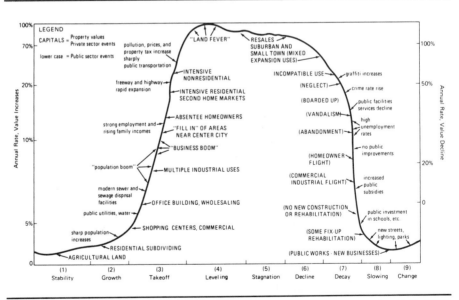

Source: Fred E. Case, *Investing in Real Estate* (Englewood Cliffs, N.J.: Prentice-Hall, 1978), p. 57.

matures (the leveling stage) and vacant land becomes scarce, the risk tends to decline, but so do the returns. Depending on the investor's return–risk preferences, he or she should choose to invest during one of the first four neighborhood stages. Real estate values will increase during these periods, although the rate of increase will fall as the neighborhood approaches the stage of stagnation. As a general rule, most real estate advisers tell investors to avoid investing in neighborhoods that are in the declining stages. On the other hand, at the end of the cycle, when the neighborhood enters a period of change and renewal, new real estate opportunities appear for the high-risk-oriented investor.

Investors should be careful to choose neighborhoods within a city that are consistent with their return and risk objectives. Ideally, they should rank-order acceptable neighborhoods and search for investment opportunities accordingly.

Property-Specific Cycles. Different types of properties are subject to different demand and supply relationships. As a result, each city has a unique set of property-specific cycles in apartments, office buildings, retail and shopping center properties, industrial buildings, and so on. Although the office building market in city A is becoming overbuilt this year and will remain so for the next two years, its market for shopping centers may have a relatively well-balanced supply and demand and prospects for continued high absorption over the next two years. The exact reverse may be true in city B. It is for this reason that diversification by property type and location is popular among portfolio builders.

Michael Halpin identifies two common types of property-specific cycles that result in market overkill cycles.[51]

1. *A new–concept–overkill cycle.* The booming cycle of the swinger apartments in the 1970s is a good example of a new–concept–overkill cycle. When first introduced, these apartments offered a new concept in living to singles and were very popular. They became a good place for single men or women to get into the swing and meet one another. However, as time passed, too many developers jumped into this market. The quality of the residents deteriorated; management problems developed, and swinger apartments gained a negative image in many markets. Swinger apartments often became problem properties. In the 1980s, the new market attracting developers is housing for the retired and elderly, which will go through a similar cycle.

---

[51]Michael C. Halpin, *Profit Planning for Real Estate Development* (Homewood, Ill.: Dow Jones–Irwin, 1977), pp. 105–108.

2. *A hot-market–overkill cycle.* When more and more large corporations were getting into real estate in the late 1960s and 1970s, they reshaped industry patterns and economics. The trend was toward large, multimarket producers and investors who were anxious to expand into new markets. Expansion-minded companies systematically researched regional and local statistics throughout the country and attached growth labels to certain cities. Unfortunately, many of the resulting corporate strategies tended to be first self-fulfilling and then self-destroying. The cycle, thus, is as follows: forecasts reveal an opportunity, investors and developers rush in to exploit it, and competitive overkill follows and destroys profit opportunities. This cycle was repeated during the 1980s; however, the players are now major institutional investors, public fund syndicators, and multistate builders creating far more real estate space than was demanded.

Seasonal Cycles. The timing of real estate transactions with respect to the month or season significantly affects a property's marketability, selling price, and terms of purchase and sale. It was common before the Tax Reform Act of 1981 for real estate tax shelter syndication activity to increase sharply before the end of the year, when wealthy investors realized that they had too much taxable income and needed to shelter some of it. Many syndicators who specialized in tax-shelter-oriented investments geared their operations for frenzied activity in the weeks leading up to December 31, hoping to take advantage of the often emotional tax avoidance syndrome that develops at this time of the year. Although recent tax reforms have eliminated most allowable year-end deductions, this seasonal trend persists in some cases. Annual tax law changes in the 1980s introduced turbulence in tax planning. The Tax Reform Act of 1986 continued this uncertainty and cyclical impact.

Most real estate investment activity shows some seasonal tendencies. For example, investors in single-family homes are aware that in most geographic areas both marketability and price will tend to be highest during the spring and summer months. The seasonal fluctuations differ by region and are most notable in the Northeast; nevertheless, median home prices tend to rise through the summer months and decline toward the end of the year.

Property, Ownership and Investor Life Cycles. Chapter 2 discussed the property, ownership, and investor life cycles at some length. Property life cycles were conceptualized by an eight-stage pyramid that encompassed the entire development and holding period—from the idea inception stage through the demise or abandonment of the project at the end of its useful economic life. The ownership life cycle is a particular period within the property life cycle encompassing the holding period experienced by one ownership group, from the day the investment is purchased through the disposal of the property at the end of the holding period. The investor life cycle is related to the types and amounts of returns and risks sought by the investor at different stages of life (usually related to age). Again, the analysis of every real estate investment should recognize and reflect these life cycles, which affect the return–risk relationships on which investment decisions are based.

Popularity Cycle. Also referred to as the bandwagon or herd cycle, the popularity cycle typically occurs during boom-and-bust periods of real estate activity and is stimulated by the news media. If investors are currently successful in a particular type of property, location, or field, many others are attracted until the market becomes glutted. After a while those who cannot compete successfully drop out of the market. A new cycle begins when another attractive opportunity occurs. Central to the existence of this cycle is the effect of the news media on the attitudes and emotions of consumers and investors. During the upswing of the cycle, the news media exaggerate information on investment opportunities and potential profits, creating many false expectations and much unwarranted enthusiasm. On the downside the reverse occurs.

The bandwagon tendency is evident even among sophisticated investors. The rise and fall of large firms in the tax shelter syndication business in the early and mid 1980s are testimony to this fact.

Social Change Cycles. A real estate investor must continually analyze the basic social and cultural changes occurring in society and their possible effects on changing real estate needs, returns, and risks. Increasingly, investors and developers are designing properties for flexible use as a method of coping with rapid social change. Minitheaters are constructed in shopping centers. Their seating capacities are relatively small and they are built on a level floor. If such use becomes unprofitable, the lease can be canceled and the space converted into a store.

Rapid social change creates cycles in property values. One study was performed concerning the impact of so-called hippies on property values.[52] It concluded that hippies affect values both negatively and positively. "Good" hippies spend money, do not destroy property, and cause property values to increase. However, they are often followed by "bad" hippies, who are panhandlers, do not spend money, and steal to support their drug habits, thereby causing property values to decline. This property value cycle can occur within a very short time, as it did in areas like Wells Street and Old Town in Chicago in the late 1960s.

---

[52] Anthony Downs, "Current Economic Trends: Impact upon Appraisal of Real Estate," *The Appraisal Journal*, April 1971, pp. 169–170.

Strategies for Dealing with Cycles

Many of the strategies developed early in the chapter for coping with inflation cycles apply equally well to all the cycles discussed. Among the basic tenets are the following.

1. *Identify important cycles.* Which cycles affect your investments? The investor must be constantly on the alert to identify new cycles and their implications.

2. *Research their effects on investment variables.* What short- and long-run impacts will these cycles have on rents, expenses, property values, financing variables, and capitalization rates? Be careful not to project trends indefinitely or use assumptions that are static and do not allow for change.

3. *Develop an investment strategy to cope with them.* The possible impact of cycles should be included in the investor's cash flow projections and the resulting measures of investment return and risk. The concepts of designing a flexible portfolio, diversifying to reduce risk, timing investments correctly, and choosing investments that will let you sleep at night apply to all real estate cycles.

It is important that the investor learn to develop his or her forecasting abilities and then have a systematic and logical method of processing the information developed through a DCF model. Too many variables must be dealt with to leave this process to intuitive management techniques.

Sensitivity to the Law of Contrary Opinion. Successive investors recognize that they are operating in a highly cyclical environment in which most average investors guess wrong a large percentage of the time. What appears to be right to the average investor often has a high probability of being wrong, for the many reasons that have been given throughout this chapter. Excellence can be achieved only by those who are strong enough to follow a path contrary to that of the masses. To remain with the masses and do what everyone else is doing is to be mediocre at best. To achieve excellence, the investor must be sensitive to real estate cycles at all levels of the economy and have the courage to venture away from the consensus and lead the masses. Investments must be bought and sold before cyclical trends are fully reflected in real estate prices and activity (see Exhibit 14-16).

Surviving the Downside, Preparing for the Upside. At a minimum, every investor should be financially prepared to survive a serious real estate recession. The keys to such survival are liquidity and tight accounting controls. Cash and cash resources, including prearranged lines of credit, should be sufficient to avoid insolvency. Unnecessary spending can be reduced to a minimum. If the investor correctly forecasts a serious real estate

EXHIBIT 14-16. The Real Estate Cycle

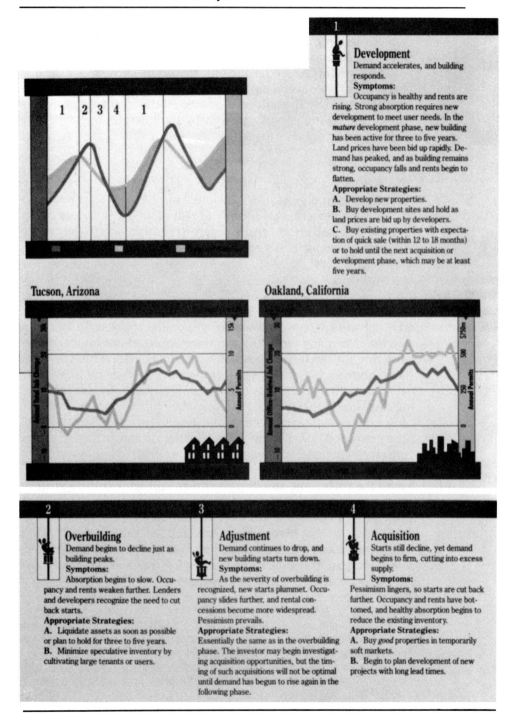

1

Development
Demand accelerates, and building responds.
Symptoms:
Occupancy is healthy and rents are rising. Strong absorption requires new development to meet user needs. In the *mature* development phase, new building has been active for three to five years. Land prices have been bid up rapidly. Demand has peaked, and as building remains strong, occupancy falls and rents begin to flatten.
Appropriate Strategies:
A. Develop new properties.
B. Buy development sites and hold as land prices are bid up by developers.
C. Buy existing properties with expectation of quick sale (within 12 to 18 months) or to hold until the next acquisition or development phase, which may be at least five years.

Tucson, Arizona

Oakland, California

2

Overbuilding
Demand begins to decline just as building peaks.
Symptoms:
Absorption begins to slow. Occupancy and rents weaken further. Lenders and developers recognize the need to cut back starts.
Appropriate Strategies:
A. Liquidate assets as soon as possible or plan to hold for three to five years.
B. Minimize speculative inventory by cultivating large tenants or users.

3

Adjustment
Demand continues to drop, and new building starts turn down.
Symptoms:
As the severity of overbuilding is recognized, new starts plummet. Occupancy slides further, and rental concessions become more widespread. Pessimism prevails.
Appropriate Strategies:
Essentially the same as in the overbuilding phase. The investor may begin investigating acquisition opportunities, but the timing of such acquisitions will not be optimal until demand has begun to rise again in the following phase.

4

Acquisition
Starts still decline, yet demand begins to firm, cutting into excess supply.
Symptoms:
Pessimism lingers, so starts are cut back further. Occupancy and rents have bottomed, and healthy absorption begins to reduce the existing inventory.
Appropriate Strategies:
A. Buy *good* properties in temporarily soft markets.
B. Begin to plan development of new projects with long lead times.

Source: G. Ronald Witten, "Riding the Real Estate Cycle," *Real Estate Today,* August 1987, pp. 44–45.

recession, properties can be sold at the top of the cycle, before the market reflects the downturn. The wise investor knows when to slow an aggressive investment expansion program and begin a consolidation period in which planning for the next upside of the cycle is emphasized; he or she has a cool head and a sense of balance and acts in moderation.[53]

The economy and inflation will always be cyclical. At the bottom of the cycle the investor finds opportunities to take advantage of excellent investments created by the failure of others. At the top of the cycle other types of opportunities are present. Exhibit 14-16 illustrates one expert's opinion on the "appropriate strategies" to implement during different phases of the real estate cycle.

An Art, Not a Science. The process described here is not simple and cannot be mastered quickly.[54] Much like mastering the art of karate, developing and implementing a successful real estate cycle strategy requires much study, time and effort, and an aggressive approach to the problem. But the expected returns relative to the risks may be great.

SUMMARY

This chapter introduced the complex subjects of inflation and real estate cycles. The many facets of each were arranged in a logical framework consistent with the techniques and concepts developed in the previous chapters. Important aspects of that framework include (1) identifying the inflation and other real estate cycle variables that influence returns and risks; (2) measuring their short- and long-run effects on rents, vacancies, operating expenses, financing costs and terms, property values, and the investor's required IRR; (3) processing the data through conventional DCF, sensitivity, and risk analysis models; and (4) developing an investment strategy that will provide decision rules for shifting the investor's portfolio over the cycle. The analysis presumes (1) that investors wish to maximize their investment returns relative to risks; (2) that real estate cycles do exist, can be estimated, and do have a dramatic impact on investment returns and risks; (3) that investors can develop forecasting ability that will enable them to measure the relationships between specific cycles and cash flow variables; and (4) that shifting between real and financial assets over the cycle is a viable investment alternative.

[53]Halpin, *Profit Planning*, p. 114.

[54]For example, see James E. Gibbons, "The Fear of Forecasting," *The Appraisal Journal*, October 1984, pp. 616–623; Albert R. Wildt and Russell S. Winer, "Modeling and Estimation in Changing Market Environments," *The Journal of Business*, July 1983, pp. 365–388; however, see Hugh O. Nourse, "Improve Investment Decisions by Breaking the DCF Habit," *Real Estate Review*, Winter 1986, pp. 75–80, who proposes a contrasting viewpoint.

Since cycles are perceived to be the most important variables influencing investment returns and risks, emphasis is placed on the development of strategies for coping with them. Failure to cope successfully with any one of these cycles can result in financial disaster.

APPENDIX TO PART 3

SOURCES OF MARKET DATA FOR REAL ESTATE INVESTORS

I. NATIONAL TRENDS

(*Note:* For trends relating to specific property types see end-of-chapter bibliographies in Part 6.)

Government and Quasi Government Publications

1. *National Economic Trends*
   Federal Reserve Bank of St. Louis
   P.O. Box 442
   St. Louis, Missouri 63166
   (monthly)
2. *Census of Population and Housing (1980)*
   (Population and housing characteristics of cities by census tracts, published by the U.S. Department of Commerce, Bureau of Census)
   Superintendent of Documents
   U.S. Government Printing Office
   Washington, D.C. 20402
   (request by state and MSA)
3. *Construction Review*
   Superintendent of Documents
   U.S. Government Printing Office
   Washington, D.C. 20402
   (bimonthly)
4. *Economic Indicators*
   Council of Economic Advisors
   Superintendent of Documents
   U.S. Government Printing Office
   Washington, D.C. 20402
   (monthly)
5. *Economic Report of the President*
   Superintendent of Documents
   U.S. Government Printing Office
   Washington, D.C. 20402
   (annual)
6. *Federal Reserve Bulletin*
   Publication Services
   Board of Governors of the Federal Reserve System
   Washington, D.C. 20551
   (monthly)

7. *Housing Characteristics*
U.S. Department of
Commerce, Bureau of Census
Superintendent of Documents
U.S. Government Printing
Office
Washington, D.C. 20402
(irregular)

8. *MGIC Newsletter*
MGIC Plaza
Milwaukee, Wisconsin 53201
(monthly)

9. *Monthly Review*
Federal Reserve Bank of San
Francisco
P.O. Box 7702
San Francisco, California
94120
(monthly)

10. *Review*
Federal Reserve Bank of St.
Louis
P.O. Box 442
St. Louis, Missouri 63166
(monthly)

11. *Quarterly Review*
Federal Home Loan Bank of
Cincinnati
200 Atrium Two, Box 598
Cincinnati, Ohio 45201
(quarterly)

12. *Survey of Current Business*
Superintendent of Documents
U.S. Government Printing
Office
U.S. Department of
Commerce
Washington, D.C. 20402
(monthly)

13. *U.S. Financial Data*
Federal Reserve Bank of St.
Louis
P.O. Box 442
St. Louis, Missouri 63166
(weekly)

14. *Statistical Abstract of the United States*
Superintendent of Documents
U.S. Government Printing
Office
Washington, D.C. 20402
(annual)

15. *County Business Patterns*
Superintendent of Documents
U.S. Government Printing
Office
Washington, D.C. 20402
(annual)

16. *Historical Chart Book Publication Services*
Board of Governors of the
Federal Reserve System
Washington, D.C. 20551
(annual)

Publications by Financial Institutions

1. *Business in Brief*
Economics Group
The Chase Manhattan Bank,
N.A.
New York, New York 10015
(bimonthly)

2. *Credit and Capital Markets*
Bankers Trust Company
P.O. Box 318, Church Street
Station
New York, New York 10015
(periodical)

3. *Life Insurance Fact Book*
American Council of Life
Insurance
1850 K Street, N.W.
Washington, D.C. 20006
(annual)

4. *Savings and Loan Sourcebook*
U.S. Savings and Loan League
111 East Wacker Drive
Chicago, Illinois 60601
(annual)

Magazines

1. *Architectural Forum*
2160 Paterson Street
Cincinnati, Ohio 45214
(ten times per year)

2. *Business Week*
McGraw–Hill, Inc.
1221 Avenue of the Americas
New York, New York 10020
(weekly)

3. *Changing Times*
The Kiplinger Washington
Editors, Inc.
Editors Park, Maryland 20782
(monthly)

4. *Forbes*
Forbes, Inc.
60 Fifth Avenue
New York, New York 10011
(biweekly)

5. *Fortune*
Time, Inc.
3435 Wilshire Boulevard
Los Angeles, California 90010
(biweekly)

6. *Housing*
McGraw–Hill, Inc.
1221 Avenue of the Americas
New York, New York 10020
(monthly)

7. *Money*
Time, Inc.
3435 Wilshire Boulevard
Los Angeles, California 90010
(monthly)

8. *Mortgage Banking*
Mortgage Bankers Association
of America
P.O. Box 37236
Washington, D.C. 20013
(monthly)

9. *Multi-Housing News*
Gralla Publications
1515 Broadway
New York, New York 10036
(monthly)

10. *Buildings*
Stamats Communications, Inc.
427 Sixth Avenue, S.E.
P.O. Box 1888
Cedar Rapids, Iowa 52406
(monthly)

11. *Industrial Development*
Conway Data, Inc.
40 Technology Park/Atlanta
Norcross, Georgia 30092
(bimonthly)

12. *National Real Estate Investor*
Communication Channels,
Inc.
6285 Barfield Road
Atlanta, Georgia 30328
(monthly)

13. *The Financial Planner*
International Association of
Financial Planners
5775 Peachtree Dunwoody
Road
Suite 120-C
Atlanta, Georgia 30342
(monthly)

Newsletters, Newspapers, Special Reports, Other

1. *Real Estate Investing Newsletter*
   H.B.J. Newsletter, Inc.
   1 East First Street
   Duluth, Minnesota 55802
   (monthly)

2. *Real Estate Investment Planning*
   Institute for Business Planning, Inc.
   IBP Plaza
   Englewood Cliffs, New Jersey 07632
   (twice-monthly updated looseleaf service)

3. *Predicasts Forecasts*
   11001 Cedar Avenue
   Cleveland, Ohio 44106
   (annual)

4. *Dodge Local Construction Potentials*
   McGraw–Hill Information System Co.
   1221 Avenue of the Americas
   New York, New York 10020
   (monthly)

5. *Real Estate Report*
   Real Estate Research Corporation
   72 West Adams Street
   Chicago, Illinois 60603
   (quarterly)

6. *The Kiplinger Washington Newsletter*
   The Kiplinger Washington Editors, Inc.
   1729 H Street, N.W.
   Washington, D.C. 20006
   (weekly)

7. *The Mortgage and Real Estate Executives Report*
   Warren, Gorham & Lamont, Inc.
   210 South Street
   Boston, Massachusetts 02111
   (twice monthly)

8. *Real Estate Financing Update*
   Warren, Gorham & Lamont, Inc.
   (monthly)

9. *Land Use Digest*
   Urban Land Institute
   1090 Vermont Avenue, N.W.
   Washington, D.C. 20005
   (monthly)

10. *Real Estate Leasing Report*
    Federal Research Press
    210 Lincoln Street
    Boston, Massachusetts 02111-2491
    (monthly)

11. *Wall Street Journal*
    Dow Jones & Co., Inc.
    200 Barnett Road
    Chicopee, Massachusetts 01021
    (five days per week)

12. *Inter-City Cost of Living Index*
    American Chamber of Commerce Researchers Association
    P.O. Box 68124
    Indianapolis, Indiana 46268
    (quarterly)

13. *The Survey of Buying Power Data Service*
    (three-volume estimates and projections)
    Sales and Marketing Management Magazine
    Market Statistics
    633 Third Avenue
    New York, New York 10017
    (annual)

14. *Home Sales: Existing and New Single-Family Apartments, Condos and Coops*
National Association of Realtors
777 14th Street, N.W.
Washington, D.C. 20005
(monthly)

15. *National Delinquency Survey*
Mortgage Banker Association of America
1125 15th Street, N.W.
Washington, D.C. 20005
(bimonthly)

II. REGIONAL DATA

(*Note:* For trends relating to specific property types, see end-of-chapter bibliographies in Part 6. Some sources cited earlier have regional, area, and city reviews and information (e.g., *National Real Estate Investor*, *Housing*).

General Sources

1. Business research bureaus.
2. Financial institutions—individual commercial banks, savings and loan associations, land title companies.
3. Office of the governor, state industrial development agencies.
4. Regional council of governments (COGs).
5. Regional real estate newspapers (e.g., *Southwest Real Estate News*).
6. Regional and state universities.
7. State builders' associations.
8. State employment commissions and comptroller's offices.
9. State associations of land title companies.
10. State mortgage bankers' associations.
11. State realtors' associations.
12. State savings and loan leagues.
13. *The Kiplinger Newsletter* (state editions).
14. U.S. government state and regional offices, and quasi-public organizations (e.g., FHA, FNMA, FHLMC).

III. CITY AND NEIGHBORHOOD INFORMATION

Location Analysis

1. Survey of business conditions and real estate activity in the area.   Research department of banks.

2. Business conditions and real estate markets.

Banks; Federal Reserve Banks; land title companies.

3. Planning reports.

Planning commissions.

4. Population, housing, and employment.

U.S. Bureau of the Census; state departments of finance, state departments of employment, state departments and chambers of commerce.

5. Deeds recorded; building permits.

County recorder; departments of building and safety.

6. Locational analysis guides.

Urban Land Institute, Washington, D.C.; research departments of financial institutions; chambers of commerce; large businesses.

7. Population, markets, family income.

Research departments of local newspapers.

Site Analysis

1. Field surveys

Own resources or consulting groups

2. Tax assessments and amounts

Tax assessor

3. Building codes

Departments of building and safety

4. Zoning, planning, land uses

Planning commissions

5. Traffic and traffic patterns

Departments of highways or streets; automotive clubs

6. Land use maps

Planning commissions; map companies; Sanborn maps

7. Sales, sales prices, terms

Land title insurance companies; ownership map and book service companies

8. Census maps and reports; block books

U.S. Bureau of the Census

9. Rents, expenses, property values, vacancies

Property management companies, brokerage companies, appraisal firms

NEGOTIATIONS, MANAGEMENT, AND TERMINATION DECISIONS

Lighton Plaza, Overland Park, Kansas.

This part of the book concludes the theoretical discussions on investment strategy, analysis, and decisions for single projects. These chapters discuss the final steps of the ten-step investment analysis and financial structuring process that was first introduced in Chapter 4: step 8—final negotiations and closing; step 9—manage the property; step 10—terminate the property. The completion of these last steps marks the end of the ownership life cycle of one property in the investor's portfolio.

Chapter 15 examines the role of negotiations in the real estate investment process and presents guidelines for successful negotiations. While often ignored in real estate investment texts, this subject is extremely important because the investor is able to influence investment structures, returns, and risks through the negotiation process. Chapter 16 presents the important subjects of property and asset (venture) management. Asset management is a relatively new subject and concept that has evolved during the last ten years as a result of the institutionalization and securitization of real estate investment, and is one of increasing importance to project and portfolio managers. Chapter 17 studies the complex subject of termination decisions and presents an analytical framework for evaluating disposition alternatives. The Appendix to Chapter 17 addresses the complex topic of tax deferred exchanges.

Picking up from the end of Chapter 10 in Part 2, sections of the Aspen Wood Apartments case study again follow each chapter. They continue to illustrate the concepts and techniques discussed in each of the chapters, as well as the associated problems and "real world" issues that every investor must address.

15

THE ART OF REAL ESTATE NEGOTIATIONS

Handling other people's mistrust is the skilled negotiator's
stock-in-trade. . . . In a successful negotiation, everyone wins.
GERARD I. NIERENBERG[1]

In Chapter 4 strategy was defined as skillful management in getting the
better of an adversary or in attaining an end. Strategy implies a plan designed to outperform the competition and maximize financial wealth. In
purchasing a specific piece of real estate, the investor seeks to achieve certain strategic goals and objectives. At the same time, the seller is also seeking to maximize his or her rate of return. Thus, negotiations should be seen
as a cooperative enterprise between wary parties in which common interests must be sought.

The ideal negotiator has developed skills useful in many careers and
tasks. In *How Nations Negotiate*, Fred Charles Ikle stated that

> The compleat negotiator, according to seventeenth and eighteenth century
> manuals on diplomacy, should have a quick mind but unlimited patience,
> know how to dissemble without being a liar, inspire trust without trusting
> others, be modest but assertive, charm others without succumbing to their
> charm, and possess plenty of money and a beautiful wife while remaining
> indifferent to all temptation of riches and women.[2]

This sexist definition may be archaic, but it clearly illustrates that skilled
negotiators are rare. Negotiation is a useful tool of human behavior and,
as such, can be mastered with study and experience.

---

[1]Gerald I. Nierenberg, *Fundamentals of Negotiating* (New York: Hawthorne Press,
1973), p. 1.
[2]Fred C. Ikle, *How Nations Negotiate* (New York: Harper & Row, 1964).

Negotiations for the acquisition of a real estate investment involve an exchange of ideas. Gathered at the conference table is a heterogeneous group of individuals with varying educational backgrounds, personalities, and levels of experience. Each of them will be influenced by his or her own subconscious emotional drives.

The ten-step investment analysis process requires that negotiations begin with the basic parameters of a transaction—including price, financial terms, and tax considerations—as early as step 4, in which the buyer seeks an early meeting of minds with the seller. By step 8—the final negotiations—the buyer should be in a position to take advantage of both the buyer's and the seller's perceived preferences and biases to increase returns. An investor should not proceed to final negotiations without knowing what he or she is willing to forgo in return for what can be achieved at the final bargaining session. The final purchase contract and the closing of the deal should conform to both the buyer's and the seller's expectations.

The success or failure of real estate negotiations depends on following the strategic plan, knowing all the underlying assumptions, being fully prepared, spotting the effects of human behavior on the process, and finally recognizing that negotiation is the process of need fulfillment.[3]

THE ROLE OF NEGOTIATIONS

When buying a six-pack of beer, no one dickers over the price at the checkout counter. Nor does an investor negotiate with the broker over the price of a common stock on the New York Stock Exchange. Real estate, however, is a different kind of commodity. When a parcel of real estate is placed on the market, the terms of sale can only be estimated. This uncertainty over price and other terms stems from the unique attributes of real estate as an economic good. The buyer is contemplating a purchase that will provide cash flow benefits over a relatively long period. The seller is terminating an ownership period and seeks to maximize the disposition returns. Both parties are operating in a market in which the quality of in-

[3]Several books on real estate negotiations have been published in recent years. For example, see Tony Hoffman, *How to Negotiate Successfully in Real Estate* (New York: Simon & Schuster, 1984); Richard L. Huff, *The Art of Persuasion in Selling Real Estate* (Chicago: National Association of Realtors, 1984); and Roger Dawson, *You Can Get Anything You Want, But You Have to Do More Than Ask* (New York: Simon & Schuster, 1987); Bert Holtje and Don Christman, *Successful Real Estate Negotiation Strategy* (New York: Wiley, 1982).

formation is poor. Real estate markets are highly stratified, and even in a seller's market, buyers may be few and not easy to find. The one major advantage that buyer and seller have is that they have found each other.

The buyer is concerned with such matters as price, down payment requirements, required escrows, financing, closing costs, personal liability, the timing of the closing, and other items that affect the nature of the deal and the costs of the transaction. But the nature of real estate markets is such that the buyer must also be concerned with the location and marketability of the property. Since it takes time to research such information, the seller, if he or she is in a hurry, must be willing to provide representations and warranties concerning zoning, the existence of adequate utilities, highway access, land and roads, the absence of condemnation or other adverse proceedings, and other critical matters that affect value. The buyer must be aware of the need to verify information and will often attempt to negotiate the right to terminate the transaction if the seller fails to provide information or if negative information is found.

The seller and his or her counsel need assurance that once the terms of the contract have been agreed on, it will be fully executed and binding on the parties. The seller usually prefers to limit exposure after closing to contracted contingencies.

In effect, although the negotiation for the purchase and sale of a parcel of real estate is an adversarial relationship, both buyer and seller should realize that they can derive mutual benefit by minimizing conflict and seeking mutual accommodation to achieve a successful acquisition and sale.

Cooperative Bargaining versus Confrontation. Real estate negotiation is an interpersonal process. Ideally, each negotiator works for the other party's needs as well as his or her own. Despite the innate urge to win, the investor should replace the win–lose approach with a search for creative alternatives by which both parties can win. There are many solutions to a problem—some better and some worse—but they should all be examined by each of the parties concerned in order to find the one that provides the greatest mutual advantage. Using computer software programs to pretest "what if" scenarios and performing sensitivity analysis of alternative outcomes *prior* to holding negotiating sessions is good preparation.

During the negotiations the investor may reduce the defensiveness of the other side by communicating a willingness to consider and experiment with alternative behaviors, attitudes, ideas, and options. Questions often produce defensiveness. A person who appears to be taking a tentative attitude rather than a hard line on an issue may seem to be problem solving rather than debating the questions. Fact finding is also an adaptive procedure.

Jack R. Gibb cites six pairs of defensive and supportive categories.[4]

Defensive Behavior	Supportive Activities
1. Evaluation.	1. Description.
2. Control.	2. Problem orientation.
3. Strategy.	3. Spontaneity.
4. Neutrality.	4. Empathy.
5. Superiority.	5. Equality.
6. Certainty.	6. Provisionalism.

Keep in mind that *negotiating provides room to bargain and compromise.* Confrontation freezes positions, which can put an end to bargaining and to the deal.

Satisficing versus Maximizing. Although some scholars claim that businesspeople always seek to maximize profits, others argue that they are really "satisficing." Satisficing is necessary because it is impossible or impractical to attain the level for each variable that produces the greatest possible satisfaction. Instead, decision makers seek a solution that provides an acceptable level of usefulness, realizing that this may be the price of complexity and uncertainty. Thus, although the objective in real estate investing is to maximize wealth, the investor is more likely to achieve this long-term objective by following a "satisficing" strategy.

Keys to Successful Preliminary Negotiations. As the investor approaches the negotiation table, tension normally increases. Since the negotiations are the culmination of a long screening process, there is a natural tendency for emotions to override reason. The prospect of having to drop the target property and search for another one will tend to make the investor willing to accept a deal that would normally be considered undesirable. Thus, the investor is wise to keep in mind the systematic rules of the investment strategy process. Following are some control mechanisms that will tend to make negotiations more successful.

1. *The strategic plan should control the investor's behavior.* The strategy is to achieve the investment objectives. Although the basic screening criteria were used to target the property, preliminary negotiations may indicate that this property should be dropped from consideration. On the other hand, the investor should be aware of and open to creative alternatives.

---

[4]Jack R. Gibb, *Leadership and Interpersonal Behavior* (L. Petrulb and B. M. Bass, 1961).

2. *The basic financial feasibility model should be used.* The basic financial feasibility model structures and tests the basic economics of the project, the financing alternatives that appeared to be available, and the investment value range for the property. The seller should not be allowed to seduce the buyer into accepting terms outside his or her basic investment range, unless hard facts indicate that the preliminary analysis was inaccurate. New information produced by the negotiation process may require a reanalysis of the property using the basic financial feasibility model. An investor who is prepared to do some on-the-spot calculations may be able to determine quickly whether or not negotiations for a particular property should be continued.

3. *Careful preparation is essential.* Earlier, the need for understanding the political, legal, economic, and sociological assumptions built into the detailed feasibility research was explored. Many other kinds of implicit and explicit assumptions are part of the negotiating process. Too often they are ignored and the venture fails during the ownership cycle because the property was purchased under assumptions different from those that were actually realized. Psychiatrists explain that people rationalize, project, displace, and role-play, or they unconsciously repress thoughts, react to externalities, and engage in other behavior that affects the negotiations.

The more options that are available for handling the needs of the opposing party in a negotiating situation, the greater the chances of success. Understanding these needs is essential to success as a negotiator, who must combine the scientific attitude of the financial analyst with the cunning of a gumshoe detective to dig up facts and figures. Before negotiations even begin, the investor should contact bankers, brokers, attorneys, and property managers to get a feel for the opponent's personality.

The opponent's previous real estate sales should be investigated. Is the opponent litigious? Does he or she keep promises? Contacts in the community may provide information on deals that the opponent has failed to consummate successfully. A careful analysis of why certain deals fell through will offer the investor a good understanding of the opponent's thought processes and approach to negotiating.

Careful preparation also requires that the investor carefully reappraise his or her own motivations and goals. Unconscious drives have a powerful effect on individual actions. Irrational drives, such as the need for status, pride of ownership, or wanting to win the game, can subvert a conscious investment strategy. Just as the opponent's needs were carefully considered, the negotiator should reconsider why the target property was originally desirable. The negotiator should also reconsider the minimum acceptable levels for critical negotiating items, the resistance points, and the levels that would constitute unabridged success: the targets. For each critical item, the resistance point and target level, an aspiration zone should be designed. If the potential investor is not as well prepared as the opponent, he or she may have the disadvantage during the negotiations.

4. *Preparation should be made for mutual accommodation.* The variations in data produced by imperfect real estate markets create the possibility of differing views of reality. Thus, the rational mind is applying logic to a perceived reality that may be inaccurate. The ability to arrive at creative alternatives is basic to successful negotiation. If a proposed change in position can be supported by subsequent feasibility studies, compromise and concessions are not necessarily a loss.

THE PSYCHOLOGY OF NEGOTIATIONS

Like corporate acquisitions, mergers, and tender offers, real estate transactions are similar to a high-stakes game, and equity positions are usually highly leveraged. Negotiations thus are carried out in an emotionally charged atmosphere. It therefore behooves both parties to convert a potentially antagonistic atmosphere into a cooperative enterprise. To do this, the opposing parties must know human nature, be able to analyze the roles being played by the negotiating parties, and seek to have even the site of the negotiations conducive to good bargaining. The buyer and seller should also control the use of brokers, CPAs, and attorneys, and effectively use other team members, such as partners, in the negotiating process. The use of negotiating strategies must be carefully considered.

Know Human Nature and Cultural Traits

In negotiations, it is important to acknowledge differences in cultural heritage and social stratum. For example, in the New York area it is customary to get down to business immediately and bother very little with the "nonsense" of social niceties. Many Southerners, however, take time to discuss the weather, family, and friends before proceeding to bargain. To them, social interaction is part of the negotiating process. In the United States a man generally places himself 18 to 20 inches away when conversing face to face with another man. When talking with a woman, he usually backs off an additional 4 inches. In contrast, Hispanic–American men may feel quite comfortable at 13 inches. In the North Central part of the United States, unacceptable offers are usually rejected promptly and emphatically in an unambiguous manner, but in the Southeast many real estate negotiators will respond with an indirect, soft response designed to avoid hurt feelings. It is not uncommon for negotiations to break down because of cultural differences. Local brokers and attorneys may be quite useful in bridging these cross-cultural differences; and a show of congenial goodwill and a sense of humor will often go far to restore a cooperative attitude to the bargaining process.

Roles Played by Negotiating Parties

Every person has an image of himself or herself, and personal decisions are often made either to protect the self-image or to enhance it. It would seem that if how a person regards himself or herself were known, assumptions could be made about that person's underlying motivations and how he or she will react to the negotiation process. Role playing should be expected by both parties in the negotiating process. The kinds of behavior shown in acting out a role are usually based on previous experiences and on the extent to which they succeeded.

Robert Ringer, in his book, *Winning Through Intimidation*, holds that there are only three types of roles played by negotiators. Ringer's theory seems to see the negotiating process as a struggle for dominance and control rather than as mutual accommodation. His theory is apparently based on the useful but too simplistic premise that no one can be trusted.[5]

Type one is a person who indicates from the outset that he or she is out to get all the chips, and follows through by attempting to do exactly that. Experience shows that many people who play this role do it in a very smooth, sophisticated, and friendly manner; others, apparently uncomfortable in projecting such an image, do it in a hostile and too-aggressive way.

Type two makes assurances at the outset that he or she is interested only in getting a fair share. However, the person's actions are clearly directed toward getting as much as possible. Careful preparation prior to negotiating may indicate whether this type of person is unethical and dishonest or simply a hard bargainer. Unfortunately, good properties may on occasion be owned by bad and dishonest bargainers. Such slippery people should be controlled during every step of the bargaining process with legally enforceable language in signed and initialed documents. On the other hand, a negotiator should not irritate an ethical hard bargainer by trying to docment every move prior to final settlement. With such people everything will be aboveboard, but it can be a fast track, and the losers are usually those who are poorly prepared.

Probably the most difficult opponent to negotiate with is Ringer's *type three*. Unfortunately, the majority of people probably fall into this class.

[5]Robert J. Ringer, *Winning Through Intimidation* (Greenwich, Conn.: Fawcett Publications, 1974). See also William A. Thau, *Negotiating the Purchase and Sale of Real Estate*, Real Estate Review Portfolio, No. 8 (Boston: Warren, Gorham & Lamont, 1975); and Alvin Arnold and Owen Smith, *Negotiating the Commercial Lease*, Real Estate Review Portfolio No. 1 (Boston: Warren, Gorham & Lamont, 1973).

Although a type three person makes assurances that he or she is not interested in getting *any* unfair or undue chips, the person's conduct indicates that he or she is trying to get *all* the chips. The reasons for this contradictory conduct are myriad. Lack of self-knowledge and lack of familiarity with good business conduct are among them—or the person may sincerely make a deal that is not legally binding and then be persuaded by a professional to reopen negotiations. Such people may be difficult to deal with, but it is not uncommon for them to own desirable real estate.

The mutually accommodative bargaining process described in this chapter is more likely to bring about successful negotiation with all three types of opponents than any other method—including trying to win through intimidation.

The Negotiation Site

Should the investor meet in his or her own office or go to the opponent's home ground? Would a neutral territory serve better? (Banks and savings and loan associations often make meeting rooms available without charge as a courtesy.) There are advantages to meeting on one's own ground. (1) It allows for quick approval of unanticipated problems; (2) it makes it discourteous for the other side to terminate the negotiations abruptly or prematurely by leaving; (3) other matters can be dealt with and familiar facilities are available while the negotiations are in progress; (4) it provides a psychological advantage; and (5) it saves on money and traveling time. On the other hand, going to the opponent's home base also has advantages. (1) The investor can be totally devoted to negotiation without the distractions and interruptions of his or her office; (2) information can be withheld with the assertion that it is not immediately available; (3) if necessary, it may be possible to go over the opponent's head to someone in higher management; and (4) the burden of preparation is on the opponent, who will not be free from other duties.

The physical arrangements of the room, such as the lighting, the color, and the seating, also have a potential effect on the negotiations. Some people still consider the head of the table the leadership seat and will listen more intently to or accede to suggestions made by the person who occupies that seat. Some people find an advantage in intentionally sitting on the opponent's side of the table in order to minimize the adversary atmosphere.

Other physical considerations are (1) a telephone, (2) an adequately sized room, large enough to hold all the participants comfortably, (3) adequate ventilation, and (4) chairs that are comfortable but not too comfortable. It has been suggested that negotiations tend to be more successful in cheerful, bright-colored rooms. Although deals made on the back of an envelope or scribbled on a napkin at a cocktail bar are legendary, care in the selection of the site of negotiations will improve the chances of success.

Using Professionals to Assist in Negotiations

Professionals can be useful in negotiations.[6] There are times when it is desirable simply to increase the number of participants on your side of the negotiating table. But real estate investment is a complex, multifaceted process, and the typical general-practice lawyer, certified public accountant (CPA), or broker is not necessarily qualified to handle all phases of it. Indeed, many investors use one lawyer to do investment tax planning and to put real estate deals together, and another to handle closings. A CPA may be competent in the field of tax planning but is not necessarily well trained in real estate financial analysis. Many brokers are real estate marketing specialists but have little knowledge of the intricacies of real estate investment analysis. The key to using professionals is to define carefully the limits of the function you want the selected professional to serve.

Brokers can serve a vital function. They can serve as an antenna in the field for improving an investor's market data base; they can provide information on new or alternative sources of financing; and they can assist in gathering the documents that are necessary to close the transaction. When tempers flare, the broker can act as an intermediary and aid in reestablishing a negotiating atmosphere. Because of their professional stature, attorneys and CPAs can lend credibility to hard positions that must be taken concerning tax and legal considerations such as zoning, occupancy permits, and code violations. The investor should make an effort to use attorneys and CPAs who specialize in real estate.

Using Other Partners in Negotiations

Obviously, on both sides of the transaction there should be someone in charge of the negotiations. If there are partners, it is wise to give one of them the authority to negotiate within carefully thought-out parameters. If other partners are to be present, their roles should be carefully defined. Arrangements should be made so that partners can leave the room and settle any differences they have during the bargaining session.

ACHIEVING THE OBJECTIVES OF THE NEGOTIATING PARTIES

If buyer and seller are to estimate the appropriate range of offers and counteroffers, they must, prior to negotiations, properly characterize the submarket for the property. To get what they are bargaining for, both parties

---

[6]Choosing the right professionals to aid in the negotiation process is important. How the investor handles and negotiates with each of these people will greatly affect the success of a transaction. For example, see Hoffman, *How to Negotiate Successfully in Real Estate*, pp. 205–215.

must be prepared to make assurances to each other that will move the proceeding toward a final settlement and closing.

The main objective of any negotiations is a legally enforceable contract at mutually acceptable terms. A legally enforceable contract is merely a written expression of the mutually acceptable terms arrived at by buyer and seller. It is essential that both parties know the limits of their bargaining power. The negotiation tactics for bringing about an exchange are quite different from those used in a foreclosure. Negotiating long-term leases requires intensive bargaining because each clause may vary the economic returns of the package. The negotiator's aim should never be to get the last possible dollar; the danger of going too far is not worth the risk.

Establishing Market Conditions. Is it a buyer's market or a seller's market? As discussed in Chapter 14, there are cyclical swings in buyer or seller dominance of the marketplace. In preparing for negotiations, both the buyer and the seller should satisfy themselves that their market information is current. Good characterization of the marketplace can help them greatly in estimating the appropriate range for offers and counteroffers.

Gross Rent Multipliers, Cap Rates, and Square-Foot Prices. Many real estate markets are influenced by rule-of-thumb pricing. Obviously, if transactions in a submarket are frequently based on gross rent multipliers (GRMs), negotiations are going to be significantly influenced by the multiplier for the target property. On the other hand, properties in some regions are traditionally exchanged on capitalization rates. Under no circumstances, though, should a prudent investor pay more than an investment value that will produce the minimum acceptable rate of return. A buyer should not be pressured to pay a price that is excessive by financial analysis, even if it can be justified by recent comparable sales. Irrational GRMs square-foot prices, or cap rates may indicate that negotiations should be dropped because the property does not meet the investor's criteria. Holding funds in short-term liquid notes is better than making a bad long-term investment.

Unique Predicaments of Buyers and Sellers. Even though special circumstances dictate prices outside the usual range, sellers and buyers may be willing to go along in order to bring about a sale or an acquisition of a property. However, there is the danger that the investor will accept at face value the reason given by the seller for why he or she is selling; the investor may not investigate the situation as thoroughly as recommended. Even though the seller presents a doctor's report saying that he or she must sell the property now, the real reason could be that impending changes in zoning will substantially diminish the area's growth possibilities. Sellers may need to raise cash for taxes; buyers may be under time pressure to invest funds or to make a real estate investment within the tax year; and public agencies exercising eminent domain may be under time pressure to gain possession of the property. Careful investigation before negotiating may reveal information that can increase a negotiator's resistance to unreasonable demands by the opposing party.

Using Market Value, Most Probable Selling Price, and Investment Value. Swings in the economic base, business cycles, and other external factors cause substantial disequilibrium in real estate markets. A careful and imaginative negotiator can put the variance among most probable selling price, market value, and investment value to use. The buyer prefers to negotiate on the basis of the investment value. By discussing its relation to the current market and the most probable selling price, the opposing parties are more likely to gain an understanding of the underlying economics of the proposed deal. However, buyers should be aware that there are other investors who lack financial sophistication and therefore are willing to offer a higher price. This competitive activity cannot be ignored.

Estimating the Range of Offers and Counteroffers

Preliminary offers should be within the range developed by the basic financial feasibility model. Before entering into negotiations, the investor should conduct a sensitivity analysis to determine the effect of variances in price, financing terms, tax planning, and other factors on the acquisition offer. This step is strongly encouraged because such information can prove very helpful in setting minimum and maximum offers. The effect of non-price concessions on the return–risk relationship should also be estimated. Some of the possibilities to be considered are the following.

1. The seller agrees to defer the date of settlement without changing the price, thereby absorbing some interest costs and other cash outlay.
2. The seller agrees to finance all or part of the debt at terms better than those obtainable in the marketplace.
3. The seller provides warranties that are better than normal expectations.
4. Leases provide better-than-expected escalation clauses for such items as real estate taxes and insurance.
5. The seller accepts an exculpatory clause (nonrecourse mortgage loan) minimizing the risk for the buyer.
6. The seller agrees to assume more than a prorated share of the transaction costs and fees.

Having estimated the range within which an acceptable offer can be made, the investor should proceed to unfold the negotiating strategy. Certainly it is easier to deal with an experienced negotiator than with an inexperienced one, but it is rare to discover that an opponent is eager, intelligent, reasonable, well informed, and experienced. Even if the opponent is all these things, he or she may have limited authority, and therefore the negotiations should be treated as preliminary. An inexperienced negotiator may have to be educated during the process to see the opponent's needs as well as his or her own. Moreover, if a position is revealed too quickly, it may be interpreted as excessive eagerness to buy. It is a better strategy to present the facts before moving into an offer position.

Occasionally an opponent will quote a price that is outside the range of acceptable offers. If the property is good and intuition suggests that the price is only a preliminary position, it may be appropriate to make a counteroffer that is outside the range of reasonable offers in the opposite direction. The function of this sort of tactic is to turn the discussion toward a reasonable consideration of both negotiators' minimum needs. Since the seller is taking the time to negotiate at all, he or she is most likely seeking a successful sale.

Some people feel that the party who initiates the negotiations should set the price of the first offer. Many sellers feel that they should entertain an offer but not make a counteroffer. It is probably most advantageous for the buyer to let the offerer begin by attempting to sell him or her on why a certain proposition should be accepted. This procedure has the advantage of allowing the investor to gain more information on the property and demonstrate an accommodating attitude. In many successful negotiations the initial asking price is simply set aside and negotiations are shifted to nonprice concessions in order to clarify the underlying structure of the deal.

Getting What You Bargained For

As negotiation proceeds to the final contract and the closing, the understanding is that the deal has been structured for the most favorable tax consequences and an acquisition price that fits the investment strategy. A real estate sales contract is designed to make a closing a certainty. Obviously, the purchaser wants as many agreed-on conditions in the contract as possible to ensure that at the closing the property will meet his or her requirements in every respect. On the other hand, the seller will generally not want any conditions whatsoever limiting the sale. The negotiations at this point should focus on limiting unilateral exit clauses for either party.

On the whole, a real estate sales contract should not be unconditional, because the costs of examining title and preparing the closing documents should be deferred until the acquisition appears to be a reasonable certainty. On the other hand, since most loan officers will not review an application without an executed sales agreement in hand, the parties will usually find it mutually beneficial to enter into a legally enforceable contract. The following are some of the conditions that the negotiating parties normally expect to be made part of a real estate sales contract.

Conditions Required by the Seller. The seller has less need for conditions than the buyer. His or her primary objective is to seek a firm price with clearly specified time and method for receipt of the cash. The closing documents can provide the remedies for any default. Usually the seller seeks to avoid any further obligation after the date of final settlement. It is appropriate for the seller to seek assurance that the buyer (individual, partnership, or corporation) has the legal power to close the transaction and that the person or persons acting on behalf of the buyer have been duly authorized to do so.

Conditions Required by the Purchaser. Objective standards should be set forth to define the purchaser's right to terminate. In order for a purchaser to use nonoccurrence of a condition precedent as a reason for not closing the contract, he or she must prove due diligence in attempting to make the condition come about. For example, if the purchaser wants to retain the right to withdraw because of an unsatisfactory feasibility report, he or she must make a "best effort" to investigate the location, market, and legal and political environment of the property. Other properties require the purchaser's best effort—seeking a building permit, a soil engineer's report, FHA approval of the development plan, and the like.

If possible, the purchaser should obtain seller's representations and warranties for conditions that must be fulfilled prior to or at the time of the closing of the transaction. Some typical representations and warranties are the following.

1. The property will not be threatened or adversely affected as a result of acts of God or municipal authorities, disaster, condemnation, and so forth on the closing date. This is a self-operating condition that can serve as an exit clause.

2. The seller shall provide for inspection prior to the closing date of all executed tenants' leases, along with their phone numbers and places of employment. Such leases are to be properly assigned at the closing.

3. The seller shall provide at the time of the closing a bill of sale for all personal property, furniture, fixtures, and equipment that are *not* attached and affixed to the realty. The seller shall also provide an adequate description of the structure, mentioning all fixtures attached, affixed, dedicated, and annexed to the realty and made part of the transaction.

4. The seller should warrant the adequacy and availability of all utility services. (This may be critical in commercial and industrial installations.)

5. The seller should warrant the structure to be sound and in good operating condition.

6. The seller should warrant any unique attributes of the property that are essential and prerequisite to the property's gross possible income.

7. The seller should provide an affirmative covenant to assure the purchaser's right to use the property for the purposes intended. On occasion occupancy permits are required by local law.

8. The seller should acknowledge that he or she continues to bear the risk of loss when the property is damaged through acts of God, casualty, or acts of the government or private parties during the period before the closing of the transaction. The seller should warrant that all special assessments and existing liens and taxes will have been paid prior to the closing. (In contrast to item 1, this is a guaranty clause that the buyer may exercise subject to litigation.)

9. The buyer should have protection against any defects in title to the property. Some kind of warranty deed is typically required.

10. The purchaser should be provided with covenants that will limit the effect of the doctrine of merger by deed. Otherwise, in many jurisdictions, the warranties and representations of the seller made before the conveyance will be a nullity and no longer enforceable immediately after the deed of conveyance has been recorded. The buyer should have the right to physical inspection of the property without waiver of the enforceability of the warranties and representations made by the seller and without eliminating the right to justifiable reliance under the doctrines of fraud, deceit, and misrepresentations.

Since some jurisdictions require time-is-of-the-essence clauses in real estate contracts unless the parties have stipulated otherwise, and since many of the requirements in the preceding list require time and effort, the contract should provide for an orderly way to handle delays and postponement of the closing date.

Conditions Required by Both Parties. Both parties should provide for a specific fixing of liability for all closing costs, rather than depending on vague customs and traditions that vary from one locality to another. The purchase contract should also define who is to pay the finder's fees, the broker's commission, financing fees, points, and so forth, and should provide for the proration of real estate taxes, rents, interests, insurance, and expenses relating to the property as of a specified date. It is not desirable in many transactions to use the closing date as the date of proration, although it may be preferred by the attorneys, because delays in the closing date act to the disadvantage of the seller and can cause a carefully negotiated deal to fall through.

Both parties will find it desirable to provide for severability of good contract clauses in the event of amendments to the contract, and in the event of a material mutual mistake or other specified surprise events, such as a national emergency, credit rationing, or unexpected condemnations. The investor should keep in mind that he or she purchases investment properties for economic return and not to win a contest. Therefore, it is better to provide for specified remedies and liquidated damages for breach of contract than to consume management skills in frustrating litigation. In some jurisdictions it may be preferable to consider an arbitration clause to handle such disputes.[7]

Both parties should be willing to specify the nature of the seller's duty to deliver a good and marketable title. In some jurisdictions certain entities are barred by law from using a general warranty deed that provides conditions tantamount to a good and marketable title, free and clear of all liens and encumbrances. It is recommended that the contract include a so-called Mother Hubbard clause to the effect that the description includes all the property owned by the seller at the location or, if appropriate, that it includes all real property owned by the seller in the particular city or county.

An accurate description of the property should be obtained and included in the contract. Appropriate sources of legal descriptions include current surveys, copies of the seller's warranty deed or title policy, a current title report or title binder. The purchaser should not rely blindly on the description of the property furnished by the seller. To be enforceable, a contract must furnish a means of determining with reasonable certainty the property intended to be conveyed by it.

Both parties should mutually agree on and enumerate the duties that the purchaser is to assume at the time of the closing (e.g., the duty to pay the price in cash). Some transactions use complex, creative forms of financing, such as purchase money mortgages and purchase–leasebacks. Since such clauses shift the risk of loss and gain back and forth, they are critical to the implementation of the investment strategy and should be negotiated carefully.

No one can prepare a real estate sales contract that will anticipate every possible problem and contingency. However, investors should not use a mortgage document or other contract form as part of the negotiations without being fully knowledgeable about the duties and obligations assumed by the parties and their economic effects on the investment. Buyers should be particularly wary of a switch to another document as negotiations progress; the so-called fine print may actually be effectively changing the understanding between the parties.

ENDING THE NEGOTIATIONS—FINAL SETTLEMENT AND CLOSING

The ten-step investment analysis model presented here should enable the investor to reach the final negotiation and closing stage with greater likeli-

---

[7]Edgar H. Hemmer and Mary C. Hotopp, "It's Better to Arbitrate Than to Litigate," *Real Estate Review*, Winter 1986, pp. 85–89.

hood of success than a less orderly approach to real estate acquisition.[8] However, the investor should be fully aware that the opposing parties are human beings who may arrive at the closing not fully prepared to complete the transaction. It is not uncommon for one or the other of the parties not to have fulfilled certain conditions. However, if the investor is to make a successful acquisition, the contract documents should be a guide to final settlement and not a tool for litigation.

Being unable to compromise is one of the handicaps of many real estate entrepreneurs. The investor should not accommodate an unethical bargainer and should not deviate from the investment strategy or go outside the range of acceptable prices and terms. Nor should the investor hesitate to abort a closing and reset the closing date if the other party has failed to fulfill some essential condition, even though it is claimed to be trivial. Many unethical bargainers, operating under the premise that anything is worth a try, use this tactic to squeeze the deal for an extra few dollars. The opposing party must defend by quietly insisting on fulfillment of the contractual obligations. This can be done in an amiable but firm manner.

In a complex transaction, phone communications may be necessary to complete the transaction. It is not uncommon for the purchaser to require that the seller provide an agent so that the premises can be inspected simultaneously with the closing to verify that all personal property, furniture, and equipment are present on the site. The seller should be willing to notify all tenants in writing of the change in ownership and direct them to pay future rents to the purchaser. Keys to the property should be transferred before witnesses. The parties should proceed to change over the utilities with dispatch, and the buyer should in fact take possession by means of an actual personal inspection as soon as possible after the closing. Finally, both parties should immediately deposit all cash and checks. Many sellers will not even permit checks to be drawn on out-of-state or out-of-town banks, and require that they be either cashier's or certified checks.

A successful legal closing often depends on the particular skills of an attorney who specializes in such transactions. Even attorneys who are knowledgeable in syndication and complex financing transactions are often not very well qualified to handle the complexities of a closing in a particular jurisdiction, and an investor is well advised to bear the costs of the services of a closing attorney recommended by trusted advisers.

---

[8] Articles on achieving successful results in real estate negotiations now appear in several magazines and journals on a regular basis. Such articles appear in the features section of *Real Estate Review*, for example. See John Oharenko and Mark Lindsay, "Negotiating Real Estate Financing Fees," *Real Estate Review*, Winter 1986, pp. 108–111; A. Haynes, "Real Estate Dealing: Negotiating Higher Yields," *Real Estate Review*, Spring 1983, pp. 10–12; R. Bell, "Negotiating the Real Estate Joint Venture," *Real Estate Review*, Fall 1983, pp. 34–44. Another example is Clarence S. Barasch, "Negotiating Real Estate Brokerage Agreements," *Real Estate Law Journal*, Winter 1980, pp. 240–254.

SUMMARY

Real estate transactions are complex because each parcel is unique, and negotiation priorities vary from one transaction to the next. A successful negotiator can identify and define the issues, evaluate the opponent's position to determine strengths and weaknesses, engage in mutual accommodation, and justify his or her position in reasonable terms. A negotiator should also be thoroughly prepared to offer and handle the compromises and concessions that are necessary to produce the agreement.

The following is a convenient checklist for the real estate negotiation process.

CHECKLIST
Guide to Real Estate Negotiations

The Role of Negotiation: Satisfying Needs

1. Engage in cooperative bargaining rather than confrontation.
   a. Try to satisfice, not maximize.
   b. The goal is a basic meeting of minds.
2. Control behavior with the strategic plan.
   a. Use the basic financial feasibility model.
   b. Fact finding is essential to defining the issues.
   c. Careful preparation means understanding the assumptions.
   d. Determine the strengths and weaknesses of both sides.
3. Be prepared for mutual accommodations.

The Psychology of Negotiation

1. Know your "audience."
   a. Whom are you trying to please?
   b. Whom is the opponent trying to please?
   c. To whom are the negotiating parties accountable?
   d. Know relevant human and cultural traits.
2. Be aware of the roles played by negotiating parties.
   a. Be wary of rigid types.
   b. Be wary of high rollers.
   c. "Don't trust me—I'm out to get you."
   d. "Trust me—I'll be fair."
   e. "Trust me—I only want what's coming to me."
3. Know your self-concept.
   a. Control the desire to control others.
   b. Be aware of the need to win and achieve.
   c. Avoid being overly trusting or overly suspicious.
   d. Avoid being manipulative and exploitive.
4. Be informed about the opponent's self-concept.
5. Carefully consider the physical factors that affect negotiations.
   a. The location—your place or mine or a neutral place?
   b. The setup—where to sit, colors, air-conditioning, and other comfort factors.
   c. What are the time limits?
6. Use professionals to assist in negotiations.

7. Be wary of using other partners in negotiations.
   a. Who's in charge here?
   b. What are the limits on each partner's authority and flexibility?

Arriving at Mutually Acceptable Terms

1. Properly characterize the market activity.
   a. Is it a seller's market?
   b. Is it a buyer's market?
   c. Is it a normal market?
2. Be careful in using GRMs, cap rates, square-foot prices, and so on.
3. Be aware of unique predicaments of buyers or sellers.
4. Make effective use of the market value, most probable selling price, and investment value concepts.
5. Estimate the range of your offers and counteroffers in advance.
6. Consider in advance the nonprice factors that can affect your return–risk relationships.

Getting What You Bargained For

1. For the buyer: What are the necessary conditions?
2. For the seller: What conditions do you require to close?
3. Identify the conditions both parties need for reassurance.
4. Provide for specified remedies and liquidated damages, if possible.

Ending Negotiations—Final Settlement and Closing

1. Be prepared to compromise within the strategic plan.
2. Cordially and respectfully demand fulfillment of return–risk expectations within any contract provision.
3. Use an attorney who has experience in closings within the jurisdiction.
   a. Require an inspection.
   b. Require lease assignments.
   c. Do not waive essential warranties and representations that must survive the closing.
   d. Take hard positions when rights and duties were unmistakably clear in the real estate contract.
   e. Cooperate with your closing attorney, but make your own business policy decisions.
   f. Do not be afraid to abort and reschedule a closing if *essential* terms are not being fulfilled.
4. Do not squeeze for the last buck! If it is still a good deal, be willing to close.

ASPEN WOOD APARTMENTS

THE FINAL SALES CONTRACT

Previous chapters have described various stages of negotiation that occurred from July 1974 to November 1974, when the final purchase structure was established. The bargaining position of the seller had been substantially reduced over time as a result of severe property management and operating problems and pressure from local commercial banks to repay short-term loans used to finance capital improvements and operating losses. The sellers readily accepted the major parameters of the restructured financial package described in Chapter 9, including a selling price of $1,003,400 and a favorable wraparound mortgage, and substantial tax shelter in the year of purchase.

The final sales contract, signed on December 6, 1974, reflected the outcome of extensive negotiations and compromises by both parties. It included the following provisions.

Description of Parties and Property. Charles Davidson, trustee, was the designated purchaser acting on behalf of the joint venture, and the three general partners of the limited partnership acted on behalf of the seller. Davidson and Boomer were concerned that the designated general partners did not have the legal authority to sign the sales contract, and demanded a copy of the limited-partnership agreement for review and verification by their attorney. In addition, the real and personal property items involved in the sale were carefully described to prevent any misunderstandings. Nevertheless, subsequent to the signing of the contract a disagreement arose over numerous pieces of expensive furniture in the sales office. The seller claimed that they were the personal property of an employee of one of the general partners. Negotiation and compromise ensued to resolve the disagreement.

Consideration for the Transaction. The total amounts of equity and debt and the timing of all payments were detailed. The purchaser was to pay $10,000 as earnest money to a local title company to secure the contract, and the additional equity cash at closing. Because of the depressed local investment economy, as well as the occupancy and operating problems that developed in the fall of 1974, Davidson and Boomer were not able to raise the full $150,000 in cash that was due the seller at closing (equity of $210,000 less $10,000 earnest money and $50,000 commission). To solve the problem, the seller agreed to accept a non-interest-bearing, nonrecourse note of $10,500 for one year, representing a one-half-share equity interest in the property. It was agreed that the note would be retired as soon as D&B sold the remaining half-share. The provisions of the wraparound mortgage note of $793,400 were to be administered by a local commercial bank that would act as a trustee for both the seller and the purchaser; the bank would be empowered to collect all payments on the wraparound note, make the debt service payments on the underlying mortgage notes, and deposit the remaining balance in the seller's account.

The total project cost also included two mortgage points (2 percent of the original loan balance), $59,505 of prepaid interest, and a real estate commission of $50,000 to D&B Associates, D&B would not receive the $50,000 commission until all remaining equity shares were sold, which occurred in April 1975.

Provisions of the Wraparound Mortgage. The contract specified that the sellers were to obtain any consents or waivers of provisions in any of the underlying notes and deeds of trust that would restrict in any manner D&B's ability to purchase the property or to transfer the title at some future time. The sellers bargained for a due-on-sale clause in the wraparound mortgage, but Davidson and Boomer insisted on waiver of such a clause; in return for that concession, it was agreed that the seller had the option to substitute another mortgage for the wraparound mortgage after five years, under specific conditions that would leave the new owners in an unchanged financial condition. A trust agreement was to be entered into by the buyer, the seller, and the bank trustee; Davidson and Boomer, who were in the driver's seat at this stage, appointed their bank as the designated trustee.

Proration of Closing Costs. The seller was to furnish the buyer, at its cost, a title policy in the full amount of the purchase price, a survey, and a set of building plans and specifications within fifteen days of the contract signing. Taxes and insurance were to be prorated as of the date of closing, and based on year-end actuals rather than estimated amounts. Legal costs and recording fees related to the closing were divided equally between seller and buyer (see the closing statement, Exhibit 15-A).

Conditions Necessary to the Purchaser. D&B was obligated to consummate the purchase only if (1) the seller provided an acceptable title policy and survey and (2) all mechanical equipment was in good working condition at the time of closing. For any other reason, D&B could terminate the contract and lose only its $10,000 earnest money. The final draft of the contract explicitly recognized defective roof conditions and water heater malfunctions that could not be corrected prior to closing. Additional moneys were to be escrowed by the seller to guarantee payment for roof repairs and provide a warranty fund for one year on the project's four central hot-water heaters. The risk of any loss or damage was not to pass to D&B until delivery and recording of the general warranty deed, and until the insurance policies were transferred to the buyer. In addition, D&B required a specific performance clause in the contract requiring the seller to deliver the property to the purchaser at closing. Finally, the seller was to provide to the buyer at closing a general warranty deed and bills of sale for all personal property involved in the transaction.

Conditions Necessary to the Seller. The main consideration of the seller–general partners was to get to a closing, receive as much of the $150,000 cash payment as possible, retire the bank loans, and get the limited partners off their backs. As described in Chapter 9, they did insist on a refinancing clause that would allow them to substitute another loan for their wraparound loan, thereby

EXHIBIT 15-A.   Aspen Wood Closing Statement

CITY TITLE COMPANY, INC.
500 GRANDE
AUSTIN, TEXAS 78767

PURCHASER/BORROWER'S STATEMENT

Purchaser/Borrower Charlie Davidson, Trustee
Seller/Contractor Sellers Ltd.
Address of Property Aspen Wood Apts.   *Closing Date* 11/1/74
Lender   *Closer* Smith   *GF*

Purchase/Contract Price		$878,027.00
CLOSING COSTS		
Appraisal or Examination Fee	$	
Credit Report	$	
Photographs (for Mortgage Company)	$	
Loan/Finance Fee	$	
Survey	$	
Attorney's Fees		
Preparation of Note and Deed of Trust	$ 70.00	
	$	
Recording Fees to County Clerk	$ 16.00	
Interim Construction Title Policy Binder	$	
Owner's Title Policy	$	
Mortgagee's Title Policy	$	
Transfer Fee	$	
Processing Fee	$	
Tax Information	$	
2% of Note	$ 15,868.00	
One-year's Prepaid Interest	$ 59,505.00	
Total Closing Costs		$ 75,459.00
PREPAID ITEMS		
Hazard Insurance (one year in advance)	$	
FHA Mutual Mortgage Fee (one month in advance)	$	
*_____ Taxes	$	
*_____ Hazard Insurance	$	
Interest (for balance of current month)	$	
Total Prepaid Items		$ —0—
TOTAL CLOSING COSTS AND PREPAID ITEMS		$ 75,459.00
TOTAL DUE FROM PURCHASER/BORROWER		$953,486.00
CREDITS		
Downpayment held in escrow by	$	
Loan from Seller	$793,400.00	
Second lien	$	
Loan balance assumed at	$	
Tax proration	$	
Note	$ 2,125.00	
Rent deposit and expense adjustment as per attached statement	$ 12,487.64	
Total Credits		$808,012.64
BALANCE PAID to/by PURCHASER/BORROWER		$145,473.36
Amount paid as per contract (balance pd. by Seller)		$

* Deposited in escrow account with above-mentioned Mortgage Company. Tax deposit based on estimated annual taxes of $_____ and is subject to future adjustment. Pro rata taxes collected from Seller in the sum of $_____ and deposited in Purchaser's escrow account.

This is to certify that the foregoing is a true and correct statement of fees and charges to Purchasers herein named.

Received of _____ the above mentioned sum of $_____ representing loan to me/us; and I/we hereby approve payment of the items charged above.

I/We further certify that the above purchase price is the true and correct consideration paid to the Seller for this property.

CITY TITLE CO., INC   _____

By *Fred N. Route*   _____
        Closing Officer/Attorney

Estimated monthly payment:
Principal & Interest: First payment due:
Tax escrow:
Insurance escrow:

releasing to them the equity remaining in the wraparound loan. This clause was necessary if certain limited partners were to approve the sale.

Closing Date. The final contract specified a closing date on or before December 10, 1974, but all prorations of income and expenses were to be made effective November 1, 1974, in order to achieve the desired financial results for the new investors. In fact, the closing was not completed and deeds fully recorded until December 28, 1974, because of additional problems that occurred in mid-December. The on-site property management was so poor that tenants were deserting their units, suing the owners for property damage caused by their failure to make necessary roof repairs, and discouraging potential renters from signing leases. Under threat of contract termination, the seller reluctantly agreed to guarantee rents and expenses at the pro forma projection levels for the months of November and December. Despite these problems, D&B believed it could release most of the units by the middle of January, the following month, and achieve the projected pro forma results in 1975.

Another source of delay was the requirement that the general partners receive the consent of a majority of the limited partners regarding the essential terms of the sale. Because of the complex and dynamic nature of the changes taking place and the negotiations that ensued, that consent was difficult to obtain and was discouraging to all the parties in the transaction. Persistence and patience on the part of all concerned resulted in a closing on December 28. The property management (the subject of the following chapter) took over the property on the afternoon of that day and was expected to salvage a near-disaster occupancy and tenant morale situation.

16

PROPERTY AND ASSET MANAGEMENT

FRANK & ERNEST

THE PURPOSE OF PROPERTY MANAGEMENT

For many newcomers to the world of real estate investment, property management may appear to involve little more than property supervision: collecting rents, maintaining the property, filling vacancies. It is sad to note that this limited perspective of building management is often found even in the property management industry itself. However, there is real need for a careful look at the role of property management both before investment decisions are made and after the real estate purchase.

The purpose of property management is to implement appropriate strategies with the long-term goal of maximizing the desired return from the investment throughout the life of the property. The significant life of a property is determined by the length of time the investor–owner plans to hold that property; the desired return is determined by the owner before purchase, with the consultation of a local professional management firm whenever possible. On the basis of this information, strategies are developed and stated in a management plan prepared jointly by the owner and the firm or individual who will manage the property.

A real estate investment can be structured to generate one or more of several types of returns: cash flow to investors, appreciation of investor capital, and shelter of cash flow and other income from taxation. Once the investor has specified the type of return desired, its mix, and its expected timing, an appropriate management plan can then be developed. Planning, with its resulting control, is the foundation of effective property management.

If, for example, an owner were seeking to maximize cash flow during a two- to three-year period, with the goal of selling the real estate at the end of the period, the property manager would probably plan to defer as much maintenance and repair as possible. Considering the short period of time, the manager might reasonably assess that maintenance deferral would have only a limited impact on the property's resale value. If, on the other hand, the owner were expecting to hold the property over a long term, the property manager would probably design a strong preventive maintenance program and give corrective maintenance high priority, thus preventing significant deterioration of the investment over time.

THE MANAGEMENT FUNCTION

Meeting the management demands of the various types of real estate requires a diversity of property management staffing, structure, compensation, and information and decision-making systems. The need for a carefully constructed plan cannot be over-emphasized. Although the day-to-day tasks of property management may lack the excitement of negotiating and closing a transaction, poor or inept management can undermine the potential gains, or increase the losses, of any property. Even undeveloped land requires attention to such management-related issues as site hazards, local development trends, taxes, and legal codes.

If any such issues are allowed to follow an uncharted course, it becomes difficult to make the necessary modifications or changes in direction when problems arise. The result is a lack of control that can quickly develop into reactive, ineffective, and often expensive management by crisis. It should be noted that adherence to a management plan does not preclude flexibility. Meeting the management demands of the various types of real estate requires ongoing reevaluation of decisions on insurance, repairs and maintenance, staffing, and other aspects of property management.

Property management encompasses a broad range of activities which can be broken down into five basic areas of responsibility, some of which overlap. Each of these is detailed later in the chapter.

1. *Prepurchase consultation.* A professional property manager familiar with the intricacies of the local market can prove to be a valuable

asset during the decision-making process by evaluating the possible returns on specific properties.

2. *Market promotion and leasing.* The property manager performs market research, implements a merchandising strategy, selects tenants, and prepares leases.

3. *Operation of the property.* Managing the physical asset and tenant management are broad definitions for a vast array of both long- and short-term responsibilities. Capital improvements, employee selection, and supervision of the maintenance and administrative staffs and of independent contractors, tenant relations, rent collections, and evictions are all integral components of property management.

4. *Administrative responsibilities, including financial reporting and controls.* The property manager prepares the operating budget, keeps detailed records, maintains accounts, develops an insurance program, administers a maintenance plan, and sees that the property complies with federal, state, and local laws. Fortunately, this age of computer technology has simplified many of these tasks and others necessary in operating a property.

5. *Counseling and communicating with the investor.* Counseling does not end with the purchase of the property but presupposes an ongoing evaluation of the local market and its trends. Owners and investors must be kept up-to-date on the performance of the property and its management, on methods of enhancing the value of the real estate, and on refinancing, capital improvements, and selling.

THE NEED FOR QUALITY PROPERTY MANAGEMENT

Managing the property is an essential cost of operation during the ownership years of a real estate investment cycle. Therefore, property owners must pay close attention to the management function to ensure that any deficiencies are corrected before they have a negative effect on the investment. Similarly, management itself must be more responsive to owners' requirements than ever before.

A property manager is any person—an owner, an employee, a general or special agent, or an independent contractor—who has the power to direct and control the real estate or to advise the investor with respect to management of the property. However, because of the critical and long-term nature of the management function, consideration should be given to the variety and depth of good property management.

In the past, investors were often satisfied with real estate investments that performed in accordance with original projections, unaware that their gains were frequently a result of inflationary economic conditions, not good management. With the increasing acceptance of real estate as a desirable pension fund investment and with the tremendous growth of syndications, however, the positive effects of good property management began to receive increased attention. These trends combined with the real estate investment trusts (REITs) crisis of the mid-1970s to reinforce the need for effective property management.[1]

During the early 1970s, real estate appeared to be such a solid investment that investment bankers, commercial banks, and other financial conglomerates were able to make an abundance of loans using large pools of capital funds created specifically for investing in real estate or real estate mortgage loans. The ready availability of these REIT loans to developers soon brought about a period of overbuilding. By the mid-1970s, the supply of available rental units exceeded demand. When occupancy levels fell below the percentage needed to pay the interest on these loans, the marketplace became imbalanced and many properties were foreclosed. The properties that survived the crisis could attribute much of their success to having given adequate attention to management.

The proliferation of real estate investment vehicles now in operation has made it easier than in the past to compare overall investment returns and has helped to establish the importance of property management capabilities as a prerequisite for the continued success of an investment. Experience has proved that the quality of management is often critical in determining the ultimate success or failure of an investment.

PROFESSIONAL PROPERTY MANAGEMENT VERSUS SELF-MANAGEMENT

This chapter explores the variety of management functions necessary to ensure the success of any real estate investment. Meanwhile, entire books have been written on the subject in great and necessary detail. The real estate investor should know and understand the critical and multifaceted requirements of property management, but it is not always necessary that he or she personally manage the properties. The choice between professional and self-management is largely dependent on the financial circumstances of the owner, the number and types of properties owned, and a number of personal preferences.

Defining the scope of management services required by specific types of real estate is the first course of action, because the very nature of the property may determine the extent of, and therefore the appropriate person for, its management. For example, an eight-unit apartment building prob-

---

[1]Paul D. Lapides, *Managing Residential Real Estate* (Boston: Warren, Gorham & Lamont, 1986), p. 1.3. Also see Austin J. Jaffe, *Property Management in Real Estate Investment Decision-Making* (Lexington, Mass.: Lexington Books, Heath, 1979).

ably needs no more than a part-time resident manager, either the investor or a tenant who is paid through a reduction in rent. The investor would do the budgeting, accounting, and other administrative tasks, and the manager would collect rents, select tenants, handle tenant complaints, and so on. Moving up the scale in terms of property size would eventually justify contracting the services of an independent property manager (at, say, 24 units) as well as maintaining a person on the site. Some large investors have enough projects within one MSA to justify an in-house property management organization.

Whoever accepts the responsibility for management should be able to meet the performance projections on which the investor's purchase decision was based. David W. Walters has analyzed how changes in certain variables can affect a typical apartment project's IRR.[2] Although Walters's analysis deals with only one project, it appears that the investor should give high priority to competent, creative property management.

Good property management cannot be taken for granted. Not only can skillful management have a significant impact on rate of return,[3] but a good manager can also do much to obtain optimal market rents, keep tenants satisfied, achieve lower turnover, and provide up-to-date financial information. Factors such as a low purchase price can do much to improve projected returns, but an experienced property manager also considers the need for capital improvements, deferred maintenance, and other possibilities. Consequently, seeking a property manager's judgment during the preacquisition stage could prove invaluable during negotiations and development of the management plan and merchandising strategy.

If professional property management is chosen over self-management, the authority of the manager and the scope and nature of the services to be performed for the specific property should be carefully defined.[4] The authority of the investor over asset and venture management and other functions specifically reserved to him or her should also be clearly understood.

[2]David W. Walters, "Just How Important Is Property Management?" *The Journal of Property Management*, July–August 1978, pp. 164–168. See also Don W. Carlson, "Professional Property Management: The Real Estate Key to a Successful Real Estate Venture," *The Journal of Property Management*, November–December 1977, pp. 295–297; and Don D. Rake, "Optimization of Property Value Through Professional Management," *Commercial Investment Real Estate Journal*, Winter 1985, pp. 41–44, 48.

[3]James R. Cooper and Stephen A. Pyhrr, "Forecasting the Rates of Return on an Apartment," *The Appraisal Journal*, July 1973, pp. 312–337; see also Austin J. Jaffe, "The Property Manager: Foremost among the Decision-Makers," *The Journal of Property Management*, November–December 1977, pp. 288–290; and George W. Gau, "Real Estate Investment Returns: Implications for Management," *The Journal of Property Management*, July–August 1982, pp. 10–11.

[4]David W. Walters, "Negotiating the Property Management Agreement," *The Journal of Property Management*, November–December 1977, pp. 291–294; John McMahan, *Property Management* (New York McGraw-Hill, 1976).

CONSIDERATIONS FOR THE FORM OF MANAGEMENT

Time investment. The primary difficulty in self-management of property is a matter of the time consumed, because property management requires extraordinary attention to detail and follow-through to avoid a variety of potential crises. Roof repairs, tenant complaints, and changes in property laws, for instance, often require immediate attention. Such demands can interfere with the investor's primary career or other objectives, or rob him or her of time that could be more profitably devoted to such investment management functions as new acquisitions and refinancing.

Individual preference. Much depends on the nature of the individual investor, many of whom by nature prefer a passive involvement; REITs are required by law not to manage property. A person seeking to be an idle capitalist does not have the time to perform the property management function adequately.

Knowledge of an expert. An obvious argument for the professional property manager is often critical need for expertise in real estate management. For example, many investors are lulled into a sense of security by 100 percent occupancy and the achievement of budget objectives, but an agent with an eye on market trends could warn that it is time to sell or raise rents before market trends have fully developed.

Approach. Too often, institutional investors such as REITs and life insurance companies view the property management function as akin to bond "coupon clipping"—as though rents were simply interest payments. Independent professional management should be the policy of institutional investors unless they hold a large enough portfolio within one MSA to justify a separate management subsidiary with *independent*, semiautonomous authority.

Training. The key skills in managing a property require that the property manager be a generalist rather than a specialist. Although it is not uncommon for CPAs, engineers, and commercial real estate brokers to become property managers, new and demanding skills must be developed to manage a large complex or many different projects.

Cost. To some, the retention or saving of management fees rather than payment to third parties is a primary advantage of self-management. Some even include the management fees produced by the equity investor's "sweat" as part of the return on investment. Beginning investors are often forced to take on the burdens of management in order to gain entry into real estate investing. Because of diseconomies of scale, it is difficult to justify professional, independent property management for any real estate investment with fewer than twenty units or a gross effective income of $50,000. Group equity investing could be a good alternative because it spreads the risk to more than one location and provides the opportunity for third-party professional management as desired. Indeed, one possibility is to invest in a project in which a professional manager has purchased a share as part of the syndicate and has also made a commitment to act as manager, as in the Aspen Wood Apartments case study.

As an agent of the owner's quest to maximize rents, minimize expenses, and conserve the asset so as to protect and enhance its value, the manager generally receives a carefully laid-out system of performance-oriented compensation and incentives.[5] These represent funds that would otherwise line the investor's pockets. Incentives may also be paid for new leases, renewals, and the achievement of a level of rent receipts that exceeds budgeted expectations. Information on typical fees and commissions is usually available through local lenders, appraisers, and other investors. This information can then be used as a guideline for negotiated compensation. (Uniform fee schedules are a violation of antitrust laws.)

Delegation of authority. As previously mentioned, the property manager must have a certain amount of authority in order to perform properly. Many individuals may not feel comfortable delegating such responsibility to another or placing beyond their immediate control factors that may prove to be the difference between the success and failure of a property. This is one reason why effective communications between investor and manager are so essential, if the professional management route is chosen.

In any contract for professional management services, practicality suggests an enabling clause that states the delegation of authority in enough scope and detail to make clear that the manager is the steward of the asset and the custodial caretaker of it as long as he or she is the agent, independent contractor, or employee. Practicality also suggests that the investor establish a limited power of attorney to the full-time manager, who should also have (1) the right to execute and terminate leases; (2) the right to meet the state and federal filing requirements for tax payments (e.g., withholding, FICA) and to ensure that standards of the Occupational Safety and Health Act (OSHA), workers' compensation, civil rights, building codes, and litigation regarding the property are all complied with; (3) the power to distribute net operating income to debt service and periodic cash distributions to various owners; (4) the authority to deal with any emergency-

---

[5]On the other hand, a strong argument can be made for basing management commissions on a property's net operating income (NOI). For example, see Austin J. Jaffe, "A Reexamination of the Problem of Management Fee Assessment," *The Journal of Property Management*, January–Februrary 1979, pp. 339–347.

fire, panic, safety, sanitation, electricity, plumbing, water, or heat; and (5) the power to hire, fire, and supervise personnel.

Although some investors deliberately seek to avoid dealing with such details themselves, others view such delegation of responsibility as a loss of control. Again, it is a matter of personal preference.

Other details. When the owner relies on professional management, along with this delegation of authority he or she assumes new responsibilities. Depending on the size of the project, an owner may be required to provide fidelity bonding, errors and omissions insurance, and so forth. In addition, a save-harmless (or hold-harmless) clause should be negotiated. There are other contingencies and risks to be taken into consideration, and no contract can provide for all possible circumstances. However, a long-term manager must feel free to exert his or her best good-faith effort without fear of reprisal for honest errors of judgment.

SELECTION OF A PROPERTY MANAGER

The selection of an appropriate manager often depends on his or her subjective qualities, yet a great deal rides on the choice. Personal, direct negotiations with the person whose expertise will determine so much of the investment performance is a sine qua non (prerequisite) of good selection. The investor should look for personality attributes that are compatible with the property management functions, some of which are listed here.

1. Capacity to handle many small details.
2. Ability to negotiate with suppliers, subcontractors, owners, tenants, and employees.
3. Assertiveness, decisiveness, and energy.
4. Entrepreneurial skills coupled with the ability to work within an organized structure.
5. Professional commitment to truth, purpose, responsibility, and trust, coupled with a continuing interest in professional education.
6. Capacity to be an officer, to supervise employees, to give direction to the business, and to enhance the value of the investment.

In *The Practice of Property Management*, William Walters, Jr. provides job descriptions that can help the investor match the necessary behavioral attitudes with the kind of property management required by a specific investment.[6]

---

[6]William Walters, Jr., *The Practice of Property Management* (Chicago: National Association of Realtors, Institute of Real Estate Management, 1979). See also William M. Shenkel, *Modern Real Estate Principles* (Dallas: Business Publications, 1984), Chap. 18;

Property management is a relatively new profession. Through the Institute of Real Estate Management (IREM), individuals can now become certified property managers (CPMs) upon completion of a course of study, examinations, and specific experience. In addition, IREM accredits on-site managers with the accredited resident manager (ARM) designation, and business organizations can be designated as Approved Management Organizations (AMOs). Other designations are possible as well. All members are expected to meet standards of professional conduct, as defined by the IREM code of ethics and regulated by local chapters and the national organization.[7] If at all possible, an investor should obtain up-to-date comments on the competence of prospective managers from local lenders, appraisers, bankers, and other investors.

It is suggested that investors utilize professional property managers unless they have enough real estate assets to operate profitably an "in-house," full-time property management division, or have the skill and desire to self-manage. In the balance of the chapter, an independent property management is assumed.

Generally, the relationship between an independent property manager and the investor is defined in a written contract which (1) fully describes the property; (2) enumerates the scope, nature, and extent of the manager's authority; and (3) considers the length of agreement, resolution of disputes, termination of the contract, and causes for discharge. Provision should be made for the owner's right to terminate in the event that specified profit or occupany objectives are not met. However, property managers who take over projects with special problems should be allowed ample time to achieve occupancy and cash flow objectives.

PREPURCHASE CONSULTATIONS

Property Manager's Prepurchase Advice

By engaging the services of a property manager during the prepurchase decision-making phase, an investor can attain an expert evaluation of the property's niche in the market and its most effective use.[8] The property

---

Alfred A. Ring and Jerome Dasso, *Real Estate Principles and Practice*, 9th ed. (Englewood Cliffs, N.J.: Prentice–Hall, 1985), Chaps. 25–26; Alvin L. Arnold, Charles H. Wurtzebach, and Mike E. Miles, *Modern Real Estate* (Boston: Warren, Gorham & Lamont, 1987), Chap. 8; Albert J. Lowry, *How to Manage Real Estate Successfully in Your Spare Time* (New York: Simon & Schuster, 1977); C. W. Bailey, "Do You Need a Professional Management Company?" *The Journal of Property Management*, May–June 1976, pp. 150–154.

[7]James C. Downs, Jr., *Principles of Real Estate Management* (Chicago: Institute of Real Estate Management, 1980), p. 25.

[8]Alvin A. Arnold, *Real Estate Syndication Manual* (Boston: Warren, Gorham & Lamont, 1984), pp. 9–12 through 9–14.

manager's skills may be used (1) to evaluate the existing design, layout, and physical condition of a prospective investment, (2) to estimate the revenue and expenses likely to be produced from the highest and best use, or (3) to estimate the cost of conversion to a higher or better use and the return–risk relationship implicit in such a change. The prepurchase consultant need not be the same person who ultimately managers the property, if outside management is chosen.

Before a decision to purchase is made, a management plan should be developed—at least in general terms—and planning for space should be included as a crucial first step. The investor must clearly identify the user in order to match the property management services with the user's needs. Property managers who work daily in the user's market are best equipped, once the user profile has been identified, to give the investor the best estimates for market rent schedules. In addition, property managers are often consulted on such questions as whether or not a property should be modernized, rehabilitated, converted to another use, or, conceivably, demolished to minimize taxes.

It should be noted that to the skilled property manager, modernization, rehabilitation, and conversion are technical terms with specific meanings.

1. *Modernization* (remodeling) consists of an effort to overcome functional obsolescence and extend the economic life of a building by replacing worn-out equipment. Generally, there is no change in use. However, room layouts may be improved, and outmoded heating equipment, lighting fixtures, and plumbing may be replaced.

2. *Rehabilitation* is the process of restoring a structure to like-new condition, giving it new economic life without significant change in the design or present use.

3. *Conversion* is succession to a different use. Some conversions are physical in nature, such as changing an old warehouse into a shopping complex. Others may be primarily a change in concept, such as converting from rental to condominium ownership.

IREM has designed a management plan that provides a comprehensive economic analysis of income property for prepurchase evaluation.[9] Much of the work performed by certified property managers (CPMs) is similar to that performed by MAIs (member, Appraisal Institute), senior real estate analysts (SREAs), or other appraisers. The CCIM (certified commercial investment member) designates of the Realtors National Marketing Institute (RNMI) may also do such work. Whoever prepares such a survey should relate the use of the space to a preliminary operating statement, a marketability analysis, and competitive surveys. This enables the investor to develop a comprehensive plan for capital additions and a maintenance

---

[9]Downs, *Principles*, pp. 157–167.

policy, both of which may affect either the acquisition price or the decision to purchase.

Predicting Maintenance and Capital Additions Costs

Before property is acquired, provisions should be made for a reserve for capital improvements, to cover rehabilitation and other capital expenditures. Although there is no clear-cut line separating capital expenditures from normal maintenance, both must be provided for in the management plan and operating budget because of their impact on extending the ordinary operating efficiency of an asset over its useful life.

According to the Internal Revenue Service, a capital addition is an item completed or installed to add value, extend useful life, or adapt the asset to a different use. Maintenance, on the other hand, is generally continuous and routine and is done to prevent the disruption of service. Repairs are a form of maintenance performed when service is disrupted. Under this definition, "patching" leaks and replacing a "limited" number of shingles are considered repairs, whereas the addition of a new roof or replacements covering a "major" area are considered capital additions. It is easy to imagine the possible disagreements between the IRS and taxpayers on whether an item is a repair to be expensed and deducted or a capital addition to be capitalized and depreciated. Careful accounting records can help prove the distinction between maintenance and capital additions.

MARKET PROMOTION AND LEASING

Real estate investors operate a business, and marketing or merchandising the product is an essential function of that business. An empty building can be managed by any janitor or watchman; the real test of a property manager's skills is whether he or she can fill that space with appropriate users at market rents and keep it filled with a minimum of turnover and bad debts.

The primary purpose of leasing and marketing efforts is to attract good prospective tenants to the property and have them sign leases at market rents. Some of the factors that contribute to achieving this end include the property's appearance and location, the reputation of the property and the management company, the rental structure and amenities, and the appearance, attitude, and training of the staff. The first step is to determine appropriate rental rates and a tenant profile, which requires that the manager be aware of occupancy trends and employment changes in the market area, competition, and numerous other factors that affect rentals in the area. Ideally, these factors will have been determined before purchase.

Generally, the manager of a real estate product need not "sell" in the sense that a salesperson creates a need and then closes the transaction. An exception would be someone who is introducing a new concept of using space (e.g., office condominiums or time-sharing of a recreational facility). As a merchandiser, the property manager has three functions: (1) inducing customers targeted by the marketability analysis to see the property, (2) selling these prospective tenants on the space in preference to competitive alternatives, and (3) selecting good tenants.

Promoting the Project

Inducing the prospective tenants to see the project is the objective of advertising, public relations, and other promotional activities.

A carefully conceived and implemented merchandising strategy can be developed for any real estate product, although time and budget constraints will vary depending on the type, size, and location of the property. One simple approach to successful promotion is the development of a thematic image. The image can be achieved by capitalizing on architectural style or location, or by consistently using a name, logo, or symbols in promotional materials and activities designed to get prospects to the site. Once a thematic image has been selected, the property manager should establish a structured promotional program, of which signs and advertising are important elements.

Promotional, directional, informational, and permanent identification signs are valuable tools for building traffic to the site. Brochures also should maintain the thematic image, but should not be expected to sell the space. The possible exceptions to this rule are properties such as time-share condominiums and new office complexes or industrial spaces, which some decision makers may not visit.

The best advertisement is the project itself and a point-of-sale vacancy or "For Sale" sign. Over 50 percent of the people who sign leases do so because they liked what they saw when they drove by. The primary purpose of advertising is to attract prospects. A rule of thumb suggests that, on average, about five prospects are required for every lease. *When* to spend for advertising depends on the level of occupancy. *How much* to spend is a function of the size of the project and how well established the thematic image is in the target market. A typical budget guideline is 3 to 5 percent of gross effective income for overall promotional activities, including advertising.

Advertising media include radio and television; daily, weekly, and neighborhood newspapers; direct mail; yellow pages; classified ads; and bulletin boards, for example, in nearby supermarkets. Whatever advertising medium is used, a careful count should be made of the number of prospects generated per dollar expended. To make each advertising dollar effective, either the investor or, preferably, the property manager should be expert in the use of the promotional budget.

Another effective tool is public relations, which encompasses all interaction with the public as well as editorial coverage in newspapers and magazines to establish visibility and public identity. Examples of public relations activities designed to attract tenants are grand openings, direct mailings, and involvement in community affairs. Giveaway premiums for signing leases should be avoided because they encourage retaliatory competition that can substantially reduce net operating income.

Selecting Tenants

On the one hand, a tenant is potentially a stable and adequate income stream—that is, a person who will continue to pay the rent, possibly renew the lease, and use the property in accordance with the terms of the lease as long as the landlord upholds the standards of the lease. On the other hand, a tenant may be a source of bad debts, pilferage, vandalism, ignorant or irresponsible usage of the premises, discord among other tenants, litigation costs through eviction, and other problems that will diminish the owner's cash flow.

Ideally, the real estate product is sufficiently competitive to allow some choice of tenants, thereby minimizing bad debts and other problems. The Institute of Real Estate Management and competent local property managers have application forms that can be used as checklists to ensure that enough information is obtained for a prompt evaluation of the prospect before lease is executed. In evaluating the quality of would-be tenants, the manager should consider such criteria as credit worthiness, compatibility of tenants, and permanence potential. Just as careful tenant selection is important to maintaining the property's integrity, so is diplomacy. As part of the marketing and merchandising phase, it, too, creates an impression of the property. Consequently, care should be taken that even those who are turned away retain a favorable image of the real estate product.

Negotiating the Lease

The skilled property manager is fully aware that lease terms establish the rules of the game for a continuing relationship with the prospective tenant. Although it is a matter of judgment when the manager should make an issue of specific lease clauses, a discussion of lease terms is an excellent technique for eliciting prospect responses and revealing true motives. In the case of commercial–industrial properties, negotiating skills are especially critical because lease clauses can be used to shift risk between investors–owners and users–lessees.

The following is a brief discussion of some of the more typical lease terms that affect return and risk.

The Lease. A carefully conceived, fair, and equitable lease is essential to a good image and efficient property management. It also encompasses the rights and obligations of the owner and tenants within the law of the jurisdiction. In the United States there is a wide range of judicial decisions and statutory laws, and therefore a great variance in the terms that are enforceable locally. The standard-form leases of local owner–manager associations are a good starting point for choosing and developing a lease that is appropriate to the real estate property. Such leases may even be preferable because they have passed the test of local litigation. For some properties, however, it may be necessary to seek the advice of a lawyer and a property manager to determine the proper vehicle for controlling the landlord–tenant relationship.

The landlord should also be acquainted with the possible effects of antitrust laws, building codes, land use controls, crime and security regulations, pollution controls, and the rights and duties of the parties to the lease relationship.

Types of Leases and Lease Clauses

Gross versus net leases. Traditionally, residential leases have consisted of tenants paying a flat rate and the landlord maintaining responsibility for all costs. Such agreements are known as *gross leases.* In some cases, however, residential property managers have preferred a fixed-base rent with a schedule of base operating expenses (e.g., sanitation fees, common-area utilities, water and sewage, and real estate taxes), with the tenant paying for any increases over the base that occur during the lease period. In areas where tenant resistance to this technique is high, property managers have been changing to shorter-term (six-month) leases. The fixed-base lease with a proportional sharing of operating increases is also applied to retail, office, and industrial leases where occupancy levels are high.

The term *net lease* is a confusing misnomer, although the concept itself is simple. Under a net lease, some operating costs are shifted to the tenant. It is necessary to look at the specific lease to determine its "netness." For the base period, the landlord usually receives a fixed rent that is adjusted annually on the basis of an index; the tenant pays for all increases in real estate taxes and insurance and for specified maintenance and repair costs above the base-year amounts. Some leases require that the tenant also pay for all interior and exterior structural repairs for the replacements of building improvements should they be destroyed by fire or other casualty.

The investor should be aware, however, that the greater the burden of management, leasehold improvement, and capital additions placed on the tenant, the greater the possibility that the IRS may deem the relationship a sale rather than a lease, or the net lease an investment rather than the operation of a business. This may have an adverse impact on the investor's rights to deductions for depreciation and favorable tax treatment. Net leases are often for long terms and are usually made with lessees who have strong credit ratings.

Percentage leases. Many leases, particularly those for commercial tenancies, provide for a base rent related to a specified level of gross receipts, to be paid on a monthly basis for the rights of possession. Whenever gross sales rise above the base-rent threshold point, a percentage clause automatically takes effect, and the rent due is based on the formula set forth in the clause. The amount by which the percentage rent exceeds the base rent is the *overage.*

A percentage lease should clearly spell out the landlord's right to audit the tenant's records for business at that specific location. It is preferable for the percentage to be based on gross receipts rather than "net profits" or "gross margins." Gross margins and net profits are potentially troublesome because they are difficult to confirm.

Escalation clauses. Escalation clauses provide a formula for adjusting the rent on the basis of a change in a specified economic indicator. They maintain the yield on the lease by adjusting for changes in monetary values and costs. The most commonly used indicators are the wholesale commodity index and the consumer price index, although it is preferable to use a regional index in order to minimize distortions. It is advisable to include an escalation clause in any lease to guard against possible inflation trends. On the other hand, high rates of inflation may cause some resistance to using actual index changes without negotiation.

Reappraisal clauses. The negotiation of a long-term relationship between the lessor and the lessee often embroiders the lease with special clauses, such as options to purchase, renewal options, and lessee's rights to first refusal in the event of sale during the term. Since the parties to the negotiation of the original lease are usually conversant with the relation of gross rents to the yield and to the value of the property, it is best to include a reappraisal clause to be triggered by such contingencies as renewal and exercise of options. Indeed, if the rent has been caculated on the basis of a percentage of property value, the clause should call for adjustment of that value at periodic intervals through reappraisal by independent fee appraisers. The typical appraisal clause provides for the lessor and the lessee each to appoint qualified appraisers, who then seek to agree on the value. In the event that they cannot agree, the clause provides that the appraisers appoint a third appraiser to arbitrate the value. Although this will not eliminate disputes, it does provide for orderly resolution of the conflict.

OPERATION OF THE PROPERTY

The successful operation of a property includes physical maintenance, staff maintenance, and maintenance of good tenant relationships, all of which enable the property to retain—or better still, enhance—its value.

Managing the Physical Asset

Managing the physical asset basically involves capital additions and maintenance. As a guide to the property manager in performing this function, a capital additions policy, agreed on by the manager and owner, is advisable and should include the limits to the former's authority to undertake certain capital additions. For example, the installation of smoke alarms in each unit of a 400-unit project is a matter over which the investor may wish to retain control. A practical approach may be to agree on a list of items that cannot be replaced without the approval of the investor or, alternatively, a dollar limit for any single expenditure.

When major construction work is required, the property manager is often the appropriate person to ensure that contractors comply with material and job specifications. The nature of real estate construction is such that many sins can be covered by paint, plaster, and other exterior coatings. Property managers are not usually engineers or architects, so they should have the authority to obtain consultation and inspection services from qualified personnel for major construction projects. Managers should also have the power to approve or disapprove payments in order to control the quality and cost of improvements.

Maintaining the Physical Asset

Most well-managed businesses are aware of the need for a policy on capital additions, but consideration must also be given to maintenance of the physical asset. The property manager, who needs to be skilled in the selection and supervision of employees and independent contractors, should develop a plan for replacing short-lived items. Crisis management, the inefficient and costly approach to emergency repairs taken day by day, can be avoided by conducting annual and seasonal inspections and routine repairs. Other benefits of such a preventive approach are volume discounts and specialization of labor for installation when low-cost, short-lived items, such as exhaust fans and garbage disposals, are replaced throughout the project on a sequential cycle. A comprehensive maintenance plan should also anticipate high-cost repairs, such as roof replacement and repair, during the ownership cycle.

Assuming that the lease places on the owner the responsibility for maintaining the building, fixtures, equipment, and other improvements, he or she must be prepared to react promptly and competently. If not properly fulfilled, the legal responsibility for fire prevention, sanitation, panic control, and security can turn a property into a capital-eating white elephant for the owner.

When investors minimize maintenance and repair, choosing instead to "milk" the property to maximize net operating income, a typical result is a lower capital gain upon the termination of the property. A responsible maintenance program, on the other hand, conserves and enhances the value of the real estate product. Still, outside factors, such as the enforcement of rent controls that decrease net cash flow, may force the owner to defer maintenance or shift the duty to the tenants.

Maintenance of the physical asset, as discussed in this chapter, is an ongoing process that can be broken down into five principal categories.[10]

1. *Preventive maintenance* requires a schedule of regular inspections for the repair or replacement of items before problems occur. Since preventive maintenance reduces the probability of emergencies by anticipating wear and the changes that the property, building, and equipment undergo, it is one of the most important tools in operating a property successfully.

The objective is to develop an annual maintenance schedule that can serve as a calendar of activity for the maintenance personnel. Schedules can ensure that preventive maintenance tasks are performed in a timely manner. Sources such as manufacturers' instruction booklets are useful for determining when maintenance should be performed on mechanical equipment.

The strategy is to avoid a continual stream of crises and, instead, to program periodic maintenance tasks. Careful and regular preventive maintenance will eliminate many corrective and emergency repairs later on. Although many investors consider preventive maintenance a poor use of cash, and some managers claim to have no time for it, the truth is that preventive maintenance eventually saves both money and time.

2. In *corrective maintenance* an item is repaired and restored after problems are indicated but before a major breakdown occurs. This type of maintenance can never be eliminated.

3. *Deferred maintenance* is needed maintenance that will not or cannot be performed until some later time.

4. *Emergency maintenance* is performed when a serious breakdown or malfunction requires immediate response, whether during regular hours, on weekends, or after hours. Both corrective and emergency maintenance are usually more expensive than preventive maintenance because the damage is usually greater. Emergency maintenance must often be performed at overtime rates.

5. *Custodial maintenance* consists of routine, day-to-day housekeeping and cleaning activities.

[10]Lapides, *Managing*, p. 3.2.

All maintenance service contracts secured by the property manager should be approved by the investor. These contracts may cover such services as trash removal, cleaning, security, landscaping, painting, and heating and air-conditioning. As the agent responsible for ensuring the service contracts are properly and promptly fulfilled, the property manager should be thoroughly familiar with the scope of each work project as well as the terms of the service contract. However, the maintenance of some buildings is a profession in itself. Skyscrapers and other high rises, for example, require the highly specialized skills of stationary engineers, computer technicians, mechanical engineers, and the like. Consequently, competent managers should continuously monitor maintenance requirements and keep abreast of changes in technology and conservation practices.

Employee Management

Quality employees, good training, compensation, and supervision also contribute to the probability that a property will meet its owner's objectives. It is the property manager's responsibility to give employees the training and tools necessary to perform their jobs well and to be sure that the staff is large enough to perform all management and maintenance duties efficiently. A strong personnel management program reflects the knowledge that the personnel function has an impact on every aspect of the management process and emphasizes the importance of effectively managing employee time and talent.[11] Gathering the best staff requires timely interviewing, recruiting, hiring, training, supervising, and directing of on-site employees, plus all the related payroll and insurance responsibilities.

Tenant Relations

As a service industry, property management is strongly affected by public image. Physical and personnel management are particularly important because they reflect management attitudes toward tenants. Equally critical is effective communication between management and tenants. Part of the manager's effort to establish a healthy, professional tone for lessor–lessee relationships entails a joint inspection and inventory of the premises at the time the tenant takes possession or vacates. This procedure fixes responsibility for abuse or neglect, helps avoid false claims of ownership, and minimizes disputes. It can also serve as the tenant's acknowledgment that there were no building violations, that the premises were habitable, and, for retail and industrial uses, that utility entrances were adequate.

An effective, consistent rental collection process is also important to tenant relations, as well as to the property's profitability. Since rental in-

[11]Lapides, *Managing*, p. 12.3.

come is often a means to meet operating expenses, a delay or decrease in this income could greatly jeopardize management's effectiveness. Good collections are a function of organized and accurate record keeping, clear collection policies, and a firm collection attitude. Should circumstances ever warrant them, eviction procedures should be clearly explained before the lease is executed.

Since tenants have a number of rights and obligations, generally determined by local jurisdictions, all parties to the lease should be aware of these in order to avoid later confusion or discrepancies. Other contingencies with which the manager–landlord should be acquainted are the possible effects of antitrust laws, building codes, land use controls, crime and security regulations, and pollution controls on the rights and duties of the parties to the lease.

ADMINISTRATIVE RESPONSIBILITIES

Accounting and Record Keeping

Fundamental to the property manager's administrative responsibilities is the preparation of a budget, the plan for meeting revenue and expenditure goals.[12] Once the budget is established, accounting enables the investor to monitor management performance and the operating income and expenses of the project. Skill in the prompt preparation and interpretation of operating results and budgets is generally expected of property managers.

A monthly cash flow statement reflecting expenditures and charges such as real estate taxes, insurance, or seasonal utility bills permits planning for spending needs. This monthly statement can also reflect debt service payments, thereby enabling the investor to monitor cash flow returns to the equity investment.

Insurance. To provide the property with adequate protection, the property manager should be familiar with the various types of insurance coverage. Being overinsured serves no function, and being underinsured can ruin the investor.

Taxes. The investor benefits when the property manager thoroughly understands real estate and personal property taxes. These taxes are based on the "assessed value" of the property, the determination of which can be complicated and somewhat subjective. A tax specialist should usually be employed to determine whether the value and rates are correct and to identify any avenues that might reduce the tax assessment.

[12]Arnold, *Real Estate Syndication*, pp. 9.40–9.43.

Security. Both tenants and management are concerned with security and safety. Two of the major property management objectives are to maintain a safe environment for the people and personal property in the building and to protect the owner's investment.

Emergency. The geographic location and type of building dictate the nature and type of emergency procedures to be formulated and distributed to employees and tenants. Typical emergency procedures address building evacuation in the case of fire or bomb threat and might include procedures for hurricanes, tornadoes, earthquakes, or floods.

Other considerations. Among the non-budget-related items for which record keeping and compliance are essential are antidiscrimination and wage and hour laws, OSHA requirements, license laws and notice requirements (e.g., real estate brokerage, elevators, and workers' compensation), and building codes. In addition, careful records must be kept of lease contracts and tenant files (especially evictions), building code violations, and correspondence concerning the property.

In addition to the direct impact on the budget of all recurring income and expense items, a good property manager will also consider the "multiplier effect" of any adjustments to these items.[13] All too often more attention is given to negotiating one-time "high-ticket" items (like casualty insurance) than to smaller, recurring costs which in the long run might generate more savings if eliminated.

For example, although a $5,000 reduction on an insurance premium produces a one-time savings of $5,000, a $10-per-month increase in rents or decrease in expenses (e.g., lowering utility costs for each unit in a multifamily housing development) can have a significantly greater impact. The latter, for a 380-unit building, would generate additional income of $45,600 per year. Moreover, the resale value of the building would increase by $570,000 in the market if the overall capitalization rate is 8 percent. Assuming a building purchase price of approximately $11,400,000 ($30,000 per apartment unit) with an equity cash investment of $2,850,000 (25 percent), the immediate equity appreciation return resulting from the $10 change would be 20 percent ($570,000/$2,850,000), and the annual increase in the ROE would be 1.6 percent ($45,600/$2,850,000). The greater the size of the property in square footage and units, the greater the impact of the multiplier effect. Its importance is enhanced even further when the property manager considers its application to all properties under management as the company's real estate management portfolio grows.

---

[13]Lapides, *Managing,* p. 4.6.

Standardization of operation. To manage real estate efficiently and effectively, a manager needs to establish a formalized standard for property management operations. This can be accomplished by creating an operations manual designed to help standardize the policies and procedures under which the company operates.

COUNSELING AND COMMUNICATING WITH THE INVESTOR

Counseling

Because of day-to-day involvement with the property as well as with the marketplace, a property manager can be a valuable asset to the investor for evaluating the ongoing success of the property. It is not uncommon for the manager to provide consulting functions that include

- Periodic review of insurance policies to ensure that the owner is continuing to receive cost-effective coverage against fire, casualty, public liability, and other risks of loss.
- Periodic review of real estate taxes to ensure that they are fair, proportionate, and nondiscriminatory to the property.
- Periodic review of the quality, adequacy, and remaining economic life of all short-lived items.
- Periodic review of the neighborhood, competitive properties, and tenants' profiles and activities.

The supplemental value of consulting services is such that an owner should not expect them to be performed as part of the ordinary management duties for the usual compensation. We suggest that a per diem compensation be agreed on in advance for such work, or that it be left for negotiation when the request for service is made.

Communicating

Within the normal parameters of property management, regular and systematic reports, including reviews of the manager's performance, should constitute the ongoing communication process between owner and manager. Any investor is consistently interested in the overall performance of his or her property, regardless of the extent of personal involvement in its daily operations, and will have more confidence in a manager who maintains close communication. In addition, periodic special reports, some of which overlap regular ones, might be prepared in response to owner requests for counseling services. They may include reports on physical conditions and maintenance problems, vacancy and bad-debt experience, changes in tenant profiles and tenant relations; reports on competitive properties and recent comparable sales; reports on the economic outlook of the MSA and mortgage market conditions; and recommendations for capital additions, replacements, selling, refinancing, and the like.

Other components to be communicated are the operating statement summary, cash information report, statement of operations, and balance sheet, examples of which are shown in the Aspen Wood Apartments case at the end of this chapter (see Exhibits 16-A to 16-D). Operating statements differ depending on the type of property. The representative statement exhibited includes items typically budgeted for residential property management. (Various chapters in Part 6 of this book give operating statements for other types of properties.) Exhibit 16-1 demonstrates how an operating statement can be used to identify the break-even point and the amount of cash flow before tax (equity income) that can be generated by an efficient manager.

In order to promote trust and mutual accommodation, the investor should fully disclose to the manager the intention to use a specific performance audit system. This may include periodic inspections of the property and interviews with tenants (see Exhibit 16-2). These audits are best performed at least annually. If third-party contractors are to perform these functions, the property manager should know who the contractors are and approximately how often the audits will take place.

Periodic conferences between the investor and the manager form a solid foundation for communication and may occur annually, quarterly, or as

EXHIBIT 16-1.   Identifying the Break-Even Point

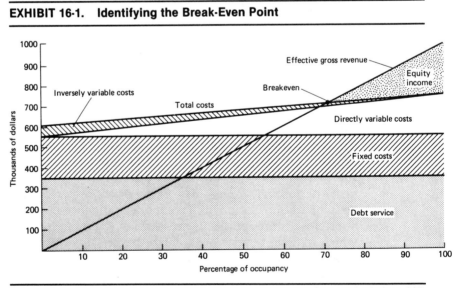

Source: John McMahan, *Property Development* (New York: McGraw-Hill, 1976), p. 365.

EXHIBIT 16-2.   A Performance Audit Checklist for Evaluating the Property Manager

---

1. Periodic inspection of the physical condition of the property by the investor: review of turnaround time of maintenance complaints, direct reports from selected tenants.

2. Periodic reports on tenants' level of satisfaction: review of tenant activity reports and interviews with selected tenants.

3. Periodic review of neighborhood and metromarket conditions: this might be performed by a third-party consultant, such as an appraiser or another independent property manager. It would include a report on employment rates, the economic outlook, a comparative analysis of competitive projects, and reports on rent level changes, utility rates, and so on.

4. An independent audit of all cash reserves, such as security deposits, debt service reserves, cash on hand, petty cash, and spot audits of invoices for repairs and supplies.

---

often as the investor or manager deems necessary. There should at least be an annual conference—with discussions guided by the management agreement, operating budget, and previously adopted policies—during which the forthcoming budget is reviewed.[14] For optimum results, the investor should be directly involved in the development of the original budget and all subsequent annual budgets. Each budget should be supplemented by a narrative statement that sets forth realistic, measurable, and specific goals. Many investors prefer to base such meetings on two management principles: *management by objectives* and the *exception principle*. Management by objectives is a system for motivating the property manager by using the principle of setting goals. Management by exception is a control technique that gives the property manager the full authority of the investor, except in clearly defined areas that have been agreed on in advance. Application of the exception principle can free the manager to take action and free the investor from worry about problems that do not exist.

Other subjects for consideration at the annual conference include

1. A comparison of yield experience with budget objectives.

2. A discussion of goals and objectives for the forthcoming year.

3. Decision making on major changes (e.g., capital additions, refinancing, possible sale or exchange, changes in management agreement, changes in marketing strategy or management plan).

4. Mutual agreement on the budget for the forthcoming fiscal year.

[14]Peter F. Drucker, *Management* (New York: Harper & Row, 1974); John B. Miner and George A. Steiner, *Management Policy and Strategy* (New York: Macmillan Co., 1977), pp. 260–262.

ASSET AND VENTURE MANAGEMENT

The terms asset and venture management have been used interchangeably in this text. In Chapter 1 we defined asset (venture) management as the structuring of the investment package for the purchase of an existing or new property and managing the investment over the ownership period. We stated that the managing equity investor, the key personality analyzed throughout the chapters of this text, was responsible for performing these duties; in addition, the managing equity investor is responsible for property management but generally contracts with a third-party firm to actually perform these duties. Two other terms, "investment management" and "partnership management," have also evolved in the real estate literature over the past ten years and tend to be used interchangeably with the terms asset and venture management. We will use these terms interchangeably unless otherwise noted.

Definition of Asset Management

Real estate asset management is a relatively new profession in the United States and has become widely recognized only in the middle and late 1980s. Asset management has been defined in several ways.

- Asset management describes the process of adding value to real estate investments. In this context, real estate profits are created in three basic ways: buying extremely well, operating a property to maximize annual income, and selling at the right time. The asset manager oversees all this activity on behalf of individual or institutional investors and, in effect, serves as a de facto property owner.[15]
- Asset management is the art of combining the management of the physical property and the management of the asset to achieve the owners' financial goals. If there is a higher use for the property or a way in which the property can produce a better return, the asset manager's job is to find it and develop the property to its full potential.[16]
- Asset management is the manipulation of all the various financial alternatives for a property in order to achieve its highest and best use and earn the highest and best after-tax returns for the investor.[17]

[15]Richard Kateley and M. Leanne Lachman, "Asset Management: The Key to Profitable Real Estate Investment," *Commercial Investment Real Estate Journal*, Fall 1986, pp. 46–53. See also Richard G. Meloy, "An Asset Management Framework for Corporate Real Estate," *Real Estate Review*, Spring 1982, pp. 99–103.

[16]Eugene J. Burger, "Asset Managers: Why the Demand," *The Journal of Property Management*, November–December 1981, pp. 309–312; also in the same issue is a panel discussion entitled "Asset Management: Wave of Your Future."

[17]Gary Langendoen, "The Asset Manager," *The Journal of Property Management*, March–April 1980.

The need for specialized asset management services originated in the 1970s when pension funds, life insurance companies, commercial banks, and public syndications began holding real estate portfolios, and the nature of real estate investment became increasingly more complex. With new capital market and financing vehicles bringing large quantities of capital into the real estate equity markets, a new breed of investment manager was needed to assume the role of managing equity investor on behalf of passive investors who were far removed from any participation in the real estate process. Professional asset managers were needed to act as fiduciaries in a highly regulated and securitized investment environment that had not previously existed. Thus, the "managing equity investor" operating in the private entrepreneurial arena has been redefined as an "asset manager" operating in an institutional and securitized arena; both are responsible for maximizing the wealth of the passive investors within the strategy framework discussed throughout this book.

Asset Management Functions

Asset management can be broken down into the eight key functions outlined in Exhibit 16-3: acquisition, property management, performance monitoring and control, retenanting and rehabilitation, peripheral development, financing, restructuring ownership, and disposition. It is the systematic and coordinated execution of all these fundamental functions that actually define asset management.

Unlike property management, asset management is concerned with the relative performance of real estate assets and the relationship of individual properties to the overall portfolio mix. Many decisions—to refinance, buy out a partner, undertake major renovation, or sell—are made on the basis of portfolio considerations rather than on property-level concerns. In addition, asset management focuses on the after-tax returns to the equity investors, as contrasted with property management which focuses primarily on before-tax returns and the actual operating performance of the property. Asset managers are more concerned with financial, tax, and investor matters; property managers are more concerned with physical, personnel, and leasing matters. In a typical chain of command, a property manager reports to an asset manager, who in turn reports to the investor–owners.

Asset Management Review Process. Most asset management resources are directed toward the ongoing review and evaluation of property performance. Asset managers must identify value-adding and profit-making opportunities by systematically reviewing property performance and market positioning. This review process consists of three systems—monitoring, budgeting, and strategic review—as explained in Exhibit 16-4.

EXHIBIT 16-3.   Asset Management Functions

---

1. *Acquisition*
   Participate in review of acquisition candidates.
   Review performance projections.
   Assess future retenanting and rehabilitation opportunities.

2. *Property management*
   Select and supervise on-site managers.
   Authorize operating expenditures.
   Review and approve leases.
   Monitor local market conditions.

3. *Performance monitoring and control*
   Generate management information at monthly, quarterly, and annual
      intervals.
   Make periodic site visits.
   Perform regular strategic review of the property's potential.
   Prepare long-term capital budgets.
   Analyze and appeal property tax assessments.

4. *Retenanting and rehabilitation*
   Design and carry out planned retenanting and rehabilitation.

5. *Peripheral development*
   Review assets for expansion opportunities.
   Prepare development plans.
   Carry out additional construction or sell or lease part of the property.

6. *Refinancing*
   Monitor national financial market and techniques.
   Renew mortgages advantageously.
   Design new financing to reduce equity or fund improvements.

7. *Restructuring ownership*
   Consider sale–lease of partial ownership.
   Evaluate buy-out options in joint venture.

8. *Disposition*
   Monitor the property's life-cycle position for optimum sale.
   Consider selling if the local market position is threatened.
   Evaluate all unsolicited offers.

Source: Richard Kateley and M. Leanne Lachman, "Asset Management: The Key to Profitable Real Estate Investment," *Commercial Investment Real Estate Journal*, Fall 1986, p. 47.

The Asset Management Team

Asset management services and fees will vary according to the needs and structure of the ownership. Some property management firms, particularly national or regional firms, provide these services as part of the basic management contract, in addition to overseeing on-site and local property managers. Other firms contract themselves out to serve solely for one large portfolio, while many institutional and portfolio managers have developed in-house asset management departments or divisions. In-house asset management departments often consist of a team of specialists in each of the areas that affect real estate values and the property owners.

Exhibit 16-5 discusses the asset management team and the broad range of skills necessary to effectively manage investment-grade real estate. The larger the investment portfolio, the more likely the asset management firm will cover these functions and skills with in-house personnel and expertise.

EXHIBIT 16-4. The Asset Manager's Review Process

Most asset management resources are directed toward ongoing review and evaluation of performance. Monitoring the costs of operation, planning for improvements, and upgrading building systems at appropriate intervals are all asset management functions.

Maintaining and enhancing revenue and seeking opportunities to replace existing leases with more favorable ones is as important as creative cost control. Goals in these critical areas are established by the asset manager and are implemented by the property manager.

Asset managers can better identify value-adding and profit-making opportunities by systematically reviewing property performance and market positioning. This review process consists of three systems: monitoring, budgeting, and strategic review.

Monitoring. Monitoring the asset includes monthly reporting from the property manager on operations and performance. Such reports typically feature an analysis of variances from the established budget. Monitoring also requires regular visits to the site by the asset manager to gather intelligence not only about the property but also about the condition of the local market and the project's position within it.

Budgeting. Budgeting for each asset takes two forms—an annual operating budget and an annual or longer-term (three to ten years) capital budget. The operating budget is typically prepared and reviewed periodically by the property manager and the asset manager, who discuss short-term needs and prospects. Capital budgeting has some input from the property manager but depends heavily on broader resource allocation decisions by the asset manager.

Strategic review. A strategic review of each real estate asset should be done at least annually. This is the qualitative, forward-looking analysis that focuses on the property's marketing plan and creatively identifies any potential actions that could materially improve returns. Often, specialists on the asset management team are brought into the strategic discussions. These discussions, moreover, are the point at which sale of properties is usually considered.

Source: Richard Kateley and M. Leanne Lachman, "Asset Management: The Key to Profitable Real Estate Investment," *Commercial Investment Real Estate Journal,* Fall 1986, p. 51.

EXHIBIT 16-5.   The Asset Management Team

To act effectively on behalf of owners of investment-grade real estate, any large-scale asset management team must have access to experienced professionals with the broad range of skills listed below. Few firms have in-house specialists covering all these subject areas, so outside consultants are used heavily. Just as some companies use external legal counsel exclusively, others contract all their on-site property management. Accounting and financial analysis are almost always handled in-house, whereas independent brokers are usually hired to lease large office projects.

An extensive in-house or consultant team is mandatory to perform the diverse asset management functions. Individual asset managers rely on multiple experts, and they in turn serve as expert, integral members of the portfolio management team that reviews the broader picture of real estate trends, matches investor objectives and portfolio composition, and oversees acquisitions and dispositions.

Skills Needed on an Asset Management Team

- Legal
- Engineering
- Financial analysis
- Accounting
- Appraisal
- Environmental analysis
- Market research
- Insurance and risk management
- Tax specialist
- Brokerage
- On-site management

Source: Richard Kateley and M. Leanne Lachman, "Asset Management: The Key to Profitable Real Estate Investment," *Commercial Investment Real Estate Journal,* Fall 1986, p. 52.

Example of Asset Management Advice. Exhibit 16-6 provides an example of how an asset manager might advise a shopping center owner who is interested in short-term profit and has a heavy debt load, as compared with recommendations for an all-cash pension fund owner of a shopping center. The asset manager must provide the necessary return and risk analysis to make solid recommendations based on each owner's objectives.

EXHIBIT 16-6.   How the Asset Manager Advises

Asset managers constantly measure the trade-offs of investment choices in light of owners' objectives. The following example draws the distinction between what an asset manager might advise for a shopping center owner who is oriented toward short-term profit and has a high debt load, as compared with recommendations for an all-cash pension fund owner of a shopping center.

A 6,000–square-foot space is vacant with two parties willing to lease the space. One tenant is a furniture retailer willing to pay $10 per square foot with no tenant allowance for a fifteen-year lease. The second tenant is a res-

EXHIBIT 16-6.   Continued

taurateur willing to pay $14 per square foot with a $150,000 tenant allowance for a fifteen-year lease.

The recommendation to the short-term owners would most likely be to take the $10 per square foot and immediately add $60,000 cash flow to the bottom line. This will ease the pressure on making the mortgage payment and will, it is hoped, allow a direct and immediate return to the investors.

The recommendation to the pension fund owner would be to take the $14 per square foot and give the $150,000 tenant allowance. The first-year cash flow will be reduced by $90,000, but in the subsequent fourteen years cash flow will be increased by $84,000 per year as compared to $60,000. The long-term return on investment is more than acceptable, and the value of the property, using an 8 percent capitalization rate, would immediately be increased by $300,000 for a $150,000 expenditure.

Although the figures in this example are oversimplified, they illustrate the process that a quality asset manager would follow. The manager does not merely watch the property; he or she provides the necessary financial analysis to make a solid recommendation based on the owner's objectives.

Decision-making factors. Properties purchased because they have potential for market repositioning, rehabilitation, or significant upgrading demand entrepreneurial efforts that far exceed those required for effective management of more stable properties.

It should be mentioned that major repositioning need not be occasioned by a shrewd purchase: the prior owner could have undertaken similar improvements. There are points, however, at which properties in the first risk category become ripe for large-scale improvement. Then, the asset manager has to decide whether to (1) move the property into the second category and assume the added risks of market repositioning in order to generate greater returns; (2) sell the property to another company that will make the change; or (3) continue to operate the property for steady but not spectacular returns.

In rental housing, considerable money has been made over the years by owners who recognized that because of the attractiveness of the surrounding neighborhood, older but reasonably well-maintained buildings could be moderately rehabilitated and then generate significantly higher rents. Again, this kind of renovation can usually be done as units turn over. Thus, cash flow continues while the rehabilitation is completed in eighteen to twenty-four months. The building can then be sold for a profit, refinanced, or held for its attractive cash flow.

Cost reduction can also play a major role in rehabilitation. The most obvious example is the energy retrofitting that occurred after the energy crisis of the 1970s. Many apartments were individually metered, and offices were switched from oil to gas or electricity. Today, energy improvements are rarely the sole impetus for major rehabilitation, but they still provide substantial operating cost savings in real estate projects of all types.

Highest-risk investments. The real estate investments with the highest risk are development of new properties, total or gut rehabilitation of older buildings, and workouts of troubled existing properties. Workouts find solutions for properties that are not leased or that are having major operating problems.

In the case of new construction, there is usually a joint-venture partner responsible for the actual development. This category of real estate activity is intensely entrepreneurial and requires single-minded commitment on the part of the developer. Such projects extend beyond the scope of asset managers, although overseeing joint-venture development partners certainly does not.

Source: Richard Kateley and M. Leanne Lachman, "Asset Management: The Key to Profitable Real Estate Investment," *Commercial Investment Real Estate Journal,* Fall 1986, p. 50.

Venture and Partnership Management

In addition to performing the asset management functions described, venture and partnership managers are responsible for managing the affairs of the partnership or legal entity that owns the property, for administering the complex regulatory and accounting procedures prescribed by law, and for carrying out the ownership agreements that bind the parties. Various issues relating to fee structures, audited financial statements, commingling of funds, conflicts of interest, record keeping during the underwriting period, interparty loans between ownership entities, and owner default conditions are the subject of considerable interest and debate among academic and industry professionals; they are issues of venture and partnership management, but they do not appear in the list of asset management functions as presented earlier.[18]

Perhaps the most important activity of venture and partnership managers is communication with the owners of the property. Once an entity begins operations, the venture or partnership manager's (or sponsor's) most important asset will be his or her ability to communicate with the investors. Since the real estate investor, unlike the corporate shareholder, cannot check his or her investment in the daily newspaper, frequency of communication is at least as important as the information actually conveyed. Frequency of communication becomes even more important if the property or investment program is having difficulties.

SUMMARY

Property management should be considered a separate field unto itself, with its own set of required skills and functions. Individual investors are often involved in management when the real estate portfolio is small or when close involvement is among the objectives of ownership. The decision for self-management should be based on the investor's ability to meet the performance objectives on which the purchase decision was based, his or her financial circumstances, the number and types of properties owned, and a number of personal preferences. Preacquisition consultation with knowledgeable local management firms and agents eases the investment decision-making process.

[18]For example, see Harris E. Lawless, "Living with the Deal, or How to Manage the Real Estate Syndicate," *Real Estate Review*, Winter 1974, pp. 84–88; Stephen E. Roulac, "Planning for Computerized Real Estate Management," *The Journal of Property Management*, January–February 1974; J. P. Regan, "Fees for Real Estate Portfolio Management," *Pension World*, June 1983, pp. 25–27; Michael E. Solt and Norman G. Miller, "Management Incentives: Implications for the Financial Performance of Real Estate Investment Trusts," *Journal of the American Real Estate and Urban Economics Association*, Winter 1985, pp. 404–423; George W. Gau, "Real Estate Investment Returns: Implications for Management," *The Journal of Property Management*, July–August 1982, pp. 10–11; and Stephen E. Roulac, "How to Structure Real Estate Investment Management," *Journal of Portfolio Management*, Fall 1981, pp. 32–35.

In the realm of property management, control of its complexities is paramount to attaining the highest possible rate of return, even for undeveloped land. Control is established via a management plan that gears appropriate strategies toward the long-term goal of maximizing the desired return from the investment throughout the life of the property. The management plan should consider all the issues discussed in this chapter; otherwise, the possibility increases that an "unforeseeable" disaster or disasters will occur and cause the property investment to fail or, at least, reduce potential returns. In the best of circumstances, these considerations are addressed before the property is acquired.

Even after a management decision has been made and a management plan prepared, performance of all related activities and the plan itself must be evaluated periodically to ensure that the manager remains current with all requirements for the proper functioning of the property. Just as in any other endeavor, property management requires the flexibility to recognize and react to needed changes while exercising long-term vision and still attending to the plethora of small details. Among the manager's goals are optimal market rents, a high occupancy rate, low turnover, tenant satisfaction, a good reputation for the care of both tenants and property, quality, well-trained employees, standardization of operations, positive monthly cash flows, accurate prediction of capital additions needs, an effective maintenance plan, compliance with local, state, and federal laws, adequate insurance protection, a workable annual budget, and good communications with the owner. The list goes on, but the underlying standard for all the manager's goals is the attainment of the owner's objectives. The details are the means to that end. At first glance, it may appear impossible to track and meet all the secondary goals of a manager, but in fact they can be categorized more simply into six fundamental areas of activity: preacquisition consultation, market promotion and leasing, operation of the property, administrative responsibilities, and other counseling and communication functions. By breaking down these areas of responsibility, the property manager in conjunction with the asset manager can develop a management plan. By means of the plan, control can be exerted over the performance of the property; exerting control allows the investor's long-term goals to be attained.

The final section of the chapter discusses the subject of asset and venture management. Simply stated, asset management is the process of adding value to real estate investment through various types of strategies administered during the ownership life cycle. The concept of asset management has evolved as a result of the institutionalization and securitization of real estate investment; it involves nothing more than the systematic application of the principles and concepts discussed throughout this book. Asset management is much broader in scope than property management and is a term that is used interchangeably with the terms venture management, partnership management, and investment management.

ASPEN WOOD APARTMENTS

PROPERTY AND ASSET MANAGEMENT

The Aspen Wood joint-venture agreement empowers D&B Associates to provide complete asset (venture) and property management services. Although Charlie Davidson is designated as the manager of the venture, in actual practice Clyde Boomer is in charge of day-to-day management. They have the following privileges, duties, and obligations.

1. The manager shall open and maintain a bank account upon which he shall be authorized to draw checks and into which all joint-venture moneys shall be deposited.

2. The manager shall maintain or cause to be maintained true and accurate books of account of the joint-venture operations, which books of account shall be readily available to the co-owners for inspection and audit.

3. The manager shall cause to be rendered monthly a statement reflecting income and expense for the month, such statements to be in the hands of the co-owners by the twentieth day of the following month. He shall, after accumulating a reasonable contingency reserve, issue and disburse with each such monthly statement the excess of cash income over expenses for the previous month, if any, to the participating parties in accordance with their proportionate interests.

4. The manager shall cause to be rendered annually a statement reflecting the financial operations of the joint venture for the previous year and the current financial condition of the joint venture. Such statements shall cover the calendar year, or part thereof, and shall be in the hands of the co-owners by March of the succeeding year.

5. The manager is authorized and obligated to manage the operation of the project, including obtaining tenants, collecting rents, depositing rents and deposits, paying bills and obligations, and handling repairs, maintenance, cleaning, and any other matter concerning operation. He is expressly authorized to hire (and discharge) resident managers of the apartment projects and to delegate to them such duties as he may desire, and shall determine the salary to be paid resident managers.

6. The manager shall be paid monthly for his services an amount equal to 5 percent of the gross income of the joint venture for the previous month. All other expenses, including advertising, of the project are classified as those of the joint venture.

7. Neither the manager nor resident managers shall be held liable to the joint venture or any co-owner for any loss or expense incurred by them in connection with the prudent discharge of their duties.

THE MANAGEMENT ORGANIZATION

One of the keys to D&B's success in real estate syndication is its excellent property management and maintenance services. A property management division handles all details of preventive and rehabilitative maintenance, including landscaping, gardening, refurbishing, and furnishing. The availability of maintenance personnel on a day-to-day basis ensures prompt attention to emergency problems, which is a major contribution to resident satisfaction and low vacancy rates.

A computer information management system is used extensively to analyze property performance. The system not only assists in coordinating and controlling the property management activities but also provides a data base for financial analyses of proposed new ventures. The D&B investment division works closely with the property management division to establish operating and capital expenditure budgets. After the cash flow budgets have been established, the property management division is held accountable for delivery of the amounts projected.

PROPERTY MANAGEMENT AT ASPEN WOOD

On December 20, 1974, D&B's property management division officially took charge of all property management activities at Aspen Wood. Before that date D&B worked closely with the on-site manager to arrange all the details of the takeover and design a leasing and maintenance program to turn the property around. On December 28 there were twenty-four vacancies, and the leasing, maintenance, and financial records were a disaster. The roofs were leaking, the central hot-water heaters were malfunctioning, and the utility company was threatening to shut off common-area electricity because of payment delinquencies. The university students had left town for the holidays, and it was not certain how many would return on January 10 to honor their lease contracts, which expired on May 31, 1975.

Despite these problems, the 1974 operating performance was guaranteed through rent–expense provisions in the contract (described in Chapter 15). As a result, the cash flow and tax losses realized by the investor for the remainder of 1974 were close to pro forma projections:

	Amounts Projected (RE004 Analysis)	Amounts Realized (2 months, 1974)
Cash flow	$ 8,889	$ 8,163
Tax loss	$99,493	$106,229

Although the cash flow realized was about $800 less than projected, tax losses exceeded projections by almost $7,000. Because of the operating problems that the property would be facing in 1975, Davidson and Boomer chose not to disburse the cash flow realized; it would be used as working capital to weather the early-1975 storm.

MONTHLY REPORTS TO INVESTORS

Several reports are sent to the joint-venture partners each month, including (1) an operating statement summary, (2) a cash information report, (3) a detailed statement of operations and capital expenditures, and (4) a balance sheet. These are illustrated in Exhibits 16-A through 16-D. Exhibits 16-A and 16-B are investor-oriented reports that provide summaries of the cash flow from operations, taxable income, and the sources and uses of cash. Exhibits 16-C and 16-D are full information reports used for analysis by property managers. All income and expense items in the detailed reports are shown as dollar amounts, percentages of gross possible income, dollars per square foot of leasable area, and actual versus budget amounts. This presentation method permitted easy comparison between projects managed by D&B Associates and data published by trade associations.

Each month, Boomer prepared a cover letter with the accounting reports, highlighting the developments of the past month and discussing items that may affect future performance. Periodically, Davidson included a letter discussing important partnership matters, developments in the marketplace, and current activities of the investment division. Major decisions that must be made by the venture, such as capital expenditures, refinancing, and sale, were also presented to the partners by Davidson.

OPERATING HISTORY OF THE PROPERTY

During 1975 Aspen Wood Apartments did not achieve its cash flow return objectives. The roofs were repaired and the central hot-water heaters were replaced. The building and the individual apartments were gradually raised to higher standards. The resident managers were replaced, and marketing efforts were made to change the poor image of the complex. Nevertheless, more than a year passed before occupancy reached the projected 95 percent level, and a working-capital loan was arranged from a local bank to finance unbudgeted capital expenditures. Operating expenses for the first three years ran in the range of 47 to 50 percent of gross possible income, as contrasted with the 42 to 45 percent budgeted amount.

The operating history of Aspen Wood from 1974 through 1981 is shown in Exhibit 16-E. Actual amounts realized are compared to the 1974–1979 financial forecast (which was presented in Chapter 10). The subsequent operating history for years 1982 through 1987 is discussed in the following chapter.

The first three years were disappointing from an operating viewpoint but produced a favorable tax shelter. The next three years were excellent from the standpoint of cash flow but produced declining tax shelter. In 1980 and 1981 the property produced a taxable income of $25,349 and $55,564, respectively, and the investors became anxious to take some action to relieve the rising income tax burden and realize some of their appreciation gains. In 1981 various alternatives for the disposition of Aspen Wood Apartments were considered; these are analyzed in the next chapter.

EXHIBIT 16-A. Aspen Wood Operating Statement Summary, Period Ended December 31, 1980

| | % | | | To Date |
	Month	YTD	December	(12 Months)
STATEMENT OF CASH FLOW				
Gross Possible Income				
Gross possible rent	95.7	95.9	$22,290.00	$239,560.00
Other income	4.3	4.2	1,009.40	10,373.99
Gross possible income	100.0	100.0	$23,299.40	$249,933.99
Vacancy and collection loss	.5	3.6 –	113.11	8,999.77 –
Gross effective income	100.5	96.4	$23,412.51	$240,934.22
OPERATING EXPENSES				
Tax and insurance accrual/expense	8.9	9.9	$ 2,071.00	$ 24,852.00
Maintenance and repairs	12.5	12.9	2,911.47	32,226.59
Gas	6.4	4.3	1,497.61	10,858.44
Electricity	.0	1.0	.00	2,535.07
Water/wastewater	.0	3.1	.00	7,804.65
Other utilities	1.4	1.7	322.40	4,145.89
Professional management	5.0	4.8	1,170.63	12,046.71
Resident management	5.9	6.0	1,363.11	15,080.28
Advertising and promotion	.1	1.0	26.20	2,417.86
Other	1.3	1.1	290.24	2,689.67
Total operating expenses	41.4	45.9	$ 9,652.66	$114,657.16
Net Operating Income	59.1	50.5	$13,759.85	$126.277.06
DEBT SERVICE				
Principal and interest payment	24.7	27.6	$ 5,751.83	$ 69,021.96
Total debt service	24.7	27.6	$ 5,751.83	$ 69,021.96
Cash Flow from Operations	34.4	22.9	$ 8,008.02	$ 57,255.10
STATEMENT OF TAXABLE INCOME				
Net operating income			$13,759.85	$126,277.06
Interest expense			4,502.00 –	54,525.85 –
Depreciation/amortization			3,806.41 –	45,676.92 –
Depreciation/current-year improvements			28.64 –	725.65 –
Taxable Income			$ 5,422.80	$ 25,348.64

EXHIBIT 16-B.   Aspen Wood Cash Information Report, Period Ended December 31, 1980

	December	To Date (12 Months)
Beginning Cash Balance	$2,338.43	$ 1,336.62
Cash flow from operations	8,008.02	57,255.10
Accounts payable	.00	185.00 –
Prepaid rent	.00	445.00 –
Owner withdrawals	4,000.00 –	28,206.00 –
Capital expenditures	286.39 –	7,256.35 –
Reversal and tax and insurance accrual	2,071.00	24,852.00
Tax and insurance escrow payment	1,657.79 –	19,848.48 –
Tax and insurance cash payments accrued	3,021.09 –	3,930.71 –
Cash to/from investment account	1,000.00 –	21,066.93 –
Employee advances	29.65	23.42 –
Net change in cash	143.40	1,145.21
Ending Cash Balance	$2,481.83	$ 2,481.83

Note: Sources are plus; uses are minus.

EXHIBITS 16-C and 16-D *(see following pages)*

EXHIBIT 16-E.   Aspen Wood Operating History

	CASH FLOW DISTRIBUTED		TAXABLE INCOME (LOSS)	
	Forecast[a]	Actual	Forecast[a]	Actual
1974	$ 8,889	0	($99,493)	($106,229)
1975	18,824	0	(69,643)	(104,650)
1976	20,421	0	(54,619)	(63,853)
1977	21,948	0	(47,808)	(47,208)
1978	23,393	$20,000	(32,558)	(32,653)
1979	21,741	21,176	(13,607)	(4,136)
1980	N.A.	28,206	N.A.	25,349
1981	N.A.	40,000	N.A.	55,564
1982–1987	Discussed in following chapter.			

[a]Financial projections assumed a holding period ending in 1979.

EXHIBIT 16-C.   Statement of Operations, Aspen Wood, Twelve Months Ended as of December 31, 1980

	%		MONTH			YEAR TO DATE			Per	Sq. Ft.
	Month	YTD	December	Budget	November	December	Budget	12-31-79	Month	YTD
RENT ANALYSIS										
Gross possible	100.0	100.0	$22,290.00	$19,953	$22,290	$239,560.00	$239,436	$209,705	$5.01	$4.49
Vacancy	1.1	3.5 –	250.00	600 –	250 –	8,342.88 –	7,200 –	5,074 –	.06	.16 –
Collection losses	.6 –	.3 –	136.89			656.89 –			.03 –	.01 –
GROSS EFFECTIVE INCOME										
Rent collections	100.5	96.2	$22,403.11	$19,353	$22,040	$230,560.23	$232,236	$204,630	$5.04	$4.32
Attorney collections	.0	.1	.00			281.53		56	.00	.01
Parking	.8	.8	167.00		157	1,845.83		1,500	.04	.03
Forfeited deposits	.5	.3	100.00			671.72		721	.02	.01
Vending concessions	1.3	1.4	290.95		296	3,249.50		2,717	.07	.06
Special charges	.4	.2	80.00		5	353.75		300	.02	.01
Interest income	1.7	1.5	371.10		299	3,680.74		1,715	.08	.07
Other income	.0	.1	.35			290.92		19 –	.00	.01
Gross effective income	105.0	100.6	$23,412.51	$19,353	$22,797	$240,934.22	$232,236	$211.170	$5.27	$4.52
OPERATING EXPENSES										
Taxes and Insurance										
Personal property tax accrual	.3	.4	$ 75.00		$ 75	$ 900.00		$ 840	$ .02	$ .02
Real property tax accrual	7.1	8.0	1,590.00		1,590	19,080.00		17,220	.36	.36
Property insurance accrual	1.8	2.0	406.00		406	4,872.00		3,600	.09	.09
Total taxes and insurance	9.3	10.4	$ 2,071.00	$ 2,071	$ 2,071	$ 24,852.00	$ 24,852	$ 22,860	$ .47	$ .47

EXHIBIT 16-C. Continued

	% Month	% YTD	MONTH December	MONTH Budget	November	YEAR TO DATE December	Budget	12-31-79	Per Month	Sq Ft YTD
Maintenance and Repairs										
Maintenance wages	4.6	4.0	$ 1,018.00		$ 818	$ 9,591.86		$ 6,859	$ .23	$ .18
Maintenance overhead	.8	.7	182.35		152	1,585.66		1,145	.04	.03
Pest control	.4	.5	84.00		84	1,105.10		525	.02	.02
Grounds	.1	.2	30.00		45	549.83		1,422	.01	.01
Buildings and exterior	.2	.6	33.66		41	1,447.36		1,188	.01	.03
Heating and air conditioning	.7	1.7	161.25		510	4,007.24		4,056	.04	.08
Plumbing	2.3	1.9	514.78		329	4,653.89		3,999	.12	.09
Appliances	1.3	.6	298.59		358	1,492.99		1,870	.07	.03
Doors, windows, locks, and keys	.1	.3	19.33		4 –	661.04		1,207	.00	.01
Pool cleaning and supplies	.1	.2	26.20		110	515.99		1,001	.01	.01
Pool repair	.0	.1	.00			183.62		523	.00	.00
Electrical	1.9	.9	425.00		54	2,033.22		1,078	.10	.04
Supplies	.1	.1	30.64			310.24		534	.01	.01
Fire prevention	.0	.1	7.72			143.85		97	.00	.00
Signs	.0	.1	.00			161.75		102	.00	.00
Total maintenance and repair	12.7	11.9	$ 2,831.52	$ 2,100	$ 2,497	$ 28,443.64	$ 25,200	$ 26,137	$ .64	$ .53
Unit Makeready										
Cleaning	.0	.1	$ .00		$	$ 171.00		$ 121	$ .00	$ .00
Painting and patching	.2	.5	52.01		29	1,274.62		1,655	.01	.02
Carpets and drapes	.0	.8	.00		91	1,887.45		1,243	.00	.04
From deposit account	.1	.0	27.94		46	5.12		824	.01	.00
Total unit makeready	.4	1.4	$ 79.95	$ 420	$ 166	$ 3,338.19	$ 5,040	$ 4,411	$ .02	$ .06
Furniture expense										
Moving furniture	.0	.1	$ .00		$ 11	$ 218.01		$ 218	$ .00	$ .00
Furniture repair	.0	.1	.00			226.75		109	.00	.00
Total furniture expense	.0	.2	$ .00	$ 84	$ 11	$ 444.76	$ 1,008	$ 432	$ .00	$ .00
Utilities										
Gas	6.7	4.5	$ 1,497.61	$ 1,050	$ 1,021	$ 10,858.44	$ 12,600	$ 10,520	$ .34	$ .20
Electricity	.0	1.1	.00	250	183	2,719.06	3,000	2,555	.00	.05

Water	.0	2.1	.00	378	4,905.56	441	4,536	4,348	.00	.09
Wastewater	.0	1.6	.00	372	3,710.21	369	4,464	3,214	.00	.07
Trash	.8	1.0	181.00	190	2,281.00	201	2,280	1,887	.04	.04
Telephone	.1	.1	27.52	25	311.97	23	300	250	.01	.01
TV cable	.6	.7	129.45	130	1,558.40	129	1,560	1,422	.03	.03
Long distance	.1 –	.0	15.57 –		5.48 –	6		49	.00	.00
Total utilities	8.2	11.0	$ 1,820.01	2,395	$ 26,339.16	2,373	$ 28,740	$ 24,245	$ .41	$ .49
General and Administrative										
Managers' wages	3.4	3.3	$ 752.35		$ 7,840.72	571		$ 7,360	$ .17	$ .15
Employee bonus	.2	.2	34.44		558.31	138		164	.01	.01
Rental allowance	1.8	1.7	390.00		4,168.00	390		4,200	.09	.08
Employee taxes	.3	.3	75.16		800.33	65		788	.02	.01
Employee insurance	.5	.4	111.16		949.39	97		795	.03	.02
Manager electricity	.0	.2	.00		586.62	30		590	.00	.01
Manager training	.0	.1	.00		207.50	21		242	.00	.01
Management fees	5.3	5.0	1,170.63		12,046.71	1,139		10,604	.26	.23
Locator fees	.6	.3	130.00		741.25			1,330	.03	.01
Advertising	.1	.9	26.20		2,254.54	74		1,488	.01	.04
Promotion	.0	.1	.00		163.32			68	.00	.00
Legal and accounting	.6	.7	125.00		1,660.88	125		1,352	.03	.03
Dues and subscription	.0	.0	10.0		10.00			85	.00	.00
Office supplies	.1	.1	24.29		276.59			325	.01	.01
Bank charges	.0	.0	.95		.95			9	.00	.00
Total general and administration	12.8	13.5	$ 2,850.18	2,772	$ 32,265.11	2,650	$ 33,264	$ 30,053	$ .64	$ .60
Total Operating Expenses	43.3	48.3	$ 9,652.66	9,842	$ 115,682.86	9,768	$ 118,104	$ 108,138	$ 2.17	$ 2.17
NET OPERATING INCOME	61.7	52.3	$ 13,759.85	10,011	$ 125,251.36	13,029	$ 120,132	$ 103,032	$ 3.09	$ 2.35
INTEREST AND DEPRECIATION										
First-mortgage interest	20.2	22.8	$ 4,502.00		$ 54,525.86				$ 1.01	$ 1.02
Depreciation allowance	17.1	19.1	3,806.41		45,676.92				.86	.86
Depreciation/current-year improvements	.1	.3	28.64		725.65				.01	.01
Total interest/depreciation	37.4	42.1	$ 8,337.05		$ 100,928.42				$ 1.88	$ 1.89

EXHIBIT 16-C.　Continued

| | % | | MONTH | | | YEAR TO DATE | | | Per | Sq Ft |
	Month	YTD	December	Budget	November	December	Budget	12-31-79	Month	YTD
TAXABLE INCOME	24.3	10.2	$ 5,422.80			$ 24,322.94			$1.22	$ .46
CAPITAL IMPROVEMENTS										
Capital replacement	.0	.1	$　　.00			$　　157.93			$ .00	$ .00
Furniture purchase	.0	1.3	.00			3,081.95			.00	.06
Appliance replacement	.4	.1	77.50			112.50			.02	.00
Drape replacement	.0	.2	.00			431.64			.00	.01
Hot-water heater replacement	.0	.7	.00			1,642.76			.00	.03
Casualty loss/recovery	.0	.1 –	.00			334.90 –			.00	.01 –
HVAC replacements	.9	.9	208.89			2,164.47			.05	.04
Total capital improvements	1.3	3.0	$ 286.39			$ 7,256.35			$ .06	$ .14

EXHIBIT 16-D. Aspen Wood Balance Sheet, as of December 31, 1980

	Balance 12-31-80	Balance 12-31-79	NET CHANGE December	To Date
ASSETS				
Owners cash balance	$ 1,456.13	$ 1,336.62	$ 143.40	$ 119.51
Taxes and insurance escrow	22,008.81	2,160.33	1,657.79	19,848.48
Operating invested cash	35,156.21	14,089.28	1,000.00	21,066.93
Employee advances		23.42 –	29.65 –	23.42
Land	84.027.00	84,027.00		
Buildings, 5–7 years	173,619.60	173,619.60		
Buildings, 8–10 years	155,047.93	155,047.93		
Buildings, 25–30 years	461,239.50	461,239.50		
Equipment	68.75	68.75		
Personal property	59,174,21	59,174.21		
Accumulated depreciation	453,030.70 –	406,628.13 –	3,835.05 –	46,402.57 –
Total assets	$538.767.44	$544,111.67	$1,063.51 –	$ 5,344.23 –
LIABILITIES AND EQUITY				
Liabilities				
Prepaid rent		$ 445.00		$ 445.00 –
Accounts payable		185.00		185.00 –
Taxes and insurance payable	$ 20,921.29		$ 950,09 –	$20,921.29
First-mortgage payable	719,069.49	733,565.60	1,249.83 –	14,496.11 –
Total liabilities	$739,990.78	$734,195.60	$2,199.92 –	$ 5,795.18
Equity				
Owner's equity	$210,000.00	$210,000.00		
Owner's withdrawals	69,377.01 –	41,171.01 –	$4,000.00 –	$28,206.00 –
Retained earnings	341,846.33 –	358,912.92 –	5,136.41	17,066.59
Total equity	$201,223.34 –	$190,083.93 –	$1,136.41	$11,139.41 –
Total liability and equity	$538,767.44	$544,111.67	$1,063.51 –	$ 5,344.23 –

17

TERMINATION OF
THE INVESTMENT

Terminating the investment is the last step in the ownership cycle. Methods of disposal are limited only by the imagination, the law, and economic and financial feasibility. The transfer of ownership rights may be brought about by, among other things, sale, exchange, gift, will or intestacy, condemnation, foreclosure, and casualty loss. For convenience, the terms *disposal*, *disposition*, and *termination* will be used interchangeably, although some terminations are voluntary and others involuntary.

Generally, an investor disposes of real estate because his or her investment goals and objectives have been achieved, because those goals have not been achieved, or for personal reasons. Since good investment strategy requires that disposal—whether voluntary or involuntary—be planned, the first objective of this chapter is to investigate the role of disposal in real estate investment analysis.

DISPOSAL AS PART OF THE INVESTMENT CYCLE

Disposal of the investment produces a net reversion to the equity holder (net sales proceeds). When the investment is in raw land, disposal may bring the only significant capital inflow during the entire ownership cycle. When the disposal is an abandonment, it may stop the flow of operating losses but yield no capital inflow. In the strategic planning process (see Chapter 4), terminating the property is defined as (1) making the decision

Acknowledgment: The authors are grateful for the assistance of James R. Webb, professor of real estate and finance, University of Akron, who coauthored the revision of this chapter.

to sell, (2) reviewing tax considerations, (3) negotiating price and terms, (4) closing the venture, and (5) beginning the next investment cycle. This chapter is limited to the mechanics of selling, pertinent tax planning, the closing transaction, and other techniques for deciding if, when, and how to terminate the investment.

Effect on Rate of Return. To monitor investment returns during the ownership cycle, the investor considers the sources of the returns and the certainty or uncertainty of projected future cash flows. This is done to ensure that the property is continuing to meet investment goals and objectives. In addition, changes in the investor's personal financial position could affect the pattern of returns. If a detailed sensitivity analysis indicates that a greater return would be gained from disposing of the property, care must be taken to arrange the disposition so that the rate-of-return objective is achieved.

Effect of Transaction Costs. Transaction costs diminish the net equity reversion realized from the disposal of the asset. Ignoring termination transaction costs overstates the net proceeds from the reversion. Although transaction costs vary, depending on the nature of the disposition, typical items include proration of real estate taxes, insurance, and final month's interest; the deed preparation fee; special assessments; seller's points to the lender; the transfer tax; releases from record; title insurance; and the broker's commission. These costs may amount to 8 to 10 percent of the total selling price for smaller properties. Since the disposition produces a net after-tax cash flow only after payment of the mortgage balance and federal and state income taxes, transaction costs may cut deeply into the net sale proceeds in a marginal situation.

Effects on Exposure to Risk. Disposition, of course, ends risk. While the acquisition planning process involves projecting earnings from operations, actual experience in the market may be quite different because of the dynamics of the economy, the neighborhood, and the location. Thus, all real estate investors must consistently monitor the timing of the disposition. Adherence to a preconceived plan can be disastrous. The investor must be prepared to respond to changes in market conditions as they affect both the timing of the disposal and the most probable selling price.

Need for Liquidity. Wise investors provide a liquidity reserve in assets other than real estate in order to avoid forced disposition. Adverse changes in interest rates, droughts in mortgage credit, threats of condemnation, and other external factors can prevent a planned disposition, or at least throw off its timing. Real estate investors are well advised to expect the actual time of disposition to be subject to considerable variance, diverging by many months—or even years—from the planned termination date.

Trading on the Equity. Trading on the equity, also called "flipping" a property, is a speculative technique by which a buyer contracts to purchase real estate with the intention of selling and assigning the contract rights to a third-party purchaser before the date of closing. The buyer is "trading on the equity" in his or her good-faith earnest-money deposit and attempting to profit from superior knowledge of market value trends. Obviously, the risk is that the buyer will not find a third party and will have to forfeit his or her rights in the down payment. Dealing with such speculators can waste valuable time for the investor and even result in the loss of a good alternative transaction. Careful credit checks and lenders' references can help investors avoid such abortive transactions.

GUIDELINES FOR DISPOSITION STRATEGY

The factors that impel investors to dispose of property are many; some are voluntary, others involuntary. Efforts should be made to anticipate possible reasons for disposition and to respond with the appropriate sell or hold decision.

Generally, the purpose of a *voluntary* disposition is to optimize the ownership or property life cycles, and to adjust the portfolio. For instance,

- Financial analysis indicates that it is time to convert amortized equity buildup into cash. Analysis may demonstrate that taxes are having a negative effect on profitability.
- A neighborhood is changing, either for the better or for the worse.
- An owner who "milked" a property because of financial difficulties discovered that overcoming the conditions of deferred maintenance are beyond his or her resources.
- Realization of a gain or loss for some reason—perhaps an unexpected offer—is necessary in order to adjust the portfolio and reinvest in another opportunity.

Estate and family planning considerations may result in transfers for reasons of love and affection, charitable gifts, or arm's-length "bargained" sales within the family with the goal of effectively conserving accumulated equity (wealth). Sales may also be made for very personal preferences, such as the desire to end a self-management role.

The reason for *involuntary* disposition is generally forced liquidation because of default on the mortgage, condemnation, or insolvency or bankruptcy from external causes. A primary-career change may force a move

---

EXHIBIT 17-1. Possible Decision Alternatives[a]

1. Cash sale.
2. Do nothing—continue to hold.
3. Refinance and hold.
4. Refinance and installment sale.
5. Refinance and restructure equity.
6. Terminate by one or a combination of methods discussed in this chapter.

---

[a]See the Aspen case study for a demonstration of some of these outcomes and the framework for their analysis.

to a remote location and the investor may be unable to find competent management. Other situations calling for liquidation include divorce, health problems, resignation, or death.

Evaluation of the Decision to Sell

The investment analysis and financial structuring process model makes it clear that through step 9 the investor monitors the property through financial reporting and the application of investment management principles. Therefore, before reaching a decision to sell, an investor generally should consider (1) the urgency of the need to sell relative to optimizing the ownership cycle; (2) the alternatives; (3) the "ripeness" of the market; (4) the tax effects; and (5) whether or not the time is right for beginning another reinvestment cycle. Each year during the holding period, the investor should analyze the decision alternatives (see Exhibit 17-1).

Optimizing the Ownership Cycle. The results of a disposition are greatly affected by the timing relative to tax planning considerations. Consideration must be given to problems arising from recapture of excess depreciation, capital gains, and minimum tax provisions. For example, Jack Friedman rates the following eleven important variables that can affect the so-called optimum holding period of a property.[1]

1. The overall rate of return, or the ratio of net operating income to the selling price at the time of purchase and resale.
2. The loan-to-value ratio. This ratio will change over time.
3. The mortgage interest rate (may change depending on the type of mortgage).

---

[1]Jack Friedman, "When Should Real Estate Be Sold," *Real Estate Issues,* Summer 1979, pp. 68–77; see also Austin Jaffe, "Critique," *Real Estate Issues,* Summer 1979, pp. 79–82; and "Reply to Jaffe," *Real Estate Issues,* Summer 1979, pp. 82–83; also William M. Russell, "When Do You Sell Real Estate," *Pension World,* June 1985, pp. 20–21.

4. The amortization term of the mortgage(s).
5. The owner's marginal income tax bracket.
6. The minimum tax on preference income.
7. The improvement ratio and cost of various assets.
8. The depreciation method used.
9. The depreciable life (or lives) claimed for income tax purposes.
10. Forecast changes in net operating income.
11. Forecast changes in property value.

The number of possible combinations and permutations of these variables is quite large. Thus, it is dangerous to use any general rule to identify the optimum time to terminate the ownership cycle of a property. Friedman suggests that the powerful, combined effects of depreciation changes and mortgage principal payments create two turning points in the ownership cycle that should be carefully observed. His study indicates that a property might be held at least until principal payments exceed depreciation charges. Before that time, the amount of taxable income would be less than the amount of the cash flow and at least some of the annual cash flow would not be subject to tax. Of course, refinancing can also mitigate the situation.

Friedman's second turning point seems to indicate that property should be sold when after-tax cash flows from operations turn negative, for at that point the owner is paying cash to retain the property. Although greater after-tax proceeds may be realized from a sale if property is held beyond this point, the fact that annual outlays continue pending the sale may make deferral of disposition a poor choice because of the effects of the time value of money.

However, as Friedman points out, distress situations, the need to settle estates, and the *rate of return on alternative investments*, among other circumstances, also impact the question of when to sell. Cooper and Pyhrr believe that appreciation in value, the need to renovate, and the "opportunity to pyramid" may be more powerful influences on the time to sell than those listed by Friedman.[2] However, the ultimate decision to sell or hold should rest on the anticipated future income of the asset (a subjective forecast) compared with alternative investment opportunities (another subjective judgment).

Individual investors should also consider whether or not a sale, at the time in question, is appropriate in view of personal objectives and obligations. Disposition usually requires time for preparing the property, negotiations, marketing, and making plans for reinvesting in the next ownership

[2]James R. Cooper and Stephen A. Pyhrr, "Forecasting the Rates of Return on Apartments: A Case Study," *The Appraisal Journal*, July 1973, pp. 312–337.

cycle. Some people prefer paying the opportunity costs of a lower rate of return rather than suffer the burden of selling at an inconvenient time. In effect, although a hold strategy may be irrational on the basis of financial analysis, it may be appropriate in view of overall life objectives.

Considering the Alternatives to Selling. Intelligent tax planning includes the evaluation of the many alternative methods of disposing of a property other than a cash sale. Planning for termination should include an evaluation of refinancing, installment sales, exchanges, gifts for reasons of love and affection, charitable contributions, and short-term trusts. Alternatives for a corporate owner include merger, liquidation, or reorganization of the corporation. In addition, the use of an option may enable the seller to use effectively the time and energy of a diligent would-be purchaser to achieve the seller's desired price with a minimum of personal effort.

Analyzing the "Ripeness" of the Market. The investor should consider whether the market is ready for the property. There may be a drought in mortgage credit or interest rates may be at a peak. The dynamics of neighborhood change may have a significant effect on the readiness of the market; and construction cycles in relevant submarkets must be evaluated for the impact they may have. If the investor has been complying with good investment management principles, continual monitoring of the property management and financial reports should indicate the external factors that might affect a sale.

Exhibit 17-2 shows a simple technique for making an annual analysis of whether or not it is time to sell.

Tax Planning

Investors in real estate consider the effects of taxes in relation to the potential capital gain or loss arising out of a disposition.

For example, if the property value has appreciated as a result of inflation and the tax basis has been significantly reduced by depreciation deductions, the investor might want to consider a proper tax deferral technique, such as an exchange. On the other hand, realization and recognition of a capital gains tax should not be thought of as unwise, particularly if the disposition produces substantial cash after taxes. It may also be worthwhile to time a sale to take advantage of the passive-loss limitation rules. As noted in Chapter 10, disallowed passive losses are carried forward and allowed in subsequent years against passive-activity income. The suspended losses are allowed in full against taxable gains from the disposition of property. Consequently, an investor can minimize taxes by selling a property and recognizing a large passive income that can be used to offset suspended passive losses.

EXHIBIT 17-2.   Annual Analysis of Conditions That Could Call for Sale of a Property

---

1. ANALYZE THE CURRENT RATE OF CASH RETURN ON THE PROPERTY

Since rate of return is a projected average return over a future period, each year one should analyze the marginal return–risk relationships:[a]

$$\frac{\text{Current annual cash flow (cash throw-off)}^a}{\text{Current-year equity value (original equity + equity buildup)}^a} = \% \text{ current annual rate of cash return}$$

2. CONSIDER ALTERNATIVE TERMINATION OR HOLD STRATEGIES

Should you hold, sell and reinvest, refinance and disburse, refinance and rehabilitate, exchange, make an installment sale, sell and liquidate, or give to a trust? Make after-tax cash flow projections for each alternative. Computer simulations that consider projected apreciation or depreciation for a future holding period should be used. Also do a risk analysis.

3. CONSIDER THE RESULTS OF THE ANALYSIS OF ALTERNATIVES

Choose the alternative that best fits the investor's objectives, and that appears to maximize returns relative to risks.

---

[a]These analyses ignore appreciation or depreciation of value and tax effects.

It is also possible, with good timing, for a capital loss to be advantageous. For example, the owner of a property that has an unrecognized passive loss would be wise to dispose of the property, recognize the loss, and take the deduction from income in a year in which he or she has experienced a surge in passive income from other properties. (See Chapter 10 for a discussion of the passive-income and passive-losses rules.)

Timing the Closing

Sellers today do not necessarily seek the highest sales price obtainable in the market. Instead, their objective is to retain the largest number of after-tax dollars, or possibly the equivalent in other things of measurable worth. They often seek to time the sale so that they pay the lowest tax on any profit; alternatively, they may seek to maximize the tax benefit from a loss. The most widely accepted view is that a sale is a consummated event for tax purposes when there has been substantial performance by both parties to the agreement. Passage of title is usually the significant event.[3] The

---

[3]Comm'r v. Segall, 114 F. 2d 706 (1940); see also Donald Borelli, T. C. Memo 1972-178.

holding period begins on the day *after* the property is purchased and ends *on the day* the property is sold.[4] Normally, the IRS will follow state law. It is necessary to check the local jurisdiction, however; a minority of states have held that execution and delivery of the contract of sale results in a consummated sale.

Defining the Nature of the Gain or Loss

A sale of real property may result in any one of the following.

- An ordinary gain or loss.
- A gain or loss from disposition of an asset used in a trade or business (Section 1231 asset).
- An involuntary conversion (casualty or condemnation).
- A capital gain or loss.

It is crucial for investors to maintain good documentation to support the kind of classification they intend to use at the time of disposition. Separate records should be maintained for property held for investment, for business, for personal use, for inventory, or for development purposes.

Computation of the Selling Price. The gross selling price is generally the sum of

- The cash received,
- Any other amounts received (e.g., notes or mortgages),
- The fair market value of any other property received,
- Any liens against the property that the buyer has assumed.[5]

The net selling price is computed by deducting the expenses of the transaction. State and local transfer taxes are usually deductible in the year of the sale rather than being considered a reduction of the selling price.

Calculating the Gain or Loss. Gain and loss are two separate and distinct concepts. First, one must calculate taxable gain or loss to determine the capital gains tax, if any. Second, one must determine the *after-tax cash flow* resulting from the sale. The latter is usually called *net equity reversion* or *net sale proceeds.* Under current tax law, computation is relatively straightforward.

Basis

In order to determine the tax effects of a sale, it is necessary to understand the adjustments to *basis* that have occurred. The gain or loss upon sale or

[4]Arthur Andersen & Co., *Federal Taxes Affecting Real Estate*, 4th ed., supp. (1978), p. 144.
[5]Crane v. Cobb, 331 US 1 (1947).

other disposition of realty is calculated on the basis and not on the difference between the selling price and the mortgage balance. Using depreciation to achieve tax shelter effects in the early years of ownership decreases the basis. Thus, the artificial losses that may provide attractive tax savings in the early years may also substantially increase capital gains and the taxes at the time of disposition. Real estate investors should understand both original basis and adjustments to basis for effective tax planning.

Original Basis. The original basis of property is its historical cost. Cost is usually the price paid plus any acquisition expenses. Note that the actual cash paid at the time of purchase includes items that are not part of the acquisition price but, are instead expenses—for example, prorated real estate taxes, prepaid insurance, and utility deposits. On the other hand, some charges are added to the purchase price and capitalized: broker's commissions, appraisal fee, survey costs, attorney's fees, title charges, tax stamps, option payment, the cost of outstanding leases, and costs of condition precedent zoning changes.

Adjusted Basis. To calculate adjusted basis, sum the following.

- Original purchase price (or fair market value, whichever is lower).
- Miscellaneous acquisition costs.
- Additional paid-in capital.
- Any capital improvements to the property.

From this figure, subtract depreciation and distributions of capital to owners. (Note: The depreciation allowable under the tax laws reduces the basis *whether or not it is actually taken.* When allowable depreciation is not taken, the straight-line method is used to determine the actual adjusted basis at the time of sale. The tax benefit of depreciation allowed but not taken is lost unless the prior years' returns can be amended.) Under the Tax Reform Act of 1986, the IRS would probably impute the 27.5- and 31.5-year life for residential and commercial property, respectively.

In addition, whenever there is an acquisition of improved real estate, it is necessary to allocate the total purchase price between depreciable items and the nondepreciable (e.g., land) portion of the property. The evidence that is most acceptable to the IRS is value as determined by independent third parties, such as qualified appraisers. In certain situations it is possible to establish the market value of the land in the contract of sale. However, the investor should keep in mind that artificial values with unrealistic tax results will not pass an IRS audit.[6]

---

[6]Institute for Business Planning (IBP), *Real Estate Investment Planning* (reporting service), Vol. 1, paragraphs 55,010.1, 55,010.2.

When Mortgage Is Greater Than Basis. Expert legal advice and tax counseling is required when a mortgage is greater than the basis, which usually occurs when accelerated depreciation has reduced the basis of the property below the outstanding mortgage, which is being amortized according to a long-term schedule. However, it can also happen with straight-line depreciation if a property's value has appreciated and refinancing has occurred.

The tax trap in such situations is the possibility of a "phantom" taxable gain. For example,

1. When the investor is personally liable on the mortgage debt, a transfer to the mortgagee with a release of liability would produce a gain or loss equal to the difference between the mortgagor's basis and the amount of mortgage discharged.
2. On the other hand, if the investor has no personal liability, the loss would be limited to the adjusted basis in the property and would be deductible in the year of the foreclosure. If the sales price of the property exceeds the adjusted tax basis on the property, there will be a realized gain. This is so even though such excess was paid directly to the mortgagee in reduction of the debt.

Before a debtor gives up a troubled project and allows the mortgagee to foreclose, both parties should consider the possibility of a taxable phantom gain. (Review the discussion of abandonment and reduction and cancellation of a mortgage as alternatives to foreclosure; see also the discussion of foreclosure in this chapter.)

Generally, adjustments to the debt structure may be a way out of this tax trap. Extending the mortgage term, adding unpaid interest to the mortgage balance, and establishing a moratorium on principal payments, or a more liberal amortization schedule, are all ways of avoiding foreclosure and phantom gains. Of course, this assumes a viable project for which sound management, favorable economic conditions, and increasing demand will produce a turnaround.

METHODS OF DISPOSITION

Exhibit 17-3 outlines the various methods of disposing of a property.

Disposition by Sale

A sale is a contract by which a seller transfers real property or an interest in real property to a purchaser. To constitute an enforceable sale, the agreement must meet the usual requirements of contract law in the *local* jurisdiction.

The interest in the real property subject to the sale may be fee simple absolute or any fractional interest permitted by public policy and the law.

EXHIBIT 17-3. Methods of Disposition

SALE

- Straight sale.
- Conditional sale.
- Buy–sell agreement.
- Sale and leaseback.
- Land contract.
- Installment sale.
- Deferred-payment sale.
- Resyndication.
- Auction.
- Partial disposition.

OTHER

- Exchange.
- Charitable contribution.
- Will or descent.
- Gift.
- Trust.
- Options.
- Abandonment.

INVOLUNTARY

- Condemnation.
- Personal and financial problems (e.g., divorce).
- Casualty losses.
- Foreclosure.

A sale may be absolute or conditional. It may be a voluntary agreement, fairly bargained and entered into by mutual assent of the parties, or it may be under judicial decree (e.g., sheriff's sale, receiver's sale). The seller should try to avoid warranties and representations that may survive a closing. It is best to plan the disposition.

Is the title insurable to the purchaser? Can the seller convey a good and marketable title, free and clear of all liens and encumbrances, except for the assumable mortgage and acceptable easements? Sellers must make a judgment about whether any clouds on the title should be satisfied in some way before negotiations are commenced.

Is the property physically ready for inspection by a buyer? Sellers should avoid providing negotiation ammunition for the opposing party!

Painting, fixing, cleaning, trimming, pruning, and so forth should be done to give the property a facelift. The books should be in good order. The tenants' lease files should be up to date. Warranty certificates on appliances and termite and pest control guarantees should be readily assignable.

Are market conditions favorable? Will mortgage market conditions support the intended sale, or will it be necessary to provide financing for the would-be purchaser? Since seller financing will reduce the cash produced by the sale, there should be sufficient liquidity reserves to handle the tax liabilities.

Straight Sale. Sales contracts, deeds, and all the other symbolic rituals that are absolutely necessary to the disposition of an interest in real estate are adequately discussed in most real estate principles textbooks.[7] (See these for examples of closing documents and settlement statement transactions.)

In a straight sale, the investor receives the dollar value equity interest in the year of the sale. The taxable gain or loss on the sale is also recognized in the year of the sale. Whether or not there are any cash proceeds, of course, depends on the size of the equity interest.

Conditional Sale. Generally, in a conditional or contingent sale title will not pass until one or more specific events have occurred. Examples are rezoning, delivery of financial statements, delivery of leases, ratification by probate court, submission of engineering studies proving physical feasibility of the proposed use, and so forth. In such a sale, the contract may even make the price subject to specified adjustments depending on future contingencies.

Buy–Sell Agreement. A buy–sell agreement provides the remaining participants in a business venture with an opportunity to purchase the interest of a retiring or deceased participant. Generally, the agreement does not force a sales transaction but, instead, provides for the retiring participant to offer the fractional share to the remaining participants, who may or may not buy.

A typical agreement will provide for the price to be an appraised "most probable selling price," with the appraisers selected according to a specified method. (The American Arbitration Association provides model contracts.) Insurance programs are sometimes set up to provide the necessary cash to carry out the agreement.

---

[7]See, for example, Charles H. Wurtzebach and Mike E. Miles, *Modern Real Estate*, 3rd ed. (New York, Wiley, 1987), pp. 117–149.

Sale and Leaseback. Although a sale and leaseback is generally thought of as a form of real estate financing, it may well be a means of disposing of important rights of the investor. Sale–leasebacks of improvements are used by developers who are willing to sacrifice future appreciation in value, equity buildup, and depreciation and interest deductions in order to cash out their equity interest and move on to other developments while still retaining control of the site. Such users as commercial, industrial, and other business concerns may sell the property to institutional investors (and lease it back) in order to free up working capital and obtain the 100 percent deductibility of rent payments rather than the partial deductibility of debt service.[8] (See Chapter 9 for more details.)

Financing the Purchaser to Facilitate the Sale

Even though some foreign investors prefer tangible assets to American dollars, and thus pay cash for real estate assets—and some institutional investors do the same—most investors finance a large proportion of the total purchase price. When market and economic conditions are good, most sellers can expect a creditworthy buyer to obtain his or her own financing. Sometimes, however, there are tax benefits to be realized by not receiving all the cash proceeds in the year of the sale.

Purchase Money Mortgages

A purchase money mortgage may or may not be a first mortgage. Because a purchase money mortgage is considered to be an intrinsic part of the sales transaction, in some jurisdictions it may take priority over previous money judgments. In some states purchase money mortgages are not subject to usury ceilings on mortgage interest rates, and the interest rate and the principal amount are subject to negotiation between the buyer and the seller. Those who use purchase money mortgages should take care to be knowledgeable about the special characteristics of such seller-to-buyer mortgages within the *local* jurisdiction.

Purchase money mortgages are a valuable tool in three particular circumstances.

1. Under conditions of mortgage drought.
2. When neighborhood or site conditions cause institutional lenders to reject loan applications, although such conditions may be tolerable to a buyer, when for example, the use is illegal under zoning regulations but it is known that the government authorities are doing nothing about it.

---

[8]Chip Conley, "The Explosion in Leveraged Sale-Leasebacks," *Real Estate Review*, Fall 1984, pp. 56–60.

3. When the interest rate that can be obtained on the purchase money mortgage makes it an attractive long-term investment. Someone who is retiring, for example, might prefer a purchase money mortgage to cash.

Land Contract or Contract for Deed

A land contract or contract for deed is a method of sale by which the seller finances the purchaser. The key element is that, until the purchase price is fully paid, the seller retains title and provides the purchaser with the right of possession and use. In the event that the buyer defaults in making installment payments or in the performance of other mandatory duties, such as paying real estate taxes or insurance, or maintaining the assets, the seller declares the contract forfeited and may simply evict (eject, in some states) and reenter and take possession without the use of foreclosure proceedings or judicial sale, as would be the process with a purchase money mortgage.

Some states have passed remedial legislation to make the repossession and forfeiture more equitable. Land contracts have become more popular in recent years for raw-land sales, recreational sites, properties to be rehabilitated, and farms, and in urban areas where lenders are reluctant to provide conventional financing.

Installment Sales

An installment sale is a method of disposal that provides for tax minimization under Section 453 of the IRS Code. Installment sales allow sellers to finance buyers.

In an installment sale a designated portion of the purchase price is paid when title is transferred; then the unpaid balance is paid to the seller by means of installment notes or purchase money mortgage financing. The seller must elect to use the installment method of reporting gain on the tax return for the year in which the real estate is sold.

The installment sales method provides an attractive advantage to investors (but no longer to dealers) because taxes on a gain can be spread over future years rather than being paid in full in the year in which the sale occurred. Under the 1987 Revenue Act, dealers may not use the installment method of tax reporting. The objective of an installment sale is to avoid calls for cash, particularly when a large profit results from the sale but the buyer will not provide the necessary funds. Since installment payments tend to level out the receipts, there is an additional advantage for cash method taxpayers of lowering the marginal tax rates as compared with the ascending effect of a large receipt in the year of the sale. Also, spreading the gain out over the years reduces the amount that is subject to tax preference and minimum tax computations.

In the past, taxpayers encountered serious problems in planning the handling of installment sales. However, the IRS Code was changed in

1980. Starting with sales made in that year, the initial-payment limitation was eliminated; there is now no restriction on the size of the payment that may be received in the year of the sale. The 1980 law also eliminated the restriction on installment reporting if more than 30 percent of the total sale was received in the year of the sale. Another significant change is the elimination of the "two-payment rule." A sale is eligible for installment reporting even if the purchase price is paid in a single lump sum amount, provided that the payment is made in a year subsequent to the taxable year in which the sale is made. Thus, no installments are actually required. Another important change is that installment sale reporting is automatic for qualified sales, *unless* the taxpayer elects not to have the provision apply with respect to the deferred-payment sale. A seller may avoid installment reporting by electing to have the entire gain taxed in the year of sale in which he or she has capital losses, a net operating loss, or loss carryovers to offset the gain.

Tax law changes have placed greater restrictions on sales between related parties. In sales of depreciable property to a spouse or controlled party, all installment payments are treated as received in the year of the sale unless it can be demonstrated that the sale was not made for purposes of tax avoidance. Second sales of nondepreciable assets between family members may be treated as sales to the original seller when the second sale occurs.

It is worth noting that an investor may subsequently borrow against the buyer's installment obligation, using the notes as collateral, thereby realizing cash without accelerating the deferred installment payments. However, the rules are very complex, and the tax laws changed dramatically in 1986 and 1987.[9]

Exhibit 17-4 is a simple example of a sale by the installment method. The economic consequences include

1. The series of payments represented as interest at $16,600 are taxed as portfolio income in the year of receipt.
2. The principal payments as received represent a complex mix of (a) a return of adjusted tax basis; (b) tax due on the capital gain as a result of the sale; and (c) the net profit, if any received. Assuming that the

[9]See Rich Robinson, "Report on Revenue Act of 1987," *Talking Taxes*, January 11, 1988, pp. 1–4, for a detailed discussion of this aspect and the post-1987 rules. For general background and additional discussion, see Alvin L. Arnold, *Real Estate Investments after the Tax Reform Act of 1986* (Boston: Warren, Gorham & Lamont, 1987); Rudolph S. Lindbeck and Charles P. Edmonds, "The Advantages of Tax-Free Swaps under New Tax Law," *Real Estate Review*, Summer 1987, pp. 61–64; Joel E. Miller, "Coexisting with the 1986 Code's 'Proportionate Disallowance of the Installment Method,'" Winter 1988, pp. 115–123; and Gerald J. Robinson, "Installment Reporting for Real Estate: Complexification after the Tax Reform Act of 1986," *The Journal of Real Estate Taxation*, Spring 1987, pp. 264–274.

EXHIBIT 17-4.   An Example of a Sale by the Installment Method

---

Selling date: December 1, 1988
Price: $100,000; adjusted basis: $27,000
Down payment: $10,000
Contract interest rate: 8% per annum on remaining balance, due with principal
   payment
Installments due: end of year 1—$10,000
                   end of year 2—$40,000
                   end of year 3—$40,000

Schedule of Receipts by Seller Pursuant to the Contract

Year	Unpaid Balance, Beginning of Year	Interest on Unpaid Balance	Principal Payments Received	Total Received at End of Year, Principal + Interest
0	$100,000	0	$ 10,000	$ 10,000
2	90,000	$ 7,200	10,000	17,200
3	80,000	6,400	40,000	46,400
4	40,000	3,200	40,000	43,200
		$16,600	$100,000	$116,600

Analysis of Yearly Income from Sales

Each year the interest on the unpaid balance constitutes portfolio income as actually received. Thus, the $16,600 indicated above will all be portfolio income.

Allocation of principal payment as received:

$$\frac{\text{Gross profit}}{\text{Total contract price}} = \frac{\text{price} - \text{adjusted basis}}{\text{total contract price}}$$

$$= \frac{\$100,000 - \$27,000}{\$100,000} = .73$$

Gross profit percentage ratio (.73) × $10,000 received first year = $7,300, which
is taxed as capital gain. The remaining part of the principal received ($2,700) is
not taxed, for it is a return of capital. All other things being equal, the capital
gains tax will be $7,300 × the individual's marginal income tax rate.

---

sale qualifies and installment reporting is elected, the seller must report as gain the same portion of the total cash actually received each
year that the *gross profit* is to the total contract price.

The IRS concept of *gross profit* requires some explanation, because the
gross profit portion of the cash that is received each year as principal will
be taxable as a capital gain. The IRS defines the *gross profit percentage* as

the amount resulting from dividing realized gain (gross profit) by the contract price. Realized gain is the selling price minus the adjusted basis minus costs of sale. The contract price is the selling price minus the amount of any mortgages assumed by the buyer. Remember, if a buyer assumes a mortgage that is greater than the adjusted basis, the *excess* must be added to the basis.

Exhibit 17-4 illustrates a method of determining (1) whether or not the sale qualifies for installment reporting and (2) how much of the installment received represents reportable capital gain to be taxed in the usual way. In our example calculations for adjusted basis are simplified in that the annual depreciation deductions have been deleted. In a typical case accumulated depreciation would be deducted to arrive at the adjusted basis.

Open-End Sales Contracts

When the entire price is contingent on future events, such as the success of a development, the parties should avoid the installment sales method and consider using an open-end or contingent-price sales contract. These methods are useful, for example, for a subdivider who is selling lots to a builder in a situation in which the price may vary, depending on the degree of success of speculative building. In this way the seller can recover the entire cost basis before reporting profits because the fair market value of the contingent sale is priced indeterminately. Sellers using this method should consult tax experts.

Deferred-Payment Sales

Another means of postponing recognition of gain on a sale is to defer the payment. With this method no gain is recognized until payments received plus fair market value of other property received, including obligations of the buyer, *exceed* the adjusted basis.[10]

The key to determining whether or not this method is useful is to analyze the spread between the face value and the fair market value of the buyer's obligation. Only the spread can be deferred. Deferred-payment sales are beyond the scope of this book. Therefore, investors should seek legal and tax counsel for further information concering the nature of such sales and their appropriateness for terminating a property.

The Problem of Imputed Interest

Some sellers have attempted to manipulate the principal and interest in artificial ways in order to avoid taxes. In effect, if by increasing the price, the seller could report what would have been interest as a capital gain, the buyer would also benefit from a higher basis. Because some uncommonly low interest rates were appearing on purchase money mortgage transac-

---

[10]See Caruth, 411 F. Supp. 604 (1976).

tions, the IRS persuaded Congress to stop this form of so-called avoidance. Under current law, the original issue discount (OID) rules require imputing a market rate of interest to purchase money mortgages if the stated interest rate is below the market rate. (See Chapter 10 for further discussion of the tax implications of these laws.)

Auctions

Auctions are frequently used to dispose of hard-to-sell properties, farms, and other rural land, although this technique is being used more frequently in urban areas. An auctioneer does not make offers; bids are invited from those present, but no bid becomes binding until it has been accepted by the auctioneer. The seller may by preannouncement reserve the right to reject unsatisfactory offers.

In real estate auctions, since sales usually require substantial deposits, the seller must be in a position to prove good and marketable title and have the documentation on hand immediately after the auction in order to make settlement. Federal and state laws dealing with full disclosure and consumer protection must be complied with.

Resyndication

In resyndication property is transferred from one set of investors to another. However, many of the buyers of the new syndication may also be the sellers of the former syndication. Therefore, depreciation starts at the new basis, and the buyer (who is also the seller) receives an asset that has a known track record. Typical candidates for resyndication would be ten-year-old subsidized housing projects.[11] The Aspen Wood case study appearing at the end of the chapter, presents a detailed analysis of such a resyndication.

Partial Dispositions

Fractional Interests. Generally, it is difficult to find a market for stock in a closely held corporation, for a partnership interest, or for a tenancy in common when it constitutes less than a controlling interest in the property. On the whole, those who buy a fractional interest in a real estate investment should understand at the outset that they are in it to stay. Liquidation of a fractional interest prior to disposition of the entire property

---

[11]See Jeb Brooks and Mark Thompson, "Resyndication: Complex Restructuring," *Mortgage Banking*, November 1982, p. 53; idem, "Spotlight on Resyndication Potentials," *Mortgage Banking*, January 1984, p. 42; and idem, "Resyndicating Government-Subsidized Housing: An Overview," *Real Estate Review*, Spring 1983, pp. 35–38.

will be done in a buyer's market. The use of buy–sell agreements is a relatively efficient way to facilitate such a withdrawal.

Subdivision Lot Sales. Subdivision development is beyond the scope of this book. However, these few comments are appropriate.

A land developer is similar to a manufacturer or a retailer in that profit generated by selling lots is usually taxed as ordinary income. However, developers face a longer cash flow cycle, and as a result they can apportion acquisition and improvement costs and report sales according to special IRS rules. They also can write off some expenses against ordinary income or choose to capitalize certain expenses.

Section 1237. A special provision of the tax code, Section 1237, is designed to protect investor status in a few subdivision situations. The regulations permit taxpayers who qualify under it to sell real estate from a single tract for investment without the income being treated as ordinary income merely because of the subdivision of the tract or because of active efforts to sell it.[12] Generally, the investor must have held the property for five years (unless it was acquired by inheritance) and may not make improvements that will substantially enhance its value. Surveying, clearing, construction of all-weather access roads, filling, and draining are not considered substantial improvements. However, construction of hard-surface roads and installation of utilities and street lighting are considered substantial improvements. Competent tax and legal advice should be sought by investors who want to meet the requirements.

Air and Subsurface Rights and Profit à Prendre. A partial disposition can also be accomplished by severing the fee into fractional interests—air and subsurface rights or mineral and timber rights. In some situations conveyance of a fractional interest makes possible the highest and best use of the property. The Pan Am building in New York City is an outstanding example of the use of air rights. At other times such partial disposition is for all practical purposes a disposition of the economic value of the property for the foreseeable future (e.g., deep strip mining in Wyoming).

Disposition by Exchange

An exchange of real property can defer federal and state income taxes on all or part of the capital gain resulting from a disposition. Under IRS rules no gain or loss is recognized if property held for productive use in a trade or business or for investment is exchanged solely for property of a *like*

[12]See Malat v. Riddell, 383 US 569 (1966), for an important discussion of dealer versus investor status; see esp. Biedenharn Realty Co., Inc. v. US 526 F. 2d 409 (5th Cir. 1976) in re-subdivision sales.

kind. In addition to tax-free treatment, an exchange can result in a step-up of basis for depreciation purposes for some of the parties. In theory, a series of exchanges could defer taxable gain indefinitely, and if the exchange cycle lasted until the investor's death, a "stepped-up basis" could be achieved for the heirs and the tax on the basis at death might be permanently avoided.[13] In any event, exchanges are an inviting disposal alternative that has increased in popularity since the Tax Reform Act of 1986. Exchanges are discussed in greater detail in the Appendix to this chapter.

Charitable Contributions

Some taxpayers may reap much more substantial tax shelter benefits from a charitable contribution than could be realized from a sale. When a property is located in a declining neighborhood, putting it on the market may not attract a buyer except at a sharply reduced "distress" price that would probably result in a long-term capital loss, but a transfer by gift to a charity may have much more profitable tax effects. A fair and ethical appraisal may indicate a market value far in excess of the current most probable selling price. In such a case, and assuming that the property is producing some cash throw-off after debt service, a charity may be willing to accept a gift and assume the mortgage.[14] Tax counseling should be sought in such cases.

Sale of a Personal Residence

Since the tax effects of the disposition of a personal residence are adequately discussed in most principles textbooks, they are not discussed here. It is assumed that the reader is acquainted with the partial rollover rights that permit deferral of capital gain when a home is sold. (Recently a yacht with bath and cooking facilities qualified as a replacement residence.) There is also a one-time, post-age fifty-five rule that permits exemption of up to $125,000 of gain from taxation. This tax policy is intended to promote homeownership. In general homeownership will continue to be preferable to renting as long as owners can deduct interest expense and real estate taxes from their personal income taxes.

---

[13]See IBP, *Real Estate Investment Planning*, paragraphs 55,150.10. See also *Taxation and Exchange Techniques*, 2nd rev. ed. (Chicago: National Institute of Real Estate Brokers, 1972), and *Real Estate Tax Shelter Techniques*, Real Estate Portfolio No. 13 (Boston: Warren, Gorham & Lamont, 1977), pp. 45–53; Donald J. Valachi, "The Tax-Deferred Exchange: Some Planning Considerations," *The Appraisal Journal*, January 1979, pp. 76–85; William J. Tappan, *Real Estate Exchanges* (Englewood Cliffs, N.J.: Prentice–Hall, 1979); M. W. Weinstein, "Tax Ideas—How to Approach Real Estate Exchanges," *Real Estate Law Journal* 306 (1976).

[14]IRC Sec. 1011 (b).

Disposition by Will or Descent and Transfers for Reasons of Love and Affection

As noted earlier, there are many disposition methods, some voluntary, others involuntary. For each the impact of state and federal tax laws and IRS rules and regulations, which may differ in important respects, must be considered.

Gift. A gift is a transfer of property by a donor to a donee without the receipt of value or other consideration in return. The two essential elements of an effective gift are the intention of the donor to make the gift and delivery of the property constituting the gift. When the gift is real estate and other large items, for which physical delivery is impossible or impractical, delivery is made by means of a document of title (e.g., a deed).

Gift in contemplation of death. Any gift in excess of the annual $10,000 exclusion made within three years of a decedent's death is no longer to be included in the decedent's estate for tax purposes, whether or not the gift was made in contemplation of death.

Trust. A trust is an arrangement by which the party creating the trust (the settlor–grantor) places legal title to property (*the corpus*) in the hands of a *trustee* with the objective of having the property administered for the benefit of the *beneficiary*, who has the rights to the benefit of the property during the term of the trust.[15] (Various kinds of trusts are discussed in Chapter 5).

Gift or Trust and Leaseback. An upper-bracket taxpayer may dispose of property as a gift or trust to benefit members of the family. The gift or trust is coupled to a leaseback of the property to the settlor. The rent payments made by the settlor–taxpayer become a necessary and ordinary deductible business expense and are income to the beneficiaries of the trust (presumably at lower marginal rates). Although the IRS will threaten litigation, the tax courts have found for the taxpayers as long as the gift met four tests.

1. The settlor must not retain the same control over the property prior to the gift.
2. The leaseback should require market rents. An independent appraiser's opinion may be desirable for IRS audit purposes.
3. The leaseback must have a bona fide business purpose such as the use by the lessee–settlor in his profession or business.

[15]See also E. William Carr, *Short-Term Trusts* (Englewood Cliffs, N.J.: Prentice–Hall, 1973), and Sanford J. Schlesinger and S. Timothy Ball, "Estate Planning for Real Estate Interests," *Trusts and Estates*, May 1984, pp. 29–38.

4. The settlor must not retain (during the lease term) a disqualifying "equity" in the property, such as a vested right to regain ownership.[16]

Options

Options are an extremely important technique in both acquisition and disposal. An option is a written contract by means of which an optionor grants, for good and valuable consideration, the optionee the exclusive right to buy, sell, or lease a particular parcel of real estate at a specified (or determinable) price during a specified period. In effect, the property is sold on a condition to be performed.

Options allow the option holder to tie up the property until financial analysis and market research have been completed. An option holder can control large parcels of property with only small cash outlays at risk. Purchase contracts may also be used for this purpose. An optionor should provide that the cash consideration to be forfeited is sufficient to pay for the time value of the investment and the loss of other opportunities during the option period. This, of course, is a matter of negotiation.

Options may take several forms. The simplest is the *fixed option*, which entitles the optionee to buy the property for a fixed price during the option period. *Step-up options* require the purchase price to increase periodically over time, often at the time of renewal. Step-up options are frequently used in rolling and long-term options.

Rolling options are commonly used by developers of subdivisions. The option normally covers a number of contiguous tracts, rolling from one tract to another as the developer progresses with the building of the subdivision. The option price usually steps up over time so that the landowner can share in the success of the venture, and to protect against loss in value from inflation and the passage of time.

A *full-credit option* credits the optionee with 100 percent credit for the consideration paid for the option against the purchase price of the real estate when the option is ultimately exercised. A *declining-credit* option provides an inducement for early exercise of the option because the percentage of the option consideration that may be applied to the purchase price declines over time in accordance with a negotiated schedule until it is extinguished by forfeiture at the end of the term.

Receipt of the proceeds from granting an option is not a taxable event for either the buyer or the seller.[17] No sale or purchase has been made. On the other hand, if an option is exercised, the seller treats the option pro-

---

[16] *The Arnold Encyclopedia of Real Estate* (Boston: Warren, Gorham & Lamont, 1979), p. 853. See also IRC Secs. 1239 (a), 267 (annotated), and Mathews, 61 TC 12 (1973). *Caveat:* Some circuit courts of Appeal disagree.

[17] Lucas v. North Texas Lumber Co., 281 US 11 (1930); Rev. Rul. 69–93, 1969–1 CB 139.

ceeds as part of the selling price of the property and the purchaser adds the consideration paid to the basis.

The distinction between a contract of sale and an option is critical. If the option consideration is substantial and full credit is granted toward the purchase price, the IRS may argue that the date of the sale was the date on which the option was granted, and this could adversely affect installment sale rights. It is important to take care that title remains with the seller until settlement.

If an option expires, the payments retained by the optionor become ordinary income in that tax year. For the optionee, the forfeiture of the option price is considered a sale of the option and, if it is a capitalized asset, will result in a capital loss. If it is a Section 1231 asset, it can be treated as an ordinary loss. Dealer status requires that the loss be treated as an ordinary loss.

An option holder may sell or exchange an option for a gain. This can be an exceptionally profitable method of disposal for a promoter who sells to a syndicate.[18]

Abandonment

Abandonment is the act by which an owner voluntarily relinquishes all right, title, and interest in a property. Under federal income tax laws, abandonment may give rise to an abandonment loss that may be used to offset ordinary income.

Abandonment is an important risk avoidance tactic of disposition for distressed debtors. Recently some lenders have encouraged the formation of "takeout" partnerships, which take over the ownership of troubled projects with the intention of abandoning them after a few years. This action may provide the lender with a respite until conditions change; however, it may be labeled a sham or abusive tax shelter by the IRS. Abandonment may also be viewed as an unethical desertion by the mortgagee.

Although the law on the subject is too complex for this book, it should be noted that abandonment is more than simply a failure to pay real estate taxes. There must be evidence that the owner vacated the property with no intention of ever returning to claim it.

A carefully planned and executed abandonment can successfully terminate a property with a deductible loss without the risk of "mortgage forgiveness," which is a dangerous tax event. The key is to achieve abandonment without a discharge of the indebtedness. One way to abandon is by means of a voluntary conveyance of title without consideration to the mortgagee. A quitclaim deed may suffice. In effect, it must be a surrender of the property without a discharge of the debt.[19]

---

[18]See IBP, *Real Estate Investment Planning*, paragraph 55,070.2; IRC Sec. 1234-1.

[19]Crane, 331 US 1 (1947); Aberle, 121 F.2d. 1726 (1941); Tanforan Co., Inc., US 313 F. Supp. 766 (1970).

Tax Deeds

After an owner has abandoned land, a tax deed may be issued. The usual procedure is to enter a lien for unpaid taxes on the public record of the local jurisdiction. If the lien is not satisfied within a specified period, the land is sold at a public action. The buyer pays the bid price to the sheriff or other public official and receives a tax deed, which may or may not ripen into a title. The defaulting taxpayer is given a specified period in which to redeem the property by paying the purchase price plus costs, penalties, and interest. (It is important to understand that such tax liens are state and local jurisdiction claims. The federal tax lien is a general lien, and although it applies to all the delinquent taxpayer's property, liens for real estate taxes and assessments specific to the property usually have priority over all other liens, including the federal lien.)

Investors who buy at such tax sales often seek quitclaim deeds from the former owners for a nominal sum and then file for quiet-title action in order to clear title and bring the property to marketable condition. Investment in tax deeds can be quite profitable, but it is akin to speculation and requires a thorough knowledge of local law and custom.

Involuntary Conversions

An owner may have to convert property involuntarily when it is condemned or destroyed by casualty. An involuntary conversion may result in a loss, a gain, or a partial loss or gain. The gain or loss is computed on the excess of the proceeds over the adjusted basis of the property at the time of the conversion. Since the owner of such property has little or no control over the conversion, special rules are provided to alleviate the inequity of recognizing a gain under the circumstances in which replacement property is obtained.

The law has partitioned the rules in relation to involuntary conversions. Those resulting from condemnation or threat of condemnation are treated differently from other involuntary conversions.

Condemnation or Threat of Condemnation. Condemnation is defined as an exercise of legal power by government to take privately owned property for necessary public use with or without the owner's consent, but upon payment of a reasonable price (fair market value) to the owner.[20] Mere notice by a public official that a decision has been made to acquire the property is deemed a sufficient threat, as long as the property owner had reasonable grounds to believe the condemnation would take place.

When property is lost through condemnation, the kinds of property that are eligible for replacement are much more liberally interpreted. In

[20]U.S. Department of the Treasury, "Condemnation of Private Property for Public Use," Publication 549 (Washington, D.C., rev. to date).

general, when properties are subject to eminent domain or threat of eminent domain, the investor can elect to invest in a wide variety of "like-kind" properties.

The replacement period for property subject to condemnation ends three years after the date on which the converted property was disposed of or the date of imminence of condemnation, whichever comes earlier.[21]

Other Forms of Involuntary Disposition. The possibilities for an involuntary disposition are virtually unlimited. A squatter's adverse possession in a remote rural area, such as Alaska, may ripen to a proper claim of title; a disgruntled co-tenant may force a judicial partition; divorce, death, insanity, disabling accident, or illness may terminate the ownership cycle. When the owner has financial problems, the property may be sold to meet a judgment.

Casualty losses. The rules about the nature of the replacement property for casualties and the duration of the replacement period are more restrictive for involuntary conversions other than condemnation.[22] Generally, for an owner to successfully elect nonrecognition of a gain, the proceeds of an involuntary conversion (e.g., insurance proceeds from a fire) must be reinvested either in replacement property "similar to or related in service or use" to the property converted or in acquisition of the controlling stock interest of a corporation holding such property. The *replacement period* generally ends two years from the close of the taxable year in which *any* gain from the involuntary conversion is realized. Extensions may be applied for, however.

The long ownership period characteristic of real estate requires contingency planning. Preplanning can change a crisis-producing event into an orderly transition of ownership. Involuntary conversions are seldom the disasters they appear to be at first glance. Even if the property was an ideal "cash cow" with a stable future, conversion permits commencement of a new ownership cycle with the substitute property without the impact of capital gains taxes.[23]

Foreclosure

Foreclosure is the process of law by which a mortgagee, or others with an interest in the debt instrument, may compel a mortgagor–debtor who has violated one of his or her mortgagor duties to redeem the pledge of pay-

---

[21]Rev. Rul. 63-221, 1963-2 CB 332; Creative Solutions, Inc., 3-20 F. 2d 809 (5th Cir. 1963); S&B Realty Co., 54 TC 863 (1970).

[22]Rev. Rul. 76-319, 1976-2 CB 242.

[23]See Arthur Andersen & Co., *Federal Taxes*, pp. 233–243.

ment promptly or eventually forfeit right to the property. In many states the mortgagee may sell a property under a power of sale contained in the mortgage itself. In other states the mortgagee must apply to courts of equity for a court-supervised process resulting in a decree of foreclosure and a sale.

Generally, the proceeds of a sale of mortgaged property are applied first to indebtedness secured by the mortgaged property—assuming that it has priority on the record—and to foreclosure expenses, and then, in order of priority, to junior lien holders, with the remaining balance, if any, paid to the mortgagor–debtor.

If foreclosure is insufficient to satisfy the secured debt, the mortgagee may proceed to seek satisfaction of the deficiency from other assets of the mortgagor. However, in the past it has been unusual for mortgagee–creditors to pursue satisfaction of a deficiency. In fact, it is not uncommon for the mortgagor and the mortgagee to have agreed at the time of origination to a nonrecourse loan. Although foreclosure is deemed a creditor's remedy by the law, debtor–mortgagors may force the creditor to act, thus using foreclosure as a tactic for disposition of unwanted property.

Mortgage foreclosure presents a variety of tax consequences for both the mortgagor and the mortgagee. Even though the mortgagor–investor suffers the loss of property, a foreclosure sale is treated as a disposition for tax purposes. Thus, it may result in a gain or loss to the mortgagor as well as to the mortgagee. The nature of such a gain or loss depends on the character of the property—capital asset, business asset, dealer property, or personal residence—and is measured by the difference between the net proceeds of the transaction and the mortgagor's adjusted basis in the mortgage debt.

To keep the reduction or cancellation of the mortgagor's indebtedness from becoming taxable income, the investor must carefully plan the transaction to qualify it under one of the following exceptions.[24]

1. The cancellation or reduction is made pursuant to the orders of bankruptcy or reorganization proceedings.
2. A purchase money mortgagor voluntarily reconveys to the mortgagee, or the purchase money mortgagee voluntarily reduces the original price of the property.
3. The mortgagee makes a gift of the reduction to the mortgagor.
4. The mortgagor can prove insolvency both before and after the debt is discharged.

---

[24]Foreclosure as sale: Hamel, 311 US 504 (1941); discharge or reduction as phantom gain: Regs. 1.61-12; debt reduction as gift: Liberty Mirror Works, 3 TC 1018 (1944) (Acq.); purchase money mortgage reduction: Killian Company, 128 F.2d 433 (1942); insolvency: Dallas Transfer, 70 F.2d 95 (1934); election to reduce basis: Regs. 1,108(a) 1, 1.1017-1(a); also Hotel Astoria, 42 BTA 759 (1940) (Acq.); for Abandonment, see note 18.

5. The mortgagor *ex ante* elects to have the amount of the debt cancellation reduce the basis of the property and thus be excluded from income.

6. The mortgagor abandons the property to the mortgagee without discharge of the debt. Thus, there is no sale or exchange.

Foreclosure is usually thought of as an ancient remedy encrusted with embellishments from debtor–creditor battles through the centuries. Under the commerce clause, Congress could pass remedial legislation to simplify and unify legal precedent instead of allowing mortgage and foreclosure procedures to be peculiar to local jurisdictions.

There are many ramifications of foreclosure, such as equity of redemption, statutory redemption, foreclosure by sale, and deeds in lieu of foreclosure. Any real estate investor with a substantial portfolio should be knowledgeable about mortgage law in appropriate jurisdictions.[25]

An important note of caution concerns the possibility of phantom gain resulting in taxable income for partners in real estate investments. Generally, an increase in a partner's share of partnership liabilities will increase the basis of his or her interest.[26] The opposite will occur when the partner is relieved of a personal obligation.[27] Partnerships may anticipate some of these problems through mutual agreement about special allocations of capital gains and losses.[28] Usually limited partners may increase their basis and still limit their liability by using nonrecourse debt, an obligation that can be satisfied only by partnership assets. However, since partnership allocations of income, gains, losses, deductions, or credits will be followed for tax purposes only if they have a "substantial economic effect," reduction and cancellation of mortgage debt must be carried out with great care by an attorney and an accountant.[29]

THE ANALYTICAL FRAMEWORK

Some real estate investment analysts argue that the termination decision results from a portfolio revision analysis (individual or institutional).[30] If

---

[25]See Robert Kratovil and Raymond J. Werner, *Real Estate Law*, 7th ed. (Englewood Cliffs, N.J.: Prentice–Hall, 1979); see also R. Kratovil, *Modern Mortgage Law and Practice* (Englewood Cliffs, N.J.: Prentice–Hall, 1972).

[26]IRC Sec. 752(a) (annotated).

[27]IRC Sec. 752(b) (annotated).

[28]IRC Sec. 704(c)(2) (annotated).

[29]See Arthur Andersen & Co., *Federal Taxes*, p. 354; see also S. C. Orrisch, 55 TC 395 (1970), aff'd per curiam, 31 AFTR2d 73-1069 (9th Cir. 1973) for related matter.

[30]Richard J. Curcio and James P. Gaines, "Real Estate Portfolio Revision," *Journal of the American Real Estate and Urban Economics Association*, Winter 1977, pp. 399–410.

the investment portfolio is monitored on a continuous basis (annually or more often), the dynamic asset allocation problem is

1. How much of which asset classes should be bought or sold?
2. Within the asset class (i.e., bonds, common stocks or real estate), how much of which asset subclass should be bought or sold? (Subclasses for real estate are residential real estate, business real estate, and farmland. Each of these subclasses can be broken into smaller categories. Business real estate can be separated into office buildings, retail, warehouses, hotel–motel, industrial, etc.)
3. What specific assets should be bought or sold?

For large institutional portfolios, this problem can become very complicated (virtually unsolvable) very quickly. However, for most individual portfolios, the problem readily collapses to manageable proportions. Most individuals do not hold well-diversified mixed-asset portfolios (i.e., cash or equivalents, bonds, common stocks, real estate). And when only real estate is considered, as it is for this chapter, the real estate portfolios of most individuals are very small.

If a portfolio has but a few specific real estate assets (is not well diversified), the risk of the portfolio is greater than that of a real estate portfolio with more assets. Therefore, periodic reevaluation becomes even more important.

Analytic Methodology

The individual real estate investment should be reevaluated annually in most cases. This process can be very simple and take minutes or very complex and take days. The easiest method is simply to reexamine the analysis done previously to justify the acquisition (purchase) of the property. If none of the inputs to that analysis has changed, the decision would be to continue to hold. However, some financial variables within the property change over time and will have impact on the realized rate of return. Because investments are made on the basis of expected incomes (cash flows, tax benefits, mortgage amortization, and property appreciation), the incomes realized by an individual real estate investor often do not match the expected incomes. Some realized amounts are smaller than those expected, but some may be larger than expected. Of course, if realized incomes are less than expected, the rate of return on the investment is less than expected.

However, an investment's failure to perform as expected for part of the holding period does not mean it should necessarily be terminated. The relevant period of analysis is the future. Rarely does any investment underperform or overperform realistic expectations for long periods. Expectations must be adjusted as additional and new information becomes available.

Each year the expected rate of return should be recalculated from anticipated future incomes (with expectations adjusted as necessary) and the current after-tax equity. The current after-tax equity of a real estate investment sold in year t should be defined as

$$E_t = P_t - S_t - M_t - T_t$$

where E_t = net after-tax equity in year t
P_t = probable selling price
S_t = selling expenses
M_t = unpaid mortgage
T_t = all taxes incurred
t = year of sale

The result is sale proceeds that are net of selling expenses, the unpaid mortgage, and all taxes paid. If the asset is sold, this is the net dollar amount the seller will retain for use in alternative investments.[31]

So now the internal-rate-of-return (IRR) equation is as follows,

$$E_t = \frac{\text{ATCF}_{t+1}}{1 + r} + \frac{\text{ATCF}_{t+2}}{(1 + r)^2} + \frac{\text{ATCF}_{t+3}}{(1 + r)^3} + \cdots + \frac{\text{ATCF}_n}{(1 + r)^n} + \frac{\text{NATER}_n}{(1 + r)^n}$$

where E_t = net after-tax equity at time t
ATCF_{t+1} = after-tax cash flow for the first year
NATER_n = net after-tax equity reversion
n = the holding period
r = the internal rate of return (IRR)

Using the IRR equation just given, which is the same as used earlier to evaluate properties for potential acquisition, the r is calculated. Then r, the IRR, is compared to the IRR on alternative investments and ranked from most profitable to least profitable. A similar approach can be developed using the NPV model. The standard decision rules for IRR and NPV are then applied, and a choice is made to sell or to continue holding the property being analyzed.

The possible decisions, including the numerous methods of disposition discussed in this chapter, can be readily adapted to this analytical procedure. Some of the timing and characteristics of the cash flows may change from one method to another. But, the same analytical framework can be applied.

---

[31]See Norman G. Miller and Michael A. Sklarz, "Pricing Strategies and Residential Property Selling Prices," *The Journal of Real Estate Research*, Fall 1987, pp. 12–26, for possible pricing strategies.

SUMMARY

Competent investors are familiar with the wide variety of techniques used to facilitate sale and maximize after-tax returns, such as conditional sale contracts, buy–sell agreements, sale–leasebacks, land contracts, auctions, installment sales, and exchanges.

Many of the techniques discussed in this chapter require that the investor be knowledgeable about local law as well as the Internal Revenue Code for trusts, wills, and transferrals for love and affection. Options, tax deeds, foreclosures, involuntary conversions, and air and mineral rights all pose risk and return trade-off opportunities that can greatly affect the success or failure of attempts to acquire significant wealth over an investor's life cycle.

Exchanges are one of the major areas of opportunity for wealth accumulation in real estate investing. Although Section 1031 transactions are complex, exchanges give the investor an opportunity for deferral of capital gains tax, offer some investors a chance to acquire a stepped-up basis with a minimum cash outlay, and provide an opportunity to replace a property that no longer satisfies investment objectives. Exchanges are discussed in detail in the Appendix to this chapter.

Although this chapter discusses many different disposition techniques, only one can be used for any given transaction. The choice of a specific method depends on the investor's goals and objectives. In effect, terminating the property investment is part of the investor's overall strategy. As indicated in Chapter 16, one aspect of disposition is to keep your house in order: in real estate investing one should always be ready to move to negotiation rapidly when the right offer comes along.

Finally, once the termination process starts, the principals should agree to keep the lines of communication open. Wise investors seek solutions rather than emphasizing problems.

APPENDIX 17A. EXCHANGES

Taxes act as a deterrent to many people who want to dispose of their property. The Internal Revenue Code allows an escape from this binding situation for those who wish merely to exchange investment properties rather than converting property into cash or other assets. If two or more owners exchange like-kind properties of equal value, all taxes from the transaction are deferred until there is an actual sale. When the properties are not of equal value or the parties' equities in their properties are unequal, the parties balance out the exchange with cash or other property (the so-called *boot*), with an existing mortgage on one of the properties, or with a combination of these adjustments. Although exchanges of this type are frequently referred to as "tax-free," they are not, for the following reasons.

1. Taxes on the realized gains are merely deferred until the occurrence of a taxable event.
2. To the extent that unlike assets (such as cash) are included in the transaction to offset unequal property values, a portion of the transaction will be taxable.
3. In multiple exchanges, some parties to the transaction may not be eligible for tax deferment.

A tax-deferred exchange may be made any time two or more investors with real property decide to change their holdings. As long as the intention of the parties is exchange (rather than liquidation), a transaction that is eligible for tax deferment may take any of several forms.

Section 1031 Exchanges.

Generally, a broker identifies opportunities for multiple transactions among his or her current listings. Nationwide, computerized, multiple-listing services like the NAR National Property Exchange Section of the Realtors Marketing Institute may facilitate the setting up of multiple exchanges.

The advantage of a multiple exchange is the greater probability that all parties will achieve their particular objectives in the transaction. For example, a developer may trade a completed project to the owner of raw land, who exchanges the project for a more mature income-producing property. Even more flexibility is introduced by the fact that some parties in the exchange may qualify under Section 1031 and others do not. Although an owner who wants to liquidate an investment may receive no direct tax advantages, he or she may benefit by receiving a higher price than would be possible from a straight sale. The property may be more valuable to a purchaser making an exchange than it would be otherwise.

Why Exchange?

Tax benefits may be achieved if a property disposition is arranged as an exchange. For the transaction to make sense, however, there must be some economic advantage besides tax savings to the parties making the exchange.

Changes in Investor Objectives. Provided that a transaction for a desirable parcel can be arranged, an exchange can permit an investor to improve his or her portfolio without loss of equity or investment continuity. For example,

1. An investor who wants to reduce management responsibilities may exchange property used in his or her business for income property upon retirement.
2. A property owner who is relocating to another city may want to find a replacement investment close at hand.
3. An investor who wants to sell or refinance may find that the present parcel is not ideally suited to these purposes. An exchange, however, may be used to acquire another parcel that can be sold outright.
4. An investor may want to exchange non-income-producing real estate (e.g., raw land) for income-producing property.
5. Changes in an investor's income may increase the need for tax shelter. If an exchange increases the depreciable basis of a property, it also increases depreciation deductions. Exchanges may be arranged to obtain properties with higher debt (to increase interest expense and total value), a higher building-to-land allocation, or a shorter useful life, or properties of a type that is eligible for accelerated-depreciation methods.

Changes in Investment Performance. Risk, income, and other investment features may change dramatically over the ownership cycle. Therefore, investors may want to replace properties that no longer satisfy investment objectives. For example,

1. A developer may want to exchange a completed project for new development sites.
2. A farmer may want to exchange land that is suitable for development for new farm land.
3. A large-scale developer may want to consolidate land inventory into one contiguous parcel.
4. An investor may want to improve cash return by leveraging accrued equity buildup and value appreciation.
5. An investor may want to convert a portion of equity into cash.

Advantages of Exchange. If an exchange can be arranged, much or all of the capital gains tax levied on a sale may be postponed. This tactic provides several benefits.

1. *Conservation of equity.* The portion of capital gains that is not taxed in an exchange is forwarded to the new property in the form of a reduced tax basis. Therefore, when property received in an exchange is eventually sold, more of the gain will be capital gain than if the property had been purchased. Moreover, since this tax is not due until eventual sale, an investor may use the entire amount of the increasing equity to acquire new investments.

Postponing the taxes benefits in two ways: in the income production and value appreciation of a larger project and, when the taxes eventually come due, payment with less valuable future dollars. In effect, Section 1031 provides an interest-free loan from the time of exchange until the time of eventual sale.

2. *Continuity of investment.* Since an exchange is consummated as one transaction, the investor may keep funds continually active over the transaction period; thus, income is not lost during the time required to dispose of one property and acquire a new one.

3. *Estate building.* Exchange can be an effective means of estate building. Contributions to the investment program may be confined to carrying costs (debt service and property taxes) and occasional broker's fees. Capital gains taxes may be deferred indefinitely, with the investor receiving the full benefits of an expanding equity. Of course, cash may be necessary to balance the equities of the transaction.

Taxes deferred through exchange may be escaped entirely upon death and transfer of the estate to devisees; then the basis of the inheritance will be adjusted to current market value. Thus, if the property is sold at the right time, capital gains would be zero.

Disadvantages of Exchanges. Although exchange can be a useful procedure, it should be entered into with a full understanding of its repercussions. Treatment under Section 1031 cannot be elected. A transaction with the characteristics of a tax-deferred exchange must be treated as a 1031 exchange. Therefore, an investor who does not desire tax deferment must be careful to structure the deal to avoid designation as an exchange.

Why avoid 1031 status? Section 1031 provides for nonrecognition not only of gains but of losses as well. Should one of the parties in an exchange dispose of property at a value below the basis, the loss could not be written off.

An investor who wants to increase depreciation deductions and tax savings may also wish to avoid Section 1031. Under the law, the basis of acquired property is reduced by an amount equal to the unrecognized (deferred) gain. A taxpayer may prefer to pay capital gains taxes immediately in order to start a new property life cycle and thus a new depreciation cycle.

Basic Considerations in Structuring an Exchange

In most exchanges only a technically qualified broker can arrange the deal to the satisfaction of all parties. Sometimes it is necessary to find additional property owners to enlarge the number of exchanges and provide each participant with the best available match.

In any exchange transaction the following points should be considered.

1. The transaction must be intended as an exchange and must comply with Section 1031. This test must be applied to each party, since some may achieve tax deferment while others do not.
2. In order to minimize taxable gains, properties should be matched to minimize the need to exchange unlike properties (boot).
3. Parties who realize a capital loss must be isolated from the transaction in order to allow recognition of the loss.
4. The property received by each party should represent a sound investment vis-à-vis his or her own objectives.

Legal Qualification for Section 1031 Treatment. Exchange transactions must follow both the letter and the spirit of the law. It is not uncommon for exchanges to be disqualified on technicalities. In *Halpern* the court upheld a disqualification with the remark that "there is no equity in tax law; conformity to the law is the requirement."[32]

Actual Exchange of Properties. For an exchange to occur, the parties in the transaction must simultaneously convey properties to which they hold title in exchange for other properties that they did not originally own. A bona fide exchange need not be as simple and pure as the case in which several property owners agree to swap. Often what begins as a sale may be converted into an exchange. However, the conversion must be handled precisely to avoid disqualifying results. For example, in *Alderson*[33] a sale was converted into an exchange by requiring the purchaser to acquire a new property (chosen by the Aldersons) to trade for their property. This arrangement was ruled acceptable on the grounds that the Aldersons *stipulated* their preference for an exchange and the potential buyer actually took title to the new property prior to the exchange.

[32] B. Halpern, 286 F. Supp 255 (1968).
[33] Alderson, 317 F.2d 790 (1963).

The procedure used in the exchange can be crucial. In the case of *Carlton*[34] a development company that wanted to acquire the taxpayer's property agreed to find a replacement property for exchange. To save title transfer taxes, however, the company merely assigned the contract to the taxpayer at the closing. The transaction was ruled a separate sale and purchase, since the company never took title to the new property.

In a multiparty exchange, it is often necessary to require a party to take title to property temporarily and pass it on to another party. It is important that these "conduits" actually take title and that each part of the exchange be made contingent on all other parts. In *Halpern*[35] these procedures were not explicitly followed and the transaction separated into an exchange and a consequent sale.

Timing is also important for an exchange to be valid. Under Section 1031 there is no provision for a reinvestment period. The exchange must usually be simultaneous. However, this requirement was successfully circumvented in *Starker II*,[36] in which an exchange of property for a promise to deliver property in the future was found to qualify because it was pivotal to the transaction's occurrence. Subsequent tax cases also support this precedent.

Relationship of the Parties. If one of the parties in the transaction is acting as an agent of another party, any exchange between the two does not qualify for Section 1031 treatment. The key test of this agency relationship is *who bears the risk of loss* for the new property *prior* to exchange. If a second party in the exchange arranges for property to be used in the transaction *but bears no ownership responsibility*, he or she may be deemed an agent. The courts, however, have made clear that for the exchange to be invalid, the agency relationship must exist in the particular transaction at hand. In *Baird*[37] a broker participated in an exchange by providing a replacement building. This was ruled valid, since the broker was not acting for Baird in the acquisition of the replacement property. In *Coupe*[38] the taxpayer's attorney participated, but the exchange was upheld since the attorney was not acting in an agency capacity.

Qualifying Properties in an Exchange. Section 1031 applies to only two classes of real property: that held for productive or business use (e.g., a farm, office space, factory, or resort) and that held for investment (both income-producing and non-income-producing property). Property held as inventory to be sold is not eligible. For the transaction to qualify as a tax-

---

[34]Carlton, 385 F.2d 238 (5th Cir. 1967).
[35]See Halpern (note 32).
[36]Starker II, 602 F.2d 1341 (1979).
[37]Baird Publishing Co., 39 TC 608 (1962), (Acq.) CB 1963-2, 4.
[38]Coupe, 52 TC 394 (1969), (Acq.) CB 1970-1 XV.

deferred exchange, both the property conveyed and the property received must be eligible. Trading business property for investment property is permissible.

A property is disqualified when it is judged to be held primarily for sale. It is the owner's intention, as indicated by his or her actions, that determines disqualification. This judgment is based on two factors: the use of the property while it is held by the taxpayer and the timing of its consequent sale. Both points were used to uphold disqualification in *Bernard*.[39] The court upheld the IRS because Bernard did not use the land but listed the property for sale immediately after the exchange.

Property acquired in exchange frequently has been purchased by the other party solely for the exchange. This practice does not jeopardize qualification for the receiving party if that party intends to hold the property for an eligible purpose. Thus, in *Alderson* the taxpayer retained eligibility even though the other party had acquired the property solely for the transaction.

Exchange of Like-Kind Properties. Section 1031 applies only to exchanges of like-kind properties. This does not mean that each property must be of the same type or grade, nor that they must be held for the same purpose. The like-kind criterion refers to the type of ownership rights in the realty. Thus, a fee title in any eligible property may be exchanged for a fee title in any other eligible property.

In most cases, a less than fee title may be exchanged for a similar interest. Some examples of interests that must be exchanged for similar interests are leaseholds, life estates, and partnership interests. (A general partnership and a limited partnership are not of like kind.) In *Starker*, 1,843 acres of timberland were exchanged for the recipient's promise to provide Starker with suitable real estate within five years or pay the balance at that time in cash. Thus, Starker exchanged for future rights to transfers of entitlement to property.

Some partial interests have been ruled to be of like kind with fee titles. The following qualify.

1. Long-term leaseholds (greater than 30 years).
2. Leased fee interests (long or short term).
3. Mineral and water rights.

Boot. Often some form of unlike-kind property is included in an exchange to balance the equities exchanged. This property, which may be cash, equipment, other personal property, or relief from mortgage obligations, is termed *boot*. The presence of boot does not disqualify the entire transaction from Section 1031 treatment. It does, however, affect the amount of

---

[39]Bernard, TC Memo 1967-176.

realized gain that may be deferred, and may result in some capital gains tax on the exchange. The mechanics of calculating this effect are presented at the end of this section.

Effect of Disqualification of One or More Participants. Failure of all parties to qualify does not affect the ability of any one party to claim benefits. Indeed, if this were not true, very few exchanges would be practical.

In multiparty exchanges it may also be possible that part of the transaction will qualify as a Section 1031 exchange and other parts will be considered sales. This may be so even though one of the parties is involved in both transactions. In *Halpern* one exchange was converted by the IRS into a sale and exchange. Although the exchange portion qualified under Section 1031, Halpern was forced to pay taxes on the boot.

Valid Purpose. Even though the investor follows the letter of the regulations in conducting an exchange, the transaction may still be disqualified if the procedure lacks a valid business purpose. If an actual sale is arranged to appear as an exchange purely for tax benefits, this is viewed as a sham use of Section 1031, and the courts have upheld the IRS's attempts to invalidate it. An example is *Smith*.[40] Smith sold his interest in one property primarily to purchase a second property. The transaction, though procedurally correct, was disallowed. Somewhat similar situations can qualify, however, as long as they are correctly labeled and occur in the proper order. In the *Alderson* exchange, after the contract on a straight cash sale had been made, Alderson found land that he preferred. The putative cash buyer (Alloy) agreed to amend the agreement, prior to settlement, to provide that Alloy would acquire the land and exchange it for Alderson's property. If the exchange did not take place as contemplated, the original cash sale would be carried out as previously planned. Ultimately, Alloy took title to the property bought for Alderson, paid the balance of the purchase price in cash (boot), and exchanged (traded in) the property acquired to Alderson, who in turn acquired his land. The Ninth Circuit Court relied on *intention* and legal obligation. It found that Alderson's intent from the beginning had been to make a tax-free exchange transfer if possible. (Such intent must be provable from the record.) In addition, it found that Alloy was legally bound, by the amendment prior to closing, to pay cash or its equivalent (i.e., the property sought by Alderson). The court made it clear that acquiring property solely for the purposes of facilitating an exchange transaction was perfectly proper. As in *Coupe*, mentioned earlier, an outsider who was not acting as an agent arranged the exchange.

Generally, it is more conservative to arrange for the exchange property prior to the closing, although the *Starker II* case in 1979 raised new possi-

[40]Juhl Smith, 76-2 USTC 9541 (8th Cir.) 1976.

bilities. In 1984, however, Congress restricted the use of delayed-property-purchase exchanges by the creation of relatively short time limits (e.g., 180 days) within which replacement properties must be identified and transferred.[41] Since finding exchange properties is so critical, interested parties have organized exchange clubs in many metropolitan areas. The Realtors National Marketing Institute (RNMI) has an International Traders Club that lists exchanges.

Evaluating the Exchange

Evaluating an exchange entails determining the taxable gains and the adjusted basis of the new property. At least one of the parties will have taxable gains if unlike-kind properties are included in the exchange. Gains that are not taxed but deferred affect the basis of the new property and, consequently, future depreciation deductions and capital gains at a future sale. The entire process is simplified by the use of readily available forms (see Exhibit 17-5).

Calculating Realized Gain. The gain realized from an exchange is determined in exactly the same manner as for a sale. The gain is the difference between market value (as indicated in the transaction) and adjusted basis. Transaction costs—commissions and loan fees—may be capitalized by being added to the adjusted basis.

Balancing Equities. When properties that are unequal in value are exchanged, additional consideration must be included to balance the transaction. This "boot" is equal to the difference between the values of the two properties represented by the owners' equity. For unencumbered properties, the equity is the market value subject to the exchange. Commonly, the properties are exchanged subject to or by assumption of existing mortgages. Therefore, equity is market value minus the outstanding mortgage balance.

As an example, assume that properties A and B are exchanged. Both are valued at $100,000, but A has an outstanding mortgage of $50,000 and B has one of $40,000. The owner of property A, with an equity of $50,000, must provide boot of $10,000 in exchange for the $60,000 equity in property B. The $10,000 boot may expose the owner of B to income tax on the exchange. (Boot may be eliminated by either party's adjusting the outstanding debt prior to the exchange.)

Calculating Recognized Gain. Each party to the exchange is subject to capital gains taxation on recognized gain. *The gain recognized is either the*

---

[41]Alvin L. Arnold, *Real Estate Investments After the Tax Reform Act of 1986* (Boston: Warren, Gorham & Lamont, 1987), pp. 96–97.

EXHIBIT 17-5.   **Worksheet for Basis Adjustments and Calculations**

Exchange Basis Adjustment

Name _____ Date _____

Property Conveyed _____

	LINE NO.		(1) PROPERTY		(2) PROPERTY		(3) PROPERTY		(4) PROPERTY	
INDICATED GAIN	1	Market Value of Property Conveyed								
	2	Less: Adjusted Basis								
	3	Less: Capitalized Transaction Costs								
	4	INDICATED GAIN								
	5	Equity Conveyed								
	6	Equity Acquired								
BALANCE EQUITIES	7	Difference								
	8	Cash or Boot Received								
	9	Cash or Boot Paid								
DETERMINE RECOGNIZED GAIN	10	Old Loans								
	11	Less: New Loans								
	12	NET LOAN RELIEF								
	13	Less: Cash or Boot Paid (L9)								
	14	Recognized Net Loan Relief								
	15	Plus: Cash or Boot Received (L8)								
	16	TOTAL UNLIKE PROPERTY RECEIVED								
	17	Recognized Gain LESSER OF L4 or L16								

Transfer of Basis

	LINE NO.									
TRANSFER OF BASIS	18	Adjusted Basis (L2)								
	19	Plus: New Loans (L11)								
	20	Plus: Cash or Boot Paid (L9)								
	21	Plus: Recognized Gain (L17)								
	22	Total Additions								
	23	Less Old Loans (L10)								
	24	Less: Cash or Boot Received (L8)								
	25	NEW ADJUSTED BASIS								

SAMPLE

New Allocation and Depreciation

	LINE NO.									
ALLOCATION	26	Land Allocation								
	27	Improvement Allocation								
	28	Personal Property Allocation								

	LINE NO.		PP	IMP	PP	IMP	PP	IMP	PP	IMP
DEPRECIATION	29	Estimated Useful Life in Years								
	30	Depreciation Method								
	31	ANNUAL DEPRECIATION IMPROVEMENTS								
	32	ANNUAL DEPRECIATION PERSONAL PROPERTY								

NATIONAL ASSOCIATION OF REALTORS® developed in cooperation with its affiliate, the ©REALTORS NATIONAL MARKETING INSTITUTE® 1975. 1-75-F604

The statements and figures presented herein, while not guaranteed, are secured from sources we believe authoritative.   Prepared by _____

Source: Courtesy of Realtors National Marketing Institute.

realized gain or the total unlike-kind property received, whichever is less. Therefore, a taxpayer who either realizes no gain or receives no unlike-kind property pays no tax on the exchange.

Unlike-kind property includes both net mortgage relief and boot. Net mortgage relief is the amount of the old mortgage minus the amount of the assumed mortgage. Negative mortgage relief is ignored. The total value of unlike-kind property is arrived at by subtracting any boot paid out and adding any boot received. The result is recognized gain if this figure is less than the gain realized. It is important to note that someone who is "trading up" in an exchange cannot offset the recognition of boot received by taking on a greater amount of mortgage debt.

Adjusting the Basis of the New Property. Taxes that are deferred in the exchange offset the basis of the new property. Property owners generally desire as high a basis as possible, since this increases the depreciation deductions allowed and the gains recognized on sale. Therefore, the cost of deferring taxes is a reduced basis.

The starting point for determining the basis of the acquired property is the adjusted basis of the old property. To this are added the assumed mortgage, the boot paid out, and any recognized gain. From this figure are subtracted the old mortgage and the boot received. A good general rule when analyzing basis in an exchange is that the aggregate basis of all qualifying and nonqualifying property, other than cash, received in the exchange should equal the basis of all qualifying and nonqualifying property and cash transferred.

To demonstrate how the deferred gains are deducted from the basis, consider a simple exchange involving no boot and, therefore, no recognized gain. All realized gains are deferred.

	Property A	Property B
Market value	$30,000	$50,000
Basis	25,000	35,000
Mortgage	20,000	40,000

The equities are identical, $10,000, so no boot is required. If each property were sold, the recognized gain on A would be $5,000 and that on B would be $15,000. The new owners could take as basis the market value of the properties. No gain is recognized in the exchange of the properties, but the basis to the new owners must be adjusted as shown in Exhibit 17-6.

Allocation of the New Basis. Before the adjusted basis of the new property may be used for depreciation, it must be allocated between the land and depreciable assets. This is done by allocating the new basis in the same proportions as the old basis. For example, assume that the investor received property A in the preceding example. The old basis of $25,000 was

EXHIBIT 17-6.   Basis Calculations in a Real Estate Exchange

	A	B
Basis of old property	$25,000	$35,000
Plus: New mortgage	40,000	20,000
Plus: Boot paid	0	0
Plus: Recognized gain	0	0
Less: Old mortgage	− 20,000	− 40,000
Less: Boot received	0	0
New basis	$45,000	$15,000

allocated $15,000 (60 percent) to the building and $10,000 (40 percent) to the land. The new basis, $15,000, is allocated in the same proportions: 60 percent, or $9,000, to buildings and 40 percent, or $6,000, to land. If the investor receives several properties in one exchange, he or she must first split the unallocated basis among the properties (in proportion to their old basis) and then allocate each piece to land and buildings.

A Final Note on Exchanges

Exchanges epitomize the strategic objective that dispositions of real estate should be structured to benefit each party to the transaction. However, at present exchanges are so complex that many people are discouraged from using this technique. The development of conversational computer software programs should do much to make it easier to evaluate exchanges. In addition, professional assistance from a broker, attorney, or CPA can be cost effective. Careful documentation and proper labeling of each step along the way are essential to a successful exchange. The key is to accept the rigid reality of Section 1031 and to comply strictly with its requirements. Finally, the rules are always subject to change.[42] Although the 1986 and 1987 tax acts treated 1031 exchanges favorably, future tax laws may reverse the trend if too many investors start using the technique to defer taxes and, as a result, revenue to the federal government decreases noticeably. Investors considering the use of exchanges should first consult an expert.

[42]See William Celis III, "Property Swaps Would Lose Luster under House Proposal," *The Wall Street Journal*, November 11, 1987, p. 21; Richard A. Goodman, "How the New Starker Case Has Revolutionized Exchanges," *Real Estate Review*, Summer 1980, pp. 78–83; and Arnold, *Real Estate Investments After the Tax Reform Act of 1986*, pp. 86–100.

ASPEN WOOD APARTMENTS

TERMINATION OF THE INVESTMENT

In 1980 the taxable income from Aspen Wood Apartments turned positive. In May 1981 Charlie Davidson and Clyde Boomer projected a taxable income of $55,500 for the year. Cash flow before tax was expected to increase to over $68,791 in 1981; however, the property needed substantial capital improvements to replace components that were nearing the end of their useful life. Boomer undertook a five-year capital budget study. The results showed a five-year schedule of capital expenditures as follows.

Year	Required Capital Expenditures
1982	$63,500
1983	62,500
1984	36,000
1985	10,500
1986	0

D&B commissioned a local MAI appraiser to estimate the current market value of the property at the end of 1981. On the basis of local market conditions, the most probable selling price was estimated at $1.6 million if the majority of the capital improvements shown in the above table were made prior to sale. Alternatively, a refurbishment reserve of approximately $100,000 would have to be deducted from the $1.6 million selling price to arrive at an "as is" selling price, under the assumption that the new owner would prefer to undertake the capital expenditure program. The net proceeds from the sale of the property for investors in the 50 and 70 percent tax brackets were estimated as shown in Exhibit 17-A. Also shown is an IRR and present-value calculation based on historical cash flows and a required IRR of 20 percent.

If a sale with the assumptions shown in Exhibit 17-A were negotiated, the investment in Aspen Wood would prove to be a highly profitable one. The focus now must therefore be on marginal additional return.

TERMINATION ALTERNATIVES

Since nothing can be done to alter past events, the focus should be on possible future occurrences over which the investor has some control. On the basis of prevailing economic and market conditions as well as physical and locational

EXHIBIT 17-A. Analysis of Sale: December 31, 1981

	50 Percent Tax Bracket	70 Percent Tax Bracket
Estimated selling price	$1,600,000	$1,600,000
Less: Refurbishment reserve	100,000	100,000
Less: Selling expenses	90,000	90,000
Net selling price	1,410,000	1,410,000
Less: Capital gains tax	168,936	236,510
Less: Recapture tax	5,997	8,395
Less: Mortgage balance	718,853	718,853
Net Proceeds from Sale	$ 516,214	$ 446,242

Internal Rate of Return/Present-Value Analysis

Equity investment, December 1974	$210,000	$210,000
Cash flows after tax		
1974 (Nov.–Dec.)	$53,115	$74,360
1975	52,325	73,255
1976	31,927	44,697
1977	23,604	33,042
1978	36,326	42,857
1979	23,244	24,071
1980	16,990	12,504
1981	20,752	14,653
Net proceeds from sale, December 1981	$516,214	$446,242
Internal Rate of Return	34.2%	45.1%
Net Present Value (at 20%)	$106,241	$144,106

characteristics specific to the Aspen Wood Apartments complex, five alternatives that were generally appealing to the partners were isolated for consideration.

1. Sell the property and reinvest the proceeds in another investment that would earn the required IRR.
2. Sell the property on an installment basis, providing the new buyer with a wraparound mortgage.
3. Refinance the property; then sell the property on an installment basis and encourage the selling investors to participate in a new venture.
4. Make required capital improvements; continue to hold.
5. Refinance the property; make required capital improvements; continue to hold.

Although refinancing a property was not generally a viable alternative in the 1981 mortgage market (interest rates of 15 to 19 percent), the existing wraparound mortgage (at 7.5 percent) on the Aspen Wood property could itself be wrapped. A local savings and loan association was willing to provide wraparound financing to the present venture if they agreed to continue to hold the property, or if D&B agreed to become partners in a new venture that bought the property. This made possible alternatives 3 and 5 of the list.

An investment time horizon of five years was chosen for the analysis of all the alternatives. The amount of equity investment available for any alternative was considered to be the amount of after-tax dollars that could be realized from a straight sale of the property as described; that is, the investor's opportunity cost was measured in terms of the net proceeds of sale: $516,214 for the investor in the 50 percent tax bracket and $446,242 for the investor in the 70 percent tax bracket (from Exhibit 17-A). Only if an alternative produced an IRR greater than 20 percent on these equity dollars would this alternative be considered superior to a straight sale.

ANALYSIS OF THE ALTERNATIVES

A complete rate-of-return, ratio, and risk analysis was performed for each of the five alternatives listed. The techniques described throughout Chapters 5 to 17 were utilized to weigh the risk and cash flow return characteristics of each alternative, and to consider systematically the nonfinancial objectives of the investors in the aggregate. The financial analysis resulted in a ranking of the alternatives as follows.

1. Refinance; sell on an installment basis; encourage the selling investors to buy shares in a new venture.
2. Sell on an installment basis; provide the new buyer with a wraparound mortgage.
3. Refinance; make required capital improvements; continue to hold.
4. Make required capital improvements; continue to hold.
5. Sell the property; reinvest the proceeds in another investment that would earn the required IRR (this is the "base case" against which other alternatives are compared).

Alternatives 1 through 4 all produced IRRs greater than the required IRR of 20 percent and therefore were superior to the straight-sale alternative, in which the funds would be reinvested at the required IRR. Davidson and Boomer recommended these alternatives to the investors in the order shown, sending each investor a copy of the investment analysis and supporting documentation.

THE TERMINATION DECISION

Davidson and Boomer called a partnership meeting in August 1981. As expected, few of the investors had studied or understood the elaborate analysis provided or the performance measures on which the analysis was based (IRR, FMRR, and NPV were calculated for each alternative). Although the explanations were clear, the investors needed to have each alternative explained again, and the pros and cons summarized and debated again. A five-hour evening meeting concluded with the investors approving D&B's recommendation to accept the first alternative—refinance and sell.

DELAYED CLOSING AND RESYNDICATION

The local savings association that agreed to provide wraparound financing suffered a major management turnover in September 1981. The new management and D&B could not agree on a wraparound loan yield and terms that would meet the objectives of both parties. In addition, the first lien holder would not agree to provide the savings and loan with an "estoppel letter," permitting the savings and loan to wrap around their loan. Without this legal assurance, the savings and loan was not willing to make the wraparound loan. As a result, the refinance and resyndication proposal approved by the partners was not consummated in 1981. Mortgage loan rates of over 15 percent prevailed on new-loan originations (the inflation rate averaged over 10 percent for 1980 and 1981) and eliminated from consideration a straight refinancing of the property.

The partners agreed to put the "refinance and sell" alternative on the "back burner" until inflation rates declined and mortgage rates decreased to make refinancing economically feasible. Thus, by default, alternative 4 (make required capital improvements; continue to hold) became the agreed-on solution for the interim period until mortgage market conditions improved. The wraparound loan from the original sellers (November 1974) was not due and payable until November of 1984. Capital improvements could be staged and paid for by the cash flow from the project.

By May of 1983, mortgage rates had fallen to the 13 to 14 percent range, and mortgage financing was readily available. Davidson and Boomer made new cash flow projections and believed that it was time to restructure the venture. They proposed a three-step process to their partners:

1. The existing indebtedness will be refinanced and all underlying liens will be retired.
2. The current venture, which can be referred to as Aspen Wood I, will sell the property at market value, using the installment sale technique to defer the tax gains over several years.
3. The property will be sold to a new venture called Aspen Wood II. This venture can consist of members of Aspen Wood I, but must have 21 percent new investors. The 21 percent was needed to validate, for tax purposes, the sale of the property to the new venture.

The stated objectives of this termination proposal was to (1) refinance while loan terms were reasonable and money was available, (2) give those partners who wished to sell, the opportunity to do so, (3) increase leverage (decrease equity) with a larger loan (refinancing proceeds are not taxable), and (4) raise the basis for greater depreciation and tax shelter.

The partners approved the proposal. The old loans were paid off in September of 1983. A new loan for $1,054,000 at 13.5 percent, thirty-year amortization, with a ten-year term (balloon) was originated with a local savings institution. Four points were paid to the lender at closing ($42,150). Refinancing proceeds of $320,850 were distributed to the investors (original investment of $210,000). Aspen Wood I sold the property to Aspen Wood II for $2,100,000, subject to a wraparound loan of $1,625,000. A down payment of $475,000 was paid to Aspen Wood I, and a capital expenditure reserve of $150,000 was funded by Aspen Wood II; the total equity investment by Aspen Wood II was $625,000.

Exhibit 17-B presents the combined financial results for a partner participating in both ventures (Aspen Wood I and Aspen Wood II) if the property is held for ten years. The property was restructured and closed as of September 1, 1983. Assumptions used for the ten-year "most likely" projection included rents increasing at 6 percent annually, expenses increasing at 7 percent annually, property appreciating at 5 percent annually (9 percent capitalization rate applied to NOI in year of sale), and a 50 percent investor tax bracket.

Exhibit 17-C shows a comparison between the resyndication of Aspen Wood (combined Aspen Wood I and Aspen Wood II) and a refinance-and-hold strategy. The analysis shows that the resyndication alternative would produce a higher present value for all discount rates considered (8 percent, 12 percent, and 15 percent) and is the superior strategy.

About 90 percent of the investors in the selling venture (Aspen Wood I) chose to become investors in the purchasing venture; they purchased a 75 percent interest in the new venture. The other 10 percent of the original investors chose to utilize their refinancing and sale proceeds in other ways. New investors in Aspen Wood II projected an IRR of approximately 17 percent, based on the assumptions for the "most likely" scenario. Required IRRs of investors had decreased from the 18 to 20 percent level stated in 1974 when the project was originally purchased. Nevertheless, there was a substantial number of individuals seeking to purchase the available shares in Aspen Wood II. The local economy was booming; inflation had decreased from the 13.5 percent rate in 1980 but was still substantial and was causing property values to rise rapidly. Substantial tax shelter benefits were available to investors, and no serious discussion of tax reform was taking place in Congress.

CURRENT SITUATION

The Austin economy became severely overbuilt in 1985 and 1986. The Tax Reform Act of 1986 substantially curtailed tax shelter benefits and had an adverse impact on property values. The Texas economy went into a depression (1985–1987) caused by a downturn in energy, real estate, and high-tech industries. Inflation rates decreased to 2 to 5 percent levels and were no longer a force supporting property values. The overall apartment market in Austin hit an economic occupancy level of 75 percent in the summer of 1987. Aspen Wood II suspended cash distributions to partners in the spring of 1986, although actual distributions were ahead of projections for the two years after its resyndication (1984, 1985). Apartment foreclosures throughout Austin in 1986 and 1987

EXHIBIT 17-B. Aspen Wood Restructuring—Aspen Wood I and II Combined

If a partner stays in both ventures, this is how the two are estimated to operate.

Year	Cash Flow			Taxable Income		
	AI	AII	Total	AI	AII	Total
1983						
Jan.-Aug.	$ 48,000			$ 32,200		
Refinance	320,850					
Sept.-Dec.		$ 33,000			$(10,600)	
Sale	385,000	(625,000)		125,800		
Total 1983	$753,850	$ (592,000)	$ 161,850	$158,000	$(10,600)	$147,400
1984	0	37,700	37,700	2,840	(93,800)	(90,960)
1985	0	46,900	46,900	3,250	(84,730)	(81,480)
1986	0	56,500	56,500	3,720	(75,240)	(71,520)
1987	0	66,600	66,600	4,250	(65,320)	(61,070)
1988	6,680	70,200	76,880	7,250	(58,960)	(51,710)
1989	20,030	68,200	88,230	16,230	(51,450)	(35,220)
1990	20,030	79,800	99,830	18,500	(38,870)	(20,370)
1991	20,030	88,900	108,930	18,630	(25,670)	(7,040)
1992	20,030	104,500	124,530	18,810	(11,820)	6,990
1993						
Jan.-Aug.	13,350	80,400		10,870	(8,820)	
Loan Payoff	583,230					
Sale		1,544,200		481,430	436,110	
Total 1993	$596,580	$1,624,600	$2,221,180	$492,300	$427,290	$919,590

EXHIBIT 17-C. Aspen Wood Restructuring—Comparison

How does Aspen Wood I and II combined compare to Aspen Wood if we only refinance?

	Cash Flow		Taxable Income	
Year	AI and AII	Refinance Only	AI and AII	Refinance Only
1983	$161,850	$392,850	$147,400	$71,500
1984	37,700	7,700	(90,960)	7,300
1985	46,900	16,900	(81,480)	18,800
1986	56,500	26,500	(71,520)	35,800
1987	66,600	36,600	(61,070)	51,400
1988	76,880	45,200	(51,710)	60,800
1989	88,230	53,200	(35,220)	74,800
1990	99,830	69,800	(20,370)	87,100
1991	108,930	81,900	(7,040)	100,100
1992	124,530	94,500	6,990	113,800
1993	2,221,180	2,241,400	919,590	1,303,700
Total	$3,089,130	$3,056,550	$654,610	$1,925,100

After-Tax Cash Flows Compared

	After-Tax Cash Flows	
Year	AI and AII	Refinance Only
1983	$102,890	$364,250
1984	74,080	4,780
1985	79,490	9,280
1986	85,100	12,180
1987	91,030	16,040
1988	97,560	20,880
1989	102,320	28,400
1990	107,980	34,960
1991	111,750	41,500
1992	121,730	48,980
1993	1,853,340	1,602,390
Total	$2,827,270	$2,183,640
Present Values at		
8%	1,433,060	1,147,900
12%	1,064,840	881,400
15%	867,830	740,850

caused rent rates to decrease approximately 20 percent. In the summer of 1987, the apartment market hit the bottom of its cycle and began to recovery slowly in the fall and winter of 1987 and throughout 1988.

How Aspen Wood II has fared as the market continues its recovery in Austin and progresses through the next set of real estate cycles will be addressed in the next revision of this text.

CONCLUSION

The Aspen Wood investment has now passed through each of the investment phases at least once—origination, operation, and termination—as described in the ten-step investment analysis and financial structuring process. This case study illustrates the many principles, concepts, and techniques that the investor must understand and systematically apply in order to be a successful managing equity investor in a dynamic and cyclical real estate environment.

PART 5

PORTFOLIO STRATEGY AND INVESTMENT OUTLOOK

Owings Mills Mall, Owings Mills (Baltimore County), Maryland.

The fifth section of this text is devoted to three important and emerging topics of interest: (1) institutional real estate portfolios, (2) developing a personal portfolio including real estate, and (3) the real estate investment outlook.

Chapter 18 presents an overview of modern portfolio theory, its application to real estate investing, and its impact on large institutional real estate funds: pension funds, REITs, and public limited partnerships. Chapter 19 examines portfolio problems from the view of the individual seeking to accumulate wealth through the stages of his or her life. Both topics usually receive scant attention in most investment texts, possibly because, until recently, there has been little academic research on the subjects and few reliable data on the performance of real estate portfolios. Involvement in these fields has grown, however, and various economic and political factors have elevated the importance of these issues to investors.

It is also important for investors to develop scenario-planning techniques as a method of dealing with increasing levels of uncertainty. Chapter 20 thus presents the authors' opinions on the market outlook and their expectations for specific property types through the early 1990s. Students and professionals are urged to further their investment education through the use of case studies and computer applications and to assume more global and holistic attitudes toward real estate investment decisions in the future.

18

INSTITUTIONAL REAL ESTATE PORTFOLIOS

The emergence of the real estate investment trusts (REIT), the enactment of the Employees Retirement Income Security Act (ERISA), financial deregulation, and changes in general economic conditions have served to redirect the focus of real estate investment. The change has been to pay less attention to the evaluation of individual real estate projects and more to the portfolio impact of real estate investment. The portfolio approach emphasizes the synergistic effects of a single investment on the total package of assets held by the investor. Before exploring further the concept of portfolio decision making, however, it is important to understand how REITs, ERISA, and the changing economic climate have brought about this shift in investor attitudes.

Real Estate Investment Trusts

REITs were organized under a 1961 revision of the Internal Revenue Service Code.[1] Originally they were authorized to provide a "real estate mutual fund" for small investors. The early REITs invested in real estate equities and provided their shareholders with higher-than-average dividend yields but lower appreciation potential. In the late 1960s REITs began to diversify into long-term mortgages, wraparound mortgages, sale–leasebacks, and construction loans. Through increased use of debt, REITs grew

[1]Public Law 86-779, which revised the Internal Revenue Service Code by adding Secs. 856, 857, and 858 to include REITs. For a good history of the REIT, see Kenneth Campbell, *Real Estate Investment Trusts: America's Newest Billionaires* (New York: Audit Investment Research, 1971).

substantially, offering shareholders high dividend yields and appreciation. When the REIT bubble burst in 1975, the industry had grown from $2 billion to $21 billion in five years.[2]

The equity REITs (EREITs), which invested almost exclusively in property ownership, with only a small proportion of assets allocated to mortgages, fared exceptionally well through the recession years. Many of the EREITs, such as General Growth, Real Estate Investment Trust of America, and Hubbard, continued to pay dividends throughout the recession. However, the mortgage REITs, especially short-term mortgage trusts, the construction and development or C&D trusts, lacked the necessary diversification of assets and were seriously hurt when developers were forced to terminate projects prior to completion and defaulted on their construction loans.

Two important lessons can be learned from the REIT experience. First, real estate portfolios were not only practicable but even desirable commodities, as is evidenced by the relatively successful performance of EREITs. Second, real estate securities were not necessarily valued by the securities markets in the same way that real estate assets were valued by the real estate markets. The REIT experience indicated again the need for sophisticated project analysis and evaluating project acquisition in terms of the entire portfolio, not simply at the project level.

Employee Retirement Income Security Act (ERISA)

ERISA was enacted in 1974 as a sort of "centralization of regulation" of the management of pension funds. It directed pension fund managers to diversify investments in order to minimize the risk of large losses. Before the enactment of ERISA, very few pension funds had significant real estate holdings. The requirement for full diversification has been a major spur to the pension fund industry, which has expanded its holdings of real estate from less than 1 percent of assets to between 3 and 5 percent of assets since 1974.[3] Because federal regulation permits such funds to invest up to 10 percent of their assets in real estate, most funds are actively pursuing investment policies with this objective. During the high interest rates of the early 1980s—substantially higher than at any other time in the past—many funds suspended investment in all media save real estate. As the decade progressed, however, reduced inflation and the decline in interest rates caused the large funds to lose some of their interest in real estate. Then, during the later 1980s, pension funds once again renewed their infatuation with real estate.

---

[2]*REIT Fact Book, 1978* (Washington, D.C.: National Association of Real Estate Investment Trusts, 1978).

[3]*Life Insurance Fact Book, 1977* (Washington, D.C.: American Council of Life Insurance, 1977).

Pension fund investing has brought a higher level of sophistication to the real estate business and a strong sense of competition for quality projects. The demand for investment-grade real estate of sufficient magnitude—large funds have minimum investment limits of around $1 million per project—continues to increase the need for sophisticated project analysis and for developing methods of rapidly evaluating and selecting suitable projects. As these funds approach their statutory investment limit, the importance of a portfolio approach to solving investment analysis and selection problems will increase.

Recent Changes in Economic Conditions

From 1974 through 1984, the U.S. economy experienced a topsy-turvy period of recession, increasing inflation and unemployment, rising interest rates and tighter money, and increasing governmental regulation. Characterized as a "stagflation" economy, it brought a new "type" of investor to the real estate market—one who is more concerned with future appreciation and capital preservation than with cash flow and current income. Properties with low or even negative current yields, with a much greater mortgage constant than a "free and clear" yield, were purchased. In many instances the prices paid seemed out of line with those estimated using conventional appraisal techniques. Although the very depressed economic conditions of 1974 to 1980 have vastly improved, the attitudes of investors have been conditioned to tax shelters and capital appreciation. Not until 1985 was there any indication that investor attitudes might shift back to an interest in current yields and adequate cash flows. Since the passage of the 1986 Tax Reform Act, real estate investment has readjusted to the concept of an economically sound investment, rather than one dependent on tax strategy and inflation for its return.

Perhaps the primary stimulus for portfolio analysis has been Wall Street's discovery of real estate "securitization." The securitization of real estate has had the greatest influence on the increasing interest in applying portfolio analysis to real estate assets. Investment vehicles such as real estate limited partnerships (RELPs), mortgage-backed securities, and master limited partnerships (MLPs) have stimulated Wall Street's interest in real estate.[4]

In summary, these factors combined with many others (e.g., financial deregulation) have changed the focus of real estate investment to the "portfolio" approach emphasizing sophisticated methods of project analysis and selection in a multiproperty context. The balance of this chapter

[4]Mark Conroe, "Mortgage-Backed Securities Come of Age," *Real Estate Research*, Fall 1985, pp. 46–50. Also Steven D. Kapplin and Arthur L. Schwartz, Jr., "An Analysis of Recent Rates of Return and the Secondary Market for Real Estate Limited Partnerships," *Journal of Real Estate Research*, Fall 1986, pp. 33–44.

will be devoted to examining the theory and techniques of a portfolio approach to real estate investment. It should be noted, however, that this is one of the fastest-changing facets of real estate research. Thus, concepts and techniques illustrated here, although they are certainly at the heart of portfolio analyses, belong to an ever-changing universe.

PORTFOLIO CHOICE

At the simplest level the portfolio approach is the theory that you should not put all your eggs into one basket (although there is a contradictory theory—that you *should* put your eggs into one basket and watch the basket very closely!). In simple terms, diversification means purchasing many investments rather than one, or purchasing several smaller projects rather than one large project. This approach is often referred to as naive diversification and is essentially a "safety in numbers" concept. Naive diversification lacks a theoretical justification, and in 1952 Markowitz challenged this approach in an article that has become the classic work of modern portfolio theory.[5] Markowitz distinguished between naive diversification, safety in numbers, and *efficient* diversification. The essence of efficient diversification lies in the trade-off between investment returns and risks. Modern portfolio theory stresses a scientific approach to the selection of portfolio assets that produces an efficient combination of assets—one that maximizes investment returns for a given level of investment risk.

Markowitz argued that little could be done to reduce the inherent risk of any single project, but a portfolio or combination of properly selected assets could be devised in which portfolio risk could, theoretically, be eliminated. To comprehend fully the impact of Markowitz's theory, it is important to understand, thoroughly, two elements: *expected* return and risk. Markowitz's theory is predicated on the proposition that all investors guide their investment choices by these two parameters.

Definition of Expected Return and Risk. The expected return on investment, $E(R)$, is the most likely return when the investor is uncertain about the actual return the investment will produce. It is the *weighted average* of all possible returns, where the weights are the probabilities of occurrence.

As observed in Chapter 8, risk may be defined in many ways: (1) as the probability of loss; (2) as the probability of not receiving what is expected; (3) as the difference (or potential variance) between expectation and realization; (4) as the possible variance of return relative to the expected or most likely return; and (5) as the chance, or probability, that the investor will not receive the expected or required rate of return. From a project

---

[5]Harry Markowitz, "Portfolio Selection," *The Journal of Finance*, March 1952, pp. 77–91.

view, it was argued that the best operational definition of risk is the last one. In contrast, the literature on portfolio theory and analysis has generally adopted the fourth definition—that is, that risk is measured by the *variance of returns* (σ^2), or the standard deviation (σ) of possible returns about the expected return $E(R)$.[6]

Markowitz's theory of portfolio choice is based on the recognition that returns on one asset are interrelated with those on other assets. The degree to which one asset's return varies with that of another asset is called *covariance*. Intuitively, investors can see that if a decline in the return on one asset is offset by a rise in the return on another asset, the variance of the combination will be less than the variance of either asset held singly. This intuitive assumption is representative of efficient portfolio diversification. The assets provide less risk in combination than when held singly. Efficient diversification, in contrast to naive diversification, can reduce or eliminate risk.

Covariance and Portfolio Characteristics. Covariance measures how one asset's return varies with that of another asset. Algebraically, covariance is found, in a two-asset portfolio, by

$$\sigma_{ij} = \sigma\, P_{ij}\, \sigma_i\, \sigma_j \tag{1}$$

where σ_{ij} = covariance
σ_i = standard deviation for the ith investment
σ_j = standard deviation for the jth investment
P_{ij} = correlation coefficient

Calculating the covariance requires first calculating the standard deviations of each investment and then determining the correlation coefficient for the two investments. Correlation coefficients range from -1 to $+1$. A correlation coefficient of $+1$ means that the two assets are *perfectly positively* correlated; as investment A's return rises, investment B's return will also rise. A correlation coefficient of -1 means that the two assets are *perfectly negatively* correlated: a rise in one investment's return will bring about a decline in the return of the other. A zero correlation means that the returns on the investments are not interdependent and a change in one will not cause a change in the other.

---

[6]For most portfolio models, the holding-period return (HPR), IRR, or geometric mean return (GMR) are commonly used. As discussed in Chapter 8 some controversy exists concerning the "correct" measure of rate of return. For an excellent discussion of the IRR and FMRR, see Stephen Messner and M. Chapman Findlay III, "Real Estate Investment Analysis: IRR versus FMRR," *The Real Estate Appraiser*, July–August 1975, pp. 5–20. The use of HPR and GMR has received widespread attention in many portfolio texts, for example, Harry Latane, Donald Tuttle, and Charles Jones, *Security Analysis and Portfolio Management* (New York: Ronald Press, 1975).

The portfolio's return and risk characteristics are a combination of the return, risk, and covariance of the assets based on the proportion of each asset held in the combination. The portfolio's expected return is the weighted average of the expected returns of all the assets, where the weights are the proportion of each asset in the portfolio. Thus, for the two-asset portfolio,

$$E(R_p) = W_A\, E(R_A) + W_B\, E(R_B) \qquad (2)$$

where $\quad E(R_p)$ = portfolio expected return

$E(R_A), E(R_B)$ = expected returns of assets A and B, respectively

W_A, W_B = proportions (for the two asset portfolio $W_A + W_B = 1.0$)

The portfolio's variance is defined as

$$\text{VAR}_2 = W_A^2 \sigma_A^2 + W_B^2 \sigma_B^2 + 2W_A W_B \sigma_{AB} \qquad (3)$$

where VAR_p = portfolio variance

$\sigma_{A,B}$ = covariance (from equation 1)

W_A, W_B = proportions of assets A and B, respectively

A careful look at equations 2 and 3 will reveal that when the correlation coefficient is positive, the term $2W_A W_B \sigma_{A,B}$ in equation 3 will be positive and will add to the total variance of the portfolio combination. When the correlation coefficient is zero, the last term drops off. When the correlation coefficient is negative, this term becomes negative and *reduces* the total portfolio variance. Graphically, we can depict how the portfolio's $E(R_p)$ and VAR_p vary with changing proportions, W_A and W_B, for different assumptions about the correlation coefficient. Exhibit 18-1 depicts such relationships.

When the correlation coefficient is positive, the covariance will be positive. The portfolio combination becomes a linear combination of investments A and B, as depicted by line *AB* in Exhibit 18-1. When the correlation coefficient is zero, the covariance is zero and the portfolio combination is depicted as line *ACB*. The combination found at point *C* has a lower risk at a given level of return than a similar combination of positively correlated investments. Line *ADB* depicts the combinations in which the correlation coefficient is negative. Here the combination at *D* provides a positive $E(R_p)$ and a VAR_p of zero.

Exhibit 18-1 illustrates the importance of Markowitz's portfolio selection theory. By choosing negatively correlated assets, the investor can design a portfolio that eliminates risk. Markowitz demonstrated that among all possible combinations of risk and return, only certain combinations are efficient, that is, maximize return for a given level of risk. Through efficient diversification, portfolios that include assets with low or negative

EXHIBIT 18-1.   Effects of Three Values of Correlation Coefficients on Portfolio Return and Variance

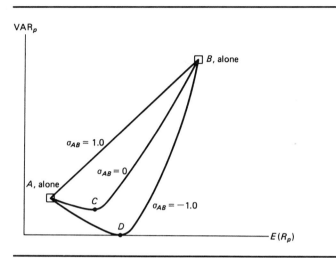

covariances can be selected, thereby reducing the portfolio's overall risk, although the investor cannot affect the risk of any single project.[7]

Modern Portfolio Theory

In 1964 William F. Sharpe published his classic article, "Capital Asset Prices: A Theory of Market Equilibrium under Conditions of Risk."[8] Sharpe provided an extension of Markowitz's portfolio theory to a general theory of market equilibrium. Sharpe theorized that inherent in the rate of return of an asset were two prices: the price of time and the price of risk. The price of time was awarded to all investors on the basis of the *maturity* of investments. The price of risk was the investor's premium for bearing the uncertainty associated with investments in capital. Sharpe proposed that risk entailed two aspects: market-related risk and business-related risk. Business-related risk is internal to the firm and reflects such elements as management, financial leverage, and production delays. (Note the difference between this definition and the one espoused in Chapter 8 of this

---

[7]The illustration assumes only a two-asset portfolio problem. In the more general *N*-asset problem, the solution cannot be effected simply but requires computer assistance. Multiasset solutions are generally solvable using modern integer programming techniques.

[8]William Sharpe, "Capital Asset Prices: A Theory of Market Equilibrium under Conditions of Risk," *The Journal of Finance*, September 1964, pp. 425–442.

EXHIBIT 18-2. The Characteristic Line for a Typical Security

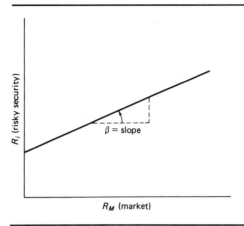

text.) Market risk refers to the impact of securities market activity on the prices of a firm's securities. In the Markowitz framework, risk is the covariance of a single security with the entire securities market.

Business-related risk, Sharpe argued, could be diversified away, as Markowitz demonstrated, by selecting securities with low or negative covariances. But some risk, market-related risk, would remain. In Sharpe's theory, therefore, only market-related risk was compensated in the rate of return. Sharpe provided a method for evaluating market-related risk by measuring the covariance of an individual security with a "perfectly" diversified portfolio—the market portfolio.[9] The method is a two-asset portfolio analysis in which one asset is the individual security and the other is the perfectly diversified market portfolio. A measure of relative risk, called beta (β), is derived from this analysis. Beta quantifies the sensitivity of an individual security's return to the return of the market portfolio. Sharpe proved that the rate of return required for a risky security in equilibrium is a linear combination of the price of time, called the riskless rate, and a risk premium. The risk premium is the market portfolio's risk premium multiplied by the security's beta. Thus, the relation between the required return on the security and the market portfolio return is a straight-line relationship, as shown in Exhibit 18-2.

[9] There has been some substantial criticism of the capital asset pricing theory that focuses on the market portfolio. For additional discussion see Stephen A. Ross, "The Current Status of the Capital Asset Pricing Model (CAPM)," *The Journal of Finance*, June 1978, pp. 885–901; and Richard Roll, "A Critique of the Asset Pricing Theory's Tests, Part I: On Past and Potential Testability of the Theory," *The Journal of Financial Economics*, March 1977, pp. 129–176.

The line is called a characteristic line, and the security's beta (β) is the measure of the slope of the characteristic line. The equation that defines the line is $Y = \alpha + \beta X + \epsilon$, where Y is the required return on the risky security, X is the market portfolio's return, ϵ is a random error term, with an expected value of zero, and α is the security's unique rate of return.

The importance of Markowitz and Sharpe's contributions to modern portfolio theory cannot be overstated. According to modern theory decisions of the investor (utility-maximizing decisions) have essentially two parameters: expected return and variance. Portfolio decisions are based on schemes that will maximize an investor's expected return at a given level of risk. This risk is composed of two elements: business-related risk (known as *unsystematic risk*) and market risk (called *systematic risk*). An asset's variance actually measures both risks. Because business or unsystematic risk may be eliminated through efficient diversification, à la Markowitz, only market risk is borne by the investor, and it is compensated for by additional return over the price of time (riskless rate of return), à la Sharpe. Market risk, an asset's beta coefficient, measures the amount of additional return required over the market return for the risk taken. An investor may now select a portfolio that eliminates unsystematic risk through diversification and is equally tailored to provide maximum return for a given level of market or systematic risk.

The selection of an optimal portfolio is based on the individual investor's attitude toward risk and return. If all investors seek to maximize return for a given level of risk (or minimize risk at a given level of return), then selecting an optimal portfolio requires superimposing the investor's utility function on the curve that defines the set of all possible efficient portfolios, called the *efficient frontier.* The efficient frontier consists of the set of efficiently diversified portfolios that provide maximum return at specified levels of risk. In Exhibit 18-1 the curve segment labeled *ACB* describes such a frontier for a two-asset portfolio. In general, the efficient frontier and total opportunity set may appear as illustrated in Exhibit 18-3. The segment labeled *ABCDEF* is the efficient frontier. All portfolios on this frontier dominate all other portfolios in the opportunity set in that they will provide either greater return at a given level of risk or less risk at a given level of return. The curves marked U_1, U_2, and U_3 are investor utility curves, called *isoquants.* Superimposing the investor's utility curves on the efficient frontier allows selection of a portfolio from the efficient set that is touched by a utility curve running tangent to the efficient frontier. This point, labeled *C,* is on utility curve U_2. By selecting this portfolio, the investor can attain the level of utility defined by utility curve U_2.

REAL ESTATE INVESTING AND MODERN PORTFOLIO THEORY

The preceding discussion provides the background of modern portfolio theory, but it should be noted that this theory has developed exclusively in

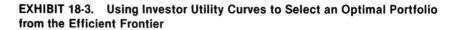

EXHIBIT 18-3.   Using Investor Utility Curves to Select an Optimal Portfolio from the Efficient Frontier

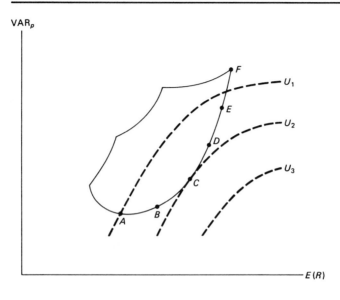

the context of securities markets where the assumptions of a "perfectly" diversified market portfolio and the efficiency of securities markets are more acceptable. Real estate markets are very different, however. They tend to be highly localized rather than national, so that information about transaction prices is lacking. Furthermore, there is a much lower incidence of transactions in real estate markets than in securities markets. In addition, real estate transfers usually have complex financing structures, and often the participants lack the sophistication of securities traders. Despite these and numerous other contrasts, applications of modern portfolio theory to real estate investing are being developed. This development has of course stemmed in part from the growing number of real estate portfolio investors: REITs, pension funds, and large limited-partnership offerings. Consequently, the informality of real estate investment decision making in the past has given way to the sophistication of computerized project simulations, which require the investor to "know" much more about projects and to make many more decisions than were required in the past.[10] As for

[10] *Study on Tax Considerations in Multi-Family Housing Investment* (Washington, D.C.: U.S. Department of Housing and Urban Development, 1972). See also Robert J. Wiley, "Real Estate Investment Analysis: An Empirical Study," *The Appraisal Journal,* October 1976, pp. 586–592.

EXHIBIT 18-4. Illustrative Components of a Typical Project Cash Flow Statement

Gross possible income	$10,000
Less: vacancy and collection loss	− 500
Effective gross income	9,500
Less: operating expenses	− 3,000
Net operating income	$ 6,500

security investments, analyzing real estate investments in a portfolio context requires the ability to develop measures of expected returns and variances.

Developing Measures of Expected Return and Variance

Computer simulation models like the one presented in Chapter 8 permit an analyst to develop a sophisticated project analysis that can produce estimates of expected return and variance. Computer simulations of real estate projects typically follow one of two avenues. The model developed by Pyhrr and illustrated in Chapter 8 is based on the use of independent continuous probability distributions for input variables. These distributions are used in a Monte Carlo simulation process to generate output distributions for the expected equity internal rate of return after tax, as well as other output parameters. From the output data generated, the analyst estimates the mean and standard deviation of the return.

The second avenue uses a Bayesian approach and assumes that probabilities of certain future events (for, say, a multiyear project evaluation) are dependent on the outcomes of certain past events. Thus, if an analyst assumed that gross revenue in the *first* year of a project had a 40 percent chance of being $10,000, the probability of gross revenue being $10,000 in the *second* year would depend on whether gross revenue was $10,000 in the first year.

This approach, the use of Bayesian analysis, was initially demonstrated in a real estate simulation by Pellatt.[11] A simple example should demonstrate the essential difference between these approaches. Exhibit 18-4 depicts some assumptions about three components of a typical real estate cash flow statement: (1) gross revenue, (2) vacancy loss, and (3) operating expenses. For this analysis subjective estimates of the probabilities of oc-

---

[11] Peter G. K. Pellatt, "A Normative Approach to the Analysis of Real Estate Investment Opportunities under Uncertainty and the Management of Real Estate Investment Portfolios," unpublished Ph.D. dissertation, University of California, Berkeley, 1970.

EXHIBIT 18-5.   Subjective Estimates of Distributions and Assigned Probabilities for Typical Project Cash Flows

	Middle Value (Prob.)	Highest Value (Prob.)	Lowest Value (Prob.)
Gross revenue	$10,000 (.5)	$15,000 (.2)	$7,000 (.3)
Vacancy allowance	5% (.6)	10% (.2)	2% (.2)
Operating expenses	3,000 (.7)	5,000 (.2)	2,000 (.1)

currence are assigned to each variable. These estimates of low, median, and high values are shown in Exhibit 18-5, with the assigned probabilities in parentheses.

In the first type of simulation discussed, each year's pro forma would be derived by randomly selecting one value for each variable out of the specified distribution. For, as an example, 100 simulations, gross revenue could be $10,000 fifty times, $15,000 twenty times, and $7,000 thirty times. The expected value of gross revenue for 100 simulations is ($10,000 × .5) + ($15,000 × .2) + ($7,000 × .3), or $10,100. A similar result can be expected for each year of a multiyear forecast with the assumption that each year's results are independent of the results of the preceding period and that no growth rates were built into the analysis.

However, when it is assumed that the outcomes in the second year are dependent on the outcomes in the first year, the problem takes on a different perspective. If gross revenue is $10,000 in the first year, the likelihood of its being $7,000 in the second year may be less than the 30 percent probability previously assigned. Exhibit 18-6 shows the branches specified for years 1 and 2. In year 1 the probabilities are as assigned in the original example. In the second year, however, the analysis presumes that if the $10,000 level of gross revenues is achieved in the first year, revenues in year 2 will have the distribution illustrated for year 2. Now, the probability of achieving $15,000 in year 2 is higher than it was for year 1, and the probability of $7,000 in year 2 is lower than it was for year 1.

Insofar as simulation models of either type are actually extrapolations from reality, it may be difficult to argue that one approach is more correct than the other. Furthermore, it is possible to combine the best elements of both methods and design a conditional probability distribution network between input variables over time by using the Monte Carlo framework. In such a model, for example, the probability distribution for gross possible income in year 2 would be dependent (conditional) on the outcome simulated in year 1. Although such a model is difficult to design and implement, it appears to be more theoretically precise than the two described.[12]

[12]Such a model was developed by Mike E. Miles in "A Conceptual and Computer Model for the Analysis and Management of Risk in Real Property Development," Ph.D. disserta-

EXHIBIT 18-6.   Tree Diagram Showing Distribution of Gross Revenue for Two Periods from Typical Project Cash Flows

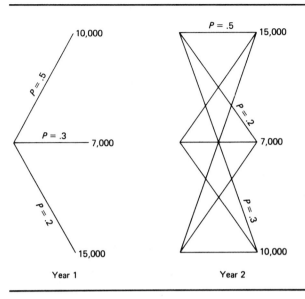

Year 1   Year 2

In addition to the stochastic models just described, there are *deterministic* models (described in Chapter 8) that use sensitivity analysis to evaluate risk. Sensitivity analysis is essentially one of deriving elasticities for certain important measures of project performance. Several models using sensitivity analysis have been developed by Wendt,[13] Hemmer,[14] Decisionex, Inc.,[15] and Graaskamp and Robbins.[16] Although sensitivity analysis is of particular value for individual project analysis, the elements of modern portfolio theory as described earlier dictate the use of expected

---

tion, The University of Texas at Austin, August 1976. The model was subsequently refined and presented by Stephen A. Pyhrr and Mike Miles in a paper entitled, "A Framework and Computer Model for Risk Analysis and Risk Management in Real Property Development," for the annual meeting of the Financial Management Association, Montreal, Canada, October 1976 (available from the authors).

[13]Paul Wendt, REAL III, described in Paul Wendt and Alan R. Cerf, *Real Estate Investment Analysis and Taxation*, 2nd ed. (New York: McGraw–Hill, 1979), pp. 63–88.

[14]Edgar H. Hemmer, "A Valuation Model for Investments in Real Estate," unpublished Ph.D. dissertation, Purdue University, 1972.

[15]Decisionex, Inc., QUICK, presented at the 1978 Colloquium on Computer Applications in Real Estate, Georgia State University, November 27–29, 1978.

[16]MRCAP, developed at University of Wisconsin by Dr. James Graaskamp and Michael Robbins. For additional discussion of these and other models, see Paul Wendt and Janet Tandy, "Evaluation of OCF Computer Models in Real Estate Investment Analysis," paper presented at the annual meeting of the American Real Estate and Urban Economics Association, Dallas, December 1975.

EXHIBIT 18-7.   Subjective Estimates of the Internal-Rate-of-Return Distribution for Two Projects

PROJECT A		PROJECT B	
IRR	Probability of Occurrence	IRR	Probability of Occurrence
− .05	.05	− .20	.05
+ .05	.15	− .05	.15
+ .15	.30	+ .15	.30
+ .20	.50	+ .30	.50

return and variance for developing efficient portfolios. Consequently, risk simulation models like Pyhrr's or Pellatt's lend themselves more specifically to portfolio selection and analysis.

Real Estate Portfolio Selection: An Illustration

By incorporating simulation models like those illustrated in the previous discussion with the basic framework proposed by Markowitz, we are able to derive efficient real estate portfolios. The methodology has been amply demonstrated by numerous authors in the field.[17] There are four basic steps in the process of developing an efficient two-asset portfolio.

1. Derive estimates of rates of return and corresponding probabilities of occurrence of each project.
2. Compute expected returns, $E(R)$, and variances for each project.
3. Compute covariance for both projects.
4. Compute or graphically derive the optimal combination.

The derivation of such a two-asset portfolio might proceed as follows:

STEP 1. Each project's cash flow data are analyzed through the use of a probabilistic model for the projected holding period, and estimates of rates

---

[17]Steven D. Kapplin, "Financial Theory and the Valuation of Real Estate under Conditions of Risk," *The Real Estate Appraiser*, September–October 1976, pp. 28–37. See also Michael S. Young, "Comparative Investment Performance: Common Stock versus Real Estate—A Proposal on Methodology," *Real Estate Issues*, Summer 1977, pp. 30–46; Richard J. Curcio and James P. Gaines, "Real Estate Portfolio Revision," *Journal of the American Real Estate and Urban Economics Association*, Winter 1977, pp. 399–410; M. Chapman Findlay III, Carl W. Hamilton, Stephen O. Messner, and Jonathan S. Yormack, "Optimal Real Estate Portfolios," *Journal of the American Real Estate and Urban Economics Association*, Fall 1979, pp. 298–317; George W. Gau and Daniel B. Kohlhepp, "Estimation of Equity Yield Rates Based on Capital Market Returns," *The Real Estate Appraiser and Analyst*, November–December 1978, pp. 33–39.

EXHIBIT 18-8.   Computation of Expected Return and Variance for Project A

(1) Probability of Occurrence	(2) R_A	(3) Col. 1 × Col. 2	(4) $[R_A - E(R_A)]$	(5) (Col. 4)^2	(6) Col. 1 × Col. 5
.05	− .05	− .0025	− .1900	.0361	.00181
.15	+ .05	.0075	− .0900	.0081	.00122
.50	+ .15	.0750	.0100	.0001	.00005
.30	+ .20	.0600	.0600	.0036	.00108
		$E(R_A) =$ .1400			$\text{VAR}_A =$ .00416
					$\sigma_A =$ .0645

of return and their corresponding probabilities of occurrence are derived. For simplicity, Exhibit 18-7 summarizes the results of such an analysis.

STEP 2. The $E(R)$ for the project and variances are calculated. Exhibits 18-8 and 18-9 show the required format and computations. Project A has an $E(R_A)$ and variance of .14 and .00416, respectively. Project B has an $E(R_B)$ and variance of .2275 and .02987, respectively. Upon inspection, project B appears to be the riskier investment.

STEP 3. The covariance between projects A and B can be calculated using equation 1 when the correlation coefficient is known. The format illustrated in Exhibit 18-10 can be used where the correlation coefficient is not known.[18] Because the covariance is positive, the optimal combination of projects A and B will not provide complete elimination of risk.

STEP 4. Determine the optimal combination by graphing the risk versus return of the portfolio combinations, using equations 2 and 3 to compute portfolio $E(R_p)$ and variance. Exhibit 18-11 and the accompanying graph

---

[18]See equation 1. Note that the sign of the correlation coefficient will be positive if projects have a positive covariance and negative if covariance is negative. Compare Exhibits 18-10 and 18-14.

EXHIBIT 18-9.   Computation of Expected Return and Variance for Project B

(1)	(2)	(3)	(4)	(5)	(6)
.05	− .20	− .0100	− .4275	.18276	.00914
.15	− .05	− .0075	− .2775	.07701	.01155
.50	+ .25	.1250	.0225	.00051	.00025
.30	+ .40	.1200	.1725	.02976	.00893
		$E(R_B) =$ .2275			$\text{VAR}_B =$ .02987
					$\sigma_B =$ .17283

EXHIBIT 18-10.   Computation of Covariance for Projects A and B

(1) Probability of Occurrence	(2) $[R_A - E(R_A)]$	(3) $[R_B - E(R_B)]$	(4) Col. 2 × Col. 3	(5) Col. 1 × Col. 4
.05	−.1900	−.4275	.08123	.00406
.15	−.0900	−.2275	.02048	.00307
.50	.0100	.0225	.00023	.00011
.30	.0600	.1725	.01035	.00311
			$COV_{A,B} =$	.01035

EXHIBIT 18-11.   Computation of Portfolio $E(R_p)$ and Portfolio Variance for Various Combinations of Projects A and B

Proportions		Portfolio Return	Portfolio Variance
W_A	W_B	$E(R_p)$	VAR_p
.10	.90	.21875	.0261
.25	.75	.20563	.0209
.50	.50	.18375	.0137
.75	.25	.16188	.0081
.90	.10	.14875	.0055

EXHIBIT 18-12.   Graph of the Efficient Frontier Derived from Data in Exhibit 18-11

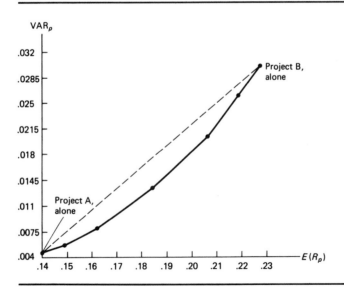

EXHIBIT 18-13. The Revised IRR Distribution for Project A

R_A	Probability of Occurrence
+.20	.05
+.15	.15
+.05	.50
−.05	.30

in Exhibit 18-12 illustrate that no combination of projects A and B reduces risk below the risk level of the least risky project. This suggests that the correlation coefficient for projects A and B is significantly positive. In fact, the correlation coefficient can be calculated as $COV_{A,B}/(\sigma_A \times \sigma_B) = .9285$. Investors seeking to minimize risk could choose between a portfolio of A and B with a small amount of B or simply invest in project A only. (This assumes that investments are made in cash and without debt.)

A slight alteration of the preceding example illustrates the impact of selecting projects with low correlations. Project A's characteristics are modified as shown in Exhibit 18-13. The $E(A_A)$ and variance are recomputed and found to be .0425 and .0056, respectively. Exhibit 18-14 shows the calculation of covariance. In this example the covariance is *negative* and the calculation of the correlation coefficient shows a value of −.908. Projects A and B are now very negatively correlated rather than very positively correlated. The results of reconstructing Exhibit 18-11 are summarized in Exhibits 18-15 and 18-16.

In this example, project A is negatively correlated with project B and an optimal portfolio combination is found that contains approximately 75 percent of project A and 25 percent of project B. The combination has an $E(R_p)$ and variance of .089 and .0006, respectively. Exhibit 18-16 depicts

EXHIBIT 18-14. Computation of the Revised Covariance for Projects A and B

(1) Probability of Occurrence	(2) $[R_A - E(R_A)]$	(3) $[R_B - E(R_B)]$	(4) Col. 2 × Col. 3	(5) Col. 1 × Col. 4
.05	.1575	−.4275	−.0673	−.00337
.15	.1075	−.2275	−.0245	−.00367
.50	.0075	.0225	.00017	.00008
.30	−.0925	.1725	−.01596	.00479
			$COV_{A,B}$ =	−.01174

EXHIBIT 18-15.   The Revised Portfolio $E(R_p)$ and Variance for Various Combinations of Projects A and B

Proportions		Portfolio Return	Portfolio Variance
W_A	W_B	$E(R_p)$	VAR_p
.10	.90	.2090	.0221
.25	.75	.1813	.0124
.50	.50	.1350	.0030
.75	.25	.089	.0006
.90	.10	.061	.0027

how the proper selection of negatively correlated projects provides for the elimination of risk from the portfolio.

This section presented a simplified illustration of optimal portfolio combinations for a two-asset portfolio. Four basic steps for deriving the optimal portfolio were given, with an example of how positively and negatively correlated assets affect return, risk, and the efficient combination. The difference between the efficient combinations for positively and negatively correlated assets is starkly evident in the contrast between the efficient frontiers graphed in Exhibits 18-12 and 18-16.

EXHIBIT 18-16.   Graph of Efficient Frontier Derived from Data in Exhibit 18-14

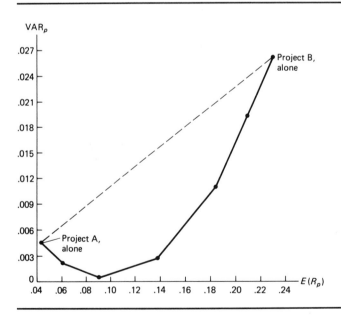

This illustration of portfolio development demonstrates both the formal process of portfolio design and the computation steps of that process. However, the discussion has been limited to the two-asset portfolio. Although the two-asset portfolio is a useful representation of modern portfolio theory and design, it is fairly unrealistic. Large real estate or mixed-asset portfolios are more likely to contain many assets than to contain only two. The illustration also points up some other problems in applying Markowitz portfolio theory to real estate portfolios. First, it is difficult to devise a real estate portfolio that consists of "75 percent investment A and 25 percent investment B," because real estate acquisitions are usually an all-or-nothing proposition. (This is not a rigid requirement, for an investor could purchase proportional shares of real estate by buying participation interests in a limited partnership.) Second, the discussion has excluded any consideration of the use of leverage. Because an investor may lend (invest) or borrow, debt can be viewed as an alternative investment that has certain return–risk and covariance characteristics. What would be positively correlated if acquired as an investment would be negatively correlated if acquired as a debt. Third, multiasset selection models tend to be extremely complicated and difficult to implement (and costly to solve).

AN EXTENDED DEVELOPMENT OF PORTFOLIO THEORY

Extending the two-asset-portfolio analysis to the more general problem of the N-asset portfolio is too complex for this discussion. The N-asset problem requires linear programming with the object of maximizing the difference between expected portfolio return and variance. The functional form is that of calculus maximization of an objective function:

$$\text{Maximize } Z = \lambda E_p - V_p \tag{4}$$

where $E_p = \sum_{i=1}^{N} E(R_i) W_i$

$$V_p = \sum_{i=1}^{N} \sum_{j=1}^{N} W_i W_j \sigma_{ij}$$

subject to

$$\sum_{i=1}^{N} W_i = 1.0$$

Adaptations of the *N*-Asset Calculus Model to Real Estate

Several adaptations of the calculus model just given have been made for real estate. These were developed to overcome some serious difficulties that are peculiar to real estate investment.

1. Real estate acquisitions usually require all-or-nothing decisions. That is, the investor purchases either the entire project or nothing because there are no fractional interests. (Limited partnerships, REIT shares, and so forth may present alternatives and ease the restriction of all-or-nothing acquisition.)

2. Real estate purchases are frequently leveraged. The inclusion of borrowed funds complicates the optimal selection inasmuch as debt has the effect not only of increasing expected equity rates of return but also of increasing the variance of equity rates of return.

3. Most portfolio optimization models are single-period models. Real estate is a multiperiod commitment that does not usually permit the investor to restructure the portfolio at the end of the period.

One of the most interesting portfolio models for use with real estate was developed by Pellatt.[19] Pellatt's model incorporated several innovative design characteristics. It was designed to generate an efficient frontier for real estate assets that includes financing decisions as part of the model's specification, permits an all-or-nothing acquisition criterion, and is predicated on a multiperiod decision horizon. This was accomplished using net present value and the variance of NPV in lieu of rate of return and variance of returns. The general structure of the model is similar to that described in equation 4:

$$\max E(\text{NPV}) = \sum_{i=1}^{N} (\text{PVAL}_i) W_i + \sum_{i=1}^{N} (\text{MVAL}_i)^{Y_i/P_i}$$

subject to

$$1. \ \text{CAP} = \sum_{i=1}^{N} (W_i - Y_i)(\text{COST}_i) \leq \text{CAPMAX}$$

$$2. \ \text{VAR} = \sum_{i=1}^{N} \sum_{j=1}^{N} W_i W_j \sigma_{ij} \leq \text{VARMAX}$$

3. $0 \leq Y_i \leq P_i W_i$ for all $i = 1$ to N

4. $0 \leq W_i \leq 1$ for all $i = 1$ to N

where $E(\text{NPV})$ = expected NPV of portfolio

N = number of properties being considered

PVAL_i = expected NPV of property i

MVAL_i = net present value of maximum mortgage allowable on property i

Y_i = proportion of total cost of property i provided by mortgage funds

---

[19]Pellatt, "Normative Approach."

P_i = maximum proportion of total cost of property i that can be provided by mortgage funds

CAP = required total investment capital

$COST_i$ = acquisition cost of property i

CAPMAX = externally imposed limit on size of portfolio

VAR = variance of NPV for investment portfolio

σ_{ij} = covariance of NPVs for ith and jth properties, respectively

VARMAX = externally imposed upper limit on portfolio variance

Pellatt's model includes an optimal financing decision, Y_i/P_i, in which the model selects a proportion of total cost to be provided through mortgage debt subject to a stipulated maximum loan-to-value ratio, P_i. The efficient frontier is subject to maximum capital constraints, CAPMAX, and a maximum variance constraint, VARMAX. When we relax the VARMAX constraint, the entire efficient frontier is generated. The imposition of a VARMAX constraint limits the portfolio to what is optimal within the VARMAX limit.

The model was designed to provide such limits on the proportion of each investment selected that the portfolio generated either includes an asset or excludes it. No fractional part of an asset can be selected. This limitation can be relaxed by the user. Pellatt devised several overlapping computer programs that provide the means of generating efficient frontiers for up to four properties. Of course, a close look at Pellatt's model specification indicates that it is a specialized case of the calculus model that incorporates some of the unusual characteristics of real estate assets. Perhaps what is most unusual about Pellatt's model is that it was developed before 1970.

It was not until 1977 that another model was formulated. In that year Curcio and Gaines[20] proposed a model that was based on the general optimization model but modified slightly to provide for a multiperiod decision horizon. Curcio and Gaines assumed that in a pure "real estate" portfolio the initial optimal portfolio needed to be revised periodically. Their model did not differ from Pellatt's, however, except that Pellatt's model maximized E(NPV), whereas Curcio and Gaines's maximized terminal wealth. Insofar as Curcio and Gaines's model was based on the concept of terminal wealth, the financing decision was external to their formulations, whereas Pellatt made the financing decision an explicit component of the model.

Later, Findlay, Hamilton, Messner, and Yormack presented a model similar to Curcio and Gaines's, but structured to be more easily solved

[20]Curcio and Gaines, "Real Estate Portfolio Revision"; Findlay et al., "Optimal Real Estate Portfolios."

using current computer programming technology.[21] More in keeping with the standard portfolio model, Findlay and his colleagues use expected returns and variances rather than terminal wealth or NPV criteria. To adapt their model to the multiperiod features of real estate investment, they proposed the use of the financial management rate of return (FMRR) rather than IRR because FMRR incorporates reinvestment rate parameters and makes possible the inclusion of uninvested portions of capital in the optimal portfolio. They claim that the ability to include uninvested portions of the total capital in the optimum portfolio makes the comparison of portfolios more legitimate. In their model the use of the FMRR makes possible an assumption that uninvested capital may be invested in a risk-free asset. This essentially makes each generated portfolio a combination of risky real estate assets with a risk-free asset.

The formulation of the Findlay model is interesting and is presented here for comparison with Pellatt's model:

$$\min Z = \frac{1}{b^2} \sum_{i=1}^{N} \sum_{j=1}^{N} W_i C_i \sigma_i P_{ij} \sigma_j C_j W_j$$

subject to

1. $r_0 + \dfrac{1}{b} \sum_{j=1}^{N} U_j W_j \geq Y$

2. $\sum_{j=1}^{N} C_j W_j \leq b$

3. $W_j = 0, 1, 2, \ldots, N$

where b = total capital funds constraint
      Y = externally imposed minimum return constant
      C_j = acquisition cost for project j
      W_j = proportion of capital invested in project j
    σ_i, σ_j = standard deviations of expected FMRRs for projects i and j, respectively
      P_{ij} = correlation coefficient of projects i and j, respectively
      r_0 = risk-free rate

It is interesting to note the essential similarities of these portfolio models. Furthermore, all three are basically derivatives of the original Markowitz and Sharpe models. The critical elements of a real estate portfolio model—its multiperiod nature, the need for discrete project selection, and the need to include financing—are addressed in each model, but in a somewhat different fashion. Pellatt attempted to resolve the problem by

---

[21]Findlay et al., "Optimal Real Estate Portfolios," pp. 298–317.

using NPV rather than rate-of-return (i.e., IRR) criteria. Pellatt assumed that by so doing one makes the financing decision an explicit element of the designated cost of capital (which is identical to NPV applications in corporate cost of capital problems). Therefore, financing alternatives could be explored by noting their impact on the discount rate. Curcio and Gaines addressed the multiperiod nature of real estate by formulating the portfolio model to include balance sheet changes and the use of dynamic programming. However, they did not tackle the leverage problem. Findlay and his colleagues utilized the FMRR concept because they felt that its multiperiod formulation and ability to handle reinvestment and the inclusion of cash as a risk-free asset are well adapted to both the multiperiod and leverage problems. All three models utilized modern programming algorithms to handle the problem of multiple assets and discrete project selection.

A Simplified Approach to Portfolio Selection

A major stumbling block to the solution of portfolio models of the types illustrated in the previous section is the need to specify the correlation coefficients (the covariance matrix) for all project pairs in the set of projects from which the efficient frontier will be generated. All three of the models described require that these inputs be generated subjectively. In fact, the limitation of Pellatt's model to four properties was predicated in part on the difficulty faced by an analyst who must generate a matrix of subjective joint probabilities (i.e., generate the matrix of correlation coefficients or covariance).

Sharpe proposed an alternative formulation of the basic Markowitz model (on which the three real estate models are based), which he called the diagonal or single-index model.[22] Sharpe's formulation of a security's characteristic line was presented in Exhibit 18-2. The development of the characteristic line was based on the assumption that risk contains two distinct elements: systematic and unsystematic risk. The latter is eliminated through portfolio diversification, but the former is undiversifiable. Systematic risk is the risk associated with the impact of changes in the market for all securities on the return for any individual security. The measure of this risk is beta (β). The security's characteristic line, as stated earlier, was formulated as $Y = \alpha + \beta K + \epsilon$, where Y is the security's forecasted return, α is the security's unique rate of return, and ϵ is an error term. In the general terminology of portfolio theory, portfolio return was defined as

$$E(R_p) = \sum_{i=1}^{N} W_i E(R_i)$$

[22]William F. Sharpe, "A Simplified Model for Portfolio Analysis," *Management Science*, January 1963, pp. 277–293.

where W_i is the proportion of the portfolio invested in the ith security and $E(R_i)$ the expected return on the ith security. From the equation for the characteristic line, $E(R_i)$ was defined as

$$E(R_i) = \alpha_i + \beta_i X + \epsilon_i$$

and therefore portfolio return was defined as

$$E(R_p) = \Sigma\, W_i E(\alpha_i + \beta_i X + \epsilon_i)$$

The term X is the return on the market as represented by some market index—for example, the index for the S&P 500 or the Dow Jones industrial average. Carrying this one step further, we have

$$E(R_p) = \sum_{i=1}^{N} W_i E(\alpha_i + \epsilon_i) + \sum_{i=1}^{N} W_i(\beta_i X)$$

Sharpe redefined portfolio return as involving an investment in two components.

1. An investment in the "basic characteristics" of each security $(\alpha_i + \epsilon_i)W_i$.
2. An "investment" in the market index—$W_i(\beta_i X)$.

The variance of this portfolio is

$$\mathrm{VAR}(R_p) = \sum_{i=1}^{N+1} W_i^2 \mathrm{VAR}(R_i)$$

Sharpe's simplified model results in a covariance matrix with zeroes in each position other than the diagonal. This simplifies the computation requirements and makes possible the generation of an efficient frontier with less difficulty than when using the Markowitz model. The data requirements are also simplified in that only periodic return data on each security and on the market index are needed. Through the use of simple linear regression the values for α, ϵ, and β can be generated.

The adaptation of Sharpe's simplified model to real estate portfolio selection is hampered in particular by the lack of an index. Several studies have been done in which real estate assets were compared with an index. Kapplin illustrated the creation of an artificial index based loosely on state preference theory in which a project's expected performance is tied to the analyst's subjective opinion of how a change in economic conditions (state of nature) might affect a project's rate of return.[23] By using an analysis similar to that used for the two-asset-portfolio problem, the analyst can calculate the covariance of the project's return with the "state of nature" and estimate a beta for the project.

---

[23]Kapplin, "Financial Theory," pp. 28–37.

Larry Wofford and Edward Moses used an interesting technique to create an index utilizing data on REITs.[24] Using regression analysis and the proportion of REIT assets invested in the type of project under consideration, they were able to generate estimates of the beta coefficient for specific types of property investment. However, the range of the beta estimates was quite substantial. In their example for shopping centers, beta estimates ranged from .135 to .921 for an 80 percent confidence interval. Despite the statistical problems, the technique does offer a possible method of creating an index.

Harris Friedman used GNP growth as a superindex in his innovative study of real estate, stock, and combined portfolios.[25] However, such an index may have questionable relevance to real estate investment performance. When real estate returns are regressed against such an index, as would be required in the simplified portfolio model, there would be a low correlation between real estate and an index like GNP. Because unexplained variance is assumed to be unsystematic and, hence, diversifiable, the index may be erroneously interpreted as meaning low portfolio risk.

Michael Young demonstrated the use of the NYSE index as a comparative index for evaluating the performance of a portfolio combining real estate assets and common stock.[26] His technique was essentially a replication of the Sharpe model using two assets: a real estate portfolio and a security portfolio. Portfolio returns were regressed against the NYSE index to derive the appropriate data inputs.

Hoag attempted to devise a specific real estate index, but his efforts did not catch on.[27] Recently, the Frank Russell Company, a firm specializing in rating portfolio managers, devised the FRC Property Index. This index tracks properties sampled from a major real estate fund (or funds). The FRC index begins in 1978 and runs through the current year. Data are provided on property returns classified by geographic region and by property type. Returns are decomposed into cash flow and appreciation components.[28]

---

[24]Larry E. Wofford and Edward A. Moses, "The Relationship Between Capital Markets and Real Estate Investment Yields: Theory and Application," *The Real Estate Appraiser and Analyst*, November–December 1978, pp. 51–61.

[25]Harris C. Friedman, "Real Estate Investment and Portfolio Theory," *Journal of Financial and Quantitative Analysis*, March 1971, pp. 861–874.

[26]Young, "Comparative Investment," pp. 30–46.

[27]J. Hoag, "Toward Indices of Real Estate Value and Return," *The Journal of Finance*, May 1980, pp. 569–580.

[28]Frank Russell Company, *FRC Commercial Property Index* (Tacoma, Wash.: Frank Russell Company). Commercially available performance indices for real estate investment are not widely available; however, two that are currently available through subscription service are *Australian Property Index*, Part 1 Melbourne 1970–1984 (Richard Ellis Pty Ltd., 60 Collins St., Melbourne, Australia 3000, (telephone 654-3333); and *Real Estate Syndication Pooled Data Base* (Stanley E. Saeks & Associates, 2201 Pacific Ave., San Francisco,

Many other studies have attempted to illustrate real estate's performance vis-à-vis other investment media as well as devise performance indices. These various studies illustrate the general applicability of modern portfolio models to the problem of selecting optimal real estate portfolios. The index (diagonal) models are simplifications of Markowitz's model of portfolio selection that tend to reduce both data requirements and computational complexity. However, there are still basic limitations in the general applicability to real estate. These include (1) inability to handle discrete project selection, (2) failure to incorporate optimal financing decisions, (3) inability to handle many projects, and (4) lack of an acceptable index for real estate. The fourth problem may be the easiest to solve. With the major involvement of large pension funds and institutional investors in the real estate market, the development of a generally accepted index of real estate performance is probably not too far away.

IMPACT OF PORTFOLIO THEORY ON LARGE INSTITUTIONAL INVESTORS

Thus far the discussion has focused on the development of a body of theory and its application to a portfolio approach to investment decision making. This section presents an overview of the research that has applied these theories to real estate investing, followed by a discussion of the historical evidence regarding the evolution and performance of large institutional investors.

Although there have been many studies of real estate and its performance within a portfolio context, a complete discussion of those studies would be out of place here. However, a historical overview of the research provides a perspective and illustrates the directions of research.

Most early research was limited to analyses of real estate performance vis-à-vis other investment media, particularly common stock.[29] These

---

Calif. 94115, (telephone 415-929-0668). Saeks and Associates should have a regular index on syndication performance available at this time. (Since the first edition of this text, Mr. Saeks has been employed by Liquidity Fund of Emeryville, Calif.) For additional information on syndication performance see *The Stanger Report* and *The Stanger Register* (Robert A. Stanger & Co., P.O. Box 7490, 1129 Broad St., Shrewsbury, N.J. 07701, (telephone 201-389-3600).

[29] See Stephen Roulac, "Can Real Estate Returns Outperform Common Stocks?" *The Journal of Portfolio Management*, Winter 1976, pp. 26–43; Paul F. Wendt and Sui N. Wong, "Investment Performance: Common Stocks Versus Apartment Houses," *The Journal of Finance*, December 1965, pp. 633–646; Dennis G. Kelleher, "How Real Estate Stacks Up to the S. & P. 500," *Real Estate Review*, Summer 1976, pp. 60–65; R. Bruce Ricks, "Imputed Equity Returns on Real Estate Financed with Life Insurance Company Loans," *The Journal of Finance*, December 1969, pp. 921–937.

studies looked at measurements of return and compared real estate's performance to those of common stocks, bonds, or other financial assets. As research progressed risk measurements were also made using the Markowitz mean–variance model.[30] Real estate generally outperformed financial assets, providing higher returns and lower risk. But these early studies looked primarily at individual properties rather than at portfolios. Given the premise that real estate assets provided better return–risk trade-offs than securities, research began to focus on the portfolio aspects. Rather than measuring return and risk on individual properties, for which data were difficult to obtain, researchers concentrated on measuring performance of real estate portfolios. Real estate investment trusts (REITs) and commingled real estate funds (CREFs) were used as sources of data. These studies compared real estate portfolios with portfolios of stocks, bonds, or both.[31]

As research progressed into the second half of the 1980s new questions were examined: better methods of measuring return and risk, derivation of efficient portfolios, diversification issues, and issues of market efficiency.[32] Diversification has become an important topic of study since 1984. Efficient diversification and the proper criteria for maximizing diversification benefits are being examined.[33] Recently, research has focused on the role of real estate in a mixed-asset portfolio, questioning what constitutes an efficiently diversified mixed-asset portfolio of which real estate is a component.[34]

Despite the proliferation of research, current knowledge is insufficient to answer the many questions relevant to sound investment decisions. Several major issues remain open to further investigation. These include

[30]Mike Miles and Michael Rice, "Toward a More Complete Investigation of Real Estate Investment Yield to the Rate Evidenced in the Money and Capital Markets: The Individual Investor's Perspective," *The Real Estate Appraiser and Analyst*, November–December 1978, pp. 8–19; C. F. Sirmans and James A. Webb, "Investment Yields in the Money, Capital and Real Estate Markets: A Comparative Analysis for 1951–1976," *The Real Estate Appraiser and Analyst*, November–December 1978, pp. 40–46; Walter H. Chudleigh III and Lawrence E. Brown, "Real Estate Investment Yield as Correlated to the Rate Shown in Money and Capital Markets," *The Real Estate Appraiser and Analyst*, November–December 1978, pp. 47–50.

[31]Mike Miles and Tom McCue, "Historic Returns and Institutional Real Estate Portfolios," *Journal of the American Real Estate and Urban Economics Association*, Summer 1982, pp. 184–199.

[32]Austin J. Jaffe and C. F. Sirmans, "The Theory and Evidence on Real Estate Financial Decisions: A Review of the Issues," *Journal of the American Real Estate and Urban Economics Association*, Fall 1984, pp. 378–400.

[33]David Hartzell et al., "Diversification Categories in Investment Real Estate," *Journal of the American Real Estate and Urban Economics Association*, Summer 1986, pp. 230–254.

[34]James R. Webb, Richard J. Curcio, and Jack H. Rubens, "Diversification Gains from Including Real Estate in Mixed-Asset Portfolios," *Decision Sciences*, 1988.

(1) improved measurements of return and risk,[35] (2) diversification issues,[36] and (3) market efficiency and the applicability of traditional models to real estate assets.[37]

Institutional Real Estate Portfolios: Characteristics and Performance

The success of large investment funds is typically judged by how well the fund has met its stated goals and objectives. The fund's investment policies are stipulated with respect to several criteria: risk control, returns, diversification, consistency of performance, and provision of adequate but not excessive operating expenses. This section provides a brief overview of the background and investment performance of the three major institutional real estate investors: pension funds, real estate investment trusts (REITs), and large, publicly offered real estate limited partnerships (RELPs).

Pension Funds. Pension fund investment in real estate has grown dramatically since 1976. In 1976 only 10 percent of pension funds was invested in real estate, a percentage which grew to 42 percent by 1984.[38] According to Goldman, Sachs and Company, Prudential's Property Investment Separate Account (PRISA) produced an average return of 11.6 percent from 1970 to 1984, an average return exceeding the returns on common stocks, bonds, and Treasury bills for the same time period.

Brueggeman, Chen, and Thibodeau analyzed the performance of two commingled real estate funds (CREFs) and found an average annual return of 11.6 percent for the period from 1972 to 1983.[39] Mike Miles and Tom McCue found returns averaging nearly 16 percent for a sample of properties taken from one CREF. The period of analysis was 1973 to 1981.[40] These returns parallel the performance of PRISA's fund and coincide well

---

[35]Joseph W. O'Connor, "Real Estate Development: Investment Risks and Rewards," in *Real Estate Investing* (New York: Dow Jones–Irwin, 1985), pp. 53–62.

[36]Hartzell et al., "Diversification Categories."

[37]Dennis W. Draper and M. Chapman Findlay, "Capital Asset Pricing and Real Estate Valuation," *Journal of the American Real Estate and Urban Economics Association*, Summer 1982, pp. 152–183; also George W. Gau, "Weak Form Tests of the Efficiency of Real Estate Investment Markets," *Financial Review*, November 1984, pp. 301–320, and "Public Information and Abnormal Returns in Real Estate Investment," *Journal of the American Real Estate and Urban Economics Association*, Spring 1985, pp. 15–31.

[38]Meyer Melnikoff, "The Attractiveness of Real Estate Investments for Pension Funds," in *Real Estate Investing* (New York: Dow Jones–Irwin, 1985), pp. 5.

[39]William H. Brueggeman, A. H. Chen, and Thomas G. Thibodean, "Real Estate Investment Funds: Performance and Portfolio Considerations," *Journal of American Real Estate and Urban Economics Association*, Fall 1984, pp. 333–354.

[40]Mike Miles and Tom McCue, "Commercial Real Estate Returns," *Journal of the American Real Estate and Urban Economics Association*, Fall 1984, pp. 355–377.

EXHIBIT 18-17.   Comparison of Composition of Various CREFs by Property Type, Region, and Property Size

Property Type (Percent)

Type	M&M Sample	M&E Sample	FRC Index Sample
Industrial	27.6	25.6	30.3
Office	51.0	28.9	42.3
Retail	16.7	33.3	20.9
Residential	2.6	4.4	3.2
Hotel/motel	1.9	7.7	3.3

Regional (Percent)

Region	M&M Sample	M&E Sample	FRC Index Sample
East	34.4	22.0	23.7
Midwest	17.6	25.0	23.7
South	22.3	31.0	20.5
West	25.7	21.0	33.9

Property Size (Percent)

Size	M&M Sample	M&E Sample	FRC Index Sample
Under $1 million	29.3	10.0	9.7
$1 Million to 2.5 million	30.7	23.0	32.1
$2.5 Million to 5 million	18.3	25.0	31.1
$5 Million to 10 million	11.0	20.0	16.7
$10 Million to 20 million	6.0	23.0	5.3
Over $20 million	4.7	N.A.	4.5

Source: Mike Miles and Tom McCue, "Commercial Real Estate Returns," *Journal of the American Real Estate and Urban Economics Association*, Fall 1984, pp. 360–361.

with earlier studies of pension fund performance done before 1982.[41] The makeup of the CREF funds is illustrated in Exhibit 18-17. These data were taken from the Miles and McCue study. The second column represents the date from the Miles and McCue (M&M) study; the third column contains

[41] See Peter C. Aldrich and King Upton, "The Pension Funds Finally Move into Real Estate," *Real Estate Review*, Winter 1978, pp. 30–35; Alvin L. Arnold, ed., *Mortgage and Real Estate Executives Report*, June 15, 1980, p. 8; Mike Miles and Janelle Langford, "Bank Trust Department Operations of Commingled Real Estate Funds," *Real Estate Issues*, Winter 1978, pp. 62–73; Mike Miles and A. S. Estey, "Performance Evaluation of Commingled Real Estate Funds," *The Journal of Portfolio Management*, Winter 1981.

data taken from an earlier study by Miles and Estey (M&E), and the last column contains data from the FRC Property Index sample. For contrast, Exhibits 18-18 and 18-19 illustrate similar information taken from PRISA's annual report.[42]

Pension fund investment has been quite successful. The performance results illustrated by the studies just cited and by PRISA's performance indicate returns that generally exceeded those of competing investments. The growth of pension fund investment has been profound. However, in recent years competition for investment-grade real estate has also increased. Thus, yields are being bid down.

Furthermore, developers anxious to build products for the pension fund investors have overbuilt most major real estate markets. Therefore, a de-

[42]Prudential Asset Management Group, *PRISA Annual Report 1986*, pp. 14, 18–19.

EXHIBIT 18-18.   Investment Results Page from PRISA's Annual Report

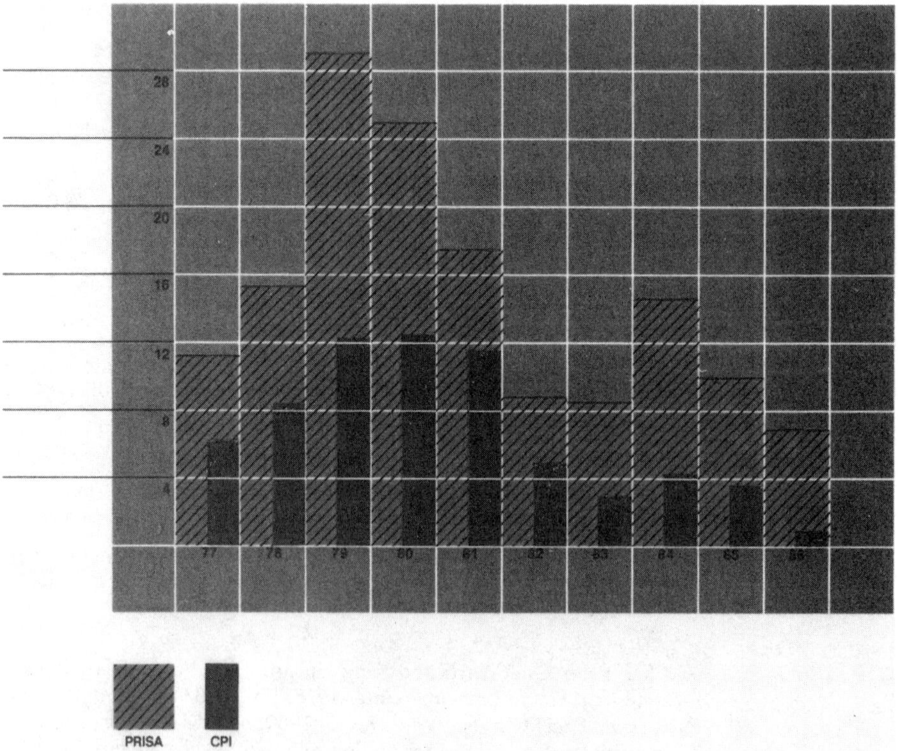

Source: PRISA Annual Report 1986, p. 14. With permission of the Prudential Insurance Company of America.

EXHIBIT 18-19. Portfolio Composition by Geographic Location and Class of Property

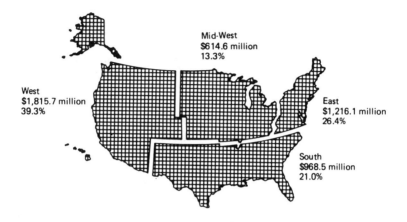

Class	Office	Retail	Industrial	Hotel	Apartment	Land	Agricultural	Total
West	22.6%(20)	4.4%(12)	6.7%(38)	1.3% (0)	3.8% (6)	0.4% (2)	0.1% (2)	39.3% (80)
South	9.4 (28)	6.5 (15)	2.9 (34)	1.1 (6)	0.4 (3)	0.0 (2)	0.7 (5)	21.0 (93)
Mid-West	5.4 (15)	3.3 (13)	3.9 (71)	0.0 (0)	0.5 (2)	0.1 (4)	0.1 (1)	13.3 (106)
East	14.8 (13)	3.3 (3)	1.4 (7)	6.2 (5)	0.0 (0)	0.7 (2)	0.0 (0)	26.4 (30)
Total	52.2%(76)	17.5%(43)	14.9%(150)	8.6%(11)	4.7%(11)	1.2%(10)	0.9% (8)	100.0%(309)

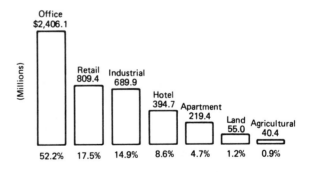

Source: PRISA Annual Report 1986, p. 18. With permission of the Prudential Insurance Company of America.

cline is expected in property prices with a reduction in pension fund returns while markets remain soft.

Real Estate Investment Trusts. REITs are perhaps the oldest group of institutional real estate investors. They date from before the 1960s, although their existence became formalized in 1960. The industry has had its booms and busts and has now settled down to a conservative future. Originally realty trusts were organized to invest in equities through a vehicle that permitted most of the tax benefits of individual ownership while offering a fractionalized investment in the form of a share of beneficial interest (SBI). Small investors were able to obtain ownership in a diversified portfolio of real estate properties by purchasing shares in an REIT with a portfolio and objectives corresponding to those of the investor, but without requiring the large cash outlay of direct ownership.

REIT assets were more than $21 billion before the economic recession of 1974–1975.[43] The industry assets now total more than $10 billion. Dividend yields have improved from an average of 7.5 percent in the 1977–1978 period to over 9 percent in 1983.[44] REITs have provided excellent returns in recent years, outperforming the FRC Property Index except in the years 1978 and 1981. From 1982 to 1987 REITs have provided an average return of 13.3 percent per year. REIT share performance, however, may be more the result of general growth in securities markets during the past five years.

Since 1984 a new variation of the REIT has come to market, the finite-life REIT (FREIT). This vehicle resembles a REIT in most respects except that it has a finite life, similar to a RELP. FREITs were created to compete with the rapidly growing limited-partnership market by providing a vehicle that would terminate and distribute capital gains from property dispositions. The passage of the 1986 Tax Reform Act eliminated the significant distinguishing feature of the RELP: its tax-sheltering benefits from the pass-through of losses. Without the pass-through of losses, the FREIT and RELP become fairly similar. However, REITs and FREITs have better liquidity than RELPs, although this characteristic may be changing, as we shall see in the next section.

Although REIT performance plummeted during the 1974–1975 recession, the REIT industry retrenched and rebuilt itself in the 1980s. Today REITs are more soundly managed; they also have sounder investment policies and better-diversified portfolios. No longer promoted as vehicles for rapid appreciation, REITs have pursued a policy of producing a stable income. Dividend returns have consistently outperformed those of common stock, and total returns have generally outperformed returns of other insti-

---

[43] *REIT Fact Book, 1979,* p. 8 (see footnote 2).
[44] *REIT Fact Book, 1983,* p. 18 (see footenote 2).

tutional real estate investment vehicles. REITs also provide excellent liquidity. As the economy has grown, REIT asset values have also increased and share prices have risen.

Limited Partnerships. Until 1981 little was known about the scope of the real estate limited-partnership (RELP) market. Even today any knowledge is primarily limited to publicly offered RELPs. Data on private partnerships are not available in quantities large enough for study and analysis. The public RELPs are registered with the SEC and are generally sold through major brokerage houses such as Merrill–Lynch, Oppenheimer, E. F. Hutton, and Shearson–Lehman Brothers. Interests are also available from the RELP's general partner–sponsor. The general partner–sponsor is the organizer who creates and manages the RELP for the limited partners.[45] Public syndications have raised more than $30 billion of equity since 1981. Most of the RELPs formed between 1981 and 1986 were tax-shelter-oriented programs, designed to produce maximum pass-throughs of losses to the limited partners. Until 1981 a larger proportion of RELPs were income-oriented, as they became again after the passage of the Tax Reform Act of 1986.

In the late 1980s, the master limited partnership (MLP) became a very popular investment vehicle. Although the first MLP was organized in 1981, most MLPs have been issued only since 1985.[46] More than $5 billion of equity was raised from 1985 to 1987. In June 1987, thirty-two MLPs were listed as operating in real estate. Unlike RELPs, these thirty-two MLPs trade on a major securities exchange—the bulk are listed on the New York or the American stock exchange—and are bought or sold like any share of stock. RELPs, on the other hand, have no organized exchange; therefore, the secondary market for RELP interests is comparatively small.[47] MLPs have been around for such a short period of time that little analysis of their performance is available. Average yields, based on current market prices, are around 9 percent, but many MLPs are today selling for much lower prices than when originally issued. In a recent study MLPs were found to provide returns which exceeded those of REITs, RELPs, and the overall stock market from 1982 to 1985. However, MLP performance was lackluster during the 1986 to 1987 period.[48]

[45]For a general reference on real estate limited partnerships see Stephen P. Jarchow, *Real Estate Limited Partnership Syndications.* (New York: Wiley, 1985).

[46]Robert Stanger Co., *The Stanger Register,* June 1987, p. 151.

[47]Steven D. Kapplin and Arthur L. Schwartz, Jr., "Public Real Estate Limited Partnerships: A Preliminary Comparison with Other Investments," *Journal of the American Real Estate and Urban Economics Association,* Spring 1988.

[48]Robert Stanger Co., *The Stanger Register,* June 1987, p. 151. Also see Steven D. Kapplin and Arthur L. Schwartz, Jr., "Investor Considerations and Recent Returns of Real Estate Master Limited Partnerships," *Journal of the American Association of Individual Investors,* September, 1988.

RELPs have had a much longer history than MLPs. In a study done in 1983, Liquidity Fund, a secondary market investor in RELP interests, reported that RELPs in their portfolio yielded better than 13 percent after tax during the period from 1970 to 1981.[49] A somewhat later study by Ronald Rogers and James Owers indicated an average return of only 6 percent after tax for a similar study period.[50] However, their study was somewhat flawed, as was the Liquidity Fund study. Both studies used estimated terminal values for the RELPs in their respective samples. In 1986 Kapplin and Arthur Schwartz used secondary-market resales to evaluate RELP returns and found an average after-tax return of less than 4 percent for the period from 1974 to 1985.[51] However, most of the poorly performing RELPs were formed after 1980. RELPs formed before 1981 provided average returns of nearly 8 percent after tax.[52]

The performance of RELPs has been somewhat checkered. Although data are still not available in sufficient quantity, it appears that RELPs provided better returns prior to the 1981 tax reform, but have done poorly since 1981. Coincidentally, this time period marked the shift from income- to tax-oriented RELPs. In addition, the period before 1981 was one of high inflation and rapid appreciation. Early RELPs very likely benefited greatly from the inflationary period from the mid-1970s through 1981.

The decade of the 1970s saw the emergence of the large institutional investor. Tax law changes and high rates of inflation, together with the creation of ERISA, provided the impetus for the growth seen from 1970 to 1980. Strong economic growth in the 1980s has allowed this impetus to continue. The 1980s has also seen the "securitization" of real estate and Wall Street's entrance into real estate markets. Investors now have a wide range of alternative real estate securities: REITs, FREITs, RELPs, MLPs, and pension fund units for Keogh and IRA plans. The Tax Reform Act of 1986 created a new vehicle for investment in large mortgage-backed investment pools: real estate mortgage investment certificates (REMICs). The future appears to have much in store for investors.

Present Problems and Future Prospects

Institutional investment in real estate has grown more rapidly than ever anticipated. This growth has given rise to the "securitization" of real estate securities markets. Unfortunately, investors purchasing these new securi-

---

[49]Liquidity Fund, *The Performance of Public Real Estate Limited Partnerships Formed Between 1971–1980*, unpublished report, available from Liquidity Fund, Emeryville, Calif.

[50]Ronald C. Rogers and James E. Owers, "The Investment Performance of Real Estate Limited Partnerships," *Journal of the American Real Estate and Urban Economics Association*, Summer 1985, pp. 153–166.

[51]Kapplin and Schwartz, "Analysis of Recent Rates of Return," p. 40.

[52]Ibid., p. 42.

ties are not well informed. Real estate securities are risky investments, as are investments in the underlying assets. It is not yet known how closely the performance of a real estate security matches the performance of the underlying assets. In Sharpe's language, the difference between unsystematic and systematic risk remains unknown.

Recent research has indicated that real estate assets should be included in investment portfolios, but this research also suggests that real estate return–risk benefits tend to dominate other investment media. No one has yet concluded that investment in the real asset itself is preferable to investment in a real estate security. Diversification benefits are definitely available, but evidence is inconclusive about how the total portfolio should be constructed and about how the real estate portfolio should be diversified (e.g., geographically, property type, property size) Real estate securities will certainly simplify portfolio development by making real estate as easy to add to the portfolio as a phone call to one's broker.

However, researchers are still far from fully understanding real estate assets. Lack of data, localized real estate markets, and a variety of other problems plague researchers' ability to comprehend real estate returns and risks fully, and to measure them correctly.

Research evidence has not shown conclusively what benefits of diversification may be derived in the real estate portfolio (viewed as a separate entity), but it certainly demonstrates that real estate assets reduce portfolio risk when combined with other assets, such as common stock. It would seem that portfolio managers and researchers should continue to focus on developing models of portfolio selection that concentrate on the real estate portfolio. Currently lacking a definitive operational model, the portfolio manager is left with the intuitive appeal of a geographic dispersion and "safety in numbers" approach to asset selection and portfolio management. The index problem discussed earlier is also a major snag in developing simpler approaches to portfolio selection. No "special" real estate index is currently being used, but the FRC Property Index could be applied successfully if it were universally accepted.

The application of portfolio theory to real estate has exciting implications and is still in its infancy. The state of the art is very dynamic. Sharpe's capital asset theory of equilibrium was based on four assumptions.

1. Investors choose portfolios that are perceived as mean–variance-efficient.
2. All investors have similar *ex ante* beliefs vis-à-vis expected return and variance.
3. The "perfectly" diversified market portfolio is mean–variance-efficient.
4. The risk premium for any asset is a linear function of its covariance with the market portfolio (as measured by beta).

Recently these assumptions have been seriously questioned through empirical research.[53]

SUMMARY

This chapter has presented an overview of modern portfolio theory and its application to real estate investing and property selection. The contrast between individual project analysis and portfolio strategy was discussed, and the need to consider real estate in a portfolio context was stressed. The concept of diversification was presented, and the difference between naive and efficient diversification was discussed. The concept of covariance was introduced, as was the development of efficient portfolios through the proper selection of assets on the basis of their covariance. Assets that covary negatively enable the investor to develop a portfolio in which variance is eliminated or substantially reduced.

The application of portfolio theory to real estate investment was illustrated and the contrast between real estate markets and security markets was stressed. The use of high leverage, the localized nature of real estate markets, the general lack of transaction information, and the lack of sophistication on the part of participants make it difficult to use modern portfolio theory in the development of real estate portfolios. Methods of developing input data were presented, and the application of a portfolio model to the two-asset portfolio was given as an example. Four steps are required to develop a two-asset portfolio.

1. Derive estimates of rates of return and associated probabilities.
2. Calculate $E(R)$ and variance for each project.
3. Calculate covariance.
4. Calculate and graph the efficient frontier.

Later, the arithmetic solution model for the two-asset portfolio model was expanded to the general N-asset case. Finally, the simplified "diagonal" model was presented.

Although research in real estate portfolio analysis has grown in sophistication and scope, the rapid growth of large institutional investors—pension funds, large public limited partnerships, corporate real estate investment—and the securitization of real estate assets have provided the impetus for additional research. During the next decade research in this field will surely make dramatic progress, and the extensive use of portfolio selection models for real estate portfolio management is sure to become a reality.

---

[53]See Ross, "Current Status," and Roll, "Critique," for a full discussion of the status of capital asset pricing theory (footnote 9).

19

DEVELOPING A PERSONAL PORTFOLIO WITH REAL ESTATE

The prudent application of knowledge enhances the accumulation and preservation of wealth.

GEORGE M. HILLER

This chapter examines the process of personal financial management with a look at the role of real estate investments in the financial planning process. The chapter focuses on the creation and use of a written financial plan as a tool for achieving personal financial goals and objectives and presents six distinct steps in creating, implementing, and reviewing a personal financial plan.

THE PURPOSE OF FINANCIAL PLANNING

Financial planning is the practical application of analysis, strategies, and planning methodology to a personal financial situation. Financial planning can be considered both a science and a process. It is a science in the sense that it is the observation, identification, description, investigation, and explanation of financially related data, events, strategies, and objectives. It is a process in the sense that it is ongoing, dynamic, adaptive, proactive, and reactive. The science and process of financial planning come together in practical application directed to (1) the achievement of personal and financial objectives; (2) the efficient utilization of financial

Acknowledgment: The authors are grateful for the assistance of George M. Hiller, George M. Hiller Wealth Planning, Atlanta, Georgia, who coauthored the revision of this chapter.

661

resources; and (3) the enhancement of financial benefits over time. This process of comprehensive financial planning can be delineated into six distinct steps.[1] Each step is necessary to formulate an adequate plan for the achievement of personal financial goals over time and to carry out the plan. The six steps are the following.

1. Clarifying the investor's present financial situation by *collecting and assessing all relevant personal and financial data.*

2. Determining the investor's long-term desires by *identifying both financial and personal goals and objectives.*

3. *Analyzing the financial situation and identifying financial problems* that might hinder the achievement of personal and financial goals.

4. *Developing a written financial plan* that specifies the changes, actions, or decisions needed to help reach stated personal and financial goals.

5. *Implementing needed financial changes or actions or decisions* developed in the written financial plan.

6. Periodically *reviewing, revising, and updating the financial plan* to account for changes in personal goals, financial goals, and economic conditions, and to monitor performance over time.

COLLECTING AND ASSESSING PERSONAL AND FINANCIAL DATA

The comprehensive financial planning process begins with collecting and assessing all relevant personal and financial data. Exhibit 19-1 presents a list of documents and financial data to gather in preparation for the planning process. In addition, a document locator page should be prepared listing important financial documents and where they are located. An important step in the financial planning process is the creation of current financial statements, which reveal the investor's current financial position. The current financial statements required to make an adequate assessment of the investor's financial situation are (1) statement of assets, liabilities, and net worth, (2) current-year tax projection, (3) sources and uses of funds statement, (4) statement of annual living expenses, and (5) estate tax projection.

Statement of Assets, Liabilities, and Net Worth. Also known as the personal balance sheet, the statement of assets, liabilities, and net worth begins with a listing of all assets divided into three categories.

---

[1] These six steps have been identified by The Registry of Financial Planning Practitioners as essential to the comprehensive financial planning process. The Registry is a program of the International Association for Financial Planning (IAFP), a nonprofit professional trade association. The Registry seeks to identify financial planners who meet its standards and practice the comprehensive financial planning process as their primary vocation.

EXHIBIT 19-1.   List of Documents and Financial Data to Gather

---

1. Previously prepared financial statements.
2. Personal income tax returns for the last three years.
3. Description and information on investment holdings, their cost basis, and their fair market value.
   a. Stocks.
   b. Bonds.
   c. Real estate.
   d. Precious metals.
   e. Collectibles.
   f. Other.
4. Insurance policies.
   a. Life insurance.
   b. Disability insurance.
   c. Health insurance.
   d. Homeowner's or renter's insurance.
   e. Auto insurance.
   f. Liability insurance.
5. Information on retirement plan benefits and employee benefits.
   a. IRAs, Keoghs, SEP-IRAs.
   b. Profit-sharing and pension plans.
   c. Deferred compensation plans.
   d. Section 401(K) plans.
6. Wills.
7. Trusts in which the investor is a grantor or beneficiary.
8. Important financial agreements
   a. Employment contracts.
   b. Buy–sell agreements.
   c. Agreements related to the marriage relationship:
      ▪ prenuptial,
      ▪ alimony or child support.
9. Annual living expense summary.
10. Other documents or reports that have a significant bearing on the investor's financial situation.

---

1. *Debt-based assets.* Debt-based assets consist of amounts of capital loaned to others. They include such items as checking accounts, money market funds, certificates of deposit, and corporate bonds.
2. *Equity-based assets.* Equity-based assets consist of any capital invested in an ownership position—common stocks, real estate, precious metals, and closely held business interests.
3. *Nonworking assets.* Nonworking assets are of a personal nature as opposed to an investment nature, although they may in fact be good

investments. They include personal residence, household furnishings, automobiles, and jewelry.

Once all assets are listed, all liabilities are divided into two categories and listed.

1. *Working liabilities.* The liabilities incurred to finance investment assets.
2. *Nonworking liabilities.* The liabilities incurred to finance personal assets or purchases.

In addition, it is often useful to create certain schedules that supplement the statement of assets, liabilities, and net worth. For example, supplemental schedules giving more detailed information about stock, bond, and real estate holdings are often helpful and necessary to the financial planning process. They generally contain information on the cost basis of investments, date of purchase, fair market value, and terms of outstanding indebtedness.

Personal net worth is determined by subtracting total liabilities from total assets. This is the one figure most often used to assess an individual's financial wealth. Another key figure is employed capital, a measure of the capital available to the investor for achieving his or her personal financial goals. This is the sum of debt-based plus equity-based assets minus the amount of working liabilities. An important ratio is that of liabilities to assets, computed by dividing total liabilities by total assets. It indicates the degree to which leverage is used in the individual's capital structure.

Current-Year Tax Projection. The current-year tax projection provides an estimate of federal and state income tax exposure for the current year. With an estimation of current-year income tax liabilities, the investor can better plan for income tax reduction and management. Before projecting income tax liability, the investor should be familiar with the various income tax laws that are applicable to his or her situation. However, because of the complexity of income tax laws, consultation with a professional is advisable.

Sources and Uses of Funds Statement. The sources and uses of funds statement indicate the movement of cash resources. Cash sources typically include earned income, interest, dividends, rental income, the sale of assets, and gifts, and cash uses typically include living expenses, federal, state, and social security taxes, and investments. If cash sources exceed cash uses for the year, there is a cash surplus; if cash uses exceed cash sources, there is a deficit.

Statement of Annual Living Expenses. The statement of annual living expenses shows the cost of living for one year and the amount spent on particular living expenses. Generally, house or rental payments and food and groceries constitute major elements of the statement of annual living expenses. Once annual living expenses are estimated, a budget can be developed and implemented.

Estate Tax Projection. The estate tax projection is a statement that estimates the potential tax liability of an estate at a person's death. The amount of the estate tax depends on the size of the estate, the disposition of the estate—whether by will or intestacy—and the application of estate and gift tax laws to the particular circumstances. Large estates can be subject to an estate tax rate of up to 55 percent of the fair market value of estate assets. Proper estate tax planning can provide significant savings, and a professional advisor may prove especially helpful or necessary.

IDENTIFYING PERSONAL AND FINANCIAL GOALS AND OBJECTIVES

The next step in the comprehensive financial planning process is to identify personal and financial goals and objectives. There are eleven possible goals that can be achieved during a person's lifetime; the optimal combination of goals will vary with each individual.

1. *Financial independence goal.* Financial independence is defined as the ability to maintain a desired standard of living without having to rely on earned income. Typically, a person may desire to be financially independent by age 50 with income equivalent to $5,000 per month in current purchasing power.
2. *Net worth goal.* A typical person might wish his or her net worth to grow an average 8 percent per year.
3. *Income tax reduction and management goal.* A general goal is to reduce income taxes.
4. *Debt reduction and debt management goal.* Another general goal is to reduce or eliminate debt or to reduce the cost of borrowing.
5. *Major purchase goals.* Examples of major purchases are a new house, a car or boat, a European vacation.
6. *Career and personal goals.* Examples of career and personal goals are starting a new business, becoming debt free, working on a Ph.D., taking a year off to spend time with the family.
7. *Charitable and social goals.* Many people wish to give a percentage of their income or time to charitable organizations and worthwhile causes.
8. *Education of children.* With the cost of education constantly rising, it is important to consider such expenses early.

9. *Provide financially for dependent parents, relatives, or others.* How much money will be required to support dependents?

10. *Risk management objectives.* It is important to be adequately insured against the risk of loss resulting from death, disability, medical problems, liabilities, and damage to home, automobile, and personal property.

11. *Defensive plan.* Home and living standards should be protected from law suits, severe financial difficulties, and severe economic upheaval—a stock market crash, a depression, hyperinflation.

ANALYSIS OF FINANCIAL SITUATION AND IDENTIFICATION OF FINANCIAL PROBLEMS

The analysis of one's financial situation and identification of financial problems are the heart of the financial planning process because at this step problems are identified and actions needed to achieve personal and financial goals are determined. This is accomplished within a framework of eight distinct areas of planning: (1) review of current financial position, (2) income tax planning, (3) cash flow management, (4) financial independence or retirement planning, (5) education planning, (6) investment planning, (7) risk management, and (8) estate planning.

Review of Current Financial Position

The review of an investor's financial position involves examining in detail the statement of assets, liabilities, and net worth (personal balance sheet). Each asset on the balance sheet should be divided by the total assets in order to determine its relative percentage weight to total assets; also the investor should determine the relative percentage weight of all debt-based assets, equity-based assets, and nonworking assets to total assets. It is also important to determine the relative percentage weights of all working liabilities and nonworking liabilities to total liabilities. This examination can reveal four types of problems: problems of liquidity, of inappropriate asset allocation, of diversification, and of leverage.

Liquidity. A frequent problem or weakness in current financial positions is lack of liquidity. A reserve of at least three to six months of living expenses is a reasonable buffer against unforeseen contingencies. This liquidity reserve serves three purposes.

1. *Emergency funds* to meet unexpected emergencies or expenses. These might be loss of earned income from disability or termination of employment, medical bills, major automobile or home repairs, and so on.

2. *Opportunity funds* to take advantage of unusual opportunities. For example, an investor may need $15,000 immediately to take advantage of a profitable real estate acquisition opportunity.

3. *Transactions funds* to cover day-to-day living expenses. Funds in a personal checking account are the most typical example.

Although there are exceptions, liquid assets generally fall into two categories: *cash equivalents*—checking account, savings account, short-term bank CDs, and money market funds; and *marketable securities*—publicly traded stocks, bonds, and mutual funds. In addition to reserving at least three months of living expenses in cash equivalents, an investor's portfolio should include three months of living expenses in marketable securities. This portion should be allocated toward lower-risk, lower-volatility securities.

Asset allocation. A second frequent problem is improper or inappropriate asset allocation; it generally manifests itself in three ways.

1. An investor's allocation of assets may be incongruent with his or her financial objectives. For example, an investor may have a financial objective of maximizing current income but have assets largely in investments producing little or no income.

2. Allocation of assets may not be compatible with stated risk preferences. An investor may prefer low-risk conservative investments but actually have assets in aggressive or speculative investments.

3. Assets may be insufficiently diversified. Diversification will be discussed in greater detail because it is of such importance to good financial planning that it ranks as a third common problem encountered in a review.

Diversification. The benefit of diversification is that it spreads the risk of loss over many investments, reducing the overall level of risk for the investor. If there is a cardinal rule to good financial planning, it is to diversify financial capital. Too often an investor's total wealth is concentrated in one or a few areas—in a closely held business, or in a real estate holding, or in a favored stock or security.

Academic studies indicate that the risks of insufficient diversification are significantly reduced by investing in at least fifteen to twenty different holdings. In the securities market investment capital of $75,000 to $100,000 may often be required to achieve proper diversification. But with the use of mutual funds a small investor can achieve proper diversification with investments of $1,000 or less. For proper diversification in the real estate market, it may be necessary to invest in fifteen to twenty different properties, which is beyond the means of most individuals. Investments in public real estate partnerships are typically $5,000, however, and in REITs $1,000.

Leverage. The fourth problem frequently identified during a review of current financial position is leverage. Leverage or debt problems are typically manifested in two ways.

1. *Inappropriate amount of debt.* Many individuals have excessive debt in their capital structure. This causes financial pressures and increases the risk of default on the debt. A general rule of thumb of many financial planners is that the liability-to-assets ratio should not exceed 50 percent.

2. *Too high cost of debt.* Individuals may have credit card debt with effective interest rates of 18 to 21 percent or more. Or their home may have been financed during a period of high interest rates. Attention should be given to paying off high-interest debt or refinancing at a lower rate.

Defining Level of Risk in Financial Position. Investors should classify the level of risk in their financial positions and determine whether it is congruent with their desired level of risk and stage in the life cycle. A simple procedure is to evaluate debt-based and equity-based holdings by how personal capital has been positioned: conservative, lower risk; moderate, moderate risk; aggressive, higher risk. In general, the level of risk in the financial position should reflect the investor's stage in the life cycle, which was discussed in Chapter 2.

Ownership Analysis. Another important aspect of the review of financial position is ownership analysis. The ownership of property falls into one of three categories.

1. Separate property is property interest owned in the investor's own name. No one else has an ownership in this interest.

2. Joint property is property owned with one or more other parties. A joint owner may or may not be a marriage partner. Joint ownership takes two forms.
   a. Tenants in common. The joint tenant's ownership passes at death according to the instructions of the will.
   b. Joint tenants with right of survivorship. A joint tenant's interest in property passes to the surviving joint tenant automatically at death. The property interest does not pass under the will, but by operation of law.

3. Community property is acquired during marriage by spouses domiciled in a community property state. Community property resembles joint ownership in many respects, but there are important distinctions.

How property is owned can have an important bearing on income tax planning, estate planning, defensive planning, and the rights of marital partners in property. For married couples, the liquidity reserve (three to six months of living expenses) should be held in joint tenancy with right of survivorship. For those with large estates, that is, taxable estates in excess of $600,000, the ownership of assets can be very important in estate planning. Proper estate planning with respect to asset ownership can help assure that avoidable estate taxes are eliminated, thereby reducing the total estate tax liability.

Asset ownership also has important considerations with respect to defensive planning, that is, protecting assets and living standards against the risk of law suits, malpractice or creditor action, severe financial difficulties, and severe economic upheaval. The investor can guard against such contingencies by holding assets in the name of a spouse or by creating trusts, such as an education trust.

Tax Planning

Effects of Taxation on Investment Growth. Because taxation represents a major constraint, one strategy for accumulating wealth over time is to utilize investment methods for deferring taxation. The least desirable method to accumulate capital is to use methods whereby both the contributions to an investment fund and the investment earnings on the fund are subject to taxation. Exhibit 19-2 dramatically illustrates the different outcomes that an investor might expect using three ways of accumulating capital. As the chart plainly shows, an investor who can make capital contributions free of tax and can compound investment earnings free of tax is able to attain a much larger amount of capital than would otherwise be possible.

Tax Advantage Investments. Investments that are given certain tax advantages or tax incentives under our tax laws should be considered in overall tax-planning efforts. Investments in real estate, oil and gas, and equipment leasing are examples. Recent changes in tax law have done away with many of the tax shelters that were formerly available for such investments, but significant tax benefits which can enhance investments with economic merit are still available.

Real estate is by far the most significant recipient of capital invested for tax advantages; the major benefit is tax-sheltered cash flow. For example, a public real estate partnership may generate a partially or fully sheltered cash return of 6 to 8 percent or more for several years plus the benefit of potential capital appreciation on the properties in the partnership.

Direct investments by an individual in real estate offer additional tax benefits. For example, an individual who invests directly in rental properties and actively manages the properties may take a tax write-off of up to $25,000 per year within certain limitations. A tax loss in real estate is one

---

EXHIBIT 19-2. Effects of Taxation on Investment Growth

Assumptions
1. Growth–interest rate: 10.00%
2. Federal marginal income tax bracket: 28.00%
3. Annual investment reflected in columns 1 through 3: $2,000
4. Single investment reflected in columns 4 through 6: $10,000
5. Columns 1 and 4: No taxability of principal or interest (e.g., qualified plan)
6. Columns 2 and 5: Taxability of principal payments (e.g., tax-deferred annuity)
7. Columns 3 and 6: Taxability of principal and interest (e.g., CD)

	$2,000 Annual Outlay			$10,000 Single Outlay		
Year	(1)	(2)	(3)	(4)	(5)	(6)
1	$ 2,200	$ 1,584	$ 1,544	$ 11,000	$ 7,920	$ 7,718
5	13,431	9,670	8,913	16,105	11,596	10,193
10	35,062	25,245	21,531	25,973	18,675	14,430
15	69,899	50,328	39,394	41,722	30,076	20,429
20	126,005	90,724	64,683	67,275	48,438	28,922
25	216,364	155,782	100,485	108,347	78,010	40,945
30	361,887	260,559	151,171	174,494	125,636	57,966

Source: This format was created by International Financial Data Systems, Atlanta, Ga.

of few that can be used to offset other income such as earned income or interest and dividend income.

Tax law allows a like-kind exchange of real estate without recognition of taxable gain. For example, the owner of appreciated real estate may be able to trade it for real estate of like kind without recognizing the appreciation for tax purposes. (For a discussion of other tax-planning benefits associated with real estate investments, see Chapter 10.)

Income Tax Deductions. To minimize income taxes, investors should use all allowable income tax deductions. By carefully planning tax-deductible expenses, the investor can maximize the value of such tax savings.

One basic tax-planning strategy is to accelerate and lump certain deductible expenses into one tax year in order to realize greater tax benefits. For example, some investors reap current tax year savings by accelerating to the end of the current year the payment of charitable contributions and other deductible items that would otherwise be paid later. If an investor in a 28 percent tax bracket accelerates the payment of deductible expenses amounting to $1,000 before the year's end, he or she will save $280 in current-year taxes. Some investors combine deductible medical expenses into one year whenever possible in order to exceed the 7.5 percent of adjusted gross income limitation on the deduction of medical expenses.

A second basic tax-planning strategy is to defer income whenever possible. For example, an appreciated investment holding may be sold in January instead of December in order to reduce the recognition of income and taxes for the current year.

Generally, to recognize the opportunities for planning income taxes, investors must be knowledgeable about income tax laws; in addition the most experienced investors may also consult with a professional income tax advisor.

Cash Flow Management

Review. Management of cash flow begins with a review of the current sources and uses of funds statement and an examination of the various sources of income: earned income, interest, dividends, rents, gifts, and sale of assets. Typically, the largest source of funds for most individuals is earned income, a fact which points out two important considerations.

First, investors need to protect themselves, their source of earned income, usually with disability income insurance. Second, investors need to reduce reliance on earned income for maintaining their standard of living. The ultimate goal is to achieve financial independence by developing additional sources of capital and income, typically through retirement plans, savings, and investment planning. The investment capital may be either income-producing or capable of becoming income-producing at the appropriate time. Sources of income can also be increased by repositioning investment capital into assets with higher current yield, but only within acceptable risk parameters.

Next, investors should examine how they use their funds, including the percentage of total funds spent on living expenses, taxes, savings and investments, and other items. The rate of savings should be compared to total sources of income. A general rule of thumb is to allocate at least 10 percent of total sources of income to savings and investment.

The investor should review his or her major living expenses and discretionary expenses. This information can form a basis for creating a budget to improve the management of cash expenses. Exhibit 19-3 is a sample budget form. Budgeting living expenses and maintaining the budget are fundamental to successful financial planning.

Unfortunately, not everyone ends the year with a cash surplus. An investor who projects a cash deficit should consider the following alternatives.

1. Increase sources of funds:
   - increase earned income,
   - increase interest,
   - increase dividends,

EXHIBIT 19-3.   Form for an Annual Personal Budget

CATEGORY	1. Monthly Budget	2. Jan.	3. Feb.	M...	12. Nov.	13. Dec.	14. This Yr. Total	15. Last Yr. Total	16. This Yr. Est.
Deposits in savings accounts									
Vacation (or other) fund									
State Income Tax									
Federal Income Tax									
F.I.C.A. (Social Security)									
Property tax on home									
Medical insurance									
Life insurance									
Disability insurance									
Home insurance									
Auto insurance									
Home mortgage or rent									
Auto Licenses									
Church contributions									
Other contributions									
Domestic help									
F.I.C.A. for domestic help									
Electricity									
Water									
Gas									
Heating fuel									
Telephone									
Home maintenance & repair									
Gardener									
Garden supplies									
Pest control									
Supermarket									
Pharmacy									
Cleaners & laundry									
Clothing									
Bank credit cards									
Gasoline, etc.									
Auto repairs									
Auto club									
Local transportation & cabs									
Membership clubs									
Education									
Doctors & dentists									
Subscriptions									
Entertainment (est.)									
Liquor									
Safe deposit box									
Tax accountant									
Attorney fees (est.)									
Payments on other loans									
Cash gifts to children for birthdays & Christmas									
TOTALS									

Source: Richard K. Rifenbark, *How to Beat the Salary Trap—8 Steps to Financial Independence* (New York: McGraw-Hill, 1978), p. 59.

- increase rents,
- increase gifts,
- increase sales of assets,
- reduce the cost of borrowing through refinancing,
- borrow funds, increase debt.
2. Reduce uses of funds:
   - reduce living expenses,
   - reduce taxes if possible,
   - reduce repayment of debt,
   - reduce savings and investment,
   - reduce other uses of funds.

By quantifying the expected deficit and making informed decisions about how to decrease it, investors can reduce the potential damage to their financial condition.

Record Keeping. Keeping a record of all receipts and disbursements of income is helpful in a number of ways. It identifies the sources of funds and, more importantly, how they are spent. Record keeping enhances the investor's ability to manage cash flow wisely and may reveal potential problems, prompting the investor to take corrective action before the problems fully develop. Good records allow the investor to qualify income tax deductions that might otherwise be forgotten and to substantiate the deductions in the event of an IRS audit. They also allow the investor to measure performance over time, such as annual growth rate in income and living expenses.

Five-Year Projections of Current Financial Statements. Once current financial statements have been created and carefully reviewed, five-year projections should be made to indicate how the investor's financial condition might be expected to change over time.

A five-year projection of assets, liabilities, and net worth includes estimates of the following.

- Additions to net worth from savings and investments (including qualified retirement plans).
- Increases or decreases in specific asset values over time. For example, an investor's personal residence may be expected to increase in value by 6 percent per year, and the values of common stock investments are expected to increase by 10 percent per year.
- Amortization of mortgages and other liabilities over time.

A five-year projection of federal income taxes includes estimates of

- increases in earned income,

- changes in other sources of taxable income,
- deductions for home mortgage interest, charitable contributions, and other itemized deductions,
- contributions to IRA or Keogh accounts.

A five-year projection of sources and uses of funds statement includes estimates of

- changes in earned income,
- changes in other sources of income,
- increases in living expenses,
- changes in taxes,
- changes in other uses of funds,
- the cumulative effect of annual cash surpluses or deficits.

These projections provide a reasonable basis for examining expected increases over time in personal net worth, income tax liabilities, and cash surplus or deficit. In addition, these projections allow investors to anticipate the downstream impact of investments and future commitments of capital. "What if" projections (i.e., sensitivity analyses) may help investors make informed decisions about future allocations of financial resources. These projections are particularly important in deciding on investments in real estate properties, which generally require a long-term commitment of funds.

Financial Independence and Retirement Planning

Planning for financial independence and retirement is particularly critical. As an investor grows older, earned income tends to reach a peak and then decline. It is important to plan adequately for such a decline so that desired living standards are not impaired.

Most individuals today are concerned that they may not have enough financial resources in their later years for a secure and comfortable life. This concern is well founded in light of the following statistics.

- Only two out of a hundred people reaching retirement age are financially independent.
- Seventy-five percent of retirees depend on social security or relatives and friends as their only source of income or support.
- Total liquid assets per capita of persons sixty-five years of age and over are approximately $4,000, according to the National Council on Aging.[2]

[2]"Financial Strategies for Financial Planners," *Financial Strategies and Concepts*, Fall 1987, p. 6.

These statistics demonstrate the important need for a lifetime of savings in order to supplement retirement benefits.

Most people have a goal of achieving financial independence at some time; investors should consider their financial independence or retirement-planning objectives in terms of monthly income needed by a certain age. What is a reasonable and realistic goal depends on each individual.

A primary consideration in planning for financial independence and retirement is the impact of inflation on purchasing power over time. Exhibit 19-4 shows how inflation affects the increasing dollar quantity required to

---

EXHIBIT 19-4. Effect of Inflation on Purchasing Power

It would be shortsighted to overlook the effect of inflationary pressures in projecting the requirements for financial independence. In this exhibit figures have been based on a 6.00 percent rate of inflation. The effect of inflation at this level on a financial independence goal of $3,000 per month is indicated by the following table.

Year	Dollar Quantity Required	Fixed-Income Equivalent
1	$3,000	$3,000
2	3,180	2,830
3	3,371	2,670
4	3,573	2,519
5	3,787	2,376
6	4,015	2,242
7	4,256	2,115
8	4,511	1,995
9	4,782	1,882
10	5,068	1,776
11	5,373	1,675
12	5,695	1,580
13	6,037	1,491
14	6,399	1,407
15	6,783	1,327
16	7,190	1,252
17	7,621	1,181
18	8,078	1,114
19	8,563	1,051
20	9,077	992
21	9,621	935
22	10,199	882
23	10,811	833
24	11,459	785
25	12,147	741

Source: This format was created by International Financial Data Systems, Atlanta, Ga.

maintain a given level of current purchasing power. The exhibit also shows how inflation causes purchasing power at a fixed-income level to decline over time.

The Elements in the Financial Independence Equation. There are three elements in the financial independence equation: the saving element, the time element, and the yield element. The relation is

Sufficient savings + sufficient time + sufficient yield = financial independence

The savings element is basic to financial independence. Without setting aside savings in some form, there is no opportunity for capital accumulation. As noted earlier, a good objective is to save 10 percent of income, which is generally sufficient for the investor to enjoy a comfortable life in later years. Time also plays an important role in achieving financial independence. The sooner a program of disciplined savings is begun, the more likely will financial independence be achieved; more time provides more opportunity for funds to compound and accumulate. Yield is the third element of the financial independence equation. Basically, the higher the yield on investment capital, the faster it will grow. Time and yield interact and determine the investor's rate of progress toward achieving financial independence.

Financial Independence Calculation: The Capitalization Method. There are several methods of calculating progress toward and requirements for achieving financial independence. A relatively simple and straightforward calculation technique is the capitalization method. By this method the amount of capital needed for financial independence beginning at a certain age is determined. Then sources of capital are estimated. If projected sources of capital exceed the estimated capital required, the individual is on track toward achieving financial independence. If projected sources of capital are less than the estimate, the amount of monthly savings needed to be on track can be established. Exhibit 19-5 provides an example of the capitalization method.

Accumulation of Retirement Capital. Tax-planning strategies can play an important role in reducing the level of taxation on capital. A principal strategy is to utilize retirement plans to reduce the exposure of retirement capital to taxation. Two primary retirement-planning arrangements are individual retirement accounts (IRAs) and qualified retirement accounts.

Education Planning

Next to buying a home, the second most major financial investment that the average American family makes is educating their children. Putting

---

EXHIBIT 19-5. Financial Independence Calculation: Capitalization Method

---

Assumptions
1. Monthly purchasing power desired in current dollars: $4,000
2. Inflation rate: 6.00%
3. Age attained at point of financial independence: 55
4. Number of years in which to attain objective: 30
5. Employed capital less certain qualified plan balances: $50,000
6. Growth rate on employed capital: 10.00%
7. Capitalization rate: 10.00%

Monthly income needed at age of financial independence	$ 22,974
Capital equivalent of purchasing power needed	$2,756,876
Less:	
Amount to which employed capital could grow	$ 872,470
Capital equivalent of qualified retirement plans	184,680
Capital equivalent of social security benefit	95,760
Net amount still needed or overage (−)	$1,604,966
Monthly payment required to accumulate capital at 10.00%	$ 710

Source: This format was created by International Financial Data Systems, Atlanta, Ga.

two children through a four-year undergraduate program might be compared to buying a new car every year for eight years. Families that plan for this expense will most likely be able to deal with it more successfully.

Exhibit 19-6 shows an estimate of the cost of sending two children to college assuming current costs of $8,000 per year per child and cost increases of 8 percent per year.

It often makes sense from a tax-planning standpoint to shift income within the family in order to reduce total taxes paid by the family. Of course, there may be valid nontax reasons for not shifting income to children or for limiting the amount of income shifted. Intrafamily income shifting is one way of planning for educational expenses.

Outright Gifts of Income-Producing Property. An outright gift of income-producing property is generally sufficient to shift the taxable income generated by the property to the donee. For example, if an investor were to gift a child $10,000 of XYZ stock which paid a yearly dividend of $1,000, the child would be taxed on the dividend income (subject to "kiddie tax" limitations). Outright gifts of income-producing property to a child are the easiest and most flexible income-shifting strategy to implement, but the method may not be desirable for children who cannot maturely handle financial resources.

Uniform Gifts to Minors Act. The Uniform Gifts to Minors Act allows a parent to gift property to a child without the child's acquiring control dur-

---

EXHIBIT 19-6.   Summary of Education Cost Estimates

Assumptions
1. First child (A) will start college in ten years.
2. Second child (B) will start college in fourteen years.
3. College costs (currently $8,000 per year) will increase 8 percent per year.

Year	Child	Current Dollars	Future Dollar
10	A	$8,000	$17,271
11	A	8,000	18,653
12	A	8,000	20,145
13	A	8,000	21,757
14	B	8,000	23,497
15	B	8,000	25,377
16	B	8,000	27,408
17	B	8,000	29,600
Gross need:		$64,000	$183,708
Net need:			$183,708
Monthly payment needed if funds earn 10.00 percent			$904.86
Lump sum needed today if funds earn 10.00 percent			$18,471

Source: This format was created by International Financial Data Systems, Atlanta, Ga.

ing his or her minority. Under this act a custodianship is created for the benefit of the minor child. A custodian is appointed to manage the property gifted to the child; the child is taxed on the income produced by the gifted property. Any property remaining in the custodianship when the child reaches legal age must be turned over to the child.

An advantage of using a custodianship under the Uniform Gifts to Minors Act is that a fiduciary income tax return need not be filed. A disadvantage is that the provisions of the custodianship are governed by statute; therefore, this mechanism provides less flexibility than a trust.

Investment Planning

Will Rogers once said, "I'm not as concerned with the return on my money as I am with the return of my money." Many times an investment opportunity is missed because an investor is not financially prepared to respond to the opportunity or to evaluate it adequately. At other times an investor may recognize a good investment opportunity, may have the financial means to participate in it, and may have evaluated it to his or her satisfaction, but must still decline to participate because he or she lacks the time to manage and supervise the investment property. More often, investors are unsure about how their investment portfolio should be composed. In order to arrive at workable solutions, investors should have an investment plan and model.

The Asset Allocation Model. The asset allocation model is a framework for allocating investment capital among different asset categories. It is an especially useful tool for ensuring diversification of investment capital. In its basic form assets are assigned to different categories such as the following.

1. Cash equivalents: money market funds, short-term certificates of deposit, short-term treasury securities.
2. Debt-based assets: intermediate and longer-term corporate and government bonds, notes, and mortgages receivable.
3. Equity-based assets: stocks and stock mutual funds.
4. Real-estate-based assets.
5. Precious-metals-based assets and other assets.

Within the different categories other classifications can be made, such as liquid assets or nonliquid assets and domestic-based assets or international-based assets.

As an example, a model portfolio might allocate assets along the following lines:

Asset Category	Percentage Allocation
Cash equivalents	20
Debt-based assets	25
Equity-based assets	25
Real estate	20
Precious metals and other assets	10
	100

Such a portfolio would offer a degree of protection against a collapse in a financial market since declines in one asset area would tend to be offset by increases or relative stability in other asset areas.

The asset allocation model is flexible in that financial resources can be allocated differently, depending on financial objectives and changing economic conditions over time.

The Investment Pyramid. A useful tool for making asset allocation decisions is the investment pyramid, as shown in Exhibit 19-7. Unlike the asset

EXHIBIT 19-7.   The Investment Pyramid

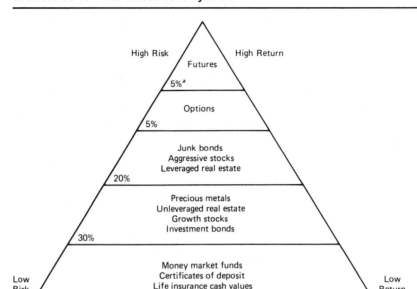

ᵃThe percents are hypothetical percentage allocations of investment capital.

allocation model, which bases asset decisions on the need for appropriate diversification, the investment pyramid bases asset decisions on the management of investment risk. The financial planning concept illustrated by the investment pyramid is that an investor should allocate the foundation of his or her investment capital among low-risk–low-return assets and build up to higher-risk–higher-return assets. Then, as the investor progresses through the investment pyramid, the percentage of total investment capital allocated to higher-risk–higher-return assets becomes less. This strategy helps to protect the investor from positioning too high a percentage of investment capital in investments with a significant potential for loss.

The Role of Real Estate in Asset Allocation Decisions. Historically, real estate has offered attractive investment returns. Exhibit 19-8 compares annualized returns on real estate to those of stocks, bonds, and cash equivalents over the fifteen-year period of 1971 to 1985. But real estate investments can also be used to reduce the level of volatility in a mixed-asset

EXHIBIT 19-8. A comparison of the Nominal Returns of Real Estate with Those of Stocks, Bonds, and Cash Equivalents for the Fifteen Years Ended December 31, 1985

Year	Real Estate	Stocks	Bonds	Cash Equivalents
1971	9.2%	14.3%	10.6%	4.4%
1972	7.5	19.0	8.1	3.8
1973	7.5	−14.8	2.3	6.9
1974	7.2	−26.5	0.2	8.0
1975	5.7	37.3	12.3	5.8
1976	9.3	23.6	15.6	5.1
1977	10.5	−7.4	3.0	5.2
1978	15.9	6.5	1.2	7.1
1979	20.6	18.5	2.3	10.0
1980	17.9	32.5	3.1	11.4
1981	16.6	−5.0	7.2	14.2
1982	9.3	21.6	31.1	11.0
1983	13.3	22.5	8.0	8.9
1984	12.9	6.2	15.0	9.9
1985	9.8	31.7	21.3	7.4

ANNUALIZED RETURNS

	Real Estate	Stocks	Bonds	Cash Equivalents
Last three years	12.0%	19.6%	11.6%	8.7%
Last five years	12.4	14.6	16.2	10.2
Last ten years	13.6	14.2	10.4	9.0
Last fifteen years	11.5	10.4	9.1	7.9
Standard deviation of annual return (15 years)	2.4%	16.6%	8.5%	1.4%

Sources: Real estate: FRC property index for 1978–1985 and Frank Russell Company con-mingled-fund data for 1971–1977. Stocks: S & P 500-stock index. Bonds: Shearson Lehman government–corporate bond index for 1973–1985. A proxy for this index based on Salomon Brothers high-grade corporate bond index for 1971–1972. Cash equivalents: 30-day U.S. Treasury bills.

portfolio. Exhibit 19-9 compares the stability of annualized returns for stock, bonds, and real estate over the fifteen-year period of 1971 to 1985.

Real-estate-based assets offer an important element of diversification and potentially enhanced investment returns for the individual investor. A study by Bailard, Biehl, and Kaiser concludes that over the twenty-year period from 1965 to 1985, a well-diversified portfolio including 20 percent real estate would have outperformed the Standard and Poor's 500-stock index and the average performance of professionally managed balanced

EXHIBIT 19-9.   Stability of Annualized Returns: 1971–1985

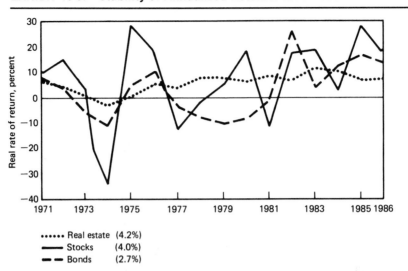

••••• Real estate (4.2%)
—— Stocks   (4.0%)
– – Bonds   (2.7%)

Sources: Frank Russell Company, S & P 500-stock index, Shearson Lehman government–corporate bond index, Salomon Brothers high-grade corporate bond index.

stock and bond portfolios, as shown in Exhibit 19-10.[3] These studies conclude that it is prudent to include real estate investments as part of the investment portfolio.

Risk Management

In developing a personal portfolio, the investor may seek other methods of risk management in combination with those discussed in Chapter 8. The purpose of these more personal tools is to help protect the investor against the risk of loss, whether to life, health, or property, or the risk of liabilities resulting from the investor's actions or those of people under his or her authority. Among these methods are life insurance and disability planning.

---

[3]The investment performance summary compares average returns over a specified period of time for the U.S. stock market (Standard and Poor's 500-stock index), the average performance of balanced stock and bond portfolio managers (SEI Corporation median), and a diversified portfolio including equal weighing of U.S. stocks, foreign stocks, U.S. corporate and government bonds, real estate and Treasury bills (Bailard, Biehl, and Kaiser). There are other factors that must be considered when comparing different types of investments, such as relative degree of risk, liquidity, marketability, whether the investment is insured, and quality of management.

EXHIBIT 19-10. Advantages of a Diversified Portfolio

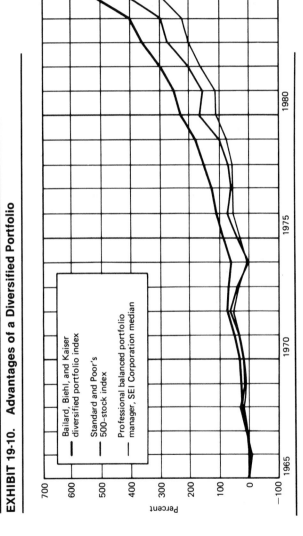

Source: Bailard, Biehl, and Kaiser Inc., San Mateo, Calif.

Life Insurance. There are many different kinds of life insurance available, but they fall into two basic groups. Whole life insurance is designed to be permanent. The consumer generally pays a fixed premium for the coverage, part of which builds the cash surrender value of the policy, and the rest reflects the cost of the insurance coverage. Therefore, whole life insurance is really partly an investment (in the form of cash surrender value) and partly an expense for protection. Term insurance is not considered permanent. Instead of fixed premiums, the consumer pays increasing premiums over time. The entire premium goes for insurance protection; term insurance has no cash surrender value. There are also many hybrid varieties, which have characteristics of the two types.

In general, life insurance should at least provide for the survivor income needs of spouse and dependent children, taking into account other sources of income they may have at the investor's death. With large estates life insurance is sometimes used as a strategy for the transfer of wealth at the lowest possible transfer cost, as well as providing for survivor income. An irrevocable life insurance trust makes it possible to exclude life insurance proceeds from being taxed in the estate of the decedent.

Disability Planning. The permanent disability of the principal income provider often causes the family a much greater financial hardship than had the person died. Not only must the family support itself, but it must also support the disabled person. Many families fail to insure adequately against the risk of disability.

For a person who depends on earned income to maintain his or her standard of living, a general rule of thumb is to purchase disability insurance that would provide a monthly benefit equal to 60 percent of the income currently earned; a breadwinner earning $4,000 per month should have disability insurance of $2,400 per month. In the event of a complete disability, either physical or mental, other questions present themselves, such as who should handle business affairs, make investment decisions, and provide for the family. A durable power of attorney is a good planning mechanism for dealing with the contingency of physical or mental disability.

Estate Planning

Effective estate planning has two primary objectives. First, the estate plan should accomplish testamentary objectives, which usually are to provide adequately for the surviving members of the family and, for many investors, to denote property to charitable organizations and to others. Second, the estate plan should minimize exposure of the estate to estate taxation. Without proper planning, not only may the accumulated assets of a lifetime be seriously and unnecessarily depleted by estate taxes, but the beneficiaries of an estate may not share in it as the owner had intended.

Estimate of Estate Value. The first step in estate planning is to estimate the value of an estate. A quick estimate can be made by adding total assets plus life insurance proceeds included in the estate, minus total liabilities, final expenses, and charitable bequests.

The Federal Estate Tax. The federal estate tax is based on unified estate and gift tax rates, so that the same tax rates are used to determine both estate taxes and gift taxes. When a person dies, all property in which he or she has any interest is included in the estate. Moreover, certain gifts made by the decedent during life may be added back into the estate for purposes of determining the estate tax. From the gross estate are subtracted liabilities and other deductions to arrive at an adjusted gross estate. Other deductions are then allowed, and what is left is the sum of the taxable estate. The unified estate and gift tax rates are then applied to arrive at a tentative estate tax.

The tentative estate taxes that would be imposed on estates of different sizes are as follows.

Size of Estate	Tentative Estate Tax	Estate Tax Rate (Percent)
$ 100,000	$ 23,800	30
$ 500,000	$ 155,800	37
$1,000,000	$ 345,800	41
$3,000,000	$1,290,800	55

In certain instances it may be possible to defer the payment of the estate tax over a lengthy period of time, but in general the estate tax must be paid nine months after the death of the decedent. Since most estates are not readily liquid, a forced sale of estate assets may be necessary to pay the estate tax bill. After payment of the estate tax a reduced estate is left for the heirs, but with proper planning literally thousands of dollar in estate taxes, sometimes hundreds of thousands of dollars, can be avoided.

Unified Credit and Marital Deduction Planning. A basic concept in effective estate planning is wise use of the unified credit, which is given to every person by the tax law. This credit can be used to offset estate and gift taxes. Remember that a credit can be applied directly against a tax liability. Thus, a unified credit of $100,000 would reduce estate taxes by $100,000. The unified credit and the equivalent amount of property that are allowed by the unified credit to pass free of estate taxes are

Unified Credit	Equivalent Amount of Property
$192,800	$600,000

In other words, up to $600,000 of a decedent's estate could pass completely free of federal estate taxes. Obviously, from the standpoint of minimizing the estate tax, it makes good sense to utilize the unified credit, but maximum use of it should not be at the expense of other estate-planning objectives.

The estate tax law allows for an unlimited marital deduction, which means that a decedent spouse can leave his or her entire estate to the surviving spouse and, no matter how large the estate, no estate tax will be imposed. When the surviving spouse dies, without having remarried, whatever property is in the spouse's estate, including property that was inherited under the marital deduction at the death of the predeceasing spouse, is subject to estate taxes.

Coordination of the unified credit with the marital deduction makes significant estate tax savings possible, both in terms of the amount of estate taxes imposed on a couple's estate and in terms of the time value of deferring estate taxes at the death of the predeceasing spouse. Conceptually, the planning strategy operates in the following manner. At the death of the predeceasing spouse, estate assets are first used to fund the unified credit. Thus, up to $600,000 of estate property would pass under the unified credit. This property can be passed in any manner other than what qualifies as the marital deduction for the surviving spouse. For example, the property could go into a trust for the children or into a trust in which the surviving spouse has a right to income for life, a right to principal to the extent necessary for adequate support, and a special power of appointment to delegate the property at his or her death to anyone other than the estate or the creditors of the estate.

If the property in the estate exceeds the amount allowed to pass under the unified credit, the remaining property can be given to the surviving spouse under the marital deduction. On the death of the predeceasing spouse, no matter how large the estate, there would be no estate tax.

Estimate of Ultimate Estate. It is important to realize that even a relatively modest rate of growth in estate size can result in significant estate taxes. An estate that is currently estimated at $250,000 and grows 6 percent per year would be $2,571,429 in forty years, and would ultimately be subject to a 50 percent marginal estate tax rate under current laws.

Other Estate-Planning Strategies. For individuals with estates of more than $600,000, there are other estate-planning strategies that should be considered. These are basic techniques for reducing the size of an estate, thus reducing the amount of the estate subject to estate taxes.

Annual gifting program. A provision of the tax law, known as the annual exclusion, allows for gifts of up to $10,000 per donee per year without any gift tax. In addition to removing the gifted property from the estate, the provision also removes from the estate any subsequent appreciation in the gifted property. If a spouse joins in a gift, up to $20,000 per year to each donee can be given without any gift tax.

Property should be gifted only if the investor can afford to gift. If there is a possibility that the property might be needed for personal support, the investor would be wise not to gift the property. Otherwise, it makes good sense for estate tax savings to utilize an annual gifting program to remove property out of the estate.

Inter vivos gifting of the unified credit. In some situations it may make sense to give large amounts of property to children during life. Generally, gifts in excess of the annual exclusion ($10,000 per donee) are subject to a gift tax. However, the taxpayer's unified credit is applied to the gift tax so that there is no actual out-of-pocket tax on the gift during life until the taxpayer's unified credit is fully used up. Thus, a donor may gift up to $600,000 plus the annual exclusion amounts to donees without having an out-of-pocket gift tax.

Two preconditions should be verified before making large gifts of this nature. First, as with annual exclusion gifts, the donor should be sure that the property he or she anticipates giving will not later be needed for personal support. Second, the property that is gifted should be property expected to appreciate substantially during the remaining years of the donor's life. The following example illustrates the benefits of this strategy. A father gifts property to a child valued at $600,000. Some years later the father dies. At the time of the father's death the property has a fair market value of $2,000,000. By making the gift during life, the father has been able to exclude $1,400,000 from his estate. At a 50 percent estate tax rate, this is an estate tax savings of $700,000.

IMPLEMENTING STRATEGIES, RECOMMENDATIONS, AND SOLUTIONS

The next step in the comprehensive financial planning process is to implement recommended actions. The investor should begin this stage with an action plan that summarizes the recommendations developed by the planning process. The action plan should have specific recommendations for dealing with the factors outlined in Exhibit 19-11.

The plan of action should have specific recommendations for which implementation is feasible. Financial and time constraints may limit the feasibility of implementing all recommendations; therefore, the implementation must follow a priority schedule. In general, needs for adequate insurance coverage and liquidity reserves should be addressed first. Then asset allocation decisions should be made. Certain items, such as IRA contributions, may have time deadlines within which action must be taken. Other items will need to be followed up on over time. The plan of action

---

EXHIBIT 19-11. Factors to Be Covered in the Action Plan

Current financial position
- Liquidity needs.
- Diversification need.
- Leverage problems.
- Asset reallocation needs for income, capital growth and so on.

Measures to reduce income tax
- Use of qualified retirement plan arrangements.
- Use of tax deferred and tax advantage investments including real estate.
- Use of tax deductions and tax credits.
- Use of income shifting and deferral or acceleration of income and expense items.

Cash flow management
- Use of budgeting and record keeping.
- Establishment of savings goal.
- Recommended asset sales.
- Financing and refinancing needs.

Financial independence and retirement planning
- Definition of financial independence goal.
- Use of retirement planning.
- Determination of savings needed and required yield to reach financial independence goal.

Education planning
- Definition of education costs.
- Use of education-funding strategies.

Investment planning
- Developing an asset allocation model.
- Recommendations on specific investments, taking into account needs for liquidity, diversification, income, risk tolerance, leverage, income tax reduction, education planning, financial independence goals, and asset ownership.

Risk management
- Definition of survivor income needs and disability income need.
- Specific recommendations on type and amount of life insurance, disability insurance, and health, homeowner's, auto, and excess liability insurance.

Estate planning
- Determination of potential estate tax liability.
- Review of wills and trusts, asset ownership, and needed actions.
- Use of lifetime and testamentary gifting strategies.

---

should provide a checklist format for dating implementation of certain recommendations and making notations on time scheduling, priorities, and so on.

PERIODIC REVIEW AND REVISION

The written financial plan should be reviewed periodically and revised if need be. An overall review of the plan on an annual basis should suffice, but investment positions should be monitored more frequently, preferably each quarter, especially publicly traded securities. Review of personal income tax exposure should be undertaken in the latter part of the tax year in order to take advantage of year-end opportunities for tax planning. A review of the written financial plan may also be necessary should there be significant changes in economic conditions, tax laws, or personal financial position.

Current financial statements should be updated at least annually and compared to previous statements for purposes of measuring performance over time and comparing expected results with actual results. The periodic review and revision of the financial plan allows the investor to stay on tract toward achieving his or her personal and financial objectives and keeps the plan adjusted to changing conditions.

SUMMARY

This chapter examines the process of developing and implementing a strategy for a personal portfolio containing real estate properties. The process of comprehensive financial planning is defined as six distinct steps: 1) collecting and assessing all relevant personal and financial data; 2) identifying both financial and personal goals and objectives; 3) analyzing the financial situation and identifying financial problems; 4) developing a written financial plan; 5) implementing needed financial changes, action and decisions; and 6) periodically reviewing, revising, and updating the financial plan. Each step is necessary for developing a successful plan and portfolio for achieving the personal financial goals of the investor over time.

This process is difficult for some individuals because developing a personal portfolio with real estate forces divergence from the conventional financial wisdom that all the attributes of an investment can be systematically compressed within two variables: return and risk. Also, although most individuals do not define wealth accumulation or maximization as the transcendent life goal, most individuals do state a desire to be financially independent by the time they retire. This chapter provides a framework for achieving such a goal and examines the role of real estate within such a broad personal framework.

20

THE REAL ESTATE INVESTMENT OUTLOOK

Real estate investments are for the long term. In this book, a time horizon ranging from five to fifteen years is recommended. Real estate investment projects are also related to the life cycle of the individual investor and the portfolio management problems of the institutional investor. However, the primary focus up to this chapter has been on the analysis of specific projects and an ownership cycle that is usually shorter than the remaining economic life of the improvements to the project itself. This text emphasizes that decision analysis should focus in part on a study of real estate market cycles, which operate independently of the business cycles. Parts 1 through 4 develop a method for strategic planning and decision making in real estate investing and tools for analyzing various types of property.

We recognize that managers of large portfolios and developers and investors in satellite new towns and large industrial projects must be future planners in the true sense of the word. The study of such periodicals as *Science News*, *The Technology Review*, and *Futurist* and the works of the Hudson Institute and the Rand Corporation, among others, are recommended for this purpose.

Unfortunately, the year 2000 and the twenty-first century are beyond the scope of this chapter. Although real estate as an asset is highly illiquid, real estate decision making takes place in a very dynamic short-run environment. Therefore, we will limit the discussion of the outlook for real estate investing to the next five years.

Assuming a five-year time horizon for investment decisions (current economic and social uncertainty precludes longer-range predictions), what philosophy should guide the investor's strategy, goals, and objectives and their implementation? All real estate investments are based on forecasts and projections, so we are forced to adopt an outlook about the future and be flexible in response to changing economic conditions and competitive threats. This chapter provides an investment outlook for the next few years, in order to establish a scenario that will enable readers to develop their own real estate investment outlooks. The idea is to predict the economic environment of real estate investment decision making within a constitutional culture that takes the rights of capitalism and democracy seriously. The first step is to consider global attitudes.

GLOBAL ATTITUDES

The French newspaper *Le Monde* commented in March 1987:

> Is the United States losing its place as the world leader? In 1986 its external trade deficit broke all records at $170 billion due to inadequate industrial exports as well as excessive imports. There are entire sectors of the domestic consumer economy—television receivers and appliances, for example— whose disappearance seems inevitable. We must hope that the United States can regain its equilibrium without resorting to a massive devaluation of the dollar, which to really be effective would have to reach half its current rate against the franc.

Consider this statement from the Japanese press (from *The World Press Review*, March 1987).

> It is ironic that Japan's ability to withstand sacrifice brings criticisms which are rooted in recognition of the troubled Japan–United States economic relationship. The gargantuan trade imbalance between the two is attributable to mismanagement in the United States, especially the uncontrollable federal budget deficit. . . . The real cause of the deficits in the U.S. economy is theirs—especially personal domestic consumption. No nation in the world has yet succeeded in reducing its external deficits without holding down domestic demand. . . . This means that Americans must accept a decline in their standard of living to relieve the U.S. economic woes. . . . The country which has played the role of unchallenged leader of the postwar world must now move from its catatonia, admit its mistakes and seek the initiative to correct its problems.

NATIONAL CONSIDERATIONS

Inflation

In 1982, when the first edition of this book was published, the most important uncertainty for the subsequent five years was the rate of inflation. In 1988, following the stock market peak in late August 1987, more than a trillion U.S. dollars of market value in paper assets vanished. Previously, consumers had lowered their savings to less than 3 percent because appreciating assets appeared likely to meet future needs without diversions from current income. This is no longer the case. The savings rate should now rise, we may hope, to a normal level. However, we must take into account a generation—the so-called yuppies—which not only outnumbers the combined total of those under twenty-five and those over sixty-five years of age but is also extremely disinclined to save. The United States must solve the problem of increasing the propensity to save of those between ages twenty-six and fifty.

By the beginning of 1989, increased inflationary pressures may necessitate a tightening of Federal Reserve Bank activity, and the resulting recession would likely forestall these pressures—so long as the U.S. dollar can be allowed to devaluate at a nondisruptive pace. This is a very difficult task, but it could be accomplished if Japan, West Germany, Britain, France, and others cooperate; they are likely to do so because, whether we all like it or not, the U.S. dollar is their reserve currency.

Thus, although the October 1987 stock market crash was traumatic, it has caused a healthy shift of consumer and investor sentiment, which could lower interest rates and inflation to a level that otherwise would not have been reached.

In his analysis of the abrupt stock market adjustment, Dr. Donald Ratajczak of the Georgia State University Economic Forecasting Center observed that much of the short-run economic impact will fall on consumer durables such as automobiles, furniture, and carpeting. Eating out is also expected to decline slightly. As reductions in consumer spending lead to reduced economic activity and a falloff in employment opportunities, incomes will decline. Thus, actual savings rates will not rise to the desired level until the economy recovers from the consumer-induced slowdown.

In the meantime, the "black hole" of the oil patch continues, sucking up energy from the rest of the nation with its cash calls to investors. But the prolonged slump in oil and gas exploration in Texas, Oklahoma, and Colorado, for example, will eventually begin to rebound. The oil price per barrel will not recover in 1988, but Ratajczak projects that it will exceed $22 during 1989. At this point, increased exploration will be profitable, and the "oil patch" may begin to be self-supporting.

Government Policy

Because the United States is greatly influenced by "presidential economics," both fiscal and monetary policies are in effect cyclically related to the four-year terms of office and to the changing ideological commitments of those currently in power; thus, it is difficult to predict government policy in mid-1988.

Some restraint in deficit financing can be expected on the basis of the previous discussion. Growth in defense spending should slow because the

Soviet Union is acting more responsibly. It is to be hoped that the Strategic Defense Initiative ("Star Wars") will be slowed down so that scientists and engineers can devote their energies to research and development in the consumer products sector and thus restore our competitiveness with the nations that do not carry our onerous defense budget. Moreover, the net effect of anticipated reduced support for agricultural programs and for nondefense durables plus a lowering of foreign aid should be to reduce the government deficit over the forecast period to 1993.[1]

Manufacturing

"Manufacturing is the key to short-run growth. Even if consumers retreat, rebounding production can keep the United States on an even keel—and help pay the nation's debts."[2]

In 1987, U.S. manufacturing experienced an upturn. Factories hummed, hiring picked up, capacity was filled. Manufacturing had suddenly seized the leading role in the economy. In the winter of 1988 the United States was in the midst of an export boom that showed few signs of letting up, and capital spending was clearly on an upswing.

The important thing, though, is that the shift not take place too suddenly. If manufacturing were to grow too fast, capacity constraints could cause the economy to overheat, as was a real danger in the spring of 1988. But few economists in 1988 expect industry to turn in such a strong performance that it will fan inflationary fears, leading to a Federal Reserve Bank tightening and a financial crises. Although businesses are monitoring inventories much more closely through computer reporting and "just-in-time" deliveries, overoptimism may still lead to an inventory imbalance that will have to be corrected.

The "silver lining" of sorts for U.S. manufacturers is that prices are finally beginning to rise sharply on imported goods, and buyers are expected to turn increasingly to domestic products. Japan, Germany, Korea, Taiwan, Singapore, and others are likely to sell at cost or even engage in below-cost "dumping" in order to try to retain market shares recently captured. Free-market proponents, blinded by ideology, will not see that such destructive practices constitute unfair competition to American manufacturers obeying antitrust laws.

A far greater boon to U.S. manufacturers will be the strong demand coming from overseas markets. The dollar has nearly retracted its gains of the 1980s, even against the newly industrialized nations with which the

---

[1]Economic Forecasting Center, *Forecast—The Nation 1987 IV–1989 III*. Donald Ratajczak (Director, College of Business Administration, Georgia State University, Atlanta) is the source for the foregoing, along with the authors' own ideas. Any errors or omissions are our own.

[2]"Manufacturing," *Business Week*, January 11, 1988.

United States increasingly trades. This means that on the basis of relative prices alone, U.S. products are more competitive again, which is beginning to have a substantial effect on trade volumes. U.S. manufacturers are already recapturing foreign market share. Unless other countries make stunning new inroads in these markets, which is unlikely, U.S. export gains are likely to settle down in 1988 at 7 to 10 percent.

Thus, exports and capital spending are likely to be the leaders in pulling the economy through yet another year of expansion. Although industrial output may grow by only 2.5 to 3 percent—well below 1987's level—the rate is still likely to exceed that of the overall economy.

As the U.S. economy finally begins to make up for past excesses by producing more than it consumes, a process has begun that will not easily be reversed. This process will continue, although it will certainly slow down should a recession occur in 1989, as many expect. (A modest recession in fact has the potential to redress some savings and investment imbalances and diminish inflationary expectations.) "This is a structural shift that's a long-term phenomenon," says Mikey Levy, economist at Fidelity Bank in Philadelphia. "It should continue right into the 1990s." For consumers the shift may be painful, but for American industry it can only be welcome.

Some Demographic Analysis

The U.S. population is still flowing to or growing predominantly in the South and the West. Even so, a study by Blackburn and Bloom indicates that the Northeast is making a significant comeback in personal income, and that the Far West remains quite strong. The map in Exhibit 20-1 notes gains in regional population and personal income over a five-year period.[3]

As the map indicates, the strongest growth in personal income is occurring in New England south to Pennsylvania, as well as on the West Coast, primarily in California. Although the regions with the largest population gains were the Southwest (12.1 percent), the Far West (10.5 percent), and the Southeast (6.7 percent), the regions with the biggest increases in non-farm personal income were New England (46.5 percent), the Far West (43.9 percent), and the Southeast (42.2 percent). The national average gain, 38 percent, was also exceeded in New York, New Jersey, and Pennsylvania, at 39.6 percent.

The weakest growth in personal income occurred in the Rocky Mountain states (27.6 percent) and the Southwest, including Texas (28.9 percent). Blackburn and Bloom say that the Farm Belt states along the Mississippi River, as well as the manufacturing states around the Great Lakes, have a more dismal short-term outlook.

[3]McKinley L. Blackburn and David E. Bloom, "Regional Roulette," *American Demographic Magazine*, January 1988, pp. 32–37.

EXHIBIT 20-1.   How the Regions Have Grown, 1982–1987: Population and Personal Income Gains over the Five-Year Period

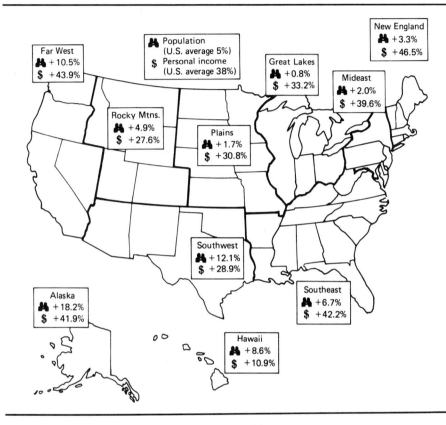

Source: Bureau of the Census, U.S. Department of Commerce.

STRATEGIC VIEW OF REAL ESTATE

Mahlon Apgar IV developed a framework for the strategic analysis of these uncertain times.[4] Investing in real estate has come to mean the acquisition, management, and disposition of specific properties on a local, deal-by-deal basis, even though national corporations are involved as financial partners and principal managers. Strategic analysis of real estate begins with an assessment of the industry's size and scope, its changing structure, and its international potential.

[4]Mahlon Apgar IV, "A Strategic View of Real Estate," *Real Estate Issues*, Fall–Winter 1986, pp. 6–11.

In 1985 almost 60 percent of the world's capital market values were based on real estate. The industry's impressive scale in the world capital markets is mirrored in the United States, where nearly 50 percent of capital market values are real-estate-related. Mortgage debt represented 44 percent of market capitalization in 1985, whereas active equity funds from pension plans, public and private syndications, and REITs amounted to less than 3 percent of the total market. The remaining 53 percent share, which exceeds $2.5 trillion, is the latent equity value of real estate assets held by corporations, other organizations, and individuals. But these assets have been outside the investable market. Securitization of real estate assets and debt is currently changing all this in exciting and disconcerting ways, as will be discussed.

Search for Hidden Assets

Equitization of corporate property assets is now a corollary to mergers and leveraged buyouts as financiers look to real estate sales–leasebacks and refinancing arrangements as a primary source for new funds. Securitization of commercial property has only scratched the surface of a $500 billion market. As owners search for hidden assets, major new opportunities are created for institutional investors with a watchful, active strategy.

Shift to Asset Management

Institutions investing in participating loans, joint ventures, and other equity positions are exposed to long-term real estate risks. Consequently, determining performance rather than deal making has become the critical investment skill. Because a property's performance has to be measured over time, a definitive strategy is essential. Good information must be collected. The flow of information is one key to increasing market efficiency and institutional performance. Recognizing the need, national institutions are undertaking cross-market data collection and research at a cost of $600 million annually, according to Apgar's private survey.

Major Corporations

In the present real estate market large companies have a major asset in their ability to supply developers and owners with a very important commodity: tenancies. Corporations also have an extraordinary opportunity to acquire an interest in real estate capital appreciation by means of the equity lease, and they can negotiate attractive deals with developers.

With the increasing popularity of securitization as a financing vehicle, corporations are becoming acutely aware that their tenancies bear strongly on project ratability, because the quality and durability of anticipated cash flows are directly related to corporate creditworthiness. Corporations should be able to negotiate some benefit as a return for providing a project with financial feasibility.

At the top of the market are high-quality, well-located buildings with substantial corporate tenancy. Corporate headquarters buildings in the central business districts of major U.S. cities are the most outstanding examples of such properties. Corporations can expect very high prices for their headquarter assets on a sale–leaseback arrangement, particularly when offshore or institutional investors are the purchasers.

Major corporations are motivated to realize the cash value both of headquarters properties and of excess real estate holdings as a defense against corporate raiders or to finance a leveraged buyout by corporate management. But it appears that there are real dangers in adopting some of these liquidation strategies in view of international conditions. It is not a time to be selling the seed corn.

SHORT-TERM OVERVIEW

The year 1988 may have marked the tail end of the longest period of sustained real estate growth in American history. Therefore, immediate prospects are only so-so, with some haziness regarding energy and inflation.

First, developers have become more experienced and more professional. They appear to be better capitalized, and investors and lenders are more aware of the need for market studies and marketability analysis. Thus, the traditional developer's entrepreneurial optimism is more likely to be tempered by rational decision making. Moreover, the U.S. system of real estate finance will become even more complex, thus providing various opportunities for participation by lenders in individual projects as an inflation hedge. However, substantial deviation from the traditional principal reduction, annual mortgage constant loan, is expected. The sources of funds will expand, and there will be more activity in the securities markets and from the pension funds.

Real Estate Is Less "Frisky"

Real estate is less frisky, but under all is the land—a real not a "paper" asset.[5] The recession of the mid-1970s merely fazed real estate. Inflation only made it stronger. Even the 1986 tax reform caused nothing more than withdrawal pains. The fundamentals require prudent action, but it looks as though the real estate industry will escape with minor damage. Home building should also bear up. During 1987, U.S. and foreign institutional investors picked up the slack. They bought properties more often than they built them, but their bankrolls buoyed the industry nonetheless. And

[5]"Real Estate Less Frisky, Still Kicking," *Business Week*, January 11, 1988, by Todd Mason, is a source, along with our own ideas. The errors and omissions are our own.

even though institutions did suspend investment after the stock crash, they now see investing in real estate as a way to deploy funds into hard rather than financial "paper" assets.

No major booms are expected in the short term. Noting that "There aren't any economic miracles taking place," Kenneth T. Rosen, research manager at Salomon Brothers, thinks that construction starts during 1988 will decline nationwide by 10 percent for retail space, by 15 percent for factories and warehouses, and by 23 percent for offices. Although this would help the industry reduce its troublesome vacancy rates, industry "bears" say the decline comes too late.

Stephen E. Roulac, managing partner of the Roulac Real Estate Consulting Group of Deloitte, Haskins + Sells in San Francisco, argues that developers have masked vacancy rates by offering deeply discounted rents. "By no means is all of the bad news out," he says. At the New York-based brokerage firm, Cushman and Wakefield, economists have another worry—that the 1980s boom in white-collar employment is ending and that an office glut will linger. "We're preparing for a national recession," reports President Arthur J. Mirante II. Even the well-heeled Japanese and the pension buyers are not providing broad support. They are buying only blue-chip office buildings and regional malls.

There is a similar impasse in the market for distressed properties. Industry executives expect to see banks, insurance companies, developers, tax shelters, and savings and loan associations begin to sell off their troubled assets. The nation's savings and loan companies alone were carrying $22.85 billion in repossessed properties as of September 1988. Sellers must be cautious, though. Fire sales could shatter prices and collateral values in depressed markets such as Dallas, Texas. The failure of the Federal Savings and Loan Insurance Corporation (FSLIC) and the Federal Asset Disposition Association (FADA) to involve highly skilled (and highly paid) negotiators, as was done for the Penn Central liquidation, is a serious mistake; it is slowing the process and creating more uncertainty. Private-sector "know-how" is seldom available at the salaries the government sector pays. As in the days of President Roosevelt's New Deal, another Reconstruction Finance Corporation is needed to refinance the FADA, FSLIC, and Federal Deposit Insurance Corporation (FDIC) sell-offs.

Home builders do not face the oversupply problem plaguing commercial developers. The National Association of Home Builders (NAHB) expects no more than a 10 percent decline in starts, to 1.45 million units. Still, apartment construction will be weak, thanks to past excesses of tax shelter promoters. NAHB economist Michael S. Carliner expects 422,000 units to be started in 1988, an 11 percent decline. Nonetheless, some institutional investors are targeting the apartment market as a safer bet than office or retail properties. The magic of real estate has been that investors find places for their capital even when opportunities shrink. Global financial jitters should keep the act going for another year.

The short-run outlook just detailed will be out of date when this book comes off the presses. It is printed here so that the reader can compare what really happened with these short-term forecasts—not to fault the predictors, but to point out the value of longer time horizon scenarios. Major structural changes are going on in the dynamic global and U.S. economies that greatly affect real estate opportunities for the future. Consider the following comments.

Outlook for Financial Services and Nonbanks

The authors join with James Jorgensen in expecting that the big winners in the more open financial marketplace will be some of American industry's best-known names: General Motors, General Electric, Ford Motor Company, and others.[6] They will do battle with such retail giants as Sears, J.C. Penney, K Mart, and 7-Eleven, whose financial clout and marketing savvy have already pushed aside many well-established financial firms. And their entry, as far reaching as it has been, is but the tip of the financial iceberg.

Jorgensen contends that thousands of financial firms will either merge into bigger money players for survival or they will die separately. A small number of megafinancial firms may spread out across the country offering one-stop financial shopping. The words "bank" and "broker" used to describe these firms may be replaced with "financial supermarkets."

One example of this anticipated trend is a pending transaction between Xerox Corporation and VMS Realty Partners. According to recent reports from real estate industry sources, as part of a $200-million transaction Xerox has agreed in principle to buy a 25 percent equity interest in the Chicago-based real estate syndication and investment firm. In addition to paying $80 million for the equity interest, Xerox will lend VMS $120 million in exchange for a new issue of subordinated debt in the closely held company. The move represents another Xerox effort to diversify product lines away from its traditional photocopier, printer, and computer systems businesses. (Its existing financial services operations include Xerox Credit Corporation, an equipment financier, and Van Kampen Merritt, an underwriter and distributor of municipal and corporate bonds and mutual funds.) For the six-year-old VMS, the cash infusion it is to obtain from Xerox will help it expand real estate acquisitions to increase its $6-billion portfolio.

Sources say that Xerox will use the extensive national sales network it has assembled for its life insurance and mutual funds to sell private and

---

[6]James Jorgensen, *Money Shock* (New York: American Management Association, 1986), pp. 186–203, is the source, along with our own ideas. Any errors and omissions are our own.

public VMS real estate syndications, which will focus on partnerships that emphasize return on investment rather than tax breaks. Until last year, Xerox was widely criticized for its diversification efforts; however, in 1986, total earnings for Crum and Forster and Xerox's other financial services units were $228 million, compared with a dismal $30 million in 1985. Even if this joint venture does not materialize, it is a schematic for the kind of changes that are taking place in the real estate financial services industry.

GTE Establishes a New Real Estate Organization

Other changes include the reorganization by some major corporations to turn their real estate departments into profit centers of major significance. The following is an excerpted mini-case study developed by Larry B. Kimbler, vice-president of corporate real estate at GTE.[7] With headquarters in Stamford, Connecticut, GTE employs about 183,000 people worldwide and ended 1985 with total revenues of almost $16 billion and assets of about $26.6 billion and growing. Some five years ago when GTE brought in its new president, Dr. Vanderslice from General Electric, there were about 60 subsidiaries analogous to loosely affiliated fiefdoms. Dr. Vanderslice immediately saw the need to centralize control and was particularly interested in real estate as a central control element. An outside consultant predicted that if GTE had a properly managed and operated central real estate function, it would not be unreasonable to expect to recoup over five years between $150 million and $200 million in capital from surplus properties and underutilized assets.

Kimbler explains the postulates upon which GTE built its new organization.

First, we determined that we should have a small organization. Our department couldn't be everything to everybody. The optimal structure would be a small staff of specialists who were highly trained in the various disciplines: construction, acquisition, disposition, finance and legal matters [Exhibit 20-2]. (I personally felt finance and legal expertise to be particularly important.)

Everything our department does is financially oriented and has great legal ramifications. We have two attorneys who are dedicated to our function, but they report to the general counsel. Corporate counsel was not easily convinced that corporate attorneys should report to the real estate department. [*Authors Note:* But it makes good sense.] Our self-contained finance group

[7]Larry B. Kimbler, "GTE Corporate Real Estate: A Case Study in Establishing Proactive Real Estate Management," *Industrial Development*, May–June 1987, pp. 9–12. See also Michael J. Kami, "Integrating Fixed Asset Management into Corporate Strategy," *Industrial Development*, November 1986; and Hugh O. Nourse, "Using Real Estate Asset Management to Improve Strategic Performance," *Industrial Development*, May–June 1986.

EXHIBIT 20-2 GTE's Corporate Real Estate Organization

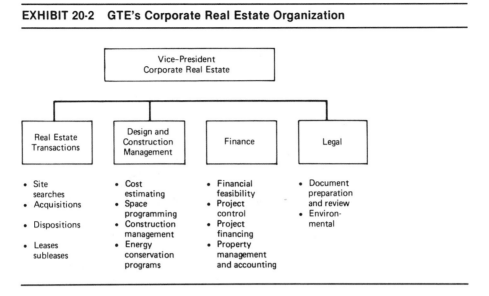

is responsible for all the financial feasibility on projects. They are responsible for project financing, project control and property management of GTE Realty's properties. We felt that the routine day-to-day matters could best be handled in the field, where our qualified people are right on top of it. . . .

The people in our department are full-service project managers, with engineering and architectural support staff, who make sure that the building is built at the right place, the right size, for the right cost, on time and on budget, and more importantly, that it will do what it is supposed to when completed. Basically, if a project costs more than $5 million, involvement of our department is mandated.

The corporate policy requiring our department's approval induced the operating divisions to get us involved early. Our department diligently scrutinized their work to ensure it was a proper transaction. We also emphasized that we wanted to control only the major transactions. We also felt it essential to include the real estate facilities function in the strategic planning process because there was absolutely no strategic planning element dealing with facilities in our typical five-year plan. . . .

Too often, the corporation would put a major facility on a 40-acre tract, do the environment impact studies, perhaps have utilities brought to the site and create tremendous value for the surrounding landowners.

GTE Realty was started to take advantage of the opportunities created by the company's own enterprise efforts, and Kimbler emphasized the importance of recruiting and retaining real estate professionals. The real estate department of GTE is careful to prove its worth to the parent corporate structure and charges other divisions for its services. Kimbler explains that

> The various units are charged for our construction-related and project management services because those costs are capitalized in the cost of the building. However, we do not charge for our real estate services, site selection, acquisition, disposition, leasing and subleasing. These services are offered gratis to make sure that our department has an opportunity to work on these projects. In my view, there is no question that a real estate department should be a profit center. It need not be a separate, autonomous consolidated or unconsolidated real estate subsidiary to be a profit center. . . . If you do not keep showing your financial performance to the corporation in your annual budget reviews and at any other opportunity, you will be perceived as being a cost center, and cost centers are very vulnerable in a decentralized mentality.

Vice-President Kimbler summarized with the observation that corporate real estate does not have a mandate for involvement. If the operating units are convinced that you can do a better job than they can for themselves, they will use you. The establishment of companywide quality, efficiency, and office standards and proactive asset management have drastically improved GTE's financial performance, he said.

The October 1987 Crash Shadows the Outlook[8]

Never was perspective more important than in evaluating how investment markets performed last year. For example, measured annually, the Dow Jones Industrial Average ended the year 2 percent above where it started twelve months earlier. But no one will remember 1987 as a year when stocks turned in a positive performance. From the opening bell January 2 through late August, stocks surged to unprecedented heights. Then in one spectacular 508-point fall on October 19, the industrial average crashed back to the level it first surpassed in March 1986. The October market crash also put the brakes on six years of runaway growth in the financial futures and options industry.[9]

Bonds, Another Market Where Point of View Made a Difference

Although bond prices fell during most of 1987 while interest rates rose, bonds lurched out of their bearish slump after the stock market crash and headed into 1988 on an upbeat. As measured by Shearson Lehman's index

---

[8] "Crash Casts a Giant Shadow on Investment Outlook," *The Wall Street Journal*, Monday, January 4, 1988, Section 2, p. 1B.

[9] Scott McMurray, "Crash Brakes Rapid Growth in the Financial Futures Market," *The Wall Street Journal*, Monday, January 4, 1988.

of government and corporate bonds, however, the total return for 1987 was little more than 2 percent—shabby indeed.

Perspective is also central to investment outlooks for 1988. Those looking at the glass half-full note that predictions of continued economic growth—albeit at a reduced rate since the stock market crash—and still-restrained inflation suggest a congenial environment for many investments. Those who see the glass half-empty observe that a recession seems likely within the next few years, and that even if it does not actually start until 1989 or beyond, investors could spend much of this year anticipating it. A "show me" skepticism about promises to stabilize the falling dollar and domestic willpower to effect significant reductions in the U.S. trade and budget deficits seems realistic. Investors must also stir in the political vinegar of a presidential election year. This mixture makes for a witch's brew that complicates the real estate investor's attempts at forecasting for the years ahead.

Municipal Bond Market Has Shrunk

In the municipal bond market, 1987 was the year that proved some Wall Street professionals were right about the effects of the 1986 Tax Reform Act. The new tax laws constricted both the size and the profitability of the business.[10] Total new-issue volume was $99.3 billion, down 33 percent from 1986, according to New York-based Securities Data Company. C. Austin Fitts, a managing director of public finance for Dillon, Read and Company, said that for issuers and brokers, 1988 could be much like 1987—including continued pruning by firms and fierce competition for a shrinking pool of new issues. Fitts noted that the limit on the amount of certain types of municipals each state could issue would fall in 1988 to $150 million, or $75 per capita, from $250 million, or $150 per capita, in 1987, and that the cap would tie municipalities' hands.

But market activity could be significantly boosted by municipal bond sales for projects such as bridge, road, and sewer repair, which generally are not subject to the volume cap. Infrastructure bonds were the market's "wild card" in 1987, according to Fitts. We must relate these infrastructure bonds to the discussion about developers' linkage fees and charges for municipal infrastructure set forth later in this outlook chapter.

Income-Producing Property: Real Estate and Overbuilding

Commercial real estate values have failed to stabilize as a consequence of overbuilding. There have been lender losses, more troubled properties, and a fall in rents. Some distressed property is selling for 35 to 40 percent

---

[10]Alexandra Peers, "Municipal Bond Industry Has Difficult Year as Field Shrinks," *The Wall Street Journal*, Monday, January 4, 1988.

of costs, compared with 50 to 60 percent a year ago. The sharpest deterioration continues in the Southwest energy belt and the West, but problems are creeping up in sections of the East.[11]

According to a survey by Frank Russell Company of Tacoma, Washington, a consultant to pension funds, the overall return for investors in such buildings was actually negative in the second quarter of 1987. Large write-downs by such investors as insurance companies and pension funds were one reason. The situation in Silicon Valley and elsewhere around the country is hurting many banks and savings and loan associations. Real estate loan losses at banks grew 38 percent in the first nine months of 1987 to $1.6 billion, and such losses at thrifts soared 43 percent to $7.2 billion. The debacle extends to many types of commercial property—hotels, shopping malls, and apartment and condominium projects.

The commercial-property glut almost certainly means that the Federal Savings and Loan Insurance Corporation will eventually need another huge capital infusion on top of the industry-financed $10.8 billion recapitalization approved by Congress in August 1987. This time, however, taxpayers may finance part of the bailout. "Where is the discipline" to stop overbuilding, wonders Blake Eagle, a real estate executive with the Frank Russell Company. "The user and the investor aren't in sync at all."

The abundance of bad decisions has worsened conditions to the point that they may finally be generating this needed discipline. Developers in some economically robust areas of the country have hopes that new demand for office space will absorb some of the excess, thereby stabilizing or raising prices and rents. However, the finance, insurance, and real estate sectors of the economy account for nearly half of office employment. Securities firms and investment banks have been hurt by the market crash; banks and real estate companies are battling slumps in their own markets. Consequently, in the winter of 1988 it appears that office employment growth is slowing dramatically.

There is another harbinger of bad times. At the end of the 1987 third quarter, the overhang of real estate that is held by banks, thrifts, and the federal deposit insurance agencies and that has been repossessed or is delinquent on loan payments rose to $96 billion. This could be an important drag on property values and rents. "Real estate owned or about to be" increased by 26 percent from $76.1 billion a year earlier. (About half of this increase resulted from a new regulation forcing more detailed disclosure of delinquent loans by thrifts.) Many of these institutions are increasingly willing to dump distressed property, depressing prices further. "The times are perilous," says John R. White, the honorary chairman of Landauer Associates of New York. "The vibrancy in financial and insur-

---

[11]"Office Glut, Binge of Overbuilding Keeps Values Falling in Commercial Realty," *The Wall Street Journal*, Monday, January 4, 1988, p. 1.

ance sectors will not be there, and office performance in general will continue on a disappointing basis."

Lack of Reliable Data

The growing problems in commercial real estate have not been lessened by the chronic underreporting of them by financial institutions. Other lenders and developers overstate the value of real estate by manipulating appraisals or lease terms; federal regulators are trying to crack down on these abuses. The American Institute of Real Estate Appraisors (AIREA), the Society of Real Estate Appraisors (SREA), and the American Society of Appraisers (ASA) among the appraisal associations are cooperating. The Appraisal Foundation is being formed to set standards for appraisal procedures and reporting.

Gluts in one-fifth of the cities surveyed in September 1987 by Coldwell Banker had worsened since September 1986. Cities in which the glut worsened include Austin, Texas, where the vacancy rate for downtown offices jumped from 19.1 to 35.8 percent, and Kansas City, where the rate rose from 18.9 to 35.4 percent. Dallas's rate increased from 20.4 to 24.6 percent and Houston's from 18.4 to 21.9 percent. Some markets, including San Diego and Los Angeles, improved moderately, but the national rate has not improved.

Dallas rents have been halved in two years. In Atlanta, concessions persist even though the vacancy rate has fallen below the national average in the past year. The tallest building in Missouri opened in Kansas City early in 1988 with major tenants receiving up to 20 percent discounts.

Managing the overhang is controversial, particularly among federal regulators who control about $15 billion in troubled property or real estate loans. Many are concerned that reducing the overhang quickly will wreck already-shaken markets, but there is pressure on the regulators from Congress and developers to sell as much as they can as soon as they can, and the pace seems to be quickening. Says Thomas Procopio, the FSLIC's southern regional director for receivership activities, "You walk a very fine line between fulfilling your mandate of winding up the affairs of the institution, and not creating disruptions in the marketplace." FSLIC's troubled real estate assets in his region mushroomed to $3 billion in 1988 from less than $1 billion in 1987.

The bargains are not all in Texas. Ford Aerospace Corporation purchased four buildings and 65 acres in North San Jose, California, for $60 million—or 25 percent less than cost, estimates Robert Eagles, the broker for Warner Communications. Chicago investor Samuel Zell acquired a foreclosed office building at about a 50 percent discount. Zell, who made a fortune buying distressed property in the mid-1970s, says that the bargains are just developing. "You are beginning to see that stuff come out of the woodwork," says Zell, who may speak for the future outlook. Those with liquidity will benefit.

1988 Back to Basics

The experts are subdued about prospects for the short term.[12] Barely half (52 percent) expect 1988 to be a better year than 1987. There are several reasons for this newfound realism. Markets are still overbuilt, and most will stay that way in 1988. It is too early for optimism, except for the prospects of a handful of cities. Competitive pressures will be intense. Developments of new projects will be slow. Lenders are more cautious, perhaps because they realize that no further building is necessary at current absorption rates. This bad news for developers is good news for investors and owners waiting for a better supply–demand balance to bail out their projects.

The multitiered market for investment-grade property is firmly in place. Top-quality projects will command even higher prices next year; good properties will also be expensive. Pricing for average buildings will decline slightly, and poor properties will not move at all. Yields, already low, will not go down much in 1988, but neither will they rise. Large organizations, well capitalized and patient, will dominate in a market of conservative, low-risk–low-reward deals. Exhibit 20-3 shows the overview of annualized percentage rates of return for office, industrial, and retail properties from 1978 to 1986. Exhibit 20-4 shows single-family housing appreciation from 1980 to 1986.

The long-term trend for unadjusted yields is clearly downward—in large part a squeezing out of inflation premiums—but real returns are still good relative to those of most other investments. Faced with sobering price and yield prospects and fewer development opportunities, the indus-

---

[12]*Emerging Trends in Real Estate: 1988* (Equitable Real Estate Investment Management, Inc., 3414 Peachtree Road, Atlanta, Ga. 30326), George Peacock and George Puskar, eds., report written by Richard Kateley, is a source for the following pages along with other sources and our own ideas. We recommend its purchase annually. The errors or omissions are our own. See also the *United States Property Report* (Richard Ellis, Inc., 527 Madison Ave., New York, N.Y. 10022); *Colliers USA Office Review* (10 Post Office Square, Boston, Mass. 02109); *Growth Market Reports* (M/PF Research, Inc., 5550 LBJ Freeway, Suite 300, Dallas, Texas 75240); *Hospitality Market Data Exchange* (372 Willis Ave., Mineola, N.Y. 11501); *Industrial Real Estate Market Survey* (SIR, 777 14th St. N.W., Washington, D.C. 20005); *International Office Market Reports* (The Office Network, 1801 Main, Suite 900, Houston, Texas 77002); *Market Trends* (Grubb & Ellis, One Montgomery St., Crocker Center—West Tower, San Francisco, Calif. 94104); *REIS Reports* (250 West 57th St., Suite 1701, New York, N.Y. 10107); *Strategic Real Estate Submarkets* and *The Robert Fuller Market Reports* (Robert Fuller Assoc., 1009 Grant St., Suite 304, Denver, Colo. 80203); *Studley Report and Spacedata* (Julien J. Studley, Inc., 625 Madison Ave., New York, N.Y. 10022); *National Real Estate Investor* and *Shopping Center World* (Communications Channels, Inc., 6255 Barfield Road, Atlanta, Ga. 30328).

EXHIBIT 20-3.   Trends in Real Estate Investment Returns, 1978–1986

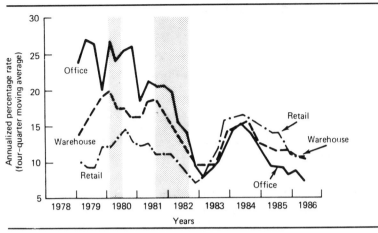

Source: Reports from Frank Russell Company and Goldman Sachs.

try is "returning to fundamentals." Those fundamentals, as one Equitable Real Estate Investment Management respondent put it, include "no gimmicks, no inflation, no tax shelter . . . real cash flow based on real rents and real tenants." Fundamentals reflect an intense interest in cash and equity, rather than returns that might be realized should all go as projected. Street talk about financial rates (e.g., cap rates of X, discounts of Y, IRRs

EXHIBIT 20-4.   Single-Family Housing Appreciation, 1980–1986

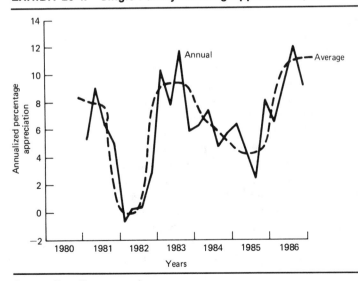

Source: Data Resources, Inc.

of Z) is often meaningless in today's markets. The difference lies in how they are applied and to what. Knowledgeable and serious investors are beginning to see rates applied to more realistic assessments of absorption, rents, expenses, renewals, reversion values, and so on; these variables, in turn, are more likely to be derived from rigorous *in-the-field market analysis* than from in-the-office assumptions. In the colorful words of Equitable staff writers,

> In those organizations with the history to have staff who predate the HP-38, there is an increasing reliance on decision criteria other than "the numbers." This does not replace systematic due diligence processes, but it brings a willingness to reject a project or forgo a deal because it doesn't make common sense.

Apprehension must be expressed that few experts seem concerned about the longer-term demand structure of real estate markets. The Real Estate Research Corporation (RERC) has strong reservations about the speed with which overbuilt markets will regain balance.

Impact of 1986 Tax Reforms

The real estate decision makers who look on real estate as their profession consider that the tax bill affected their business positively. It is making the market more responsive to supply and demand rather than artificial incentives. Others relate that the loss of tax incentives has resulted in fewer new project starts, leveled the playing field for all investors, and washed the amateurs out of the business. For those whose business was dedicated to tax shelter—and who are still in business—1988 has to look a great deal grimmer. Still, the larger or more sophisticated organizations had already seen the writing on the wall and moved into new products. MLPs, asset management, and pension fund advisory services, as well as so-called economic deals, have been their new targets. Thus, perhaps, tax reform killed the right kind of syndications but certainly not all syndicators; the best ones are out there competing for properties just as before. *Stanger Reports* predicted a multibillion-dollar year for syndications during 1987 and considers 1988 to have prospects as a modest but substantial year. Cities that appear to offer the best all-around real estate prospects for the next year and those with the least favorable prospects are listed in Exhibit 20-5.

The intensity with which the strong markets are being exploited, combined with the well-known herd mentality of real estate investors and developers, suggests that even the best areas will soon be saturated. National real estate organizations comb through even the smallest markets carefully and are continually screening for signs of unmet demand and indicators of future appreciation. Niche land uses such as mobile home parks, rental complexes for the elderly, and mini-warehouses, however, all sound more appealing as return–risk trade-offs than they really are.

EXHIBIT 20-5. Real Estate Prospects for 1988

Most Favorable Cities	Least Favorable Cities
New York	Houston
Washington, D.C.	Denver
Los Angeles	Dallas
Boston	Miami

Source: *Emerging Trends*, interviews, Summer 1987.

1988 REAL ESTATE INVESTMENT OUTLOOK

Investment prospects reflect the general mood of the industry, which is cautious but not negative. Real estate prices have generally been stable and even gone up for top-quality projects. According to RERC, Frank Russell, and professional appraisers, prices actually increased for first-tier properties in 1987 and have proved remarkable strong in the second tier of "B+" properties. For average-to-below-average, but still investment-grade, buildings, however, values and prices have fallen between 10 and 15 percent. Similar activity is expected in the short term.

Real Estate Yields

As shown in Exhibit 20-6, real estate yield and overall capitalization rate trends were sharply down in recent years. These are returns for institutional investment-grade properties, however, and do not indicate true yields on leveraged equity properties. Exhibit 20-7 demonstrates that portfolio returns have been decreasing since 1983. The total return for pooled real estate funds (upper-tier investment properties) was 14.2 percent in 1983 and 8.6 percent in 1986.

Low interest rates have offset high prices and lower occupancy on vintage buildings, but low inflation contributes to the erosion of real estate returns when leveraged with fixed-rate mortgages or with ARMs, which move to higher rates. When inflation is low, investors tend to move away from hard assets and into financial assets, especially equities. The annual income returns from real estate (cash flow) are still attractive. An important finding of RERC delphi interviews is that 82 percent of respondents believe that investors will continue to accept the lower yields that have characterized the real estate industry for the past three years.

Transaction Volumes

1988 will be a year for institutions. Their acquisition teams may be kept intact even though they are below target on closings. The level of buying

EXHIBIT 20-6. Real Estate Yield and Capitalization Rate Trends, 1979–1987

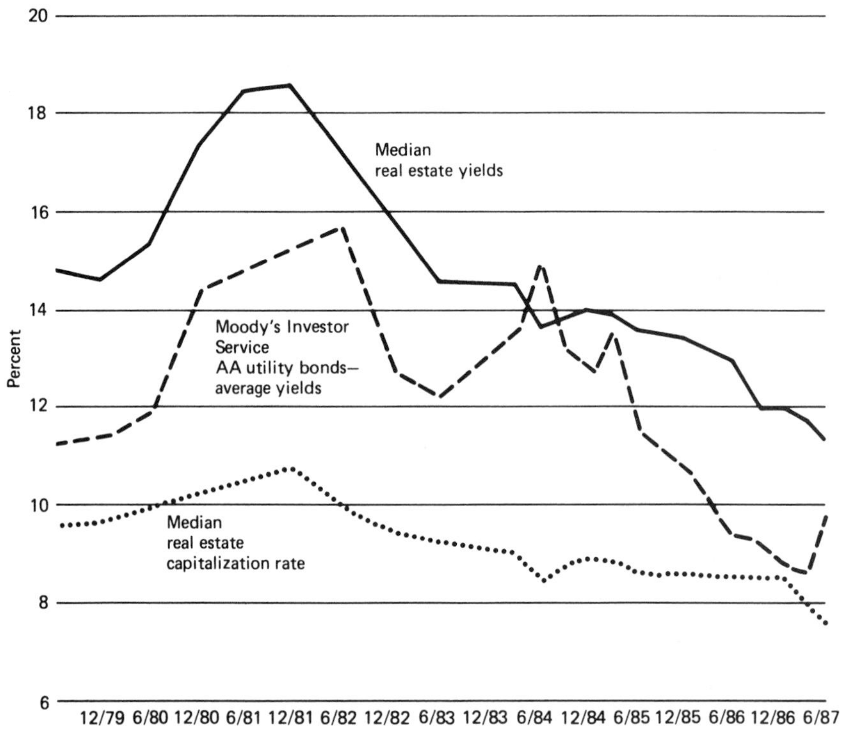

Real estate yield:

Similar to bond yield to maturity. It is a combination of the present value of anticipated annual cash flows plus the present value of a projected resale at the end of a medium-term holding period.

Real estate capitalization rate

The initial annual rate of return on market value (not a fixed rate). These are prevailing going-in capitalization rates for institutional investment-grade properties.

Source: Real Estate Research Corporation, *Quarterly Real Estate Investment Survey.*

and selling will decline in 1988 in relation to the previous several years, and for good reason: lack of product. Most of the top-quality properties have already been purchased for long holding periods by institutional and foreign investors. So the volume of transactions at this tier will be very limited. Bad properties will not move in 1988, and projects controlled by savings and loan associations, FADA, and FSLIC are of interest to only the most savvy "cycle" investors.

Prices will not be attractive except to long-hold players with plenty of patient money. Perhaps a new attribute of the American real estate mar-

EXHIBIT 20-7. **Real Estate Pooled Fund Returns, the S&P 500, and Inflation: 1975–1986**

Year	Pooled Real Estate Funds			S&P 500 Stocks			CPI
	Unrealized Appreciation	Income Return	Total Return	Unrealized Appreciation	Income Return	Total Return	
1975	1.3%	8.6%	9.9%	28.4%	4.3%	32.7%	7.0%
1976	2.4	8.8	11.2	15.1	3.8	18.9	4.8
1977	3.2	8.8	12.0	(8.4)	4.6	(3.8)	6.8
1978	8.0	9.6	17.6	3.4	5.3	8.7	9.0
1979	11.2	9.6	20.8	8.4	5.5	13.9	13.3
1980	8.9	9.3	18.2	26.4	5.3	31.7	12.4
1981	7.9	8.9	16.8	(8.2)	5.2	(3.0)	8.9
1982	0.6	8.5	9.1	11.9	5.8	17.7	3.9
1983	5.8	8.4	14.2	21.2	4.4	25.6	3.8
1984	5.3	8.4	13.7	(0.3)	4.6	4.3	4.0
1985	2.6	7.7	10.3	19.2	4.2	23.4	3.8
1986	1.4	7.2	8.6	23.7	3.5	27.2	1.1
Arithmetic mean	4.9	8.7	13.5	11.7	4.7	16.4	6.6

Sources: Real Estate Profiles, Evaluation Associates, Fourth Quarter, 1986; Standard & Poor's; U.S. Department of Labor, Bureau of Labor Statistics; Real Estate Research Corporation.

kets is emerging on the equity side. From 1988 to 1990, the pension funds, foreign investors, and individuals, through a variety of vehicles, will again be the relevant sources of capital. Many industrial projects will be built to suit and will be financed by corporations.

Pension Funds. Data showing the asset mix of the 200 largest pension funds, which represent about half the total dollars in all funds, indicate that real estate equity grew over the four-year period of 1983 to 1986 at the rapid average annual rate of 22 percent. And 1985 was the big year. In 1986, however, real estate equity increased by only a modest 7 percent ($2.3 billion), while stock and bond assets grew by 31 and 28 percent, respectively. Plan sponsors and their advisors today talk of reaching a 10 percent allocation to real estate. There is similar talk of placing an additional $50 billion into real estate assets during the next five years. Neither of these goals is realistic at this stage of the real estate cycle. To reach $10 billion per year would mean nearly tripling the estimated 1987 investment level. If the 200 largest funds were to increase their equity holdings to 10 percent of 1986 assets (up from 3.5 percent), an additional $65 billion would have to go into ownership of real estate.

Needless to say, there are not enough good-quality properties to absorb that amount of investment. There are three reasons for this view. First, many funds, especially public funds, are just beginning equity programs. Second, the asset allocation models used by virtually all funds work to sustain real estate investment even when alternatives (stocks especially) perform better. Third, a convincing three-part argument has been worked out to justify the lower returns achieved by institutional-grade real estate.

1. Real estate provides stable and reasonable current income.
2. The best properties are not vulnerable to small-area cyclical economic changes.
3. If inflation goes up, real estate will hedge, but stocks typically will not and bonds will certainly suffer.

Thus far pension funds have reduced risk by buying the best. But as the number of available "best" properties decreases and their prices increase, this strategy will be more difficult to implement. Still it is conceivable that FSLIC, FADA, and FDIC activities could change price–earnings ratios to make more of the buildings now rated "below investment grade" attractive at the lower price level that could occur.

Individual Investors. One of the revolutions in real estate finance has been the large numbers of individuals investing in both debt and equity commercial real estate. Many people are still committed to real estate, even without tax shelter benefits. Yet, the go-go days are over, and it is probably for the best.[13] With prospective investors battered by worries about tax law changes and sagging cash returns, sales of public limited partnerships plummeted in the fourth quarter of 1987. There's lots of resistance to partnerships among financial planners," said William G. Brennan, publisher of a Valley Forge, Pennsylvania, partnership newsletter. Although sales of public limited partnerships for the first nine months of 1987 ran a strong 33.8 percent ahead of 1986 sales, Robert A. Stanger, president of a Shrewsbury, New Jersey, firm that tracks partnerships, projects a 21 percent drop in sales for 1988 to about $10.7 billion overall. According to Stanger's projections, sales of master limited partnerships, which are traded on stock exchanges, will be hit especially hard, dropping as much as 74 percent to around $750 million from an estimated $2.9 billion in 1987.

Legislation passed by Congress in December 1987 subjects some new publicly traded partnerships to corporate-level federal income tax for operating businesses. In addition, it eliminates an important tax break for individual investors by reclassifying income from publicly traded partner-

---

[13]Earl C. Gottschalk, Jr., "Public Limited Partnership Sales Are Expected to Continue Slump, *The Wall Street Journal*, Monday, January 4, 1988.

ships as portfolio income instead of so-called passive income, generally defined as the income from activities for which investors do not directly participate in management. As a result, investors will not be able to use such income to offset losses from older tax shelter investments. The biggest drop in public limited-partnership sales in 1987 was in real estate, which is by far the largest partnership category. Stanger found that sales for the year fell 18 percent to $6.9 billion—a still significant volume of business. The 1988 outlook is cautious, according to Stephen E. Roulac, who forsees "sales flat to drifting downward."

Some real estate partnerships have had to reduce their cash returns because of high vacancy rates in office buildings. Other troubled real estate partnerships have delayed going into bankruptcy until 1988, when the top tax rate falls to 33 percent, so that they can ease the tax bite on investors. In the event of bankruptcy, as noted in Chapter 5, limited partners receive forgiveness of debt on their partnership investment, which may be recognized as income for tax purposes.

An additional factor weighing on partnership sales is the aftermath of the stock market crash. The nation's six largest brokerage firms account for about 50 percent of regular limited-partnership sales and, according to Stanger, the current atmosphere is not conducive to sales. Still, as indicated by Exhibit 20-8, the outlook is that there will be some business, and Stanger forecasts public partnership sales of $6.5 billion for 1988, which could indicate the purchase of about $26 billion of real estate by syndicators during 1988 on a 25 percent equity contribution basis.

Real Estate Investment Trusts. REITs raised some $4.7 billion in 1986 and about $4 billion in 1987. Because their performance is vulnerable to interest rate changes, the mortgage REITs were hurt by the mid-1987 up-tick in rates. But over longer periods, REITs have done very well—especially equity REITs, which have outperformed the S&P 500. Retirement accounts (IRA, Keogh, 401K) are also a continuing source of real estate capital that undergirds the markets.

Foreign Investment. Direct foreign investment in U.S. real estate has been dominated by five countries: the United Kingdom, the Netherlands, Japan, Canada, and West Germany. Japanese firms investing in U.S. real estate have forged close ties with a variety of American companies, ranging from investment banks and insurance companies to real estate brokers and developers.

As Japanese investors move into lesser-known territories—suburbs, second-tier cities, and perhaps B-quality properties—they will need to learn to "read" a market and compare the attributes of particular locations. Japanese lenders are offering very competitive financing packages on developments of over $80 million. Their role as lenders will continue to expand,

EXHIBIT 20-8.   Public Limited-Partnership Sales, 1986–1988

	1986	1987[a] (% Change)	1988[b] (% Change)
Real estate	$8,461[c]	$6,935 (−18.06%)	$6,500 (−6.3%)
Oil and gas	1,226	1,350 (+10.1%)	1,250 (−7.4%)
Equipment leasing	812	1,100 (+35.5%)	1,200 (+9.1%)
Other	2,639	4,195 (+59.0%)	1,750 (−58.3%)
Total	$13,138	$13,580 (+3.4%)	$10,700 (−21.2%)
Nontraded	$10,663	$10,690 (+0.3%)	$9,950 (−6.9%)
MLPs	2,475	2,890 (+16.8%)	750 (−74.0%)

Source: Robert A. Stanger & Company.
[a]Estimated.
[b]Projected.
[c]Dollar amounts are in millions.

and a more aggressive approach to convertible and participating mortgages can be expected. The authors agree with Equitable Real Estate Investment Management's projection that Japan will continue, along with pension funds and life insurance companies, to be one of the most important sources of permanent financing during the next five years.

Risk Protection. Lenders are much more aware of the complicated risk profile of today's large-scale commercial projects. Important dimensions of risk include

- Environmental issues, such as asbestos, toxic waste, impact assessment and mitigation, and indemnification of current owners.
- Lender liability.
- Interest rate volatility.

The cautious posture lenders are taking with development finance obviously helps to decrease the number of new starts as the moderating market slowly absorbs the overbuilding financed by the federal deficit.

Housing

David Maxwell, chairman and chief executive officer of FNMA, stated,

> One thing that matters most of all: Our nation must care—and care a lot—about housing problems of our less fortunate citizens. The elderly, the first-time home buyer, and, above all, the wretchedly housed poor and homeless.

Maxwell said that free-market proponents who favor the filtering theory and are against intervention base their arguments on their peer group experience as yuppie offspring of well-to-do parents, waiting for Dad and Mom to retire and finance their childrens' new condo with the capital gains tax exemption.

In fact, said Maxwell,

> The people we're talking about are policemen, hairdressers, office and factory workers, and families with two incomes who can't afford to buy a home near their jobs.

For the first time, an average American buying a conventionally financed home in 1988 had to make a mortgage payment exceeding $1,000 per month, according to *U.S. Housing Markets*, a publication of Lomas and Nettleton Company. Average payments include real estate taxes, insurance, a 20 percent down payment, and a thirty-year amortization term. According to Lomas and Nettleton's report, the average home cost $146,400 in January 1988, for which a local household needed an income of $43,000 to qualify for a mortgage loan. Clearly there is a problem of affordability. Some market place innovations, such as high quality manufactured homes and homesite rentals, may improve the situation for some individuals.

Directors of the National Association of Homebuilders have stated that the key issues today are high interest rates, the need for savings incentives for first-time buyers to accumulate down payments, and increasingly complex growth controls and linkage fees (impact fees), which push up the price of the lot and the home.[14] The National Association of Realtors' affordability index for existing housing reached its highest point in the decade in early 1987, at about the same time that mortgage interest rates reached their lowest point.

Some significant social and economic changes are having an impact on real estate use.

1. There will be more home-centered leisure pursuits, such as video tapes and games and microcomputers. Less discretionary disposable income will result in more at-home activity.

[14]Alfred L. King, "Is Housing a Luxury in America?," *Atlanta Constitution*, Saturday, January 23, 1988, Homefinder, p. 1.

2. The workweek will continue to grow shorter. Vacation time will increase slightly, but only an energy shortage would hasten the movement toward the four-day workweek.

3. The labor force will increase in size, and female participation will continue to grow. More important, employment will continue to shift from blue-collar to white-collar as automation, computer software, and other new technologies change the factory, its layout, and size.

4. The service sector of the economy will increase sharply in both absolute and relative terms. More than 90 percent of new jobs will be in the service sector. In addition, there will be rapid and major evolutionary changes in the use of office space because of word processing, CRT terminals, and microcomputers. This will translate into a continued increase in the demand for office space.

5. The commuter distances for the service worker from poverty enclaves to suburban office complexes will cause serious social problems, which will not soon be solved.

6. Crime rates will drop because a smaller proportion of the population will be of the "crime-prone ages," between fifteen and twenty-four. Further, there will be a broader adoption of victim indemnification programs, making American cities feel more secure.

Demand. Regional trends in employment and therefore in housing have shifted dramatically since the early 1980s. In the South and West, private starts—which, except for a dip in the early 1970s, had been increasing for decades—plummeted from 77.3 percent in 1983 to 62.3 percent in the first half of 1987. Construction levels in the Midwest, however, have been particularly strong since 1985, as part of that region's recovery from the deep recession of the early 1980s. With only 16 percent of U.S. households, California and Florida still claim a heavy concentration of new-home construction, accounting for 28 percent of the nation's permits in 1986. The strength of demand in the Northeast coupled with the scarcity and high cost of sites (caused in part by government restrictions) has continued to push prices up far faster than in other parts of the country.

As recently as 1983, the most costly housing markets were in California. These areas are still expensive, but median resale prices are now higher in New England cities and greater New York than they are in Los Angeles and San Diego. Between 1983 and the second quarter of 1987, median resale prices increased only 22 percent nationally, but rose 113 percent in Boston, 101 percent in Providence, 93 percent in Hartford, and 106 percent in greater New York. But with pent-up demand being satisfied and price resistance setting in, the heated pace of markets in the Northeast and Midwest is easing somewhat.

Condominiums. Nationally, condo starts decreased only 6 percent from 1985 to 1986 and many markets remain glutted. Condo conversion is virtually nonexistent in most areas. Demand has been steady, however, in selected markets such as greater New York City and New England, where condos provide distinct lifestyle and locational advantages for some households. Although empty nesters and professional couples show some preference for condo, town house, and cluster home lifestyles, Americans have not yet fully accepted neighborhood responsibility, such as homeowner associations, in the "urban village" of a condominium project. Because of this reluctance to accept association governance, presold units typically have not increased in market value to the extent that nearby detached, owner-occupied dwellings have.

Rental Apartments. Rental markets in much of the country have been weakened by a combination of high production levels (partly to beat changes in the tax laws), a decrease in demand attributable to the improved affordability of ownership, and depressed conditions in the oil-based economies. Vacancies have gone up almost everywhere, although some northeastern markets remain tight. In Boston, for example, multifamily development is difficult and condo demand is strong enough to curtail rental development. Washington and Philadelphia will probably experience their own forms of overbuilding within the next year or two and, much to the chagrin of local builders, are attracting many Texas developers.

The Texas markets are in the worst shape, with major-city vacancy rates estimated at 18 to 19 percent by Lomas and Nettleton. (Vacancy is not much lower, however, in such areas as Tampa and Denver.) Robert Sheehan, consulting economist for the National Apartment Association, reports creative concessions in Texas for new tenants: season football tickets, trips to Las Vegas, balloon rides, and groceries for a month, which of course increase operating expenses and simply play musical chairs with the tenants. Rental starts dropped by an estimated 20 to 25 percent by the end of 1987, a huge drop in construction for a one-year period. This reduction in new supply should begin to stabilize rental markets, but too late for many who were driven to bankruptcy by a free market gone wild with market failures.

The situation is actually worse than some imagine in Texas and other parts of the oil patch, in part because some investors will not realize how much returns on apartments have been cut until they file their tax returns. Moreover, despite all odds, financing remains readily available for the acquisition of desirable existing developments. Furthermore, the prices of investment-grade properties are being bolstered by the strong interest that institutional investors have in apartments. Ironically, this encourages some developers to continue building.

Retirement Housing. A retrenchment is under way in retirement housing, with some of the savviest developers cutting plans for new developments until existing projects are absorbed. RERC cautions developers to

- Analyze the trade area carefully.
- Recognize that a good location is at least as important as for other types of development.
- Plan for slow absorption.
- Avoid prices so high that only a small portion of the market can or will pay them.
- Provide for the skills and experience to handle this complex, management- and labor-intensive type of development. Food service is particularly critical, and hotel companies are ideally suited for this.
- Address the issue of health care thoroughly.
- Motivate people to reside in these developments by promoting the emphasis on fulfilling residents' needs.
- Cater to the need-driven market by building assisted-living or personal-care units that offer more intensive care than is typically provided in congregate developments.

Housing the Poor. Lower-income housing needs are being discussed much more openly in the development community than they have been for some twenty-two years. In their February 1988 report "State of the Nation's Housing," the analysts at the Joint Center for Housing Studies of Havard–MIT highlight the need for renewed funding at the federal level, regardless of which party wins the 1988 election.

Private investment in new low-income housing is virtually nil. Many analysts believe that the homeless, who are especially visible in large cities such as New York, San Francisco, and Chicago, are but the tip of an iceberg. There are in addition the "hidden homeless," two families living in a space intended for one and people living in garages and other unsuitable places.

Low- and moderate-income housing will have to be returned to a high position on the national political agenda. The best minds in the real estate industry will be needed to devise realistic approaches to affordable housing. These solutions will require federal leadership and participation.

Retail—Some Miscellaneous Comments

Specialty stores. In the remainder of the 1980s, retail chains—superstores such as Price Club and Wal-Mart, discounters such as Venture and K Mart, off-price retailers such as Mervyn's and Main Street—will become more specialized. 1988 will be the year of the designer boutique with such key players as Ralph Lauren, Calvin Klein, Valentino, and Alexander

Julian. And many specialty retailers that have become destination stores themselves will serve as "anchors" for smaller-scale urban infill shopping centers, which could help absorb some of the overbuilding that has occurred.

Department stores. Sears is planning a specialty retail approach, through either acquisitions or newly created concepts, and is researching cable television shopping as well. J.C. Penney's Telaction home shopping system has signed on such prestigious retailers as Marshall Field, Neiman-Marcus, Abercrombie and Fitch, and Hammacher Schlemmer. If this medium works well for these merchants, the prognosis for the future visibility of television and video shopping will be greatly enhanced and so will the related need for office space.

New development concepts. As the globe's leading consumers, Americans must be encouraged by producers to continue their spending spree; these buyers must be kept amused in order to maintain the present spending status quo. New concepts combining entertainment and retailing are being thought through; although the mix and scale of the West Edmonton mall in Canada would be inappropriate for most markets, many believe that such a blend of amusement and retailing is warranted. The entertainment guru, the Walt Disney Company, will begin with a forty-acre development in Burbank, California, and future plans include some joint-venture deals with developer James Rouse.

Offices

During the next few years, office markets in almost every major area will be working off the substantial oversupply. New construction will decline in the most overbuilt markets, but it will continue at a slower pace in healthier areas. Vacancies remain high for the fourth year in a row, but they will continue to fall slowly in most cities. Occupancy is stronger in downtown areas than in the suburbs, and this trend will extend through 1988. Concession packages will become increasingly complex, making effective rents even more difficult to track. In addition to enjoying periods of free rent, above-standard buildout, and the payment of moving expenses, major tenants are beginning to negotiate the purchase of their existing building or the assumption of their lease obligations, and in some instances rights in the appreciation in value of the building over the terms of their leases.

Industrial Real Estate

Industrial real estate should become a more desirable investment alternative in the future due to the growing strength of the manufacturing sector, especially the light industrial and warehouse/distribution markets in a planned industrial park atmosphere. "Industrial" encompasses quite disparate property types, and national trends mask wild performance variations in geographic markets, as noted in Chapter 25. Nevertheless, the industrial component of the Frank Russell Company Index averaged an annual 12.7 percent return from 1980 through 1986, compared with 12.2 percent for the overall index. Global and national economic forces point to moderate growth for industrial properties. There is a strong likelihood that more industrial space markets will become overbuilt, which has already happened with "high tech," research and development, and flex space. Environmental issues cut both ways with respect to industrial real estate. The specter of liability has depressed the values of some older industrial sites and in some instances the value of land near industrial sites.

In many cities, the value potential of industrial property, when it is appropriately located, lies in redevelopment. Well-sited, vacant, or underused industrial sites often have excellent development qualities. They may be near central business districts but be less expensive than other properties, be accessible to transportation or located on improving waterfronts, and be large enough for flexibility in planning and design. These sites will be prime candidates for redevelopment when the next construction cycle rolls around.

Hotels

Aggressive national hotel chains have not tempered their expansion goals despite the widespread failure of new hotels to reach projected financial goals. Target cities rarely evidence a need for more or better rooms but are selected because they add stature to the firm's existing system. Even if 1988 marks the start of a two- to three-year decline in new construction, nationwide occupancy may reach 68 percent or higher by 1990. This outlook assumes no drastic slowdown in the economy and the continuing loss of at least 35,000 obsolete rooms annually through conversion and demolition. The industry agrees that overbuilding has occurred in almost all the major U.S. markets, and lenders admit to having portfolios replete with nonperforming hotel loans on properties with current values less than the outstanding debt.

Hotel deals are not flooding the market because of the tiered nature of the ownership–management arrangements. Furthermore, ownership interests are internationally diverse. Of the hotels operated by the fifteen largest U.S. chains, fewer than 20 percent are owner-operated; the vast majority are either franchised or operated under a management contract. Except for overbuilding, however, the industry has not changed. When occupancy rises above 65 to 70 percent, owners make a little bit of money; when occupancy reaches 75 to 80 percent, they make a very good profit.

Absentee owners—some with staying power—are still dreaming and waiting.

Land Development

Many wealthy investors are aware that the timing is now right to purchase, hold, and develop land in readiness for the next construction cycle. Predevelopment land offers excellent opportunities for capital appreciation and portfolio diversification at levels of risk that can be managed by the astute investor, as discussed in Chapter 27.

In general, land positioned to take advantage of the next building cycle may be classified as follows.

1. *Raw land*, possibly in agricultural use, situated at the edge of an expanding metropolitan area but within the established path of growth of the MSA. It should be possible to supply water to this property and dispose of its sewage, and to build on the terrain.

2. *Infill sites within urbanized areas.* Infill sites are usually problem sites that were passed over years ago but, now that land values have matured, can be purchased for prices low enough to allow site corrections and development of the property in harmony with the neighborhood.

3. *Underutilized or vacant land* in or on the edge of downtown areas. Older abandoned industrial sites often fall into this category; there are also air rights and land assemblage clearance sites where new residential communities for service workers could be built. Although public health and street crime are problems, neighborhood crime watches, civic organizations, and other networking techniques can solve them. Developed, these properties yield substantial profits.

Development of raw or vacant land requires an array of skills on the part of the land developer, who must prepare and adopt a master plan, negotiate zoning and government approvals, and provide utilities, roads, and other infrastructures. This process takes years to complete, and the market risks and cost exposure can be high. Still, these functions create value and cause the land to appreciate. Chapter 27 details some risk management techniques.

CONSIDERING THE LONGER TERM

Real estate is always conceived of as a cyclical business, a boom-or-bust industry. Yet beneath the ups and downs of housing starts, tight or easy money, and high or low vacancy rates are ongoing demographic, socioeconomic, and legal regulatory dynamics that profoundly affect the type of product built, its location, and its marketability.

Demographic and Economic Factors

The U.S. population will grow slowly in the years between now and the end of the century. The baby boomers, who number about 80 million and make up a third of our population, will enter middle age in the 1990s. Employment growth will be slower, and greater economic stability is likely with fewer structural economic shifts than occurred during the 1980s. Service jobs will increase fastest, but they pay less than the manufacturing jobs they replace.

Overall, the number of households will continue to increase between 1990 and 1995, but at a slower average annual increase—about 200,000 fewer households than the rate during the late 1980s. Nonetheless, absolute growth in households will continue at a strong 1.2 million per year.

Average household size will continue to decline, and there will be as many new nonfamily male households as married-couple households. Household age demographics will also shift, with a decrease in those aged twenty to thirty-five and a significant increase in those aged forty-five to fifty-five.

Legal and Regulatory Issues

Developers, financial partners, and owners are starting to build expertise—whether they want to or not—in two legal regulatory areas: environmental hazards and development exactions, sometimes called "linkage fees" or "impact charges."

Environmental Hazards. Environmental problems can claim the equity invested in a real estate project and leave the current and past owners, tenants, and lenders liable for cleanup costs far in excess of their original investment. Toxic wastes, contaminated buildings, and various other environment problems—most notably groundwater contamination—are the areas of greatest concern. Over the past decade, the emphasis has moved from beautification and preservation of the environment to controlling the effects of dangerous substances. Numerous federal, state, and local regulations and court cases have broadened the responsibilities of developers, investors, and lenders.

- The definition of what is contaminated and what is toxic is constantly expanding, typical problems being asbestos used in electrical equipment and polychlorinated biphenyls, or PCBs, used in spray-on insulation and ceiling tiles.
- Liability for cleanup costs and damages is also more broadly defined. The EPA can sue a facility's current and past owner or its operator. Financial institutions can be held responsible for cleanup problems in a foreclosure, and owners may be fully liable for contamination caused by their tenants.

■ As investors and lenders take greater precautions to protect themselves from the cost of environmental cleanup, property inspections by environmental engineers and investigations of past property users will become standard procedures.

Special permits granted by regulatory agencies and any outstanding complaints or actions against the property may identify past users of hazardous materials, if such history can be discovered. In addition, purchasers are more often including financial protection clauses in purchase contracts, which, if nothing else, should allow withdrawal from a deal if hazards are discovered. Warranties, releases, and indemnifications are becoming more frequent.

Developer Exactions. Several different terms—including *exactions, linkage fees,* and *dedications*—are used to denote attempts by public entities to obtain additional revenues from private-sector developers to finance or improve an area's infrastructure and services. Exhibit 20-9 shows the many varieties of costs being imposed on local developers by way of typical developer exactions. Impact fees are most often applied to the improvement

EXHIBIT 20-9. Typical Developer Exactions

Type of Exaction or Fee	Example
Linkage fee	A new office building causes more traffic; the developer pays to expand highway access around the development.
Buy-in	The developer pays X dollars to connect existing sewer lines to his or her subdivision.
Pay-as-you-go	The developer pays X dollars per house to connect existing sewer lines to his or her subdivision.
Formula-based developer fee	The developer contributes $5 per square foot of space built. Funds may be used for low-income housing, new sewers, mass transit, and so on.
Negotiated exaction fee	The city and the developer determine what the developer can contribute to help achieve identified goals.
Provision of facilities, services, and equipment	The developer builds a fire station, donates a computer, provides technical advice.
Dedication of land	The developer contributes 10 acres of a 100-acre subdivision to the city for parks.

Source: Real Estate Research Corporation.

of highway and sewer–water infrastructures. The principal exceptions are in Boston and San Francisco where the fees ($6 per square foot of gross leasable area of new office space in San Francisco) are specifically targeted to provide affordable housing. These local governing-body revenue programs will proliferate over the next decade. Rather than take an "us versus them" approach, the real estate community can benefit from the lessons learned thus far. Exaction fee issues to be aware of include the following.

- Impact-free programs should be backed by the authority and predictability of legislation, as opposed to informal bargaining on a case-by-case basis.
- Proposed programs should have a link between the fee to be imposed and the infrastructure of the new development.
- Consensus building by public agencies, community groups, developers, lawyers, and financiers is essential to a successful impact-fee program.
- Fees work best when they are administered by a single public agency that can respond to changing market conditions over time.

The Sprawling Costs of Urban Containment

Conversion of prime agricultural land to urban use in areas like Iowa, Illinois, and California is conversion of a national treasure to a dubiously higher and better use.[15] Converting Corn Belt soil into middle-class subdivisions is a little like wrapping fish in the Dead Sea scrolls. However, the marketplace does not account for social costs. Because urban land uses are so highly interdependent, the price paid for an improvement does not reflect all the costs incurred to produce it. This is a basic reason for urban land use planning, an exercise of police power that has stood up well in several decades of legal testing. Americans have become more conscious of the finite nature of their space and the fact that air and water and the esthetic appeal of trees and scenery are not free.

The next five years will see increasing pressure for control of real estate investors and developers. It appears likely that proposals to develop land will meet increasing resistance from nearby owners who anticipate environmental degradation, that users of newly developed land will be made to compensate the community for social costs, and that the pace of land development will be slowed.

More and more cities and counties are obligated to act as agents of the state in enforcing environmental protection policies. Because private land development necessarily carries social costs to the surrounding commu-

[15]Wallace F. Smith, "The Sprawling Costs of Urban Containment," *California Management Review*, Spring 1976, pp. 40–45.

nity, whereas its benefits tend to accrue to buyers and users, who are often not yet members of that community, the environmental review process is loaded against the developer's pricing mechanism. In the celebrated Mt. Laurel cases, the New Jersey Supreme Court determined that a suburban community like Mt. Laurel could not regulate land use in order to carry out primarily local home rule objectives, but was required to accommodate a regional need for housing for low- or moderate-income families.

The next five years will be difficult ones for rationalizing the interests of various groups in land use planning and development.

New Risks in Developing and Investing in Metropolitan Areas

Development has always been a relatively risky business. In performing the entrepreneurial function, the developer commits substantial resources to some projects that do not come to fruition at all or, worse, take longer than expected to reach the rental phase. This phase of real estate investing has been stretched out and made more uncertain by the problems just discussed.

The very economic conditions that make new development financially unattractive make existing income-producing properties more attractive. There are reasons to expect that it will become more difficult to finance new projects to meet increasing demand in the various sectors of real estate investment. This should favor the existing stock in all real estate sectors.

However, operating costs continue to rise faster than rents in many cities. Furthermore, there seems to be a semipermanent upward shift in the cost of amortizing loans through annual debt service, with annual mortgage constants much higher than in the past. It is clear that property investment faces some serious uncertainty in the next five years as the market adjusts to the increasing burden on cash flow and to the market pressures on capitalization rates. Only if rents rise at a faster rate in the future than in the past will the value of real estate properties continue to rise as fast as they have.

The following are some general observations about the new return–risk relationships.

1. Less favorable mortgage financing will be available. Higher equity contribution ratios—say, 25 to 50 percent—should be expected.
2. As a result of inflation and the influx of new money into equity investment, gross income multipliers have risen and equity capitalization rates (cash flow before tax/equity investment) have fallen.
3. Individuals are more knowledgeable and better able to discriminate among available investments. Tax shelter is no longer a justification in and of itself; investors want to see a meaningful cash flow from a real estate venture over the holding period.

4. All the foregoing points to less opportunity for financial and tax leveraging, and indicates that in future years returns will be more dependent on appreciation of property value and rising rental income and NOIs.

In summary, equity investors will probably still be able to make higher-than-average returns in real estate relative to other investment media, but the increase in the level of knowledge and expertise in the marketplace will make it more difficult and competitive.

Who Forecasts Better, Business People or Professional Forecasters?[16]

The usefulness of training managers in strategic planning and in management by objectives and having them examine case studies and scenarios to prepare for the uncertain environment of real estate investment has been recognized for some time. Data about business conditions and government and private forecasts are readily available to business people, who often use this information to keep track of changes in the economy, as this chapter suggests should be done. Business people, however, generally use more "naive," or less rigorous, procedures to forecast than the professionals who specialize in business forecasting. Interestingly, the mathematical and statistical models used by some professionals may not necessarily ensure the success of their forecasts. Both professional forecasters and real estate decision makers must interpret and subjectively evaluate the numbers.

Most students of real estate return–risk trade-offs keep abreast of economic events at their place of employment. They read newspapers, magazines, and trade publications that report the latest business conditions. Many actually make decisions based on their anticipations of future events. However, most are quick to admit that they do no "formal" forecasting, per se, as part of their work.

Charles H. Little, director of business research at St. John's University, New York, performed a study in which he compared the professional forecasts from about 50 economists who specialize in business forecasting,[17] with forecasts made by a group of businessmen who were attending an MBA class at St. John's University. All had full-time executive jobs. Median professional forecasts were compared to the median class forecasts for the same time periods. Little's valuable conclusion follows.

The hypothesis that a person using average business techniques can forecast as well as the professional is accepted for forecasts of economic growth and unemployment. The professionals are somewhat better at forecasting infla-

[16]Charles H. Little, "Who Forecasts Better—Business People or Professional Forecasters?," *Future Research Quarterly*, Spring 1986.

[17]The sample was taken from the quarterly survey conducted by the American Statistical Association and the National Bureau of Economic Research (ASA–NBER).

tion, but their record is not as good for the other two series. An average business person with the same economic information can and does forecast future business activity, though they may not readily admit it. Plans for the future are based on such projections. As expected, the projections for eight months ahead were somewhat more accurate than those looking a year ahead. For each comparison, the forecasts were at least as accurate. The results are the same for the professionals and the businessmen.

Cause and effect are difficult to determine in a situation such as this. Business people are expected to interpret business situations similarly, and there may then be some validity to the argument that business forecasts are self-fulfilling. Reported forecasts do have an effect on the economy, which is evident when the pronouncements of a single economic "guru" one day may cause substantive changes in the stock market the next day. The argument cannot be carried too far, however, because it is difficult to determine empirically which came first, the forecast or an action by the business person.

It is clear that scenario planning is both useful and still naive. But it handles the future as well as the most sophisticated techniques currently known.

Current Problems of Scenario Planning

As an aid to those who would do scenario modeling to improve the effectiveness of real estate investing, we have set forth some of the difficulties of intellectually modeling the real estate investment as a process.

The entrepreneur is currently necessary for success in real estate investing. At least it is necessary to have such a person as a top manager in an investing group. However, an entrepreneur has difficulty playing the role of employee or subordinate in an authoritarian environment. He or she tends not to want to be accountable to anyone else. In effect, the qualities that make people successful entrepreneurs make them marginally acceptable to conventional, established business and social networks. But successful scenario planning requires that the entrepreneur cooperate with others and accept short-term subordination of personal aims. Given the quality of real estate data and the highly politicized environment of real estate decision making, such a person needs breadth of education and training, considerable social awareness, and a sense of direct involvement. The entrepreneur must have a high degree of confidence in his or her own ability and an orientation toward solving problems for the uncertain future. It is apparent that if we are to integrate strategic planning into the real estate investment process, we must also find ways to make organizations feel comfortable working with entrepreneurial personalities and to help entrepreneurs feel at home in an organizational framework.

Framing the scenario is difficult today. Generally, the problems that must be solved in the future are the following.

1. Establishing parameters for scenarios of real estate investing is an important initial task. The first research would focus on defining the problem space.

2. Setting data base requirements within time and budget constraints will be necessary to produce an appropriate information system for each scenario. Current data base requirements are a Procrustean bed. It is hoped that structuring of appropriate scenarios will make data base needs more explicit.

3. More flexible and interactive computer software, readily accessible through microcomputers (stand-alone and on-line), can facilitate the use of appropriate, well-developed scenarios. Such telecommunicating is necessary to maximize the use of an entrepreneur's thinking, as recent research has proved.

4. From the early scenarios others must be developed. Early scenarios are often hierarchically at too high a level and tend to be insensitive to inputs from, say, the local environment and neighborhood events. They tend to be either too crude to be efficient or too detailed and therefore unwieldy. More effective scenarios that are disaggregated but linked by a master scenario will be developed.

5. Many models are inadequately documented, so that only the author–user is capable of using the scenario.

6. Scenarios would be most useful if they enabled the user to forecast. Currently we tend to be limited to "most likely," "optimistic," and "pessimistic" analyses, which are often inadequate in a probabilistic environment.

7. There is a need to integrate various models—market, physical, political, and financial—into a single interactive program to enable academics and practitioners in the field to improve scenario planning.

It is to be hoped that with much dedicated research, study, experimentation, and hard work by academicians and practitioners alike, approaches and solutions to the problems just enumerated will be forthcoming in the 1990s. We encourage all of you to become involved and participate actively in this challenging process.

Have We Forgotten That Adam Smith Was a Professor of Moral Philosophy?

Before the Glass–Steagall Act is repealed, its initial purpose should be recalled. Recent insider trading, conflicts of interest, frauds, and predatory use of economic power have brought the 1930s back to haunt us. Because we are first a constitutional culture with an open, free society, we should remember that the market of democratic capitalism is supposed to serve us, not enslave us to some kind of corporate nomenclature, the corporate socialism of the future.

As the illegality and excesses in the financial community are being exposed, trust in financial structures and their viability is being seriously eroded. The questions raised by recent events should be examined from two perspectives. First, the illegal activity itself should be considered, as should the adequacy of existing laws and regulations to deal with it. Second, our securities laws aim to enforce three basic principles: (1) full disclosure of fundamental financial information, (2) equal treatment of all shareholders, and (3) nonmanipulation of the market. Both the techniques of current takeovers and present legal trends undermine these principles.

To protect themselves against raider-type takeovers, investing institutions such as those in the savings and loan industry have begun large-scale restructurings in which they assume significant amounts of additional debt in order to shrink their equity and increase the price of their stocks. These actions make them less desirable targets for raiders, but the issue is not just the behavior of the financial industry or the success or failure of a few corporate raiders. More important are the bread-and-butter issues of jobs, growth, and new investment. To compete with Japan, the United States must invest in and create new products, instead of tearing apart its industries and simply inventing new kinds of paper.

When Adam Smith spoke of the "enlightened self-interest" he expected of those who would make the market economy work in the long run, he was referring to a type of honor code. Society's seeming abandonment of such a code has prompted the authors to focus on business ethics in the closing statements of this chapter. Apparently, many have forgotten that a deregulated market economy is highly dependent on peer group enforcement of such important social values as integrity, fidelity, competence, accountability, the duty to speak out, and the paramountcy of our employers' interests.

Unfortunately, the prevailing attitude has reflected Milton Friedman's statement that "profit maximization is not the cardinal principal of corporate management, it is the only principle." According to Friedman, to talk of the "social responsibility" of corporate managers and union leaders is subversive. But he would likely be shocked by what his Chicago school of "free marketeers" and bottom-line maximizers has wrought.

Democratic capitalism must be restored. In order to play the game fairly and well, however, we first need to learn the rules against unfair and deceptive trade practices.

To avoid a financial debacle—perhaps triggered by the MLPs, REMICs, and defaults on junk bonds—the real estate appraising vocation must be made to come of age now as a profession. There is already movement in this direction, but it is focusing on FHLMC, FNMAs, GNMAs, pension funds, and problems with residential mortgages. Another sector of appraising that needs competence, accountability, and ethical standards is corporate America. Adam Smith would probably agree that the fiduciary responsibilities of all call for prudent, socially responsible action.

CONCLUSION

In reading this chapter you have discovered that, given the conditions of uncertainty that persist, the future outlook for real estate investing depends on your own world view. We hope that this text provides an information base for comprehensive planning of investment management. The short-term future should give sophisticated, systematic, opportunistic real estate investors a chance to monitor the cycles, time their moves, and earn above-average returns. It is not easy to make money in real estate, but the probability of success for the educated, rational investor is higher than in other investment mediums.

PART
6

PROPERTY SELECTION

InfoMart, Dallas, Texas.

Previous chapters of the book provide the theoretical and analytical base for analyzing real estate investments. With an investment strategy now in place, attention can be directed toward the various types of property alternatives available for consideration. As indicated in Exhibit 21-1, the scope of possible property types is expansive. Attention here is focused on the more popular types and categories of property.

Chapter 21   Property Types and Selection
Chapter 22   Apartments
Chapter 23   Shopping Centers
Chapter 24   Office Buildings
Chapter 25   Industrial Buildings and Parks
Chapter 26   Other Income-Producing Properties
Chapter 27   Land Investments

These, the final chapters of the book, provide reference material for students developing case study solutions and for professionals analyzing potential acquisitions. The information and discussions in each chapter are organized systematically by subject matter (e.g., definitions, track records and trends, advantages and disadvantages), and extensive references and suggestions for further reading are presented at the end of each chapter.

21

PROPERTY TYPES AND SELECTION

With an investment strategy in place, attention can be directed toward identifying the types of real estate that have the highest probability of satisfying the preferences articulated in the strategy. It is evident that many different types of real estate exist: apartments, office buildings, industrial buildings, shopping centers, and movie theaters, to name a few. Within each category substantial variations exist in the size, age, and quality of particular properties. However, it is possible to identify the general characteristics and tendencies of each type of real estate. These general characteristics and tendencies can help focus efforts to identify suitable real estate investments and thereby reduce the cost of search efforts and increase the probability of finding a property that achieves the investor's objectives.

The variety of possible property types is illustrated in Exhibit 21-1. An investor entering the property selection process with the strategy of looking at every investment opportunity can easily become confused and frustrated. A more reasonable approach to identifying investment properties is to realize that even seasoned real estate investors are not and cannot become experts in all types of real estate. Acquiring the specialized knowledge necessary to become such an expert is too time-consuming to afford investors that luxury. Instead, many investors identify a limited number of general property types and concentrate their efforts and learning on them.

This chapter presents an introductory discussion of the more popular types of property. The discussion is not exhaustive in breadth or depth but is intended to provide a frame of reference for studying the remainder of the book. More specific detail on apartments, office buildings, shopping centers, industrial buildings, other income-producing properties, and land investment may be found in the following chapters, as can information on tax law and financing.

EXHIBIT 21-1.   Different Property Types

LAND

Raw acreage
Recreational acreage
Subdivided lots
Farms, ranches, and groves
Oil and timber lands

RESIDENTIAL PERMANENT FACILITIES

Houses
Apartments
Townhouses
Condominiums
Cooperatives
Mobile homes
Nursing homes

RESIDENTIAL TRANSIENT FACILITIES

Motels
Hotels
Resorts
Spas
Recreational condominiums
Convalescent homes

OFFICE PROPERTY

General-use buildings
Office parks
Professional buildings
Trade centers
Condominiums

RETAIL AND SHOPPING CENTERS

Stores
Restaurants
Fast-food franchises
Gas stations
Supermarkets
Strip centers
Neighborhood, community, regional
   centers
Merchandise marts
Airport concessions
Parking lots and garages
Car washes
Laundry facilities

INDUSTRIAL

Warehouses and mini-warehouses
Factories
Industrial parks

ENTERTAINMENT AND RECREATIONAL

Theaters
Bowling alleys
Golf courses
Golf driving ranges
Miniature golf courses
Arenas
Museums
Convention centers
Marinas
Target practice ranges
Baseball batting ranges
Tennis clubs
Racketball clubs
Massage parlors
Gymnasiums
Health spas

COMPREHENSIVE DEVELOPMENT

Subdivisions
Skiing facilities
Amusement parks
Retirement communities
Urban redevelopments
Rehabilitating existing projects
New communities
New towns

PUBLIC SERVICE

Hospitals
Schools
Public buildings

OTHER

Churches
Islands
Foreign investments
Exotic properties

PROPERTY TYPES

Residential Rental Property

A popular starting point for many beginning real estate investors is a small residential rental property, such as a house, duplex, fourplex, or small apartment building. One possible strategy for a beginning investor is to turn a home into a rental property (instead of selling it) when ready to move into a second home. Also included in the residential rental property category are large apartment complexes, mobile home parks, and nursing homes. Often the last two—mobile home parks and nursing homes—are considered special-use properties and require specialized expertise as compared to houses and apartments.

Small residential properties are popular with beginning investors because most are familiar with the operation of a single-family home or apartment. Furthermore, during the past ten years these properties, especially single-family homes, have experienced very high property value growth rates—sometimes as much as 12 to 20 percent per year or more in the case of single-family rental houses. However, recent property value changes have been more modest.

In addition to the smaller residential rental properties, apartments range from garden apartments of one to three stories and any number of units, to high-rise apartments of fifty floors or more comprising an entire community. Amenities, such as swimming pools, tennis courts, clubrooms, and exercise rooms, vary with the size and price range of the property. Apartments often compete on the bases of price and amenities.

Demand for residential rental properties is directly related to population and the ability of that population to purchase or rent living space. The demand for particular types and styles of residential rental properties depends on demographics and tastes and preferences. Preferences for a particular location are predicated on accessibility to work, shopping, schools, entertainment, and other destinations of interest to households. Thus, economic and demographic data are of critical importance in making decisions about investing in residential rental property.

Another important factor affecting residential property performance is property management. Residential properties are management-intensive; that is, they take a great deal of time, care, and effort and can prove to be frustrating when tenants complain and violate lease provisions, as they often do. Calls in the middle of the night from irate tenants are not unusual. With small properties the owner usually cannot afford professional property management and must personally perform all the management duties. With larger properties the owner must interview management firms and select one. Even then, constant monitoring of the property and meetings with the professional managers are necessary if good performance is to be expected. Many investors avoid investments in apartments and other residential properties because such intensive management is needed.

Lease terms on apartments generally provide for monthly rental payments based on a rate for the entire unit, for example, $575 per month. Leases frequently are for periods of six months to one year, with a month-to-month arrangement after that. Every state has landlord–tenant laws outlining the rights of both parties to a residential lease. In some areas, rent control laws have introduced a new and important type of risk into apartment investment.

One advantage of residential rental properties is that good financing is generally available because such properties normally maintain their value and provide good collateral for a loan. In the first half of the 1980s, investors bid up the prices of most types of residential properties; as a result the cash flow yields on their equity investments fell, and investors relied more on tax shelter and appreciation to achieve their desired rates of return. In the latter half of the 1980s, prices in many communities decreased as a result of tax reform, overbuilding, and lower inflation rates, thus providing good investment opportunities.

Property value appreciation is often a prime objective of residential property investors. If a property is well located and well maintained, its value should increase in line with the income generated by the property. If rents and cash flow can be increased proportionately with the inflation rate, property values will tend to increase accordingly. Obviously, poor management can be devastating. Research has indicated that poor management is the leading source of tenant dissatisfaction, often causing tenants to terminate their leases. However, some investors have been successful at finding and purchasing poorly managed or poorly maintained properties, taking corrective action, increasing rents, and then selling them for handsome gains.

Office Buildings

Office buildings, in general, are considered to be riskier than residential properties and require more knowledge about property management and leasing, but at the same time they offer greater possible returns to the investor. Medium- and high-rise buildings, found in downtown and suburban areas of cities, and garden (low-rise) office buildings, usually limited to suburban areas, are general types of office buildings. A new investor in office buildings often begins with the purchase of suburban low-rise buildings, because they more closely resemble the ownership and operation of apartment buildings, whereas a more experienced investor may prefer a larger property.

General demand for office buildings is directly related to the level of office employment. Office employment covers a wide range of business activities such as national and regional headquarters for major corporations; administrative offices for smaller firms; work space for professionals such as doctors, lawyers, and accountants; support space for distribution, manufacturing, and research activities; and space for services such as travel agencies, real estate firms, banks, and insurance firms. The condition of the local and national economies affects the attitudes of office space users toward the number of square feet of office space allotted to each employee and the provision of extra space to allow for growth.

Office space leases are for varying lengths of time, but traditionally for a minimum of two to three years. Lease terms are quoted in terms of dollars per square foot per year—for example, $16 per square foot. Often, a tenant finish allowance stated in dollars per square foot is provided by the owner to pay for carpeting, paneling, shades and draperies, and other costs of preparing the space for occupancy. Care must be exercised in gathering lease information because in periods of excess supply office building owners often make concessions in the form of free rent or extravagant tenant finish allowances. For example, an owner may give a tenant six months free rent for signing a three-year lease at $18 per square foot. Calculating the true or "effective" rental rate can be a time-consuming and difficult task.

Another potential problem is determining the number of square feet on which rent is to be paid. At question is whether rent is paid on common areas such as hallways and bathrooms and whether office space is measured to the inside or outside of the walls. How office space is measured varies between cities and, sometimes, within a city; there can be significant differences in effective rental income for a stated rental rate. Various organizations, such as the Building Owners and Managers Association (BOMA), have developed guidelines for the measurement of space.

The elements of prestige and convenience make a good location critical for office buildings. For suburban office buildings, good location means ready access to major streets and expressways and good proximity to high-income residential areas, other offices, restaurants, hotels, and shopping facilities. Successful office buildings are frequently found near major highway intersections and adjacent to community and regional shopping centers. In many cities, office nodes (concentrations of office development) tend to develop in particularly attractive parts of the city. The prestige of an office building is directly related to the quality of its tenants. An owner of an office building may seek a prestigious tenant and name the building after that tenant in order to create a prestigious image and thereby attract other high-quality tenants to the project.

The purchase price (per square foot) for an office building is substantially greater than for a similar-sized apartment property, primarily because of higher land cost and better construction quality. On the other hand, well-located office buildings are attractive investments for lenders and represent good collateral for high loan–value ratios. As compared with apartment properties, office properties tend to attract more stable tenants, have lower tenant turnover ratios, are less subject to rent controls, and are increasingly characterized by "net leases" that shift many operating-expense uncertainties directly to tenants.

The value of well-located and well-maintained office buildings with well-written leases is likely to increase as fast as the rate of inflation and, during periods of strong demand, considerably faster. However, many poorly maintained and built buildings will be unable to attract and keep good tenants and will end up in bankruptcy. In addition, office building markets have a more dramatic boom-and-bust cycle than that of other real estate sectors.

Shopping Centers

Of the property types discussed so far, the shopping center is considered by many to be the most sophisticated and complex property type and requires the greatest management and investor expertise. Lease arrangements tend to be complicated and tenant selection difficult. Property management and leasing sophistication is essential for success. As a result the risks tend to be greater, but so are the potential rewards. Shopping centers are highly desirable properties for mortgage lenders because very few have been foreclosed in years past; moreover, they are generally owned by sophisticated and wealthy investors who have the financial resources to hold a project through adverse economic periods. There are four basic types of shopping centers: neighborhood, community, regional, and superregional.

Neighborhood Centers. A neighborhood shopping center is often referred to as a strip center and provides for the sale of convenience goods and services (food, drugs, dry cleaning, laundry, barbering, etc.). It is usually built around a supermarket or drugstore as the principal tenant, and averages about 50,000 square feet of gross leasable area (GLA) in size. It is the smallest type of shopping center.

Community Centers. In community shopping centers clothing and furniture are sold as well as the convenience goods found in neighborhood centers. There may also be banking, professional offices, and sometimes recreational facilities. The center is usually built around a junior department store, variety store, or discount department store. A typical GLA size for such a center would be about 150,000 square feet.

Regional Centers. A regional shopping center is built around one or two full-time department stores (e.g., Sears) of generally not less than 100,000 square feet each. These department stores are the "anchors" and act as traffic generators for the many smaller retail outlets in the center. These centers will have a range of 400,000 to one million square feet. They have been extremely successful in most cities and have been an excellent investment for individuals and institutional equity investors such as REITs and life insurance companies.

Superregional Centers. A superregional shopping center is found only in major metropolitan areas and is built around at least three major department stores. Its size is usually one million square feet and larger. A superregional center might be anchored by Sears, Wards, and Penneys as the major national tenants, plus two large regional-chain department stores, in addition to 100 to 200 individual stores and restaurants, providing complete lines of goods.

Successful Shopping Centers. Shopping center leases are often structured to allow the tenant and owner to share in the ability of the site to generate sales volume. This is accomplished by the use of leases providing for the payment of base rents, regardless of sales volume, and rents as a percentage of sales above a specified amount. The owner and tenant apportion the risks and returns through negotiations over the base and the percentages. Many other lease terms, such as hours of operation, freight handling, and contributions to maintaining the common areas of the center are also important. Shopping center leases are often very complex documents.

The success of a given center depends on important factors such as the size of the market area, the level and growth rate of family income in the market area, and the number of nearby competitors. The income generated by a center will depend on specific project factors such as tenant mix, length of leases, and lease terms. The ideal situation would be a growing and affluent market where

- Nonanchor tenants are selected to achieve high sales volumes and pay percentage (percentage of sales) rents.
- Lease terms permit periodic escalation of base rents.
- Lease terms provide that all tenants pay a percentage of operating expenses of the center, and these contributions increase as the owner's operating expenses increase, thus providing an inflation hedge for the owner.

Most investors seek to cover basic operating expenses and mortgage payments through the base (guaranteed) rents and make their profits through percentage rents that are tied directly to the sales volumes of the individual anchor and mall tenants. As the sales volumes of the tenants increase through inflation and growth in the retail demand in the area, the investor's cash flow increases accordingly. Investors in shopping centers are interested in substantial amounts of cash flow from operations. Cash flow automatically increases when the sales volume of the center rises, and property value increases as sales volumes and cash flows become larger.

Shopping centers are good alternatives to consider once the investor has gained investment experience with other less complicated properties. Smaller centers, however, are riskier than larger ones because they are more subject to competition from new strip centers and retail areas and, thus, are subject to substantial economic obsolescence.

Industrial Buildings

Warehouses and mini-warehouses, factories, and industrial parks are all industrial properties. Factories are special-use properties and are not easily converted to other uses. Therefore, factories tend to be very risky enterprises for the average investor and are avoided except by those who specialize in such investments. Various types of special-use properties are addressed in the following section. The industrial park—a large tract of land containing many compatible buildings which are used for a variety of light industrial uses—is a complex investment alternative that should be considered only by a sophisticated and wealthy investor. However, if an investor wishes to buy a partnership interest and leave the management and ownership problems to a managing or general partner with a good track record, this may be a viable alternative.

The most popular type of industrial property investment is the warehouse. Warehouses are really nothing more than boxes of space for the temporary storage of goods. There are very small warehouses, known as mini-warehouses, which are used by families and small businesses and are arranged in one- or two-story buildings that have been subdivided into many small cubicles. There is also the traditional warehouse, used by every major business. This large building has special loading and unloading facilities designed for the businesses who lease space.

Not surprisingly, the critical factor for good warehouses is access to key transportation arteries. Warehouses are simple to construct, have a very long economic life, require very little management effort compared with other income properties, and are popular investments for individuals who wish to avoid management hassles. Many investors seek to lease their warehouse buildings to major industrial companies under long-term net leases (the tenant pays most or all of the operating expenses) and then sit back and collect their monthly cash flow. Such investments tend to be long term, and relatively low return and low risk in nature.

However, if investors seek higher returns, including the associated higher risks, they can lease out warehouse space at a higher rent per square foot to several smaller, lower-credit tenants under short-term leases. Although such a rental means higher risk because of the possibility of vacancies, investors can charge a higher rent from the start, and possibly raise rents as the leases are renewed. This strategy, of course, means that a more intensive management and leasing effort must be expended.

Fully leased warehouses provide good collateral for a loan and are desirable properties for lenders. Consequently, good long-term financing at favorable rates is often available to investors. The cash flow from the property will be stable at a moderate rate if a long-term lease is present. Tax shelter is not a prime motive of the investor because of a high land ratio and relatively low improvement cost of warehouses.

The key to increasing property value in a warehouse investment is cash flow. If the leases are structured to lock in fixed rental rates for long periods of time, there is little hope of property value appreciation during the term of the lease. However, if leases are short term and rents can be increased periodically, or if long-term lease rates are indexed to inflation rates, cash flows and property values also increase. In addition, it would be advantageous for the investor to structure net leases to pass on expense increases directly to tenants, in order to decrease operating expense risks for the investor.

Special-Use Properties

Motels and hotels, nursing homes, hospitals, theaters, recreational facilities, fast-food franchises, and auto service stations are all special-use properties, as are most of the property types listed in Exhibit 21-1 under "residential transient facilities," "entertainment and recreational," "public service," and "other."

Unlike other property types, special-use projects have two investment elements: (1) the real estate itself, and (2) the specialized business for which the property is used. Investors purchasing special-use properties buy both and assume the risks of both. Thus, these properties should be considered only by relatively sophisticated investors who wish to specialize in analyzing and managing the unique business situation created by the special-use property. The alternative is to have blind faith and trust in others who will perform these functions.

The investor who would like to become involved in these types of properties should consider the following factors.

1. Special-use properties tend to be very risky ventures. Anyone investing in them should be able to manage the risks as well as the possible losses.

2. The successful investor of special-use properties should be a serious student of the business that occupies the real estate and have a substitute in mind should the business not be successful. The alternative businesses for a special-use property should include only those that are well understood by the investor.

3. Lenders are difficult to attract and they ask for high interest rates and substantial equity contributions. They almost always require personal loan guarantees and often demand that an investor pledge other collateral (e.g., certificates of deposit, or stock) to guarantee that loan payments will be made.

4. It may be necessary to allocate a considerable amount of time to such projects. These are the most management-intensive properties of all those we have discussed. Investors who do not plan to delegate most of these responsibilities to completely trustworthy managers or net-lease the property to a good-credit business (e.g., Pizza Hut) will have to devote much of their time to managing the affairs of the business. If such time is not available, it would be wise to forgo these opportunities despite the prospects of extraordinary cash flow returns.

Raw Land

Of all the types of real estate investments, raw-land investments will usually be the most risky. Here, a raw-land investment refers to the purchase of undeveloped acreage on the fringe of or in a city that is expected to be ready for development sometime in the future. Consequently, the investor should be sure that the land is in the path of future growth and that it will be desirable for development. Successful raw-land investors should understand such market factors as the dynamics of urban and regional growth and what makes developers do the things they do. If the raw-land investor does not understand this process, or is wrong in the timing of development activity, the land investment can turn into a financial disaster.

A number of important physical, legal, and political factors must be considered when evaluating a raw-land investment: (1) access of the property to public roads; (2) topography and soil types present; (3) current zoning of the land and the probability that it can be rezoned for a higher and better use; (4) availability of utilities, such as water and sewer, electricity, gas, and telephone; and (5) future availability of public services, such as fire, police, and sanitation. Problems with any of these factors can substantially affect the rate of return on the land investment.

Raw land is an unattractive investment from a cash flow or tax shelter perspective. Most raw-land investments experience negative cash flows each year (they have to be "fed") because the owner must pay interest, taxes, and insurance during a time when the property produces no rental income unless it is put to an interim land use, such as farming or ranching. Tax shelter is poor because land cannot be depreciated for tax purposes and interest expenses may not be deductible. Consequently, an investor who seeks tax shelter or positive cash flow as an objective would not be very interested in investing in raw land. Partly because of the lack of cash flow and partly because of the volatile nature of land values, institutional financing is usually not available for raw land. Often, the investor must depend on seller financing for the transaction.

The key factor to financial success is appreciation of property value. Only if the land value rises very quickly can the investor cover the costs of holding the property, make a substantial investment profit, and justify the risks associated with raw-land investment. One rule of thumb used by many investors is that land value must increase a minimum of 20 to 30 percent annually in order for a raw-land investment to be financially attractive. Although many have become millionaires because of such rapid appreciation in raw land, many other investors have gone broke because land values did not increase at rapid rates. Novice investors should not venture into this arena.

PROPERTY SELECTION

Selecting the property type or types that best satisfy the needs of the investor is a process similar to that used to select the ownership form. That is, it requires the simultaneous consideration of many factors, with the investor determining the minimum and maximum acceptable levels and weighting to be applied to each. A matrix approach may be developed for selecting the general types of properties for investment.

To aid in this process, Exhibit 21-2 summarizes the extent to which various property types possess selected characteristics. This exhibit should be a useful review of the ideas presented in this chapter. Used in conjunction with the investor's investment philosophy, goals, and objectives, it should permit the investor to develop an understanding of factors important in the property selection process. Later chapters provide significantly more detail about each property type.

SUMMARY

This chapter outlines the characteristics of each basic property type. Properties differ with respect to market demand for space, locational considerations, cash flow characteristics, management burden, and other factors. The selection of a property type is an important and complex decision. It has a pronounced impact on the risk and expected return associated with real estate investment.

EXHIBIT 21-2. Characteristics of Property Types

	Agricultural and Undeveloped Land	Predeveloped Land	New Apartments
Function	Agricultural, forest, and mineral production; recreation	Held for investment and speculation on successful development	Shelter, housing, amenities, and living environment
Investment characteristics			
Cash flow	Low (or negative)	Negative	Low to medium
Inflation hedge	Good	Good	Good
Operating risk	High	High	High
Liquidity	Relatively illiquid	Generally difficult to sell	Generally good for smaller units
Mortgage financing	Financing primarily by sellers and specialized government programs	Financing almost exclusively available from seller; favorable financing terms reflected in higher selling price	70 to 80 percent conventional financing, with land lease possible for developer to "mortgage out"
Ownership characteristics			
Owner's equity	Generally owned by user with increasing tendency to investment by institutional investors and partnerships	Owned primarily by individuals, partnerships, and large corporations	All types of owners, including many individuals and partnerships
Size	Can be bought in all sizes, but meaningful operating economies require substantial holdings	Can be of any size	All sizes; tend to be somewhat larger than existing apartments
Management time required	Heavy; constant supervision required if in use	Low, although it is essential that important developments be monitored, but when disposition occurs, substantial management time could be required	Extensive for initial rent-up; average to heavy for ongoing operations
Management expertise required	Very high; timing of paramount importance	Moderate, although ability to interpret—and influence—political and eco---	Average

Economies of size	With the trend to use more advanced technology and larger capital-intensive equipment, large land holdings advantageous	Large acreage can represent substantial economies of scale	Substantial economies realized with larger units
Economic characteristics			
Users	Farmers, ranchers, individuals, corporations	Large corporations, individual speculators	Families and individuals of moderate means or those who choose not to own a home (usually rents for more than an existing unit)
Term of use	Lifetime down to yearly leases	One to five years	Year leases, condominiums and cooperatives to lifetime
Demand influences	Population levels, food and other consumption levels, technology, transportation systems	Population trends, general economic conditions, land use controls, transportation systems, availability of money for development, government programs (new communities financing)	Population increases, family formation rates, social and economic changes, life-style modes, amenity packages offered
Supply influences	Water availability, transportation access, removals through development activity, fertility and soil conditions, scenic or other recreational possibilities	Land use regulations, conversion to developed status, establishment of parks and natural preserves, regional growth patterns, density and sprawl trends, volume of land promotion activity	Removals from housing stock by demolition or condemnation, availability of money for new financing, land use approval process, political environment, special government programs (FHA-subsidized housing, housing allowances)
Government controls	Crop subsidy programs, formal financing programs, land use controls	Land use controls, restrictions on marketing practices	Restrictions on condominiums, property tax assessment policies, financing availability (specialized government programs), land use regulations

EXHIBIT 21-2. Continued

	Existing Apartments	Hotel and Motel	Individual, Strip, Commercial, and Small Office Properties
Function	Shelter, housing, amenities, and living environment	Protection for travelers, home away from home for travelers, a communications-related property	Exchange goods; distribution centers; personal services; administration and management
Investment characteristics			
Cash flow	Reasonable	Possibly high	Average to good
Inflation hedge	Good	Good	Low
Operating risk	Average	High	Average to high
Liquidity	Generally good for smaller units	Harder to sell because of operating risks	Low to average
Mortgage financing	70 to 80 percent financing available from conventional sources; seller often carries back secondary financing	Financing dependent on previous operating record and strength of management	70 to 80 percent conventional sources; seller may often provide secondary financing
Ownership characteristics			
Owner's equity	All types of owners, including many individuals and partnerships	By operating companies or when owned by individuals or partnerships, generally leased to an operating company	Smaller investors, individuals, small groups
Size	All sizes; tend to be many small units available	Range from "Mom and Pop" operations to very large units	Moderate
Management time required	Average, except that "problems" can make excessive time demands	Excessive; a 24-hour operation requiring constant attention	Average to high, particularly when leases are of shorter term
Management expertise required	Average	High; the constant client contact and continual turnover, combined with	Average

the diverse array of services provided, require broad knowledge

Economies of size	Substantial economies realized with larger units	Larger units more efficient for operations	Low, unless multiple properties owned
Economic characteristics			
Users	Families and individuals of moderate means or those who choose not to own a home	Individuals, families, travelers, business	Households, small businesses, chain stores, white-collar workers
Terms of use	Month to month, some year leases, condominiums and cooperatives	Overnight, weekly	One-year to long-term leases
Demand influences	Population increases, family formation rates, social and economic changes	General economic conditions, recreation and leisure trends, transportation availability and pricing, special events (conventions, conferences, expositions)	Population levels, transportation access and technology, parking, competition
Supply influences	Removals from housing stock by demolition or condemnation, political environment, conversions to other use (condominiums), conversions from other uses (e.g., hotels), supply of new units	Removal of space of existing units from market; conversion of existing units to alternative uses; perceived demand; financing availability; land use regulations; conference, convention, and exposition demand	Land or lot availability, existence of commercial "strip," local government attitude toward transportation and strip development
Government controls	Restrictions on convertibility to condominiums, property tax assessment policies, financing availability (specialized government programs)	Restrictions on convertibility to condominiums, property tax assessment policies, financing availability (specialized government programs), land use regulations	Zoning, building codes, willingness to supply services, traffic control

EXHIBIT 21-2. Continued

	Shopping Centers	Office Buildings	Industrial Property
Function	Exchange goods, distribution centers; opportunity for concentration shopping experience	Personal services, administration and management of economic and social systems	Conversion of raw materials, production of manufactured goods, labor, land and capital meet here
Investment characteristics			
Cash flow	Average to good	Average	Average to high
Inflation hedge	Average	Average	Poor
Operating risk	Low	Average	High
Liquidity	Relatively good if leases are strong	Relatively good if leases are strong	Very difficult to sell unless there is strong long-term lease
Mortgage financing	Financing dependent on major department store as anchor tenant as well as designated percentage of leases signed	Financed often on a floor-ceiling arrangement whereby additional increments of financing depend on threshold levels of leasing being achieved	Financing depends on credit rating, often owned by occupant; if not, financing will depend on credit rating of lessee
Ownership characteristics			
Owner's equity	Tend more to be owned by larger investors including corporations, REITs, and insurance companies	Tend more to be owned by larger investors including corporations, REITs, and insurance companies	Often owned by users; otherwise, REITs and other institutional investors
Size	Some smaller investment properties available, but tend to become larger	Come in all sizes, but a number are very large and require substantial capital	Tend to be medium-sized to larger units
Management time required	High; requires constant promotion and attention to maintenance and tenant satisfaction	Average to low	Relatively low, although negotiating leases can be very time-consuming
Management expertise required	High, particularly in negotiating leases and conducting promotions	Average, although lease negotiation requires high level of sophistication and expertise	Average to high; lease negotiation can be particularly complex

Economies of size	Substantial management economies with larger centers; can enjoy joint promotion activities	Size tends to be of less concern, although it can effect certain savings	Manufacturing trend to larger facilities, although many businesses require modest amount of space
Economic characteristics			
Users	All households (particularly heavy usage in suburbs); small businesses and chain stores	White-collar workers, administrators and managers, large and small businesses	Blue-collar workers, managers, large and small corporations
Term of use	One- to fifty-year leases	One- to ten-year or longer leases	Lifetime down to short term
Demand influences	Population, density, general economic conditions, spending patterns, presence of demand "magnet" (special attraction to bring people to center)	Economy, politics, social modes, communications technology, size of work force, work technologies (space per worker, equipment per worker)	Economic conditions, business cycles in specific industry, foreign trade and tariffs, raw-material availability, technological developments, land use laws
Supply influences	Capital availability, competitors' perceptions of demand potential, department store location decisions, new housing development, economic conditions, government regulations	Corporate location decisions, financing availability, government decision (i.e., locating new facilities), corporate "image" decisions, space utilization patterns, business climate, removal of space from market, movement in direction of "urban" downtown	Land use controls, pollution regulations, technological obsolescence, changing manufacturing or service orientation of economy, conversion of space to alternative uses, removal of industrial space from market
Government controls	Property tax assessment policies, financing availability (specialized government programs), land use regulations	Restrictions on convertibility to condominiums, property tax assessment policies, financing availability (specialized government programs)	Property tax assessment policies, financing availability (specialized government programs), land use regulations, pollution emission standards

Source: Sherman J. Maisel and Stephen E. Roulac, *Real Estate Investment and Finance* (New York: McGraw-Hill, 1976), p. 470.

22

APARTMENTS

Free market, for profit, rental housing [development] cannot survive a prolonged inflation. From an investor's view, rentals must support not only the increased cost of construction and the financing but also a continuous rise in the market value of the property to match the continuous fall in the value of the dollar.

MARTIN MAYER, *The Builders*

Before World War II, fewer than 45 percent of all American households owned their residences. By 1976, almost two-thirds of American households occupied their own dwellings. Estimates are that by 1990 nearly 70 percent of all households will be owner-occupied. Furthermore, nearly 30 percent of all multifamily developments will be condominiums.

From 1970 to 1976 about 8 million single-family homes and 2.5 million rental units were added to the housing stock. New housing construction fell sharply during the period from 1976 to 1980 but was resurrected during the first half of the 1980s. The high inflation and interest costs of the last five years of the 1970s cut deeply into the construction of new rental units, but changing economic conditions in the 1980s led to an increase in multifamily rental housing construction. Thus, rental housing presents an attractive investment opportunity for the decade ahead.

The nature of rental housing in the 1980s has differed from that in the past. High interest rates and construction costs coupled with inflation and weaker markets may keep rental rates from being high enough to cover higher operating costs and debt servicing requirements and still provide rates of return equal to those in the past. It appears that adequate profitability today depends more on operating efficiencies and expected appreciation than on cash flows and tax shelter benefits. Further complicating the picture are property tax revolts and rent controls in some parts of the country. It is therefore important to monitor the political atmosphere and avoid investing where tax reform and rent controls could hinder investment in rental housing. Another major issue that is evolving is the removal or treatment of environmentally hazardous materials such as asbestos.

Definitions[1]

Rental housing is often classified partly by developmental density and partly by architectural style.

Garden apartments. Garden apartments have a relatively low density of development, typically ranging from sixteen to twenty-five units per acre. Buildings usually are two- to two-and-one-half-story walk-ups. The grounds are extensively landscaped and have such outdoor amenities as swimming pools, tennis courts, and clubhouses. Parking is provided on the grounds. The buildings, usually containing eight to sixteen units, are constructed of wooden studs and brick veneer or other siding requiring little maintenance. In warmer climates concrete block construction is common. Concerns over environmental protection have moved more developers (in cooperation with local planning ordinances) to rely on the planned unit development (PUD) concept, stressing retention of the natural landscape and integration of the development within it. There is then little need to remove natural vegetation, and site development costs are kept to a minimum. However, such developments often incur higher costs in land investment, building permits, and conformance to environmental regulation.

Walk-up (low-rise apartments). Usually consisting of four to six stories, walk-up buildings are found mostly in older cities where smaller sites necessitates high building density. Stairways or hydraulic elevators provide access to the upper floors. Because such buildings are found mostly on small sites, amenities are usually limited, although some projects supplement their offerings by locating them near public parks. Usually, laundry facilities and storage rooms are located in the basements. Parking on site is often limited.

Medium-rise apartments. Ranging in height from six to nine stories, medium-rise developments are found mostly in the inner city or nearby suburbs. Parking may be available underground; hydraulic or cable-lift elevators are located in a service core area which also includes trash depositories, meter rooms, laundry, and so on. Inside, a common hallway provides access to each unit on a floor. Some projects provide a wide range of amenities such as swimming pools, club houses, exercise rooms and sun decks, and storage facilities. The size and complexity of such buildings

[1]For more complete definitions, see Urban Land Institute, *Residential Development Handbook* (Washington, D.C.: 1978).

may require on-site service personnel as well as professional property management.

High-rise apartments. Although high-rise apartments are typically twenty- to thirty-story buildings, averaging about 240 units per building, many are much taller and offer considerably more than 750 units. High-speed elevators are common for such structures, with a ratio of about one elevator to every eight floors. The basic service core is the same as in the medium-rise building, but the supporting amenities are larger in size and scope and include receiving rooms for tenants' packages, maid and valet service, doormen (and other security measures, including sophisticated electronic security devices), garage attendants, retail outlets, and other conveniences. Some tier arrangements are provided as amenities, and it is not uncommon to offer custom work for long-term tenants. Occupants are usually upper-income empty nesters, professional couples, and families. The staff is required to have special technical training for operating and maintaining utility, elevator, and service equipment.

Townhouse complexes. The row houses making up complexes have party walls; masonry or wood stud with brick veneer construction is common. Many townhouses are also designed using a zero lot line zoning that actually provides separate ownership of the land and building rather than tenancy in common ownership of the land. Young families are attracted to townhouses as a stepping-stone to ownership of a single-family detached home. Separate entrances and patios, the illusion of privacy, and ample parking together with shared recreational facilities are major features. Townhouses usually cost less to manage than other types of complexes because typical lease arrangements provide that tenants are responsible for most day-to-day maintenance and repairs.

Condominiums. Under the condominium arrangement, occupants buy rather than lease dwellings. The deed and mortgage provide for fee ownership of the apartment (or townhouse) with a patio or balcony and some interest in the common areas, streets, parking areas, and recreational facilities. Most states have enabling legislation that controls how condominium projects are governed. Generally management control rests with the owners' association, which has responsibility for maintenance, taxes and insurance, water and sewage, and common-area amenities. In large projects, however, management is often delegated to professional management companies.

Cooperatives. Unlike condominium ownership, persons purchase shares of stock in a cooperative and occupy the individual units by lease. The cooperative is run as a not-for-profit corporation under IRS rules. Management is in the hands of the board of directors elected by the shareholder–tenants under the constitution and bylaws of the corporation. Actual management may be delegated to professional management companies. This type of ownership, which is not common in most parts of the country, seems to be concentrated in older cities of the Northeast and the North Central states.

TRACK RECORD AND TRENDS

The future productivity of an existing apartment project is not usually related to the past. For example, from 1975 to 1979 an excess supply of units in many MSAs deflated the rental market. Many complexes went into foreclosure; those that survived often did so at the cost of extensive deferred maintenance, and managers of some properties leased units to tenants who literally destroyed them. The demand for apartment housing was reborn in the early 1980s, but recently the construction of new units seems to be fueled less by increases in demand and more by the insatiable appetite of pension funds and public limited partnerships for new investment. Indeed, a 1986 survey by the National Association of Realtors found that multifamily housing projects are the most frequently traded type of real estate investment.[2]

In many cities, new units were built for sale to large institutional real estate investors at prices not justified by existing market demand and rents. The hope is that in the future demand will prop up rents, but the numbers of new units constructed and the total rehabilitation of many older units may saturate the market for many years to come.

The relevant housing market or neighborhood is the area where lessors and lessees communicate with one another for the leasing of individual dwelling units. There may be a number of geographic submarkets in the metropolitan area that compete for the same set of tenants. The demand for apartments is derived from the total demand for housing. The utility or amenity package offered by the apartment house and convenient linkages to municipal services, shopping, and so forth make up the services supplied to the household.

In broad terms, housing market analysis is concerned with the following elements.

1. Delineation of the market area within which dwelling units compete with one another.

---

[2]March–April 1986 survey by the National Association of Realtors' Economics and Research Division.

2. The area's economy—principal economic activities and basic resources.

3. Demand factors—employment, incomes, population, and family size.

4. Supply factors—residential construction, existing inventory, conversions, and demolitions.

5. Current market conditions—vacancies, unsold inventory, marketability or sales and rental units, prices, rents, building costs, mortgage defaults, foreclosures and disposition of acquired properties.

6. Quantitative and qualitative demand—prospective number of dwelling units that can be absorbed economically at various price and rent levels under conditions existing on the "as of" day.

The demand for housing since World War II has been substantially greater than the market's ability to supply housing. The government's policy of promoting ownership of single-family housing has greatly benefited this sector of the shelter industry. The government has provided aid to the low-income segment of the rental housing market but has not generally provided any assistance to the remainder of the industry. Thus, investment in housing seems "doomed" to success! In more recent times the spread between demand and supply has widened and created what some analysts call "pent-up demand," households that demand housing and are not adequately serviced either because levels of construction are too low or costs of acquisition too high. Occupancy rates appear to remain in the middle 90 percent range in many markets.[3] Condominium conversions have also kept the supply of rental housing low relative to demand, although conversion seems to have run its course, and its affect on supply will likely lessen in the future. The relatively high cost of owner-occupied housing also bodes well for the rental housing market. Many families marginally able to afford home purchases will help keep the demand for rental units strong, particularly for those built with the aura of a single-family home; these units have become increasingly attractive to today's renters. More recently, too, housing for older citizens has become more of an art form; the inclusion of attractive features and the provision of some limited care for the householders are attracting this sector to rental housing more than ever before. Rutgers University Urban Policy Research Center projected that the demand for rental units through the year 2000 would be over 9 million units.[4]

[3]U.S. Department of Commerce, Bureau of Census, *Annual Housing Survey*, (Washington, D.C.: 1975 to date, updated quarterly), see December 1987 issue, Table 15.

[4]Rutgers University, Center for Urban Policy Research, *Future Demand for Rental Housing: 1980 to 2000* (Brunswick, N.J.: Spring 1978).

INVESTING IN APARTMENTS

Advantages and Disadvantages

The primary advantages of rental housing investments are good cash flows (limited somewhat in recent years), frequent tenant turnover, which permits rents to rise quickly with inflation, reasonably good appreciation experience, and good rates of return on invested funds.

The disadvantages include the need for intensive management, the need for frequent repairs and redecoration as tenants vacate, less stable income flows, and decreasing returns over time as competition increases.

Mixed-use developments, increasingly popular in suburban sites where improvements in site utilization parallel increases in land costs, may reduce the advantages and disadvantages by diversifying the sources of return. Housing is becoming more common in mixed-use projects, which are often regulated by city governments and have as their aim extending city life beyond rush hour, providing entertainment and cultural activities for residents, and retaining office users and retail businesses in the area.

Types of Investors and Investor Motivations

The availability of tax shelter represented the basic motivating factor in apartment investment prior to the passage of the Tax Reform Act of 1986. Since then, investors have shifted attention to the "basic economics" of apartment projects, seeking adequate levels of cash flow and appreciation potential. Most institutional investors and public syndicators are "current yield" buyers who seek first year ROEs in the range of 8 to 9 percent.

The conversion of apartments into condominiums units has been highly profitable in the past, but future cycles of conversion may be marginal and the number of units offered can exceed market absorption rates. To attain full benefits of such arrangements, investors usually sell to a condominium converter–developer, if possible.

The market phenomenon in which the value of an existing apartment (capitalized NOI) is considerably less than the reproduction cost has caused many investors to buy and hold apartments for resale. Although new units provide greater utility for the tenant, investment in such units has become less attractive in many MSAs and new apartment units have been costing disproportionately more than comparable older ones. There is a reasonable expectation of more appreciation in the value of many older apartments.

A final motivating factor can be traced to the various government subsidy and assistance programs, including the section 8 rent subsidy, rehabilitation matching-grant, and low-income housing tax credit programs. Since HUD accepts both new and rehabilitated units in these programs, some investors have been purchasing older buildings and building new developments, profiting through the mortgagor–developer fees that are built into the original rehabilitation cost and then realized by mortgaging out at higher prices.

PRELIMINARY ANALYSES

Market and Marketability Analysis

Demand and Supply Analysis. A submarket for apartment investment has a particular geographic segmentation of the market and an income level and appropriate occupational mix of prospective tenants. The investor identifies the users that he or she wishes to serve and their preferences. This determination generally begins with an analysis of the following supply and demand data (also see Chapter 12 on market analysis techniques).

1. Data on trends and characteristics of the local housing stock—tenure, types of structures, rents and prices, values, quality and condition—must be collected. The analyst then proceeds to identify short-run changes, both actual and planned and including demolitions, casualty losses, conversions, mergers, and new construction activities.

2. Evaluation of access and availability of urban services, such as hospitals, shopping centers, cultural and religious activities, and schools. Access to highways and arterial roads and adequacy of police, fire, and sanitation services are also examined. The analyst then identifies various neighborhoods and their respective qualities, including utilities, parks, and recreation, civic clubs, and neighborhood planning organizations.

3. Stratified vacancy estimates are obtained by field survey together with attention to the types, values, and quality of existing housing. Economic and demographic data are used to develop user profiles and to determine household size, income and occupation mix, turnover, mobility, and any unique characteristics of the population or neighborhood.

4. In effect, a quantitative and qualitative analysis is made of the existing competitive environments and the abilities of these environments to absorb new housing construction in both owner- and renter-occupied units across various price or rental brackets. The boundaries and scope of pertinent target markets are delineated and the distribution of units for sale or lease among various price classes is noted.

The completed market study enables the analyst to identify specific target markets in which demand vacuums exist. The market study also identifies the characteristics of buyers in the target market together with a profile of their preferences and the price range that they can pay for rent. All together, the information can direct the investor to where and what product to build. Once the target market and its pertinent characteristics have been selected, the investor then proceeds with a marketability analysis, providing in detail the absorption rate for the product, its pricing, its design, and the maximization of expect revenues. (Also see Chapter 13 on this topic.)

This process may appear rather elaborate; however, much of the information required is readily available from local planning commissions, appraisal firms, and other local agencies both public and private. The most likely sources of data from the field include local associations of apartment owners and managers (AOMA), builder–developers, commercial real estate brokers, utility engineers, mortgage lenders, university real estate departments, chambers of commerce, and planning departments. Investors who put effort into getting the details of market and marketability studies correct reduce the risk of acquiring an undesirable product, an overly expensive product, or a product ahead of its time in a specific area. Good market studies can be both time-consuming and expensive, yet considerably less than the cost of holding unleasable inventory! Any investor who intends to specialize in apartments should obtain a copy of *FHA Techniques of Housing Market Analysis.*[5]

Risk Management and Control. The major operating risks associated with apartment ownership are tenant selection, tenant turnover, control of expenses, and maintenance of rents and amenities at a level competitive with those in the immediate market area. Hazard risks can be easily controlled through insurance, but loss of tenants or rapid tenant turnover, like excessive operating expenses, can usually be traced to poor management. As with such risks as functional obsolescence and neighborhood deterioration, the effect is the loss of high-quality tenants as the downside process speeds up and a chain of moves brings in lower-income users.

Physical, Legal, Political, and Environmental Analysis

Physical Factors. The functional design of the apartment building is of maximum importance to potential demand, and amenity factors have as much bearing on the value of apartment buildings and complexes as they do on that of individually owned residences, particularly for the "baby boomers" and older citizens who represent continually growing segments of the market. The typical apartment dweller looks for roomy and well-closeted living space, neatly arranged kitchens and bathrooms, exterior exposure and balconies wherever possible, and central placement of the lobby, elevators, corridors, and laundry rooms so that these services are readily accessible. The amenity package for a good complex should include a swimming pool, a clubhouse, tennis courts, laundry facilities, good landscaping, playground equipment (if it is a family complex), and

[5]*FHA Techniques of Housing Market Analysis* (Washington, D.C.: Govt. Printing Office, 1978).

adequate parking. There should be at least 1.5 parking spaces per unit, preferably two. Many of the "baby boomer" generation, wanting more than typical rental but not willing to spend the time required of home-ownership, are attracted by the best recreational and status-oriented amenities available.

Upkeep of the physical condition of units is important for extending the competitive life of the building or complex. Investors often prefer brick exteriors, even though wood can be superior for both construction and energy conservation. Certain items have rather short useful lives—such as carpets, heating and air-conditioning units, drapes, and appliances—and generally some portion is replaced each year. Roofs and exterior walls can be trouble spots if maintenance was deferred by previous owners.

Legal and Political Factors. To avoid as much long-term disappointment as possible, the investor should review in advance the quality of local government, its capital improvement program, and its budget procedures. A rating system can be developed to evaluate the adequacy and convenience of municipal services of any potential location. An investor should also be wary of the political attitudes in a locality. Some local governments are very responsive to the demands of apartment dwellers. For example, some cities have passed laws prohibiting all-adult apartment projects, condominium conversions, and tenant assessments. On the other hand, more than one foreclosure has occurred because promised bus routes never materialized. Finally, property taxes should be compared to taxes in other localities on a per-unit or per-square-foot basis.

Environmental Factors. Investors and rehabilitators are facing increasing per-unit costs because of environmental regulations. For example, many investors are being required to install water retention basins to control runoff. Rehabilitators are finding that compliance with building codes is not enough and that the standards of stringent housing codes often require changes in room layouts, closets, entries, and the like. Also, containment and removal of hazardous materials such as asbestos is becoming an increasing problem in apartment investments.

Financial Analysis

In recent years apartment investors have sought cash-on-cash returns in the range of 8 to 10 percent. After-tax discounted returns may amount to as much as 30 percent or more in some cases. The 1986 tax reform reduced the time value of depreciation benefits, but returns should not be affected too dramatically. The recent rise in public real estate syndications has created substantial demand for well-located and well-managed properties. Prices have been pushed up and yields down; the high returns experienced in the past may no longer be available because of this increased demand.

Institutional investors are seeking going-in capitalization rates of 7.5 to 9.0 percent and terminal rates of 9.0 to 10 percent. For high returns, investors may have to turn to properties that are not large enough to attract national syndications and so would not command premium prices.

Although tenant turnover may certainly affect returns, poor management seems to be the most prevalent cause of poor investment performance; the quality of management is a primary source of risk. Escalating operating costs are another source of risk, but continued high occupancy rates and reduced inflation should bolster a satisfactory margin between gross receipts and operating expenses.

Another factor is financial risk, a matter that many investors fail to consider properly. Since it is unlikely that interest rates will fall dramatically in the years to come, the cost of borrowed funds is substantially higher than it was when apartment investments provided high cash flow returns. Many investors formerly purchased apartments using seller financing, but they are now using qualified nonrecourse high-ratio institutional financing, both of which would place heavy debt-servicing loads on the investment's net operating income. Thus, financial leverage can be very high and small percentage drops in gross revenues cause large decreases in equity yield rates.

Many institutions are now more interested in the debt coverage ratio than in loan-to-value ratios. Because of the higher interest rates being charged today, maintaining an acceptable debt coverage ratio usually means a smaller amount for debt funds and a larger amount for equity funds; the larger equity investments tend to lower equity return rates.

The reduction in the margin for error created by high debt loads, increases in operating expenses, and nonprofessional property management only emphasizes the need for good investment analysis on the part of small investors. Investors in syndications must carefully analyze syndication prospectuses to be sure that front-end loads do not cause too high a price to be paid for the equity participation, thus reducing the investor's return.

Other risks include the changing tastes and preferences of renters, deterioration of neighborhoods, and the escalation of property expenses. Owners should be able to recover their increases in expenses by similar increases in rent, since most markets in the United States exhibit high occupancy levels. However, real estate cycles and divergence in the timing of these events can drastically alter the cash flow. Lease duration creates another risk. If the market has an oversupply of units, then leases are necessary to hold tenants; if, however, the demand for units is high, lease terms become a hindrance in raising rents to allow owners to recover escalating expenses.

The marketability analysis provides the investor with estimates of the number of units that will be absorbed per time period together with an estimate of unit rental rates. Gross possible income can be estimated by analyzing rentals on existing units (usually on a square footage basis) and existing vacancy rates for comparable facilities in the target market. Some experts also suggest developing a method of tying economic indicators, such as the consumer price inex, to rent as a method of coping with inflation and operational cost increases. It is difficult to project income by applying simple growth factors—a real estate cycle scenario approach (see Chapter 14) is more realistic.

A vacancy rate factor should be based on the historical experience of comparable properties, the leasing strategy of the investor, and property management expertise. Income from other sources, such as laundry income and income from vending machines, should be added. Generally, economic occupancy above 95 percent is difficult to achieve, and the resulting eighteen vacant days per year allow for cleaning, painting, and normal turnover. Evictions are another source of loss; although collection efforts will minimize bad debts, a bad-debt reserve is necessary.

Expenses can be estimated by contacting local firms that provide needed services for estimates of the annual cost of these services. Local power, gas, water, and sanitation companies can provide very detailed estimates. Another method of estimating expenses is by examining the historical costs of existing projects. A third method would be to contact several professional property managers for estimates of operating expenses based on their experience. Finally, the investor can obtain published surveys on operating expense histories from the Institute of Real Estate Management in Chicago, Illinois.[6]

The general objective of good property management is to control operating expenses and maintain competitive rent and occupancy levels. To accomplish this objective, the investor must utilize good cash management techniques, such as cash budgeting, and have a means of selecting good tenants, keeping in mind that tenants pay for comfort, safety, and quiet enjoyment of the premises. If the investor is not trained in these areas, the property should be put in the hands of a competent property manager. The cost of property management runs anywhere from 3 to 10 percent of gross receipts, depending on the size of the project and the scope of the work to be performed.

FINANCING

Apartment loans are generally considered to be somewhat riskier than office or industrial property loans, and most long-term lenders require an interest rate from about .05 to 1 percent higher than for less risky properties, such as single-family homes and industrial properties. If the property

---

[6]National Association of Realtors, Institute of Real Estate Management, *Income/Expense Analysis: Apartments* (Chicago: annual research report).

is under construction, most lenders will hold back from 10 to 20 percent of the loan funds until the project achieves a specified occupancy level (usually break-even occupancy).

For small acquisitions, local institutions such as savings and loan associations and commercial banks are the most likely sources of mortgage money. Larger projects (loans more than $500,000 to $1,000,000) are often financed through insurance companies. In most cities there are several active mortgage banking firms that specialize in this type of property.

Terms for such loans vary widely, but some common requirements include possible participations either in profits or directly in the equity position (usually in return the lender provides very high-ratio financing), relatively short maturities (five to ten years with twenty-five- or thirty-year amortization terms), and balloons. Large investments may exhibit even more unusual terms, including deferred interest for the first few years, interest-only payments at reduced interest rates with the arrearage deferred until maturity, and convertible mortgages in which the lender obtains a growing equity position during the payment period until the lender's interest in the property fully converts to that of an equity holder. Suffice it to say that "creative" techniques are being practiced by most institutional lenders as well as by sellers. Other sources of multifamily financing may include the enhanced mortgaged packages of the Federal Home Loan Mortgage Corporation and the Federal National Mortgage Association. In addition, in exchange for the rental of a specified percentage of a project's units to low- and moderate-income tenants, the Internal Revenue Code grants tax-exempt status for bonds used to finance qualified projects.

Underwriting procedures, too, have changed dramatically during the past decade. In the past lenders were often satisfied with using the loan-to-value ratio to determine the amount of the loan. Today lenders are very sensitive to the ability of a project's NOI to service a loan and often use the debt coverage ratio to estimate the maximum mortgage payment, then back into the magnitude of the loan using the mortgage constant. This second method usually results in lower loan-to-value ratios and larger equity investments than in the past. To obtain higher-ratio financing, the borrower may have to resort to participations, short maturities, balloons, and so on, and large project investors might use land sale–leasebacks to increase the financial leverage. Unfortunately, the small investor is often unable to utilize many of the aforementioned methods unless the seller is involved in the financing arrangements. Local lenders often take a somewhat conservative attitude toward small investment loans.

TAXATION

Apartments historically offered better tax benefits than other types of real estate investments. Benefits included accelerated depreciation on both new and used units under ACRS provisions, full deductibility of mortgage interest, and favorable capital gains treatment on future resale proceeds. The Tax Reform Act of 1986 significantly curtailed or eliminated many of these benefits. The method of depreciation for residential real property is limited to straight-line over 27.5 years, mortgage interest deductions may be limited, and capital gains are taxed at regular rates. Some preferential treatment is awarded to historic structures and low-income housing. (See Chapter 10 for further discussion of these tax law provisions.)

DISCOUNTED-CASH-FLOW ANALYSIS

Although any investment should be analyzed using discounted-cash-flow techniques, many investors do use rule-of-thumb methods to simplify initial investment decisions. Apartments are often evaluated using the gross rent multiplier and cash-on-cash rules. High-quality apartment buildings may sell for anywhere from six to eight times gross revenues. Smaller properties and older properties tend to have lower gross rent multipliers and higher cash-on-cash yields.

Nevertheless, a proper DCF analysis should be used to determine internal rate of return (IRR). Because of the heavy competition between syndicators and large pension funds, IRRs on medium to large apartment projects have been bid down during the last ten years. In the past, apartment investments have provided IRRs after-tax ranging from 15 to 20 percent (large tax-sheltering projects provided even higher returns for high-bracket investors). It appears, however, that IRRs on institutional grade properties decreased to a range of 10 to 15 percent in the late 1980s.

THE INVESTMENT DECISION

At the present time apartment investors appear to be seeking well-constructed, well-located projects in balanced demand-supply states and cities. Larger investors are looking for future appreciation and higher rents from relatively new properties (one to five years old) to provide profits and are purchasing properties with current yields (ROE) in the 7 to 10 percent range. Small investors often find higher returns in smaller apartment building investments because there is less competition and the sellers are generally less sophisticated. There appear to be some excellent opportunities for the small investor in somewhat older projects of twelve to fifty units that are in good condition and well located in high-demand areas.

Throughout Parts II and IV of this text, the analysis of Aspen Wood Apartments is presented; this case study provides a systematic decision framework and guide for evaluating apartment investments. The reader should refer to this material for further discussion of subjects presented here.

SELECTED REFERENCES

Trends

Apartment Market Outlook, (Washington, D.C.: National Real Estate Investor, annual).

Housing and Development Reporter, (Washington, D.C.: The Bureau of National Affairs Inc., weekly).

Multi-Housing News, monthly.

National Real Estate Index (Emeryville, Calif.: Liquidity Fund).

Silacs, Jared and Richard Roddewig, *Rehab for Profit: New Opportunities in Real Estate* (Dubuque, Iowa: Kendall/Hunt Publishing Co., 1984).

Operations

Adams, Eli, "Real Men Don't Need to Give Rent Concessions," *Professional Builder*, January 1986, p. 116.

Ardman, Harvey and Perri Ardman, *The Complete Apartment Guide* (New York: Macmillan Co., 1982).

Goodkin, Sanford R., "Dense Does Make Sense But You Have To Merchandise It," *Professional Builder*, October 1985, p. 100.

Harris, R. Lee, "Giant Multifamily Communities: Management Realities," *The Journal of Property Management*, July–August 1985, pp. 47–50.

Hierbrier, Doreen, *Managing Your Rental House for Increased Income* (New York: McGraw-Hill, 1985).

LiVolsi, Robert F., "The Criteria Sell for Leasing Apartments," *The Journal of Property Management*, January–February 1985, pp. 52–55.

Lurz, William H., "Apartments Sell Serenity With Landscape, Waterscape . . . and Paint!," *Professional Builder*, September 1986, pp. 36–40.

Miller, E. Robert, "The Laundry Room's Hidden Profits," *The Journal of Property Management*, September–October, pp. 9–10.

Rynberk, Howard J. Jr., "Developing a Successful Rent Collection Policy," *The Journal of Property Management*, March–April 1986, pp. 29–32.

Investment Performance

"The Amenity Factor in Multifamily Site Planning," *Urban Land*, February 1983, p. 29.

Arnold, Alvin L., *How to Evaluate Apartment Building Investments* (Boston: Warren, Gorham & Lamont, 1978).

Danner, John C., "Cooperative Apartments," *The Real Estate Appraiser and Analyst*, Spring 1985, pp. 45–48.

Haddow, David F., "How Feasibility Studies Benefit Apartment Builders," *Real Estate Review*, Summer 1980, pp. 64–67.

Meagher, James P., "A Year for Apartments . . . Second-home Strategy," *Barrons*, December 31, 1984, p. 37.

Meagher, James P., "How Older Syndications Perform . . . Apartments for Pension Funds?" *Barrons*, November 14, 1983, p. 65.

National Real Estate Index, (Emeryville, Calif.: Liquidity Fund, quarterly).

Shirley A. Ness, "Environmental Hazards in Real Estate," and four other featured articles on the subject, *Commercial Investment Real Estate Journal*, July-August 1988, pp. 16–38.

O'Connell, Daniel J., *Apartment Building Valuation, Finance, and Investment Analysis* (New York: Wiley, 1982).

Tarantello, Rocky, "Inflation Dependency of Leveraged Investments," *Real Estate Issues*, Fall–Winter 1985, p. 7.

Temple, Douglas M., *Investing in Residential Income Property*, revised ed. (Chicago: Contemporary Books, 1981).

Market Analysis

Boehm, Thomas P., "Inflation and Intra-Urban Residential Mobility," *Housing Finance Review*, January 1984, pp. 10–30.

Bosselman, Fred P., et al., *Downtown Linkages: Policy Education Forum Co-sponsored by the Urban Land Institute and the U.S. Conference of Mayors, New York City, April 11, 1985* (Washington, D.C.: Urban Land Institute, 1985).

Carn, Neil, Joseph Rabianski, Ronald Racster, and Maury Seldin, *Real Estate Market Analysis: Techniques and Applications* (Englewood Cliffs, N.J.: Prentice-Hall, 1988), pp. 116–171.

Casazza, John, *Condominium Conversions*, (Washington, D.C.: Urban Land Institute, 1982).

"Design of Elderly Communities Stresses Residents' Independence," *Multi-Housing News*, October 1985, p. 27.

"Developers Meet Challenges of Continuing Care Housing," *Multi-Housing News*, October 1985, p. 26.

Hare, Patrick H., *Accessory Apartments* (Chicago: American Planning Association, Planning Advisory Service, 1981).

Hodges, Samuel J. III and Ellis G. Goldman, *Allowing Accessory Apartments: Key Issues for Local Officials* (Washington, D.C.: U.S. Department of Housing and Urban Development, Office of Policy Development and Research, 1983).

Lurz, William H., "Apartments Beat Tight Site Restrictions," *Professional Builder*, January 1985, p. 106.

"Marketing of Continuing Care Projects Packages Housing, Health Services," *Multi-Housing News*, October 1985, p. 26.

"Multis, Detached Houses Sell for Similar Prices per Sq. Ft.," *Multi-Housing News*, March 1986, p. 27.

"Rental Condos Lure Tenants," *Multi-Housing News*, September 1985, p. 24.

Shafer, Paul and Jean Weiner, *Small Space Design: Remodeling Apartments for Multiple Uses* (New York: Van Nostrand Reinhold, 1984).

Shashaty, Andre, "Mixed-Use Development Takes Hold in Suburban Locations," *Multi-Housing News*, November 1985, p. 10.

Snedcof, Harold R., *Cultural Facilities in Mixed-Use Development* (Washington, D.C.: Urban Land Institute, 1985).

"Ways to Soften Density," *Professional Builder*, February 1985, pp. 148–151.

Working with the Community: A Developer's Guide (Washington, D.C.: Urban Land Institute, 1985).

Financial Analysis

Byrne, Peter and David Cadman, *Risk, Uncertainty and Decision Making in Property Development* (London, New York: E. & F. N. Spon Ltd., 1984).

Cartee, Charles P., "Testing the Feasibility of Residential Rent Indexing," *The Journal of Property Management*, January–February, pp. 21–22.

Draper, Dennis W. and M. Chapman Findlay, "Capital Asset Pricing and Real Estate Valuation," *Journal of the American Real Estate and Urban Economics Association*, Summer 1982, pp. 152–183.

Dzierbicki, Daniel J., "Federally Subsidized Apartments & Cooperative Properties—The Ad Valorem Tax Appraisal Review," *Appraisal Review Journal*, Summer 1983, pp. 32–61.

Fogler, H. Russel, Michael R. Granito, and Laurence R. Smith, "A Theoretical Analysis of Real Estate Returns," *Journal of Finance*, July 1985, pp. 711–719.

Nixon, Clair J. and I. Richard Johnson, "Tax and Financial Implications of Converting Personal Residences to Rental Property: An Application of Net Present Value Analysis," *The Real Estate Appraiser and Analyst*, Summer 1984, pp. 43–48.

O'Connell, Daniel J., *Apartment Building Valuation, Finance, and Investment Analysis* (New York: Wiley, 1982).

Smith, Lawrence B., "Rental Apartment Valuation: The Applicability of Rules of Thumb," *The Appraisal Journal*, October 1985, pp. 541–552.

"Tax-Exempt Bonds, Joint Ventures Help Finance Development of Most Senior Citizen Communities," *Multi-Housing News*, October 1985, p. 26.

Wiley, Robert J., *Real Estate Accounting and Mathematics Handbook*, 2nd ed. (New York: Wiley, 1986).

Financing and Refinancing

Fabozzi, Frank J., ed., *The Handbook of Mortgage-Backed Securities* (Chicago: Probus Publications, 1985).

Lipscomb, Joseph B., "Refinancing Real Estate Investments: A Strategy for Maximizing NPV," *The Appraisal Journal*, April 1983, pp. 255–269.

Nore, Kenneth G., *Mortgage-Backed Securities: Developments and Trends in the Secondary Mortgage Market* (New York: Clark Boardman Co., 1985).

Sirmans, C. F. and Bobby Newsome, "Mortgage-Equity Valuation and Alternative Financing," *The Appraisal Journal*, April 1983.

Vidger, Leonard P., *Borrowing and Lending on Residential Property: Fundamentals for Homeowners, Investors and Students* (Lexington, Mass.: Lexington Books, 1981).

Wride, Jeff and Richard C. Ratcliff, *Creative Financing: Avoiding the Pitfalls* (Reston, Va.: Reston Publishing, 1984).

Taxation

Allen, Roger H., *Real Estate Investment and Taxation*, 2nd ed. (Cincinnati: South-Western Publishing Co., 1984).

Arnold, Alvin L., *Real Estate Investments After the Tax Reform Act of 1986* (Boston: Warren, Gorham & Lamont, 1987).

Kau, James B. and C. F. Sirmans, *Tax Planning for Real Estate Investors: How to Take Advantage of Real Estate Tax Shelters* (Englewood Cliffs, N.J.: Prentice-Hall, 1982).

Robinson, Gerald J., *Federal Income Taxation of Real Estate: Text Forms and Tax Planning Ideas*, 4th ed. (Boston: Warren, Gorham & Lamont, 1984).

Sirmans, C. F., ed., *Research in Real Estate*, Vols. 1 and 2 (Greenwich, Conn.: JAI Press, 1982). See also Vol. 3, 1983.

SHOPPING CENTERS

The shopping center industry has become increasingly important since World War II. There were only 100 centers in the United States in 1950, but by 1985 there were an estimated 25,000. These centers encompass nearly 3.5 billion square feet of gross leasable area (GLA) and account for more than $350 billion in retail sales. In the mid-1970s, there was a softening in shopping center development as most major retail markets became saturated. Consequently, attention began to focus on smaller centers and specialty centers, causing development to shift to the smaller MSAs where shopping center development lagged behind that in large U.S. cities. In the 1980s attention was focused on renovation of the more than 16,000 centers over fifteen years old (half of which are at least twenty years old). Regional shopping center development, which slacked off during the later part of the 1970s and during the early 1980s, has grown most notably in small urban areas.

Although the overall risks have increased because of greater and more skillful competition, shopping centers are considered blue-chip investment properties by foreign and institutional investors, equity REITs, and large public syndications. In recent years, this competition has resulted in lower capitalization rates as more investors are willing to pay higher prices to obtain ownership of a site where rents are tied to retail prices (through percentage-rate overage clauses), thus providing the investor with some protection against erosion of capital by inflation. Furthermore, the recent splurge in office space development has made the shopping center more attractive as an investment with future appreciation potential.

Definitions

Throughout this section many specialized terms are used, some of which are defined here.

Shopping center. A shopping center is a group of commercial establishments that are planned, developed, owned, and managed as a unit and are related in terms of location, size, and type of shops to the trade area served by the unit. As part of the site area (the gross area within the property lines), shopping centers typically include sufficient space to provide for customer and employee parking, according to the types and sizes of shops required by the local planning agency.

A shopping center's type is usually determined by the nature of its major tenant or tenants. Neither site area nor square footage alone determines the type of center.

There are four basic types of shopping centers.

1. *Neighborhood center.* A neighborhood center provides for the sale of goods (foods, drugs, and sundries) and personal services (laundry and dry cleaning, barbering, shoe repair, etc.) for the day-to-day needs of the immediate neighborhood. It is usually built around a supermarket or drugstore as the principal tenant. The typical neighborhood center has a gross leasable area (GLA) of about 50,000 square feet and is the smallest type of shopping center. In recent years, a variation of this type of center, the neighborhood strip, has become popular. This version of the neighborhood center is usually small, from 5,000 to 15,000 square feet, and caters to local needs within a relatively small radius of the center—often only a few blocks. Strips generally do not have a discernible major tenant, but rather a number of low-credit, service-oriented tenants, such as a laundry, video store, and real estate or insurance office.

2. *Community center.* In addition to the convenience goods and personal services of the neighborhood center, a community center provides facilities for the sale of soft lines (wearing apparel for men, women, and children) and hard lines (hardware and appliances). It is built around a junior department store, variety store, or discount department store, although it may have a strong specialty store. The typical community center has about 150,000 square feet of GLA. Many "theme" centers and off-price centers are in this category.

3. *Regional center.* A regional center provides general merchandise, apparel, furniture, and home furnishings in depth and variety, as well as a range of services and recreational facilities. It is built around one or two full-line department stores of generally not less than 100,000 square feet. A typical size is about 400,000 square feet of GLA. The regional center is the second-largest type of shopping center. As such, it provides services that are typical of a business district.

4. *Superregional center.* A superregional center provides an extensive variety of general merchandise, apparel, furniture, home furnishings, as well as services and recreational facilities. It is built around at least three major department stores of generally not less than 100,000 square feet each. Although by definition the typical size is around 850,000 square feet

of GLA, in recent years superregionals have ranged from 1 million square feet and up. Only a handful of cities in the United States, mostly MSAs, have population bases large enough to support one or more superregional centers. Development of these large centers has dropped off in recent years in favor of smaller centers.

Exhibit 23-1 summarizes the characteristics of the four types of shopping centers.

Specialty or theme center. As the number of shopping centers has grown in recent years, developers have sought to build centers that would compete more effectively. The result has been the development of specialty or theme shopping centers.

Although, by definition, each specialty or theme center is different and difficult to categorize as a group, they share certain similarities. Typically, their tenant mix concentrates in imported goods, gift shops, and specialty merchandise. Stores usually cater to a high-end, expensive product line. They may also have restaurants and specialty food stores, boutiques, jewelers and high-fashion clothiers. Specialty or theme centers tend to be located in affluent neighborhoods with higher-than-average family incomes and have no anchor tenant. Examples include Ghirardelli Square in San Francisco, the Galleria in Houston, Trolley Square in Salt Lake City, and Reading Station in Philadelphia.

Another dominant characteristic of the theme center is architecture and design. Theme centers often have an unusual structural configuration (e.g., a renovated factory or trolley barn) or a dominant architectural theme, or they use extensive gardens and landscaping to create a special environment.

Anchor tenant. The anchor tenant is the key tenant (or tenants), the one that gives the center its stability and drawing power. The commitment of a well-known anchor tenant is usually required before construction financing can be arranged. A solid anchor tenant can often mean the difference between success and failure of a shopping center.

Convenience goods. Items such as groceries, shampoo, dry cleaning, and hardware that are needed immediately and often are convenience goods. Shoppers tend to look for these goods at conveniently located facilities.

Impulse goods. Some goods are not actively sought by shoppers but are purchased on impulse. Impulse goods have an indefinite trade area and are placed into the customer flow created by other businesses or within a store where people are passing by on their way to find a specifically sought item. Cosmetics and costume jewelry are examples of impulse goods.

EXHIBIT 23-1.   Characteristics of Shopping Centers

Type	Leading Tenant (Basis for Classification)	Typical GLA (Square Feet)	General GLA Range (Square Feet)	Usual Minimum Site Area (Acres)	Minimum Patron Support Required
Neighborhood	Supermarket or drugstore	50,000	30,000–100,000	3	2,500–40,000 people
Community	Variety, discount, or junior department store	150,000	100,000–300,000	10 or more	40,000–150,000 people
Regional	One or more full-line department stores of at least 100,000 sq. ft. GLA	400,000	300,000–1 million or more[a]	30–50 or more	150,000 or more people
Superregional	Three or more full-line (sometimes freestanding) department stores of at least 100,000 sq. ft. GLA	1 million	750,000–2 million	85 or more	1 million or more people in primary-tertiary trade area

Source: Urban Land Institute, *Shopping Center Development Handbook,* 2nd ed. (Washington, D.C.: ULI, 1985).
[a]Centers with 750,000 sq. ft. GLA usually include three or more department stores and hence are superregionals.

Major tenants. Major tenants have high credit ratings and substantial net worth (over $1 million). Most major tenants are national chains or well-established local businesses.

Mall. A mall is a pedestrian way between two facing strips of stores and may be enclosed or open.

Market trading area. The geographic area from which customers for a given class of goods or services are expected to be drawn is called the market trading area. The *primary* area is the immediately surrounding area, in which few competitors exist and a high market share is expected. The *secondary* area may be shared with competitors, and the *tertiary* area is expected to supply only customers who cannot find satisfactory goods in more convenient locations. The larger the shopping center, the more extensive the market trading area must be.

Merchants' association. An effective merchants' association makes a significant contribution toward the objective of a stable, profitable shopping center. The association can promote the shopping center on a collective basis more effectively than separate actions by individual tenants. It is also a forum for tenant–management relations and is helpful in formulating policies for the center and enforcing regulations that affect all tenants.

In a survey of 69 superregional centers, 98 percent had merchants' associations; 95 percent of 80 surveyed regional centers and 54 percent of 234 community centers sampled had such organizations; but merchants' associations were found in only 22 percent of 316 sampled neighborhood centers.[1]

Tenants are assessed by the association for working funds for services such as trash pickup, snow removal, air-conditioning of common areas, parking area maintenance, security, and so forth.

Multiuse center. A multiuse center is a development that incorporates residential, office, and recreational uses with the commercial retail shops.

Satellites. Satellites are small, localized tenants attracted to the center by the potential spillover of customers drawn by major tenants. Satellites are expected to pay higher rentals than majors and receive lower allowances and concessions.

Shopping goods. Larger-ticket items that are generally subject to comparison shopping are called shopping goods. Examples are pianos, appliances, stereos, microcomputers, and lawn mowers.

[1]Mary Alice Hines, *Shopping Center Development and Investment* (New York: Wiley, 1983), p. 203.

Specialty goods. Highly differentiated by brand and style, specialty goods are generally purchased after considerable shopping effort. Examples are fine jewelry, fashion clothing, imported cheese, and wine.

Strip center. A strip center is a line of stores tied together by a canopy over the sidewalk running along the store fronts.

Vertical center. Vertical centers have more than one level and are more common in Canada and Europe than in the United States.

TRACK RECORD AND TRENDS

The development of the shopping center industry has closely followed the major population and economic trends at work in the country. In the 1950s and 1960s, when the suburban and fringe areas of most large cities were growing rapidly, large regional and, later, superregional centers developed to serve these new markets. In recent years there has been a slowdown, as most major metropolitan areas have become saturated. Community resistance, expressed through restrictive zoning and environmental controls, has limited the available sites for development and has raised the cost of suitable land. Today, most of the growth has shifted to the growing southern and western states and, within these states, to the smaller market areas.[2]

The industry has developed innovations to deal with the problems imposed by land and economic constraints. There is more interest in developing downtown centers, often as part of urban renewal efforts. Renovation of older centers in profitable locations is also a major trend. More than half of all centers are at least fifteen years old.[3] The introduction of the multilevel center is another attempt to minimize land costs, for example, the three-level Galleria in Houston, Chicago's Water Tower Plaza, with six stories, and the Cumberland Mall in Atlanta (see the accompanying photographs and data).

The desire to reduce the impact of rising energy costs has added to the appeal of multiuse developments in which retail shops are combined with residential and office uses to form a self-sufficient mini-city (e.g., Allegheny County in Pittsburgh). Special shopping needs are now being catered to with the development of discount centers, in which the anchor is a major discount store, and fashion–specialty centers (e.g., Northridge Fashion Center in Northridge, California). Off-price centers bring collections of manufacturers selling products directly to the public at discount

[2]John A. Dawson and J. Dennis Lord, eds., *Shopping Center Development: Policies and Prospects* (Sydney: Croom Helm Ltd., 1985), pp. 215–222.
[3]Ibid., p. 226.

prices. The Urban Land Institute (ULI) Project Reference Files provide additional information on some of these projects, such as costs of construction, financing, design, tenant mix, and expense–revenue units.

The demand for shopping center investments remains high. Concern about inflation has led lenders and investors to seek equity positions in well-located centers. The associated high cost of debt financing has caused developers to invite greater equity participation as an alternative to highly leveraged financing techniques. Institutional lenders have participated as well. By the early 1980s, inflation was under control and reduced to rates below 5 percent per year. Whereas office construction had boomed and become burdened with increasing vacancy rates, retail facilities enjoyed high occupancy levels and a boon from increased consumer spending. Today, the shopping center is a healthy investment.

Development trends since 1984 indicate a healthy rise in total retail space. A recent survey of developers published in *Chain Store Age Executive* indicated that they experienced an average increase in GLA of 80 percent from 1984 through 1986, adding an estimated 2.1 million square feet—nearly 60 percent from new construction, 26 percent from expansion, and the balance through acquisition.[4]

Before projecting future income for an existing shopping center, the investor should answer the following questions.

1. What is the historical trend of net income from the center? The trend of rental income from individual stores?
2. Has the trade area recently been invaded by other centers offering similar merchandise? Is the area's potential, as measured by population and income, growing or declining?
3. When will existing leases expire, and do renewal options preclude raising rents?
4. What possibilities exist for expanding or renovating the center or changing the tenant–product mix? How would such changes affect the sales of existing stores?
5. What plans do the municipal or state governments have with regard to changing highway services?

INVESTING IN SHOPPING CENTERS

Advantages and Disadvantages

A well-located center can provide a relatively stable and secure return with adequate growth potential and can maintain an appreciation rate that will keep pace with or exceed the inflation rate. Security is provided by the

---

[4]*Chain Store Age Executive*, January 1985, pp. 61–66.

CUMBERLAND MALL, Atlanta, Georgia

Project Data

Site: 72 net acres

Building area (gross leasable area):
  Cumberland Mall: 325,000 sq. ft.
  Four free-standing department stores:[1] 840,000 sq. ft.
  Total gross leasable area: 1,165,000 sq. ft.

Existing parking: 5,800 spaces

Parking ratio: 5.0/1,000 sq. ft. of gross leasable area

Tenant information (other than department stores)

Classification	Number of Stores	Percent of GLA	Sq. Ft. of GLA
Food	18	12.7	41,389
Food services	4	1.5	4,971
Clothing and shoes	49	45.6	148,103
Furniture and house furnishings	4	2.8	8,939
Other retail	58	34.6	112,562
Financial	2	.8	2,600
Services	6	2.0	6,436
	141	100.0%	325,000

Sales and rent information[2]
  Total rent roll for Cumberland Mall: $9,117,700*
  Average rent/square foot: $20.85[3]**
  Operating expenses/square foot: $8.00[4]
  Estimated retail sales/square foot of GLA: $300.00
  Merchants' Association dues: $0.85/square foot

[1]Davisons: 160,000 sq. ft.; J.C. Penney: 195,000 sq. ft.; Richs: 285,000 sq. ft.; Sears: 200,000 sq. ft.
[2]Sales and rent information per tenant may be classification estimated from Urban Land Institute, *Dollars and Cents of Shopping Centers*
[3]Department stores are self-owned in fee simple. A proxy rental income could be estimated from *Dollars and Cents of Shopping Centers.*
[4]Operating expenses do not include central administrative overhead for Carter & Associates.

  *Includes operation cost reimbursements.
**(Base + average)/GLA.

Photos and data courtesy of Mr. Woodford L. Hall, General Manager, Cumberland Mall, Carter & Associates.

Lower Level

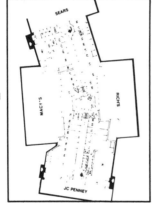

Upper Level

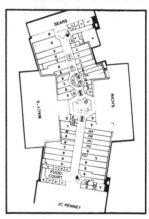

generally high credit ratings of major tenants and the minimum rent schedules in most leases. Growth potential is afforded by provisions for overages and the ability to pass along increases in expenses to the tenants through net leases and pro rata sharing of common expenses. Prospects for resale and refinancing are also good, because of the appreciation in land values and the strong investor demand for profitable centers.

Formerly, shopping centers had an advantage of strong depreciation write-offs because they had a shorter economic life through functional and locational obsolescence (median life equaled twenty-six years). The shift to ACRS lives under the tax reform acts of 1981 and 1984 increased the levels of these write-offs, but eliminated any comparative advantage over other properties. Since then, under the Tax Reform Act of 1986, depreciation benefits have been dramatically reduced for all nonresidential properties. Older centers, however, may benefit from new rehabilitation incentives under the tax reform act.

Because of strong investor demand and the difficulty of developing new centers, locating a profitable center at a price that will provide suitable returns will be difficult. The most likely candidates are smaller centers in relatively untapped market areas, such as medium-sized cities, and centers that are ripe for renovation or rehabilitation and are located in stable trading areas. Generating a competitive return depends to a great extent on the negotiating skill of the manager and his or her ability to obtain leases with provisions for income growth and tenant participation in expense increases. The owner's negotiating power, however, may be restricted by the ability of major tenants to extract favors and concessions. The value of a center is also dependent on dynamic features, such as attractiveness of design, convenience of layout, population distribution, and the quality of surrounding development. Disadvantages are, of course, found in the complexity of management and economic factors that most frequently affect centers. These factors, in order of impact, are set forth in Exhibit 23-2.

EXHIBIT 23-2. Factors That Cause Change in Shopping Center Rates of Return

- Competition entering the market
- Outdated design and layout
- Changes in trade area income levels
- Changes in population density
- Changes in highway network

Source: Institute for Business Planning, *Real Estate Investment Planning* (Englewood Cliffs, N.J.), Vol. 1, p. 57,306.

Types of Investors and Investor Motivations

Shopping centers have been attractive investments for major institutions, wealthy individuals, and development firms alike. But the motivations of investors differ. Individuals and development firms are generally interested in near-term income and tax shelter, whereas institutions, which are willing to accept lower but stable initial returns, have sought their return over the long term through appreciation. Quite often these two groups are not in direct competition, since the developers and equity partners are generally first owners, and the institutions become second-user investors or buyers after the property has been established. This is changing, though: institutions are now seeking immediate equity positions in order to enhance their returns. With the recent growth of the pension fund industry, pension fund investors have bid up the price of quality properties, in part because they are nontaxable entities and can accept a lower pretax return. However, institutional risk avoidance policies generally limit their willingness to compete for anything but prime investments. Consequently, developer–investor groups who are willing to assume greater risks may expect to earn better returns.

Foreign investors. Foreign investors' desire to place money in U.S. real estate is motivated by the need for security from governmental confiscation, plus tax advantages and the lack of better investment opportunities at home. Immediate profitability appears to be secondary; furthermore, our lower rate of inflation invites investment here to conserve capital.

Institutional investors. Insurance companies and pension funds are seeking relatively secure investments with growth potential. To achieve this potential, these sources increasingly are seeking ownership participations. The fact that these investors are often nontaxable entities makes them very competitive.

Large public syndications. Syndicators have expressed interest in smaller centers in untapped markets in order to diversify their largely residential property portfolios. Shopping centers provide them with the opportunity to generate returns large enough to bear the front-end loads necessary to syndicating, while delivering acceptable returns to the syndicate's limited partners.

Equity REITs. Some large-equity REITs specialize in shopping centers (e.g., Henry Miller REIT in Dallas and Great American Growth Properties in the Quad Cities, Iowa–Illinois area) and are quite active in the market. The 1986 Tax Reform Act may prove a boon to REIT growth in real estate investment markets.

PRELIMINARY ANALYSES

Market and Marketability Analysis

Depending on the size and type of center and population density, the primary market (trading) area will vary from a few miles to twenty or thirty miles in radius. A survey of the delineated trade area will indicate trends in population and income that are important in determining the area's potential. The market area should be segmented according to the product mix offered in the center. Convenience goods have a more immediate market range than shopping and specialty goods. Compare the tenant mix with the growth potential for each segment of buying power for the market area.

An evaluation should also be made of factors that threaten the sales potential of the center. Existing and potential competitors should be examined for proximity, duplication of product, and design advantages. Changes in the location and upgrading of access roads may affect the convenience of the location. Impending disruptions in the basic industries of the local economy could soften sales in the short term. An examination of locally prepared planning reports may uncover these trends.

Demand Analysis. Commercial retail investments are based on derived demand. Although income is provided by leasing space to stores, the demand for this space is derived from customers' demands for goods and services. Therefore, demand analysis should focus on the retail sales potential of the center.

The first step is to delineate the *trading area*. Although market analysts use intensive survey methods to measure market areas accurately, a good approximation can be made by considering the size of the center, the type of goods offered, population density, and available transportation facilities. As a guide, neighborhood centers require a market of 2,500 to 40,000 people within a 1.5-mile radius; community centers, 40,000 to 150,000 within three to five miles; and regional centers, 150,000 or more within eight to ten miles. In densely populated areas with many competing centers, these trading areas may be smaller; in rural areas with good high-speed roads, they may be expanded.

The core of the market is the primary area in which the center represents the most ready source of convenience goods. In urban areas the core may have a radius of no more than one mile. A larger, or secondary, market area is generally shared with other centers equally or slightly more conveniently located for customers. A peripheral (tertiary) area may exist for specialty and shopping goods, extending beyond the boundaries of the formal market area. Full trade area analysis will entail investigations of driving times, existing competition, physical barriers, and socioeconomic factors relating to the population surrounding the center or its proposed site.

These data will provide the analyst with the information needed to estimate the scope of the primary, secondary, and tertiary trading areas.

Once the trading areas have been delineated, the next step is to evaluate purchasing power. This process usually begins with an examination of population and income statistics within the trading area. Population data are converted to number of households and multiplied by family income to derive total purchasing power. Data from such publications as *Sales and Marketing Management's Survey of Buying Power* permit further refinement from total purchasing power to income available for shopping center goods and services (department-store-type merchandise, or DSTM). An analysis of past, current, and projected trends in purchasing power will permit a detailed evaluation of trade area purchasing power. Estimated capture rates are used to determine the specific site's market share.

The attributes of the market area also indicate the type of center that is most needed in an area. A high-income area provides a good market for specialty and luxury goods, possibly a good setting for a specialty center. Low- and moderate-income areas call for discount stores. The type of merchandise should match the purchasing habits and capabilities of consumers in the area.

Supply Analysis. Once the potential of the market area has been determined, an estimate of market penetration should be made. The key factors are the location, size, and type of competition and any competitive advantages the subject center or location may command. By analyzing the total sales potential and the number and total size of competitors, the analyst can estimate the total amount of retail space supported by the trading area and how much additional space (if any) the trade area is capable of supporting. The technique is sometimes referred to as a *vacuum* analysis. That is, if the area can support more retail space than is currently present and planned, then new facilities can enter the market and "fill in the vacuum."

More sophisticated techniques make use of complex computer models, which analyze the percentage shares of the market currently held by existing competition. Then probability analysis is used to estimate what percentage of the market could be captured by a new facility. Simulations of the market are usually made. Regardless of the technique used, the end result is an estimate of the center's capture rate, which is used to estimate the share of market purchasing power that the center is expected to command.

The center will normally draw most of its business from the immediately surrounding area, depending on the existence of independent stores in the vicinity. No more than a fractional share of the secondary trade area, and even less from the tertiary market, can be expected. Any superior features of the center, such as covered parking, well-regarded stores, or excellent exposure and access, will add to the share of customers attracted.

Financial Feasibility. If projections and analyses of the trade area indicate a net demand for new space, the next stage of analysis is a determination of financial feasibility. Shopping center income can be estimated from gross-sales forecasts. An analysis of typical lease terms will reveal the levels of minimum rents and average percentages. Most retail stores can pay a certain percentage of their gross sales for rent. An estimate of total rental income for the center is made using these percentages. This estimate can be further broken down into fixed minimum rents and percentage overages. An analysis of typical leases will reveal other terms and provisions that may affect rental income and operating expenses.

The center's income, less operating expenses, must produce sufficient NOI both to enable repayment of the loans required to construct the center and put it into operation, and to provide a reasonable return for the developer–investor.

Risk Management and Control. The most effective internal-control technique available to the shopping center investor is the tenant mix selection. Generally, investors and managers of shopping centers should be knowledgeable about retail marketing business risks and consumer buying behavior patterns. For example, the power of the retailer to influence the actual decision to buy changes as the shopper moves from convenience goods to shopping goods. The management skills of the tenants are more important with shopping goods than with convenience goods.

A certain proportion of high-credit-rated tenants will be required by the lenders in order to reduce risk. Such tenants, realizing their value to the investor, can often negotiate favorable lease terms. The satellites, though increasing the risks of turnover and bankruptcy, generally pay higher rents. This is especially true of first-time business enterprises. Reflecting the differences in risks are the lease terms offered to major and minor tenants. Majors generally enter long-term (ten- to twenty-year) leases, whereas other tenants may obtain short-term (three- to five-year) leases. Unilateral options of tenants to renew are risks that should be carefully negotiated.

Setting the level of minimum rents is another risk control measure, although minimum rents must reasonably conform to those currently charged by competition. Requiring low minimums with high percentages effectively shifts much of the risk of the tenant onto the investor, as the tenant pays high rents only when most able to do so. Small centers often are unable to attract tenants capable of paying percentage overages and are more likely to charge only fixed rents. Rent escalation clauses are used to assure an increase in rental income during periods of inflation. Large centers, on the other hand, charge minimum guaranteed rentals, which are set reasonably below the fixed rental market in order to be attractive to top tenants. The strong drawing power of large centers assures tenants of a large market potential. The center owners will in turn receive percentage overages during good economic times and periods of rising inflation.

In large centers with major-credit tenants, management may be able to purchase lease insurance to reduce the risk of loss when a major tenant leaves or goes out of business. By controlling a tenant's ability to sublet, management can prevent unregulated entry of undesirable tenants.

Physical, Legal, Political, and Environmental Analysis

Physical and Structural Factors. The center should provide design features comparable to the market standard in the area. Such features as mall enclosure, sheltered parking, attractive landscaping and facades, and mall ornamentation may add to the appeal of the center. The location of the anchors can affect their usefulness to other tenants in terms of attracting customers. Evaluate how easy and inexpensive it will be to maintain, clean, heat, air-condition, and light the center. The ease and expense will depend on the location of janitorial facilities, the construction materials, the amount of insulation and glass surfaces, the heating and air-conditioning equipment, the type of fuel used, and the amount of natural lighting. When appropriate, snow removal equipment, high-capacity air-conditioning equipment, and so forth should be checked. Consider the adequacy and quality of drainage facilities to handle rain and snow runoff.

Take note of how much space, if any, in the center is devoted to special uses, such as theaters, medical offices, and restaurants. Adequate parking should be provided for both current and potential business. Look for adequate curb cuts and ease of legal access to and from major streets.

An inspection and evaluation should be made of all components that may need repair or replacement. This should be done by technically qualified personnel. Include in this estimate a provision for adding any improvements necessary to meet market standards. These expenditures should be considered in evaluating the purchase price.

Legal and Political Factors. A study should be made of the local attitude toward shopping center operation and development. Hostile local communities may use zoning, environmental controls, or tax policy to restrict the growth of a center's profitability. Compare assessed value to appraised value to determine the possibility of an increase in taxes. A field inspection of the taxing jurisdiction may be necessary to consider whether or not the schools, roads, sewage system, and so forth are adequate. Suburban communities often sharply increase tax assessments after the subdividers have phased out, thereby leaving shopping centers to bear the brunt of delayed capital improvements. Moreover, differentials in the sales tax may affect sales volume if the rate is higher than in surrounding jurisdictions (with the greatest impact on big-ticket shopping goods). An examination of existing leases may uncover possible antitrust violations (primarily agreements to restrict competition with the center).

Many municipalities now use impact fees to help defray increases in local government costs brought about by new development. Commercial property development will usually carry larger impact fees than residential development. A large center will almost certainly require an environmental impact study to determine the scope of its impact on the local infrastructure. Both impact fees and environmental impact studies represent significant front-end costs to shopping center development.

Financial Analysis

Compared to most other commercial real estate ventures, investments in well located existing shopping centers entail relatively lower risk. The high credit ratings of major tenants (required by lenders), as well as prelease commitments, reduce the speculative aspects of development. The return–risk trade-off may be balanced by adjusting the tenant mix. Higher percentages of major tenants add to security by providing a dependable base of rental income and enhancing the drawing power of the center. However, their superior bargaining position can result in lower NOI and meager returns. Satellite tenants, on the other hand, add to profitability through the payment of higher rents and the need for fewer lease concessions.

Lenders often seek full amortization (with modest debt coverage) solely from the rent rolls of the major tenants. Enforceable leases requiring minimum levels of rent when the center is in operation are typical for new centers, and for renovation or refinancing of existing centers. Thus, the mortgagee shifts much of the primary source of equity returns to the satellite stores. In small centers without major tenants, fixed-rate leases are typical. Lenders will then require that a certain percentage of the center's space be leased before funding a loan. Equity investors in small centers must look exclusively to the fixed rents for profitability, since they cannot rely on overages as in the larger centers. For this reason the small centers must charge higher fixed rents, thus shifting some fixed-cost risk directly onto the tenant. However, with proper tenant selection, the investor can minimize the risk of tenant loss through bankruptcy.

In stable economic times shopping centers provide fairly attractive yields, ranging from 10 to 18 percent (IRR) on equity, after tax. Under inflationary conditions, these returns can be expected to increase as percentage leases provide overages and escalation clauses generate fixed-rent increases. The lower risk of shopping centers is also reflected in overall capitalization rates (ROIs), which range from 7.5 to 11 percent, before tax, on invested capital. The increase in the demand for well-located and profitable shopping centers since the late 1970s has driven prices up and yields down. Today a typical center investment may provide cash-on-cash yields of less than 8 percent. Often, in order to gain control of a property, investors may have to accept current cash-on-cash yields of 3 to 5 percent. Foreign investors are bidding prices up, because they will settle for zero current yields if the property has appreciation potential. As a result of this competition, institutional investors, pension funds, commingled real estate funds, and REITs are buying retail properties at relatively low yields.[5]

The motivations behind this activity are diverse. The individual equity investors appear to be the already-wealthy who are seeking to conserve assets. Foreign investors are moving capital out of economies that have higher inflation rates than the United States or are politically less stable; and life insurance companies are moving money out of utilities, bonds, and mortgages in an effort to protect principal against erosion from inflation. Apparently all of them believe that retail price levels will trigger rent increases and thus make shopping centers one of the best hedges against inflation. However, the decline in the rate of inflation since 1982, coupled with the strength of the stock and bond markets, may be signaling a reduction in the demand for real estate in large investment portfolios. There is every evidence in the high vacancy rates in other types of real estate that the demand for investment properties may begin to decline over the next few years. A possible result of this decline could be a drop in relative prices and an increase in yields. Lately, shopping center rents have not increased as rapidly as apartment rents, but they have outstripped increases in office space rents.

Major sources of risk include the possibility of high vacancy rates in stores for nonmajor tenants, lack of adequate growth in sales to provide overage income, bankruptcy of a major tenant, uncompensated but escalating operating costs caused by rising tax and utility bills, and the opening of new shopping centers in the trading area without concomitant increases in consumer buying power. Fortunately, lower interest rates reduce the financial risk of center ownership, but a new round of inflation could quickly bring that benefit to an end.

Analysis of Operations

Property Management and Leasing. Efficient operation of the center depends on competent management. The common areas should be well maintained and clean. The shops should be full of customers during peak shopping hours. Survey the parking areas to determine center use. Leases should be structured to provide for income growth. This will mean percentage-rent agreements in larger centers and the ability to raise fixed rents

[5]Cushman and Wakefield, Inc., *Real Estate Outlook*, May 1986.

through escalation clauses. Base rents should be raised when short-term leases expire. Look for an active merchant's association with an effective promotional campaign.

In addition to performing the normal tasks of property management—maintenance, sanitation, leasing, and paying bills—the shopping center manager is expected to collect and maintain sales records for each store in the center. Such information is important for determining overage rents and providing owners with an indication of the economic health of the center and its individual tenants. Identifying tenants who are doing poorly permits management to take action before the tenant goes bankrupt. The manager is also expected to calculate and bill tenants for any pro rata share of the expenses, according to the lease provisions.

Three types of rent structures are commonly used in shopping center leases. The *percentage-rent* structure provides that a tenant pay the *greater of two* amounts: a minimum rent or a percentage of gross sales. The percentage is negotiable. Such an arrangement provides a stable minimum income and the potential for increases as sales volume expands. Examples of percentages used in such leases are shown in Exhibit 23-3.

For tenants who are not retailers and for tenants in small centers, *graduated rents* or *indexed rents* may be used. In such leases rent payments are structured with a fixed rent, which either steps up in graduated amounts or increases on the basis of a price index, such as the consumer price index (CPI). Both types of leases assure rental increases during the life of the lease.

Major tenants often sign *net leases*. Such leases usually provide a clause that makes the base rent amount subject to an index change and has the tenant pay additional rent to cover a share of operating expenses, including common-area maintenance (CAM) fees, taxes, utility costs, and an administrative surcharge. Rate changes may be dollar-for-dollar, true-cost-related, or the base year may be subject to a specified index—the CPI, for example. The advantage of net leases is that the center generates a base NOI that increases in accordance with the index, whereas operating expenses remain fairly constant. This arrangement significantly reduces risks of operating costs rising faster than revenues and NOI being reduced during periods of high inflation. The disadvantage of such a lease is that the major tenants will never pay overages, regardless of how well they perform economically.

A sufficient lease will include, among others, the following provisions.

1. A description of the space to be leased.
2. The beginning and length of the lease term.
3. The rental agreement and payment procedures.
4. Specific required sales reports and other necessary information on tenant experience.
5. Required membership in a merchants' association, and dues.

EXHIBIT 23-3. Representative Percentage Rent Structure for a Shopping Center

Type of Business	Percentage Rental	Type of Business	Percentage Rental
Auto parts and accessories	1–3	Haberdasher	6–8
Bakery	5–7	Hosiery	7–8
Beauty shop	8–10	Jewelry	5.5–8 (exclusive); 8–10
Bookstore	6–8	Laundromat	10–20
Camera shop	4–6	Men's clothing	6–7
Candy store	10	Men's hair stylist	10–12
Card and gift shop	8.5–10	Men's ties	10
Children's wear	6–8	Millinery	15–20
Cigars and cigarettes	8	Optometrist and optical instruments	10–17
Cleaning and dyeing	8–10	Parking lot	45–50
Cocktail bar	25 (and downward)	Piano	5
Coffee shop and luncheonette	8–10	Prescription pharmacy	8
Coins and stamps	9–10	Radio, TV, stereo	4–5
Cosmetics	10 (and downward)	Record shop	6–8
Cutlery	6–8	Restaurant and cafeteria	6–8
Currency exchange	15	Shoe repair	7–10
Department store	2–3	Shoe store	6–8
Drapery and dry goods	11 (and downward)	Sporting goods	4–5
Drugstore	4–5	Stationery	5–6
Fast food	8	Supermarket	1.5–2
Florist	7–10	Trunks and leather goods	8
Furniture	4–5	Variety shop	5–6
Furs	5–7	Watch repair	20
Greeting cards	7–10 plus	Women's wear	5–6 (exclusive)

6. Restrictions on the use of the premises, including types of merchandise sold.

7. Fixing of responsibility for utility bills, repairs, insurance, and tax increases.

8. Restrictions on subletting space.

9. Conditions under which the landlord may cancel the lease.

10. Limits on the tenant's right to constructive eviction (e.g., condemnation, fire or other casualty, lease violations by other tenants, loss of parking per square foot ratio).

11. Duty to pay for share of common-area maintenance charges.

12. Requirements for security deposits.

13. Provisions triggering assessments for major center improvements, such as enclosure of the mall or renovation of the facade.

14. An arbitration clause to handle disputes in lieu of litigation.

Analysis of Current Operating Income and Expenses. Rents and vacancies can be estimated from the track record of the property (or comparable ones if new construction is involved). Average income, including overage, should be multiplied by total GLA to estimate total income. For new construction, income estimates can be derived from the projected sales volume estimated in the market analysis. Derived revenues can then be compared with rental data from comparable properties or published data sources such as the Urban Land Institute's *Dollars and Cents of Shopping Centers.* Expenses can be estimated from comparable properties or from published data sources. Expenses paid by tenants should be deducted from estimates, unless comparable properties have similar expense structures.

An investor should have available the operating history of a center for the past three to five years, if the existing center has been in operation for at least that long. Comparative analyses should be undertaken to test the validity of the data before doing a financial analysis.

Key Ratios. Sales per square foot and expense–income ratios related to GLA are useful analytical tools for prospective shopping center investors. Longitudinal trends indicating percentage changes over time are good indicators of the potential profitability of the targeted center.

The Urban Land Institute provides extensive data that enable an investor to analyze the primary sources of income and expense for a shopping center. For example, exhibit 23-4 abstracts key ratios for median sales volume and rent per square foot of GLA for different types of shopping centers.

Total rent is the income from tenants received as rent for the leased space, including the minimum guaranteed yearly rent, straight percentage rent (no minimum guarantee), and overage rent for the year.

EXHIBIT 23-4.	Space, Sales, and Rent Data for Shopping Centers by Type			
	Median GLA (Sq. Ft.)			
	Superregional	Regional	Community	Neighborhood
Department store	127,082	105,644	60,000	12,960
Variety store	ND[a]	ND	20,000	9,220
Ladies' ready-to-wear	3,900	3,750	3,000	1,700
Men's wear	3,215	3,257	2,704	2,400
Family shoes	3,256	3,290	3,073	2,880
Cards and gifts	2,516	2,485	2,440	2,250
Jewelry	1,467	1,439	1,335	1,000
Medical and dental	951	957	1,000	1,200
MEDIAN SALES VOLUME/SQ. FT. OF GLA				
Department store	93.00	89.77	83.67	95.44
Variety store	65.91	55.19	62.80	50.53
Ladies' ready-to-wear	119.85	110.30	98.62	103.15
Men's wear	134.51	131.55	101.96	119.91
Family shoes	129.58	112.43	74.28	72.65
Cards and gifts	136.85	112.60	73.54	71.75
Jewelry	343.56	264.19	185.35	128.20
Medical and dental	ND	ND	ND	ND
MEDIAN RENT/SQ. FT. OF GLA				
Department store	2.09	2.18	2.48	3.00
Variety store	3.34	2.64	2.14	2.25
Ladies' ready-to-wear	8.28	7.72	5.80	7.00
Men's wear	8.75	8.00	5.55	7.13
Family shoes	10.00	9.00	5.04	6.31
Cards and gifts	12.00	9.02	5.82	7.00
Jewelry	20.59	17.55	9.11	7.75
Medical and dental	8.44	8.00	6.31	7.48

Source: Urban Land Institute, *Dollars and Cents of Shopping Centers: 1984* (Washington, D.C.: ULI, 1984), pp. 30, 78, 124, 170.
[a]No data.

Common-area charges are collected from tenants for operating and maintenance of the common areas. Shopping center leases usually contain a clause that requires the tenant to pay a share of operation and maintenance costs for common areas. Of the ways to prorate the charges among tenants, the most common are (1) a pro rata charge based on a tenant's leased area as a percentage of the total leasable area of the center or the linear exposure in store frontage, (2) a fixed charge for a stated period, or

(3) a variable charge based on a percentage of sales. Some centers include a cost-of-living index to determine increases in common-area charges.

Other charges are income to the center under certain lease provisions, such as real estate tax and insurance escalator clauses and income from facilities like pay telephones, pay toilets, and vending machines. Full tax escalation without ceiling and recapture from overage rents is included, where such lease clauses pertain, after the initial year's assessment.

Total operating receipts are all the moneys received from rentals, common-area charges, and other income described earlier. Total operating receipts do *not* include income from furniture and equipment sold to tenants, charges collected that are to be given to another organization (e.g., merchant's association dues), or receipts from any special situations that are not directly related to the operation of the shopping center. (Total operating receipts are the same as gross receipts.)

Operating expenses can be estimated from expense information collected on the basis of functional categories and natural divisions of expenses. The functional expense categories are broad classifications that can be applied to all centers. They include expenses for building maintenance, the parking lot, the mall and other common areas, central utility systems, office area services, advertising and promotion, real estate taxes, insurance, and general and administrative functions. The definition of each functional category may be found in the *Standard Manual of Accounting for Shopping Center Operations*, published by the Urban Land Institute.

The natural divisions of expenses are the breakdowns of operating costs used for recording items within a functional category. Some of the expense divisions are interchangeable, such as payroll, management fees, contracted expenses, and professional services. For example, some centers pay an agency for management services, and others are managed by the owner. When the owner is the manager, the management cost would be considered a payroll expense to the extent that the owner pays himself or herself a salary. It is not possible, therefore, to provide a uniform comparison of the natural divisions of expenses.

The following functional expense categories are the bases of developing comparative data on operating statistics per square foot of GLA.

- *Building Maintenance.* Includes such items as painting, repairs, and uncapitalized alterations to structures.

- *Common-Area Maintenance.* Covers repair of paving and striping of the parking lot; cleaning, lighting, guard or police service, heating, ventilating, and air-conditioning (HVAC) of an enclosed mall; servicing public toilets; power used for maintenance of signs (those for which the landlord is responsible); snow and trash removal; maintenance and landscaping of grounds; and so on.

- *Office Area Services.* Include janitor service, lighting, and the like for the areas occupied by office tenants.
- *Central Utility Systems.* Include all costs of operating a central utility plant or total energy system in the center.
- *Real Estate Taxes.*
- *Insurance.* Includes fire and other damage, public liability, plate glass, and rental value (use of occupancy).
- *General and Administrative.* Includes expenses not otherwise classified, such as management of the center, communications, and office staff.

Exhibit 23-5 shows some median values for analyzing the operating statements of various kinds of shopping centers. These figures can be used for comparison with a targeted property only for the data base year (1985).[6]

Analysis of Trends and Uncertainties. Unless the center is in need of major repairs or renovation, the greatest potential for expense increases during the life of the investment is in utilities and taxes. Utility rates are tied to the cost and availability of fuels, with escalating prices expected in the future. The efficiency with which the center uses energy will help determine the impact of these higher costs. Property taxes may increase substantially in suburban areas faced with the prospect of building new infrastructures for development, and in large cities with increasing operating costs and a diminishing tax base. Popular movements for limiting property tax increases may bring tax relief for residential properties only. Tax assessors may raise the assessed value of the center to reflect the increased value of the underlying land. Although there are appeal procedures to contest tax increases, a center is somewhat vulnerable to greater property tax charges, especially if it is successful in capturing a large market share.

The Urban Land Institute's *Dollars and Cents of Shopping Centers* provides useful data on current and historical cost trends for various types and locations of centers. Projections of these trends, with modifications for expected increases as described earlier, should provide good data for comparative analysis. For pro forma purposes, all expenses billed to the center should be shown on the expense side of the statement. Contributions by the tenants to offset these expenses should be included on the revenue side. By isolating these charges, the investor may evaluate how they affect individual stores.

Net-lease provisions are the investor's protection against rising operating costs. Rapid increases in operating costs, however, may outstrip the

[6]Urban Land Institute, *Dollars and Cents of Shopping Centers: 1984* (Washington, D.C.: ULI, 1984).

EXHIBIT 23-5. Operating Statements for Shopping Centers (Median Values)

Item	Superregional $/GLA	Superregional Percentage of Receipts	Regional $/GLA	Regional Percentage of Receipts	Community $/GLA	Community Percentage of Receipts	Neighborhood $/GLA	Neighborhood Percentage of Receipts
GLA (sq. ft.)	329,214		252,615		146,774		62,525	
Operating Receipts								
Rental income—minimum	7.49	58.02	5.09	60.41	3.00	78.10	4.02	80.32
Rental income—overages	1.44	12.73	1.27	15.98	.44	10.98	.50	10.03
Total rent	9.29	72.26	6.43	79.72	3.41	90.92	4.56	90.93
Common-area charges	1.55	12.52	.84	10.53	.19	4.67	.25	4.96
Rent escalation charges	.67	4.60	.32	3.84	.13	3.22	.20	3.54
Income from utilities	1.24	8.71	.88	8.19	.43	6.49	.09	1.64
Miscellaneous income	.15	1.20	.09	.96	.04	.56	.05	.62
Total other charges	1.56	12.92	.56	8.04	.19	3.97	.20	4.05
Total Operating Receipts	12.97	NA[a]	8.27	NA	4.01	NA	5.21	NA
Operating Expenses								
Building maintenance	.12	.67	.11	1.27	.09	2.03	.10	2.12
Parking, mall, common area	1.36	10.87	.98	11.74	.24	6.22	.31	5.89
Central utility system	1.36	9.00	.69	10.23	.09	2.10	.11	2.12
Office area services	.17	.97	.11	1.10	.04	1.09	.11	1.49
Total maintenance and housekeeping	2.48	19.79	1.43	17.66	.41	10.47	.49	9.40
Advertising and promotion	.14	1.15	.12	1.31	.03	.65	.03	.40
Real estate taxes	.90	6.63	.65	7.34	.32	8.21	.41	8.22
Insurance	.10	.85	.09	1.19	.06	1.38	.08	1.39
General and administration	.80	7.08	.71	8.39	.23	5.76	.30	5.59
Total Operating Expense	4.74	40.58	3.18	39.41	1.20	29.30	1.44	27.39
Net Operating Balance	7.49	59.42	4.96	60.17	2.68	70.70	3.51	72.61

Source: Urban Land Institute, *Dollars and Cents of Shopping Centers: 1985* (Washington, D.C.: ULI, 1985), Tables 3-1, 4-1, 5-1, 6-1.
[a]Not applicable.

ability of many smaller tenants to pay pro rata shares and still maintain profitability. Such a situation will raise vacancy and turnover rates. Emphasis on energy efficiency, diligence in challenging tax increases, and more efficient maintenance and housekeeping procedures may hold down cost increases. Tenants may be further protected by establishing ceilings on their pro rata share of cost increases. These ceilings are called "stops."

FINANCING AND REFINANCING

Sources. Financing for shopping centers is available from a variety of sources. Large centers are financed mostly by insurance companies, savings and loan associations, and commercial banks. Pension funds, mortgage bankers, and public funding are next in importance, followed by foreign lenders and credit companies. Syndications and REITs make up a small but important source, particularly for small existing centers.

Rates, Terms, and Conditions. Investors should expect to pay interest rates comparable to the market rate on commercial loans. However, participations may reduce the contract rates. The amount of the loan will generally depend on the type of lender, but ranges between 70 and 80 percent of appraised value for nonparticipation loans. Under participating loan agreements, 100 percent financing is possible. The length of the loan is often tied to the life of the major anchor's lease, although in recent years there has been a tendency toward shorter-term loans—five to ten years—with long amortization periods and balloons.

Because of the importance of income from major tenants, lenders require firm commitments from a certain number of tenants with substantial credit ratings and financial substance. Typical participations may include sharing in overages, proceeds of sale or refinancing, net income, or gross income. Exhibit 23-6 gives the results of a survey of lenders who make permanent loans on shopping centers. Since 1984 interest rates have dropped dramatically and were near 8 percent for prime properties in early 1987.

Projection of Financing Costs. Debt service is usually fixed over the investment period and can be accurately projected. If escalation provisions are involved or participation agreements exist, a judgment must be made about future interest rate trends or added interest estimated from revenue and expense projections. Renegotiable rate mortgages introduce interest rate uncertainty, but they are declining in popularity in favor of shorter-term loans with balloons. Simulations can be done over the range of financing rates to test their impact on IRR.

Debt Coverage Ratio and Mortgage Constant Desired by the Lender. If a loan is assumed, debt service continues from the existing loan. Currently

EXHIBIT 23-6. Shopping Center Financing Terms (Nonparticipating Loans)

Lender	Loan Amount[a]	Interest Rate	Term[b]	Loan-to-Value Ratio	Number of Loans
Life insurance companies	$15,083	12.8%	9	76%	51
Pension funds	15,668	13.1	23	71	12
Banks	16,753	12.7	6	77	44
Savings and loans	13,037	12.6	8	80	37
Credit companies	6,249	13.5	7	78	5
Mortgage bankers	9,927	13.2	9	79	14
Public financing[c]	5,397	9.6	19	80	23
Foreign lenders	17,370	12.4	9	75	4

Source: Urban Land Institute, *Shopping Center Development Handbook*, 2nd ed. (Washington, D.C.: ULI, 1985), p. 48.
[a]Average loan amount, in millions.
[b]Term in years.
[c]Applies to projects at least partially financed by industrial revenue bonds (IRBs), urban development action grants (UDAGs), or other public programs.

available rates should be used when refinancing. Required debt coverage ratios (DCR) for shopping centers are generally based on minimum rents, often from major tenants only. Estimates of the lender's share of income participation may be added to debt service. Some computer models make it necessary to treat such equity participation as an operating expense.

Ground-rent payments may be projected in much the same way as debt service, especially if there are no graduated payments or participations. Participations should be proportioned according to the assumptions used for increases in income and resale value. If variable-rate mortgages are involved, then key assumptions must be made about the range of such variability. Of course, variable-rate mortgages may be structured so that they simply vary the size of the final payment (balloon) rather than the annual debt service, thus shifting the impact from operating income to the net-equity reversion.

The DCR has become the most important underwriting measure for commercial loans. Needless to say, the riskiness of the venture helps to determine the magnitude of the DCR. Low interest rates coupled with the lower risk associated with large shopping centers will tend to dictate DCRs ranging from 1.10 to 1.25. Participations and other lender risk-reducing features could drive the DCR even lower.

Risk Control and Management Techniques of Lenders. Market financing usually requires a varying down payment, dependent on the availability of mortgage credit, the quality of the shopping center's location, and the net worth and track record of the buyer. Down payments may vary from 10 to 30 percent without overburdening the cash flow. Debt service should be compared to minimum rents to gauge the margin of coverage.

In general, requirements are that minimum rents from major tenants (those with a net worth greater than $1 million) should be sufficient to cover debt service and operating expenses, including property taxes. The remaining term of an assumed mortgage should be long enough so that immediate refinancing is an option rather than a necessity. Examine loan terms carefully to detect any participation agreements that may be triggered by increased income. The loan agreement should be rigorously analyzed so that one can detect, for example, a possible due-on-sale clause that may trigger increased interest rates, and acceleration clauses based on external occurrences (e.g., condemnation). If assumption is a valuable right, it may be necessary to bargain aggressively with the lender as well as the seller concerning such clauses.

Lenders attempt to control their exposure to risk through two mechanisms: (1) the ratio of the amount of the loan committed to the value, and (2) requirements related to tenants. The loan amount may be based on the capitalized value of income from major tenants, possibly 60 to 70 percent of the capitalized value of total income. In addition, a maximum may be set on a "loan dollars per GLA" basis, varying with the type and location of the center.

Lenders also require that a certain proportion of the space be leased to tenants with high credit ratings under triple net leases with overages.

Specialized financing techniques are used in shopping center ventures to manage risk and structure capital. Sale–leaseback and sale–buyback arrangements are used to reduce equity contributions and maximize deductions. Joint ventures may be formed with anchor tenants for the development of new centers and freestanding parcels within multitenant centers. Other recent trends that should be mentioned are (1) the increased use of wraparound mortgages, mortgage assumptions, and various forms of lender participations; (2) the increased use of creative financing techniques, such as junior mortgages, ground leases, and spreading risk through syndication of the equity interest; and (3) the use of government financing programs such as urban development action grants (UDAGs), industrial revenue bonds (IRBs), and tax abatement and tax incentive financing.[7]

TAXATION AND TAX STRUCTURE

Tax shelter benefits are derived from the ability to defer or avoid payment of taxes ordinarily due on current income. These benefits are garnered, in part, by claiming noncash deductions to offset depreciation of wasting assets.

[7]Urban Land Institute, *Shopping Center Development Handbook*, 2nd ed. (Washington, D.C.: ULI, 1985), pp. 47–48.

Shopping centers are eligible for the 31.5 year cost recovery period under the 1986 Tax Reform Act. Only straight-line depreciation is permitted. However, under prior tax laws shopping centers could be depreciated quite differently. Under the 1981, 1982, and 1984 acts, shopping centers that were newly built could claim ACRS recovery over fifteen years (1981, 1982) or nineteen years (1984). Existing shopping centers could be depreciated only by the straight-line method, but with alternative periods of thirty-five or forty-five years, as well as the ACRS periods. Prior to 1981 the depreciation rules were somewhat more complex.

Under tax reform since 1981, shopping centers depreciated under ACRS guidelines would be subject to substantial depreciation recapture if the property was sold before the end of the asset's life. However, under the current law only straight-line depreciation is permitted. The recent changes in tax law simplify decisions relating to depreciation strategy, but the reader should, nevertheless, read thoroughly Chapter 10 for a full understanding of recent changes.

Although buildings, their structural components, and items attached, affixed to, and made part of the realty must be depreciated as a total entity, some personalty is eligible for the three- and five-year ACRS lives. Examples are snow-clearing equipment, mall furniture, artificial plants, and the like. However, personalty is no longer eligible for the investment tax credit (ITC). Tax counsel should be sought when seeking to classify as personalty any separately maintained and movable items that might be properly classified as equipment. Examples are carpeting, movable partitions, bank equipment, vending machines, fencing, window-washing equipment, leasehold improvements, and specially designed and installed HVAC and humidity control equipment.

Rehabilitation of older shopping centers should be carried out in such a way that their eligibility for new tax incentives available under the 1986 tax reform is ensured. Tax credits are available for rehabilitation of structures that are at least thirty years old or have historic significance.

If the landlord has made tenant improvements that are repaid out of rent payments, he or she may be able to specify a certain portion of rental income as repayment for the improvement and deduct this amount from taxable income. Finally, if property improvements can be legitimately scheduled as periodic repairs, the expenditures may, to some extent, be expensed as current operating costs rather than being added to the depreciable base.

For some improvement expenditures to be eligible as deductible operating costs, the improvement program might be *fractionalized* into routine repair operations, thus minimizing capital additions. Tax advantages should be weighed against any additional costs or inconvenience that may result from spreading the program over several tax years. To take advantage of tax-deductible rent proceeds for repayment of tenant-specific improvements, the landlord must identify a portion of rental income from the tenant as amortization of that expense in the lease. The portion identified as such must be based on some reasonable imputed discount rate. Such activities must have a sound business policy objective and not be carried out simply to evade taxes.

Disposition of shopping centers is also eligible for various tax deferment techniques, such as installment sales and tax-deferred exchanges. However, the 1986 and 1987 tax acts imposes new limitations on the installment sale, which may render it less desirable.

After structuring the venture for tax planning, the analyst must make assumptions about the ownership entity, marginal tax rates, and changes in those rates, and probable resale value and proceeds. These assumptions are fairly standard for all types of property and should be done in accordance with principles and concepts set forth in earlier sections of this book.

DISCOUNTED-CASH-FLOW ANALYSIS

Rate-of-Return Analysis. To calculate internal rate of return, the investor must make assumptions about the length of the holding period and the probable resale value. Projections of income, expenses, finance costs, and taxes can be extended to cover the assumed ownership cycle. The chart of accounts used for pro forma comparative analysis should follow the format shown in Exhibit 23-5.

Desired Rate of Equity Return. Equity investors in shopping centers should require an after-tax IRR of 10 to 18 percent on equity capital. This is in line with the expected returns anticipated by major property investors. However, the required rate of return is dependent on risk and current inflationary expectations. In today's market investors are buying shopping centers on "going-in" capitalization rates of 7.5 to 11 percent and selling on "going-out" capitalization rates ranging from 50 to 150 basis points higher. Higher rates should be applied to overage incomes, which are typically riskier.

Ratio and Risk Analysis. For analyzing risk, sensitivity analysis provides a good interpretive tool. Variations of average minimum rents, growth rate of overages, vacancies, and operating expenses should be tested. Variables like net cash flow, rate of return, and DCR should be used to test for risk sensitivity.

Evaluation of the Data. The key tests in the sensitivity analysis are the following.

1. The probability of negative cash flows and the ability to carry the project through such periods.

2. Dependence on overages for adequate rates of return.
3. The impact of foreseeable vacancies on the ability to cover debt service.

THE INVESTMENT DECISION

The analysis of risk and rate of return provides essential information for negotiating the purchase. The investor may use this information when negotiating the purchase price and request concessions from the seller, and when negotiating the loan with the lender and leases with major tenants. The investor should use the analysis to set limits on the amount of equity participation granted to a lender and the concessions granted to tenants.

SELECTED REFERENCES

Trends and Statistics

Advanced Monthly Retail Sales (Washington, D.C.: Gov't. Printing Office), monthly.

Annual Report, Retail Trade (Washington, D.C.: Gov't. Printing Office), annual.

"Buildings Census Highlights," *Buildings*, September 1985, p. 124.

County Business Patterns (Washington, D.C.: Gov't. Printing Office), annual, issued in separate reports by state.

Final Weekly Sales Estimates (Washington, D.C.: Gov't. Printing Office), weekly.

Monthly Retail Trade: Sales and Inventory (Washington, D.C.: Gov't. Printing Office), monthly with annual summary.

National Real Estate Index (Emeryville, Calif.: Liquidity Fund), quarterly.

"New Mixes Cater to Today's Tastes: Changing Trends in Tenanting Reported in Shopping Center Survey," *Chain Store Age Executive*, April 1987, pp. 25–26.

"Overbuilding: A Real or Imagined Issue?," *Chain Store Age Executive*, May 1987, pp. 48–50.

Parking Requirements for Shopping Centers (Washington, D.C.: Urban Land Institute, 1982).

Rogers, David, "America's Shopping Centres: A Mid-Life Crisis?," *Retail & Distribution Management*, November–December 1987, pp. 21–26.

Shopping Center Legal Update (New York: International Council of Shopping Centers, 1986).

Shopping Centers (Washington, D.C.: Urban Land Institute, 1986).

Top Shopping Centers—SMSA Markets 1–50 (Chicago: National Research Bureau, 1982).

"Trends in Mall Rents, Sales Volumes and More," *Stores*, September 1987, pp. 48–51.

Weekly Retail Sales (Washington, D.C.: Gov't. Printing Office), weekly.

Investment Performance

"Alternative Avenues: Maximizing Assets; With Fewer New Projects, Developers Reassess Existing Centers," *Chain Store Age Executive*, May 1986, pp. 53–58.

Curran, John J., "The Bright Jewels in Real Estate" (1988 Investor's Guide), *Fortune*, Fall 1987, p. 24.

"Investors Must Avoid Negative Generalizations," *National Real Estate Investor*, September 1986, p. 32.

Kevenides, Herve A., "Analyzing the Demand for Shopping Centers," *Buildings*, March 1986, p. 49.

Kowinski, William Severini, *The Malling of America: An Inside Look at the Great Consumer Paradise* (New York: William Morrow, 1985).

Lessons for States and Cities (Chicago: Real Estate Research Corp., 1982).

Shopping Center Bankruptcy: Hearing before the Subcommittee on Monopolies and Commercial Law of the Committee on the Judiciary, House of Representatives, Ninety-eighth Congress, second session on H.R. 2377 and H.R. 5187, May 17, 1984 (Washington, D.C.: U.S. Gov't. Printing Office, 1985).

Snyder, Wayne, "Shopping Centers Shape Up," *Real Estate Today*, September 1987, pp. 63–69.

Stern, Richard L. and Howard Rudnitsky, "Commercial Real Estate—The Worst Is Yet to Come," *Forbes*, January 26, 1987, pp. 64–69.

Stone, John M., "Under Variety of Names, Strip Centers Rebound," *National Real Estate Investor*, May 1985, pp. 58–59.

Therrien, Lois, "The Wholesale Success of Factory Outlet Malls," *Business Week*, February 3, 1986, pp. 92–93.

Development

"Building on a Trend," *Chain Store Age Executive*, February 1988, pp. 3A–6A.

"Commercial Development," *Builder*, October 1986, pp. 164–171.

Dawson, John A., *Shopping Center Development* (London; New York: Longman Inc., 1983).

Dawson, John A. and J. Dennis Lord, *Shopping Center Development: Policies and Prospects* (New York: Nichols Publishing Company, 1985).

Fletcher, June, "Shopping Centers," *Builder*, May 1986, pp. 158–165.

"Former Airport Is Site for Mixed-Use Project," *Chain Store Age Executive*, April 1988, pp. 48–49.

Hines, Mary Alice, *Shopping Center Development and Investment* (New York: Wiley, 1983).

Mills, David E., "Indivisibilities and Development Timing: The Shopping Center Problem," *Regional Science & Urban Economics*, February 1985, pp. 23–40.

Shopping Center Development Handbook (Washington, D.C.: Urban Land Institute, 1985).

Market Analysis

Adams, Eli, "Shopping Around for the Best Location," *Professional Builder*, August 1986, p. 72.

Carn, Neil, Joseph Rabianski, Ronald Racster, and Maury Seldin, *Real Estate Market Analysis: Techniques and Applications* (Englewood Cliffs, N.J.: Prentice-Hall, 1988).

Doyle, Margaret, "Strip Centers Shed Shoddy Image," *Building Design & Construction*, March 1988, pp. 66–73.

Friedman, Edith J., ed., "Appraisal of Shopping Centers," *Encyclopedia of Real Estate Appraising* (Englewood Cliffs, N.J.: Prentice-Hall, 1978).

Gorys, Julius M. L., "The Market Study Review Process," *Socio-Economic Planning Sciences*, July 1987, pp. 213–222.

McKeever, J. Ross and Frank H. Spink, Jr., *Factors in Considering a Shopping Center Location* (Washington, D.C.: U.S. Small Business Administration, 1980).

Ordway, Nicholas, A. Alexander Bul, and Mark E. Eakin, "Developing a Visibility Index to Classify Shopping Centers," *The Appraisal Journal*, April 1988, pp. 233–243.

Peterson, Eric C., "Market-by-Market Trends," *Stores*, September 1986, pp. 48–53.

Peterson, Eric C., "MXD-Mall Excitement," *Stores*, January 1987, pp. 144–148.

Scharfe, Thomas, "Finding Retail Success in Smaller Markets: Despite an Onslaught of Special Requirements, Mall Developers Are Entering Secondary Downtowns," *Building Design & Construction*, March 1988, pp. 56–61.

"Shoppers Rediscover Small Centers" (includes related article on management of small centers), *Chain Store Age Executive*, July 1986, pp. 69–71.

"Small Centers Grow in Numbers and Strength: Variations on the Traditional Strip Offer an Alternative to a Mall," *Chain Store Age Executive*, November 1987, pp. 72–74.

"Some Developers Opt for Middle Markets," *Chain Store Age Executive*, May 1987, p. 94.

"Theme Centers Draw Multi-Market Customers: Entertainment Plus Shopping Lures Tourists, Conventioneers, Locals," *Chain Store Age Executive*, May 1987, pp. 98–101.

"Too Big or Not Too Big? Sizing Today's Shopping Centers Requires a More Complex Formula," *Chain Store Age Executive*, August 1986, pp. 37–39.

Umesh, U. N., "Transferability of Preference Models Across Segments and Geographic Areas," *Journal of Marketing*, January 1987, pp. 59–71.

Marketability Analysis

Alexander, Alan A., "Are Percentage Rents Meaningful for Analyzing Retail Sales?" *The Journal of Property Management*, January–February 1985, pp. 22–23.

Bivins, Jacquelyn, "Personality: Can a Center Have One?," *Chain Store Age Executive*, April 1986, p. 36.

"Competition Strong for Prime Centers: Acquisition and Redevelopment of Existing Shopping Centers Are Helping Companies to Expand Their Bases," *Chain Store Age Executive*, April 1985, pp. 41–45.

"Demographics: Picking the Perfect Site for a Shopping Center," *Chain Store Age Executive*, February 1988, pp. 10A–13A.

"Developers of Small Centers Refine Marketing Techniques," *Chain Store Age Executive*, November 1985, pp. 76–79.

Dunham, Terry, "Value Retailing: A Changing Phenomenon," *Real Estate Today*, July–August 1985, pp. 20–22.

Gershman, Jerry and Herman Renfro, "Mall Renovations Inject New Life into Old Centers," *National Real Estate Investor*, May 1986, pp. 96–97.

ICSC Research Department, "Four Percent U.S. Mall Vacancy Rate Half of What's Found in Strip Centers," *Shopping Centers Today*, September 1986, p. 69.

Kroner, Kenneth, "Tests of Intraurban Central Place Theories," *Economic Journal*, March 1985, pp. 101–117.

Martin, W. B., "Estimating Retail Sales Potential for a Proposed Regional Shopping Center," *Real Estate Review*, Summer 1985, pp. 77–81.

Nevin, J. and M. Hustin, "Image as a Component of Attraction in Intraurban Shopping Areas," *Journal of Retailing*, Spring 1980.

"New Faces for Older Places: Renovations Add New Tenants and Business to Existing Centers," *Chain Store Age Executive*, June 1987, pp. 25–28.

Peterson, Eric C., "Site Selection," *Stores*, July 1986, pp. 30–34.

"Site Selection: A Computerized Approach," *Chain Store Age Executive*, August 1987, pp. 48–50.

Wood, Jeffrey G., "Shopping Centers Offer Alternatives for Investor Profits," *National Real Estate Investor*, May 1985, pp. 84–85.

Operation

Alexander, Alan A., *Shopping Center Lease Administration* (New York: International Council of Shopping Centers, 1986).

Foos, George, "Marketing Off-Price Centers," *Real Estate Today*, July–August 1985, pp. 23–24.

Glassman, Howard T., "Bankruptcy Law Amendments Aid Shopping Center Owners," *Real Estate Today*, November–December 1986, p. 51.

Greenspan, Jodi, "Solving the Tenant Mix Puzzle in Your Shopping Center," *The Journal of Property Management*, July–August 1987, pp. 27–31.

Halper, Emanuel B., "Restoration Clauses in Shopping Center Leases," *Real Estate Review*, Winter 1986, pp. 66–74.

Halper, Emanuel B., *Shopping Center and Store Leases* (New York: Law Journal Seminars Press, 1979).

ICSC Shopping Center Operating Cost Report 1984 (New York: International Council of Shopping Centers, 1984).

Kovach, Jerry, "Compensating Shopping Center Managers," *Real Estate Review*, Summer 1986, pp. 28–30.

Leech, James, "Tenants Can Frustrate Shopping Center Renovations," *Real Estate Review*, Spring 1985, pp. 61–66.

"Management, Marketing Create a 'Brand Name,'" *Chain Store Age Executive*, September 1985, pp. 31–34.

Miller, Henry S., Jr. and W. Michael Murray, "Maximizing Shopping Center Rents with Lower Minimums and Higher Percentages," *The Journal of Property Management*, March–April 1987, pp. 12–17.

Muhlebach, Richard F., "Updating the Shopping Center Lease," *The Journal of Property Management*, May–June 1986, pp. 23–29.

Peterson, Eric C., "Seeking New Niches, New Customer Bases with New Approaches to Marketing," *Stores*, January 1985, pp. 98–100.

Peterson, Eric C., "Temporary Tenants," *Stores*, January 1987, pp. 142–146.

"Shopping Centers," *The Journal of Property Management*, March–April 1988, pp. 28–31.

"Turn Good into Better: Concerned Mall Managers Keep Centers Operating at Peak Efficiency," *Chain Store Age Executive*, pp. 37–38.

Wertheimer, Jack, "Turnarounds Can Create New Market for Mall Managers," *National Real Estate Investor*, June 1985, pp. 124–126.

Financing

"Financing Comes from a Variety of Sources," *Chain Store Age Executive*, February 1988, pp. 14A–17A.

"Mega-Deals: Financing, Sales and Development," *National Real Estate Investor*, November 1986, pp. 116–123.

Olive-Tower Revitalization Project: August 1984 (Fresno: California State University, Department of Urban and Regional Planning, 1984).

"Project Financing Eases in Placid Financial Seas," *Chain Store Age Executive*, August 1985, pp. 43–46.

Razzano, Rhonda, "Firm Anchors Secure Small Center Financing: Most Major Lenders Set Stiff Rules for Obtaining Funding," *Chain Store Age Executive*, September 1986, pp. 52–56.

Switzer, Michael H., "Using Due Diligence in Shopping Center Purchases," *Real Estate Review*, Fall 1985, pp. 88–92.

"Taking a Chance on Hitting It Big: Retailing Lures Venture Capitalists as Other Industries Strike Out," *Chain Store Age Executive*, March 1986.

Wadhama, John D., "The Challenge: Financing Retail Development," *National Real Estate Investor*, May 1985, pp. 234–238.

Taxation

Jaben, Jan, "Retail Renovations Serve to Fill the Void as Tax Debate Puts Historic Building Rehabs on Hold," *National Real Estate Investor*, May 1986, pp. 108–113.

OFFICE BUILDINGS

Much of the growth in GNP since World War II has been in the service sector. Although the ratio of working-age population may have reached its peak, the reliance on a service-oriented society continues. As the amount of paperwork, computer use, and telecommunications increases, the demand for office space also continues to rise. Meanwhile, the needs of tenants are changing, too, because of their dependence on word-processing and voice-actuated terminals. "Smart" buildings are being designed and developed to accommodate current and future technological needs.

Office building construction has tended to follow the growth of financial and other service centers within a MSA, with successful projects being those chosen for their prime location. When considering the comparative advantages and disadvantages of the targeted site, the investor should seek an area that scores high on accessibility. Other factors to be considered include parking, visibility, prestige, proximity to desired amenities and related uses, accessibility to surrounding streets, and accessibility to major traffic generators. Investors in office buildings generally seek secure properties in locations with growth potential and a cash flow return from operations in the range of 6 to 9 percent. They seek an investment that can be leveraged through debt financing, appreciation of value, and tax benefits. Most of these investors rely on professional management, pay leasing commissions, and take on a minimum of maintenance and repair responsibilities. A general expectation is that gross rents will increase at better than inflationary rates to improve the expected IRR. Although historical data indicate wide cyclical fluctuations in office building returns, these properties are perceived as relatively conservative and desirable investments, especially by institutional and foreign investors.

Definitions

Competitive building. A competitive building is one that offers space to the public. The building may be completely competitive—that is, all space is under lease to nonowners—or it may be an owner-occupied building in which surplus space is leased on a competitive basis. Such a building may be identified with the name of the owner or management.

Gross building area. The gross building area, or aggregate area, is measured according to the exterior dimensions.

Office building. An office building is a structure devoted to nonretail business and service activities. A portion of the building is sometimes used for ancillary activities such as retail shops and food services.

Office park. Two or more office buildings arranged in a coordinated development that includes parking and landscaping constitute an office park.

Owner-occupied building. In an owner-occupied building, the property owner is also the principal or exclusive tenant. Owners are typically large financial institutions or corporations for which the building serves as national or regional headquarters.

Professional building. A professional building is used exclusively by professionals, for example, CPAs, attorneys, doctors, and dentists. Such a building may also contain associated drug retailers and clinics.

Net rentable area. The total area available for occupancy by tenants, is the net rentable area. Excluded are stairwells, common areas, and mechanical areas.

TRACK RECORD AND TRENDS

The future productivity of a property is partially indicated by past trends. The examination of comparative trends, relative rental rates, and the credit standing of tenants can alert an investor to a building that is filtering down toward eventual zero net demand, when it is difficult to hold tenants as current leases expire. If the surrounding area is deteriorating in quality, demand can become zero even though the property itself is holding its own; deterioration of the surrounding area may also limit the feasibility of modernization efforts.

The leasing structure of the property also influences its future profit potential. Gross, fixed-rate leases with long maturity dates obligate the owner to years of declining real income. Net leases with escalator clauses and reasonable renewal options are preferable for maintaining real returns.

There are two general categories of office properties: the low- or medium-rise buildings found in suburban locations and the familiar high-rise buildings common to downtown districts.

As population spreads to the suburbs of some cities, office development begins to decentralize. Small buildings and groups of buildings arranged in attractive office parks offer shorter commuting distances, ample parking, quiet settings, and better opportunities for smaller tenants and investors.

Downtown office development continues to grow, however—even in cities with generally declining central districts. There remains a distinct demand for large, contiguous spaces and for the prestige of large-building ownership or principal tenancy. Many professionals do not want to give up the business spirit of a downtown center and prefer proximity to clients and competition.

Both the national and the regional supply of office space has tended to follow a more dramatic boom-and-bust cycle than any other real estate sector. Builders and lenders typically overreact to demand by producing enough office space for a five- to seven-year absorption period. This short-term oversupply causes periodic depressions of rental rates; significant rent concessions are offered. A new wave of construction may not begin for another ten years. On the other hand, it can resume in less than five years if the MSA is growing rapidly.

Functional and locational obsolescence are important features to be considered when investing in office buildings. A superior location offering favorable public exposure and proximity to clients can rent to capacity. Modern design and style features also command premium rents and encourage occupancy. (For an excellent example, see the accompanying photographs and project information on Executive Park, Atlanta, Georgia.) Energy consciousness, in both the ecological and cost sense, has also become of great concern to today's office building tenants. Still, older buildings in good locations can compete successfully with new buildings if they have been modernized to provide computer-assisted elevator service, heating and air-conditioning, wiring and electrical capacity to support up-to-date automation practices, an attractive appearance, and space contiguity comparable to that provided by new buildings. Otherwise, a form of filtering takes place in which a building accommodates lower-paying tenants as it ages. Significant variations in rental rates usually coexist in each submarket, depending on location, age, obsolescence, and other functional characteristics of the particular property. The 1986 tax act provided significant competitive advantage over new development for rehabilitating buildings that were built before 1936 and have ample layouts and architectural amenities. Besides the updating of a building's features, many renovations reflect the conversion of the national work force from industry-based to service-based.

Inflation-induced economic losses have caused lenders to alter traditional mortgage arrangements, often requiring higher interest rates for

EXECUTIVE PARK

Project Data

Site: 120 acres: 8 acres dedicated streets; 3 acres private streets; 2 acres leased land

Land value: $250,000 per acre[1]

Building area
Existing offices: 1,632,109 sq. ft.
Convenience commercial: 17,193 sq. ft.[2]
Floor area ratio: .3
Parking ratio: 5 spaces/1,000 sq. ft. of gross building area[3]

Tenant Information
Total, January 1981	165
Number with less than 20,000 sq. ft.	149
Number with more than 20,000 sq.ft.	16[4]

Lease information
Leases vary from 3 to 10 years based on negotiation with tenant. All leases include escalation clause for changes in operating and maintenance costs and ad valorem taxes. All covenants include provisions for relocation for expansions.

Rates 1981: $10.50-$12.00/sq. ft. net rentable area[5]

Operating expenses projected for 1981: $4.23/sq. ft.

Building developments costs
Typical cost during 1968-1970 for 5-story, 100, 000 sq. ft. building was $26.50.[6] 1981 cost is $60.00.

[1]Includes dedicated roads and private roads, street lighting, and signing, street landscaping, utilities to sites.
[2]Includes 2-acre bank site. Cafeteria in operation. Additional uses include retail establishments to meet needs of tenants' employees. Leases signed include dress shop, beauty and barber shops, copy service, etc.
[3]Early buildings were provided with three spaces/1,000 sq. ft. gross building area.
[4]American Mutual Liability; American Oil Co., Continental Can Co., Simmons, U.S.A., National Cash Register Co., Radio Corporation of America, American Express Co., Prudential Insurance Co., Service Bureau Corp., Southern Bell T&T Co., Procter & Gamble, Texaco, Union Carbide Corp., Sentry Insurance Co., Republic Steel.
[5]Typically includes janitorial services, building and grounds maintenance, heating and air-conditioning, parking, security, and all utilities except telephone. Where a tenant occupies an entire floor, rentals are based on total floor area rather than net floor area.
[6]During that period rents ranged from $4.75-$5.25 per net foot and net square footage averaged 82-87 percent of gross square footage.

Photos and data courtesy of Mr. Thomas Eldridge, Manager, Executive Park, Taylor Mathis Management Company

shorter periods. Many lenders insist that borrowers pay points if the loan is to be assigned. Lenders who are actually partners with borrowers are becoming more common, hedging against inflation themselves and sharing in cash flow, or appreciation, or both. Because of the high cost of many office building ventures, the formation of venture partnerships has become more common.

INVESTING IN OFFICE BUILDINGS

Advantages and Disadvantages

Stable income streams are derived from well-located buildings, particularly those of high-quality construction. Standard leasing arrangements provide for periodic income increases and protect the investor against rising expenses. Office buildings have not generally been subjected to rent control. Some buildings can provide additional income from store rentals, vending and food service, and provisions for antennas, observation decks, and advertising. Demand is segmented, so older buildings may be profitable with low rental rates if they were purchased at appropriately lower prices, and modern buildings may command high rentals because of superior features. Debt financing in relatively higher ratios is often available for office buildings, especially when they are rented to high-quality tenants. The short depreciable lives of leasehold improvements and some equipment (e.g., office partitions) provide larger tax deductions.

The primary disadvantages are the large outlays needed to purchase major buildings and the nature of the competition. New high-rise buildings may cost $100 million or more. The resulting equity contributions, even with substantial leverage, are relatively large. Investors may scale down such sums by participating in investment ownership entities or, alternatively, by purchasing smaller suburban buildings. Competition from new development may not be synchronized to normal demand conditions, which are tied to local economic and demographic trends. For example, a major tenant may vacate to build its own building. Other owner–users may construct buildings and then lease the excess space, or a government office complex may be developed to accommodate agencies that currently occupy competitive space. All may be acting without regard to current vacancy rates. During the first quarter of 1986, for example, national vacancy rates reached new high levels at 16.5 percent in downtown areas and 22.5 percent in suburban areas, according to Coldwell Banker's Office Vacancy Index.[1] This is a problem that has often caused destructive competition with serious adverse affects on profitability.

---

[1]Steve Hammerick, "New Space Woes Hit Office Market," *Pensions & Investment Age,* June 9, 1986, pp. 13–15.

Types of Investors and Investor Motivations

Office buildings often have a complex split ownership. A building may have been developed as a joint venture by a builder and a user or investor. The builder may derive profits through development and rental in the early years, then eventually be phased out by the user. A ground lease may be involved, with the lessor seeking a stable, low-risk income stream and the building owner seeking residual cash flow and maximum deductions for tax purposes. Leasebacks are also common.

Many large organizations own their buildings and occupy them exclusively or lease out excess space competitively. Some of the reasons for such arrangements go beyond pure economics.

1. Control over operation, security, and maintenance.
2. Protection against loss of lease.
3. Advertising, by placing the company's name on the building's facade.
4. Creation of a monument to the organization's status and achievements.
5. Expression of architectural creativity or demonstration of the company's products.
6. Need for highly specialized facilities.
7. Lack of a high enough credit rating to command a "preferred" occupancy status in competitive buildings.

Office buildings are popular vehicles for institutional investment because ownership of the property offsets inflation and represent a relatively low management burden. Traditionally, institutional investors have sought full ownership positions, but recently they have begun to purchase leveraged properties and shared interests because the risks are better understood. Partaking in joint-venture partnerships is increasing in popularity while the costs of development continue to rise. Pension funds invest to diversify their portfolios in response to ERISA directives. For pension funds, participations offered by major financial institutions may further reduce diversification and management problems. Foreign investors have continued their involvement in office buildings because such ventures provide steady long-term returns that are safe from confiscation by their home government. Generally, they rely on prime properties purchased at low cash-on-cash rates to shelter their money and appreciate in value.

PRELIMINARY ANALYSES

Market and Marketability Analysis

The demand for office space is derived from the needs of service-related industries and the administrative functions of all types of concerns. In general, areas with manufacturing-based economies generate lower demand than areas with service-based economies. In some areas, the trend toward mixed-use zoning continues strongly, providing for offices, retail uses, and residential apartments or hotels all in a single zone. Therefore, the nature of the local economic base is a good indication of current and future needs for office space.

Occupancy rates are good indicators of current market conditions, although they may vary greatly for different types of buildings. Occupancy is better analyzed when buildings are segmented by location, age, and features. Rules of thumb, such as ratios of square feet of office space per population or service employment, may be applied to available projections to estimate future demand. A study of recent building trends in the area coupled with discussions with local construction lenders can also help the investor anticipate future additions to the competitive stock.

Demand Analysis. They key to effective demand analysis is proper stratification of the office space market, thereby enabling the investor to discover an appropriate niche to fill. There are five major segments of office demand.

1. *Major institutions.* Large financial and nonfinancial corporations seek large blocks of space in a building for use as a corporate symbol. Many of these organizations construct their own buildings, but others become key tenants under favorable lease conditions. Their primary concern is a prestigious location and building. The most prestigious locations are downtown and in the more fashionable suburban office parks near regional shopping centers. A corporation may also want the flexibility of being able to lease the space to another tenant, should it ever decide to vacate.

2. *General commercial.* Smaller tenants are more interested in good access and favorable rates. They are prime candidates for free-standing and park-based suburban buildings. Attorneys, engineers, accountants, and computer software firms are included in this category.

3. *Medical–dental.* Doctors and dentists like to be located near one another and near major medical facilities. They have very specialized needs in terms of space and facilities. This segment is decreasing as more such users purchase space cooperatively or in condominium arrangements, and as hospitals provide captive space at favorable lease rates.

4. *Quasi-industrial.* Users whose business is related to manufacturing or who seek low-cost space in industrial parks may take advantage of excess space in parks where land use controls permit a mixture of uses.

5. *Industrial.* The administrative and engineering functions of manufacturing concerns often locate their space in close proximity to the factory. Such users generally do not seek competitive office space.

The first two segments represent the chief target markets for competitive buildings, and the location and features of the subject property determine which segment is more appropriate. The investor may be supplying regional headquarters for major corporations or banks, or small office buildings for emerging companies.

Once the investor identifies the target market and the specific industry groups represented, forecasts using standard industrial code classifications should be consulted. These are generally available from Building Owners and Managers Association International (BOMA) regional offices, local planning agencies, commercial brokers, and regional U.S. Department of Commerce offices. Many of these reports are stratified by region, city (MSA), and type of physical buildings, providing useful underlying data to aid demand analysis. When these forecasts are combined with current ratios (office area occupied per employee) for each industry group, space needs can be projected. Expanding needs for space may indicate strong future demand for existing space as well as for any new space developed. Conjoint analysis, a technique developed in the mid-1960s, may provide the student with some insight into the importance of such detailed demand analysis.[2]

Supply Analysis. Just as demand is segmented, so is supply. It is beneficial to survey the existing stock of the appropriate market segment to determine rates, vacancies, and recent improvements. New construction will affect older buildings primarily through the filtering process. Without new construction, and given constant demand, all existing space tends to be at a premium.

The absorption rate for new space depends on the composite inventory of new space produced and occupied, the amount of old space vacated and converted, and the net change in vacancies. High absorption rates relative to new construction indicate continued good prospects for low vacancies and sufficient revenues. However, the process should be carefully monitored because, as previously noted, office construction occurs in waves followed by long periods of oversupply. Also, the effects of the invisible competitive supply can be determined by checking with local utility companies, lenders, and planning offices.

Exhibit 24-1 lists the factors used to evaluate the market risk for an office building location. (See also the technique for conducting a competitive survey of office locations presented in Chapter 13.) Depending on the requirements of the targeted market segment, an actual location can be rated on a scale of 1 to 10.

[2]William C. Weaver, "Forecasting Office Space Demand with Conjoint Measurement Techniques," *The Appraisal Journal*, July 1984, pp. 389–398.

EXHIBIT 24-1. Characteristics of a Good Office Building Location

---

CENTRAL CITY

Proximity to
   Other major office buildings
   Main railroad terminal
   Main suburban buses
   Mass-transit stations
   Fashionable shops
   Department stores
   Good restaurants
   Government office buildings and courts
   Financial district
   Esthetically pleasing neighborhood
   Leading quality hotels
   No objectionable neighborhood activities

SUBURBAN

Proximity to
   Major highways to central city (e.g., frontage road[a])
   Central location (relative to other major business centers such as shopping
      centers)
   Government buildings and courts
   Other new office buildings
   No objectionable neighborhood activities
   No heavy industrial buildings
   Banks
   Restaurants
   Bus service and other mass transit
   Parking
   Metropolitan airports[a]
   Industrial parks[a]

Source: Sanders A. Kahn and Frederick E. Case. *Real Estate Appraisal and Investment* (New York: Wiley, 1977), pp. 430–431.
   [a]Added by author.

Risk Management and Control Techniques. The primary risks for investing in office buildings are loss of high-quality tenants and bad-debt losses from low-quality tenants. The first is difficult to control except by providing good service and timely modernization. Some owners or managers make concessions to preferred tenants by providing prime space, rent-free periods, and allowances for remodeling. An investor's goal may be to have better tenants sign longer-term leases that include rent escalation provisions. The second problem is handled by a careful investigation of the credit histories of prospective tenants. The degree of insistence on high credit ratings, of course, depends on market conditions and the age and quality of the building.

Physical, Legal, Political, and Environmental Analysis

Physical and Structural Factors. The desirability of office space to the tenant greatly depends on the physical features of the building. Convenience and comfort are valuable amenities, as is quality interior design. Tenants expect good elevator service, temperature control, ventilation, lighting, and spacious quarters. In suburban developments, tenants look for the availability of a labor pool, a good tax rate, transportation networks, positive community attitude toward business, and often, proximity to their client base. Deviations from the standards available to tenants of the most recently developed buildings will be penalized by lower rental rates unless they are offset by a superior location.

Some of the physical characteristics to check include

1. *Poor soil conditions* or improper foundation work. The bearing qualities of the substrata are critical to the economic life of multistory buildings.
2. *Feasibility of modernization* at some future date. Can the elevator and heating–air-conditioning plant be readily updated or replaced? Can office space be internally redesigned? How adaptable is the electrical system to varying intensities of use and to changes in outlet locations?
3. *Availability of parking,* either on-site or publicly provided nearby.
4. *Floor space per floor.* Will a large tenant have to spread personnel throughout a number of floors?
5. *Preparation for contingencies.* Is there auxiliary power to run elevators during a power cutoff? Is there adequate fire protection, emergency lighting, and provision for rapid evacuation?
6. *Unnecessary architectural features* that add to maintenance costs but contribute little to value.
7. *Space efficiency for the building.* One rule of thumb is the ratio of gross area minus net leasable area to gross area (GA − NLA/ GA).Generally, it should be no more than 12 percent for a highrise building. The newer the building, the lower the ratio is likely to be.

Legal, Political and Environmental Factors. The primary legal concerns of the investor are local policies that affect operations and restrict use of the property. Local government policies may affect the demand for space by, for example, instituting tax programs or even rent control laws that reduce investment feasibility. Assessments favoring noncommercial land uses may increase operating costs and shift the competitive advantage to other locations. Conversely, a local government can substantially improve the attractiveness of a location with strong law enforcement, good public service, and effective planning and capital improvement programs.

Restrictions on use may emanate from other sources as well. Deed restrictions from private covenants or liens may prohibit conversion or partial demolition. Public ordinances can restrict the height of a building, change parking requirements, prohibit certain types of business operations (e.g., sale of liquor), and limit outside advertising and signing. The clustering of office uses may be limited in order to control traffic congestion and pollution. An older building may be placed on the national historical register, which may or may not be advantageous to the owners.

Becoming familiar with local politics is probably the best way to evaluate the probability of such occurrences.

An important legal and environmental problem that has developed during the 1980s is the identification and treatment of hazardous materials, especially asbestos, commonly found in buildings that were constructed prior to 1980. Many buildings of this vintage contain asbestos products in fireproofing and pipe-wrapping materials used.[3] Many investors and lenders will not purchase or make loans on properties that have significant asbestos problems.

Financial Analysis

In normal times, office building investors have sought a stable cash flow return of 8 to 12 percent plus an inflation premium over a ten-year period. However, the market is now fragmented by overbuilding and investors with diverse motivations. A well-located existing building designed to be periodically modernized can be a relatively stable, low-risk investment: leases can often be negotiated to offset net operating expenses, tenant turnover is low, and such properties enjoy high-leverage possibilities and tax shelter. Internal rates of return (after-tax) are often more than 20 percent for five to ten year holding periods.

The primary source of risk is overbuilding and competition from new and renovated buildings. The cyclical effects of the market may be minimized by maintaining a stable core of long-term tenants and, when possible, by the competitive advantage of a good location. (The importance of careful market analysis is especially relevant when the difference of one city block from a prime location can have great impact on the rate of re-

---

[3]Shirley A. Ness, "Environmental Hazards in Real Estate," and four other featured articles on the subject, *Commercial Investment Real Estate Journal*, July–August 1988, pp. 16–38.

turn. See Exhibit 24-1.) However, new construction generally forces owners of old buildings to modernize, and what is considered a favorable location can vary over time. A streak of tenant moves may result, accompanied by adverse effects on cash flow and returns. The owners of existing buildings, however, have one factor in their favor: the escalating cost of new development. In the mid 1980s, high-rise development costs of $100 to $125 per square foot, exclusive of site costs, requiring minimum rentals of $20 to $25 per square foot for reasonable returns, were common in many cities.

Leasing. The leasing of office space is complicated by the number of methods used to protect income against inflation and by the concessions offered to entire good tenants to the building.

Basically, three types of variable-rate leases are used. The first stipulates a fixed rental rate with pro rata contributions by the tenants to offset increased operating expenses—utilities, taxes, and insurance—which are paid by the management. Charges are made to tenants on the basis of the proportion of space occupied. The second type adjusts rental rates periodically according to changes in the consumer price index. (Regional indexes may more accurately reflect rates of change in office rents.) The third type of lease makes the tenant responsible for all expenses, including structural repairs. This arrangement takes the equity owner out of the landlord business; he or she becomes a purely passive investor.

Management. Good management is the key to maintaining high occupancy and minimizing operating costs. Large office properties generally have a professional property manager to handle leasing and overall administration, and a building engineer to supervise upkeep of the mechanical apparatus in the building. Whether either employs a staff to assist in these duties depends on the size of the property. Larger buildings may have a permanent crew for maintenance and housekeeping, but small ones often contract for such services. Large, modern buildings also utilize specialized computer systems to regulate heating and air-conditioning, operate security systems, and perform other functions. The choice is largely a matter of economics, and the purchaser should evaluate the system from the standpoints of adequacy and efficiency.

Analysis of Current Operating Income and Expenses. The operation of an office building generally includes the following expense items: staff payroll, fuel for utilities (electricity, water, and sewer), maintenance contracts, supplies and uniforms, repairs, insurance, real estate taxes, management, and reserves for mechanical replacements, alterations, tenant improvements, and lease commissions. Expenses for payroll and supplies vary, depending on whether an in-house crew is used for repairs and

EXHIBIT 24-2. BOMA Chart of General Ledger Accounts for Office Buildings

ASSETS

100 CURRENT ASSETS
101 Cash
102 Cash Fund-petty cash
110 Bank Accounts
111 General Account
112 Pay-Roll Account
113 Savings Account
119 Total Bank Accounts
120 Marketable Securities
121 Securities
  (If a variety of securities are owned, individual accounts may be kept for each kind of security.)
130 Accounts-Notes Receivable
131 Accounts Receivable-Rents and Services
132 Accounts Receivable-Alterations
133 Notes Receivable
134 Accrued Receivables
135 Reserve for Doubtful Receivables (credit)
139 Total Accounts-Notes Receivable
140 Inventory
141 Inventories-Materials
  (There may be items, such as removable partition stock, which should be carried in Inventory Accounts; however, miscellaneous supplies which will be consumed within a short time should not be included in these accounts. See also Account 261.)

150 INVESTMENTS
151 Investment in Subsidiary Companies
152 Sinking Fund Investments
159 Total Investments
199 Total Current Assets

200 FIXED ASSETS
201 Land
202 Leasehold
2021 Reserve for Amortization of Leasehold
203 Building
2031 Reserve for Depreciation of Building
204 Equipment-Building
2041 Reserve for Depreciation Equipment-Building
  (If desirable, separate accounts can be used for the various kinds of equipment numbering the accounts from 20402 to 20499 inclusive.)

31303 State Unemployment Insurance Tax
314 Accrued Property Taxes
315 Provision For Federal and State Taxes
316 Accrued Interest Payable
319 Total Accrued Liabilities
320 Other Current Liabilities
328 Total Current Liabilities

329 LONG TERM LIABILITIES
330 Bonds Payable
340 Mortgages Payable
350 Long-Term Notes Payable
358 Total Fixed Liabilities

359 DEFERRED INCOME
360 Deferred Income
361 Advance Rentals
362 Deferred Interest Income
368 Deferred Income/Credits
369 Total Deferred Income

370 RESERVES
371 Reserve for Contingencies

CAPITAL

401 CORPORATION
402 Preferred Stock
40201 Authorized
40202 Unissued
410 Common Stock
41001 Authorized
41002 Unissued
420 Surplus—Capital
430 Retained Earnings
450 Profit & Loss—Current Year

359 PROPRIETORSHIP OR PARTNERSHIP
(The following accounts should be used only in the event ownership of the building is in a partnership or sole proprietorship)
460 Capital (An account is provided for each partner)
470 Drawings (An account is provided for each partner)
480 Profit and Loss—Current Year
498 Total Capital
499 Total Liabilities—Capital

620 Electrical
621 Wages
62101 *Social Security
62102 **Compensation Insurance
62103 ***Fringe Benefits
622 Supplies/Materials
623 Contract Services
628 Miscellaneous
629 Total Electrical

630 Heating
631 Wages
63101 *Social Security Taxes
63102 **Compensation Insurance
63103 ***Fringe Benefits
632 Supplies/Materials
633 Contract Services
638 Miscellaneous
639 Total Heating

640 Air Conditioning and Ventilating
641 Wages
64101 *Social Security Taxes
64102 **Compensation Insurance
64103 ***Fringe Benefits
642 Supplies/Materials
643 Contract Services
648 Miscellaneous
649 Total Air-Conditioning-Ventilating

650 Combined Heating, Ventilating and Air Conditioning
651 Wages
65101 *Social Security Taxes
65102 **Compensation Insurance
65103 ***Fringe Benefits
652 Supplies/Materials
653 Contract Service
658 Miscellaneous
659 Total Combined Heating, Ventilating And Air Conditioning

660 Elevators
661 Wages
66101 *Social Security Taxes
66102 **Compensation Insurance
66103 ***Fringe Benefits
662 Supplies/Materials
663 Contract Service
668 Miscellaneous
669 Total Elevators

670 General Expense—Building
671 Wages (Watchman, Matron, Storekeepers, etc.)
67101 *Social Security Taxes
  (If social security taxes are not charged to each expense group on the basis of the wages charged to each, charge the entire social secu-

70801 Business Association Memberships and Dues
70802 Donations, Subscription, and Gifts
70803 Other
709 Total Administrative Expenses

720 Energy (Building Operation Only)
721 Electricity
722 Gas
723 Oil
724 Steam
725 Chilled Water
726 Coal
729 Total Energy
730 Total Operating Expense

738 ALTERATIONS—PAINTING—DECORATE
740 Alterations—Tenants' Premises (Not Charged to Tenant)
741 Wages
74101 *Social Security Taxes
74102 **Compensation Insurance
74103 ***Fringe Benefits
743 Contract Services
748 Miscellaneous
749 Total Alterations—Tenant
750 Painting or Decorating—Tenants' premises (not charged to tenants)
751 Wages
75101 *Social Security Taxes
75102 **Compensation Insurance
75103 ***Fringe Benefits
753 Contract Services
758 Miscellaneous
759 Total Painting—Decorating—Tenant
760 Total Alterations—Painting—Decorating
  (It may be desirable to segregate Accounts 740 and 750 between (a) Ground Floor Tenants (b) Office Tenants, in which case sub-accounts can be created.)

798 FIXED CHARGES
800 Insurance
801 Fire Insurance
802 Earthquake Insurance
803 Liability Insurance
805 Other Insurance
809 Total Insurance
810 Operating Taxes
811 Real Estate Taxes
812 Personal Property Taxes
819 Total Operating Taxes
829 Total Fixed Charges
830 Leasing Expense
831 Commissions

ASSETS (continued)

205 Office Furniture and Fixtures
20501 Reserve for Depreciation Furniture-Fixtures
(If more than one building is operated, separate accounts should be kept for each building. Use a capital letter prefix with the account number to distinguish the separate properties, as: 203, 204, 205.)
249 Total Fixed Assets

258 DEFERRED CHARGES
260 Deferred Charges
261 Supplies
262 Prepaid Insurance Premiums
263 Prepaid Taxes
264 Organization Expense
265 Unamortized Bond Discounts
266 Unamortized Capital Stock Discount
268 Other Deferred Charges
269 Total Deferred Charges

270 OTHER ASSETS
271 Other Assets
272 Utility Deposits
273 Deposit on Workmen's Compensation Insurance
279 Total Other Assets
299 Total Assets

LIABILITIES

300 CURRENT LIABILITIES
301 Notes and Accounts Payable
302 Notes Payable (Short Term)
303 Accounts or Vouchers Payable
306 Dividends Payable
309 Total Notes—Accounts Payable
310 Accrued Liabilities
311 Accrued Pay Roll
31101 Accrued Pay-Roll Bonuses
31110 Employee Pay-Roll Contributions
31201 Employee Old-Age Benefit Tax
31202 State Unemployment Insurance Tax
313 Employer Payroll Taxes Payable
31301 Federal Old-Age Benefit Tax
31302 Federal Unemployment Insurance Tax

INCOME

501 RENTAL INCOME
502 Rental Income
503 Office Rent (Fixed)
50301 Office Rent Escalation
504 Store Rent (Fixed)
50401 Store Rent (Overage)
50402 Store Rent Escalation
505 Storage Area Rent
506 Rent of Special Areas
507 Loss on Uncollectible Accounts
509 Total Rental Income

510 SERVICE INCOME
511 Service Income
512 Energy Sales
513 Alterations and/or Decorating for Tenant
518 Other Services
519 Total Service Income
530 Service Income
531 Service Expense
532 Energy Expense (For Resold Energy Only, Not Building Operating Energy)
533 Steam
537 Alterations—Decorating for Tenant (Billed)
538 Other Services
539 Total Service Expense
542 Total Service Income

545 MISCELLANEOUS INCOME
546 Miscellaneous Income
547 Interest Income
548 Other
549 Total Miscellaneous Income
599 Total Income (Including Net Services)

EXPENSES

600 OPERATIONS
610 Cleaning
611 Wages
61101 *Social Security Taxes
61102 **Compensation Insurance
61103 ***Fringe Benefits
612 Supplies/Materials
613 Contract Services
618 Miscellaneous
619 Total Cleaning

---

rity tax to this account and prorate to expense groups at the end of the year.)
**Compensation Insurance
67102 **Compensation Insurance
(If compensation insurance is not charged to each expense group on the basis of the wages charged to each, charge all compensation insurance expense to this account and prorate to expense groups at the end of the year.)
67103 ***Fringe Benefits
672 Supplies/Materials
673 Contract Services
674 Decorating (Public Areas)
675 Plumbing
676 Sewer
677 Water
678 Miscellaneous
679 Subtotal General Expense Building
680 Security and Life Safety
681 Wages
68101 *Social Security Taxes
68102 **Compensation Insurance
68103 ***Fringe Benefits
682 Supplies/Materials
683 Contract Services
688 Miscellaneous
689 Total Security and Life Safety
690 Landscaping & Grounds
691 Wages
69101 *Social Security Taxes
69102 **Compensation Insurance
69103 ***Fringe Benefits
692 Supplies/Materials
693 Contract Services
696 Miscellaneous
699 Total Landscaping
700 Administrative Expense
701 Salaries
70101 Management
70102 Clerical
70201 *Social Security Taxes
70202 **Compensation Insurance
70203 ***Fringe Benefits
703 Building Office Expense
70301 Supplies and Stationery
70302 Other
704 Management or Agency Fee
705 Advertising
706 Professional Fees (Legal, Etc.)
708 Miscellaneous
697 Total General Building Expense

---

832 Other Leasing Expense
839 Total Leasing Expense
840 Tenant Alteration Amortization (or Expensed)
849 Total Tenant Alteration Amortization
850 Depreciation
851 Building
852 Building Equipment
853 Office Furniture and Fixtures
859 Total Depreciation
925 Total Fixed Charges

929 FINANCIAL EXPENSES
930 Ground Rent
931 Ground Rent/Air Rent
939 Total Ground Rent
940 Organization Expense
941 Amortization of Organization Expense
942 Amortization of Capital Stock Discount
949 Total Organization Expense
950 Interest Expense
951 Interest on Notes and Mortgages
952 Bond Interest Paid
953 Amortization of Bond Discount
959 Total Interest Expense
970 Corporate Taxes
971 State and Federal Taxes (except income taxes)
972 Income Taxes
979 Total Corporate Taxes
980 Other Financial Expenses
998 Total Financial Expenses

*Social Security Taxes should be charged to each expense group, Accounts 600 to 750 inclusive, on the bases of the wages charged to each group. If Social Security Taxes cannot conveniently be segregated in this manner each month, charge all such taxes to Account 67101, Social Security Taxes, in the General Expense—Building group expenses and prorate to the proper expense group at the end of the year.

**Compensation Insurance should be charged to each expense group on the basis of the wages charged to each. If compensation insurance cannot conveniently be segregated in this manner each month, charge all such insurance to Account 67102, Compensation Insurance, in the General Expense—Building group of expenses and prorate the proper expense group at the end of the year.

***Fringe Benefits should be charged to each expense group; 600 to 750 inclusive on the basis of wages.

©

Source: Reprinted with permission from Building Owners and Managers Association International's publication, *1980 Downtown and Suburban Office Building Experience Exchange Reports.*

housekeeping. Payroll expenses also vary according to prevailing local wages and the presence of unions. Cleaning costs for the typical office building average $0.66 per rentable square foot per year (1988). Particularly in a slow market, such costs are meaningful to prospective tenants if, for example, higher lease rates but lower operating costs compare favorably to local competition.

A chart of accounts should include all income and expense items, such as any pro rata payments from tenants, which are deducted from the expense total. Typically, management is expected to provide utility services, cleaning and janitorial service, elevator operation, and building security. Also becoming common are provisions for tenant payments designed to offset increases in expenses above a base-year figure.

BOMA International has developed a method of accounting that includes a breakdown of the items required for effective fiscal management of office building properties. The BOMA chart of general ledger accounts for office buildings is illustrated in Exhibit 24-2. The balance sheet accounts—assets, liabilities, capital—are represented by the sections numbered 100–499; the profit-and-loss income and expense accounts are grouped under the sections numbered 600–999. For investment analysis purposes, the most useful items are 501–599, Income, and 600–998, Expenses. An office building company profit and loss statement, based on the BOMA standard accounting method system is depicted in Exhibit 24-3. These national standards, adopted in 1972 and later refined, allow for more accurate comparisons for purposes of leasing and operations analysis.

BOMA's *Experience Exchange Report* provides comparative data on downtown and suburban office buildings on a national and regional, calendar year basis. The basic measure of comparison is cents per square foot, and the report provides a glossary of terms that enable an analyst to compare the income and expense items of the report with the statement for a targeted investment. For effective computer simulation of an office building investment, the BOMA standard accounting system utilizes the following categories for income and expense items.

- *Building Total.* Operating costs and income in cents per square foot for total rentable area, both office and nonoffice.
- *Office Total.* Operating costs and income in cents per square foot for total rentable office area.
- *Office Rented.* Operating costs and income in cents per square foot for the office space actually rented.
- *Operating Cost Breakdown.* Wages, supplies, contract services, and other costs of operating the building.
- *Operating Ratios.* Several significant ratios calculated by the Exchange to facilitate comparison of properties.

EXHIBIT 24-3.   BOMA Office Building Company Profit and Loss Statement

Office Building Company
PROFIT AND LOSS STATEMENT
Six Months Ending June 30, 19____

Acct.	DESCRIPTION	Detail	Subtotals	Total
	RENTAL INCOME			
503	Office Rent	XXXX.XX		
504	Store Rent	XXXX.XX		
505	Storage Area Rent	XXX.XX		
506	Rent of Special Areas	XXXX.XX		
	Total Rental Income		XXXX.XX	
	MISCELLANEOUS INCOME			
542	Total Net Service Income	XX.XX		
547	Interest Income	XX.XX		
548	Other	XX.XX		
	Total Miscellaneous Income		XXX.XX	
	TOTAL RENTAL AND MISC. INCOME			XXXXX.XX
	OPERATING EXPENSES			
619	Cleaning Expense (see schedule)	XXX.XX		
629	Electrical Expense (see schedule)	XXX.XX		
639	Heating Expense (see schedule)	XXX.XX		
649	Air Conditioning and Ventilating Expense (see schedule)	XXX.XX		
650	Combined HVAC (see schedule)	XXX.XX		
669	Elevator Expense (see schedule)	XXX.XX		
699	General Expense—Building (see schedule)	XXX.XX		
709	Administrative Expense (see schedule)	XXX.XX		
729	Energy Expense (see schedule)			
	Total Operating Expense		XXXXX.XX	
	ALTERATIONS, DECORATING, AND REPAIRS EXPENSES			
749	Alterations—Tenants' Premises (see schedule)	XXX.XX		
759	Painting or Decorating—Tenants' Premises (see schedule)	XXX.XX		
	Total Alterations and Decorating		XXXX.XX	
	FIXED CHARGES			
809	Insurance Expense (see schedule)	XXX.XX		
829	Operating Taxes Expense (see schedule)	XXX.XX		
849	Tenant Alterations—Amortization/Expensed	XXX.XX		
	Total Fixed Charges Expense		XXXX.XX	
	TOTAL EXPENSES			XXXX.XX
	NET OPERATING PROFIT			XXXX.XX
939	Ground Rent (see schedule)	XXXX.XX		
949	Organization Expense (see schedule)	XXX.XX		
959	Interest Expense (see schedule)	XX.XX		
979	Corporate Taxes (see schedule)	XX.XX		
990	Other Financial Expense	XX.XX		
	TOTAL FINANCIAL EXPENSE			XXXX.XX
	FINAL NET PROFIT			XXXX.XX

(Subsidiary schedules must be prepared for each expense group
indicated in this condensed statement)

Use of Operating Statement

The Profit and Loss Statement, as it appears above, is practically the same as the Operating and Service sections of the Experience Exchange report form. By adopting this standard breakdown for your monthly and annual statements, the extra effort involved in making out your Experience Exchange return will be eliminated and the procedure simplified throughout.

The reference, "see schedule," appearing in several places, calls for a supporting memorandum which will correspond with the Analysis of Operating Costs on the reverse side of the Experience Exchange form.

The great advantage of adopting this standard operating statement is that its use enables you to make accurate comparisons with local, regional and national unit cost figures, as compiled from industry experience, thus deriving practical benefit from the authoritative information contained in the Office Building Experience Exchange Report.

Source: Reprinted with permission from Building Owners and Managers Association International's publication, *1980 Downtown and Suburban Office Building Experience Exchange Reports.*

Those who are interested in office building investments should analyze the *Experience Exchange Reports.* However, significant distortions could occur if the data being used do not conform to the BOMA uniform method of accounting and the BOMA *Experience Exchange Reports.* BOMA does provide information on the evolutionary changes of the reports for anyone who wants to make a comparison using past *Experience Exchange Reports.*

Analysis of Trends and Uncertainties. Like other properties, office buildings have the potential for significant increases in expenses. Buildings designed during periods of readily available, low-cost energy are especially vulnerable to substantial fuel and electricity cost increases, and the curtailment of heating and air-conditioning to enhance operation profitability would not be a popular solution among tenants. Energy-efficient buildings have some market advantage; for example, computer-assisted energy use control systems are producing major savings with rapid payback.

Local tax rates represent another potential cost increase. Owners of buildings developed under favorable tax assessments—provided to encourage expansion of business—may be faced with dramatic tax increases when those concessions expire. Trends pertaining to other commercial properties may be discovered through the study of the tax rolls. Tax appeal litigation may result in some relief. If the building is on a ground lease, escalation clauses should be reflected in the income and expense projections.

The projection of operating expenses is straightforward, although the application of the varying growth rates for each item, based on recent trends, usually yields more accurate estimates. Depending on the present condition of the building and the anticipated rate of new construction in the market area, the need for capital expenditure for modernization and renovation should be estimated and allocated to amortization. It is beneficial to integrate this analysis with the data of the market study and marketability analysis.

To some extent, operating expenses can be controlled through the skillful negotiation of leases, the goal being tenant absorption of the occupancy expenses. Primary constraints on this technique are the market conditions surrounding the negotiations and the quality of the building. A building that conserves energy is easier to keep clean and repaired, is likely to have cost-effective security, and may be more amenable to modernization. Features like omniflexible partition systems in open-space interiors, with zoned heating, ventilation, and air-conditioning, generally maximize the control over occupancy expenses. Architectural features that do not increase maintenance costs and are effective in producing revenue (i.e., are cost-efficient) may reduce risk by making the building more attractive to tenants.

FINANCING

Sources. Large office buildings attract capital from sources like REITs, foundations, insurance companies, and pension funds. Commercial banks and others may provide construction loans, permanent mortgages, and refinancing. Investors in smaller buildings must generally look to local sources, such as savings and loan associations. Well-located buildings with quality tenants and net leases are popular investments for major institutions, although equity ownership and income participation by the funds, even extending to ownership of leveraged properties, are becoming common. For example, PRISA, a special commingled pool of pension funds, had over 30 percent of its portfolio in office buildings in 1985.

Rates, Terms, and Conditions. Interest rates for office buildings tend to be lower, terms longer, and loan-to-value ratios higher than for other investments because they are often considered less risky and because the borrower is generally a prime, creditworthy client. In the fourth quarter of 1978, the average interest rate and term for office building loans made by a group of fifteen life insurance companies were 9.81 percent and twenty-two years, six months, respectively. In contrast, average hotel/motel loans were 10.29 percent for seventeen years, five months.

DCR and mortgage constant desired by the lender. On the basis of information from existing loans, 1.25 to 1.3 is a conservative estimate of the debt coverage for new financing. Exhibit 24-4 shows the trend in mortgage constants required by a group of life insurance companies on loan commitments of $100,000 or more on office building properties.

Lenders prefer buildings with substantial lease commitments at net or with pro rata expense sharing by high-quality tenants. The leases should be subordinated to the mortgage, thereby allowing the lender to foreclose on fully occupied buildings while requiring lessees to continue their lease obligations. Lending sources may also be amenable to sale–leaseback (see Chapter 9).

Projection of Financing Costs. Projections of financing expenses should include any participation charges required by the lender, financing adjust-

EXHIBIT 24-4. Average Annual Constants

	1985	1986	1987
January	12.9%	11.0%	9.9%
June	12.0	10.6	10.2

Source: Based on data from *The Appraiser*, June 1987.

ments necessary to fund renovations and modernization, ground-lease payments (when appropriate), allocation of points and other front-end charges, balloons, and so forth. For simulation purposes, one-time items may be capitalized, and others may be treated as projected operating expenses.

Risk Management and Control Techniques of Lenders. At one time, some new office buildings utilized bond financing, often under the sponsorship of the local government as part of the city's urban development program. Today, although federal urban development assistance grants can have favorable affects, most debt financing for competitive buildings is provided by financial institutions, especially insurance companies. The purchase of an owner-occupied building may require new financing because many carry no specific debt financing other than general-obligation debt instruments, such as debentures issued by the owner–organization. However, purchase–sale–leaseback techniques may sometimes allow for off-balance-sheet financing. Investors often can shift the risk of loss to the lender by raising the loan-to-value ratio; by avoiding personal liability, or limiting it to the top 20 to 25 percent of the loan; by eliminating prepayment penalties; by minimizing holdbacks for completion and rental achievement; by eliminating due-on-sale clauses to permit wraparounds; and the like. They also generally avoid clauses that do not permit prepayment of the loan.

Key elements to consider when evaluating an assumable financing package are the remaining life of the loan, the remaining economic life of the building, and special conditions associated with the mortgage. The remaining term should be sufficient to provide an opportunity to obtain refinancing when it is advantageous to the owner. Refinancing, in turn, depends on changes in monetary policy over the ownership period. Another factor is the relation of the contract's mortgage interest rate to interest rate trends. Depending on the current stage of the office construction cycle, rates and terms may improve in the short run. In addition, special provisions that limit changes in the physical design of the building or its use may be included in the mortgage.

The rejection of inferior loan proposals is the primary risk control technique used by lenders, who, for new buildings, often require 75 to 80 percent occupancy with high-quality lease commitments. Older buildings are judged primarily on the basis of existing leases and physical condition. Leases with escalation clauses and expense-defraying mechanisms are desired by lenders because they are concerned about the building's continued ability to produce adequate revenues and meet fixed obligations.

Financing and refinancing can be difficult under one of two conditions. First, lenders are often reluctant to take on more office building commitments during the period following a wave of overbuilding. They may persist in this policy even after the excess space has been absorbed. Second, special-purpose buildings, such as professional buildings, have more limited market appeal, which may decline rapidly after foreclosure. The financing for many of these buildings comes from noninstitutional sources, such as sale to a cooperative or condominium arrangement; syndication; a high ratio of equity contribution to loan; or, possibly, joint or several liability of the principals.

TAXATION AND TAX STRUCTURE

Office buildings have the same types of federal and state income tax advantages as other types of nonresidential properties. These include depreciation allowances, deduction of interest on the mortgage, and capital gains treatment. Office building investments often have less favorable tax effects from depreciation because of relatively high ratios of land to total property value, as compared with apartments..

Under the Economic Recovery Tax Act of 1981, office buildings were eligible for ACRS fifteen-year recovery periods; however, recovery periods of thirty-five or forty-five years could be used, depending on the type of investor. The Tax Reform Act of 1986 requires the investor to use the straight-line depreciation method and a 31.5 year useful life; any improvements to the building must also be depreciated using straight-line depreciation over 31.5 years.

Although buildings and their structural components, as well as attacted items, are treated as realty, there are items of personalty that are eligible for ACRS three- and five-year schedules. Examples are window-washing equipment, computer control systems, office furniture, sidewalk-cleaning equipment, nonattached carpeting, fencing, vending machines, bank equipment, art objects, and (possibly) free-standing, specially designed HVAC and humidity control system. Finally, leasehold improvements may be segregated by special agreement and amortized by the tenant over the term of the lease rather than being depreciated.

Under the 1981 tax act, rehabilitation was eligible for investment tax credit incentives of 15 percent for structures at least thirty years old, 20 percent for structures at least forty years old, and 25 percent for certified historic structures. Since 1986, investment tax credits are no longer allowed. (See Chapter 10 for additional discussion of tax treatment.)

Sale–leaseback arrangements may be used to shift ownership of some of the nondeductible assets. By means of a land lease, for example, the lessee may deduct 100 percent of the rental payment. If the ground lessor is a tax-free organization, it may be indifferent to the tax implications of this shift. Such an arrangement must be structured carefully, however. If the sale is based on a below-market price and the property is leased back at favorable rates with unlimited renewal options, the transaction may be interpreted as a mortgage by the IRS. This would allow for the deduction of only some depreciation and just a portion of the rental payments. The investor also must be wary of shifting federal budget priorities that result in large increases in state and local government taxes.

DISCOUNTED-CASH-FLOW ANALYSIS

Rate-of-Return Analysis. When older buildings are compared with alternative investments, present-value analysis may be a more reliable technique than rate-of-return analysis. The reason is that cash flows may be negative in years when modernization is expensed. IRR/PV analysis should be based on at least a full building cycle, and the desired rate of return should be competitive with those of comparable investments.

Desired rate of equity return. The investor's desired rate of equity return depends on yields on alternative investments and the building's age and condition. Older buildings may require extensive renovation at some future date to remain competitive, for which equity investors may need to contribute funds not accounted for in the basic feasibility model. For new buildings, equity investors may seek approximately 12 percent IRR after-taxes on equity, plus an inflation risk premium. The required shorter payback periods for older buildings may raise this figure to 15 percent or more, exclusive of the inflation premium. Risk premiums added to the minimum acceptable IRR should be considered to cover specific problems, such as the neighborhood, architecture, and lease terms. Because current conditions are so uncertain, the use of a scenario-type sensitivity analysis may aid in the selection of minimum acceptable rates of return.

Ratio and Risk Analysis. Ratios and cash-on-cash measures should reflect the cyclical overbuilding intrinsic to the office market as well as the lower risk and the steady income available. Sensitivity analysis should be applied to determine the effects of varying vacancies (e.g., 5 to 15 percent), expense growth rates (4 to 10 percent annually), and rental rate increases (e.g., 3 to 8 percent annually).

Evaluation of the Data. The investor with prior investment experience both in office buildings and in the particular submarket of the specific MSA may wish to conduct an independent evaluation. Otherwise, it would be beneficial to engage an ethical, local real estate counselor (e.g., an appraiser, property manager, or commercial broker) on a per diem basis to review data, consult, and advise.

THE INVESTMENT DECISION

Office building investors tend to be more averse to risk and more patient than most real estate investors. Consequently, their returns are often lower but more stable. Tenants are less volatile, and management is less onerous. Recently, some investors have chosen to avoid the larger MSAs. Instead, they concentrate on well-located high-rise office buildings in MSAs with populations of 300,000 to 500,000 and a record of growth, with the expectation that these areas are less likely to be threatened by new construction than are more popular, fast-growing MSAs.

SELECTED REFERENCES

Trends and Statistics

Beitler, J. Paul and Benjamin J. Randall, "The Case for the Office Condominium," *Real Estate Review*, Fall 1983, pp. 99–102.

Clevenger, Michael, "The Integration Obstacles to the 'Office of the Future,'" *Real Estate Review*, Fall 1985, pp. 83–86.

Downtown and Suburban Office Building Experience Exchange Report (Washington, D.C.: Building Owners and Managers Association, International, 1987, annual).

Friedman, Rick, "Smart Building Designed to Hone Competitive Edge," *The Office*, April 1986, pp. 69–71.

Hammerick, Steve, "New Space Woes Hit Office Market," *Pensions and Investment Age*, June 9, 1986, pp. 13–15.

Salton, Gary J., "Corporations Should Actively Develop Office Buildings," *Real Estate Review*, Winter 1986, pp. 81–84.

Schell, Theodore H., "Office Building Developers and the Communications Explosion," *Real Estate Review*," Winter 1984, pp. 44–47.

Sugarman, Alan D., Andrew D. Lipman, and Robert F. Cushman, eds., *High Tech Real Estate: Planning, Adapting and Operating Buildings in the Computer and Telecommunications Age* (Homewood, Ill.: Dow Jones–Irwin, 1985).

Wheaton, William C. and Raymond G. Torto, "Office Construction Booms: History and Prospects," *Urban Land*, July 1985, pp. 32–33.

Investment Performance

Brian, Tracy M., "Owning vs. Renting Office Space: A Financial Comparison," *Real Estate Review*, Winter 1982, pp. 86–89.

Canestaro, James C., *The Real Estate Financial Feasibility Analysis Handbook with Workbook* (Blacksburg, Va.: The Refine Group, 1982).

Donnelly, John C., "Investor Attitudes and the Appraisal of the Major Urban Center Office Building," *The Appraisal Journal*, January 1981.

Friedman, Edith J., ed., "Appraisal of Office Buildings," *Encyclopedia of Real Estate Appraising* (Englewood Cliffs, N.J.: Prentice-Hall, 1978), pp. 371–383.

Haight, G. Timothy and Deborah Ann Ford, "Renovating Older Buildings: The Recapture Dilemma," *Real Estate Review*, Winter 1984, pp. 33–36.

Hoyer, John E., "Commercial Rehabilitation for Profit," *The Journal of Property Management*, September–October 1985, pp. 6–8.

Laub, Kenneth D., "Evaluating the Office Condominium," *Real Estate Review*, Spring 1983, pp. 53–58.

Ness, Shirley A., "Environmental Hazards in Real Estate," and four other featured articles on the subject, *Commercial Investment Real Estate Journal*, July–August 1988, pp. 16–38.

Pygman, James W. and Richard Kateley, *Tall Office Buildings in the United States*, for the Real Estate Research Corp. (Washington, D.C.: Urban Land Institute, 1985).

Reed, John T., *Office Building Acquisition Check Lists* (Moraga, Calif.: The Real Estate Investor Information Center, 1982).

Schwanke, Dean and Kelley S. Roark, *Smart Buildings and Technology: Enhanced Real Estate* (Washington, D.C.: Urban Land Institute, 1985).

Development

Bakeman, Michael, *Office Development: A Georgaphical Analysis* (New York: St. Martin's Press, 1985).

Basile, Ralph J., et al., *Downtown Development Handbook*, sponsored by the Executive Group of the Urban Development/Mixed-Use Council of the Urban Land Institute (Washington, D.C.: ULI, 1980).

Black, J. Thompson, Donald P. O'Connell, and Michael J. Marino, *Downtown Office Growth and the Role of Public Transit* (Washington, D.C.: Urban Land Institute, 1982).

Cross, Frank M., *Case Study, Financial Feasibility of a Suburban Office Building* (Boston: Warren, Gorham & Lamont, 1980).

O'Mara, W. Paul, *Office Development Handbook*, sponsored by the Executive Group of the Industrial and Office Park Development Council, and the Commercial and Retail Development Council of the Urban Land Institute (Washington, D.C.: ULI, 1982).

Market Analysis

Archer, Wayne R., "Determinants of Location for General Purpose Office Firms within Medium Size Cities," *Journal of the American Real Estate and Urban Economics Association*, Vol. 9, 1981, pp. 283–297.

Barrett, G. Vincent and John P. Blair, *How to Conduct and Analyze Real Estate Market and Feasibility Studies* (New York: Van Nostrand Reinhold, 1982).

Carn, Neil, Joseph Rabianski, Ronald Racster, and Maury Seldin, *Real Estate Market Analysis: Techniques and Applications*, Chapter 12, "Techniques of Performing Office Market Analysis" (Englewood Cliffs, N.J.: Prentice-Hall, 1988), pp. 250–289.

Hollander, Richard E., "Marketing Office Space in the Suburbs," *The Journal of Real Estate Development*, Summer 1985, pp. 27–32.

Kelly, Hugh F., "Forecasting Office Space Demand in Urban Areas," *Real Estate Review*, Fall 1983, pp. 87–95.

Weaver, William C., "Forecasting Office Space Demand with Conjoint Measurement Techniques," *The Appraisal Journal*, July 1984, pp. 389–398.

White, John Robert, "How to Plan and Build a Major Office Building," *Real Estate Review*, Spring 1980, pp. 87–92.

Operation

How to Market Office Space in Your Building, Portfolio No. 10, Real Estate Portfolio Series (Boston: Warren, Gorham & Lamont).

McManus, Karen, "Survey of Leasing Techniques," *The Journal of Property Management*, May–June 1986, p. 9,

Office Building Lease Manual, compiled by BOMA International's Lease Content Task Force.

Rahm, David A., "Escalation Clauses in Urban Office Leases," *Real Estate Review*, Summer 1982, pp. 55–62.

Roberts, Duane F., "Playing the Escalation Game," *The Journal of Property Management*, May–June 1986, pp. 7–10.

Sheldon, Frank, "Developing a Tenant Improvement Construction Package," *The Journal of Property Management*, March–April 1986, pp. 26–28.

Woods, Barbara S., "Leasing in a Soft Market," *The Journal of Property Management*, May–June 1986, pp. 6–8.

Yorke, Marianne, "The Disposal of Vacant Office Space," *The Journal of Property Management*, March–April 1985, pp. 26–29.

Financing

Cymrot, Allen, Abraham Gelber, and Lynda L. Cole, "How to Invest in Office Buildings and Shopping Centers," *Real Estate Review*, Summer 1982, pp. 75–82.

Peltzer, Kenneth E., "Computerized Analysis of a Joint-Venture-Investment Office Building," *The Appraisal Journal*, October 1982, pp. 537–561.

25

INDUSTRIAL BUILDINGS AND PARKS

Industry embraces all the activities involved in the production, storage, and distribution of tangible economic goods, as opposed to intangible services. Industrial real estate is where these activities take place. Manufacturing has been defined as "the mechanical or chemical transformation of inorganic or organic substances into new products."[1] This transformation includes all the activities that go into the creation of what economists call *form utility*. Encompassed by this definition is the relatively new process of recycling worn-out, discarded, or waste materials, which are then used in the manufacture of new products.

Industry also includes research and development activities that serve the needs of manufacturing. Moreover, the facilities of transportation companies that provide terminal space and maintenance facilities as a service to industrial firms fall under this classification. These facilities house public warehousing, airport terminal services, stockyards, and packing and crating activities. Finally, such business services as publishing and printing, automobile and equipment repair, and cleaning establishments are regarded as industrial activities.

There are five basic categories of industry: (1) mineral and agricultural extractive, (2) those most oriented to sales markets, (3) those most oriented toward transportation, (4) those most oriented toward labor, and (5) nonoriented industries.[2]

[1]U.S. Office of Management and Budget, *Standard Industrial Classification Manual* (Washington, D.C.: U.S. Gov't. Printing Office, 1972), p. 37.

[2]William N. Kinnard, Jr., Stephen D. Messner, and Byrl N. Boyce, *Industrial Real Estate*, 3rd ed. (Washington, D.C.: Society of Industrial Realtors, 1979). See also Melvin L. Greenhut, *Plant Locations in Theory and in Practice; the Economics of Space* (Chapel Hill: Univ. of North Carolina Press, 1956), pp. 263–272.

Definitions

There are three types of industrial buildings; categorized according to purpose: general, special, and single.

General-purpose buildings have a wide range of alternative uses. Often, they are constructed on speculation and are generally adaptable to light manufacturing, assembly, storage, research, or service.

Special-purpose buildings have physical characteristics and facilities that are suitable to a restricted range of industrial processes.

Single-purpose buildings are adaptable to only one kind of process, sometimes only one particular firm. The more closely facilities are aligned with the particular needs of a given process or firm, the less readily they can be converted to other uses. In addition to structural attributes, physical characteristics of the site itself—size, shape, slope, or bearing characteristics—can limit its industrial uses. The site may also be severely limited in use by zoning or other land use controls, as well as by the availability of essential utility and transportation facilities.

Industrial plant. A plant is an establishment at a single location where industrial operations are performed. The total floor area of a plant includes all structures on the site, such as offices, power plants, repair shops, garages, warehouses, and laboratories.

Plant area. According to the standard method of computing plant size adopted by United States of America Standards Institute, "The gross floor area of a plant is the sum of the areas at each floor level included within the principal outside faces of exterior walls, and neglecting architectural setbacks or projections." To qualify as part of the floor area, the clear, standing headroom must be at least seven feet, six inches. Balconies and mezzanines are included in the gross floor area if they form an integral part of the building and have a minimum width of twelve feet.

Certain other structures are not properly considered part of the gross floor area. Structures with unroofed floor areas, unenclosed roof spaces, light wells, connecting passageways, and various sheds, lean-tos, and unenclosed loading platforms and silos are excluded from the gross floor area of the plant. (Industrial real estate brokers generally prefer the term *floor* rather than *story* in describing plant levels.) Some authorities have suggested a minimum ceiling height of fourteen feet as a standard measurement, but because many older buildings have lower ceilings, industrial specialists have not yet agreed on a standard ceiling height.

Plant site. The total land area within the property boundaries is expressed in either square feet or acres. The net land area excludes public easements or public roads that are not under private control.

Clear span. All open space, unobstructed by columns or posts, is considered clear span.

Fireproof building. No combustible materials were used in the construction of a fire-resistant structure. The construction is usually masonry, concrete, or concrete block, steel, and glass, with metal doors.

Floor loads. The weight that a floor can hold safely is called its floor load. In effect, it is the bearing capacity, usually measured in pounds per square foot of floor area.

Floor space per employee. The ratio of floor space per employee is expressed in square feet. It varies considerably by industry, geographic region, size of firm, and age of plant. It is a useful measure for planning for the growth of a metropolitan area.

Loading docks. A loading dock is a platform built to match the floor height of truck bed or freight car so that they can be loaded and unloaded easily.

Loading well. A loading well is a ramp built to allow trucks and trailers to back down to the floor level of a building for easy loading and unloading.

Major-shift employment. The number of employees working at the plant site during the largest daily shift and during periods of normal plant operation make up its major-shift employment. To obtain an accurate estimate of needed parking space, the term covers all employees, whether they serve in administrative, maintenance, or operating capacities. Employment densities are figured by relating the number of employees on the major shift to the land area. They are expressed as the number of employees per acre of land, or per square foot of required parking area. Estimations of parking requirements, however, commonly allow for overlap in shifts, visitors, temporary contractors, and so forth.

Mill construction. Buildings with heavy wood beams and heavy wooden, brick, or steel upright members have what is called mill construction. This type of construction was common fifty years ago, and many such buildings remain in use. They are sometimes referred to as *slow burners* because their knurled beams resist combustion.

Power wiring. Special heavy-duty wiring is brought in to service machinery that cannot be operated from average-sized power lines. Power wiring usually requires high-cost switch boxes and fittings.

Sprinklered building. A sprinklered building has an overhead sprinkler system with shower heads that are activated at a certain degree of heat. A sprinklered building is less expensive to operate because its fire insurance rates are substantially lower.

Structural density (floor–area ratio). The figure for structural density is derived by dividing the ground area of structures by the total land area. Thus, the floor–area ratio is the ratio of the total floor area of the plant to the site area. A three-story building containing 10,000 square feet per floor on a 50,000-square-foot site has a floor–area ratio of 60 percent.

TRACK RECORD AND TRENDS

The most significant trend in industry has been a migratory shift in industrial employment and activity from the traditional concentrations in the Northeast and the North Central states to the southern states, the Southwest, and the South Central and Pacific regions. The Sunbelt in particular is reporting record growth. With the southward and westward movement, there has been a marked tendency for new establishments to locate in suburban or outlying communities rather than in central cities. Sometimes there is a short-term period of high vacancies because investors have overbuilt. The chief impact of obsolescence on persons who own and invest in industrial real estate has been the need to devise means of adapting and rehabilitating the old facility.

The development of highway and expressway travel has led to greater reliance on truck transportation. The U.S. worker remains automobile-oriented, and public transportation systems in metropolitan areas have not kept pace with the outward movement of population and industry. All these developments have combined to accelerate the movement of freight-generating industries and large employers away from congested central districts.

Meanwhile, rail facilities have become less important to many industries. As we seek greater energy efficiency, a revival of rail transportation for industrial purposes may be seen by the end of the century. Air freight transportation has grown rapidly in recent years, particularly when the speed of delivery of items with high value-to-weight ratios is critical. Locations that provide air transport facilities therefore have a great comparative advantage for attracting such activities.

The shift in location from central to more outlying areas has been accompanied by a trend toward one-story buildings in which goods flow horizontally rather than vertically. Most firms prefer single-story plants because the layout and flow of goods and materials is considerably more flexible than in multistory structures. In addition, heating and ventilation can usually be handled more efficiently.[3]

For operations in which location is more important than process flows (e.g., high-fashion garment manufacturing), "vertical" industrial parks have continued to operate on a modest scale in central locations. Both manufacturing and storage processes have been significantly influenced by new methods of materials handling, such as forklifts designed to handle multilevel pallets and containers with standardized sizes and shapes. Containerization has necessitated the redesign of docking and loading facilities. Sea–land and air–land containerized facilities are now relatively common.

Also affecting industrial real estate is a long-term shift in demand in the United States that has significantly changed the employment patterns of major manufacturing industries. As new products have emerged, others have declined in market share. Investors in industrial real estate must be students of the Census of Manufacturers, last done for 1987.[4] (The next such census will be for 1992.) These selected statistics, grouped by Standard Industrial Classification (SIC), provide the investor with a better understanding of the pattern of change in the use of industrial facilities and sites. They also provide an early-warning system that permits rehabilitation and salvage of existing industrial real estate to prevent the waste of valuable assets. A sound method of rehabilitation is to put the building to other uses. The conversion of old warehouses and loft buildings into apartments or artisan villages is one imaginative example; the subdivision of old facilities into smaller areas—to be used by companies that apply microelectronics or plastic extrusion processes—is another.

The most important single development in the private sector is the planned industrial district (PID) or industrial park. Here concentrations of industrial establishments, through the economies of scale, can take advantage of the amenities offered by outlying areas with excellent access. Some are high-tech or employment parks that often offer a campuslike environment and combine several types of land use, for example, offices, manufacturing facilities, research and development laboratories, warehousing or distribution centers, retail centers, and open space as recreation areas.

Industrial renewal and rehabilitation has been thrust on many older cities as a means of offsetting their declining employment and smaller tax base. The programs have emphasized new, efficient industrial spaces in central-city locations. Because of the legal problems and expenses incurred, the rehabilitation has usually been accomplished with federal sub-

---

[3]Detroit City Planning Commission, *Industrial Study*, Master Plan Technical Report, Second Series, Detroit, 1956, pp. 27–36.

[4]U.S. Department of Commerce, Bureau of the Census, 1987 *Census of Manufacturers—Selected Statistics—Summary Series*, MC87-S-1 (Washington, D.C.: U.S. Govt. Printing Office, 1987).

sidies and state industrial-development authority bonds. The future of federal participation in such programs is uncertain. New England states, such as Massachusetts, have demonstrated that new industrial jobs can be created by a partnership of schools, states, and industries.

Finally, industrial real estate has been affected by the intense concern of many public and private groups about the effects of some industries on local environment. Although currently there is little agreement about who should pay, major steps are being taken by governments at all levels to "internalize" the costs of the more obvious and widespread forms of pollution by industrial firms. Many industrial firms had voluntarily acted to reduce pollution, even before the imposition and enforcement of public regulations. These pollution abatement activities often produce more elaborate facilities, and they tend to segregate certain necessary but polluting uses. Tallow rendering and junkyards are examples of uses that most communities try to prohibit. However, it is obvious that waste recycling must be provided for at some nearby place.

INVESTING IN INDUSTRIAL BUILDINGS AND PARKS

Advantages and Disadvantages

The market for industrial space is actually national or international; competitive properties may be widely dispersed and often spread over several MSAs. To reduce search costs, the investor may use an industrial relocation service, such as Fantus, a subsidiary of Dun and Bradstreet. Some local public utilities and railroads have developed competent real estate search departments, and a few even maintain up-to-date services reporting on the supply of industrial real estate available in their service area.

The fixed location of industrial real estate means that investors (both equity and debt) must be attracted into the market area in most instances. This requires more preacquisition planning and higher transaction costs. In addition since relatively large amounts of funds are required to effect an industrial real estate transaction, there is a tendency for investment funds to come from outside the local market area. The major centers of investment fund accumulations, such as New York City and Chicago, represent outstanding exceptions.

Industrial users are very reluctant to move both because of the actual cost of relocating machinery and equipment and because of the lost production time. Thus, even if an area is deteriorating, its effect on industrial concerns will lag. Industrial tenants are the least demanding of all; because many install large, bulky machinery and equipment, they are willing to sign long-term leases. The cost of an industrial building generally is many times higher than the cost of the land, thereby generating relatively more tax shelter and enabling the owner to take a higher depreciation base. Moreover, because tenants usually manage their own facilities, a relatively high proportion of gross income is translated into net income for the owner–landlords.

Industrial buildings, particularly those designed for manufacturing purposes, are often highly specialized and therefore more difficult to adapt to the requiirements of another user. Industrial real estate tends to be a relatively slow-moving commodity. Generally, the more specialized the facility, the less rapidly it turns over, which increases the liquidity risk. Typically, the value of the real estate itself is intimately related to the profitability of the industrial process it houses. Therefore, once equipment has been installed, it is often difficult to separate the value of the plant from that of the equipment.

Industrial real estate exhibits a higher degree of sensitivity to local taxes and other government regulations. Therefore, a particularly good working knowledge of tax impacts (realty and income), as well as of the regulatory climate, is required. Industrial buildings also have relatively high ratios of fixed charges (property taxes and insurance), whether occupied or not, which makes marketability or adaptability to other uses a major consideration.

Types of Investors and Investor Motivations

Generally, investors in industrial real estate are users, equity investors, institutional investors, small businesses using corporate surpluses, and public development agencies.

The primary investment goal for users is to pay less than the prevailing competitive price for the space. Because funds are generally more productive as working capital, there is often a financial advantage for the user to be a tenant rather than an owner, unless control of the location or wealth accumulation goals takes priority.

Equity investors in industrial real estate are usually persons with very high incomes or groups seeking higher returns through partially tax-sheltered income flows. Many such investors are willing to forgo current income for the sake of increased cash flow and capital gains in the future. Historically, they have sought a turnover of ownership after seven to twelve years. Balloon mortgage loans are particularly popular with such investors.

Life insurance companies, trusts, pension funds, and similar institutional investors make equity investments in industrial real estate, as well as mortgage loans. They are more inclined to make large, long-term investments in established industrial parks or buildings with proven good records. Short-term liquidity is rarely a primary objective. Instead, institutional investors seek greater portfolio stability and a larger average size of investment in order to reduce portfolio operating and management costs per dollar invested.

Institutional investors normally are subject to lower income tax rates than private, profit-seeking individuals or groups. Some are tax-exempt. Consequently, they have tended to emphasize the size and stability of the annual income flow rather than the prospect of capital gain. Thus, lower-risk, long-term leases with highly rated tenants are more likely to be sought by institutional investors. Their lower tax liability and long-run orientation, together with their generally greater accumulations of funds, often permit them to outbid leveraged and tax-oriented investors. Recently, some life insurance companies have made equity investments in industrial real estate and then obtained the maximum mortgage loan available from another insurance company or bank. Thus, they maximize financial leverage and seek an arbitrage between the overall rate generated and the loan rate that must be paid. Increasingly, lease guarantee insurance companies, one-bank holding companies, pension funds, and commingled funds have invested in industrial real estate.

An important source of equity investment funds is the earned surplus of smaller business corporations. Both equity and loan investments in industrial real estate represent attractive alternatives for such corporations. Such investments and loans may also be used to facilitate production and distribution relationships with suppliers or buyers.

Finally, local (and occasionally state) development agencies will often construct a plant and make it available on favorable lease terms, particularly as an incentive to attract new industry into an area that is seeking to expand or diversify its economic base. Often the plants must be general purpose and built on speculation, although they are built specifically for the tenant under a long-term lease arrangement. Both public and private money may be found in industrial development agencies. However, they are much more likely to lend money or guarantee loans than make equity investments.

PRELIMINARY ANALYSES

Market and Marketability Analysis

The market analysis for the industrial building and land is itself an application of a risk analysis technique. It must be remembered, however, that there are more frequently voids on the supply side because the private sector has lacked the creativity to lead demand rather than because it has failed to meet a known consumer need. Assumptions regarding general-lease parameters, tenant quality, and tenant mix should be based upon the market study, because ambitious MSAs often zone an excess supply of industrial land far beyond the capacity of the market to absorb in the near term. Such zoning tends to deflate land values and can result in an over-supply of general-purpose industrial buildings built on speculation. A competent market study should forewarn equity investors of such an un-fortunate phenomenon. A good risk avoidance technique would be to seek the advice of an ethical and knowledgeable industrial broker who has close ties to tenants and is familiar with competitive revenue–expense units. The use of competitive survey techniques, like those delineated in Chapter 13, is urged. Consultation with a qualified, well-connected realtor, such as a member of the Society of Industrial Realtors (SIR), can do much to mini-mize business risk.

Demand Analysis. The history of a property in terms of the credit stand-ing of tenants, relative rental rates, and comparative trends indicates a property's stage in the filtering-down process. Although industrial prop-erty is not as sensitive to neighborhood change as other types of income property, deterioration of the surroundings can cause difficulties in hold-ing tenants when current leases expire and severely limits the feasibility of modernizing the property.

The structure of the lease also can influence the economic performance of a property. Gross, fixed-rate leases with long maturity dates and no expense stops may burden the owner with years of declining real income. Leases that share or shift the risk of rising expenses and that index net in-come are preferred in order to maintain real returns.

It is important to understand the bases for site selection when analyzing demand. The decision to move or expand an industrial plant is based on two factors. (1) The plant must remain competitively productive during the period of the investment, and (2) although production and distribution methods change over time, the fundamental economic rationale for the location must remain cost-effective. Demand for industrial space may come from entirely new establishments, from firms moving in from out-side the metropolitan area, from relocations within the area, or from on-site expansion of existing establishments.

An *agglomerating* or clustering tendency develops when one type of production tends to be concentrated in one place (e.g., airframe produc-tion). Industrial services expanding to meet the needs of the dominant in-dustry create a complex that attracts other industries requiring similar services. Substantial concentrations are usually necessary before related services and supporting facilities develop to a significant degree.

However, *deglomerating* forces—for example, plant obsolescence in the dominant industry—detract from an otherwise favorable location. Tem-porarily high land prices, brought about by increased demand as a new industry influences an area, are another example.

Industrial users seek least-cost locations and consider such factors as (1) the location of competitors; (2) proximity to well-established distribu-tion centers; (3) proximity to customers, depending on the importance of direct contacts with customers; (4) the extent of the market area; (5) costs, including basic land prices, labor costs, community facilities, availability of housing, state labor laws, and the costs of materials, equipment, and transportation; and (6) active programs of industrial park development.

The steps for estimating the future space requirements of industry are as follows.

1. Determine the present number of manufacturing employees per gross acre by type of industry.
2. Estimate future industrial employment, by type of industry and size of firm.
3. Estimate future employee densities in light of changing trends in requirements for industrial space. As industries modernize plant and equipment, their output per square foot of floor space is usually greater. Offsetting this is the trend toward one-story buildings on outlying sites that contain more space for parking and for plant expansion.
4. Estimate future land requirements by multiplying the estimated square feet of land area required per worker (the industrial density) by the expected industrial employment for each use as of a given date. Employment estimates must relate to all industrial uses (rather than simply to manufacturing), or land needs for industrial purposes will be understated. A further adjustment may be necessary if nonindustrial uses are permitted in industrial zones. The estimate also should account for the community's land use regulations. Employment density analysis will have limited applicability for many commercial uses permitted in industrial zones.
5. Compare the estimated demand for industrial land with an estimate of the future supply of industrial land. A survey of the industrial land supply considers the quality of the land that is expected to be made available. Future land requirements may, for example, be dominated by demand for space with a structural density of 20 percent or less, whereas the supply of available space may consist largely of scattered, odd-sized lots.

Supply Analysis. Generalizations about supply analysis within a region are not useful because users of industrial land often consider sites scattered throughout a region and in more than one SMA. In a study by the American Trucking Association, the factors in plant location that were mentioned most often by industrial respondents, in order of frequency, were the following.[5]

1. Proximity and access to good highways.
2. Abundant industry-related labor supply.

[5] *Highways, Trucks, and New Industry: A Study of Changing Patterns in Plant Location*, prepared by the American Trucking Association, Department of Research and Transport Economics (Washington, D.C.: U.S. Govt. Printing Office, July 1963), p. 5.

3. Availability of suitable land.
4. Proximity to markets for product or services of user.
5. Availability of rail service, if relevant.
6. Availability of raw materials.
7. Favorable state and local tax structure.
8. Favorable leasing or financing.
9. Abundant water supply, if important.
10. Proximity to related industry.
11. Existence of building at site.
12. Community's cultural and recreational assets.
13. Nearby vocational training facilities.

Although many similar studies report that essentially the same factors are significant, there is variation in the priority of factors, depending on the industry, the size of the firm, or the process. For example, in a *Fortune* survey of more than 400 of the largest manufacturing firms in the United States, the following factors—in order of importance—were mentioned most frequently.[6]

1. Availability of workers of appropriate skill.
2. Proximity to customers, for minimizing transportation.
3. Proximity to raw materials, supplies, and services.
4. Ample area for future expansion.
5. A growing regional market.
6. Water supply.
7. Inexpensive power and other utilities.

The supply of industrial space is stratified or segmented by type. For example, some users are limited to sites with high-capacity, low-cost water, gas, and electricity. Others are strongly attracted to certain labor skills. In the event that improvements already exists on the site, the investor should analyze physical, legal, political, and environmental factors in order to identify competitive sites that would be of interest to the appropriate users. Particular attention should be given to the structural characteristics of the buildings in order to match these to the needs of potential users.

Centrally located sites. Land in older industrial areas is relatively scarce. Furthermore, the sites are often small and irregularly shaped; there is a limited amount of land available for parking, off-street truck loading,

---

[6]*Facility Location Decisions: A Fortune Market Survey*, conducted by Belknap Data Solutions (New York: Fortune, 1977).

or expansion. Traffic congestion is a common problem. Security may be perceived as a problem as well. Available central sites may be adversely affected by surrounding uses. Dilapidated buildings, smoke, smells, and the noise of the central district seriously limit prospects for modern industrial use. The utility service in older industrial areas may not be adequate for modern industry. Relatively high property taxes are often encountered, partly because other central-district uses normally support higher land values. A central location may also pose commuting problems for workers seeking to live in suburban communities.

However, these disadvantages must be balanced against many advantages. For some industries, a central location may be of overriding importance, particularly if such factors as delivery time or frequent customer contact are crucial to performance. The potential savings in transportation costs may justify locating warehouses and other distribution facilities in the downtown fringe area.

Besides attaining space, an industrial firm located in the central area acquires the right to use a valuable municipal infrastructure. The central area may be better served by lower-cost utilities, and other municipal services, such as police, fire protection, snow removal, are often superior. Although real estate taxes in such areas are high, they tend to rise at a slower rate than taxes in outlying areas.

Often, a downtown site is strategically located with respect to the unskilled and semiskilled labor pool. The proximity of professional consultants, suppliers, and subcontractors helps explain why some firms prefer central locations. Central industrial areas, though limited by traffic congestion, are often advantageously near major transportation terminals. Finally, for certain industries a central location with older buildings provides a means of securing space at a lower cost than is possible in the suburbs.

Suburban sites and acreage. Industrial acreage and individual sites in rural or suburban areas generally have just undergone a transition from agricultural use. Therefore, the cost of many suburban sites consists of the cost of the vacant land plus the cost of land development. Other considerations in determining whether industrially zoned land can be made into an industrial site include the topography and the load-bearing quality of the soil. The best land is level and well drained and contains no subsoil hazards.

Large sites (100 acres or more) in outlying areas permit occupants to isolate their operations from those of adjoining landowners. The dangers of explosion, heat, glare, fire, or radiation, and the nuisances of noise, smog, and smoke may be minimized by purchasing sufficient acreage. Enough land can be acquired to construct a one-story building, and still allow room for expansion and landscaping and for separation from an inharmonious industry nearby.

Although utilities are often lacking, large plants may prefer to install their own systems anyway, thereby avoiding the limitations of inadequate existing water lines, sewer mains, gas lines, and power sources. Utility companies occasionally cooperate by providing the necessary capacity and connections.

Organized industrial parks. An organized industrial park is a tract of land under proprietary control that is reserved by a master plan for the exclusive use of industry and supporting uses. Sites in industrial parks are relatively expensive compared to industrial acreage. However, the parks often have better support services and a superior location.

Site users who do not conform to the land use controls and lot sizes of the industrial district are unable to utilize such sites effectively. On the other hand, zoning and other land use problems are resolved by the park sponsor. Firms that locate in organized industrial districts avoid the time and expense necessary to negotiate and arrange for utility extensions with public authorities. Compared to uncontrolled industrial areas, the organized industrial district generally has superior highway access. (For an excellent example, see the accompanying photographs and project information on Technology Park, Atlanta, Georgia.)

The organized industrial district represents a specialized source of industrial land that is useful primarily for (1) firms that require less than ten acres and can adapt to the architectural and landscaping requirements imposed by the district, (2) distribution establishments that need superior market access, and (3) firms that require the special services and facilities of the organized industrial district.

Redeveloped land. The older areas of many cities—frequently those with mixed-use land, blighted sections, and dilapidated buildings surrounding downtown areas—have been redeveloped under federal or state programs. In these areas, privately owned land has been acquired by local public agencies, then cleared, subdivided, and offered to industrial prospects for sale or lease. Often the sites are oddly shaped, irregular, and uneconomical in size. Although the land is generally more expensive than outlying sites, it is also generally less expensive than competitive industrial sites in the same neighborhoods. Long-term land leases occasionally overcome the high cost. Prospects for renewal may be adversely affected by surrounding incompatible land uses that have not been eliminated. Still, this space is generally more convenient to urban centers and thus offers the attractions of such locations.

Redeveloped lands attract (1) industries and distribution firms that require centrally located space; (2) industries that emphasize customer service and convenience to downtown merchants, suppliers, and customers; (3) industries that must locate near labor supplies in the surrounding downtown area; (4) small plants and industries that are ancillary to major industries located in the central area; and (5) firms that can afford relatively high land prices and can comply with severe restrictions. The Urban Enterprise Zones, if promoted, provides tax incentives for industry to occupy and use urban ghetto sites and train underemployed youths. The next federal administration may encourage such subsidized central-city activity.

Physical, Legal, Political, and Environmental Analysis

Physical Analysis of Site and Improvements. Plant layout and construction are of utmost importance to industrial users and can take on numerous forms. In a *product layout*, equipment is arranged according to the particular sequence of operations needed to produce a particular product. Plants producing different but related products generally have a process layout that centralizes certain production functions.

Three construction classifications, distinguished by degree of fire resistance and quality of materials employed, are generally used for fire insurance rating.

First-class buildings are usually constructed of nonflammable materials. Exterior walls, bearing partitions, roofs, floors, doors, and window frames may be concrete, steel-covered, or aluminum. Floors are hardwood, rubber blocks, or metal strips. Vibration and noise are minimized. Alteration, expansion, and demolition costs for such buildings are relatively high.

Second-class buildings are only partially fireproof. The exterior walls—usually constructed of solid brick to a height of five or six stories—as well as the bearing partitions, stairwells, elevator shafts, and doors, are fireproof. Such buildings are exemplified by the mill-type structures erected in the late 1800s or early 1900s. The floors, roof, interior walls, columns, and all other interior construction are generally flammable. Consequently, these buildings must be served with overhead sprinkler systems (dry or wet), fire doors, fire walls, and exterior fire escapes. In general, they are suited to light or medium multiple-product operations.

Third-class buildings are of wood frame construction and are more flammable than the preceding types. Light-duty construction of one or two stories, a relatively low floor loading and bearing capacity, and high maintenance costs are characteristic. Compared to those of first- and second-class buildings, construction costs are relatively low. Third-class buildings are inexpensive to alter, expand, or remove.

Architectural design. In judging the utility of a building, the investor should relate the uses for which the building is adapted to the demand for these uses. For example, high walls with few windows are highly desirable for warehouses and general storage. Steel or galvanized iron walls are pop-

TECHNOLOGY PARK, Atlanta Georgia

Project Data

Site: 340 acres: 277.5 acres plotted; 35.4 acres right of way; 37.1 acres lake

Sales price per acre (parcel size 1 to 15 acres)
  Interior: $65,000-$80,000
  Lakefront: $80,000-$100,000

Building use (total area 850,000 sq. ft.): office, engineering production, warehouse

Open space ratio: .40; Floor area ratio: .026

Construction costs (without land)

	Sq. ft.	Built	Cost/sq. ft.
Office	27,000	1979	$40
Engineering production	40,000	1979	25
Office	44,000	1980	35

Rents and operating expenses per square foot (developer-owned buildings)

Rents
  Office: $8.50-$14.00
  Engineering production: $4.50-$8.00
Operating expenses: $2.75-$3.00

Photos and data courtesy of Technology Park/Atlanta, Georgia

Site Plan

ular in more moderate climates. Floors elevated to railroad car or truck bed levels are important for distribution purposes. Street-level floors are best for forklift truck use. Shipping floors adapted to food processing are unsuitable for most manufacturing or storage uses. Buildings with open ceilings and exposed rafters, trusses, and beams are more useful for warehousing because of their greater ceiling clearance. Multistory plants are better adapted to processing activities in which gravity flow is required. Moreover, activities that should be isolated from major functions are better located at a different level.

Adaptability. Where feasible, general-purpose buildings are preferable over the other types because they can more readily accommodate changes in industrial processes or products. A general-purpose building is usually both more salable and easier to finance.

Manufacturing and processing plants are more likely to be in special-purpose (or even single-purpose) buildings; wholesaling, distribution, and assembly activities (as well as related office and management functions) can usually be carried out in less specialized structures.

Building Analysis. As with site requirements, building characteristics tend to be user-specific. Among the items to be considered, in addition to the required amount of square footage, the type of construction material, bearing capacity, and foundations, are the following.

Electrical, gas, water, sewage, and rail installations. The proper type of electrical installation is an example of what are termed *economic* standards as opposed to *physical standards*. Many production activities, for example, require not only high-voltage and heavy-amperage electrical service, but also specialized levels or cycles of electric power. The provision of adequate power must be accompanied by a planned network of lines and circuits with sufficient capacity for maximum load. It is not uncommon for gas, water, sewage, and electrical service to be custom-designed to serve the special needs of an industrial customer. The absence of such utility services may make a site unacceptable to some industrial tenants.

Security systems. Security systems must be carefully evaluated, preferably by an experienced specialist. One potential pitfall is spending large sums to provide superadequate fencing and other devices, although protection systems and devices can be quite expensive if they must be installed later.

Fire protection and sprinkler systems. Fire protection varies with the type of activity and with local or state codes. Many industrial users have special requirements.

Elevators, lifts, and conveyors. Because of the expense of acquiring and installing elevators and conveyors, as well as the space they absorb, extreme care must be exercised to ensure that they suit their intended purpose. Correcting mistakes can be very costly, and allowance should be made for future expansion.

Heating, lighting, and ventilation. Electronics manufacturers may require a hermetically sealed environment, cooled, heated, and humidified to close tolerances. Many users require special high-speed, high-capacity ventilators equipped with pollution abatement devices.

Ceiling heights. The adequacy of ceiling heights is directly related to the intended use of the structure. The shift from bow trusses to laminated or I-beam construction has made higher, clean-span ceiling heights financially feasible and has enabled users to take advantage of the economies of new materials-handling equipment. Spans and heights tend to be in multiples of six feet for palletizing. Recently, heights in excess of thirty-two feet have been required because of improvements in forklift trucks and palletized storage facilities.

Legal, Political, and Environmental Factors. Zoning and environmental-quality regulations must be analyzed before anything else. Everyone wants jobs, but few communities want industries with pollution management problems located within their boundaries. Some enlightened communities, however, are creating industrial districts that are zoned to provide land for inharmonious but necessary uses. Conversely, the need to attract and preserve employment-generating industries is increasingly, dominating the decision making of local municipalities.

There are economic opportunities for investors in proprietary industrial parks that provide adequate land use controls, including control of environmental degradation. In recent years, militant opposition to establishing new industrial locations has given a quasi-monopoly market power to those who already own industrial land, because such sites do not have to run the ecological gauntlet to qualify. An environmental-impact analysis may be required for rehabilitation, expansion, or new-site development.[7] This analysis has grown particularly important in light of the growing trend toward making lenders and past users, as well as current users, liable for any cleanup required by activities on the site.

Financial Analysis

Industrial real estate occupancy is usually based on a long-term lease, ten or more years in duration. The typical industrial lease is more nearly net to

---

[7]Jane A. Silverman, *Environmental Factors of Real Estate Development*, Real Estate Review Portfolio No. 17 (Boston: Warren, Gorham & Lamont, 1978). See also *Environmental Comment* (Washington, D.C.: Urban Land Institute, series).

the investor than is a commercial lease, with much of the risk of changing operating expenses (e.g., utilities and property taxes) assumed by the tenant. Gross income is the annual contract rental for the space, plus any service income (e.g., from sale of electricity). When there is a long-term lease on industrial property with a well-rated tenant, potential gross income and effective gross income are often equal.

The average tenant in an industrial building makes fewer demands for services than tenants in other types of income-producing properties. The landlord pays the property taxes, but the leases contain a tax stop clause so that each tenant pays a pro rata share of any increase. The landlord pays for fire insurance on the building, but the tenants pay for liability, equipment, and inventory coverage. The tenants pay for their own separately metered utilities. However, exterior lighting is usually paid for by the landlord and prorated among the tenants. Generally, the tenant is responsible for all interior maintenance and repair, as well as for replacing broken glass. The landlord's responsibility is limited to maintenance of the roof and exterior walls, and sometimes common areas. The landlord should set up a reserve account to take care of future roof and wall maintenance.

The cost of maintaining the parking lot and common exterior grounds is borne by the landlord but passed on to the tenants on a pro rata basis. When a vacancy occurs, the landlord not only suffers the loss of rental income but also assumes other expenses that the tenant would have paid, including administrative overhead for management of the property—office expenses, bookkeeping and accounting, legal fees, telephone charges, advertising expenses, commissions, and time to resolve tenant problems. When a good management company performs these services without the responsibility for leasing, the cost is in the range of 2 to 4 percent of gross income; with leasing responsibility it may be 7 to 10 percent.

Analysis of Operations

Property Management and Leasing. The management of industrial properties is a separate specialty. Whereas maintenance and operating needs are comparatively simple (since most industrial tenants maintain the interior and often the exterior of their spaces themselves), the merchandising of industrial space requires substantial specialized knowledge about the manufacturing and distribution problems of the various enterprises to be housed.

Another reason for the specialization of industrial brokers is the national—even international—nature of the trading markets, which ties brokers into a semiconfidential communication network concerning the relocation plans of industrial businesses. It is in a broker's self-interest not to disclose the intent of a would-be tenant to change locations. Often the decision to seek an industrial site in a new region is made at a corporate headquarters a great distance from the site. Even local industries determined to move usually seek to keep their plans confidential.

One effective way for equity investors to tie into this private network is to bring an industrial broker into a joint-venture agreement or join a syndicate being organized by a broker. For such an arrangement, the broker would probably require (1) participation as property manager during the ownership cycle, (2) sales commissions, and (3) a share of the equity reversion. The extent to which a broker shares in the responsibility for providing cash equity contributions depends on negotiations, as well as the return–risk relationships implicit in the particular project. Because the broker's involvement, as described here, is fraught with possible conflicts of interest, it would behoove equity investors to investigate carefully the reputation of the would-be working partner.

The management of industrial real estate may or may not be tied to leasing. In some areas, the management fee is included in the leasing contractor's obligations and is part of the commission structure. In others, a separate management fee is charged only when there are multiple tenants.

Whatever the arrangement, there is a distinction between the functions of leasing or merchandising the space and of managing the property, which consists of collecting rents and maintaining the physical condition of the real estate in accordance with the owner's requirements and wishes. Management is an important function that must be integrated with leasing in order to keep the building completely and continuously occupied at appropriate rental levels.

A distinguishing characteristic of industrial real estate is that more of the maintenance and operation of the building tends to be automated, with the hours of service, such as heating and elevators, specified in the lease contract. Owners of multiple-tenant industrial buildings often buy utilities (especially electricity) at wholesale rates and resell them to their tenants at retail rates. Because this may be an important source of income, the lease must be analyzed to ascertain which party is responsible for services. Generally, all but first-year operating costs are borne by the lessee.

Leases and Tenant Arrangements. Landlords reduce leasing risk by attracting high-quality tenants and negotiating net leases. Smaller local tenants may be able to get lease guarantee insurance from the Small Business Administration, making them comparable to top-rated credit risks. On the revenue side, the investor can avoid the effects of inflation through a lease provision that escalates rent based on periodic evaluations of the cost of living. Reappraisal of the property is another method of determining future rental changes.

The four types of general leasing arrangements used to manage risk in industrial real estate practice are the following.

Straight lease. A straight or direct lease is used for a property that is already in existence or is being built as a general-purpose building.

Build–lease. A build–lease arrangement, also termed *build to suit*, consists of one of two situations. In the first, a property owner–developer already owns a building site in which a prospective tenant is interested. The owner constructs a building to suit the tenant. In the second situation, the investor has an arrangement with a prospective tenant to construct a building specifically for the tenant, but the investor must find and purchase a suitable site.

Frequently, a build–lease building is a special-purpose or special-use structure. The lenders therefore consider the credit of the tenant–user. As in all credit-oriented industrial real estate transactions, the higher the credit rating of the tenant, the better the tenant's bargaining position. The lessor can utilize the credit of the tenant in negotiating more favorable mortgage financing. The lender will, of course, insist on an assignment of the lease from the lessor in the event of mortgagor default.

Sale–leaseback. In a sale–leaseback transaction the buyer–lessor is often a financial institution, pension fund, or wealthy individual seeking a tax shelter. It is not necessary for the lessor to be a tax-favored or tax-exempt organization, but such status adds considerably to the attractiveness of the leases. Institutional lessor–purchasers are less interested in complex real estate development transactions than they are in "paper deals" that are easily evaluated using traditional techniques of financial analysis. Sale-leasebacks of existing facilities are readily understandable to them because the risk can be measured by familiar credit analysis methods.

Ground lease. Under this arrangement, the land is subject to a long-term lease and the lessee utilizes the leasehold estate to finance the construction of buildings on the land, or as a way to refinance partially. In effect, leasing the site is similar to obtaining a loan of 100 percent of the land value. Recently, industrial firms have been inviting investors to buy ground leases on established locations with the aim of generating working capital from an otherwise nonproductive asset.

FINANCING

Estimating Financing Costs

Debt service is generally fixed over the investment period and may be accurately projected. If loan call or escalation provisions are involved, a judgment must be made regarding future interest rates. In recent years, rising construction costs and interest rates made annual amortization costs so expensive that industrial real estate investors have sought to lower the mortgage constant. Balloon payment mortgages with amortization terms of up to thirty years are used to establish the annual mortgage constant on which the payments are based, with the balloons typically due in ten to twelve years. Another possible recourse, growing in popularity but not yet common, is the industrial condominium.

Sources of Funds

The financing of industrial real estate is more diversified than the financing of any other type of property. Within the limits set by regulations and laws, variation is found in the financing offered by different types of lenders, by one lender compared to another in the same group, and even from one loan to another by the same lender. Banks and insurance companies participate in the financing; so do pension funds, which are not hampered by the same laws and regulations that affect insurance companies and banks. As long as they comply with fiduciary responsibilities, pension funds can lend on higher loan-to-value ratios. Firms like Shell, U.S. Plywood, General Electric, and U.S. Steel, among others, have supplied funds and taken junior liens to facilitate good relations with their suppliers.

Small Business Investment Companies (SBICs) are specifically authorized to make both equity investments and long-term secured loans in order to serve borrowers who cannot qualify for conventional loans. As such, they usually demand premium rates and equity rights. In addition, estates, private trusts, university endowment funds, REITs, and wealthy individuals have an interest in industrial real estate lending. Besides offering the more conventional loans, many are willing to consider junior lien positions and subordinated land leases as well as convertible bonds. (See Chapter 9 for more details on the institutional lenders and financing techniques applicable to this market.)

Until recently, public agencies at all three levels of government offered industrial-development programs. Most public agencies at the federal, state, and local levels offer advice and assistance to industrial firms and developers. However, they do not usually make loans, with the exception of the federal government's Small Business Administration (SBA). Any manufacturing establishment with fewer than 250 employees is an eligible small business, and in some industries the limit is even higher. As a general rule, the SBA extends long-term credit secured by industrial real estate only if such credit is not available from private sources. The SBA may make a direct loan to the borrowing firm or participate in a loan by a private lender.

State and local industrial-development commissions frequently advance funds for plant construction and acquisition, particularly when private sources do not provide as much as is needed by the firm. This credit is commonly extended as junior liens, with relatively low interest rates and very favorable amortization provisions. Federal industrial-assistance programs are currently in a state of flux, but indications are that these will be restructured and that local authorities will increase their participation. In the past, state agencies and corporations have offered assistance that differs considerably from federal programs, but varies only insignificantly from region to region. The available programs range from exemptions to encourage research and development to excise tax exemptions, and tax concessions or inducements in some form are found in every state. However, it should be noted that the industrial mortgage guaranty is aptly termed the New England plan because of its heavy concentration in the New England states.

Industrial Real Estate Bonds

Mortgage bonds. Industrial corporations that are short of capital often issue mortgage bonds, which subsequently bear substantial limitations. The range of restrictive covenants is almost limitless; three of the most common provisions are (1) the "after-acquired clause" (dragnet), requiring that any other real estate acquired by the corporation following the issuance of the mortgage bonds be included as security until the bonds are retired; (2) a limitation on dividend payments until sufficient funds have been accrued to ensure continued payment of interest and principal on the bonds; and (3) a requirement that minimum working-capital ratios be maintained. Another problem is that the costs of a mortgage bond issue are considerably higher than those of placing a mortgage. Offsetting these limitations, the chief advantage of the mortgage bond is the avoidance of legal limits on the mortgages of some lenders and the possibility of borrowing 100 percent of the cost of the property.

Debentures. In contrast, debentures are simply full-faith and credit promissory notes of a corporation, secured by a loan agreement. Two types of debentures can be used to finance real estate acquisitions. First, highly rated industrial corporations may utilize their own credit in the financial markets to issue debentures, the proceeds of which pay for the acquisition of real estate. Technically, this is not real estate finance at all, but it has the advantage of being less expensive, because the interest rate on debentures of high-credit corporations is usually lower than that on mortgage bonds and even that on first mortgages in some capital markets.

Small corporations that need funds for physical expansion often issue convertible debentures. These carry the right of conversion into common or preferred stock of the issuing corporation, a "sweetener" designed to overcome the fact that the issuing corporation represents a relatively high risk. The chief difference is a legal one. Because debentures come under the heading of securities, they must comply with the securities laws, whereas a mortgage is simply a loan. The risk-taking investors or lenders most likely to be attracted to convertible debentures are SBICs and REITs.

Equipment trust certificates. A rarely utilized alternative for financing equipment and fixtures that technically may be regarded as part of the realty is the equipment trust certificate. These certificates are a form of chattel mortgage and are unusual enough to require the advice of a specialist in the Uniform Commercial Code and local law.

Major Bases of Credit. Although the credit analysis of mortgage lenders places greater emphasis on the status of occupants, the financial status of the investor–owner is not ignored.

Owner–occupant. An owner with blue-chip national credit will always command favorable terms. If the owner–occupant is a good local risk, some financial covenants may be attached to the loan agreement, such as a limit on future borrowing by the corporation until the mortgage is paid off, the establishment of working-capital ratio standards, or a limitation on the distribution of profits while the mortgage loan is outstanding.

Owner–investor. Relatively little emphasis is placed on the credit standing of the typical owner–investor, primarily because little effective recourse is possible in the event of default. Typically, institutional lenders on industrial real estate look for the notes to be endorsed without personal liability on the part of the owner and for the assignment of rents and receivership in the event of default. Many institutional lenders who are precluded from lending on unimproved property may lend on leaseholds without the land being pledged. In these situations, the real security for the mortgage is the credit of the tenants.

Tenant–owner. Ordinarily any lease on industrial real estate is conditionally assigned to the lender, in which case the tenant continues paying rent should the mortgagor default. As a further safeguard, the loan agreement normally provides for the subordination of any penalty clause or condemnation clause contained in the lease. Generally, the better the credit rating of the tenant, the more favorable the terms available to the borrower and the greater the emphasis on credit rather than real estate.

The lending institution normally pursues two avenues of investigation in evaluating the risk of either the owner–occupant or the tenant–occupant. The credit quality of a tenant or an owner–occupant depends in part on the industry in which it is operating and its place in that industry. Within the framework of its industry and its history, the credit quality of a tenant or owner–occupant also depends on its financial characteristics and earnings record. The future prospects of the firm and the quality of its management are all considered by the lender. A variety of ratios—working capital, dividend payout, capitalization—are utilized to evaluate the stability and strength of the company. Credit reports (e.g., Equifax or Dun and Bradstreet) are used to supplement earnings records. Bank references, competitors, customers, and outside auditing firms may be interviewed if permitted.

Lease Guarantee Insurance. It is not surprising that one of the most important uses of lease guarantees has been to help obtain financing for new construction. The guarantee offers an excellent form of collateral to the lender and is used to support the financing of industrial developments or investments that otherwise might not be acceptable risks to the mortgagee. Private lease guarantee companies usually insure up to 85 percent of the lease income in return for a lump sum premium that generally is treated by developers as part of the cost of project development. The typical premium might be equal to approximately six months' rent.

Debt Coverage Ratio and Mortgage Constant Desired by the Lender. Required debt coverage ratios vary significantly, depending on the owner's or tenant's credit credentials and on the location of the real estate. Generally, higher loan constants are used for industrial properties, unless there is a high-quality tenant with a "no-exit" lease that permits longer amortization than the normal fifteen to twenty years.

Loan-to-Value Ratio. Conventional industrial real estate mortgages usually carry loan-to-value ratios of between 66.67 and 75 percent of estimated market value. There are certain exceptions, such as New York State insurance companies, which loan up to 90 percent of value on "adequately secured loans." A construction loan may be granted for 75 to 80 percent of certified construction costs. A development loan might be 60 percent of development costs. In either case, the value of the land does not enter into the cost–value base. Alternatively, a "floor loan" arrangement may be employed, with the full loan commitment available when a specified level of income has been achieved.

Mortgage Loan Maturity. A new industrial building may carry a loan term of between fifteen and thirty years, whereas an older existing building might command only a ten- to fifteen-year maturity. To a large extent, leases tend to set the maturity of the mortgage. Often, the term of the mortgage will not run beyond the term of the lease. If underlying leases have very long terms (e.g., thirty-five to forty years), cannot be canceled, and are made to high-credit tenants, the terms of the mortgage can be extended accordingly. When the real estate, rather than the credit of the occupant or tenant, is the fundamental collateral, shorter terms are usually dictated by the lender's desire for safety. Guarantees of the state industrial-development authority are used to extend maturities.

TAXATION AND TAX STRUCTURE

The Tax Reform Act of 1986 requires a depreciation life of 31.5 years for industrial real estate property and three, five, seven, and ten years for various types of personal property and equipment. Real property is depreciated using the straight-line method; personal property is depreciated using the 200 percent declining-balance method. Certain other classes of personal property qualify for fifteen-year or twenty-year 150 percent declining-balance depreciation.

Depreciable, tangible personal property used as an integral part of manufacturing, production, extraction, and related research and storage functions is generally eligible for the short ACRS three-, five-, and ten-year terms. Thus, if a building is properly classified as a general-purpose building and the owner is supplying such equipment as overhead cranes, counters, racks, gasoline pumps, signs, fencing, storage bins, and special heating or air-conditioning to maintain a specific temperature or humidity, these items may be segregated out of the structural components and are eligible for the accelerated depreciation.

Improvements made for a specific tenant may enable the landlord to use a certain portion of the rental income as repayment for the capital improvement, amortizing this amount from taxable income. To take advantage of this opportunity, the landlord must identify a portion of the rental income based on some reasonably computed discount rate *ex ante* as amortization of the expense in the lease. The cautious strategy is to have an actual written agreement with the tenant.

When industrial properties are disposed of, they are eligible for various tax deferment techniques; capital gains or losses may be eligible for Section 1231 asset treatment, exchanges, or installment method sales.

The use of ACRS depreciation requires that the depreciable asset be segmented into appropriate classes, the life of which is generally statutory or regulatory. Although depreciation based on useful life has been eliminated, the ACRS lives are generous. An investor should consult an accountant, or a machinery and equipment appraiser, to determine the appropriate three-, five-, seven-, or ten-year life for items other than the real property. Trade and industrial fixtures that are not intended to be a part of the realty, even though apparently attached permanently, may be treated as personalty and thus eligible for the appropriately shorter life (see also Chapter 10). A significant percentage of the value of an industrial building may be correctly treated as personalty rather than being subject to the 31.5-year ACRS recovery period for real property.

A problem of a sale–leaseback arrangement is whether the transaction will be treated as a lease or a sale for income tax purposes. If it is truly a lease, the lessee is entitled to deduct the rental payments. The rent is ordinary income to the lessor, who is entitled to a deduction for depreciation and other expenses. Merely calling an agreement a lease does not ensure its treatment as one: the transaction may be treated as a sale, it may be taxed at ordinary rates, the sale may not be eligible for installment reporting, and the seller may have to report imputed interest income. The purchaser would receive deductions for depreciation and imputed interest. Similar problems exist for poorly drafted purchase–leaseback agreements, which may be classified as loans.

DISCOUNTED-CASH-FLOW ANALYSIS

Rate-of-Return Analysis. The most accurate estimate may be derived by estimating cash flows after taxes for the anticipated ownership cycle and discounting each to its present value, using IRR/PV methods of analysis.

Desired Rate of Return. Equity investors in industrial properties generally have required an after-tax IRR of 10 percent or higher, plus an inflation premium. This expectation is lowered significantly if the investor can purchase industrial property that has been leased for a long term by a firm with strong national credit. In recent years, as investors have tried to hedge against inflation, acceptable current cash flow yields (ROEs) have been much lower than the historic rule of thumb (10 percent ROE), plus the inflation premium on the best of the industrial properties leased to blue-chip tenants.

Ratio and Risk Analysis. Sensitivity analysis should be applied to determine the separate effects of individual expense increases, sudden vacancy, and potential rental increases as per the lease terms. In effect, an analysis should be made of the various escalator items to determine how effective they are at offsetting inflation and enhancing profitability.

THE INVESTMENT DECISION

Currently, investors seem to be aggressively seeking well-constructed industrial properties leased to strong-credit tenants on long-term net leases, or multitenant properties in established industrial parks. Also worth considering are properties for sale and leaseback to creditworthy owner–tenants. Warehousing, distribution facilities, and industrial park sites are the preferred risk investment. It appears likely that more industrial corporations are willing to sell and lease back land, plants, and equipment in order to put such assets to more productive use. As a result, more syndication of such industrial assets and increased equity investments by institutional portfolio managers can be expected.

SELECTED REFERENCES

Trends

Jackson, F. Scott and James L. Laughlin, *Business Condominiums: A Step-By-Step Approach* (Washington, D.C.: National Homebuilders Association, with Community Associations Institute, 1985).

Lyne, Jack, "There've Been Some Strange Turns on the Road to High-Tech," *Site Selection Handbook,* July–August 1986, pp. 758–760.

Melaniphy, John C., Jr., "Commercial and Industrial Condominiums Revisited," *Urban Land,* January 1983, pp. 10–13.

Operations

Baker, Don H., "Contemporary Issues in Real Estate Transactions Involving Environmental Concerns," *Industrial Development,* March–April 1986, pp. 2–3.

Frey, Stephen L., *Warehouse Operations: A Handbook* (Beaverton, Ore.: M/A Press, 1983).

"Inquiry: High-Tech Business Parks," *Urban Land,* April 1983, p. 40.

Industrial Development Handbook (Washington, D.C.: Urban Land Institute, 1978).

Kinnard, William N., Jr., Stephen D. Messner, and Byrl N. Boyce, *Industrial Real Estate,* 3rd ed. (Washington, D.C.: Society of Industrial Realtors, 1979).

Reimer, Paul, "Future High-Tech Parks: The User's View," *Urban Land,* November 1983, pp. 20–23.

Market Analysis

Miller, Darryl, "The Components of a Facility Review," *Industrial Development,* March–April 1986, p. 4.

Morrison, Constance Castle, "Industrial Marketing—A Key to Growth in the 1980s," *Urban Land,* November 1983, pp. 24–27.

Porter, Douglas R., with Linda Amato and Cheryl Siskin, *Covenants and Zoning for Research/Business Parks* (Washington, D.C.: Urban Land Institute, 1986).

Rubin, Marilyn, Ilene Wagner, and Pearl Kamer, "Industrial Migration: A Case Study of Destination by City-Suburban Origin Within the New York Metropolitan Area," *Journal of the American Real Estate and Urban Economics Association,* Winter 1978, pp. 417–438.

Site Selection Handbook (Washington, D.C.: Conway Publications Inc., 1983).

Investment Performance and Valuation

Black, J. Thomas, et al., *Mixed-Use Development Projects in North America: Project Profiles,* prepared by the Research Division, Urban Land Institute (Washington, D.C.: Urban Land Institute, 1983).

Brown, Margaret Evelyn, "Market, Design, and Financial Feasibility of the Re-use of Warehouse Buildings in Central Atlanta," a thesis presented to the faculty of the Division of Graduate Studies, Georgia Institute of Technology, June 1980.

Friedman, Edith J., ed., "Appraisal of Warehouses," and "Appraisal of Industrial Property," *Encyclopedia of Real Estate Appraising*, 3rd ed. (Englewood Cliffs, N.J.: Prentice-Hall, 1978).

Hartman, Donald J., "Industrial Real Estate—Estimating Value in Use," *The Appraisal Journal*, July 1979, pp. 340–350.

Nourse, Hugh O., "Using Real Estate Asset Management to Improve Strategic Performance," *Industrial Development*, May–June 1986, pp. 1–7.

Seymour, Charles F., "Appraising Industrial Parks," *The Appraisal Journal*, April 1979, pp. 165–176.

OTHER INCOME-PRODUCING PROPERTY

A brief analysis of three additional types of property—single-family houses, condominiums, and small apartment buildings—and two types of special-purposes properties—hotels and motels and nursing homes—will fulfill three purposes: (1) prescribe how to simplify the analytical process presented by this book when selecting a simple investment such as a single-family home, a condominium, or a small apartment property; (2) exemplify how investment in such real estate products as hotels and motels really represent a venture into a highly specialized primary business venture; and (3) present a real estate product, nursing homes, that is dominated by government regulations and special financing programs. Since none of these properties is analyzed in detail here, investors interested in a more thorough understanding and analysis should consult the references provided at the end of the chapter.

SINGLE-FAMILY HOMES, CONDOMINIUMS, AND SMALL APARTMENT PROPERTIES

Definitions

Single-family homes. A single-family home may be a detached unit on a single lot providing primary shelter for one family, or it may be a townhouse sharing common walls with contiguous units. Setbacks of the units are often varied to avoid the monotony usually associated with the single line of older row houses.

Duplexes, triplexes, and quadruplexes. Rental units found on one site usually share common walks and driveways, exterior walls, and sometimes common facilities. Duplexes, triplexes, and quadruplexes offer the advantages of rental units clustered in one neighborhood and, where the owner occupies one of the rental units, the convenient role of resident property manager. Offsetting these advantages is the fact that the owner is easily accessible for maintenance requests, which can be quite discouraging at four o'clock in the morning. Being both landlord and neighbor may become a source of friction.

Condominiums. A condominium is a form of ownership within a facility of any type of structure, from high-rise apartments to townhouses with four to six units.

Timesharing. An increasingly popular way to secure guaranteed use of high-priced resort properties and facilities, timesharing can take one of two forms: interval timesharing, in which an ownership position is taken in the property; and lease timesharing, with the right to use the property for a limited number of years. In interval-ownership timesharing (or tenancy-in-common ownership), the investor acquires an equity position by purchasing an undivided interest in the property based on some predetermined percentage, normally in proportion to the length of the time selected for personal use.

An investor in interval-ownership timesharing has

1. An equity position.
2. Security (warranty deed and title insurance).
3. The right to sell, will, rent, lend, or transfer share of ownership in the living unit, within the limits set by the owner's association.
4. The right to sell at a profit.
5. The right to take a pro rata share of tax deductions from real estate taxes and interest, provided the property is owner-occupied for more than fourteen days.
6. A voice in building management (through the owner's association), but also the responsibility for hiring a management firm and paying assessment fees.
7. Guaranteed annual use of the property for a set period.
8. A limited obligation for taxes or maintenance, based on a pro rata share of ownership.

The buyer's privileges may be encumbered by outstanding debt on the property (usually in construction loans). This debt may be offset, if the property is purchased during the development stage, by a nondisturbance clause or a trust or escrow fund set up for the retirement of outstanding obligations. If the property is purchased after occupancy has commenced, a mortgage payment certificate is desirable.

TRACK RECORD AND TRENDS

Investing in single-family (rental) houses, duplexes, small apartment buildings, and condominiums can provide a good cautious first step toward building a real estate portfolio. During the 1970s, single-family detached houses were among the best investments in income-producing properties.[1] This continued to be true in the 1980s except in certain states such as Texas, Louisiana, Oklahoma, and Colorado, which were subjected to severe overbuilding and economic downturns.

Several changes have taken place in recent years. The fixed annual mortgage constant is still available, but at a higher cost. Recent trends demonstrate the gradual changeover by lenders from the fixed-rate thirty-year mortgage because, although lenders' money costs have soared with inflation, their portfolios of fixed-rate mortgages have caused income to increase more slowly. By turning to various forms of adjustable-rate mortgages, lenders hope to pass on to investors the fluctuations in their cost of money.

Another significant destabilizing factor is the change in the characteristics of home buyers. In the past, single-family houses, which on the whole were privately owned, were a market distinguished from multifamily apartment buildings occupied by renters. During the late 1970s, more and more single-family homes were taken over by investors intent on "flipping" the properties for quick-turnover profits. More conservative investors sought tenants as interim users until market appreciation resulted in a capital gain for the medium-term future.

Another major market change has been the decrease in the number of first-time home buyers. In 1977, more than 50 percent of home buyers were first-home buyers; in 1978, such buyers accounted for 36 percent, and in 1985 they accounted for only 18 percent of the market.[2] Furthermore, first-home mortgage applicants are seeking more modest homes. According to the National Association of Home Builders, first-time buyers are sharply reducing the square footage of living space they wish to occupy. And when home mortgage lenders evaluate mortgage applications, three out of five consider energy costs a primary factor. Appraisers also are giving energy efficiency important weight in their valuations.

It appears that young couples are making major changes in life-style in order to achieve the venerable American dream. The traditional 25 percent of income allocated to housing has risen to 30 or even 40 percent. Couples are postponing childbearing in order to permit both partners to work for more years, and working couples are returning to the inner city because city homes are cheaper to own and maintain.

[1] R. Bruce Ricks, "Managing the Best Financial Asset," *California Management Review,* Spring 1976, pp. 96–102.

[2] Bernard Freidan, "For the First-Time Home Buyers: Despair, Sacrifice, Compromises," *The Wall Street Journal,* October 29, 1980, p. 31.

The National Association of Realtors has reported that the median price of existing homes increased over 400 percent since 1970: from $23,400 to $78,200 in June of 1984, to $100,000 in 1988. This upward trend is continuing (see Exhibit 26-1). During the same period, the overall consumer price index rose less than 150 percent, and it appears likely that residential construction costs will continue to rise faster than other consumer prices. Thus, the supply side cost of new production increases the value of existing stock, and speculative buying of houses by people who already own a dwelling has been another factor driving up prices. Speculative fever in the southern California housing market once caused prices to soar so unreasonably that the Federal Home Loan Bank Board in San Francisco had to threaten to stop the flow of mortgage credit. Some purchasers seem unaware that they are engaging in criminal conduct when they swear that they are buying as owner–occupants but their intent in fact is to find a tenant. Finally, occasional price deflation is one risk that results from this market churning.

Less uncertain are forecasts of the types of structures that will be built in typical residential areas. It is predicted that

1. There will be a fall in the size of homes from the current average of 1,750 square feet to around 1,500 square feet.

EXHIBIT 26-1. Sales Price of Existing Single-Family Homes, Not Seasonally Adjusted

Year	United States	Northeast	Midwest	South	West
MEDIAN					
1981	$66,400	$ 63,700	$54,300	$64,400	$ 96,200
1982	67,800	63,500	55,100	67,100	98,900
1983	70,300	72,200	56,600	69,200	94,900
1984	72,400	78,700	57,100	71,300	95,800
1985	75,500	88,900	58,900	75,200	95,400
1986	80,300	104,800	63,500	78,200	100,900
AVERAGE (MEAN)					
1981	$78,300	$ 76,000	$58,900	$75,400	$111,400
1982	80,500	75,400	60,700	78,700	114,200
1983	83,100	85,400	62,900	81,500	111,000
1984	86,000	94,800	63,700	84,000	112,700
1985	90,800	108,900	66,100	88,700	113,900
1986	98,500	128,700	71,100	92,700	122,200

Source: "Existing and New Single-Family, Apartment Condos and Co-ops," *Home Sales*, National Association of Realtors, November 1987.

2. Lot sizes will decrease.

3. Cluster houses and townhouses with densities of from fifteen to thirty units per acre may replace the detached house on a quarter-acre lot.

4. Rising energy costs will encourage builders to install more insulation and to plan for fewer cathedral ceilings, central air conditioners, and other energy-consuming luxury items.

Spurred by these and other factors, condominiums could be to the 1980s what single-family detached units were to the 1970s. It is expected that 2,614,000 condominum units will have been built in the 1980s, and as their popularity increases, so will their unit prices.[3]

The increasing popularity of condominiums may be traced to their ability to achieve high unit densities on increasingly expensive land as well as their appeal to first-time buyers and empty nesters. Condominium developments are also popular to second-home and resort home buyers. For the investor, they provide easier options in financing than do resort hotels, plus the profit potential from sales. Condominiums offer the same tax write-off advantages as single-family residences, and they offer lower monthly costs in comparison to renting or buying and maintaining a single-family detached dwelling. However, the spread of rent controls and moratoriums on condominium conversions point to the growing recognition of tenant rights and increases the risk to the investor.

INVESTMENT ADVANTAGES AND DISADVANTAGES

The initial cash investment for this type of property is usually relatively low; down payments may run from 5 to 20 percent of value. Some investors have assumed mortgages in which the seller provides a second mortgage requiring no initial cash investment. Such properties also offer the usual tax advantages, such as depreciation of the improvements; interest, real estate tax, and operating expense deductions; and capital gains treatment of profits from a sale.

Because they are based on an underlying demand for shelter and a broad market, such investments are relatively secure. Although moderately priced single-family homes are becoming scarce, demand remains relatively high and vacancy rates are usually lower than for multifamily property. In growing metropolitan areas, rental houses are among the most liquid type of real estate property, and frequent recorded sales of comparable properties allow the investor to establish a relatively reliable market value estimate. And for the new real estate investor who wants to learn

---

[3]*Fortune,* April 17, 1980, p. 1.

how to operate a property, rental houses provide a good starting point. The costs of mismanagement are relatively small; such properties are easier to manage, sell, or buy than more complex investments; and there is less governmental control than for large apartment complexes.

On the other hand, small rental properties can be time-consuming. Condominium residents require a high level of attention, but hiring a professional management company is too expensive for an investor owning several geographically scattered properties. Thus, the responsibility for leasing, collecting rents, and maintaining the property falls directly on the investor. Even a single-family home can be difficult to handle since a vacancy can eliminate operating income while expenses continue.

It is also becoming increasingly difficult to find investments that will easily provide substantial returns or break even. Because of intensive competition, capitalization rates have declined in many metropolitan areas.

PRELIMINARY ANALYSES

Market and Marketability Analysis

The best opportunities for substantial short-term gains in small rental properties are found in rapidly growing cities. Timing is important. Metropolitan areas do not grow evenly: some sections expand rapidly; some are occupied only by affluent people or only by the poor. The best place for an investment in small rental properties is a section that is in the path of the area's outward residential growth, generally on the outer fringes of metropolitan areas.

Successful investments may also be found in older sections of the inner city that are experiencing new popularity and a higher number of resales. Care should be taken to buy into an upgrading neighborhood, not a deteriorating one. A visual inspection is a good first step, perhaps with a neighborhood Realtor other than the seller's agent.

Demand Analysis. Basically, demand analysis is the same as for apartment investments (see Chapter 22). A simplified comparative market analysis form is presented in Exhibit 26-2.

A city's planning department is able to tell you what services—parks, street improvements, water—are planned for the future. The school that the children in the area must attend is an extremely important factor. Being close to parks, shopping, and churches is a great benefit for residential housing.

It also is important to determine the area's competitive rent level. This can be accomplished through discussions with professional management and realty companies or a survey of the leading city newspaper, the one with the largest classified advertisement section.

EXHIBIT 26-2.   A Comparative Analysis Form

Subject Property Address _____ Date _____

Information on other properties which are located in the same general area and have the same approximate value as the subject property:

FOR SALE NOW	Bedrooms	Bath	Den	Sq. Ft.	Mtgs.	Price	Days on Market	Terms
SOLD PAST 12 MONTHS								
EXPIRED PAST 12 MONTHS								

Source: Nothing Down. Copyright © 1980, by Robert G. Allen. Reprinted by permission of Simon & Schuster, a Division of Gulf & Western Corporation.

Supply Analysis. Consulting an area realtor, driving around the area, and keeping a record of offerings and sales can acquaint the investor with the properties of the neighborhood. In a developing area, conversations with builders will reveal what will be coming to the market. Developing a good relationship with a Realtor may also enable the investor to learn about area properties before they are formally listed.

If time is not of great concern, there are some alternative methods for finding properties in the target area.

1. Use the local newspapers. In addition to combing the classified ads, the investor can run an ad expressing interest in buying certain types of properties in certain areas.
2. Send out flyers to residents in the targeted area.
3. Send word out to other area professionals (lawyers, CPAs, doctors, etc.) that you are interested in purchasing.

As a general rule, problem properties should be purchased only after a detailed analysis has confirmed that the identified problems can be profitably solved. Other procedures that the investor can follow in making a supply analysis are discussed in Chapter 22.

Risk Management and Control. The greatest risks in small rental properties are negative cash flows and nonappreciation of the property value. The primary methods of reducing these risks are to select a good neighborhood, purchase the property at or below the market value, and arrange financing at favorable terms.

The next major risk is loss of marketability and liquidity, a problem less worrisome if guarded against during property selection. Only properties in stable, highly regarded neighborhoods that appeal to broad segments of the market should be selected.

Physical, Legal, Political, and Environmental Analysis

Unless the investor plans rehabilitation, run-down or functionally obsolescent older homes should be avoided in favor of property that looks neat and clean with locationally specific amenities. For example, houses in the Sunbelt require air-conditioning. A good rule of thumb is that if 90 percent of the houses in an area have large lots, enclosed garages, and other amenities in common, the investor should purchase only houses with such fixtures. Some desirable amenities are dishwashers, garbage disposals, trash compactors, extra insulation, and electric garage door openers.

Exhibit 26-3 provides a checklist for evaluating the physical, structural, and neighborhood aspects of a small investment property. There are few environmental consideration for such properties, except those relating to political and legal factors.

The investor should be wary of an increasing real estate tax burden. Communities with inadequate streets, water, and wastewater services or parks might be faced with property tax increases to fund the delayed capital improvements. To prevent such a surprise, the investor can compare market values to appraised values; properties with large discrepancies face the prospect of an equalizing property tax increase. It is also wise to review past trends and proposed zoning plans, which may be obtained through local planning departments.

EXHIBIT 26-3. A Small-Property Investment Checklist

NEIGHBORHOOD QUALITY

- Are property values rising?
- Are the other houses in the same price range?
- Are the property taxes in line with those in other areas?
- Is the neighborhood well maintained?
- Is there good access to public transportation?
- Is there adequate parking (on and off street)?
- Are all municipal services available and adequate?
- Is the quality of the schools good?
- Is there adequate shopping nearby?
- Are there any special noise problems?
- Are there any hazardous traffic patterns

THE SITE

- Is the size of the yard adequate?
- Is the drainage away from the foundation?
- If the house has a septic tank, has it been serviced recently?
- Are there any dead trees?
- Is the general condition of the yard good?
- Are all fences, retaining walls, and walkways in good repair?
- Does any landscaping need replacement?

THE BUILDING (STRUCTURAL AND EQUIPMENT)

- Is there any problem that will require an immediate outlay of cash?
- Is there a 220-volt line for the range and dryer?
- Is the roof watertight? Will it be in the near future?
- Is the basement free from watermarks, wet cracks, or other signs of moisture?
- Is the building structurally sound?
- Is the garage wide enough and long enough for adequate parking?
- Is the electrical service adequate?
- Are the range and oven included in the price?
- Are all floors and floor coverings in good repair?
- Is the furnace working properly?
- Does the water heater have a good remaining useful life?
- Is the condition of the exterior paint adequate?
- Is the condition of the interior paint adequate?
- Are walls and ceilings free from minor cracks?
- If there are any additions or alterations, were the necessary permits filed?
- Are kitchen countertops and cabinets in good repair?
- Do all windows have coverings or draperies, and are they in acceptable condition?
- Is there ample wall space for furniture?
- Is there adequate closet and storage space?

Financial Analysis

The four types of returns from small rental properties are cash flow, tax shelter, equity buildup, and appreciation.

Cash flow. Cash flow from small rental properties is, in most cases, either negative or negligible. The three determinants are as follows.

1. *Rental levels.* In recent times, monthly rent multipliers have increased substantially (up to 150) because, although the prices of houses have risen, rental increases have lagged far behind. Rents in many MSAs have been increasing from 10 to 15 percent per year and so offer hope that the situation may ease to stop positive cash flows from being a rarity.

2. *Financial levels.* The amount of the mortgage constant, determined by the prevailing mortgage rate, constitutes the largest drain on cash flow from rental receipts. The loan-to-value ratio may be very high for single-family residences. When these heavily leveraged positions are coupled with mortgage rates running from 10 to 12 percent, cash flow may be negative even before considering other fixed and variable costs. Liquidity reserves are virtually mandatory.

3. *Expense levels.* Such out-of-pocket expenses as maintenance, management, and repair are escalating but can be held down when the owner provides these services personally and places a low value on his own time.

Investors have historically been satisfied with nonexistent to negative cash flow from operations because (1) they have little up-front equity in the investments; (2) the amount of negative cash flow is usually small, and intelligent investors have already budgeted for this contingency; and (3) most investors realize that their major gains will come from property appreciation and tax shelter.

Tax shelter. The IRS permits the investor to deduct depreciation, interest, and necessary and ordinary business expenses for Section 1231 property on the regular federal income tax return. Straight-line depreciation over 27.5 years was authorized in 1986. Through their active participation, some investors are eligible for the special up-to-$25,000 matching of passive rental losses to business or professional services income. If so, the tax shelter may be quite significant, sharply increasing the yields.

Equity buildup. A portion of each monthly mortgage payment applies to reduction of the principal on the mortgage note balance. As each loan payment is made, the investor's equity in the property increases. Since some, if not all, of the monthly payment is made from rentals, rentals may help pay for the equity gain. This depends, of course, on stable or even increasing value.

Appreciation. Because of the rising cost of housing and its capacity to take a heavily leveraged position, the greatest returns in small rental properties have been made in appreciation. Over the last decade the price of existing houses increased, on average, at a compound rate of 10 percent a year.

The major sources of risk are (1) purchasing a property in a deteriorating neighborhood, (2) a 100 percent vacancy rate (if an investor owns one rental house, one vacancy represents a 100 percent vacancy rate), (3) liability for personal injuries that occur on the investment property, and (4) bad tenant relations. A poor tenant can easily cause more damage to the property than the security deposit will cover.

Projection of Rental Income and Vacancies. Existing selling prices and rents provide the basis for projections. The investor can obtain these data through area professionals. One method of projecting the data is to analyze the preceding five-year record for the area and calculate the yearly percentage increase in prices and rents. After new demand elements are taken into consideration and recent trends are noted, the derived growth figure can be applied to current sales and rent levels to determine what future levels might be.

Property Management and Leasing. Most investors in small rental properties self-manage their properties, particularly since finding competent property management firms for small rental properties is difficult. Furthermore, an investor–manager has a greater incentive to enhance the value of the property.

The two most important factors in managing a property are tenant relations, since better tenants keep the property in good condition, and maintenance, since the property must be well kept and maintained to attract quality tenants. In the long run, attracting quality tenants can lead to considerable savings in maintenance costs.

Generally, selecting good tenants depends on the following.

- *Previous References.* Phone calls will verify the prospective tenant's statements.
- *Steady Employment.* The existence of the claimed job and income level should be verified. A one-year record of steady employment is a good minimum cutoff point.
- *Credit Report.* It is ordinary to expect at least three credit references from the tenant. The divulgence of credit card numbers is another possible prerequisite.
- *Income-to-Rent Ratio.* The tenant must realistically be able to afford the rent payments. A good ratio is 3.5 or 4 to 1.
- *Other Specific Policies.* Other matters to be discussed and investigated are bank references, pet controls, age limit, and advance payment of rent and security deposit against cleaning and damage. Resistance to any of these is a sign of potential trouble.

Another way to cut down on the maintenance burden is to pass on as much of the responsibility and cost as possible to the tenant through the lease agreement. For example, utilities are usually paid for by the tenant. A great asset to any lease is a clause like the following.

Maintenance, Repairs, or Alteration: Tenant acknowledges that the premises are in good order and repair, unless indicated herein. Owner may at any time give Tenant an accurate written inventory of furniture and furnishings on the premises and Tenant shall be deemed to have possession of all said furniture and furnishings in good condition and repair, unless he objects thereto in writing within five days after receipt of such inventory. Tenant shall, at his own expense, and at all times, maintain the premises in a clean and sanitary manner including all equipment, appliances, furniture, and furnishings therein and shall surrender the same, at termination hereof, in as good condition as received, normal wear and tear excepted.

Tenant shall be responsible for all repairs required for exposed plumbing or electrical wiring and for damages caused by Tenant's negligence and that of his family or invitees or guests. Tenant shall not paint, paper, or otherwise redecorate or make alterations to the premises without the prior written consent of the Owner. Tenant shall irrigate and maintain any surrounding grounds, including lawns and shrubbery, and keep the same clear of rubbish or weeds if such grounds are a part of the premises and are exclusively for the use of the Tenant.

(Investors are warned that if too much property management is shifted to the tenant, the investor may lose Section 1234 status and be classed as a passive investor.)

Self-managers should point out such a clause to the tenant, explain it, and be firm in enforcing the requirements, although cooperation with reasonable tenants is important. For all major repairs, the tenant should be asked to call the owner–manager so that prompt arrangements can be made. If the repair is necessary because the tenant has been negligent or abused the property, the tenant can be billed for it.

The owner should use a written property inspection report, which generally are available from local managers. Such reports can help to minimize disputes when a tenant vacates or should there be an eviction or casualty such as fire.

Analysis of Operating Income and Expenses. An analysis of potential cash flow, expenses, and taxes is essential to enable the investor to evaluate the debt-carrying capacity of the property and the stability and adequacy of the net operating income (NOI).

However, because investors are looking to potential appreciation for virtually all their return, capitalization rates based on NOI in today's market are generally low. Mortgage equity capitalization rates that take into consideration appreciation or depreciation in value are recommended instead.

Generally, there are three reasons for a below-market capitalization rate: (1) rents are too low, (2) expenses are too high, or (3) price is too high. The last is usually the case. However, an investor can buy a property with a low market-derived capitalization rate if he or she is confident that expenses can be lowered, that rents can be raised, or that values will increase sharply over the short term.

Excluding the need for major repairs brought about by code compliance activity of the local governing body (which is usually applied only to older structures), the greatest potential for increased expense in small rental properties is in real estate taxes. Growing communities often raise property tax rates to pay for new municipal services and escalating service budgets. In addition, assessed values may be raised to reflect increasing market values. Conversations with local public officials can reveal the trend in taxes for a community.

FINANCING TECHNIQUES

High inflation rates and unpredictable interest rate fluctuations of the past have made lenders less willing to offer long-term fixed-rate loans, and the market has moved toward a type of adjustable rate by indexing. The Federal Home Loan Bank Board, the Federal National Mortgage Association, the Federal Home Loan Mortgage Corporation, the Federal Reserve Board, and others have left up to market negotiations and competition among buyers and sellers the choice of which index will control the periodic change in interest rates. The amount of the loan depends on the appraised value and the proposed use of the property; lending institutions may make loans on new owner-occupied residential property for as much as 90 to 95 percent of the property's appraised value. Investor-owned rental properties are usually eligible for 75 to 80 percent loan-to-value ratios.

In today's world of highly appreciated prices for existing structures, owner–sellers have become an important source of real estate financing through *subordination*; however, if wraparound mortgage financing is used, the investor should be wary of due-on-sale clauses. Sellers willingly accept such financing arrangements because they can then take advantage of high interest rates and receive higher prices for their properties. Investors benefit because they can increase leverage. Currently, in order for an owner–occupant to qualify for a loan, the monthly income must reach approximately three to four times the monthly debt service. The terms of the mortgages run up to thirty years. For assumptions, the term would be the remaining life of the underlying mortgage.

Conventional loans often present problems for the investor who is trying to assume them. There may be prepayment penalties for the seller or the loan may contain a due-on-sale clause. The purchaser may have to sign an affidavit, under criminal penalties, affirming status as owner–occupant.

Questionable practices are sometimes used to increase leverage positions. For example, the investor may (1) time the closing date so that the down payment comes out of the first month's rent; (2) use the tenant's security and cleaning deposits to fund part of the down payment; (3) require that the realtor lend his commission to the investor for the down payment in order to make the sale (the investor does not inform the seller of this deal); (4) use personal credit cards to purchase goods for the seller in lieu of a cash down payment; or (5) stagger the down payment. Some of these strategies are not sound business practices, particularly if they create financial obligations that the investor cannot afford, and they should be avoided. Moreover, some are unethical and sometimes even illegal or criminal.

The costs of financing such properties should be carefully considered. For a fixed-rate mortgage, debt service is normally fixed over the life of investment, whereas an adjustable-rate mortgage requires that the investor project future interest rate levels. With an assumable mortgage, the debt service may or may not be the same as the existing mortgage because interest is often adjusted to market levels.

Creative financing techniques can be used to increase the leverage position and reduce the level of monthly debt service. Examples include assumption by the buyer of an existing mortgage with a below-market rate, provision by the seller of a short-term buydown of an existing institutional rate and a first- or second-lien mortgage at below-market rates for a limited time. These techniques require that the seller provide lenient, flexible, favorable terms for the buyer, which, needless to say, is sometimes difficult to achieve and effectively place a premium on the selling price of the house. Robert G. Allen suggests the following techniques.[4]

1. Structuring a seller's note to match seasonal demand. During months when expenses are usually high, payments would be below the negotiated level. The difference would be made up with payments above the negotiated level during months when expenses are low.

2. Requiring interest-only notes. The investor does not amortize the principal amount under this arrangement. Instead, the principal (in some cases principal and interest) comes due in one lump sum at the end of the note's duration.

3. Lowering the amortization cost with a balloon payment. The monthly debt service is calculated for a note with a long term

[4]Robert G. Allen, *Nothing Down* (New York: Simon & Schuster, 1980). See also Dave Glubetich, *The Monopoly Game* (Pleasant Hill, Calif.: Impact Publishing, 1981) and Maury Seldin and Richard Swesnik, *Real Estate Investment Strategy*, 3rd ed. (New York: Wiley, 1985).

(twenty to forty years), and the remaining balance—the balloon—comes due earlier, usually in the fifth to seventh year.

4. Increasing the interest rate. The interest rate in the initial years of the note is set low. In later years, after the project is established, the rate increases.
5. Converting balloon notes into amortization notes on the due date. When the lump sum balance comes due, the investor negotiates a new amortization note for the balance due.

DISCOUNTED-CASH-FLOW ANALYSIS

The key to successful investment is price appreciation and leverage. Cash-on-cash returns for these small properties are very low or negative, making traditional methods of capitalizing income virtually worthless. The best method for ranking investments is an after-tax IRR/PV analysis. Most investors today assume that short-term appreciation will be relatively high and therefore are specifying 20 to 25 percent as the minimum acceptable after-tax IRR, including the inflation premium.

Sensitivity analysis provides a useful measure of the risk associated with different properties being considered. Key variables include rent and vacancy rates, operating expenses, and appreciation, and careful attention should be paid to their effect on cash flow. Many properties have been foreclosed because the investor was unable to accommodate negative cash flows. It is risky to rely on appreciation to bail out poor productivity.

THE INVESTMENT DECISION

Investors buy small rental properties for short-term appreciation gains and as a hedge against erosion of capital by inflation. The investor should consider purchasing property only in neighborhoods that are not expected to suffer any type of decline. A relatively high leverage position should be sought while still allowing for potential negative cash flows. Sufficient liquidity reserves may provide the only resource to meet unexpected contingencies. For DCF and sensitivity analyses, it is advantageous to use high required rates of return because of the high leverage and financial risks, the difficulty of projecting the holding period, and of providing for an appropriate inflation premium.

SPECIAL-USE PROPERTIES

Success in special-use properties—such as hotels and motels, nursing homes, hospitals, recreational facilities, fast-food franchises and service stations—depends on specialized skills in business, marketing, and promotional and financial management related to the property's primary use. Space limitations permit only a brief review of two types of special-purposes properties, each of which has its own unique analytical tools: hotels and motels and nursing homes.

A special-use property consists of undeveloped land or an existing improved property used for a specific nonindustrial business. When buying an interest in a special-use property, an equity investor must either become a serious student of the underlying business or have blind faith and trust in others. The best analysis of the investment viability of the special-purpose properties considers the following points.

Alternative Uses for the Property. A building erected for a fast-food franchise in the shape of a hot dog with mustard and pickle would be difficult to adapt to another use in the event of business failure. Many special-use properties, however, can be adapted to alternative uses. A motel may be adapted to a senior citizens' residence; a fast-food restaurant, with some cosmetic changes, might provide a good setting for a microcomputer store. The flexibility, ingenuity, and imagination of the investor in showing the lender what the possibilities are may do much to improve the underwriting risks in the mind of the lender. Exhibit 26-4 may be helpful in this regard.

The Lender's Equity Investment Requirements. Although investing in special-purpose properties is speculating on the probability of the business's success, loans must usually be obtained with higher equity-to-loan ratios than are typical of ordinary real estate investments. Loans are usually not available for more than 70 percent of the cost of construction or capitalized value, whichever is lower. However, the cushion of the higher debt coverage ratio for the lender coupled with equity capital from outside investors, can enable a superior business manager to make a satisfactory return for everyone. Since 1986, professional couples and other high-income investors have been working on active-participation arrangements in

---

EXHIBIT 26-4.   Table of Alternative Uses

Type of Property	Proposed Use	Alternate Use
Freestanding open construction	Catering hall	Supermarket or warehouse
Freestanding multirooms	Motel	Senior citizens' residence
Freestanding small shell construction	Diner	Gas station, bank, funeral home
Attached open construction	Restaurant	Office building
Attached multirooms	Office building	School

Source: Sheldon Farber, "Financing the Specialty Property," *Real Estate Review,* Winter 1975, p. 106.

which, as the business manager, they can be eligible for the up-to-$25,000 write-off against professional services income.

The Effectiveness of the Existing Operating Management. Investors planning on risking equity capital in the belief that a business manager can deliver above-average returns should take the time to study the chart of accounts, find appropriate units of comparison to evaluate performance, and understand the threats, competition, and problems peculiar to the business in question. Each industry has a literature of its own and its own trade periodicals.

Investors should require submission of pro forma and actual operating statements. It is also important to obtain a formal agreement that the business will operate according to strict accounting procedures and maintain minimum working capital ratios as well as controls on dividends and disbursements. It is not unreasonable to require that certain key management personnel be insured against death, accidental injury, and disability; the costs for such insurance should be borne by the underlying business.

Potential Need for Additional Collateral. Most investors are reluctant to burden their personal balance sheets with liens, pledges, and contingent obligations when the lender requires other sources of collateral. On the other hand, greater risk may realize greater gain, especially when special-use properties are well managed. Borrowers may sometimes agree that if the property produces a deficiency at foreclosure, the lender has recourse to other assets of the investor limited to, say, the top 20 or 30 percent of the loan. The agreement could also provide that the pledge of secondary collateral be reduced in accordance with a specific schedule as the loan is reduced. Flexibility on the part of the investor may well overcome the lender's reluctance to fund an otherwise acceptable special-purpose property.

HOTELS AND MOTELS

The motel and hotel industry employs more than 5 million people. In many states, it is one of the largest industries, although it is dependent on a derived demand that is innately cyclical in nature and subject to such external factors as gas shortages and transportation strikes.

Definitions

Hotels. A hotel is an establishment that provides transient lodging for the public and often meals and entertainment. Factors affecting the success or failure of a hotel vary according to its primary function. For example, *residential hotels* accommodate a significant number of long-term residents whose rooms are sometimes leased for a number of years. *Convention hotels*, on the other hand, cater to national, regional, and local meetings of business and other organizations and as such often provide meeting rooms and accommodations for exhibits, expositions, and related entertainment. They are generally located in the central districts of major cities and at major highway intersections. *Resort hotels* are located near vacation-related activities such as skiing, swimming, golf, tennis, sailing, and fishing, and in areas providing unusual or relaxing physical features.

Motel. A motel is an establishment located on or near a highway and is designed to serve the motor traveler. Although originally conceived to provide only transient lodging, they now more often than not provide food, entertainment, and beverages as well.

Budget motels. Budget motels are often associated with a national chain and offer modest lodgings at a low price. The management generally achieves economy by keeping rooms small and minimizing amenities.

Location. A successful hotel or motel usually has a location offering several particular advantages.

1. A good location either offers active points of interest for business and pleasure travelers or is along a busy transportation corridor at a logical stopover point. Major convention cities, large universities, and tourist attractions like Disney World offer points of interest; a place such as Lake City, Florida, located on Interstate-75 approximately one day's drive from Miami, is a logical stopover point.
2. Of utmost importance is convenient access to and from major transportation arteries, exhibit halls, auditoriums, and other points of local interest.
3. Good locations are readily visible and accessible to passers-by and out-of-town visitors.
4. Good locations are attractive, have safe surroundings, and offer sufficient entertainment and sight-seeing opportunities.

Industry experts project a growth in combined hotel and motel capacity of 60 percent in the next twenty years as various metropolitan areas grow and new MSAs come into being.

INVESTING IN HOTELS AND MOTELS

Advantages and Disadvantages

The lodging industry tends to break even on a relatively low average occupancy level of about 60 to 65 percent. Thus, properties have a great potential for high profits when fully occupied. And because hotels neither depend on long-term leases nor are subjected to rent controls, the industry as a whole is more flexible and less vulnerable to inflation. The industry also offers opportunities to add other profit-generating activities such as supplying food, beverages, and valet services; retail sales; conference accommodations; and entertainment. Frequently such ancillary facilities are operated as concessions or leased units and are thereby rental rather than business operations. Large convention and resort properties such as Disney World and Busch Gardens provide a certain measure of prestige and glamour for corporations. Under the 1986 tax act, investors who have rehabilitated older structures for income-producing properties (pre-1986) may receive favorable depreciation schedules and sizable tax deductions.

The cyclical and seasonal use of properties, changes in what is considered fashionable, and the properties' short economic lives increase their vulnerability to downside risk. Ownership of new and reviving properties requires sufficient cash reserves to cover low occupancies and heavy promotional expenses during the start-up phase. Expert and efficient management and promotion are vital. Location is of prime importance, but the appeal of one site may be destroyed by changes in local economic conditions, the quality of tourist attractions in the area, and major transportation routes. These risks have been mitigated to some extent by the integration of hotels in mixed-use developments. If such a development is well done, the hotel and the adjoining shops, offices, and entertainment facilities can benefit from offering shared services, possible higher-density zoning, name recognition, distinctive design, and better marketability. They may therefore be more successful than single-purpose projects.

Types of Investors and Investor Motivations

Independent, small-scale motel operators generally view their investment as a business opportunity providing self-employment. Individual franchise holders are attracted primarily by profit potential. Institutional investors seek to boost portfolio yields and add inflation-offsetting equity participations to the fixed returns on loans to hotel and motel properties. Many chains operate management contracts for investors or partnership arrangements or otherwise provide expertise in operation, construction, and promotion.

PRELIMINARY ANALYSES

Market and Marketability Analysis

A property should be examined on the basis of the stability of its income stream, the would-be owner's position in the long-term life cycle of the property, and its neighborhood.

EXHIBIT 26-5.   Important Factors to Consider When Selecting Hotel and Motel Locations

---

GENERAL CONSIDERATIONS

- Local, regional, and national economic trends
- Neighborhood characteristics and appearance
- Location and type of competitive lodging facilities: number of rooms, facilities, average rate, percentage of occupancy
- Availability of adequate utilities
- Location and transportation for labor force

DOWNTOWN LOCATIONS

- Traffic patterns—access and visibility
- Location of generators of visitation—offices, convention centers, tourist attractions, entertainment, etc.
- Availability of parking
- Availability of public transportation—taxi, bus, subway
- Location of restaurants and evening entertainment
- Location of convention center—size and types of events
- Effectiveness of convention and visitors' bureau
- Potential for weekend patronage
- Security of surrounding area and character of neighborhood

AIRPORT LOCATIONS

- Number of passengers per year (historic and future trends)
- Volume of airport cargo
- Number of airlines serving airport

- Usage of airport—origination, destination, transfer point
- Types of airport traffic—overseas, domestic, charter, long haul, short haul
- Purpose of airport travel—commercial, convention, vacation, etc.
- Layover point for airline crews
- Hours of airport operation
- Local weather conditions—potential for delayed flights
- Type and location of nearby business and industry
- Highway and traffic patterns
- Types of transportation to nearby hotels
- Distance of hotel from airport, travel time to downtown, convenience to terminal, restaurants, and entertainment
- Potential for weekend patronage

HIGHWAY LOCATIONS

- Traffic counts (historic and future trends)
- Highway patterns and type (interstate, U.S. highways)
- Access—both ingress and egress
- Visibility
- Origination and destination of traffic
- Types of travelers—commercial, vacation, etc.
- Periods of travel—weekly, monthly, seasonally
- Distance and travel time from major destinations
- Future changes in highway and travel patterns

Source: William Eggbeer, "What Should You Do When Foreclosure is Imminent on Your Hotel or Motel Property?" *The Mortgage Banker,* July 1978, p. 56.

Demand Analysis. The key to a successful hotel or motel investment is the location's potential for attracting and holding guests and how well the services offered are matched to the proper market segment. The following are important aspects of demand: purpose of trips, duration of visits, seasonal variations, the desired amenities, and demographic characteristics of travelers. Exhibit 26-5 presents important factors to consider when selecting hotel and motel locations. Exhibit 26-6 presents an analysis of various activities that generate "guest-days." The activities offered by the location indicate the type of guest the property is likely to attract. Exhibit 26-7 supplies a possible format for comparing features of the market segments to the features of a particular property. Activity descriptions are usually analytically adjusted to fit (attract) the most promising segment of the market.

Basic marketing strategies emphasize differentiation, the advantages of the property over those of competitors, and segmentation, its appeal to a given segment of the market. Situations that favor such emphases are shown in Exhibit 26-8.

Supply Analysis. A stratified analysis of competitive facilities generally concentrates on the clientele attracted, competitive advantages of the subject property, and customer loyalty. Nearby facilities may be serving segments of the market that are inappropriate for the subject property. When

EXHIBIT 26-6. Activity Attributes of a Motel or Hotel Location

Activity	Example
Leisure	Sun seeking, sight-seeing
Recreation	Sailing, golf, skiing, climbing, riding, spectator games, sports, displays
Culture	Interests in art, history, archeology, pageantry
Religion	Ceremonies, pilgrimages, festivals
Entertainment	Theaters, concert halls, opera houses, casinos, night clubs
Convention	Conferences, conventions, assemblies, meetings, exhibits, shows
Institutional	Visitors to institutions, hospitals, universities
Business	Business and commercial travel, executive meetings
Economic	Promotional shows, exhibitions, trade displays
Medical	Health, dietary, spa and convalescence facilities
Social	Visits by relatives, friends' societies, clubs
Travel	Overnight and staging requirements along route

Source: Fred R. Lawson, *Hotels, Motels and Condominiums: Design, Planning and Maintenance* (Boston: Cahners, 1976), p. 19.

EXHIBIT 26-7.   A Development and Design Criteria Matrix

Guest Requirements	MARKET SEGMENTS									
	COMMERCIAL–INDUSTRIAL				RECREATIONAL–PLEASURE					
	Independent		Group		Independent		Group		Inde-pendent	Local Group
	In-Transit	Ter-minal	In-Transit	Ter-minal	In-Transit	Ter-minal	In-Transit	Ter-minal		
LOCATION										
Accessibility	X		X		X		X			
Parking	X	X	X	X	X	X	X	X	X	X
Proximity	X	X	X	X	X	X	X	X	X	X
Visibility	X		X		X		X			
APPEARANCE										
Decor		X		X		X		X		
Design		X		X		X		X		
Landscaping						X		X		
Structure		X		X		X		X		
LODGING										
Capacity			X	X			X	X		
Equipment		X		X		X		X		
Rates	X	X	X	X	X	X	X	X		
Room size		X		X		X		X		
RESTAURANTS										
Capacity	X		X	X			X	X		X
Diversity		X		X		X		X	X	X
Function space				X				X		X
Hours of operation	X	X	X	X	X	X	X	X	X	X
OTHER GUEST SERVICES										
Laundry		X		X		X		X		
Shops		X		X		X		X	X	
Valet		X		X		X		X		
ENTERTAINMENT AND RECREATION FACILITIES										
Active		X		X		X		X	X	X
Sedentary		X		X		X		X		

Source: Clarence Peters, "Pre-Opening Marketing Analyses for Hotels," copyright © *Cornell H&R Administration Quarterly,* May 1978, pp. 15–22.

EXHIBIT 26-8.   Market Differentiation and Segmentation Decision Criteria

---

I. *A differentiation strategy will generally prove most appropriate where the following can be demonstrated.*
   1. The total market is demographically, geographically, and psychographically homogeneous.
   2. Market sensitivity to differences between establishments is high.
   3. The establishment is relatively new.
   4. The establishment is distinctive (e.g., architecturally, style of service).
   5. There are few competing establishments.
   6. Most competitors employ a differentiation strategy.

II. *A segmentation strategy is most appropriate when the following conditions prevail.*
   1. The total market is demographically, geographically, and psychographically diffuse.
   2. Market sensitivity to differences between establishments is low.
   3. The establishment has been in operation for several years.
   4. The establishment is not distinctive.
   5. There are several competing establishments.
   6. Most competitors employ a segmentation strategy.

Source: Peter Yesavich, "Post-Opening Marketing Analysis for Hotels," copyright © *Cornell H&R Administration Quarterly*, November 1978, pp. 70–81.

competitive properties serve the same segment, the investor would be well advised to compare room rates and occupancies.

Several factors may be used to classify competitors: rates, size, type of accommodations, location, restaurant, and meeting rooms. The competitive survey should include an evaluation of marketing strategy and management policies. Also important are proposed new facilities and expansions. Construction in this industry tends to be highly cyclical, and there is often overbuilding.

Projection of Rental Income, Expenses, and Vacancies. Income projections are complicated by the instability of the revenue stream over seasons and years. Any projection by years should be based on weighted, seasonally adjusted, average guest-days (occupancy) and room rates (considering off-season specials) during the year. For most properties, there are several distinct sources of income. According to the *Uniform System of Accounts and Expense Dictionary for Motels/Hotels* of the American Hotel and Motel Association, these sources include rooms, food, beverages, telephone, other department profits, and other income. Income from other sources, such as rental of retail space, is reported as a separate item.

Periodic recessions have a drastic impact on income, effecting travel for both business and pleasure. The effects are generally immediate for smaller transient motels but may be delayed for hotels that hold advance reservations for conventions. Such disruptions may be offset by making both pessimistic and optimistic projections and then comparing the sensitivity of the rates of return generated by each.

Physical, Legal, Political, and Environmental Analysis

The physical design and condition of the property are important from two standpoints: (1) attracting and pleasing the clientele and (2) improving operating efficiency. Architectural design is a matter of taste but generally is most effective when tailored to the target market; a design that is suitable for Miami Beach or Las Vegas might not be appropriate in Williamsburg or San Francisco. Chains that appeal to middle-class business and vacation travelers use a standard motif connoting modest but comfortable standard accommodations at reasonable prices. Beyond design appeal, certain features can add a competitive advantage, such as protection from noise and nuisance light, logical layout, connections between buildings that are protected from the elements, and adequate security and fire protection. Finally, operating efficiency may be increased by well-designed work areas and by design and materials that promote ease of upkeep.

The primary legal liabilities of hotel or motel operations are laws regulating the sale and consumption of alcoholic beverages; efforts to control within the facility such illegal activities as prostitution, sexual perversion, and gambling; and laws governing reservations and the activities of travel agents. Most problems of this type can be avoided by employing knowledgeable and experienced managers.

Financial Analysis

Analysis of Current Operating Income and Expenses. Operating statistics are available from many sources, as indicated at the end of this chapter. Many components of income and expense fluctuate because of variations in seasonal demand; seasonally adjusted averages should be used as input into the basic model. These may be derived from the recent experience of the property, moderated by information from comparable properties. Only with utmost caution should an investor accept projections of revenues and expenses for uses that have not been market-tested at the location (e.g., PLATO franchise or disco lounge).

The principal problem in estimating the trend of gross potential income is projecting seasonally adjusted guest-day units and ancillary income, such as in-house bar or restaurant. Fixed costs (amortization of debt, real estate taxes, insurance, and necessary maintenance) tend to produce a break-even point of about 60 to 70 percent. As guest-day units rise, fixed costs per unit fall. Variable costs per guest-day are subject to some significant economies of scale for large functions such as conventions, banquets, and balls. Variable costs tend to be a relatively constant proportion of projected gross revenues. Promotional costs tend to be heavier during preopening, rehabilitation, and low-occupancy periods. Some operating expenses are not subject to internal control. For example, energy costs, which doubled between 1973 and 1977, have accelerated much faster than room rates.

Making projections requires knowledge of the local motel and hotel industry. Past earnings records for the property—assuming continuation of the marketing–management plan—may be useful, as might be competitive surveys. When there are no usable current local data at the basic financial feasibility stage, judgmental projections may be made based on regional data in hotel industry sourcebooks. A field survey prior to purchase is essential.

Property Management. Effective management of operations is almost as crucial as location. A continuous effort must be made to maintain a good reputation, make the clientele feel comfortable, and encourage return business. Signs of management problems in existing properties include (1) failure to adopt the uniform system of accounts; (2) high levels of accounts payable, indicating cash management problems, underfinanced operations, or shoddy accounting; (3) neglected maintenance; (4) a high turnover of managerial personnel; and (5) recent use of giveaway promotions to bolster sagging occupancy. Giveaway promotions are properly used only in the off-season in order to retain personnel and provide amortization income.

Although many hotel and motel properties are operated by individual owners, most larger establishments are run by management chains. When the chain works under contract for a percentage fee, the cost of management is treated as a normal operating expense to the owner. Many institutional investors lease the property to specialized operators however. Lease terms provide for minimum and alternative percentage rate, typically 20 to 30 percent of room rental income, 5 to 7 percent of food income and 10 to 15 percent of income from liquor sales. Leases generally are net of all operating expenses; under this arrangement, owners can treat the lease payments as income subject only to financing and taxation costs. The important details of such contracts are beyond the scope of this book; however, it should be noted that negotiations for such contracts require a thorough knowledge of both owner and operator concerns. During the 1970s, leases on some distressed properties were negotiated to be extremely favorable to the hotel management companies in that they provided for 10 to 15 percent of gross revenues with an additional incentive percentage of cash throw-off after debt service. Such arrangements left many owners with

100 percent of the risk, including even china breakage and silver losses; the only exception was malfeasance of top management at the management company's home office. A lender who lacks the skills of hotel and motel business management pays the price of bad marketing, overbuilding, and foreclosure.

Risk Management. When ownership is in the form of partnership, there may be a tendency for fellow partners to abuse ownership privileges. This abuse can prove detrimental not only because use of facilities for free lodging, dining, and entertainment cuts into operating revenues but also because it may adversely affect management and other personnel. Pilferage and embezzlement are other chronic problems in the hotel and motel industry.

Finally, personal property tax on furnishings and inventory may form a substantial portion of the tax burden. Investors should check local rates and the seller's level of compliance. Assurances should be sought that such taxes are paid in full, with the tax for the current year prorated at settlement.

FINANCING

Lenders generally limit loans to 50 or 60 percent on operations affiliated with a franchised management chain, preferably net leased. Recently, participations on profits have been required, or the lender may obtain a partial equity interest. Hotel and motel operations lend themselves to splitting the equity contribution into several layers (the so-called Zeckendorf Hawaiian pineapple slices) with individuals, institutions, operators, and developers taking a cut based on varying return–risk trade-offs. Equity syndications are also useful for financing rehabilitations, particularly to individual investors seeking tax breaks.

Debt structure may also be leveraged by mortgaging separate components. Mortgageable assets may be separated into the management contract or lease, land, and improvements (through a junior mortgage), and furnishings (through a chattel mortgage).

Debt service projections should include provisions for participation payments (corresponding to projected income), ground rents (if any), and periodic refinancing. If the loan is short term or subject to a balloon, the remaining economic lives of the improvements should be carefully scrutinized.

TAXATION PROBLEMS

Hotel and motel properties are eligible for the usual commercial property tax treatments: accelerated three-, five-, seven-, and ten-year ACRS deductions for personal property, capital gains treatment, and tax-deferred exchange. In addition, owners may elect to form a Subchapter S corporation, thereby avoiding double taxation while retaining limited liability. The Subchapter S corporation entity can be advantageous when no partner is willing to function as the general partner in a limited partnership.

Since a significant proportion of value is represented by equipment, furniture, and other components subject to ACRS three-year and five-year lives, the lodging industry provides an opportunity for unusually short depreciation schedules for much of the overall value. Examples are swimming pool equipment, vending machines, and wall-to-wall carpeting. Most hotels and motels also have a large investment in service assets, such as linens, kitchen equipment, and crockery. Often these assets are grouped into a single account with a useful life of three years.

Finally, the 1986 Economic Recovery Tax Act has provided graduated tax credit percentages for substantial rehabilitation of pre-1936 buildings. This tax credit is in lieu of the sixty-month depreciation previously provided. Chapter 10 explains the risk involved in using accelerated depreciation methods.

DISCOUNTED-CASH-FLOW ANALYSIS

Cash flow analysis requires some knowledge of hotel and motel accounting, although uniform standards that permit useful comparisons have been adopted. After determining "house profit," the real estate analyst must allow for store rentals, financing costs, depreciation, fire insurance, and franchise, personal property, real estate, and income taxes before estimating net cash flow. Exhibit 26-9 gives an example of a statement based on uniform standards.

Of course, equity cash flows and tax effects must be divided among the ownership interests as agreed. In accordance with state laws and IRS regulations, disproportionate shares are a common practice. Investment analysis is conducted by assuming an average room rate and calculating profits on the basis of varying levels of occupancy. The level of occupancy at which cash flow to equity (cash throw-off) begins (i.e., equals zero) should be the break-even point. In normal markets it generally occurs at about 60 to 70 percent occupancy.

THE INVESTMENT DECISION

Investors are generally interested in the same ratios that are applied to other businesses: liquidity ratio, collection period, inventory turnover, and return on total assets. During normal operating periods, these ratios should compare favorably with those for other properties in the industry.

**EXHIBIT 26-9. Estimated Statement of Income and Expenses for an
Average Year at an Average Daily Rate of $39.00**

	ASSUMED OCCUPANCY LEVEL	
	70 Percent	80 Percent
Total sales and income		
Rooms (average daily room rate: $39.00)	$2,979,432	$3,405,173
Food	1,654,653	1,826,761
Beverages	534,944	627,540
Telephone	106,184	121,281
Other departmental profits	24,407	28,433
Other income	77,499	87,564
Subtotal	$5,377,119	$6,096,752
Cost of goods sold and departmental wages and expenses		
Rooms	$ 883,941	$ 996,415
Food and beverages	1,752,785	1,963,391
Telephone	152,482	172,863
Subtotal	$2,789,208	$3,132,669
Gross operating income	$2,587,911	$2,964,083
Deductions from income		
Administrative and general expenses (less management fee)	$ 272,253	$ 296,408
Advertising and sales promotion	125,810	125,810
Heat, light, and power	251,368	260,930
Repairs and maintenance	213,877	230,736
Subtotal	$ 863,308	$ 913,884
House profit	$1,724,603	$2,050,199
Plus: Store rentals	225,979	255,328
Gross operating profit	$1,950,582	$2,305,527
Less: Franchise taxes and fire insurance	22,155	24,030
Profit before real estate taxes and capital expenses	$1,928,427	$2,281,497
Less: Real estate taxes	385,000	455,000
Net cash flow to investors before provision for replacement of short-lived items	$1,543,427	$1,826,497

Because the rate of return is very sensitive to cyclical and seasonal variations, careful consideration should be given to the way in which income and expense items are estimated.

Hotel and motel properties represent somewhat speculative ventures because high occupancy depends on prosperity in both the national and local economies. The downside risk is high. Location advantages may vanish through shifts in transportation routes, and a good reputation is difficult to cultivate and maintain. New competition is a constant threat: since rooms are rented at most on a weekly basis, there is no income stability by way of long-term agreements.

Considering the speculative nature of such properties and the extraordinary management capabilities required, ownership should demand the relatively high rates of return of about 20 to 25 percent, plus an inflation premium. If much of the return depends on tax benefits, the holding period may be short and the resale value lower than would otherwise be the case. Elimination of the 50 to 70 percent marginal tax brackets (pre 1981) caused many equity investors to switch from special-use properties to less risky investments; the 1986 tax reform act, however, caused equity investors to shift their attention to "passive income generators" such as hotels and motels that promise to produce both high ROEs and taxable "passive income."

Much of the foregoing analysis applies also to fast-food and greeting card franchises, car washes, and similar properties. Each has unique business characteristics, its own chart of accounts, special locational needs, marketing problems, and the like. A potential investor must evaluate management, location, and marketing plans; success depends on the quality of the primary business operation.

NURSING HOMES

A major growth sector in urban land use from 1988 to 2000 and beyond will be custodial and domiciliary nursing homes, particularly as so-called baby boomers begin to gray in the 2010s. According to projections by the Bureau of the Census, more than one out of every five Americans will be sixty-five years or older by 2030, and even now more than 11 percent of the American population is sixty-five or older. Although there will be some tendency for new construction to concentrate in the Sunbelt states, nursing homes are expected to be constructed or rehabilitated in both urban and rural areas throughout the nation.

Currently, the problem with nursing homes is that their feasibility depends on changing government programs. Because nursing homes are not generally economically feasible but there is a need for them, they must be subsidized. A few nursing homes do provide above-average income, particularly those located where there is strong demand from upper-income families and those blessed with strong management. However, most analysts consider nursing homes to be speculative for the real estate investor because the yields are derived largely from tax effects, the cash flow is modest, and the capital gain from appreciation is uncertain. The recent change in marginal tax brackets, which lowers the maximum tax on investment income to 50 percent, makes equity positions even more speculative.

Definitions

A *nursing home* is a facility that offers living quarters, food, and skilled nursing care for convalescents, the chronically ill, and other people who need third-party domiciliary or custodial care. About 70 percent of nursing home beds are in proprietary (profit-seeking) organizations; the balance are operated by nonprofit organizations such as counties, churches, and hospitals. Facilities used as homes for the elderly and specialized clinics (e.g., rehabilitation or diagnostic) are not included in this definition.

Medicare. In 1966, Public Law 89-97 amended the Social Security Act to provide a health insurance program for the aged, and nursing homes receive financial assistance under this program if designated state agencies pronounce them eligible. A Utilization Review Committee functioning under federal guidelines and composed of the director of nursing, the nursing home administrator, and two licensed physicians reviews the record of every person seeking benefits under the Medicare program.

Medicaid. Medicaid is a program for the medically indigent. The benefits not only vary greatly from one state to another but are subject to manipulation as state budgets are formulated from year to year. Part of the Medicaid program provides nursing care for poor people, young and old. The local jurisdiction's regulations and level of reimbursement must be analyzed to determine whether or not the costs (including profit) of nursing care are fully covered. In some states, the rates are so inadequate that Medicaid patients would substantially depress the investment potential of a facility. The federal adoption of catastrophic medical care reimbursement may substantially reduce this effect on medical (hospice) facilities.

Life Safety Code. Inspection and certification for fire, safety, and panic protection are the responsibility of a state fire marshal or other designated state employee. A copy of the Life Safety Code is available from the National Fire Protection Association in Boston. All nursing homes that are insured under the FHA or are receiving federal payments for patients must comply, and compliance activity is vigorous.

Accreditation and licensure. Every state and many political subdivisions have an active licensure program. Files of the state health department and other regulatory bodies should be investigated by a would-be investor to determine whether or not the nursing home has deficiencies or violations. In addition, accreditation or recognition of a nursing home is available through the Joint Commission on Accreditation of Hospitals and Long-Term Care Facilities in Chicago. Other important forms of official recognition include certification by Medicare and the Blue Cross organizations, and approval by the Veterans Administration. Exhibit 26-10 illustrates a request for a Medicare certificate and provides some insight into the nature of nursing home facilities.

Nursing hours. The unit of nursing care is a nursing hour. An investor can compute nursing hours by dividing the total number of patient-days for a period (month or year) by the total number of nursing personnel hours for the same period. However, nursing homes are stratified by level of care and nursing hours per patient-day differ under each mode of operation: (1) minimal, (2) normal, and (3) intensive. State licensure laws generally provide for a minimum of two hours of nursing care per patient-day.

INVESTING IN NURSING HOMES

Investment Advantages and Disadvantages

Several trends fuel the expanding demand for nursing home facilities. They include the extended life span of the general population, the rapidly escalating costs of hospital care, and the establishment of government programs for people who need custodial and domiciliary medical care. In spite of expanding demand, increased public regulation and scrutiny call for exceptionally skillful management if profits are to be realized from the investment. Federal budget deficits are slowing Medicaid and Medicare payments, thus threatening the solvency of many nursing homes. Knowledgeable operation may provide substantial returns, however, and opportunities exist to add profit centers that provide patient services beyond the necessities included in the basic fee.

Nursing homes are highly regulated with few options in terms of design, operation, and rent structure. Paperwork is an ever-expanding management burden, and the operator must have extensive, detailed, and current knowledge of the legal and regulatory procedures. Occupancy during the start-up phase can be expected to be low, calling for substantial working capital in the early years. Because a nursing home is highly specialized, the market value is reduced and discourages conventional financing sources. Working capital reserves are necessary to carry accounts receivable be-

EXHIBIT 26-10. Form Requesting Medicare Certification

FORM APPROVED
OMB No. 0938-0100

DEPARTMENT OF HEALTH AND HUMAN SERVICES
HEALTH CARE FINANCING ADMINISTRATION

**LONG-TERM CARE FACILITY REQUEST FOR CERTIFICATION
IN THE MEDICARE AND/OR MEDICAID PROGRAM**

I. Identifying Information	NAME OF FACILITY		STREET ADDRESS		MEDICARE/MEDICAID PROVIDER NUMBER (N1)	STATE VENDOR NO.
	CITY, COUNTY, AND STATE		ZIP CODE	TELEPHONE NUMBER (Including Area Code) (N7)	STATE/COUNTY (N3)	STATE REGION (N4)

II. Eligibility

REQUEST TO ESTABLISH ELIGIBILITY IN

(N13) 1)☐ MEDICARE   2)☐ MEDICAID   3)☐ BOTH

RELATED PROVIDER NUMBER (N8)

III. Type of Facility (Check one) (N14)

01 ☐ Skilled Nursing Facility	04 ☐ Skilled Nursing Unit of Domiciliary Inst.	07 ☐ General ICF	12 ☐ ICF/MR Distinct Part of Hospital
02 ☐ Skilled Nursing Unit of Hospital	05 ☐ SNF Distinct Part of Skilled Nursing Facility	08 ☐ ICF Distinct Part of Skilled Nursing Facility	13 ☐ ICF/MR Distinct Part of SNF
03 ☐ Skilled Nursing Unit of Rehabilitation Center	06 ☐ Christian Science San.	09 ☐ SNF/ICF (Swing Bed)	14 ☐ ICF Distinct Part of Hospital
		10 ☐ ICF/MR	15 ☐ ICF Distinct Part of ICF
			16 ☐ ICF/MR Distinct Part of ICF/MR

IV. Type of Control (Check one) (N15)

Voluntary Non-Profit
1 ☐ Church
2 ☐ Other (Specify)

3 ☐ Proprietary

Government (Non-Federal)
4 ☐ State   6 ☐ City
5 ☐ County   7 ☐ City-County

Hospital
8 ☐ District

V. Services Provided: BY STAFF. Place a "1" in the block(s). If UNDER ARRANGEMENT, place a "2" in the block(s). (N16)

01 ☐ Nursing	08 ☐ Recreational Activities	14 ☐ Podiatry
02 ☐ Physical Therapy	09 ☐ Pharmacy	15 ☐ Ophthalmology
03 ☐ Outpatient Physical Therapy	10 ☐ Clinical Laboratory	16 ☐ Psychological Services
04 ☐ Occupational Therapy	11 ☐ Diagnostic X-ray	17 ☐ Other (Specify)
05 ☐ Speech Pathology	12 ☐ Administration and Storage of Blood	
06 ☐ Outpatient Speech Pathology	13 ☐ Dentistry	
07 ☐ Social Services		

VI. Number of Employees (Full-time equivalents) Please See Instructions

1. REGISTERED PROFESSIONAL NURSES		2. LICENSED PRACTICAL/VOCATIONAL NURSES		3. ALL OTHERS	
(N17) (a)	(b)	(N18) (a)	(b)	(N27) (a)	(b)

WHOEVER KNOWINGLY AND WILLFULLY MAKES OR CAUSES TO BE MADE A FALSE STATEMENT OR REPRESENTATION ON THIS STATEMENT, MAY BE PROSECUTED UNDER APPLICABLE FEDERAL OR STATE LAWS. IN ADDITION, KNOWINGLY AND WILLFULLY FAILING TO FULLY AND ACCURATELY DISCLOSE THE INFORMATION REQUESTED MAY RESULT IN DENIAL OF A REQUEST TO PARTICIPATE OR WHERE THE ENTITY ALREADY PARTICIPATES, A TERMINATION OF ITS AGREEMENT OR CONTRACT WITH THE STATE AGENCY OR THE SECRETARY, AS APPROPRIATE.

SIGNATURE OF AUTHORIZED OFFICIAL	TITLE	(N28) DATE

cause insurance companies and government agencies pay slowly. Recently, the expansion of nursing care facilities has been threatened by the shortage of registered nurses.

PRELIMINARY ANALYSES

Market and Marketability Analysis

Demand Analysis. Most areas have publicly employed planning personnel who routinely conduct surveys and prepare plans for health care systems. Such reports may provide an adequate basis for market and marketability studies of specific facilities. The reports may show population trends that indicate increasing demand for extrahospital patient care. There may be a prepared projection of the number of beds needed by county or by regional unit. If not, rules of thumb may be applied, for example, forty-five beds per 1000 over-sixty-five population in urban areas.

State agencies ostensibly attempt to control overbuilding through the issuance of certificates of need. Any proposed facility must obtain such a certificate before being qualified for assistance. Unfortunately, some state planning agencies are "growth"-oriented and have granted certificates far in excess of demand. When considering an existing facility, the investor should check the effectiveness of the state's program to prevent overbuilding.

Supply Analysis. Given sufficient demand, an examination of current supply will indicate whether the facility has a chance of maintaining high occupancy. Inventories of current facilities are available from local and regional health planning agencies, which may also have data on average occupancy rates. Ninety-five percent by the third year is considered a minimum to justify investment. Fieldwork should concentrate on the features offered by the competition, particularly the age and design of the structure, staffing, and auxiliary services. In addition, a competitive survey should be conducted to evaluate the comparative advantage of the subject property in terms of location and staffing.

Projection of Rental Income and Vacancies. Revenues are derived from two types of patients, private and those assisted by Medicare or Medicaid. Nationally, the average home has 45 percent private patients with 55 percent assisted. Reimbursed revenues, however, are controlled by federal and state government policies and may not equal 100 percent of the normal rate. In recent years, because some costs of operation are not allowable under accounting procedures of the Social Security Administration, it has been difficult to break even on Medicare patients. Therefore, nursing homes are reluctant to permit the ratio of Medicare patients to exceed 50 or 55 percent. An additional problem is that reimbursements are subject to postaudit and delay in payment by the Social Security Administration. Therefore, the investor would be well advised to discount expected income from Medicare patients by about 20 percent.

The best method of ascertaining the market rate is to compare private rates of similar facilities and use this figure in projections. In the past, most senior citizens paid for health care services through a single payment calculated to cover costs of lifetime health care. This means of payment is often impractical, constituting a form of insurance in which the more healthy residents support the rest, while life spans and health care costs for all have increased. An increasingly popular arrangement is the continuing care retirement center (CCRC), which provides housing, meals, and basic services, for a monthly rent plus services for a fee. A conservative vacancy factor of 7 to 10 percent covers losses attributable to bad debts and reimbursement delay. Daily rates generally cover a fixed package of services; additional services, such as therapy, medicine, haircuts, and outings, are billed separately and are ordinarily projected as additional income.

Physical, Legal, Political, and Environmental Analysis

The key aims of structural design and maintenance are to provide adequate space, fireproofing, and emergency power and to maintain high hygenic standards. State licensing laws and the Fire Safety Code include an extensive list of specifications for design and upkeep. And the fact that a subject facility is licensed to operate does not mean that it conforms to these requirements. Some nursing homes operate under grandfather clauses granting approval for existing conditions which will be deemed nonconforming whenever there is a change in ownership.

Although the industry is highly regulated, nursing home operations may be periodically subjected to public scrutiny concerning adequacy of care and level of profit. Some people feel that such operations have lower standards of sanitation and care. Investors should make themselves aware of any reports in the past exposing inadequate sanitation and fire prevention in nursing homes in the area, particularly any past scandals associated with the subject property. Many homes operate under a special-use permit rather than the sanction of proper zoning. Such permits may be revoked at any time, causing the operation to be nonconforming.

Financial Analysis

Analysis of Current Operating Income and Expenses. The best analysis segregates returns from operations. For example, the ownership entity could control the real property and receive its return via a lease to the operating entity. Such leases are net and based on an annual rate per bed. The operating entity pays rent as an operating expense with the proceeds from patient fees, reimbursements, and additional income.

The income-expense breakdown shown in Exhibit 26-11 provides a tool for comparative analysis. Before the net cash flow to the investors in the real estate can be determined, deductions must be made for fire insurance, franchise taxes, and licenses that pertain to the building and not to the nursing home operation; real estate and other local taxes; and financing costs, depreciation, and necessary reserves. Of course, disproportionate partnership allocations may be made in accordance with business risk principles that enable the equity investors to participate in income and loss from the nursing home operation subject to limitations related to material and active participation. Passive investors have lost the advantage of sheltering business and other professional income from such investments.

Property Management. The manager of a nursing home must be able to provide satisfactory patient care and a good working environment for a qualified and efficient staff, and at the same time satisfy licensing and accreditation inspectors and the supervisory medical care committee. A premium should be placed on proven experience in operating successful homes.

EXHIBIT 26-11.   Income and Expenses for a Large Nursing Home for a Twelve-Month Period

	Actual Income from Operations	Percentage of the Year's Revenue	Cost per Patient-Day[a]
Income: Patient-Days (occupancy at 89.7 percent)			
Routine services	$1,107,088	93.5	$34.40
Personal nursing (net)	8,916	0.7	.27
Incontinency care (net)	12,230	1.0	.38
Special diet	–	0.0	.00
Medical supplies (net)	17,595	1.4	.54
Pharmacy (net)	5,869	0.4	.17
Laboratory (net)	3,357	0.2	.09
Physical therapy (net)	12,321	1.5	.38
Beauty and barber (net)	1,015	0.0	.03
Equipment rental (net)	10,030	0.8	.31
Laundry and dry cleaning	6,017	0.5	.17
Other revenue (net)	(439)	0.0	(.01)
Total Revenue	$1,183,999	100.0	$36.73
Operating Expenses			
Nursing—Salary and wages	$ 393,533	33.2	$12.22
Supplies and expense	4,587	0.3	.13
Professional nursing service	–	0.0	.00
Recreational therapy—Salary and wages	10,491	0.8	.32
Supplies and expense	948	0.0	.03
Dietary—Salary and wages	77,543	6.5	2.41
Supplies and expense	13,210	1.1	.40
Food	63,448	5.3	1.97
Housekeeping—Salary and wages	23,967	2.0	.74
Supplies and expense	7,263	0.6	.22
Laundry—Salary and wages	8,916	0.7	.27
Supplies and expense	1,750	0.1	.05
Linens	1,346	0.1	.04
Plant maintenance—Salary and wages	27,014	2.2	.83
Supplies and expense	662	0.0	.01
Repair and maintenance	10,394	0.8	.32
Exterminator and trash	2,466	0.2	.07
Utilities—Electricity	19,302	1.6	.59
Fuel	8,081	0.6	.24
Water and sewer	6,714	0.5	.20
Total Operating Expenses	$ 681,635	56.6	$21.06
Gross Operating Income	$ 502,364	43.4	$15.67

EXHIBIT 26-11.   Continued

	Actual Income from Operations	Percentage of the Year's Revenue	Cost per Patient-Day[a]
Gross Operating Income	$ 502,364	43.4	$15.67
Administrative Expenses			
Salary and wages	$ 49,880	4.2	$ 1.55
Payroll taxes	44,286	3.7	1.37
Insurance employee	16,408	4.3	.50
Employee welfare	285	0.0	.00
Advertising and public relations	13,487	1.1	.42
Travel	2,611	0.2	.08
Professional fees	11,227	0.9	.34
Equipment rental	170	0.0	.00
Dues and subscriptions	2,119	0.1	.05
Telephone	3,303	0.2	.09
Supplies and printing	3,117	0.2	.09
Insurance business	5,521	0.4	.16
Employee recruiting	622	0.0	.01
Other administrative expense	2,862	0.2	.08
Total Administrative Expenses	$ 155,898	12.5	$ 4.74
Net Income before Other Expenses	$ 346,466	30.9	$10.93
Other Income and Expenses			
Add: Other income	$ 1,160	0.0	$ 0.3
Deduct: Other expense	15,269	1.3	.47
Management fee	69,454	5.8	2.15
Medical write-off	28,142	2.3	.82
Welfare write-off	10,881	0.9	.34
Other write-off	–	0.0	.00
Total Other Income and Expenses	$ 122,586	10.3	$ 3.81
Net Operating Income from Nursing Home Business	$ 223,880	20.6	$ 7.12
Property Expense			
Taxes—real estate	$ 36,003	3.0	$ 1.12
Taxes—personal property	1,553	.1	.04
Total Property Expenses	$ 37,556	3.1	$ 1.16
Net Income before Taxes and Debt Service	$ 186,324	17.5	$ 5.96

[a]A patient-day is a 24-hour period during which a patient is in the nursing facility. The number of patient-days for the year is divided into the individual revenue and cost figures to determine the revenue and cost per patient-day.

In the operation of nursing homes, ownership of the physical facility and equipment is often separated from the business of operating the home. Allocation of returns may be disproportionate but, obviously, must allow a sufficient return to provide an incentive for the manager to remain on the job. Under such an arrangement, the structuring of an active-participation role for equity investors may be manageable.

TAXATION PROBLEMS

Nursing homes are eligible for straight-line composite depreciation (31.5 year life), capital gains, deferred-tax exchanges, and the installment sales method of allocation. Very short lives for wall surfaces, floor coverings, and so on may be appropriate because, to meet state and federal hygienic requirements, such features must be replaced periodically. But to qualify for such treatment, these items must be classified as equipment, which is debatable. In any event, the tax benefits would be minimized by the capital expenditures required. Finally, many items of equipment—perhaps as much as 15 or 20 percent of total value—may be properly classified as personal property, and ACRS three-year and five-year lives can increase the amount of deductions in the earlier years.

First-time investors should be aware that many states restrict resale of nursing home properties; state approval may be required. Such restrictions may force investors into longer-than-anticipated holding periods, thus keeping capital gains, being deferred, from contributing to the rate of return as initially anticipated.

THE INVESTMENT DECISION

Operating a nursing home is a high-overhead business, but one that offers good compensation to diligent and expert management. A primary requirement is a nursing home property with high occupancy. Specifically, the subject property should have a stable or increasing occupancy rate of at least 93 percent, have operating expenses amounting to no more than 70 percent of revenues, and provide a sufficient before-tax cash flow return (ROE of 15 to 20 percent annually). The required IRR may be in the 18 to 26 percent range when an inflation premium is included.

Conventional debt coverage ratio and break-even analysis is not used because the feasibility of nursing home financing is controlled by the procedures of the Section 232 FHA-insured loan program. Such a technical analysis is beyond the scope of this book, and even return and risk analysis should not be undertaken without specialized knowledge of federal and state financing procedures and minimum property standards.

As a real estate investment, nursing homes continue to be speculative in nature and may be appropriate for only the very high marginal-tax-rate investor; the maximum-tax-rate reduction makes these properties even less attractive. Furthermore, net cash flow is a residual only after compensating management and is subject to politically inspired program changes that cause delays in payments and much uncertainty. Nursing homes are necessary, but a socially acceptable way to make them consistently viable as an investment of public or private funds has yet to be found.

SELECTED REFERENCES

HOUSES, CONDOMINIUMS, AND SMALL APARTMENTS

Trends and Track Record

Grebler, Leo and Leland S. Burns, "Construction Cycles in the United States Since World War II," *Journal of the American Real Estate and Urban Economics Association*, Vol. 10, 1982, pp. 123–151.

Hare, Patrick H., "Rethinking Single-Family Zoning: Growing Old in American Neighborhoods," *New England Journal of Human Services*, Summer 1981, pp. 32–35.

Market and Marketability Analyses

Bush, Vanessa A., *Condominiums and Cooperatives* (Chicago: Contemporary Books, 1986).

Duffy, Robert E., "Residential Land Leases Provide New Opportunities," *Journal of Real Estate Development*, Summer 1985, pp. 5–14.

Falk, Barry, "Forecasting Housing Starts Using Multivariate Time Series Methods," *Housing Finance Review*, April 1983, pp. 109–126.

Finger, Michael H., "Financing Timeshare Development," *Journal of Real Estate Development*, Fall 1985, pp. 43–51.

"Key Challenges Include Affordability, Regulation," *Professional Builder*, October 1985, pp. 160–167.

Leventhal, Kenneth, "Appraisals Must Be More Comprehensive Than Ever," *Professional Builder*, June 1986, p. 32.

McElyea, J. Richard, "The Resort and Second Home Industry," *Urban Land*, October 1983, pp. 32–33.

Opelka, F. Gregory, "Study Highlights Key Appraisal Problems," *Savings Institutions*, June 1985, p. 107.

Rohe, William M. and Lauren B. Gates, *Planning with Neighborhoods* (Chapel Hill: Univ. of North Carolina Press, 1985).

Romney, Keith B., *Condominium Development Guide*, rev. ed. (Boston: Warren, Gorham & Lamont, 1983).

Rosen, Kenneth T., *Affordable Housing: New Policies and the Housing and Mortgage Markets* (Cambridge, Mass.: Ballinger Publishing Co., 1984).

Strathman, James G., P. Barton DeLacy, and Kenneth J. Dueker, "Creative Financing 'Concessions' in Residential Sales: Effects and Implications," *Housing Finance Review*, April 1984, pp. 149–163.

Vernon, James D., "Condominium Community Analysis: A Rational Approach for Appraisers and Investors," *The Appraisal Review Journal*, Winter 1983, pp. 47–55.

Financial Analysis

Expense Analysis—Condominiums, Cooperatives, and PUDs (Chicago: Institute of Real Estate Management, annual).

Ferguson, Jerry, "Small Investment Properties and Explicit Reinvestment Rates," *The Appraisal Review Journal*, Winter 1985, pp. 60–64.

Resort Real Estate and Timesharing (Philadelphia: American Law Institute—American Bar Association Committee on Continuing Professional Education, 1986).

Seale, Leady Jr., "Appraising Condominium and PUD Units for Freddie Mac," *The Appraisal Review Journal*, Winter 1984, pp. 27–31.

Webb, James R., "Negative Cash Flows: A Current Appraisal Problem," *The Appraisal Journal*, January 1981, pp. 96–101.

Operation

The Owner's and Manager's Guide to Condominium Management (Chicago: Institute of Real Estate Management of the National Association of Realtors, 1984).

Romney, Keith B., *Condominium Development Guide* (Boston: Warren, Gorham & Lamont, 1983).

Financing and Refinancing

Clauretie, Terren M., "Do Single-Family House Prices Always Reflect the Value of Creative Financing?" *The Appraisal Review Journal*, Fall 1983, pp. 62–71.

"The Current Boom of Mortgage Customers Won't Last Forever," *Savings Institutions*, July 1986, pp. 30–31.

Ferreira, Eurico J. and G. Stacy Sirmans, "Assumable Loan Value in Creative Financing," *Housing Finance Review*, April 1984, pp. 139–147.

Guttentag, Jack M., "Recent Changes in the Primary Home Mortgage Market," *Housing Finance Review*, July 1984, pp. 221–255.

Langdon, William H., "Home-Equity Conversion and the Appraiser," *The Appraisal Review Journal*, Summer 1984, pp. 32–37.

Pesando, James E. and Stuart M. Turnbull, "The Time Path of Homeowner's Equity Under Different Mortgage Instruments: A Simulation Study," *Housing Finance Review*, January 1985, pp. 483–504.

"Resurgence of Fixed Rate Loans Hurts Borrower and Lender," *Savings Institutions*, February 1985, pp. 37–39.

Rosen, Kenneth T., *Affordable Housing: New Policies and the Housing and Mortgage Markets* (Cambridge, Mass.: Ballinger Publishing Co., 1984).

Rosen, Kenneth T., "Creative Financing and House Prices: A Study of Capitalization Effects," *Housing Finance Review*, April 1984, pp. 119–127.

Schwartz, Arthur L., "Valuing Seller-Financed Homes," *Appraisal Review & Mortgage Underwriting Journal*, Winter 1986, pp. 54–57.

Siegel, Jeremy J., "The Mortgage Refinancing Decision," *Housing Finance Review*, January 1984, pp. 91–97.

Sirmans, C. F., "The Refinancing Decision for Income-Producing Real Estate," *The Appraisal Journal*, January 1985, pp. 41–43.

Sirmans, G. Stacy, "Seller Financing and Selling Price of Single-Family Homes," *Appraisal Review & Mortgage Underwriting Journal*, Summer 1985, pp. 24–27.

Taxation

Rutledge, John K., "Is Tax Reform Good For Real Estate?" *Pension World*, August 1986, pp. 14–24.

Yablon, Jeffery L. and Allen J. Klein, "Income-Producing Property and the New Tax Law," *Bottomline*, September 1987, pp. 47–49.

HOTELS AND MOTELS

Track Record and Trends

Brener, Stephen W., *Census of the Motor Hotel Industry in the U.S.* (New York: Helmsley-Spear, periodic).

Resort Real Estate and Timesharing (Philadelphia: American Law Institute-American Bar Association Committee on Continuing Professional Education, 1986).

U.S. Lodging Industry (New York: Laventhol & Horwath, annual).

Voss, Glenn B., *Hotel Condominiums* (Chicago: Contemporary Books, 1986).

Investment Performance

DeLuca, Michael, "Era of Uncertainty: Developers, Lenders Rethink Traditional Beliefs," *Hotel and Motel Management*, March 17, 1986, p. 2.

Mellor, Michael J. W. and Robert Witherspoon, "Focus on Hotels in Major Projects," *Urban Land*, September 1985, pp. 8–11.

Development

Dervon, Ron, "Hotels: Achieving the Competitive Edge," *NAIOP News*, National Association of Industrial and Office Parks, December 1985, pp. 13–15.

Geller, Laurence, "Hotels in the Mixed-Use Development," *The Journal of Real Estate Development*, Summer 1986, pp. 59–64.

Hotel/Motel Development (Washington, D.C.: Urban Land Institute, 1984).

Market and Marketability Analyses

Brookes, Philip J., "Mid-Sized Hotels Are an Investment Opportunity," *Real Estate Review*, Summer 1981, pp. 89–92.

Brookes, Philip J., "Repositioning Old Hotels for New Markets," *The Journal of Real Estate Development*, Summer 1986, pp. 26–31.

Eberhart, Cheryl, "Rehabilitation Project Gives New Life to St. Louis Union Station," *Hotel and Motel Management*, June 30, 1986, pp. 40–41.

Feiertag, Howard, "Giveaways Aren't Needed For Effective Hotel Marketing," *Hotel and Motel Management*, September 1, 1986, p. 18.

Gamoran, A. Carmi, *How to Provide a Hotel in a Development and Benefit Both* (Boston: Warren, Gorham and Lamont, 1979).

Yarnell, Michael C., *The Marketing of Timeshare Condominiums* (Santa Monica, Calif.: Delphi Information Sciences Corp., 1980).

Operation

Blagden, Nellie, *The Complete Condo and Co-Op Information Book* (Boston: Houghton Mifflin, 1983).

Drath, Lawrence, "Remember 'Events of Default' When Negotiating Lease," *Hotel and Motel Management*, June 30, 1986, p. 18.

Eyster, James J., "Managing the Negotiations in Hotel Management Contracts," *Real Estate Review*, Spring 1981, pp. 120–128.

Residential Condominium and Cooperative Development (New York: Practising Law Institute, 1982).

Uniform System of Accounts and Expense Dictionary for Small Hotels and Motels (East Lansing, Mich.: Educational Institute of the American Hotel and Motel Association, 1981).

Financial Analysis

Barash, Samuel T., *Encyclopedia of Real Estate Appraising Forms and Model Reports* (Englewood Cliffs, N.J.: Prentice–Hall, 1983).

Timesharing II (Washington, D.C.: Urban Land Institute, 1982).

Wilder, Jeff, "Liability Insurance Hassles Can Hinder Hotel Investment," *Hotel and Motel Management*, September 1, 1986, p. 16.

Financing

Corgel, John B., "Hotel/Motel Properties vs. Other Real Estate: A Comparison of Mortgage Terms," *Real Estate Finance*, Spring 1986, pp. 104–107.

Huff, Nadine F., "Rehab Spurred by Equity Syndication," *Urban Land*, February 1983, pp. 28–29.

NURSING HOMES

Track Record and Trends

Brecht, Susan B., "Lifecare Comes of Age," *Urban Land*, August 1984, pp. 14–17.

Chellis, Robert D., J. F. Seagle, Jr., and B. M. Seagle, eds., *Congregate Housing for Older People: A Solution for the 1980s* (Lexington, Mass.: Lexington Books, 1982).

"Consumer Reports Guide on Housing Options for Older Americans," *Aging,* July 1985, p. 42.

Finkelstein, Alex, "Lifecare Communities, by Any Name, Are Flourishing," *South Florida Business Journal,* June 10, 1985, p. 24.

Hare, Patrick H. and Margaret Haske, "Innovative Living Arrangements: A Source of Long-Term Care," *Aging,* December 1983, pp. 3–9.

Heumann, Leonard and Duncan Boldy, *Housing for the Elderly: Planning and Policy Formulation in Western Europe and North America* (New York: St. Martin's Press, 1982).

Howland, Libby, "Changing Characteristics of the Elderly Population," *Urban Land,* April 1985, pp. 32–33.

Kosterlitz, Julie, "The Graying of America Spells Trouble for Long-Term Health Care for the Elderly," *National Journal,* April 13, 1985, pp. 798–801.

LaGory, Mark, "The Age Segregation Process: Explanation for American Cities," *Urban Affairs Quarterly,* September 1980, pp. 59–80.

Lifecare Industry in the United States, annual report.

McCarthy, Kevin F., *The Elderly Population's Changing Spatial Distribution: Patterns of Change Since 1960* (Santa Monica, Calif.: Rand Corporation, 1983).

Mintz, Anita, "Health Care for Elderly Is Almost Next Door," *Builder,* August 1984, pp. 56–60.

Parket, Rosetta E., "The Future of Elderly Housing," *The Journal of Property Management,* May–June 1984, pp. 12–16.

Shipp, Audrey, ed., *The National Nursing Home Survey: 1977 Summary for the United States* (Hyattsville, Md.: National Center Health Statistics, 1979).

Stockman, Leslie E. and June Fletcher, "A Maturing Market," *Builder,* June 1985, pp. 70–73.

Topolnicki, Denise M., "The Broken Promise of Life-Care Communities," *Money,* January 1984, pp. 88–91.

Development

Adams, Eli, "Rehab Transforms Mansion to Congregate Home" (Graying of America), *Professional Builder,* September 1985, pp. 76–78.

Blackie, Norman K., "Alternative Housing and Living Arrangements for Independent Living," *Journal of Housing for the Elderly,* Spring–Summer 1983, pp. 77–83.

Breger, William N. and William R. Pomeranz, *Nursing Home Development: A Guide to Planning, Financing and Constructing Long-Term Care Facilities* (New York): Van Nostrand Reinhold, 1985).

Carstens, Diane Y., *Site Planning and Design for the Elderly: Issues, Guidelines and Alternatives* (New York: Van Nostrand Reinhold, 1985).

"Designing for Aging," *Real Estate Today,* June 1985, pp. 14–15.

Franz, J., "Profits Can Bloom From Unused Land," *Modern Healthcare,* October 1983, p. 96.

Graskie, Margaret, "Sheltered Independence: Life After 65" (Building Types Study: Housing for the Elderly), *Architectural Record,* February 1985, pp. 95–97.

Haynes, William E., "Cypen Tower: A Design for Retirement Living," *Aging*, January–February 1983, pp. 18–22.

Henderson, Michael J. "Lifestyles for the Elderly: Best of Both Worlds," *Mortgage Banking*, December 1985, pp. 27–41.

Huth, Mary Jo, "A Seminary Becomes A Residence and Community for the Elderly," *Aging*, December 1983, pp. 22–26.

Lesser, Robert C., "Developing for the Over-50s Market," *Urban Land*, February 1984, pp. 2–7.

Pave, Irene and Kimberley Carpenter, "What's Putting New Life Into Life Care Communities," *Business Week*, March 3, 1986, p. 108.

Investment Performance

Coyne, Deidre C., "Lewinsville Center Residence: A New Horizon for the Elderly," *Virginia Town & City*, April 1985, pp. 9–11.

Friedman, Stephen B., "Opportunities in Continuing Care Facilities for the Elderly," *Journal of Property Management*, July–August 1986, pp. 30–33.

Hunt, Michael E., *Retirement Communities: An American Original* (New York: Haworth Press, 1984).

"Life-Care Retirement Homes: What They're Like, What They Cost; They're Not Nursing Homes, They're Not Old-Folks Homes and They're Not Senior Villages," *Changing Times*, October 1982, p. 28.

Petse, Peter, "Marketers Mine for Gold in the Old," *Fortune*, March 31, 1986, p. 70.

Wood, Stephen F., "Nursing Home Investment: Growing Opportunities," *Mortgage Banking*, December 1985, pp. 26–32.

Operation

Adams, Eli, "Lifecare Includes Healthcare Services" (Graying of America), *Professional Builder*, September 1985, pp. 72–82.

Adams, Eli, ed., "Meeting the Varied Market for the Graying of America," *Professional Builder*, April 1986, pp. 68–98.

Goodkin, Sanford R., "Graying America Has Special Needs," *Professional Builder*, September 1984, p. 56.

Laing, Susan and Linda F. Little, "The Management of Federally Subsidized Housing for Elderly Residents," *The Journal of Property Management*, November–December 1985, pp. 9–12.

Miller, Dulcy B. and Jane T. Barry, *Nursing Home Organization and Operation* (New York: CBI Publications, 1979).

Nelton, Sharon, "A New Kind of Retirement Home," *Nation's Business*, January 1986, pp. 77–78.

Patterson, Dorothy Brown, *Nursing Home Administration* (Springfield, Ill.: C. C. Thomas, 1982).

Posyniak, Henry, *Guide to Accounting Principles, Practices and Systems for Nursing Homes* (St. Louis, Mo.: Catholic Hospital Association, 1984).

Market and Marketability Analyses

Adams, Eli, "Attract Active Retirees with Outdoor Amenities" (Graying of America), *Professional Builders*, September 1985, pp. 66–70.

Adams, Eli, "Children Help Decide Where Parents Live" (Graying of America), *Professional Builder*, September 1985, pp. 70–71.

Adams, Jerry, "An Older Market Opens New Doors," *American Banker*, October 22, 1985, pp. 33–34.

Diez, Roy L., "Learn How to House the New World of Graying Americans: Builders Marketing Variety of Products," *Professional Builder*, September 1985, p. 7.

Golant, Stephen M., *Location and Environment of Elderly Population* (New York: Wiley, 1979).

Golant, Stephen M., *A Place to Grow Old: The Meaning of Environment in Old Age* (New York: Columbia Univ. Press, 1984).

"Housing: Increasing Aged Population to Increase Housing Demand," *USA Today*, December 1983, p. 2.

Kauffman, Gadi, "Selling to Seniors: It Is a Lively Market," *Real Estate Today*, June 1985, pp. 10–13.

Nelton, Sharon, "A New Kind of Retirement Home," *Nation's Business*, January 1986, pp. 77–78.

Page, Clint, "Coping with the Housing Needs of the Elderly: Community Groups Plan New Approaches," *Nation's Cities Weekly*, September 13, 1982, p. 3.

Power, Kandance, "Posh Is the Name of the Game at New Living Centers," *New Orleans City Business*, June 24, 1985, pp. 18–20.

Sachs, Martha, "CSI: A Successful Senior Housing Cooperative," *Aging*, March–April 1983, pp. 14–17.

Smart, J. Eric, ed., *Housing for a Maturing Population* (Washington, D.C.: Urban Land Institute, 1983).

Trupp, Beverly, "Merchandising for Graying America," *Professional Builder*, December 1984, pp. 40–42.

Warnes, A. M., ed., *Geographical Perspectives on the Elderly* (New York: Wiley, 1982).

Financial Analysis

Hogan, John O., "The Valuation of Nursing Homes," *The Appraisal Journal*, April 1979, pp. 185–194.

Williams, Thomas P. and John A. Rasmussen, "Feasibility and Valuation of a Continuing Care Retirement Community," *The Appraisal Journal*, July 1985, pp. 354–370.

Financing

Blocker, Mark D., "Nursing Care Finance: The Structure," *Mortgage Banking*, March 1983, pp. 51–57.

Gabler, William J. and Terry W. McKinley, "Selected Financing Options for Elderly Housing," *The Journal of Real Estate Development*, Winter 1986, pp. 35–41.

Henderson, Michael J., "Nursing Care Finance: The Limitations," *Mortgage Banking*, March 1983, pp. 47–50.

Jeck, Allister M. and June E. Carlson, "Retirement Housing: Exploring the Gray Area of Housing's Gray Market," *Real Estate Finance*, Winter 1986, pp. 57–68.

Mallet, R. Christopher, "Lending to Nursing Homes," *Journal of Commercial Bank Lending*, February 1986, p. 23.

Merger, William and William Pomerang, "Facility Financing for Nursing Homes: Use of the Tax-Exempt Bond Market," *Economic Development and Law Center Report*, May–June 1980, pp. 1–8.

Pastalan, Leon A., "The Role of the State Housing Finance Agencies in Providing Housing for the Elderly: A Review of Past Performance," *Journal of Housing for the Elderly*, Spring 1984, pp. 65–68.

Wared, M. E., "Congregate Living Arrangements: The Financing Option," *Topics in Health Care Financing*, Spring 1984, pp. 34–45.

27

LAND INVESTMENTS

Buy land! They aren't making it anymore. Gene Autry believed that, and he's a very wealthy man today. . . . I knew a muleskinner, he was really big! . . . He had mule trains! . . . He believed that about land. . . . Eventually he lost all his asses.

Anonymous land trader

Buying land to make a profit is much like playing a game of Monopoly. The buyer seeks to purchase a parcel with a minimum of holding costs and a maximum of financial leverage in the hope that the land will change quickly from a lower use to a higher one, thereby producing a large profit. Many people who buy land seem to expect that the weedy ground will soon be covered with a regional shopping center, or that they will find a person with a fool's faith and hope willing to purchase or lease the land.

Land developers and interstate land-marketing companies came under severe attack during the 1970s by many groups crying out against premature land development and land waste. The consequent regulation should help ensure that socially responsible, ethical development becomes the rule. Heading into the 1990s, the competent, successful land investors are those who work in cooperation with the environment and local planners to provide for orderly growth.

Although many believe that land always increases in value, raw-land speculation and investing entail implicit risks that can destroy such expectations. It is not for the risk-averse because there is little chance of cash inflows from the property, and equity buys only the right to risk a capital gain by way of the reversion.

Fred Case, a respected scholar of real estate, has suggested that land requires a very high rate of price increase over the ownership cycle, primarily because the annual cost of holding the land is high, and substantial earnings are required on money invested in order to achieve profit objectives. In the example provided by Case, these earning objectives have been converted into percentages of market price, assuming a one-year holding period.[1]

	Annual Rate Required (Percent)
1. Earning on the down payment (10% earnings × 10% down)	1
2. Interest on the loan (12% × 90%)	11
3. Real estate taxes	3
4. Improvements	2
5. Overall profit on total investment	15
6. Transaction costs (commissions, legal, etc.)	12
	44

Note: Some of these figures have been adjusted to reflect current (1988) rates and are therefore not those found in the cited reference.

Although transfer costs and improvements could be stretched out over a longer ownership cycle, whatever the assumptions, the land must earn relatively high returns by way of higher prices. In addition, higher rates of return should be expected for riskier investments, *ceteris paribus.* Clearly, the lack of interim income places a heavy burden on the reversion and on the investor's pocketbook during the holding period. It should be kept in mind that the foregoing example does not include the effects of taxes on the gain. Nevertheless, people can make large profits with superior market knowledge and a little good luck!

TRACK RECORD AND TRENDS

In the post–World War II period, farmers, developers, land bankers, and land investors reaped large gains from rising land values on the urban fringes of growing MSAs. In less than fifty years the population had grown by more than 100 million and the GNP increased more than sixfold. The main problems now faced by a land speculator are (1) the extent to which slower growth implies slower rates of gain in land values and (2) the extent to which future growth has already been capitalized into the asking price of the current owner.

Obviously, many other factors affect land value, such as interregional migration, the shift from manufacturing to service industries, and the current trend of population movement away from large MSAs to smaller ones. Many large MSAs are suffering from energy problems and water problems, and in-filling (filling up land that was skipped over) is occurring

[1]Fred E. Case, *The Investment Guide to Home and Land Purchase* (Englewood Cliffs, N.J.: Prentice–Hall Spectrum Books, 1977), pp. 154–155.

in MSAs that have suffered from rapid growth and overcrowding. It appears that the period of rapid growth for this nation is over. We have "settled in" and in general have selected the locations of all our metropolitan areas.

Many people who have studied the rate of suburban conversion relative to land prices believe that current land values have largely anticipated the next possible use, given the holding costs and current discount rates.[2] Thus, opportunities for above-average returns required by land speculation are less likely to occur any time soon in most MSAs, with the following exceptions.

1. Large gains will be realized when speculators guess correctly on changes in zoning, master plans, and other government controls, and buy before the transition becomes common knowledge.

2. High profits will be realized by those who benefit from the "windfall" of improved highway access, mass transit, airport facilities, and rail and sea terminals. However, sharp increases in the value of privately owned land tend to occur only for parcels that are very close to these uses and their corridors. Values drop sharply as one moves away from the immediate vicinity.

3. Speculative gains will be obtained by those who can anticipate the effects of the actions of OPEC or other commodity cartels on essential minerals, foods, and fossil fuels. For example, the oil shales of Colorado and the tar flats of Alberta, Canada, have been traded back and forth for years. When the time is right for actual development, because the world price of oil has risen enough to justify the costs of extracting shale oil, the owner who is holding such land will probably make a large gain. (However, recent events concerning world oil prices and supplies seem to preclude such an opportunity until the late 1990s.)

4. Speculators will perform a useful function when they "take out" landholders with parcels that have been passed over by urban growth and who need to cash out for some reason. The speculator will believe that the metropolitan area will in-fill the site with an appropriate use in three to five years.

5. High returns will be obtained by some speculators who can anticipate that a metropolitan area has grown to the point at which it is ready to break through to more intensive land uses than it has supported in the past, particularly when the speculator can forecast the most likely locations for these uses.

6. Some land values will continue to be affected by population and employment. In the United States, for example, seacoasts, skiing areas,

---

[2]See Marion Clawson, *Suburban Land Conversion in the United States* (Baltimore: Johns Hopkins Press, 1971); *Real Estate Reports* (issued monthly) (Chicago: Real Estate Research Corporation); *The Wall Street Journal*, various articles.

oil–gas lease lands, crossover points of interstate highways, and other locations are appropriate for speculative activity because it is difficult to guess when the next most probable use will in fact take place. The demand for beach and lakefront properties continues to increase as more people compete to gain control of this desirable amenity. However, one should be cautious in considering factors such as travel time from metropolitan areas to the recreational sites. There are beautiful seacoast areas in the United States that simply are not convenient to enough people to warrant sharp increases in land value in the short term. Hilton Head, South Carolina, was an example of such premature development. The capture rate was based on travel times and trip costs that did not anticipate the 55-mph speed limit and the rising cost of gasoline. Now that trip time radii have improved, however, the investment performance of Hilton Head and other localities has also improved.

INVESTING IN LAND

Advantages and Disadvantages

Investing in raw land may offer a higher potential for gain than investing in income property. Through the use of options and low down payments with purchase money mortgages or installment land contracts with favorable terms, it is possible for the investor to gain control of the property at a relatively low cost. Some land investors couple the lower capital requirement with diversification of location to minimize market risk. They buy scattered sites in the area or systematically buy alternate parcels to achieve a checkerboard effect, hoping that their "hold-out negotiating power" over the next buyer will enable them to get a premium price. As long as investor status can be maintained, there are also the advantages of classifying profits as capital gain rather than ordinary income, and receiving installment sale tax treatment.

Other risks associated with raw land investments are the following:

1. Throughout the ownership period there are cash outlays for real estate taxes, liability insurance, and property maintenance; additional potential costs include mortgage principal and interest payments and site improvement programs to create a more marketable product.

2. Inflationary effects on price levels may or may not work to the investor's advantage, depending on the mortgage–equity ratio and the rate of gain in value relative to the rate of inflation.

3. Mortgage contract terms usually require loss of all equity in the event of default (installment sales contracts). Exercise of the equity of redemption, if available, is unlikely.

4. Lack of liquidity is a feature of owning raw land and other rural properties.

5. The uncertainty of timing makes financial analysis quite problematical. If the market does not develop as expected, the time value of money, inflationary effects on the dollar, and additional cash outlays for carrying costs will reduce the rate of return quickly, unless prices increase faster than expected.

6. Increasing public scrutiny makes the political, legal, and physical risks of land development greater than in the past.

7. Classification as portfolio and investment interest limitation apply to most raw-land investment debts. Land investments cannot easily be classified as a trade or business unless the person is growing Christmas trees, operating a golf driving range, farming, or ranching. In effect, an investment with no interim business use encounters the problems of tax preference and alternative tax if investment interest from such investments is equal to $5,000 or more per year.

Types of Investors and Investor Motivations

Most investors lack the risk-taking aggressiveness, the liquidity, and the ability to handle the uncertainty that land investment requires. As a general rule, land investing is for those who have accumulated wealth or who have little concern about losing what wealth they have accumulated. Corporate pension funds have sometimes been invested in land. For those with the wealth and proper motivations, buying land as an investment for future generations makes sense economically. Of course, land speculation on a small scale in an overall plan may be a justifiable strategy, especially considering the current rate of inflation relative to typical rates of return from other investment forms.

Recently, another kind of land investment arrangement has come into the market: joint ventures that couple established developers with both individual and institutional investors, with the investors holding the property for the developer, who acts as a captive market. Such arrangements evolved because large-scale developers cannot afford to have their borrowing capacity or working capital tied up in banking land at the current cost of money. On the other hand, they need to have the land inventory in "friendly hands" in order to perform rational production scheduling. This niche in the market may open up to land syndications as the practice spreads to smaller, stable, well-capitalized developers.

PRELIMINARY ANALYSES

Market and Marketability Analysis

Supply and Demand Analysis. The land investor who is an expert on the patterns of growth and land uses in the metropolitan areas in which he or she is active can forecast the next possible use for selected vacant parcels of real estate. The investor's task is to find *nodes* of activity just before they actually occur; this generally requires analyses of market segmentation and geographic zones in an effort to find underpriced land that could be developed within a relatively short time. An example is the general shift in the location of auto dealers during the past few decades away from the central business districts (CBDs) to perimeter highways. Another example is the Hallmark Center in Kansas City, an office-retail-condominium built about twelve blocks away from the older CBD. The area between was deteriorated, with mixed low-intensity uses. Eventually, a higher-intensity corridor created a dumbbell-shaped layout in which the CBD and Hallmark Center merged. The investor has to be concerned with the timing of the anticipated events. The longer the waiting period, the less likely the events are to occur; furthermore, if they do occur, the investor's profit rate may be lessened and his holding costs increased. It is axiomatic that market analysis for the land buyer is a predevelopment decision process similar to that conducted by a developer when the right time for construction is some years away. Ideally, the investor identifies a use in search of a site, and the site is the targeted investment.

Experience indicates that speculators seldom analyze market sectors or geographic zones to discover a site for specific use. Instead, they monitor overall growth trends and respond to offers from the network of brokers and owners with whom they have working relationships. They then do an analysis of the offered site. However, better opportunities are found by making systematic analyses and then seeking to buy a site that is well suited to the expected demand.

Holding Costs During Ownership Period. During the market analysis stage, it is appropriate to project any interim income and to estimate holding costs. These estimates are often based on the investor's experience or, when the investor is inexperienced, on the advice of knowledgeable professionals.

Generally, no income is anticipated from raw land except by way of resale proceeds. However, if the site is particularly well suited to some interim use, it may be possible to generate interim cash flows through, for example, parking lots, mobile home parks, golf driving ranges, Christmas tree lots, drive-in theaters, nurseries, builders' supplies storage, and many more. Renting the land also may aid in protecting tax status as a Section 1231 investor rather than as a dealer. Some landowners, pleased with their status, prefer to lease rather than sell land to developers. For developers, this decreases the project's cost relative to cash flow from the early years of operations, and owners receive regular stipends. Such a ground lease may be either subordinated—the owner mortgages his or her land as security, thereby inciting the lender to a larger investment; or unsubordinated—the land is not subject to the lien of the mortgage. However, a lease arrangement can sometimes render a property useless for years, because developers require time to organize a deal before the project even approaches reality.

Expenses usually have such predictable sources as real estate taxes, property maintenance, mortgage principal and interest payments, possible additional local assessments, site improvement costs (grading, paving, etc.), and fees for legal and engineering work. Most or all of these expenses can be reasonably estimated or determined. In addition, good financial planning includes a contingency fund to handle unexpected costs or costs larger than anticipated.

Risk Management and Control

A good way to be a loser in land investment is to pay too much, underestimate holding costs, hold for a year or two longer than expected, or sell for a little less than expected. The investor must complete a thorough decision process that identifies the rate of growth and the areas where such growth is likely to occur. Assuming that several alternative parcels within a geographic zone have been identified—we will call them parcels A, B, C, D, and E—several techniques may be used to minimize risk.

- *Checkerboard Technique.* Instead of buying only C, buy A, C, and E.
- *Parimutuel Technique.* Join with other speculators and buy fractional shares in C.
- *Combination of the Two.* Join with other speculators in buying fractional shares of sites in a checkerboard pattern.

There are many variations on these techniques. Suppose, for instance, analysis indicates that the next possible use may leapfrog to one of several submarkets in different neighborhoods. There are now a number of possible sites in each of several neighborhoods:

I—A, B, C, D, and E.
II—F, G, and H.
III—I, J, K, and L.

The risk reduction strategy might be as follows:

Alternative 1: Buy I-C, II-H, and III-L.
Alternative 2: Join with other speculators in buying a checkerboard in each of the three areas.

In recent years, some land traders have created syndications to "lay off" the risk by acting as general partners for a number of separate deals. Another way for risk-averse land investors to use reinsurance or the layoff maneuver is to sell off fractional interests when a land investment does not mature as rapidly as expected and when it represents problems with both the time value of money and liquidity. This reduces the magnitude of gains or losses, and, more importantly, frees capital for another investment. Interestingly, the reinsurance tactic should be attractive to the buyer because his or her time horizon for the profitable sale of the land is shorter than that of the original investor, enabling the buyer to realize higher returns.

Investors should confront the issue of the effect of time on price during negotiation. The farther into the future they expect the next probable use to occur, the more aggressive they should be in negotiations because of the time value of money and the uncertain timing of the resale. Pension fund managers and the like often rely on registered qualified professional asset managers who, together with development managers, study various land investments and explore the basic project possibilities. Generally, the various possibilities should be studied as thoroughly as prospects for development of a specific project would be studied.

Physical, Legal, Political, and Environmental Analysis

Physical Factors. Physical factors are critical when evaluating the future potential of undeveloped land, because the existing and potential site conditions and size must be matched with projected needs. On-site conditions should be carefully checked by field inspection. Engineering studies may be essential to check the geology and bearing characteristics of the soil and determine whether the topography will be suitable for the intended future use. Other relevant factors may include drainage, erosion, slope, shape of site (i.e., not too long and thin), usable acres (vs. gross acres), natural hazards, and vegetation. Any or all of these factors could have an effect on potential future uses. An inventory map may be called for to present the property's natural resources and relate them to the land's physical or economic productivity. Such estimations can help determine an area's potential for urban development.[3]

The capacity of and access to off-site improvements such as railroads, highways, and urban transportation should be adequate. Also to be considered is the feasibility of obtaining sewage and water services from the local municipality or whether it will be necessary to build wells and septic tanks at the time of development. Access to other municipal services and utilities should also be studied. The investor could conclude that areas of the site unsuitable for building or paving might be used for treatment facilities or water retention systems. The cost of clearing and grading the site and the legal and administrative costs of potential zoning changes should be considered, as necessary.

[3]Marion E. Everhart, *Land Classification for Rural and Urban Uses—Management and Valuation* (Scottsdale, Ariz.: Todd Publishing Co., 1983).

Legal Factors. Legal considerations may constitute either opportunities or pitfalls for land speculators. Land traders know that it is not enough to make a thorough investigation of the public record for easements, liens, zoning regulations, building code violations, unpaid taxes, mineral rights, and the like. Unrecorded claims that may cloud the title also should be checked, as should whether the seller will provide a full-warranty deed and proper title protections such as title insurance. Investors should exercise extreme care before finally taking title to property. Claims made after the purchase and before the future development of the property could cost the investor not only his or her profit, but possibly the entire investment!

Political Factors. Political uncertainty always exists, and predicting its possible impact on land use is difficult at best, although prevailing attitudes toward development will provide some indication. Even in cities with generous zoning ordinances (or cities with "no zoning," such as Houston), there are influential groups that have much to say about what types of land use are acceptable. John Rahenkamp and his associates have provided one methodology by which investors may predict the chances of obtaining zoning approval.[4]

Environmental Factors. Land investors make money on changes in land usage, which raises the concern of the public about environmental quality. The removal of trees and other vegetation, for example, may destroy wildlife habitats. The new use also may affect air and water quality in an adverse way. Furthermore, if the development is large enough, it may require an environmental-impact study.

The land investor must therefore be environmentally sensitive and should be well informed about which locations within the metropolitan area are "officially" sensitive and so avoid purchasing in those areas. It is important that a land investor maintains a good reputation with regulators and leaders of environmental groups. Environmental groups can generate bad publicity and hostility toward the landowner and prospective developers. Finally, delays caused by expensive environmental-impact studies could substantially diminish the rate of return.

FINANCING

The nature of raw land does not make it attractive to institutional lenders unless the purchaser has substantial assets and a track record. Because

---

[4]The assimilation capacity model was developed by John Rahenkamp, Kathleen McLeister, and Robert Ditmer for the firm of Rahenkamp, Sachs, and Wells, Philadelphia; for reports on the models see *House and Home*, August 1972 and August 1976.

land usually produces no continuous stream of income, lenders are naturally concerned with how the loan will be repaid. Moreover, it is difficult to appraise raw land, because its potential use is not germane and would be ignored by financial institutions as too speculative. However, the unfortunate history of REITs indicates that institutions will make loans on the basis of "as-developed" appraisals. Many of these lenders lost considerable amounts of money on such loans, but often institutional lenders fail to learn lessons from history!

A farmland investor who intends to continue productive farming until the property "ripens" to its potential use may qualify for a farmland loan from the Federal Land Bank. Small commercial banks and savings and loan institutions in rural areas may also make loans on productive farmland, although such loans tend to be for relatively short terms.

Life insurance companies usually limit their land loans to farms and short-term land development loans that provide them with important lending opportunities for large-scale real estate development projects. Land investors per se are of little interest to them, whereas a developer with a well-established record who is going to produce a large-scale project would be of interest. Recently, life insurance companies have been interested in some joint ventures and other forms of direct participation.

Seller financing is usually the key to high-leverage financing of land purchases, with installment land contracts being the most common method. Sellers usually accept low down payments and offer attractive interest rates and terms. Now that all sales are considered installment sales by the IRS, purchase money mortgages can be used in lieu of the land contract. The land contract does not convey title until the terms of the contract have been fully satisfied. With a purchase money mortgage, the title passes to the buyer upon closing. Obtaining title may be important in the future when development loans are needed, because the development lender usually seeks a first lien on the land. The true speculator, who simply trades in land, prefers high-leverage seller financing with interest-only payments, hoping to resell the property before the principal payments begin.[5]

In theory, options provide the land investor with the greatest leverage and flexibility. If the option can be obtained for a reasonable period and at a low price, the investor's only monetary risk may be the price of the option. If the investment fails, the investor loses only the option's cost. If the investment succeeds, the investor has two alternatives: (1) purchase the land at the option's striking price, then resell for profit or develop; or (2) sell the option to another investor at a profit. The option's profit would

[5]Jack Friedman, "How to Value Variable Payment Mortgages," *Real Estate Review*, Fall 1975, pp. 92–96.

be the difference between the option striking price and the current market value.

Obviously, the financial arrangements are a crucial part of the land investment. They certainly affect the holding costs, may affect resale opportunities, and may affect rate of return. Because it is more difficult to make financial arrangements for land purchases than for income-producing properties, it is important to work closely with sellers or their agents.

TAXATION AND TAX STRUCTURE

A prime attraction of land investment is that the payments made to hold the land are largely tax-deductible, because they generally consist of real estate taxes, operating expenses, and interest. Of course, substantial improvements may have to be capitalized, and legal expenses, engineering services, surveying, and the like are generally considered capital expenditures.

A problem with most raw-land investments is the classification as portfolio income and the investment interest limitation,[6] which restricts the deductibility of interest from passive investment to an amount equal to net investment income, and permits no offset of investment interest against the long-term capital gains preference. Suffice it to say that holding land is much less attractive to an investor for whom interest deductibility is important. It is well to note that calculation of the investment interest is cumulative within a tax year—in that one sums investment interest from all sources except personal residence interest and interest expenses on trade or business investments—and there are carryover rights.[7] (See also Chapter 10.)

Another serious problem for land traders, discussed in more detail in Chapter 10, is the position of the IRS on dealer versus investor status for land traders. In brief, a real estate trader may preserve the right to a capital gain provided that he or she can prove a particular parcel was bought primarily for investment purposes. The IRS is skeptical when there are frequent sales, quick turnover, and prompt reinvestment of the proceeds into other properties. Exchanging is an ideal way of avoiding the dealer taint because there is no realization of gain. Otherwise, if the investor is classified as a dealer, capital gains income from the land deal is treated as ordinary income and installment sale tax treatment is not permitted.

---

[6] IRS Sec. 93; see also Coopers Lybrand, *Tax Planning for Real Estate Transactions* (Chicago: National Association of Realtors, Institute of Farm and Land Brokers, 1978), pp. 92–95.

[7] Ibid.

DISCOUNTED-CASH-FLOW ANALYSIS

A land investor deals in a simple future expectancy. Projected return is realized only if the land appreciates in price to produce the specified rate of return. The only inflows for the land investor usually consist of the net cash proceeds of sale, unless the property produced some periodic income during the holding period.

Often, an investor seeking a 10 percent IRR on the venture must anticipate that the property will be sold for 155 percent more than the purchase price at the end of five years. This represents an 11 percent simple annual rate of appreciation, or a 9.2 percent compounded rate, which may be difficult to achieve in the average market.

Conclusion. Although each land investment situation must be evaluated in terms of its unique financial and tax characteristics, the analysis illustrates the substantial rate of appreciation required to achieve merely a normal return. A very large return will require much more dramatic price increases. Indeed, the advice that the Red Queen in *Alice in Wonderland* gave to Alice is particularly apt as a basic principle of land speculation: "You must run as fast as you can just to stay in the same place. If you want to get ahead, you must run at least twice as fast."

THE INVESTMENT DECISION

In 1988, with advantageous seller terms, mortgage rates are likely to be at least 12 percent, whereas IRRs of 20 percent and higher would be required in present market conditions because of the speculative nature of land investment. With the declining inflation rates prevalent today, land investors must evaluate carefully if they are to achieve the annual appreciation rates necessary to provide rates of return commensurate with risk.

SELECTED REFERENCES

Property Analysis

Asabere, Paul K. and Barrie Harvey, "Factors Influencing the Value of Urban Land: Evidence from Halifax-Dartmouth, Canada," *Journal of the American Real Estate and Urban Economics Association*, 1985, pp. 361–377.

Bateman, Michael, *Office Development: A Geographical Analysis* (New York: St. Martin's Press, 1985).

Case, Fred E., *The Investment Guide to Home and Land Purchase* (Englewood Cliffs, N.J.: Prentice–Hall, 1977).

Ciandella, Don, "Overlooking Site Factors in Industrial Park Locations," *Site Selection Handbook*, February 1984, pp. 898–901.

"Investing in Raw Land," *Real Estate Review Portfolio Number 3* (Boston: Warren, Gorham & Lamont, 1974).

Kirk, John E., *How to Build a Fortune Investing in Land* (Englewood Cliffs, N.J.: Prentice-Hall, 1973).

Middlebrook, William C., "Appraisal Review Certificate—Unimproved Lands," *The Appraisal Review Journal*, Winter 1984, pp. 80–83.

Nicely, Glen, *How to Reap Riches From Raw Land: Guide to Profitable Real Estate Speculation* (Englewood Cliffs, N.J.: Prentice-Hall, 1974).

Paulson, Morton C., *The Great Land Hustle* (Chicago: Henry Regnery, 1972).

Roulac, Stephen E., "Anatomy of a Land Deal," *Real Estate Review*, Winter 1975, pp. 93–96.

Shackleford, J. Cooper, "Preliminary Site Studies," *Site Selection Handbook*, February 1984, pp. 243–319.

Seldin, Maury, *Land Investment* (Homewood, Ill.: Dow Jones–Irwin, 1975).

Risk Management

Abrahams, Frank, "Real Estate Development: Risk Can Be Reduced," *Pension World*, February 1986, pp. 22–24.

Halper, Emanuel B., "People and Property: To Buy or Not to Buy," *Real Estate Review*, Summer 1983, pp. 78–87.

Koch, James H., *Profits from Country Property: How to Select, Buy, Maintain, and Improve Country Property* (New York: McGraw-Hill, 1981).

Smart, Eric, *Making Infill Projects Work* (Washington, D.C.: The Urban Land Institute in collaboration with the Lincoln Institute of Land Policy, 1985).

Market Analysis

Barr, Gary K. and Richard Brockmeyer, *How to Evaluate an Investment in Agricultural Real Estate* (Boston: Warren, Gorham & Lamont, 1980).

Gabe, Vernon D., "Outline of a Corporate Site Location Procedure," *Site Selection Handbook*, 1984, pp. 318–319.

Heinly, David, "Developers, Again, Will Have Their Day in Court," *Professional Builder*, January 1986, p. 52.

Kearsky, Joseph E., *Complete Real Estate Exchange and Acquisition Handbook* (Englewood Cliffs, N.J.: Prentice-Hall, 1982).

Kolman, J., "The Boom in Real Estate Development Funds," *Institutional Investor*, November 1984, p. 165.

Miles, C. W. N. and W. Seabrook, *Recreational Land Management* (London: E.&F.N. Spon Ltd., 1978).

Porter, Douglas R. and Frank Schnidman, "Sales of Excess Federal Property: Bonanza or Boondoggle?" *Urban Land*, February 1983, pp. 24–27.

"A Property Bust to Follow the Oil Slide?" *Economist*, March 30, 1985, pp. 83–84.

Working with the Community: A Developer's Guide (Washington, D.C.: Urban Land Institute, sponsored by the ULI's Executive Group of the Development Regulations Council, 1985).

APPENDIX A

THE TIME VALUE OF MONEY: PROBLEMS FOR THE STUDENT

1. What is the value today of $10,000 paid in 7 years if the investor's desired rate of return is 7%?
2. What is the present value of $1 million to be received in 15 years if the investor's discount rate is 12%?
3. An investor has an opportunity to purchase an investment that will provide $10,000 at the end of the third year and $50,000 at the end of the fifth year. It is anticipated that the property may be sold at the end of the sixth year for $200,000. If the investor expects a 15% yield, what should he pay for the investment today?
4. To what amount will $1,000 accumulate in 10 years at 10% interest, with monthly payments?
5. Five thousand dollars is placed in a savings account today at 7% interest compounded monthly. An additional $10,000 will be placed in the account at the end of the sixth year. To what amount will the account have compounded at the end of the tenth year?
6. What is the monthly payment required for $100,000 to accumulate in a savings account at the end of the fifteenth year at 10% interest?
7. A lender makes a $100,000 mortgage at 9% interest, 25 years, with monthly payments.
   a. What is the monthly debt service required?
   b. What is the schedule for the principal and interest components of debt service for the first 3 months?
   c. What is the remaining mortgage balance at the end of the third year?
8. A borrower takes a loan for $250,000 for 30 years at 8% interest, with monthly payments. What are the monthly debt service payments?

9. An investor has a chance to purchase an apartment building that will provide estimated net operating income as shown in the following table. It will have an estimated resale value at the end of the third year of $38,000. If the investor wants a 12% return on the investment, what should be paid for the property?

End of Year	Payment
1	$12,000
2	10,500
3	25,500

10. Property under a step-up lease has the following payments due:

Year	Annual Rent, Paid at Beginning of Year
1–10	$50,000
11–15	55,000
16–20	75,000

When the lease terminates in 20 years, the market value is expected to be $600,000.

What is the justified investment price of the property if the investor expects an 18% rate of return?

11. An investor has an opportunity to purchase land for $50,000 and thinks it may be sold for $110,000 in 8 years. What is the internal rate of return, disregarding holding costs?

12. Land is expected to double in value in 10 years. What is the internal rate of return?

13. An investor has an opportunity to purchase a $10,000 annuity paid annually for 10 years for $60,000. What yield (IRR) will be received?

14. A property is available for $200,000 and is generating net operating income of $30,000. If the estimated resale value of the property in 7 years is $250,000,
   a. What yield will the investor receive?
   b. What portion of the $30,000 in periodic returns is return *of* investment and what part is return *on* investment?

15. A man purchased a commercial lot and is paying monthly interest only of $183.33. At an annual simple interest rate of 11%, what is the principal owed?

16. If you paid $30,000 for your house five years ago and its value has appreciated at an annual compound interest rate of 10%, what would it be worth today?

What will the purchasing power of $1 be worth 50 years from now if inflation continues at an annual compound rate of 6%?

17. You have been offered a 30% interest in a partnership that plans to net $100,000 on the sale of a property at the end of 4 years. What would

you pay for this interest if you wanted to earn 14% on your investment, compounded annually?

18. Some apartments that you own will need a complete renovation in 7 years. You estimate the total renovation cost to be $40,000. How much must you deposit monthly into an account earning 6%, compounded monthly, in order to have the money for renovation at the end of 7 years?

19. How much will you owe on a $55,000, 30-year mortgage at the end of 12 years, assuming a 12% interest rate compounded monthly?

   What percent of a mortgage will be unpaid at the end of 15 years on a 20-year mortgage? Assume a 10% annual interest rate with *annual* compounding.

20. A seller offers a small office building for the price of $100,000. The equity required from the buyer at closing is $30,000. Thus, the existing first-mortgage balance is $70,000. The existing mortgage is payable monthly for the 21 years remaining at an 8% interest rate. Negotiations occur. The seller agrees to take back a wraparound of $85,000, 10% interest rate for 21 years.

   a. Compute the true yield (IRR) on the wraparound mortgage to the seller. Assume that the full mortgage balances are repaid in accordance with their terms.

   b. Evaluate the transaction. Is it good from the seller's viewpoint? From the buyer's?

APPENDIX B
Selected Compound Interest Tables

6.00% MONTHLY COMPOUND INTEREST TABLES 6.00%
EFFECTIVE RATE 0.500

	1 AMOUNT OF $1 AT COMPOUND INTEREST	2 ACCUMULATION OF $1 PER PERIOD	3 SINKING FUND FACTOR	4 PRESENT VALUE REVERSION OF $1	5 PRESENT VALUE ORD. ANNUITY $1 PER PERIOD	6 INSTALMENT TO AMORTIZE $1	
MONTHS							
1	1.005000	1.000000	1.000000	0.995025	0.995025	1.005000	
2	1.010025	2.005000	0.498753	0.990075	1.985099	0.503753	
3	1.015075	3.015025	0.331672	0.985149	2.970248	0.336672	
4	1.020151	4.030100	0.248133	0.980248	3.950496	0.253133	
5	1.025251	5.050251	0.198010	0.975371	4.925866	0.203010	
6	1.030378	6.075502	0.164595	0.970518	5.896384	0.169595	
7	1.035529	7.105879	0.140729	0.965690	6.862074	0.145729	
8	1.040707	8.141409	0.122829	0.960885	7.822959	0.127829	
9	1.045911	9.182116	0.108907	0.956105	8.779064	0.113907	
10	1.051140	10.228026	0.097771	0.951348	9.730412	0.102771	
11	1.056396	11.279167	0.088659	0.946615	10.677027	0.093659	
12	1.061678	12.335562	0.081066	0.941905	11.618932	0.086066	
YEARS							MONTHS
1	1.061678	12.335562	0.081066	0.941905	11.618932	0.086066	12
2	1.127160	25.431955	0.039321	0.887186	22.562866	0.044321	24
3	1.196681	39.336105	0.025422	0.835645	32.871016	0.030422	36
4	1.270489	54.097832	0.018485	0.787098	42.580318	0.023485	48
5	1.348850	69.770031	0.014333	0.741372	51.725561	0.019333	60
6	1.432044	86.408856	0.011573	0.698302	60.339514	0.016573	72
7	1.520370	104.073927	0.009609	0.657735	68.453042	0.014609	84
8	1.614143	122.828542	0.008141	0.619524	76.095218	0.013141	96
9	1.713699	142.739900	0.007006	0.583533	83.293424	0.012006	108
10	1.819397	163.879347	0.006102	0.549633	90.073453	0.011102	120
11	1.931613	186.322629	0.005367	0.517702	96.459599	0.010367	132
12	2.050751	210.150163	0.004759	0.487626	102.474743	0.009759	144
13	2.177237	235.447328	0.004247	0.459298	108.140440	0.009247	156
14	2.311524	262.304766	0.003812	0.432615	113.476990	0.008812	168
15	2.454094	290.818712	0.003439	0.407482	118.503515	0.008439	180
16	2.605457	321.091337	0.003114	0.383810	123.238025	0.008114	192
17	2.766156	353.231110	0.002831	0.361513	127.697486	0.007831	204
18	2.936766	387.353194	0.002582	0.340511	131.897876	0.007582	216
19	3.117899	423.579854	0.002361	0.320729	135.854246	0.007361	228
20	3.310204	462.040895	0.002164	0.302096	139.580772	0.007164	240
21	3.514371	502.874129	0.001989	0.284546	143.090806	0.006989	252
22	3.731129	546.225867	0.001831	0.268015	146.396927	0.006831	264
23	3.961257	592.251446	0.001688	0.252445	149.510979	0.006688	276
24	4.205579	641.115782	0.001560	0.237779	152.444121	0.006560	288
25	4.464970	692.993962	0.001443	0.223966	155.206864	0.006443	300
26	4.740359	748.071876	0.001337	0.210954	157.809106	0.006337	312
27	5.032734	806.546875	0.001240	0.198699	160.260172	0.006240	324
28	5.343142	868.628484	0.001151	0.187156	162.568844	0.006151	336
29	5.672696	934.539150	0.001070	0.176283	164.743394	0.006070	348
30	6.022575	1004.515043	0.000996	0.166042	166.791614	0.005996	360
31	6.394034	1078.806895	0.000927	0.156396	168.720844	0.005927	372
32	6.788405	1157.680906	0.000864	0.147310	170.537996	0.005864	384
33	7.207098	1241.419693	0.000806	0.138752	172.249581	0.005806	396
34	7.651617	1330.323306	0.000752	0.130691	173.861732	0.005752	408
35	8.123551	1424.710299	0.000702	0.123099	175.380226	0.005702	420
36	8.624594	1524.918875	0.000656	0.115947	176.810504	0.005656	432
37	9.156540	1631.308097	0.000613	0.109212	178.157690	0.005613	444
38	9.721296	1744.259173	0.000573	0.102867	179.426611	0.005573	456
39	10.320884	1864.176825	0.000536	0.096891	180.621815	0.005536	468
40	10.957454	1991.490734	0.000502	0.091262	181.747584	0.005502	480

SOURCE: Paul Wendt and Alan R. Cerf, *Tables for Investment Analysis* (Center for Real Estate and Urban Economics, 1966; reprinted by the Institute of Business and Economic Research, 1977, 1979 and 1981, University of California, Berkeley).

6.00%   ANNUAL COMPOUND INTEREST TABLES   6.00%
                                     EFFECTIVE RATE 6.00

	1 AMOUNT OF $1 AT COMPOUND INTEREST	2 ACCUMULATION OF $1 PER PERIOD	3 SINKING FUND FACTOR	4 PRESENT VALUE REVERSION OF $1	5 PRESENT VALUE ORD. ANNUITY $1 PER PERIOD	6 INSTALMENT TO AMORTIZE $1
YEARS						
1	1.060000	1.000000	1.000000	0.943396	0.943396	1.060000
2	1.123600	2.060000	0.485437	0.889996	1.833393	0.545437
3	1.191016	3.183600	0.314110	0.839619	2.673012	0.374110
4	1.262477	4.374616	0.228591	0.792094	3.465106	0.288591
5	1.338226	5.637093	0.177396	0.747258	4.212364	0.237396
6	1.418519	6.975319	0.143363	0.704961	4.917324	0.203363
7	1.503630	8.393838	0.119135	0.665057	5.582381	0.179135
8	1.593848	9.897468	0.101036	0.627412	6.209794	0.161036
9	1.689479	11.491316	0.087022	0.591898	6.801692	0.147022
10	1.790848	13.180795	0.075868	0.558395	7.360087	0.135868
11	1.898299	14.971643	0.066793	0.526788	7.886875	0.126793
12	2.012196	16.869941	0.059277	0.496969	8.383844	0.119277
13	2.132928	18.882138	0.052960	0.468839	8.852683	0.112960
14	2.260904	21.015066	0.047585	0.442301	9.294984	0.107585
15	2.396558	23.275970	0.042963	0.417265	9.712249	0.102963
16	2.540352	25.672528	0.038952	0.393646	10.105895	0.098952
17	2.692773	28.212880	0.035445	0.371364	10.477260	0.095445
18	2.854339	30.905653	0.032357	0.350344	10.827603	0.092357
19	3.025600	33.759992	0.029621	0.330513	11.158116	0.089621
20	3.207135	36.785591	0.027185	0.311805	11.469921	0.087185
21	3.399564	39.992727	0.025005	0.294155	11.764077	0.085005
22	3.603537	43.392290	0.023046	0.277505	12.041582	0.083046
23	3.819750	46.995828	0.021278	0.261797	12.303379	0.081278
24	4.048935	50.815577	0.019679	0.246979	12.550358	0.079679
25	4.291871	54.864512	0.018227	0.232999	12.783356	0.078227
26	4.549383	59.156383	0.016904	0.219810	13.003166	0.076904
27	4.822346	63.705766	0.015697	0.207368	13.210534	0.075697
28	5.111687	68.528112	0.014593	0.195630	13.406164	0.074593
29	5.418388	73.639798	0.013580	0.184557	13.590721	0.073580
30	5.743491	79.058186	0.012649	0.174110	13.764831	0.072649
31	6.088101	84.801677	0.011792	0.164255	13.929086	0.071792
32	6.453387	90.889778	0.011002	0.154957	14.084043	0.071002
33	6.840590	97.343165	0.010273	0.146186	14.230230	0.070273
34	7.251025	104.183755	0.009598	0.137912	14.368141	0.069598
35	7.686087	111.434780	0.008974	0.130105	14.498246	0.068974
36	8.147252	119.120867	0.008395	0.122741	14.620987	0.068395
37	8.636087	127.268119	0.007857	0.115793	14.736780	0.067857
38	9.154252	135.904206	0.007358	0.109239	14.846019	0.067358
39	9.703507	145.058458	0.006894	0.103056	14.949075	0.066894
40	10.285718	154.761966	0.006462	0.097222	15.046297	0.066462
41	10.902861	165.047684	0.006059	0.091719	15.138016	0.066059
42	11.557033	175.950545	0.005683	0.086527	15.224543	0.065683
43	12.250455	187.507577	0.005333	0.081630	15.306173	0.065333
44	12.985482	199.758032	0.005006	0.077009	15.383182	0.065006
45	13.764611	212.743514	0.004700	0.072650	15.455832	0.064700
46	14.590487	226.508125	0.004415	0.068538	15.524370	0.064415
47	15.465917	241.098612	0.004148	0.064658	15.589028	0.064148
48	16.393872	256.564529	0.003898	0.060998	15.650027	0.063898
49	17.377504	272.958401	0.003664	0.057546	15.707572	0.063664
50	18.420154	290.335905	0.003444	0.054288	15.761861	0.063444

7.00%   MONTHLY COMPOUND INTEREST TABLES   7.00%
EFFECTIVE RATE 0.583

	1 AMOUNT OF $1 AT COMPOUND INTEREST	2 ACCUMULATION OF $1 PER PERIOD	3 SINKING FUND FACTOR	4 PRESENT VALUE REVERSION OF $1	5 PRESENT VALUE ORD. ANNUITY $1 PER PERIOD	6 INSTALMENT TO AMORTIZE $1	
MONTHS							
1	1.005833	1.000000	1.000000	0.994200	0.994200	1.005833	
2	1.011701	2.005833	0.498546	0.988435	1.982635	0.504379	
3	1.017602	3.017534	0.331396	0.982702	2.965337	0.337230	
4	1.023538	4.035136	0.247823	0.977003	3.942340	0.253656	
5	1.029509	5.058675	0.197680	0.971337	4.913677	0.203514	
6	1.035514	6.088184	0.164253	0.965704	5.879381	0.170086	
7	1.041555	7.123698	0.140377	0.960103	6.839484	0.146210	
8	1.047631	8.165253	0.122470	0.954535	7.794019	0.128304	
9	1.053742	9.212883	0.108544	0.948999	8.743018	0.114377	
10	1.059889	10.266625	0.097403	0.943495	9.686513	0.103236	
11	1.066071	11.326514	0.088288	0.938024	10.624537	0.094122	
12	1.072290	12.392585	0.080693	0.932583	11.557120	0.086527	
YEARS							**MONTHS**
1	1.072290	12.392585	0.080693	0.932583	11.557120	0.086527	12
2	1.149806	25.681032	0.038939	0.869712	22.335099	0.044773	24
3	1.232926	39.930101	0.025044	0.811079	32.386464	0.030877	36
4	1.322054	55.209236	0.018113	0.756399	41.760201	0.023946	48
5	1.417625	71.592902	0.013968	0.705405	50.501993	0.019801	60
6	1.520106	89.160944	0.011216	0.657849	58.654444	0.017049	72
7	1.629994	107.998981	0.009259	0.613499	66.257285	0.015093	84
8	1.747826	128.198821	0.007800	0.572139	73.347569	0.013634	96
9	1.874177	149.858909	0.006673	0.533568	79.959850	0.012506	108
10	2.009661	173.084807	0.005778	0.497596	86.126354	0.011611	120
11	2.154940	197.989707	0.005051	0.464050	91.877134	0.010884	132
12	2.310721	224.694985	0.004450	0.432765	97.240216	0.010284	144
13	2.477763	253.330789	0.003947	0.403590	102.241738	0.009781	156
14	2.656881	284.036677	0.003521	0.376381	106.906074	0.009354	168
15	2.848947	316.962297	0.003155	0.351007	111.255958	0.008988	180
16	3.054897	352.268112	0.002839	0.327343	115.312587	0.008672	192
17	3.275736	390.126188	0.002563	0.305275	119.095732	0.008397	204
18	3.512539	430.721027	0.002322	0.284694	122.623831	0.008155	216
19	3.766461	474.250470	0.002109	0.265501	125.914077	0.007942	228
20	4.038739	520.926660	0.001920	0.247602	128.982506	0.007753	240
21	4.330700	570.977075	0.001751	0.230910	131.844073	0.007585	252
22	4.643766	624.645640	0.001601	0.215342	134.512723	0.007434	264
23	4.979464	682.193909	0.001466	0.200825	137.001461	0.007299	276
24	5.334930	743.902347	0.001344	0.187286	139.322418	0.007178	288
25	5.725418	810.071693	0.001234	0.174660	141.486903	0.007068	300
26	6.139309	881.024426	0.001135	0.162885	143.505467	0.006968	312
27	6.583120	957.106339	0.001045	0.151904	145.387946	0.006878	324
28	7.059015	1038.688219	0.000963	0.141663	147.143515	0.006796	336
29	7.569311	1126.167659	0.000888	0.132112	148.780729	0.006721	348
30	8.116497	1219.970996	0.000820	0.123206	150.307568	0.006653	360
31	8.703240	1320.555383	0.000757	0.114900	151.731473	0.006591	372
32	9.332398	1428.411024	0.000700	0.107154	153.059383	0.006533	384
33	10.007037	1544.063557	0.000648	0.099930	154.297770	0.006481	396
34	10.730447	1668.076622	0.000599	0.093193	155.452669	0.006433	408
35	11.506152	1801.054601	0.000555	0.086910	156.529709	0.006389	420
36	12.337932	1943.645569	0.000514	0.081051	157.534139	0.006348	432
37	13.229843	2096.544450	0.000477	0.075587	158.470853	0.006310	444
38	14.186229	2260.496403	0.000442	0.070491	159.344418	0.006276	456
39	15.211753	2436.300456	0.000410	0.065739	160.159090	0.006244	468
40	16.311411	2624.813398	0.000381	0.061307	160.918839	0.006214	480

7.00%   ANNUAL COMPOUND INTEREST TABLES   7.00%
                              EFFECTIVE RATE 7.00

	1 AMOUNT OF $1 AT COMPOUND INTEREST	2 ACCUMULATION OF $1 PER PERIOD	3 SINKING FUND FACTOR	4 PRESENT VALUE REVERSION OF $1	5 PRESENT VALUE ORD. ANNUITY $1 PER PERIOD	6 INSTALMENT TO AMORTIZE $1
YEARS						
1	1.070000	1.000000	1.000000	0.934579	0.934579	1.070000
2	1.144900	2.070000	0.483092	0.873439	1.808018	0.553092
3	1.225043	3.214900	0.311052	0.816298	2.624316	0.381052
4	1.310796	4.439943	0.225228	0.762895	3.387211	0.295228
5	1.402552	5.750739	0.173891	0.712986	4.100197	0.243891
6	1.500730	7.153291	0.139796	0.666342	4.766540	0.209796
7	1.605781	8.654021	0.115553	0.622750	5.389289	0.185553
8	1.718186	10.259803	0.097468	0.582009	5.971299	0.167468
9	1.838459	11.977989	0.083486	0.543934	6.515232	0.153486
10	1.967151	13.816448	0.072378	0.508349	7.023582	0.142378
11	2.104852	15.783599	0.063357	0.475093	7.498674	0.133357
12	2.252192	17.888451	0.055902	0.444012	7.942686	0.125902
13	2.409845	20.140643	0.049651	0.414964	8.357651	0.119651
14	2.578534	22.550488	0.044345	0.387817	8.745468	0.114345
15	2.759032	25.129022	0.039795	0.362446	9.107914	0.109795
16	2.952164	27.888054	0.035858	0.338735	9.446649	0.105858
17	3.158815	30.840217	0.032425	0.316574	9.763223	0.102425
18	3.379932	33.999033	0.029413	0.295864	10.059087	0.099413
19	3.616528	37.378965	0.026753	0.276753	10.335595	0.096753
20	3.869684	40.995492	0.024393	0.258419	10.594014	0.094393
21	4.140562	44.865177	0.022289	0.241513	10.835527	0.092289
22	4.430402	49.005739	0.020406	0.225713	11.061240	0.090406
23	4.740530	53.436141	0.018714	0.210947	11.272187	0.088714
24	5.072367	58.176671	0.017189	0.197147	11.469334	0.087189
25	5.427433	63.249038	0.015811	0.184249	11.653583	0.085811
26	5.807353	68.676470	0.014561	0.172195	11.825779	0.084561
27	6.213868	74.483823	0.013426	0.160930	11.986709	0.083426
28	6.648838	80.697691	0.012392	0.150402	12.137111	0.082392
29	7.114257	87.346529	0.011449	0.140563	12.277674	0.081449
30	7.612255	94.460786	0.010586	0.131367	12.409041	0.080586
31	8.145113	102.073041	0.009797	0.122773	12.531814	0.079797
32	8.715271	110.218154	0.009073	0.114741	12.646555	0.079073
33	9.325340	118.933425	0.008408	0.107235	12.753790	0.078408
34	9.978114	128.258765	0.007797	0.100219	12.854009	0.077797
35	10.676581	138.236878	0.007234	0.093663	12.947672	0.077234
36	11.423942	148.913460	0.006715	0.087535	13.035208	0.076715
37	12.223618	160.337402	0.006237	0.081809	13.117017	0.076237
38	13.079271	172.561020	0.005795	0.076457	13.193473	0.075795
39	13.994820	185.640292	0.005387	0.071455	13.264928	0.075387
40	14.974458	199.635112	0.005009	0.066780	13.331709	0.075009
41	16.022670	214.609570	0.004660	0.062412	13.394120	0.074660
42	17.144257	230.632240	0.004336	0.058329	13.452449	0.074336
43	18.344355	247.776496	0.004036	0.054513	13.506962	0.074036
44	19.628460	266.120851	0.003758	0.050946	13.557908	0.073758
45	21.002452	285.749311	0.003500	0.047613	13.605522	0.073500
46	22.472623	306.751763	0.003260	0.044499	13.650020	0.073260
47	24.045707	329.224386	0.003037	0.041587	13.691608	0.073037
48	25.728907	353.270093	0.002831	0.038867	13.730474	0.072831
49	27.529930	378.999000	0.002639	0.036324	13.766799	0.072639
50	29.457025	406.528929	0.002460	0.033948	13.800746	0.072460

8.00%   MONTHLY COMPOUND INTEREST TABLES   8.00%
                              EFFECTIVE RATE 0.667

	1 AMOUNT OF $1 AT COMPOUND INTEREST	2 ACCUMULATION OF $1 PER PERIOD	3 SINKING FUND FACTOR	4 PRESENT VALUE REVERSION OF $1	5 PRESENT VALUE ORD. ANNUITY $1 PER PERIOD	6 INSTALMENT TO AMORTIZE $1	
MONTHS							
1	1.006667	1.000000	1.000000	0.993377	0.993377	1.006667	
2	1.013378	2.006667	0.498339	0.986799	1.980176	0.505006	
3	1.020134	3.020044	0.331121	0.980264	2.960440	0.337788	
4	1.026935	4.040178	0.247514	0.973772	3.934212	0.254181	
5	1.033781	5.067113	0.197351	0.967323	4.901535	0.204018	
6	1.040673	6.100893	0.163910	0.960917	5.862452	0.170577	
7	1.047610	7.141566	0.140025	0.954553	6.817005	0.146692	
8	1.054595	8.189176	0.122112	0.948232	7.765237	0.128779	
9	1.061625	9.243771	0.108181	0.941952	8.707189	0.114848	
10	1.068703	10.305396	0.097037	0.935714	9.642903	0.103703	
11	1.075827	11.374099	0.087919	0.929517	10.572420	0.094586	
12	1.083000	12.449926	0.080322	0.923361	11.495782	0.086988	
YEARS							**MONTHS**
1	1.083000	12.449926	0.080322	0.923361	11.495782	0.086988	12
2	1.172888	25.933190	0.038561	0.852596	22.110544	0.045227	24
3	1.270237	40.535558	0.024670	0.787255	31.911806	0.031336	36
4	1.375666	56.349915	0.017746	0.726921	40.961913	0.024413	48
5	1.489846	73.476856	0.013610	0.671210	49.318433	0.020276	60
6	1.613502	92.025325	0.010867	0.619770	57.034522	0.017533	72
7	1.747422	112.113308	0.008920	0.572272	64.159261	0.015586	84
8	1.892457	133.868583	0.007470	0.528414	70.737970	0.014137	96
9	2.049530	157.429535	0.006352	0.487917	76.812497	0.013019	108
10	2.219640	182.946035	0.005466	0.450523	82.421481	0.012133	120
11	2.403869	210.580392	0.004749	0.415996	87.600600	0.011415	132
12	2.603389	240.508387	0.004158	0.384115	92.382800	0.010825	144
13	2.819469	272.920390	0.003664	0.354677	96.798498	0.010331	156
14	3.053484	308.022574	0.003247	0.327495	100.875784	0.009913	168
15	3.306921	346.038222	0.002890	0.302396	104.640592	0.009557	180
16	3.581394	387.209149	0.002583	0.279221	108.116871	0.009249	192
17	3.878648	431.797244	0.002316	0.257822	111.326733	0.008983	204
18	4.200574	480.086128	0.002083	0.238063	114.290596	0.008750	216
19	4.549220	532.382966	0.001878	0.219818	117.027313	0.008545	228
20	4.926803	589.020416	0.001698	0.202971	119.554292	0.008364	240
21	5.335725	650.358746	0.001538	0.187416	121.887606	0.008204	252
22	5.778588	716.788127	0.001395	0.173053	124.042099	0.008062	264
23	6.258207	788.731114	0.001268	0.159790	126.031475	0.007935	276
24	6.777636	866.645333	0.001154	0.147544	127.868388	0.007821	288
25	7.340176	951.026395	0.001051	0.136237	129.564523	0.007718	300
26	7.949407	1042.411042	0.000959	0.125796	131.130668	0.007626	312
27	8.609204	1141.380571	0.000876	0.116155	132.576786	0.007543	324
28	9.323763	1248.564521	0.000801	0.107253	133.912076	0.007468	336
29	10.097631	1364.644687	0.000733	0.099033	135.145031	0.007399	348
30	10.935730	1490.359449	0.000671	0.091443	136.283494	0.007338	360
31	11.843390	1626.508474	0.000615	0.084435	137.334707	0.007281	372
32	12.826385	1773.957801	0.000564	0.077964	138.305357	0.007230	384
33	13.890969	1933.645350	0.000517	0.071989	139.201617	0.007184	396
34	15.043913	2106.586886	0.000475	0.066472	140.029190	0.007141	408
35	16.292550	2293.882485	0.000436	0.061378	140.793338	0.007103	420
36	17.644824	2496.723526	0.000401	0.056674	141.498923	0.007067	432
37	19.109335	2716.400273	0.000368	0.052330	142.150433	0.007035	444
38	20.695401	2954.310082	0.000338	0.048320	142.752013	0.007005	456
39	22.413109	3211.966288	0.000311	0.044617	143.307488	0.006978	468
40	24.273386	3491.007831	0.000286	0.041197	143.820392	0.006953	480

	1 AMOUNT OF $1 AT COMPOUND INTEREST	2 ACCUMULATION OF $1 PER PERIOD	3 SINKING FUND FACTOR	4 PRESENT VALUE REVERSION OF $1	5 PRESENT VALUE ORD. ANNUITY $1 PER PERIOD	6 INSTALMENT TO AMORTIZE $1
YEARS						
1	1.080000	1.000000	1.000000	0.925926	0.925926	1.080000
2	1.166400	2.080000	0.480769	0.857339	1.783265	0.560769
3	1.259712	3.246400	0.308034	0.793832	2.577097	0.388034
4	1.360489	4.506112	0.221921	0.735030	3.312127	0.301921
5	1.469328	5.866601	0.170456	0.680583	3.992710	0.250456
6	1.586874	7.335929	0.136315	0.630170	4.622880	0.216315
7	1.713824	8.922803	0.112072	0.583490	5.206370	0.192072
8	1.850930	10.636628	0.094015	0.540269	5.746639	0.174015
9	1.999005	12.487558	0.080080	0.500249	6.246888	0.160080
10	2.158925	14.486562	0.069029	0.463193	6.710081	0.149029
11	2.331639	16.645487	0.060076	0.428883	7.138964	0.140076
12	2.518170	18.977126	0.052695	0.397114	7.536078	0.132695
13	2.719624	21.495297	0.046522	0.367698	7.903776	0.126522
14	2.937194	24.214920	0.041297	0.340461	8.244237	0.121297
15	3.172169	27.152114	0.036830	0.315242	8.559479	0.116830
16	3.425943	30.324283	0.032977	0.291890	8.851369	0.112977
17	3.700018	33.750226	0.029629	0.270269	9.121638	0.109629
18	3.996019	37.450244	0.026702	0.250249	9.371887	0.106702
19	4.315701	41.446263	0.024128	0.231712	9.603599	0.104128
20	4.660957	45.761964	0.021852	0.214548	9.818147	0.101852
21	5.033834	50.422921	0.019832	0.198656	10.016803	0.099832
22	5.436540	55.456755	0.018032	0.183941	10.200744	0.098032
23	5.871464	60.893296	0.016422	0.170315	10.371059	0.096422
24	6.341181	66.764759	0.014978	0.157699	10.528758	0.094978
25	6.848475	73.105940	0.013679	0.146018	10.674776	0.093679
26	7.396353	79.954415	0.012507	0.135202	10.809978	0.092507
27	7.988061	87.350768	0.011448	0.125187	10.935165	0.091448
28	8.627106	95.338830	0.010489	0.115914	11.051078	0.090489
29	9.317275	103.965936	0.009619	0.107328	11.158406	0.089619
30	10.062657	113.283211	0.008827	0.099377	11.257783	0.088827
31	10.867669	123.345868	0.008107	0.092016	11.349799	0.088107
32	11.737083	134.213537	0.007451	0.085200	11.434999	0.087451
33	12.676050	145.950620	0.006852	0.078889	11.513888	0.086852
34	13.690134	158.626670	0.006304	0.073045	11.586934	0.086304
35	14.785344	172.316804	0.005803	0.067635	11.654568	0.085803
36	15.968172	187.102148	0.005345	0.062625	11.717193	0.085345
37	17.245626	203.070320	0.004924	0.057986	11.775179	0.084924
38	18.625276	220.315945	0.004539	0.053690	11.828869	0.084539
39	20.115298	238.941221	0.004185	0.049713	11.878582	0.084185
40	21.724521	259.056519	0.003860	0.046031	11.924613	0.083860
41	23.462483	280.781040	0.003561	0.042621	11.967235	0.083561
42	25.339482	304.243523	0.003287	0.039464	12.006699	0.083287
43	27.366640	329.583005	0.003034	0.036541	12.043240	0.083034
44	29.555972	356.949646	0.002802	0.033834	12.077074	0.082802
45	31.920449	386.505617	0.002587	0.031328	12.108402	0.082587
46	34.474085	418.426067	0.002390	0.029007	12.137409	0.082390
47	37.232012	452.900152	0.002208	0.026859	12.164267	0.082208
48	40.210573	490.132164	0.002040	0.024869	12.189136	0.082040
49	43.427419	530.342737	0.001886	0.023027	12.212163	0.081886
50	46.901613	573.770156	0.001743	0.021321	12.233485	0.081743

9.00%   MONTHLY COMPOUND INTEREST TABLES   9.00%
                                        EFFECTIVE RATE 0.750

	1	2	3	4	5	6
	AMOUNT OF $1 AT COMPOUND INTEREST	ACCUMULATION OF $1 PER PERIOD	SINKING FUND FACTOR	PRESENT VALUE REVERSION OF $1	PRESENT VALUE ORD. ANNUITY $1 PER PERIOD	INSTALMENT TO AMORTIZE $1

MONTHS
1	1.007500	1.000000	1.000000	0.992556	0.992556	1.007500
2	1.015056	2.007500	0.498132	0.985167	1.977723	0.505632
3	1.022669	3.022556	0.330846	0.977833	2.955556	0.338346
4	1.030339	4.045225	0.247205	0.970554	3.926110	0.254705
5	1.038067	5.075565	0.197022	0.963329	4.889440	0.204522
6	1.045852	6.113631	0.163569	0.956158	5.845598	0.171069
7	1.053696	7.159484	0.139675	0.949040	6.794638	0.147175
8	1.061599	8.213180	0.121756	0.941975	7.736613	0.129256
9	1.069561	9.274779	0.107819	0.934963	8.671576	0.115319
10	1.077583	10.344339	0.096671	0.928003	9.599580	0.104171
11	1.085664	11.421922	0.087551	0.921095	10.520675	0.095051
12	1.093807	12.507586	0.079951	0.914238	11.434913	0.087451

YEARS   MONTHS
1	1.093807	12.507586	0.079951	0.914238	11.434913	0.087451	12
2	1.196414	26.188471	0.038185	0.835831	21.889146	0.045685	24
3	1.308645	41.152716	0.024300	0.764149	31.446805	0.031800	36
4	1.431405	57.520711	0.017385	0.698614	40.184782	0.024885	48
5	1.565681	75.424137	0.013258	0.638700	48.173374	0.020758	60
6	1.712553	95.007028	0.010526	0.583924	55.476849	0.018026	72
7	1.873202	116.426928	0.008589	0.533845	62.153965	0.016089	84
8	2.048921	139.856164	0.007150	0.488062	68.258439	0.014650	96
9	2.241124	165.483223	0.006043	0.446205	73.839382	0.013543	108
10	2.451357	193.514277	0.005168	0.407937	78.941693	0.012668	120
11	2.681311	224.174837	0.004461	0.372952	83.606420	0.011961	132
12	2.932837	257.711570	0.003880	0.340967	87.871092	0.011380	144
13	3.207957	294.394279	0.003397	0.311725	91.770018	0.010897	156
14	3.508886	334.518079	0.002989	0.284991	95.334564	0.010489	168
15	3.838043	378.405769	0.002643	0.260549	98.593409	0.010143	180
16	4.198078	426.410427	0.002345	0.238204	101.572769	0.009845	192
17	4.591887	478.918252	0.002088	0.217775	104.296613	0.009588	204
18	5.022638	536.351674	0.001864	0.199099	106.786856	0.009364	216
19	5.493796	599.172247	0.001669	0.182024	109.063531	0.009169	228
20	6.009152	667.886870	0.001497	0.166413	111.144954	0.008997	240
21	6.572851	743.046852	0.001346	0.152141	113.047870	0.008846	252
22	7.189430	825.257358	0.001212	0.139093	114.787589	0.008712	264
23	7.863848	915.179777	0.001093	0.127164	116.378106	0.008593	276
24	8.601532	1013.537539	0.000987	0.116258	117.832218	0.008487	288
25	9.408415	1121.121937	0.000892	0.106288	119.161622	0.008392	300
26	10.290989	1238.798494	0.000807	0.097172	120.377014	0.008307	312
27	11.256354	1367.513924	0.000731	0.088839	121.488172	0.008231	324
28	12.312278	1508.303750	0.000663	0.081220	122.504035	0.008163	336
29	13.467255	1662.300631	0.000602	0.074254	123.432776	0.008102	348
30	14.730576	1830.743483	0.000546	0.067886	124.281866	0.008046	360
31	16.112406	2014.987436	0.000496	0.062064	125.058136	0.007996	372
32	17.623861	2216.514743	0.000451	0.056741	125.767832	0.007951	384
33	19.277100	2436.946701	0.000410	0.051875	126.416664	0.007910	396
34	21.085425	2678.056697	0.000373	0.047426	127.009850	0.007873	408
35	23.063384	2941.784473	0.000340	0.043359	127.552164	0.007840	420
36	25.226888	3230.251735	0.000310	0.039640	128.047967	0.007810	432
37	27.593344	3545.779215	0.000282	0.036241	128.501250	0.007782	444
38	30.181790	3890.905350	0.000257	0.033133	128.915659	0.007757	456
39	33.013050	4268.406696	0.000234	0.030291	129.294526	0.007734	468
40	36.109902	4681.320272	0.000214	0.027693	129.640902	0.007714	480

	1 AMOUNT OF $1 AT COMPOUND INTEREST	2 ACCUMULATION OF $1 PER PERIOD	3 SINKING FUND FACTOR	4 PRESENT VALUE REVERSION OF $1	5 PRESENT VALUE ORD. ANNUITY $1 PER PERIOD	6 INSTALMENT TO AMORTIZE $1
YEARS						
1	1.090000	1.000000	1.000000	0.917431	0.917431	1.090000
2	1.188100	2.090000	0.478469	0.841680	1.759111	0.568469
3	1.295029	3.278100	0.305055	0.772183	2.531295	0.395055
4	1.411582	4.573129	0.218669	0.708425	3.239720	0.308669
5	1.538624	5.984711	0.167092	0.649931	3.889651	0.257092
6	1.677100	7.523335	0.132920	0.596267	4.485919	0.222920
7	1.828039	9.200435	0.108691	0.547034	5.032953	0.198691
8	1.992563	11.028474	0.090674	0.501866	5.534819	0.180674
9	2.171893	13.021036	0.076799	0.460428	5.995247	0.166799
10	2.367364	15.192930	0.065820	0.422411	6.417658	0.155820
11	2.580426	17.560293	0.056947	0.387533	6.805191	0.146947
12	2.812665	20.140720	0.049651	0.355535	7.160725	0.139651
13	3.065805	22.953385	0.043567	0.326179	7.486904	0.133567
14	3.341727	26.019189	0.038433	0.299246	7.786150	0.128433
15	3.642482	29.360916	0.034059	0.274538	8.060688	0.124059
16	3.970306	33.003399	0.030300	0.251870	8.312558	0.120300
17	4.327633	36.973705	0.027046	0.231073	8.543631	0.117046
18	4.717120	41.301338	0.024212	0.211994	8.755625	0.114212
19	5.141661	46.018458	0.021730	0.194490	8.950115	0.111730
20	5.604411	51.160120	0.019546	0.178431	9.128546	0.109546
21	6.108808	56.764530	0.017617	0.163698	9.292244	0.107617
22	6.658600	62.873338	0.015905	0.150182	9.442425	0.105905
23	7.257874	69.531939	0.014382	0.137781	9.580207	0.104382
24	7.911083	76.789813	0.013023	0.126405	9.706612	0.103023
25	8.623081	84.700896	0.011806	0.115968	9.822580	0.101806
26	9.399158	93.323977	0.010715	0.106393	9.928972	0.100715
27	10.245082	102.723135	0.009735	0.097608	10.026580	0.099735
28	11.167140	112.968217	0.008852	0.089548	10.116128	0.098852
29	12.172182	124.135356	0.008056	0.082155	10.198283	0.098056
30	13.267678	136.307539	0.007336	0.075371	10.273654	0.097336
31	14.461770	149.575217	0.006686	0.069148	10.342802	0.096686
32	15.763329	164.036987	0.006096	0.063438	10.406240	0.096096
33	17.182028	179.800315	0.005562	0.058200	10.464441	0.095562
34	18.728411	196.982344	0.005077	0.053395	10.517835	0.095077
35	20.413968	215.710755	0.004636	0.048986	10.566821	0.094636
36	22.251225	236.124723	0.004235	0.044941	10.611763	0.094235
37	24.253835	258.375948	0.003870	0.041231	10.652993	0.093870
38	26.436680	282.629783	0.003538	0.037826	10.690820	0.093538
39	28.815982	309.066463	0.003236	0.034703	10.725523	0.093236
40	31.409420	337.882445	0.002960	0.031838	10.757360	0.092960
41	34.236268	369.291865	0.002708	0.029209	10.786569	0.092708
42	37.317532	403.528133	0.002478	0.026797	10.813366	0.092478
43	40.676110	440.845665	0.002268	0.024584	10.837950	0.092268
44	44.336960	481.521775	0.002077	0.022555	10.860505	0.092077
45	48.327286	525.858734	0.001902	0.020692	10.881197	0.091902
46	52.676742	574.186021	0.001742	0.018984	10.900181	0.091742
47	57.417649	626.862762	0.001595	0.017416	10.917597	0.091595
48	62.585237	684.280411	0.001461	0.015978	10.933575	0.091461
49	68.217908	746.865648	0.001339	0.014659	10.948234	0.091339
50	74.357520	815.083556	0.001227	0.013449	10.961683	0.091227

10.00%   MONTHLY COMPOUND INTEREST TABLES   10.00%
                                   EFFECTIVE RATE 0.833

	1 AMOUNT OF $1 AT COMPOUND INTEREST	2 ACCUMULATION OF $1 PER PERIOD	3 SINKING FUND FACTOR	4 PRESENT VALUE REVERSION OF $1	5 PRESENT VALUE ORD. ANNUITY $1 PER PERIOD	6 INSTALMENT TO AMORTIZE $1	
MONTHS							
1	1.008333	1.000000	1.000000	0.991736	0.991736	1.008333	
2	1.016736	2.008333	0.497925	0.983539	1.975275	0.506259	
3	1.025209	3.025069	0.330571	0.975411	2.950686	0.338904	
4	1.033752	4.050278	0.246897	0.967350	3.918036	0.255230	
5	1.042367	5.084031	0.196694	0.959355	4.877391	0.205028	
6	1.051053	6.126398	0.163228	0.951427	5.828817	0.171561	
7	1.059812	7.177451	0.139325	0.943563	6.772381	0.147659	
8	1.068644	8.237263	0.121400	0.935765	7.708146	0.129733	
9	1.077549	9.305907	0.107459	0.928032	8.636178	0.115792	
10	1.086529	10.383456	0.096307	0.920362	9.556540	0.104640	
11	1.095583	11.469985	0.087184	0.912756	10.469296	0.095517	
12	1.104713	12.565568	0.079583	0.905212	11.374508	0.087916	
YEARS							**MONTHS**
1	1.104713	12.565568	0.079583	0.905212	11.374508	0.087916	12
2	1.220391	26.446915	0.037812	0.819410	21.670855	0.046145	24
3	1.348182	41.781821	0.023934	0.741740	30.991236	0.032267	36
4	1.489354	58.722492	0.017029	0.671432	39.428160	0.025363	48
5	1.645309	77.437072	0.012914	0.607789	47.065369	0.021247	60
6	1.817594	98.111314	0.010193	0.550178	53.978665	0.018526	72
7	2.007920	120.950418	0.008268	0.498028	60.236667	0.016601	84
8	2.218176	146.181076	0.006841	0.450821	65.901488	0.015174	96
9	2.450448	174.053713	0.005745	0.408089	71.029355	0.014079	108
10	2.707041	204.844979	0.004882	0.369407	75.671163	0.013215	120
11	2.990504	238.860493	0.004187	0.334392	79.872986	0.012520	132
12	3.303649	276.437876	0.003617	0.302696	83.676528	0.011951	144
13	3.649584	317.950102	0.003145	0.274004	87.119542	0.011478	156
14	4.031743	363.809201	0.002749	0.248032	90.236201	0.011082	168
15	4.453920	414.470346	0.002413	0.224521	93.057439	0.010746	180
16	4.920303	470.436376	0.002126	0.203240	95.611259	0.010459	192
17	5.435523	532.262780	0.001879	0.183975	97.923008	0.010212	204
18	6.004693	600.563216	0.001665	0.166536	100.015633	0.009998	216
19	6.633463	676.015601	0.001479	0.150751	101.909902	0.009813	228
20	7.328074	759.368836	0.001317	0.136462	103.624619	0.009650	240
21	8.095419	851.450244	0.001174	0.123527	105.176801	0.009508	252
22	8.943115	953.173779	0.001049	0.111818	106.581856	0.009382	264
23	9.879576	1065.549097	0.000938	0.101219	107.853730	0.009272	276
24	10.914097	1189.691580	0.000841	0.091625	109.005045	0.009174	288
25	12.056945	1326.833403	0.000754	0.082940	110.047230	0.009087	300
26	13.319465	1478.335767	0.000676	0.075078	110.990629	0.009010	312
27	14.714187	1645.702407	0.000608	0.067962	111.844605	0.008941	324
28	16.254954	1830.594523	0.000546	0.061520	112.617635	0.008880	336
29	17.957060	2034.847259	0.000491	0.055688	113.317392	0.008825	348
30	19.837399	2260.487925	0.000442	0.050410	113.950820	0.008776	360
31	21.914634	2509.756117	0.000398	0.045632	114.524207	0.008732	372
32	24.209383	2785.125947	0.000359	0.041306	115.043244	0.008692	384
33	26.744422	3089.330596	0.000324	0.037391	115.513083	0.008657	396
34	29.544912	3425.389448	0.000292	0.033847	115.938387	0.008625	408
35	32.638650	3796.638052	0.000263	0.030639	116.323377	0.008597	420
36	36.056344	4206.761236	0.000238	0.027734	116.671876	0.008571	432
37	39.831914	4659.829677	0.000215	0.025105	116.987340	0.008548	444
38	44.002836	5160.340305	0.000194	0.022726	117.272903	0.008527	456
39	48.610508	5713.260935	0.000175	0.020572	117.531398	0.008508	468
40	53.700663	6324.079581	0.000158	0.018622	117.765391	0.008491	480

10.00%   ANNUAL COMPOUND INTEREST TABLES   10.00%
                                        EFFECTIVE RATE 10.00

	1 AMOUNT OF $1 AT COMPOUND INTEREST	2 ACCUMULATION OF $1 PER PERIOD	3 SINKING FUND FACTOR	4 PRESENT VALUE REVERSION OF $1	5 PRESENT VALUE ORD. ANNUITY $1 PER PERIOD	6 INSTALMENT TO AMORTIZE $1
YEARS						
1	1.100000	1.000000	1.000000	0.909091	0.909091	1.100000
2	1.210000	2.100000	0.476190	0.826446	1.735537	0.576190
3	1.331000	3.310000	0.302115	0.751315	2.486852	0.402115
4	1.464100	4.641000	0.215471	0.683013	3.169865	0.315471
5	1.610510	6.105100	0.163797	0.620921	3.790787	0.263797
6	1.771561	7.715610	0.129607	0.564474	4.355261	0.229607
7	1.948717	9.487171	0.105405	0.513158	4.868419	0.205405
8	2.143589	11.435888	0.087444	0.466507	5.334926	0.187444
9	2.357948	13.579477	0.073641	0.424098	5.759024	0.173641
10	2.593742	15.937425	0.062745	0.385543	6.144567	0.162745
11	2.853117	18.531167	0.053963	0.350494	6.495061	0.153963
12	3.138428	21.384284	0.046763	0.318631	6.813692	0.146763
13	3.452271	24.522712	0.040779	0.289664	7.103356	0.140779
14	3.797498	27.974983	0.035746	0.263331	7.366687	0.135746
15	4.177248	31.772482	0.031474	0.239392	7.606080	0.131474
16	4.594973	35.949730	0.027817	0.217629	7.823709	0.127817
17	5.054470	40.544703	0.024664	0.197845	8.021553	0.124664
18	5.559917	45.599173	0.021930	0.179859	8.201412	0.121930
19	6.115909	51.159090	0.019547	0.163508	8.364920	0.119547
20	6.727500	57.274999	0.017460	0.148644	8.513564	0.117460
21	7.400250	64.002499	0.015624	0.135131	8.648694	0.115624
22	8.140275	71.402749	0.014005	0.122846	8.771540	0.114005
23	8.954302	79.543024	0.012572	0.111678	8.883218	0.112572
24	9.849733	88.497327	0.011300	0.101526	8.984744	0.111300
25	10.834706	98.347059	0.010168	0.092296	9.077040	0.110168
26	11.918177	109.181765	0.009159	0.083905	9.160945	0.109159
27	13.109994	121.099942	0.008258	0.076278	9.237223	0.108258
28	14.420994	134.209936	0.007451	0.069343	9.306567	0.107451
29	15.863093	148.630930	0.006728	0.063039	9.369606	0.106728
30	17.449402	164.494023	0.006079	0.057309	9.426914	0.106079
31	19.194342	181.943425	0.005496	0.052099	9.479013	0.105496
32	21.113777	201.137767	0.004972	0.047362	9.526376	0.104972
33	23.225154	222.251544	0.004499	0.043057	9.569432	0.104499
34	25.547670	245.476699	0.004074	0.039143	9.608575	0.104074
35	28.102437	271.024368	0.003690	0.035584	9.644159	0.103690
36	30.912681	299.126805	0.003343	0.032349	9.676508	0.103343
37	34.003949	330.039486	0.003030	0.029408	9.705917	0.103030
38	37.404343	364.043434	0.002747	0.026735	9.732651	0.102747
39	41.144778	401.447778	0.002491	0.024304	9.756956	0.102491
40	45.259256	442.592556	0.002259	0.022095	9.779051	0.102259
41	49.785181	487.851811	0.002050	0.020086	9.799137	0.102050
42	54.763699	537.636992	0.001860	0.018260	9.817397	0.101860
43	60.240069	592.400692	0.001688	0.016600	9.833998	0.101688
44	66.264076	652.640761	0.001532	0.015091	9.849089	0.101532
45	72.890484	718.904837	0.001391	0.013719	9.862808	0.101391
46	80.179532	791.795321	0.001263	0.012472	9.875280	0.101263
47	88.197485	871.974853	0.001147	0.011338	9.886618	0.101147
48	97.017234	960.172338	0.001041	0.010307	9.896926	0.101041
49	106.718957	1057.189572	0.000946	0.009370	9.906296	0.100946
50	117.390853	1163.908529	0.000859	0.008519	9.914814	0.100859

11.00%   MONTHLY COMPOUND INTEREST TABLES   11.00%
                               EFFECTIVE RATE 0.917

	1 AMOUNT OF $1 AT COMPOUND INTEREST	2 ACCUMULATION OF $1 PER PERIOD	3 SINKING FUND FACTOR	4 PRESENT VALUE REVERSION OF $1	5 PRESENT VALUE ORD. ANNUITY $1 PER PERIOD	6 INSTALMENT TO AMORTIZE $1	
MONTHS							
1	1.009167	1.000000	1.000000	0.990917	0.990917	1.009167	
2	1.018417	2.009167	0.497719	0.981916	1.972832	0.506885	
3	1.027753	3.027584	0.330296	0.972997	2.945829	0.339463	
4	1.037174	4.055337	0.246589	0.964158	3.909987	0.255755	
5	1.046681	5.092511	0.196367	0.955401	4.865388	0.205533	
6	1.056276	6.139192	0.162888	0.946722	5.812110	0.172055	
7	1.065958	7.195468	0.138976	0.938123	6.750233	0.148143	
8	1.075730	8.261427	0.121044	0.929602	7.679835	0.130211	
9	1.085591	9.337156	0.107099	0.921158	8.600992	0.116266	
10	1.095542	10.422747	0.095944	0.912790	9.513783	0.105111	
11	1.105584	11.518289	0.086818	0.904499	10.418282	0.095985	
12	1.115719	12.623873	0.079215	0.896283	11.314565	0.088382	
YEARS							MONTHS
1	1.115719	12.623873	0.079215	0.896283	11.314565	0.088382	12
2	1.244829	26.708566	0.037441	0.803323	21.455619	0.046608	24
3	1.388879	42.423123	0.023572	0.720005	30.544874	0.032739	36
4	1.549598	59.956151	0.016679	0.645329	38.691421	0.025846	48
5	1.728916	79.518080	0.012576	0.578397	45.993034	0.021742	60
6	1.928984	101.343692	0.009867	0.518408	52.537346	0.019034	72
7	2.152204	125.694940	0.007956	0.464640	58.402903	0.017122	84
8	2.401254	152.864085	0.006542	0.416449	63.660103	0.015708	96
9	2.679124	183.177212	0.005459	0.373256	68.372043	0.014626	108
10	2.989150	216.998139	0.004608	0.334543	72.595275	0.013775	120
11	3.335051	254.732784	0.003926	0.299846	76.380487	0.013092	132
12	3.720979	296.834038	0.003369	0.268747	79.773109	0.012536	144
13	4.151566	343.807200	0.002909	0.240863	82.813859	0.012075	156
14	4.631980	396.216042	0.002524	0.215890	85.539231	0.011691	168
15	5.167988	454.689575	0.002199	0.193499	87.981937	0.011366	180
16	5.766021	519.929596	0.001923	0.173430	90.171293	0.011090	192
17	6.433259	592.719117	0.001687	0.155442	92.133576	0.010854	204
18	7.177708	673.931757	0.001484	0.139320	93.892337	0.010650	216
19	8.008304	764.542228	0.001308	0.124870	95.468685	0.010475	228
20	8.935015	865.638038	0.001155	0.111919	96.881539	0.010322	240
21	9.968965	978.432537	0.001022	0.100311	98.147856	0.010189	252
22	11.122562	1104.279485	0.000906	0.089907	99.282835	0.010072	264
23	12.409652	1244.689295	0.000803	0.080582	100.300098	0.009970	276
24	13.845682	1401.347165	0.000714	0.072225	101.211853	0.009880	288
25	15.447889	1576.133301	0.000634	0.064734	102.029044	0.009801	300
26	17.235500	1771.145485	0.000565	0.058020	102.761478	0.009731	312
27	19.229972	1988.724252	0.000503	0.052002	103.417947	0.009670	324
28	21.455242	2231.480981	0.000448	0.046609	104.006328	0.009615	336
29	23.938018	2502.329236	0.000400	0.041775	104.533685	0.009566	348
30	26.708098	2804.519736	0.000357	0.037442	105.006346	0.009523	360
31	29.798728	3141.679369	0.000318	0.033558	105.429984	0.009485	372
32	33.247002	3517.854723	0.000284	0.030078	105.809684	0.009451	384
33	37.094306	3937.560650	0.000254	0.026958	106.150002	0.009421	396
34	41.386816	4405.834459	0.000227	0.024162	106.455024	0.009394	408
35	46.176050	4928.296368	0.000203	0.021656	106.728409	0.009370	420
36	51.519489	5511.216961	0.000181	0.019410	106.973440	0.009348	432
37	57.481264	6161.592447	0.000162	0.017397	107.193057	0.009329	444
38	64.132929	6887.228627	0.000145	0.015593	107.389897	0.009312	456
39	71.554317	7696.834582	0.000130	0.013975	107.566320	0.009297	468
40	79.834499	8600.127195	0.000116	0.012526	107.724446	0.009283	480

11.00%   ANNUAL COMPOUND INTEREST TABLES   11.00%
                             EFFECTIVE RATE 11.00

	1	2	3	4	5	6
	AMOUNT OF $1 AT COMPOUND INTEREST	ACCUMULATION OF $1 PER PERIOD	SINKING FUND FACTOR	PRESENT VALUE REVERSION OF $1	PRESENT VALUE ORD. ANNUITY $1 PER PERIOD	INSTALMENT TO AMORTIZE $1
YEARS						
1	1.110000	1.000000	1.000000	0.900901	0.900901	1.110000
2	1.232100	2.110000	0.473934	0.811622	1.712523	0.583934
3	1.367631	3.342100	0.299213	0.731191	2.443715	0.409213
4	1.518070	4.709731	0.212326	0.658731	3.102446	0.322326
5	1.685058	6.227801	0.160570	0.593451	3.695897	0.270570
6	1.870415	7.912860	0.126377	0.534641	4.230538	0.236377
7	2.076160	9.783274	0.102215	0.481658	4.712196	0.212215
8	2.304538	11.859434	0.084321	0.433926	5.146123	0.194321
9	2.558037	14.163972	0.070602	0.390925	5.537048	0.180602
10	2.839421	16.722009	0.059801	0.352184	5.889232	0.169801
11	3.151757	19.561430	0.051121	0.317283	6.206515	0.161121
12	3.498451	22.713187	0.044027	0.285841	6.492356	0.154027
13	3.883280	26.211638	0.038151	0.257514	6.749870	0.148151
14	4.310441	30.094918	0.033228	0.231995	6.981865	0.143228
15	4.784589	34.405359	0.029065	0.209004	7.190870	0.139065
16	5.310894	39.189948	0.025517	0.188292	7.379162	0.135517
17	5.895093	44.500843	0.022471	0.169633	7.548794	0.132471
18	6.543553	50.395936	0.019843	0.152822	7.701617	0.129843
19	7.263344	56.939488	0.017563	0.137678	7.839294	0.127563
20	8.062312	64.202832	0.015576	0.124034	7.963328	0.125576
21	8.949166	72.265144	0.013838	0.111742	8.075070	0.123838
22	9.933574	81.214309	0.012313	0.100669	8.175739	0.122313
23	11.026267	91.147884	0.010971	0.090693	8.266432	0.120971
24	12.239157	102.174151	0.009787	0.081705	8.348137	0.119787
25	13.585464	114.413307	0.008740	0.073608	8.421745	0.118740
26	15.079865	127.998771	0.007813	0.066314	8.488058	0.117813
27	16.738650	143.078636	0.006989	0.059742	8.547800	0.116989
28	18.579901	159.817286	0.006257	0.053822	8.601622	0.116257
29	20.623691	178.397187	0.005605	0.048488	8.650110	0.115605
30	22.892297	199.020878	0.005025	0.043683	8.693793	0.115025
31	25.410449	221.913174	0.004506	0.039354	8.733146	0.114506
32	28.205599	247.323624	0.004043	0.035454	8.768600	0.114043
33	31.308214	275.529222	0.003629	0.031940	8.800541	0.113629
34	34.752118	306.837437	0.003259	0.028775	8.829316	0.113259
35	38.574851	341.589555	0.002927	0.025924	8.855240	0.112927
36	42.818085	380.164406	0.002630	0.023355	8.878594	0.112630
37	47.528074	422.982490	0.002364	0.021040	8.899635	0.112364
38	52.756162	470.510564	0.002125	0.018955	8.918590	0.112125
39	58.559340	523.266726	0.001911	0.017077	8.935666	0.111911
40	65.000867	581.826066	0.001719	0.015384	8.951051	0.111719
41	72.150963	646.826934	0.001546	0.013860	8.964911	0.111546
42	80.087569	718.977896	0.001391	0.012486	8.977397	0.111391
43	88.897201	799.065465	0.001251	0.011249	8.988646	0.111251
44	98.675893	887.962666	0.001126	0.010134	8.998780	0.111126
45	109.530242	986.638559	0.001014	0.009130	9.007910	0.111014
46	121.578568	1096.168801	0.000912	0.008225	9.016135	0.110912
47	134.952211	1217.747369	0.000821	0.007410	9.023545	0.110821
48	149.796954	1352.699580	0.000739	0.006676	9.030221	0.110739
49	166.274619	1502.496534	0.000666	0.006014	9.036235	0.110666
50	184.564827	1668.771152	0.000599	0.005418	9.041653	0.110599

12.00%   MONTHLY COMPOUND INTEREST TABLES   12.00%
                                EFFECTIVE RATE 1.000

	1 AMOUNT OF $1 AT COMPOUND INTEREST	2 ACCUMULATION OF $1 PER PERIOD	3 SINKING FUND FACTOR	4 PRESENT VALUE REVERSION OF $1	5 PRESENT VALUE ORD. ANNUITY $1 PER PERIOD	6 INSTALMENT TO AMORTIZE $1	
MONTHS							
1	1.010000	1.000000	1.000000	0.990099	0.990099	1.010000	
2	1.020100	2.010000	0.497512	0.980296	1.970395	0.507512	
3	1.030301	3.030100	0.330022	0.970590	2.940985	0.340022	
4	1.040604	4.060401	0.246281	0.960980	3.901966	0.256281	
5	1.051010	5.101005	0.196040	0.951466	4.853431	0.206040	
6	1.061520	6.152015	0.162548	0.942045	5.795476	0.172548	
7	1.072135	7.213535	0.138628	0.932718	6.728195	0.148628	
8	1.082857	8.285671	0.120690	0.923483	7.651678	0.130690	
9	1.093685	9.368527	0.106740	0.914340	8.566018	0.116740	
10	1.104622	10.462213	0.095582	0.905287	9.471305	0.105582	
11	1.115668	11.566835	0.086454	0.896324	10.367628	0.096454	
12	1.126825	12.682503	0.078849	0.887449	11.255077	0.088849	
YEARS							**MONTHS**
1	1.126825	12.682503	0.078849	0.887449	11.255077	0.088849	12
2	1.269735	26.973465	0.037073	0.787566	21.243387	0.047073	24
3	1.430769	43.076878	0.023214	0.698925	30.107505	0.033214	36
4	1.612226	61.222608	0.016334	0.620260	37.973959	0.026334	48
5	1.816697	81.669670	0.012244	0.550450	44.955038	0.022244	60
6	2.047099	104.709931	0.009550	0.488496	51.150391	0.019550	72
7	2.306723	130.672274	0.007653	0.433515	56.648453	0.017653	84
8	2.599273	159.927293	0.006253	0.384723	61.527703	0.016253	96
9	2.928926	192.892579	0.005184	0.341422	65.857790	0.015184	108
10	3.300387	230.038689	0.004347	0.302995	69.700522	0.014347	120
11	3.718959	271.895856	0.003678	0.268892	73.110752	0.013678	132
12	4.190616	319.061559	0.003134	0.238628	76.137157	0.013134	144
13	4.722091	372.209054	0.002687	0.211771	78.822939	0.012687	156
14	5.320970	432.096982	0.002314	0.187936	81.206434	0.012314	168
15	5.995802	499.580198	0.002002	0.166783	83.321664	0.012002	180
16	6.756220	575.621974	0.001737	0.148012	85.198824	0.011737	192
17	7.613078	661.307751	0.001512	0.131353	86.864707	0.011512	204
18	8.578606	757.860630	0.001320	0.116569	88.343095	0.011320	216
19	9.666588	866.658830	0.001154	0.103449	89.655089	0.011154	228
20	10.892554	989.255365	0.001011	0.091806	90.819416	0.011011	240
21	12.274002	1127.400210	0.000887	0.081473	91.852698	0.010887	252
22	13.830653	1283.065278	0.000779	0.072303	92.769683	0.010779	264
23	15.584726	1458.472574	0.000686	0.064165	93.583461	0.010686	276
24	17.561259	1656.125905	0.000604	0.056944	94.305647	0.010604	288
25	19.788466	1878.846626	0.000532	0.050534	94.946551	0.010532	300
26	22.298139	2129.813909	0.000470	0.044847	95.515321	0.010470	312
27	25.126101	2412.610125	0.000414	0.039799	96.020075	0.010414	324
28	28.312720	2731.271980	0.000366	0.035320	96.468019	0.010366	336
29	31.903481	3090.348134	0.000324	0.031345	96.865546	0.010324	348
30	35.949641	3494.964133	0.000286	0.027817	97.218331	0.010286	360
31	40.508956	3950.895567	0.000253	0.024686	97.531410	0.010253	372
32	45.646505	4464.650519	0.000224	0.021907	97.809252	0.010224	384
33	51.435625	5043.562459	0.000198	0.019442	98.055822	0.010198	396
34	57.958949	5695.894923	0.000176	0.017254	98.274641	0.010176	408
35	65.309595	6430.959471	0.000155	0.015312	98.468831	0.010155	420
36	73.592486	7259.248603	0.000138	0.013588	98.641166	0.010138	432
37	82.925855	8192.585529	0.000122	0.012059	98.794103	0.010122	444
38	93.442929	9244.292938	0.000108	0.010702	98.929828	0.010108	456
39	105.293832	10429.383172	0.000096	0.009497	99.050277	0.010096	468
40	118.647725	11764.772510	0.000085	0.008428	99.157169	0.010085	480

12.00%

ANNUAL COMPOUND INTEREST TABLES
EFFECTIVE RATE 12.00

12.00%

	1 AMOUNT OF $1 AT COMPOUND INTEREST	2 ACCUMULATION OF $1 PER PERIOD	3 SINKING FUND FACTOR	4 PRESENT VALUE REVERSION OF $1	5 PRESENT VALUE ORD. ANNUITY $1 PER PERIOD	6 INSTALMENT TO AMORTIZE $1
YEARS						
1	1.120000	1.000000	1.000000	0.892857	0.892857	1.120000
2	1.254400	2.120000	0.471698	0.797194	1.690051	0.591698
3	1.404928	3.374400	0.296349	0.711780	2.401831	0.416349
4	1.573519	4.779328	0.209234	0.635518	3.037349	0.329234
5	1.762342	6.352847	0.157410	0.567427	3.604776	0.277410
6	1.973823	8.115189	0.123226	0.506631	4.111407	0.243226
7	2.210681	10.089012	0.099118	0.452349	4.563757	0.219118
8	2.475963	12.299693	0.081303	0.403883	4.967640	0.201303
9	2.773079	14.775656	0.067679	0.360610	5.328250	0.187679
10	3.105848	17.548735	0.056984	0.321973	5.650223	0.176984
11	3.478550	20.654583	0.048415	0.287476	5.937699	0.168415
12	3.895976	24.133133	0.041437	0.256675	6.194374	0.161437
13	4.363493	28.029109	0.035677	0.229174	6.423548	0.155677
14	4.887112	32.392602	0.030871	0.204620	6.628168	0.150871
15	5.473566	37.279715	0.026824	0.182696	6.810864	0.146824
16	6.130394	42.753280	0.023390	0.163122	6.973986	0.143390
17	6.866041	48.883674	0.020457	0.145644	7.119630	0.140457
18	7.689966	55.749715	0.017937	0.130040	7.249670	0.137937
19	8.612762	63.439681	0.015763	0.116107	7.365777	0.135763
20	9.646293	72.052442	0.013879	0.103667	7.469444	0.133879
21	10.803848	81.698736	0.012240	0.092560	7.562003	0.132240
22	12.100310	92.502584	0.010811	0.082643	7.644646	0.130811
23	13.552347	104.602894	0.009560	0.073788	7.718434	0.129560
24	15.178629	118.155241	0.008463	0.065882	7.784316	0.128463
25	17.000064	133.333870	0.007500	0.058823	7.843139	0.127500
26	19.040072	150.333934	0.006652	0.052521	7.895660	0.126652
27	21.324881	169.374007	0.005904	0.046894	7.942554	0.125904
28	23.883866	190.698887	0.005244	0.041869	7.984423	0.125244
29	26.749930	214.582754	0.004660	0.037383	8.021806	0.124660
30	29.959922	241.332684	0.004144	0.033378	8.055184	0.124144
31	33.555113	271.292606	0.003686	0.029802	8.084986	0.123686
32	37.581726	304.847719	0.003280	0.026609	8.111594	0.123280
33	42.091533	342.429446	0.002920	0.023758	8.135352	0.122920
34	47.142517	384.520979	0.002601	0.021212	8.156564	0.122601
35	52.799620	431.663496	0.002317	0.018940	8.175504	0.122317
36	59.135574	484.463116	0.002064	0.016910	8.192414	0.122064
37	66.231843	543.598690	0.001840	0.015098	8.207513	0.121840
38	74.179664	609.830533	0.001640	0.013481	8.220993	0.121640
39	83.081224	684.010197	0.001462	0.012036	8.233030	0.121462
40	93.050970	767.091420	0.001304	0.010747	8.243777	0.121304
41	104.217087	860.142391	0.001163	0.009595	8.253372	0.121163
42	116.723137	964.359478	0.001037	0.008567	8.261939	0.121037
43	130.729914	1081.082615	0.000925	0.007649	8.269589	0.120925
44	146.417503	1211.812529	0.000825	0.006830	8.276418	0.120825
45	163.987604	1358.230032	0.000736	0.006098	8.282516	0.120736
46	183.666116	1522.217636	0.000657	0.005445	8.287961	0.120657
47	205.706050	1705.883752	0.000586	0.004861	8.292822	0.120586
48	230.390776	1911.589803	0.000523	0.004340	8.297163	0.120523
49	258.037669	2141.980579	0.000467	0.003875	8.301038	0.120467
50	289.002190	2400.018249	0.000417	0.003460	8.304498	0.120417

13.00%   MONTHLY COMPOUND INTEREST TABLES   13.00%
EFFECTIVE RATE 1.083

	1 AMOUNT OF \$1 AT COMPOUND INTEREST	2 ACCUMULATION OF \$1 PER PERIOD	3 SINKING FUND FACTOR	4 PRESENT VALUE REVERSION OF \$1	5 PRESENT VALUE ORD. ANNUITY \$1 PER PERIOD	6 INSTALMENT TO AMORTIZE \$1	
MONTHS							
1	1.010833	1.000000	1.000000	0.989283	0.989283	1.010833	
2	1.021784	2.010833	0.497306	0.978680	1.967963	0.508140	
3	1.032853	3.032617	0.329748	0.968192	2.936155	0.340581	
4	1.044043	4.065471	0.245974	0.957815	3.893970	0.256807	
5	1.055353	5.109513	0.195713	0.947550	4.841520	0.206547	
6	1.066786	6.164866	0.162210	0.937395	5.778915	0.173043	
7	1.078343	7.231652	0.138281	0.927349	6.706264	0.149114	
8	1.090025	8.309995	0.120337	0.917410	7.623674	0.131170	
9	1.101834	9.400020	0.106383	0.907578	8.531253	0.117216	
10	1.113770	10.501854	0.095221	0.897851	9.429104	0.106055	
11	1.125836	11.615624	0.086091	0.888229	10.317333	0.096924	
12	1.138032	12.741460	0.078484	0.878710	11.196042	0.089317	
YEARS							MONTHS
1	1.138032	12.741460	0.078484	0.878710	11.196042	0.089317	12
2	1.295118	27.241655	0.036708	0.772130	21.034112	0.047542	24
3	1.473886	43.743348	0.022861	0.678478	29.678917	0.033694	36
4	1.677330	62.522811	0.015994	0.596185	37.275190	0.026827	48
5	1.908857	83.894449	0.011920	0.523874	43.950107	0.022753	60
6	2.172341	108.216068	0.009241	0.460333	49.815421	0.020074	72
7	2.472194	135.894861	0.007359	0.404499	54.969328	0.018192	84
8	2.813437	167.394225	0.005974	0.355437	59.498115	0.016807	96
9	3.201783	203.241525	0.004920	0.312326	63.477604	0.015754	108
10	3.643733	244.036917	0.004098	0.274444	66.974419	0.014931	120
11	4.146687	290.463399	0.003443	0.241156	70.047103	0.014276	132
12	4.719064	343.298242	0.002913	0.211906	72.747100	0.013746	144
13	5.370448	403.426010	0.002479	0.186204	75.119613	0.013312	156
14	6.111745	471.853363	0.002119	0.163619	77.204363	0.012953	168
15	6.955364	549.725914	0.001819	0.143774	79.036253	0.012652	180
16	7.915430	638.347406	0.001567	0.126336	80.645952	0.012400	192
17	9.008017	739.201542	0.001353	0.111012	82.060410	0.012186	204
18	10.251416	853.976825	0.001171	0.097548	83.303307	0.012004	216
19	11.666444	984.594826	0.001016	0.085716	84.395453	0.011849	228
20	13.276792	1133.242353	0.000882	0.075319	85.355132	0.011716	240
21	15.109421	1302.408067	0.000768	0.066184	86.198412	0.011601	252
22	17.195012	1494.924144	0.000669	0.058156	86.939409	0.011502	264
23	19.568482	1714.013694	0.000583	0.051103	87.590531	0.011417	276
24	22.269568	1963.344717	0.000509	0.044904	88.162677	0.011343	288
25	25.343491	2247.091520	0.000445	0.039458	88.665428	0.011278	300
26	28.841716	2570.004599	0.000389	0.034672	89.107200	0.011222	312
27	32.822810	2937.490172	0.000340	0.030467	89.495389	0.011174	324
28	37.353424	3355.700690	0.000298	0.026771	89.836495	0.011131	336
29	42.509410	3831.637843	0.000261	0.023524	90.136227	0.011094	348
30	48.377089	4373.269783	0.000229	0.020671	90.399605	0.011062	360
31	55.054699	4989.664524	0.000200	0.018164	90.631038	0.011034	372
32	62.654036	5691.141761	0.000176	0.015961	90.834400	0.011009	384
33	71.302328	6489.445641	0.000154	0.014025	91.013097	0.010987	396
34	81.144365	7397.941387	0.000135	0.012324	91.170119	0.010969	408
35	92.344923	8431.839055	0.000119	0.010829	91.308095	0.010952	420
36	105.091522	9608.448184	0.000104	0.009516	91.429337	0.010937	432
37	119.597566	10947.467591	0.000091	0.008361	91.535873	0.010925	444
38	136.105914	12471.315170	0.000080	0.007347	91.629487	0.010914	456
39	154.892951	14205.503212	0.000070	0.006456	91.711747	0.010904	468
40	176.273210	16179.065533	0.000062	0.005673	91.784030	0.010895	480

	1	2	3	4	5	6
	AMOUNT OF $1 AT COMPOUND INTEREST	ACCUMULATION OF $1 PER PERIOD	SINKING FUND FACTOR	PRESENT VALUE REVERSION OF $1	PRESENT VALUE ORD. ANNUITY $1 PER PERIOD	INSTALMENT TO AMORTIZE $1
YEARS						
1	1.130000	1.000000	1.000000	0.884956	0.884956	1.130000
2	1.276900	2.130000	0.469484	0.783147	1.668102	0.599484
3	1.442897	3.406900	0.293522	0.693050	2.361153	0.423522
4	1.630474	4.849797	0.206194	0.613319	2.974471	0.336194
5	1.842435	6.480271	0.154315	0.542760	3.517231	0.284315
6	2.081952	8.322706	0.120153	0.480319	3.997550	0.250153
7	2.352605	10.404658	0.096111	0.425061	4.422610	0.226111
8	2.658444	12.757263	0.078387	0.376160	4.798770	0.208387
9	3.004042	15.415707	0.064869	0.332885	5.131655	0.194869
10	3.394567	18.419749	0.054290	0.294588	5.426243	0.184290
11	3.835861	21.814317	0.045841	0.260698	5.686941	0.175841
12	4.334523	25.650178	0.038986	0.230706	5.917647	0.168986
13	4.898011	29.984701	0.033350	0.204165	6.121812	0.163350
14	5.534753	34.882712	0.028667	0.180677	6.302488	0.158667
15	6.254270	40.417464	0.024742	0.159891	6.462379	0.154742
16	7.067326	46.671735	0.021426	0.141496	6.603875	0.151426
17	7.986078	53.739060	0.018608	0.125218	6.729093	0.148608
18	9.024268	61.725138	0.016201	0.110812	6.839905	0.146201
19	10.197423	70.749406	0.014134	0.098064	6.937969	0.144134
20	11.523088	80.946829	0.012354	0.086782	7.024752	0.142354
21	13.021089	92.469917	0.010814	0.076798	7.101550	0.140814
22	14.713831	105.491006	0.009479	0.067963	7.169513	0.139479
23	16.626629	120.204837	0.008319	0.060144	7.229658	0.138319
24	18.788091	136.831465	0.007308	0.053225	7.282883	0.137308
25	21.230542	155.619556	0.006426	0.047102	7.329985	0.136426
26	23.990513	176.850098	0.005655	0.041683	7.371668	0.135655
27	27.109279	200.840611	0.004979	0.036888	7.408556	0.134979
28	30.633486	227.949890	0.004387	0.032644	7.441200	0.134387
29	34.615839	258.583376	0.003867	0.028889	7.470088	0.133867
30	39.115898	293.199215	0.003411	0.025565	7.495653	0.133411
31	44.200965	332.315113	0.003009	0.022624	7.518277	0.133009
32	49.947090	376.516078	0.002656	0.020021	7.538299	0.132656
33	56.440212	426.463168	0.002345	0.017718	7.556016	0.132345
34	63.777439	482.903380	0.002071	0.015680	7.571696	0.132071
35	72.068506	546.680819	0.001829	0.013876	7.585572	0.131829
36	81.437412	618.749325	0.001616	0.012279	7.597851	0.131616
37	92.024276	700.186738	0.001428	0.010867	7.608718	0.131428
38	103.987432	792.211014	0.001262	0.009617	7.618334	0.131262
39	117.505798	896.198445	0.001116	0.008510	7.626844	0.131116
40	132.781552	1013.704243	0.000986	0.007531	7.634376	0.130986
41	150.043153	1146.485795	0.000872	0.006665	7.641040	0.130872
42	169.548763	1296.528948	0.000771	0.005898	7.646938	0.130771
43	191.590103	1466.077712	0.000682	0.005219	7.652158	0.130682
44	216.496816	1657.667814	0.000603	0.004619	7.656777	0.130603
45	244.641402	1874.164630	0.000534	0.004088	7.660864	0.130534
46	276.444784	2118.806032	0.000472	0.003617	7.664482	0.130472
47	312.382606	2395.250816	0.000417	0.003201	7.667683	0.130417
48	352.992345	2707.633422	0.000369	0.002833	7.670516	0.130369
49	398.881350	3060.625767	0.000327	0.002507	7.673023	0.130327
50	450.735925	3459.507117	0.000289	0.002219	7.675242	0.130289

14.00%

MONTHLY COMPOUND INTEREST TABLES
EFFECTIVE RATE 1.167

14.00%

	1 AMOUNT OF $1 AT COMPOUND INTEREST	2 ACCUMULATION OF $1 PER PERIOD	3 SINKING FUND FACTOR	4 PRESENT VALUE REVERSION OF $1	5 PRESENT VALUE ORD. ANNUITY $1 PER PERIOD	6 INSTALMENT TO AMORTIZE $1	
MONTHS							
1	1.011667	1.000000	1.000000	0.988468	0.988468	1.011667	
2	1.023469	2.011667	0.497100	0.977069	1.965537	0.508767	
3	1.035410	3.035136	0.329475	0.965801	2.931338	0.341141	
4	1.047490	4.070546	0.245667	0.954663	3.886001	0.257334	
5	1.059710	5.118036	0.195387	0.943654	4.829655	0.207054	
6	1.072074	6.177746	0.161871	0.932772	5.762427	0.173538	
7	1.084581	7.249820	0.137934	0.922015	6.684442	0.149601	
8	1.097235	8.334401	0.119985	0.911382	7.595824	0.131651	
9	1.110036	9.431636	0.106026	0.900872	8.496696	0.117693	
10	1.122986	10.541672	0.094862	0.890483	9.387178	0.106528	
11	1.136088	11.664658	0.085729	0.880214	10.267392	0.097396	
12	1.149342	12.800745	0.078120	0.870063	11.137455	0.089787	
YEARS							**MONTHS**
1	1.149342	12.800745	0.078120	0.870063	11.137455	0.089787	12
2	1.320987	27.513180	0.036346	0.757010	20.827743	0.048013	24
3	1.518266	44.422800	0.022511	0.658646	29.258904	0.034178	36
4	1.745007	63.857736	0.015660	0.573064	36.594546	0.027326	48
5	2.005610	86.195125	0.011602	0.498601	42.977016	0.023268	60
6	2.305132	111.868425	0.008939	0.433815	48.530168	0.020606	72
7	2.649385	141.375828	0.007073	0.377446	53.361760	0.018740	84
8	3.045049	175.289927	0.005705	0.328402	57.565549	0.017372	96
9	3.499803	214.268826	0.004667	0.285730	61.223111	0.016334	108
10	4.022471	259.068912	0.003860	0.248603	64.405420	0.015527	120
11	4.623195	310.559535	0.003220	0.216301	67.174230	0.014887	132
12	5.313632	369.739871	0.002705	0.188195	69.583269	0.014371	144
13	6.107180	437.758319	0.002284	0.163742	71.679284	0.013951	156
14	7.019239	515.934780	0.001938	0.142466	73.502950	0.013605	168
15	8.067507	605.786272	0.001651	0.123954	75.089654	0.013317	180
16	9.272324	709.056369	0.001410	0.107848	76.470187	0.013077	192
17	10.657072	827.749031	0.001208	0.093834	77.671337	0.012875	204
18	12.248621	964.167496	0.001037	0.081642	78.716413	0.012704	216
19	14.077855	1120.958972	0.000892	0.071034	79.625696	0.012559	228
20	16.180270	1301.166005	0.000769	0.061804	80.416829	0.012435	240
21	18.596664	1508.285522	0.000663	0.053773	81.105164	0.012330	252
22	21.373928	1746.336688	0.000573	0.046786	81.704060	0.012239	264
23	24.565954	2019.938898	0.000495	0.040707	82.225136	0.012162	276
24	28.234683	2334.401417	0.000428	0.035417	82.678506	0.012095	288
25	32.451308	2695.826407	0.000371	0.030815	83.072966	0.012038	300
26	37.297652	3111.227338	0.000321	0.026811	83.416171	0.011988	312
27	42.867759	3588.665088	0.000279	0.023328	83.714781	0.011945	324
28	49.269718	4137.404360	0.000242	0.020296	83.974591	0.011908	336
29	56.627757	4768.093468	0.000210	0.017659	84.200641	0.011876	348
30	65.084661	5492.970967	0.000182	0.015365	84.397320	0.011849	360
31	74.804537	6326.103143	0.000158	0.013368	84.568442	0.011825	372
32	85.975998	7283.656968	0.000137	0.011631	84.717330	0.011804	384
33	98.815828	8384.213826	0.000119	0.010120	84.846871	0.011786	396
34	113.573184	9649.130077	0.000104	0.008805	84.959580	0.011770	408
35	130.534434	11102.951488	0.000090	0.007661	85.057645	0.011757	420
36	150.028711	12773.889539	0.000078	0.006665	85.142966	0.011745	432
37	172.434303	14694.368869	0.000068	0.005799	85.217202	0.011735	444
38	198.185992	16901.656479	0.000059	0.005046	85.281792	0.011726	456
39	227.783490	19438.584900	0.000051	0.004390	85.337989	0.011718	468
40	261.801139	22354.383359	0.000045	0.003820	85.386883	0.011711	480

14.00%   ANNUAL COMPOUND INTEREST TABLES   14.00%
                         EFFECTIVE RATE 14.00

	1 AMOUNT OF $1 AT COMPOUND INTEREST	2 ACCUMULATION OF $1 PER PERIOD	3 SINKING FUND FACTOR	4 PRESENT VALUE REVERSION OF $1	5 PRESENT VALUE ORD. ANNUITY $1 PER PERIOD	6 INSTALMENT TO AMORTIZE $1
YEARS						
1	1.140000	1.000000	1.000000	0.877193	0.877193	1.140000
2	1.299600	2.140000	0.467290	0.769468	1.646661	0.607290
3	1.481544	3.439600	0.290731	0.674972	2.321632	0.430731
4	1.688960	4.921144	0.203205	0.592080	2.913712	0.343205
5	1.925415	6.610104	0.151284	0.519369	3.433081	0.291284
6	2.194973	8.535519	0.117157	0.455587	3.888668	0.257157
7	2.502269	10.730491	0.093192	0.399637	4.288305	0.233192
8	2.852586	13.232760	0.075570	0.350559	4.638864	0.215570
9	3.251949	16.085347	0.062168	0.307508	4.946372	0.202168
10	3.707221	19.337295	0.051714	0.269744	5.216116	0.191714
11	4.226232	23.044516	0.043394	0.236617	5.452733	0.183394
12	4.817905	27.270749	0.036669	0.207559	5.660292	0.176669
13	5.492411	32.088654	0.031164	0.182069	5.842362	0.171164
14	6.261349	37.581065	0.026609	0.159710	6.002072	0.166609
15	7.137938	43.842414	0.022809	0.140096	6.142168	0.162809
16	8.137249	50.980352	0.019615	0.122892	6.265060	0.159615
17	9.276464	59.117601	0.016915	0.107800	6.372859	0.156915
18	10.575169	68.394066	0.014621	0.094561	6.467420	0.154621
19	12.055693	78.969235	0.012663	0.082948	6.550369	0.152663
20	13.743490	91.024928	0.010986	0.072762	6.623131	0.150986
21	15.667578	104.768418	0.009545	0.063826	6.686957	0.149545
22	17.861039	120.435996	0.008303	0.055988	6.742944	0.148303
23	20.361585	138.297035	0.007231	0.049112	6.792056	0.147231
24	23.212207	158.658620	0.006303	0.043081	6.835137	0.146303
25	26.461916	181.870827	0.005498	0.037790	6.872927	0.145498
26	30.166584	208.332743	0.004800	0.033149	6.906077	0.144800
27	34.389906	238.499327	0.004193	0.029078	6.935155	0.144193
28	39.204493	272.889233	0.003664	0.025507	6.960662	0.143664
29	44.693122	312.093725	0.003204	0.022375	6.983037	0.143204
30	50.950159	356.786847	0.002803	0.019627	7.002664	0.142803
31	58.083181	407.737006	0.002453	0.017217	7.019881	0.142453
32	66.214826	465.820186	0.002147	0.015102	7.034983	0.142147
33	75.484902	532.035012	0.001880	0.013248	7.048231	0.141880
34	86.052788	607.519914	0.001646	0.011621	7.059852	0.141646
35	98.100178	693.572702	0.001442	0.010194	7.070045	0.141442
36	111.834203	791.672881	0.001263	0.008942	7.078987	0.141263
37	127.490992	903.507084	0.001107	0.007844	7.086831	0.141107
38	145.339731	1030.998076	0.000970	0.006880	7.093711	0.140970
39	165.687293	1176.337806	0.000850	0.006035	7.099747	0.140850
40	188.883514	1342.025099	0.000745	0.005294	7.105041	0.140745
41	215.327206	1530.908613	0.000653	0.004644	7.109685	0.140653
42	245.473015	1746.235819	0.000573	0.004074	7.113759	0.140573
43	279.839237	1991.708833	0.000502	0.003573	7.117332	0.140502
44	319.016730	2271.548070	0.000440	0.003135	7.120467	0.140440
45	363.679072	2590.564800	0.000386	0.002750	7.123217	0.140386
46	414.594142	2954.243872	0.000338	0.002412	7.125629	0.140338
47	472.637322	3368.838014	0.000297	0.002116	7.127744	0.140297
48	538.806547	3841.475336	0.000260	0.001856	7.129600	0.140260
49	614.239464	4380.281883	0.000228	0.001628	7.131228	0.140228
50	700.232988	4994.521346	0.000200	0.001428	7.132656	0.140200

15.00%   MONTHLY COMPOUND INTEREST TABLES   15.00%
                                   EFFECTIVE RATE 1.250

	1	2	3	4	5	6
	AMOUNT OF $1 AT COMPOUND INTEREST	ACCUMULATION OF $1 PER PERIOD	SINKING FUND FACTOR	PRESENT VALUE REVERSION OF $1	PRESENT VALUE ORD. ANNUITY $1 PER PERIOD	INSTALMENT TO AMORTIZE $1
MONTHS						
1	1.012500	1.000000	1.000000	0.987654	0.987654	1.012500
2	1.025156	2.012500	0.496894	0.975461	1.963115	0.509394
3	1.037971	3.037656	0.329201	0.963418	2.926534	0.341701
4	1.050945	4.075627	0.245361	0.951524	3.878058	0.257861
5	1.064082	5.126572	0.195062	0.939777	4.817835	0.207562
6	1.077383	6.190654	0.161534	0.928175	5.746010	0.174034
7	1.090850	7.268038	0.137589	0.916716	6.662726	0.150089
8	1.104486	8.358888	0.119633	0.905398	7.568124	0.132133
9	1.118292	9.463374	0.105671	0.894221	8.462345	0.118171
10	1.132271	10.581666	0.094503	0.883181	9.345526	0.107003
11	1.146424	11.713937	0.085368	0.872277	10.217803	0.097868
12	1.160755	12.860361	0.077758	0.861509	11.079312	0.090258

YEARS							MONTHS
1	1.160755	12.860361	0.077758	0.861509	11.079312	0.090258	12
2	1.347351	27.788084	0.035987	0.742197	20.624235	0.048487	24
3	1.563944	45.115506	0.022165	0.639409	28.847267	0.034665	36
4	1.815355	65.228388	0.015331	0.550856	35.931481	0.027831	48
5	2.107181	88.574508	0.011290	0.474568	42.034592	0.023790	60
6	2.445920	115.673621	0.008645	0.408844	47.292474	0.021145	72
7	2.839113	147.129040	0.006797	0.352223	51.822185	0.019297	84
8	3.295513	183.641059	0.005445	0.303443	55.724570	0.017945	96
9	3.825282	226.022551	0.004424	0.261419	59.086509	0.016924	108
10	4.440213	275.217058	0.003633	0.225214	61.982847	0.016133	120
11	5.153998	332.319805	0.003009	0.194024	64.478068	0.015509	132
12	5.982526	398.602077	0.002509	0.167153	66.627722	0.015009	144
13	6.944244	475.539523	0.002103	0.144004	68.479668	0.014603	156
14	8.060563	564.845011	0.001770	0.124061	70.075134	0.014270	168
15	9.356334	668.506759	0.001496	0.106879	71.449643	0.013996	180
16	10.860408	788.832603	0.001268	0.092078	72.633794	0.013768	192
17	12.606267	928.501369	0.001077	0.079326	73.653950	0.013577	204
18	14.632781	1090.622520	0.000917	0.068340	74.532823	0.013417	216
19	16.985067	1278.805378	0.000782	0.058875	75.289980	0.013282	228
20	19.715494	1497.239481	0.000668	0.050722	75.942278	0.013168	240
21	22.884848	1750.787854	0.000571	0.043697	76.504237	0.013071	252
22	26.563691	2045.095272	0.000489	0.037645	76.988370	0.012989	264
23	30.833924	2386.713938	0.000419	0.032432	77.405455	0.012919	276
24	35.790617	2783.249347	0.000359	0.027940	77.764777	0.012859	288
25	41.544120	3243.529615	0.000308	0.024071	78.074336	0.012808	300
26	48.222525	3777.802015	0.000265	0.020737	78.341024	0.012765	312
27	55.974514	4397.961118	0.000227	0.017865	78.570778	0.012727	324
28	64.972670	5117.813598	0.000195	0.015391	78.768713	0.012695	336
29	75.417320	5953.385616	0.000168	0.013260	78.939236	0.012668	348
30	87.540995	6923.279611	0.000144	0.011423	79.086142	0.012644	360
31	101.613606	8049.088447	0.000124	0.009841	79.212704	0.012624	372
32	117.948452	9355.876140	0.000107	0.008478	79.321738	0.012607	384
33	136.909198	10872.735858	0.000092	0.007304	79.415671	0.012592	396
34	158.917970	12633.437629	0.000079	0.006293	79.496596	0.012579	408
35	184.464752	14677.180163	0.000068	0.005421	79.566313	0.012568	420
36	214.118294	17049.463544	0.000059	0.004670	79.626375	0.012559	432
37	248.538777	19803.102194	0.000050	0.004024	79.678119	0.012550	444
38	288.492509	22999.400698	0.000043	0.003466	79.722696	0.012543	456
39	334.868983	26709.518627	0.000037	0.002986	79.761101	0.012537	468
40	388.700685	31016.054774	0.000032	0.002573	79.794186	0.012532	480

15.00%   ANNUAL COMPOUND INTEREST TABLES   15.00%
                                      EFFECTIVE RATE 15.00

	1 AMOUNT OF $1 AT COMPOUND INTEREST	2 ACCUMULATION OF $1 PER PERIOD	3 SINKING FUND FACTOR	4 PRESENT VALUE REVERSION OF $1	5 PRESENT VALUE ORD. ANNUITY $1 PER PERIOD	6 INSTALMENT TO AMORTIZE $1
YEARS						
1	1.150000	1.000000	1.000000	0.869565	0.869565	1.150000
2	1.322500	2.150000	0.465116	0.756144	1.625709	0.615116
3	1.520875	3.472500	0.287977	0.657516	2.283225	0.437977
4	1.749006	4.993375	0.200265	0.571753	2.854978	0.350265
5	2.011357	6.742381	0.148316	0.497177	3.352155	0.298316
6	2.313061	8.753738	0.114237	0.432328	3.784483	0.264237
7	2.660020	11.066799	0.090360	0.375937	4.160420	0.240360
8	3.059023	13.726819	0.072850	0.326902	4.487322	0.222850
9	3.517876	16.785842	0.059574	0.284262	4.771584	0.209574
10	4.045558	20.303718	0.049252	0.247185	5.018769	0.199252
11	4.652391	24.349276	0.041069	0.214943	5.233712	0.191069
12	5.350250	29.001667	0.034481	0.186907	5.420619	0.184481
13	6.152788	34.351917	0.029110	0.162528	5.583147	0.179110
14	7.075706	40.504705	0.024688	0.141329	5.724476	0.174688
15	8.137062	47.580411	0.021017	0.122894	5.847370	0.171017
16	9.357621	55.717472	0.017948	0.106865	5.954235	0.167948
17	10.761264	65.075093	0.015367	0.092926	6.047161	0.165367
18	12.375454	75.836357	0.013186	0.080805	6.127966	0.163186
19	14.231772	88.211811	0.011336	0.070265	6.198231	0.161336
20	16.366537	102.443583	0.009761	0.061100	6.259331	0.159761
21	18.821518	118.810120	0.008417	0.053131	6.312462	0.158417
22	21.644746	137.631638	0.007266	0.046201	6.358663	0.157266
23	24.891458	159.276384	0.006278	0.040174	6.398837	0.156278
24	28.625176	184.167841	0.005430	0.034934	6.433771	0.155430
25	32.918953	212.793017	0.004699	0.030378	6.464149	0.154699
26	37.856796	245.711970	0.004070	0.026415	6.490564	0.154070
27	43.535315	283.568766	0.003526	0.022970	6.513534	0.153526
28	50.065612	327.104080	0.003057	0.019974	6.533508	0.153057
29	57.575454	377.169693	0.002651	0.017369	6.550877	0.152651
30	66.211772	434.745146	0.002300	0.015103	6.565980	0.152300
31	76.143538	500.956918	0.001996	0.013133	6.579113	0.151996
32	87.565068	577.100456	0.001733	0.011420	6.590533	0.151733
33	100.699829	664.665525	0.001505	0.009931	6.600463	0.151505
34	115.804803	765.365353	0.001307	0.008635	6.609099	0.151307
35	133.175523	881.170156	0.001135	0.007509	6.616607	0.151135
36	153.151852	1014.345680	0.000986	0.006529	6.623137	0.150986
37	176.124630	1167.497532	0.000857	0.005678	6.628815	0.150857
38	202.543324	1343.622161	0.000744	0.004937	6.633752	0.150744
39	232.924823	1546.165485	0.000647	0.004293	6.638045	0.150647
40	267.863546	1779.090308	0.000562	0.003733	6.641778	0.150562
41	308.043078	2046.953854	0.000489	0.003246	6.645025	0.150489
42	354.249540	2354.996933	0.000425	0.002823	6.647848	0.150425
43	407.386971	2709.246473	0.000369	0.002455	6.650302	0.150369
44	468.495017	3116.633443	0.000321	0.002134	6.652437	0.150321
45	538.769269	3585.128460	0.000279	0.001856	6.654293	0.150279
46	619.584659	4123.897729	0.000242	0.001614	6.655907	0.150242
47	712.522358	4743.482388	0.000211	0.001403	6.657310	0.150211
48	819.400712	5456.004746	0.000183	0.001220	6.658531	0.150183
49	942.310819	6275.405458	0.000159	0.001061	6.659592	0.150159
50	1083.657442	7217.716277	0.000139	0.000923	6.660515	0.150139

16.00% MONTHLY COMPOUND INTEREST TABLES 16.00%
EFFECTIVE RATE 1.333

	1 AMOUNT OF $1 AT COMPOUND INTEREST	2 ACCUMULATION OF $1 PER PERIOD	3 SINKING FUND FACTOR	4 PRESENT VALUE REVERSION OF $1	5 PRESENT VALUE ORD. ANNUITY $1 PER PERIOD	6 INSTALMENT TO AMORTIZE $1	
MONTHS							
1	1.013333	1.000000	1.000000	0.986842	0.986842	1.013333	
2	1.026844	2.013333	0.496689	0.973857	1.960699	0.510022	
3	1.040536	3.040178	0.328928	0.961043	2.921743	0.342261	
4	1.054410	4.080713	0.245055	0.948398	3.870141	0.258389	
5	1.068468	5.135123	0.194737	0.935919	4.806060	0.208071	
6	1.082715	6.203591	0.161197	0.923604	5.729665	0.174530	
7	1.097151	7.286306	0.137244	0.911452	6.641116	0.150577	
8	1.111779	8.383457	0.119283	0.899459	7.540575	0.132616	
9	1.126603	9.495236	0.105316	0.887624	8.428199	0.118649	
10	1.141625	10.621839	0.094146	0.875945	9.304144	0.107479	
11	1.156846	11.763464	0.085009	0.864419	10.168563	0.098342	
12	1.172271	12.920310	0.077398	0.853045	11.021609	0.090731	
YEARS							MONTHS
1	1.172271	12.920310	0.077398	0.853045	11.021609	0.090731	12
2	1.374219	28.066412	0.035630	0.727686	20.423539	0.048963	24
3	1.610957	45.821745	0.021824	0.620749	28.443811	0.035157	36
4	1.888477	66.635803	0.015007	0.529527	35.285465	0.028340	48
5	2.213807	91.035516	0.010985	0.451711	41.121706	0.024318	60
6	2.595181	119.638587	0.008359	0.385330	46.100283	0.021692	72
7	3.042255	153.169132	0.006529	0.328704	50.347235	0.019862	84
8	3.566347	192.476010	0.005195	0.280399	53.970077	0.018529	96
9	4.180724	238.554316	0.004192	0.239193	57.060524	0.017525	108
10	4.900941	292.570569	0.003418	0.204042	59.696816	0.016751	120
11	5.745230	355.892244	0.002810	0.174057	61.945692	0.016143	132
12	6.734965	430.122395	0.002325	0.148479	63.864085	0.015658	144
13	7.895203	517.140233	0.001934	0.126659	65.500561	0.015267	156
14	9.255316	619.148703	0.001615	0.108046	66.896549	0.014948	168
15	10.849737	738.730255	0.001354	0.092168	68.087390	0.014687	180
16	12.718830	878.912215	0.001138	0.078624	69.103231	0.014471	192
17	14.909912	1043.243434	0.000959	0.067069	69.969789	0.014292	204
18	17.478455	1235.884123	0.000809	0.057213	70.709003	0.014142	216
19	20.489482	1461.711177	0.000684	0.048806	71.339585	0.014017	228
20	24.019222	1726.441638	0.000579	0.041633	71.877501	0.013913	240
21	28.157032	2036.777427	0.000491	0.035515	72.336367	0.013824	252
22	33.007667	2400.575011	0.000417	0.030296	72.727801	0.013750	264
23	38.693924	2827.044294	0.000354	0.025844	73.061711	0.013687	276
24	45.359757	3326.981781	0.000301	0.022046	73.346552	0.013634	288
25	53.173919	3913.043898	0.000256	0.018806	73.589534	0.013589	300
26	62.334232	4600.067404	0.000217	0.016043	73.796809	0.013551	312
27	73.072600	5405.444997	0.000185	0.013685	73.973623	0.013518	324
28	85.660875	6349.565632	0.000157	0.011674	74.124454	0.013491	336
29	100.417742	7456.330682	0.000134	0.009958	74.253120	0.013467	348
30	117.716787	8753.759030	0.000114	0.008495	74.362878	0.013448	360
31	137.995952	10274.696396	0.000097	0.007247	74.456506	0.013431	372
32	161.768625	12057.646856	0.000083	0.006182	74.536375	0.013416	384
33	189.636635	14147.747615	0.000071	0.005273	74.604507	0.013404	396
34	222.305489	16597.911700	0.000060	0.004498	74.662626	0.013394	408
35	260.602233	19470.167508	0.000051	0.003837	74.712205	0.013385	420
36	305.496388	22837.229117	0.000044	0.003273	74.754498	0.013377	432
37	358.124495	26784.337116	0.000037	0.002792	74.790576	0.013371	444
38	419.818887	31411.416562	0.000032	0.002382	74.821352	0.013365	456
39	492.141422	36835.606678	0.000027	0.002032	74.847605	0.013360	468
40	576.923018	43194.226354	0.000023	0.001733	74.870000	0.013356	480

16.00% ANNUAL COMPOUND INTEREST TABLES 16.00%
EFFECTIVE RATE 16.00

	1 AMOUNT OF $1 AT COMPOUND INTEREST	2 ACCUMULATION OF $1 PER PERIOD	3 SINKING FUND FACTOR	4 PRESENT VALUE REVERSION OF $1	5 PRESENT VALUE ORD. ANNUITY $1 PER PERIOD	6 INSTALMENT TO AMORTIZE $1
YEARS						
1	1.160000	1.000000	1.000000	0.862069	0.862069	1.160000
2	1.345600	2.160000	0.462963	0.743163	1.605232	0.622963
3	1.560896	3.505600	0.285258	0.640658	2.245890	0.445258
4	1.810639	5.066496	0.197375	0.552291	2.798181	0.357375
5	2.100342	6.877135	0.145409	0.476113	3.274294	0.305409
6	2.436396	8.977477	0.111390	0.410442	3.684736	0.271390
7	2.826220	11.413873	0.087613	0.353830	4.038565	0.247613
8	3.278415	14.240093	0.070224	0.305025	4.343591	0.230224
9	3.802961	17.518508	0.057082	0.262953	4.606544	0.217082
10	4.411435	21.321469	0.046901	0.226684	4.833227	0.206901
11	5.117265	25.732904	0.038861	0.195417	5.028644	0.198861
12	5.936027	30.850169	0.032415	0.168463	5.197107	0.192415
13	6.885791	36.786196	0.027184	0.145227	5.342334	0.187184
14	7.987518	43.671987	0.022898	0.125195	5.467529	0.182898
15	9.265521	51.659505	0.019358	0.107927	5.575456	0.179358
16	10.748004	60.925026	0.016414	0.093041	5.668497	0.176414
17	12.467685	71.673030	0.013952	0.080207	5.748704	0.173952
18	14.462514	84.140715	0.011885	0.069144	5.817848	0.171885
19	16.776517	98.603230	0.010142	0.059607	5.877455	0.170142
20	19.460759	115.379747	0.008667	0.051385	5.928841	0.168667
21	22.574481	134.840506	0.007416	0.044298	5.973139	0.167416
22	26.186398	157.414987	0.006353	0.038188	6.011326	0.166353
23	30.376222	183.601385	0.005447	0.032920	6.044247	0.165447
24	35.236417	213.977607	0.004673	0.028380	6.072627	0.164673
25	40.874244	249.214024	0.004013	0.024465	6.097092	0.164013
26	47.414123	290.088267	0.003447	0.021091	6.118183	0.163447
27	55.000382	337.502390	0.002963	0.018182	6.136364	0.162963
28	63.800444	392.502773	0.002548	0.015674	6.152038	0.162548
29	74.008515	456.303216	0.002192	0.013512	6.165550	0.162192
30	85.849877	530.311731	0.001886	0.011648	6.177198	0.161886
31	99.585857	616.161608	0.001623	0.010042	6.187240	0.161623
32	115.519594	715.747465	0.001397	0.008657	6.195897	0.161397
33	134.002729	831.267059	0.001203	0.007463	6.203359	0.161203
34	155.443166	965.269789	0.001036	0.006433	6.209792	0.161036
35	180.314073	1120.712955	0.000892	0.005546	6.215338	0.160892
36	209.164324	1301.027028	0.000769	0.004781	6.220119	0.160769
37	242.630616	1510.191352	0.000662	0.004121	6.224241	0.160662
38	281.451515	1752.821968	0.000571	0.003553	6.227794	0.160571
39	326.483757	2034.273483	0.000492	0.003063	6.230857	0.160492
40	378.721158	2360.757241	0.000424	0.002640	6.233497	0.160424
41	439.316544	2739.478399	0.000365	0.002276	6.235773	0.160365
42	509.607191	3178.794943	0.000315	0.001962	6.237736	0.160315
43	591.144341	3688.402134	0.000271	0.001692	6.239427	0.160271
44	685.727436	4279.546475	0.000234	0.001458	6.240886	0.160234
45	795.443826	4965.273911	0.000201	0.001257	6.242143	0.160201
46	922.714838	5760.717737	0.000174	0.001084	6.243227	0.160174
47	1070.349212	6683.432575	0.000150	0.000934	6.244161	0.160150
48	1241.605086	7753.781787	0.000129	0.000805	6.244966	0.160129
49	1440.261900	8995.386873	0.000111	0.000694	6.245661	0.160111
50	1670.703804	10435.648773	0.000096	0.000599	6.246259	0.160096

18.00%   MONTHLY COMPOUND INTEREST TABLES   18.00%
                              EFFECTIVE RATE 1.500

	1 AMOUNT OF $1 AT COMPOUND INTEREST	2 ACCUMULATION OF $1 PER PERIOD	3 SINKING FUND FACTOR	4 PRESENT VALUE REVERSION OF $1	5 PRESENT VALUE ORD. ANNUITY $1 PER PERIOD	6 INSTALMENT TO AMORTIZE $1	
MONTHS							
1	1.015000	1.000000	1.000000	0.985222	0.985222	1.015000	
2	1.030225	2.015000	0.496278	0.970662	1.955883	0.511278	
3	1.045678	3.045225	0.328383	0.956317	2.912200	0.343383	
4	1.061364	4.090903	0.244445	0.942184	3.854385	0.259445	
5	1.077284	5.152267	0.194089	0.928260	4.782645	0.209089	
6	1.093443	6.229551	0.160525	0.914542	5.697187	0.175525	
7	1.109845	7.322994	0.136556	0.901027	6.598214	0.151556	
8	1.126493	8.432839	0.118584	0.887711	7.485925	0.133584	
9	1.143390	9.559332	0.104610	0.874592	8.360517	0.119610	
10	1.160541	10.702722	0.093434	0.861667	9.222185	0.108434	
11	1.177949	11.863262	0.084294	0.848933	10.071118	0.099294	
12	1.195618	13.041211	0.076680	0.836387	10.907505	0.091680	
YEARS							MONTHS
1	1.195618	13.041211	0.076680	0.836387	10.907505	0.091680	12
2	1.429503	28.633521	0.034924	0.699544	20.030405	0.049924	24
3	1.709140	47.275969	0.021152	0.585090	27.660684	0.036152	36
4	2.043478	69.565219	0.014375	0.489362	34.042554	0.029375	48
5	2.443220	96.214652	0.010393	0.409296	39.380269	0.025393	60
6	2.921158	128.077197	0.007808	0.342330	43.844667	0.022808	72
7	3.492590	166.172636	0.006018	0.286321	47.578633	0.021018	84
8	4.175804	211.720235	0.004723	0.239475	50.701675	0.019723	96
9	4.992667	266.177771	0.003757	0.200294	53.313749	0.018757	108
10	5.969323	331.288191	0.003019	0.167523	55.498454	0.018019	120
11	7.137031	409.135393	0.002444	0.140114	57.325714	0.017444	132
12	8.533164	502.210922	0.001991	0.117190	58.854011	0.016991	144
13	10.202406	613.493716	0.001630	0.098016	60.132260	0.016630	156
14	12.198182	746.545446	0.001340	0.081979	61.201371	0.016340	168
15	14.584368	905.624513	0.001104	0.068567	62.095562	0.016104	180
16	17.437335	1095.822335	0.000913	0.057348	62.843452	0.015913	192
17	20.848395	1323.226308	0.000756	0.047965	63.468978	0.015756	204
18	24.926719	1595.114630	0.000627	0.040118	63.992160	0.015627	216
19	29.802839	1920.189249	0.000521	0.033554	64.429743	0.015521	228
20	35.632816	2308.854370	0.000433	0.028064	64.795732	0.015433	240
21	42.603242	2773.549452	0.000361	0.023472	65.101841	0.015361	252
22	50.937210	3329.147335	0.000300	0.019632	65.357866	0.015300	264
23	60.901454	3993.430261	0.000250	0.016420	65.572002	0.015250	276
24	72.814885	4787.658998	0.000209	0.013733	65.751103	0.015209	288
25	87.058800	5737.253308	0.000174	0.011486	65.900901	0.015174	300
26	104.089083	6872.605521	0.000146	0.009607	66.026190	0.015146	312
27	124.450799	8230.053258	0.000122	0.008035	66.130980	0.015122	324
28	148.795637	9853.042438	0.000101	0.006721	66.218625	0.015101	336
29	177.902767	11793.517795	0.000085	0.005621	66.291930	0.015085	348
30	212.703781	14113.585393	0.000071	0.004701	66.353242	0.015071	360
31	254.312506	16887.500371	0.000059	0.003932	66.404522	0.015059	372
32	304.060653	20204.043526	0.000049	0.003289	66.447412	0.015049	384
33	363.540442	24169.362788	0.000041	0.002751	66.483285	0.015041	396
34	434.655558	28910.370553	0.000035	0.002301	66.513289	0.015035	408
35	519.682084	34578.805588	0.000029	0.001924	66.538383	0.015029	420
36	621.341343	41356.089520	0.000024	0.001609	66.559372	0.015024	432
37	742.887000	49459.133342	0.000020	0.001346	66.576927	0.015020	444
38	888.209197	59147.279780	0.000017	0.001126	66.591609	0.015017	456
39	1061.959056	70730.603709	0.000014	0.000942	66.603890	0.015014	468
40	1269.697544	84579.836283	0.000012	0.000788	66.614161	0.015012	480

18.00%   ANNUAL COMPOUND INTEREST TABLES   18.00%
                                    EFFECTIVE RATE 18.00

	1	2	3	4	5	6
	AMOUNT OF $1 AT COMPOUND INTEREST	ACCUMULATION OF $1 PER PERIOD	SINKING FUND FACTOR	PRESENT VALUE REVERSION OF $1	PRESENT VALUE ORD. ANNUITY $1 PER PERIOD	INSTALMENT TO AMORTIZE $1
YEARS						
1	1.180000	1.000000	1.000000	0.847458	0.847458	1.180000
2	1.392400	2.180000	0.458716	0.718184	1.565642	0.638716
3	1.643032	3.572400	0.279924	0.608631	2.174273	0.459924
4	1.938778	5.215432	0.191739	0.515789	2.690062	0.371739
5	2.287758	7.154210	0.139778	0.437109	3.127171	0.319778
6	2.699554	9.441968	0.105910	0.370432	3.497603	0.285910
7	3.185474	12.141522	0.082362	0.313925	3.811528	0.262362
8	3.758859	15.326996	0.065244	0.266038	4.077566	0.245244
9	4.435454	19.085855	0.052395	0.225456	4.303022	0.232395
10	5.233836	23.521309	0.042515	0.191064	4.494086	0.222515
11	6.175926	28.755144	0.034776	0.161919	4.656005	0.214776
12	7.287593	34.931070	0.028628	0.137220	4.793225	0.208628
13	8.599359	42.218663	0.023686	0.116288	4.909513	0.203686
14	10.147244	50.818022	0.019678	0.098549	5.008062	0.199678
15	11.973748	60.965266	0.016403	0.083516	5.091578	0.196403
16	14.129023	72.939014	0.013710	0.070776	5.162354	0.193710
17	16.672247	87.068036	0.011485	0.059980	5.222334	0.191485
18	19.673251	103.740283	0.009639	0.050830	5.273164	0.189639
19	23.214436	123.413534	0.008103	0.043077	5.316241	0.188103
20	27.393035	146.627970	0.006820	0.036506	5.352746	0.186820
21	32.323781	174.021005	0.005746	0.030937	5.383683	0.185746
22	38.142061	206.344785	0.004846	0.026218	5.409901	0.184846
23	45.007632	244.486847	0.004090	0.022218	5.432120	0.184090
24	53.109006	289.494479	0.003454	0.018829	5.450949	0.183454
25	62.668627	342.603486	0.002919	0.015957	5.466906	0.182919
26	73.948980	405.272113	0.002467	0.013523	5.480429	0.182467
27	87.259797	479.221093	0.002087	0.011460	5.491889	0.182087
28	102.966560	566.480890	0.001765	0.009712	5.501601	0.181765
29	121.500541	669.447450	0.001494	0.008230	5.509831	0.181494
30	143.370638	790.947991	0.001264	0.006975	5.516806	0.181264
31	169.177353	934.318630	0.001070	0.005911	5.522717	0.181070
32	199.629277	1103.495983	0.000906	0.005009	5.527726	0.180906
33	235.562547	1303.125260	0.000767	0.004245	5.531971	0.180767
34	277.963805	1538.687807	0.000650	0.003598	5.535569	0.180650
35	327.997290	1816.651612	0.000550	0.003049	5.538618	0.180550
36	387.036802	2144.648902	0.000466	0.002584	5.541201	0.180466
37	456.703427	2531.685705	0.000395	0.002190	5.543391	0.180395
38	538.910044	2988.389132	0.000335	0.001856	5.545247	0.180335
39	635.913852	3527.299175	0.000284	0.001573	5.546819	0.180284
40	750.378345	4163.213027	0.000240	0.001333	5.548152	0.180240
41	885.446447	4913.591372	0.000204	0.001129	5.549281	0.180204
42	1044.826807	5799.037819	0.000172	0.000957	5.550238	0.180172
43	1232.895633	6843.864626	0.000146	0.000811	5.551049	0.180146
44	1454.816847	8076.760259	0.000124	0.000687	5.551737	0.180124
45	1716.683879	9531.577105	0.000105	0.000583	5.552319	0.180105
46	2025.686977	11248.260984	0.000089	0.000494	5.552813	0.180089
47	2390.310633	13273.947961	0.000075	0.000418	5.553231	0.180075
48	2820.566547	15664.258594	0.000064	0.000355	5.553586	0.180064
49	3328.268525	18484.825141	0.000054	0.000300	5.553886	0.180054
50	3927.356860	21813.093667	0.000046	0.000255	5.554141	0.180046

APPENDIX C
Coefficients for Present Value of $1

$$\text{Coefficient} = \frac{1}{(1+i)^n}$$

To be received at the end of

Discount Rate

Period	1%	2%	3%	4%	5%	6%	7%	8%	9%	10%	12%	14%	15%
1	.990	.980	.971	.962	.952	.943	.935	.926	.917	.909	.893	.877	.870
2	.980	.961	.943	.925	.907	.890	.873	.857	.842	.826	.797	.769	.756
3	.971	.942	.915	.889	.864	.840	.816	.794	.772	.751	.712	.675	.658
4	.961	.924	.889	.855	.823	.792	.763	.735	.708	.683	.636	.592	.572
5	.951	.906	.863	.822	.784	.747	.713	.681	.650	.621	.567	.519	.497
6	.942	.888	.838	.790	.746	.705	.666	.630	.596	.564	.507	.456	.432
7	.933	.871	.813	.760	.711	.665	.623	.583	.547	.513	.452	.400	.376
8	.923	.853	.789	.731	.677	.627	.582	.540	.502	.467	.404	.351	.327
9	.914	.837	.766	.703	.645	.592	.544	.500	.460	.424	.361	.308	.284
10	.905	.820	.744	.676	.614	.558	.508	.463	.422	.386	.322	.270	.247
11	.896	.804	.722	.650	.585	.527	.475	.429	.388	.350	.287	.237	.215
12	.887	.788	.701	.625	.557	.497	.444	.397	.356	.319	.257	.208	.187
13	.879	.773	.681	.601	.530	.469	.445	.368	.326	.290	.229	.182	.163
14	.870	.758	.661	.577	.505	.442	.388	.340	.299	.263	.205	.160	.141
15	.861	.743	.642	.555	.481	.417	.362	.315	.275	.239	.183	.140	.123
16	.853	.728	.623	.534	.458	.394	.339	.292	.252	.218	.163	.123	.107
17	.844	.714	.605	.513	.436	.371	.317	.270	.231	.198	.146	.108	.093
18	.836	.700	.587	.494	.416	.350	.296	.250	.212	.180	.130	.095	.081
19	.828	.686	.570	.475	.396	.331	.276	.232	.194	.164	.116	.083	.070
20	.820	.673	.554	.456	.377	.312	.258	.215	.178	.149	.104	.073	.061
25	.780	.610	.478	.375	.295	.233	.184	.146	.116	.092	.059	.038	.030
30	.742	.552	.412	.308	.231	.174	.131	.099	.075	.057	.033	.020	.015

Period	16%	18%	20%	24%	28%	32%	36%	40%	50%	60%	70%	80%	90%
1	.862	.847	.833	.806	.781	.758	.735	.714	.667	.625	.588	.556	.526
2	.743	.718	.694	.650	.610	.574	.541	.510	.444	.391	.346	.309	.277
3	.641	.609	.579	.524	.477	.435	.398	.364	.296	.244	.204	.171	.146
4	.552	.516	.482	.423	.373	.329	.292	.260	.198	.153	.120	.095	.077
5	.476	.437	.402	.341	.291	.250	.215	.186	.132	.095	.070	.053	.040
6	.410	.370	.335	.275	.227	.189	.158	.133	.088	.060	.041	.029	.021
7	.354	.314	.279	.222	.178	.143	.116	.095	.059	.037	.024	.016	.011
8	.305	.266	.233	.179	.139	.108	.085	.068	.039	.023	.014	.009	.006
9	.263	.226	.194	.144	.108	.082	.063	.048	.026	.015	.008	.005	.003
10	.227	.191	.162	.116	.085	.062	.046	.035	.017	.009	.005	.003	.002
11	.195	.162	.135	.094	.066	.047	.034	.025	.012	.006	.003	.002	.001
12	.168	.137	.112	.076	.052	.036	.025	.018	.008	.004	.002	.001	.001
13	.145	.116	.093	.061	.040	.027	.018	.013	.005	.002	.001	.001	.000
14	.125	.099	.078	.049	.032	.021	.014	.009	.003	.001	.001	.000	.000
15	.108	.084	.065	.040	.025	.016	.010	.006	.002	.001	.000	.000	.000
16	.093	.071	.054	.032	.019	.012	.007	.005	.002	.001	.000	.000	
17	.080	.060	.045	.026	.015	.009	.005	.003	.001	.000	.000		
18	.069	.051	.038	.021	.012	.007	.004	.002	.001	.000	.000		
19	.060	.043	.031	.017	.009	.005	.003	.002	.000	.000			
20	.051	.037	.026	.014	.007	.004	.002	.001	.000	.000			
25	.024	.016	.010	.005	.002	.001	.000	.000					
30	.012	.007	.004	.002	.001	.000	.000						

Coefficients for Present Value of a $1 Annuity

$$\text{Coefficient} = \sum_{n=1}^{n} \frac{1}{(1+i)^n}$$

Received at the end of each period for:

Discount Rate

Period	1%	2%	3%	4%	5%	6%	7%	8%	9%	10%
1	0.990	0.980	0.971	0.962	0.952	0.943	0.935	0.926	0.917	0.909
2	1.970	1.942	1.913	1.886	1.859	1.833	1.808	1.783	1.759	1.736
3	2.941	2.884	2.829	2.775	2.723	2.673	2.624	2.577	2.531	2.487
4	3.902	3.808	3.717	3.630	3.546	3.465	3.387	3.312	3.240	3.170
5	4.853	4.713	4.580	4.452	4.329	4.212	4.100	3.993	3.890	3.791
6	5.795	5.601	5.417	5.242	5.076	4.917	4.766	4.623	4.486	4.355
7	6.728	6.472	6.230	6.002	5.786	5.582	5.389	5.206	5.033	4.868
8	7.652	7.325	7.020	6.733	6.463	6.210	5.971	5.747	5.535	5.335
9	8.566	8.162	7.786	7.435	7.108	6.802	6.515	6.247	5.995	5.759
10	9.471	8.983	8.530	8.111	7.722	7.360	7.024	6.710	6.418	6.145
11	10.368	9.787	9.253	8.760	8.306	7.887	7.499	7.139	6.805	6.495
12	11.255	10.575	9.954	9.385	8.863	8.384	7.943	7.536	7.161	6.814
13	12.134	11.348	10.635	9.986	9.394	8.853	8.358	7.904	7.487	7.103
14	13.004	12.106	11.296	10.563	9.899	9.295	8.745	8.244	7.786	7.367
15	13.865	12.849	11.938	11.118	10.380	9.712	9.108	8.559	8.060	7.606
16	14.718	13.578	12.561	11.652	10.838	10.106	9.447	8.851	8.312	7.824
17	15.562	14.292	13.166	12.166	11.274	10.477	9.763	9.122	8.544	8.022
18	16.398	14.992	13.754	12.659	11.690	10.828	10.059	9.372	8.756	8.201
19	17.226	15.678	14.324	13.134	12.085	11.158	10.336	9.604	8.950	8.365
20	18.046	16.351	14.877	13.590	12.462	11.470	10.594	9.818	9.128	8.514
25	22.023	19.523	17.413	15.622	14.094	12.783	11.654	10.675	9.823	9.077
30	25.808	22.397	19.600	17.292	15.373	13.765	12.409	11.258	10.274	9.427

Period	12%	14%	16%	18%	20%	24%	28%	32%	36%
1	0.893	0.877	0.862	0.847	0.833	0.806	0.781	0.758	0.735
2	1.690	1.647	1.605	1.566	1.528	1.457	1.392	1.332	1.276
3	2.402	2.322	2.246	2.174	2.106	1.981	1.868	1.766	1.674
4	3.037	2.914	2.798	2.690	2.589	2.404	2.241	2.096	1.966
5	3.605	3.433	3.274	3.127	2.991	2.745	2.532	2.345	2.181
6	4.111	3.889	3.685	3.498	3.326	3.020	2.759	2.534	2.339
7	4.564	4.288	4.039	3.812	3.605	3.242	2.937	2.678	2.455
8	4.968	4.639	4.344	4.078	3.837	3.421	3.076	2.786	2.540
9	5.328	4.946	4.607	4.303	4.031	3.566	3.184	2.868	2.603
10	5.650	5.216	4.833	4.494	4.193	3.682	3.269	2.930	2.650
11	5.938	5.435	5.029	4.656	4.327	3.776	3.335	2.978	2.683
12	6.194	5.660	5.197	4.793	4.439	3.851	3.387	3.013	2.708
13	6.424	5.842	5.342	4.910	4.533	3.912	3.427	3.040	2.727
14	6.628	6.002	5.468	5.008	4.611	3.962	3.459	3.061	2.740
15	6.811	6.142	5.575	5.092	4.675	4.001	3.483	3.076	2.750
16	6.974	6.265	5.669	5.162	4.730	4.033	3.503	3.088	2.758
17	7.120	5.373	5.749	5.222	4.775	4.059	3.518	3.097	2.763
18	7.250	6.467	5.818	5.273	4.812	4.080	3.529	3.104	2.767
19	7.366	6.550	5.877	5.316	4.844	4.097	3.539	3.109	2.770
20	7.469	6.623	5.929	5.353	4.870	4.110	3.546	3.113	2.772
25	7.843	6.873	6.097	5.467	4.948	4.147	3.564	3.122	2.776
30	8.055	7.003	6.177	5.517	4.979	4.160	3.569	3.124	2.778

APPENDIX D
Mortgage Constant: Monthly Payment in Arrears

Description: This table shows the percent of the principal amount of a loan needed each year to pay off the loan when the actual payments are monthly and are paid in arrears. Divide the percent by 12 to get the level monthly payment per $100 that includes both interest and principal.

Example: The Constant Annual Percent needed to pay off a 15%, 30 year loan if payments are made monthly and in arrears is 15.18%. Divide by 12 to get the actual monthly payment. The constant annual payment for a $50,000 loan is $7,590. The monthly payment is $632.50.

INTEREST RATE	5 yr	6 yr	7 yr	8 yr	9 yr	10 yr	11 yr	12 yr	13 yr	14 yr	15 yr	16 yr	17 yr	18 yr	19 yr	20 yr
4.00	22.10	18.78	16.41	14.63	13.25	12.15	11.26	10.51	9.88	9.35	8.88	8.48	8.12	7.81	7.53	7.28
4.25	22.24	18.92	16.55	14.77	13.40	12.30	11.40	10.66	10.03	9.49	9.03	8.63	8.28	7.96	7.68	7.44
4.50	22.38	19.05	16.69	14.91	13.54	12.44	11.55	10.81	10.18	9.65	9.18	8.78	8.43	8.12	7.84	7.60
4.75	22.51	19.19	16.83	15.05	13.68	12.59	11.69	10.95	10.33	9.80	9.34	8.94	8.59	8.28	8.01	7.76
5.00	22.65	19.33	16.97	15.20	13.83	12.73	11.84	11.10	10.48	9.95	9.49	9.10	8.75	8.44	8.17	7.92
5.25	22.79	19.47	17.11	15.34	13.97	12.88	11.99	11.25	10.63	10.11	9.65	9.26	8.91	8.60	8.33	8.09
5.50	22.93	19.61	17.25	15.48	14.12	13.03	12.14	11.41	10.79	10.26	9.81	9.42	9.07	8.77	8.50	8.26
5.75	23.07	19.75	17.39	15.63	14.26	13.18	12.29	11.56	10.94	10.42	9.97	9.58	9.24	8.94	8.67	8.43
6.00	23.20	19.89	17.54	15.77	14.41	13.33	12.45	11.72	11.10	10.58	10.13	9.74	9.40	9.10	8.84	8.60
6.25	23.34	20.03	17.68	15.92	14.56	13.48	12.60	11.87	11.26	10.74	10.29	9.91	9.57	9.27	9.01	8.78
6.50	23.48	20.18	17.82	16.07	14.71	13.63	12.75	12.03	11.42	10.90	10.46	10.07	9.74	9.44	9.18	8.95
6.75	23.63	20.32	17.97	16.22	14.86	13.78	12.91	12.19	11.58	11.07	10.62	10.24	9.91	9.62	9.36	9.13
7.00	23.77	20.46	18.12	16.37	15.01	13.94	13.07	12.35	11.74	11.23	10.79	10.41	10.08	9.79	9.54	9.31
7.25	23.91	20.61	18.26	16.52	15.16	14.09	13.22	12.51	11.91	11.40	10.96	10.58	10.25	9.97	9.71	9.49
7.50	24.05	20.75	18.41	16.67	15.32	14.25	13.38	12.67	12.07	11.56	11.13	10.75	10.43	10.14	9.89	9.67
7.75	24.19	20.90	18.56	16.82	15.47	14.41	13.54	12.83	12.24	11.73	11.30	10.93	10.61	10.32	10.08	9.86
8.00	24.34	21.04	18.71	16.97	15.63	14.56	13.70	12.99	12.40	11.90	11.47	11.10	10.78	10.50	10.26	10.04
8.25	24.48	21.19	18.86	17.12	15.78	14.72	13.87	13.16	12.57	12.07	11.65	11.28	10.96	10.69	10.44	10.23
8.50	24.62	21.34	19.01	17.28	15.94	14.88	14.03	13.33	12.74	12.24	11.82	11.46	11.14	10.87	10.63	10.42
8.75	24.77	21.49	19.16	17.43	16.10	15.04	14.19	13.49	12.91	12.42	12.00	11.64	11.33	11.06	10.82	10.61
9.00	24.92	21.64	19.31	17.59	16.26	15.21	14.36	13.66	13.08	12.59	12.18	11.82	11.51	11.24	11.01	10.80
9.25	25.06	21.78	19.46	17.74	16.42	15.37	14.52	13.83	13.25	12.77	12.36	12.00	11.70	11.43	11.20	11.00
9.50	25.21	21.93	19.62	17.90	16.58	15.53	14.69	14.00	13.43	12.95	12.54	12.18	11.88	11.62	11.39	11.19
9.75	25.35	22.09	19.77	18.06	16.74	15.70	14.86	14.17	13.60	13.12	12.72	12.37	12.07	11.81	11.58	11.39
10.00	25.50	22.24	19.93	18.21	16.90	15.86	15.03	14.35	13.78	13.30	12.90	12.56	12.26	12.00	11.78	11.59
10.25	25.65	22.39	20.08	18.37	17.06	16.03	15.20	14.52	13.96	13.48	13.08	12.74	12.45	12.20	11.98	11.78
10.50	25.80	22.54	20.24	18.53	17.23	16.20	15.37	14.69	14.14	13.67	13.27	12.93	12.64	12.39	12.17	11.99
10.75	25.95	22.69	20.39	18.69	17.39	16.37	15.54	14.87	14.31	13.85	13.46	13.12	12.84	12.59	12.37	12.19
11.00	26.10	22.85	20.55	18.86	17.56	16.54	15.72	15.05	14.50	14.03	13.64	13.31	13.03	12.79	12.57	12.39
11.25	26.25	23.00	20.71	19.02	17.72	16.71	15.89	15.23	14.68	14.22	13.83	13.51	13.23	12.98	12.78	12.60
11.50	26.40	23.15	20.87	19.18	17.89	16.88	16.07	15.40	14.86	14.41	14.02	13.70	13.42	13.18	12.98	12.80
11.75	26.55	23.31	21.03	19.34	18.06	17.05	16.24	15.58	15.04	14.59	14.21	13.89	13.62	13.39	13.18	13.01
12.00	26.70	23.47	21.19	19.51	18.23	17.22	16.42	15.77	15.23	14.78	14.41	14.09	13.82	13.59	13.39	13.22
12.25	26.85	23.62	21.35	19.67	18.40	17.40	16.60	15.95	15.42	14.97	14.60	14.29	14.02	13.79	13.60	13.43
12.50	27.00	23.78	21.51	19.84	18.57	17.57	16.78	16.13	15.60	15.16	14.80	14.49	14.22	14.00	13.80	13.64
12.75	27.16	23.94	21.67	20.01	18.74	17.75	16.96	16.32	15.79	15.36	15.00	14.68	14.42	14.20	14.01	13.85
13.00	27.31	24.09	21.84	20.17	18.91	17.92	17.14	16.50	15.98	15.55	15.19	14.88	14.63	14.41	14.22	14.06
13.25	27.46	24.25	22.00	20.34	19.08	18.10	17.32	16.69	16.17	15.74	15.39	15.09	14.83	14.62	14.44	14.28
13.50	27.62	24.41	22.16	20.51	19.26	18.28	17.50	16.87	16.36	15.94	15.58	15.29	15.04	14.83	14.65	14.49
13.75	27.77	24.57	22.33	20.68	19.43	18.46	17.68	17.06	16.55	16.13	15.78	15.49	15.25	15.04	14.86	14.71
14.00	27.93	24.73	22.49	20.85	19.61	18.64	17.87	17.25	16.75	16.33	15.99	15.70	15.45	15.25	15.08	14.93
14.25	28.08	24.89	22.66	21.02	19.78	18.82	18.05	17.44	16.94	16.53	16.19	15.90	15.66	15.46	15.29	15.15
14.50	28.24	25.05	22.83	21.19	19.96	19.00	18.24	17.63	17.14	16.73	16.39	16.11	15.87	15.68	15.51	15.36
14.75	28.40	25.22	22.99	21.37	20.14	19.18	18.43	17.82	17.33	16.93	16.60	16.32	16.09	15.89	15.72	15.59
15.00	28.55	25.38	23.16	21.54	20.31	19.37	18.62	18.02	17.53	17.13	16.80	16.53	16.30	16.11	15.94	15.81
15.25	28.71	25.54	23.33	21.71	20.49	19.55	18.80	18.21	17.73	17.33	17.01	16.74	16.51	16.32	16.16	16.03
15.50	28.87	25.71	23.50	21.89	20.67	19.73	18.99	18.40	17.93	17.53	17.21	16.95	16.72	16.54	16.38	16.25
15.75	29.03	25.87	23.67	22.06	20.85	19.92	19.19	18.60	18.12	17.74	17.42	17.16	16.94	16.76	16.60	16.48
16.00	29.19	26.04	23.84	22.24	21.04	20.11	19.38	18.79	18.33	17.94	17.63	17.37	17.16	16.98	16.83	16.70
16.25	29.35	26.20	24.01	22.42	21.22	20.29	19.57	18.99	18.53	18.15	17.84	17.58	17.37	17.20	17.05	16.93
16.50	29.51	26.37	24.18	22.59	21.40	20.48	19.76	19.19	18.73	18.36	18.05	17.80	17.59	17.42	17.27	17.15
16.75	29.67	26.53	24.35	22.77	21.58	20.67	19.96	19.39	18.93	18.56	18.26	18.01	17.81	17.64	17.50	17.38
17.00	29.83	26.70	24.53	22.95	21.77	20.86	20.15	19.59	19.14	18.77	18.47	18.23	18.03	17.86	17.72	17.61
17.25	29.99	26.87	24.70	23.13	21.95	21.05	20.35	19.79	19.34	18.98	18.69	18.45	18.25	18.08	17.95	17.84
17.50	30.15	27.04	24.88	23.31	22.14	21.24	20.54	19.99	19.55	19.19	18.90	18.66	18.47	18.31	18.17	18.06
17.75	30.31	27.21	25.05	23.49	22.33	21.43	20.74	20.19	19.76	19.40	19.11	18.88	18.69	18.53	18.40	18.29
18.00	30.48	27.37	25.23	23.67	22.51	21.63	20.94	20.39	19.96	19.61	19.33	19.10	18.91	18.76	18.63	18.52
18.25	30.64	27.54	25.40	23.86	22.70	21.82	21.14	20.60	20.17	19.82	19.55	19.32	19.13	18.98	18.86	18.76
18.50	30.80	27.71	25.58	24.04	22.89	22.01	21.34	20.80	20.38	20.04	19.76	19.54	19.36	19.21	19.09	18.99
18.75	30.97	27.89	25.76	24.22	23.08	22.21	21.54	21.01	20.59	20.25	19.98	19.76	19.58	19.44	19.32	19.22
19.00	31.13	28.06	25.93	24.41	23.27	22.41	21.74	21.21	20.80	20.47	20.20	19.98	19.81	19.67	19.55	19.45
19.25	31.30	28.23	26.11	24.59	23.46	22.60	21.94	21.42	21.01	20.68	20.42	20.21	20.03	19.89	19.78	19.69
19.50	31.46	28.40	26.29	24.78	23.65	22.80	22.14	21.63	21.22	20.90	20.64	20.43	20.26	20.12	20.01	19.92
19.75	31.63	28.57	26.47	24.96	23.84	23.00	22.34	21.84	21.43	21.11	20.86	20.65	20.49	20.35	20.24	20.16
20.00	31.80	28.75	26.65	25.15	24.04	23.20	22.55	22.04	21.65	21.33	21.08	20.88	20.72	20.58	20.48	20.39
20.25	31.96	28.92	26.83	25.34	24.23	23.39	22.75	22.25	21.86	21.55	21.30	21.10	20.94	20.82	20.71	20.63
20.50	32.13	29.10	27.01	25.52	24.42	23.59	22.96	22.46	22.08	21.77	21.53	21.33	21.17	21.05	20.95	20.86
20.75	32.30	29.27	27.20	25.71	24.62	23.80	23.16	22.68	22.29	21.99	21.75	21.56	21.40	21.28	21.18	21.10

SOURCE: *Thorndike Encyclopedia of Banking and Financial Tables*, Rev. Ed. (Boston: Warren, Gorham & Lamont, 1980), pp. 1–2 and 1–3.

Mortgage Constant: Monthly Payment in Arrears

INTEREST RATE	21 yr	22 yr	23 yr	24 yr	25 yr	26 yr	27 yr	28 yr	29 yr	30 yr	31 yr	32 yr	33 yr	34 yr	35 yr	40 yr
4.00	7.05	6.85	6.66	6.49	6.34	6.20	6.07	5.95	5.84	5.73	5.64	5.55	5.47	5.39	5.32	5.02
4.25	7.21	7.01	6.83	6.66	6.51	6.37	6.24	6.12	6.01	5.91	5.81	5.73	5.65	5.57	5.50	5.21
4.50	7.37	7.17	6.99	6.83	6.67	6.54	6.41	6.29	6.18	6.09	5.99	5.91	5.83	5.75	5.68	5.40
4.75	7.54	7.34	7.16	7.00	6.85	6.71	6.58	6.47	6.36	6.26	6.17	6.09	6.01	5.94	5.87	5.59
5.00	7.71	7.51	7.33	7.17	7.02	6.89	6.76	6.65	6.54	6.45	6.36	6.28	6.20	6.13	6.06	5.79
5.25	7.87	7.68	7.50	7.34	7.20	7.06	6.94	6.83	6.73	6.63	6.54	6.46	6.39	6.32	6.25	5.99
5.50	8.04	7.85	7.68	7.52	7.37	7.24	7.12	7.01	6.91	6.82	6.73	6.65	6.58	6.51	6.45	6.19
5.75	8.22	8.03	7.85	7.70	7.55	7.42	7.31	7.20	7.10	7.01	6.92	6.85	6.77	6.71	6.65	6.40
6.00	8.39	8.20	8.03	7.88	7.74	7.61	7.49	7.39	7.29	7.20	7.12	7.04	6.97	6.91	6.85	6.61
6.25	8.57	8.38	8.21	8.06	7.92	7.80	7.68	7.58	7.48	7.39	7.31	7.24	7.17	7.11	7.05	6.82
6.50	8.75	8.56	8.39	8.24	8.11	7.98	7.87	7.77	7.68	7.59	7.51	7.44	7.37	7.31	7.25	7.03
6.75	8.93	8.74	8.58	8.43	8.30	8.17	8.06	7.96	7.87	7.79	7.71	7.64	7.58	7.52	7.46	7.25
7.00	9.11	8.93	8.76	8.62	8.49	8.37	8.26	8.16	8.07	7.99	7.91	7.85	7.78	7.72	7.67	7.46
7.25	9.29	9.11	8.95	8.81	8.68	8.56	8.46	8.36	8.27	8.19	8.12	8.05	7.99	7.93	7.88	7.68
7.50	9.47	9.30	9.14	9.00	8.87	8.76	8.65	8.56	8.47	8.40	8.32	8.26	8.20	8.15	8.10	7.90
7.75	9.66	9.49	9.33	9.19	9.07	8.96	8.85	8.76	8.68	8.60	8.53	8.47	8.41	8.36	8.31	8.12
8.00	9.85	9.68	9.53	9.39	9.27	9.16	9.06	8.97	8.88	8.81	8.74	8.68	8.63	8.57	8.53	8.35
8.25	10.04	9.87	9.72	9.59	9.47	9.36	9.26	9.17	9.09	9.02	8.95	8.90	8.84	8.79	8.75	8.57
8.50	10.23	10.07	9.92	9.79	9.67	9.56	9.47	9.38	9.30	9.23	9.17	9.11	9.06	9.01	8.97	8.80
8.75	10.43	10.26	10.12	9.99	9.87	9.77	9.67	9.59	9.51	9.45	9.38	9.33	9.28	9.23	9.19	9.03
9.00	10.62	10.46	10.32	10.19	10.08	9.97	9.88	9.80	9.73	9.66	9.60	9.55	9.50	9.45	9.41	9.26
9.25	10.82	10.66	10.52	10.39	10.28	10.18	10.09	10.01	9.94	9.88	9.82	9.77	9.72	9.68	9.64	9.49
9.50	11.01	10.86	10.72	10.60	10.49	10.39	10.31	10.23	10.16	10.10	10.04	9.99	9.94	9.90	9.86	9.73
9.75	11.21	11.06	10.93	10.81	10.70	10.60	10.52	10.44	10.38	10.31	10.26	10.21	10.16	10.13	10.09	9.96
10.00	11.41	11.26	11.13	11.01	10.91	10.82	10.73	10.66	10.59	10.54	10.48	10.44	10.39	10.36	10.32	10.19
10.25	11.62	11.47	11.34	11.22	11.12	11.03	10.95	10.88	10.82	10.76	10.71	10.66	10.62	10.58	10.55	10.43
10.50	11.82	11.68	11.55	11.43	11.34	11.25	11.17	11.10	11.04	10.98	10.93	10.89	10.85	10.81	10.78	10.67
10.75	12.03	11.88	11.76	11.65	11.55	11.46	11.39	11.32	11.26	11.21	11.16	11.12	11.08	11.05	11.02	10.91
11.00	12.23	12.09	11.97	11.86	11.76	11.68	11.61	11.54	11.48	11.43	11.39	11.35	11.31	11.28	11.25	11.14
11.25	12.44	12.30	12.18	12.08	11.98	11.90	11.83	11.77	11.71	11.66	11.62	11.58	11.54	11.51	11.48	11.38
11.50	12.65	12.51	12.40	12.29	12.20	12.12	12.05	11.99	11.94	11.89	11.85	11.81	11.77	11.74	11.72	11.62
11.75	12.86	12.73	12.61	12.51	12.42	12.35	12.28	12.22	12.16	12.12	12.08	12.04	12.01	11.98	11.95	11.87
12.00	13.07	12.94	12.83	12.73	12.64	12.57	12.50	12.44	12.39	12.35	12.31	12.27	12.24	12.22	12.19	12.11
12.25	13.28	13.16	13.05	12.95	12.87	12.79	12.73	12.67	12.62	12.58	12.54	12.51	12.48	12.45	12.43	12.35
12.50	13.50	13.37	13.26	13.17	13.09	13.02	12.96	12.90	12.85	12.81	12.78	12.74	12.71	12.69	12.67	12.59
12.75	13.71	13.59	13.48	13.39	13.31	13.24	13.18	13.13	13.09	13.05	13.01	12.98	12.95	12.93	12.91	12.84
13.00	13.93	13.81	13.71	13.62	13.54	13.47	13.41	13.36	13.32	13.28	13.25	13.22	13.19	13.17	13.15	13.08
13.25	14.14	14.03	13.93	13.84	13.77	13.70	13.64	13.59	13.55	13.51	13.48	13.45	13.43	13.41	13.39	13.32
13.50	14.36	14.25	14.15	14.07	13.99	13.93	13.87	13.83	13.79	13.75	13.72	13.69	13.67	13.65	13.63	13.57
13.75	14.58	14.47	14.37	14.29	14.22	14.16	14.11	14.06	14.02	13.99	13.96	13.93	13.91	13.89	13.87	13.81
14.00	14.80	14.69	14.60	14.52	14.45	14.39	14.34	14.30	14.26	14.22	14.19	14.17	14.15	14.13	14.11	14.06
14.25	15.02	14.92	14.82	14.75	14.68	14.62	14.57	14.53	14.49	14.46	14.43	14.41	14.39	14.37	14.36	14.30
14.50	15.24	15.14	15.05	14.98	14.91	14.86	14.81	14.77	14.73	14.70	14.67	14.65	14.63	14.61	14.60	14.55
14.75	15.47	15.37	15.28	15.21	15.14	15.09	15.04	15.00	14.97	14.94	14.91	14.89	14.87	14.86	14.84	14.80
15.00	15.69	15.59	15.51	15.44	15.37	15.32	15.28	15.24	15.21	15.18	15.15	15.13	15.12	15.10	15.09	15.04
15.25	15.92	15.82	15.74	15.67	15.61	15.56	15.51	15.48	15.45	15.42	15.40	15.38	15.36	15.34	15.33	15.29
15.50	16.14	16.05	15.97	15.90	15.84	15.79	15.75	15.72	15.69	15.66	15.64	15.62	15.60	15.59	15.58	15.54
15.75	16.37	16.28	16.20	16.13	16.08	16.03	15.99	15.95	15.93	15.90	15.88	15.86	15.85	15.83	15.82	15.79
16.00	16.59	16.50	16.43	16.37	16.31	16.27	16.23	16.19	16.17	16.14	16.12	16.09	16.08	16.07	16.07	16.03
16.25	16.82	16.74	16.66	16.60	16.55	16.50	16.47	16.43	16.41	16.38	16.36	16.35	16.33	16.32	16.31	16.28
16.50	17.05	16.97	16.89	16.83	16.78	16.74	16.71	16.67	16.65	16.63	16.61	16.59	16.58	16.57	16.56	16.53
16.75	17.28	17.20	17.13	17.07	17.02	16.98	16.94	16.92	16.89	16.87	16.85	16.84	16.82	16.81	16.80	16.78
17.00	17.51	17.43	17.36	17.31	17.26	17.22	17.19	17.16	17.13	17.11	17.10	17.08	17.07	17.06	17.05	17.02
17.25	17.74	17.66	17.60	17.54	17.50	17.46	17.43	17.40	17.38	17.36	17.34	17.33	17.32	17.31	17.30	17.27
17.50	17.97	17.90	17.83	17.78	17.74	17.70	17.67	17.64	17.62	17.60	17.59	17.57	17.56	17.55	17.55	17.52
17.75	18.20	18.13	18.07	18.02	17.97	17.94	17.91	17.88	17.86	17.85	17.83	17.82	17.81	17.80	17.79	17.77
18.00	18.44	18.37	18.31	18.26	18.21	18.18	18.15	18.13	18.11	18.09	18.08	18.06	18.05	18.05	18.04	18.02
18.25	18.67	18.60	18.54	18.49	18.45	18.42	18.39	18.37	18.35	18.34	18.32	18.31	18.30	18.29	18.29	18.27
18.50	18.90	18.84	18.78	18.73	18.69	18.66	18.64	18.61	18.60	18.58	18.57	18.56	18.55	18.54	18.54	18.52
18.75	19.14	19.07	19.02	18.97	18.94	18.90	18.88	18.86	18.84	18.83	18.81	18.80	18.80	18.79	18.78	18.77
19.00	19.37	19.31	19.26	19.21	19.18	19.15	19.12	19.10	19.09	19.07	19.06	19.05	19.04	19.04	19.03	19.02
19.25	19.61	19.55	19.50	19.45	19.42	19.39	19.37	19.35	19.33	19.32	19.31	19.30	19.29	19.28	19.28	19.26
19.50	19.85	19.79	19.74	19.69	19.66	19.63	19.61	19.59	19.58	19.56	19.55	19.55	19.54	19.53	19.53	19.51
19.75	20.08	20.02	19.98	19.94	19.90	19.88	19.86	19.84	19.82	19.81	19.80	19.79	19.79	19.78	19.78	19.76
20.00	20.32	20.26	20.22	20.18	20.15	20.12	20.10	20.08	20.07	20.06	20.05	20.04	20.03	20.03	20.02	20.01
20.25	20.56	20.50	20.46	20.42	20.39	20.36	20.34	20.33	20.32	20.30	20.30	20.29	20.28	20.28	20.27	20.26
20.50	20.80	20.74	20.70	20.66	20.63	20.61	20.59	20.57	20.56	20.55	20.54	20.54	20.53	20.53	20.52	20.51
20.75	21.03	20.98	20.94	20.90	20.88	20.85	20.84	20.82	20.81	20.80	20.79	20.78	20.78	20.77	20.77	20.76

INDEX

Abandonment, 596
Aberle case, 596**n.**
Abrams, Daniel S., 142**n.**
Absorption phase of property life cycle, 49
Absorption rate, 439–442
Accelerated basis, 235
Accelerated cost recovery system (ACRS), depreciation and, 334–341, 762, 776, 794, 819, 851, 881, 891
Accelerated depreciation, 230**n.**, 332–333, 336
Accessibility, 403
Accounting controls, 266
Accounting methods:
  accrual method, 346–348
  cash method, 346–348
Accounting rate of return, 243
Accounting and record keeping by property managers, 551–553
Accredited resident manager (ARM), 541
Accrual method of accounting, 346–348
Acquisition phase of ownership life cycle, 51
Active income, 337
Active investors, 16–18
Adams, John S., 383**n.**, 404**n.**
Add-on, 282
Adjustable-rate mortgage (ARM), 284
Adjusted gross income (AGI), 327
Adler and Lenz, 310**n.**
Administrative responsibilities of property manager, 535, 551–553
Advertising, 544
Aerial photographs, land use patterns analyzed through, 402–403, 404–405
Aetna, 46
After-tax cash flow, **see** Cash flow after tax
After-tax internal rate-of-return model, 74–75
Age composition of the population, 389, 390
Agglomerating tendency of industrial buildings, 834
Aging process of property life cycle, 50
Agricultural land, impact of inflation on, 467–468. **See also** Raw land
Air and subsurface rights, 542
Alderson case, 607, 610
Aldrich, Peter C., 477**n.**, 653**n.**
Allen, Roger G., 54, 868
Alternative minimum tax (AMT), 342–343
American Arbitration Association, 585
American College Dictionary, 86**n.**
American Hotel and Motel Association, 877
American Institute of Real Estate Appraisers (AIREA), 41, 55**n.**, 705
  Textbook Revision Subcommittee, 41**n.**, 42**n.**
American Society of Real Estate Counselors (ASREC), 55**n.**, 705
American Trucking Association, 835
Amortization, 231
  method of, 280–281
  terms of, 280
Analysis of a property, **see** Investment analysis
Anchor tenant, 769
Andrews, Richard B., 400**n.**
Annualized net present value (ANPV), 254
Annual living expenses, statement of, 664–665
Annual reevaluation of real estate investments, 600–602
Annual U.S. Economic Data, 482
Apartment owners and managers associations (AOMAs), 757
Apartments, 750–762. **See also** Lease(s); Small apartment buildings
  advantages and disadvantages of investing in, 755
  Aspen Wood, **see** Aspen Wood Apartments
  categories of, 751–753
  characteristics of, as investments, 735–736, 744–747
  discounted-cash-flow-analysis, 761
  financing, 760–761
  inflation's impact on, 470–471
  investment decision, 762
  outlook for, 717
  preliminary analyses, 756–760
    financial, 758–760
    market and marketability, 756–757
    physical, legal, political, and environmental, 757–758
  taxation, 761–762
    depreciation method for, 336, 762
    investment interest limitations, 345
    passive income rules, 337, 340
    small buildings, **see** Small apartment buildings
  track record and trends, 753–754
  types of investors and investor motivations, 755–759
Apgar, Mahlon, IV, 7**n.**, 8**n.**, 267**n.**, 695
Applebaum, William, 417**n.**, 419**n.**
Appraisal, **see** Real estate appraisal
Appreciation, 12–13, 864–865
Appreciation leverage, 277–278
Approved Management Organizations (AMOs), 541
Arbitrage pricing theory (APT), 80
Archer, Dr. Wayne R., 228**n.**
Architecture:
  engineering and, study of, 40
  of hotels and motels, 878
  of industrial buildings, 839–842
  of shopping centers, 769
Arnold, Alvin L., 33**n.**, 277**n.**, 284**n.**, 290**n.**, 293**n.**, 304**n.**, 324**n.**, 336**n.**, 350**n.**, 517**n.**, 541**n.**, 588**n.**, 611**n.**, 614**n.**, 653**n.**
Arthur Andersen & Co., 149**n.**, 598**n.**, 600**n.**
Artificial accounting losses, 233, 340
Aspen Wood Apartments, 119–124
  basic financial feasibility model applied to, 204–209
  capital expenditures, 361–363
  cash flow analysis, 364–365, 366
  computer analysis, 228–239
  depreciation schedules, 363
  description of the property, 119–121
  detailed feasibility research, 270–272

discounted-cash-flow analysis, 225–239, 272–273, 278, 367–369
final sales contract, 529–532
financing for, 269, 279, 290–291, 317–321
introduction, 119
investment strategy, 119–124
  basic screening criteria, 124
  investment objectives and criteria, 123–124
  investment philosophy, 122–123
  investment plans and policies, 124
loan schedules, 363
negotiations with the seller, 269–270
net cash position analysis, 365–367
operating assumptions, 364, 365
ownership decision model applied to, 167–169
projection of net sale proceeds, 367, 368
property and asset management, 564–573
ratio analysis and final investment decision, 369
return-risk evaluation, 272–273
termination of investment in, 615–622
Asset allocation model, 679
Asset management, **see** Venture (asset) management
Assets, personal, 662–664
  allocation of, review of, 667
Assumption base ratios, 244–245
"At-risk" rules, 289, 291–292, 341–342
Auctions, 591
Audit by IRS, 350–351
Axial-growth theory, 401

Babcock, Guilford C., 223n.
Bailard, Biehl, and Kaiser, Inc., 681–682
Bailey, C. W., 541n.
Bailey, John B., 415n.
Baird case, 608
Baker, James A., 228n., 361n.
Balance sheet, personal, 662–664
Balbach, Rachel, 459n.
Ball, S. Timothy, 594n.
Balloon loan, 280–281
Bank America, 10
Barasch, Clarence S., 526n.
Bargains, 59
Barlowe, Raleigh, 400n.
Barr, Gary K., 307n., 308n.
Barrett, G. Vincent, 380n., 400n., 415n., 427n.
Bartlett, William W., 461n.
Basic financial feasibility model (BFFM), 170–203, 253
  application of, 189–197
    analyzing rent and expense variability, 191–193
    to Aspen Wood Apartments, 204–209
    completion and changing property usage, 195–196
    conclusion, 197
    multiple loans and joint ventures,

193–195
    concepts, principles, and techniques related to, 171–182
    developing a detailed one-year pro forma, 197–202
      how current NOI can be distorted, 198–201
      other sources of data, 201–202
    the model, 182–189
      formulas in, 187
      illustration of, 183–186
      restructuring the financial package, 186–189
    preliminary negotiations using, 515
Basic screening criteria, 106–108
  of Aspen Wood Apartments, 124
Basis, 581–583
  adjusted, 582
  of exchanged property, 611–614
  in general partnership, 137
  in limited partnership, 143–144
  mortgage greater than, 583
  original, 582
Bayesian analysis, 635
Beaton, William R., 70n.
Before-tax cash flow, **see** Cash flow (before tax)
Before-tax internal-rate-of-return model, 74
Belknap Data Solutions, 836n.
Bell, David E., 432n.
Bell, Robert, 289n., 526n.
Bernard case, 609
Bernstein, Joel H., 304n.
Best-fit approach, 69–71
Better-than-market operating results, 175
Betts, Richard M., 400n.
Biases and irrational preferences, 108–110
Birthrates, 388
Blair, John P., 380n., 400n., 415n., 427n.
Blank check syndication offerings, 310–311
Blazer, Sheldon M., 470n.
Blind pool syndication offerings, 310–311
Bloom, David E., 694n.
Bloomberg, Barbara S., 419n.
Blue Cross, 885
"Blue-sky laws," state, 315
Bockl, George, 54, 57–58, 69
Body, Zvi, 476n.
Boehm, Thomas P., 469n.
Bona fide tenants, 200
Bonds:
  industrial real estate, 848–849
  outlook for, 702–703
Boot, 609–610
Born, Waldo L., 314n., 409n., 432n., 448n., 449n., 451n., 462n.
Bottom-line, 234
Boundaries for marketability analysis, establishing, 428–429
Bower, D., 80n.
Bower, R. S., 80n.
Boyce, Byrl, 38n., 410n., 426n., 826n.
Break-even leverage, 181
Break-even ratio (point), 76, 178, 179, 243, 554

Brealey, Richard, 451n.
Breeden, D. T., 80n.
Brennan, William G., 712
Brenner, Michael J., 287n.
Brigham, Eugene F., 180n., 216n., 220n., 221n., 451n.
Britton, James A., Jr., 171n., 264n.
Brokers:
  industrial, 844–845
  role in negotiations of, 519
Brooks, Jeb, 591n.
Brown, Gordon T., 484n.
Brown, Lawrence E., 651n.
Brueggeman, William, 80, 652
Brummer, J., 417n.
Bucklin, L., 417n.
Budget motels, 872
Budget preparation, 551–552
Builder-developer, 18
Building Owners and Managers Association (BOMA), 453, 737
  Experience Exchange Reports, 816–818
  International, 809, 815, 817n.
Building phase, 115–116
Build-lease (build to suit), 846
Bureau of the Census, 374–375, 376, 384, 394, 432, 754n., 830n., 883
Bureau of Economic Analysis, 381, 392, 396, 432n.
Bureau of Labor Statistics, 432n., 453n., 454
Burger, Eugene J., 556n.
Burgess, Ernest, 400–401
Burns, Leland S., 489n.
Business cycle, general, and real estate cycle, 489–490
Business risk, 250–252.
Buy-sell agreement, 585

CACI Inc., 432, 433–437
Cady, K. B., 248n.
Cambon, Barbara R., 13n., 450n.
Campbell, Kenneth, 625n.
Canadian rollover, **see** Renegotiated rate mortgage (RRM)
Capital appreciation, 12–13, 864–865
Capital assets, 329, 330, 331
  defined, 32
Capital budgeting approaches, **see** Modern capital budgeting approaches
Capital expenditures:
  Aspen Wood Apartments, 361–363
  forecasts of, 444
  vs. maintenance expenses, 543
  vs. operating expenses, 348, 358
  policy for, 548
  predicting necessary, 543
  property needing substantial, 199
Capital gains taxes, 235, 325, 327, 329–334, 579, 581
  capital gains **vs.** ordinary income, 329–334
  conditions for long-term capital gain treatment, 329–332

depreciation capture, 332–334
exchange of properties and, 611–613
installment sales and, 289, 332, 359, 587–591, 909, 910
selection of ownership form and, 129, 136, 146–147, 151, 153
Capitalization of expenses, improper, 199
Capitalization method for financial independence calculation, 676, 677
Capitalization rate trends, 709, 710
Capital outlay requirements, ownership form and, 131, 147
Capture rates, 442–444, 520
Carliner, Michael S., 698
Carlson, Don W., 537**n.**
Carlton case, 608
Carn, Neil, 378**n.**, 415**n.**, 422**n.**, 426**n**, 443**n.**
Carr, E. William, 594**n.**
Carr, Jack L., 473**n.**
Caruth case, 590**n.**
Case, Fred E., 96**n.**, 400**n.**, 484–485, 489**n.**, 494**n.**, 810**n.**, 900–901
Cash, Stephen L., 136**n.**
Cash equivalents, 667
Cash flow analysis, Aspen Wood Apartments, 364–365, 366
Cash flow from operations, **see** Cash flow (before tax)
Cash flow statement, 171–172
Cash flow (after tax), 581
to initial equity, 241
plus equity buildup to initial equity, 242
plus equity buildup plus appreciation to initial equity, 242–243
Cash flow (before tax), 34. **See also** Discounted-cash-flow (DCF) models
to initial equity, 241
management of personal, 671–674
from small rental properties, 864
Cash flow to total capital after tax, 234
Cash method of accounting, 346–348
Cash-on-cash return, **see** Rate of return, on equity (ROE)
Cash throw-off, **see** Cash flow (before tax)
Cash throw-off rate, **see** Rate of return, on equity (ROE)
Casualty losses, 598
C corporation(s), 126, 129, 130, 146–150
collapsible, 150
multiple, 149–150
Ceiling heights of industrial buildings, 843
Celis, William, III, 614**n.**
Census of Manufacturers, 830
Census of Population and Housing, 432
Central business district (CBD), 401, 402
Centrally located industrial sites, 836–837
Central utility systems, costs of, 789
Cerf, Alan R., 75**n.**, 97**n.**, 450**n.**
Certified Commercial Investment Member (CCIM), 55
Certified Mortgage Banker (CMB), 55
Certified Property Manager (CPM), 55, 541, 542
Certified public accountant (CPA), 519

Chain Store Age Executive, 773
Charitable contributions, 593
Cheatham, Christopher, 282**n.**
Checkerboard technique, 906
Chen, A. H., 80, 652
Chicago Title and Trust Company, 159**n.**
Childs, Barbara J., 188**n.**, 359**n.**
Christman, Don, 512**n.**
Chudleigh, Walter H., III, 651**n.**
Cirese, Robert C., 254**n.**, 267**n.**
Cities, **see** Urban analysis
City and urban area cycles, 493–494
Clapp, John M., 378**n.**, 415**n.**, 439**n.**, 440**n.**
Clark, William Dennison, Jr., 277**n.**
Clawson, Marion, 902**n.**
Clean Air Act Amendment of 1970, 6
Clear span, 828, 843
Closed-end syndicates, 311
Closing, 94, 525–526
Aspen Wood Apartments, 369, 531, 532
timing of, 580–581
Coastal Zone Management Act of 1974, 6
Coates, C. Robert, 86**n.**
Coefficient of variation (CV), 263
Cognitive processes in real estate investment decisions, 110, 111
Cohen, Jerome B., 44**n.**
Cohen, Martin, 24**n.**
Coldwell Banker Company, 96, 705
Vacancy Index, 806
Collapsible corporations, 150
Collateralized loans, 294–295
Colwell, Peter F., 66**n.**, 67**n.**
Coming Boom in Real Estate, The (Wenzlick), 484
Commercial second mortgage, 289
Commitment fees, mortgage, 281–282
Common-area charges, shopping center, 787–788
Common-area maintenance, 788
Communication with the investor:
by property manager, 535, 553–555
by venture and partnership managers, 562
Community development block grants, 287
Community shopping centers, 738, 768, 770
Compatibility study, 40
Competition, field survey of, 438–439, 440–441
Competitive building, 801–802
Compound interest, 56–59, 455
theory of, 56–57
Compound interest and control approach, 58–59
Computer generated economic and demographic profiles, 432–438
Concentric-ring theory, 400–401
Condemnation or threat of condemnation, 597–598
Conditional sale, 585
Condominiums, 752, 855–869
conversions, 754, 755
definition of, 856
discounted-cash-flow analysis, 869
financing of, 867–869

investing in, 859–860
investment decision, 869
outlook for, 717
preliminary analyses, 860–867
financial, 864–867
market and marketability, 860–862
physical, legal, political, and environmental, 862–863
track records and trends, 857–859
Conduit theory, 57–58
Conley, Chip, 586**n.**
Conroe, Mark, 627**n.**
Conservative forecasts, 76
Consolidated metropolitan statistical area (CMSA), 375, 376
Consolidated mortgage obligations (CMOs), 161
Construction cycles, 490–492
Construction lender, 20
Construction loans, 461
Construction period interest, 348
Consumer price index (CPI), 453–454
Consumption-capital asset pricing model (consumption-CAPM), 80
Contingent-price sales contract, 590
Continuing care retirement center (CCRC), 887
Continuity, selection of ownership form and, 130, 137, 138, 140, 142, 147, 150, 156
Contracts:
for deed, 587
land, 266, 587
legal complexity of, 15
maintenance service, 550
negotiation of, **see** Negotiations
open-end sales, 590
with property manager, 541
real estate sales, 522–525
Aspen Wood Apartments, 529–532
Control variables, 258
Convenience goods, 769
Convention hotels, 872
Conversion, 542
Conway, Dan, 419**n.**
Cooley, Phillip E., 279**n.**
Cooley, Phillip L., 180**n.**
Cooper, James R., 6**n.**, 97**n.**, 258**n.**, 450, 537**n.**, 578
Cooperative apartments, 752–753
Coopers and Lybrand, 336**n.**, 910**n.**
Copeland, Thomas E., 451**n.**, 456**n.**
Corporation(s), 341
alternative minimum tax on, 343
general (C), 126, 129, 130, 146–150
nominee, dummy, or straw, 152–153
S, 126, 131, 150–152, 881
as sole general partner of limited partnership, 142
tax formula for, 329
tax year for, 346
Counseling of the investor, property manager's, 535, 553
Counselor of Real Estate (CRE), 55
Coupe case, 608, 610

Covariance and portfolio characteristics, 629–631, 639–641

Coyne, Thomas J., 450**n.**

Crane case, 596**n.**

Creative Solutions, Inc. case, 598**n.**

Credit analysis of industrial building investor, 849–850

Credit tenant, 115

Cumberland Mall, Atlanta, 772, 774–775

Cummings, Jack, 299**n.**

Cumulative cash flow before tax and after tax, 234

Curcio, Richard J., 80, 600**n.**, 647

Current-year tax projection, 664

Cushman and Wakefield, 698, 783**n.**

Dallas Transfer case, 599**n.**

Daly, Maurice T., 14

Dasso, Jerome, 378**n.**, 380**n.**, 411**n.**, 483, 541**n.**

Data on properties (nonowner), sources of, 201–202

Davies, R. L., 419**n.**

Dawson, John A., 772**n.**

Dawson, Roger, 512**n.**

Day, Theodore E., 476**n.**

Dealer in real estate, capital gains tax rules for, 329, 330–332, 910

Death rates, 388

Debentures, 848–849

Debt, 33–34

Debt coverage ratio (DCR), 76, 172–173, 175, 243, 462
  for industrial buildings or parks, 859
  for office buildings, 819
  risk and, 177–178, 179
  for shopping centers, 791–792

Debt financing, **see** Financing, debt

Debt service, 34
  annual, 172, 173, 174, 175

Debt-to-equity ratio, 34, 174

Decision criteria, 100–103, 104–105

Decisionex, Inc., 637

Declining balance depreciation, 336, 338–339

Default point, **see** Break-even ratio (point)

Deferred-payment sales, 590

Deficit Reduction Act of 1984, 210, 211

Deflation, **see** Disinflation

Deglomerating forces for industrial buildings, 834

Del Casino, Joseph J., 258**n.**

Delegation of authority to property managers, 539–540

Demand. **See also** Supply
  analysis of:
    for apartments, 756–757
    for hotels and motels, 874–877
    for industrial buildings and parks, 834–835
    for land, 904–905
    for nursing homes, 886–887
    for office buildings, 808–809
    relationship and supply and, 421–423
    for shopping centers, 778–779

for small rental properties, 860–861
  effective, capture rates and, 442–444
  estimation of present and future, 415–418
  models of, 415–418
  net, 420, 421–423
  potential, absorption rate and, 439–442
  real estate cycles and, 485–489

Demise phase of property life cycle, 50

Demographic analysis:
  long-term, 722
  national, 694–695
  profile of immediate area and site, 432, 433, 436–438
  urban, 384–395

Department of..., **see** U.S. Department of...

Department stores, 718

Depreciation, 228–230, 582. **See also** Tax shelters; **specific types of properties, e.g.,** Apartments; Office buildings
  accelerated, 230**n.**, 332–333, 336
  accelerated cost recovery system and, 334–341, 762, 776, 794, 819, 851, 881, 891
  for Aspen Wood Apartments, 363
  beginning basis for, 228–230
  declining balance, 336, 338–339
  depreciable basis, 335
  excess, 230
  recaptured, 230, 332–334
  straight-line, 230**n.**, 329, 332, 335, 336, 338–339
  straight-line basis for, 230, 230**n.**
  sum-of-the-years' digits, 336, 338–339
  Tax Reform Act of 1986 and, 230, 325, 335, 336, 582, 762, 794, 819, 851
  tax shelters and, 352–357, 358
  undepreciated balance, 230
  of value, 13–15

Deregulation, financial, 23

Deterministic models, 75, 256, 637

Detroit City Planning Commission, 830**n.**

Developer, 18–19
  builder-, 18

Developer exactions, 723–724

Development agencies, public, industrial buildings, and parks financed by, 833, 847–848

Diamond, Douglas B., 470

Dickers, Thomas L., 136**n.**

Direct utility approach, 76

Disability planning, 684

Discounted-cash-flow (DCF) analysis:
  after-tax analysis, 300–303
  for apartments, 762
  applied to refinancing decision, 300–303
  for Aspen Wood Apartments, 225–239, 272–273, 278, 367–369
  financial management rate of return (FMRR), 223–224, 646, 647
  for hotels and motels, 881, 882
  for industrial buildings and parks, 852
  inflation and, 480–482

internal-rate-of-return, **see** Internal rate of return
  for land investments, 911
  modified (adjusted) internal rate of return (MIRR), 220–224
  for office buildings, 822
  for shopping centers, 795–796
  for small rental properties, 869

Discounted-cash-flow (DCF) models:
  internal-rate-of-return (IRR) model, 51, 74–75, 477
  present value (PV) model, 51, 72–74, 477

Discount loan, 282

Discount rate, 211

Disinflation, 15, 448, 459, 461–462, 466, 468, 470. **See also** Inflation and inflation cycle

Disintermediation, 493

Disposal of the investment, **see** Termination of the investment

Ditmer, Robert, 908**n.**

Diversification:
  of institutional portfolios, 628, 629, 633, 651, 652, 659
  of personal investments, review of, 667
  of a public real estate partnership, 116
  refinancing for portfolio, 298
  selection of ownership form and, 131, 147
  static risk eliminated by, 251, 266

Dodge, F. W., 419**n.**, 421**n.**

Donnelley Marketing Information Service, 432**n.**

Dormant mortgage, 281

Downs, Alvin A., 541**n.**

Downs, Anthony, 24**n.**, 38**n.**, 274**n.**, 460**n.**, 497**n.**

Downs, James C., Jr., 450**n.**, 541**n.**

Draper, Dennis W., 652**n.**

Drucker, Peter, 555**n.**

Due-on-encumbrance clause, 284

Due-on-sale clause, 284, 867

Dummy corporation, 152–153

Duplexes, 856

Dynamic risk, 251

Eagle, Blake, 704

Eagles, Robert, 705

Economic conditions:
  investment outlook for real estate, 690–730
  long-term outlook, 722
  urban economic analysis, 378–384

Economic profile of immediate market area and site, 432–438

Economic Recovery Tax Act of 1981, 210, 334–335, 458, 821

Economic standards, 842

Edmonds, Charles P., 588**n.**

Edson, Charles L., 343**n.**

Education, 15–16

Education planning, 676–678

Edwards, Charlie E., 180**n.**, 279**n.**

Edwards, Ward, 108**n.**

Effective marginal tax rate, 327, 328
Effective mortgage constant, 231
Efficient frontier, 633
Eggbeer, William, 874n.
Elasticity coefficient to measure risk, 256
Elevators, lifts, and conveyors for industrial buildings, 842–843
Ellis, Robert M., 96n.
Ellwood, L. W., 65, 417n.
Ellwood valuation model, 65–66
Emergency procedures, 552
Emerging Trends in Real Estate, 25n.
Employee management, 550
Employee Retirement Income Security Act (ERISA), 160, 626–627
Employment rate, changes in, 391
Enever, Nigel, 14n.
Englebrecht, T. D., 277n.
English, Wilke D., 419n.
Entrepreneurial leverage theory, 58
Environmental analysis of prospective investments:
    apartment buildings, 758
    hotels and motels, 878
    industrial buildings and parks, 843
    land, 908
    nursing homes, 888
    office buildings, 812
    shopping centers, 782
    small rental properties, 862
Environmental hazards, 722–723, 758
EPIC syndication operation, 470n.
EQK Realty Investors, 154
Equipment trust certificates, 849
Equitable Real Estate Investment Management, 707, 714
Equitization of corporate property assets, 8
Equity buildup in small rental properties, 864
Equity cash flow after tax, 233–234
Equity cash flow before tax, 233, 234
Equity-cash flow valuation model, 64–65
Equity cost, 239
Equity dividend, **see** Cash flow (before tax)
Equity dividend rate, **see** Rate of return, on equity
Equity financing, 303–309
    compensation schemes for investors, 307–309
    creative structures for, 305–306
    form of ownership and, 303–304
    sources of, 304–305
Equity investment, 33
Equity investor, 49
    defined, 33
    in industrial real estate, 832
    managing, **see** Managing equity investor
    relationship to lender, 34–35
    strategy of, 178–179
Equity participations or kickers, 282–283
Equity REITs (EREITs), 155, 626, 777
Equity value, 238
Equity yield (rate of return), 69
Erler, Raymond L., 277n.
Escalation clauses, 547, 784
Escrow accounts, mortgage, 284

Estate building, 11
    selection of ownership form and, 131, 142
Estate planning, 684–687
Estate tax(es), 129, 325, 594, 684–687
    projection of, 665
Estey, Arthur S., 69n., 653n., 654
Estoppel statements, 200
Ethics, 728–729
Etter, Wayne E., 279n., 314n.
Everhart, Marion E., 907n.
Exchange of property, tax-free, 359, 579, 592–593, 604–614
    basic considerations in structuring, 607–611
    evaluating, 611–614
    reasons for, 605–607
    Section 1031 exchanges, 604–614
Executive Park, Atlanta, 803, 804–805
Expected return on investment, **see** Rate of return
Expenses, **see specific types of expenses,** e.g., Operating expenses
Exposure, 403–406
External financial risk, 252

Fabozzi, Frank J., 452n.
Fair market value, deductions based on price in excess of, 349–350
Fama, Eugene F., 450–451, 467n.
Family partnership, 126, 138–139
Fantus, 831
Farber, Sheldon, 870n.
Farmers Home Administration (FmHA) rural housing, Title V, 287
Farmland, impact of inflation on, 467–468. **See also** Raw land
Farragher, Edward J., 101n.
Feasibility analysis, 30–31, 38–41, 93
    vs. investment analysis, 30–31, 38, 39–40
    model for, **see** Basic financial feasibility model
    types of reports, 40–41
Feasibility research, 267. **See also** Basic financial feasibility model
    Aspen Wood Apartments, 270–272
Federal Deposit Insurance Corporation (FDIC), 698, 712
Federal Home Loan Bank Board, 858, 867
Federal Home Loan Mortgage Corporation (Freddie Mac), 288, 761, 867
Federal Housing Administration (FHA), 287, 288
Federal Land Bank, 909n.
Federal National Mortgage Association (Fannie Mae), 288, 761, 867
Federal Reserve Bank(s), 396, 692
    of St. Louis, 482
Federal Reserve Board, 867
Federal Savings and Loan Insurance Corporation (FSLIC), 698, 704, 705, 710, 712
Federal Water Pollution Control Act of 1972, 6
Feedback, 28

Fee simple ownership, 6
Fertility rates, 388
FHA Techniques of Housing Market Analysis, 757
Field survey of competition, 438–439, 440–441
Financial analysis of prospective investments. **See also specific forms of financial analysis,** e.g., Discounted-cash-flow (DCF) analysis; Financial ratio analysis
    apartments, 758–760
    hotels and motels, 878–880
    industrial buildings and parks, 843–844
    nursing homes, 888–891
    office buildings, 812–818
    shopping centers, 782–783
    small rental properties, 864–867
Financial decision approaches, **see** Traditional financial decision approaches
Financial-economic study, 40
Financial factors in best-fit approach, 71
Financial feasibility model, **see** Basic financial feasibility model
Financial feasibility of shopping center investment, 780
Financial independence, planning for, 674–676, 677
Financial management rate of return (FMRR), 223–224, 646, 647. **See also** Internal rate of return
Financial planning, personal, **see** Personal portfolio, developing, with real estate
Financial ratio analysis, 76, 239–245
    Aspen Wood Apartments, 369
    assumption base ratios, 244–245
    profitability ratios, 239–243
    risk ratios, 243
Financial risk, 251–252.
Financial services firms, outlook for, 699
Financing, 274–321. **See also** Leverage; Mortgage(s)
    of apartment loans, 760–761
    for Aspen Wood Apartments, 269, 279, 290–291, 317–321
    debt, 276–297, 586–591
        collateralized loans, 294–295
        erosion of leverage benefits, 279
        first-mortgage financing alternatives, 284–286
        government-sponsored loan and grant programs, 286–288
        high-credit-lease loan, 295
        illustration and comparison of methods, 295–297
        junior mortgage financing alternatives, 288–293
        leverage decision, 277–279
        personal loans, 295
        sale-buyback, 294, 296
        sale-leaseback, 293–294, 586, 819, 846, 851–852
        sandwich lease, 294
        variables in terms of, 279–284

decision model, 275–276
equity, 303–309
    compensation schemes for investors,
        307–309
    creative structures for, 305–306
    form of ownership and, 303–304
    sources of, 304–305
of hotels and motels, 880
of industrial buildings, 846–850
of land, 908–910
of office buildings, 819–821
refinancing, 297–303
    alternatives for, 298–299
    illustration of, 300–303
    impact on returns and risks, 299–300
    objectives of, 297–298
    tax shelters and, 355, 356
of shopping centers, 791–793
of small rental properties, 867–869
syndication offerings, 309–315
    federal and state regulation of, 312–
        315
    types of, 309–312
Findlay, M. Chapman, III, 80, 223n., 225n.,
    625n., 638n., 646, 647, 652n.
Finite life real estate investment trusts
    (FREITs), 118, 155, 656
Fireproof building, 828
Fire protection and sprinkler systems, 842
Fire safety code, 888
First-class buildings, 839
Fiscal year, 345–346
Fischhoff, Baruch, 108n.
Fisher, Irving, 456n.
Fisher, Ted L., 277n.
Fisher effect, 480
Fitts, C. Austin, 703
Fitzgerald, Michael L., 145n.
Five-year projections of current financial
    statements, 673–674
Fixed option, 595
Flexibility and selection of ownership form,
    129–130, 136, 139
"Flipping" a property, 576, 857
Floor loads, 828
Floor space per employee, 828
Fogler, H. Russel, 80n., 476n., 477n.
Forecasters, business **vs.** professional, 726–
    727
Forecasts of revenue and revenue-related ex-
    pense, 444
Foreclosure, 598–600
Foreign investment, 24–25, 713–714, 777
Forest land, impact of inflation on, 467–468.
    See also Raw land
Form utility, 826
Fortune, 836, 857n.
401 (k)s, 160
Fractional interests, 591–592
Framework for real estate investment
    studies, 25–28
    analysis, 26–28
    decisions, 26–28
    feedback, 28
    investment transaction, 28

strategy, 26
Frank Russell Company, 649, 704, 709, 720
FRC Property Index, 649, 659
Freeman, Robert, 36n.
FREITs (finite life real estate investment
    trusts), 118, 155, 656
Friedan, Bernard, 857n.
Friedman, Harris C., 80, 649
Friedman, Jack, 577, 578, 909n.
Friedman, Milton, 729
Fringe benefits of corporate form of owner-
    ship, 148, 151
Full-credit option, 595
Fully amortizing mortgage, 281
Functional obsolescence, 13–15
Furbush, Ann Blair, 135n.
Future value, 212

Gaines, James P., 600n., 638n., 647
Gains:
    capital, **see** Capital gains taxes
    in exchange of properties, 611–614
    ordinary, 581
Galleria, Houston, 769, 772
Garden apartments, 751
Garrigan, Richard T., 188n.
Gau, George W., 224n., 258n., 537n., 562n.,
    638n., 652n
Generalized model of investment value, 63–
    64
General partnership, 126, 130, 135–138
General-purpose industrial buildings, 827
General-use property, 115
Genetski, Robert J., 452n., 457n.
Georgia State University Economic Forecast-
    ing Center, 692
Ghirardelli Square, San Francisco, 769
Gibb, Jack R., 514
Gibbons, James E., 14, 43n., 500n.
Gibbons, M. R., 80n.
Gifts, 359, 594–595
    annual gifting program, 686–687
    education planning and, 677–678
    inter vivos gifting of the unified credit,
        687
    and leaseback, 594–595
Gift taxes, 159, 327, 686–687
Gitman, Lawrence J., 254n., 255n.
Globalization of real estate investment, 24–25
Glubetich, Dave, 868n.
Goal congruency, 307
Goals, **see** Investment objectives
Gobar, Al, 465n.
Goggans, Travis P., 277n.
Goldberg, Daniel L., 136n., 336n.
Goldberg, Harry F., 142n.
Goldman, Sachs and Company, 652
Goldstein, Richard S., 343n.
Goldstrucker, J. C., 419n.
Goodman, Richard A., 614n.
Gottschalk, Earl C., Jr., 712n.
Goulet, Waldemar M., 450n.
Government fiscal and monetary policy, 692–
    693
Government National Mortgage Association

(Ginny Mae), 288
Government-qualified, low-income residential
    properties, capital gain and deprecia-
    tion on, 334
Government regulation, 10, 15
    selection of ownership form and, 130,
        139
    of syndicates, 312–315
Government-sponsored loan and grant
    programs, 286–288
Graaskamp, James A., 3, 5n., 38–39, 40n.,
    64n., 72n., 250n., 264n., 411n, 419n.,
    637
Graduated-payment mortgage (GPM), 285
Graduated rents, 784
Graduate Realtors Institute (GRI), 55
Granito, Michael R., 476n.
Grantor-trust, **see** Revocable trust
Grayson, C. Jackson, Jr., 248n.
Great American Growth Properties, Quad
    Cities, 777
Grebler, Leo, 489n.
Greenberg, Michael, 393n.
Greenfield, Harry I., 452n.
Greenhut, Melvin L., 826n.
Greer, Gaylor E., 277n.
Grissom, Terry V., 39n.
Gross building area, 802
Gross leasable area (GLA), 738
Gross leases, 546, 846
Gross national product (GNP), real estate as
    sector of, 7
Gross profit, 589
Gross profit percentage, 589–590
Gross rent multiplier approach, 71–72, 244–
    245, 520
Ground floor stage of property life cycle, 48
Ground lease, 846, 905–906
Group equity investing, 539
GTE, 700–702
Guide to Feasibility Analysis (Graaskamp),
    38–39
Guntermann, Karl L., 6n.

Haig, Robert Murray, 400n.
Hallmark Center, Kansas City, 905
Halper, Emanuel B., 283n.
Halperin, Jerome Y., 287n.
Halpern case, 607, 608, 610
Halpin, Michael C., 451n., 495–496, 500n.
Hamel case, 599n.
Hamilton, Carl W., 80, 638n.
Hammerick, Steve, 806n.
Hammond, James H., Jr., 284n.
Hanford, Lloyd D., Sr., 38n., 70n.
Hanrahan, Michael J., 228n.
Haroldsen, Mark Oliver, 58–59, 60n.
Harris, Chauncy D., 401
Harris, Jack E., 449n.
Hartzell, David, 651n., 652n.
Hayes, Perry, 297n.
Haynes, A., 526n.
Heating of industrial buildings, 843
Heilburn, James, 400n.
Hemmer, Edgar H., 525n., 637

Hennessey, Sean F., 419**n.**
Henry Miller REIT, Dallas, 777
Hertz, David B., 260**n.**
High-credit-lease loan, 295
High-rise apartments, 752
Hilton, Hugh G., 470**n.**
Hilton Head, South Carolina, 903
Hines, Mary Alice, 97**n.**, 771**n.**
Hirsch, Werner Z., 380**n.**
Historic structures, tax credit for rehabilitation
　　of certified, 343
Hoag, J., 649
Hoffmann, Tony, 512**n.**, 519**n.**
Holding costs of land investments, 905–906
Holland, A. Steven, 473**n.**
Holthouse, Philip J., 359**n.**
Holtje, Bert, 512**n.**
Holzman, Lee J., 126**n.**
Homeowners, impact of inflation on, 468–470
Hoover, Edgar M., 380**n.**, 383**n.**
Hotel Astoria case, 599**n.**
Hotels and motels, 871–883
　　advantages and disadvantages of in-
　　　　vesting in, 872–873
　　characteristics of, as investments, 746–
　　　　749
　　definitions of, 871–872
　　discounted-cash-flow analysis, 881, 882
　　financing, 880
　　the investment decision, 881–883
　　outlook for, 720–721
　　preliminary analyses, 873–880
　　　　financial, 878–880
　　　　market and marketability, 873–878
　　　　physical, legal, political, and environ-
　　　　　　mental, 878
　　taxation problems, 880–881
　　types of investors and investor motiva-
　　　　tions, 873
Hot-market-overkill cycle, 496
Hotopp, Mary C., 525**n.**
Household composition, 390, 391, 722
Housing, 1988 outlook for, 715–718
Housing and Urban Development, U.S.
　　Department of (HUD), 99, 286, 396,
　　470, 755
Housing Development Action Grant
　　(HoDAG), 287
**How I Turned $1,000 into Five Million in
　　Real Estate** (Nickerson), 54
How Nations Negotiate (Ikle), 511
How Real Estate Fortunes Are Made
　　(Bockl), 54
Hoyt, Homer, 400**n.**, 401, 483, 492**n.**
Hudson, Ray, 431**n.**
Huff, David, 417**n.**, 432**n.**
Huff, Richard L., 512**n.**
Hughes, Connie O., 384**n.**
Hughes, James W., 384**n.**
Hybrid REITs, 155

Ibbotson, Roger G., 7**n.**, 450**n.**, 476**n.**
Ikle, Fred C., 511
Illiquidity of real estate, 13
Immediate market area analysis, 429–430

Immigration, 389
Implicit price deflator, 453
Impulse goods, 769
Income and expense statement, 197
Income taxes, **see** Tax(es); Tax law; Tax plan-
　　ning; Tax shelters
Incorporated pocketbook, 149
Indexed rents, 784
Individual ownership, 126, 130, 133, 345–346
Individual Retirement Accounts (IRAs), 160,
　　676
Industrial brokers, 844–845
Industrial buildings and parks, 826–852
　　advantages and disadvantages of in-
　　　　vesting in, 831–832
　　categories of, 827
　　characteristics of, as investments, 740–
　　　　741, 748–749
　　definitions, 827–829
　　discounted-cash-flow analysis, 852
　　financing, 846–850
　　　　estimating costs of, 846–847
　　　　sources of funds, 847–850
　　inflation's impact on, 471–472
　　the investment decision, 852
　　outlook for, 719–720
　　preliminary analyses, 833–846
　　　　financial, 843–844
　　　　market and marketability, 833–839
　　　　operations, 844–846
　　　　physical, legal, political, and environ-
　　　　　　mental, 839–943
　　taxation and tax structure, 851–852
　　track record and trends, 829–831
　　types of investors and investor motiva-
　　　　tions, 832–833
Industrial real estate bonds, 848–849
Inflation and inflation cycle, 15, 32, 35, 211,
　　448–483, 675–676
　　framework for analyzing, 449–457
　　　　measures of inflation, 452–457
　　　　return-risk framework and, 451–452
　　　　the unanalyzed factor, 449–451
　　impact on investors and properties of,
　　　　457–472
　　　　on commercial properties, 471–472
　　　　on existing properties, 463–466
　　　　on homeowner, 468–470
　　　　on leverage strategy, 459–462, 463
　　　　mathematics of wealth transfer, 458–
　　　　　　459
　　　　on multifamily income properties,
　　　　　　470–471
　　　　on new properties, 462
　　　　on unimproved land, 467–468
　　　　winners and losers, 457–458
　　investment strategy and, 472–483
　　　　capital-budget approach, 477–479
　　　　an inflation cycle strategy, 473–477
　　　　mathematical estimation of inflation's
　　　　　　impact on project variables,
　　　　　　478–483
　　protection against, 12–13, 691–692
Information:
　　for decision-making, 9, 15

sources of, for investors, 482–483, 502–
　　507
In-house data on similar properties, 201
Installment sales, 587–591, 596
　　taxes and, 289, 331, 359, 587–591,
　　　　909, 910
Institute of Business Planning, 139**n.**, 776**n.**
Institute of Real Estate Management (IREM),
　　55**n.**, 541, 542, 545, 760
Institutional investors, 24, 49, 341, 777
　　in industrial real estate, 832–833
　　life cycle of, 46
　　in office buildings, 807
　　portfolio of, **see** Institutional real estate
　　　　portfolios
Institutionalization, 23–24
Institutional real estate portfolios, 625–660
　　ERISA and, 626–627
　　extended development of portfolio
　　　　theory, 643–650
　　　　adaptations of **N**-asset calculus
　　　　　　model to real estate, 643–647
　　　　simplified approach to portfolio selec-
　　　　　　tion, 647–650
　　history of REITs and, 625–626
　　impact of portfolio theory on large in-
　　　　stitutional investors, 650–660
　　portfolio choice, 628–633
　　　　covariance and portfolio charac-
　　　　　　teristics, 629–631
　　　　definitions of expected risk and
　　　　　　return, 628–629
　　　　modern portfolio theory, 631–633
　　real estate investing and modern
　　　　portfolio theory, 633–643
　　　　measures of expected return and
　　　　　　variance, 635–638
　　　　portfolio selection: an illustration,
　　　　　　638–643
　　recent changes in economic conditions
　　　　and, 627–628
Institutional second mortgages, 289
Insurance, 265, 551, 684, 789
　　lease guarantee, 850
Insured-mortgage partnerships, 117–118
Interest-only loan, **see** Straight-term
　　mortgage
Interest rates, 35
　　compound, 56–59, 455
　　effective, 282
　　inflation and, 459–461
　　mortgage, 274, 280, 358
　　on purchase money mortgages, 590–
　　　　591
　　real, 459–460
　　simple, 280, 455
Interim stage of property life cycle, 48
Internal financial risk, 251–252
Internal rate of return (IRR), 179, 216–220
　　annual recalculation of, 602
　　for apartments, 762
　　of Aspen Wood Apartments, 237–239
　　calculation of, 217–218
　　decision rule, 220
　　defined, 216–217

Internal rate of return (IRR) **(Continued)**
    financial management rate of return
        (FMRR), 223–224, 646, 647
    for industrial buildings and parks, 852
    for land improvements, 911
    modified (adjusted) (MIRR), 220–223
    for office buildings, 822
    problems with, 220–221
    real **vs.** normal, 455–457
    relationship to business and financial
        risk, 252
    risk analysis by partitioning, 253–254
    for shopping centers, 795
    for small rental properties, 869
    with unequal cash flow streams, 218–
        219
Internal-rate-of-return model, 51, 74–75, 477
Internal Revenue Service (IRS). **See also**
    Tax(es)
    audit by, 350–351
    on capital additions **vs.** maintenance,
        543
    on capital **vs.** operating expenses, 348–
        349
International Association of Financial Plan-
    ning (IAFP), 662n.
International business developments and
    real estate cycle, 490
International Council of Shopping Centers,
    453
International real estate trading markets, 414
In-the-field market analysis, 708
Intuitive abilities, 109
Investment, defined, 32
Investment analysis, 26–28, 32–38
    capital assets, 32
    debt, 33–34
    defined, 32
    equity, 33
    vs. feasibility analysis, 30–31, 38, 39–
        40
    maximization of wealth, 36, 37
    net operating income, 34
    overview of, 33
    relationship of lender to equity investor,
        34–35
    return and risk management, 36–38
Investment analysis and financial structuring
    process, 89–95
    basic assumptions, 89–91
    analyze property using basic financial
        feasibility models, 92
    complete financial and tax structuring,
        93
    determine an investment strategy, 91
    do detailed feasibility study, 93
    final negotiation and closing, 94
    generate alternatives, 92
    manage the property, 94
    negotiate basic terms with seller, 92
    perform a discounted-cash-flow
        analysis, 93
    tax considerations in, 322–323
    terminate the property, 94–95
Investment cost, defined, 63

Investment criteria, 100–103, 104–105
    Aspen Wood Apartments, 123–124
    defined, 89
Investment decisions, 28, 30–81
    for apartments, 762
    approaches to, 54–81
        modern capital budgeting, 55, 62, 72–
            81
        popular "how to," 54, 55–62
        traditional financial, 54–55, 62–72
    feasibility analysis, 30–31, 38–41
    for hotels and motels, 881–883
    for industrial buildings and parks, 852
    investment analysis, 32–38
    investment **vs.** speculation, 31–
        32
    for land investments, 911
    for nursing homes, 891–892
    for office buildings, 822–823
    overview of process of making, 30–53
    real estate appraisal, 41–44
    for shopping centers, 796
    for small rental properties, 869
    time horizons for, or life cycles, 44–52
Investment interest limitations, 344–345, 910
Investment objectives, 10–16, 97–100
    of Aspen Wood Apartments, 123
    defined, 89
    financial **vs.** nonfinancial, 99–100
    identifying personal, 665–666
    for investment in public real estate
        partnership, 112–114
    ranking, 100
    short run **vs.** long run, 99
    unrealistic, 99
    written, 98–99
Investment outlook for real estate, 690–730
    global attitudes, 691
    longer term, 721–729
        current problems of scenario plan-
            ning, 727–728
        demographic and economic factors,
            722
        legal and regulatory issues, 722–724
        metropolitan areas, 725–726
        moral and social responsibility, 728–
            729
        professional **vs.** business
            forecasters, 726–727
        urban containment, 724–725
    national considerations, 691–695
    for 1988, 709–721
        hotels, 720–721
        housing, 715–718
        industrial real estate, 719–720
        land development, 721
        offices, 719
        retail, 718–719
        transaction volumes, 709–714
        yields, 709
    short-term overview, 697–709
    strategic view of, 695–697
Investment philosophy, 95–96
    of Aspen Wood Apartments, 122–123
    defined, 88

Investment planning, 678–682
Investment plans, 103–106
    of Aspen Wood Apartments, 124
    defined, 89
Investment policy, 106, 107
    of Aspen Wood Apartments, 124
    defined, 89
Investment principles, 96–97
Investment pyramid, 679–680
Investment strategy, 26, 85–110
    Aspen Wood Apartments, 119–124
    defined, 86, 88
    developing an, 95–110
        basic screening criteria, 106–108
        decision criteria, 100–103
        decision-making biases and irrational
            preferences, 108–110
        investment objectives, 97–100
        investment philosophy, 95–96
        investment plans and policies, 103–
            106, 107
        investment principles, 96–97
    framework for an, 86–89
    inflation cycles and, 472–483
    investment analysis and financial struc-
        turing process, 89–95, 110
    terminology for, 87–89
Investment tax credits, (ITCs), 325, 343, 821
Investment termination, **see** Termination of
    the investment
Investment transactions, 28
Investment value, 43
    defined, 63
    Ellwood valuation model, 65–66
    equity-cash flow valuation model, 64–65
    generalized model of, 63–64
Investment value approach, 63–66
Investment value decision rule, 63
Investor:
    in apartments, 755–759
    equity, **see** Equity investor
    in hotels and motels, 873
    in industrial buildings and parks, 832–
        833
    information sources for, 482–483, 502–
        507
    institutional, **see** Institutional investors
    in land, 904
    life cycle, 44–46, 52, 497
    managing equity, **see** Managing equity
        investor
    objectives of, 10–16, 97–100
    in office buildings, 807
    passive equity, 16, 21, 22, 49, 866
    role of, determining, 95
    in shopping centers, 776
Involuntary dispositions, 598–600
IRAs (Individual Retirement Accounts), 160,
    676
Irrational preferences and biases, 108–110
Irrevocable trust, 159
Isoquants, 633

Jaffe, Austin J., 36**n**, **97n.**, 180**n.**,216**n.**,
    277**n.**, 451**n.**, 536**n.**, 537**n.**, 539**n.**,

577n., 651n.
Jaffe, Jeffrey, 476n.
Japan, investment in U.S. real estate by, 25, 71, 713–714
Jarchow, Stephen, 137n., 153n., 314n., 657n.
Jean, William H., 220n.
Jerrimad, B., 469n.
Johnson, Robert, 211n.
Joint Center for Housing Studies of Harvard-MIT, 718
Joint Commission on Accreditation of Hospitals and Long-Term Care Facilities, 885
Joint tenancy, 126, 131, 133–134, 668, 669
Joint-venture (partner), 20, 35, 48, 126, 131, 145–146, 283
    basic financial feasibility model applied to, 193–195
Jones, Charles, 629n.
Jorgensen, James, 699
Junior mortgage financing, 188, 288–293, 295–296

Kahn, Sanders A., 810n.
Kahneman, Daniel, 108n.
Kamath, Ravindra, 286n.
Kami, Michael J., 700n.
Kaplan, Howard M., 467n.
Kapplin, Steven D., 75n., 248n., 627n., 638n., 648, 657n., 658
Kateley, Richard, 556n., 559n., 560n., 561n., 706n.
Kay, James B., 354
Keeling, Kermit, 130n.
Keeney, Ralph L., 432n.
Kelleher, Dennis G., 450n., 470n., 650n.
Kelley, Hugh F., 419n.
Kelting, Herman, 251n.
Keogh plan, 131, 160–161
Kerwood, Lewis O., 171n., 264n.
Key decision makers, 18–22
    construction lender, 20
    developer, 18–19
    joint-venture partner, 20
    managing equity investor, 21–22
    passive equity investor, 16, 22
    permanent lender, 20–21
Killan Company case, 599n.
Kimball, J. R., 419n.
Kimbler, Larry B., 700–702
King, Alfred L., 715n.
King, Donald A., Jr., 85n.
Kinnard, William N., Jr., 826n.
Kintner regulations, 138, 141
Kirby, Robert O., 216n., 221n.
Klein, Robert, 31n., 457n., 474
Klein, Roger, 452n.
Knight, F. H., 248n.
Kohlhepp, Daniel B., 224n., 258n., 638n.
Kopcke, Richard W., 477n.
Korpacz, Peter F., 41n.
Kosarowich, John T., 159n.
Kratovil, Robert, 600n.
Kraus, Egon H., 291n.
Krueckeberg, Donald A., 393n.

Kuhle, James L., 126n., 310n.
Kusnet, Jack, 33n., 126n, 290n.

Labor market area, 375
LaBrecque, Mort, 108n.
Lachman, M. Leanne, 556n., 559n., 560n., 561n.
Laden, Ben E., 467n.
Landauer Associates, 704–705
Land, raw, **see** Raw land
Land contract, 266, 587
Land development, outlook for, 721
Land leasebacks, subordinated, 292–293
Land rent, 292, 293
Land trusts, 159
Land use theories, 400–403
    analysis of, 402–403, 404–405
Langendoen, Gary, 556n.
Langford, Janelle, 653n.
Lapides, Paul D., 536, 549n., 550n.
Latane, Harry, 629n.
Lawless, Harris E., 562n.
Lease(s), 535, 543, 545–547
    gift or trust and leaseback, 594–595
    for hotels and motels, 879–880
    for industrial buildings and parks, 740–741, 845–846
    for land, 905–906
    long-term, with escalation clauses, 265–266
    negotiation of, 545–547
    for office buildings, 737, 813
    -purchase contracts, 349
    for residential rental properties, 736
    risk of public real estate partnerships and, 115
    sale-leaseback, 293–294, 586, 846, 851–852
    sandwich, 294
    for shopping centers, 739, 780–781, 782, 783–786, 787
    for small rental properties, 866
    special concessions in, 200
    standard form, 546
    subordinated land leasebacks, 292–293
    tenant selection, 545
    types of, and lease clauses, 546–547, 846
Lease guarantee insurance, 850
Legal analysis of prospective investments:
    apartments, 758
    hotels and motels, 878
    industrial buildings and parks, 843
    land, 908
    nursing homes, 888
    office buildings, 811–812
    shopping centers, 781–782
    small rental properties, 862
Legal environment of urban area, analysis of, 395–396
Legal-political barriers, 428
Legal study, 40
Leider, Arnold, 290n.
Lender(s):
    permanent, 20–21

relationship to equity investor, 34–35
Lesser, Daniel H., 419n.
Letter of credit, 282
Leverage, 12
    appreciation, 277–278
    approaches to real estate decisions and, 59–60
    break-even, 181
    defined, 180
    erosion of benefits from, 279
    favorable, 180–182, 239, 241
    inflation's impact on, 459–462, 463
    operations, 277–279
    of public real estate partnerships, 112–114, 115
    review of current financial position for, 668
    tax, 277–278
    tax shelters and, 356, 358
    unfavorable, or negative, 180–182
Leveraged partnerships, 116–117
Levi, Donald R., 314n.
Levy, Mikey, 694
Liabilities, personal, 664
Liability:
    at-risk rules and personal, 341–342
    mortgage provision, 283
    selection of ownership form and, 129, 133, 134, 137–138, 139, 140–141, 145, 147, 150, 152, 156
Liberty Mirror Works case, 599n.
Lichtstein, Sarah, 108n.
Life cycles, **see** Real estate cycles
Life insurance, 684
Life insurance companies, 909
Life Safety Code, 884
Lighting of industrial buildings, 843
Limited partnerships, 126, 129, 131, 139–144, 265. **See also** Master limited partnerships; Real estate limited partnerships
    sales of public, 712–713, 714
Lincoln Properties, 49
Lincoln (N.C.) Realty Fund, Inc., 154
Lindbeck, Rudolph, 588n.
Lindeman, J. Bruce, 467n.
Lindsay, Mark, 526n.
Lipsey, Robert H., 342n.
Liquidity:
    disposition of property and, 575–576
    review of current financial position for, 666–667
Liquidity Fund study, 658
Little, Charles H., 726–727
Little, John D. C., 432n.
Litzenberger, R. H., 80n.
Living trust, **see** Revocable trust
Loading docks, 828
Loading well, 828
Loan amortization schedule, Aspen Wood Apartments, 363
Loan balance as percentage of original cost, 243

Loan balance as percentage of property value, 243
Loan commitment stage of property life cycle, 49
Loans, **see** Financing
Loan term, 280
Loan-to-value (L/V) ratio, 115, 461–462
    for industrial real estate mortgages, 850
Local real estate markets, 414
Local taxes, 326
Location, 266–267
    concepts, 403–406
    depreciation of value and, 13
    of hotels and motels, 872, 874, 875
    of office buildings, 809, 810
Logue, D. E., 80n.
Lomas and Nettleton Company, 715
Long, Clarence D., 492n.
Lord, J. Dennis, 772n.
Loss:
    capital, **see** Capital gains taxes
    ordinary, 581
Love, Kathryn S., 476n.
Lowenstern, Hugo H., 322
Low-income housing, 754
    outlook for, 718
    tax credits for investment in, 343–344
Low-rise (walk-up) apartments, 751
Lowry, Albert J., 541n.
Lucas **vs.** North Texas Lumber Co., 595n.
Lusht, Kenneth M., 180n., 277n., 450n., 470n.
Lynn, Theodore S., 142n.
Lyon, Victor L., 74n., 220n., 223n.

McCue, Tom, 651n., 652
McIntosh, Willard, 101n., 103n., 104n., 105n.
McKenzie, Dennis J., 400n.
McKenzie, Joseph A., 469n.
McKinley, L. Blackburn, 694n.
McLeister, Kathleen, 908n.
McMahon, John, 439n., 450n., 537n.
McMurray, Scott, 702n.
Macro real estate cycle, 483–485
Maginn, John L., 44n.
Maintenance, 548–550
    vs. capital expenditures, 543
    corrective, 549
    custodial, 549
    deferred, 549
        by seller, 198–199
    emergency, 548, 549
    predicting necessary, 543
    preventive, 549
    of shopping centers, 788
    of small rental properties, 865–866
Maisel, Sherman J., 15n., 451n., 485n., 749n.
Major-shift employment, 828
Major tenants, 771, 780–781, 782
Management plan, 446–447
Management, property, **see** Property management
Management by exception, 555

Management by objectives, 555
Management plan, property, 542–543
Managing equity investor, 21–22
    compensation of, 307–309
Mandelker, Gershon, 476n.
Mandell, L., 417n.
Manning, Christopher A., 244n., 310n.
Manufacturing, outlook for, 693–694
Mao, James C. T., 220n.
Maps, land use, 402–403, 404–405
Marchitelli, Richard, 41n.
Marketability, selection of ownership form and, 129
Marketability analysis, 425–447
    absorption rate and potential demand, 439–442
    for apartments, 756–757
    capture rates and effective demand, 442–444
    establishing the boundaries, 428–429
    field survey of the competition, 438–439
    guidelines for a, 427–428
    for hotels and motels, 873–878
    immediate market area (neighborhood) analysis, 429–430
    for industrial buildings and parks, 833–839
    for land, 904–906
    management plan, 446–447
    vs. market analysis, 408–410
    marketing strategy, 444–446
    for nursing homes, 886–887
    for office buildings, 807–811
    revenue and revenue-related expense forecasts, 444
    scope of, 425–427
    for shopping centers, 778–781
    site and property analysis, 430–438
        economic and demographic profile, 438–439
    for small rental apartments, 860–862
Marketable securities, 667
Market absorption rate, 422
Market analysis, 40, 408–424
    analysis of relationship between supply and demand, 421–423
    for apartments, 753–754, 756–757
    development of demand and supply models, 415–418
    elements of a, 411–413
    estimation of present and future supply and demand, 420–421
    for hotels and motels, 873–878
    for industrial buildings and parks, 833–839
    for land investments, 904–906
    limitations of, 412
    vs. marketability analysis, 408–410
    market area definition, 419–420
    nature, scope, and depth of, 410
    for nursing homes, 886–887
    for office buildings, 807–811
    real estate markets, 412–414
    for shopping centers, 778–781

    for small rental properties, 860–862
    summary of salient facts and conclusions, 423–424
Market and marketability studies, 202
Market area definition, 419–420
Market data sources, listing of, 502–507
Market growth index (MGI), 435
Market potential index (MPI), 435
Marketing strategy, 444–446
Market promotion function, 535, 543–545
Market study, **see** Market analysis
Market trading area, 771
Market value, 41–42
    defined, 41–42, 63
    problems with traditional appraisals based on, 43–44
Markowitz, Harry, 79, 80, 628–629, 632, 633, 638, 643, 646
Marquandt, Raymond, 456n., 476n.
Marshall, Richard D., 460n.
Martin, William B., 419n.
Mason, J., 417n.
Master limited partnerships (MLPs), 24, 126, 144–145, 312, 627, 712
Master prospectus, 311–312
Maturing process of property life cycle, 49
Maximization of wealth, 2, 36, 37
Maximum loan formula, 175–177
Maxwell, David, 715
Medicaid, 884, 885, 887
Medicare, 884, 885, 886, 887
Medium-rise apartments, 751–752
Mellon Participating Mortgage Trust, 154
Melnikoff, Meyer, 652n.
Meloy, Richard G., 556n.
Member of the Appraisal Institute (MAI), 55, 542
Merchandising study, 40
Merchants' associations, 771, 784
Merrill-Lynch, 23
Messner, Stephen D., 38n., 74n., 80, 220n., 223n., 225n., 410n., 629n., 638n., 826n.
Metropolitan area(s). **See also** Urban analysis
    definition of, 374–378
    new risks in developing and investing in, 725–726
Metropolitan Life Insurance, 46
Metropolitan statistical area (MSA), 375, 376
Michaelson, Connie, 393n.
Middle-aged investor, 45
Migration, 391–393
    as indicator of change in demand for real estate, 391–393
Miles, Mike E., 69n., 541n., 585n., 636n.–637n., 651n., 652–654
"Milking" the property, 200
Mill construction, 828
Miller, Norman G., 562n., 602n.
Milne, Robert D., 44n.
Miner, John B, 86n., 555n.
Mirante, Arthur J., II, 698
MLPs, **see** Master limited partnerships
Moderate-income housing, 754

Modernization, 542

Modern capital budgeting approaches, 55, 62, 72–81

to inflation cycle strategy, 477–479

internal-rate-of-return model, 74–75, 477

present-value model,, 51, 72–74, 477

risk analysis models, 75–81

Modified accelerated cost recovery system (MACRS), 335

Modified (adjusted) internal rate of return (MIRR), 220–223. **See also** Internal rate of return

Monetary Trends, 482

Monte Carlo risk simulation approach, 76–79, 258–261, 635

Montgomery, J. Thomas, 36**n.**, 37**n.**, 41, 264**n.**

Moore, Geoffrey H., 452**n.**

Moorehead, Josef D., 310**n.**

Morrison, Cathy A., 258**n.**

Mortgage(s), 35, 188, 295–296, 857

amortization method, 280–281

amortization term, 280

amount of, 266, 279

for Aspen Wood Apartments, 269, 279, 290–291

dormant, 281

first, types of, 284–286

greater than basis, 583

inflation and, 461, 470

junior, types of, 188, 288–293, 295–296

market-indexed, avoiding, 265

nonrecourse, 265, 289, 342

purchase money, 289–290, 295–296, 586–587, 590–591, 901

terms of, 266, 279–284, 290, 850

Mortgage and Real Estate Executives Report, 198**n.**, 482

Mortgage Bankers Association of America (MBA), 55**n.**

Mortgage bonds, 848

Mortgage constant (**K**), 171, 172, 173–174, 175, 239

for industrial buildings and parks, 850

leverage and, 180–182, 241

for office buildings, 819

Mortgaged-out project, 279

Mortgage equity techniques, 65–66

Mortgage interest deductions, 325, 327

Mortgage market, health of real estate market and conditions in, 423

Mortgage money cycle, 493

Mortgage REITs, 155

Moses, Edward, 649

Most probable selling price, 42

Motels, **see** Hotels and motels

MSA (metropolitan statistical area), 375, 376

Multiclass equity structures, 305–306

Multiple corporations, 149–150

Multiple loans, basic financial feasibility model applied to, 193–195

Multiple-nuclei theory, 401–402

Multiple-property syndication offerings, 309–310

Multiplier effect, 552

Multiuse center, 771

Municipal bonds, 703

Myers, Stewart, 451**n.**

National Association of Home Builders (NAHB), 698, 715, 857

National Association of Realtors (NAR), 55**n.**, 453, 715, 753, 858

National Property Exchange Section, 604

National business development and real estate cycle, 490

National Decision Systems, 432**n.**

National Environment Policy Act of 1969, 6

National Fire Protection Association, 884

National Life Real Estate Pension Fund Management Company, 160

National real estate trading markets, 414

Natural barriers, 428

Negotiations, 92, 266, 511–528

achieving objectives of negotiating parties, 519–525

conditions in real estate contract, 522–525

estimating the range of offers and counteroffers, 521–522

general guidelines, 519–521

Aspen Wood Apartments, 269–270, 369

checklist, 527–528

final settlement and closing, 94, 369, 512, 525–526

psychology of, 516–519

human nature and cultural traits, 516–517

negotiation site, 518

role of partners, 519

role of professionals, 519

roles played by negotiators, 517–518

role of, 512–516

cooperative bargaining **vs.** confrontation, 513–514

keys to successful preliminary negotiations, 514–516

satisficing **vs.** maximizing, 514

Neighborhood analysis, 429–430

Neighborhood cycles, 494–495

Neighborhood shopping centers, 738, 768, 770

Nelson, Charles N., 476**n.**

Nelson, Richard L., 417**n.**

Ness, Shirley A., 430**n.**, 812**n.**

Net cash position analysis, Aspen Wood Apartments, 365–367

Net demand, 420

direct estimation of, for space, 4210422

other indicators and measures of, 422–423

Net equity reversion, 581

Net income after debt service, **see** Equity demand

Net-leased property, 115, 345

Net leases, 546–547, 784, 789

Net operating income (NOI), 34

Aspen Wood Apartments, 232–233

developing a detailed one-year forma, 197–202

how NOI can be distorted, 198–201

other sources of data, 201–202

ratio of, to property value, 244

ratio of, to total property cost, 239–241

Net present value (NPV), 74, 215, 216, 238, 602, 646, 647

Net rentable area, 802

Net sale proceeds, 581

Aspen Wood Apartments, projection of, 367, 368

Net selling price, 235

Net tax payable, 328

Net worth, personal, 664. **See also** Equity investment

New concept-overkill cycle, 495–496

New-job formation, rate of, 391

Nickerson, William, 54, 56–57, 61–62

Nierenberg, Gerald I., 511**n.**

Nodes of activity, land investment and, 905

Nominal **vs.** real rate of return, 455–457

Nominee corporation, 152–153

Nonrecourse mortgages, 265, 289, 342

Nonresidential property. **See also specific forms of nonresidential property**

capital gain and depreciation recapture on, 333

depreciation method for, 336, 776

investment interest limitations on rental property, 345

North, Lincoln W., 31**n.**

Northridge Fashion Center, 772

Nothing Down (Allen), 54

Nourse, Hugh O., 500**n.**, 700**n.**

Nursing homes, 883–892

advantages and disadvantages of investing in, 885–886

definitions, 884–885

the investment decision, 891–892

preliminary analyses, 886–891

financial, 888–891

market and marketability, 886–887

physical, legal, political, and environmental, 888

taxation problems, 891

Nursing hours, 885

OBERS report, 381

O'Connor, Joseph W., 652**n.**

Occupational Safety and Health Act (OSHA), 539

Office area services, 789

Office buildings, 801–823

advantages and disadvantages of investing in, 806–807

characteristics of, as investments, 736–738

definitions, 801–802

discounted-cash-flow analysis, 822

financing, 819–821

inflation's impact on, 471–472

the investment decision, 822–823

outlook for, 719

preliminary analyses, 807

Office buildings (**Continued**)
  financial, 812–818
    market and marketability, 807–811
    physical, legal, political, and environmental, 811–812
  taxation and tax structure, 821–822
  track record and trends, 802–806
  types of investors and investor motivations, 807
Office park, 802
Offshore trusts, 159–160
Oharenko, John, 277**n**., 304**n**., 526**n**.
Older investor, 45–46, 58
O'Neil, Cherie J., 152**n**.
"100 Times Formula," 59–60
Open-end sales contracts, 590
Open-end syndicates, 311
Operating assumptions, Aspen Wood Apartments, 364
Operating deductions, 348–350, 358
Operating expenses:
  forecasts of, 444
  hotel and motel, 879
  inflation and, 461
  nursing home, 888, 889–890
  office building, 813–818
  ratio of, to gross effective income, 245
  ratio of, to gross possible income, 245
  shopping center, 786, 788–790
  small rental apartments, 864, 867
Operating income:
  hotel and motel, 877–879
  nursing home, 887, 888, 889–890
  office building, 816–818
  shopping center, 786, 790
  small rental property, 866–867
Operating statement, 554
  office building, 816–818
Operational period, 116
Operation of the property, 535, 548–551
Operations analysis:
  industrial buildings and parks, 844–846
    leases and tenant arrangements, 845–846
    property management and leasing, 844–845
  shopping center, 783–791
    current operating income and expenses, 786
    key ratios, 786–788
    property management and leasing, 783–786
    trends and uncertainties, 789–791
Operations leverage, 277–279
OPM (other people's money) approach, 59
Opportunity cost, 211
Options, 595–596, 909–910
Ordinary annuity tables, 214
Ordinary gains and losses, 581
Ordinary income, 129
  capital gains **vs.**, 329–334
Organized industrial parks, 838
Overage, 547
Overall capitalization rate, 244

Overbuilding of commercial property, 703–705
Owers, James E., 658
Owner-occupied buildings, 802, 807
Owner's cash investment, **see** Equity investment
Ownership, forms of, 6, 125–166, 303–304
  Aspen Wood Apartments, 167–169
  corporations, 146–152
    regular (C), 126, 129, 130, 146–150
    S, 126, 131, 150–152, 881
  decision model, 126–127, 128
  making the decision as to, 125
  matrix approach to, 163–166
  noncorporate, 126, 132–146
    family partnerships, 126, 138–139
    general partnership, 126, 130, 135–138
    individual, 126, 130, 133
    joint tenancy, 126, 131, 133–134, 668, 669
    joint venture, 126, 131, 145–146
    limited partnerships, 24, 126, 129, 130, 139–144, 265
    master limited partnerships, 126, 144–145
    tenancy in common, 126, 132, 134–135, 668
  REMIC, 24, 161–162
  review of personal financial position and, 668–669
  selection criteria, 127–132
    assigning relative weights to, 132
  syndication, **see** Syndication
  trusts, 152–161
    individual retirement accounts, 160–161
    irrevocable, 158–159
    Keogh plans, 131, 160–161
    offshore, 159–160
    pension, 126, 129–130, 131, 160
    real estate investment (REITs), 24, 126, 127, 129–130, 131, 153–158, 536
    revocable, 158–159
Ownership life cycle, 44, 50–51, 52, 93, 496–497

Packager-syndicator, 18
Page, Daniel E., 101**n**., 104**n**., 105**n**.
Parimutuel technique, 906
Parisse, Alan, 312**n**.
Partial dispositions, 591–592
Partially amortizing mortgage, 280–281
Participants in the investment process, 16–25
  interrelationship of decision-making roles, 22–23
  key decision makers, 18–22
  real estate investor roles, 16–18
  structural changes in the marketplace, 23–25
Participating mortgage loan partnerships, 117
Participations or equity kickers, 283
Partnerships, 519

  family, 126, 138–139
  general, 126, 130, 135–138
  hotel/motel, 880
  joint ventures, 20, 35, 48, 126, 131
  limited, 126, 129, 130, 139–144, 265, 712–713, 714
  management, 562
  master limited, 24, 126, 144–145, 312, 627, 712
  public real estate, 112–118
  real estate limited, 627, 656, 657–658
  tax year for, 345–346
Passive equity investors, 16, 22, 49, 866
  vs. managing equity investor, 21–22
Passive income, 233, 325, 336–341, 365, 579–580, 712–713
  impact on investment structures, 340–341
  inability to deduct real economic losses, 340
  phase in rule, 337–340
  special rule for rental real estate, 340
Passive-income generator (PIG), 341
Payback, 235
Payback decision rule, 75
Payback period approach, 72
Peers, Alexandra, 703**n**.
Peiser, R. B., 75**n**., 258**n**.
Pellatt, Peter G. K., 80, 262**n**., 635, 638, 646–647
Pension funds:
  ERISA and, 626–627
  performance of real estate invested, 652–656
  real estate holdings of, 711–712
Pension trusts, 126, 129–130, 131, 160
Percentage leases, 547, 783, 784, 785
Performance audit checklist for evaluating property manager, 555
Permanent lenders, 20–21
Personal control over real estate assets, 11
Personal holding company, 149
Personal interviews with owners, 201–202
Personal (unsecured) loans, 295
Personal portfolio, developing, with real estate, 661–690
  cash flow management, 671–674
  collecting and assessing personal and financial data, 662–665
  education planning, 676–678
  estate planning, 684–687
  financial independence and retirement planning, 674–676
  identifying financial and personal goals and objectives, 665–666
  implementing recommended actions, 687–689
  investment planning, 678–682
  periodic review and revision, 689
  purpose of financial planning, 661–662
  review of current financial position, 666–669
  risk management, 682–684
  tax planning, 669–671
Personal residence, sale of, 593

Personal use and occupancy, real estate for, 11
Peters, Clarence, 876**n.**
Pettygrove, C. S., 248**n.**
Pfouts, Ralph, 378**n.**
"Phantom" taxable gains, 583, 600
Physical analysis of prospective investments:
    apartments, 757–758
    hotels and motels, 878
    industrial buildings and parks, 839–843
    land, 907–908
    nursing homes, 888
    office buildings, 811
    shopping centers, 781
    small rental properties, 862–863
Physical standards, 842
Picconi, Mario J., 450**n.**
Pittenger, D., 393**n.**
Plan, **see** Investment plans
Planned industrial district (PID) or industrial park, **see** Industrial buildings and parks
Plant, industrial, 827
    area of, 827
    site of, 827
Points, mortgage, 281–282
Policies, **see** Investment policies
Political analysis of prospective investments:
    apartments, 758
    industrial buildings and parks, 843
    land, 908
    nursing homes, 888
    office buildings, 811–812
    shopping centers, 781–782
Political environment of urban area, analysis of, 395–396
Political-legal barriers, 428
Popular "how to" approaches to real estate investment decisions, 54, 55–62
    compound interest and control, 58–59
    conduit theory and entrepreneurial leverage theory, 57–58
    critique of, 60–62
    leverage, superleverage, and bargains, 59–60
    pyramiding with other people's money, 56–57
    view of risks in real estate investment, 60
Popularity cycle, 497
Portfolio:
    analysis of, 79–81, 83, 110
    institutional, **see** Institutional real estate portfolios
    personal, developing a, **see** Personal portfolio, developing, with real estate
Portfolio income, 337
Power wiring, 828
Prepayment provisions, mortgage, 283–284
Prepurchase consultations, 534–535, 542–544
Present-value (PV), 212–216
    of Aspen Wood Apartments, 237–238
    decision rule, 215
    with equal cash flow streams, 213–215

net (NPV), 74, 215, 216, 238, 602, 646, 647
    profitability index (PI), 215–216, 238
    with unequal cash flow streams, 213
Present-value model, 51, 72–74, 477
Present value of one per period tables, 214
Price:
    in excess of market value, deductions based on, 349–350
    location decision and, 406
    purchase, 266
    sale, 359
Price, Donald, 456**n.**, 476**n.**
Price-level-adjusted mortgage (PLAM), 285
Pride of ownership, 11
Primary metropolitan statistical area (PMSA), 375, 376
PRISA (Prudential Property Investment Separate Account), 98, 652, 654, 819
Pritchett, Clayton P., 449**n.**
Privacy, selection of ownership form and, 130, 131, 134–135, 139–140, 152
Probabilistic models, 75
Procopio, Thomas, 705
Producer price index (PPI), 453
Product layout, 839
Professional building, 802
Profitability index (PI), 63, 215–216, 238
Profitability ratios, 239–243
Profit a prendre, 905
Profit potential study, 423
Pro forma, developing a detailed one-year, 197–202
Promotional activities, 535, 543–545
Property analysis, 430–431
Property life cycle, 44, 46–50, 52, 496
    downside of, 47, 49–50
    upside of, 46–47, 48–49
Property management, 13, 18, 21, 94, 201, 266, 533–555
    administrative responsibilities, 535, 551–553
    Aspen Wood Apartments, 564–573
    compensation of managers, 307, 538–539
    consideration in determining form of, 538–540
    counseling and communication with investor, 535, 553–555
    of hotels and motels, 878–880
    of industrial buildings and parks, 844–845
    investment philosophy, 95, 534
    leasing, 535, 543, 545–547
    the management function, 534–535
    management plan, 446–447
    market promotion, 535
    need for quality, 535–536
    of nursing homes, 888–891
    of office buildings, 813
    omission of expenses for, 201
    operation of the property, 535, 548–551
    prepurchase consultations, 534–535, 542–544

professional **vs.** self-management, 536–537
    purpose of, 533–534
    selection of a manager, 540–541
    selection of ownership form and, 130, 133, 140–141, 147, 150–151, 155, 156
    of shopping centers, 783–784
    of small rental properties, 865–866
Property selection, property types and, 743–749
Property-specific cycles, 495–496
Property types, 733–743
    industrial buildings, 740–741
    listing of, 734
    office buildings, 736–738
    property selection and, 743–749
    raw land, 742–743
    residential rental property, 735–736
    shopping centers, 738–740
    special-use properties, 741–742
Property taxes, 326, 327, 789, 862, 867, 880
Property value at end of each year, 235
Prudential-Bache, 10, 23, 46
Prudential Life Insurance Company, 98
    Property Investment Separate Account, 98, 652, 654, 819
Public image, selection of ownership form and, 130, 139, 147, 151
Public real estate partnerships, selecting, 112–118
    assessing risk, 114–116
    deciding on investment objectives, 112–114
    understanding investment alternatives, 116–118
Public relations, 544–545
Purchase money mortgages, 586–587, 590–591, 909
    as junior mortgage, 289–290, 295–296
Pyrrh, Stephen A., 36**n.**, 75**n.**, 78**n.**, 171**n**, **228n.**, 258**n.**, 361**n.**, 450, 537**n.**, 578**n.**, 635, 637**n.**, 638
Pyramiding with other people's money, 56–57

Quadruplexes, 856
Qualified nonrecourse financing, 342
Quince, James R., 430**n.**
Quirin, G. David, 247**n.**
Quitclaim deeds, 596, 597

Rabianski, Joseph, 378**n.**, 415**n.**, 422**n.**, 426**n.**, 443**n.**
Rabinowitz, Alan, 484**n.**, 485**n.**, 492**n.**
Racster, Ronald, 378**n.**, 415**n.**, 422**n.**, 426**n.**, 443**n.**
Rahenkamp, John, 908
Raimer, Russell B., 286**n.**
Rake, Don D., 537**n.**
Ratajczak, Dr. Donald, 692, 693**n.**
Ratcliff, Richard n., 30, 42**n.**, 76, 400**n.**
Ratcliff, Richard U., 258**n.**

Rate of return, 12
  disposition of property and, 575
  on equity (ROE), 68, 69, 179–180, 852
    after tax, 241
    leverage and, 180–182, 239
  internal, **see** Internal rate of return
  outlook for real estate investment, 709, 710
  portfolio theory and expected, 628–633, 638–642
  real estate cycles and analysis of, 451–452
  real **vs.** normal, 455–457
  relationship to risk, 2, 249
  required, estimation of, 69
  on total capital (ROI), 68, 179
    leverage and, 180–182, 239
  wealth maximization, 36, 37
Rate-of-return approach, 66–69
Rate-of-return calculation models, 68–69, 179–180
Rate-of-return decision rule, 68
Ratio analysis, **see** Financial ratio analysis
Raw land, 900–911
  advantages and disadvantages of investing in, 903
  characteristics of, as an investment, 742–743, 744–745
  discounted-cash-flow analysis, 911
  financing, 908–910
  inflation's impact on, 467–468
  the investment decision, 911
  investment interest limitation on, 345, 910
  preliminary analyses, 904–908
    market and marketability, 904–906
    physical, legal, political, and environmental, 907–908
    risk management and control, 906–907
  taxation and tax structure, 910
  track records and trends, 901–903
  types of investors and investor motivations, 904
Reading Station, Pennsylvania, 769
Real estate:
  asset allocation decisions and role of, 680–682
  defined, 3–8
    as a dynamic relationship, 4–5
    as part of wealth portfolio, 7–8
    as space and money over time, 4
    as a stewardship, 6
  environment, 9–10
  inflation, measures of, 454–455
  investment outlook for, **see** Investment outlook for real estate
  investor motivations, 10–16. **See also specific investments, e.g.** Apartments; Office buildings
  investment advantages and returns, 10–13
  investment disadvantages and risks, 13–16
  weighing advantages and disadvantages, 16

Real estate appraisal, 41–44
  market value, 41–42
  most probable selling price, 42
  problems with traditional market value, 43–44
Real Estate Appraisal Terminology, 42
Real estate brokers:
  industrial, 844–845
  role in negotiations of, 519
Real estate cycles, 10, 15, 451, 520
  causes and dynamics of, 485–489
  construction cycle, 490–493
  general business cycle and, 489–490
  inflation and, **see** Inflation and inflation cycle
  integration of, 51–52
  investor life cycle, 44–46, 52, 497
  macro, 483–485
  mortgage money cycle, 493
  neighborhood cycles, 494–495
  ownership life cycle, 44, 50–51, 52, 93, 496–497
  popularity cycle, 497
  property life cycle, 44, 46–50, 52, 496
  property-specific cycles, 495–496
  return-risk analysis and, 451–452
  seasonal cycles, 496
  social change cycles, 497
  strategies for dealing with, 498–500
  urban area and city cycles, 493–494
Real Estate Investing Letter, 482
Real estate investment trusts (REITs), 24, 126, 127, 129–130, 131, 153–158, 536
  advantages of, 156–157
  disadvantages of, 157–158
  eligibility requirements for conduit tax treatment, 154–156
  equity (EREIT), 155, 626, 777
  finite-life (FREIT), 118, 155, 656
  history of, 625–626, 656
  1988 outlook for, 713
  performance of, 656–657
Real estate limited partnerships (RELPS), 627, 656, 657–658
Real estate markets, 412–414
  importance of submarkets, 413
  trading markets, 413–414
Real estate mortgage investment conduits (REMICs), 24, 161–162, 658
Real Estate Research Corporation (RERC), 708, 709
Real Estate Review, 312n., 313n.
Real estate sales contract, 522–525
  Aspen Wood Apartments, 529–532
Realtors National Marketing Institute (RNMI), 55n., 542
  International Traders Club, 611
Real **vs.** nominal rate of return, 455–457
Reappraisal clauses, 547
Recaptured depreciation, 230, 332–334
Reconstruction Finance Corporation, 698
Record keeping:
  and accounting by property manager, 551–553
  personal, 673

Redeveloped land as industrial sites, 838–839
Redford, K. J., 86n.
Reed, John T., 299n., 330n., 345n.
Refinancing, 297–303
  alternatives for, 298–299
  illustration of, 300–303
  impact of returns and risks, 299–300
  objectives of, 297–298
  of shopping centers, 791–793
  tax shelters and, 355, 356
REF Symposium, 24n.
Regan, J. P., 562n.
Regional real estate trading markets, 414
Regional shopping centers, 738–739, 768, 770
Registry of Financial Planning Practitioners, 662n.
Regularity of return, selection of ownership form and, 131
Regulation, **see** Government regulation
Rehabilitation, 340, 344, 542, 873, 881
Reiling, William S., 304n.
Reilly, Frank K., 456n., 476n.
Reinsurance, 906–907
REITs, **see** Real estate investment trusts
Remaining principal, 231
REMICS (Real estate mortgage investment conduits), 24, 161–162, 658
Renegotiated-rate mortgage (RRM), 284–285
Rental apartments, **see** Apartments
Rental income:
  forecasts of, 444
  for hotels and motels, 877–878
  inflation and, 461
  for office buildings, 816–818
  for shopping centers, 786, 790
  for small rental property, 464, 465
Rental property. **See also** Lease(s); specific types of rental properties
  nonresidential, investment interest limitations on, 345
  residential, 337, 735–736
    depreciation method for, 336, 762
    investment interest limitations, 345
    passive income rules, 337, 340
Rent-up guarantee, 308
Rent-up period, 116
RE001 computer model, 228, 256
RE004 computer model, 361
Replacement period for gain from involuntary conversion, 598
Replacement reserves, inadequate, 199
Reporting system, 266
Research Institute of America, 324n.
Reserves, replacement, inadequate, 199
Residential hotels, 872
Residential property. **See also specific forms of residential property**
  capital gain and depreciation recapture on, 332–333
  rental property, 337, 735–736
    depreciation method for, 336
    investment interest limitations, 345
    passive income rules, 337, 340

Resort hotels, 872
Resyndication, 591
  Aspen Wood Apartments, 615–622
Retailers, outlook for real estate of, 718–719
Retail trading areas, 375–378
Retirement fund, 131, 160–161, 676
  selection of ownership form for, 148
Retirement housing, 754
  outlook for, 718
Retirement planning, 674–676, 677
Return, **see** Internal rate of return; Rate of
  return; Regularity of return
Revenue Act of 1987, 332, 587
Revenue forecasts, 444
Reverse annuity mortgage (RAM), 285
Reversion cash flow, 235–237
Review, 482
Revocable trust, 158–159
Rhind, David, 431**n.**
Rice, Michael, 651**n.**
Ricks, R. Bruce, 450**n.**, 469, 650**n.**, 857**n.**
Ring, Alfred A., 483, 541**n.**
Ringer, Robert J., 517–518
Risk, 211, 628–629. **See also** Risk analysis
  avoiding or eliminating, 265
  in commercial projects, 714
  debt coverage ratio and, 177–178
  defined, 248–249
  disposition of property and, 575
  "how to" approaches' view of, 60
  life cycles and, **see** Real estate life
    cycles
  management and control of, 36–38,
    264–267, 682–684
    in apartment investments, 757
    Aspen Wood Apartments, 272–273
    in hotels and motels, 880
    in land investments, 906–907
    in office building financing, 820–821
    in office building investments, 810–
      811
    in shopping center financing, 792–
      793
    in shopping center investments, 780–
      781
    in small rental properties, 862
  portfolio theory and, 628–633, 639–642
  of public real estate partnerships, 114–
    116
  reducing the remaining, 266–267
  relationship to return, 2, 249
  reviewing financial position for level of,
    668
  in small rental properties, 865, 869
  transferring or shifting, 265–266
  types of, 250–252
  vs. uncertainty, 248–249
  wealth maximization, 36, 37
Risk absorption (RA) ratio, 254–255
Risk-adjusted discount rate, 75–76
Risk analysis:
  Aspen Wood Apartments, 272
  for industrial buildings and parks, 852
  levels of, 253–264
  models for, 75–81

nature and definition of risk, 247–249
  for office buildings, 822
  real estate cycles and, 451–452
  for shopping centers, 795
  for small rental properties, 869
  types of risk, 250–252
Risk index (RI), 263–264
Risk premium, 249, 251
Risk ratios, 243
Ritchie, Karen, 359**n.**
Robbins, Michael, 637
Robertson, Terry, 70**n.**
Robert Stanger Co., 657**n.**
Robichek, Alexander A., 248**n.**
Robinson, G. D., 431**n.**
Robinson, Gerald J., 135**n.**, 588**n.**
Robinson, Rich, 588**n.**
Rockefeller Center Properties, Inc., 154
ROE, **see** Rate of return, on equity
Rogers, D. S., 419**n.**
Rogers, Ronald C., 658
ROI, **see** Rate of return, on capital
Roll, Richard, 80**n.**, 632**n.**, 660**n.**
Rolling options, 595
Rose, Clarence C., 152**n.**
Rosen, Kenneth T., 419**n.**, 698
Rosenberg, Menachem, 223**n.**
Ross, S. A., 80**n.**, 660**n.**
Roulac, Stephen E., 15**n.**, 16**n.**, 35**n.**, 51**n.**,
  85**n.**, 92, 99, 254**n.**, 267**n.**, 306**n.**,
  307**n.**, 311**n.**, 313**n.**, 451**n.**, 485**n.**,
  562**n.**, 650**n.**, 698, 713, 749**n.**
Rouse, James, 719
Rubens, Jack H., 80
Rushing, Philip J., 66**n.**, 67**n.**
Rushmore, Stephen, 14
Russell, William M., 577**n.**
Rutgers University Urban Policy Research
  Center, 754
Rystrom, David, 470**n.**

Sacks, Mason J., 330**n.**
Safe harbor rules, 142, 314
Sale of property:
  alternatives to, 579
  analysis of conditions that might war-
    rant, 579, 580
  calculation of net proceeds from, 235–
    237
  disposition by, 583–592
    auctions, 591
    financing the purchaser to facilitate,
      586–591
    partial dispositions, 591–592
    resyndication, 591
  evaluating decision to sell, 577–579
  personal residence, 593
  tax planning and, 579–583
Sale-buybacks, 294, 296
Sale-leaseback of property or building, 293–
  294, 586, 819, 821, 846, 851–852
**Sales and Marketing Managment's Survey
  of Buying Power,** 779
Sales potential profile, 434–345, 437
Salomon Brothers, 24–25, 698

Sandwich lease, 294
Satellites, shopping center, 771, 780, 782
Scenario planning, current problem of, 727–
  728
Scheduled net, 200
Schlesinger, Sanford J., 594**n.**
Schreiber, Irving, 74**n.**, 220**n.**, 223**n.**
Schumpeter, J. A., 248**n.**
Schwab, Bernhard, 76, 258**n.**
Schwartz, Arthur L., Jr., 627**n.**, 657**n.**, 658
Schwert, G. William, 450–451, 476**n.**
S corporation, 126, 131, 150–152, 881
Scoular, Robert F., 430**n.**
Screening criteria, 106–108
  of Aspen Wood Apartments, 124
Sears Financial Network, 23
Seasonal cycles, 496
Secondary financing, 288–293, 295–296
Second-class buildings, 839
Section 8 housing program, 287
Section 202 housing program, 287
Section 1031 exchanges, **see** Exchange of
  property, tax-free
Section 1231 property, 329, 330, 331, 581,
  596, 864
Section 1237 of the tax code, 592
Sector theory, 401
Securities Acts of 1933 and 1934, Regulation
  D, 162, 313–315
Securities and Exchange Commission
  (SEC), 310, 312, 314
  Regulation A, 315
  Rule 146 (Safe Harbor Act), 142, 314
  Rule 147 (Safe Harbor for Intrastate Ex-
    emption), 314
Securities Data Company, 703
Securitization of commercial property, 8, 627
  by general corporation, 148
  of limited partnership, 140
Security of capital, 12
Security deposits, 349
Security of the property, 552
  industrial buildings, 842
Seldin, Maury, 46**n.**, 107**n.**, 378**n.**, 415**n.**,
  422**n.**, 443**n.**, 450**n.**, 451**n.**, 868**n.**
Selection of property, property types and,
  743–749
Self-liquidating loan, **see** Fully amortizing
  mortgage
Self-management of property,. **See also**
  Property management
  considerations in deciding on, 538–540
  vs. professional management, 536–537
  small rental properties, 865–866
Seller financing, 289–290, 867
Selling price, 581
Senior citizens, housing for, 754
  outlook for, 718
Senior Real Estate Analyst (SREA), 55, 542
Senior Real Property Appraiser (SRPA), 55
Sensitivity analysis, 76, 255–257, 521, 657
  for industrial buildings and parks, 852
  for office buildings, 822
  for small rental properties, 869
  for shopping centers, 795–796

Sewel, Murphy A., 432**n.**
Shafer, Thomas W., 400**n.**
Shared-appreciation mortgage (SAM), 285
Sharpe, William, 79, 80, 631–632, 646, 647–648, 659
Sheahan, Joseph W., 430**n.**
Shenkel, William M., 540**n.**
Shlaes, Jared, 41**n.**
Shopping centers, 767–796
  advantages and disadvantages of investing in, 773–776
  categories of, 738–739, 768–769, 770
  characteristics of, as investments, 738–740, 748–749
  definitions, 767–772
  discounted-cash-flow analysis, 795–796
  financing and refinancing, 791–793
  inflation's impact on, 471–472
  the investment decision, 796
  preliminary analyses, 778–791
    financial, 782–783
    market and marketability, 778–781
    operations, 783–791
    physical, legal, political, and environmental, 781–782
  taxation and tax structure, 793–795
    depreciation, 776, 794
  track records and trends, 772–773
  types of investors and investor motivations, 776
Shopping goods, 771
Short, James L., 277**n.**
Siegel, Laurence P., 7**n.**, 450**n.**, 476**n.**
Sills, Richard P., 330**n.**
Silverman, Jane A., 843**n.**
Simple interest, 280, 455
Simplified probability approach, 261–262
Single-family homes, 855–869
  definition, 855
  discounted-cash-flow analysis, 869
  financing of, 867–869
  inflation's impact on homeowners, 468–470
  investing in, 859–860
  investment decision, 869
  preliminary analyses, 860–867
    financial, 864–867
    market and marketability, 860–862
    physical, legal, politital, and environmental, 862–863
  track record and trends, 857–859
Single-property syndication offerings, 310
Single-purpose industrial buildings, 827
Sirmans, C. F., 36**n.**, 97**n.**, 354, 450**n.**, 451**n.**, 651**n.**
Site analysis, 431–432
  economic and demographic profile, 432–438
Siteline, 433
Site-Potential system, 434–435
Sklarz, Michael A., 602**n.**
Slovic, Paul, 108**n.**
Small apartment buildings, 855–869
  definitions, 856
  discounted-cash-flow analysis, 869

financing of, 867–869
investing in, 859–860
investment decision, 869
preliminary analyses, 860–867
  financial, 864–867
  market and marketability, 860–862
  physical, legal, political, and environmental, 862–863
  track record and trends, 857–859
Small rental properties, **see** Condominiums; Single-family homes; Small apartment buildings
Small Business Administration, 845, 847
Small Business Investment Companies (SBICs), 847
Smith, Adam, 729
Smith, Halbert C., 276**n.**
Smith, Lawrence B., 473**n.**, 476**n.**–477**n.**
Smith, Owen, 517**n.**
Smith, Wallace F., 724**n.**
Smith case, 610
Social change cycles, 497
Social Security Act, 884
Social Security Administration, 887
Society of Industrial Realtors (SIR), 834
Society of Real Estate Appraisers (SREA), 55**n.**, 705
Sole proprietorship, **see** Individual ownership
Solt, Michael E., 562**n.**
Sources and uses of funds statement, 664
Southmark Corporation, 154
Special allocations, 137, 142–143, 152
Specialist in Real Estate Securities (SRS), 55
Special-purpose industrial buildings, 827
Specialty goods, 772
Specialty shopping centers, 769
Specialty stores, 718–719
Special-use properties, 115, 869–892. **See also** Hotels; Motels; Nursing homes
  characteristics of, as investments, 741–742
  points to consider before investing in, 870–871
Speculation, investment **vs., 31–32**
Spellman, Lewis J., 450
Speltzer, Carl S., 260**n.**
Spieker, A. M., 431**n.**
Spies, P. F., 415**n.**
Sprinkel, Beryl W., 452**n.**, 457**n.**
Sprinklered building, 829
Square-foot prices, 520
Staged equity investment techniques, 309
Standard Industrial Classification (SIC) code, 380–381, 382, 830
Standardization of operation, 553
Standard Manual of Accounting for Shopping Center Operations, 788
Standard loan, **see** Straight-term mortgage
Stanger, Robert A., 712, 713
Stanger Reports, 163, 708
Stanley, Thomas J., 432**n.**
Starchild, Adam, 159**n.**
Starker II case, 608, 609, 610–611
State "blue-sky laws," 315
State taxes, 326

State variables, 258**n.**
Static risk, 250–251
Steele, Robert W., 61**n.**
Steiner, George A., 86**n.**, 555**n.**
Step-up options, 595
Sternlieb, George, 384**n.**
Stephen Roulac & Associates, 163
Stevenson, Howard W., 471**n.**
Stock market, 702, 713
"Stops," 791
Straight lease, 846
Straight-line basis, 230, 235
Straight-line depreciation, 230**n.**, 332, 333, 335, 336, 338–339
Straight-rate mortgage loan funds, 117–118
Straight sale, 585
Straight-term mortgage, 280
Strategy, **see** Investment strategy
Strategy of analysis, defined, 89
Strategy study, 40
Straw corporation, 152–153
Strip center, 772
Strobel, Caroline, 188**n.**, 359**n.**
Structural density (floor-area ratio), 829
Subdivision lot sales, 592
Subordinated land leasebacks, 292–293, 296
Suburban industrial sites and acreage, 837–838
Sumichrast, Michael, 451**n.**
Summation estimating technique, 442–443
Sum-of-the-years' digits (SOYD) depreciation, 336, 338–339
Superleverage, 60
Superregional shopping centers, 739, 768–769, 770
Supply. **See also** Demand
  analysis of:
    of apartments, 756–757
    of hotels and motels, 875–877
    of industrial buildings and parks, 835–839
    of land, 904–905
    of nursing homes, 887
    of office buildings, 809–810
    relationship between demand and, 421–423
    of shopping centers, 779–780
    of small rental properties, 860–861
  estimation of present and future, 415–418
  models of, 417
  real estate cycles and, 485–489
Svoboda, Karla D., 432**n.**
Swesnik, Richard H., 46**n.**, 107**n.**, 450**n.**, 868**n.**
Syndication, 126, 162–163, 777, 906. **See also** Packager-syndicator
  compensation of sponsors of, 307–309
  federal and state regulation of, 312–315
  as form of financing, 309–315
  types of offerings, 309–312
Systematic risk, 251, 633

Takeout letter, 282
Tandy, Janet, 637**n.**

Tanforan Co., Inc. case, 596n.
Tappan, William J., 593n.
Tarantello, Rocky, 462n.
Tatom, John A., 478n.
Tax(es), 93
    for apartment buildings, 336, 337, 340,
        345, 761–762
    Aspen Wood Apartments' tax structure,
        269–270
    capital gain, **see** Capital gains taxes
    current-year tax projection, 664
    estate, **see** Estate tax(es)
    exchanges and, **see** Exchange of
        property, tax-free
    gift, 159, 325
    for hotels and motels, 880–881
    for industrial buildings and parks, 851–
        852
    for land, 910
    for nursing homes, 891
    for office buildings, 821–822
    property, 326, 327, 789, 862, 867, 880
    property maanger's knowledge about,
        551
    on sale of property, calculating, 235, 236
    selection of ownership form and, 127–
        129, 133–146, 148, 149–152, 153,
        154, 156, 157, 159–
        160
    for shopping centers, 776, 793–
        795
    on subordinated land leasebacks, 292
    wraparound morgages and, 291
Taxable income, 233, 234
    tax rate schedules and, 327–328
Tax credits, 328, 340, 343–344, 358
Tax deeds, 597
Tax-free exchanges, **see** Exchange of proper-.
    ty, tax-free
Tax law, 325–345, 356. **See also individual
    laws**
    alternative minimum tax, 342–343
    "at-risk" rules, 289, 291–292, 341–342
    on capital gains, **see** Capital gains taxes
    on depreciation, **see** Depreciation
    on general partnerships, 135–136
    income tax formula, 326–329
    on installment sales, 587–590
    investment interest limitations, 344–345
    passive-loss limitation rules, 325, 336–
        341. **See also** Passive income
    types of leases and, 546–547
Tax leverage, 277–278
Tax planning, 322–369
    disposition of property and, 579–583
    IRS audit, 350–351
    operating deductions, 348–351
    ownership and, **see** Ownership, forms of
    personal financial planning and, 669–
        671
    tax law and, **see** Tax law; **specific laws**
    tax reform and real estate investment,
        324–325
    timing of income, 345–348, 670–671
Tax Planning for Real Estate Investors

(Kay and Sirmans), 354
Tax rate schedules, 325, 327–328, 358
Tax Reform Act of 1986, 50, 98, 163, 210,
    211, 354, 458, 627, 658, 703
    capital gains treatment, 129, 325, 329
    on capital **vs.** operating expenses, 348
    on depreciation, 230, 325, 335, 336,
        582, 762, 776, 794, 821, 851
    exchanges and, 593
    on investment interest limitations, 345
    on IRAs and Keoghs, 160
    on loan points and commitment fees,
        282
    overview of, 324–325
    passive-loss limitation rules, 325, 336–
        341, 365
    real estate professionals' view of, 708
    on REMICs, 161–162
    on sale-leasebacks, 293–294
    on tax credits, 343–344, 873, 881
    on tax losses, 233
Tax shelters, 12, 98, 137, 351–359
    comparison of cash flow and taxable in-
        come statements, 352–353
    concepts of, 351–356
    game plan of investor, 353–354
    pitfalls of, 355–356
    property life cycle and, 50
    public real estate partnerships as, 112–
        113
    refinancing to increase, 298
    small rental properties as, 864
    stages of, 354–355
    strategy checklist, 356–359
Tax year, 345–346
Technology Park, Atlanta, 838, 840–841
Tenancy in common, 126, 132, 134–135, 668
Tenancy state of property life cycle, 49
Tenants:
    anchor, 769
    bona fide, 200
    major, 771
    mix of shopping center, 780
    relations with, 550–551, 865
    selection of, 545, 865
    in small rental properties, 865
Terminal-value IRR, **see** Modified (or ad-
    justed) internal rate of return
Termination of the investment, 94, 574–622
    analytical framework for, 600–602
    Aspen Wood Apartments, 615–622
    guidelines for disposition strategy, 576–
        583
        evaluating decision to sell, 577–579
        tax planning, 579–583
        voluntary and involuntary disposi-
            tions, 576–577
    methods of disposition, 583–600
        abandonment, 596
        by charitable contributions, 593
        involuntary conversions, 598–600
        by exchange, 592–593, 604–614
        options, 595–596
        by sale, 583–592, 593
        tax deeds, 597

by will or descent and transfers for
    reasons of love and affection,
    594–595
    as part of investment cycle, 574–576
    transaction costs, 575
Thal, Lawrence S., 76n.
Thau, William A., 517n.
Theme shopping centers, 769
Thibodeau, T. G., 80, 652
Thielen, Richard n., 307n.
Third-class buildings, 839
Thompson, Mark, 591n.
Time horizons for investment decisions, 44–
    52
Time preferences and biases, faulty, 106
Timesharing, 856
Title V Farmers Home Administration
    (FmHA) rural housing, 287
Total down payment, **see** Equity investment
Total rent, shopping center, 786
Townhouse complexes, 752
Trading areas, shopping cneter, 778–779
Trading markets, real estate, 413–414
Trading on equity, 576
Traditional financial decision approaches, 54–
    55, 62–72 ,
    best-fit approach, 69–71
    gross rent multiplier approach, 71–72
    investment value approach, 63–66
    rate-of-return approach, 66–69
    payback period approach, 72
Trammell Crow, 18–19, 49
Transferability of interest, selection of owner-
    ship form and, 129, 134, 136, 137, 140,
    141, 147, 152, 153, 156
Trimble, Harold G., 38n., 410n.
Triplexes, 856
Trolley Square, Salt Lake City, 769
Trusts, 126, 130, 140n., 359, 594–595
    IRAs, 160–161
    irrevocable, 159
    Keogh plans, 131, 160–161
    and leaseback, 594–595
    offshore, 159–160
    pension, 126, 129–130, 131, 160
    real estate investment, **see** Real estate
        investment trusts
    revocable, 158–159
Tschappatt, Carl J., 276n.
Tuttle, Donald L., 44n., 629n.
Tversky, Amos, 108n.

Ullman, Edward L., 401
Uncertainty, inability to deal with, 108–109
Unified credit, 685–686
    inter vivos gifting of the, 687
Uniform Gifts to Minors Act, 677–678
Uniform Limited Partnership Act (ULPA), 139,
    140
Uniform Partnership Act, 136
**Uniform System of Accounts and Ex-
    pense Dictionary for Motels/Hotels,**
    877
U.S. Department of Agriculture, 467

U.S. Department of Commerce, 381, 396, 454**n.**, 460**n.**, 809
  Bureau of the Census, 374–375, 376, 384, 394, 432, 754**n.**, 830**n.**, 883
  Bureau of Economic Analysis, 381, 392, 396, 432**n.**
U.S. Department of Housing and Urban Development (HUD), 99, 286, 396, 470, 755
U.S. Department of Labor, Bureau of Labor Statistics, 432**n.**, 453**n.**, 454
U.S. Department of Transportation, 396
U.S. Department of the Treasury, 597**n.**
U.S. Financial Data, 482
U.S. Housing Markets, 715
U.S. Industrial Outlook, 381
United States of America Standards Institute, 827
U.S. Office of Management and Budget, 826**n.**
Unleveraged real estate partnerships, 117
Unsystematic risk, 633
Updegrave, Walter L., 305**n.**
Upton, King, 653**n.**
Urban analysis, 373–407
  defining a metropolitan area, 374–378
  demographic analysis, 384–395
    checklist for, 398–399
    demand indicators for urban space use, 393–394
    migration, 391–393
    of other aspects of the population, 387–391
    population projections, 386–387
  economic analysis, 378–384
    checklist for, 398–399
    classifying economic activity, 380–381, 382
    competition and interdependence of metropolitan areas, 383–384
    economic-base analysis, 378–380
    indicators of stability, 383
    limits of urban growth, 381
  patterns of urban growth, 397–406
    location concepts, 403–406
    theories of land use, 400–403, 404–405
  political and legal considerations, 395–396
  secondary data for, sources of, 396–397
Urban area and city cycles, 493–494
Urban containment, 724–725
Urban Decision Systems Inc., 432**n.**
Urban Development Action Grants (UDAGs),

287
Urban Enterprise Zones, 839
Urban fringe, 375
Urbanized area, 375
Urban land, impact of inflation on unimproved, 467
Urban Land Institute, 751**n.**, 770**n.**, 786, 787**n.**, 788, 789
  Project Reference Files, 773
Urban place, 375
Usury ceilings, 493
Utilities for industrial buildings, 842
Utility approach, direct, 76

Vacancies:
  forecast of rates of, 444
  provision for, 200
  in small rental properties, 865
  vacancy rate factor, 760, 783
Vacuum analysis, 779
Valachi, Donald J., 188**n.**, 220**n.**, 253**n.**, 299**n.**, 593**n.**
Value factors in best-fit approach, 70–71
Variable-rate mortgages, 470
Ventilation of industrial buildings, 843
Venture (asset) management, 21, 22, 94, 556–562
  advice given by asset managers, 560–561
  Aspen Wood Apartments, 564–573
  definition of, 556–557
  functions of, 557–558
  review process, 557, 559
  team for, 558–560
  venture and partnershp management, 562
Vernor, James D., 415**n.**
Vertical center, 772
Veterans Administration, 885
Vitt, Lois A., 304**n.**
VMS Realty Partners, 699–700

Walk-up (low-rise) apartments, 751
Waller, Neil G., 223**n.**
Walters, David W., 537
Walters, William, Jr., 540
Walther, Carl H., 126**n.**
Ward, Robert L., 38**n.**, 74**n.**, 220**n.**, 223**n.**, 410**n.**
Ward, William L., 288**n.**
Warehouses, 840–841
Water Tower Plaza, Chicago, 772
Wealth maximization, 2, 36, 37
Wealth-pyramiding process, 56–57

Weaver, William C., 419**n.**, 809**n.**
Webb, James R., 80, 101**n.**, 103**n.**, 104**n.**, 105**n.**, 279**n.**, 450**n.**, 574**n.**, 651**n.**
Webster's Third International Dictionary, 31**n.**
Weicher, John C., 470**n.**
Weinstein, M. W., 593**n.**
Weitzman, M. K., 415**n.**
Welch, Russell, 183**n.**, 212**n.**
Wendt, Paul F., 66**n.**, 75**n.**, 97**n.**, 450**n.**, 467**n.**, 470**n.**, 637, 650**n.**
Wenzlick, Roy, 484
Werner, Raymond J., 600**n.**
Westby, D. K., 248**n.**
Weston, Fred, 216, 220**n.**, 451**n.**, 456**n.**, 461**n.**
Wheaton, William C., 484**n.**
White, John R., 41**n.**, 704–705
Whitson, B. A., 419**n.**
Wilbur, Robert W., 277**n.**
Wildt, Albert R., 500**n.**
Wiley, Robert J., 101**n.**, 410**n.**, 634**n.**
Winer, Russell S., 500**n.**
Winning Through Intimidation (Ringer), 517**n.**
Withers, William C., 342**n.**
Witten, G. Ronald, 499**n.**
Wofford, Larry E., 85**n.**, 108**n.**, 110**n.**, 254**n.**, 255**n.**, 260**n.**, 649
Wolman, William, 34**n.**, 452**n.**, 457**n.**, 474**n.**
Wong, Sui N., 450**n.**, 470**n.**, 650**n.**
Woods, Donald H., 260**n.**, 426**n.**
World economy, real estate in, 7, 8
World view of real estate investment outlook, 691
Wraparound mortgage, 188, 290–292, 867
Wurtzebach, Charles H., 223**n.**, 541**n.**, 585**n.**

Xerox, 699–700

Yesavich, Peter, 877**n.**
Yield, **see** Rate of return
Yormack, Jonathan S., 80, 638**n.**
Young, Michael S., 224**n.**, 258**n.**, 638**n.**, 649
Young investor, 44–45, 57–58

Zeckendorf, William, 86, 281, 306
Zeikel, Arthur, 44**n.**
Zell, Samuel, 705–706
Zerbst, Robert H., 13**n.**, 180**n.**, 253**n.**, 450**n.**
Zero-coupon bond, 281
Zinbarg, Edward D., 44**n.**
Zoning, **see** Legal analysis of prospective investments